MASTERING UNREAL® TECHNOLOGY

The Art of Level Design

Jason Busby, Zak Parrish, Joel Van Eenwyk

EPIC GAMES

Sams Publishing, 800 East 96th St., Indianapolis, Indiana, 46240 USA

Mastering Unreal Technology: The Art of Level Design

International Standard Book Number: 0-672-32692-2

Library of Congress Catalog Card Number: 2004095071

Printed in the United States of America

First Printing: November 2004

07 06 6 5

Trademarks

Unreal is a registered trademark of Epic Games, Inc. All terms mentioned in this book that are known to be trademarks or service marks have been appropriately capitalized. Sams Publishing cannot attest to the accuracy of this information. Use of a term in this book should not be regarded as affecting the validity of any trademark or service mark.

Warning and Disclaimer

Every effort has been made to make this book as complete and as accurate as possible, but no warranty or fitness is implied. The information provided is on an "as is" basis. The authors and the publisher shall have neither liability nor responsibility to any person or entity with respect to any loss or damages arising from the information contained in this book or from the use of the DVD or programs accompanying it.

Bulk Sales

Sams Publishing offers excellent discounts on this book when ordered in quantity for bulk purchases or special sales. For more information, please contact

U.S. Corporate and Government Sales
1-800-382-3419
corpsales@pearsontechgroup.com

For sales outside of the U.S., please contact

International Sales
international@pearsoned.com

Associate Publisher
Michael Stephens

Acquisitions Editor
Michael Stephens

Development Editor
Sean Dixon

Managing Editor
Charlotte Clapp

Senior Project Editor
Matthew Purcell

Copy Editor
Lisa M. Lord

Indexer
Chris Barrick

Proofreader
Cindy Long

Publishing Coordinator
Cindy Teeters

Multimedia Developer
Dan Scherf

Cover Designer
Jason Busby

Interior Designer
Gary Adair

Page Layout
Stacey Richwine-DeRome

Graphics
Tammy Graham
Laura Robbins

Contents at a Glance

Table of Contents

About the Authors

Jason "Buzz" Busby is the president/CEO of 3D Buzz, Inc., a company dedicated to teaching the world the arts and skills behind today's hottest 3D industries, including gaming, film, and visualization. Through his website, www.3DBuzz.com, Buzz distributes his signature Video Training Modules (VTMs), which contain hours of training content that is professional, informative, and entertaining. Buzz is also the Director of Animation at The Renaissance Center in Dickson, Tennessee, where he offers his students a unique insight into the world of Alias Maya and Discreet 3ds max.

Zak Parrish is currently an animation instructor at The Renaissance Center, where he teaches both Alias Maya and Discreet 3ds max. For the past two years, he has worked with Jason Busby and 3D Buzz, Inc. to help provide top-quality education to students across the world. His work can be seen on many of the 3D Buzz VTMs as well as in the UT2004 Special Edition training video series. In what little spare time he manages, he is also seeking his bachelor of fine arts degree at Austin Peay State University.

Joel Van Eenwyk grew up in China, where his parents both work as teachers. He attended public school in China for four years and was then homeschooled by his mother. Joel developed an interest in computer programming and was soon writing programs to help with his homework. At 17, Joel traveled to the United States to further his education at a community college in Kansas. During that time, he attended an intensive four-week training program on Alias Maya, instructed by Jason Busby. After completing a one-year internship with 3D Buzz, Joel is currently seeking his computer science degree at the University of Kansas.

Dedication

Jason:

This book is lovingly dedicated to my beautiful wife, Angela; my two wonderful daughters, Heather and Meagan; and my loving mom, Belinda, who was always there to support me just when I needed it the most.

Zak:

I dedicate this book to my parents, Don and Carolyn; to my three brothers, Josh, Micah, and Daniel; but most especially to my girlfriend, Robyn, without whose love and patience I would be truly lost.

Joel:

I dedicate this book to my Mom, Dad, and brother, who have been a never-ending flow of support, and to all my friends who have encouraged me to follow my dreams.

Acknowledgments

Jason: I would like to thank my family and my mom for putting up with me throughout this project and providing the love and support that allowed me to get the job done. I'd like to thank Zak for dealing with me through all my ups and downs and using his incredible writing talent to help make this book run as smoothly as possible. I would also like to thank Joel, whose unbelievable level of focus and determination never ceased to amaze me. No matter the task or situation, he took every job with a smile and always returned amazing results.

Zak: I would like to thank Jason for seeing potential in me and helping me see it in myself. Without his vision and insight, I could never have learned or achieved so much. I want to thank Joel for being a friend and confidant and always giving me that chuckle I needed to make it through the day. Last, I very much want to thank Robyn, who kept my feet on the ground, my heart in the clouds, and the rest of me wrapped around her little finger.

Joel: First and foremost, I would like to give a huge thank you to my family for supporting me through the arduous task of writing this book. When all seemed hopeless, they were always there to encourage me and give me the confidence to continue. I would also like to thank Zak for doing such an excellent job of proofing my writing. Big thanks to Buzz for giving me the opportunity to be a co-author of this book and for being such an honest critic of my work, despite my sometimes hostile response. Through his encouragement and help, I've learned more about Unreal, 3D, and programming than I ever dreamed possible. If it wasn't for all these people, I would never have completed this book and would have lost the little sanity I had left.

All Authors: The three of us would like to send a most heartfelt thank you to Logan Frank, without whose technical wizardry and deep understanding of the Unreal Engine much of this book would not have been possible. For countless hours, he sat in turn with each one of us, helping us better understand and better explain every facet of Unreal. We would also like to sincerely thank Ian Blackford for his personal support of our work, his incredible design talents, and the wonderful artwork he composed for the cover of this book. Also, we would like to send a massive thank you to David Aguilar for his absolutely awesome drawings that you'll find in Chapter 2 of the book. He was able to produce beautiful results on very short notice and with little instruction.

We would also like to thank Mark Rein for making this book a reality as well as Tim Sweeney for designing the Unreal Engine and starting this awesome phenomenon. Finally, we would like to give a very large thanks to the Unreal Community, which has been a massive source of support and inspiration in all our Unreal projects.

We Want to Hear from You!

As the reader of this book, *you* are our most important critic and commentator. We value your opinion and want to know what we're doing right, what we could do better, what areas you'd like to see us publish in, and any other words of wisdom you're willing to pass our way.

As an associate publisher for Sams Publishing, I welcome your comments. You can email or write me directly to let me know what you did or didn't like about this book—as well as what we can do to make our books better.

Please note that I cannot help you with technical problems related to the topic of this book. We do have a User Services group, however, where I will forward specific technical questions related to the book.

When you write, please be sure to include this book's title and author as well as your name, email address, and phone number. I will carefully review your comments and share them with the author and editors who worked on the book.

Email: feedback@samspublishing.com

Mail: Michael Stephens
Associate Publisher
Sams Publishing
800 East 96th Street
Indianapolis, IN 46240 USA

For more information about this book or another Sams Publishing title, visit our Web site at www.samspublishing.com. Type the ISBN (0672326922) or the title of a book in the Search field to find the page you're looking for.

Introduction

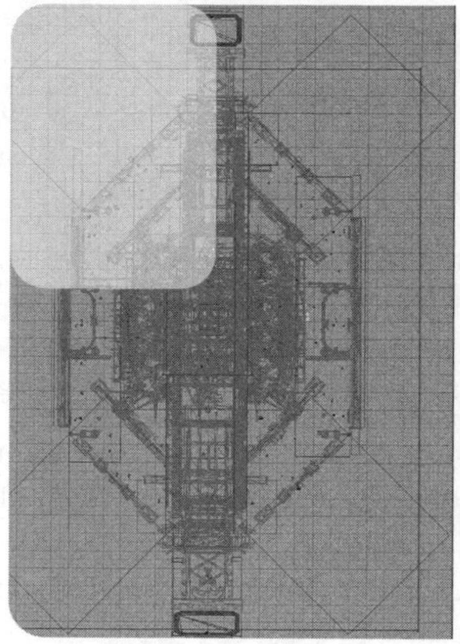

Welcome to *Mastering Unreal Technology: The Art of Level Design*. You're going to take an exciting journey through the rich world of game design, using the Unreal Engine. This book is dedicated to the aesthetic aspects of game design, such as level design creation, character development, and static mesh design. On the other hand, this book does not cover many game design topics from the programmer's perspective, meaning there isn't much emphasis on programming the Unreal Engine through its native programming language, UnrealScript.

Who Is This Book For?

This book has been designed for a wide range of people, actually. The first group is aspiring mod makers or fledgling game designers. This book is also aimed at anyone who has ever wondered exactly what kind of work goes into making his or her favorite game.

Beyond gamers, however, this book can be a great resource for those in the fields of architecture or construction visualization. With the Unreal Engine, you can offer your clients real-time flythroughs and simulations that they can view *and* explore. How to apply the Unreal Technology that drives today's cutting-edge games is limited only by your imagination.

How to Use This Book

This book is designed to be read from start to finish, although this isn't necessarily the best way for everyone to complete this book. You'll find that each chapter has a robust selection of information about each relative topic; however, the book has been designed to be flexible enough so that you can start with the areas of game design that interest you the most.

Whatever your motive, this book is your resource, so use it as you will. However, keep in mind that game design is an interconnected field, in that many of its aspects are directly connected to each other. You might not want to be a level designer or static mesh constructor, but you'll make yourself far more valuable to a prospective employer (or mod team) by knowing about each field of game design.

How This Book Is Organized

Part I: The Unreal Universe

This first part of the book focuses on a general introduction to level design for the Unreal Engine with its native editing system, UnrealEd. It begins with a brief history of Unreal and quickly moves on to a thorough introduction to how the Unreal Engine functions.

From there, Part I walks you through creating your first Unreal Level. You see how to carve your own environments into the Unreal world, how to texture and light them, and how to add the elements that make them aesthetically pleasing and still fun to play. The topics covered include creating indoor and vast outdoor environments, creating and controlling your level's physics through the use of volumes, and generating a variety of lighting effects. Part I wraps up with an in-depth look at material and texture creation and how to create interactive level elements, such as moving doors and controllable elevators.

Part II: Advanced Design Techniques

Part II opens the doors to more high-end features of the Unreal Engine. Beginning with an introduction to working with real-time particle systems and effects, Part II also brings you face to face with the Karma physics engine, explaining how it can be used to create realistic simulations based on the laws of physics. Next, the chapter covers the techniques for controlling the behavior of Unreal's artificially intelligent players, known as "bots."

Part II then moves on to cover Matinee, UnrealEd's integrated system for creating in-game cinematics—animated clips and films—with the game engine. Next, Part II discusses how to create scripted in-game sequences to create exciting events that pull players deeper into the action. This part closes with a look at optimizing your levels to keep gameplay as fast as possible, while pulling as much power as you can from the engine.

Part III: External Design

Part III introduces you to creating3D game elements with Alias's Maya. This part begins with an introduction to Maya from the beginner's perspective. You're quickly brought up to speed on navigating the software, learning techniques for polygon modeling, creating static meshes for use as decorative elements in your levels, and preparing your models for the application of texture.

Next, Part III explains techniques for creating full character models. This part then covers how you can turn that model into a digital puppet so that it can be animated and eventually used as a playable character in your Unreal game.

Special Features

This book contains a series of in-depth tutorials, outlining each major concept introduced. To assist you in following these tutorials, the book includes a CD packed with all the necessary assets, the Unreal Runtime Engine demo, and Maya Personal Learning Edition 5.0. The book also includes an appendix that serves as a user's guide for UnrealEd and another that lists the pertinent properties for Unreal's most important in-game assets.

Part I

The Unreal Universe

Chapter 1

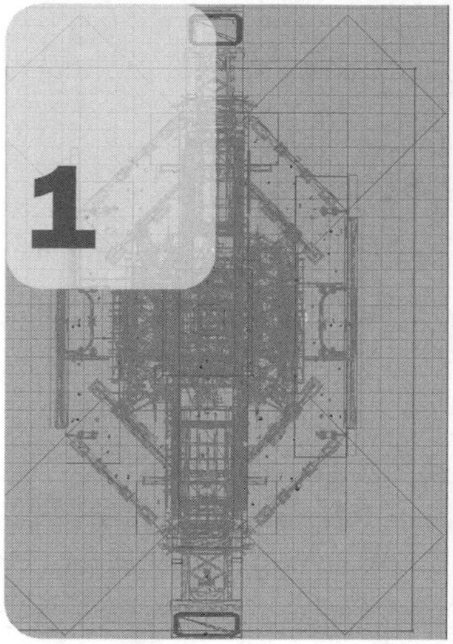

Unreal Technology: The Big Picture

This chapter is intended to give you a broad overview of Unreal Technology as a whole, with a discussion of Unreal's history, the Unreal Engine and its components, the various assets that make up a modern Unreal-based game, and how all these assets and components are brought together to give you a quality real time experience. In this chapter, you also learn about some of the tools you need to create your own content for Unreal and some general points to keep in mind when creating content. However, this chapter does not go deeply into technical details of creating assets; this topic is discussed in future chapters.

1

Unreal and Its History

The saying goes that the Roman Empire wasn't built in a day, and neither was Unreal. The following sections show a timeline of Unreal history and some of the most important moments in its development so that you can see what it took to get this far.

Date: June 1998

Event: Unreal is launched with a warm welcome from the PC gaming community. It's the first game to ever use the Unreal Engine and is arguably one of the best-looking games released at that time. The game's lush environments and beautiful graphics take gamers by storm. Who can forget that first encounter with the Skaarj? The game also had a robust multiplayer mode that could be played against artificially intelligent "bots," players controlled by the computer rather than by human players.

The game's development laid the foundation for the Unreal Engine. Its modular design allowed Epic, or its licensees, to easily customize parts of the engine without needing to rewrite the entire program. The game also made it possible for mod makers (those who edit pre-existing games) to insert their own UnrealScripts to enhance and customize their gaming experiences.

FIGURE 1.1 Unreal is released in 1998 and is an immense success.

Date: November 1999

Event: Unreal Tournament is launched on the PC and ported to the Sony PlayStation 2 and Sega Dreamcast console gaming systems. The game was originally intended to be an expansion pack for the original Unreal. Focused on multiplayer gameplay, it also offered an intense single-player gaming experience by implementing some of the most advanced bot AI ever to be used in a game. Unreal Tournament was also backward-compatible with maps from the original Unreal.

FIGURE 1.2 Unreal Tournament is released in 1999 and is ported to multiple platforms.

Date: March–July 2001

Event: The Unreal Developer Network (UDN) website goes online, giving the world a central location for finding documentation and tutorials for content creation and other aspects of the Unreal Engine. To this day, licensees and mod makers use the site regularly, and it remains one of the most respected resources for information on the Unreal Engine and its development:

`http://www.udn.epicgames.com`

UNREAL developer network

FIGURE 1.3 The UDN logo.

Date: September 2002

Event: Unreal Championship is launched on the Xbox, followed closely by Unreal Tournament 2003 on the PC. Both games focus mainly on multiplayer gameplay, with Unreal Championship being one of the flagship games for the debut of the Microsoft Xbox Live! broadband online system. Digital Extremes assists Epic with content creation for the games.

1

The new Unreal games sport a wide variety of new engine features, including the implementation of powerful particle systems, terrains, and the Karma physics engine. The game also includes Matinee, an embedded system for generating in-game movies and cutscenes. Finally, the revolutionary static mesh is introduced, which allows levels to be populated with more geometric detail than had ever been seen before, while maintaining extremely fast gameplay and animation frame rates.

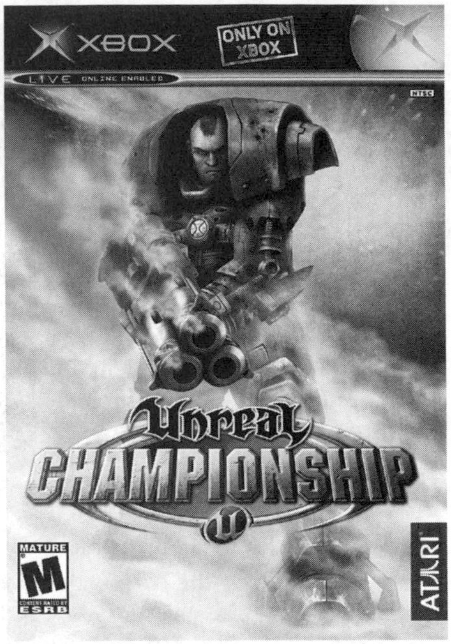

FIGURE 1.4 Unreal Championship is released for the Xbox in 2002.

Date: February 2003

Event: Unreal 2: The Awakening is launched. It's the first Unreal game to focus on single-player gaming since the release of the original, almost five years earlier. The game pushes the limits of the Unreal Engine even further, showing an unprecedented amount of onscreen detail in a fast-paced game with a deep plot and intriguing nonplayer characters (NPCs). The game also supports the use of static meshes, terrains, the Matinee movie system, the Karma physics engine, materials, and particles and was supplemented by the Golem animation system from Legend Entertainment.

FIGURE 1.5 Unreal 2: The Awakening is released in 2003.

Date: March 2004

Event: Unreal Tournament 2004 is released. This game marks yet another leap in the gaming experience that Unreal players have come to expect. With the new Onslaught game type and the introduction of vehicles, players are no longer limited to simple levels. They now have vast terrains, skies, and even outer space.

Date: The Present

Event: <Your Name Here> begins a quest into the world of game design. This date is sure to be marked as one of the most significant dates in the history of the Unreal Technology, as on this day, one of the greatest game designers ever took his or her first steps toward changing the way the world will look at gaming in the future, using the Unreal Engine as the preferred medium.

FIGURE 1.6 Unreal Tournament 2004, released in March 2004.

The Unreal Engine

This section introduces you to the components that make up the Unreal Engine. So what exactly *is* the Unreal Engine? If you were to ask a bona-fide Unreal programmer that question, you'd likely get bombarded with a barrage of technical terminology, descriptions of code, and all sorts of details that would confuse someone who had never worked with the engine. The intent of this section is to put into understandable terms precisely what the Unreal Engine and all its components are doing so that you understand how it affects and controls the many elements of your game.

Introduction to the Unreal Engine

The Unreal Engine is a system that sorts through level maps, textures, static meshes, and other artistic aspects of a game and combines them fluidly into a seamless, interactive masterpiece. Of course, that's a simple way to describe a complex system. Several elements compose the Unreal Engine, such as the graphics engine, the sound engine, and the physics engine, and each element functions independently of the others. All these independent systems tie into a single core engine, allowing them to work together in synchronized harmony. These separate parts, along with the core, form what's called the Unreal Engine. **FIGURE 1.7** shows how data maps to the elements of the Unreal engine.

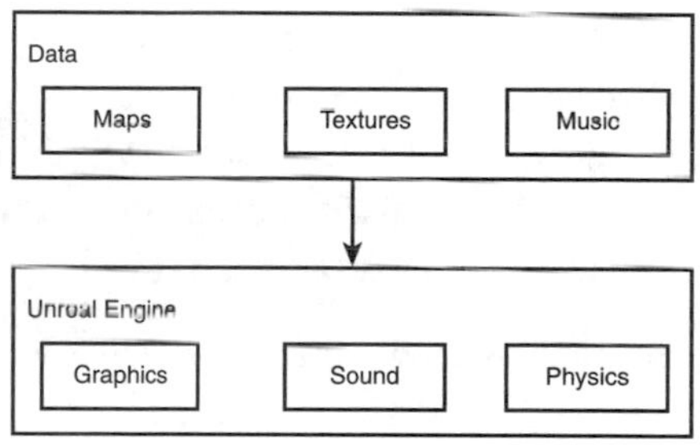

FIGURE 1.7 Unreal Engine flow.

The Components

The following subsections introduce you to each component of the Unreal Engine, starting with the graphics engine, which controls what you see, and the sound engine, which controls what you hear. From there, you learn about the Unreal Engine's physics engine, Karma, which is used to create dynamic simulations in the game based on physical laws such as gravity, friction, and more. Next is the input manager, which reads all input from the user or player and translates it into commands sent to the core and to the Unreal Engine's network infrastructure.

The Graphics Engine

The *graphics engine* in the Unreal Engine is the component that makes it possible to see what's going on in the game. It's responsible for what you actually see on your computer screen or television. In Unreal Tournament 2004, as a game character is running across a room blasting everything in sight, it's the graphics engine that produces the images of what the character is doing in its surrounding environment. Without the graphics engine, that same scene would simply exist as a series of attributes, such as the character's health, location in the world, any items he or she might be carrying, and more. In their simplest form, these values are just a list of numbers. Naturally, lists of numbers could make for an uninteresting game. Fortunately, the graphics engine is capable of reading all this data and instantly translating it into something you can actually see onscreen, allowing for real-time visualization (see **FIGURE 1.8**).

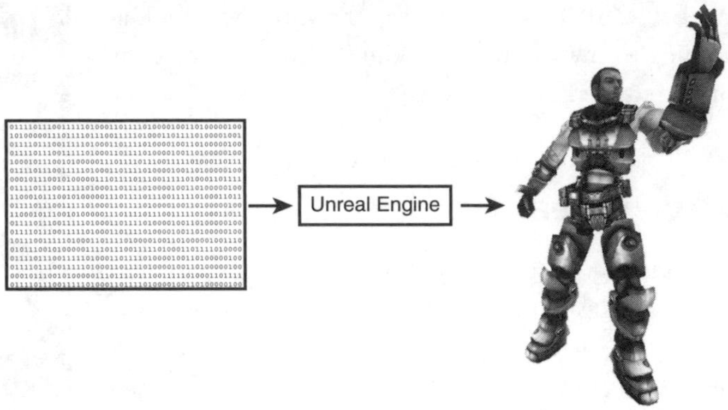

Figure 1.8 The graphics engine transforms data into images.

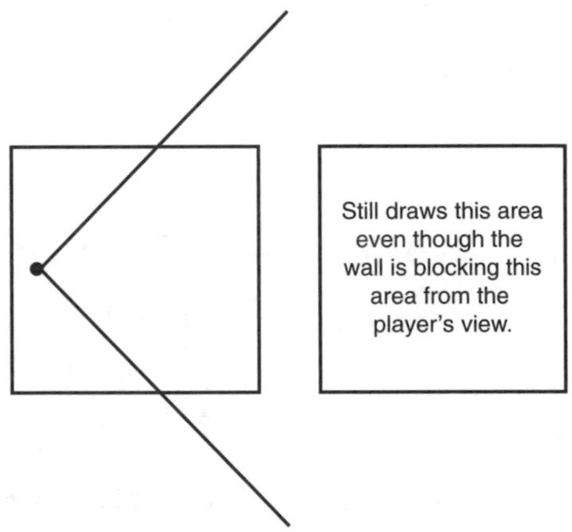

FIGURE 1.9 Draw calculation.

Beyond just governing what's displayed onscreen, the graphics engine is also responsible for a wide variety of behind-the-scenes tasks for controlling what aspects of a level the engine is rendering (calculating). You might be surprised to know that the graphics engine is also responsible for more than what you see; it handles elements that other objects occlude, or hide.

By default, the graphics engine renders everything within a player's field of view. Say, for example, that you have a map composed of two rooms, which are separated by a wall with no doors or windows. Now say that a player is looking directly at the wall that divides these rooms. Obviously, players cannot see the next room because the wall is blocking their view, but is the graphics engine still rendering that second room? The answer is yes. In fact, the graphics engine is rendering all polygons that would fall in the field of view, except for polygons that would form the *back* of the wall you're looking at (see **FIGURE 1.9**). This rendering is based on Binary Space Partition (BSP) calculation, which is covered in detail in Chapter 4, "Advanced Brush Techniques."

Naturally, because the graphics engine, by default, renders occluded objects, your levels would become noticeably slower and less efficient as they become larger and more detailed. Level designers can remedy this problem by implementing a set of techniques that tell the graphics engine when to render various parts of the level and when to exclude them. These techniques are covered in detail in Chapter 15, "Level Optimization (Zoning) and Distribution."

The Sound Engine

As game technology has progressed, sounds have played a more vital role in defining the game experience. Gone are the days when sounds were a series of electronic beeps backed up by simple MIDI music. Today, players are so accustomed to hearing every aural nuance of a game that it's easy to take full-fledged sound for granted. Games are filled to the brim with high-quality sound effects, from action/reaction sounds, such as bullets firing, rockets exploding, and tires screeching, to ambient noises, such as falling rain, humming motors, and howling wind. Modern games also incorporate a soundtrack of beautifully orchestrated music, which can accentuate a particular mood during parts of a game.

The *sound engine* is what makes all these effects possible. The engine combines all your built-in sound effects and ambient noises, and then re-creates them as accurately as possible with the audio hardware installed on your computer. The best part is that the sound engine is so well designed that it has become one of the simplest aspects of the Unreal Engine. All you have to do is create your sound effects, compose your music, set a few properties, and then tell the engine where and when to play your sound.

The Physics Engine

One of the most exciting ways to add realism to a game is by simulating real-world physics. In the real world, when you push an object and knock it over, you see a reaction based on the laws of physics. The object bounces and rolls, or even knocks something else over. You can simulate these events in Unreal through the *physics engine*, which handles all calculations for real-time physics.

Unreal's native physics engine, called *Karma* or sometimes the *Math Engine*, is what handles these reactionary forces in the game. It enables you to create falling objects that respond accurately on impact; reactive obstacles, such as springboards and swinging lights; and even the rag-doll effects you see when a player dies in the game (see **FIGURE 1.10**). Beyond

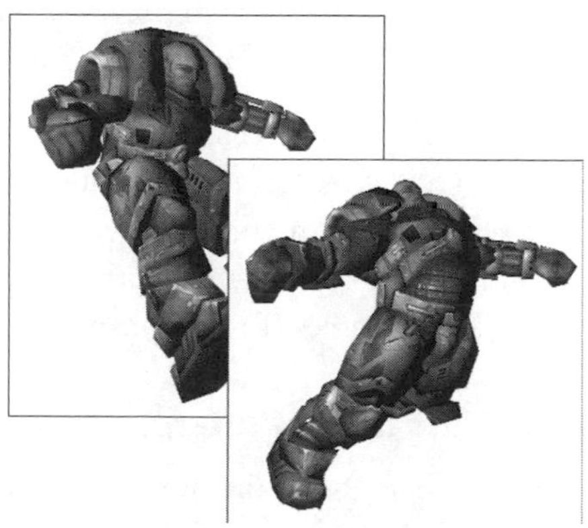

FIGURE 1.10 Rag dolls responding to motion from an outside force.

this, it also controls the physics behind any vehicle in the game, automating how its shocks function or even how its tires slide.

The Input Manager

To actually have a game, you need some sort of interaction. If you can't control what you see onscreen, you might as well be watching television. This is where the *input manager* comes in. This engine component reads all input from the mouse, the keyboard, the joystick, the gamepad, and so forth. It then communicates information to other parts of the system that change a corresponding aspect of the game. For example, when you move the mouse to the left, your player looks to the left; if you click the left mouse button, the player fires its weapon.

What the input manager actually does is set a series of properties that are sent to the graphics engine, which then reflects this information to the user by displaying different parts of the level, making it possible to see a weapon's trajectory, for example. At the same time, information is also sent to the sound engine to play the correct sound effect when, for example, a weapon is fired. All this communication between the input manager and the other components happens quickly—so quickly, in fact, that you almost never notice a delay. The input manager is so flexible that game developers can alter it completely so that they have full control over what types of properties are changed through a player's input devices.

Network Infrastructure

The Unreal Engine includes a well-developed *network infrastructure* that facilitates a client-server relationship. During networked gameplay, client computers (usually the players' computers) communicate with another computer that acts as a server. This computer can be a dedicated server, which means the host computer isn't actually being used to play the game, or it can be a server computer that's also running a client, which allows someone at the host machine to join the game. As you play the game, only the information needed to represent your characters' activities and the immediate response of their environment is sent across the network, keeping network speeds and game response times running at optimum levels.

Over the years, this system has been optimized so that it still runs impressively fast, even on slower networks. It also allows tremendous amounts of data to be exchanged quickly between clients and the server to help accommodate newer games with more players. The infrastructure can also be customized to facilitate network play of many types of games, including first-person shooters, role-playing games (RPGs), racing games, or anything else you might want to create.

The UnrealScript Interpreter

UnrealScript, one of the most revolutionary aspects of the Unreal Engine, is an object-oriented programming language similar in syntax to C++ that provides access to almost every component of the Unreal Engine. UnrealScript makes additions and customizations to the Unreal Engine easy. The best part of the language, however, is that despite its ease of use, it retains immense power, so few, if any, modifications could be made to the engine's actual source code that couldn't be done with UnrealScript (see **FIGURE 1.11**).

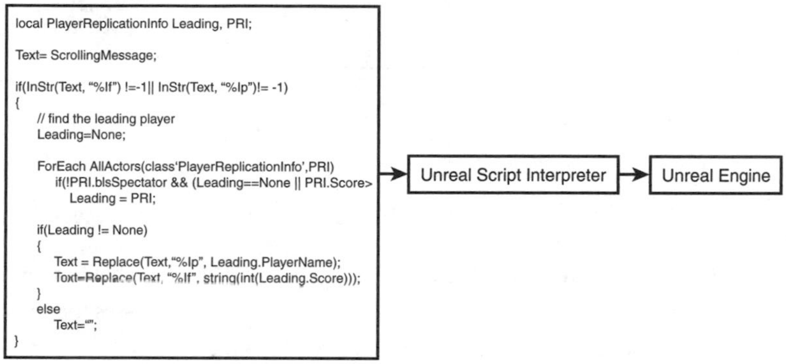

local PlayerReplicationInfo Leading, PRI;
Text= ScrollingMessage;
if(InStr(Text, "%lf") !=-1|| InStr(Text, "%lp")!= -1)
{
// find the leading player
Leading=None;
ForEach AllActors(class'PlayerReplicationInfo',PRI)
if(!PRI.bIsSpectator && (Leading==None || PRI.Score>
Leading = PRI;
if(Leading != None)
{
Text = Replace(Text,"%lp", Leading.PlayerName);
Text=Replace(Text, "%lf", string(int(Leading.Score)));
}
else
Text="";
}
Unreal Script Interpreter
Unreal Engine

FIGURE 1.11 UnrealScript interpreter.

Overview of Component Interaction

Now that you know the components of the Unreal Engine, you're ready to take a brief look at what's going on under the hood of the Unreal Engine, so to speak.

At the core of most games you'll find what's referred to as a *game loop*. This part of the program constantly repeats itself throughout the game to ensure that everything is updated correctly (see **FIGURE 1.12**). Within this loop, checks (such as yes or no questions) are made to see whether a player has jumped, fired his weapon, lost his health, and so forth. In addition to these checks, many game loops include common tasks, such as redrawing the screen, playing sounds, or even sending and receiving information across the network. Game loops give you a linear-based system with a simple series of checks, which means every aspect has the same priority so that all tasks are always addressed in the same order the programmers originally set.

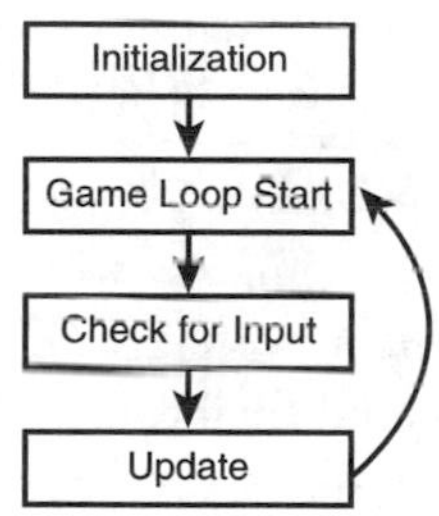

FIGURE 1.12 The game loop.

The Unreal Engine uses a game loop, but is also an event-driven system. This means the game contains a queue that holds a series of events, which components of the engine need to address. These events are created by many important game elements, such as input from a player when a key is pressed or when engine components try to communicate with one another. So how does the core engine know the order in which to handle these events? Each event is given a certain priority, and events with higher priorities are processed before events with lower priorities.

1

To make the event process more clear, take a look at an example. At any particular moment during gameplay, the queue is filled with a variety of different events and tasks, each with different priority levels. When a player shoots a gun, events are generated, and several tasks, such as shooting a projectile and playing a gunfire sound, are sent into the queue. Of these tasks, firing a projectile obviously has the higher priority because it clearly affects gameplay. The gunfire sound, in contrast, hardly affects gameplay at all. In fact, if the sound weren't played, no other parts of the game would be affected. Therefore, the Unreal Engine fires the projectile first and then plays the sound. The central idea of an event-based system is that the engine processes the most critical activities before going on to the less important ones (see **FIGURE 1.13**).

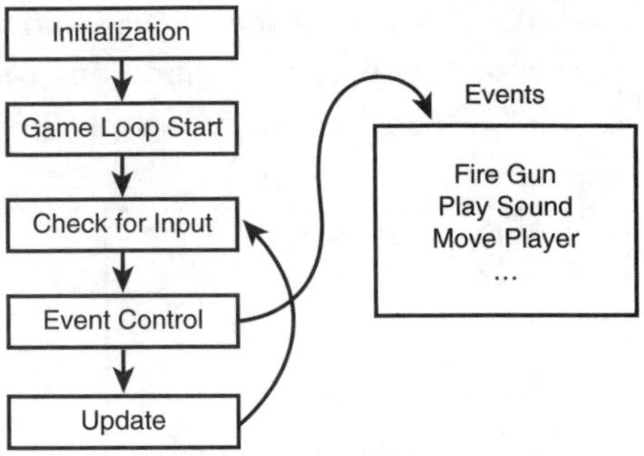

FIGURE 1.13 Event-based system.

The Components in Action

Now that you have an understanding of this event-based system, it's time to take a look at what all these components are doing while the game is running. When you start Unreal, all the individual components are *initialized*. It's much like the process of starting your car and letting it warm up; the car hasn't gone anywhere yet, but it's ready for the driver to put it in gear, press the gas pedal, or any other event a car can handle. In the case of Unreal, initialization is where the game usually begins.

FIGURE 1.14 shows how different parts of the engine communicate with the engine core. At startup, the engine core has initialized the graphics engine, the sound engine, the physics engine, and the UnrealScript interpreter. As this happens, the core engine begins sending commands to each component. Some components, such as the physics engine, even send responses back to the engine core so that everything is kept in sync. Now that all the engine components have been initialized, the user interface is displayed and the engine awaits input from the user.

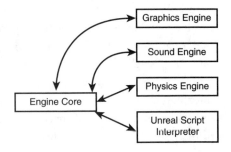

FIGURE 1.14 Component interaction.

When the user starts a game, a level is loaded that contains several types of assets, such as textures, sounds, static meshes, animations, and scripts. The information for each asset is routed to the proper engine component. Then, when gameplay begins, the message queue comes alive with hundreds of events. At this point, the core starts to route information between the different components for handling, based on the priority of each event sent to the queue. The script interpreter, for example, takes all the scripts needed in the level, processes them when required, and, in turn, sends that information to the engine core, so appropriate commands can then be sent to the other system components.

The following is a numerical listing of this process, with each step written both in general terms and in language describing how it would apply to Unreal Tournament 2004:

1. Game initialization (starting Unreal Tournament 2004)
   a. The core engine initializes all system components.
   b. Components begin to send information back to the core for synchronization.
   c. Game is ready for user input.
2. Game launch (choosing and starting a level)
   a. A map is loaded, containing all game assets and their corresponding properties.
   b. Each asset's information is routed to its respective engine component. For example, sounds are sent to the sound engine and textures to the graphics engine.
3. Gameplay (artistic use of the Shock Rifle, Flak Cannon, Rocket Launcher, and so on)
   a. Each component sends events and tasks to the message queue.
   b. Unreal's game loop runs, evaluating each event by priority and performing the tasks with highest priority first.

Engineering New Worlds with the Unreal Engine

Now that you know what components go into actually running the game and what happens to them as the game runs, you should have a better understanding of exactly how the Unreal Engine works. From here, you're ready to begin creating your own virtual worlds for use in your games, mods, and other projects. Remember that the Unreal Engine is an open-ended system that can accommodate the needs of nearly any real-time project. Although, at its heart, the system has been developed for games, its power and flexibility make it a perfect tool for many tasks, including the visualization industry.

Imagine going to a meeting where you're trying to get a bid on a building contract. A competing company has brought a nice prerendered flythrough of its project. You, on the other hand, have put together a beautiful flythrough using the Unreal Engine. Your presentation can now be in two parts: a Matinee movie in which you use Unreal to play a prerecorded flythrough, and the opportunity for your potential client to use the computer to fly around the building. Which project would *you* find more impressive?

Game Assets

Nearly all the data Unreal uses is stored in a series of *packages*. You can think of a package as a collection of data, such as texture information, static meshes, animations, and so on (see **FIGURE 1.15**). Typically, packages are separated by the kind of information they contain. For example, one package holds static meshes, another package holds textures, and so forth. Keep in mind that not all game assets are stored in packages. Levels, for example, are stored in maps. In the next few sections, you take a look at some of these assets and see how the Unreal Engine uses them.

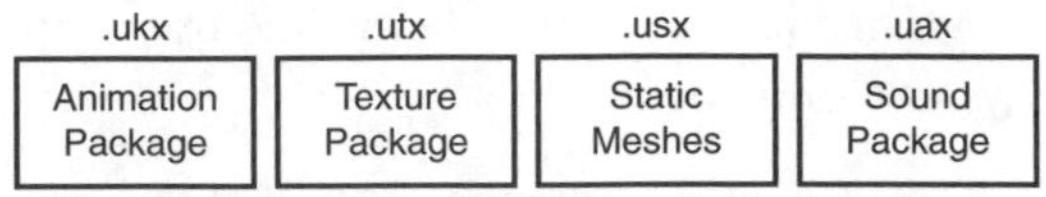

FIGURE 1.15 These are the type of assets found in packages with the standard file extensions.

> **NOTE**
>
> Although Unreal packages come with several different file extensions, the extension itself—`.ukx`, for example—doesn't control the type of data in the package. All packages are essentially stored in the same format, and the different extensions merely make it possible to determine the types of assets in each package more easily.

Maps

Maps, or levels, are the one major asset type not stored in packages. They are the environments in which your game will take place (see **FIGURE 1.16**). Technically speaking, a map is a collection of many game elements, as mentioned earlier. Artistically, however, a map is a medium you can use to evoke different feelings or moods in your players and enhance their gaming experiences. There can never be enough planning for a good map. Don't be afraid to share your ideas for a level with other members of your team or the online community. You'll definitely benefit from the experience, opinions, and ideas of others who eventually play your level.

FIGURE 1.16 A screenshot of the map Gael from Unreal Tournament 2004.

A map contains many elements, or *assets*, all of which are necessary to convey the visual effect you want and to make sure your map is both playable and enjoyable. Some of these elements include textures to "color" the surfaces of your level, static meshes to add the major physical detail, and sound effects, including ambient noises (see **FIGURE 1.17**). The map inserts these assets into your level by referencing them from their corresponding packages. For example, if you delete a texture package that a specific map uses, those textures don't appear the next time the map is played.

Textures

Textures come in packages that, by default, are denoted by the extension `.utx`. You can think of textures as "paint" or "stickers" that cover the surfaces in your maps (see **FIGURE 1.18**). Textures are generated in an external software package, such as Photoshop or UPaint. You can get textures from a variety of sources: They can be created from scratch, retrieved from a digital photograph, or acquired with a scanner. For example, say you need a carpet texture for the floor of your map. You could draw one, you could take a snapshot of one with your digital camera, or you could even place a piece of carpeting on a flatbed scanner.

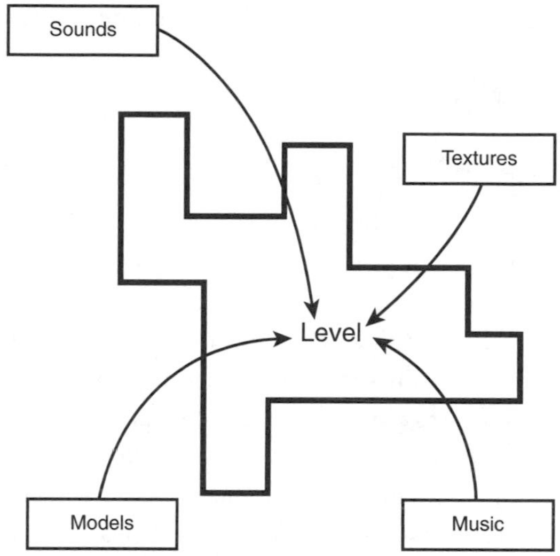

FIGURE 1.17 Assets used in a level.

FIGURE 1.18 Different kinds of textures, one generated in Photoshop and the other taken from a digital camera.

Sounds

Like textures, *sounds* are created in an external software application or might come from audio files you already have. Sounds in a map are played in response to specific events in your level, such as firing a weapon or opening a door. Some sounds, such as ambient noises, play when a character is within a certain range. The sounds included with most Unreal Engine–based games are stored in a package with the extension `.uax`.

Don't forget to consider music when developing sounds for your map. Modern games are cinematic and reflect much of the movie-going experience. You can use music to create a feeling of

1

suspense, intensity, dread, victory, and much more. Although music might not be necessary for what you have in mind, a musical score can definitely add drama and excitement to just about any game or project.

Static Meshes

Static meshes are highly optimized polygonal models imported into your game from external 3D packages, such as Maya or 3ds max. They enable you to create numerous instances of a single polygonal mesh in your maps, with virtually no more overhead (frame rate loss) than if you had inserted only a single copy. For example, a map with 50 copies of a static mesh would run just as fast as another map that only had one copy. Your maps can include any kind of object you need—chairs, shelves, doors, stairs, pictures, and so on. In modern games, static meshes are also used for larger objects, such as sections of buildings, and stationary vehicles, such as a wrecked automobile. Static meshes are saved in packages with the file extension `.usx`. **FIGURE 1.19** demonstrates how computer performance drops with the increase of static meshes in your level.

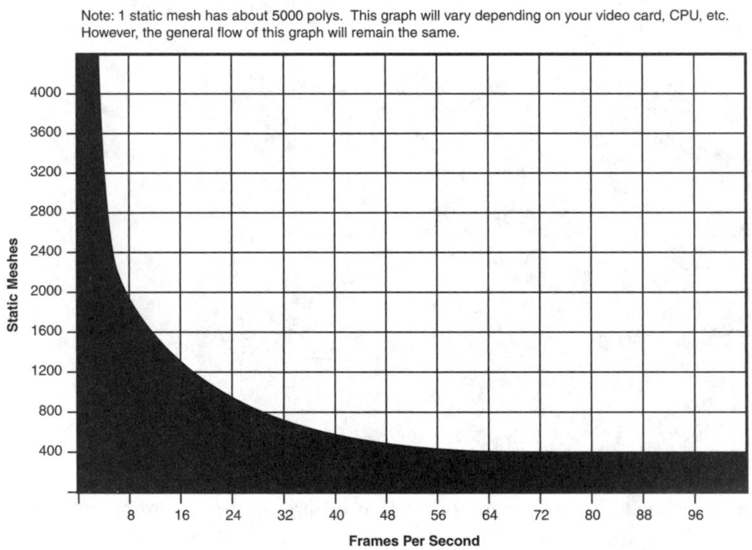

FIGURE 1.19 Performance graph.

Static meshes play a vital role in game creation, as they are the main source of physical detail. In fact, many maps in modern Unreal Engine–based games, such as Unreal Tournament 2004, would look quite barren if you removed all the static meshes. However, you must remember that static meshes are intended to be instanced, or copied, numerous times throughout your map. Therefore, if you constructed a map with thousands of different static meshes, you would quickly lose the benefit of their architecture. In this situation, it's best to consider static meshes as a decoration for elements that typically appear several times in your map.

Animation Packages

Animation packages, denoted with a `.ukx` file extension, store information for all animated assets in Unreal. They include a wide variety of game elements, such as characters, vehicles, and weapons. Animation packages store two separate files for each of these elements: the textured model and the object's animation. The package contains these two files so that you can apply different animations to separate models. For example, in many games, several different characters move in precisely the same manner because the same animation file can be applied to many characters. Reusing animation files saves tremendous amounts of time because the number of separate animations for game characters can be huge. Many characters in UT2004 have a total of more than *80* different animations for their walking, running, jumping, swimming, and taunting animation cycles.

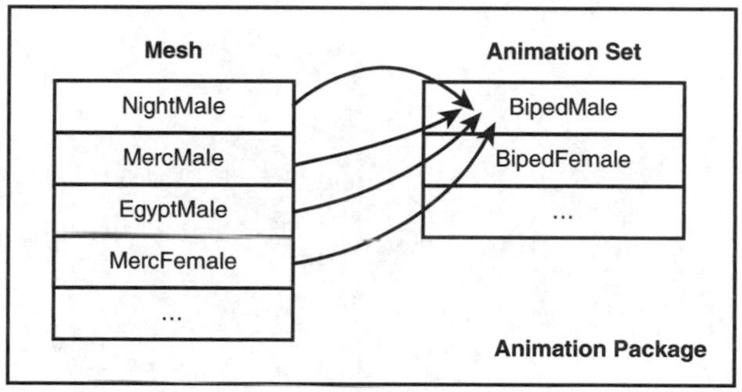

FIGURE 1.20 Animation package.

The Tools

You now know the different types of assets the Unreal Engine uses. This section discusses the tools, or software applications, you need to create these assets. As mentioned, many of the assets needed for your maps must be created with external software, and this section discusses some of these applications. Keep in mind that this discussion is not an all-inclusive list; many different applications could be used to create some of these assets. The programs discussed here are mentioned only as suggestions, but you're more than welcome to use others.

UnrealEd

UnrealEd is the primary system for creating or controlling all the content for your project. It's capable of creating maps for your projects, importing content, and managing asset packages. It's also the only program you can use to open and examine the contents of an Unreal package.

You can't use UnrealEd, however, to create 3D content, such as static meshes or character models, paint custom textures, or record sound effects. For this reason, you have to incorporate third-party software packages, such as those listed in the following sections, to generate content that might not be available with the Unreal Runtime Engine, included with this book.

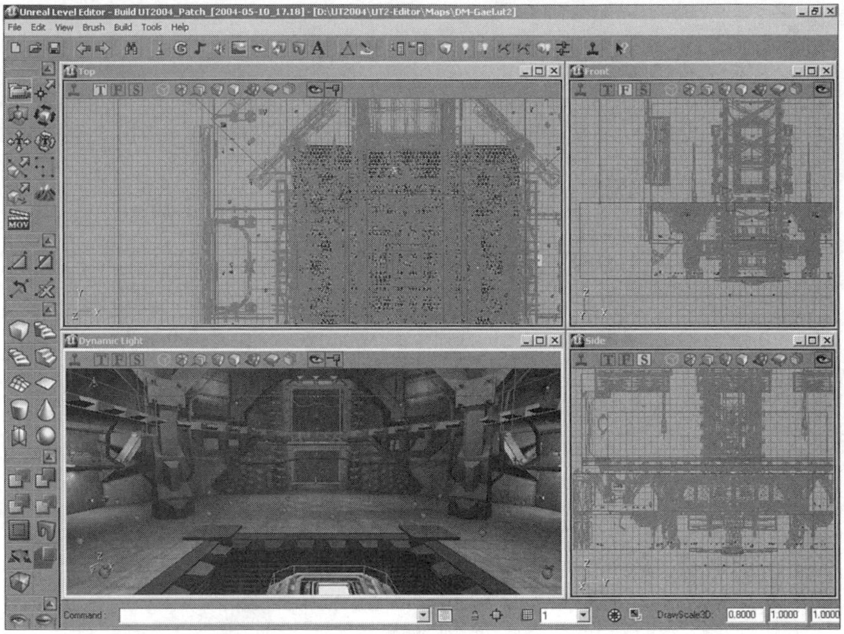

FIGURE 1.21 The UnrealEd user interface.

UCC

> **NOTE**
>
> Although UCC is an important application for generating Unreal content, much of its use involves programming and UnrealScript. As such, it's not covered in this book.

The *Unreal execution environment* (*UCC*) is a command-line program that allows for low-level package editing. With it, you can change package settings that are unavailable in UnrealEd, such as whether data in the package can be downloaded from server to client. It's capable of compressing and decompressing files, compiling packages, exporting data from packages, and many more tasks. Its most common function is compiling UnrealScript.

3D Applications

For just about any project, game-related or otherwise, you need a 3D application of some sort to create custom content. A wide variety of 3D applications, from many different vendors, are on the market. Maya, from Alias, and 3ds max, from Discreet, are two of the most popular applications for 3D game content development. You can find out more about these programs and download trial versions at `www.alias.com` and `www.discreet.com`.

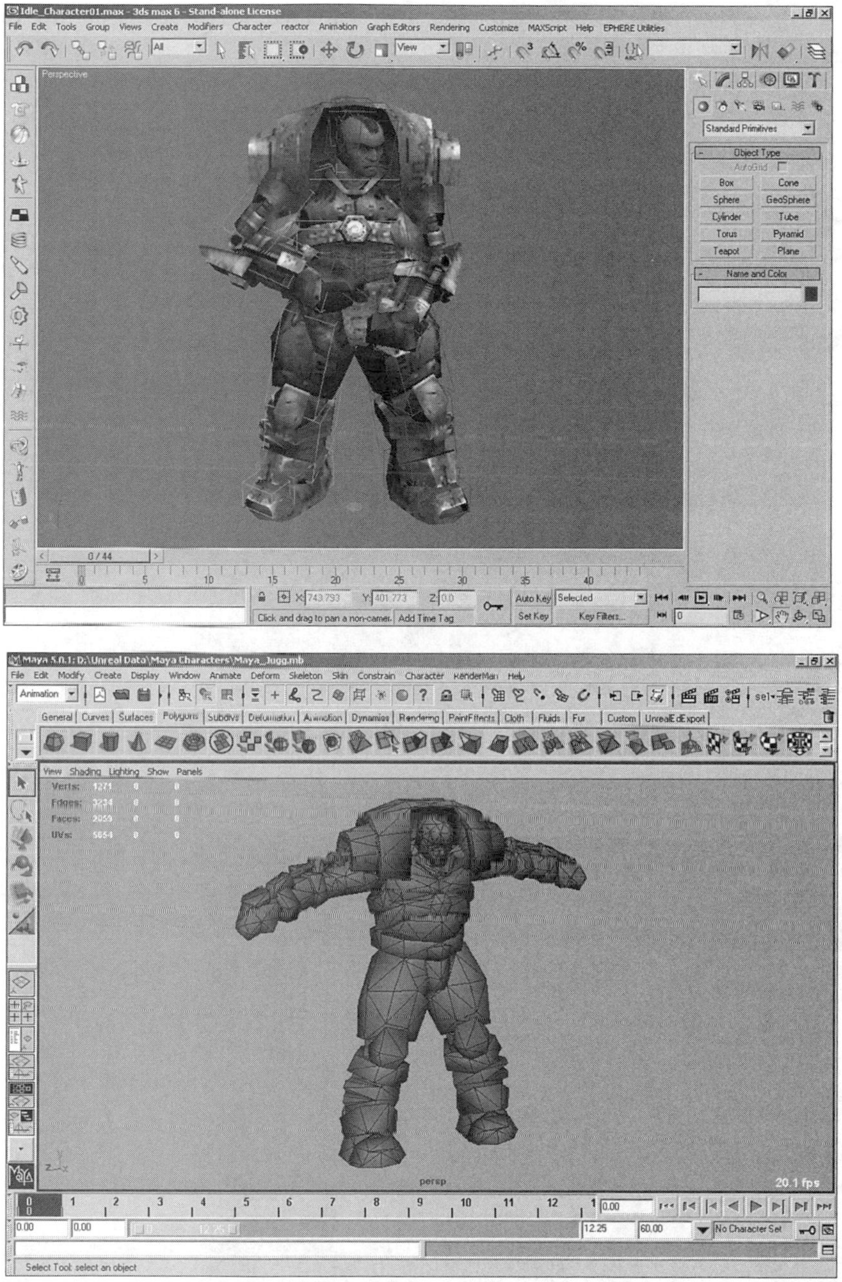

FIGURE 1.22 3D applications.

Using a 3D application can be difficult at first. If you need help, you can find two excellent sources of online training at `www.3Dbuzz.com` and `www.MasteringUnreal.com`. At these sites, you can find a wide variety of *free* downloadable tutorials for many of today's hottest 3D applications, including Maya and 3ds max.

FIGURE 1.23 Online training websites.

Paint Programs

> **NOTE**
>
> **No matter what 3D application you go for, make sure you can find the correct plug-ins to export your data into a format that UnrealEd can read.**

Games such as UT2004 include a robust library of texture packages, but eventually you'll probably want to create your own. To do this, you need to use a separate 2D paint program, such as Adobe Photoshop or Corel Painter. Both applications give you a wide range of flexibility when designing the look of your game assets. You might also need to use a 3D paint application, such as Deep Paint 3D or Deep Character by Right Hemisphere. A special Unreal-based version of Deep Character, known as *UPaint*, is included with UT2004. With these programs, you can import a 3D model so that you can paint directly on its surface.

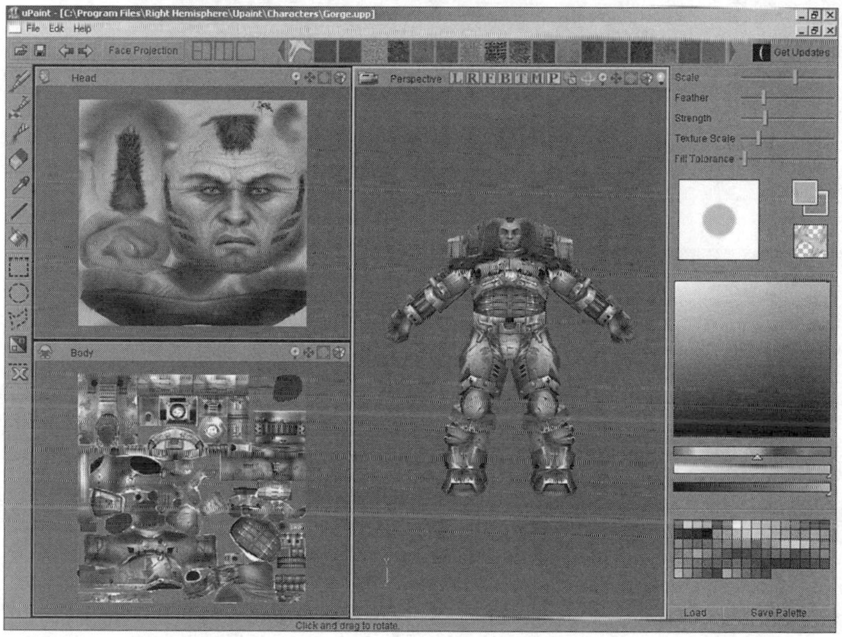

FIGURE 1.24 **The UPaint user interface.**

Sound Programs

Because you can't record audio in UnrealEd, you need an external sound composition program to produce your own sound effects or music for your games. Many different programs enable you to do this, such as Sonic Foundry's Sound Forge and Twelve Tone Systems' Cakewalk. When choosing a program, keep in mind that you need to be able to edit the sound's waveform so that you can remove any slight pauses that happen before a sound effect and any dead time after the audio in the file. Also, remember that Unreal accepts only WAV (`.wav`) files for sound effects and OGG Vorbis (`.ogg`) files for music.

1

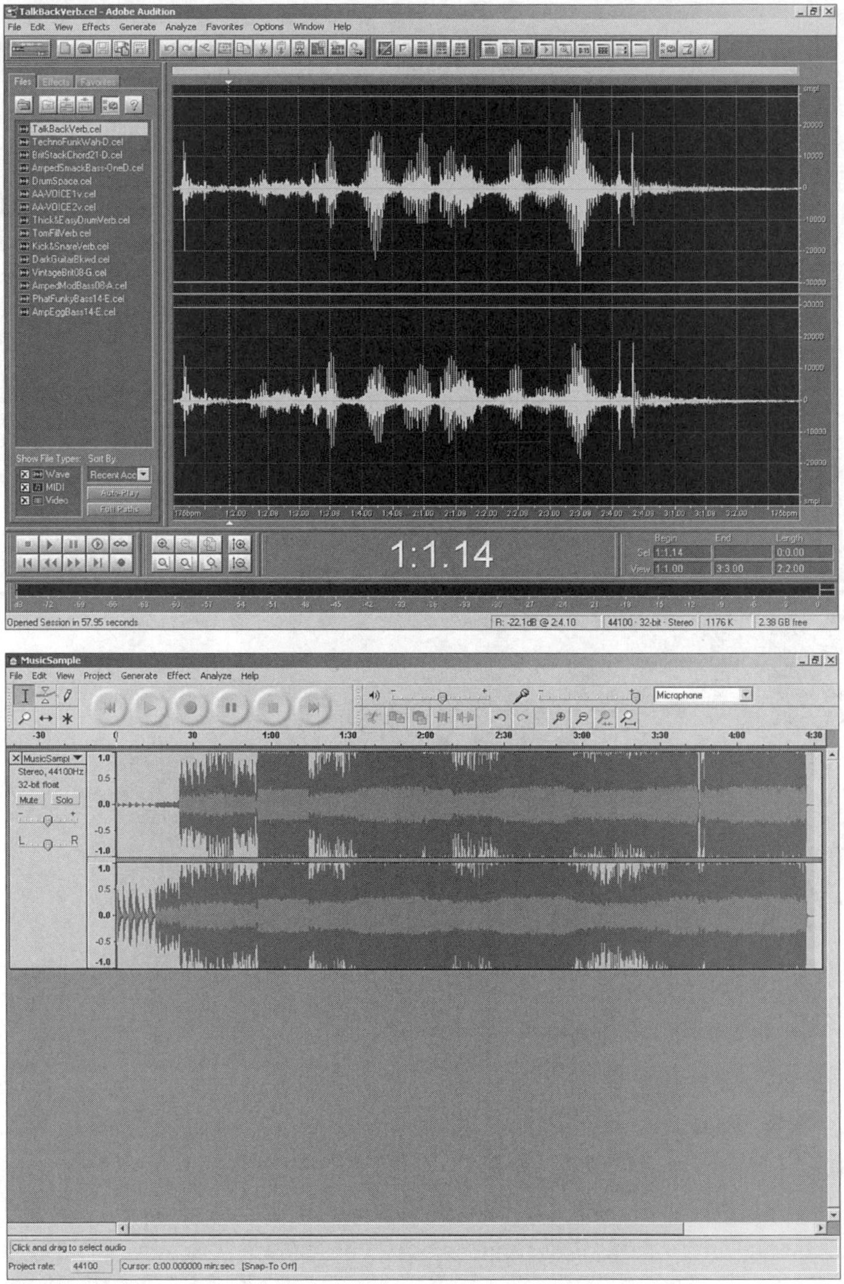

FIGURE 1.25 Sound programs.

Summary

You should now have a better idea of what's involved in creating a project using the Unreal Engine. You have learned how Unreal has developed and grown, what the Unreal Engine is, what components it encompasses, and how it works. You have also seen the many assets that are needed when creating real-time content for Unreal and some of the tools you need when generating these assets.

At this point, you're probably eager to start creating your own content. Before you do that, however, you need to review some guidelines for taking on any large-scale project involving the Unreal Engine. Chapter 2 introduces the fundamental concepts behind game development and offers some strategies to make your project run more smoothly and come together more quickly.

Chapter 2

The Process of Game Development

At this point, you should have a good idea of what components and assets you need to produce for your game or project. So now you might be asking "How do I go about acquiring all this new content?" In that respect, you're lucky because this book is designed to tell you how to construct each major asset to complete your game. However, even after you have learned how to produce all your material, you might still ask yourself the infinitely more difficult question "Where do I begin?"

This chapter presents a basic schedule and planning system for game content development. You are more than welcome to use it as a framework for your development process, or you can design your own based on your specific needs and your project's requirements. Much of what's presented in this chapter is designed for first-time developers who might need some guidance in developing their game. Everyone has a different workflow, so be sure to use the methods that work best for you, especially if you already have experience in the field of game development.

Building Your Foundation: Before Production

You need to consider many factors before you jump into game development. If you're a gamer, try to think of the number of people you've heard say "Hey, I've got a great idea for a game!" Sometimes, the ideas really are good. You might have heard one or two that would make successful games. Perhaps you've even had such an idea yourself.

Just thinking of a good idea, however, is not enough in the game development world. The best ideas out there will probably never see the light of day. What you need is a detailed plan of action in which you've considered all the possibilities and pitfalls you might encounter throughout the course of the project. Creating this plan can seem overwhelming at first, but with enough time, effort, and planning, just about anything can be accomplished in the game world.

In the following sections, you get a taste of some guidelines you need to keep in mind to turn a good idea for a game or project into a reality. The sections in this chapter are designed to guide inexperienced game developers and to paint a complete picture of the game development process.

Developing Your Idea

You might want to develop your idea after you have formed a team, but usually it's better to have a solid idea and plan of attack in place when you approach prospective team members. Make sure you think your idea through to its end. The more you know about your project, the easier it is to select your team. Take into account the volume of assets you need to create versus the timeframe in which you need to finish them. This factor helps you decide how large your team needs to be. If your plan is a small-scale one that doesn't require a team, getting insight and feedback on your idea from others who understand games or game modding is still a good idea.

Your idea should be as original as possible to set it apart from other games in the genre. The game design world is a competitive environment, where new games always try to outdo the old. Game graphics have become more sophisticated, but this factor isn't always enough to attract customers. You have to come up with a way to make the game fun and playable, regardless of its graphics. Try to come up with something that hasn't been done before in a game, or at least put a new spin on a popular game element. The following example has been divided into three sections: the story, the player's perspective, and the pitch.

The Story:

Many games have some sort of plot or story to help push the action along. Even though the game doesn't yet exist, a story is an important part of your idea because it helps you determine the type of assets your game is going to need. The following paragraphs outline an opening story from a yet-to-be-developed game called Eternal Exodus: The Fall of the Creators.

Project:

Single-player first-person shooter/space flight game (some multiplayer elements)

Working Title:

Eternal Exodus: The Fall of the Creators

Plot Introduction:

It is the year 2359. Humans have destroyed their homeworld of Terra through overmining and pollution. They have since escaped to the stars and established numerous colonies across their native galaxy. They have scoured deep space in vain searching for planets as abundant in resources as their fallen home planet. As their industry devours whatever materials they find on their travels, the corporations driving those industries have become ultimately powerful, superseding or supplanting all governments and regulations. The most powerful of these corporations is the Lathius TransGalactic Corp., which holds a monopoly on all interspace travel.

From the decadence of society has risen a relatively small but quickly growing resistance movement known as Fidus Terrenus. This activist militia focuses on the belief that humanity is destined to be more than interstellar parasites and that what's happening to colonial planets is the highest atrocity. The Fidus Terrenus have been known to engage in anti-corporate activities, and most corporate governments have officially labeled them as terrorists.

During a skirmish between an FT fighter group and a Lathius deep-space gas mining fleet, a large disruption happened. Two small ships of unknown design entered the fray, quickly destroying all other craft in the engagement. One of the FT ships was able to send out a distress signal that included an incomplete scan of one of these ships.

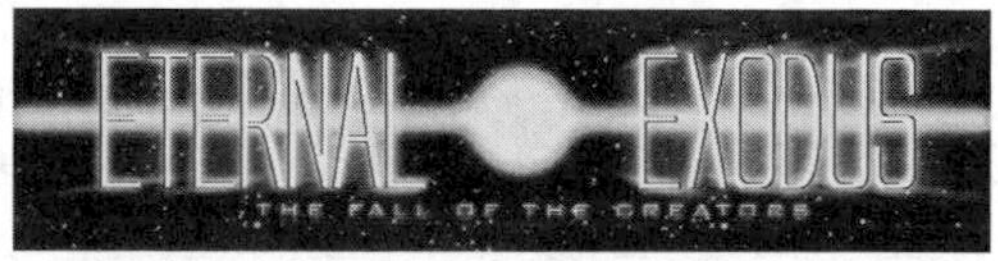

FIGURE 2.1 Eternal Exodus: Fall of the Creators.

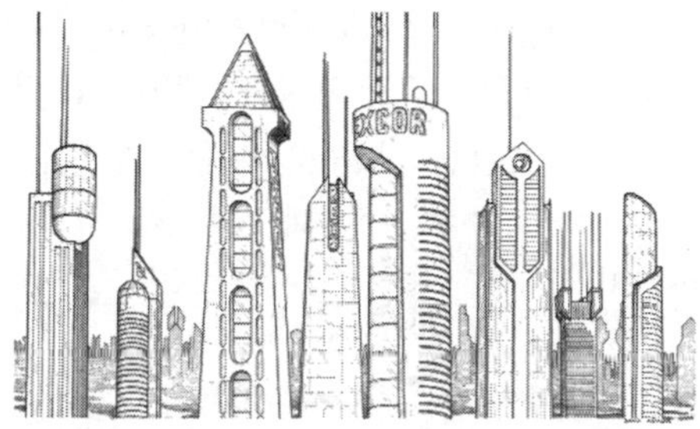

FIGURE 2.2 Corporate buildings, circa 2359.

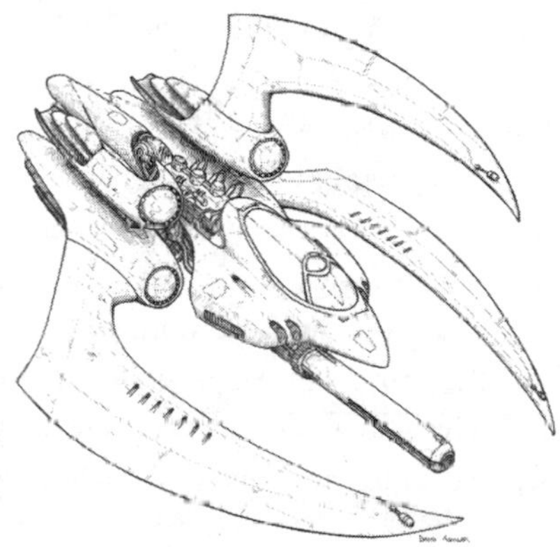

FIGURE 2.3 Lathius TransGalactic Interceptor ship.

FIGURE 2.4 Fidus Terrenus troops.

Days later, a massive signal was transmitted to virtually every Terran colony. The signal's force was so intense that only the most powerful receiving stations were able to monitor it without overloading. The transmission was translated via supercomputer within just a few hours, suggesting that the source of the transmission wanted it to be understood quickly.

The message was simple but enigmatic: "We come to put an end to that which we have begun."

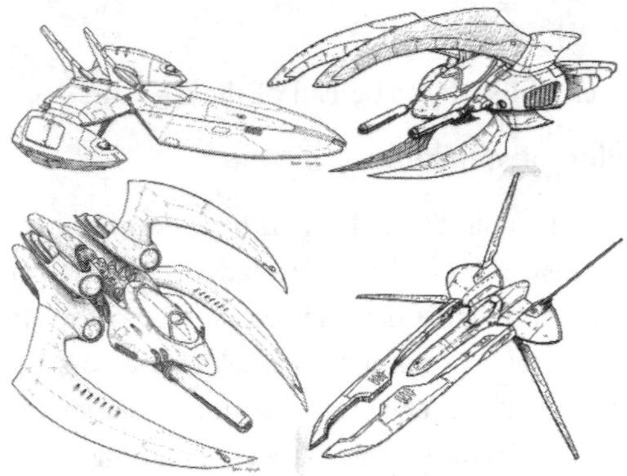

FIGURE 2.5 Ships from Lathius TransGalactic and Fidus Terrenus.

The Player's Perspective

After you have a story, drafting out how your players are exposed to the plot throughout gameplay is a good idea. This step can be a little difficult to nail down, so take your time. Also, don't be too surprised if your idea is forced to adapt to changes that arise as your game is developed. This draft doesn't need to include every single level and nuance of your game, but it should give your development staff an idea of how the game will progress. The following sections give you an overview of how players experience the story of this make-believe game.

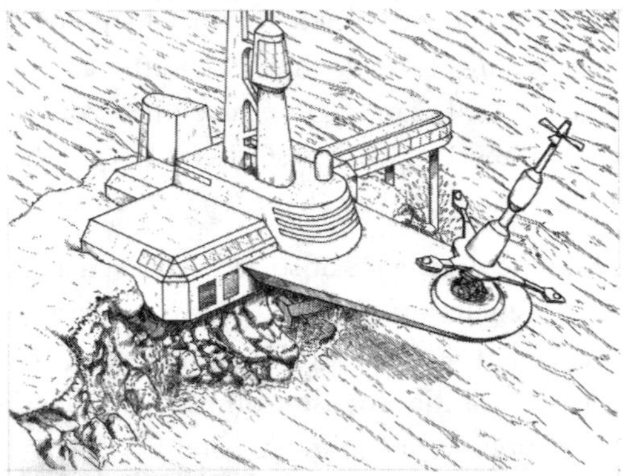

FIGURE 2.6 Receiving station where the original message was intercepted.

Overview of Game Plot from the Player's Perspective

The game begins with the player known as Jace Delaroix controlling the main character. Jace is a contracted escort fighter pilot and corporate bodyguard for some middle-to-upper management of Lathius TransGalactic. The message from the alien race, who call themselves "The Creators," was received months ago, and several of the outlying Terran colonies have been destroyed.

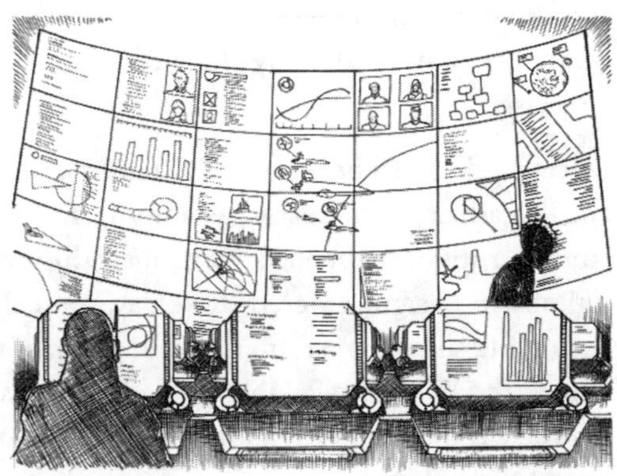

FIGURE 2.7 Control room of the receiving station.

The first few missions of the game include the player acting out the role of corporate bodyguard, in space and on foot. It's a time of turmoil, and smuggling, looting, and piracy are running rampant. Basically, players will have their hands full completing each task.

FIGURE 2.8 Player character Jace Delaroix.

Eventually, Fidus Terrenus approaches Jace, asking him to abandon the corporation. The player can accept or refuse, and this decision determines the next several missions. If the player chooses to join Fidus Terrenus, Jace will have to complete such tasks as smuggling runs and skirmish assaults against corporate establishments. If, on the other hand, the player sticks with the corporation, Jace will combat the FT, trying to cut their supply lines and end their reign of terror over the colonies.

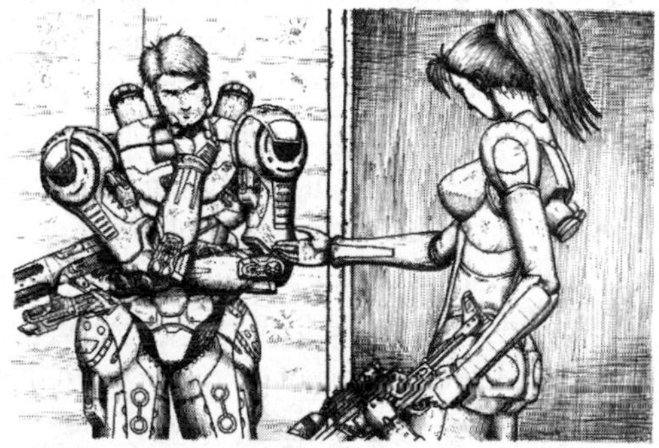

FIGURE 2.9 Jace approached by Fidus Terrenus.

Either way, the Creators' threat eventually spreads to the player's location, and a massive battle ensues between The Creators and the planet's colonial inhabitants. Battle is on foot at first and then in space, as Jace tries to escape the planet and avoid the imminent doom brought on by the Creators. The only hyperspace-capable transport belongs to Fidus Terrenus, and Jace is forced to join their ranks if he wants to survive.

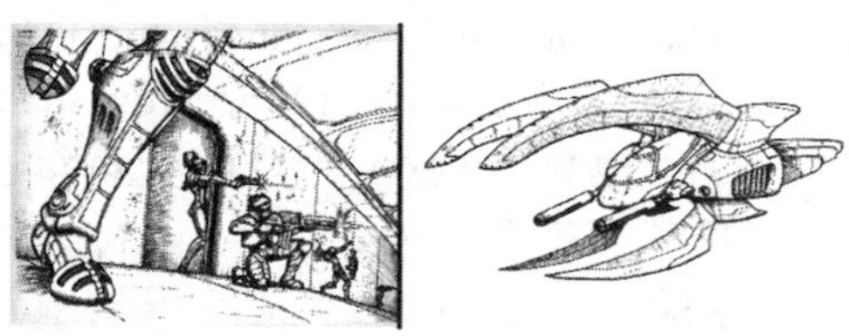

FIGURE 2.10 The battle begins, and the player is right in the middle of it.

Jace is then taken to FT headquarters, where he finds out that a plan has been put into motion to retaliate against the Creators. At first, the plan requires capturing some of the Creators' ground forces, an exceptionally difficult task, as they have a tendency to self-destruct when defeated or overcome. Jace helps with these missions and eventually leads an assault to capture a Creator ship. During these missions, Creator technology is used to create new weapons and defenses.

The FT then learns that the Creators are a race of beings who found a rare kind of planet, which soon became Terra, and spawned mankind as an experiment, losing contact soon after developing a race now known as the Egyptians. During the next several thousand years, mankind achieved space travel, destroyed its homeworld, and began to spread like a virus across the stars. Mankind became the Creators' greatest failure, so the Creators have come to destroy mankind once and for all and put an end to their "experiment."

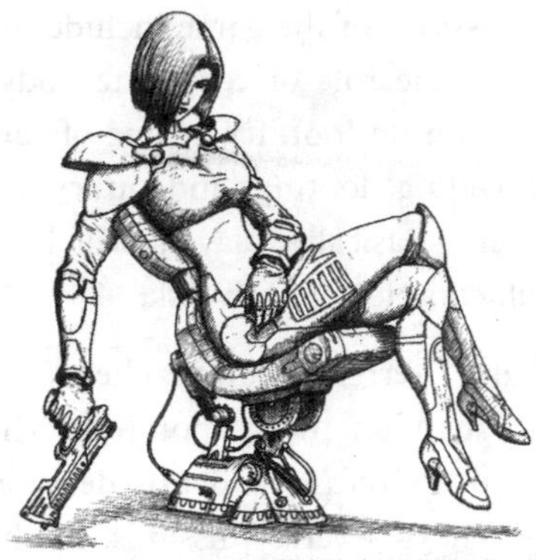

FIGURE 2.11 Jace meets the leader of Fidus Terrenus, Shelia Sorenson.

The FT also discovers that the Creators know of a planet similar to Terra, which is accessible only through an unstable wormhole. The remainder of the game consists of missions revolving around running from the Creators, getting the remnants of the FT to this planet, and destroying the wormhole, effectively removing the threat of extinction. The game ends with a sequence in which players find out that the Creators actually created the wormhole leading to this planet. This discovery suggests that the FT might have an encounter with them in the future, should the Creators choose to construct another wormhole.

FIGURE 2.12 Planet exploding as a result of the Creators' attack.

The game has multiplayer aspects as well, including ground-based skirmish levels, such as FT forces fighting Lathius battle squads. Space fights with ships are also included, which could be team based or free-for-all. Finally, the multiplayer aspect could include a cooperative mode so that at least two players could move through the single-player campaign.

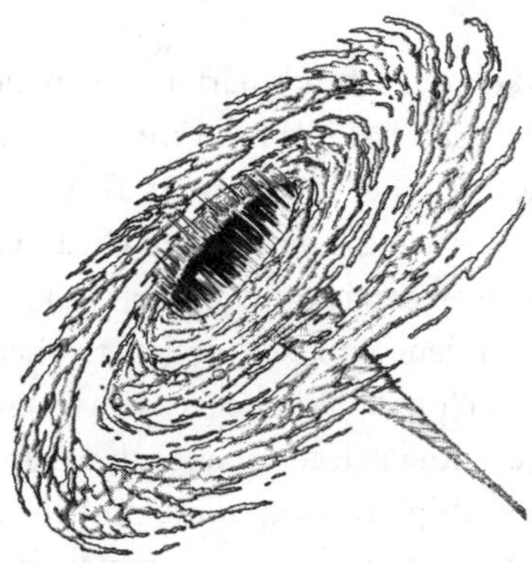

FIGURE 2.13 Space shot of wormhole.

The Pitch:

If your game or project is more than just a hobby, the pitch is the most important part of your plan. To convince others to be involved in production, you need to persuade them (at least on some level) to participate. You need to form a sales pitch to help people get as fired up about your idea as you are. Developing a pitch is also a good time to figure out whether your idea is a good one. Keep in mind that if you can't sell someone on your game's concept, you probably won't be able to sell anyone the final result. Remember that not everyone shares your ideas of what's cool or exciting. Your pitch needs to present the project in such a way that most people can see why your idea is marketable.

Gathering the Team

Gathering your team is a more important step than many people realize. If you have ever tried to work with a group of people to accomplish a goal, you know exactly how important this step is. Working with a group to finish a project is often like trying to order a pizza that satisfies everyone. You have to take into account personal schedules, emergencies, obligations, and other day-to-day stuff that pops up for people who live in the real world. The following sections explain what factors you should consider when trying to get a team together.

Know Who You Need on Your Team

Take some time to figure out exactly what kind of jobs are necessary to complete your project. It's pointless to seek out team members until you have done this step. Remember, however, that when working with a small group, often team members can fill more than one role. On the other hand, if your project has complex tasks, such as extensive modeling, you might need to sign on more than one person to complete those tasks.

The following list describes some possible positions for members of your team:

- *Concept artist*—This person provides all the drawings and sketches needed for your project, such as characters, weapons, vehicles, and map layouts. For example, the earlier sections in this chapter about the story for Eternal Exodus included several pieces of what could be considered concept art. Naturally, concept artists need to exhibit exceptional skill at creating 2D art based on ideas and descriptions. Having a good design sense, too, is a tremendous help in enhancing the final look and feel of the game's elements.

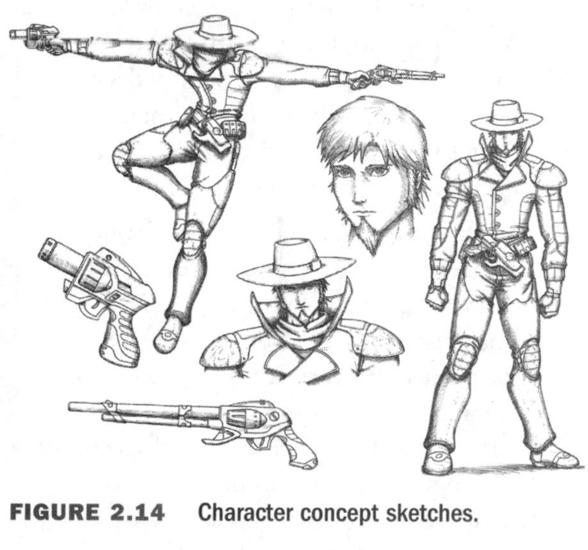

FIGURE 2.14 Character concept sketches.

- *Level designer*—You need someone on your team who knows how to design and create maps for your game or project. That's where the level designer comes in. This team member should have a thorough knowledge of UnrealEd as well as what can and cannot be done in a game map. Level designers need to have a good overall understanding of game design, such as what look is popular in today's games and what will look best for your specific idea. They also need a good aesthetic sense of interior design for placing lighting, decorating levels, and making certain that the overall look of each map is consistent throughout the game.
- *Modeler*—This team member converts the concept artist's 2D artwork into 3D assets that can be imported into your game. Typically, modelers' work needs to be relatively low in polygon count, depending on the amount of physical detail your project needs. Modelers need to be familiar with the polygonal modeling tools in your chosen 3D package and should be ready to work closely with concept artists to make sure their work follows the original designs. Modelers must also stay in close contact with level designers so that they're modeling all the necessary static meshes for each map.
- *Texture artist*—The tactile look of your game elements are left to the texture artist, who is the team member responsible for making sure your project's objects seem to be made of the correct materials and have appropriate colors and shading. Texture artists must have extensive knowledge of 2D computer art applications, such as Photoshop, and know where to find sources of real-world textures.

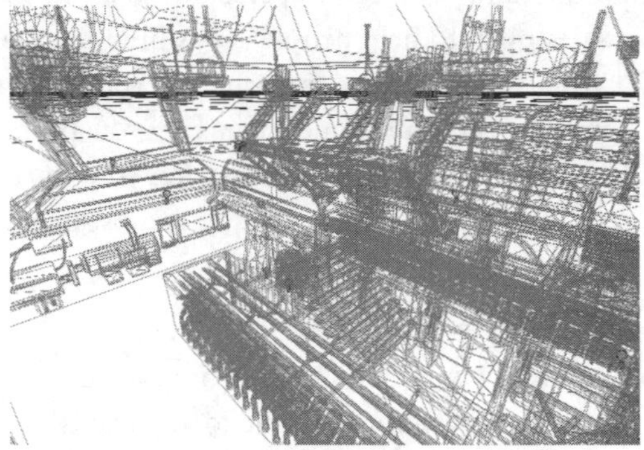

FIGURE 2.15 Wireframe image of a level.

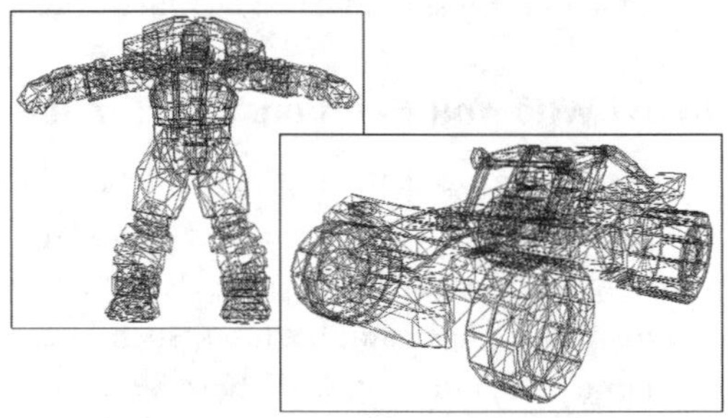

FIGURE 2.16 Vehicle and character wireframes.

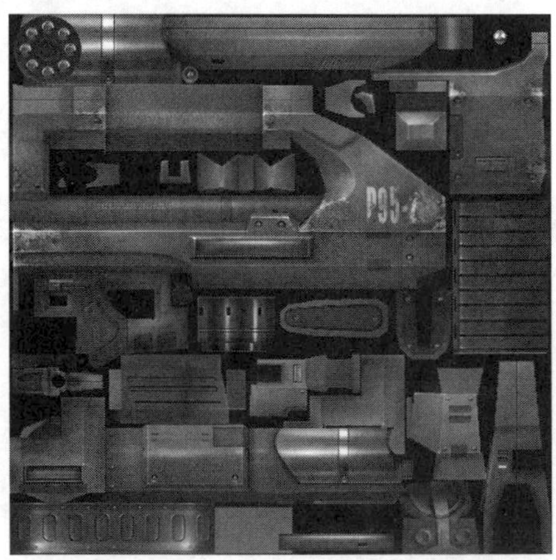

FIGURE 2.17 Assault rifle texture.

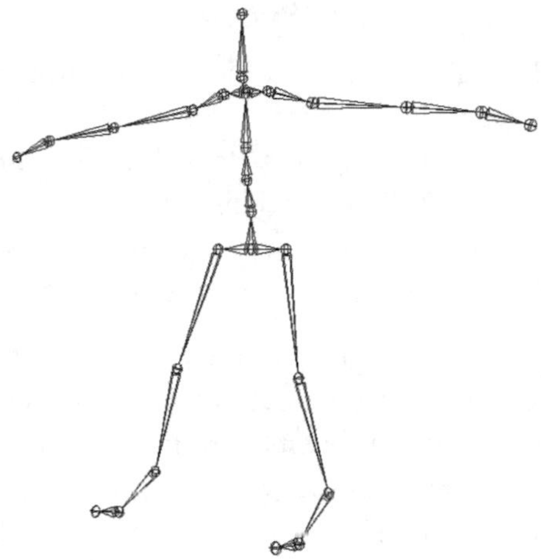

FIGURE 2.18 Bones for a game character.

- *Creature setup technician*—This team member is responsible for creating the control system that turns your character models into digital puppets that the animator can later set to move. Creature setup technicians need to have a thorough understanding of character rigging techniques in the 3D package you have decided to use for the project, such as Maya or 3ds max. Often, especially on smaller teams, this person doubles as an animator.
- *Animator*—When motion is needed, the animator is the one to call. The animator not only understands animation methods in your selected 3D animation software, but also has a thorough knowledge of the way objects move, especially their timing. If the animator isn't doing the creature setup, you should make sure the creature setup technician and animator work together closely so that there are no conflicting ideas about how control systems should be designed.
- *Programmer/coder*—This team member knows how UnrealScript works and how to use it to integrate the necessary functionality into the game or project. In most cases, programmers also understand many of the fundamental concepts that drive the Unreal Engine, so don't be afraid to go to them for advice on your idea. Good programmers should also understand the capabilities of the UnrealScript language so that they can judge the difficulty—or even the possibility—of integrating a new idea into the system.
- *Project manager*—This person doesn't usually create any of the game's elements, but still plays a vital role by making sure each part of the project is being completed on time and any internal problems are solved. In many cases, this team member might turn out to be you. If, however, you don't feel comfortable with or capable of keeping your workers on schedule, you should probably consider finding someone else for the job. If you have someone other than yourself in this position, make sure you stay in close contact with him or her throughout the project so that you're informed of the project's progress.
- *Web designer*—The web designer can be any member of the team who has experience in creating web pages, but you might want to bring in a person dedicated strictly to designing a site and keeping it maintained and updated. Get other online game community sites and forums to mention your game or project so that people check out your site and get excited about its release. Promoting your project is an important aspect of its success. An easy way to get your game noticed is to design a web page that informs the public about your project and offers updates on the progress of its development.

Choose the Right People

Find recruits who are reliable and hard-working. This advice cannot be emphasized enough. You need people for your project who are just as serious as you are about seeing it through to the end. Don't be afraid to reject potential team members who don't seem as though they can stick with the project. If you don't think someone is cut out for the project, be honest and explain why you feel that way. Your honesty might even provoke him or her into "proving you wrong" by working hard and becoming a strong member of the team.

Find people who enjoy working on jobs such as your project and are willing to dedicate time to it. Remember that a lot of people think game design is cool and will jump at the chance to get involved, but they might not realize the tremendous amount of time and work involved. You need to find team members who understand the difficulties ahead and are willing to work through them.

Know Their Capabilities

Don't add someone to the team as an animator unless you know this person can animate well. Ask to see references or past work. Depending on the professional level of your project, you might request a formal resume, demo reel, or documentation of previous related work. Ask people who have worked with your potential team member in the past so that you have a better idea what to expect of his or her work and attitude. At the very least, make sure you know whether this person is capable of the work and skill level needed for the project.

Define the Roles Clearly

Many problems that happen in a team occur when the boundaries between different team members' roles blur. This can happen when lines of authority aren't clearly drawn or when your team hasn't been thoroughly informed about the tasks for which they are responsible. Head these problems off before they occur by letting people know ahead of time who their supervisor is supposed to be, whether it's you or someone else. Don't allow team members to step on each other's toes. For instance, if your animator is spending time editing a character model that your modeler said was finalized, you have a problem that needs to be addressed immediately.

Make Sure They Are Willing to Listen

There's no point in adding a team member who doesn't listen to directions. Make certain your workers respect authority, are willing to listen to whomever is in charge of their work, and follow the instructions given to them. At the same time, don't bring in team members who can't accept criticism of their work from you or other team members. Acknowledging problems is the first step in repairing them, and if one of your workers can't tolerate being told that he or she has done something wrong, you might want to reconsider keeping this person on the project.

Compatibility Is Important

Choose team members who can work well with others and have a positive attitude toward the project. In a perfect world, even people who don't see eye-to-eye can still work together. In reality, however, this isn't always the case. If a team member's attitude is detrimental to the rest of the team, that person should go. Of course, you can't *make* all your team members like each other, but you can let popular opinion help you with decisions. For instance, if a potential team member just can't get along with most of your group, make sure this person is working closely with those who *can* tolerate him or her, or perhaps just drop this person from your team.

Honesty Is Still the Best Policy

Be honest with people from the start. If you know the schedule will be tough, let your team members know when they sign on. If team members aren't working up to your standards, tell them immediately, but remember to be fair in your criticism of their work. Fairness and honesty go a long way toward preventing conflicts. Your honesty can help your team members trust you and place more value on your opinions.

Keep Personal Schedules in Mind

Make sure you know what personal obligations your team members have. For example, if a team member must attend a weekly meeting, make sure to fit your schedule around that meeting, if possible. At the same time, remember that you can't have an effective team if everyone needs time off at different points throughout the week. Be sure you speak with your entire team and find a schedule that everyone can agree on. Note that finding a workable schedule isn't always as simple as it seems.

Compensating Team Members

Not everyone on your team can work for free. To anyone who has worked for a company or corporation, this statement seems obvious, but the subject of compensation seldom comes up with nonprofessional projects, games, or mods, as self-promotion or recognition from the game community is quite often the goal. However, you might have a team member who can't donate his or her time to your project but would be a tremendous asset to production. For example, you might know a professional programmer who could cut your coding time in half, so you might want to make that person's involvement in your project worth his while. Whatever the case, be sure that you carefully weigh costs versus benefits when compensating your team members.

Refining Your Ideas with the Team

Now that you have signed people on to help you achieve your vision, you should meet with them and gather feedback on your project. Take advantage of your increased base of ideas. There's a good chance that a team member will think of something new, and its implementation could prove worthwhile. At the same time, be open to the possibility that some aspects of your plan might not flow as well as you thought, and be willing to accept opinions and feedback on what to do. Also, meet with team members individually and hear what they have in mind for their part of the project. For example, you might want to speak with your concept artist to see how he or she envisions the characters and objects in your project, or make sure your level designer has a clear idea of your project's look.

Generate a printout or an email that covers your idea in its entirety and give each team member a copy. After they read it, encourage them to write down ideas they think would enhance the original concept. You can then share these ideas with the group and come to a consensus on whether to include them. Having these meetings is also a good way to find out whether your team is capable of completing every aspect of the project or you need to bring in additional help.

Creating a Production Schedule

Few things are more discouraging to a project's participants than falling off schedule. Keep in mind that during production, delays are bound to happen, and you and your team should be ready to strive to maintain the set schedule. During the project, remember to make the most of your project manager's skills to keep your team's progress on time.

How do you set up a workable schedule for your project? It takes close communication between you and your team members to make sure they know exactly what they need to do and the order in which to do it. They also need to let you know how fast they can complete each task. With that knowledge, it's much easier for team members to have a schedule they're able to maintain without undue pressure.

Scheduling is not a quick process, so don't rush it. Creating an individual schedule for each team member is probably a good idea; this schedule should state specific details for each task the person needs to do and outline precisely when the task should be completed. You should base this schedule on the team member's capabilities and availability.

After you have created these individual schedules, you should bring them together to form a master schedule. Team members can refer to this generalized schedule at any time to check on the progress of other departments, without having to see the specific details of each task to be completed.

Beginning Construction: During Production

Now that you know exactly what's going to happen during your production and when each task is going to take place, it's time to get to work! Production is a process that you should find fulfilling and rewarding. Nevertheless, you will probably encounter a variety of problems during your project. Although the intention of this chapter is not to cover every possible problem, a few situations that commonly arise are discussed as well as how you might go about solving or reacting to them.

Maintaining the Schedule

After production has officially begun, the schedule is of maximum importance. Make sure your project manager follows the progress of all team members or departments and keeps everyone on schedule (or as close to it as possible). Often this job can be quite challenging for your project manager, so be sure to offer advice or try to help as much as you can.

The project manager needs to keep team morale in mind, too. Remember the difference between constructive and destructive criticism: Constructive criticism points out problems yet encourages team members to keep trying to improve. Destructive criticism only shames, alienates, insults, and, in the end, drives your team members away from the project. For example, telling a team member that his recent work isn't up to his usual high standard and could improve with some extra effort goes much farther than simply calling his work "a pathetic excuse for game content." Sometimes there's a fine line between these two types of criticism, so try to keep team members' overall morale in mind when criticizing their work, but remember to stay honest at all times. This guideline is especially important for team members who are volunteering their time because only their morale and enthusiasm will keep them from leaving your team.

Dealing with Delays

Remember that delays happen. They can occur for a variety of reasons, from personal crises to software issues. The key is not to let delays bring you or your team down. Try to get back on schedule, or if that isn't possible, form a new schedule that takes your delay into account. However you deal with a delay, make sure you inform the public, regardless of the disappointment this announcement might generate. In the game development world, delays are common, but this doesn't mean they should be taken lightly. A project with zero delays is probably never going to happen, but a project with too many delays can lose the interest of an eager public.

Bringing It Together

After you have enough project assets completed, it's time to integrate them into a functional game. This task is usually the work of the level designer and the coder, as they have the clearest idea of how the Unreal Engine works. This step includes developing the functionality of game assets and making sure all assets work correctly when combined. They also need to ascertain how the game, mod, or project plays when it's finished.

The Unreal Engine is extremely powerful and capable, but you might still need it to perform tasks it doesn't do in an existing game, such as UT2004. If you're experimenting with the Unreal Engine, you'll find that even simple functionality, such as weapon firing and behavior, needs to be added to the system's code for use in your project. Your programmer needs to establish this functionality even before assets are put into place in the project.

For example, when playing a first-person shooter game, one of the simplest functions is firing a weapon. When playing, you press a button, your Shock Rifle fires an energy beam, and the beam strikes something and causes damage. This sequence sounds simple from a player's perspective, but internally, a lot of things are going on. First, an UnrealScript weapon script is making a call to a weapon-firing script, which then initiates a projectile script. As the projectile script runs, it keeps track of whether the fired projectile strikes something. If it does, it implements the damage function of the object being hit, which responds by taking note of what type of projectile just hit it and how much damage the object suffered as a result.

Sound complex? That's just a small taste of the kind of functionality needed to make a game behave properly. On top of that, there's the behavior of bots and vehicles and how physics work in your level—the list goes on and on. Don't be surprised if integration takes a while or if certain aspects need to be reworked into the project during the development process.

Testing and Acquiring Feedback

After you have integrated enough of the game that it's playable, it's a good time to begin testing. In nearly all professional projects, testing begins long before the project is completed. The process is fairly simple: Have someone play the game, knowing which parts have been completed and which haven't, and make sure those completed elements are working correctly. You can get the whole team involved in this process, or if they are too busy, call in some extra help. Usually, little effort is needed to convince a fellow gamer to play-test a new game. Testing typically comes in two phases: alpha testing and beta testing. The following sections describe each phase and explain how this testing can be used to help finish your project and maintain its quality.

Internal Testing: Alpha

Alpha testing is usually done in house, among the team members. Depending on the size of your staff, however, you might need to recruit outside testers. Your testers should be aware of how the project development process is progressing and precisely which elements have and have not been fully implemented. In most cases, you don't want to release an alpha edition of your software to the public because you're sure to get plagued with a barrage of emails from people who have no idea how your game is being created. Make sure security is tight for your alpha testing phase, and ensure that your team members aren't revealing it to the web community.

Say, for example, that someone leaked your game's alpha version onto the Internet. At this point in your production, you have integrated player mobility and weapon functionality for only 2 of your 26 weapons. In addition, none of your vehicles have been programmed completely, so trying to enter one of them causes the game to crash because of the incomplete code. When alpha testers play the game, they know ahead of time exactly what they can and cannot do, so a game crash isn't a problem for them. The general public, on the other hand, won't be able to understand your project's current limitations. If they see your incomplete game, they could start generating bad publicity for your project based on their judgment of an incomplete game.

Alpha testing is a good way to collect data, make changes to your project, tweak functionality, and streamline the various aspects of your game. Eventually, you have each element of your project fully integrated and working correctly. Then you're ready to move on to the next level, beta testing.

External Testing: Beta

Beta testing essentially works the same as alpha testing, but it's performed on an almost complete project. In most cases, you won't want to release your beta version to the public either. Your beta version will eventually become the finalized game or project, so you don't want it to be freely downloaded before the official release.

Be careful who you choose as a beta tester. Security is always a concern. Also, it's not enough for beta testers to just be gamers. They also need to be interested in helping you with your project by looking for problems that gamers could find, such as "holes" in the maps, nonfunctioning elements, and incompatibility with certain hardware or software. Also, make sure your beta testers are prompt with their feedback and aren't just taking advantage of you to play your new game.

In many cases, you should take applications for your beta testers. An application doesn't need to be formal, but it should ask potential testers what kind of experience they've had with beta testing, what kind of games they like to play, and what kind of computer they have. This last question can be important because you want to make sure your game or project is tested across a wide variety of platforms and video cards.

Remodeling and Closing: Ending Production

You've built your game and are in the middle of the final tests, getting ready to release your project. At this phase, you should be wrapping up your beta testing, getting your web designer to start promoting the launch date, and finalizing all parts of the project. But what do you do with all this beta test data and, more important, when do you quit beta testing?

What to Do with Beta Test Info

The purpose of beta testing is to get feedback from a larger base of users to find and fix any nonfunctional aspects of your game or project. Collect as much data as you can from your testers and cross-reference it with other testers to see what the biggest problems are. Use this data to fix your game's most important problems. Processing all this data is a major task, and you will likely want to get your entire team involved. In the end, much of the repair work will probably fall on the level designer and the programmer, so try to keep them from getting tied up with other tasks.

Feedback from your beta testers is vital to finishing your project. You need to know what kind of video cards your game supports, what kind of drivers are needed, and so on. This feedback can also help you discover and repair the small (but still important) problems that arise in most game development. Beta testers can often tell you where loopholes are in your project.

For instance, say your map has a section guarded by two massive creatures, and it's supposed to be difficult for players to pass. As it turns out, in a previous part of the map, players can drive a tank and, with just the right driving skills, drive it all the way to where the two monsters wait. Players can then use the tank's cannon and eradicate the monsters with practically no effort, thereby avoiding a challenge that's been carefully crafted for them. Avoiding obstacles in this manner isn't cheating, really. It's just a section of your map that needs to be tweaked. With your testers' feedback, you need to edit the map so that perhaps a large obstacle prevents the tank from being used on the monsters. You need to remedy as many of these problems as possible.

Keep in mind that your project will likely go through several beta versions. After you finish repairing many of the problems that come up, make a new version available to your testers to help narrow down the number of problems even more before the project is released.

When to Stop Beta Testing

Remember that a game can be like a work of art. Often, it's difficult to tell exactly when it's finished. When deciding whether your project is finished, you need to take a few factors into account. First, take a look at the kind of feedback coming in from your beta testers. The number of severe issues should be winding down. More important, remember your schedule! Don't go too far off schedule during the tweaking process.

Keep in mind, too, that most games (excluding console-based games for systems such as the Xbox or PlayStation) aren't released in what most gamers might consider to be a fully completed state. Despite developers' valiant efforts, bugs or glitches can often slip by the testing process and wind up in the final game. This is the reason that many games offer patches and post-release fixes for problems. You want to make sure your game is as clean as you can make it and that no errors exist that could hinder or cripple gameplay. Realistically, however, it's likely that you won't be able to think of everything before the project is released.

Finalizing and Releasing

Congratulations! You've made it through the course of production, and now it's time to make your project available to customers. This time could prove to be busy, depending on the size of your project. At this point, your game could "go gold," which means it's being manufactured on CD, or your mod or project could be made available for download to the online community. Your project is officially finished, but the work isn't over for the entire crew. You still need to support your game by creating and releasing game patches for any technical problems that come up. Plus, you want to continue promoting your game to the community!

Summary

This chapter has covered many different topics to consider before launching into a major gaming project. Although it's a given that some of your projects might be so small that you don't need to use all the techniques and ideas presented here, eventually you might want to try your hand at a project with a larger scale. Also, this chapter has been designed to give you a better idea of some of the work that goes into even the simplest games. At this point, you should have a better understanding of the hurdles that await those who want to take on a serious game development project.

Chapter 3

Creating Your First Level with UnrealEd

This chapter introduces you to UnrealEd, the development application included with Unreal Tournament 2004 (UT2004). You begin with an explanation of what UnrealEd is and an overview of the fundamental concepts that differentiate UnrealEd from other level design packages. By the end of the chapter, you should have a solid understanding of the UnrealEd user interface, the anatomy of an Unreal level, and the skills required to construct simple custom levels. **FIGURE 3.1** shows a completed Unreal level.

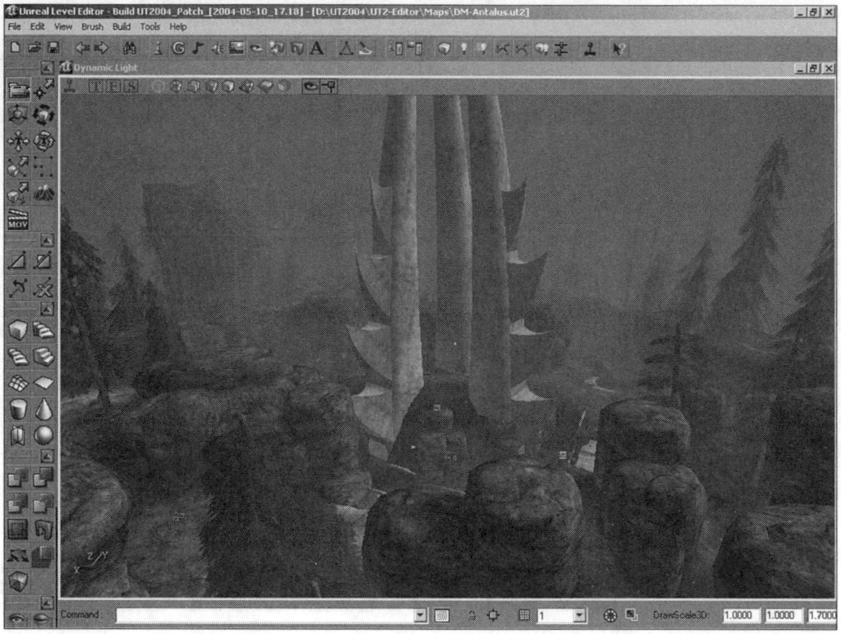

FIGURE 3.1 An Unreal level.

What Is UnrealEd?

UnrealEd is the primary application level designers use to create Unreal levels. Originally introduced in 1998, UnrealEd was the first game editor to give users real-time feedback. Its most distinguishing factor was that the Unreal Engine was directly integrated into UnrealEd, so level designers could instantly see exactly what their levels would look like during gameplay without needing to actually start the game. Before this innovation, level designers were forced to construct their levels primarily with two-dimensional views. The only three-dimensional view offered in level editors was merely an interpretation of what the level would probably look like in the game. Then the level editor converted this interpretation into a playable level, a process typically known as "compiling," just so that level designers could test it out. Compiling made level creation tedious because the process could easily take minutes, hours, or even days, in extreme cases.

The Subtractive Method of Level Creation

Another aspect of UnrealEd that separated it from the crowd was the manner in which its levels were developed. Before the introduction of UnrealEd, game levels were created in much the same way that architectural structures are constructed in the real world: creating a floor first, then adding walls, and finally installing a ceiling. Even a simple cube-shaped room required creating and placing no less than *six* polygonal objects. You could think of this method as an *additive* way of creating enclosed areas, much like building a box from sheets of plywood. This means that objects were added into the empty void of the game's world to create a level. During this process, level designers had to be extremely careful to make sure each piece was aligned correctly to remove any gaps between the wall and the floor, at a corner where two wall sections met, and so on. If these gaps remained, players could see "outside" the level, resulting in a graphics error known as the Hall of Mirrors (HOM) effect.

Levels used to be constructed this way because older games were composed of levels that existed within a void of empty space. In essence, levels floated in an infinitely open volume, like a vacuum. This is why, in some older games, it's sometimes possible to "fall off the level" and watch your character seem to fall forever as the game level recedes into the distance above your character.

The advent of Unreal changed all this by reversing the empty void situation. Instead of a game world that was an infinite vacuum, Unreal levels were created within a world of infinite solid mass. The creation method was turned into a *subtractive* one rather than the additive methods used in the past. Essentially, all Unreal levels begin by subtracting volume from the game world's solid mass, much like carving a box-shaped room out of the center of a mountain. This method has two distinct advantages over the additive approach. First, the speed of level creation increases dramatically. For instance, creating a simple cube-shaped room with the additive approach means the level designer would need to create six separate objects to serve as the floor, walls, and ceiling and make sure that all objects were perfectly aligned with each other. With Unreal's new subtractive approach, you could create the same cube-shaped room in a single step by subtracting a single cube from the game world, without worrying about how the sides are aligned.

The second advantage is the reduced risk of the HOM effect because walls require no alignment to work as a level. From the player's perspective, the difference between the two methods is zero. Think about it: The inside of a box looks exactly the same, whether it's in deep space or 20 miles underground.

The subtractive method for level creation does not, however, mean you can't add more details to your level. In UnrealEd, you can subtract matter *and* add it back in. Essentially, you always begin level creation in Unreal by subtracting the basic shapes and areas of your level from the world's infinite mass, and then adding various types of detail. For more "open range" levels, such as outdoor environments, you can begin level creation by subtracting an enormous box or cylinder, and then adding the rest of your detail, such as terrain, back in.

NOTE

Producing HOM effects is still possible in Unreal. Typically, this HOM effect happens if you create a simple box-shaped room in UnrealEd, and then add a texture containing an alpha channel (in other words, a texture with some transparency) to one wall, such as a grate-like texture. When you look at that wall during gameplay, voilà! You get a stomach-churning version of the HOM effect. Techniques for texture application are covered in "Adding Textures," later in this chapter.

Rebuilding

During level creation in UnrealEd, often you need to update the changes you make to the level's base geometry. This process is known as *rebuilding*. Essentially, rebuilding compiles all the shapes you have added and subtracted to form a playable level. At the same time, it generates the necessary light maps for your level, which creates areas of light and shadow within your level based on the location of your light Actors. Fortunately, this process is many times faster than the old-fashioned method of compiling.

So technically, what is UnrealEd doing when it rebuilds your levels? First, it checks the location of all *Binary Space Partitioning* (*BSP*; discussed in depth in Chapter 4, "Advanced Brush Techniques") brushes in the level. After calculating the position of all brushes, UnrealEd uses those brushes to construct the level's geometry. From there, it calculates the properties of lights in your level, such as location, intensity, and color, and uses them to generate light maps for the surfaces of the level's geometry. Finally, it recalculates any navigation paths that have been built for bots in your level. Light maps and lighting techniques are discussed in Chapter 7, "Lighting in Unreal." Bot paths and AI navigation are discussed in Chapter 12, "Advanced Bot/AI Navigation."

Although these tasks sound high in calculation difficulty, UnrealEd is capable of performing them quickly, even in larger levels. You can also speed up the process even more by rebuilding only the necessary aspects of your level. For example, say you've adjusted some lights in your level and need only your light maps recalculated. You can select the Rebuild Lights or even Rebuild Changed Lights option.

The Anatomy of an Unreal Level

At this point, you're probably eager to jump in and create your first level. Before you dive in, however, you need a basic understanding of the types of objects you generally find in a level. Many different objects can exist in a level, but they can be classified into one of two categories: world geometry or Actors.

World Geometry

You can think of *world geometry* as the shell of your level. World geometry is what creates the subtracted spaces inside the solid mass of the Unreal world. Without this geometry in place, only the solid mass would remain; your level would be more like a cavern that has yet to be dug out than an actual level. The subtracted space that forms your level is known as world geometry, or *constructive solid geometry* (*CSG*). The only steps needed to complete a functional level are subtracting space, adding a Player Start, and placing a light (provided you'd like to see the level, of course). Naturally, for most of your levels, you then add some mass back into the subtracted areas.

So how is world geometry actually created? Everything in a level can be classified as world geometry or an Actor. World geometry is created through a series of CSG operations using special

Actors known as BSP brushes. These brushes are used to define a specific volume that needs to be added or subtracted from the level. Although BSP brushes are *technically* classified as Actors, their close relationship to world geometry makes discussing them in this section more logical.

Several types of BSP brushes are available in UnrealEd. The two most commonly used are the additive and subtractive brushes. As their name implies, level designers use these brushes to define where mass is to be added to or subtracted from the Unreal world. For example, when you create a subtractive BSP brush, the area of that brush is removed from Unreal's solid mass. UnrealEd then processes these added and subtracted areas during rebuilding to produce world geometry. **FIGURE 3.2** shows a level with only the world geometry visible. Later in this chapter, you see how to create and use these brushes, but first, you need to learn about other Actors.

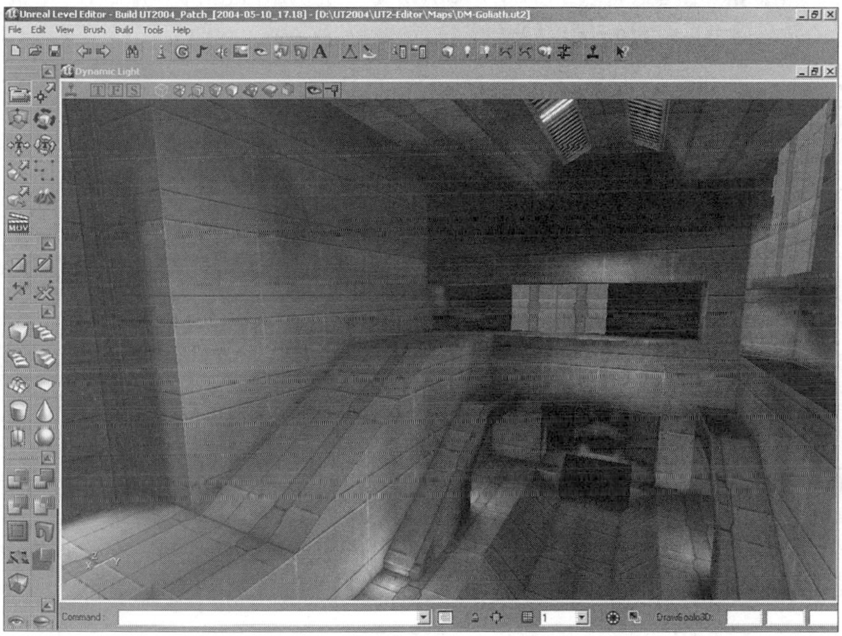

FIGURE 3.2 A level showing only the world geometry.

Actors

After your world geometry is established, every other object placed in your level (or already there by default) is an *Actor*. Actors can be brushes, triggers, players, lights, and anything else in your level that's not world geometry. As you've learned, world geometry forms the basic shell of your level. Obviously, a proper level consists of more than just a series of walls. This leaves you with a long list of objects that fall into the category of Actors. Actors themselves, however, can be classified into two subcategories: placeable and non-placeable.

Placeable Actors Versus Non-placeable Actors

Many types of Actors are classified as *placeable*, such as Player Start positions, teleporters, lights, jump pads, and movers. With placeable Actors, a level designer must manually add them into a level and then set properties to control their behavior and make them perform as desired. For example, a level designer would add a teleporter to a level at the precise position where he needs it to appear and then set parameters to control the teleporter's destination (where it sends players who enter it). Similarly, level designers must place a Player Start in a specific location to control exactly where a player spawns into the level.

Placeable Actors are always visible in UnrealEd. Each type of Actor has a different visual representation, or icon, drawn in the viewports. For instance, lights in UnrealEd are represented as light bulb icons and player starts are displayed as joystick icons; static meshes, on the other hand, are displayed by using the mesh's actual geometry. **FIGURE 3.3** shows examples of icons and a static mesh.

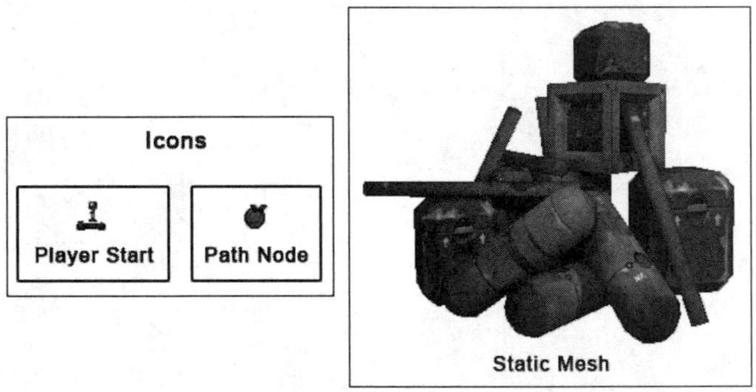

FIGURE 3.3 Examples of icons and a static mesh in UnrealEd.

Non-placeable Actors, conversely, aren't intended to be placed into a level manually during its creation. Examples include weapon projectiles; the game's heads-up display (HUD); game types, which control the rules of the game; and Mutators, which change various aspects of gameplay. Think about it: Projectiles, such as rockets or lasers, are objects created while the game is taking place. As such, they spawn into a level only when a player fires a weapon. As soon as a projectile strikes its target, that projectile's purpose has been served, and it usually ceases to exist. Because there's no reason for level designers to place these objects into their levels during construction, UnrealEd doesn't flag weapon projectiles as placeable.

All Actors used by the Unreal Engine are derived from UnrealScript, so you can examine and alter any Actor's functionality in the Unreal Engine. This capability is evidence of the Unreal Technology's flexibility. In many traditional games, most non-placeable Actor types are hard-coded into the game, which means mod makers are severely limited in their ability to modify or customize that aspect of the game.

Some Assembly Required

As mentioned in Chapter 1, "Unreal Technology: The Big Picture," a successful level has many aspects. Creating world geometry is just the first step. From there, you need to populate your levels with static meshes and apply textures to the surface of your world geometry. You might also want to add animated elements, scripts, sound, and music.

A Quick Tour Around the User Interface

In this section, you take a brief look at the UnrealEd user interface (UI). This overview is general, not a button-by-button exploration of the program. For more in-depth details on each part of UnrealEd, see Appendix A, "The UnrealEd Manual."

The Main Menu Bar

UnrealEd's main menu bar, located at the top of the application window, provides nearly all the functionality available in other parts of the UI in a typical drop-down format. This functionality ranges from standard-issue commands, such as opening, saving, and importing files, to adjusting the program's viewports, controlling the rebuilding process, and more.

The Toolbar

The toolbar, located directly beneath the main menu bar, includes a series of icons for many of the common tasks you need to perform during level design. These tasks include opening and saving files, opening browsers, rebuilding certain aspects of your level, and running Unreal to play-test your level.

The Toolbox

The toolbox, a vertical toolbar on the left side of the UnrealEd window, gives you access to a wide variety of functions used frequently during level creation. These functions include adjusting the camera's mode, editing BSP brushes, adding or subtracting mass, adding special Actors, and much more. The toolbox is divided into six collapsible sections to optimize space, so only the tools you need at the moment are visible.

The Viewports

The viewports are likely the most crucial aspect of UnrealEd, as they give you a "window" into the level you're building. Viewports come in two distinct flavors: *perspective* and *orthographic*. Perspective viewports provide a three-dimensional sense of depth, and orthographic viewports are two-dimensional, like a set of blueprints. You can toggle a variety of modes, such as Wireframe, Textures Only, and Dynamic Lighting, for the perspective viewport, based on which part of the level you're focusing on at the moment.

The Console Bar

The console bar at the bottom of the UnrealEd window offers such features as access to a command line, which can be used to enter commands to the Unreal Engine. You can also use the console bar to adjust the snapping and grid size of your viewports and to scale Actors within the level.

The Browsers

Several different browsers are available in UnrealEd to give you many of the game assets needed for a game level (see **FIGURE 3.4**). Each asset type has a separate browser: Texture, Actor Classes,

Mesh, Animation, Static Mesh, Prefab, Group, Sound, and Music. You can find more information on these browsers in Appendix A.

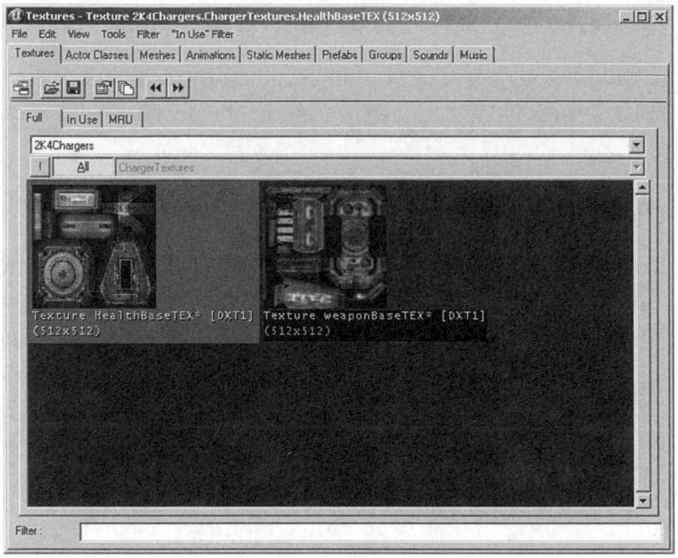

FIGURE 3.4 Along the top of the Texture browser are tabs for access to other available browsers in UnrealEd.

Property Windows

Several types of property windows are available in UnrealEd. They are used to control various parameters for objects. They are used to control various parameters for objects. The following sections give you an overview of some of the most important property windows.

Actor Properties

The Actor Properties window in UnrealEd is available through a variety of means, including using the main menu or merely double-clicking the object. This window is fundamentally the same for each Actor, but displays a different set of properties corresponding to the type of Actor that's selected. For example, the Camera Properties window shows a different list of properties than the ones that would be listed for a static mesh (see **FIGURE 3.5**). Each property window is arranged in collapsible sections so that you don't have to scroll through pages of properties.

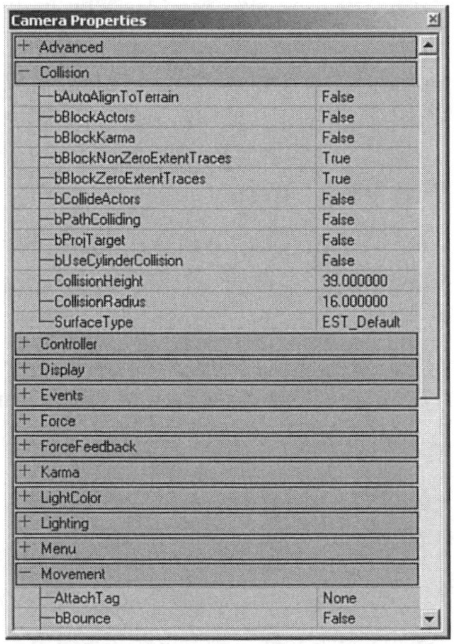

FIGURE 3.5 The Camera Properties window.

Surface Properties

The Surface Properties window enables you to change several aspects that affect what the surfaces of your levels look like in the game (see **FIGURE 3.6**). For example, you can select a wall in your level and adjust how textures are placed on it. These adjustments might include the texture's rotation, scale, and tiling. You can also change a surface's flags, which handle any special properties the surface might have, and control the resolution of light maps on the surface.

Properties for Primitives

You use the Properties window for primitives to change the dimensional properties of a BSP brush before its shape is added to or subtracted from your level (see **FIGURE 3.7**). You can access this window by right-clicking any primitive object icon in the toolbox. The window's name and the available properties vary depending on which primitive object you selected. For example, for a cube, the window is called CubeBuilder, and its properties would include width, height, and breadth.

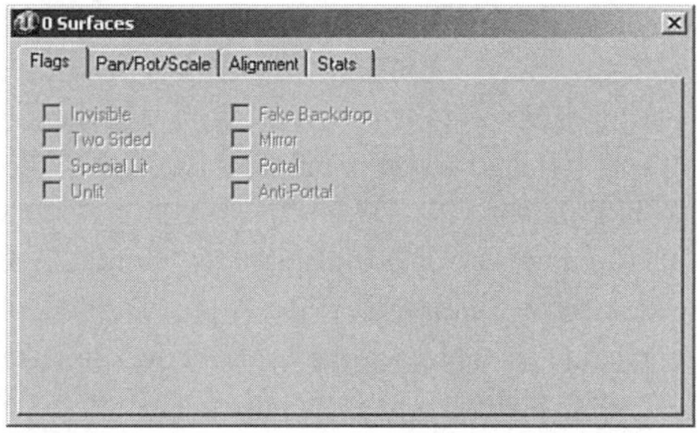

FIGURE 3.6 The Surface Properties window.

Build Options

You use the Build Options dialog box to change options for the rebuilding process (see **FIGURE 3.8**). In this dialog box, you have a high degree of control over how to generate the BSP of your level, how to create light maps, which Actors should be considered in the rebuilding process, and more.

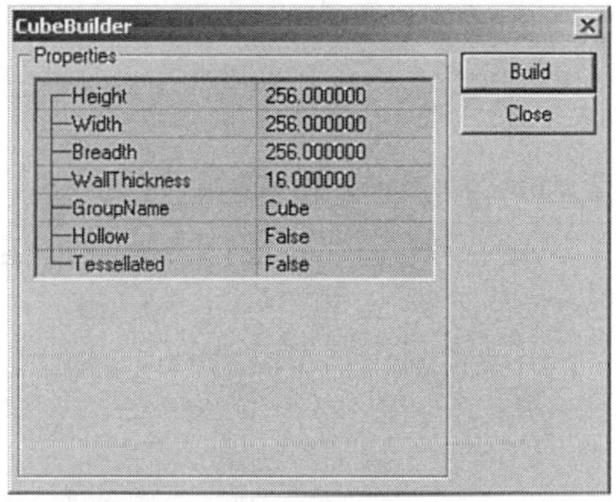

FIGURE 3.7 Primitive options for a cube.

Working in 3D Space

The Unreal Engine is designed to power today's hottest 3D games, so creating levels with this engine requires working in three-dimensional space to construct a 3D world.

2D Versus 3D

You can think of a two-dimensional system as a simple grid. A 2D grid, such as latitude and longitude, runs in two separate directions, meaning that these grids have two *axes* (pronounced *ax-eez*). One axis runs horizontally, or from side to side. The second axis runs vertically, or up and down. On standard grids, the horizontal axis is known as the *X-axis*, and the vertical axis is known as the *Y-axis*. Therefore, you could pinpoint the position of any part of the grid by using two numbers: a value for X and a value for Y.

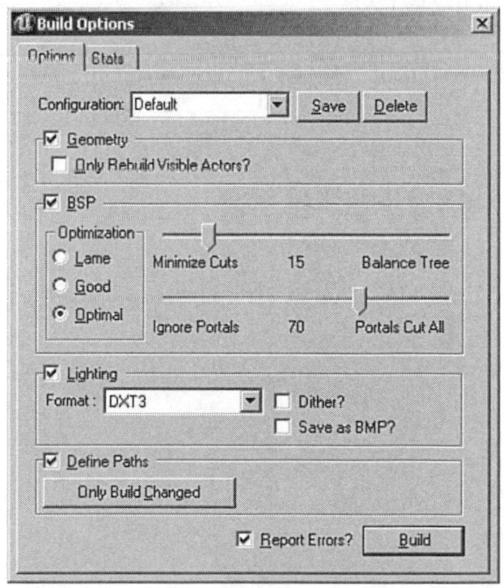

FIGURE 3.8 The Build Options dialog box.

A three-dimensional grid, on the other hand, adds a new value to your coordinates. To picture a 3D grid, imagine placing a 2D grid on the ground and standing on it. The Y-axis would run forward and backward, the X-axis would run left and right, and a new axis, the *Z-axis,* would run up and down. Locating a single position in 3D space requires three values: X, Y, and Z. If a 2D grid looks like a plane, such as a piece of paper, a 3D grid looks like a cube. **FIGURE 3.9** is a representation of a 3D grid.

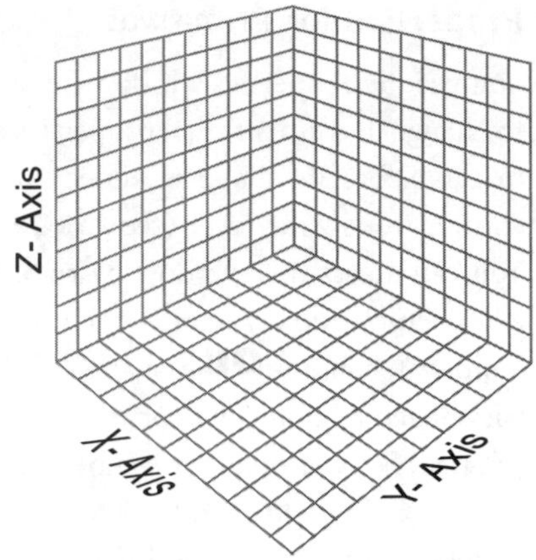

FIGURE 3.9 A 3D grid.

When working in UnrealEd, you can imagine that you're within a massive 3D grid. As you position objects in the world, you give them coordinates based on this 3D world, meaning they have position values for X, Y, and Z.

Positive and Negative Directions

Now that you're familiar with the three axes of a 3D world, you need to learn about positive and negative directions. When working in 3D space, technically there's no up, down, left, right, forward, and backward. The center of a 3D grid, including in UnrealEd, is called the *origin*, and its coordinates in 3D space are zero for X, Y, and Z (often written as 0,0,0). When you move away from the origin, you can go left, right, forward, backward, up, or down. This means every axis has two directions, which are considered to be positive and negative.

Imagine that you're standing at the origin of UnrealEd's 3D grid and looking down the Y-axis. The following list designates the positive and negative directions for each axis (see **FIGURE 3.10**):

- Along the X-axis

  Positive = left

  Negative = right
- Along the Y-axis

  Positive = forward

  Negative = backward
- Along the Z-axis

  Positive = up

  Negative = down

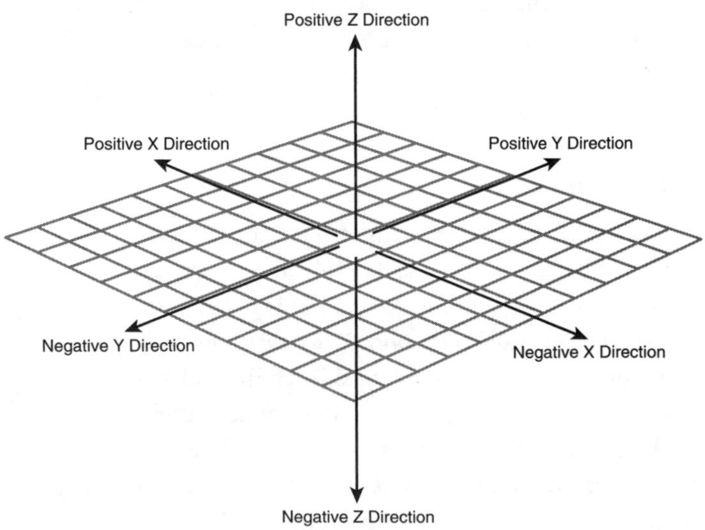

FIGURE 3.10 A 3D grid with positive and negative directions.

In the lower-left corner of the 3D viewport in UnrealEd, you can see an icon that shows the three axial directions. This icon displays three lines, one for each axis, with a letter at the end of each line signifying which axis it represents. The lines point in the positive direction of each axis. With these concepts in mind, you should have a better understanding of precisely where each of your Actors exists in the Unreal world.

Creating Your First Room

> **NOTE**
>
> When working in Unreal Tournament 2004, your level size is limited to 524,288 Unreal units in X, Y, and Z. That averages out to about six miles in each direction, or 216 cubic miles.

Now that you have taken a quick look at UnrealEd and the anatomy of a level, it's time to get busy! In this section, you use UnrealEd to construct a simple level that you can load and explore. This simple level gives you some hands-on experience at creating levels with UnrealEd and a base of knowledge to expand on in future tutorials. As you go through this chapter, the level gradually becomes more complex, until you finally wind up with a space fighter hangar for a sci-fi level (see **FIGURE 3.11**). When you're finished, you can load the level into the UE2 Runtime Engine included with this book or into Unreal Tournament 2004, depending on which editor you use to construct the level. Please note that levels created with the Unreal Runtime Engine aren't compatible with Unreal Tournament 2004, and vice versa.

FIGURE 3.11 The completed hangar.

Subtracting Out Space: How Tall?

Before you begin creating the mass of your Unreal level by subtracting and adding shapes, you need to establish a size perspective. At first, you might ask "How large should my rooms be?" or "How big is my player?" Few things are as frustrating as spending hours designing the perfect level, only to discover that your character is ant-sized or so monstrous that it can't pass through any doors.

The Technicalities of Scale

If you want to get technical about where a player can and cannot go by default, you must consider two vital properties: `CollisionHeight` and `CollisionRadius`. Essentially, these properties define a cylindrically shaped volume around your player (see **FIGURE 3.12**). This volume is used to calculate any collisions your player might have with its surrounding environment. These are the default settings for these properties:

`CollisionRadius`: 25

`CollisionHeight`: 44

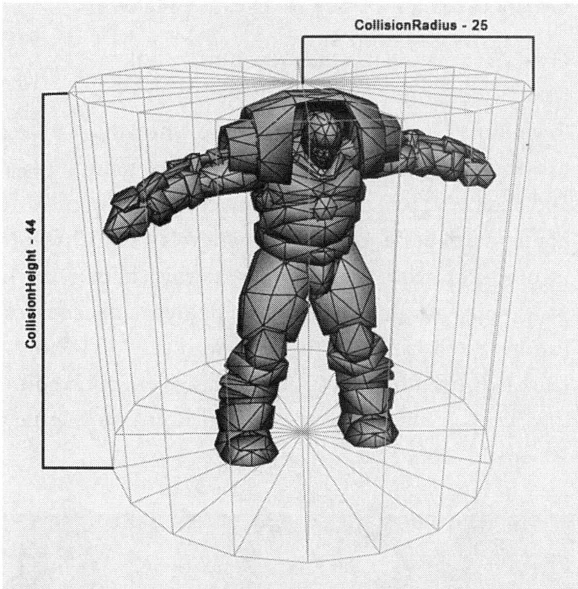

FIGURE 3.12 A collision cylinder surrounding a character.

These settings don't mean, however, that a player could pass through a doorway that was 25 units wide and 44 units tall. Remember that the `CollisionRadius` property defines the radius for a cylinder, meaning that it must be doubled to achieve that cylinder's width, or diameter. On top of that, you need to add *at least* 2 units to the cylinder's diameter to create an opening wide enough for a character to pass through. Using this method, a character could pass through a door or corridor, provided it was at least 52 units wide ($25 \times 2 + 2$). Keep in mind, however, that a width of 52 units is *just* enough for one character, and even that amount is tight.

The `CollisionHeight` property works in a similar manner. At a glance, you might think that if your `CollisionHeight` is 44 units, and your ceiling is 46 units tall, your character could easily pass through the room. Unfortunately, this is not so. The height of your room must be *twice* the `CollisionHeight`, plus at least 2 units. This means that at a `CollisionHeight` of 44 units, your ceiling would need to be at least 90 units tall for a character to pass through the room. Like `CollisionRadius`, even this amount would mean that space is tight. When using `CollisionHeight` or `CollisionRadius`, a good rule of thumb is to double the property's value, and add at least 5 units.

The Aesthetics of Scale

You need to consider another factor when determining the size of your levels: how big it should *look*. Obviously, a large room looks more ominous than a small one, but what do you need to know to make objects seem to be the *proper* size? There's a formula you can use for Unreal Engine models that you can even translate to your own games or projects.

First, note that *most* characters in UT2004 are modeled to the following parameters (see **FIGURE 3.13**):

Height when standing: 96 units

Height when crouching: 64 units

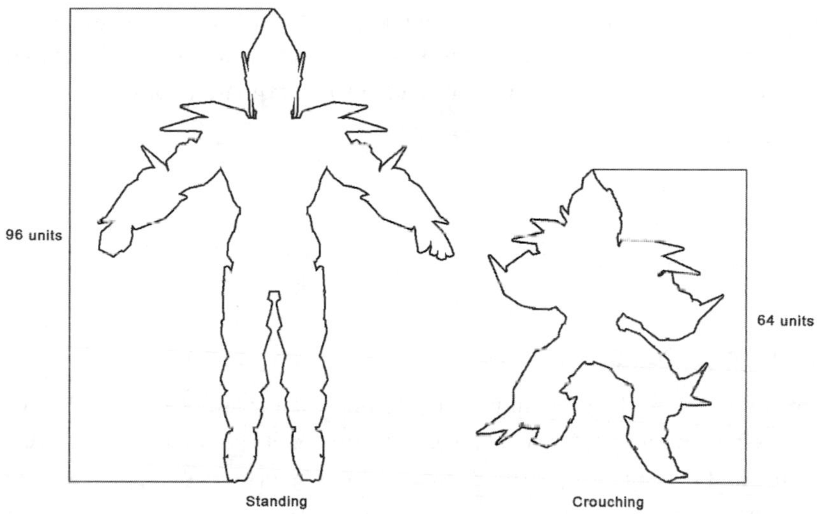

FIGURE 3.13 A character in the crouching and standing positions.

Given, these parameters have a small range of flexibility, but in general you can assume these heights are standard. Incidentally, this means you can use these parameters when judging the height of your ceilings, and you'll never have a problem with UT2004 characters.

So if you assume that a character is 96 units tall in Unreal, and that it would be 6 *feet* tall in the real world, use the following formula:

$$96 \div 6 = 16$$

This formula shows you that 16 Unreal units are equal to one foot in the real world. All you have done is divide the number of Unreal units by the character's assumed height in the real world. Now you have a means of converting real-world measurements to Unreal units. So if you had to create a computer desk for an Unreal level, and you knew it was 3.5 feet tall, you could use the following equation to convert it to Unreal units:

$3.5 \times 16 = 56$ units

There's a catch, however. You must keep one exception in mind, especially when building levels for Unreal Tournament 2004. Objects in UT2004 are bulky. Take the Unreal character Gorge, for example. If you saw Gorge in the real world, and he was about 6 feet tall, he would also be about 4 feet *wide*! Remember this factor when trying to judge the size of your levels and meshes, and make them a bit oversized. A general rule of thumb is to take the size of the object in feet, multiply it by 16, and then add 10%.

When playing Unreal Tournament 2004, you might want to consider some other scales. As you play the game, you often find yourself jumping and dodging quite a lot. For your convenience, you can refer to the following list of some jump and dodge distances to help you out. Note that these distances are all under standard gravity conditions and are approximate values:

Jump height: 64 units

Double-jump height: 132 units

Dodge distance: 320 units

Dodge-jump distance: 720 units

Using the Grid to Manage Scale

The drag grid in UnrealEd is one of the most important factors when creating a level. All your Actors, especially BSP brushes, should always be placed exactly on the grid lines. In fact, this rule is so important that UnrealEd automatically snaps Actors to the drag grid by default. The term *snap* or *snapping* simply means the program allows you to place an object into the level only if its location is based precisely on the grid. As you begin building levels in UnrealEd, you'll see how snapping works as you begin to move objects around the viewports. Instead of being able to drag an object smoothly from one side of the scene to another, your object seems to jump from one grid intersection to another. This is the result of snapping and is an essential part of keeping your levels precise in measurement and free from BSP errors, such as the HOM effect.

However, you do have control over how and whether snapping occurs. At the bottom of the UnrealEd window, in the console bar, is the Drag Grid Size combo box where you can adjust the grid's resolution to control the number of possible points that can be snapped to on the grid, thereby controlling the snap's precision (see **FIGURE 3.14**). For example, at a Drag Grid Size of 16, you can move an object only in increments of 16 units. At a Drag Grid Size of 64, the object snaps in increments of 64. You can set this resolution as high as 4096 units and as low as 1 unit.

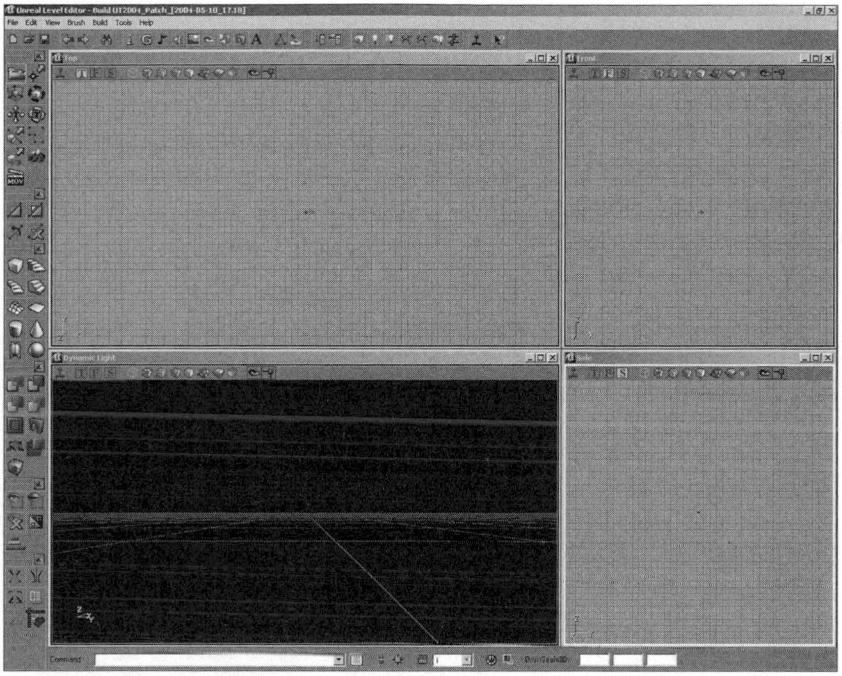

FIGURE 3.14 Drag grid.

You can deactivate snapping if you like, but this isn't recommended. Snapping is important because of the high possibility of errors when positioning objects by hand. Creating your level's world geometry is a precision process. UnrealEd calculates which areas of your level have open subtracted space or solid space, based on the location of a series of BSP brushes. If these brushes aren't aligned properly, a few serious errors can result. For example, say you have created two subtractive brushes, and you need them to be aligned together, or touching, so that they result in a single open space. If they aren't snapped together precisely, you will have problems. If they are overlapping, you could end up with BSP errors, such as the HOM effect, at the seam where they overlap. If there's any space between them, no matter how small, you'll have a very thin wall between the two rooms. Aligning these objects by hand is difficult and pointlessly tedious; for this reason, you should never switch off the drag grid.

The drag grid is also important when placing static meshes in your level. Many static meshes are designed to act as walkways or sectional level components that are placed end to end so that they appear to be a single unit. For example, you might have a 32-unit static mesh pipe section that you could place on your level's wall. If you positioned several instances, or copies, of this static mesh, one directly after the other, one long pipe would seem to run along the wall, as long as you positioned each section accurately. You could try to position these sections yourself, making sure each one was moved only 32 units, not 32.01, for instance. If you're looking for fast results, this process could become quite the headache. Instead, you can reactivate the drag grid and set it to 32 units. Then, as you move your object in the 2D views, you can see it automatically snaps to 32 units exactly, and your static meshes will be positioned perfectly with far less effort on your part.

> **NOTE**
>
> Keep in mind that some Actors, such as lights and triggers, do not snap because they don't need to be placed with extreme precision.

Brushes in Depth

Before you cut loose and begin constructing your first level, you need to learn about brushes. As mentioned earlier in this chapter, BSP brushes are used to calculate your level's world geometry. You've learned a little about using subtractive and additive brushes for level creation in UnrealEd, but the most important brush is the Builder brush. The following sections cover these brush types in more detail and give you some tips concerning brush workflow.

The Builder Brush

The Builder brush is displayed as a red wireframe object in your UnrealEd viewport (see **FIGURE 3.15**). It can have many different shapes based on the primitive object you have selected in the toolbox, including Cubes; Curved, Spiral, and Linear Staircases; BSP Terrains; Sheets; Cylinders; Cones; Volumetrics; and Tetrahedrons. For more information on these primitive objects, please refer to Appendix A, "The UnrealEd Manual." You can also edit the dimensions of these primitives by right-clicking the corresponding primitive icon.

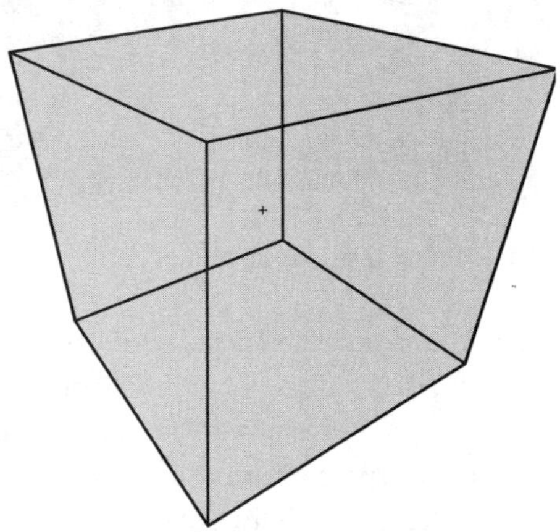

FIGURE 3.15 The Builder brush.

The Builder brush is the most important because it defines the shape from which all other brushes are defined. You can think of it as a template used to create your subtractive, additive, intersection, and deintersection brushes. For example, if you right-click the Cube icon and set its dimensions for width, height, and breadth to 128, and then click the Add icon, you would end up with an additive brush that has those same dimensions. The idea is that you set the Builder brush's shape and size, and then use it to create other types of brushes.

The Builder brush is always present in your level, even when you first start UnrealEd. At first, it exists merely as a vertex and remains so until you define a new shape for it. In fact, if you opened any map included with Unreal Tournament 2004, you would most likely find the Builder brush tucked somewhere out of the way. However, the brush isn't rendered in the game; therefore, after you complete your level or map, the brush's position is irrelevant. Most level designers simply move it away from the map, just so it's not in the way in the Perspective viewport. You can never get rid of it completely, but you can set it to a cube with dimensions of, say, 0.1 for width, height, and breadth to make it almost disappear.

Subtractive Brushes

Subtractive brushes are covered before additive brushes because they are almost always the first kind of brush you create in your levels. As mentioned, these brushes carve out an area from the solid mass of the Unreal world, giving your player a space to move around (see **FIGURE 3.16**). To create a subtractive brush, first select a primitive shape for the Builder brush, and then click the Subtract button in the toolbox. The result is a new brush with the same shape as the Builder brush, but it's displayed in a yellow wireframe instead of red. You can also see that the shape the Builder brush defined has now been turned into a "room" in the UnrealEd Perspective viewport. Furthermore, the sides of this new subtracted shape have a texture applied to each side, which is the default texture or the most recently selected texture from the Texture browser.

FIGURE 3.16 A subtracted room.

Additive Brushes

When you need some mass added back into your levels, reach for additive brushes. To create an additive brush, first select a primitive shape and size for the Builder brush, and then click the Add button in the toolbox. The additive brush, which is the same size and shape as the Builder brush, is displayed in the viewport with a blue wireframe. You use additive brushes often when creating walls, stairs, and raised areas in floors. **FIGURE 3.17** shows a cube added to a subtracted room.

FIGURE 3.17 A subtracted room with a cube added in the middle.

Working with Brushes

When working with BSP brushes in UnrealEd, you should always keep some workflow guidelines in mind. First is the location of each brush's *pivot*. The pivot can best be described as a brush's center of movement (see **FIGURE 3.18**). When you're snapping to the grid, this pivot determines the point at which the brush snaps. The pivot is also used as a point of rotation. For example, say you have a cube-shaped brush with its pivot precisely at the center of the cube. If you rotate the brush, you would see the cube appear to spin in place. However, you can relocate the cube's pivot, even place it *outside* the brush. If you rotated the cube again with its pivot moved far to the left, the cube would seem to move in a circle because its pivot is the point of rotation.

Brush order is another important factor in level construction. Say you've constructed a level of a multistory building. You began by subtracting a massive cube to represent the area outside your building, and then created the building from a series of additive brushes within this subtracted area. After you're done, you realize that a cylinder, rather than a cube, would have been a more appropriate shape for your first subtraction. Your first impulse is to delete the existing cube and create a large cylindrical subtractive brush that completely surrounds your building. The problem is that after you rebuild and play-test the level, you find the entire building gone. This happens because the brushes are created in the wrong order. Think about it: If the *last* operation you perform is a massive subtraction, then all the additive brushes within that subtraction would be removed. However, you can change the order in which each brush is calculated. If you tell UnrealEd to calculate the enormous cylindrical subtraction *first*, the building would still exist in the game because Unreal would subtract the large cylindrical area *before* it calculated the parts of the building, not vice versa. To change a brush's order, right-click the brush, and choose Order from the context menu. You then see commands for calculating a brush first or last or for swapping its brush order with another selected brush.

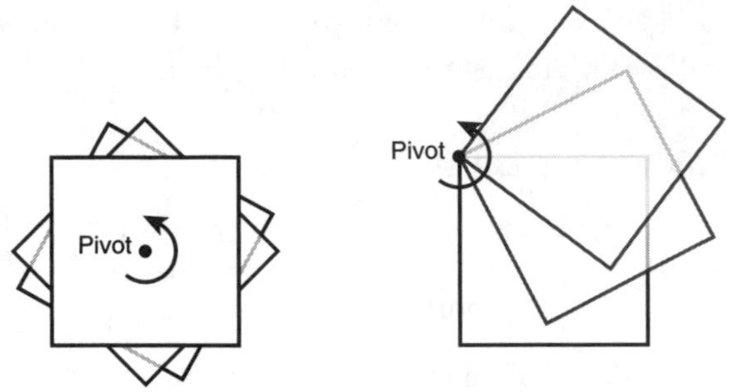

FIGURE 3.18 The effect of changing the pivot's location.

Navigation in UnrealEd

When UnrealEd first starts, Camera Movement mode (the default mode) is enabled in the toolbox. Although moving the camera in other modes is possible, this mode enables you to move Actors rather than rotate or scale them. You will probably use this mode for most of your work in UnrealEd. The Camera Movement mode icon toggles the viewport so that you can move only the camera.

Viewport navigation in UnrealEd is fairly straightforward, but might take some getting used to if you come from other 3D applications. Also, the navigation controls work differently depending on whether you're in a perspective or orthographic view. If you're completely new to UnrealEd, you would do well to practice with them until their use becomes second nature.

Perspective viewport controls:

- Holding down the left mouse button (LMB) while moving the mouse forward and back moves the camera forward and back. Moving to the left and right while holding down the LMB turns the camera left and right. The effect is similar to driving the camera around like a car.
- Holding down the right mouse button (RMB) while moving the mouse enables you to rotate the camera, much like the way you turn your head. Left and right movements

rotate the camera in those directions, and moving the mouse forward and back rotates the camera up and down, respectively.

- Holding down the LMB and RMB simultaneously facilitates camera panning. As you move the mouse left and right, the camera seems to slide or strafe in those directions. Moving the mouse forward and back pans the camera up and down.

Orthographic viewport controls:

- Holding down the LMB or RMB causes the camera to pan around the scene. This method moves the camera along the same plane as the viewport.
- Holding down the LMB and RMB together enables you to zoom in to and out of a viewport.

Moving Actors

In this section, you're going to examine how you can move Actors around your levels in UnrealEd. For example, you'll move the Builder brush around in the level so that you can see how to move and rotate Actors.

In **TUTORIAL 3.1**, you see how to move and rotate the Builder brush. Keep in mind that these techniques can be used to manipulate any placeable Actor:

TUTORIAL 3.1: Positioning Brushes and Actors in 2D and 3D

1. In the toolbox, click the Cube icon. Select the Builder brush in the Top view (see **FIGURE 3.19**).

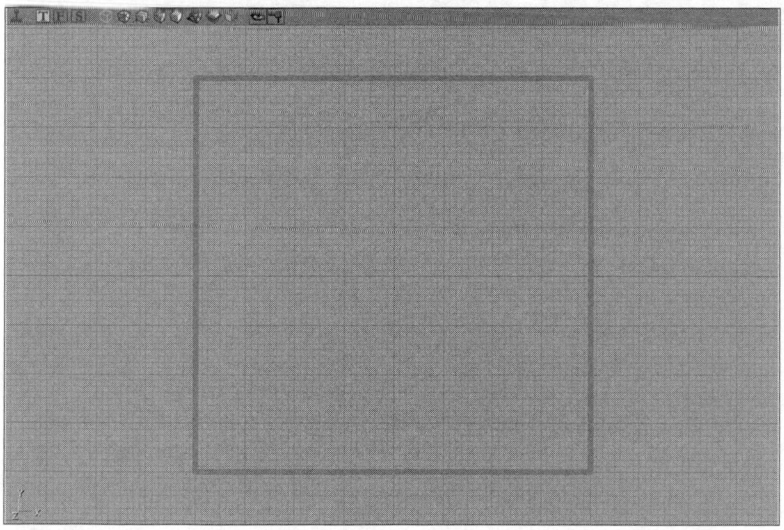

FIGURE 3.19 Cube-shaped Builder brush.

2. Holding down the Ctrl key, drag the Builder brush with the LMB. Notice that the Builder brush moves with you, snapping to the increments of the current Drag Grid Size setting. Also note that if you check the Side view, the brush hasn't moved up or down in the Z-axis. You can move objects only in the X- and Y-axes in the Top view.

3. Using the same technique, move the Builder brush in the Side view. Again, you're moving only in the Y- and Z-axes. Similarly, when you're moving the Builder brush in the Front view, movement is allowed only in X and Z.

4. In the Top view, press Ctrl and drag left and right while holding down the RMB. The Builder brush rotates perpendicularly to the camera (see **FIGURE 3.20**). The same holds true for the other two 2D viewports.

> **NOTE**
>
> Rotation is influenced by the rotation grid, which enables you to snap to precise angles. This feature, which makes rotation easy, is on by default. If you want to switch it off, however, click the Toggle Rotation Grid icon in the console bar.

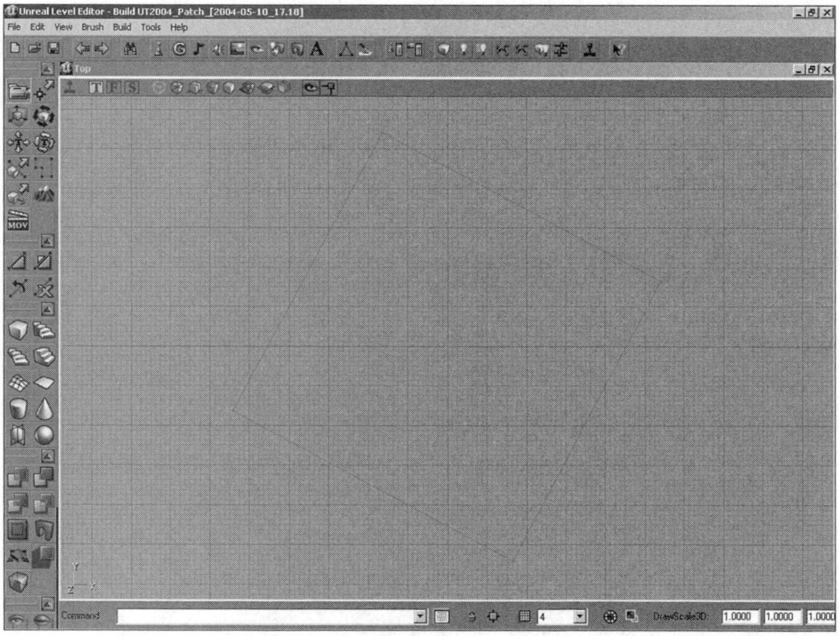

FIGURE 3.20 A rotated Builder brush.

5. Now see how movement works in the 3D view. Navigate the view so that you can see the entire Builder brush, and then press Ctrl and drag with the LMB. The brush moves along the X-axis.

> **NOTE**
>
> You cannot rotate Actors in the 3D view unless you have activated Actor Rotate mode in the toolbox. Also, all rotations are lost if you build a new primitive brush.

6. Try dragging while holding down Ctrl and the RMB, and then with Ctrl and LMB+RMB. The movement you see can be described as follows:

   - Ctrl and LMB: X-axis
   - Ctrl and RMB: Y-axis
   - Ctrl and LMB+RMB: Z-axis

END TUTORIAL 3.1

Creating Your First Map

Now that you know all these important aspects of level design, it's time to do some real level construction. The following tutorials introduce you to a variety of fundamental concepts and tasks that you need to understand before you're ready to complete your own levels. You'll begin simply by subtracting out a box-shaped room, and then "paint" it with texture, add some lights, and go on from there. **FIGURE 3.21** shows the completed level you will end up with after completing the tutorials in this chapter.

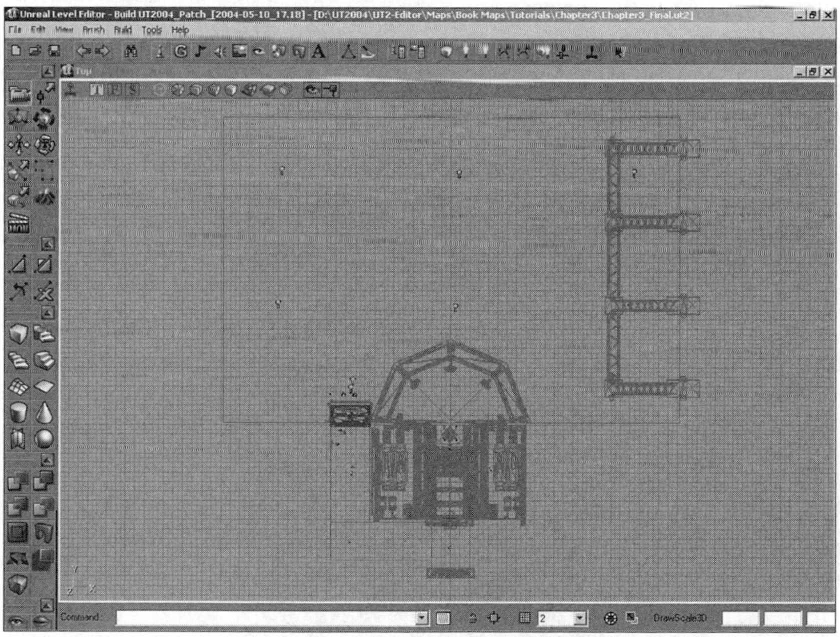

FIGURE 3.21 A completed level.

Subtracting the First Room

TUTORIAL 3.2 shows you what you need to know to create your first open space from Unreal's world of infinite solid mass:

TUTORIAL 3.2: Subtracting a Simple Room

3

1. Start UnrealEd, and begin a new scene by choosing File > New from the menu.

2. You need to define the shape and size of your Builder brush so that you can create a subtractive brush of the correct dimensions. Open the CubeBuilder dialog box by right-clicking on the Cube primitive in the CSG section of the toolbox.

3. In the CubeBuilder dialog box, enter the following settings (see **FIGURE 3.22**), and then click the Build button. When you do, you'll notice that you can see the Builder brush as a red cube of the dimensions you selected. You can then close this dialog box.

   Height: 384

   Width: 636

   Breadth: 1024

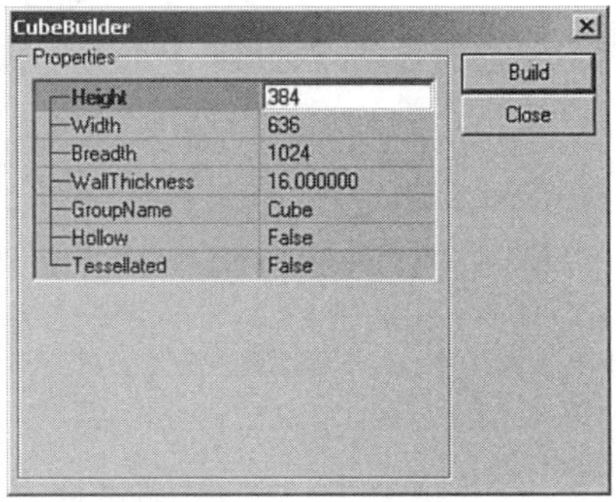

FIGURE 3.22 Dimension settings in the CubeBuilder dialog box.

4. Click the Subtract button in the toolbox. You have just created the first subtracted space of your map (see **FIGURE 3.23**).

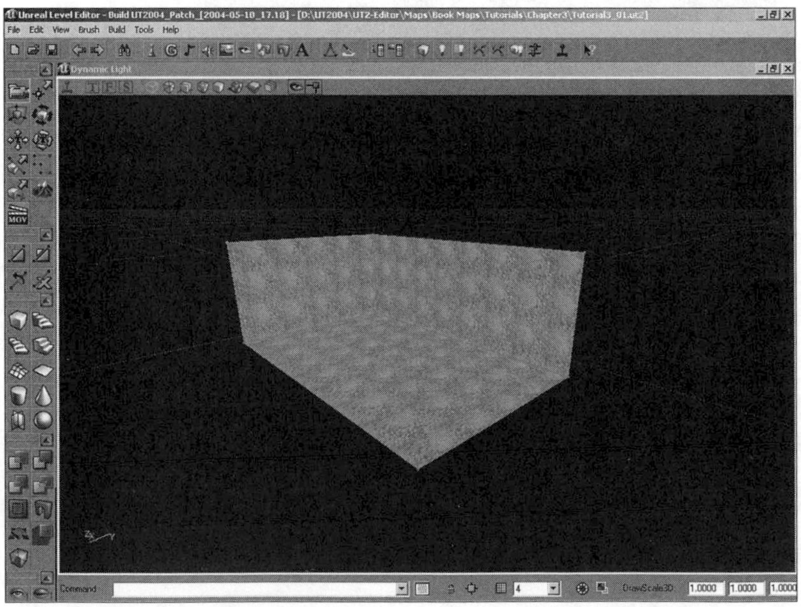

FIGURE 3.23 A subtracted room.

END TUTORIAL 3.2

Adding Textures

Right now, the textures on your room's surfaces look rather bland because they're covered with the default texture. If you don't select a texture from the Texture browser before adding or subtracting mass in your map, the surfaces of the resulting brush are covered with the default texture, a greenish bubbly surface. Selecting a texture from the Texture browser *before* adding or subtracting is a good idea. If you forget to do this, you can still change those textures by using the Texture browser.

To open the Texture browser, click its icon  on the toolbar of the UnrealEd window. You can use this browser to view textures included in texture packages and to filter the number of displayed packages by selecting specific groups (see **FIGURE 3.24**). You can find out more about the menus and features of the Texture browser in Appendix A.

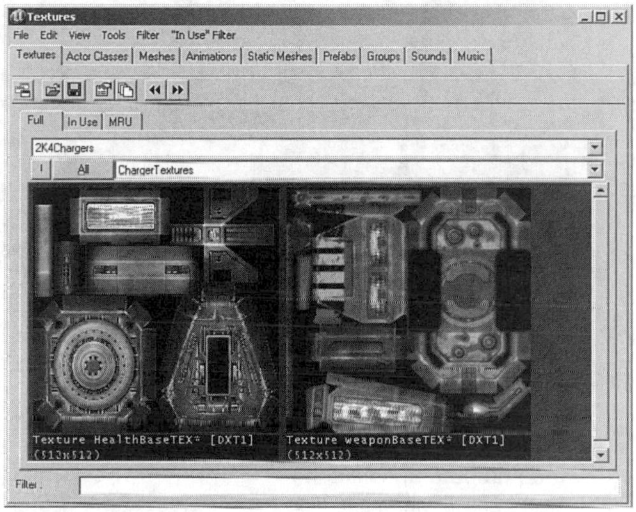

FIGURE 3.24 The Texture browser.

TUTORIAL 3.3 demonstrates how to select textures for the walls, floor, and ceiling of your room. The textures you need are stored in a package, so first you need to load that package.

TUTORIAL 3.3: Texturing the Room

1. Notice that if you click on any surfaces in your room, they turn blue to indicate they are selected. Before you begin texturing, make sure no surfaces are selected (see **FIGURE 3.25**). If a surface is selected, click it again to deselect it.
2. Open the Texture browser using the method described at the beginning of this section.
3. From the browser's menu bar, choose File > Open and select the `Chapter3_tex.utx` file (see **FIGURE 3.26**). This package contains several textures, divided into the following groups: Base, Ceilings, Floors, Wall, and Glass. You can switch between these groups by using the drop-down list next to the All button. Click the All button to see all textures in the package, regardless of what group they're in.

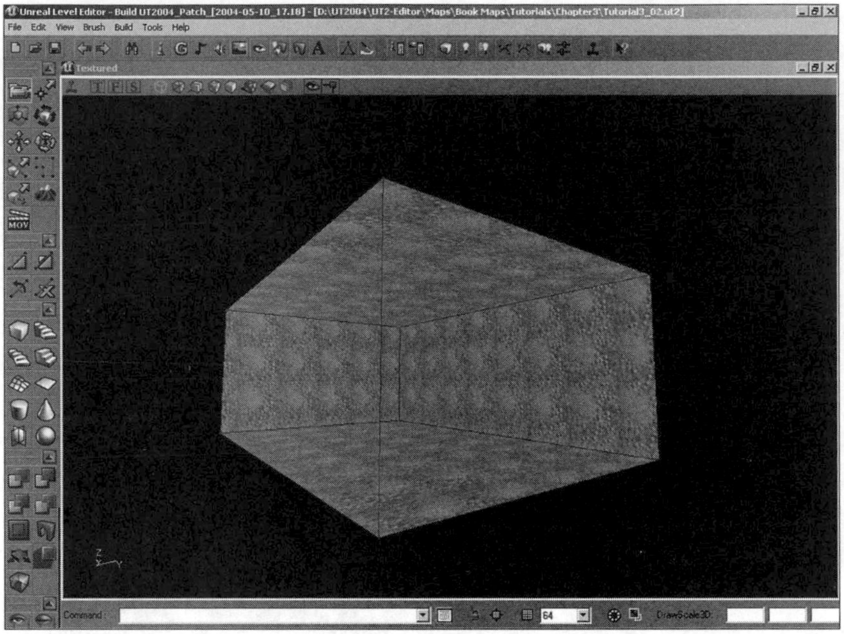

FIGURE 3.25 The room before texturing.

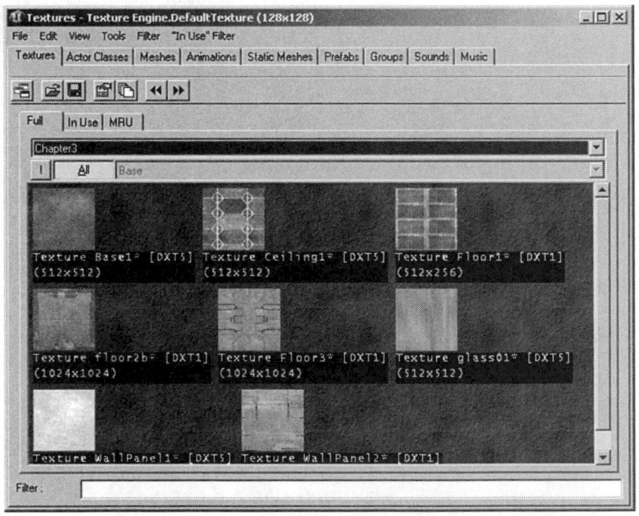

FIGURE 3.26 The Texture browser with the `Chapter3.utx` file loaded.

4. Click the list arrow next to the Add button, select the Walls group, and click the `WallPanel1` texture. The selected texture isn't applied to any surfaces in the level because no surfaces are selected.

5. Select the four walls in the room by Ctrl-clicking each one in the 3D viewport.

6. Click the `WallPanel1` texture again in the Texture browser. Notice that the texture is then applied to all walls (see **FIGURE 3.27**).

7. In the 3D viewport, select the floor surface.

8. In the Texture browser, select the Floors group and click the `Floor2b` texture (see **FIGURE 3.28**).

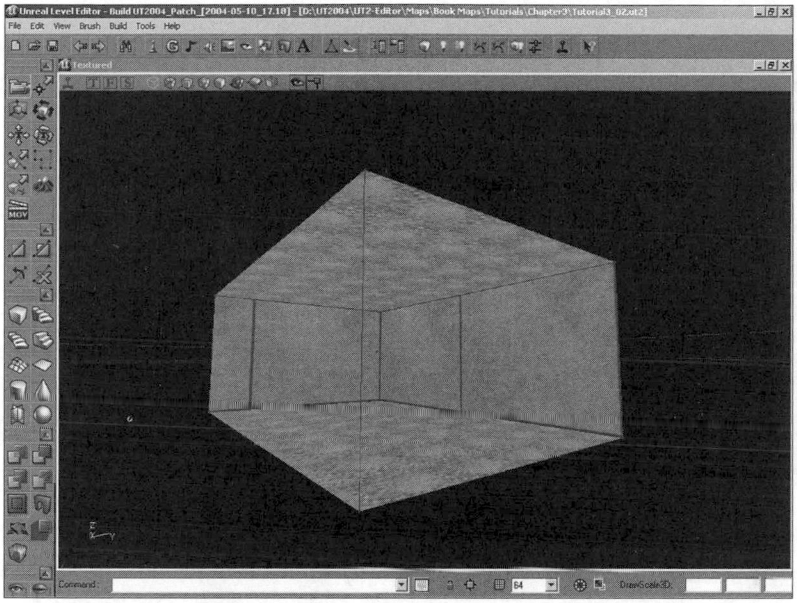

FIGURE 3.27 Walls with the `WallPanel1` texture applied.

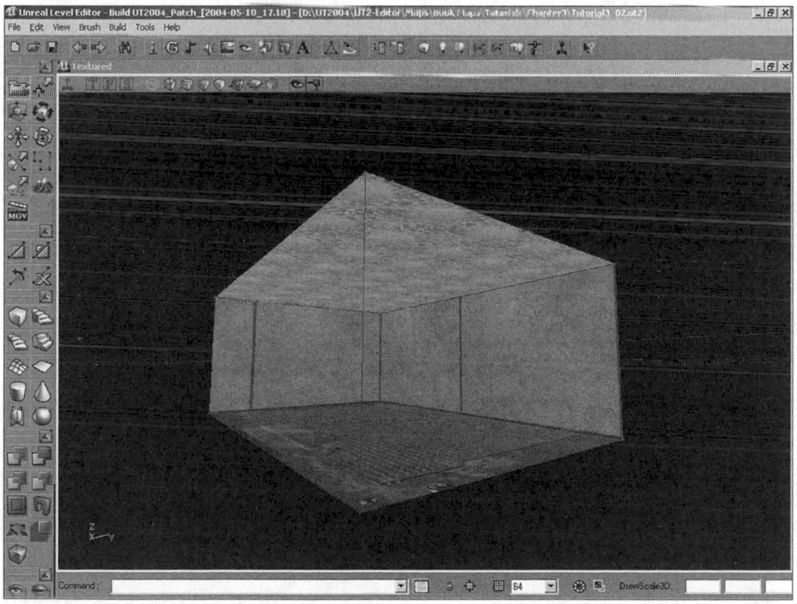

FIGURE 3.28 The floor texture applied.

9. Use the methods in steps 7 and 8 to select the ceiling surface and apply the `Ceiling1` texture (see **FIGURE 3.29**).

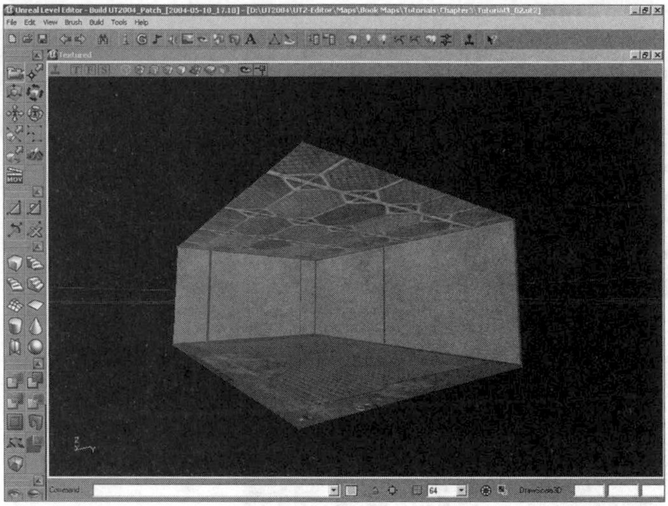

FIGURE 3.29 Textured room.

END TUTORIAL 3.3

Texture Fitting

You have now applied textures to your level, but they don't seem to be placed well. Using the Surface Properties window, you can adjust how the textures appear on each surface by using the surface's UV coordinates. A surface's UVs are a two-dimensional coordinate system for controlling the placement of a texture on a surface. In most cases, U is in the horizontal direction, and V is in the vertical.

You can type numeric values in the Surface Properties window instead of adjusting these coordinates interactively. The Surface Properties window also gives you access to special alignment tools not found in the toolbox. In **TUTORIAL 3.4**, you take a look at how to adjust textures in your level. Note that many of the numeric values given in this tutorial were derived through experimentation.

TUTORIAL 3.4: Fitting the Textures

1. Select the four walls in the room.
2. Click the Surface Properties button or press F5.
3. In the Surface Properties window, select the Alignment tab, set the following options (see **FIGURE 3.30**), and then click the Align button:

   Alignment (list box at the left side of the window): Planar

   UTile: 4.02

   VTile: 4.02

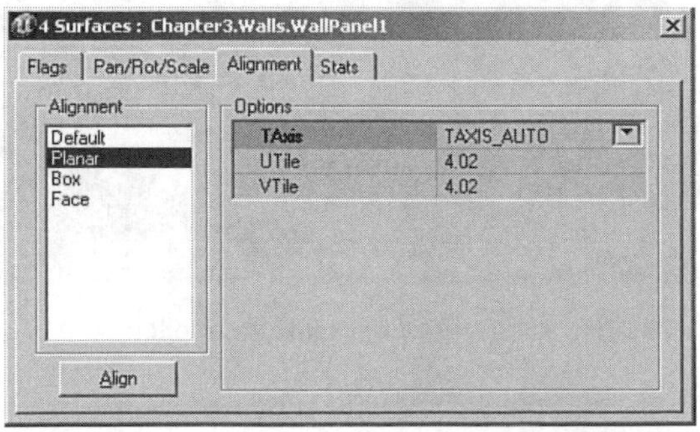

FIGURE 3.30 Alignment tab of the Surface Properties window.

4. The wall appears to have tiles, but the alignment is still off because the tiles at the edges of each surface look cut off. To fix this problem, in the Surface Properties window, select the Pan/Rot/Scale tab (see **FIGURE 3.31**).

5. As you can see, the textures need to be moved vertically to align correctly with the floor and ceiling. With all four walls still selected, click the Pan V 64 button four times. You can see the textures move downward 64 units each time you click the button. Four clicks should make everything align with the top and bottom of the walls.

6. You're almost finished, but you can see that the two short walls need their textures aligned horizontally. Go ahead and select these two walls now.

7. Click the Pan U 64 button four times. The walls should then be aligned correctly (see **FIGURE 3.32**).

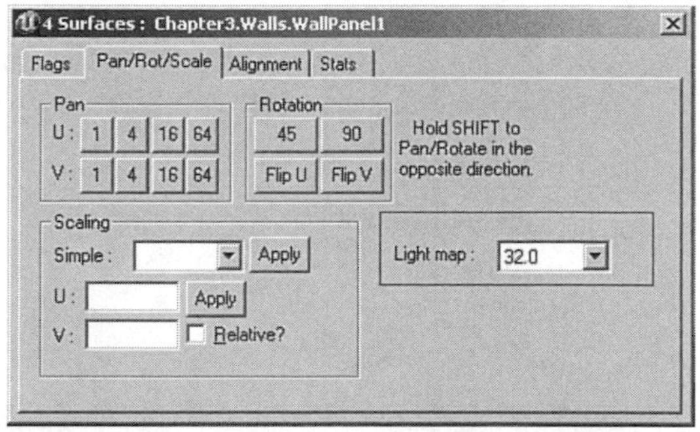

FIGURE 3.31 Pan/Rot/Scale tab of the Surface Properties window.

> **NOTE**
>
> You can pan in V in a downward direction simply by clicking any of the incremental buttons. Pressing Shift while clicking pans the texture back up. This is, of course, in relation to the surface you're facing.

> **NOTE**
>
> If all four walls are still selected, you can simply Ctrl-click the two longer walls, thereby deselecting them.

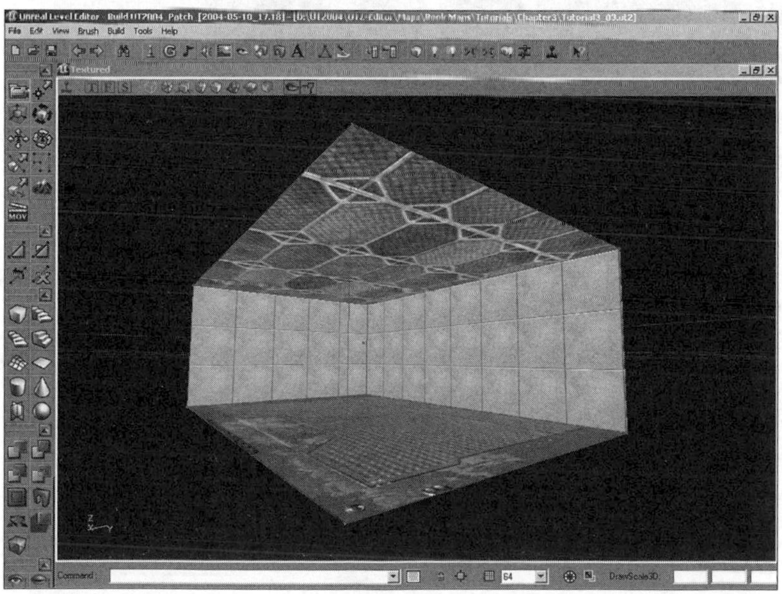

FIGURE 3.32 Correctly aligned walls.

8. For the ceiling and floor alignments, the following are the recommended alignment numbers. Using the technique demonstrated earlier in this tutorial, see if you can get everything aligned correctly. **FIGURE 3.33** shows an example.

Floor	Ceiling
Alignment: Planar	Alignment: Planar
UTile: 8.0	UTile: 2.0
VTile: 8.0	VTile: 2.0

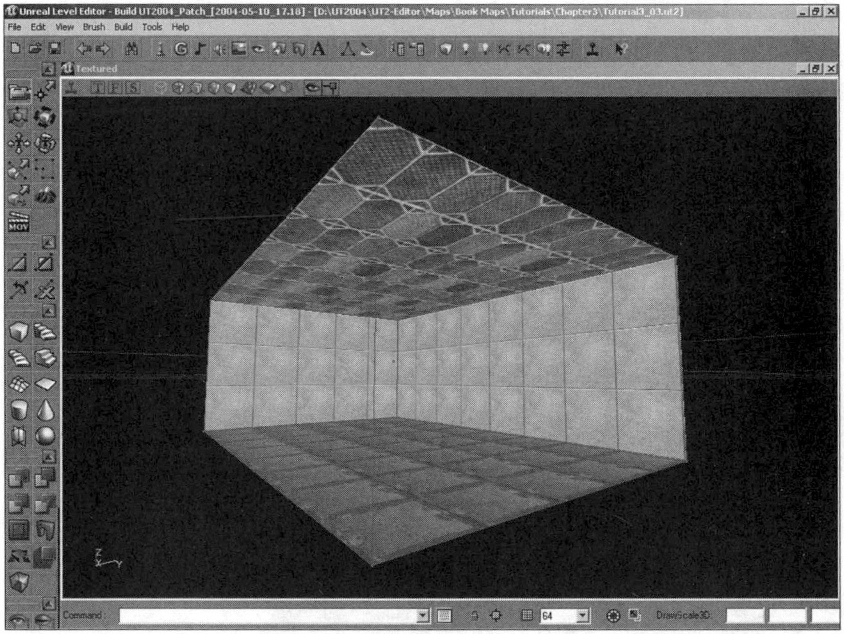

FIGURE 3.33 Correctly aligned floor and ceiling.

END TUTORIAL 3.4

Making the Level Functional

Lights, as you might imagine, are essential to your levels. Lightless game levels look much like a room with the lights turned off. Obviously, playing a lightless game would be quite difficult. Lights are used not only to allow players to *see* your level, but also to create mood, add color, and control the dramatic "feel" of each area of the map. In the following tutorial, you make your level playable by learning how to place lights and rebuild the level to generate light maps for creating areas of light and shadow.

Before you can jump in and actually run around this map in the game, you need to add a few missing items. The first item, as mentioned, is a light source of some kind. The second is a Player Start Actor, which gives your map a point of entry for any characters that want to play it. Finally, you must rebuild the level to calculate its world geometry and generate the light maps that make surfaces seem to be illuminated.

TUTORIAL 3.5: Making the Level Functional

1. First, add a light. Right-click on the center of the ceiling surface in the 3D viewport, and choose Add Light Here from the context menu. A light bulb icon is displayed to represent the light's position (see **FIGURE 3.34**).

> **CAUTION**
>
> **Forgetting to rebuild before testing a level often results in your characters dying as soon as they enter the game! If you run into this problem, be sure to rebuild your level's geometry.**

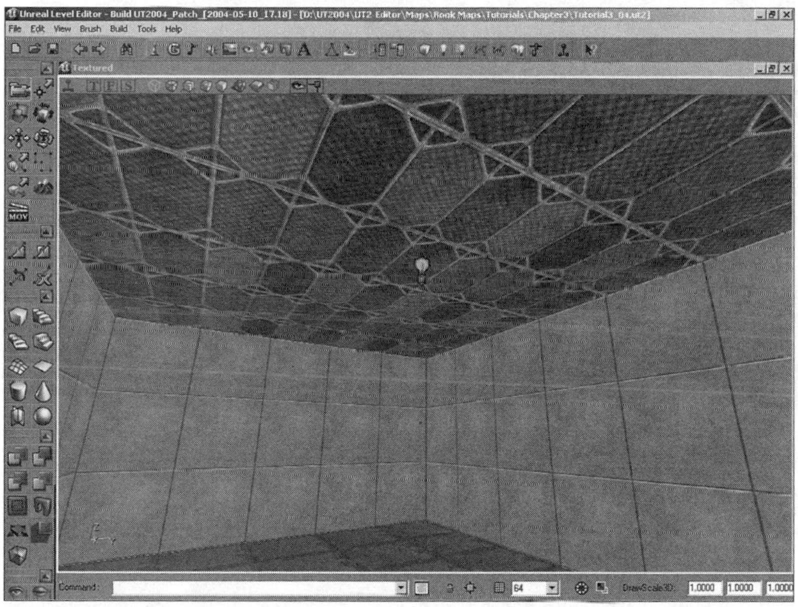

FIGURE 3.34 Newly created light.

2. At first, you probably won't see much change in the level. To see what the light will look like in the room, you must rebuild the level. Click the Rebuild All button on the toolbar.

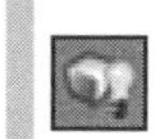

   You can see some dim lighting with quite realistic softened shadows in the corners (see **FIGURE 3.35**). The lighting conditions in the room are affected by several things:

   - Light position
   - Light settings (brightness and color)
   - Number of lights in the room
   - Object placement and the shadows created by those objects

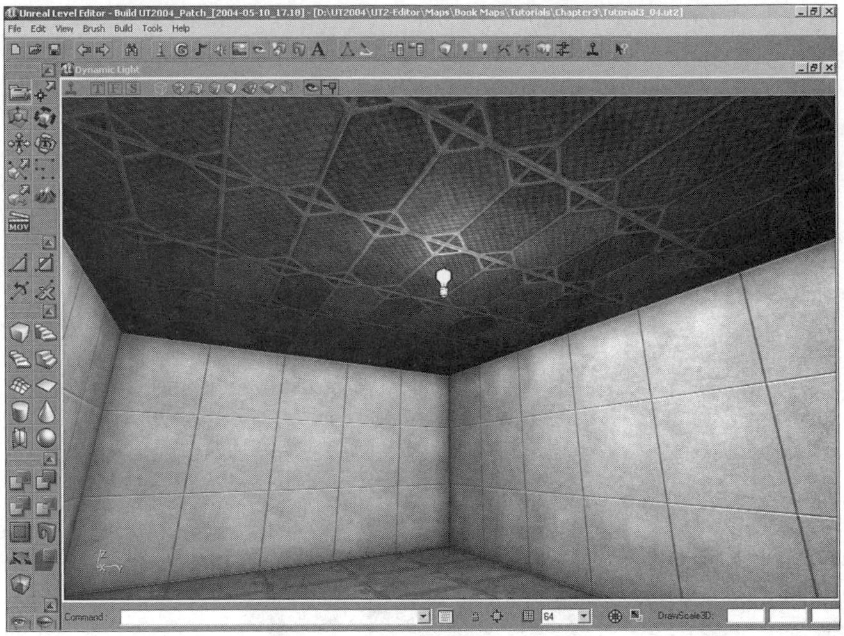

FIGURE 3.35 Room with lighting.

3. With the light selected, click the Actor Properties button on the toolbar or double-click the light's icon.

4. In the Light Properties dialog box, expand the LightColor section and set the `LightBrightness` property to 128 (see **FIGURE 3.36**). You'll notice the room get brighter, but this isn't an accurate representation of the new value. To see an accurate representation, you need to rebuild the level again. Do so now.

5. Now it's time to add a Player Start. Right-click on the floor surface, somewhere near its center, and choose Add Player Start Here from the menu.

   A joystick icon is displayed to represent where the player starts (see **FIGURE 3.37**). When you click the icon, an arrow indicates the direction the player will be facing when he or she spawns into the map.

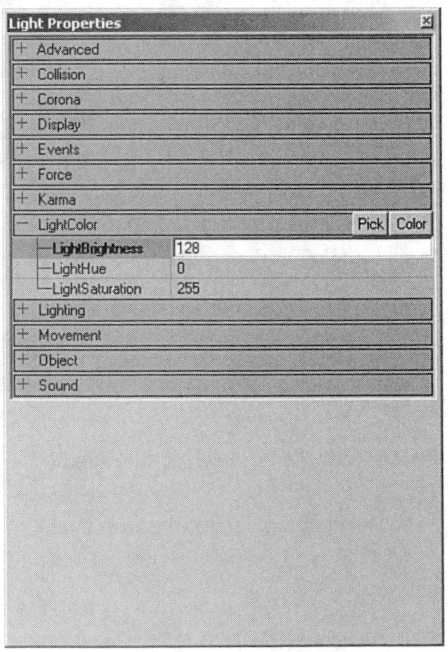

FIGURE 3.36 The Light Properties dialog box.

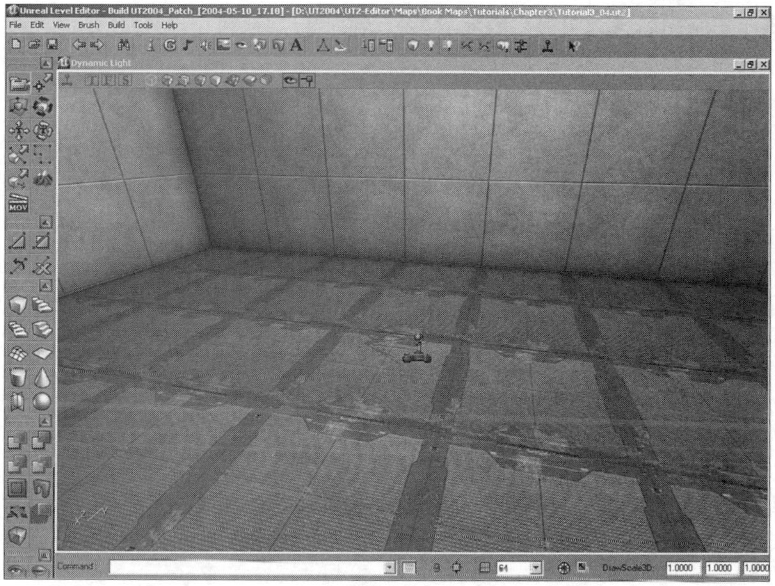

FIGURE 3.37 A Player Start icon with visible arrow.

6. Time to play! There's no need to rebuild a level after adding a Player Start. You can simply click the Play Map! button on the toolbar and check out your new level (see **FIGURE 3.38**). Congratulations! You've finished a basic level!

7. When you're finished playing, press the tilde (~) key to close the console, and type **`exit`**. This immediately closes the game and sends you back to your desktop.

> **NOTE**
>
> You can also click the Build Lights button or the Build Changed Lights button on the toolbar for the same effect.

FIGURE 3.38 A completed level.

END TUTORIAL 3.5

Expanding the Level: Creating Objects and Adding Lights

You've completed a basic room, but obviously it's not enough to make for an exciting level. You need to enhance and build on what you have so far and change it into a level rich with detail. To begin, you add a window to the control room, followed by a hangar room beyond it. Next, you add a hallway that leads from the hangar to the control room.

The Window and Hangar

In **TUTORIAL 3.6**, you create the window that leads from the existing control room into the hangar, which has yet to be created.

TUTORIAL 3.6: Creating a Window

1. Create a Cube Builder brush and enter the following property settings in the CubeBuilder dialog box:

   Height: 256

   Width: 16

   Breadth: 1024

> **TIP**
>
> By making the dimensions of your rooms divisible by 16, you won't have to make changes to the grid as often, and proper snapping is much easier to achieve.

2. In the Top viewport, position the Builder brush so that its bottom edge aligns with the top edge of the control room (see **FIGURE 3.39**). Notice how this alignment seems impossible because of snapping? You need to lower the Drag Grid Size setting for this to work. Set Drag Grid Size to 2 in the console bar.

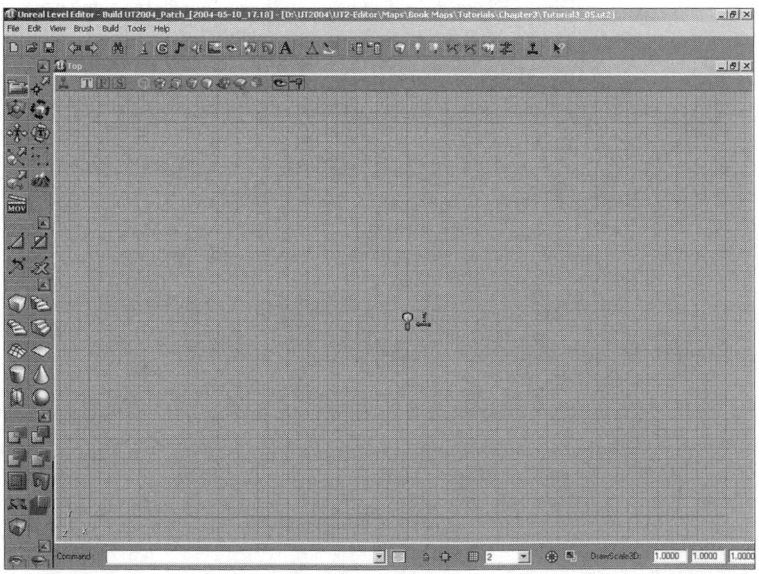

FIGURE 3.39 Top view showing the alignment of brushes.

3. In the Side viewport, position the Builder brush so that its top aligns with the top of the control room (see **FIGURE 3.40**).

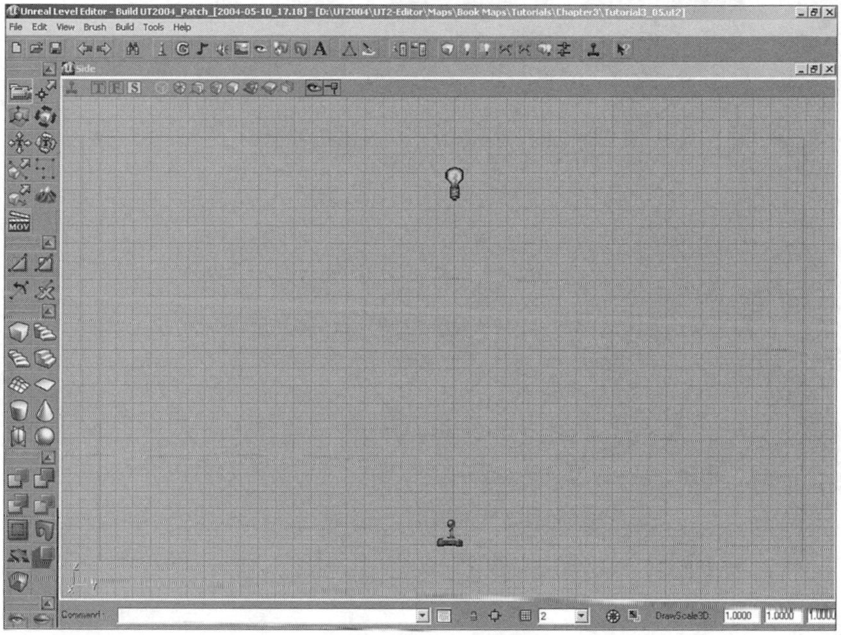

FIGURE 3.40 Side view showing the alignment of brushes.

4. Before subtracting the space, select a texture. Open the Texture browser and select the Base1 texture from the Base group of the Chapter3_tex.utv package.

5. Subtract the space for the window and rebuild the map as you did for the first room. You have created a recession in the wall, which will soon act as a window into the hangar (see **FIGURE 3.41**).

> **NOTE**
>
> If necessary, you can temporarily set Drag Grid Size back to 16, which should make it easier to center the new hangar brush in the control room, and then reset it to 2 so that you can snap against the window.

6. Next, you need to subtract the space for the hangar. Create a Cube Builder brush and enter the following property settings in the CubeBuilder dialog box:

   Height: 1152

   Width: 2048

   Breadth: 3072

7. As you did earlier, align the Builder brush in the Top viewport so that the bottom edge is aligned with the top edge of the window brush. Make sure to keep the center of the Builder brush aligned with the center of the control room, as shown in **FIGURE 3.42**.

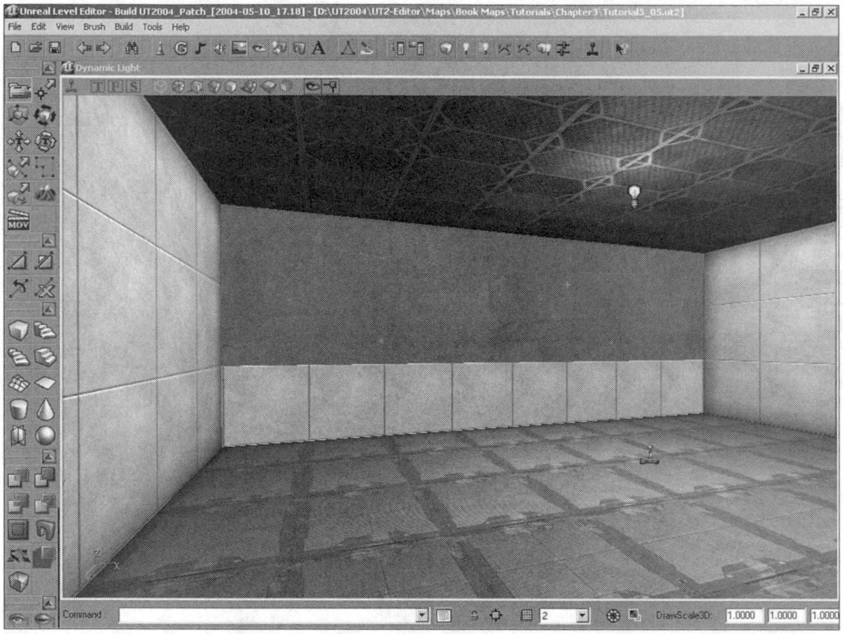

FIGURE 3.41 3D view showing the newly subtracted space.

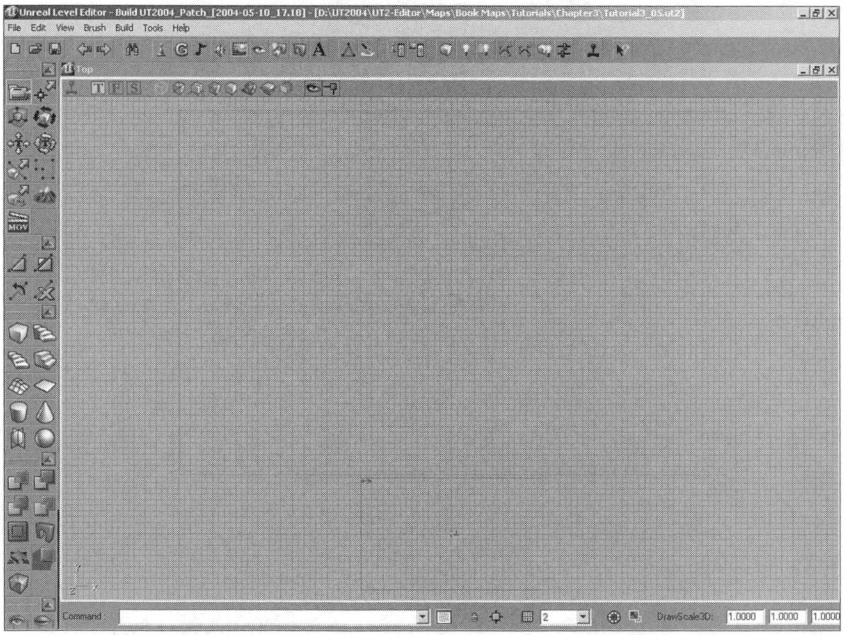

FIGURE 3.42 The brushes for the window, aligned in the Top view.

8. In the Side viewport, align the Builder brush so that the top edge aligns with the window and the control room brush's top edge.

9. Subtract the space for the hangar (see **FIGURE 3.43**).

> **TIP**
>
> **If you can't snap a brush to the grid, you can force-snap the brush to the active grid settings by Ctrl+RMB-clicking on any vertex of the brush. This method force-snaps the entire brush back to the grid, based on the nearest grid intersection to the vertex you clicked.**

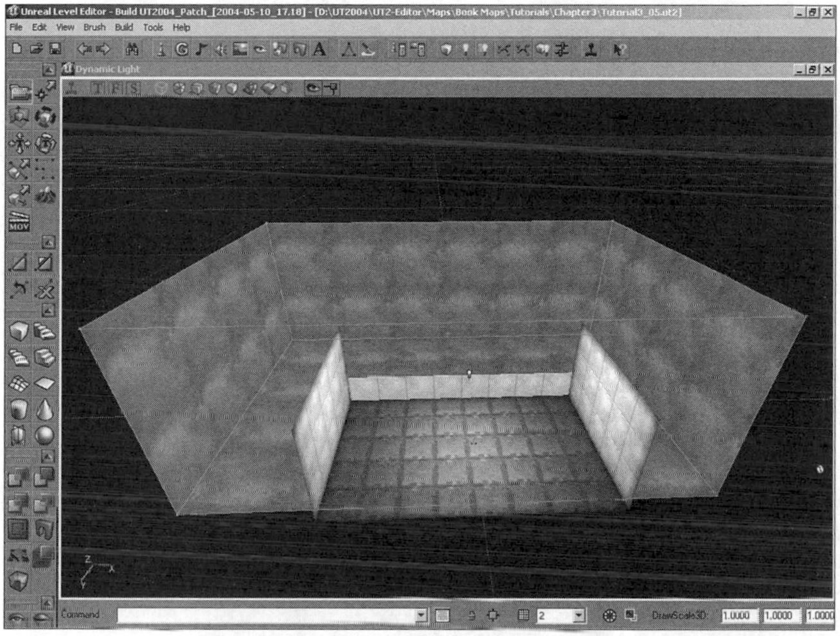

FIGURE 3.43 **3D view of newly subtracted hanger.**

10. Rebuild the level. As you might have expected, the hangar is dark. You need to add some lights so that you can see into the hangar. You'll do this in the next tutorial.

11. Choose File > Save from the main menu, and name the file `myHangar.ut2`.

END TUTORIAL 3.6

In **TUTORIAL 3.7**, you see how to duplicate Actors to quickly create a series of lights, instead of adding each one individually. Keep in mind that the duplication methods discussed in this tutorial can be used on any Actor.

TUTORIAL 3.7: Lighting the Hangar

1. In the Perspective viewport, navigate the camera into the hangar. It's currently a bit dark and rather difficult to see what's going on. To help you see what you're doing, you can switch the viewport to a Textured Only mode by clicking the icon of that name on the 3D viewport's toolbar. This mode illuminates all surfaces of the level evenly, removing any shadows that might be hampering your visibility.

2. Right-click anywhere on the ceiling surface and choose Add Light Here (see **FIGURE 3.44**).

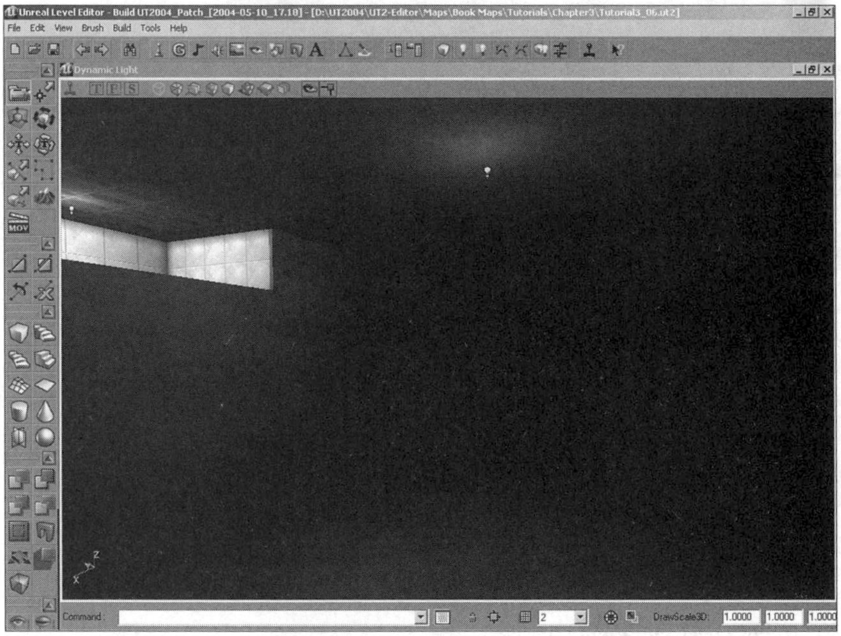

FIGURE 3.44 The hanger with one light.

3. Because this room is so big, move the light halfway down to the floor to get adequate lighting (see **FIGURE 3.45**).

4. Now you need to duplicate the light twice. With the light selected, press Ctrl+W to copy the light. The new light is automatically selected. Notice that the new light is slightly offset from the first, making it easier to discern the original from the copy.

5. Using the same technique, make one more copy of the light and position the new lights so that they form a vertical straight line along the left side of the hangar brush in the Top viewport. See the image in **FIGURE 3.46** if you need help.

> **NOTE**
>
> The scale of the light bulb icons has been increased so that you can see the lights better.

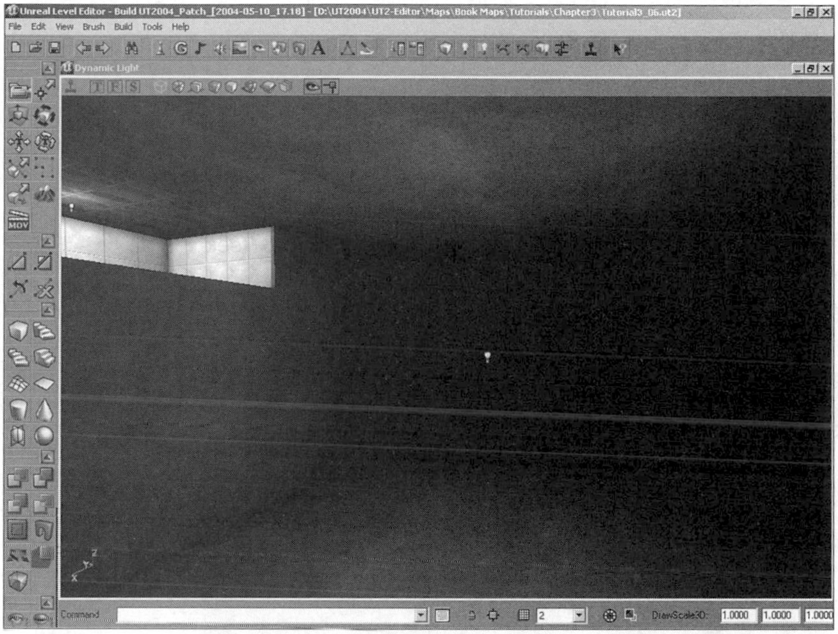

FIGURE 3.45 The hanger with one light in the center of the room.

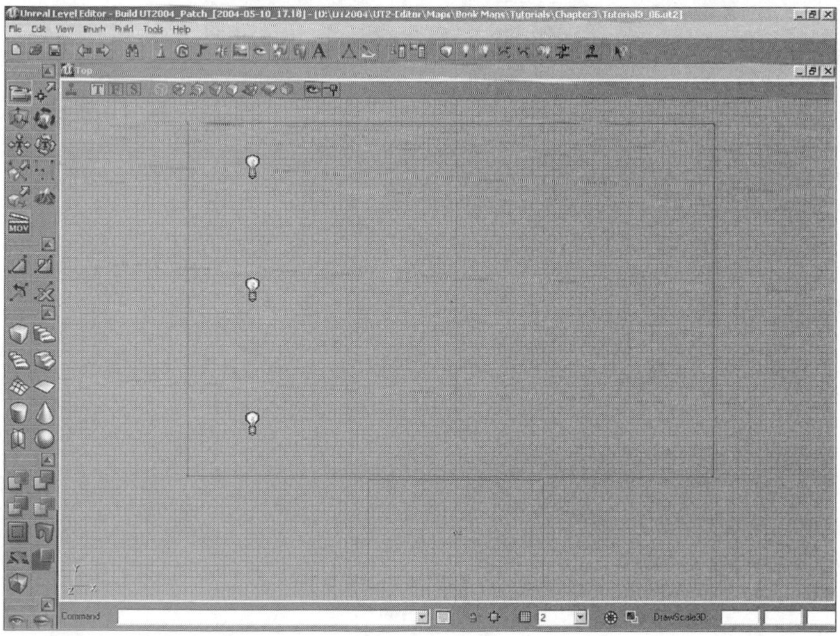

FIGURE 3.46 Top view of the three lights.

6. Select all three lights. Press Ctrl+W and move the new lights to the center of the room. Notice how the three lights move as one unit. Finally, duplicate the three lights again and position them near the right-hand wall. **FIGURE 3.47** shows a top view of the nine lights.

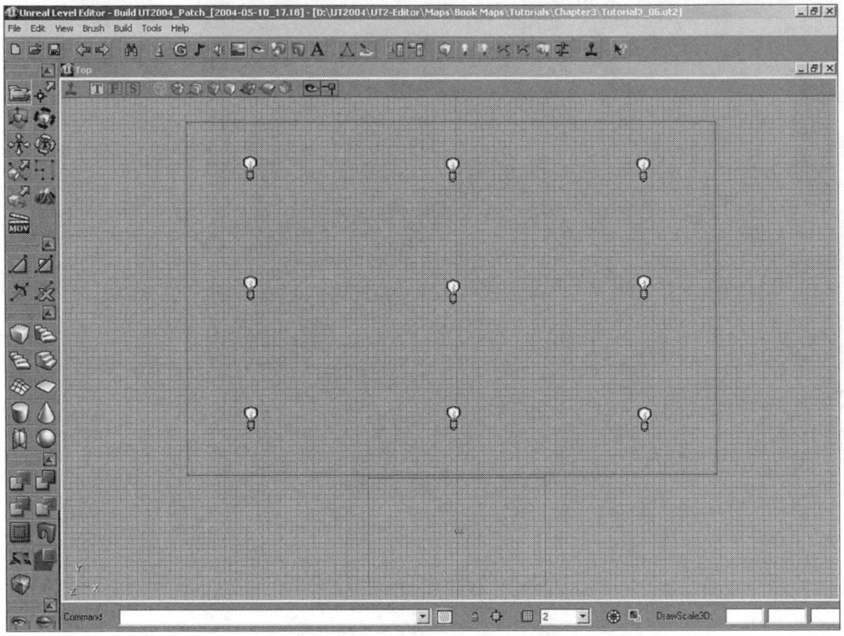

FIGURE 3.47 **Top view of the nine lights.**

7. Rebuild the level and change the Perspective viewport back to Dynamic Lighting mode so that you can see what type of illumination is in the hangar area (see **FIGURE 3.48**).

Keep in mind that any lights you add to the level at this stage are only temporary, intended to give you a general idea of basic illumination. You'll replace these lights after you have added all the light fixtures. If it helps, think of them as work lights.

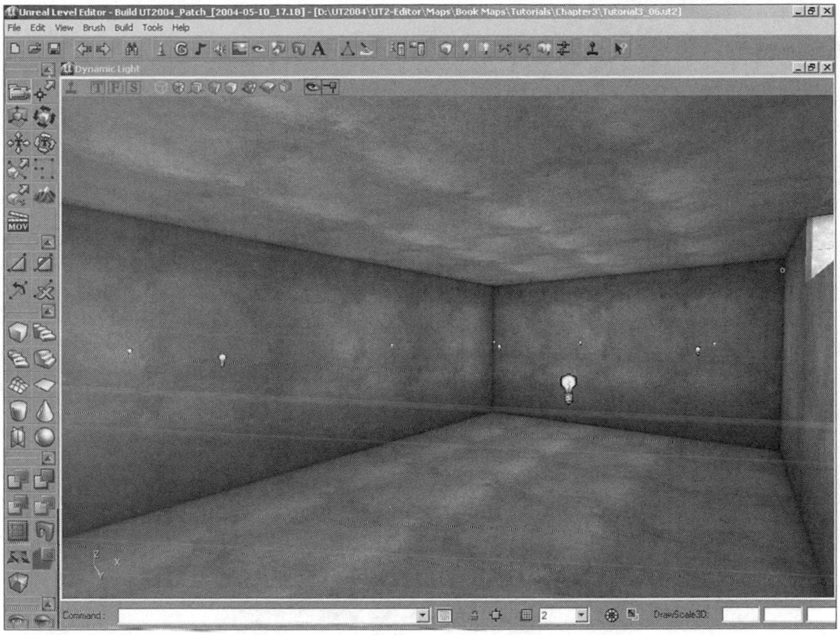

FIGURE 3.48 3D view of the properly lit hangar.

END TUTORIAL 3.7

TUTORIAL 3.8: Creating the Passageway That Connects the Hangar to the Control Room

1. Create a Cube Builder brush with the following settings:

   Height: 256

   Width: 656

   Breadth: 256

> **NOTE**
>
> **Moving the brush in this way creates a 32-unit gap between this new hallway and the hangar. You'll deal with that gap momentarily.**

2. Position the brush in the Top viewport so that it's aligned with the control room at the top and 16 grid spaces (with Grid Size set to 2) over from the left side (see **FIGURE 3.49**).

3. In the Side viewport, make sure the top of the hallway is aligned to the top of the other rooms (see **FIGURE 3.50**).

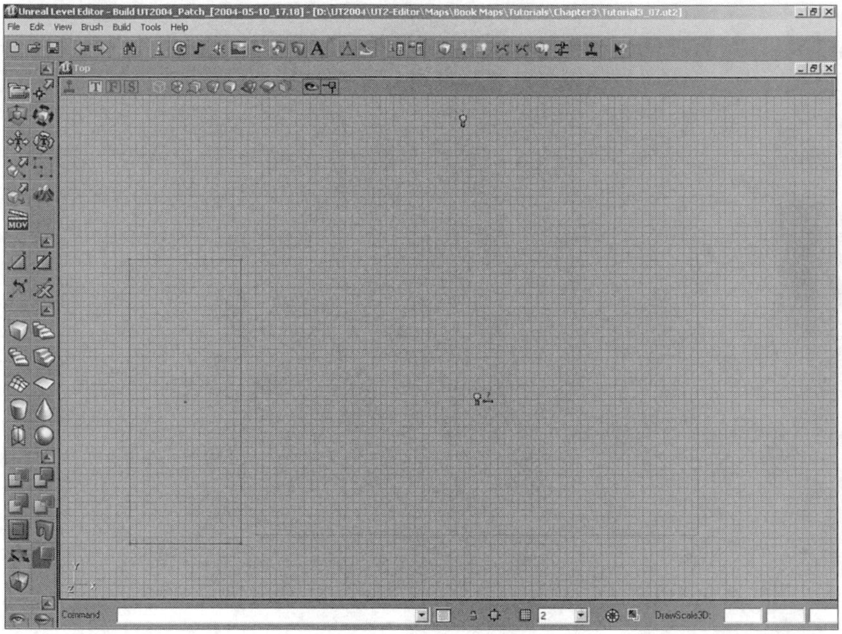

FIGURE 3.49 Top view of the Builder brush.

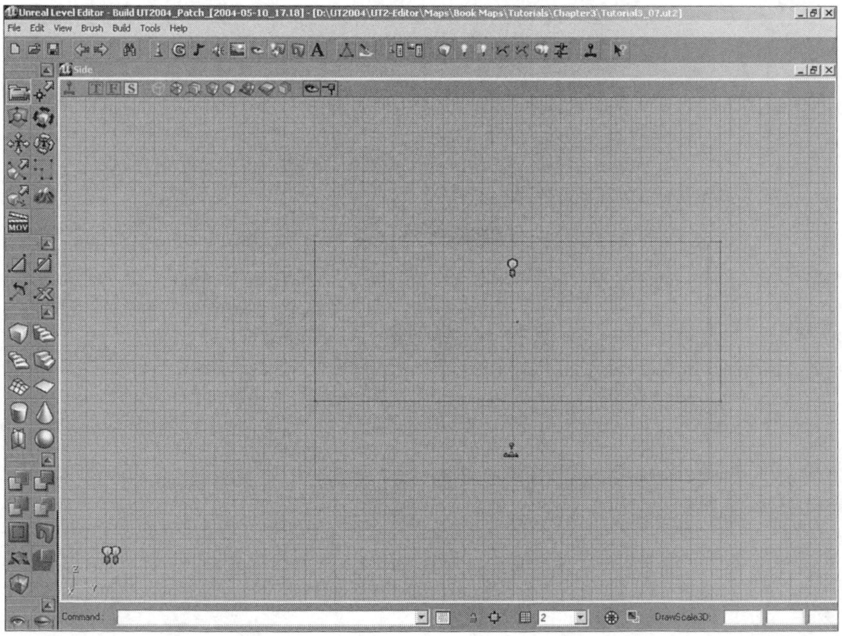

FIGURE 3.50 Side view of the Builder brush.

4. Subtract the space to form the hallway (see **FIGURE 3.51**). You don't need to rebuild at this stage, but you can if you like.

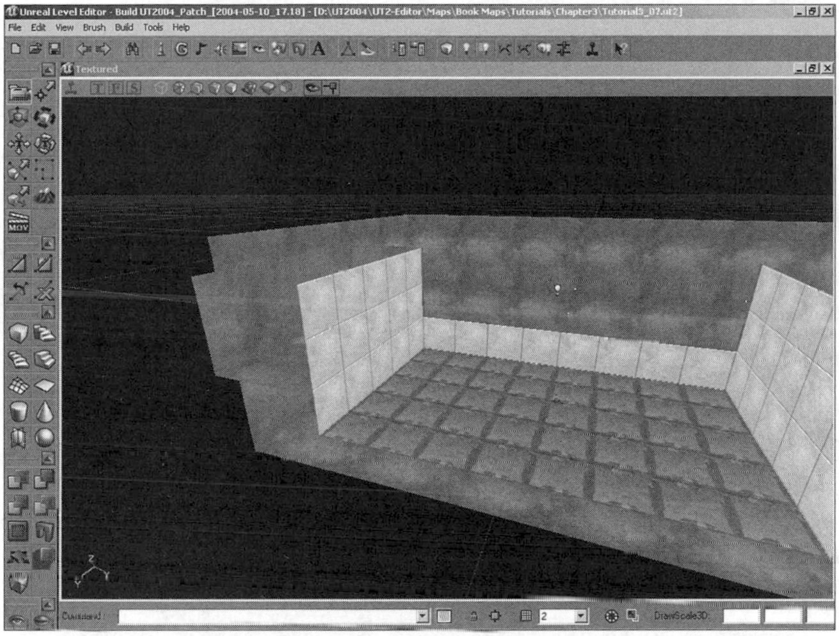

FIGURE 3.51 3D view of subtracted passageway.

5. To connect the hallway to the hangar, you're going to create an indented section that later serves as an elevator shaft. To do this, first create a Cube Builder brush with the following settings:

   Height: 1152

   Width: 16

   Breadth: 256

6. Position the brush in the Top view so that it's aligned against the top edge of the newly created hallway (see **FIGURE 3.52**). Make sure it's also aligned with the bottom of the hangar's floor in the Side view. It should perfectly fit the 32-unit gap mentioned earlier. This gap serves as an indentation in the hangar wall to make it easier to add an elevator later (see **FIGURE 3.53**).

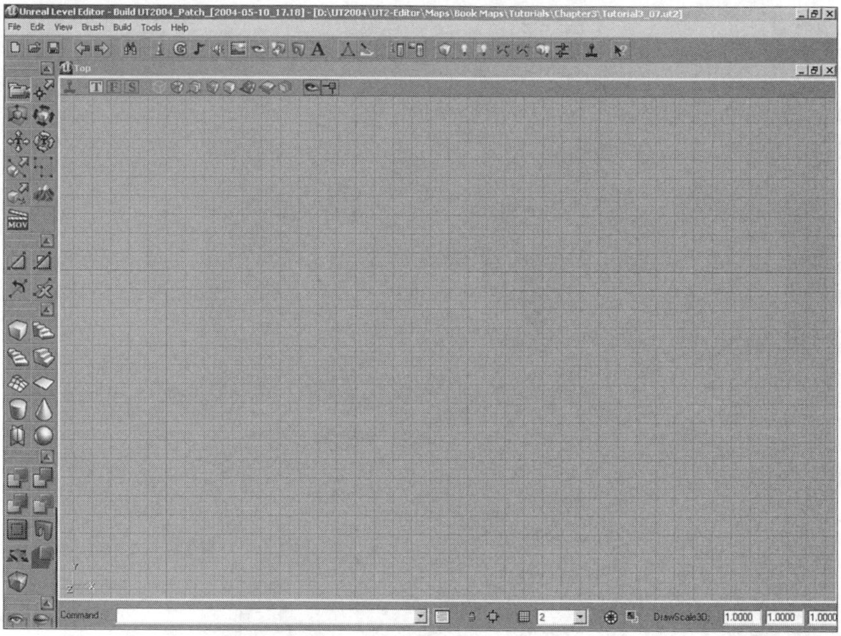

FIGURE 3.52 Top view of the Builder brush.

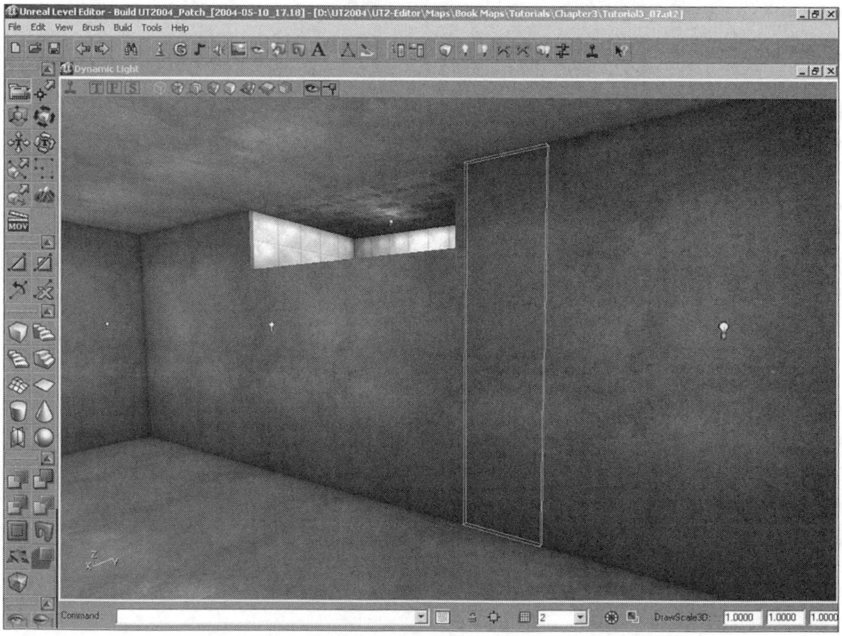

FIGURE 3.53 3D view of the Builder brush.

7. Subtract the space for the elevator shaft. Add a couple of lights in the hallway and rebuild the level. Your room should look similar to **FIGURE 3.54**.

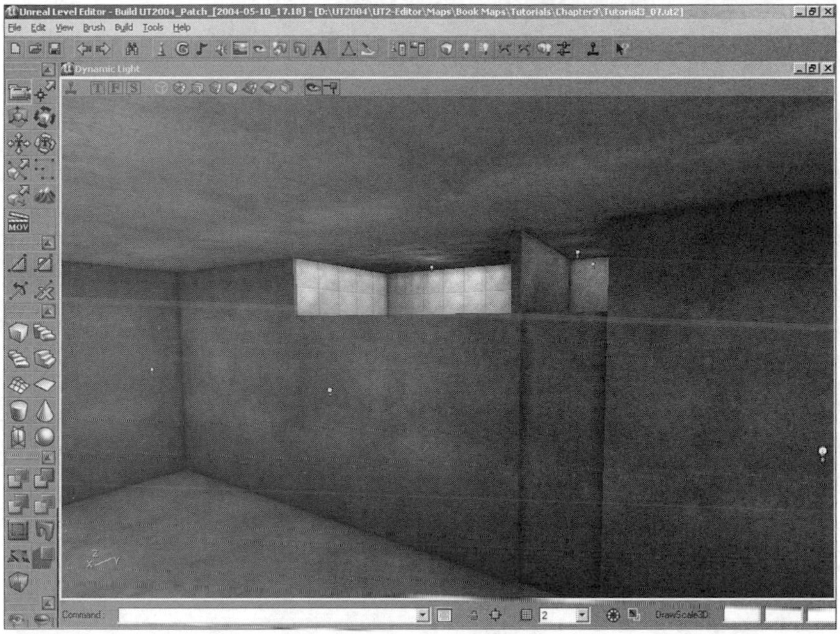

FIGURE 3.54 3D view of the hallway with lights.

8. To attach the hallway to the control room, you need to subtract two more sections. Create another Cube Builder brush with the following settings:

   Height: 256

   Width: 256

   Breadth: 672

9. Align the brush at the bottom of the first hallway brush in the Top view so that it creates a 90-degree turn in the hallway. **FIGURE 3.55** shows the 3D view of this brush.

10. Subtract the space for the connecting hallway.

11. Create one final Cube Builder brush with the following settings:

    Height: 256

    Width: 384

    Breadth: 256

12. Align the brush so that it's flush with the end of the last hallway and flush with the control room (see **FIGURE 3.56**).

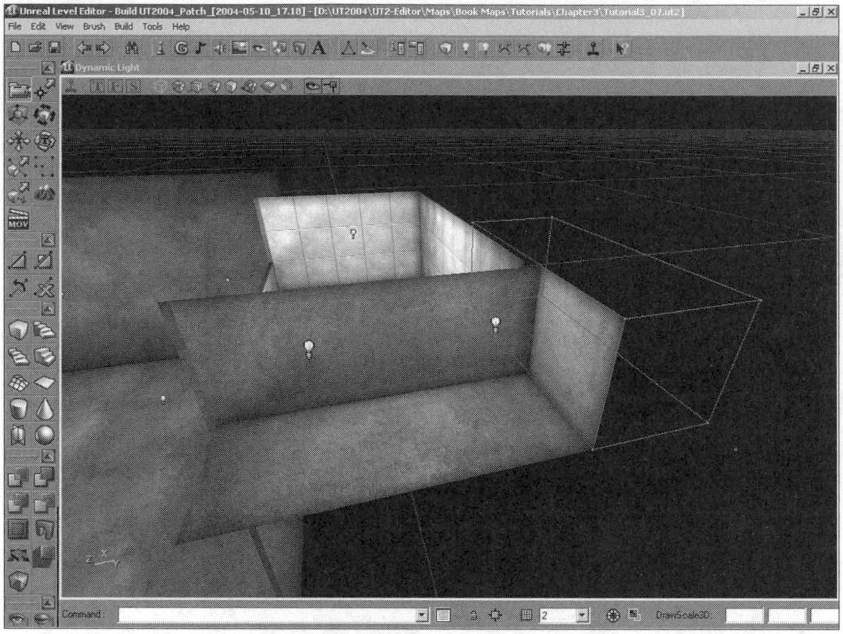

FIGURE 3.55 3D view of hallway Builder brush.

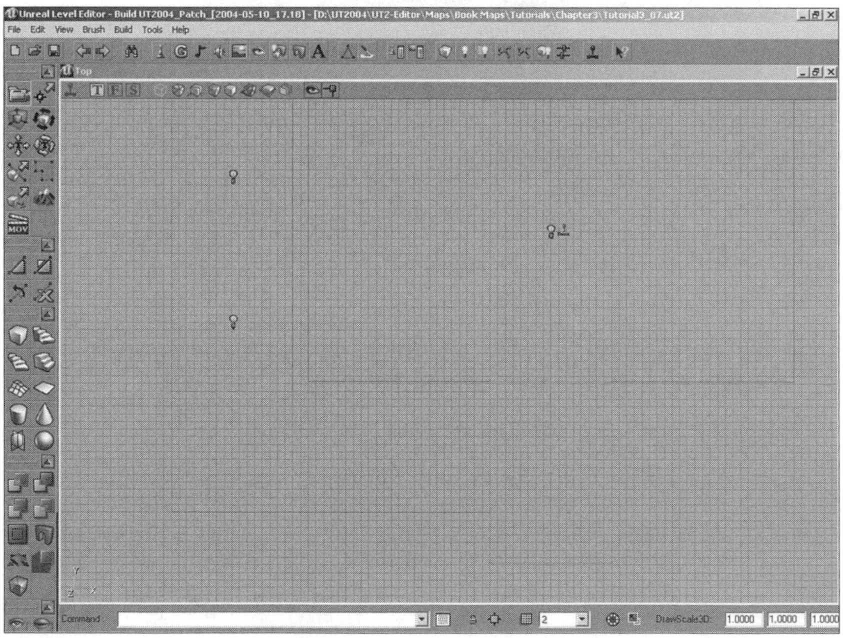

FIGURE 3.56 Top view of the connecting hallway.

13. Subtract the space. Add some lights in the hallway and rebuild the level. You should have something similar to **FIGURE 3.57**.

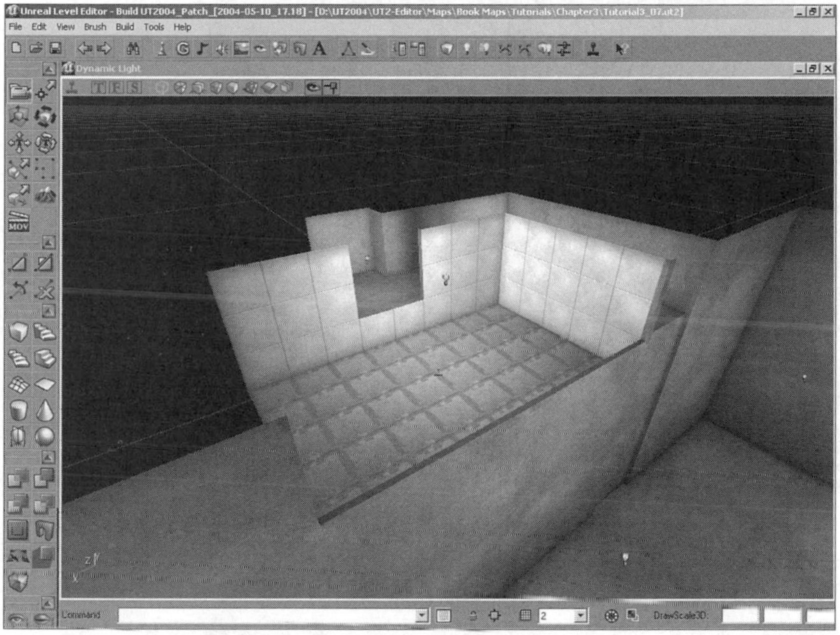

FIGURE 3.57 3D view of hallways and the control room.

14. Next, you add a window between the control room and the eastern hallway (see **FIGURE 3.58**). Create a Cube Builder brush with the following settings:

Height: 128

Width: 596

Breadth: 32

FIGURE 3.59 shows the 3D view of the subtracted window.

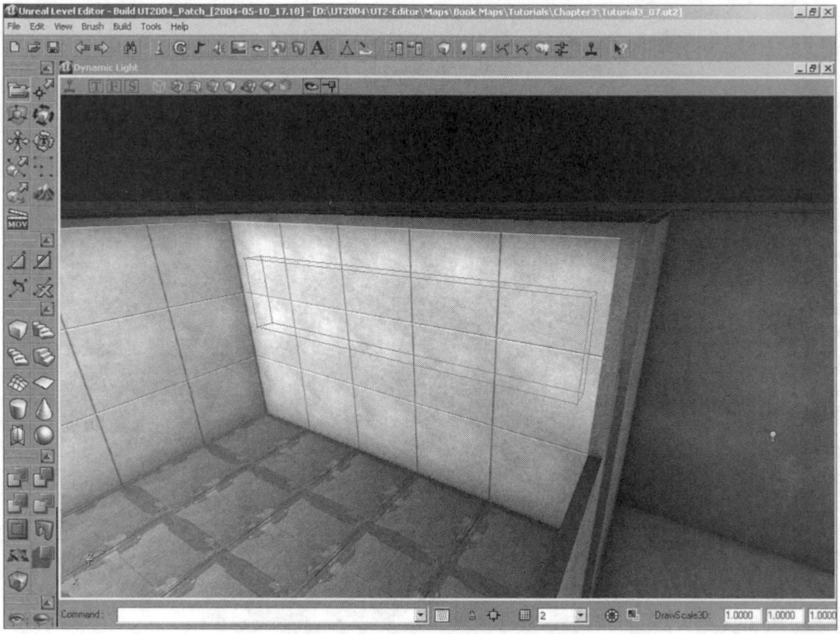

FIGURE 3.58 3D view of the window Builder brush.

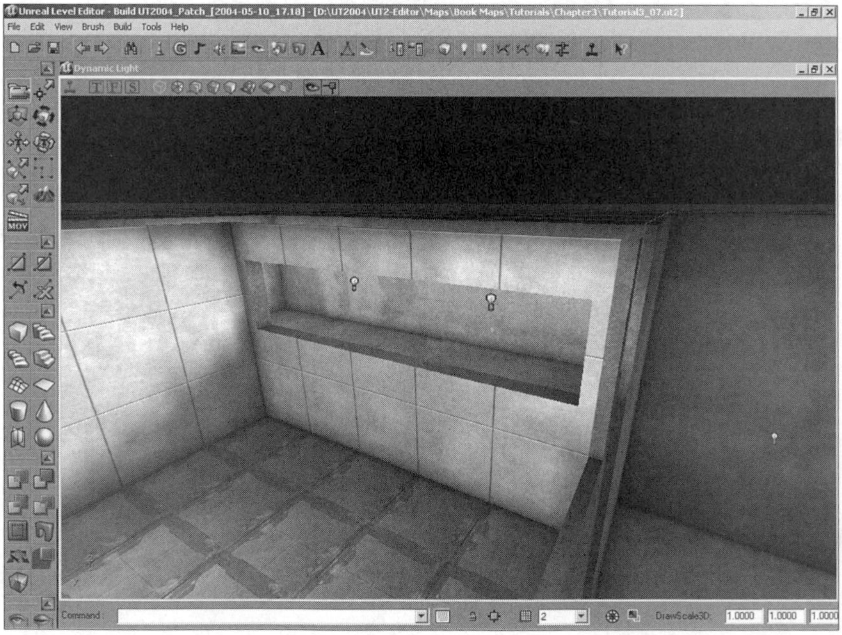

FIGURE 3.59 3D view of the subtracted window.

END TUTORIAL 3.8

Excellent work! After rebuilding, you will have all the map's world geometry in place and be ready to place the static meshes in the level. Save your work.

Adding Detail: Static Meshes

At the moment, your level still looks a little boring. To make it more attractive, you're going to add some static meshes. The first static meshes you add serve a practical purpose: to create a bridge across the control room and a window/observation deck in the control room to look out into the hangar. You then add stairs in the "pit" of the control room as well as rails to keep people from falling off and hurting themselves. Before you do that, however, have a look at the Static Meshes browser.

The Static Mesh Browser

To open the Static Mesh browser, click its icon on the toolbar or choose View > Show Static Mesh Browser from the menu. This browser has a layout similar to the Texture browser (see **FIGURE 3.60**). You can choose from any packages that might be loaded as well as groups within a package. On the left is a list of all static meshes in your selected group, and in the center is a large viewport that you can navigate in the same manner as the 3D viewport in UnrealEd.

You can open packages of static meshes in this browser, select a group, choose a specific mesh, and navigate around it. You can also edit the textures on a static mesh, and save your changes to a new or existing package. After you have selected a static mesh, right-click anywhere in your level and choose Add Static Mesh: *Some.Static.Mesh*. The italicized words are the name of the static mesh you have selected in the browser. For more information on the Static Mesh browser and its functionality, be sure to refer to Appendix A.

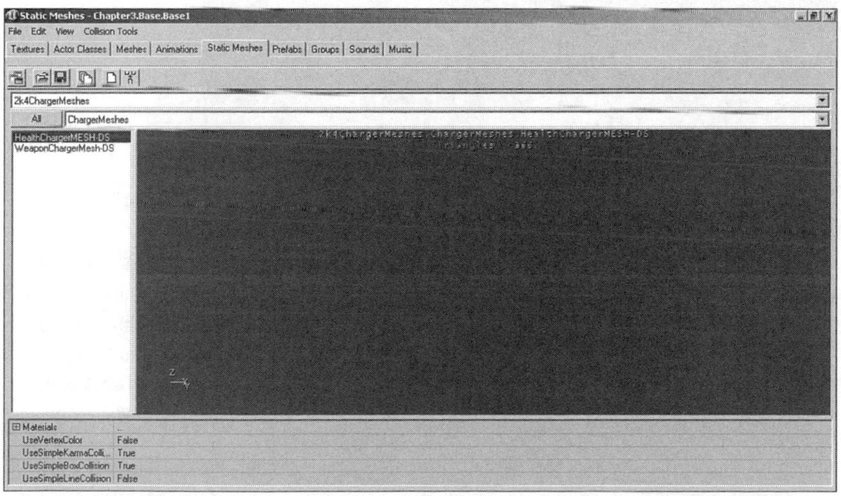

FIGURE 3.60 The Static Mesh browser.

Placing Static Meshes

In the next section, you're going to take a look at placing static meshes in your map. Later, after you have a clearer idea of how to add static meshes, you try more advanced techniques on your own to add some decorative static meshes for completing the map.

Adding the Control Room Window

TUTORIAL 3.9 shows you how to add a window to your control room.

3

TUTORIAL 3.9: Adding the Control Room Window

1. Open the Static Mesh browser and load the `Chapter3_sm.usx` package by choosing File > Open from the browser menu.
2. Change the group to FrameWork and select the `Control_Room` static mesh (see **FIGURE 3.61**). You use this static mesh to cover the window from the control room into the hangar.

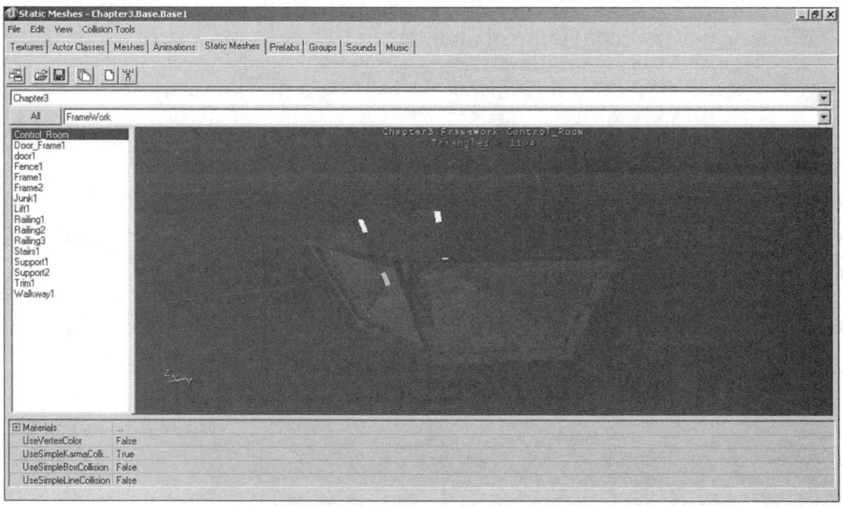

FIGURE 3.61 The Control_Room static mesh.

3. Right-click anywhere in your level (it's best to do it close to where the static mesh is going to be placed) and choose Add Static Mesh to place the new FrameWork mesh in your level.

> **TIP**
>
> A Drag Grid Size of 32 makes the alignment in step 4 much easier. Remember that aligning any Actors, including static meshes, is easier if you always use the highest possible Drag Grid Size settings.

4. Align the static mesh so that it fills in the large window in the control room. It should be aligned with the hangar's wall and ceiling and completely cover the window into the control room. **FIGURE 3.62** and **3.63** show the 3D view of the FrameWork static mesh from inside and outside the control room, respectively.

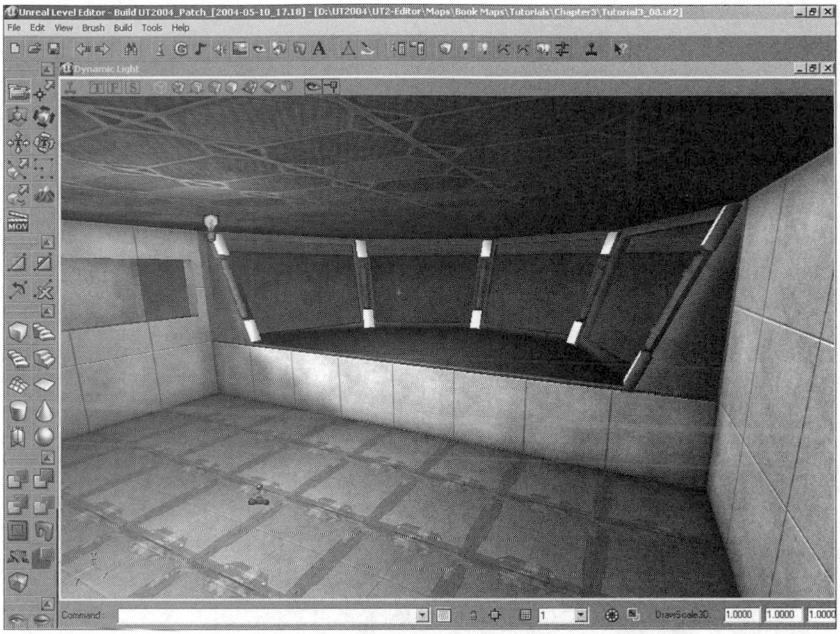

FIGURE 3.62 3D view of the FrameWork static mesh from inside the control room.

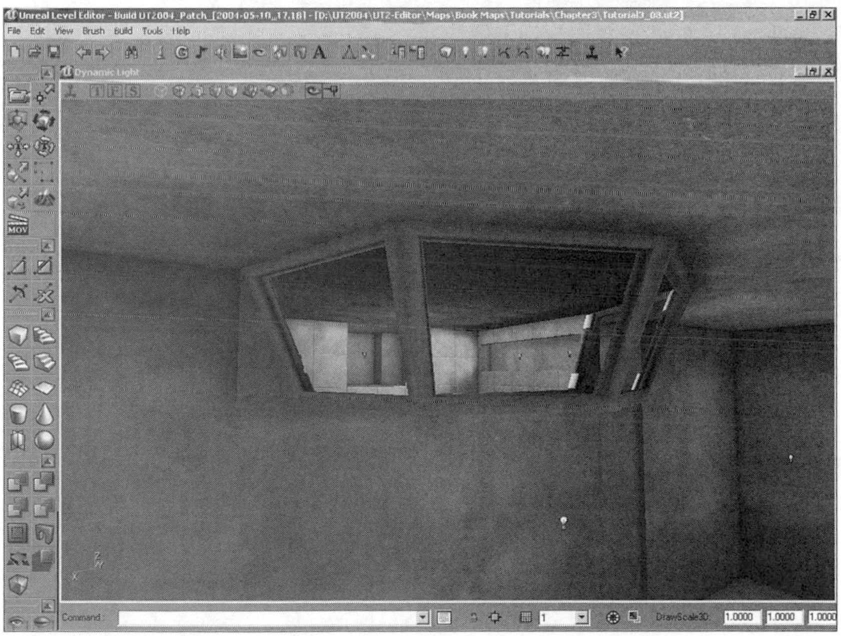

FIGURE 3.63 3D view of the FrameWork static mesh from outside the control room.

END TUTORIAL 3.9

Adding the Bridge

You need a bridge crossing the "pit" or work area of the control room. However, the static mesh you select at first is too large to fit if you simply copy it. You need to adjust its scale by using the DrawScale3D tool.

TUTORIAL 3.10: Adding the Bridge

3

1. In the Static Mesh browser, select `Walkway1` (see **FIGURE 3.64**).

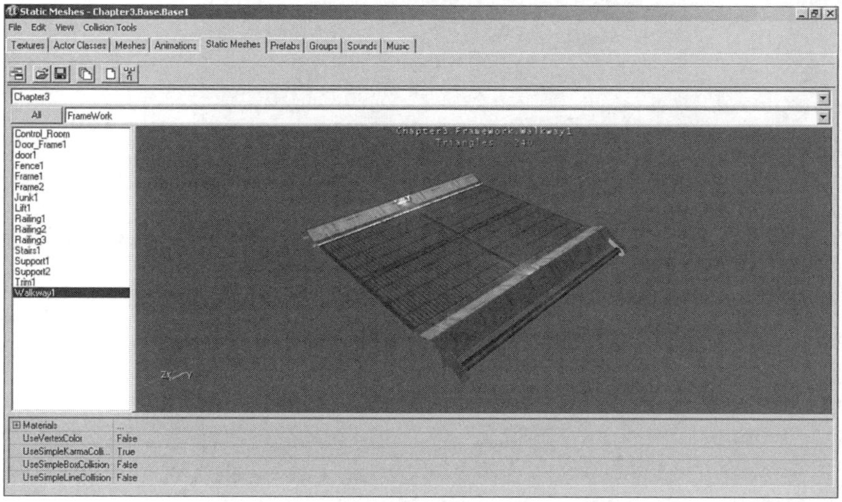

FIGURE 3.64 `Walkway1` **static mesh.**

2. Right-click in the 3D viewport to add the static mesh to the map.

3. Set the DrawScale3D Y (found in the console bar) value to `0.50`. You should enter this number in the *second* text box. The three numbers displayed in this area correspond to X, Y, and Z, from left to right (see **FIGURE 3.65**).

4. Position the static mesh on the end with the control room. It should be centered on the control room and aligned with the edge of the window in the Top and Side views (see **FIGURE 3.66**). Adjust your Drag Grid Size setting accordingly. **FIGURE 3.67** shows the 3D view of the first piece of the bridge.

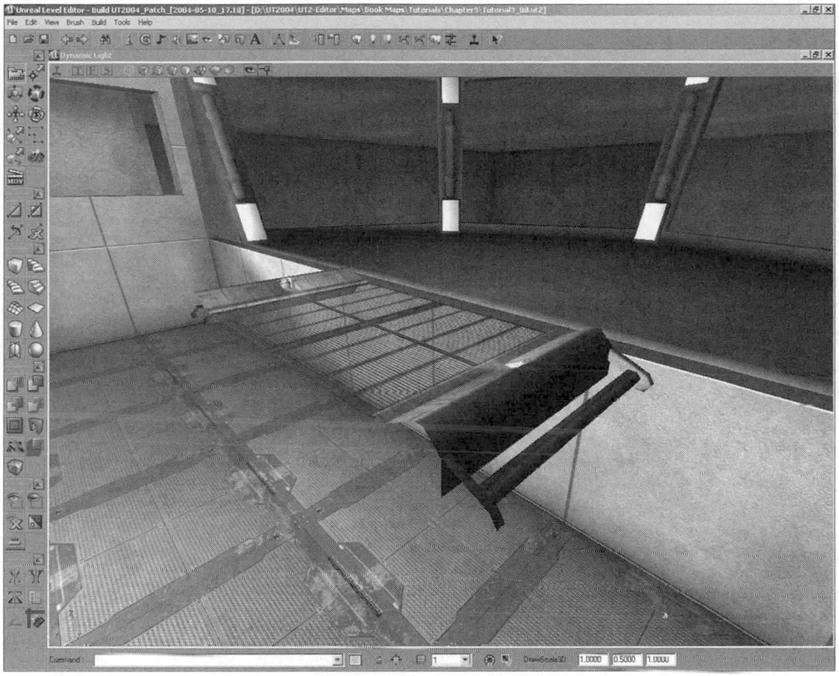

FIGURE 3.65 DrawScale3D settings.

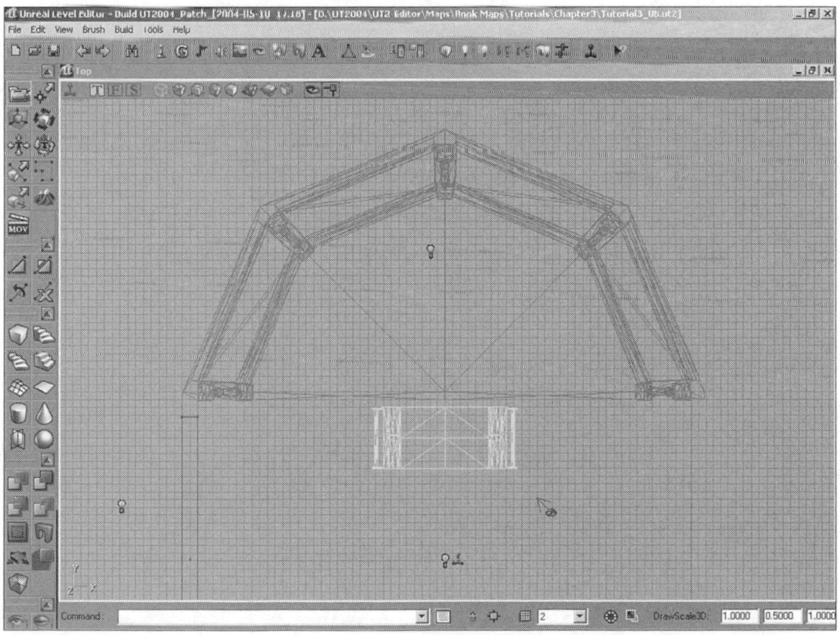

FIGURE 3.66 Top view of the first piece of the bridge.

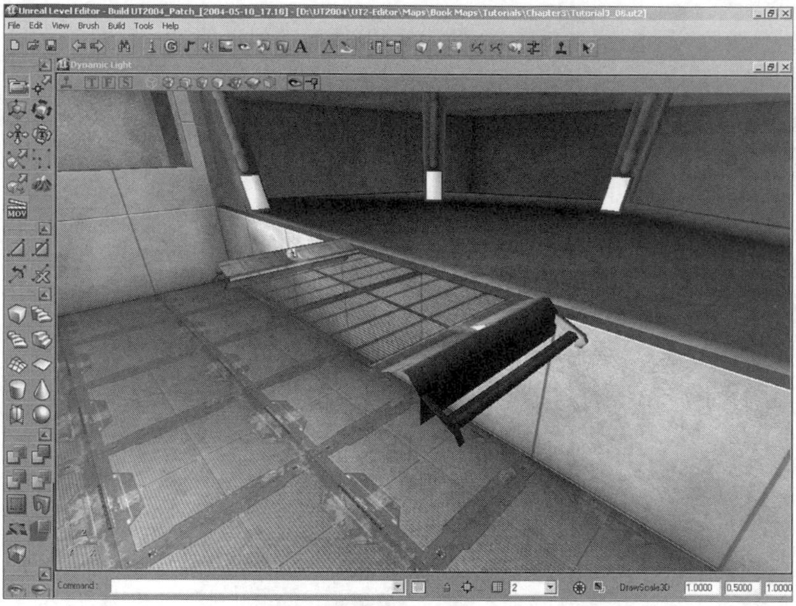

FIGURE 3.67 3D view of the first piece of the bridge.

5. Press Ctrl+W to duplicate the static mesh walkway. Move the new copy back so that it aligns with the other walkway mesh (see **FIGURE 3.68**).

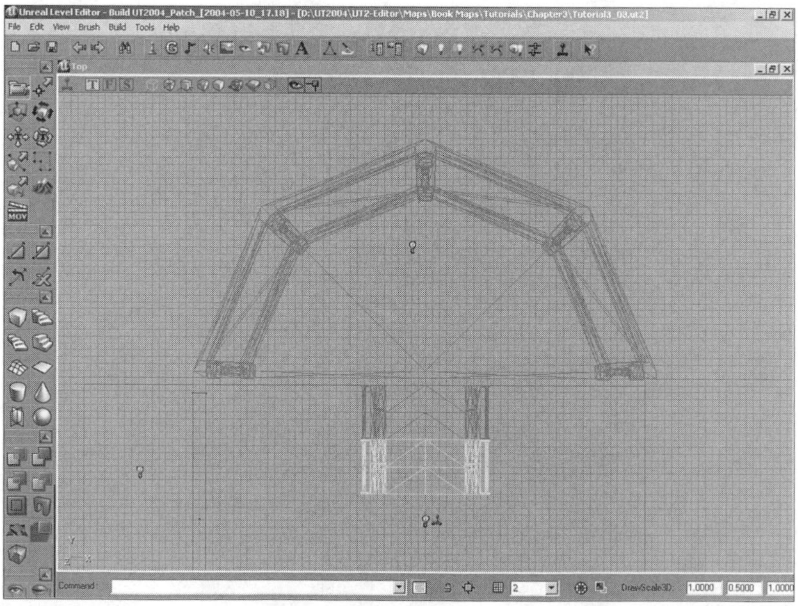

FIGURE 3.68 Top view of the second piece of the bridge.

6. Duplicate the walkway three more times, and align each one with its predecessor. The fifth static mesh might overlap slightly into the wall, but this is acceptable (see **FIGURE 3.69**).
7. In the Static Mesh browser, select the `Railing1` mesh (see **FIGURE 3.70**).

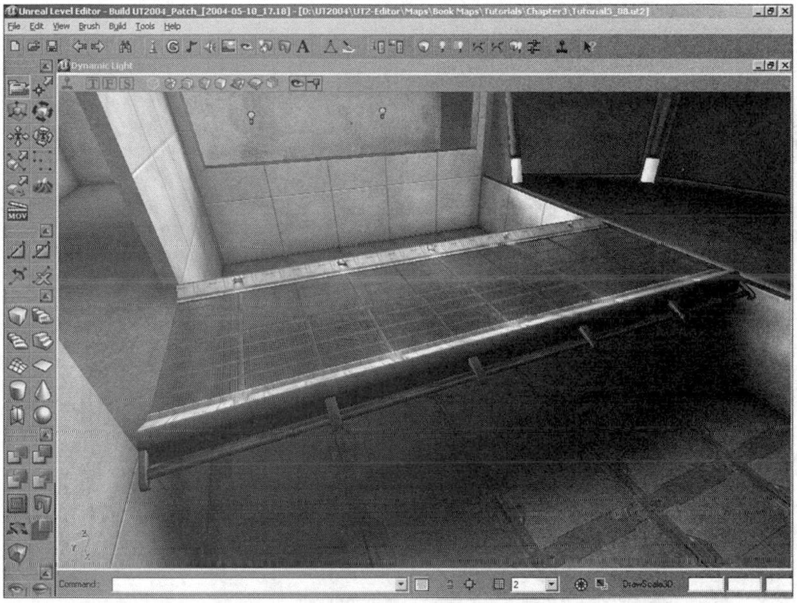

FIGURE 3.69 3D view of the entire bridge.

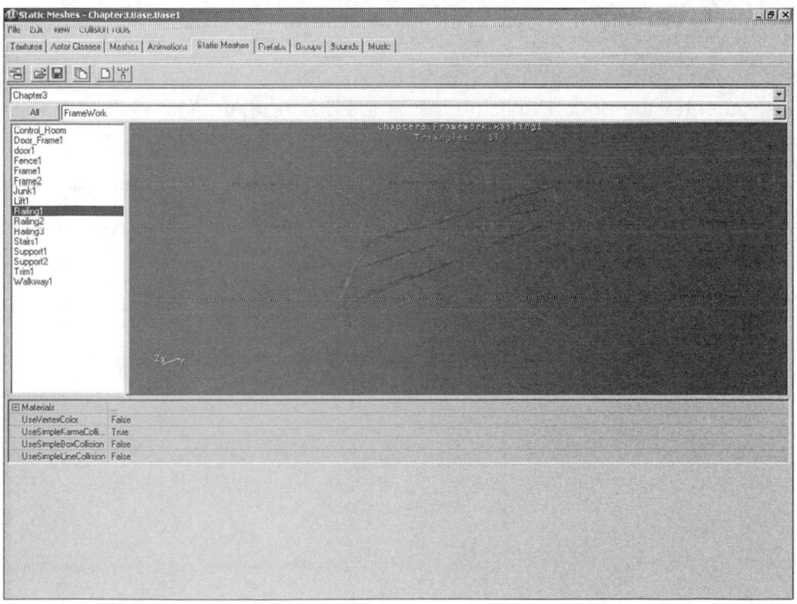

FIGURE 3.70 Railing1 static mesh.

8. Add and align the Railing1 static mesh, and then duplicate it until you have two railings on each side of the bridge and one on each side of the control window (see **FIGURE 3.71**). You need to add a total of six static meshes to the level. Be sure to leave some spacing at the beginning of the walkway for the stairs, which are added next.

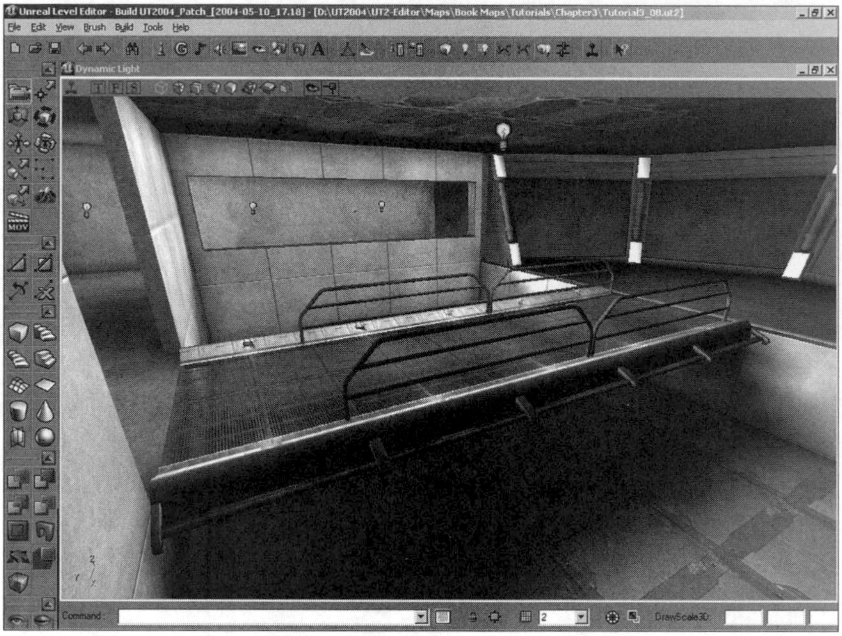

FIGURE 3.71 Four railings for the bridge.

9. Add the Stairs1 static mesh to the level. Align the mesh so that you can climb down from the walkway just as you enter the door. Duplicate the stairs, rotate them 180 degrees, and position them on the opposite side of the walkway, as shown in **FIGURE 3.72**.

10. As before, rebuild all your lighting and play-test the level. Make sure your meshes not only appear to be positioned well, but also serve their designated functions.

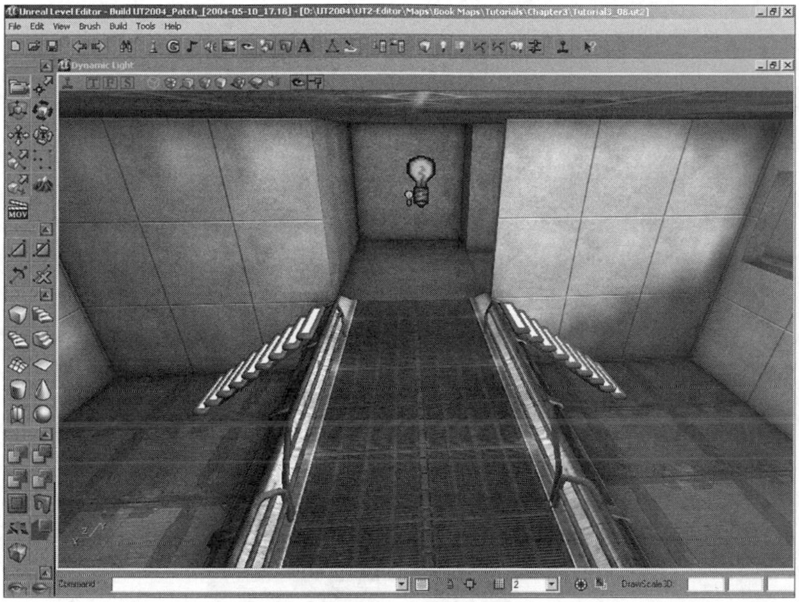

FIGURE 3.72 Stairs added to the walkway.

END TUTORIAL 3.10

Decorating with Static Meshes

You have now placed all the functional static meshes in your level, but overall it's still dull. You need to add more static meshes to fill the level with physical detail. However, instead of stepping through placing what could be hundreds of instances of static meshes, you have the opportunity to practice what you've learned by completing the room on your own. **FIGURE 3.73** shows what this room is intended to look like, with some additional objects. Read over the following sections, examine the collection of static meshes in the `Chapter3_sm.usx` package, and have fun!

Control Room Treatment

The control room consists of a bridge-like walkway that extends over a bay filled with computers and monitoring equipment. These computers should be underneath the bridge and along the walls. However, they should be positioned so that there's a clear passage between the two sides of the pit. The control room needs several monitors and screens to help keep track of information being sent to it from the hangar.

Because the hangar might need to depressurize in an emergency, you need to add some sort of heavy ventilation equipment to move large quantities of air quickly so that the control room environment isn't compromised. Along the wall opposite the hallway window, you should add some pipework and braces to help support sections of the ceiling. You need to add light fixtures on the ceiling, too. **FIGURE 3.74** shows the completed control room.

FIGURE 3.73 Completed level.

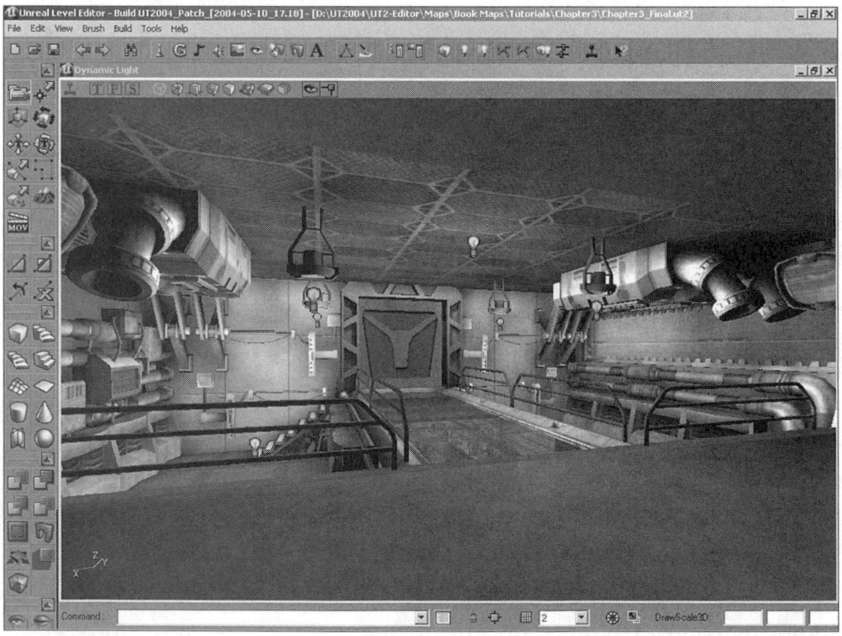

FIGURE 3.74 A completed version of the control room.

Completion Challenge

Beneath the walkway across the control room, you should add a staircase that moves down and away from the direction of the hangar into a smaller room. This room houses the main electronics of the control room's computer systems. It needs a power core, several transistor units, and a main CPU.

FIGURE 3.75 shows you some ideas for finishing the room. Feel free to experiment, and build the map in your own image. Be patient—level design is not a quick process. When you're finished, rebuild and play-test the map. Congratulations! You have just finished your first Unreal map.

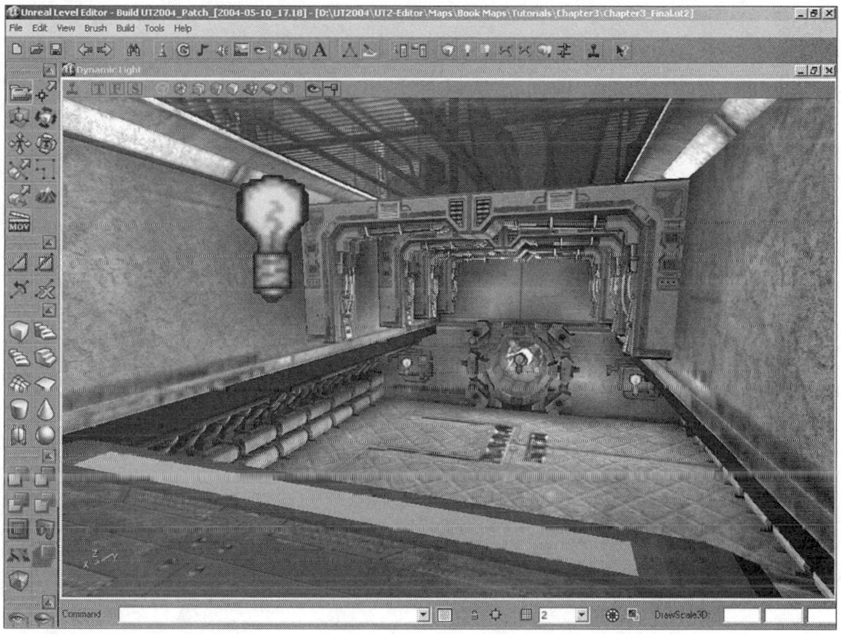

FIGURE 3.75 The Control room with more decorative static meshes.

Summary

This chapter has covered navigation in three-dimensional space, how to create and manipulate your Actors, how to use BSP brushes, and how to subtract spaces from the Unreal world.

You have also learned how to use brushes to create world geometry, place textures onto the surfaces of that geometry, and add lighting and practical and decorative static meshes to your level.

With the skills you have learned, you can now create a wide variety of levels in the Unreal Engine. In Chapter 4, "Advanced Brush Techniques," you learn more about BSP brushes and their advanced functions.

Chapter 4

Advanced Brush Techniques

By now, you should have a general understanding of how Binary Space Partitioning (BSP) brushes are created and used in level design. In this chapter, you supplement that knowledge by learning the fundamental theory behind BSP and a variety of advanced techniques you can use to take full advantage of how BSP works. This chapter also covers Intersect and De-Intersect brushes and the 2D Shape Editor, which is an invaluable tool for those without access to a 3D application, such as Maya or 3ds max. Next, you learn how to save the brushes you create for future use and how to export your brushes from UnrealEd.

This chapter's coverage focuses on helping you understand how the geometry of your levels works so that you can make your levels operate more efficiently and complete them in a more timely fashion. For example, when building objects in your levels from BSP brushes, you *can* use just simple brushes and primitives, but this method could create unnecessary detail in your level. For example, say you wanted to create a pillar with crossbeam supports coming out of it, as in **FIGURE 4.1**.

For this example, a cylinder primitive was used for the central pillar and added to the level with an additive brush. For the crossbeams, you *could* simply make them with additive brushes as well so that they intersect not only with each other, but also with the central pillar. **FIGURE 4.2** shows the effect in the Top viewport.

FIGURE 4.1 Room with central pillar and crossbeams.

This method might seem to work, but it's actually creating unnecessary geometry, which could eventually result in BSP errors, such as a Hall of Mirrors (HOM) effect. The problem is that the lines inside the cylinder shouldn't exist because separate pieces of world geometry shouldn't be allowed to pass through each other. To fix this, you can perform an action called *intersection*, which modifies the Builder brush so that the additive geometry of the crossbeams doesn't pass through the cylinder. Intersection is discussed more in "The Intersect Tool," later in this chapter, but if you performed this action on both crossbeams, the result would look similar to **FIGURE 4.3.**

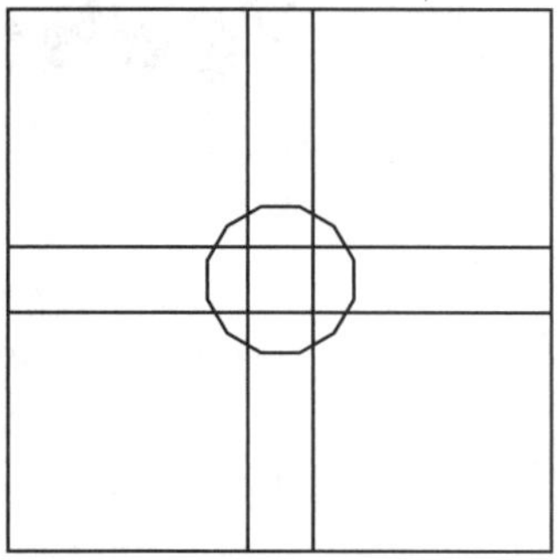

FIGURE 4.2 Crossbeams created with simple additive brushes.

This technique might look more visually complex, but it's actually easier for the computer to calculate because of the nature of BSP. The next section discusses the fundamental workings of BSP, how the Unreal Engine uses it to control how BSP brushes are used, and how the world geometry surfaces in your levels are rendered.

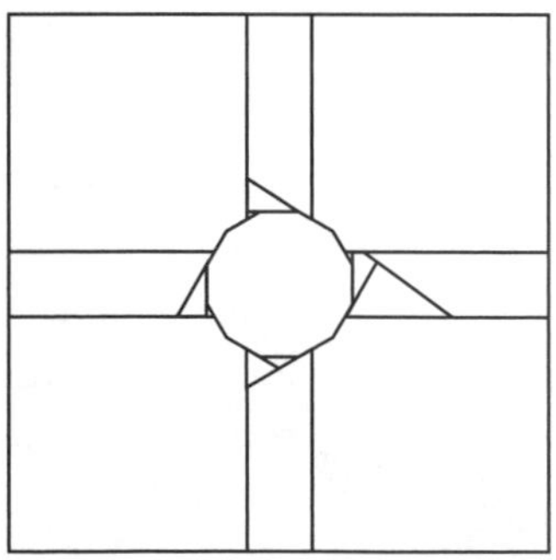

FIGURE 4.3 Crossbeams are made by using an intersection before creating the additive geometry.

BSP Theory

When you start combining brushes in complex situations, you might get results that seem strange at first, such as the cuts in the crossbeams of the example in the previous section. These cuts are caused by BSP. After you understand how BSP works, the purpose behind these cuts and divisions will be clear. Please keep in mind that the theory behind BSP can be difficult to understand at first, so don't get frustrated if it takes a few tries to fully grasp. After you understand how the graphics engine uses BSP, you'll have a much better handle on what's going on behind the scenes of your maps and levels.

Polygons

Before you go any further, however, take a quick look at polygons, as they are the basis for why BSP calculations take place on three edges. All polygons in Unreal are triangles, and every polygon has a positive and a negative side that you can think of as the front (the positive side) and back (the negative side). "Positive" and "negative" in this context, however, aren't relative terms based on a viewer's perspective. The positive and negative sides of a polygon are constant, regardless of the angle from which you're seeing the polygon. A good analogy is describing the sides of a polygon as the head and tail sides of a coin. No matter how you flip a coin or move around it, the head and tail sides are constant in relation to the coin.

The front and back of a polygon are significant for two reasons. First, they are used in creating BSP trees, which are described in the next section. Second, the graphics engine doesn't draw the negative side of a polygon. Therefore, if you're looking at a wall with no depth (a simple 2D plane) in Unreal, you could look at it only if you were facing its positive side. As soon as you move around behind the wall and try to look at it, it's no longer visible because you're looking at the negative side of the polygon that makes up that wall. The reason you can actually see both sides of a wall when in the game is that the wall has thickness. After you add thickness to a plane, it effectively becomes a cube, which has six faces. When you're looking at the back of a wall in an Unreal map, you're actually looking at the *positive* side of a polygon on the *back* of a cube. Note: You can force the rendering engine to draw the negative side of a polygon by placing a two-sided material on it. Materials are discussed in Chapter 8, "Creating Materials in Unreal."

BSP Trees

Now that you understand what polygons are, you can learn how BSP calculations are made by creating *BSP trees*. A BSP tree is nothing more than a method of arranging polygons so that the graphics engine draws them in the right order.

Draw Order

The order in which the graphics engine draws polygons is vital to what rendered scenes look like. Imagine standing at the end of a hallway, with three walls dividing it, as shown in **FIGURE 4.4.**

When you're trying to see the end of the hall, Wall 1 blocks your view, and you can't see Wall 2 or Wall 3. This problem happens in the real world because of *occlusion*—one object blocking the view of another.

In a graphics engine, however, this problem occurs because of the order in which polygons are drawn. In Unreal, polygons are drawn from far to near, meaning that the polygon farthest away from the player is drawn first, then the next closest, then the next closest, and so on. The effect is the same as placing several stickers on a piece of paper, overlapping them one atop the other. The last sticker you place is the one in "front," and the first sticker placed is in the "rear." If polygons are drawn in the incorrect order, it's extremely difficult to tell which surfaces are nearest to you and which ones are farther away in the game. In **FIGURE 4.5**, you can see the results of draw order and how they apply to the example of Walls 1, 2, and 3. On the left is the result of incorrect draw order, meaning that the nearest wall was drawn first. The draw order in that case is Wall 1, then Wall 2, and then Wall 3. On the right is the same scene drawn in the correct order, starting with the farthest wall first: Wall 3, then Wall 2, and then Wall 1.

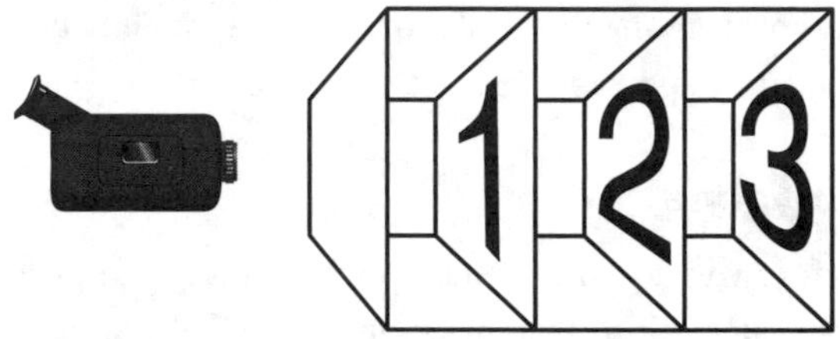

FIGURE 4.4 Occlusion that blocks the view of Wall 3.

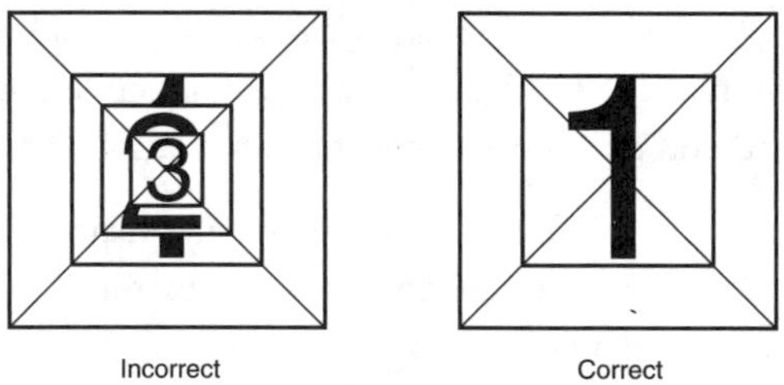

FIGURE 4.5 Correct and incorrect draw order.

Tree Creation

The graphics engine uses BSP trees to determine the order in which these walls, or polygons, are drawn. The BSP tree is formed by an algorithm, which begins by designating a single polygon as a point of reference. This polygon, called the *origin polygon*, goes at the top of the tree. The algorithm then moves on to the next polygon it finds and places it in the tree beneath the first polygon. If the second polygon is on the same side as the front (positive side) of the origin polygon, this new polygon is placed, say, on the right side of the tree. If the polygon is on the same side as the *back* (negative side) of the origin polygon, it's placed on the *left* side of the tree. The next polygon is placed below the second, using the same system to determine whether it's placed to that polygon's right or left.

At the same time this calculation is going on, the engine is checking to see where cuts need to be made in the BSP. This is done by testing whether a polygon would cut into any other polygons if you extended it to infinity. If it does, the polygon being cut would technically exist on both sides of the first polygon. This makes it impossible to determine on which side of the BSP tree to place it. Therefore, that polygon is going to be split in half. Those two new polygons are then processed, with the half on the positive side going on the right side of the tree and the half on the negative side going on the left side of the tree. The algorithm then continues this pattern until it has accounted for every polygon in the level. The resulting shape is a tapered network, with the origin polygon at the top, forming a tree-like shape.

To see how tree creation works, take a simple two-dimensional level, shown in **FIGURE 4.6**, and create a BSP tree for it.

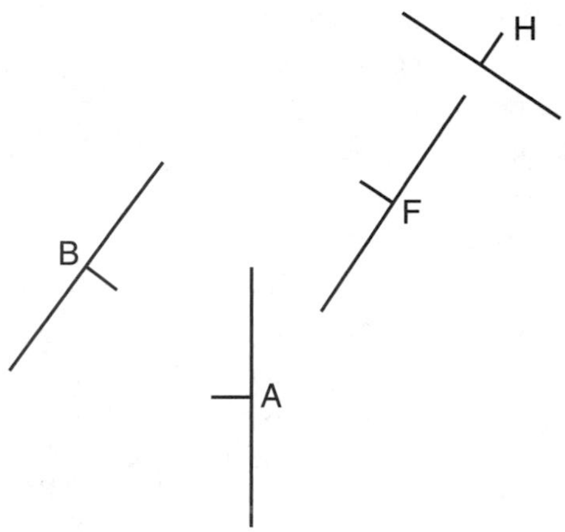

FIGURE 4.6 A two-dimensional level represented with lines.

Each polygon, or line, is given a name. The little lines protruding from each polygon line are called the *normals*. They designate the polygon's positive and negative sides: The side with the normal protruding from it is considered positive.

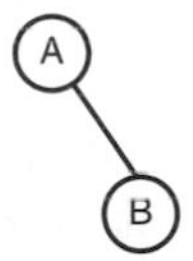

FIGURE 4.7 First step in constructing the BSP tree.

Start by picking a line to be the origin polygon. For this example, use line A, and start by processing the positive side. B is the only polygon on the positive side of A, so place it on the right side of the tree (see **FIGURE 4.7**).

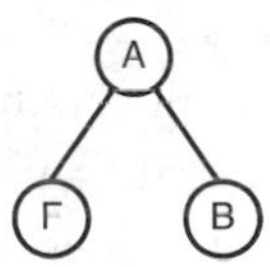

FIGURE 4.8 Second step in constructing the BSP tree.

Two polygons are on the negative side of A. For this simple demonstration, it doesn't matter which polygon you choose, so begin with F, which is on the negative side of A. This means it's placed on the left side of the tree (see **FIGURE 4.8**).

If you extended line F to infinity, it would intersect H. Technically, this means H is not placed on the positive or negative side of F, so you have to split H into H1 and H2. Now H1 is on the positive side of F and H2 is on the negative side. When you place them under the tree, they both go underneath F, with H1 on the right and H2 on the left. **FIGURE 4.9** shows the final BSP tree.

Now that this tree has been created, the graphics engine can use it as a diagram of the polygon's relationships to each other based on their relation to the origin polygon. This diagram can then be used to determine in which order polygons should be drawn. Here's how it works: If the player is looking at the origin polygon and its positive side is facing away from the player, meaning the player is facing the negative side, the engine would go down the *right* side of the tree. Think about it: You've already established that all polygons on the *positive* side of the origin are placed on the *right* side of the BSP tree. Therefore, if the positive side of the origin is pointed *away* from the player, all polygons on the right side of the BSP tree must be on the opposite side of the origin polygon, from the player's perspective.

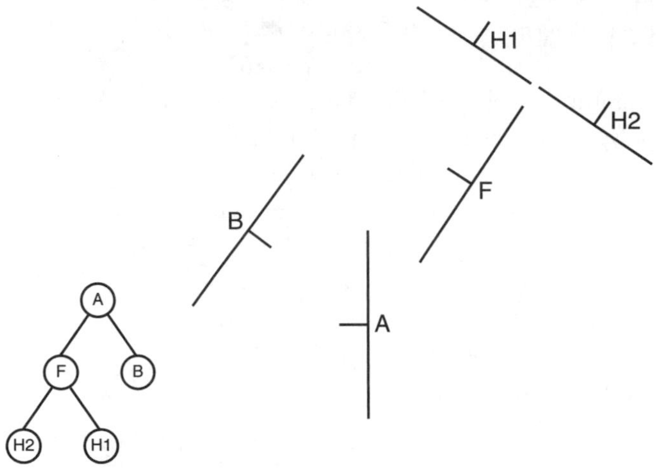

FIGURE 4.9 Final BSP tree along with the 2D level where line H is now split.

As you move down the right side of the tree, you're effectively moving away from the player. When you reach the end of the "branch," you're at the farthest polygon from where the player is standing. The graphics engine then draws these polygons, starting at the end of this branch and moving back up to the top, all the way to the origin polygon. The result is that all the polygons are drawn in the correct order, with the farthest polygon from the player being drawn first and the nearest polygon being drawn last. This causes the polygons closest to the player to appear to be *in front* of the polygons that are farther away.

Perhaps the best part of this algorithm, however, is that it's calculated *before* the game is even played, which speeds the game up dramatically during runtime. Note, too, that BSP can also be used as a method for determining whether the graphics engine even calculates polygons completely outside the player's view. This method, however, is an unreliable way to gauge whether to render polygons. To solve this problem, level designers can implement *portals* and *zones* to determine what parts of a level are calculated and what parts are not. These techniques are covered in Chapter 15, "Level Optimization (Zoning) and Distribution."

Brushes from Other Brushes

When creating your levels, at times you need brushes with special shapes that you can't produce by using simple primitives. Say, for instance, that you need a half-sphere brush. The primitive brushes have no setting for this shape, but often, you can achieve unusual shapes by basing your brush on geometry already in the level. The following sections explain a pair of tools in UnrealEd called Intersect and De-Intersect. These tools perform special operations on your Builder brush to create new brushes based on existing level geometry. Creating brushes with these tools helps keep your world geometry efficient and prevent BSP errors.

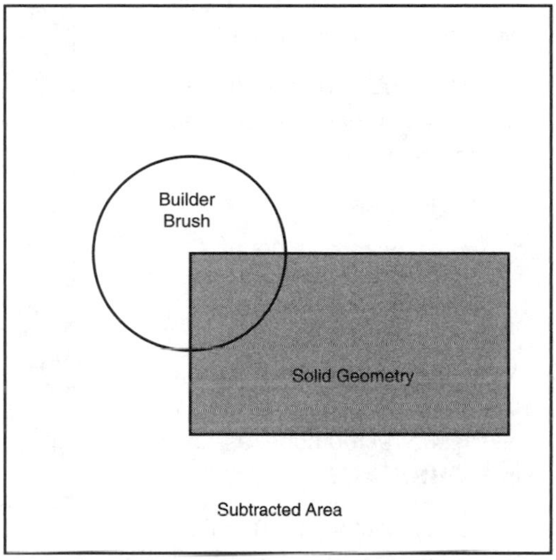

FIGURE 4.10 Before intersection.

The Intersect Tool

The Intersect tool  removes all areas of your Builder brush that are *not* inside solid geometry. The following figures demonstrate how this tool works. Before intersection, you would have what's shown in **FIGURE 4.10**.

After intersection you would get what's shown in **FIGURE 4.11**.

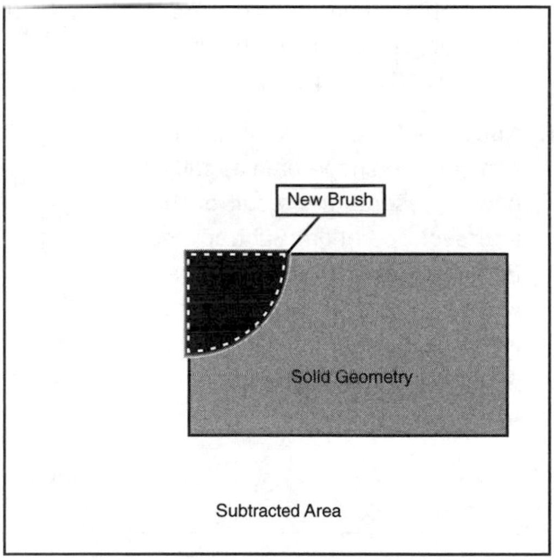

FIGURE 4.11 After intersection.

Your Builder brush is now a quarter-cylinder. Keep in mind that your Builder brush has been modified, nothing else. At this point, you're ready to create an additive or subtractive brush to build geometry based on the new shape. To see what happens when you use the Intersect tool, try it out on a simple box-shaped room.

TUTORIAL 4.1: Using the Intersect Tool

1. Start UnrealEd and choose File > New from the main menu.
2. Create a Cube brush with the following settings, and subtract it from the world:

   Height: 256

   Width: 256

   Breadth: 256

3. Move the Builder brush so that it overlaps the top-right corner of this newly subtracted cube, as shown in **FIGURE 4.12**.

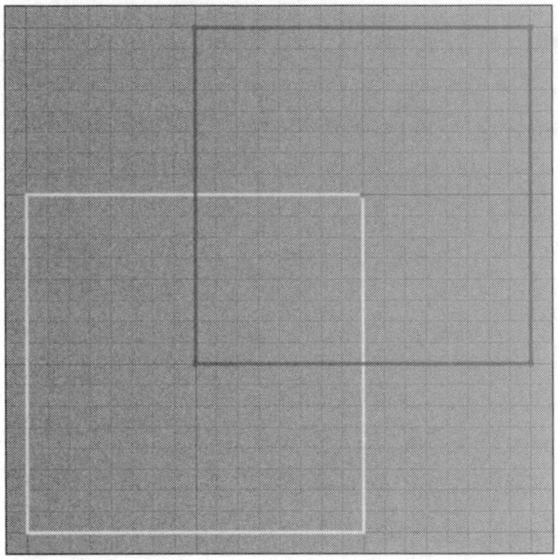

FIGURE 4.12 Top view of the Builder brush positioned over the top-right corner of the subtracted cube.

4. If you subtracted the Builder brush from the world at this point, you would have two subtractive brushes overlapping. This can lead to BSP errors such as the HOM effect. Instead, click the Intersect button in the toolbox (see **FIGURE 4.13**).
5. Notice that the Builder brush has changed its shape dramatically. It now represents the result of the Intersect operation. Subtract the Builder brush from the world, and you'll have much more efficient world geometry than you would by simply subtracting the original cube.

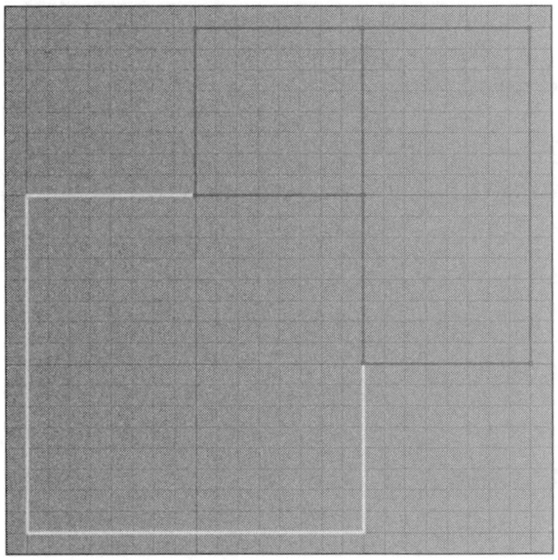

FIGURE 4.13 Top view of the Builder brush after an intersection with the subtracted cube.

END TUTORIAL 4.1

Intersections can also be used in more complex situations, such as subtracting a corridor into a curved surface while maintaining proper geometry. Remember that using this tool is always better than having two BSP brushes overlap each other.

The De-Intersect Tool

Think of the De-Intersect tool as the opposite of the Intersect tool. As with intersecting, the operation edits the shape of the Builder brush. However, the resulting shape is calculated by removing the area of the Builder brush that's *inside* solid geometry and leaving the rest. Using the previous example, you would begin **FIGURE 4.14**.

After using the De-Intersect tool, you would have what's shown in **FIGURE 4.15**.

To better understand how the De-Intersect tool works, use it to create a half-cylinder in **TUTORIAL 4.2**.

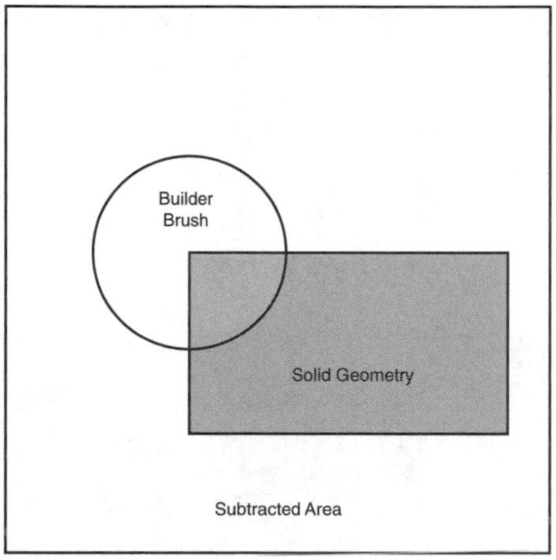

FIGURE 4.14 Before deintersecting.

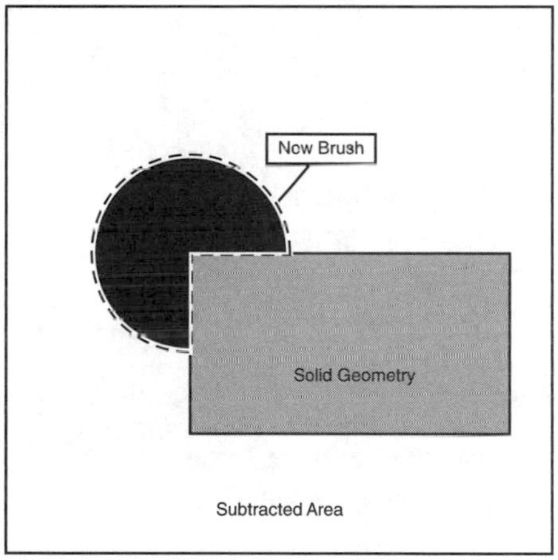

FIGURE 4.15 After deintersecting.

TUTORIAL 4.2: Using the De-Intersect Tool

1. Start UnrealEd and choose File > New from the main menu.
2. Create a cylinder with the following properties:

   Height: 512

   OuterRadius: 256

   Sides: 16

3. Subtract this brush from the world.

4. Now create a cube with the following properties:

   Height: 512

   Width: 512

   Breadth: 512

5. Place this new cube brush over half the cylinder, as shown in **FIGURE 4.16**.

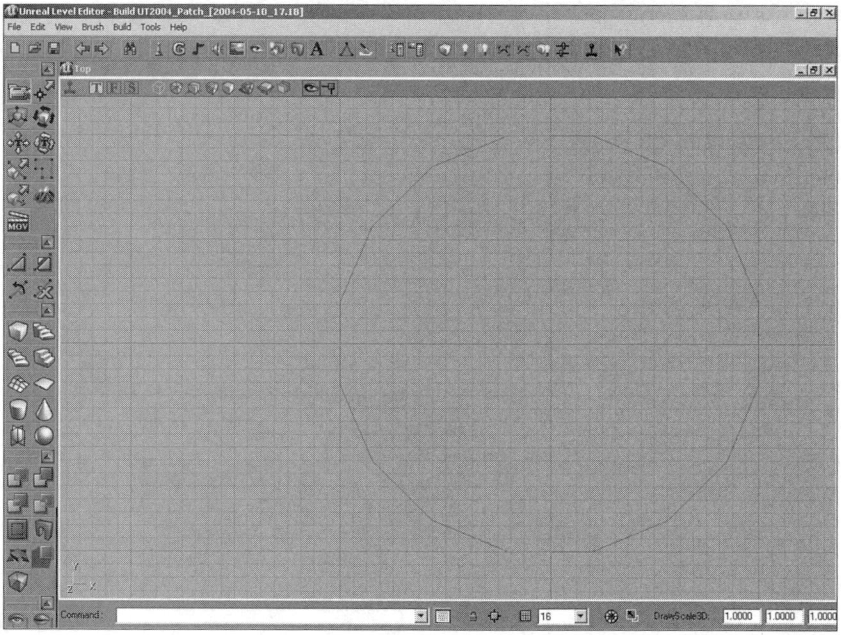

FIGURE 4.16 **Top view of cube brush over half the cylinder.**

6. Click the De-Intersect button. You should now have a perfect half-cylinder brush with a radius of 256 (see **FIGURE 4.17**).

4

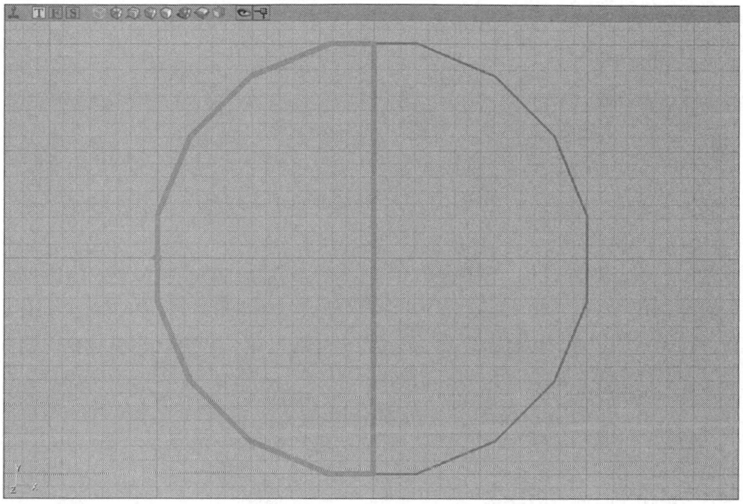

FIGURE 4.17 Top view of the half-cylinder brush.

END TUTORIAL 4.2

With just these two tools, you can make many different brush shapes. Remember to use these tools whenever you need to create world geometry based on shapes already in your level.

Brush Manipulation

Although the Intersect and De-Intersect tools certainly add tremendous flexibility to the shapes you can create in UnrealEd, at times you need more power to edit your brushes. UnrealEd offers three ways to directly change the shape of your brushes: Vertex Editing mode, Face Drag mode, and Brush Clipping mode. The following sections discuss these modes and explain how to use them to create more advanced brush shapes.

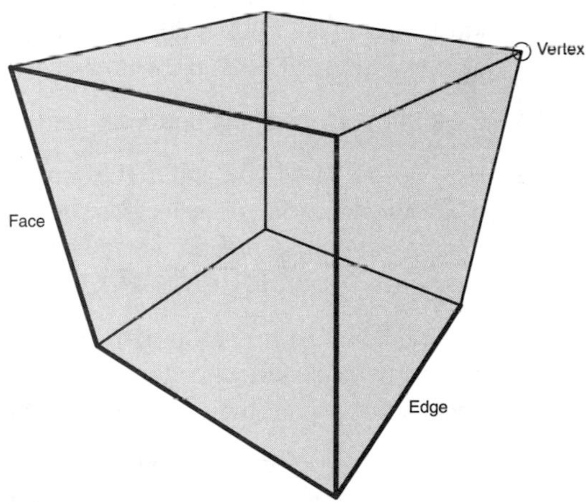

FIGURE 4.18 Visual representation of polygon components.

World geometry in Unreal is composed of polygons, which are shapes with many sides. When you're working in 3D, a polygon is a surface composed of vertices, edges, and at least one face. Before you see how these components can be used to edit your brushes, take a moment to review these components, which are illustrated in **FIGURE 4.18**:

- A *vertex* is defined as a point in space. For a polygonal shape, it's a point where two or more edges meet. You can think of a vertex as a dot in a three-dimensional connect-the-dots game.

- An *edge* is a line between two vertices. For example, the lines between the corners of a polygonal cube are classified as edges.
- A *face* is a surface stretched between three or more edges. For a cube, it's one entire side of the cube.

Vertex Editing

Vertex Editing mode enables you to move the vertices of a polygon object around in space. Doing this changes the shape of your brush and makes it possible to create shapes that would be difficult, if not impossible, to create with the Intersect or De-Intersect tools. The following tutorial shows how you can use Vertex Editing mode to drastically alter the shape of your brushes, without needing to create extra brushes for intersection operations.

TUTORIAL 4.3: Vertex Editing in UnrealEd

1. Start UnrealEd and choose File > New from the main menu.
2. Create a cube with the following properties, and subtract it from the level:

   Height: 256

   Width: 256

   Breadth: 256

3. Move your Builder brush out of the way, and select the remaining subtractive brush. Make sure you select it in an orthographic view so that you aren't just selecting the surfaces.
4. Click the Vertex Editing button in the toolbox.
5. Hold down the Alt key, and in the Top view, click the vertex at the upper-right corner of the box. Note that you can select vertices only in the orthographic views. Keep in mind that this operation has actually selected *two* vertices: one on top of the cube and another on the bottom (see **FIGURE 4.19**).
6. While holding down the Ctrl key, drag with the LMB and notice how the vertex is moved around the viewport, changing the brush shape (see **FIGURE 4.20**). You can also see the original position of the vertex designated by a small point.
7. You can also select multiple vertices in Vertex Editing mode. Holding down the Ctrl and Alt keys, drag with the LMB to draw a box around all the vertices on the left side of the brush.
8. Move these vertices while holding down the Ctrl key. Experiment and see what sort of interesting shapes you can make, just from starting with a simple cube.

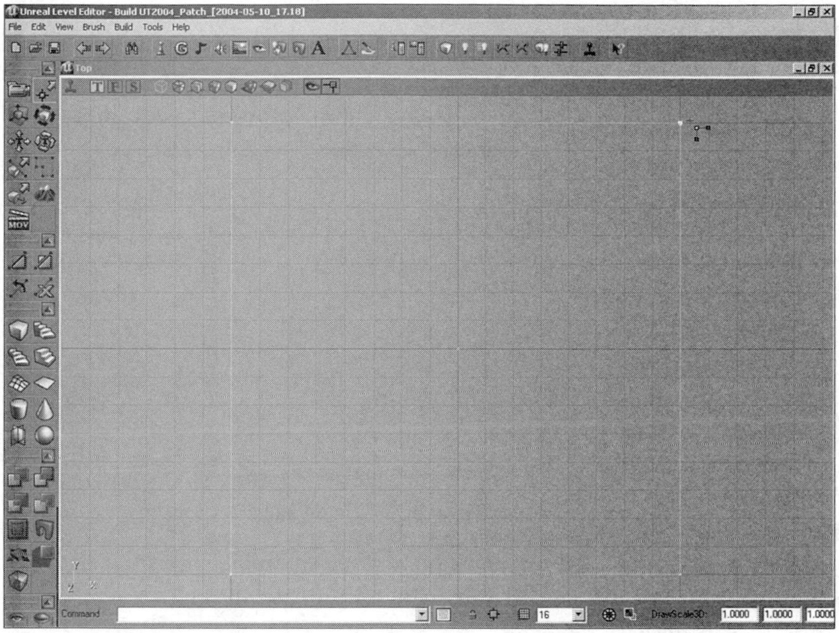

FIGURE 4.19 Top view of the two vertices selected.

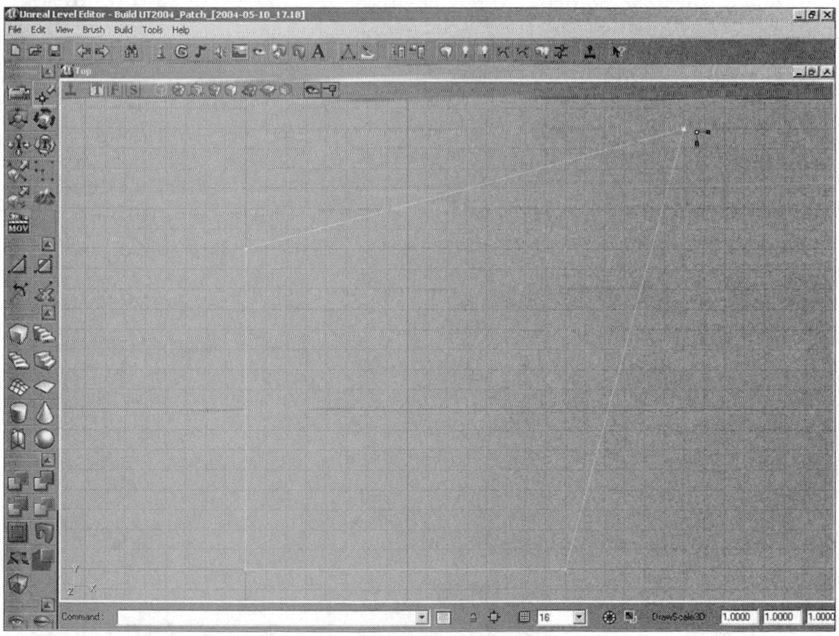

FIGURE 4.20 Top view of the deformed (altered) shape.

END TUTORIAL 4.3

Face Dragging

Face Drag mode enables you to manipulate entire faces of your brush to reshape it. It works similarly to Vertex Editing mode, but enables you to quickly select a face that contains multiple vertices.

> **NOTE**
>
> At the time of this writing, Face Drag mode loses functionality when more than one brush is added to the level. Instead, you can use Vertex Editing mode, and select all the vertices surrounding a face.

To use Face Drag mode, simply move the mouse pointer near an edge and drag the mouse as shown in **FIGURE 4.21**.

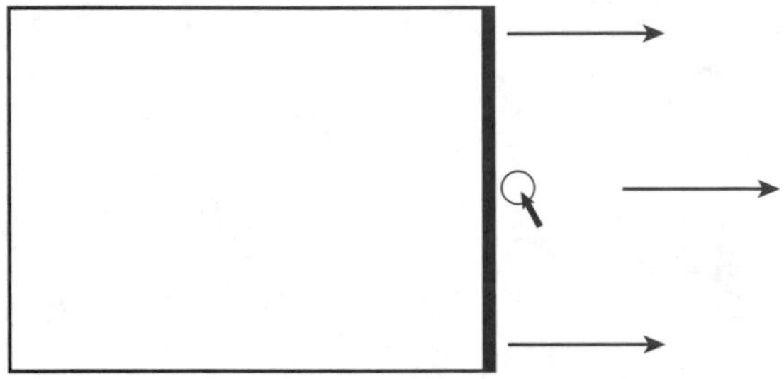

FIGURE 4.21 Using Face Drag mode.

Brush Clipping (2D and 3D)

Brush Clipping mode enables you to split a brush by using a plane. You can use this tool in two modes: 2D and 3D. Clipping a brush in 2D is similar to placing a ruler on a piece of paper and using a razor blade to cut along the ruler. Clipping in 3D is like cutting a log with a chainsaw. In both cases, you can keep both of the resulting pieces or keep only one.

Brush clipping is done by creating *clipping markers*, which are points in space that designate the plane at which the clip will occur. Placing two markers creates a 2D clip; adding a third marker results in a 3D clip. To see how these methods work, try **TUTORIAL 4.4**, which uses Brush Clip mode to add character to an ancient ruin.

TUTORIAL 4.4: Using Brush Clipping

1. Start UnrealEd and choose File > Open from the main menu. Open the `Chapter4` folder from your installation folder, and select `Tutorial4_04_Start`. You'll see a level with a Greek-style ruin that, frankly, is in excellent shape for a ruin (see **FIGURE 4.22**). You'll use the Brush Clipping tools to clip a column of this temple so that you can add some character to it.

FIGURE 4.22 A level with a Greek-style ruin.

2. Open the Texture browser. In the Chapter4.utx package, find and click the `base08AL` texture. This texture will be applied to new faces during a clip.

3. In the Top viewport, select the column in the lower-right corner (see **FIGURE 4.23**). The column is an additive Semi-Solid brush. (This brush type is covered in "Brush Solidity," later in this chapter.)

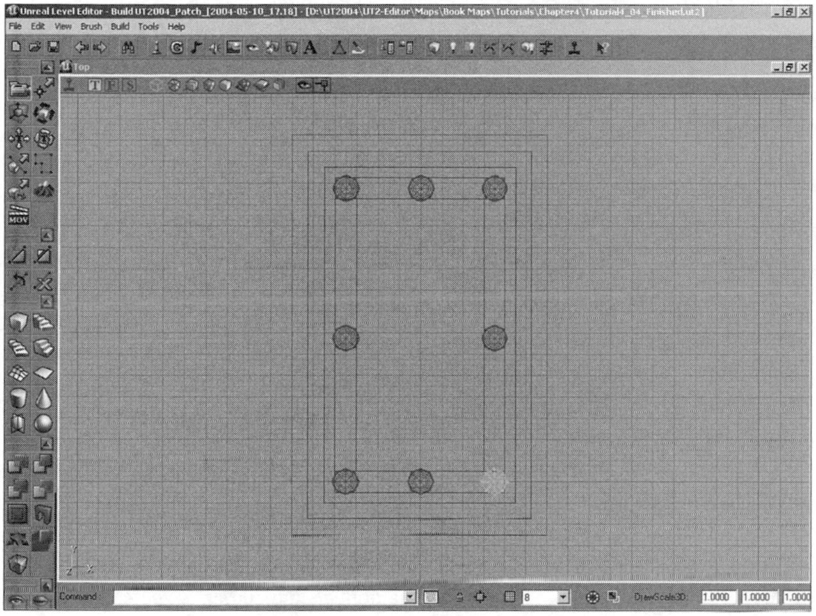

FIGURE 4.23 Top view of the selected pillar.

4. Click the Brush Clipping button in the toolbox.

5. Hold down the Ctrl key and right-click in the Side viewport. For this example, you're placing only two clipping markers to generate a 3D plane that's perpendicular to the Side viewport (see **FIGURE 4.24**).

6. Notice a line between the two clipping markers, which indicates where the column will be clipped (cut). Think of this line as a cutting laser that slices all the way through your brush. Another line that's perpendicular to the line connecting the two points is called the *clipping normal*. It points to the piece of your brush that will be removed when you clip the brush. After placing the clipping markers, you can then use any of the four clipping commands in the following list:

   - *Clip Selected Brushes* —This command removes the part of the brush that's on the same side of the clipping plane as the clipping normal.

   - *Split Selected Brushes* —This command divides the brush along the clipping plane, but doesn't delete either side.

   - *Flip Clipping Normal* —This command reverses the place the clipping normal on the opposite side of the clipping plane.

   - *Delete Clipping Markers* —This command removes all clipping markers from the level.

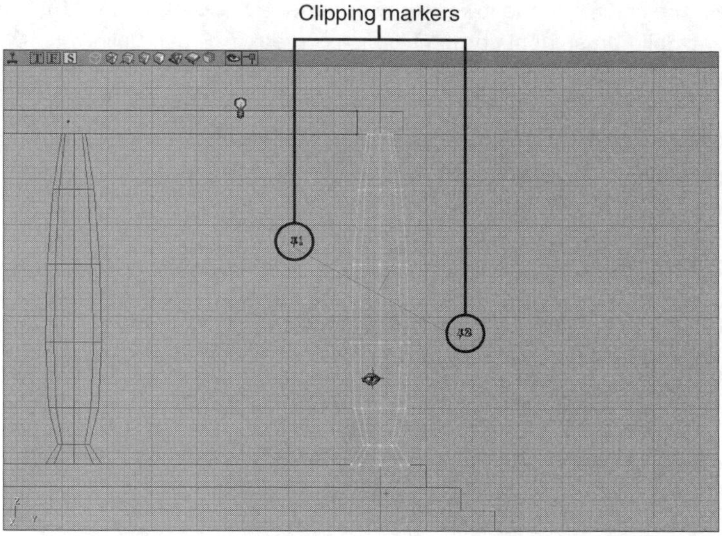

FIGURE 4.24 Side view of clipping markers.

7. For this example, you want the top of the column to be removed, not saved. Therefore, you need the perpendicular line to be flipped. To do this, the clipping normal must point at the upper half of the column. If necessary, click the Flip Clipping Normal button. It not only flips the clipping normal, but also reverses the numbering of the two clipping markers.

> **NOTE**
>
> **If you create your clipping points in a left-to-right direction, the normals face down. If you create them right to left, the normals face upward.**

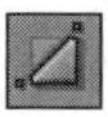

8. Now click the Clip Selected Brushes button, and rebuild your geometry and lighting. Notice that the top half of the column is gone (see **FIGURE 4.25**).

9. Next, you clip a second column, but first you need to remove the current clipping markers. Click the Delete Clipping Markers button in the toolbox.

10. Create two more clipping markers in the Front viewport that clip another column, as shown in **FIGURE 4.26**. Make sure the clipping normal points toward the top of the column again.

11. Instead of clipping the column, however, you're going to use the Split Selected Brushes command. Splitting the brush divides it into two separate brushes along the clipping plane. Click the Split Selected Brushes button in the toolbox.

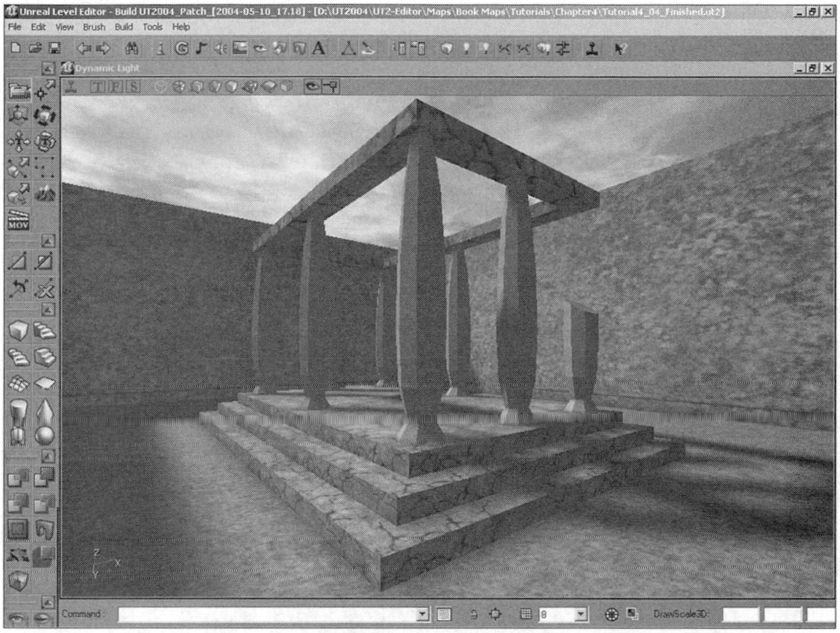

FIGURE 4.25 3D view of new column.

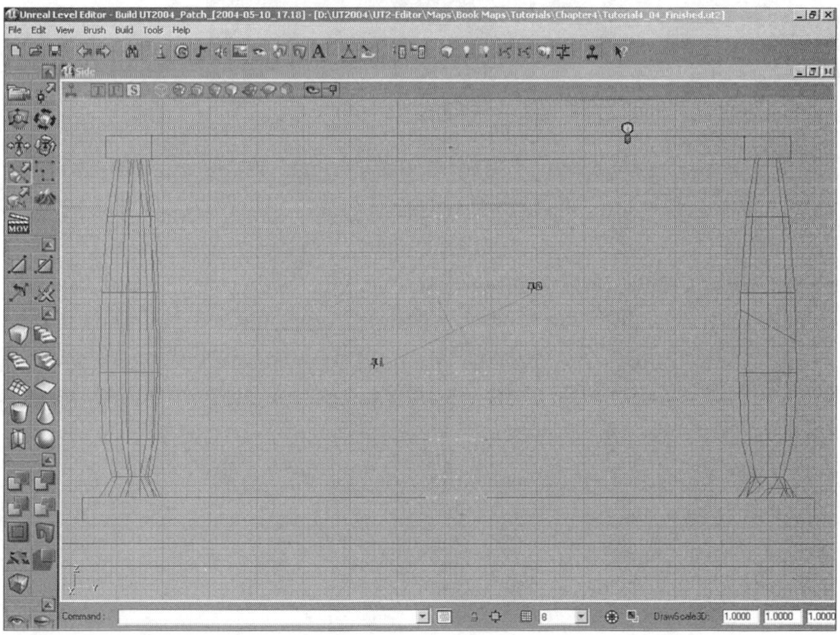

FIGURE 4.26 The clipping markers in the Front view.

12. You now have two halves of the column. Using the skills you learned in Chapter 3, "Creating Your First Level with UnrealEd," move and rotate this new brush to place it somewhere in the level, as shown in **FIGURE 4.27**. Remember to rebuild your lighting to see the effect.

> **NOTE**
>
> **You can clip the Builder brush, but you can't split it, as that would result in two Builder brushes.**

FIGURE 4.27 Final columns.

END TUTORIAL 4.4

In most cases, 2D clipping in one of the orthographic viewports gives you enough control to create the shape you need. However, at times you might need more control over the clipping plane. In these cases, you can use 3D clipping, which is done by simply adding a third clipping marker. Remember that three points in space define a plane. Therefore, you can move the three clipping markers to adjust the clipping plane's orientation.

In **TUTORIAL 4.5**, you add more cuts to the Greek ruins.

TUTORIAL 4.5: Improving the Look of the Ruins

1. In the Top view, hold down the Ctrl key and right-click to create three clipping markers, forming a triangle between the columns in the lower-right corner of the temple (see **FIGURE 4.28**). When you're done creating the third marker, notice that the perpendicular line seems to disappear. However, what really happens is the normal is now pointing up in the Z-axis, so you can't see it from the Top viewport. You can see the normal clearly in the 3D view.

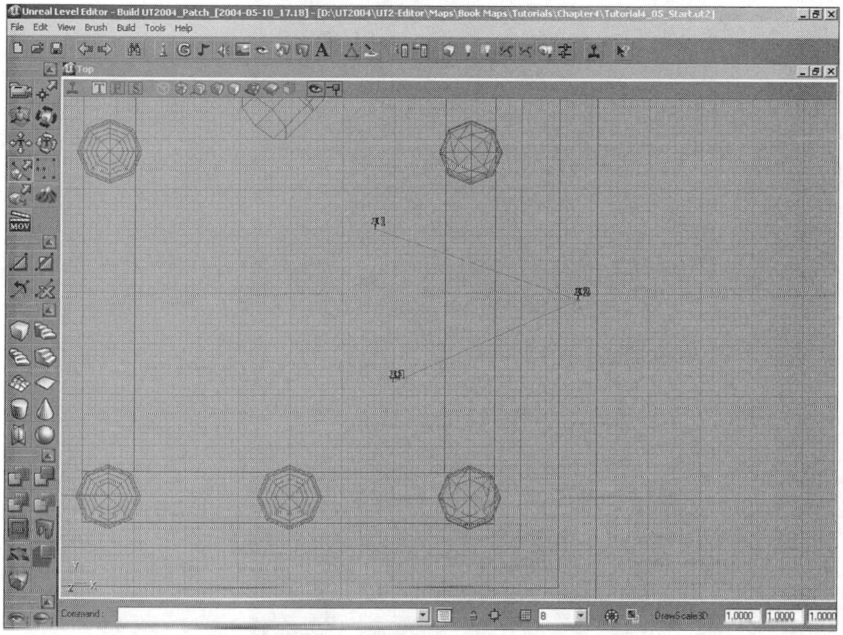

FIGURE 4.28 Top view of the three clipping markers.

2. Now move the clipping markers in the 3D viewport so that they define a plane that cuts through the temple's entablature (the series of blocks laid across the top of the columns) at an interesting angle (see **FIGURE 4.29**). Notice the direction of the normal and how the clipping plane rotates as you move any of the clipping markers. The three clipping markers don't need to surround the brush.

3. Select the brush you'll be clipping. In the Top viewport, it's the right side brush of the temple's entablature. Click the Clip Selected Brushes button, and rebuild your level. You should get something similar to **FIGURE 4.30**.

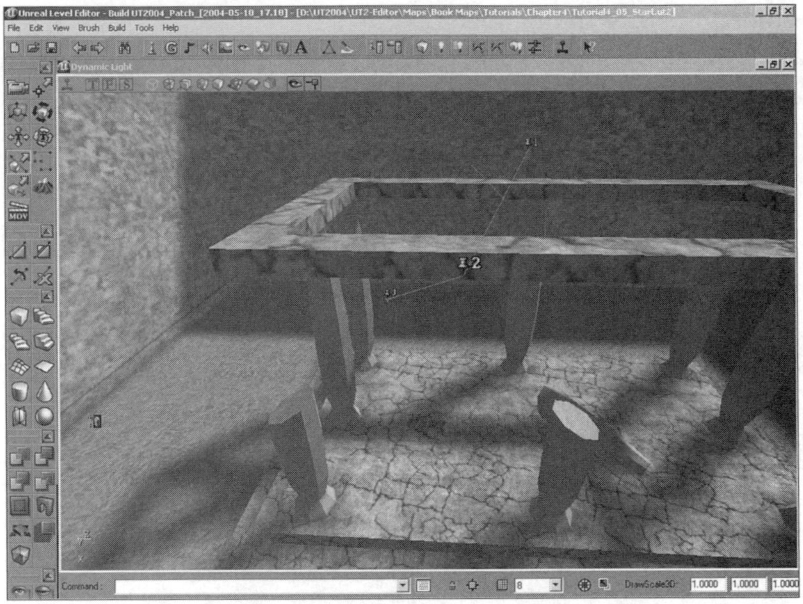

FIGURE 4.29 3D view of the three clipping markers.

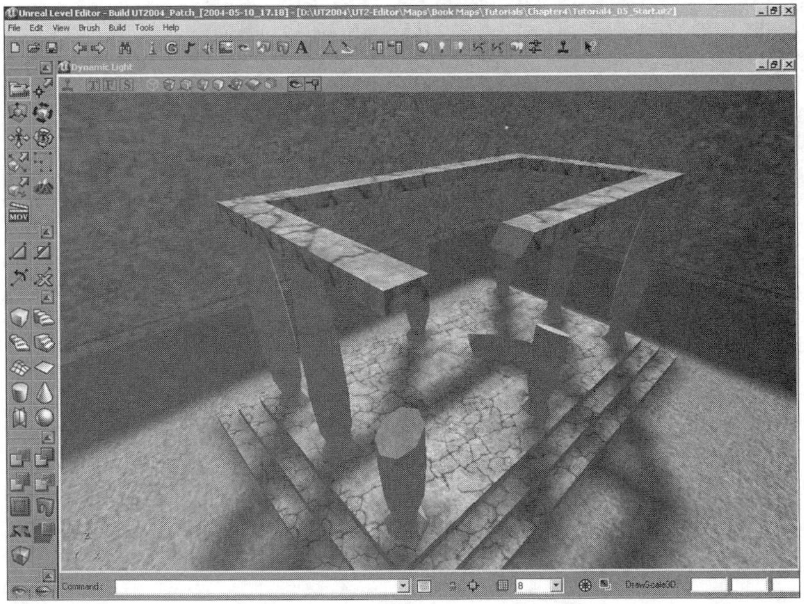

FIGURE 4.30 3D view of clipped entablature.

4. Save your work as `RuinedTemple`.

END TUTORIAL 4.5

You can now create brush clips at any angle you like, which makes it possible to create more irregularly shaped brushes. The clipping tools are extremely useful for generating interesting brushes when a simple primitive won't do. Use the skills you have learned so far to make more cuts in the temple for a more realistic aged look. If you like, open the `Tutorial4_05_Enhanced.ut2` file and see a fully ruined temple (see **FIGURE 4.31**).

FIGURE 4.31 Fully ruined temple.

Freehand Polygon Drawing

With the Freehand Polygon Drawing tool, you can create BSP brushes by placing your own vertices, thereby designating your own custom shape. This tool is simple to use and makes it possible to create irregularly shaped brushes quickly. All you need to do is draw a few vertices in a connect-the-dots fashion, and then choose the height you need the shape to have. In this section, you see how to create an irregular brush with this tool for use in your Greek ruins level.

TUTORIAL 4.6: Using the Freehand Polygon Drawing Tool

1. In the Greek ruins level, click the Freehand Polygon Drawing button .
2. Make sure the `base08AL` texture is still selected in the Texture browser.
3. Holding down the Ctrl key, right-click in the Top viewport, somewhere off to the side of the temple. This action places a vertex in the viewport, which appears as a red cross with a green circle around it (see **FIGURE 4.32**).
4. Place at least three vertices in this manner. Notice as you place the second vertex that a line appears connecting the two vertices. You can continue placing vertices as long as you like. There is no need to close the shape by placing the final vertex on the first point (see **FIGURE 4.33**). The shape automatically closes when you create the brush.
5. When you're satisfied with the shape, release the Ctrl key, right-click in the Top viewport, and choose Create Brush from the context menu.

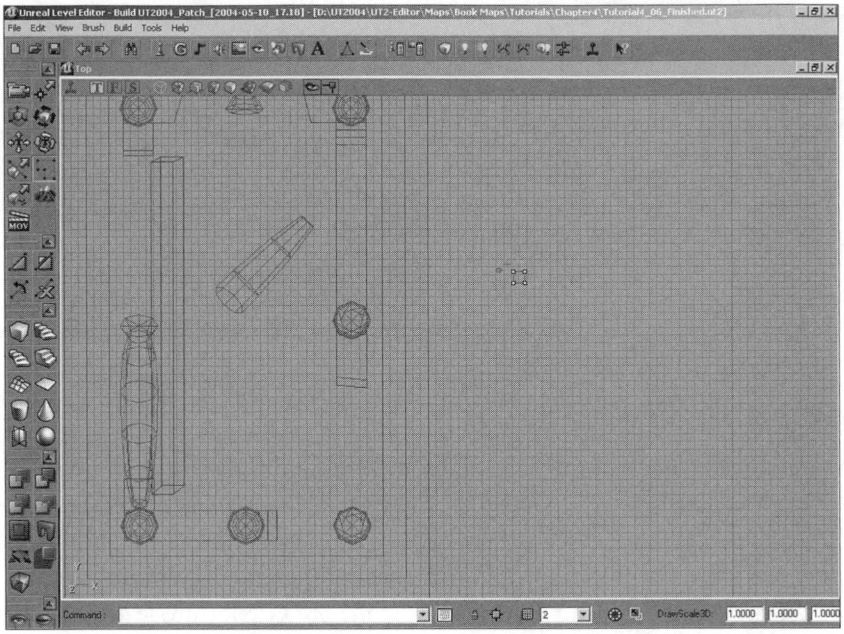

FIGURE 4.32 Top view of the newly placed vertex.

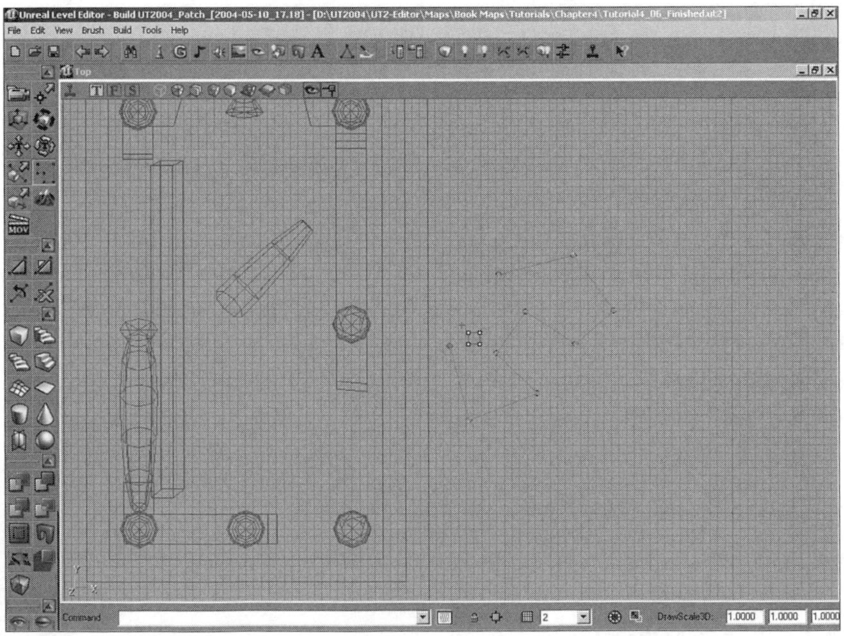

FIGURE 4.33 Top view of the shape.

6. In the Depth dialog box, enter 128 for the depth (256 is the default value), as shown in **FIGURE 4.34**. Click OK when finished. This setting controls how deep the shape becomes.

7. Position the new brush on the ground near the temple, and add it to the world (see **FIGURE 4.35**).

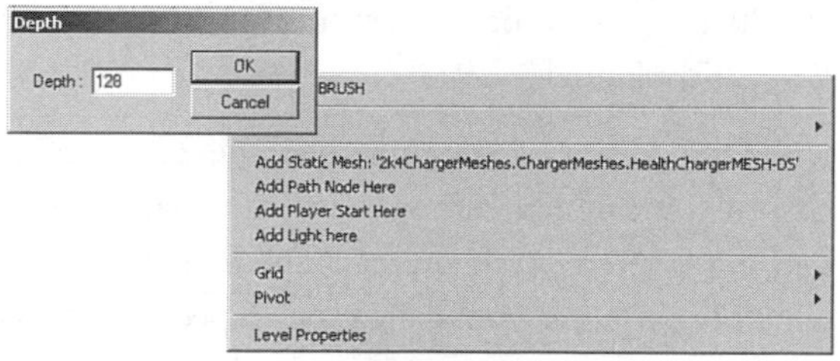

FIGURE 4.34 The Depth dialog box.

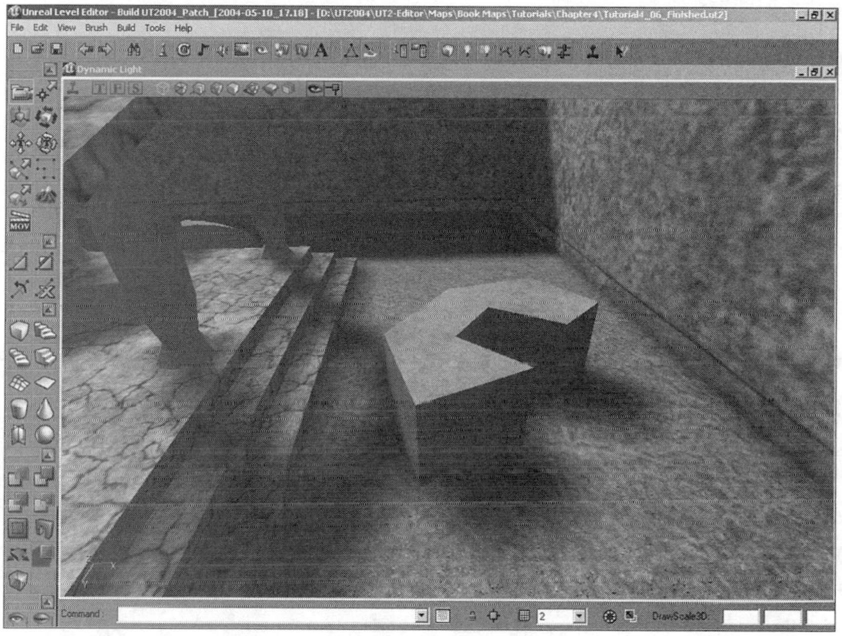

FIGURE 4.35 Newly created piece of rubble.

END TUTORIAL 4.6

As you can see, the Freehand Polygon Drawing tool is a fast and efficient way to create oddly shaped brushes for your levels. However, be careful not to add too many vertices, which could make your object unnecessarily complex and result in excessive BSP cuts in your shape.

The 2D Shape Editor

You can use the 2D Shape Editor to create custom 3D brushes from 2D curves. With this tool, you can quickly create interesting shapes that would otherwise be impossible with primitives and clipping. This section is designed to give you a general overview of the 2D Shape Editor, its options, and its uses. For more in-depth information on this tool's functions, refer to Appendix A, "The UnrealEd Manual."

Since the advent of static meshes, the 2D Shape Editor hasn't been used as often. Most of the shapes you can generate with the 2D Shape Editor can easily be created in an external package and imported as static meshes. The final result of the 2D Shape Editor is to create a BSP brush, which is perfect if you're creating a specially shaped room. However, static meshes are far more efficient for decorations. Using the 2D Shape Editor is recommended only for specially shaped rooms, and use it for decorative brushes only if you don't have access to a 3D application such as Maya or 3ds max.

User Interface Overview

4

To access the 2D Shape Editor, choose Tools > 2D Shape Editor from the menu or click the triangle icon on the toolbar. The 2D Shape Editor window includes a single orthographic view, a toolbar, and a menu bar (see **FIGURE 4.36**). By default, the current shape is a square, but you can edit this shape by moving and adding vertices and then perform one of the available operations to convert it into a 3D brush for use in your level. The next two sections give you an overview of the user interface for the 2D Shape Editor.

Menu and Toolbar

At the top of the 2D Shape Editor window is the menu bar, which gives you access to all operations that can be performed on the current shape. Many of the common commands used in the editor are also available on the toolbar, which gives you fast single-click access to operations such as rotating, flipping, scaling, and adding and removing vertices. The toolbar also has buttons for operations to convert your 2D shape into a 3D brush. You can use both the menu bar and toolbar to save and open your shapes for later reuse or editing.

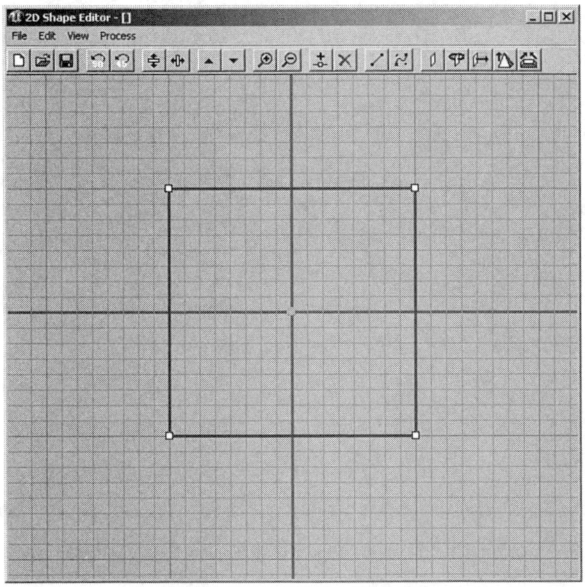

FIGURE 4.36 2D Shape Editor window.

Viewport

Navigating the viewport is as simple as dragging with the RMB. The response is similar to navigation in UnrealEd's orthographic viewports. Note that dragging doesn't move the shape around;

it merely pans the camera. To zoom in and out, use the magnifying glass icons on the toolbar, or choose View > Zoom In or Zoom Out from the menu.

Right-clicking in the viewport gives you access to several commands that are available in the Edit menu. This context menu also includes the Set Origin command, which relocates your shape's origin to the position where you click the mouse button. (The importance of the origin is explained shortly in the "Components" section.

Shape Editing

Now that you have a basic knowledge of the 2D Shape Editor's interface, you can learn how to edit the shape and create objects. The first step is understanding the components that make up each shape. The following sections familiarize you with the shape components and how they can be used to alter and customize your shape.

Components

The small white boxes at the corners of the default square are vertices, which form the foundation of your shape. When you connect these vertices, you see black lines to indicate the shape's edges. When you select a vertex, its corresponding edge becomes thicker, meaning that it's also selected.

At the center of the shape are two small squares. They might be difficult to see at first because they are right on top of each other. The orange square is your shape's *center point*. This square is actually just a handle used to relocate your shape. It always stays in the exact center. You can click and drag on it to move your object around the viewport. You can have multiple shapes in this viewport at once, and these center points make moving them much easier.

Just behind this orange square is a green square, which is your shape's *origin*. No matter how many shapes are available in your viewport, you can have only one origin. The origin serves as a reference point for revolving, discussed in Tutorial 4.10, later in this chapter. **FIGURE 4.37** shows the components of the 2D Shape Editor.

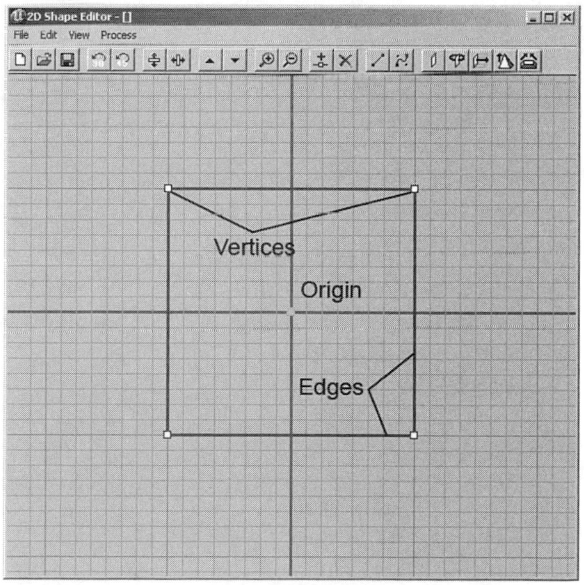

FIGURE 4.37 **2D Shape Editor components.**

Moving and Adding Detail

You can edit a shape's look by simply clicking and dragging the vertices around with the LMB. However, you'll quickly notice that the default square doesn't allow you to make anything especially interesting. To create a more complex shape, you have to add more vertices.

To add vertices, first select the vertex for a specific edge. For example, when you click the vertex at the upper-right corner of the default square, the edge on the right side of the square is highlighted. To add a new vertex, you need to split this edge. There are several ways to do this:

- Choose Edit > Split Side from the menu.
- Press Ctrl+I.
- Right-click on the vertex, and choose Split Side.

TUTORIAL 4.7: Using the 2D Shape Editor

1. Open the 2D Shape Editor by using its toolbar button.
2. In the 2D Shape Editor's viewport, click the vertex at the upper-right corner of the default square shape (see **FIGURE 4.38**).
3. Using the LMB, drag the vertex around the viewport to change the shape's look (see **FIGURE 4.39**). Notice that the orange center point relocates to stay at the center of the object.
4. Right-click the selected vertex, and choose Split Side from the context menu. Note the new vertex that appears (see **FIGURE 4.40**).

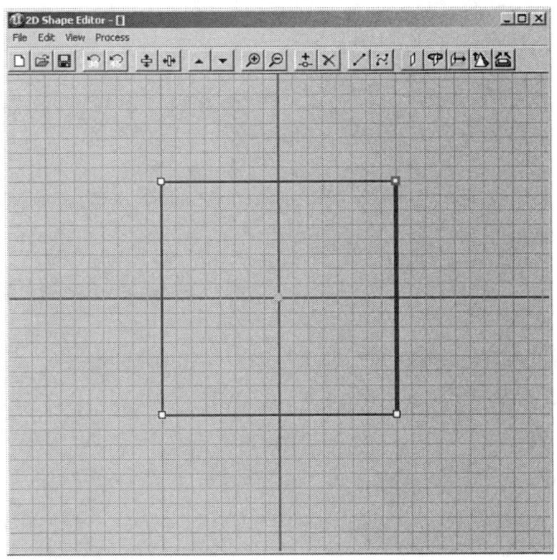

FIGURE 4.38 **Upper-right vertex selected in the 2D Shape Editor.**

Now you have another vertex that you can use to edit the shape. You can add as many vertices as you like, but remember that you should keep your detail level as low as possible.

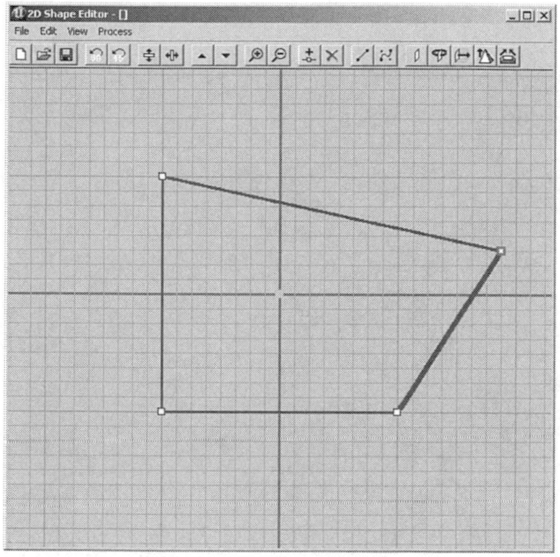

FIGURE 4.39 The upper-right vertex moved.

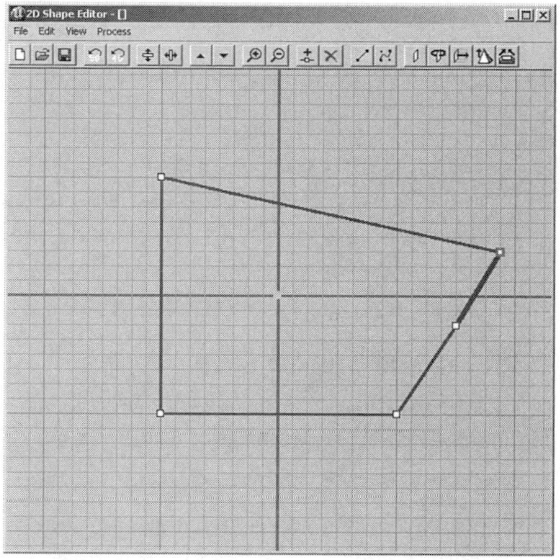

FIGURE 4.40 2D Shape Editor showing the split side.

END TUTORIAL 4.7

Bezier Segments

One advantage of the 2D Shape Editor is that you can use it to create curved shapes (see **FIGURE 4.41**). By default, each edge, or segment, comes together in a "corner." This means your segments are *linear*. You can change them to Bezier segments to create a smooth curvature.

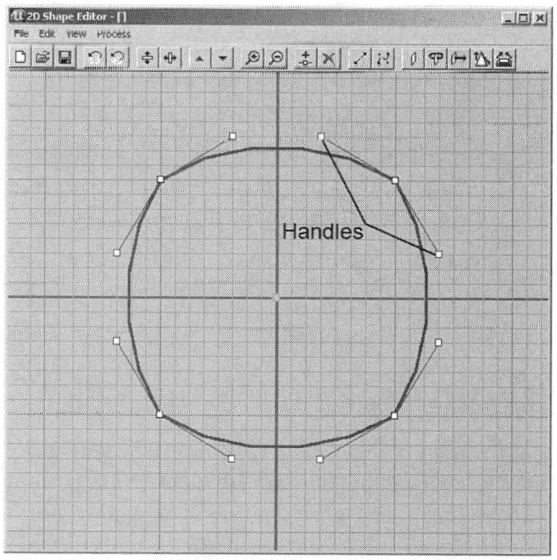

FIGURE 4.41 Bezier segments.

However, keep in mind that the result of the 2D shape is a 3D brush. As mentioned earlier, brushes are made of polygons, and as a rule, a polygon cannot be curved. Because of this, the curved line you see when using Bezier segments is actually made up of several smaller segments. You can change the number of segments that create your curvature, thereby controlling how smooth the curve looks. Keep in mind that adding more segments requires more calculation, and you should always keep your detail level as low as possible.

TUTORIAL 4.8: Creating Bezier Segments

1. Open the 2D Shape Editor by using its toolbar button.
2. Select a vertex/edge, and choose Edit > Segment > Bezier. You can also use the right-click menu in the viewport. The new blue boxes that appear are the Bezier handles (see **FIGURE 4.42**).
3. Click and drag the Bezier handles around the viewport, noting the change in the segment's shape (see **FIGURE 4.43**).
4. Next, you need to adjust the segment's detail level. First, adjust your Bezier handles to point in opposite directions to form an S-curve, as shown in **FIGURE 4.44**.
5. Right-click on the vertex, and choose Segment > Detail Level > 20. Notice that the segment seems to have much smoother curvature.
6. You can also set the detail level to a custom setting. Right-click on the segment again, and choose Segment > Detail Level > Custom. In the Detail Level dialog box, enter a value of 6, as shown in **FIGURE 4.45**, and click OK. Notice that the curve of the segment is now made of six separate lines.

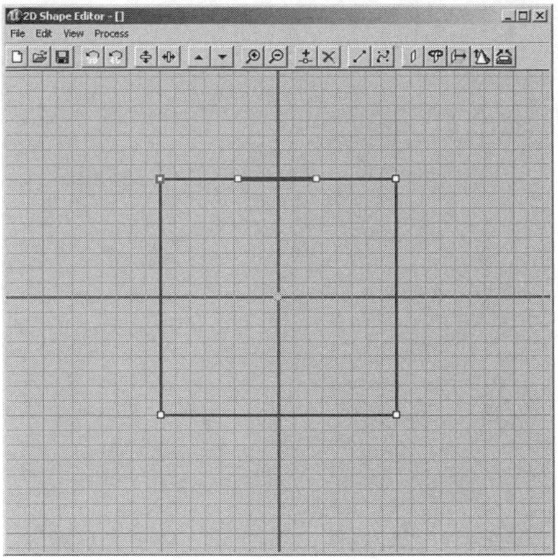

FIGURE 4.42 Segment converted to a Bezier segment.

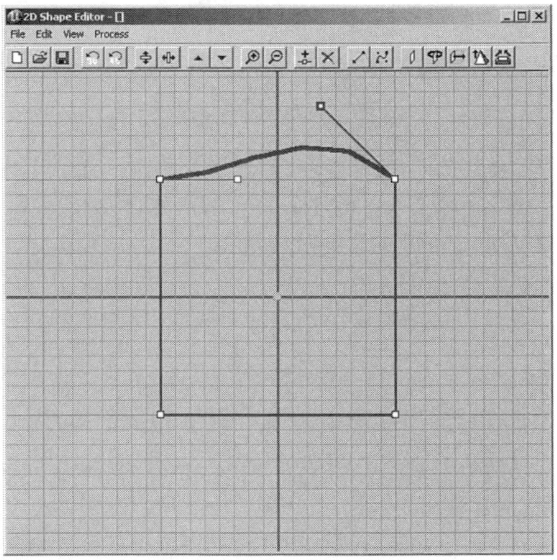

FIGURE 4.43 Modified Bezier segment.

> **NOTE**
>
> At the time of this writing, you must take care not to close any windows in the 2D Shape Editor (such as the Detail Level dialog box) by clicking the Close button in the upper-right corner. Doing so locks the 2D Shape Editor, and you have to restart it by clicking its button on the toolbar. You will also lose your work if you haven't saved it. Make sure you click the OK button instead.

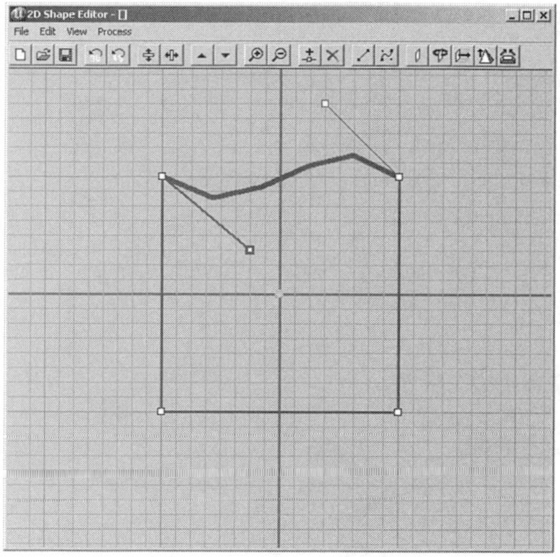

FIGURE 4.44 The segment now forms an S-curve.

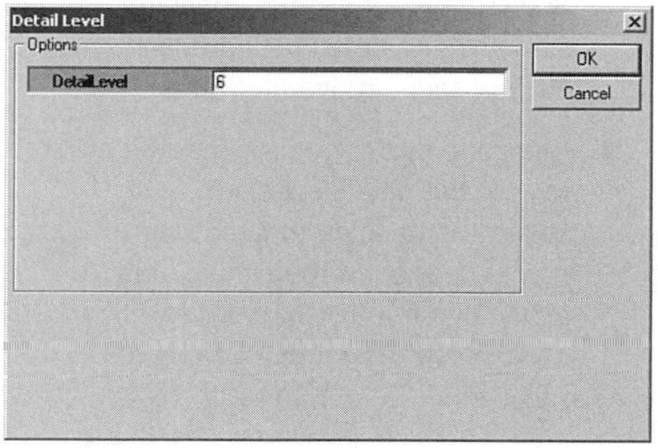

FIGURE 4.45 Entering a custom setting in the Detail Level dialog box.

END TUTORIAL 4.8

Processing Shapes

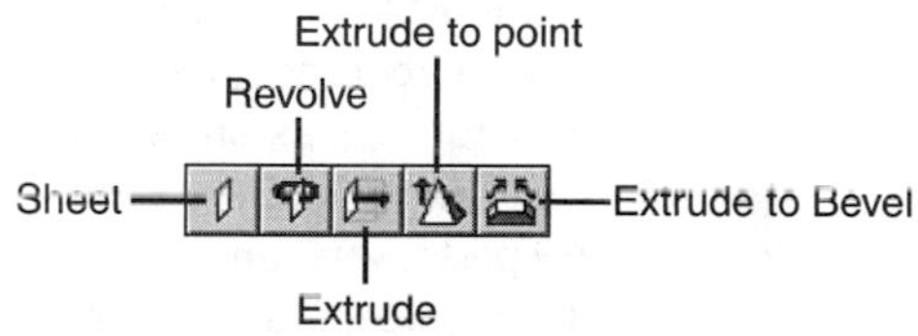

FIGURE 4.46 The Process toolbar.

To create a 3D brush with the 2D Shape Editor, you use one of a group of processes: Sheet, Revolve, Extrude, Extrude to Point, and Extrude to Bevel, as shown in **FIGURE 4.46**. Each process creates a brush in a unique manner. Keep in mind that your 2D shape is irrelevant in UnrealEd until you have applied one of these processes to it. This section covers only Sheet, Revolve, and Extrude. For information on the other processes, please refer to Appendix A.

The Sheet process converts your 2D shape into a flat plane by stretching a polygonal surface across the segments of your shape. This process is especially useful for creating custom-shaped windowpanes. In the following tutorial, you use the Sheet process to make an arched pane for a stained glass window.

4

TUTORIAL 4.9: Creating a Windowpane

1. Open the 2D Shape Editor.
2. Select the vertex in the upper-left corner of the default square, and set the segment type to Bezier.
3. Using the skills you have learned so far, set the detail level to 5, and adjust the handles to form a curve across the top of the shape. This action creates a windowpane with basic curvature without getting too detailed.
4. Move both Bezier handles straight up, and make sure they are directly across from each other. The result is a nice arch at the top of the window. Refer to **FIGURE 4.47** if you need help.
5. Click the Create a Sheet button on the 2D Shape Editor toolbar. Leave the axis set to Y, as shown in **FIGURE 4.48**, and click OK. In the UnrealEd viewports, you can see your arched windowpane appear as a plane. You can then create an additive brush from this plane.

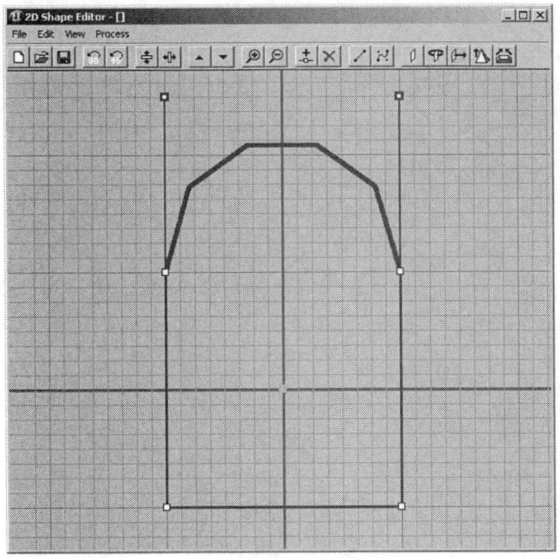

FIGURE 4.47 Archway created by Bezier segments.

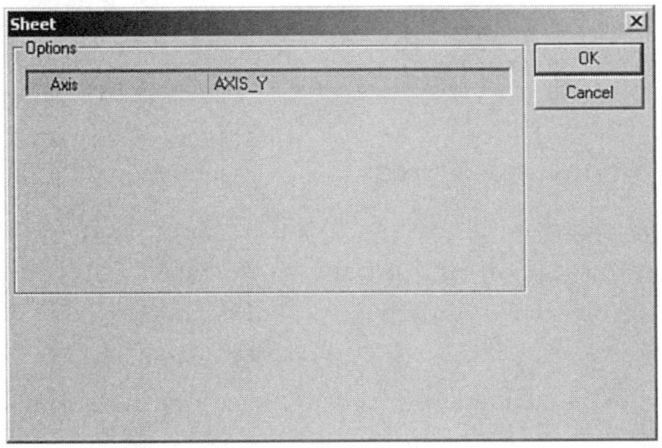

FIGURE 4.48 Sheet options.

END TUTORIAL 4.9

One of the most useful options available in the 2D Shape Editor is the Revolve process. This process converts your 2D shape into a 3D brush by revolving it around the pivot. A Revolve is perfect for creating cylindrically shaped objects, such as columns and silos.

TUTORIAL 4.10: Revolving with the 2D Shape Editor

1. Open the 2D Shape Editor.
2. Using the skills you have learned, create the half-silo shape shown in **FIGURE 4.49**.
3. Next, check the origin. For revolving purposes, the origin must always be placed on the leftmost or rightmost side of the shape. Right-click the leftmost segment of the shape, and choose Set Origin to place the origin directly on the shape's left side.
4. Click the Revolved Shape button on the toolbar. In the dialog box that opens, you will choose the following attributes:

   Sides: 12

   SidesPer360: 12

   Axis: AXIS_Y

   For more information on these settings, see Appendix A.

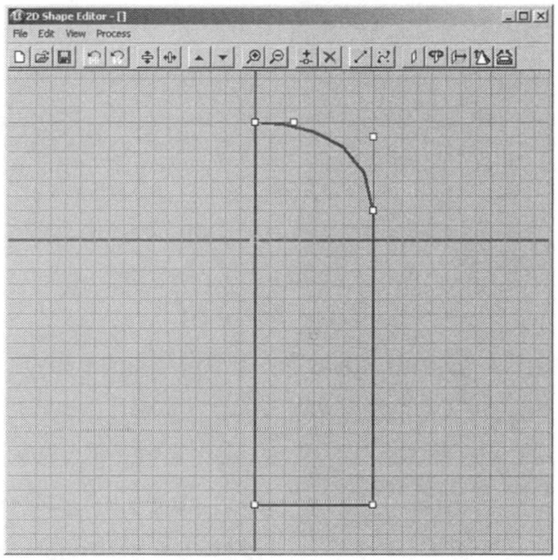

FIGURE 4.49 Half-silo shape.

> **NOTE**
>
> When using the 2D Shape Editor, the Y-axis points up. In the UnrealEd viewport, the Z-axis points up. Keep that in mind when selecting the axis for the Revolve process.

5. Click OK. You now have a rounded silo shape in your 3D viewport (see **FIGURE 4.50**). You can subtract it from your level to produce an interestingly shaped room.

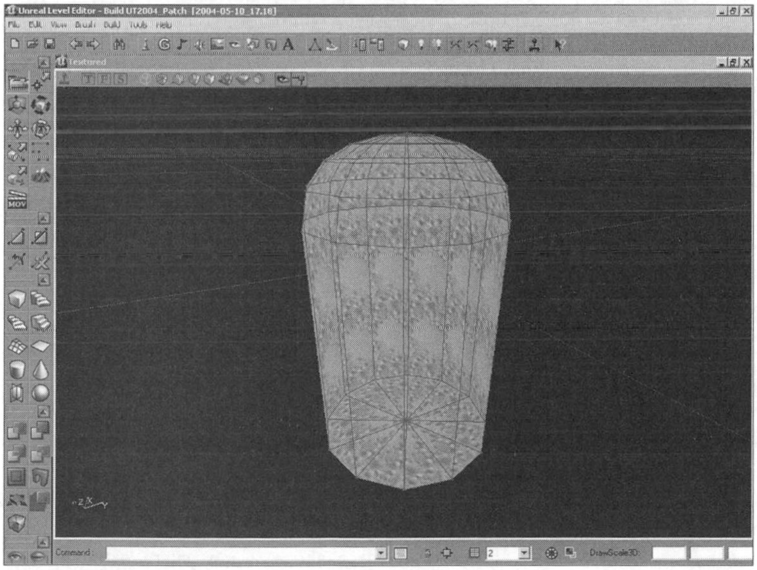

FIGURE 4.50 3D view of subtracted silo.

END TUTORIAL 4.10

Using the 2D Shape Editor to Create a Simple Level

Although static meshes might have replaced much of the 2D Shape Editor's capabilities, this tool does enable you to create a basic one-story level quickly. Using a technique similar to creating an architect's floor plan, you can use the 2D Shape Editor's Extrude process to create a basic level. The following sections explain how to use this process to quickly visualize a level's layout.

Room

To create the basic space of your level, you're going to draw a shape similar to a floor plan, and then extrude it upward. In this example, you create this floor plan from scratch. You can create a floor plan based on an actual image, such as a set of blueprints, if you like. To do this, choose File > Image > Open From Disk from the menu to place the selected image in the background of the 2D Shape Editor.

NOTE

You can place only BMP files in the 2D Shape Editor as images.

TUTORIAL 4.11: Creating a Level with the 2D Shape Editor

1. Open the 2D Shape Editor.
2. Choose Edit > Grid > 64 from the menu to set the current grid size to 64 units per grid space. With the setting this high, making a level large enough for you to navigate will be easier.
3. Using the skills you have learned so far, create a shape similar to the one in **FIGURE 4.51**. You can deviate from this example if you want, but try to have at least one curved wall. In this example, the Bezier segments' detail level is set to 4.

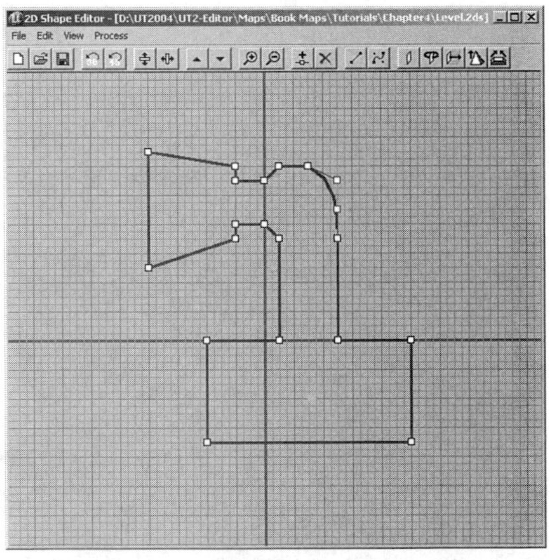

FIGURE 4.51 Level shape.

4. When you're satisfied with the shape of your floor plan, choose File > Save from the menu. Save the shape as `level.2ds` and click OK.
5. Next, you extrude the shape to create a 3D brush. Click the Extrude button on the 2D Shape Editor's toolbar, and set the following attributes:

   Depth: 256

   Axis: AXIS_Z

NOTE

Unlike revolving a shape, when you're extruding a shape, the Z-axis points upward.

6. Select a texture, subtract the brush, and place a few lights. **FIGURE 4.52** shows an example of where the lights have been placed.

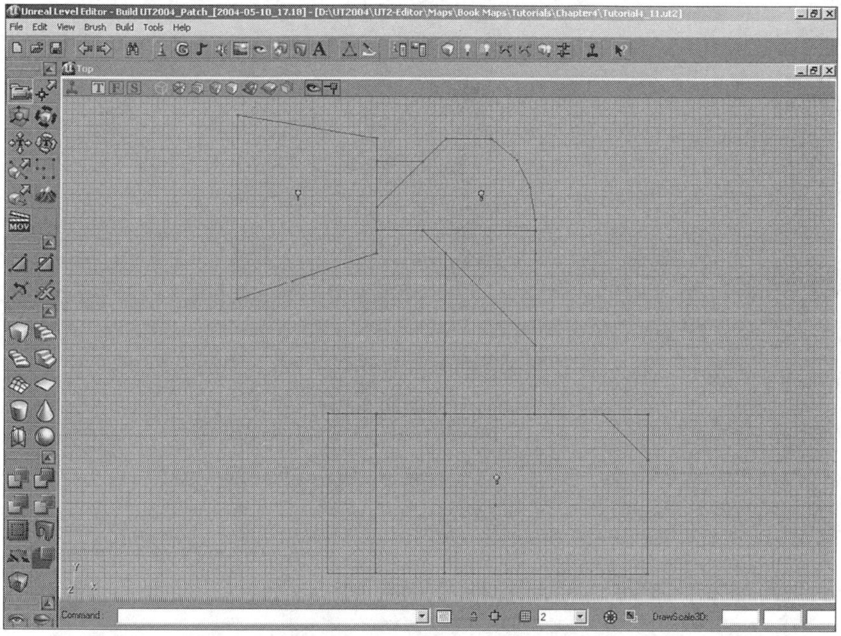

FIGURE 4.52 Light positions in the level.

7. Rebuild and play-test the new level.

END TUTORIAL 4.11

Although this method of level creation is fast, notice in the Top view that it results in some strange BSP cuts. This problem isn't serious in this example, but it could become severe with a more complex shape. Keep in mind that this method is best suited for prototyping a level quickly rather than making a large series of aligned brushes.

Pillars

The 2D Shape Editor really shines in creating objects such as pillars. With its Bezier controls, you can create beautiful columnar shapes that can be revolved easily. In this example, you create some pillars to place in the trapezoidal room you created at the end of the level.

> **NOTE**
>
> As mentioned at the beginning of this section, static meshes have almost completely replaced the 2D Shape Editor. When adding decorations such as pillars to your level, using static meshes is far more efficient than BSP brushes. For more information on how to create static meshes, turn to Chapter 20, "Static Meshes."

TUTORIAL 4.12: Creating a Column

1. Open the 2D Shape Editor, and set the grid size to 16.
2. Create a half-column shape similar to the one shown in **FIGURE 4.53**. Remember that your room is 256 units tall, and construct your shape accordingly.
3. When finished, save your shape as `pillar.2ds`.
4. Revolve the shape using the following settings:

   Sides: 12

   SidesPer360: 12

   Axis: Y_Axis

5. Add the brush to your level, making sure you align it with the floor and ceiling (see **FIGURE 4.54**).

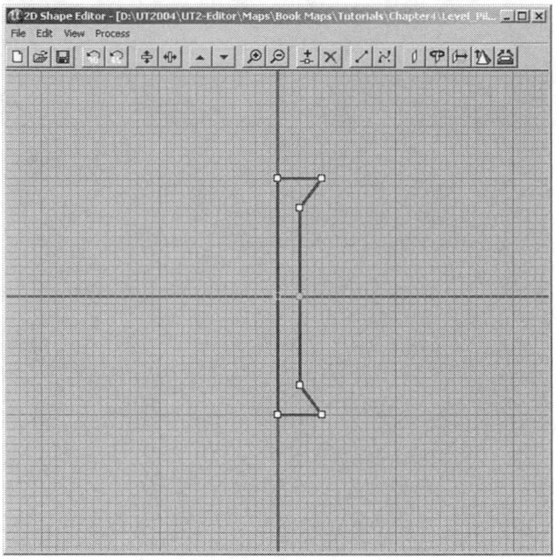

FIGURE 4.53 Column shape.

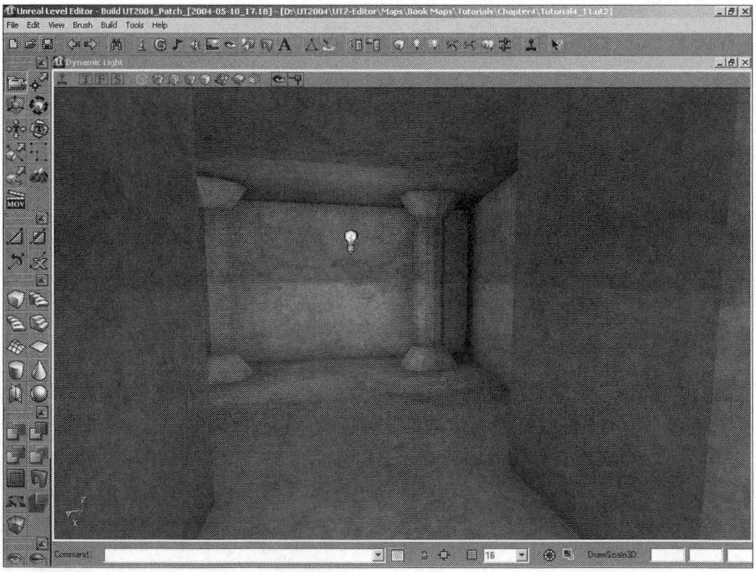

FIGURE 4.54 3D view of pillar.

6. Rebuild and test the map.
7. When you're finished, exit Unreal, and save the map as `TestMap1`.

END TUTORIAL 4.12

Brush Solidity

Earlier in this chapter, you learned about the importance of BSP and BSP cuts. Now it's time to see how brush solidity can affect your level's BSP cuts. In Unreal, brushes can be created with three different levels of solidity: Solid, Semi-Solid, and Non-Solid. The following sections explain these solidity levels and how they affect the makeup of your maps. Each brush type is available as a Special brush, which you can add by clicking the Add Special button. For more information on the Special brushes not mentioned here, refer to Appendix A.

Solid Brushes

Solid brushes are the standard brush used in Unreal. If you have been doing the tutorials in this book up to this point, you have used nothing but Solid brushes. Solid brushes have the following main properties:

- Solid brushes block players and projectiles in the game. This means you can't run through them or shoot through them.
- Solid brushes can be additive or subtractive.
- Solid brushes create BSP cuts in their surrounding world geometry.

Of the three properties, the third is the most important. When you place a Solid brush into a level so that it's touching another Solid brush, both brushes exhibit BSP cuts. Take a look at an example of this phenomenon in the following tutorial.

TUTORIAL 4.13: Creating BSP Cuts with Solid Brushes

1. Start a new level by choosing File > New from the UnrealEd main menu.
2. Create a 256×256×256 cube, and subtract it from the world. Add a light for good measure, and rebuild the level.
3. Switch to Zone/Portal mode in the 3D viewport (keyboard shortcut: Alt+2). This mode shows you all the BSP cuts in your level. At the time of this writing, BSP Cuts mode is nonfunctional, so you must use Zone/Portal mode to view cuts in your BSP.

   Take a moment to look around the room in the 3D viewport (see **FIGURE 4.55**). Notice that each face of the room is a consistent shade of blue, which indicates that these faces currently have no BSP cuts.
4. Create a new cube with dimensions 128×128×128, and align it with the floor in the Side viewport. Add it to your level. Although the effect is immediate, go ahead and rebuild your geometry.

   Notice that the room's floor now has distinct divisions with different shades of blue (see **FIGURE 4.56**). These divisions are BSP cuts in your level's world geometry. For this cube, they are rather minor. Take a look at what happens in the next step when you add a more complex shape.

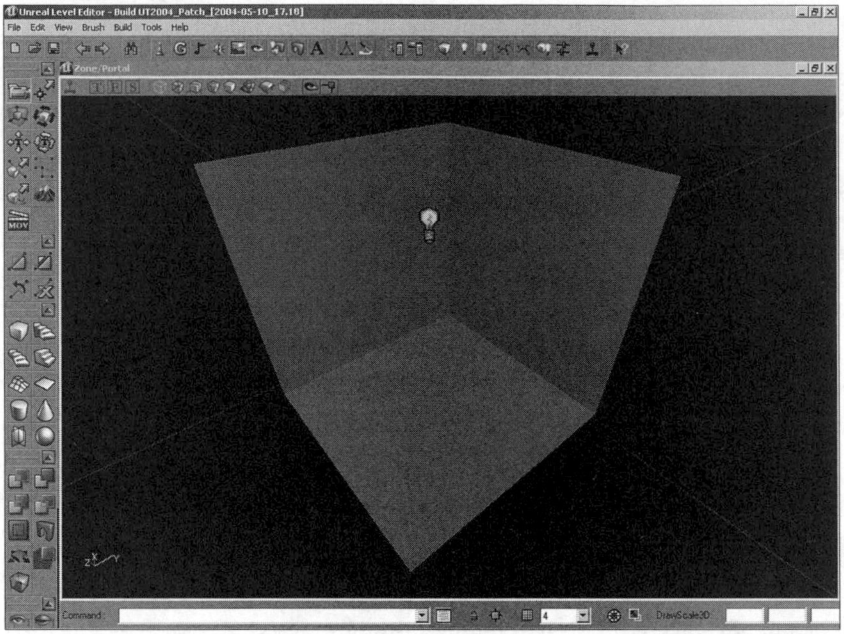

FIGURE 4.55 3D view in Zone/Portal mode of the subtracted cube.

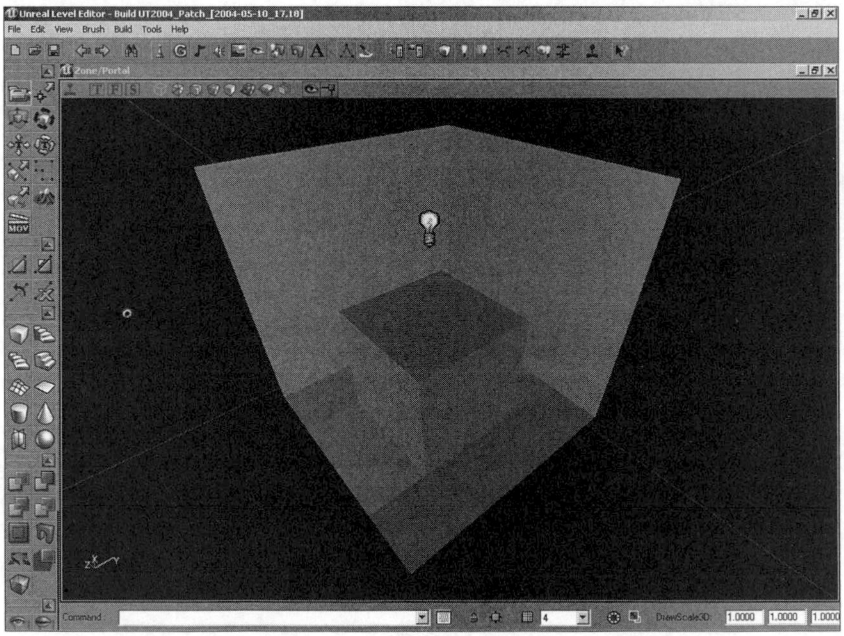

FIGURE 4.56 The floor shows the divisions because of the BSP cuts.

5. Select the added cube brush and delete it. In its place, add a cylinder with the following settings:

    Height: 128

    OuterRadius: 32

    Sides: 12

> **NOTE**
>
> **Make sure the cylinder is aligned with the ground.**

6. As soon as you add the brush, you'll see the pattern of cuts created on the level's floor. In the Top viewport, select this additive brush, and move it to one side of the level. Duplicate the cylinder, and move the duplicate to the opposite side of the level.

7. Rebuild your geometry, and look at the complex cuts created on the floor of your level (see **FIGURE 4.57**).

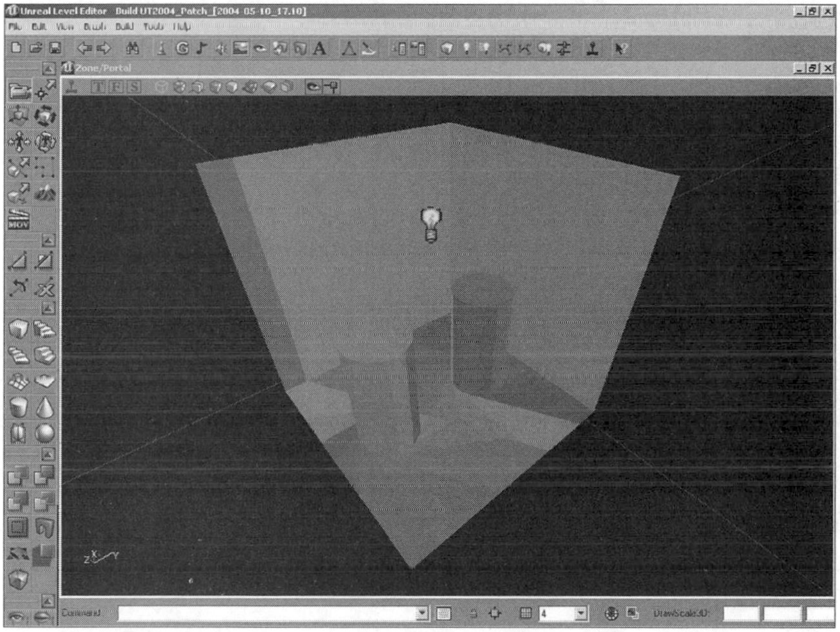

FIGURE 4.57 **Pattern of cuts caused by the two cylinders.**

8. Save your scene when finished.

END TUTORIAL 4.13

These cuts are adding precious calculation time to your level without helping to add any physical detail. To keep your levels as efficient as possible, you want to avoid this problem by using a Semi-Solid brush, discussed in the next section.

Semi-Solid Brushes

With Semi-Solid brushes, you can place brushes into a level without adding any BSP cuts to the surrounding world geometry. This is a tremendous benefit when adding decorations to your levels, such as pillars, beams, and light fixtures. The following is a list of the key attributes of Semi-solid brushes:

- Semi-Solid brushes block players and projectiles, just as Solid brushes do.
- Semi-Solids can *only* be additive, never subtractive.
- Semi-Solids don't leave BSP cuts in their surrounding world geometry.

The following tutorial shows you an example of how these brushes affect their surrounding environment. In this example, you add a pair of cylinders to a cube room, as you did in the previous tutorial.

TUTORIAL 4.14: Using Semi-Solid Brushes

1. Open the level you saved at the end of Tutorial 4.13, and delete the two cylinders. If you don't have this level, create a 256×256×256 cube, select a texture, and subtract the cube from the level. Add a light and rebuild your geometry.
2. Create a cylinder with the following settings:

   Height: 128

   OuterRadius: 32

   Sides: 12

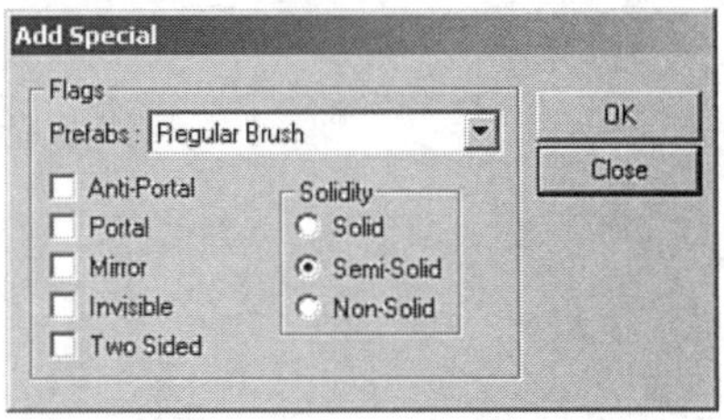

FIGURE 4.58 The Add Special dialog box.

3. Align the cylinder with the floor, and click the Add Special button.
4. In the Add Special dialog box shown in **FIGURE 4.58**, select the Semi-Solid option button, and click OK.
5. Change the 3D viewport mode to Zone/Portal, and notice there are no BSP cuts on the floor of your level (see **FIGURE 4.59**).
6. Save your level.

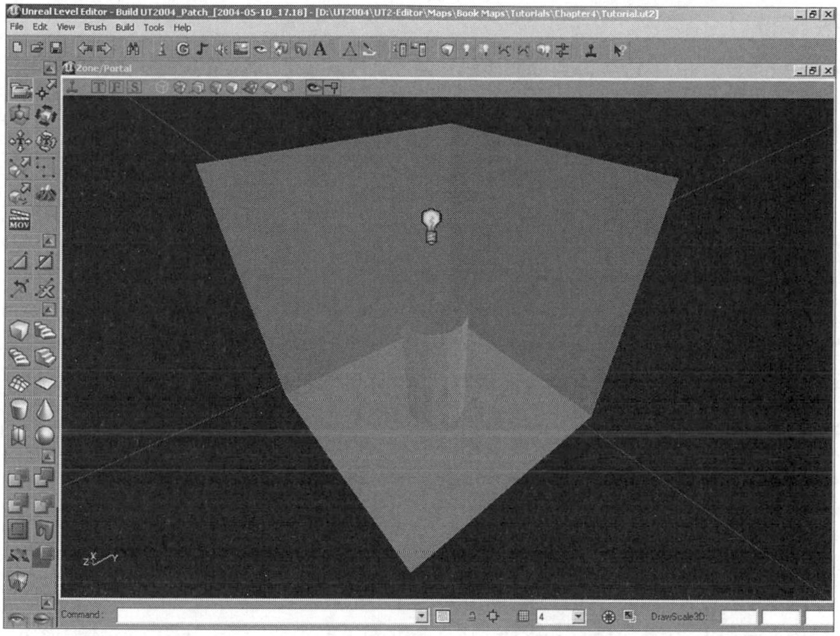

FIGURE 4.59 No cuts were made because a Semi-Solid brush was used.

END TUTORIAL 4.14

Because Semi-Solid brushes don't disturb their surrounding world geometry, they are perfect for decorative additions to your level. However, you should be careful that you don't use them to replace static meshes. For example, say you need a room lined with columns. You could make a pillar with the 2D Shape Editor as you did earlier in this chapter, and then make a series of Semi-Solid brushes from it. However, creating the pillar in an external 3D package and importing it as a static mesh is far more efficient.

> **NOTE**
>
> Be careful not to let your Semi-Solid brushes overlap or touch other Semi-Solid or Non-Solid brushes, as BSP errors could result.

Non-Solid Brushes

With Non-Solid brushes, you can create level geometry that behaves similarly to a hologram. A player can see it, but can't collide with it. Non-Solids can be used anywhere you need to *see* geometry, but not *touch* it. Their practical uses are slightly limited for aesthetic purposes, but they are used heavily when optimizing your level. Anti-portals and level optimization are discussed in Chapter 15, "Level Optimization (Zoning) and Distribution."

On the other hand, you can use Non-Solid brushes to make devious traps and hidden passages. When you rebuild a Non-Solid, it still creates a light map. During gameplay, your Non-Solid brush is indistinguishable from Solid brushes until a player runs into it or tries to shoot it. The following tutorial shows you an example.

TUTORIAL 4.15: Using Non-Solid Brushes

1. Open the level saved at the end of Tutorial 4.14, and delete the cylinder. If you don't have this level, create a 256×256×256 cube, select a texture, and subtract the cube from the level. Add a light, and rebuild your geometry.
2. Create a cylinder with the following settings:

   Height: 128

   OuterRadius: 32

   Sides: 12

3. Align the cylinder with the floor, and click the Add Special button.
4. In the Add Special dialog box, select the Non-Solid option button, and click OK.
5. First, notice that the floor still has no BSP cuts. Rebuild the level, add a Player Start Actor, and test it out by trying to run into the cylinder.

4

END TUTORIAL 4.15

The cylinder *looks* normal, but you can't collide with it, nor can your projectiles bounce off it. Non-Solid brushes are a great way to hide objects and passages in your levels.

Saving Brushes (u3d Files)

Using the techniques explained so far in this chapter, you can create BSP brushes that you want to save for later use. Under the Brush menu of UnrealEd's main menu, you'll find the Open Brush and Save Brush As commands.

TUTORIAL 4.16: Saving Brushes

1. Open the 2D Shape Editor, and open the `pillar.2ds` file you saved in Tutorial 4.12. If you don't have this file, simply create an interesting shape of your own.
2. Revolve the shape to create a pillar-like brush.
3. With the Builder brush selected (it should currently look like a pillar), choose Brush > Save Brush As from UnrealEd's main menu.
4. Save the brush as `pillarBrush.u3d`, and click OK.
5. Click the Cube primitive to change the Builder brush into a cube.

6. From the main menu, choose Brush > Open Brush. Click the `pillarBrush.u3d` file you just saved, and click Open. Notice that the Builder brush transforms back into your original pillar shape.

This technique is quite useful when you want to create archives of your most frequently used brushes.

END TUTORIAL 4.16

Importing/Exporting Brushes

At times, you might want to edit a brush you have made in UnrealEd with an external 3D package. Alternatively, you might need to import an object that you modeled in a 3D package into UnrealEd. You can do this with UnrealEd's Import and Export brush functionality. These import and export processes have been demonstrated in the following tutorial, assuming that you don't have a 3D package at your disposal.

TUTORIAL 4.17: Importing and Exporting Brushes

1. Open the `pillarBrush.u3d` file saved in Tutorial 4.16.
2. With the brush selected, choose Brush > Export from the UnrealEd main menu.
3. Save the brush as `pillarExport.t3d`. Be sure to change the file type to the t3d format.
4. Click the Cube primitive to change the Builder brush into a cube.

> **NOTE**
>
> The available import types are t3d, dxf, asc, and ase. The available export types are t3d and obj.

5. From the main menu, choose Brush > Import, and select the `pillarExport` file you just created. Click Open, and click OK in the Import Brush dialog box. Watch the Builder brush change back into a pillar.

END TUTORIAL 4.17

Summary

This chapter has covered the theory behind BSP and explained several techniques you can use to make your levels more efficient. You have learned several methods for creating specially shaped brushes to add more detail to your levels, especially if you do not have access to static meshes. You should now be ready to create a variety of different environments while making the most out of the different brushes. Practice the tutorials in this chapter so that you can more easily identify which brush to use in different situations. Remember that brushes form the foundation of your levels, and the more you know about how to use them, the more efficient your levels will be.

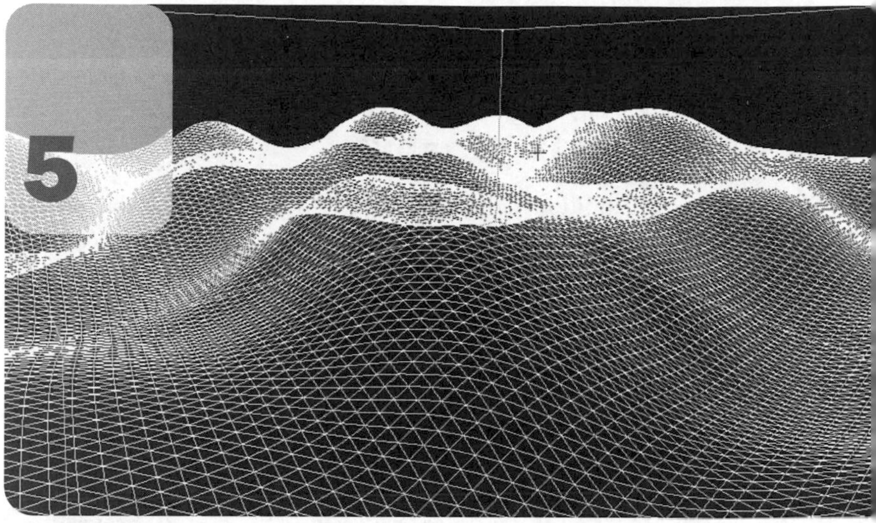

Chapter 5

Terrain

Thus far, the content of this book has focused on the construction of interior-based, or indoor levels. The Unreal Engine, however, does not restrict you to having only tightly enclosed levels. In fact, many of today's hottest Unreal-based games, including UT2004, also cover vast landscapes. In this chapter, we will discuss UnrealEd's powerful terrain generation system, and how it can be used to create your own open-ranged landscapes, both native and alien.

We will begin with a general discussion of exactly what terrain *is*, including the components involved in its creation. We will then look at the Terrain Editing dialog, which encompasses the suite of tools used for working with terrain. When you have a basic understanding of terrain and the tools used to develop it, we will move on to a series of tutorials, which will take you through creation of your own terrains. We will discuss how these terrains can be edited with UnrealEd's conventional system. From there, we will begin painting textures on our terrain, in order to give the look of dirt, rock, and grasses. We will then demonstrate how you can use decoration layers to enhance the look of your terrains by adding decorations such as trees, grasses, rocks, or any static mesh object.

What Is Terrain?

By definition, *terrain* is an area of land or a particular geographic area. Within UnrealEd, this is really only the beginning, as there are several components that all come together to generate the landscape you see in-game. At its heart, terrain is a highly *tessellated* piece of geometry, meaning that it is made up of hundreds if not thousands of polygons. The geometry's shape is driven by a height map. More specifically, the Z-axis location of each of the geometry's vertices is defined by either an 8- or 16-bit grayscale image. Darker shades will define lower elevations of the terrain, whereas brighter shades will create higher elevations. In **FIGURE 5.1**, you see a simplified height map, demonstrating how light and dark areas can define elevations.

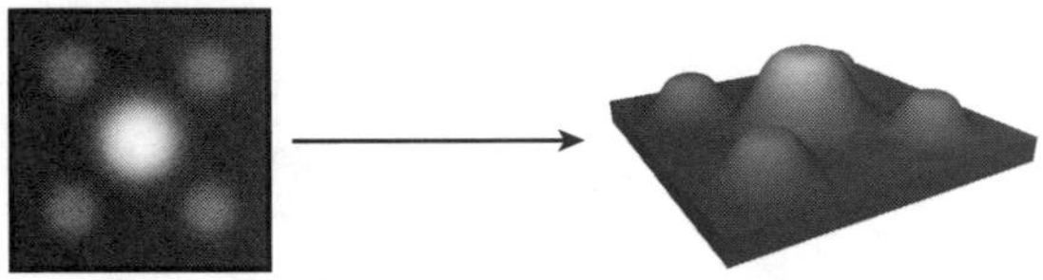

FIGURE 5.1 2D Texture used as a height map.

The Components of Terrain

As mentioned earlier, terrain consists of several components. In this section, we will take a close look at each of the Actors required to create terrain and how the different assets of the game are used in conjunction with these Actors to give us rich landscapes for use in our levels.

Terrain Zoning with the ZoneInfo Actor

The first component required is the ZoneInfo Actor. This Actor is responsible for defining, or *zoning*, the area in which terrain can exist. If you were to attempt to create terrain in an area that had not been properly zoned, you would not see it at all. When adding the ZoneInfo Actor into subtracted space, all connecting subtractions will also be considered zoned. This allows our terrain to flow through multiple subtracted spaces that are all connected together without using multiple ZoneInfo Actors.

With the ZoneInfo Actor, only a single property adjustment is required for terrain to exist: the `bTerrain` property. Setting this property to `True` creates a zone that is conditioned to contain and render terrain.

The ZoneInfo Actor offers a few features that work well when designing outdoor scenes. One of the most important features is the ability to create and control distance fog. Although there are many things to understand about zones, not every aspect of the Actor will be discussed in this chapter. Rather, we will focus only on those properties that are pertinent to terrain and landscape creation. Later in the book, we cover in greater detail the concepts behind zoning as well as the benefits of proper zoning.

Using the TerrainInfo Actor

After the ZoneInfo Actor has been added to the level, the designer can proceed with the creation of the terrain. Generating the terrain geometry is done through the TerrainInfo Actor. It is this Actor that references the various texture maps used to define the way the terrain will look. The Actor also houses all of the properties used to define specific attributes of the terrain that will be rendered at runtime. One can easily say that the TerrainInfo Actor is the heart of the terrain system. Multiple TerrainInfo Actors can be added into a level, even into the same zone. This can be helpful in creating effects like a cave-type ceiling above the ground, in which you would need one terrain object to act as the cave floor, and another to form the ceiling.

The textures used by the TerrainInfo Actor can be divided into three categories: the Height Map and Layer textures, and DecoLayer textures.

Controlling Terrain with the Height Map

The Height Map texture is arguably the most important texture, as it is used to define the elevation and contour of the terrain through the variation of grayscale colors. As mentioned earlier, dark areas of the height map will create valleys, whereas lighter areas will become hills. It should be noted, however, that this system works on a pixel-to-vertex level, meaning that the color of a single pixel will change the height of one vertex on the terrain's geometry. Without a height map, the rendering engine would not be able to draw the terrain at all. Conversely, using a height map of a single solid color would result in a flat terrain, as there would be no differentiation to cause elevation changes.

When creating a height map externally, one important thing to keep in mind is the final file format in which the texture will be saved. Three formats are accepted by the terrain system:

- 8-bit grayscale
- 16-bit grayscale—The map type generated by UnrealEd
- The Alpha channel of a 32-bit image

If you plan on using the Terrain Editing dialog to interactively paint the textures used to drive the height, you will need to use the G16 format. This is not a problem when the texture is created from the Terrain Editing dialog, but importing textures from other applications requires a bit more planning. If the format is not G16, the editing tools will not function.

Height maps play another important role with terrain; they determine the terrain's physical dimensions in X and Y. There is a formula that can be used to find what the size will be:

```
Resolution X * Terrain Scale X – Terrain Scale X
Resolution Y * Terrain Scale Y – Terrain Scale Y
```

The default scale for a terrain is 64 in all axes. Therefore a height map of 128 × 128 would result in the following:

```
Width: 128 * 64 – 64 = 8128
Breadth: 128 * 64 – 64 = 8128
```

Although this equation may seem strange in that the terrain scale is subtracted after the resolution and scale are multiplied, this is how the terrain generation system will internally calculate the size of your terrain.

Layers

Although the height map determines the shape of the terrain, it does not have any effect on the terrain's surface appearance, such as its color. Control of the visual aspects of terrain is handled by *layers*, which provide the look of dirt, rock, grass, and so on. The TerrainInfo Actor can have a maximum of 32 layers, each with its own texture, assigned to the terrain. Each layer in the TerrainInfo Actor contains two texture maps, the first being the color map that will be visible on the surface, and the second being an alpha map, which controls the transparency and blending from one texture to another. As textures are added, they are stacked on top of one another. If the alpha map associated with the new layer added is completely white, nothing below that layer is visible. Alpha maps control how textures blend together from layer to layer.

5

> **NOTE**
>
> **About the layer's alpha format: The actual texture information for the alpha is an 8-bit grayscale image. This can be by itself as a P8 texture, or the alpha channel of an RGBA8 texture. The Terrain Editing dialog will create an RGBA8.**

When defining a new layer from the Terrain Editing dialog, two things happen: First, a selected texture is assigned to supply the layer with color. Second, a new texture is created in which all color information will be ignored, and which will only be used for its alpha channel. It is this alpha channel that will determine how the created layer blends with the subsequent layers beneath it (see **FIGURE 5.2**).

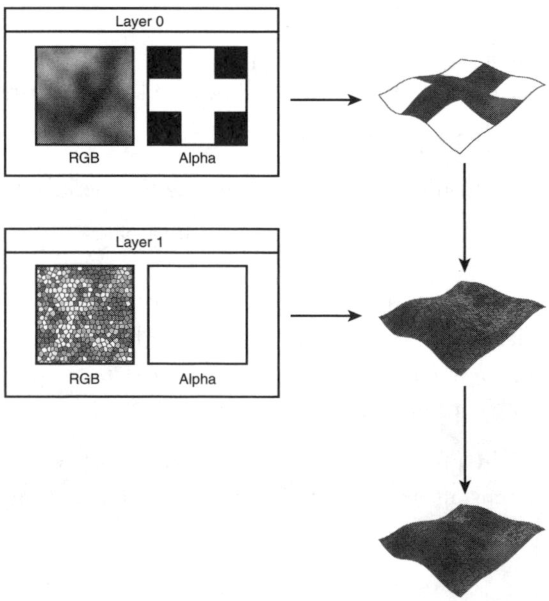

FIGURE 5.2 **Layers blend to form the final terrain.**

DecoLayers

Finally, the decoration layer (DecoLayer) textures are used to drive the placement of decoration objects on the terrain, such as blades of grass, trees, and shrubs. These objects will consist of static meshes, whose physical and location data will be based on a series of texture maps. There are three types of texture maps associated with a DecoLayer: the density map, the color map, and the scale map. We will cover how each of these components is used to drive the decorations across the terrain later in this chapter. **FIGURE 5.3** shows how each of these maps is used to control the density, color, and scale of the static meshes used within the DecoLayer.

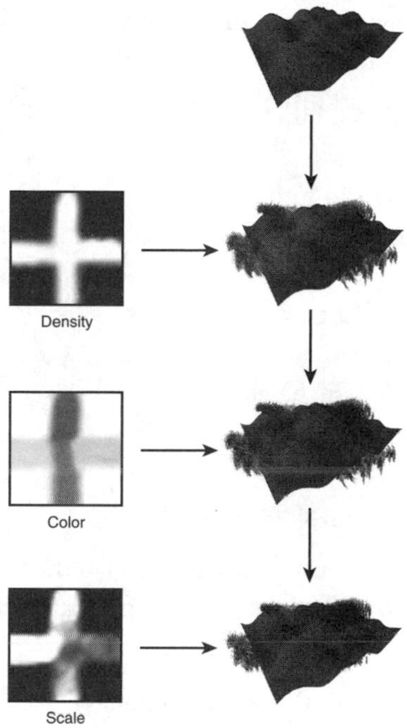

FIGURE 5.3 The construction of a DecoLayer.

Altering Terrain with the Terrain Editing Dialog

As mentioned before, textures play a large role in the creation of terrain, from defining our terrain's physical contours to controlling how the visible surface textures such as dirt, grass, and rock blend together to give the final look. We also use textures to define the location and density of terrain decorations such as trees, shrubs, rocks, and so on.

You can go about the creation and manipulation of these textures in two ways: by the use of external painting applications such as Photoshop and Paint Shop Pro, or through UnrealEd's built-in Terrain Editing dialog. Although it is possible to create all of your terrain without the use of the editor, the process is not nearly as intuitive, as you will not see the results of your work immediately. In order to expedite the terrain creation process, the Terrain Editing dialog provides a suite of tools that make creating, selecting, and painting these textures both fast and easy. Without these tools, the level designers would find themselves repeatedly jumping from their painting application into UnrealEd, in order to view any tweaks or changes made to their textures.

The Terrain Editing dialog provides four primary functions:

- Creation and manipulation of height maps
- Assignment and blending control of texture layers
- Assignment and manipulation of DecoLayers
- Automatic terrain generation

FIGURE 5.4 shows the Terrain Editing dialog, which you can access by clicking the Terrain Editing icon from the toolbox.

The dialog is divided into two key areas: Tools and Miscellaneous. In the Tools panel, we have access to a suite of tools used for terrain editing as well as a way to control which textures we are editing, whether they are for the height map, one of the texture layers, or DecoLayers. The Miscellaneous panel provides a means for automatic terrain generation.

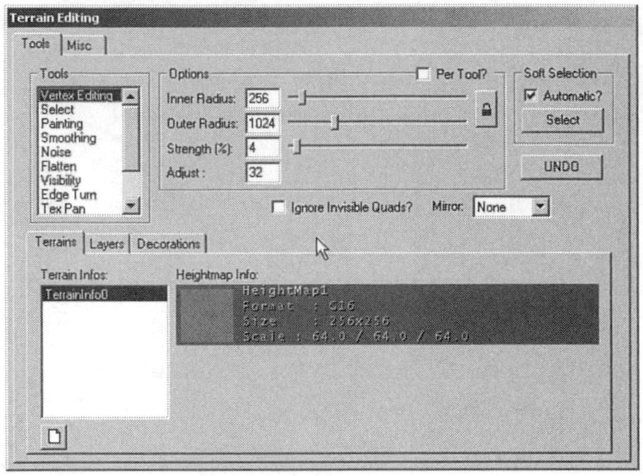

FIGURE 5.4 Terrain Editing dialog.

Throughout this chapter, we will explore all of the features and tools available in the Terrain Editing dialog. We will also take a look at creating terrain without this editor, using Adobe Photoshop.

In **TUTORIALS 5.1** and **5.2**, we will walk you through the steps required to create simple terrain. We will begin with the creation of a large room. From there we will add the ZoneInfo Actor and designate the room as a place where terrain can exist. When the room has been properly flagged to allow terrain, we will then use the Terrain Editing tools to create a simple flat surface.

TUTORIAL 5.1: Preparing an Area for Terrain

1. In UnrealEd, start a new level and load the Ch5_Terrain texture package into the Texture browser.
2. Select the MossWalls texture.
3. Subtract a cube with the following dimensions:

    Height: 4096

    Width: 8128

    Breadth: 8128

4. From the Actor Class browser, choose Actor > Info > ZoneInfo (see **FIGURE 5.5**).
5. In the Top viewport, right-click near the middle of the level and select Add ZoneInfo Here from the context menu (see **FIGURE 5.6**).

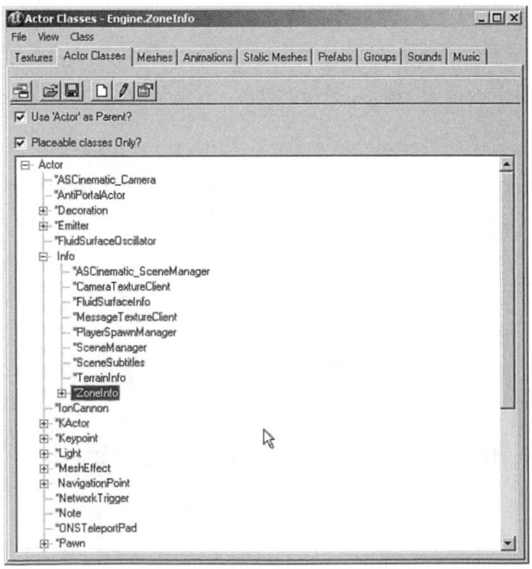

FIGURE 5.5 ZoneInfo selected in the Actor Class browser.

6. Open the Properties dialog for the ZoneInfo by double-clicking the Actor's icon.
7. In the ZoneInfo property section, set `bTerrainZone` to `True` (see **FIGURE 5.7**).
8. Save your map.

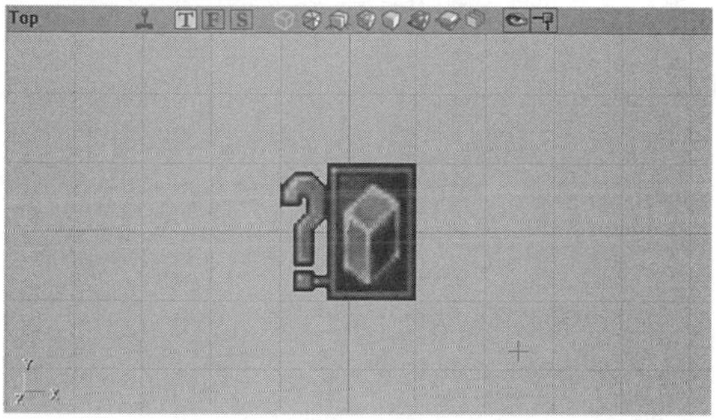

FIGURE 5.6 The ZoneInfo icon prepares the zone to handle terrain.

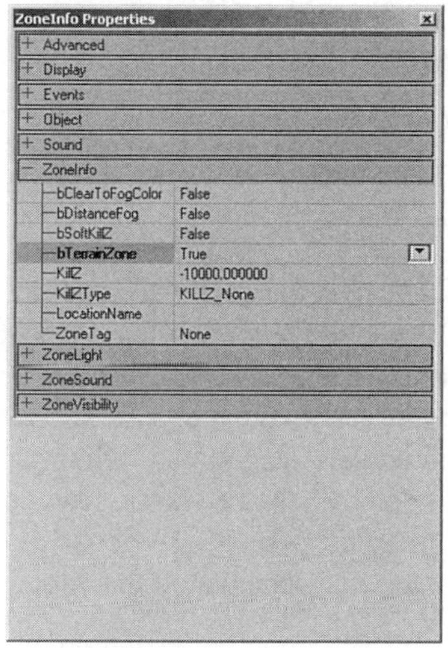

FIGURE 5.7 Setting the `bTerrainZone` property of the ZoneInfo Actor.

END TUTORIAL 5.1

You now have a zone that has been conditioned to render terrain. You will not see the terrain at this point as it has yet to be created. In **TUTORIAL 5.2**, we will see how a TerrainInfo Actor is used to create the terrain.

We will create two important components of terrain: the TerrainInfo Actor and its associated height map. As mentioned previously, there are two ways to go about this; you can create the TerrainInfo Actor manually through the Actor Class browser and then assign a height map that you created in Photoshop, or you can use the Terrain Editing dialog to create both the Actor and map in a single step. In **TUTORIAL 5.2**, we will use the Terrain Editing dialog.

TUTORIAL 5.2: Creating a Basic Terrain Using the Terrain Editing Dialog

1. Open the file saved in **TUTORIAL 5.1**. Continuing from where we left off, switch to Terrain Editing mode by clicking the Terrain icon in the toolbox. This will open the Terrain Editing dialog (see **FIGURE 5.8**).

2. Click the New button located in the lower-left corner of the Terrain Editing dialog.

3. In the New Terrain dialog, set the following parameters (see **FIGURE 5.9**):

   Package: myLevel

   Group: Heightmaps

   Name: Heightmap1

   XSize: 128

   YSize: 128

   Click OK. Two things are created: the TerrainInfo Actor and the associated height map. The new height map has a resolution of 128 × 128 pixels and is being stored within the level. **FIGURE 5.10** shows how the Terrain Editing dialog will appear once you have completed this step.

4. With the exception of the TerrainInfo Actor appearing in the viewport, it appears that nothing has happened. Rebuild the level. The level should go dark because there are no lights in the scene. In the 3D viewport, switch to the Textured view (no lighting) by clicking the icon.

5. In the 3D viewport, you will notice that a new type of cursor moves under your mouse. This is the Terrain Editing tool. At the moment you cannot see any terrain. This is because we must have at least one texture layer created. Without a texture, the terrain appears invisible.

6. In the Texture browser, select the Dirt texture.

7. In the Terrain Editing dialog, make sure Heightmap1 is selected (it will be highlighted with a dull green) and then click the Layers tab.

8. Select the first Undefined slot (see **FIGURE 5.11**); you will see a small

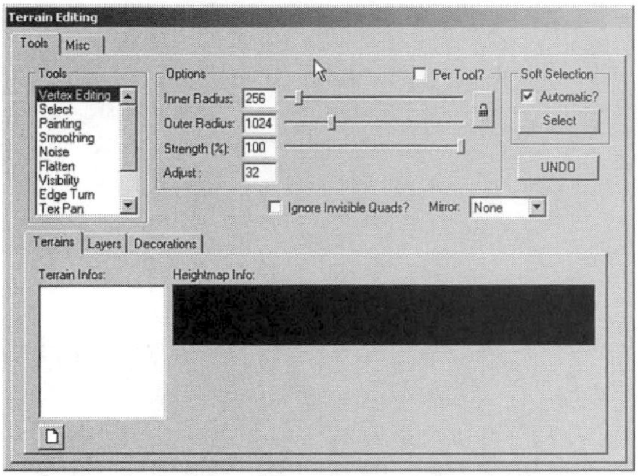

FIGURE 5.8 Terrain Editing dialog showing no height map.

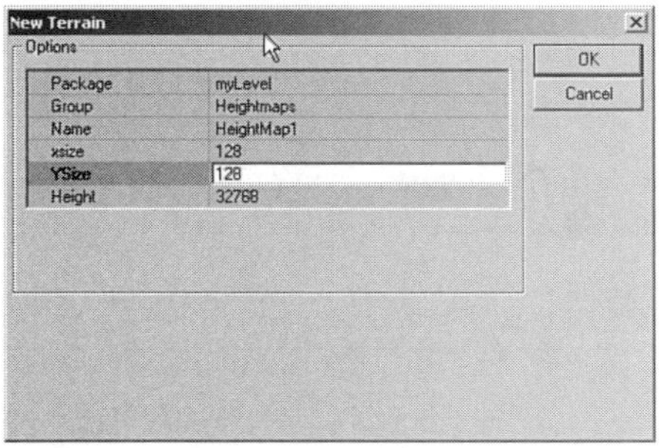

FIGURE 5.9 New Terrain dialog allows you to set parameters for your terrain.

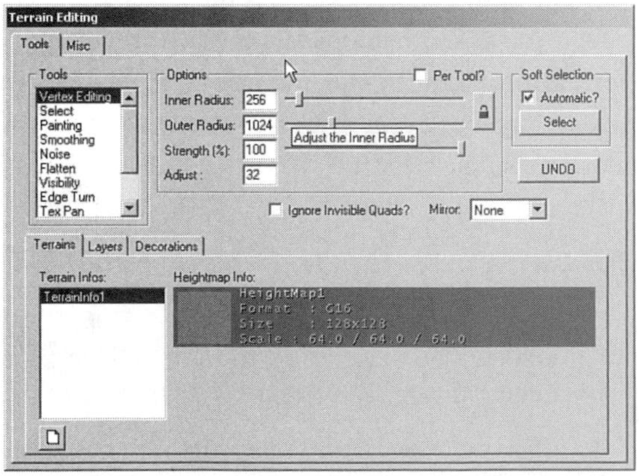

FIGURE 5.10 Terrain Editing dialog after creating the new terrain.

highlight appear around the undefined layer when you select it.

9. Click the New button. In the New Layer properties dialog, set the following settings (see **FIGURE 5.12**):

   Package: myLevel

   Group: TerrainLayers

   Name: DirtLayer1

   AlphaHeight: 128

   AlphaWidth: 128

   AlphaFill: Set the color to white.

   UScale: 8

   VScale: 8

   Click OK.

10. You have now created basic terrain (see **FIGURE 5.13**). Obviously, it is not the most exciting landscape in the world, but you can add a player start and a light or two, and then rebuild and run the game. You'd have no problem running around on the terrain.

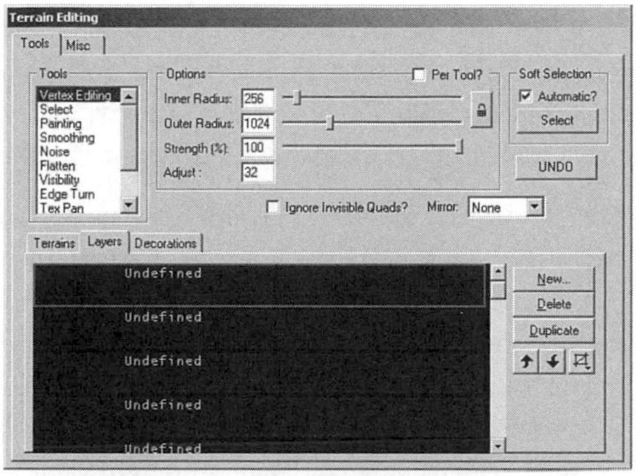

FIGURE 5.11 First Undefined slot selected.

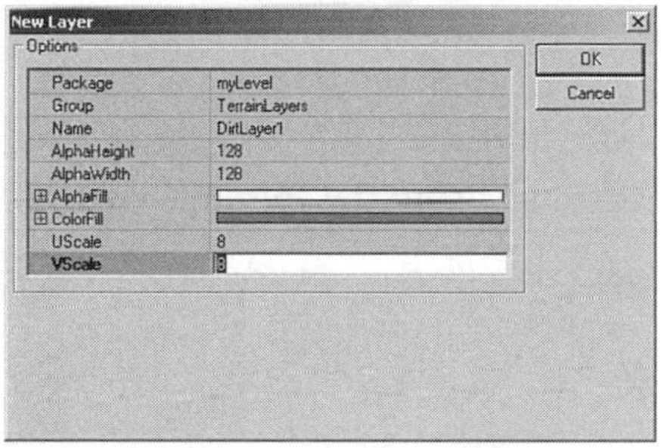

FIGURE 5.12 New Layer dialog.

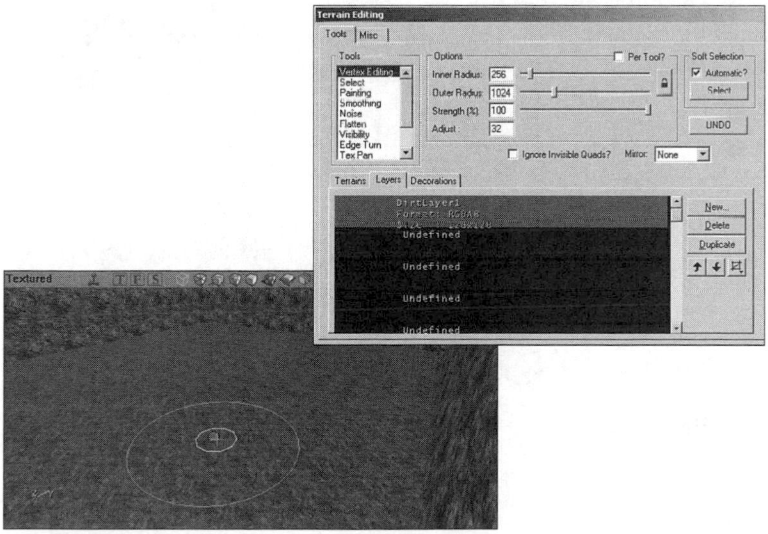

FIGURE 5.13 You can now see the terrain with the dirt texture applied.

END TUTORIAL 5.2

Now that we have terrain in our level, it's time to see if we can make it a little more visually interesting. To give the terrain a more appealing look, we will need to vary its altitude. This is done by editing the height map. There are two main ways that we can go about this; we can either use the tools in the Terrain Editing dialog, or we can use the Terrain Generation feature that is built into the editor.

The Terrain Generator is a great way to quickly create randomized terrain. Although the terrain's contour is random, the designer does have a level of control over what is generated. The Select tool can be used to specify a certain area to randomize, or you can simply have the generator randomize the entire terrain plane. Furthermore, control over the peaks and valleys is provided through the Steps and Strength settings. In its simplest form, you can think of Steps as a way to control the number of hills, whereas the Strength setting controls the magnitude, or steepness, of the hills being generated. Higher Strength values will produce steeper hills, whereas lower values can be used to produce more of a rolling hills effect.

In **TUTORIAL 5.3**, you will use the Terrain Generator to give you a quick starting point with your terrain.

TUTORIAL 5.3: Using the Terrain Generator

1. You can continue from the end of the last tutorial, or open the file `Tutorial5_03_Start.ut2`.

2. Make sure you are still in Terrain Editing mode and select the Select tool (see **FIGURE 5.14**). You are not required to use this tool, but it must be selected before the Terrain Generator will work.

3. Highlight the Heightmap and click the Misc tab at the top of the dialog.

4. Set the following options in the Terrain Generation section (see **FIGURE 5.15**):

   Steps: 5

   Strength: 40

   Check the Use Entire Heightmap option.

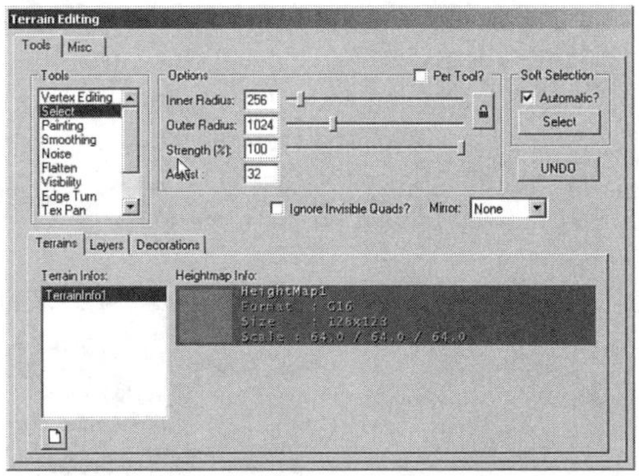

FIGURE 5.14 The Select tool selected from the Tools list.

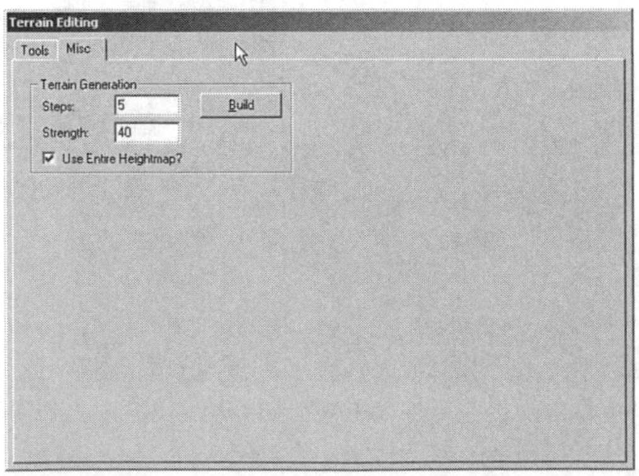

FIGURE 5.15 Terrain Generation section.

5. Click Build. Your terrain will now have a random set of hills and valleys, as shown in **FIGURE 5.16**.
6. Continue to adjust the Steps and Strength settings and rebuild the terrain until you achieve an interesting look.
7. Save the map.

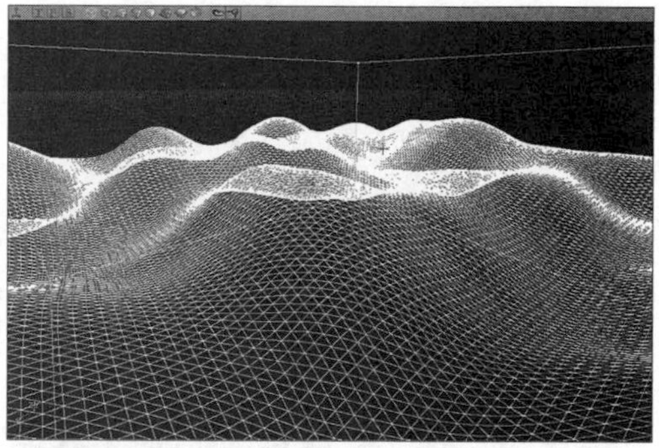

FIGURE 5.16 Wireframe view of the results from the Terrain Generator.

END TUTORIAL 5.3

Lighting Terrains with Sunlight

When you are creating terrain, lighting plays an important role in making things look realistic. Without shadowing, varying elevations of your terrain will be difficult to distinguish. Here you see our current level, and it is very hard to make out what is going on. To correct this, we will add a Sunlight Actor.

Until now we have only worked with lights that appear to come from a specific point in space, such as the standard Light Actor. If we were to light our terrain with this approach, it would be difficult to simulate the type of light effects one sees when outdoors. In the real world, our sun (and moon for that matter) is so large and so far away that by the time the light reaches us, the light rays appear to be parallel to one another. Think about it—the next time you are standing in a parking lot during the day, look at the shadows cast by the light posts. Even though the light posts are separated by some distance, their shadows are all pointing in the same direction, meaning that they are in parallel to one another.

In Unreal, we can reproduce this effect with the Sunlight Actor. This Actor will produce parallel rays of light appearing to come from infinitely far away. The effect is very similar to the lighting effect provided by the sun on a clear day. In **TUTORIAL 5.4**, we will take a look at how to set up a Sunlight Actor as well as how to make it illuminate our rather washed-out landscape.

TUTORIAL 5.4: Adding Sunlight

1. You can continue from the end of the last tutorial, or open the file `Tutorial5_04_Start.ut2`.
2. In the Actor Class browser, choose Actor > Light > Sunlight.
3. In the 3D viewport, right-click on the ceiling of your level and select Add Sunlight Here from the context menu (see **FIGURE 5.17**).

4. Rebuild the level and switch the 3D viewport back to the Dynamic Lighting mode so that you can see the effects of the light on the terrain. After you have done this, you will notice that everything is black; it appears that the light had no effect at all. Remember, this type of light is not emitted from the point of the Actor. To make the light work properly, we will need to flag the ceiling as a Fake Backdrop. This will cause the light to appear as if it were coming in through the ceiling of the level.

5. In your 3D viewport, select the ceiling. Press F5 to open the Surface Properties dialog (see **FIGURE 5.18**). Check the Fake Backdrop option and close the dialog.

6. Rebuild the level once more. This time you should see light somewhere. Most likely you will need to orient the light. This can be done quickly by using the Lock to Selected Actor mode.

7. Click the Lock to Selected Actor icon in the 3D viewport. Click the Sunlight Actor in the 3D view. The camera has now been snapped to the sunlight, and as you move/rotate your camera view in the 3D viewport, it will move/rotate the sunlight with you. Because the light seems to originate from infinitely far away, the location of the Sunlight Actor is irrelevant. All you will need to do is find the best rotation of the light. You will need to rebuild the lighting to see the effects of the new orientation. When you are satisfied with the placement

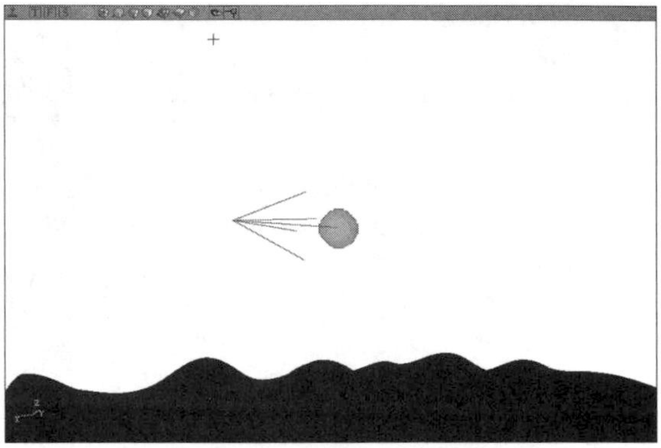

FIGURE 5.17 Sunlight Actor placed in the level. The sunlight is viewed without the textured background to make it easier to see.

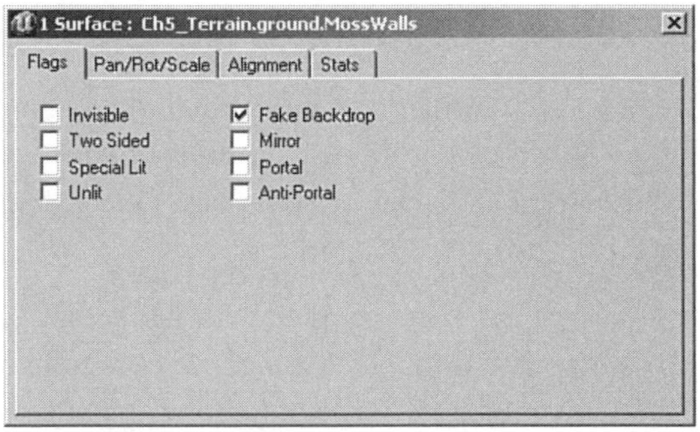

FIGURE 5.18 Set the Fake Backdrop option in the Surface Properties dialog.

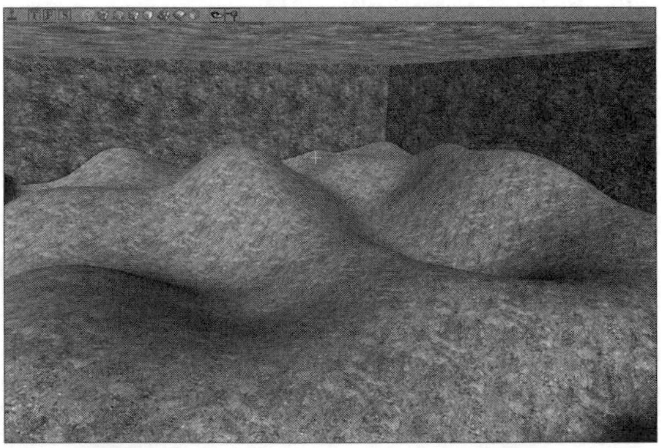

FIGURE 5.19 The terrain has a much more natural feel after the Sunlight Actor is added.

of the sunlight, click the Lock to Selected Actor icon again to release the light's constraint. **FIGURE 5.19** shows the result of the Sunlight Actor on the terrain's surface.

> **TIP**
>
> **You may find it necessary to open the properties for the sunlight and set Light Brightness to a higher value, such as 100. This will boost the contrast between the areas of light and shadow.**

END TUTORIAL 5.4

You will notice that light does not reach all of the terrain. The only way to make this happen through manipulation of the light's orientation would be to point it straight down, which would result in a sort of high-noon effect, eliminating virtually all of our terrain's shadows. Instead, we will later turn the side walls into fake backdrops as well. This will create a much better distribution of light. However, we still have a small problem. Our terrain appears to be lit by a sun, and yet it exists indoors. To make the level appear more realistic, we will need a sky from which our sunlight can shine. In the next section, we will take a look at how we can create a sky for our level.

The Skybox

With the ability to create vast outdoor areas with terrain, we must naturally be able to compliment them with realistic-looking skies. Without a sky, we would simply have an outdoor area that was enclosed in a box, which would obviously look out of place. Unfortunately, the subtractive nature of the Unreal Engine prevents us from making infinitely open skies. We can, however, fake the effect of an open sky using what is called a *skybox*. In this next section we are going to take a look at skyboxes, the setups used to create the illusion of open skies. We will begin with a discussion of what a skybox is and how it works. From there we will move into a tutorial that will step you through adding a skybox to our terrain level.

What Are Skyboxes?

A skybox is nothing more than subtracted space (generally a box) that is separated from the rest of the level. The objective of the skybox is to create the illusion of objects, such as clouds, suns, moons, and so on, off in the far distance. The illusion that these objects are so far away becomes apparent as you navigate around the level. The objects viewed in the skybox look stationary, similar to the way stars seem to stay still as you drive around in a car. Skyboxes are great for creating cloudy skies, night scenes, or even futuristic space scenes.

A skybox can be set up in various ways, depending on the workflow preferred by the level designer or dependent on a specific look that you are trying to achieve (see **FIGURE 5.20**). The most common skybox is the shape of a box, but occasionally you will find cylinders and even spheres used to house the sky environment.

FIGURE 5.20 Skybox example.

How Does a Skybox Work?

As mentioned earlier, a skybox is an area subtracted from the level that is isolated from the rest of the map. So, how does a player see this sky if it is completely separated from the level? This is done through the use of a SkyZoneInfo Actor, which must be added near the center of the skybox. This Actor is responsible for causing the skybox to render around the entire level. Of course by default the players would not see the walls of the skybox because the level walls are blocking their view, and the skybox itself is detached from the level. But, with UnrealEd, we have the ability to flag a wall as a "fake backdrop." Doing this causes the rendering engine to not render this wall. If the wall is not rendered, we will see the skybox.

An interesting way to visualize this is to picture your entire level fitting into the SkyZoneInfo Actor. This would result in the skybox completely encompassing the level. Any surface flagged as a fake backdrop would not render, resulting in the player seeing out into the skybox. In our case, the ceiling was previously flagged as a fake backdrop so that we could have our sunlight illuminate our level from that surface. But after we add a skybox into the level, we will no longer see the texture on our ceiling. Instead, that surface will basically vanish, resulting in the player seeing out into the skybox. Because the SkyZoneInfo is a stationary Actor, when the player moves, the sky remains in place, giving the illusion that it is quite vast and some distance away, which is exactly the effect we're chasing.

Throughout the design of a level, textures play an enormous role. This is no different with skyboxes. Skyboxes can be textured with any image you see fit, in order to give the visual effect you are after. In most cases, you will find some sort of open sky or outer space texture. Working with textures on a skybox, however, can be a bit tricky. If the skybox is not properly textured, seams can result, meaning that the player would be able to see that the sky was actually a large box overhead. This quickly breaks the illusion of a massive skyline. Numerous methods have been developed to help keep the seams from showing. The following are some of the more common methods employed:

- Create five textures that fit together seamlessly on a box (see **FIGURE 5.21**). The sixth texture (the floor texture) is not necessary in most cases as the players should never see the floor of the skybox (otherwise, they'd have to see through the ground). After applying these textures to the skybox, the designer carefully aligns the textures so that the transition from surface to surface is seamless.

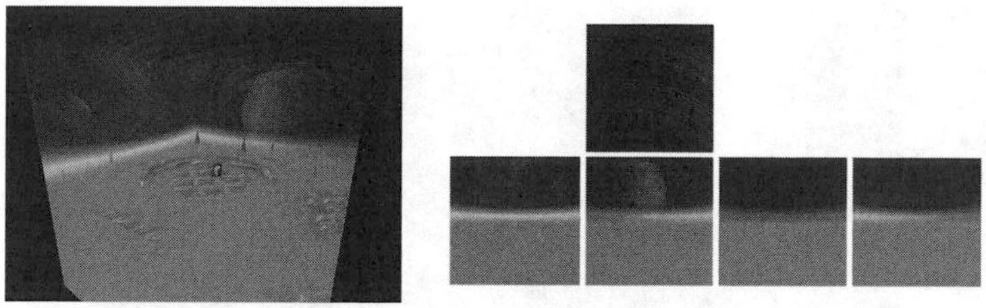

FIGURE 5.21 The inside of a skybox, along with the six images used to decorate the sides of the skybox cube.

- A cylinder static mesh is used to surround the SkyZoneInfo with a texture. The texture applied to the cylinder is a gradient that is affecting transparency. This makes the sky appear to be fading out, thereby faking the look of a distant horizon (see **FIGURE 5.22**).
- Texture only the ceiling, and then surround the SkyZoneInfo with static mesh objects such as mountains, buildings to create a cityscape, and so on (see **FIGURE 5.23**). The idea is that the player should not be able to see the sides of the skybox.

FIGURE 5.22 The gradient of transparency on the cylinder.

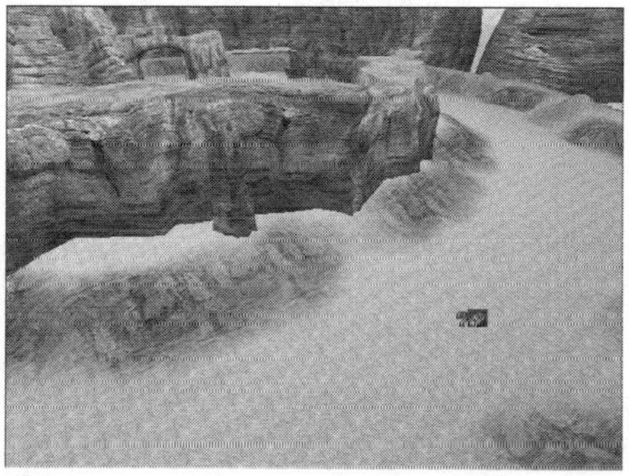

FIGURE 5.23 Static meshes of mountains or cliffs can be placed in the skybox around the ZoneInfo Actor to create the illusion that your level is surrounded by massive and distant landforms.

- Place a TerrainInfo Actor in the skybox and create hills/mountains in such a way that the outer walls are blocked by the terrain (see **FIGURE 5.24**). This is the approach we will be using in our tutorial.
- Finally, and this method can be added with any of the other methods presented in this list: Enable distance fog! By applying fog in the skybox, we can have the walls of the skybox hidden by the fog (see **FIGURE 5.25**). This generally gives a nice result, and we will also be using it in our tutorial.

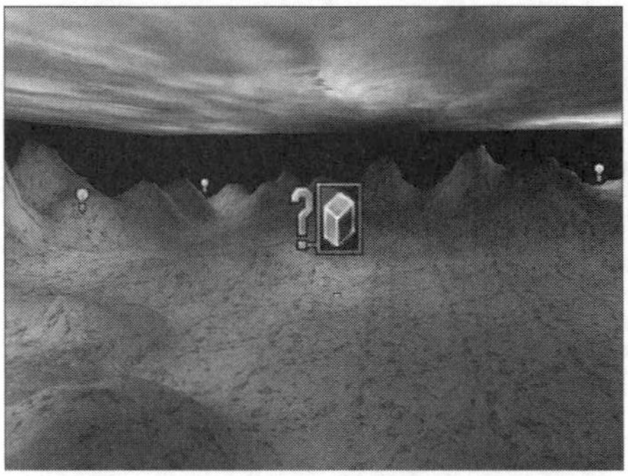

FIGURE 5.24 The result of placing a TerrainInfo actor into the skybox, creating a second terrain within the skybox. The effect is like a large range of mountains surrounding the level.

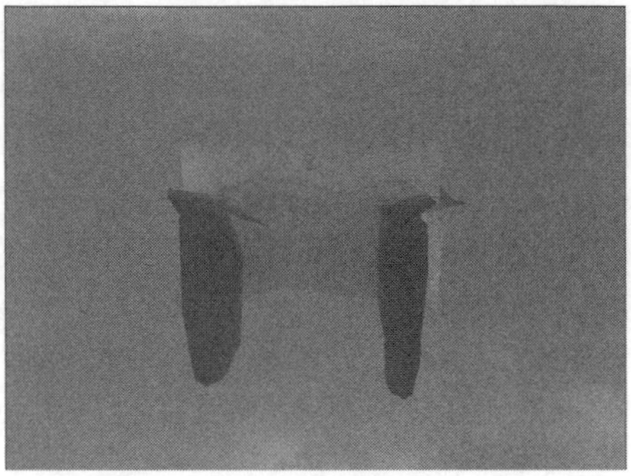

FIGURE 5.25 This figure shows how fog can be used to obscure distant areas of the skybox.

Skyboxes can be further enhanced by using sheets textured with materials of panning clouds. This provides the player with the illusion of a more dynamic environment as the skies are seen to move above them. In **TUTORIAL 5.5**, we will add a skybox to our level.

TUTORIAL 5.5: Enhancing the Look of Our Terrain by Adding a Skybox

1. You may continue from the end of the last tutorial, or you can open the file `Tutorial5_05_Start.ut2`.
2. Open the Textures browser and select the texture Sky1 from the Sky group.
3. Subtract a cube from the level that is in no way connected to the area you have been working on (see **FIGURE 5.26**). Use the following dimensions:

   Height: 2048

   Width: 4096

   Breadth: 4096

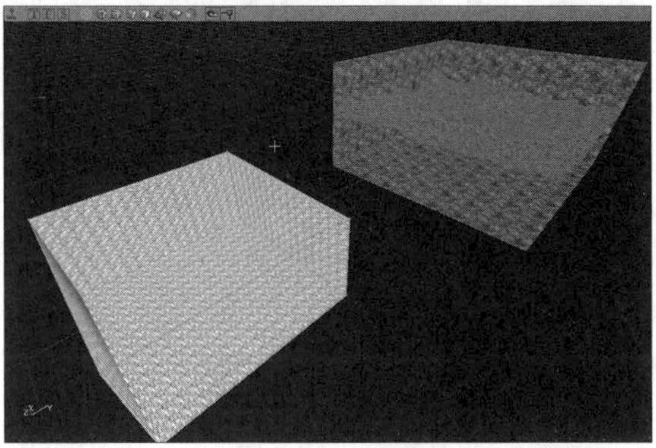

FIGURE 5.26 The newly subtracted skybox. Notice how it does not connect with the main level.

4. Select all of the walls in the skybox with the exception of the ceiling. Apply the texture named Black from the sky group (see **FIGURE 5.27**). This setup will keep us from having to deal with seams caused by misaligned textures.

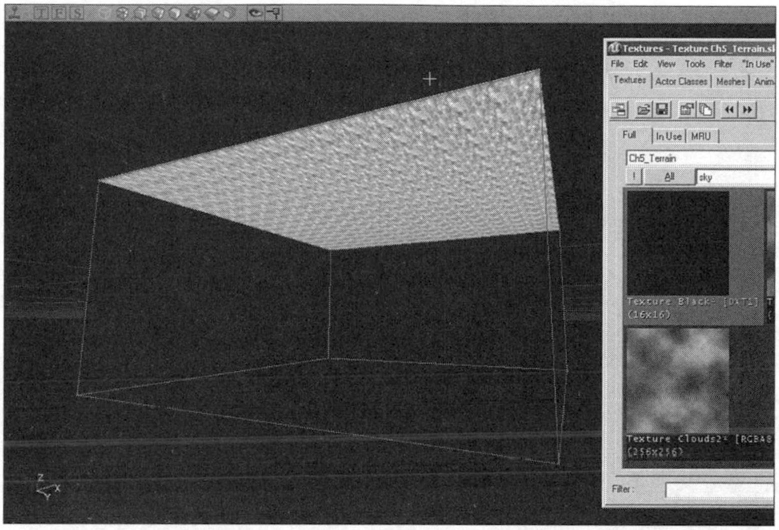

FIGURE 5.27 The walls and the floor have been assigned the Black texture.

5. Select the ceiling surface and open the Surface properties dialog (see **FIGURE 5.28**). From the Alignment tab, select Face alignment and set the UTile and VTile options to 2. Click the Align button.

> **TIP**
>
> You may need to pan the texture if you are able to see a visible seam due to the tiling.

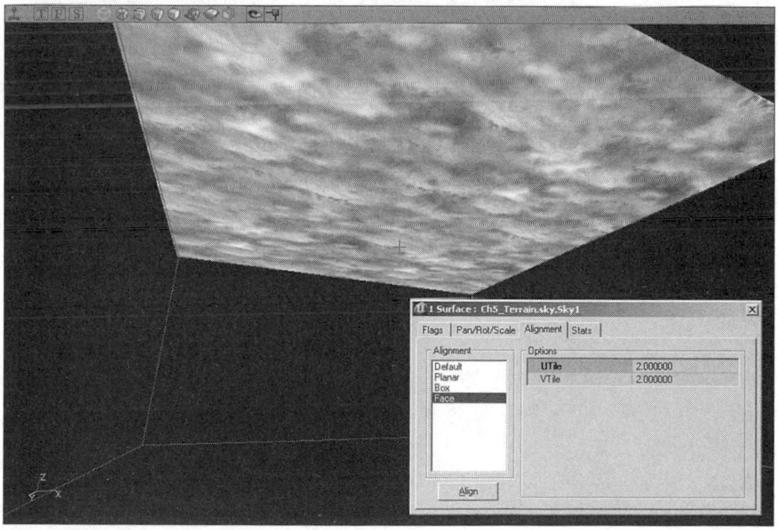

FIGURE 5.28 The sky texture has been tiled twice for a better appearance.

6. Now it is time for us to add the SkyZoneInfo Actor. Open the Actor Class browser and choose Actor > Info > ZoneInfo > SkyZoneInfo. In the Top viewport, right-click in the center of the skybox and add the Actor. In the perspective viewport (or a side view), move the SkyZoneInfo up so that it is approximately somewhere in the middle of the box (see **FIGURE 5.29**).

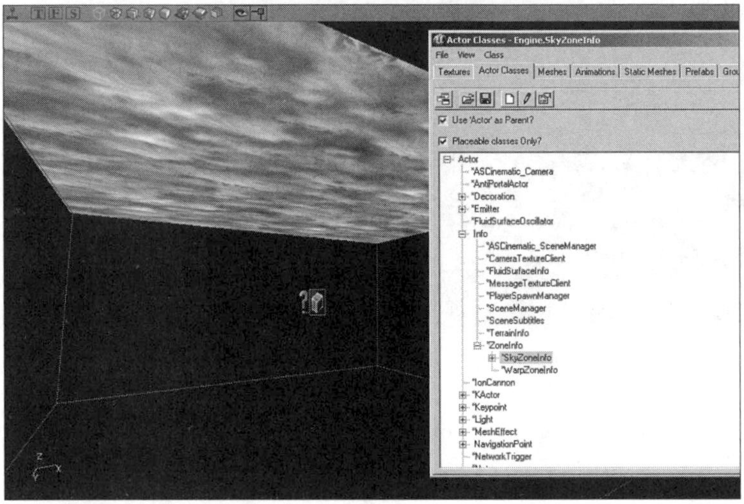

FIGURE 5.29 The SkyZoneInfo Actor has been added to the skybox.

7. So that our players are able to see the skybox, we will need to light it. After all, the box is completely separate from our main level, so there is no way for lighting to seep into it. Lighting can make or break a skybox, and the objective of this lesson is not to turn you into an expert lighting artist. Using the techniques you learned in Chapter 3, "Creating Your First Level with UnrealEd," add about eight lights to the skybox. The trick is to space the lights out enough to create an evenly lit sky. Varying the color and brightness of the lights will result in a more dynamic and interesting sky. After adding the lights, do not forget to rebuild geometry and lights (see **FIGURE 5.30**).

FIGURE 5.30 The skybox after adding numerous lights.

8. In your perspective viewport, navigate back to the main area of the level (where your terrain is). At this point you will not see any of the skybox. Fortunately, we can see the effects of a skybox without going into game. You can right-click on the toolbar across the

perspective viewport and choose View > Show Backdrop or you could use the hotkey K (see **FIGURES 5.31** and **5.32**).

9. Although we do have a functional skybox, obviously the results are not extremely convincing. We need to devise a way of hiding the black walls. In our case, we will use a combination of two techniques: distance fog and a secondary terrain system. Select the SkyZoneInfo Actor and open its properties. Set ZoneInfo > `bDistanceFog` to `True`. Expand the ZoneLight property category and set the following settings:

    `DistanceFogColor` (R: 125, G: 176, B: 185)

    `DistanceFogEnd`: 1575

    `DistanceFogStart`: 400

    You can also move the SkyZoneInfo Actor closer to the ceiling in the skybox. This will also help improve the effect (see **FIGURE 5.33**).

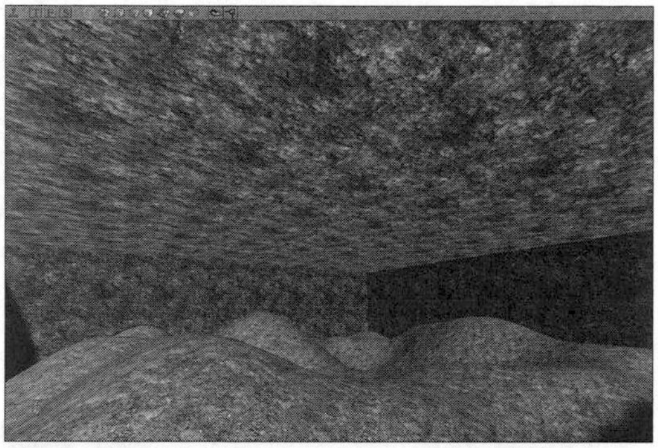

FIGURE 5.31 The main level with Show Backdrop turned off.

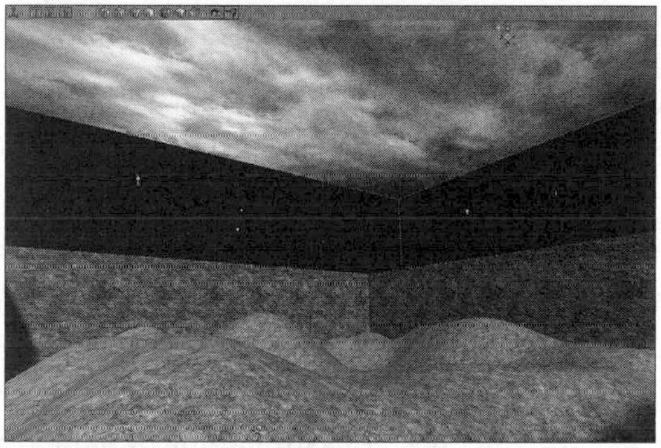

FIGURE 5.32 The main level with Show Backdrop turned on.

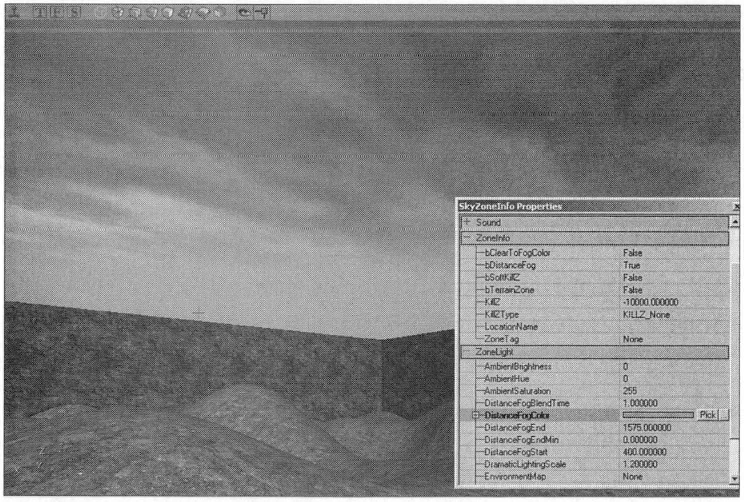

FIGURE 5.33 The effects of the skybox after adding fog and adjusting the SkyZoneInfo Actor's height.

10. The skybox is starting to take shape, but what about the walls? And we still have the hard shadows created by two of the walls. Select the four walls around your level and flag them as Fake Backdrops just as you did with the ceiling. Rebuild the level. **FIGURE 5.34** shows the result.

11. Save your level.

FIGURE 5.34 The outer walls have been flagged as Fake Backdrops.

END TUTORIAL 5.5

We are still left with the problem of seeing walls at the edges of our level. Most often, you will find that level designers will simply add some sort of obstruction to block the player from seeing the walls housing the terrain. These objects can be cliff walls, rock piles, buildings, and so on. Careful placement of these objects can do a great job of hiding the fact that the player is at the outer edge of the level.

With our level, we will use a similar approach, but instead of using static meshes or textures to fake an ongoing landscape, we will use a secondary terrain that is placed in our skybox. For this to work, we will need to make the remaining walls around our level into fake backdrops. By doing this, we will not only create the illusion of our terrain going on into the distance, but we will even out the lighting caused by the sunlight. We will be creating this backdrop during this chapter, but first, we need to take a look at the tools available to us to control the look of terrain.

A Closer Look at Terrain Editing

At this point, you know just the basics: You can make terrain, place a texture on it, and create a light and environment for it. Now, we need to see how we can customize, alter, and bring out the full potential of our virtual landscapes. To do this, we will need to access the Terrain Editing tools, located within the Terrain Editing dialog.

The Terrain Editing dialog offers a wide range of tools for developing terrain. The effects caused by these tools vary depending on what you are manipulating, be it the shape of the terrain itself (height map), the color of the terrain (texture layers), or the objects scattered across it (DecoLayers).

Before we start, a word of warning: Although UnrealEd's terrain editing system is extremely powerful and easy to use, it is always possible to make a simple mistake. Unfortunately, UnrealEd's undo functionality is not always dependable. You could see very unpredictable results, and its usefulness when painting is limited. Because of this, it is recommended to save often when working with terrain.

Terrain Editing User Interface

We've already taken a glance at the Terrain Editing dialog, so now let's have a more in-depth look at its functionality, as it is truly the center of the terrain control system. In this section, you will be introduced to the full user interface of the Terrain Editing dialog for the purposes of shaping and texturing our landscape. Later, we will discuss how to apply and control DecoLayers to scatter collections of static meshes across the surface of your terrain. **FIGURE 5.35** shows the Terrain Editing dialog.

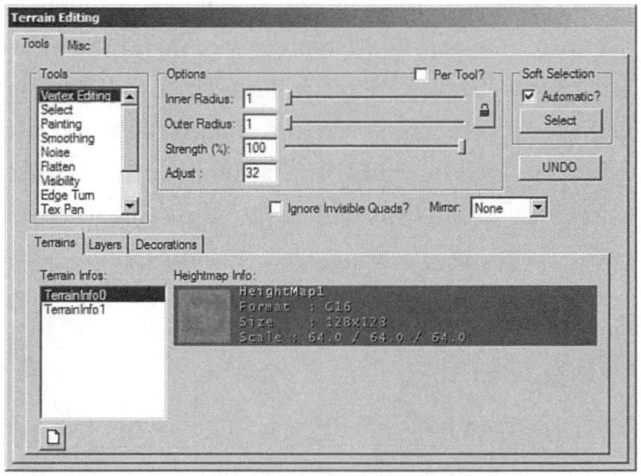

FIGURE 5.35 The Terrain Editing dialog.

Earlier in the chapter, we covered the Terrain Generation system, which makes up the main functionality of the Miscellaneous tab. We will focus on the Tools tab, and take a look at the capabilities found therein.

The Tabs

We will begin at the bottom of the window, with the three tabs for Terrain, Layers, and Decorations. These are some of the most important areas of the window, as they allow you to select which area you want to edit. One of the biggest problems beginners have when working with terrain is that you must remember to have the item you are editing selected in this window before any changes will take place. For example, if you want to alter the height map of your terrain, you must select that height map in this window before the brush will have any effect. The same goes for texture layers. You must have the texture you want to edit selected before the tools will affect it at all. Through these tabs, you will be able to sort through and select any of the elements of your terrain.

The Terrains Tab

The Terrains tab allows you to sort through the height maps of the various TerrainInfo Actors that you have available in your level. At the bottom of the tab, you will see a button that allows you to create new TerrainInfo Actors, in case you need more than one area of terrain in your level. For example you may have one terrain that is the floor of a cave, and another for the cave's ceiling. Keep in mind, though, that you can only have one height map per TerrainInfo Actor.

Just above this, you will see a list of all of the TerrainInfo Actors in your scene. You can use this list to select a specific TerrainInfo for editing. Keep in mind, though, that this list does not always update; if you delete a TerrainInfo Actor from your level, and then try to select that Actor from the list, UnrealEd will likely crash.

As you select each TerrainInfo, you will see its Height Map texture to the right of the list. This is the texture that you are editing to control the physical shape of the terrain. The texture begins as a flat grey. Darker areas on the texture will denote depressions in the landscape, whereas lighter areas will create rises. When you use the Painting tool to change the shape of your terrain, a technique covered later in this chapter, it is this texture that you are actually updating. Keep in mind that in order to adjust the shape of your texture with the Painting tool, you will need to have this texture selected, meaning that you must actually click on it to highlight it. Note: To select this texture, you will usually need to click on the top of the bar to the right of the TerrainInfo list.

The Layers Tab

Next to the Terrains tab, you will see the Layers tab, which is where you can add, select, and arrange your texture layers. Be aware that this list is evaluated from the top down, meaning that the lowest layer of the terrain is actually at the top of the list. Therefore, if you were to place a grass texture beneath a dirt texture in the list, your terrain would be completely covered in grass, and your dirt would be invisible.

To edit a texture, you must have that texture selected in this tab. You can only edit the texture that you currently have selected. As with the height map in the Terrains tab, selecting the texture usually requires that you click on the top of the appropriate bar. We'll be discussing texture editing shortly.

To the right of the texture layer list, you will see three buttons. The first is the New button, which allows you to create new texture layers. The Delete button will obviously remove unwanted texture layers, whereas the Duplicate button will copy an existing layer into the next slot down.

Below these three buttons you will see three smaller buttons. The first two allow you to rearrange the position of a texture in the texture layer list. For example, you can select a texture and click the Up arrow, and the texture will swap places with the texture directly above it. The Down arrow, conversely, will swap the texture with the layer directly underneath the selected layer. The third button is the Grid Options button, which opens a drop-down list that gives you access to a grid for specific layers. This grid allows you to more easily see where textures are visible on a terrain. For example, your grass texture may be so sparse that it is hard to see where you painted it. If, however, you switch on the grid for the grass texture layer, you will see a bright white grid on all areas of the terrain where the grass texture is at all visible. This is a great guide to see where textures have been placed on your terrain.

The Editing Tools

At the top left of the window, we see the Tools group. This contains a list of 11 tools that will allow you to edit an aspect of terrain in some way. Not all of the tools work with all terrain components, though some will work with more than one. For example, the Painting tool will work with height maps, allowing you to edit the elevation of a certain area of terrain. However, it functions differently for textures, in that it allows you to control the value of your alpha channel to show one texture through another.

We will present these tools to you not in the order in which they are listed, but rather in the order of an efficient terrain workflow. We will begin by shaping our height map, while demonstrating all of the tools that affect and control the shape of terrain. Next, we will move on to placing texture on our terrain, discussing each of the necessary tools for controlling the placement and look of our texture layers. Later, in a separate section, you will be introduced to the creation and control of DecoLayers, in order to add static mesh decorations to your terrain such as grass, rocks, debris, and so on.

The Brush

Before we begin, we need to discuss the Terrain Editing brush (not to be confused with a BSP brush). Most of the tools available through the Terrain Editing dialog are represented by a brush that appears on the surface of the terrain, which can only be seen when the Terrain Editing mode is active. It appears as two circles, an inner and an outer, at the location of the mouse. The inner circle applies the full strength of the tool, determined by the designer, to the terrain. The effect drops off between the inner and outer circles. At the center of the brush you will see a red dot, indicating the brush's center. **FIGURE 5.36** shows the option group in the Terrain Editor.

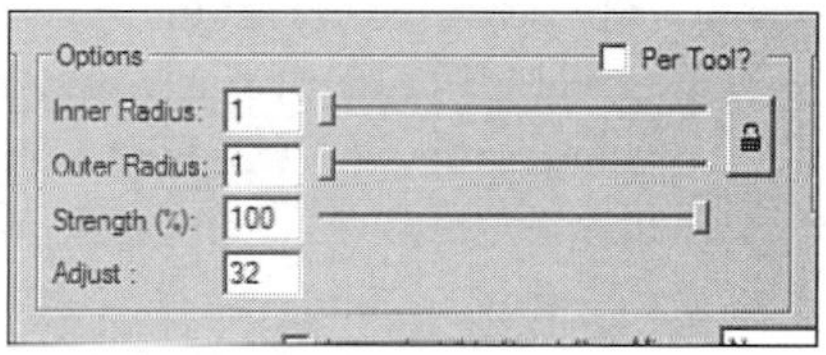

FIGURE 5.36 The Options group in the Terrain Editor.

Inner and Outer Radius

The Inner and Outer Radius sliders determine the size of the brush. It is within the inner radius that the maximum strength for the selected tool is applied. The effect of the selected tool diminishes between the inner radius and the outer radius to an effect of zero when the outer radius is achieved.

Lock Icon

Clicking the Lock icon will cause the Inner radius setting to become locked. It will retain its offset from the outer radius. When the outer radius is adjusted, the inner radius will move in tandem automatically. When the inner radius reaches a value of one, it will remain there as the outer radius value continues to fall, but the tool will remember the offset so that when the outer radius value increases past the amount of the offset, the inner radius will begin to move again.

Per Tool

The Per Tool check box will allow the level designer to give each tool a different brush setting. Each option set in the Tool Options section will be independent for each tool. If Per Tool is turned off, the global tool options will be used. The Per Tool settings are not lost when the option is turned off. When Per Tool is enabled again, the old individual setting will still be valid.

Strength

The Strength option is used to determine the amount of effect a particular tool will have. Not all tools will use the Strength option. The Strength setting is a percentage value ranging from 0 to 100%. The value of this strength is applied to the inner radius of the brush.

Adjust

The Adjust option is a multiplier value added only to the Painting and Noise tools. By default this is set to a value of 32. Increasing this value will make your paint strokes and noise values much more dramatic. Be aware that extreme values can cause this tool to behave wildly, and usually result in undesired effects.

Ignore Invisible Quads

The Ignore Invisible Quads option is a setting reserved for DecoLayers. Its purpose is to prevent static meshes from being scattered across invisible quads. For example, you may need to make an area of your terrain invisible in order to carve a cave or bunker into it. If you had a DecoLayer of grass across most of the terrain, you wouldn't want it to be on the area of a cave entrance, as it would appear to be floating in air. In such cases, you would want this option to be activated.

Mirror

The Mirror option offers a drop-down that allows you to choose an axis (or pair of axes) across which to mirror the brush. This is especially useful when trying to make a symmetrical area, perhaps for a Capture the Flag map. You can mirror across the X or Y axes, or you may mirror across both, which will result in four brushes, all working in double symmetry.

Height Map Editing Tools

To begin, let's take a look at how we can control the shape of our terrain by adjusting our height map. The Terrain Editing dialog offers several tools that allow us to physically alter our terrain's surface in a variety of ways. This section describes all of the tools you can use to edit your height map, along with a description of how they work. Remember that in order to make any of these tools work, you must physically select the height map you want to edit in the Terrains tab.

Vertex Editing

The Vertex Editing tool allows you to adjust your height map by physically selecting and moving groups of vertices either up or down. Raising a selection will lighten that area of the height map, whereas lowering a selection will darken it. Along with this tool comes the ability to use Soft Selection, an option located in the Soft Selection group, found in the upper-right corner of the Terrain Editing dialog (see **FIGURE 5.37**). Within this group is a check box that allows you to switch on Automatic soft selection.

The Vertex Editing tool always works with some level of soft selection. The Automatic check box simply offers you a way to automatically expand a soft selection by clicking a second area. While Automatic is deactivated, the behavior of vertex selection is as follows: Ctrl+clicking the surface will allow you to make a selection of vertices, based on the inner and outer radii of your brush (see **FIGURE 5.38**). Vertices that fall within the inner radius of the brush will receive the strength value found under the Strength percentage. Any selections that are made after the first will only add individual vertices to the selection.

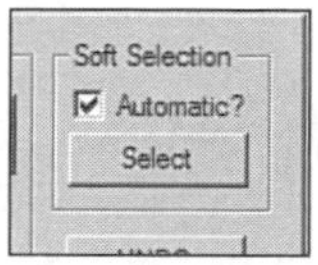

FIGURE 5.37 Soft Selection group.

> **CAUTION**
>
> **When adding individual vertices to the Vertex Editing tool, you must be extremely careful that you do not move the mouse *at all* as you click subsequent vertices. The slightest motion will cause UnrealEd to create a new soft selection, essentially starting you over from square one!**

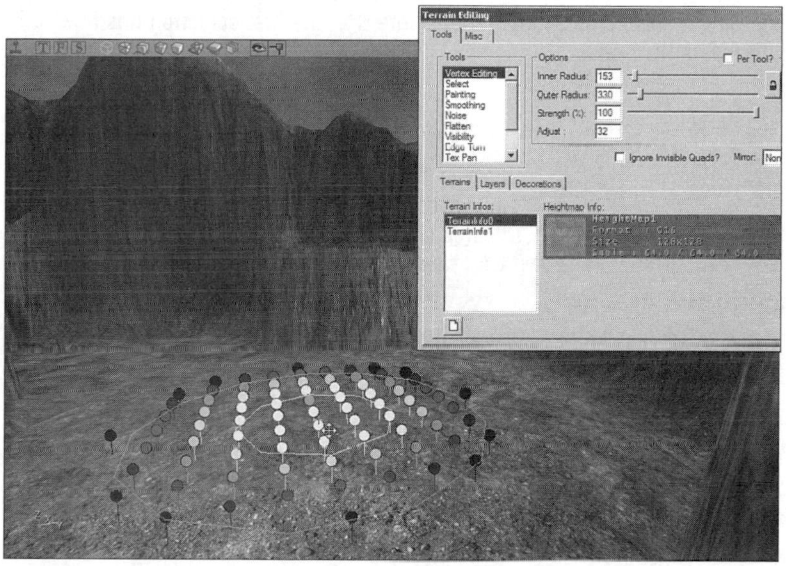

FIGURE 5.38 Image showing selected vertices.

If you activate the Automatic check box for soft selection, any subsequent selections you make will expand the radius of all previous selections made. For example, if you Ctrl+click on an area of the terrain, you will have a single soft selection, based on the side of your inner and outer radii. If you then Ctrl+click an area outside the current selection, the radius of the original selection will expand to include the second click (see **FIGURE 5.39**).

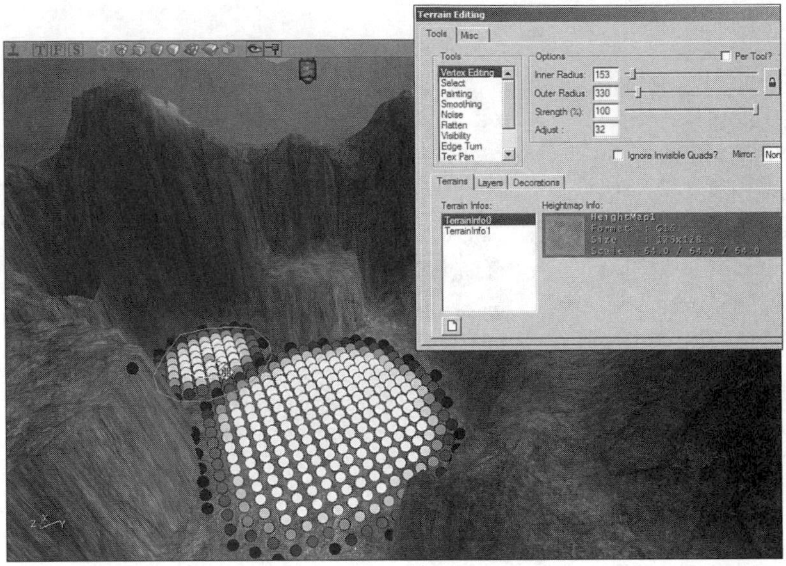

FIGURE 5.39 **Image showing a second selection added. Note that the first selection has now expanded because Automatic was turned on.**

After you have made a vertex selection, you can then move the selected vertices either up or down by holding the Ctrl key and both the left and right mouse buttons, and then moving the mouse up or down (see **FIGURE 5.40**). The motion will be based on the amount of falloff of your selection. You can see this falloff in the viewport by looking at the color-coded vertices. White vertices will receive 100% of the motion of the mouse, whereas black vertices receive virtually none. All shades of grey in between will receive varying levels of strength, resulting in a softened effect as you move the vertices up and down. This is a great way to create perfectly circular hills or pits in your terrain, or to have fluid control over moving an entire area up or down.

> **NOTE**
>
> Keep in mind that making multiple selections with the Automatic check box enabled can cause long calculation times, as UnrealEd determines exactly which vertices should be included in the selection.

> **TIP**
>
> Although it is possible to select vertices without holding down the Ctrl key, doing so is far more reliable, as the slightest mouse movement while not holding Ctrl will cause the camera to move.

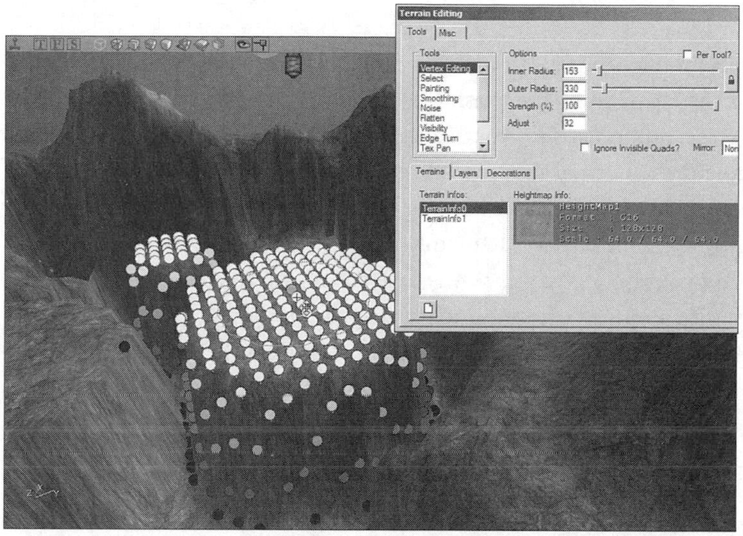

FIGURE 5.40 While you hold down the left and right mouse buttons, you can move the selected vertices up or down as seen here.

The Select Tool

This tool is primarily used for the Terrain Generator. You will make a squared selection on your terrain, and the Terrain Generator will rebuild only the terrain within the selection (see **FIGURE 5.41**). If, however, you have the Use Entire HeightMap option checked in the Terrain Generator, the entire landscape will be rebuilt, regardless of the selection.

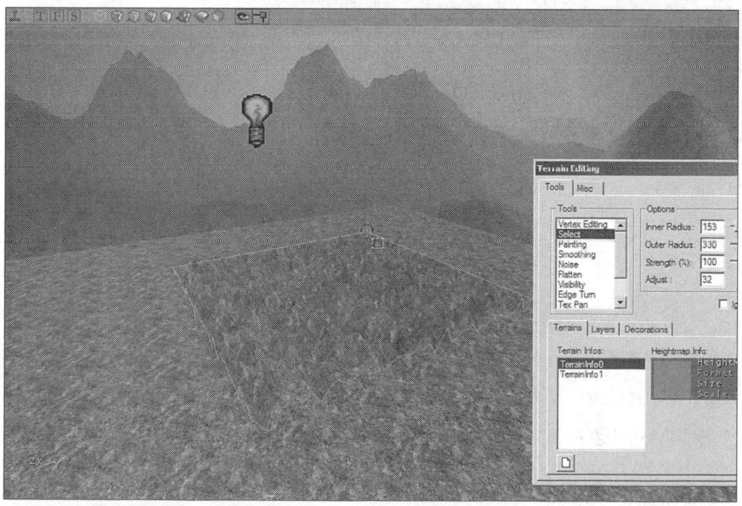

FIGURE 5.41 You can see a selected area that is being edited by the Terrain Generator.

Painting

This is the primary tool for height map editing. This is a very intuitive tool that allows you to raise and lower areas of the terrain just by painting the brush across them. Its use is very simple. Merely select a strength and brush size, and perhaps set your Adjust value for fine control. As you hold down Ctrl and left-drag across the surface of the terrain, you will raise the terrain wherever you paint. Dragging with the right mouse button while holding the Ctrl key will lower the terrain, so that you are creating depressions in the surface. Remember that it is usually best to leave your strength relatively low, and add your brush strokes slowly, one atop the other, to create your final terrain. You can also use the mirror option with this tool to keep your painted strokes symmetrical across a given axis or axes. **FIGURE 5.42** shows a terrain object that is being edited through painting.

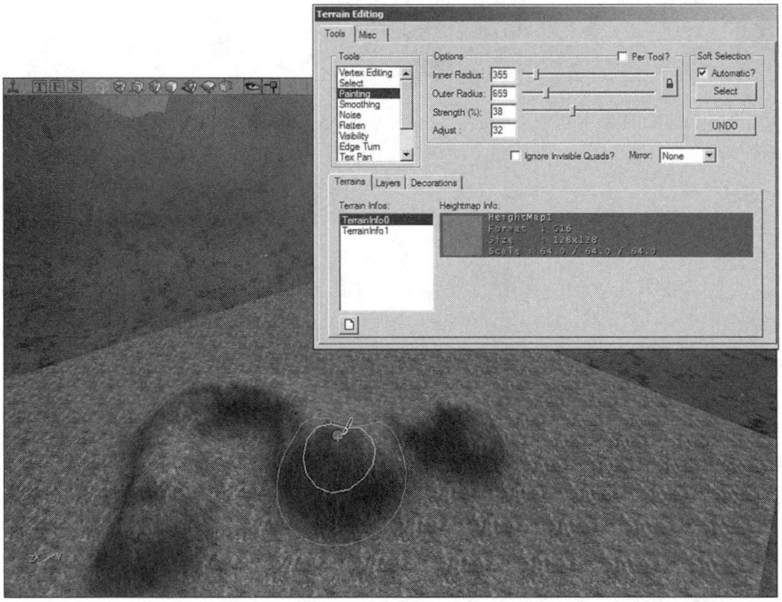

FIGURE 5.42 You can see an area of terrain that is being edited using the Paint tool.

Smoothing

This tool allows you to take out any harsh contrasts in your height map. This, in effect, smooths out your terrain by removing harsh edges (see **FIGURE 5.43**). This is a perfect tool to make your terrain look less jagged, especially when adding features such as rolling hills. Technically, the tool is taking the lowest point average of the grayscale pixel values within the radius of the brush. You will usually want the strength value to be relatively low when using this tool, as it is easy to "melt" away the detail that you have been working on.

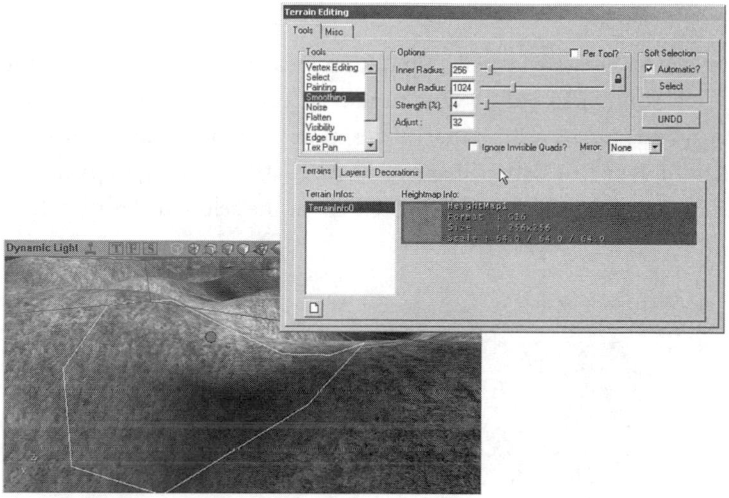

FIGURE 5.43 The area painted in was once a sharp point, but has now been smoothed out.

Noise

The Noise tool applies a noise value to your height map, which has the effect of creating patches of "lumpy" areas of terrain. A grayscale noise appears to be a patchy conglomeration of dark and light areas. When this is added to an existing height map, the result is a closely placed group of raised and lowered areas. Use of noise combined with low-strength smoothing can result in very realistic terrain features (see **FIGURE 5.44**).

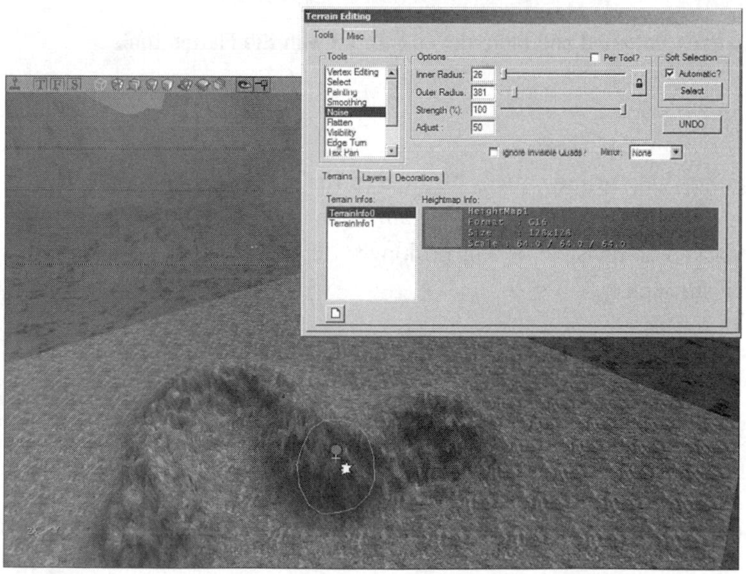

FIGURE 5.44 Noise has now been added to the hill.

Flatten

The Flatten tool, as its name suggests, allows you to flatten out an area. This is especially useful for carving roads and other such landmarks out of your terrain. It can also be used to create plateaus, mesas, and buttes in your terrain. Its use is remarkably simple. Just move the mouse over an area that is the desired height of your new flattened area, and then Ctrl+left-drag to paint. All of the terrain within the outer radius of the brush will be forced flat at the selected elevation (see **FIGURE 5.45**).

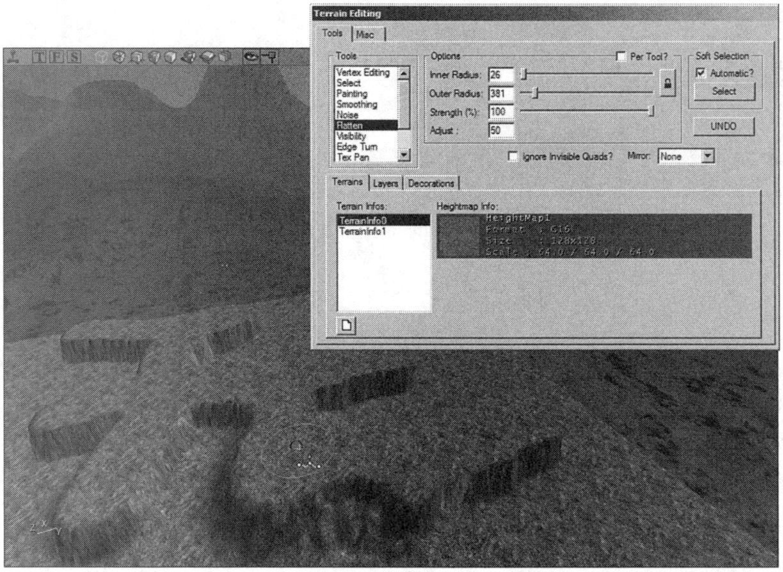

FIGURE 5.45 **The hill has been flattened and more ridges created with the Flatten tool.**

Visibility

The Visibility tool allows you to show or hide quads of the terrain (see **FIGURE 5.46**). This is especially useful when you need to open holes in your terrain, such as for a cave or bunker-type building. When a quad is marked as invisible, it will no longer detect collisions with a player, meaning that a player can fall through it.

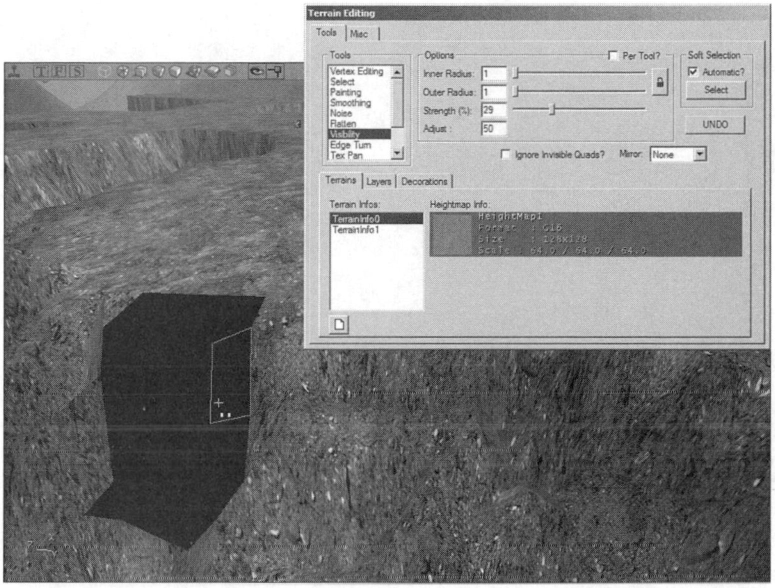

FIGURE 5.46 The Visibility tool was used to cut this opening into the terrain.

Edge Turn

The Edge Term tool allows you to modify the topology of your terrain by flipping the triangle edge of a quad. Terrain geometry is composed of a series of four-sided polygons, or quads, each divided into two right triangles. The direction of the triangle edge determines how the surface will bend. You can use this tool to flip the triangle edges of quads in your terrain so that it is deforming properly. It works in a paintbrush fashion, changing the edge of faces that you paint over. **FIGURES 5.47** and **5.48** show the result of using the Edge Turn tool.

Applying the Terrain Editing Tools

Now that we have taken a closer look at the editor and the tools available for shaping terrain, it's time to turn our attention back to the terrain we've been creating in this chapter. Until now, the only thing we have done to our terrain was to use the Terrain Generator to give some life to the landscape. Although the generator can be a great way to produce a starting point, it does not give us the absolute control needed to sculpt the landscapes we need for our games, simulations, and so on. **TUTORIAL 5.6** will focus on using the tools we have discussed to shape our terrain.

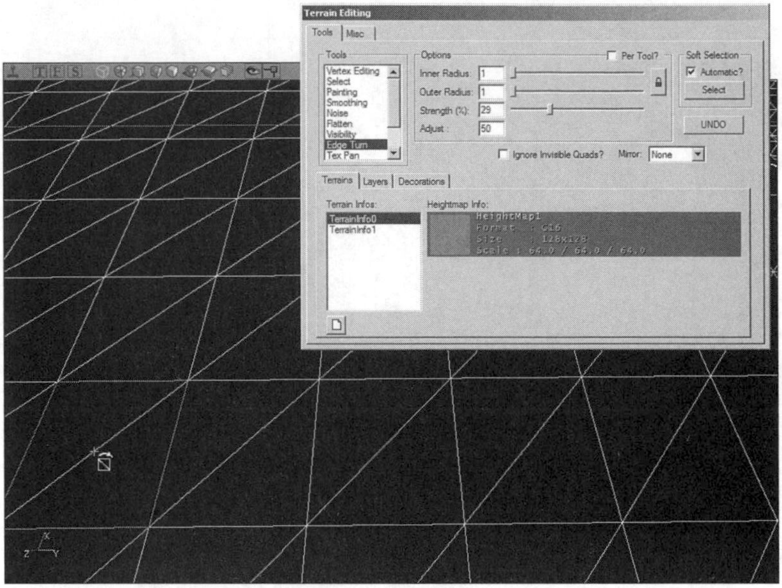

5

FIGURE 5.47 Before using Edge Turn.

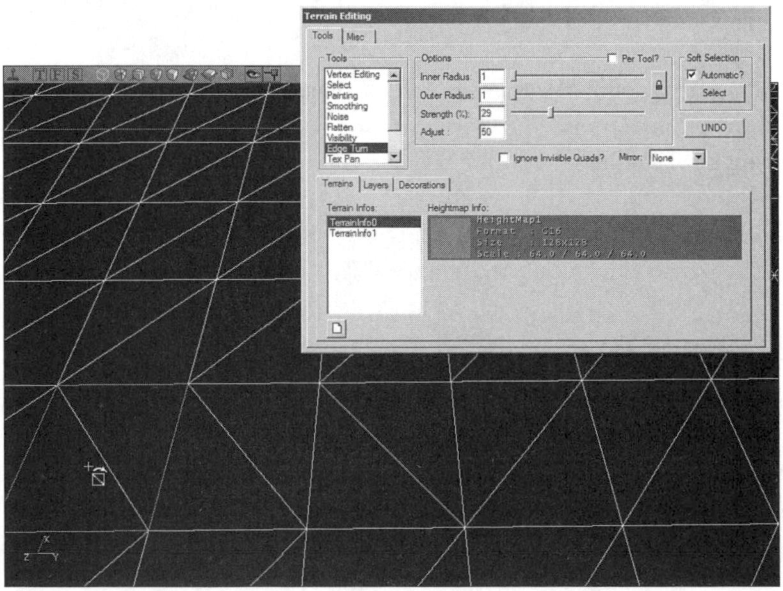

FIGURE 5.48 After using Edge Turn.

TUTORIAL 5.6: Shaping Your Own Landscapes

1. Open the file `Tutorial5_06_Start.ut2`. You will see the terrain and skybox we completed earlier with the Terrain Generator. We will now rebuild our terrain by hand. To make the most of our height map, we will push down and pull up detail to create a range of mountains separating two bases.

2. To begin, we will flatten out the entire terrain. The fastest way to do this is to choose the Select tool from the list, and then switch over to the Miscellaneous tab. In the Terrain Generation group, enter a Steps value of 1, and a Strength value of 1. Check Use Entire Heightmap, and click the Build button. Rebuild the lighting when finished to remove any unwanted shadows.

3. We first need to build the outer hills that will prevent the player from seeing the edge of the terrain. We're doing this to prevent the player from running off the edge of the map. Later, you will be able to supplement these hills with blocking volumes, which are invisible brushes that will behave like walls, preventing the player from getting to the top of these hills. You will learn more about volumes in Chapter 6, "Working with Volumes."

   To start, select the height map in the Terrain layer, and then choose the Painting tool. Set the following settings for your brush:

   Inner Radius: 330

   Outer Radius: 684

   Strength: 44

   Adjust: 32

   Mirror: XY

   > **TIP**
   >
   > **When finished, you may want to set the Mirror back to None, in order to add some asymmetry to your map.**

   We're setting the Mirror value to XY so that each stroke is copied across the X and Y axes (see **FIGURE 5.49**). This means that you can paint each of the corners of the map, and your strokes will be mirrored.

   Paint around the edges of your map to create the hills that will surround your terrain.

4. We're going to create a setup that will allow for two bases, one on each corner of the map. Make sure that Mirror is set to None, and use the Paint tool to create two depressions at opposite corners of the map (see **FIGURE 5.50**).

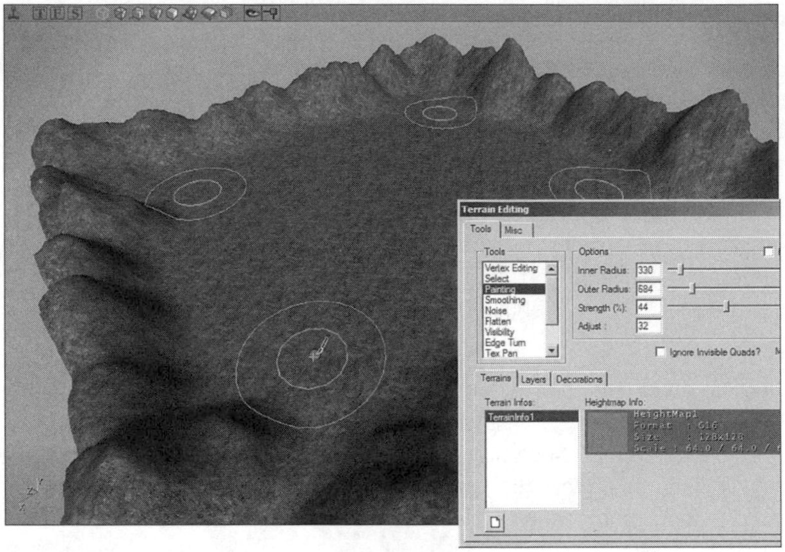

FIGURE 5.49 Painting with mirror set to XY.

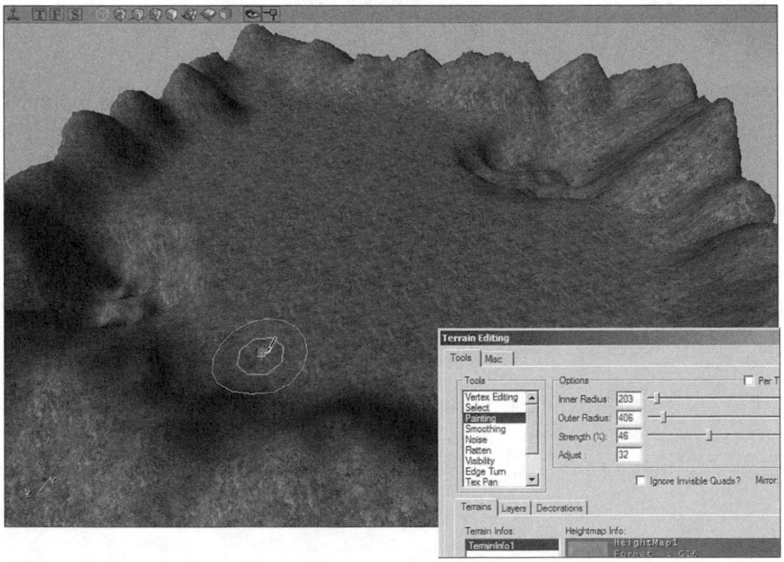

FIGURE 5.50 Sinking two areas in the terrain for bases.

5. Select the Flatten tool. Move the brush over one of the lower areas of one of the depressions. Ctrl+left-drag to flatten the entire depression to that elevation, as shown in **FIGURE 5.51**. Be careful that you do not cut too far into the hills behind the base area.

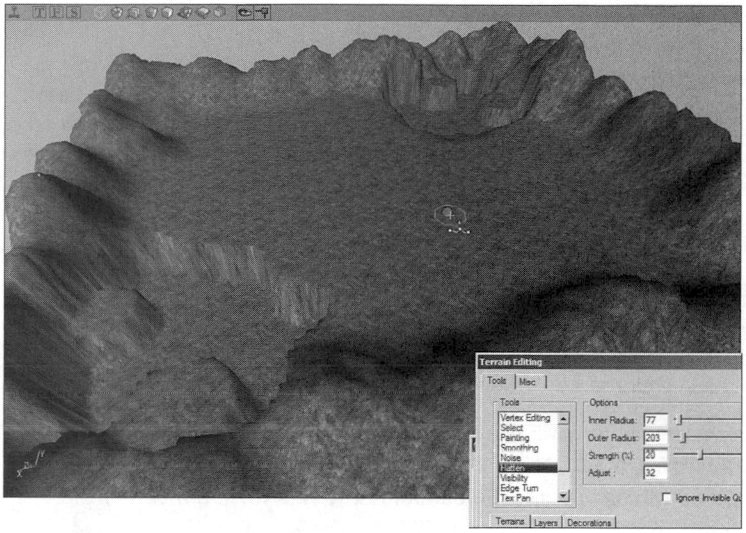

FIGURE 5.51 Flatten the two base areas.

6. Now, using the Painting tool, create a series of hills and mountains in the middle of the map. Adjust the inner and outer brush radii as necessary. Remember that if you keep your brush too small, your hills will be very tight, which will not look natural. Also, don't be shy about adjusting the strength. It is almost always better to use lower-strength strokes and layer your strokes on top of one another. Use **FIGURE 5.52** if you need help.

> **TIP**
>
> **You can also choose higher areas around the base, such as in the surrounding hills, and use the Flatten tool to create perfect areas to place turrets.**

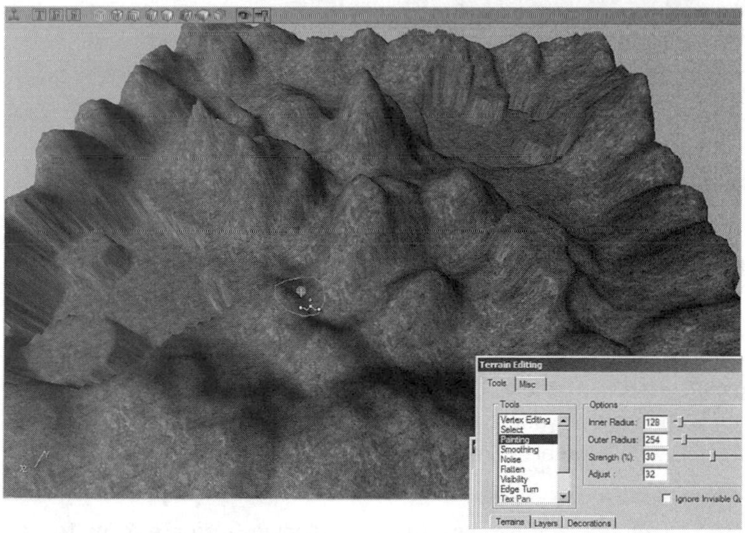

FIGURE 5.52 Using the Paint tool to add mountains into the scene.

> **TIP**
>
> **While modeling your terrain, try to imagine how you could use your terrain for areas such as hidden bases, power-up areas, special defense areas, and so on. Also, watch your geography very closely to make sure that it stays useful. If you want your characters to be able to climb to the top of a hill, make sure its slope is not too steep to prevent climbing.**

7. Let's create some roads for our map to connect one base to the other. We will keep these relatively small. Use the following settings on the brush for now:

   Outer Radius: 102

   Select the Flatten tool. Move the brush to an area that is just above the level of one of your bases, and begin using the tool to carve in a road. Lead the road around the fringe of the level, just inside the surrounding mountains. Pause from time to time to create a raised or lowered area from which to continue the road. This will keep your road from being perfectly flat from one end to the other.

   Have fun with this step. Basically, you will need two roads, each connecting one base to the other, as shown in **FIGURE 5.53**. Aside from that, you're free to create your own paths through the hills, or anything you like. Be careful not to destroy too much of the landscape you've created.

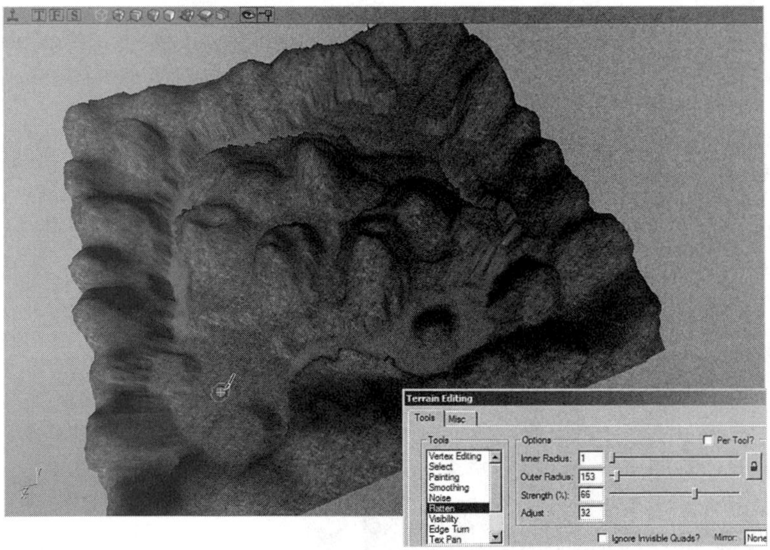

FIGURE 5.53 Using the Flatten tool to cut roadways into our terrain. The roads have been painted here to make viewing easier.

8. Switch to the Smoothing tool. Set the strength to a relatively low percentage, and smooth out the areas of sharp cliffs on either side of the roads. You will also want to smooth out any places where the road changed elevation, in order to create a "ramp" from one level to the other. While you're at it, you can also smooth out any areas around your bases that are a little too sharp.

   It could help to switch to a wireframe and see how things are looking. We are trying to avoid having polygons that are stretched too far, as shown in **FIGURE 5.54**.

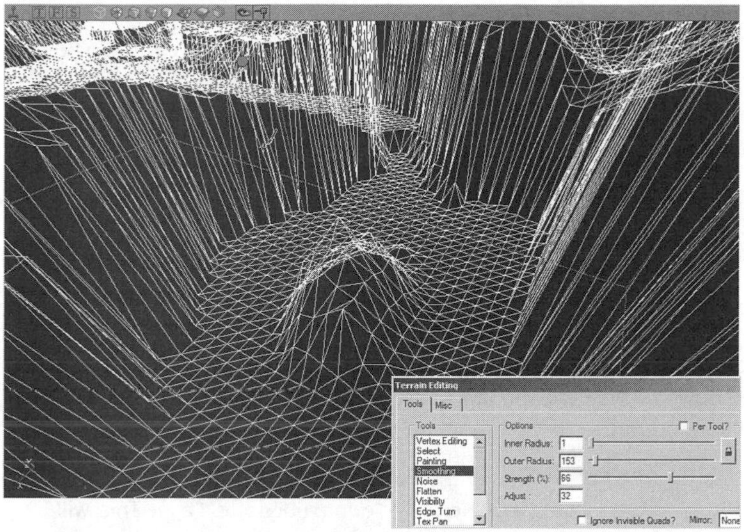

FIGURE 5.54 Before smoothing. Notice how far the polygons are being stretched?

After smoothing, you will notice that the triangles are more appropriately spread across the surface, making it easier to see the texture across it, as in **FIGURE 5.55**.

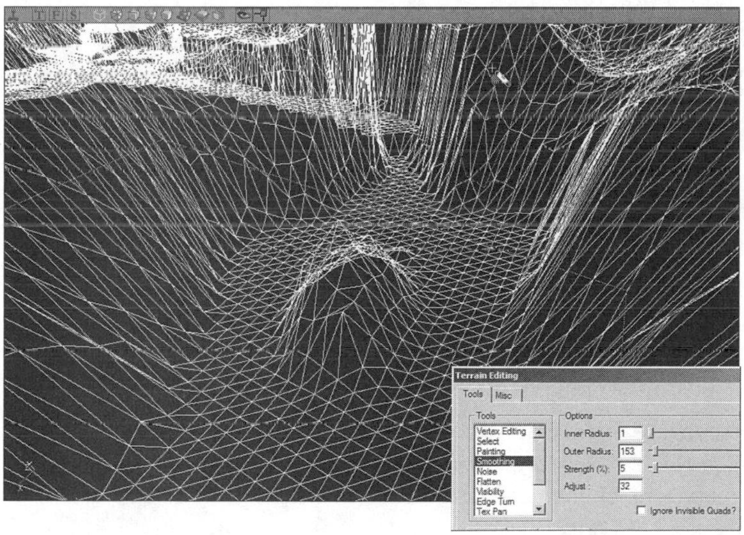

FIGURE 5.55 After smoothing. We now have more detail on the sides.

9. Make any tweaks and adjustments you like until you are satisfied with the look of the level. When finished, be sure to save your level. You may find it handy to play-test the level to make sure that areas you create are accessible and will work properly for your ideas.

END TUTORIAL 5.6

Now that our terrain is created and we have a Skybox in place, we can make the surrounding environment much more interesting by adding a second terrain system into the skybox in **TUTORIAL 5.7**.

TUTORIAL 5.7: Adding Terrain to The Skybox

1. Continue from the last tutorial, or open the file `Tutorial5_07_Start.ut2`. We will now supplement our skybox and add a little more character to our level by creating a second terrain system inside the skybox. This will produce the illusion that our level is surrounded by vast mountains far out in the distance.

2. Double-click the Search For Actor icon. In the search line, start typing **`SkyZoneInfo`** until the Actor list is filtered down to the SkyZoneInfo Actor. When you see it in the list, double-click it, and click the Close button.

   This will select the SkyZoneInfo Actor and move the camera to its position. Open the properties window. Expand the ZoneInfo category, and set `bTerrainZone` to `True`. This will allow a TerrainInfo Actor to be placed and terrain to be visible in the skybox.

3. In the Terrain Editing dialog, go to the Terrains tab and click the New Terrain button. In the New Terrain dialog, input the following:

   Package: myLevel

   Group: Heightmaps

   Name: HeightMap2

   Xsize: 128

   Ysize: 128

   This will create a new TerrainInfo Actor at the position of the camera, which should be near the center of the skybox.

4. Right now, the terrain is too big. Open the properties for the new TerrainInfo Actor that was created in the skybox. Expand the TerrainInfo category, and go to the `TerrainScale` property. Set the X and Y values to 32. This should cause the terrain to fit nicely into the skybox.

5. Using the skills that you have learned, place the same texture used on the original terrain onto the new terrain. Rebuild as necessary. When finished, use the height-map editing tools to pull up some mountains on the outsides of the terrain. Leave the middle area sunken down like a valley.

6. Move the camera into the main area of the level and press the K key to view the skybox. You should be able to see your new terrain surrounding your level. If necessary, move the SkyZoneInfo Actor down lower to make the mountains surrounding the level appear taller. Keep in mind that you may also need to relight the skybox terrain, as it is not affected by

the Sunlight Actor. Also, be aware that if you pull the mountains up so that they cover any of the lights that were in the skybox, those lights will no longer be visible, resulting in a darker sky. To alleviate this problem, reposition the lights as necessary.

7. Test and tweak the results until you are satisfied (see **FIGURE 5.56**). Keep in mind that your skybox terrain may not be visible from some of the lower areas of your level. When finished, save your map.

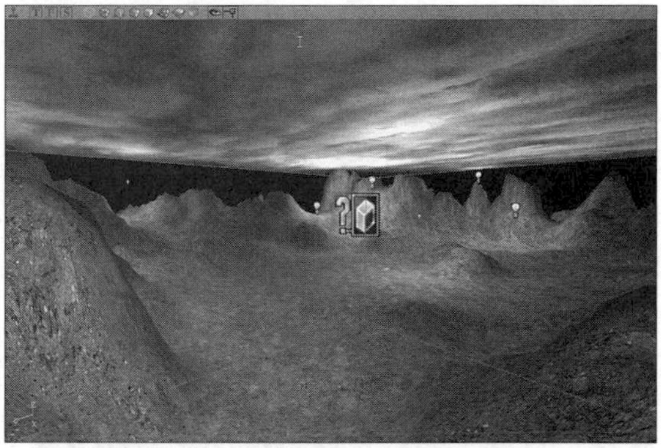

FIGURE 5.56 Through another TerrainInfo Actor, we've added mountains into our skybox.

END TUTORIAL 5.7

TerrainInfo Properties

There are several properties for TerrainInfo Actors that will come in handy when controlling the shape and behavior of your terrain. **TABLE 5.1** describes each of these properties.

TABLE 5.1 TerrainInfo Properties

`bKCollisionHalfRes`	Typically, Karma uses the actual triangles of your terrain as the collision mesh. Setting this property to `True` will cause the number of triangles to be divided by two for the collision mesh, resulting in simpler (read *faster*) collisions.
`DecoLayerOffset`	This property will offset your DecoLayer meshes from the surface of the terrain. If the `AlignToTerrain` property (found under DecoLayers) is set to 0, the meshes will simply offset by moving up the number of units specified in the `DecoLayerOffset` property. If `AlignToTerrain` is set to 1, the meshes will offset in a direction perpendicular to the direction of the triangle upon which the mesh was placed.
`DecoLayers`	**See Table 5.3, later in this chapter.**
`Inverted`	Terrain is viewed from one side only. Setting this property to true will invert the terrain such that you can only see it if you were standing below it. This is an excellent way to add in rocky ceilings as if you were in some sort of natural underground cavern.
`Layers`	**See Table 5.2, later in this chapter.**
`TerrainMap`	This is the Height Map texture. This is the texture responsible for determining the altitudes of the terrain.

TABLE 5.1 Continued

`TerrainScale`	This property allows you to control the three-dimensional scale of the terrain.
`TerrainSectorSize`	This is mainly used for optimization. As terrain stops rendering, it will disappear segments at a time. For example, if you set this to 16, the terrain will be divided into sectors that are 16 quads by 16 quads.
`VertexLightMap`	This allows you to specify your own light map texture for your terrain.

Texture Layer Editing Tools

In this section, we will describe the tools that can be used for texture layer editing. Some of these tools were already used for height map editing, but will function differently after we select a texture layer. Always remember that for any of these tools to function, you must have the texture layer you want to edit selected in the Layers tab.

Painting

This tool is really only effective when you have more than one texture layer. If you add a new texture layer with an `AlphaFill` value of black, you will not see the new texture at all, as a black value denotes complete transparency. You can then paint the texture onto specific areas of the terrain using this tool. When painting texture onto your landscape, you are actually editing the Alpha channel of the texture. Ctrl+left-dragging will paint white areas onto the Alpha channel, making your topmost texture visible only on the areas you are painting. Ctrl+right-dragging will remove value from the alpha channel (similar to painting black, if you prefer), which results in removing or erasing the top-most texture. For example, let's say that you have a single dirt texture all across your terrain. You then add a new texture layer with a snow texture, but set the `AlphaFill` property to black. You won't see the snow anywhere, but as you Ctrl+left-drag with the Painting tool, you will add snow to the areas you paint. You could then Ctrl+right-drag over the snow, and "erase" it away, back to the dirt texture. **FIGURE 5.57** demonstrates how this process works.

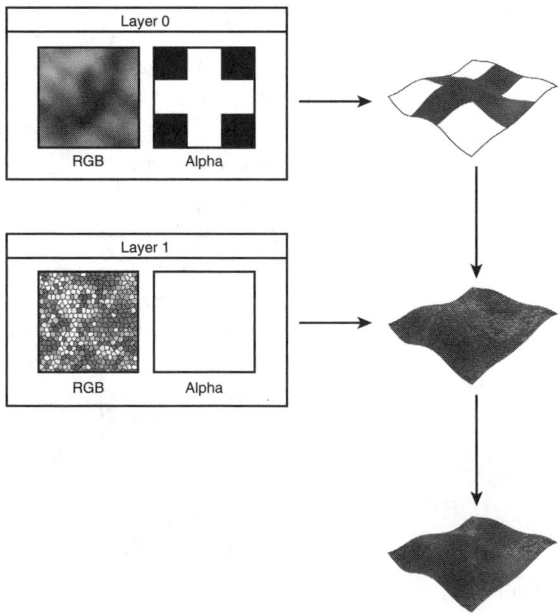

FIGURE 5.57 Image showing how the alphas work by allowing you to show one texture through another, such as showing a dirt texture through a layer of snow.

Smoothing

Smoothing is another tool that works for texture layers as well as height maps. In this case, its function is very similar. This will smooth out the values between areas of your alpha channel, which, in effect, smooths out distribution of a texture (see **FIGURE 5.58**). For example, if you have painted on a texture, and the contrast from one texture to another is very sharp, you could easily use the Smoothing tool to soften the edges between the two visible textures.

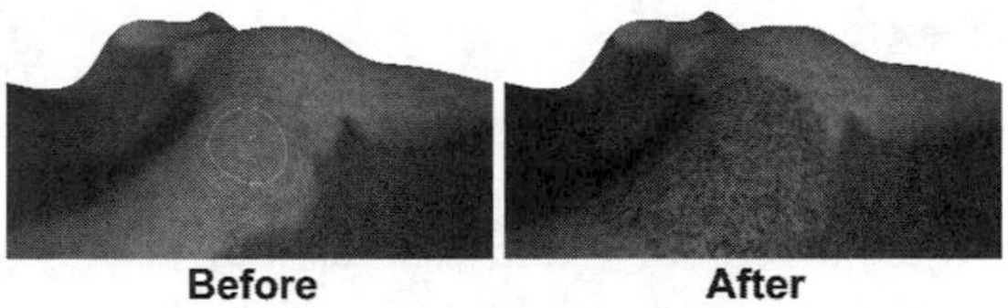

FIGURE 5.58 Left: Before smoothing. Right: After smoothing.

Noise

The Noise tool works for texture layers similar to the way it works for height maps. However, rather than making raised and lowered patches of elevation, it creates areas of light and dark areas in your alpha channel, making your topmost texture visible only in patches. It is a great tool to create sparse areas of grass or stone on your terrain (see **FIGURE 5.59**).

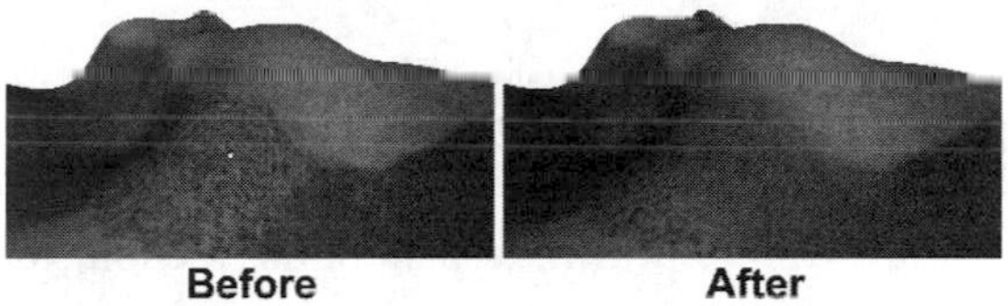

FIGURE 5.59 Left: Before noise is applied. Right: After noise is applied.

Tex Pan

This tool allows you to adjust the position of textures on your terrain in the U and V direction. First, you must select the texture in your Layers tab that you want to adjust. Next, hold the Ctrl key, and then drag with one of the mouse buttons. Dragging with the left mouse will move the texture in the U direction, whereas dragging with the right mouse button will move the texture in the V direction.

Tex Rotate

The Tex Rotate tool, as you might imagine, allows you to rotate the selected texture. This is an excellent tool for adjusting the look of textures on specific surfaces. The pivot of texture rotation will be the origin of your level (0,0,0). The tool works in a similar fashion to the other tools available in the Terrain Editing dialog. Holding Ctrl and dragging with either mouse button will cause the texture to rotate. Dragging to the left will cause a counterclockwise rotation, whereas moving to the right will cause a clockwise rotation (see **FIGURE 5.60**).

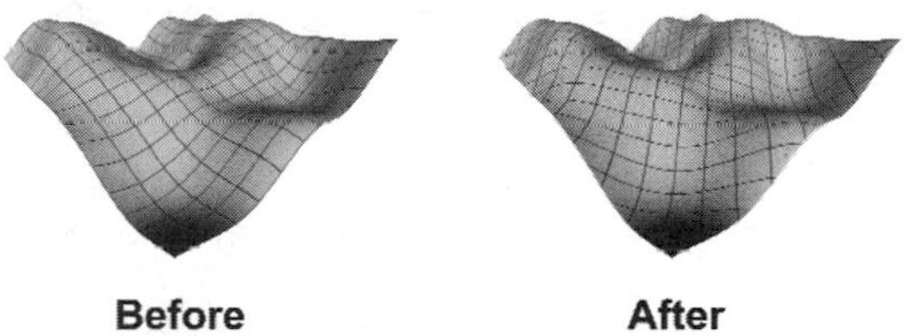

FIGURE 5.60 Left: Terrain before texture is rotated. Right: Terrain after texture is rotated.

Tex Scale

This tool allows you to scale your texture in the U and V directions. This is very handy when trying to get your texture to line up without it being apparent that the texture is tiling across your terrain. Holding Ctrl and left-dragging will scale the texture in U, whereas right-dragging will cause the texture to scale in the V direction (see **FIGURE 5.61**).

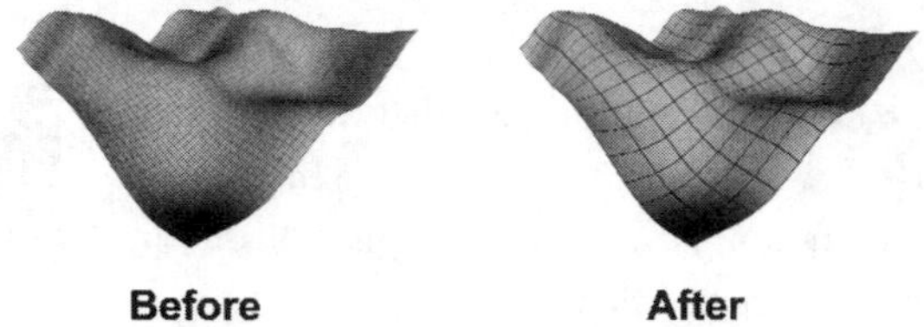

FIGURE 5.61 Left: Terrain before texture is scaled. Right: Terrain after texture is scaled.

Editing Terrain Texture

Now that you know the tools involved in editing terrain texture, you are ready to try your hand at texturing your own terrain. In this section, you will create and edit textures on a terrain system, as well as have a look at the properties for texture layers. To begin, **TUTORIAL 5.8** introduces you to creating and editing a basic texture on your terrain.

5

TUTORIAL 5.8: Texturing Your Terrain

1. Continue from the last tutorial, or open the file `Tutorial5_08_Start.ut2`. We will now add some texture layers. Before you start, make sure that TerrainInfo0 is selected in the Terrains tab, so that you are painting on the proper terrain. Make sure the Texture browser is open, and that the Ch5_terrain package is open.

   In this tutorial, we will be bringing the texture of our terrain to life. We currently have a simple dirt-like texture applied to the entire terrain, just for construction purposes. We will add more layers to this to create a complete texture system.

   In this case, we will be going for a very cold feeling level. It is always a good idea to get an idea of the type of terrain you're making, be it desert, jungle, tundra, or other types. Our terrain will have harsh rocks, a little moss, and snow-capped peaks, giving the feel that the environment is not quite freezing, but very cold. We will supplement this effect by altering the fog color to accentuate the feel of the environment.

2. In the Texture browser, from the Ch5_Terrain package, select the Rocks texture. Go to the Terrain Editing dialog. Make sure that TerrainInfo0 is selected in the Terrains tab. In the Layers tab, click on the Undefined slot beneath the DirtLayer1 texture that you added earlier, verifying that it is selected. The slot *must* be selected in order to create the new texture. Click the New button, and enter the following settings into the dialog:

   Package: myLevel

   Group: TerrainLayers

   Name: Rocks

   AlphaHeight: 128

   AlphaWidth: 128

   AlphaFill: Set color to White

   UScale: 8

   VScale: 8

When you create a new layer, the texture that was selected in the Texture browser is applied to the terrain. A new texture is also created, which is an RGBA8. The alpha channel of this new texture will be used to control the blending between this texture and the texture directly above it in the Layer list.

You will also notice that we set the alpha color to white. This will make our new layer completely opaque, meaning that we will not be able to see our original texture at all. We will then use a subtractive painting method to blend back to the original dirt layer. This is not unlike "cutting holes" to reveal our original texture.

3. Select the Painting tool, and make sure that the Rocks layer is selected in the Layers tab. Dragging with the right mouse button while holding the Ctrl key, remove the rock texture in the areas of your roads. You will probably want to set your strength to a moderately low level, and use multiple strokes to carve away the rock texture. Use additive and subtractive strokes to create areas of soft blending between the dirt and rock layers, in order to keep the contrast from one texture to the next from being too harsh (see **FIGURE 5.62**). Don't be afraid to cut away from the rock very lightly all throughout the map, just so that the terrain doesn't feel unbalanced.

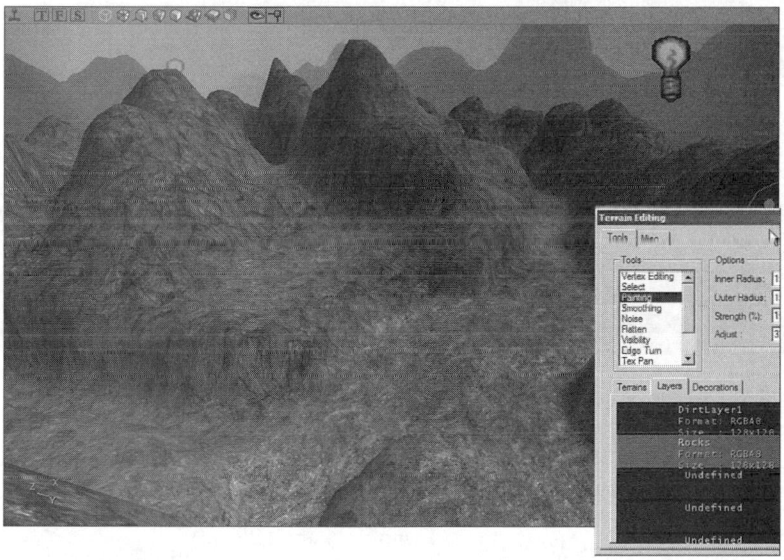

FIGURE 5.62 **Blending so that you can see a mixture of dirt and rock.**

4. Now, go back to the Layers tab, and select the next Undefined layer. Select the MossWalls texture in the Texture browser. Click the New button, and enter the following values into the dialog:

Package: myLevel

Group: TerrainLayers

Name: Grass

AlphaHeight: 128

AlphaWidth: 128

AlphaFill: Set color to Black

UScale: 8

VScale: 8

This time, our AlphaFill color is set to black, meaning that the texture itself is invisible when created. We will then paint it on in an additive fashion.

Naturally, grass should only appear on relatively level areas that are not trod on very much. This pretty much rules out roads and steep slopes, though you may want to lightly border your roads with some of the texture. As before, you can achieve a very nice balanced look by setting the strength of the brush very low and adding soft spots of the grass texture across the level (see **FIGURE 5.63**). You could also use the Noise tool with a very low strength to help with this effect.

> **TIP**
>
> **You can create soft blending quickly by first using the Noise tool, and then follow up with the Smoothing tool.**

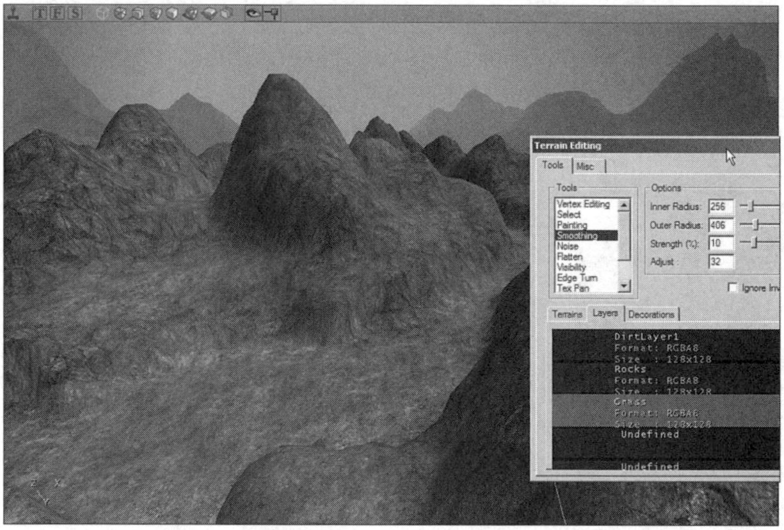

FIGURE 5.63 Blending in grass.

5. In the Texture browser, select the SnowRocks texture. Select the next Undefined layer, and click the New button. Use the following settings:

Package: myLevel	AlphaWidth: 128
Group: TerrainLayers	AlphaFill: Set color to Black.
Name: Snow	UScale: 8
AlphaHeight: 128	VScale: 8

Using the same techniques you've used thus far, add the snow to the peaks of the hills on your map, and also softer patches of it to areas throughout your map (see **FIGURE 5.64**). Remember that the terrain needs to appear cold. A light dusting of this texture will make the environment look much more harsh, so don't hesitate to patch it lightly in places.

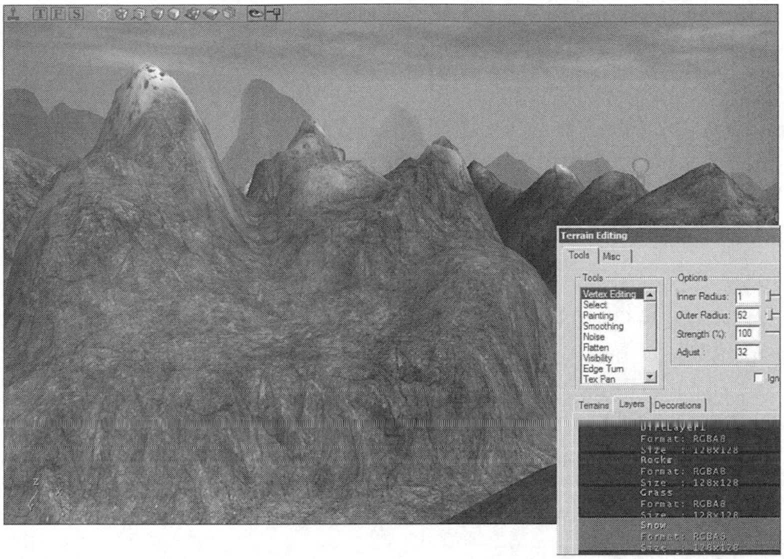

FIGURE 5.64 **Adding snow to the top of the mountains.**

6. With that, the texture is basically done. Feel free to take a while to sift back through the layers making tweaks and adjustments. When finished, apply the same techniques to create texture layers for the terrain in the skybox, as in **FIGURE 5.65**. Save your map when finished.

FIGURE 5.65 **Adding snow to the skybox mountains for a more balanced look.**

END TUTORIAL 5.8

When working with terrain, you may notice some problems where textures are stretching, such as on cliff edges. This problem can be alleviated by creating a new texture layer, painting onto the problem areas, and adjusting a single property of the layer. In the properties window of the TerrainInfo you're working on, you will see the TerrainInfo category. Within, you will see the Layers array, where you will find Layers 0 through 31. You will need to expand the proper element for the layer you just created.

That element will have a property called the `TextureMapAxis`. This property allows you to change the projection plane of the texture. For example, if the surface you are trying to fix is near to being parallel to the XZ plane, you would want to set this property to `TEXMAPAXIS_XZ`.

Layers have a variety of properties that can be used to control their behavior and appearance. **TABLE 5.2** describes each of these properties.

TABLE 5.2 Layer Properties

[0] – [31]	These are the 32 indexes for your texture layers.
`AlphaMap`	This is the texture map that controls the blending of the texture layer.
`KFriction`	This property is currently not implemented.
`KRestitution`	This property is currently not implemented.
`LayerRotation`	Pitch/Roll/Yaw: This property attempts to rotate the texture in 3D space, based on Unreal rotation units.
`Texture`	This is the visible texture that will be applied to the terrain surface.
`TextureMapAxis`	This is the plane upon which the texture will be projected. Useful to prevent texture stretching on sheer faces such as cliffs.
`TextureRotation`	This rotates the texture in Yaw.
`UPan`	This pans the texture in the U direction.
`UScale`	This scales the texture in the U direction.
`VPan`	This pans the texture in the V direction.
`VScale`	This scales the texture in the V direction.

DecoLayers

Now that you have seen how to create, edit, and texture terrain, let's take a look at how we can add objects such as blades of grass, trees, and rocks. In Unreal, these objects are referred to as terrain decorations. Adding these objects is done within the terrain editing system through the use of DecoLayers. DecoLayers are similar to texture layers in that they are represented in a list fashion, but in the case of DecoLayers, each layer represents an object (static mesh) being used for decoration. Also, unlike texture layers, you can have as many decoration layers as you need, rather than being limited to just 32. **FIGURE 5.66** shows a grass static mesh used for a DecoLayer.

FIGURE 5.66 Grass is a common decoration that is often found scattered across terrain.

When you are adding a decoration layer, there are a total of four components that drive what the player will see: the static mesh, the density map, the color map, and the scale map. The static mesh is a given; this is the object the current layer represents and is what will be displayed on the terrain. The density map is one of several controlling factors that determine where and how closely these objects are scattered across the terrain. The color map gives the level designer an extra level of control over the color of the static meshes being added, and the scale map allows an unprecedented level of control over the scale of the objects in each of its individual axes (see **FIGURE 5.67**).

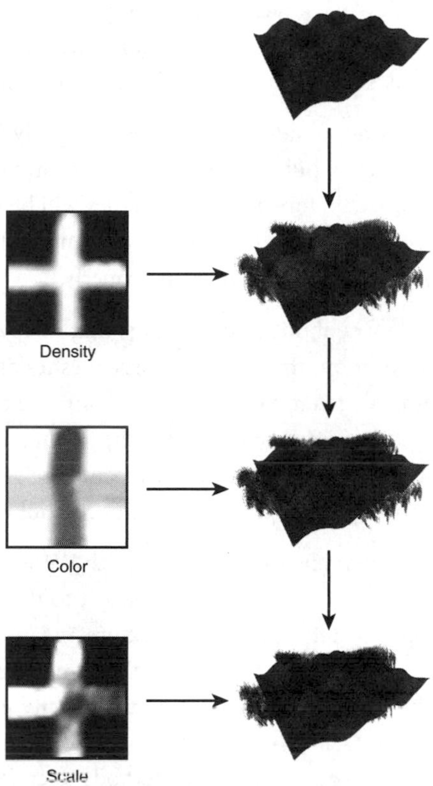

FIGURE 5.67 **Create an image that shows how the three maps affect the decorations.**

The density map is used to drive the concentration of static meshes on the layer. Anywhere that the layer's color is black, there will be no static meshes. Wherever the texture contains the color white, you will have the maximum number of static meshes. You then have other methods of controlling this density, including the `DensityMultiplier` property and a property that controls the maximum number of meshes per quad. A *quad*, in this case, refers to the geometric area between four vertices. Although these two properties will be discussed in detail later in this chapter, for now, you can visualize the density control of static meshes in a DecoLayer with the following equation:

grayscale value (0 – 255) × DensityMultiplier value × MaxPerQuad = Final Density

The Color Map texture allows us to combine colors with our static mesh objects being added to the terrain. This provides us with a method to override the static mesh's default color when adding them to the terrain. This is an exceptionally powerful feature when it becomes necessary to alter static mesh colors in specific areas of the terrain. For instance, a color map can be used to alter the color of grass in specific areas to produce the effect of grass that has been burned by a fire or even dried out to a color of brown.

The Scale Map provides a way of scaling the associated static meshes in specific areas. Through the use of the map, we not only control where the scaling occurs, but in which axis and by how much. The color black has no effect on scale, whereas the colors red, green, and blue will cause static meshes in the region of that color to be scaled in the X, Y, or Z axis respectively. Naturally, any of the gray shades between black and white will result in a uniform scaling of the mesh.

There are two ways to add a DecoLayer: manually through the TerrainInfo Actor's properties, or by clicking the New button while on the Decorations tab. Either way will require the setting of various properties before any static meshes will be seen on the terrain. In the following tutorials, both of these methods will be discussed, along with the various properties that need to be set in order for the DecoLayer to function properly.

An interesting fact about DecoLayers is that once created, they do not automatically generate a density map. Without this map, the static meshes of the DecoLayer will not display on the surface of the terrain. We *could* go into an external image editing package such as Adobe Photoshop and create a grayscale texture to be used as the texture map. However, there is a clever workaround we can use that not only allows us to work completely in UnrealEd, but also gives us the ability to use the texture editing tools such as the Painting tool to edit the density map.

Here's a brief overview of how this works: We will create an extra texture layer on our terrain, which we will hide from sight by moving it to the top of the layer list. This will hide the texture behind our completely opaque base texture, meaning that the texture we use is irrelevant. We will then use the RGBA8 grayscale texture that is used to control this new layer's blending as our density map. This means that we can edit the density map using the Painting, Smoothing, and Noise tools if we want, allowing for a much more intuitive way to control the density map. In **TUTORIAL 5.9**, we will use these methods to create decorations on our terrain.

TUTORIAL 5.9: Adding Decorations Through DecoLayers

1. Continue from the last tutorial, or open the file `Tutorial5_09_Start.ut2`. You should have a completely sculpted and textured terrain, ready for decoration meshes.
2. Open the Static Mesh browser and load the Ch5_TerrainSM package. Locate and select the Grass1 static mesh.
3. From the Terrain Editing dialog, verify that the TerrainInfo0 is selected. Switch to the Decorations tab and click the New button. This will create the first DecoLayer.
4. Right-click on the new DecoLayer and select Set Static Mesh from Current from the context menu. Now we have a static mesh associated with this layer. Notice that we cannot currently see any copies of the static mesh. This is because the DecoLayer currently has no density map. We will now create a new texture layer and use its blending texture as a density map.
5. Switch to the Layers tab. In the Texture browser, select any texture from the Ch5_Terrain package. As mentioned earlier, the texture is irrelevant, but the new RGBA8 texture that gets generated will become very important. Create a new layer in the first Undefined slot

using the following settings (see **FIGURE 5.68**):

Package: myLevel

Group: DecoLayers

Name: DecoLayer1_Grass

AlphaHeight: 128

AlphaWidth: 128

AlphaFill: Black (This will prevent any static meshes from appearing on the terrain.)

U and VScale have no effect.

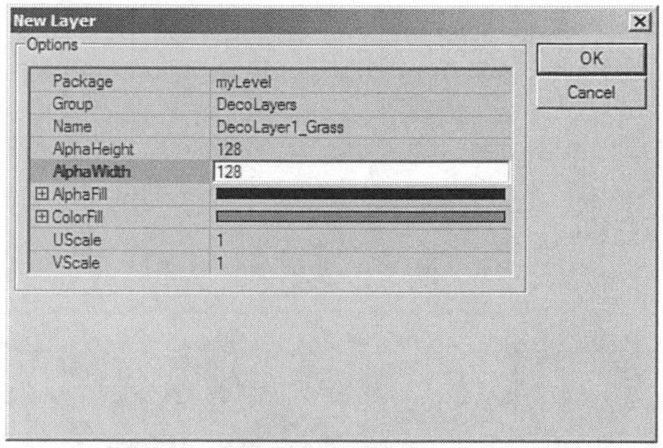

FIGURE 5.68 Creating a new texture layer.

6. Select the new DecoLayer1_Grass layer that has been added to the Layers stack and use the Up Arrow icon to the right to move this layer to the very top of the stack. The layer should now appear above DirtLayer1 in the stack and will not render on the landscape because of the opaque alpha channel on the DirtLayer1 (see **FIGURE 5.69**).

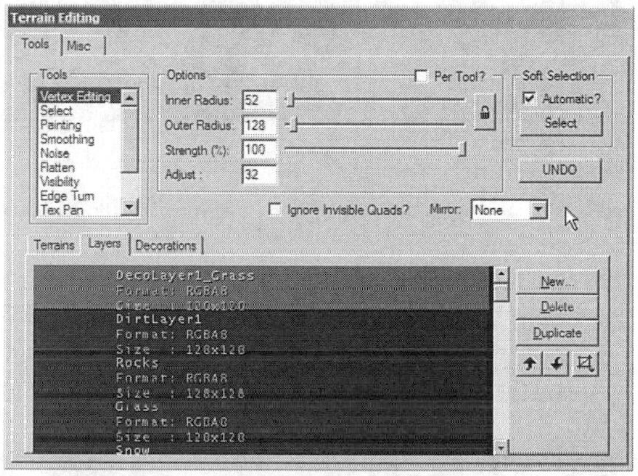

FIGURE 5.69 The texture layers that will be used for the DecoLayers should be moved to the top of the stack to prevent them from rendering their associated textures.

7. In the Textures browser, switch over to the myLevel package. Select the DecoLayer1_Grass texture (see **FIGURE 5.70**). This is the RGBA8 texture that was created to control the blending of the texture layer.

8. In the Terrain Editing dialog, switch back to the Decorations tab. Right-click on the DecoLayer and select Set Density Texture from Current. We now have a texture that will drive the placement of objects (grass in this case) on our terrain.

9. Now that we have a texture assigned, you would think that we could begin painting grass onto our terrain, but there is still one more thing that must be set; the Min and Max `FadeoutRadius`. These two properties determine how far we can see decorations before they begin to fade out and then finally disappear. This is in effect for both the editor and in-game. Use Search for Actors and select the TerrainInfo Actor to which you have added the DecoLayer. Expand the TerrainInfo category, and then locate and expand the `DecoLayers` property. Within, you will see index [0], and underneath this you will find the `FadeoutRadius`. Set the following:

   Max: 5000

   Min: 1000

   This means that you will be able to see the grass objects for 1000 units. Between 1000 and 5000 units the grass will simply fade out. This value would change based on the size of your level and how far you would be able to see across it. Now that we have a texture in place and have adjusted the appropriate properties, we are ready to paint.

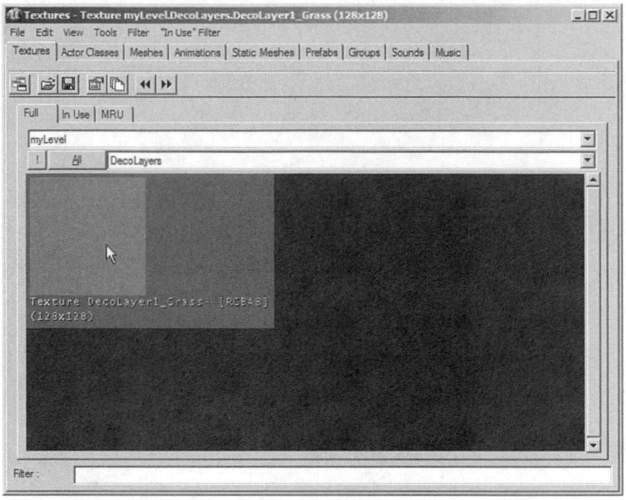

5

FIGURE 5.70 Selecting the new RGBA8 files that will be used as the density map.

10. Switch back to the Layers tab and select the DecoLayer1_Grass layer. Select the Painting tool, adjust the Inner and Outer Radius settings, and paint some grass on the terrain (see **FIGURE 5.71**). You may want to paint the grass in areas that you have added green to in **TUTORIAL 5.8**. Use the left mouse to add grass, right mouse to remove grass.

FIGURE 5.71 Painting static meshes on the terrain.

END TUTORIAL 5.9

TUTORIAL 5.10 assumes that you have access to Adobe Photoshop. If you do not, virtually any image editing software should work as well, though the process will not be the same.

TUTORIAL 5.10: Using Color Maps to Adjust DecoLayer Colors

1. Continue from the last tutorial, or open the file `Tutorial5_10_Start.ut2`. You might notice that the grass is still very green for a cold, snowy area. We will correct the colors of the grass with a color map.
2. Maximize the top viewport in UnrealEd. Right-click on an empty area in the viewport's toolbar, and from the context menu, choose View > Show Terrain. Alternatively, press the T key. You will now see a bird's-eye view of your terrain. Notice that all of the grass that you scattered across the terrain is displayed as white patches. We will use this to our advantage as we create our color map (see **FIGURE 5.72**).

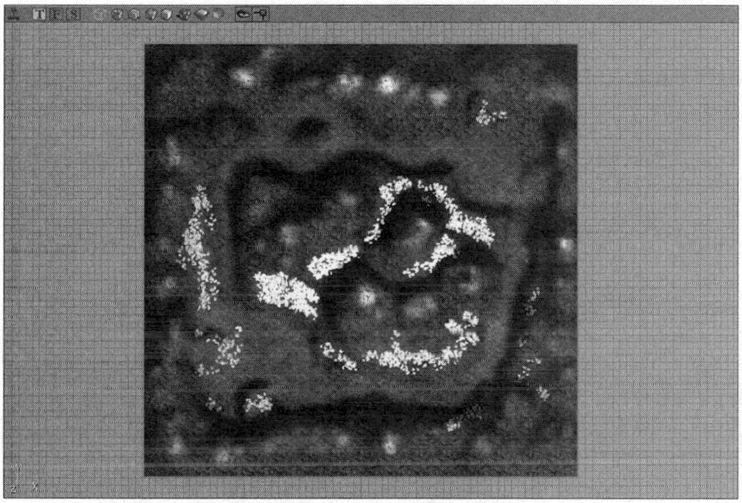

FIGURE 5.72 Using the Top view to generate a reference image for creating our color map.

3. Press Shift+Print Screen. This will copy the image of the screen to the clipboard so that you can paste it into another program such as Photoshop.
4. Launch Adobe Photoshop, and choose File > New. Verify that the pixel dimensions of the new document match the current resolution of your monitor. Also verify that the mode is set to RGB Color (see **FIGURE 5.73**). Click OK when done.

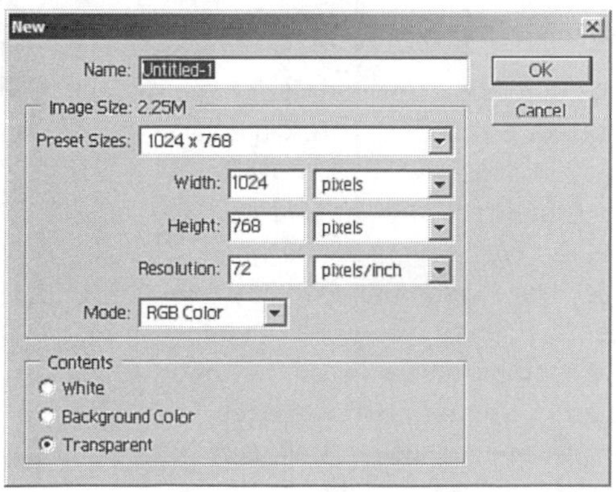

FIGURE 5.73 Creating the new color map in Photoshop.

5. Press Ctrl+V to paste the screen-captured image onto your new document. When this is done, select the Crop tool. At the top of the window, set the Crop width and height to 128 px. Putting the "px" at the end will verify that the crop will be measured in pixels. Drag a selection around the terrain image from the top view, and use the handles to make sure that the crop selection is right against the image of the terrain (see **FIGURE 5.74**).

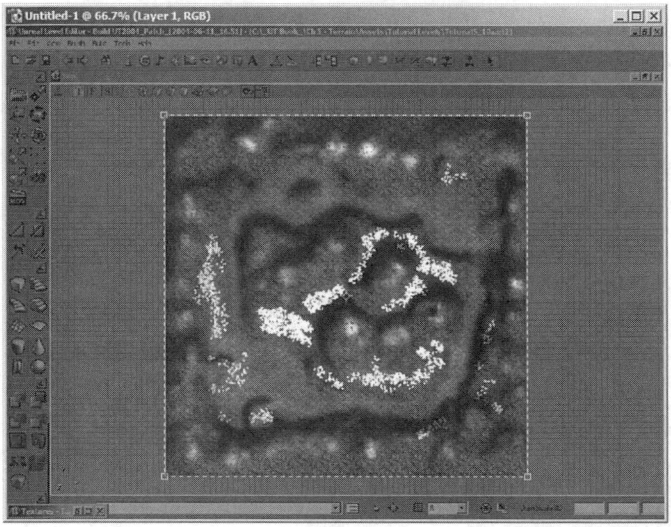

FIGURE 5.74 Cropping out the appropriate area.

Press Enter when done.

6. The image now consists of just the top view of the terrain, which has been resized to 128 × 128 pixels, the same size as our other texture maps (see **FIGURE 5.75**). Now, create a new layer for the document, and name the layer Color.

7. Make sure the color layer is selected. Set your foreground color to any shade you like, and use the Paintbrush tool to paint your selected color wherever the white DecoLayer meshes appear. For realistic dead grass, you would probably want a yellowish-brown, but for testing and demonstration purposes, you can use any color at all (see **FIGURE 5.76**).

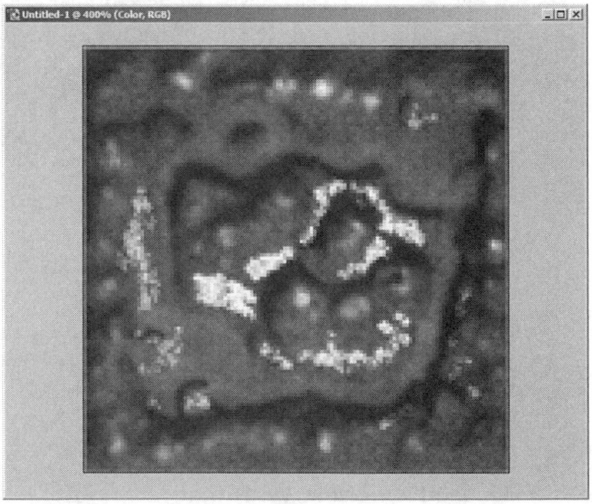

FIGURE 5.75 The image has now been cropped and resized to 128 × 128.

8. Select Layer 1, and set your foreground color to White. Choose Edit > Fill, and set Use to Foreground Color and Blending Mode to Normal. Click OK when done. Your paint strokes should now appear to be on a white background, as in **FIGURE 5.77**.

> **NOTE**
>
> **When this texture is added back as the color map, the hue information will be added to our static meshes in a special way. White areas of the texture will not affect the meshes at all. Grey areas will darken the meshes, and any color you paint will be added to the existing color of the mesh.**

9. Save the file as a 32-bit Targa, under the name `ColorMap.tga`.

10. Back in UnrealEd, go to the Texture browser, and Import the texture into the myLevel package, under the group DecoLayers. Set the name to ColorMap. Uncheck the Generate MipMaps check box. Click OK when done, and select the new texture from the browser.

11. In the Terrain Editing dialog, go to the Decorations tab, right-click on the DecoLayer, and choose Set Color Texture from Current from the context menu that appears.

12. Save your work and test your map. Notice that the colors of your Color Map texture have been applied to the corresponding static meshes. This is a great way to recolor DecoLayer meshes to add realism, or to help designate areas such as the blue and red bases.

END TUTORIAL 5.10

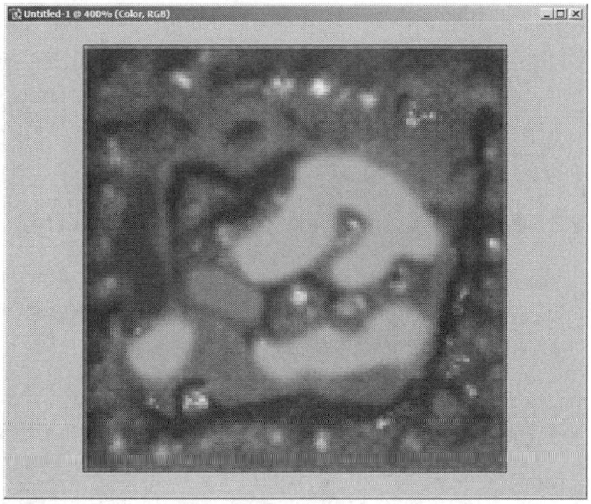

FIGURE 5.76 Painting our color map using the image as a reference.

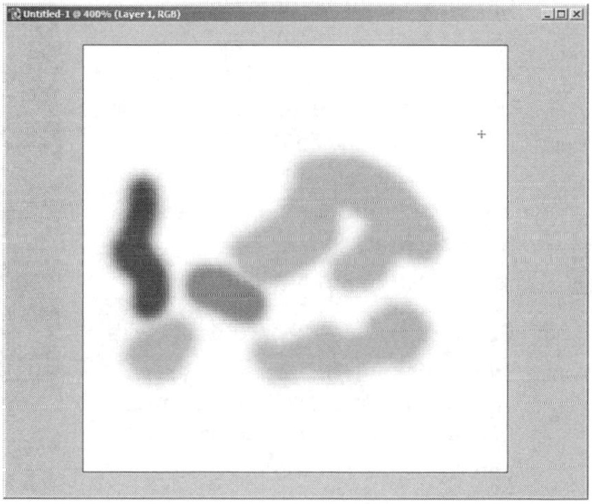

FIGURE 5.77 Now that the background has been flooded, we are ready to save.

> **NOTE**
>
> **If you don't immediately see the results of the color map in the viewport, you can open the properties of the TerrainInfo Actor, expand the TerrainInfo category, and expand the DecoLayers category. Expand index [0], and click the Use button on the `ColorMap` property.**

Our terrain is almost finished. As a final addition to our terrain, we will add an underground structure into our level. This will require that we create a hole in our terrain through which players can move from the surface and into the structure. **TUTORIAL 5.11** will introduce the methods necessary to do this.

TUTORIAL 5.11: Carving Bases into Terrain

1. Continue from the last tutorial, or open the file `Tutorial5_11_Start.ut2`. We will now create an additive BSP-based structure into the terrain. To do this, we will have to create a "hole" in our terrain.

   In order to create any sort of base in our terrain, we must add mass back into the subtracted space of our level. As you recall, the world of Unreal is a space of mass, from which you carve out areas with BSP brushes. Any sort of structures you want to create within these subtracted areas must then be added back in through the use of an additive brush. In this case, we will be adding a brush into our level, and then subtracting *from* that brush to form an open room that is accessible from the surface of our terrain.

5

2. Create an additive brush with dimensions of 512 × 1024 × 1024 in the flattened area of one of your bases. Use a concrete texture, such as the one included in the Ch5_Terrain package. Move the brush up so that it slightly protrudes from the terrain, as in **FIGURE 5.78**. Edit the terrain's height map if necessary.

3. Create a new subtractive brush with dimensions of 448 × 960 × 960. This should be placed in the exact middle of the additive brush. This can be verified in the front, side, and top viewports.

FIGURE 5.78 Adding the brush that our interior space will be carved out from.

4. Our hollowed cube now needs an entrance. Create a new subtractive brush with dimensions of 32 × 128 × 128. Place this in the thickness between the additive and subtractive brushes, at the top. Rebuild your geometry. You should now have a box-like room carved into the additive brush with a small squared opening. Note: You will not currently be able to see completely into the room, as the terrain is in the way. To fix this, we will now hide the faces of the terrain that protrude into the room.

5. Open the Terrain Editing dialog. Select TerrainInfo0 in the Terrains tab, and select the Visibility tool. Set your brush size to a small value, and paint with Ctrl+right mouse to remove the quads of the terrain geometry that are in the way of the hole (see **FIGURE 5.79**).

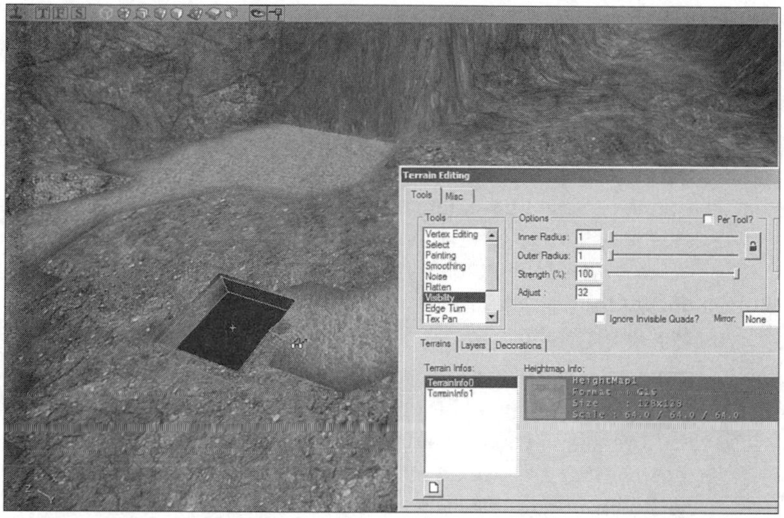

FIGURE 5.79 The Visibility tool is used to cut away terrain revealing our doorway into the new room.

6. Place a light in your new bunker to illuminate it. Edit the shape of your bunker to blend properly into your new terrain, for example to fix areas where the terrain seems to float over the top of the bunker. You could then use the Flatten tool to evenly cover the terrain across the top of the bunker so that only the hole is showing (see **FIGURE 5.80**). Generally, it's a good idea to surround such holes with static meshes of doorways, rocks, and so on in order to cover the areas where the terrain suddenly ceases to exist.

FIGURE 5.80 Static meshes are commonly used to hide problem areas when hiding terrain.

END TUTORIAL 5.11

There are some properties for DecoLayers that allow you to affect how your decorations appear on the terrain's surface. **TABLE 5.3** describes how all of the properties inherent to DecoLayers could be used.

> **NOTE**
>
> **The actual number of meshes visible on the surface of your terrain is achieved with the following formula:**
>
> Value of Density Map × DensityMultiplier × MaxPerQuad
>
> **This is how you keep track of the number of meshes available on the surface.**

TABLE 5.3 DecoLayer Properties

`[0] -`	DecoLayers are housed in a dynamic array. Layers are added as needed without a given limit to a total number.
`AlignToTerrain`	This property controls the alignment of the static meshes on the terrain surface. A value of 0 will result in all static meshes pointing straight up, whereas a value of 1 will result in the static meshes aligning with the normal of the terrain surface upon which it was generated. This also can help prevent meshes that appear to float above the surface in areas where the contour changes dramatically.
`ColorMap`	RGBA8 is the required file type for this property. The map fits the terrain. The idea is for it to add color to the static meshes. For example, if you had a part of the map colored red, any static mesh in that area would also receive the color red. This is very helpful if you are looking to make some areas of grass appear burnt, or even dead, whereas other areas are green.
`DensityMultiplier`	Min/Max This property allows the randomization of how many static meshes will be visible. The density of the static meshes used will be determined by the Density Map texture multiplied by this value. Setting different numbers for the Min and Max values will generate a random number between the two.
`DisregardTerrainLighting`	This property is responsible for controlling whether the static mesh will use the quad lighting information from the terrain or will ignore that information. If the information is ignored (this property is set to 1), the static mesh will appear.
`DrawOrder`	This property is used to determine the order in which decorations for a given layer are drawn. Options are as follows: `SORT_BackToFront`: This option will cause the decorations furthest away to be drawn first. The closest decorations to the player's view will be drawn last. This is the most common setting, as the other settings tend to lean toward less realistic results. `SORT_NoSort`: Uses no specific order. `SORT_FrontToBack`: This option draws the opposite of `SORT_BackToFront`.

TABLE 5.3 Continued

`FadeoutRadius`	Min/Max Determines the point at which static mesh decorations begin to fade out and the point at which they are no longer visible. By default, this property has a Min/Max value of 0, resulting in no visible static meshes when painting on the DecoLayer occurs.
`LitDirectional`	A value of 1 will force static meshes to use sunlight.
`MaxPerQuad`	This determines the number of static meshes that can exist in a quad on the surface. A typical value is 1.
`RandomYaw`	By default, all decoration objects are aligned via rotation in the same direction (around the Z-axis). Setting this property to a value of 1 will cause all of the decoration objects to be randomly rotated along the Z-axis. This helps to break up any tiling appearance that is caused by the objects being all rotated the same way.
`ScaleMap`	The `ScaleMap` is an RGBA8 texture that is used to determine the size of the static meshes on a terrain. The size is generated through the scale of the objects on an individual axis basis. The red channel will affect the scale of width (X-axis), the green channel affects the length (Y-axis), whereas the blue channel will affect the height (Z-axis). The overall scale effect (final size) is determined by the scale map color multiplied by the `ScaleMultiplier` property settings.
`ScaleMultiplier`	X (Min/Max)/Y (Min/Max)/Z (Min/Max) The `ScaleMultiplier` generates a random scale factor for the X, Y, and Z components of a decoration static mesh. The designer enters a minimum and maximum value for each axis. When the static meshes are rendered, the meshes affected by the `ScaleMap` (see `ScaleMap` in the immediately preceding item) are then multiplied by the random number generated between the Min and Max settings of this property. The final result is then applied to the decoration resulting in the object's final size.
`Seed`	This property is used to generate the random placement used for static meshes. Although density is controlled through other properties, the placement of static meshes within the designated areas is randomly generated. If the density is correct but the level designer is not happy with the grouping of the static meshes, the `Seed` property can be changed until the desired look is achieved.

TABLE 5.3 Continued

ShowOnInvisibleTerrain	This property determines whether a decoration will render if it has been painted onto an area that has been flagged invisible. Setting this value to 1 will cause the static mesh to render, which then looks like a floating decoration. In most cases, you would leave this set to False, but effects like spider webs or vines would require this property set to True.
ShowOnTerrain	This property determines whether the static meshes will display on the terrain. A value of 0 results in all static meshes associated with this DecoLayer being hidden. A value of 1 will make all static meshes for this DecoLayer visible.
StaticMesh	This property is used to specify which static mesh will be rendered for the given DecoLayer.

Summary

In this chapter, we have discussed a great variety of techniques to create and control virtual landscapes in your Unreal Engine projects. We discussed the general creation of terrain, the implementation of skyboxes, how to edit the shape of your terrain, and how to change and edit its texture. We then covered how you can create layers of decoration using groups of static meshes. At this point, you should be ready to create a variety of environments for your Unreal worlds, whether they are indoor or outdoor.

Chapter 6

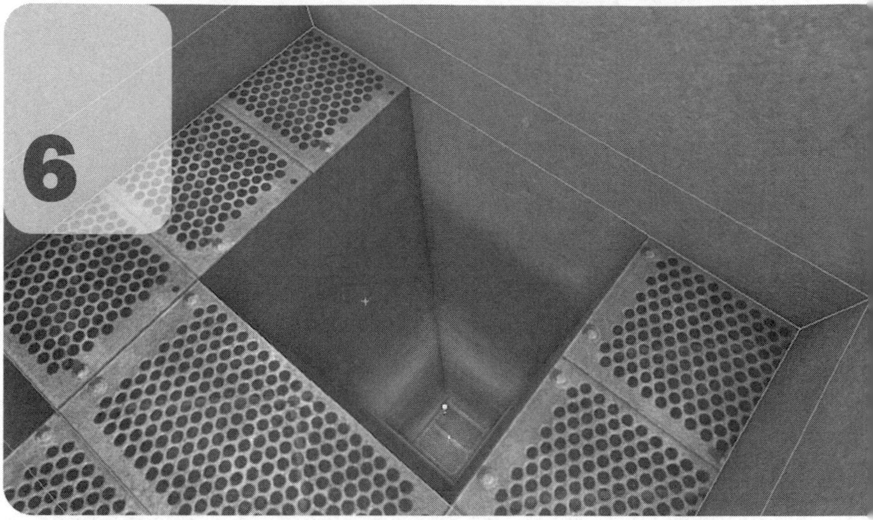

Working with Volumes

This chapter explains volumes in Unreal and how to use them. *Volumes* are used to bend the rules of the natural Unreal environment to create such things as water, lava, and slime. This chapter starts with a simple discussion of the concepts behind volumes and explains how they are designed to work by giving some simple examples of how to use them in your Unreal levels. Next, you then learn about volume properties, focusing on the `PhysicsVolume`. From there, the chapter branches off to show how fluids are created and how you can use the `FluidSurfaceInfo` Actor to create a wavy, fluid-like surface for your liquid volumes. Finally, you see how to use volumes to simulate the effect of a climbable ladder in the game.

Concept of Volumes

As mentioned, you can use volumes to create objects such as water, lava, slime, and ladders. To be precise, a volume is an area that's "aware" of when a player enters or exits. Within this volume, you can change the physical properties of your Unreal worlds, including gravity, terminal velocity, friction, and much more.

By default, a single volume encompasses your entire level: the *DefaultPhysicsVolume*. Each time a new Actor is placed in your level, it's placed within this default volume and remains there until it enters another volume you have created.

To access the properties of the `DefaultPhysicsVolume`, choose Edit > Search for Actors from the main menu. In the Name text box, enter `DefaultPhysicsVolume`. The list of available volumes narrows down to `DefaultPhysicsVolume0` long before you finish entering the text. Double-click the Actor's name to select it, and open the Actor Properties window by clicking the Actor Properties icon on the main toolbar. In this window, you could, for example, change the gravity of your entire level.

If you want variation, however, you need to create your own volumes by using the Builder brush to define the boundaries of a volume's area. You don't add or subtract this brush from your level. Instead, you click the Volume icon to select the type of volume you want to create. **TABLE 6.1** charts the available volumes.

TABLE 6.1 Volume Types

Volume Type	Description
`BlockingVolume`	Use this volume to create a collision area. Typically, it's an invisible volume that deflects players but not projectiles.
`Volume`	This basic volume is essentially an area that keeps track of when players enter or exit, but by default has no effect on gameplay.
`LadderVolume`	This volume defines an area that a player can "climb" like a ladder.
`PhysicsVolume`	This volume enhances the basic `Volume` and gives you more control over the environment.
`DefaultPhysicsVolume`	This default volume encompasses the entire level and is used wherever a volume is not defined.
`WaterVolume`	This volume is basically a `PhysicsVolume` with a series of default properties that create the effect of entering a mass of water.
`SnipingVolume*`	You can use this volume to set locations where bots actively target and snipe enemies.
`LavaVolume`	This volume is simply a `PhysicsVolume` with default properties set to inflict damage to the player when entering the area.

TABLE 6.1 Continued

Volume Type	Description
XFallingVolume*	This PhysicsVolume has default properties geared toward a bottomless-pit look. This volume kills your character when it enters the area.
LimitationVolume*	This simple volume limits the entrance of objects such as projectiles, translocators, and so on.
HitScanBlockingVolume*	This subset of a BlockingVolume blocks projectiles.
PressureVolume	At the time of this writing, this volume is nonfunctional.

*Denotes that volume is available only in UT2004

FIGURE 6.1 graphs the relationship of the available volumes and shows how they relate to a standard volume.

To create any of these volumes, simply define a brush shape, such as a cube, click the Volume icon, and select the type of volume you want to use. The next section explains the properties you can change to customize how the volume behaves when your characters enter it.

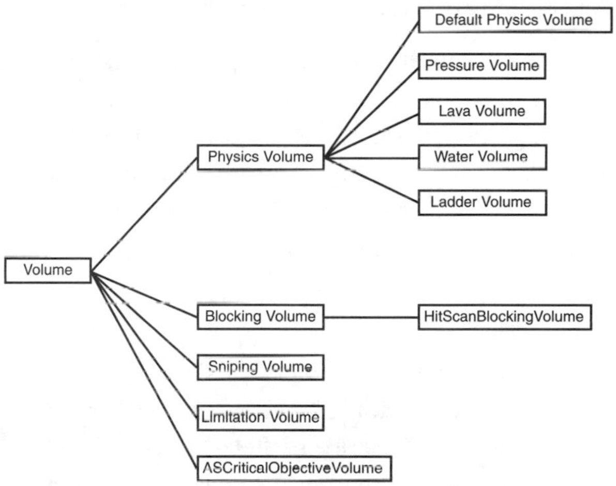

FIGURE 6.1 Volume relationships.

Basic Volumes

By itself, a basic volume doesn't have much functionality. It's simply a foundation for all the other volume types to build on. In this basic form, a volume is nothing more than an Actor that keeps track of when players enter or exit its area. Volumes can, however, be used to designate a location with a specific name or be used along with the DecorationList Actor, which is discussed later in the "DecoList" section.

Volume Properties

Under the Volume category of a volume's Properties window, you'll find a series of important properties that can be altered to change the effect players experience when they enter the volume. Two properties define your location: LocationName and LocationPriority. LocationName is the name you give to a particular volume. This property can be quite useful for team-based levels because you can use it to get constant feedback on player locations. For example, if you had two bases in your map, one for each team, you could create one massive volume around each base. For one of the volumes, you could set the `LocationName` property to Base 1, and the other could be set to Base 2. As players entered or exited either base, you could see their locations on your game's heads-up display.

`LocationPriority` is useful when you have two or more volumes overlapping each other. If a player is standing in an area with two intersecting volumes, the volume with the higher priority is used to designate the player's location, as shown in **FIGURE 6.2**.

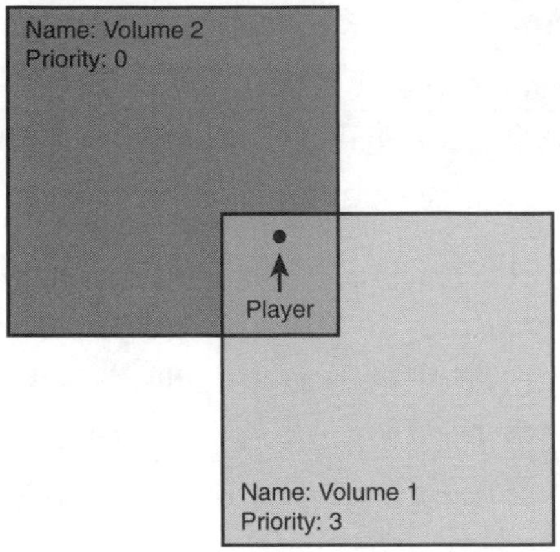

FIGURE 6.2 The player is considered to be in Volume 1 because that volume has a higher priority.

Specifying a volume priority is important because a player can be in only one volume at a time, so only the properties of the higher priority volume are applied. A volume's effects are not amplified or influenced by other volumes when two or more volumes are layered or intersecting.

6

`DecoList`

A volume's `DecoList` property is used with a `DecorationList` Actor. This Actor enables you to create a group of static meshes that are placed somewhat randomly within the volume. However, static meshes are always projected onto the ground.

To use the `DecoList` property, you simply specify which `DecorationList` Actor the volume will use. After placing a `DecorationList` Actor (choose Actor > Keypoint > DecorationList from the menu) in your scene, open its Properties window, where you'll notice a List category (see **FIGURE 6.3**). This category contains the `Decorations` property, which begins simply as an empty array. When you click the Add button next to Decorations, you see a series of properties you can adjust.

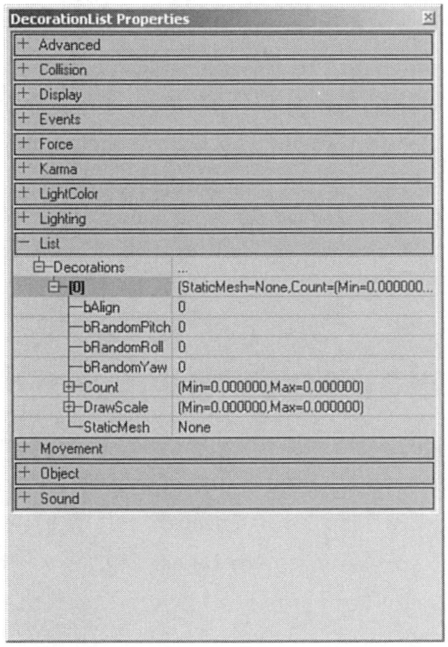

FIGURE 6.3 The DecorationList Properties window.

The most important property in this list is `StaticMesh`, which specifies which static mesh is used for duplication in the volume. The rest of the properties are explained in **TABLE 6.2**.

> **NOTE**
>
> **The "b" in many of these properties specifies that the property holds a Boolean value, meaning it can store only the values `True` and `False`.**

TABLE 6.2 `DecorationList` **Properties**

Property	Description
`bAlign`	This true/false (1 or 0) property determines whether static meshes are going to be aligned with the ground's curvature.
`bRandomPitch`	This true/false (1 or 0) property determines whether to have random rotation in the X-axis.
`bRandomRoll`	This true/false (1 or 0) property determines whether to have random rotation in the Y-axis.
`bRandomYaw`	This true/false (1 or 0) property determines whether to have random rotation in the Z-axis.
`Count`	This property contains Min and Max values for setting the range of how many static meshes to place inside the volume.
`DrawScale`	This property contains Min and Max values for generating a random number within that range. This random number is used to set the `DrawScale` of individual static meshes.

TUTORIAL 6.1: Using the `DecoList` Property

1. Create a 512×512×512 room and subtract it from the world (see **FIGURE 6.4**). Apply a simple texture to the room, place a light, and add a Player Start.
2. Create a new brush that's 128×128×128 and center it in the room. **FIGURE 6.5** shows this new brush in the Top view. At this point, you could move the brush to rest on the floor, but keeping it above the floor won't make much difference because the volume projects static meshes onto the ground anyway.

> **NOTE**
>
> **If you run into a situation in which static meshes aren't duplicating, try increasing the size of the level where the volume exists. This problem should happen only if the area containing your volume is smaller than the volume itself.**

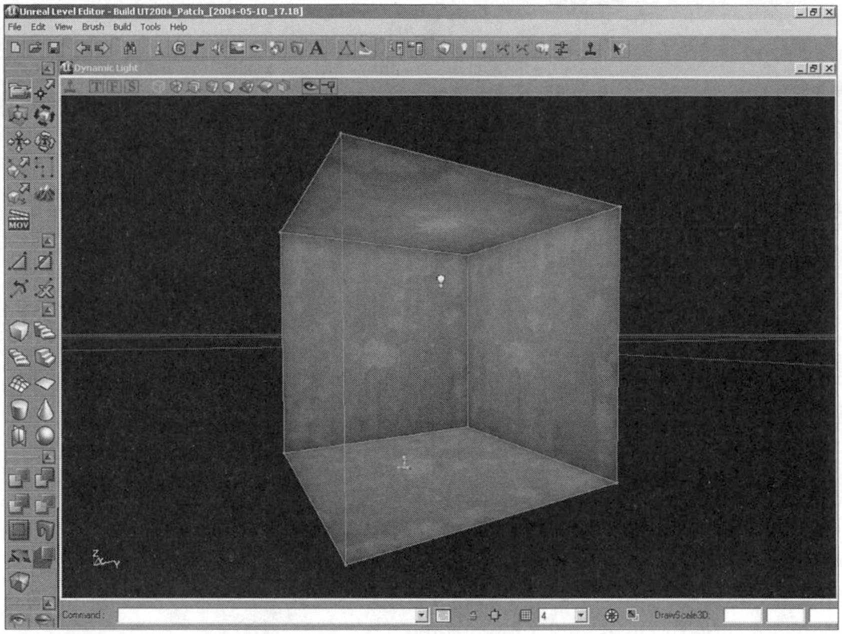

FIGURE 6.4 Newly subtracted room.

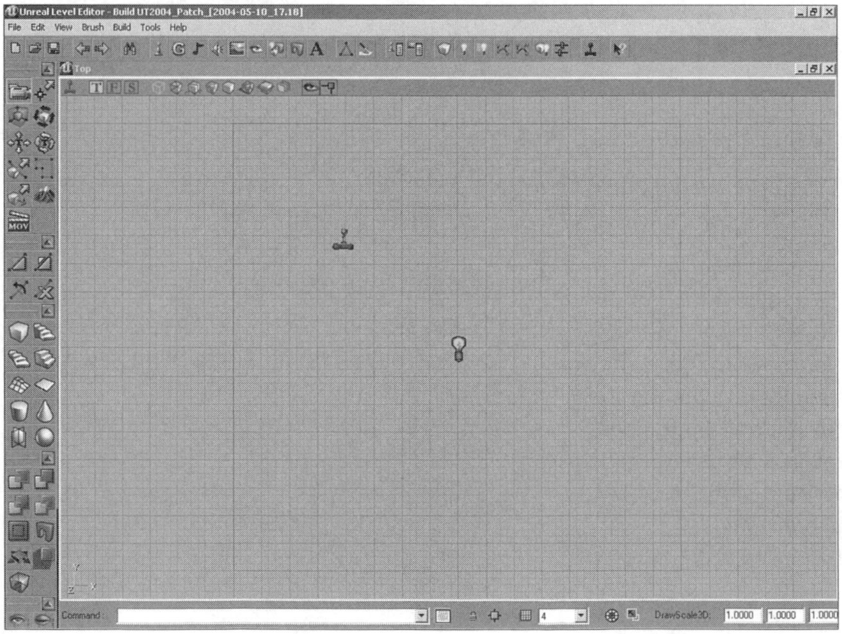

FIGURE 6.5 Top view of new brush.

3. Now go to the Volumes icon set and click Volume. You won't see a noticeable difference at this time, but a basic volume has been created.
4. Move the Builder brush out of the way, and you can see a grayish-pink cube in its place.
5. Next, open the Actor Classes browser and click Actor > Keypoint > DecorationList. Place this Actor in the level and double-click it to open its Properties window. Under the List category, click the Add button next to the `Decorations` property (see **FIGURE 6.6**).
6. Next, you need to set the `StaticMesh` property. Open the Static Mesh browser and load the Chapter6 package. Under the Tree group, select Cone. Back in the DecorationList Properties window, select the `StaticMesh` property and click Use (see **FIGURE 6.7**).
7. To make all duplicated items the same size, set the `DrawScale` property's Min and Max values to `1`. For the `Count` property, set the Min value to `10` and the Max value to `15` so that the volume creates a range of duplicates from 10 to 15.
8. In the volume's Properties window, go to the Volume category and select the `DecoList` property. Click the Find button and then click the DecorationList Actor icon in your level (see **FIGURE 6.8**). Your `DecoList` property is now working. Rebuild the level and try running it.

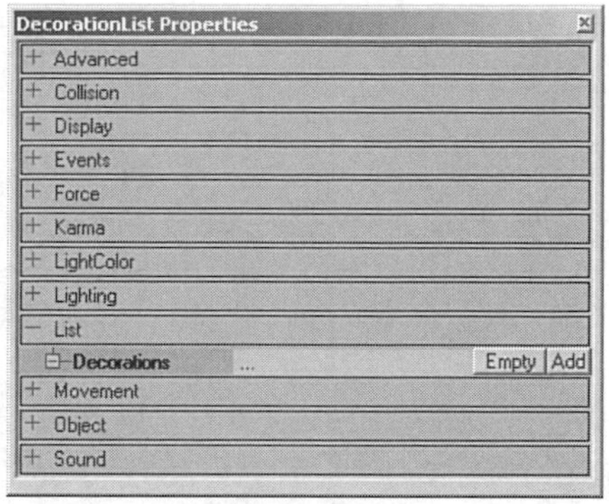

FIGURE 6.6 Add the `Decorations` property.

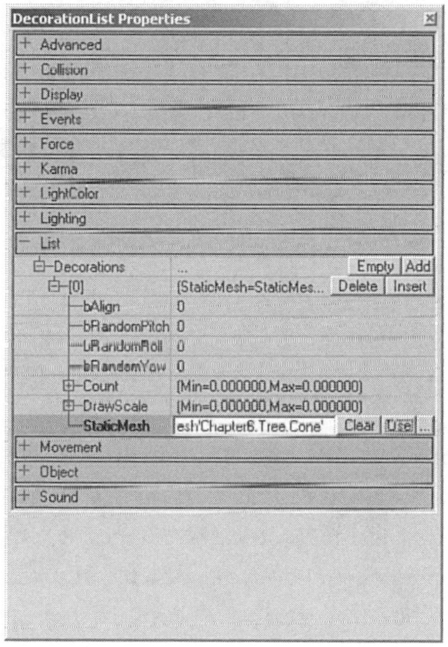

FIGURE 6.7 Setting the `StaticMesh` property of the `DecorationList`.

NOTE

Keep in mind that you will *not* be able to see the effects of this `DecoList` unless you rebuild and run your level.

FIGURE 6.8 `DecoList` in action.

END TUTORIAL 6.1

`BlockingVolume`

`BlockingVolumes` are essentially just volumes used to block certain objects, such as players. You can think of a `BlockingVolume` as an invisible wall. It has three extra properties in addition to the basic volume properties: `bBlockActors`, `bBlockZeroExtentTraces`, and `bBlockKarma`. These properties, however, can be left untouched because the `BlockingVolume` changes them by default. **TABLE 6.3** describes each of these properties.

TABLE 6.3 `BlockingVolume` **Properties**

Property	Description
`bBlockActors`	When set to True, this property "blocks" actors from entering the volume (default: True).
`bBlockZeroExtentTraces`	When set to True, this property "blocks" projectiles (bullets, grenades, and so on) from entering the volume (default: False).
`bBlockKarma`	When set to True, this property "blocks" Karma Actors and causes them to interact with the `BlockingVolume` (default: True).

It might seem strange that bBlockZeroExtentTraces is set to False, meaning that the volume doesn't block projectiles. However, there's a good reason for this default setting. Typically, BlockingVolumes are used as collision meshes for highly detailed static meshes. You could, for example, create a simple cylindrical BlockingVolume around a spiked sphere to effectively prevent players from running into the sphere and getting caught up in the spikes. It would also prevent Unreal from having to calculate per-polygon collisions, which is more processor intensive. However, you still want the projectiles shot at the spiked sphere to have accurate collisions with it. With bBlockZeroExtentTraces set to False, the BlockingVolume doesn't stop projectiles.

If you want to have the BlockingVolume block projectiles as well, you could simply set bBlockZeroExtentTraces to True. Aternatively, you could use a second volume to do the trick. The HitScanBlockingVolume is specifically designed for projectile deflection. It's simply an extension to the basic BlockingVolume that sets bBlockZeroExtentTraces to True.

Under the BlockingVolume category are three properties unique to BlockingVolumes: bClampFluid, bClassBlocker, and BlockedClasses. When bClampFluid is set to true, FluidSurfaceInfo Actors take this BlockingVolume into account when *clamping*, or limiting the action of, fluid surface vertices. This concept is discussed more thoroughly in the "FluidSurfaceInfo" section, later in this chapter.

The bClassBlocker and BlockedClasses properties work hand in hand. When bClassBlocker is set to True, all the classes specified in BlockedClasses collide with the BlockingVolume; nothing else will. These properties are an excellent way to control the types of collisions you get from your volume.

TUTORIAL 6.2: Using a BlockingVolume

1. Create a 512×512×512 room and subtract it from the world. Apply a simple texture onto the room, place a light, and add a player start.
2. Open the Static Mesh browser, and from the Chapter6 package under the BlockingVolume group, select Spikes. Place this static mesh in the middle of the room (see **FIGURE 6.9**).
3. If you run the level at this point, all collisions with the Spikes static mesh would be per-polygon, which means calculating the collisions would be slower. More important, it means the player could easily get "stuck" in the Spikes. Even with only a single polygon in the player's path, the player would be held by the Spikes, even though that polygon might be so small that you can't see it.
4. Therefore, you're going to add a BlockingVolume around this static mesh and remove all collisions from the Spikes. Start by creating a cylinder with Height set to 64 and OuterRadius set to 32.

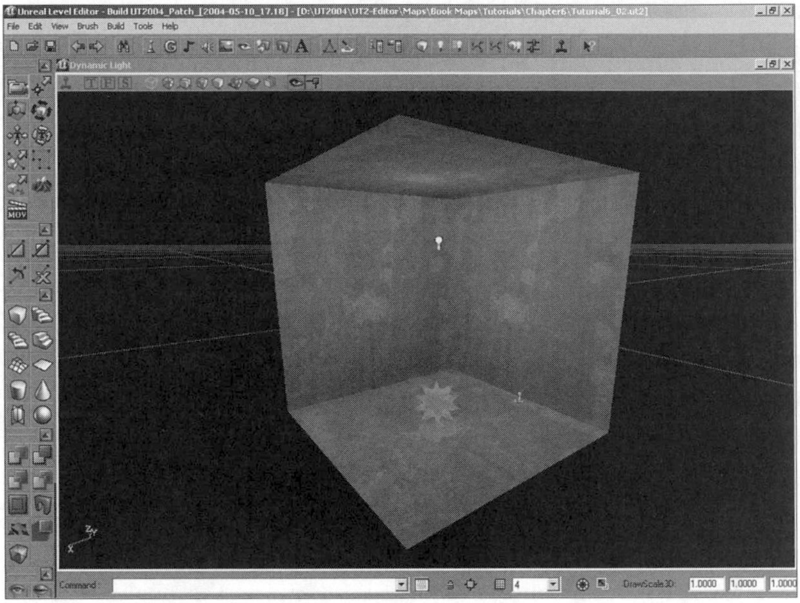

FIGURE 6.9 Place the Spikes static mesh in the middle of the room.

5. This cylinder will be slightly smaller than the Spikes static mesh, but in this case, that's good because it allows the player to get closer to the Spikes without noticing the `BlockingVolume`. Place the cylinder around the Spikes, click the Volume icon, and select `BlockingVolume` (see **FIGURE 6.10**).

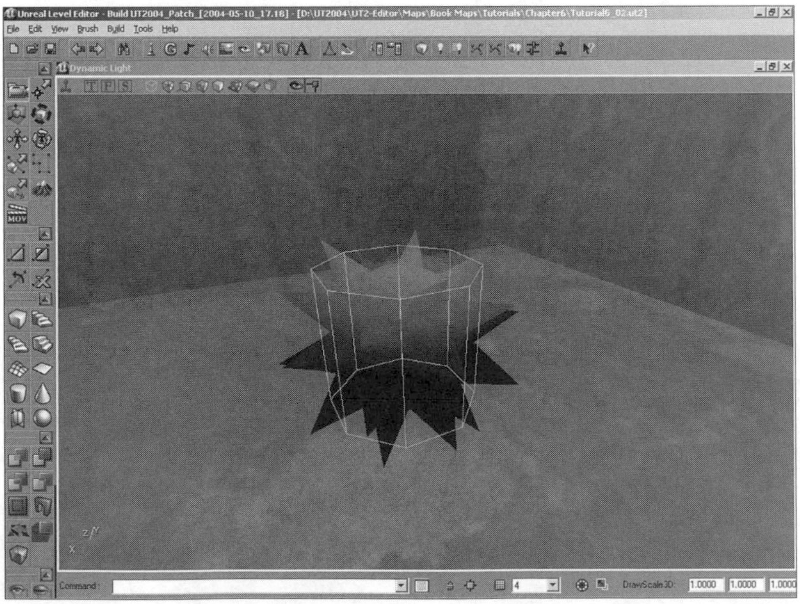

FIGURE 6.10 Place a `BlockingVolume` around the Spikes static mesh.

6. If you run the level at this point, everything would seem to work fine. However, the player is still calculating collisions with the Spikes, so you need to change this to remove any excess calculation overhead. Open the Properties window for the Spikes static mesh and go to the Collision category. Set `bBlockNonZeroExtentTraces` to False to effectively remove collisions between players and this static mesh. However, leave `bBlockZeroExtentTraces` set to True because you want projectiles to continue colliding with it.

7. Run the level. The player should now be colliding with the `BlockingVolume` instead of the Spikes static mesh.

END TUTORIAL 6.2

PhysicsVolume

As mentioned earlier in this chapter, `PhysicsVolumes` are a subset of volumes that add a variety of properties so that you can manipulate the environment's physics within that volume. This volume has two property categories in addition to the basic volume properties: `PhysicsVolume` and `VolumeFog`. The Volume tab includes the same options as for a basic volume. **FIGURE 6.11** shows the PhysicsVolume Properties window.

These properties are covered later in this section as they become relevant. For now, start with a look at how to create a slippery floor by taking advantage of the `GroundFriction` property.

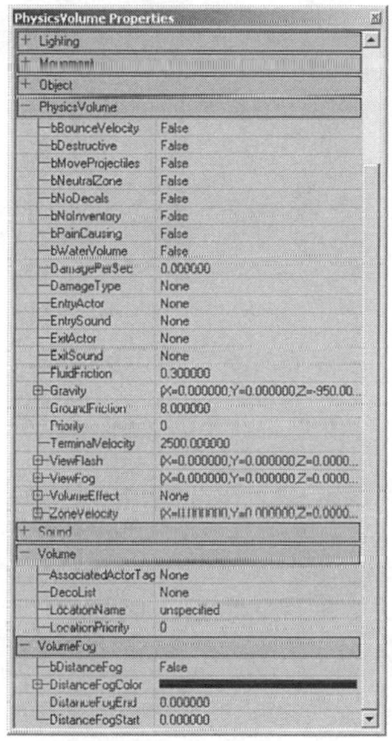

FIGURE 6.11 The PhysicsVolume Properties window.

TUTORIAL 6.3: Creating a Slippery Floor

1. Open `Tutorial6_03_Start.ut2`. You're going to make the floor around the pit at the end of the room slippery. **FIGURE 6.12** shows the empty room.

2. Create a cube and set its Height to `64`, Width to `384`, and Breadth to `512`. Place it at the end of the room over the pit. Click the Volume icon and create a `PhysicsVolume` (see **FIGURE 6.13**).

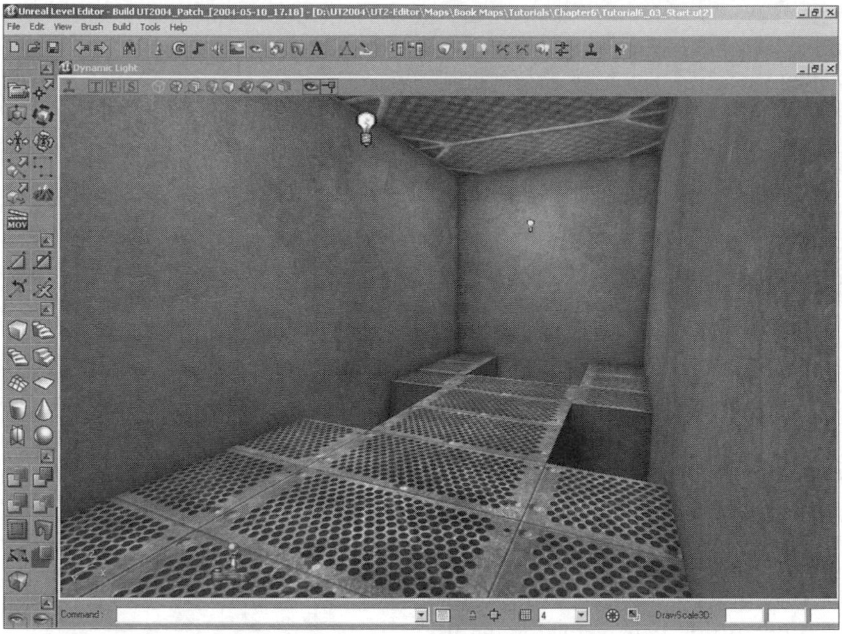

FIGURE 6.12 Empty room.

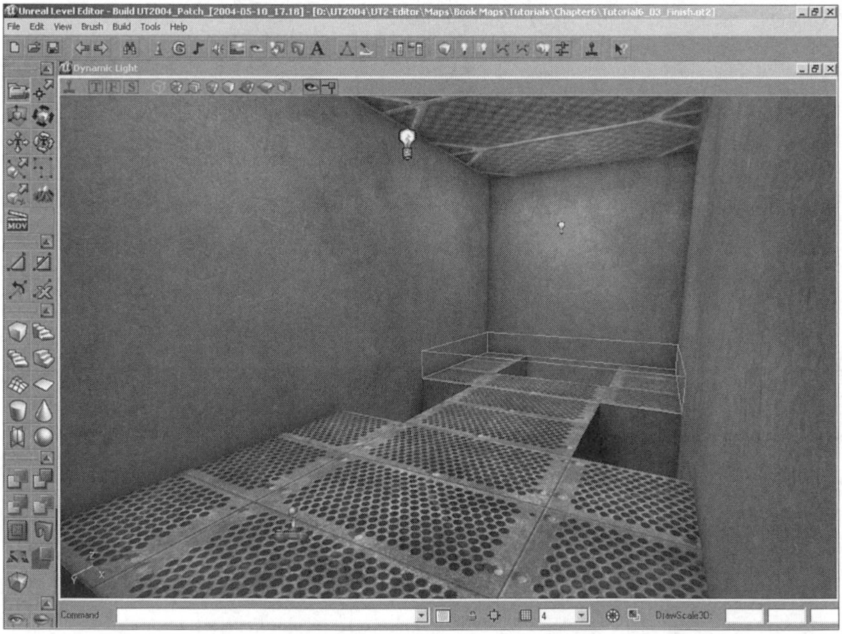

FIGURE 6.13 `PhysicsVolume` covering the hole at the end of the room.

3. Open the Properties window for the `PhysicsVolume`. Under the PhysicsVolume category, you'll see the `GroundFriction` property. The default value is 8, which means that after pressing one of the direction keys and letting go, the player stops immediately. If you decrease this value, the player starts sliding on the surface more. Set this property to `0.2`. Now, after pressing a direction key and letting go, the player will continue moving for a bit, as though sliding on ice.

4. Save the level and run the game. You should now have a slippery floor.

END TUTORIAL 6.3

All uses of `PhysicsVolumes` are similar to **TUTORIAL 6.3**. It's simply a matter of setting a few properties and knowing exactly what those properties do. **TUTORIAL 6.4** shows you how to use the `TerminalVelocity` property to prevent a player from suffering excessive damage after a long drop.

TUTORIAL 6.4: Using the `TerminalVelocity` Property

1. Open `Tutorial6_04_Start.ut2`. At the moment, the pit at the end of the room, shown in **FIGURE 6.14**, can cause serious damage to unsuspecting players who fall into it. To prevent this danger, you'll place a `PhysicsVolume` at the very bottom of the pit to prevent speeds over a certain rate.

FIGURE 6.14 The pit of inevitable doom.

2. Create a 128×256×256 cube and place it on the very bottom of the pit. Create a `PhysicsVolume` (see **FIGURE 6.15**).

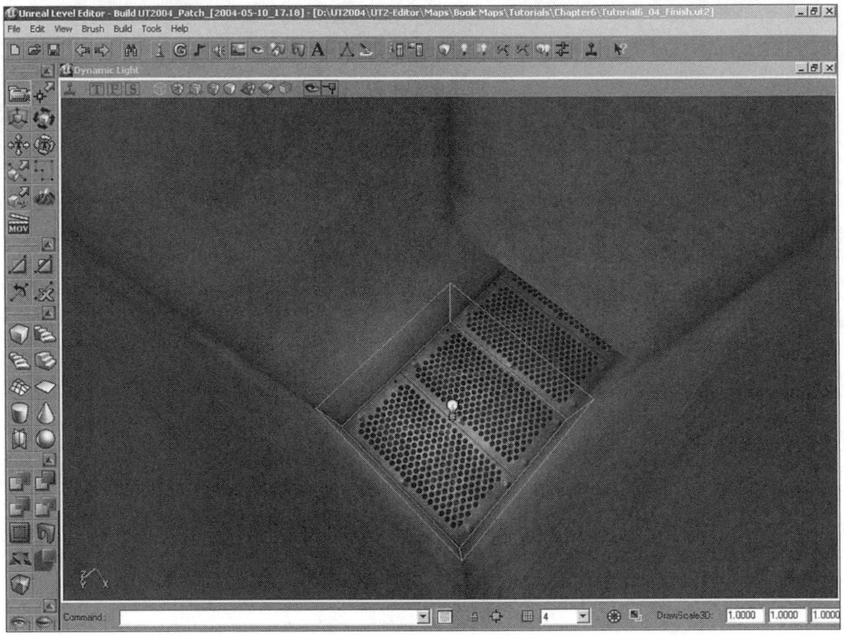

FIGURE 6.15 Place a `PhysicsVolume` in the pit.

3. Open the Properties window for the `PhysicsVolume` and go to the PhysicsVolume category. Change the `TerminalVelocity` property to `1000`.
4. Rebuild and run the map. Now if players fall into the pit, they don't suffer any damage.
5. Save the map.

END TUTORIAL 6.4

Because you changed only the `TerminalVelocity` property, the area at the very bottom of the pit still functions properly when a player jumps, dodges, or performs any other common moves.

`WaterVolume`

A `WaterVolume` is used to create areas that you want to fill with a fluid of some sort so that players can swim in that area. It's basically just a `PhysicsVolume` with a few changes to the default properties. In fact, changing a `PhysicsVolume`'s `bWaterVolume` property to True makes the volume act like water. **TABLE 6.4** shows the properties changed in a `WaterVolume` and the purpose of each.

TABLE 6.4 WaterVolume **Properties**

Property	Purpose
KExtraAngularDamping	This property determines the amount of force applied to decrease the amount of angular movement (rotation) for Karma Actors while they are in the volume (default: 0.1).*
KExtraLinearDamping	This property determines the amount of force applied to decrease linear movement for Karma Actors while they are in the volume. The higher the number, the slower the movement (default: 0.8).*
PhysicsVolume	
bWaterVolume	This true/false property determines whether a volume acts like water (default: True).
EntrySound	This property sets the sound played when entering the volume. When using a WaterVolume, however, changing this property makes no difference because a default water sound is used.
ExitSound	This property sets the sound played when leaving a volume. Like EntrySound, changing this property for a WaterVolume makes no difference.
FluidFriction	If bWaterVolume is set to True, this property sets the amount of hindrance to a player's movement in the water (default: 2.4). Setting this value to somewhere between 0 and 0.5 means players can move easily in the water. The higher the number, the harder it is to move around. However, increasing the number to, say, 60,000 causes some interesting effects. Movement in that area becomes inverted: Forward becomes backward, left becomes right, and so forth.

*Karma Actors are discussed in Chapter 11, "The Karma Physics Engine."

Aside from the properties in **TABLE 6.4**, another set of properties enables you to produce fog. Although these properties are available in a regular PhysicsVolume, the discussion of water makes it a perfect time to explain them in detail. Adding fog limits a player's visible range when inside the volume. This effect can be immensely useful when creating water effects to add murkiness to the water or to limit a player's view with a fog effect. A blue fog is often used with WaterVolumes.

Under the VolumeFog category are four properties: bDistanceFog, DistanceFogColor, DistanceFogEnd, and DistanceFogStart. Setting bDistanceFog to True activates fog inside that volume. DistanceFogColor sets the fog color. DistanceFogStart defines where your fog begins based on the distance from your player in Unreal units. `DistanceFogEnd` determines where the fog ends. Everything after the point set by `DistanceFogEnd` is pure dense fog with the color the `DistanceFogColor` property designates. **FIGURE 6.16** demonstrates how `DistanceFogStart` and `DistanceFogEnd` work.

With that understood, now you can try your hand at creating a simple area of water in **TUTORIAL 6.5**.

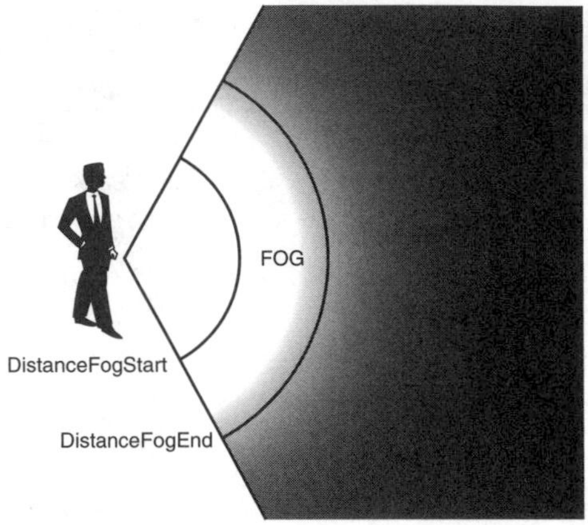

FIGURE 6.16 This diagram demonstrates the result of Distance Fog.

TUTORIAL 6.5: Creating Water

1. Open `Tutorial6_05_Start.ut2`.
2. Create a cube and set its Height to 512, Width to 256, and Breadth to 128. Using the skills you have learned, place a `WaterVolume` so that it rests on the bottom of the pool at the left (see **FIGURE 6.17**).

FIGURE 6.17 A `WaterVolume` in place.

3. Build and run the level. Although you don't see anything in the pool at the left, it's now filled with water. To make the water visible, you could just place a special Non-Solid brush at the same location as the `WaterVolume` and apply a water-like texture to it, but this method makes the fluid look quite stagnant. That's where the `FluidSurfaceInfo` Actor (discussed in the following section) comes into play.

4. Save the map.

END TUTORIAL 6.5

FluidSurfaceInfo

The `FluidSurfaceInfo` Actor is a plane of geometry that has noise deformation applied across the surface over time, meaning that it's a sheet of triangles that ripple like liquid. You can find it in the Actor Classes browser under Actor > Info > FluidSurfaceInfo. Because a `FluidSurfaceInfo` is simply for decorative purposes, setting it up is quite easy. Simply place the Actor in your level, set its size, adjust a few properties, and you're done. **TUTORIAL 6.6** shows you how to add a `FluidSurfaceInfo` to the level you've been working on.

TUTORIAL 6.6: Adding a Surface to the Water

1. Open the `Tutorial6_06_Start.ut2` map.

2. Place a `FluidSurfaceInfo` into the map (see **FIGURE 6.18**).

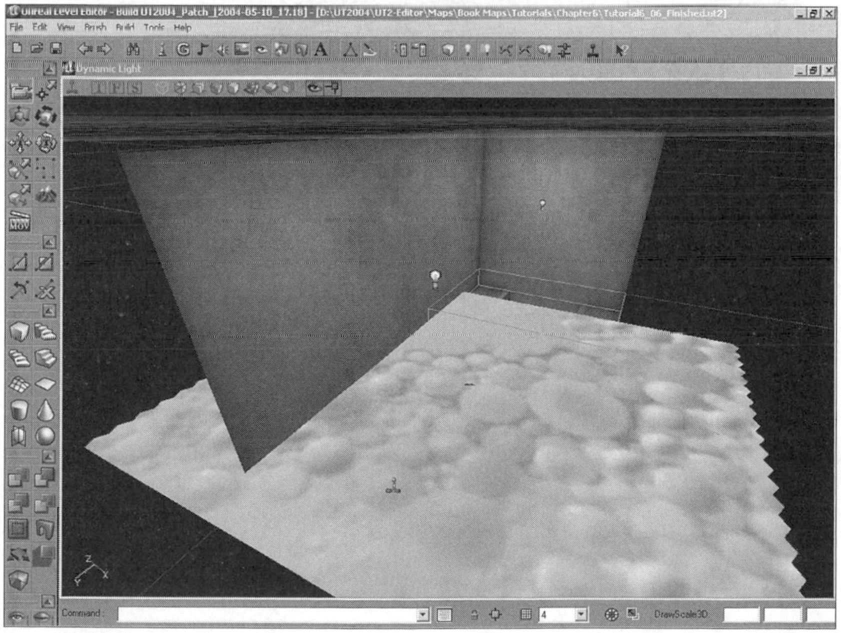

FIGURE 6.18 3D view of `FluidSurfaceInfo`.

3. For your purposes, this `FluidSurfaceInfo` Actor is far too big. Open its Properties window and click the FluidSurfaceInfo tab. To modify its size, change `FluidXSize` to `8` and `FluidYSize` to `16` (see **FIGURE 6.19**). It's a good practice to always make these values powers of 2. Each grid's size is determined by `FluidGridSpacing`, which is, by default, set to 24. Therefore, this grid fills approximately (8-1) × 24, or 168 units. (You subtract one because the grid size is zero based.) Right now, `FluidGridType` is set to `FGT_Hexagonal`, which specifies how the individual vertices are arranged. This setting causes the grid to take up a little more space than your calculated value. In fact, it would take up 180 units, which is 168 plus half the `FluidGridSpacing` setting. Place this on the top of the `WaterVolume`. If you can't see it in the Side view, turn on the Realtime Preview for a moment. This feature causes some deformation on the `FluidSurfaceInfo` so that you can see it in the viewport.

6

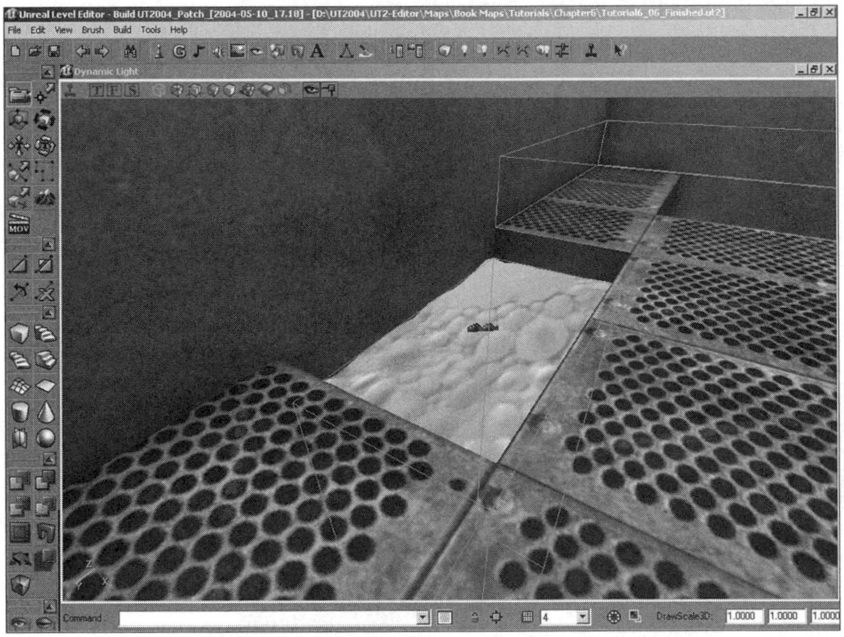

FIGURE 6.19 `FluidSurfaceInfo` **resized to fit the pool space.**

4. Obviously, the default material for this surface isn't appropriate. Open the Texture browser and select AWGlobal.utx > OceanGlass. To apply this texture to the surface, open the Properties window for the `FluidSurfaceInfo` and go to Display > Skins. Add a new entry to the list, and click the Use button on index 0. You now have a water-like surface that ripples (see **FIGURE 6.20**).

5. Rebuild and play the map. When you're done, save the map.

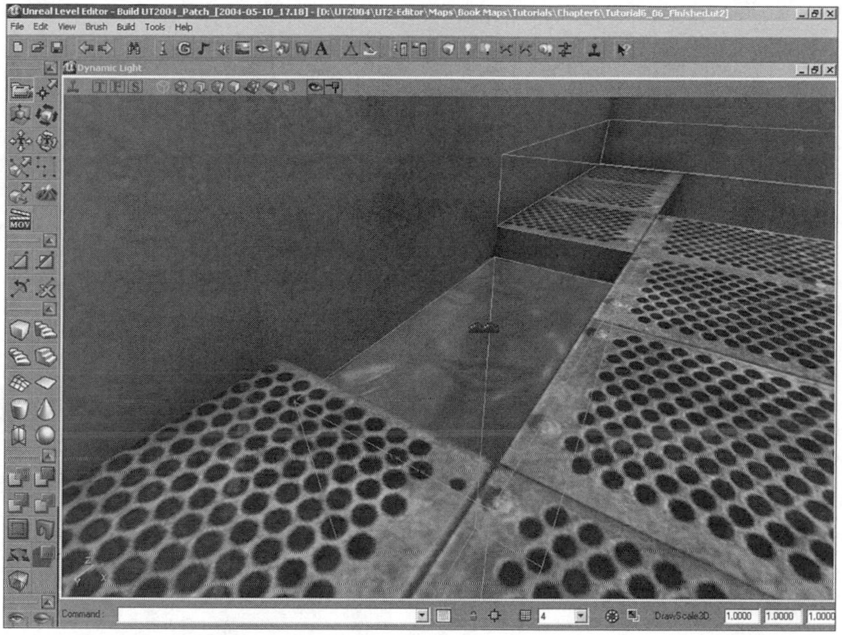

FIGURE 6.20 **The `OceanGlass` material applied to the `FluidSurfaceInfo`.**

END TUTORIAL 6.6

The properties for the `FluidSurfaceInfo` are quite daunting at first glance. However, **TABLE 6.5** explains the important properties.

TABLE 6.5 `FluidSurfaceInfo` **Properties**

Property	Purpose
`FluidColor`	This property determines the color of the surface in a wireframe view. It doesn't actually change the surface during gameplay.
`FluidHeightScale`	This property sets the size of the waves. The larger the number, the taller the waves.
`FluidNoiseFrequency`	This property can be thought of as the randomness of the fluid's movement. The higher the number, the more "frequent" the ripples are.
`FluidNoiseStrength`	This property determines the size or amplitude of the noise. The amplitude can be anywhere between the Min and Max values.
`FluidSpeed`	This property controls the speed of the noise, but also affects the way in which the noise changes.
`FluidTimeScale`	This property also controls the speed of the noise, but it has no effect on the way in which the noise changes. It simply controls how fast it fluctuates.

FluidSurfaceOscillator

The FluidSurfaceOscillator Actor is used to add ripples to your FluidSurfaceInfo. You can find it in the Actors browser under Actor > FluidSurfaceOscillator. To use this Actor, simply place it in your level on the FluidSurfaceInfo where you want the ripples to originate. Then, in the Properties window for your FluidSurfaceOscillator, go to the FluidSurfaceOscillator tab. Click the Find button and select the FluidSurfaceInfo you want to add the ripples to. Now it's just a matter of tweaking a few settings. **TABLE 6.6** lists the properties and their uses.

TABLE 6.6 FluidSurfaceOscillator Properties

Property	Purpose
Frequency	This property sets the number of ripples the FluidSurfaceOscillator generates every second.
Phase	This property enables you to change the phase of the oscillator. You might want to give each oscillator influencing the same FluidSurfaceInfo a different phase to keep the fluids from canceling out each other's motion.
Radius	If you consider the oscillator as a pebble being thrown repeatedly into the FluidSurfaceInfo, this property determines the size of the pebble.
Strength	This property controls the amount of force that goes into each ripple.

LavaVolume

A LavaVolume is a PhysicsVolume that behaves like lava. The main difference is that it causes damage. This volume introduces three properties that haven't been covered yet: DamagePerSec, DamageType, and bPainCausing.

After you set bPainCausing to True, entering the volume causes a certain amount of damage every second; this value is controlled by DamagePerSec. The default value is 40, which means 40 units of damage take place every second. You can, however, control the type of damage that's applied. By default, DamageType is set to FellLava, which means that after a player dies in the lava, he'll turn into a skeleton and fall into the pit of doom.

TUTORIAL 6.7: Using a LavaVolume

1. Open Tutorial6_07_Start.ut2.

2. Right-click the WaterVolume and choose Polygons > To Brush. Now the Builder brush is the same size as the WaterVolume you worked with in **TUTORIAL 6.6**. Move the Builder brush over the pit at the right. Use the skills you have learned to create a LavaVolume (see **FIGURE 6.21**).

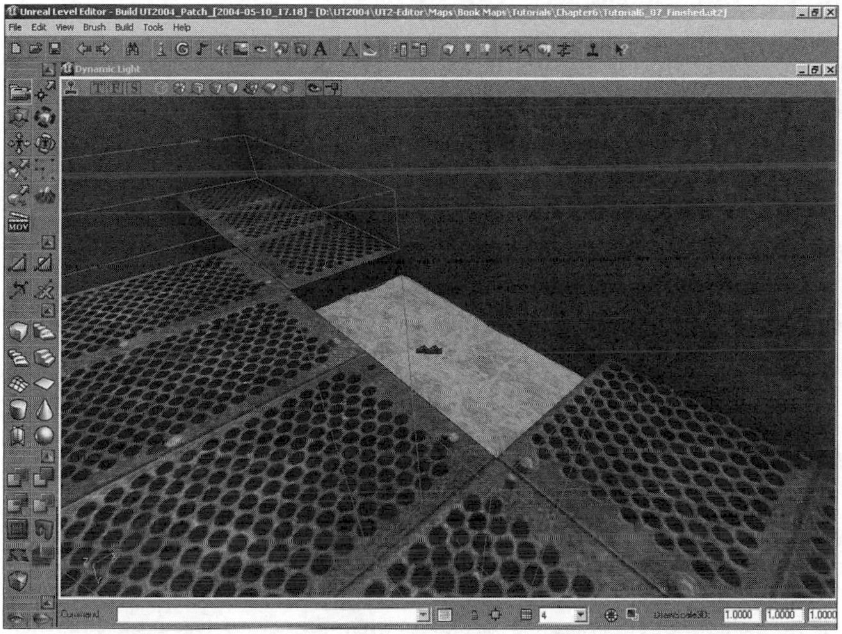

FIGURE 6.21 The LavaVolume in place.

3. At this point, the lava should work correctly, but you won't see it. Therefore, you need to add a FluidSurfaceInfo with a lava texture applied to it. Select the water's FluidSurfaceInfo, duplicate it, and move it over the pit on the right. Open the Texture browser and select the TexOscillator1 texture from the SC_Volcano_T.utx texture package. Open the Properties window for the new FluidSurfaceInfo and go to the Display category. Click the Use button on index 0 of the Skins property (see **FIGURE 6.22**).

4. Rebuild the map and run it. You should now have damage-causing lava. When you're done, save the map.

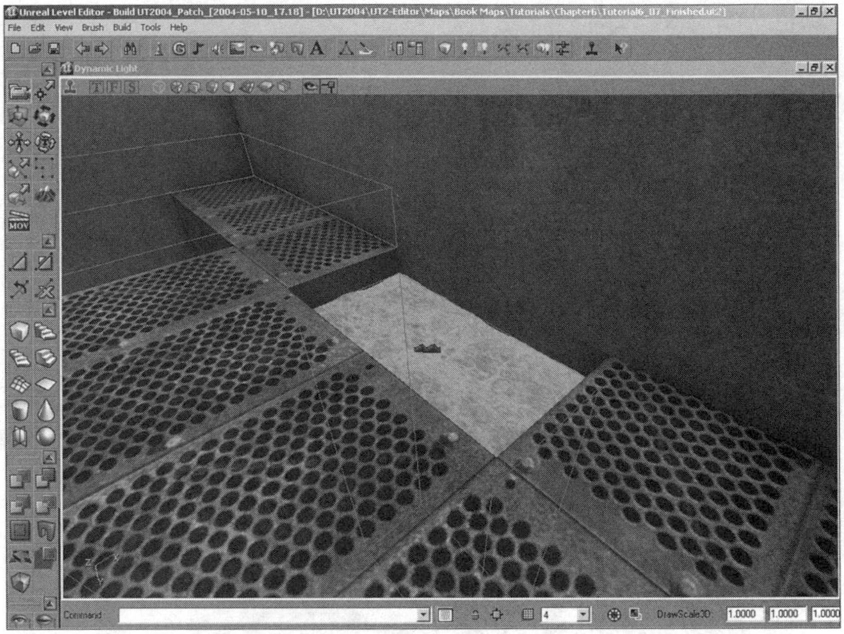

FIGURE 6.22 A Magma texture applied to the `FluidSurfaceInfo`.

END TUTORIAL 6.7

XFallingVolume

The `XFallingVolume` is almost identical to the `LavaVolume` except that the damage type and amount of damage per second have changed. This volume kills players when they enter it, so it's useful when you want to simulate a pit or similar trap. To use it, just create the volume as you have created all the other volumes. **TABLE 6.7** shows the important properties and their default values.

TABLE 6.7 `XFallingVolume` **Properties**

Property	Default Value
`DamagePerSec`	100
`DamageType`	class'Fell'
`bPainCausing`	True

LadderVolume

In many games, especially single-player games, often you want to have ladders for players to climb. You can do this easily with the `LadderVolume`. After entering the volume, you can "walk" up and down the ladder by moving forward and backward and jump off the ladder by using the jump button. Note, however, that going back down the ladder can be hard after you're at the top.

TUTORIAL 6.8: Creating a LadderVolume

1. Load the Tutorial6_08_Start.ut2 map, which contains a tall room with a little shelter at the top (see **FIGURE 6.23**). This shelter is accessible only through the currently nonfunctional ladder.

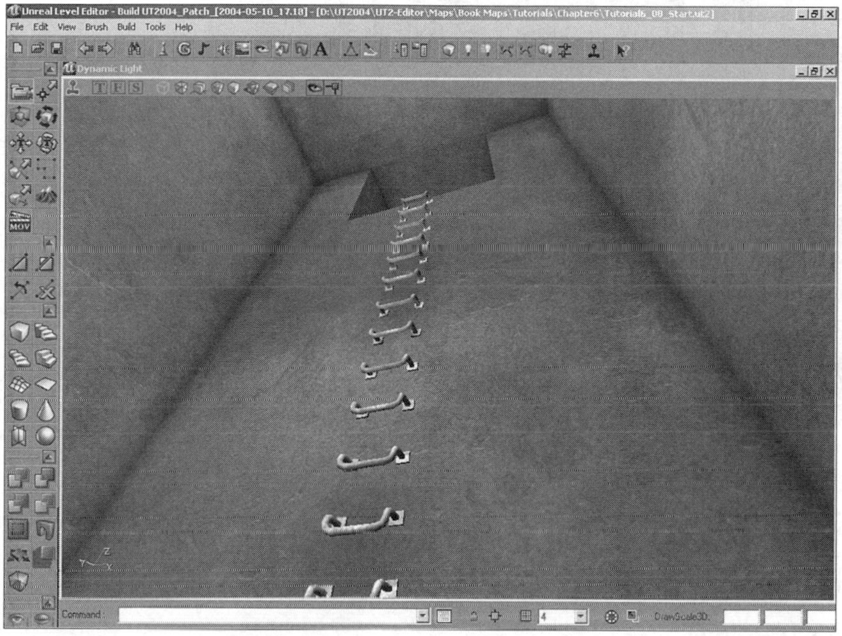

FIGURE 6.23 Room with a ladder.

2. Create a brush and set its Height to 808, Width to 64, and Breadth to 64.
3. Align this brush with the wall and ground. Click the Volume icon, and create a LadderVolume at this location (see **FIGURE 6.24**).

> **NOTE**
>
> For purposes of bot navigation, a LadderVolume should be 40 units higher than the top of the area to be climbed. For more information on bot navigation, please refer to Chapter 12, "Advanced Bot/AI Navigation."

4. You've created the ladder, but notice that an arrow is pointing east out of the LadderVolume. This arrow needs to be pointing toward the wall, in the direction the player would have to face to climb the ladder.
5. In the Properties window for the LadderVolume, look under the LadderVolume category to find the WallDir property. This property is used to set the direction your player needs to face to climb the ladder, typically toward the wall. In this case, you want the arrow to be pointing north, which requires setting Yaw to 49152. **TABLE 6.8** shows the values you need to use for each direction.

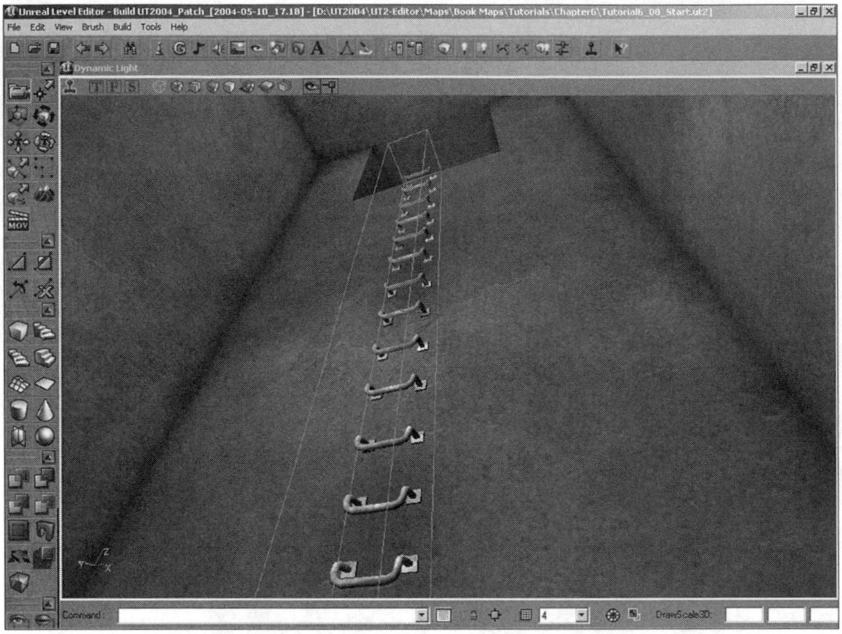

FIGURE 6.24 A `LadderVolume` placed in the right position.

6

TABLE 6.8 Rotation Settings for the Cardinal Directions

Yaw	Direction
49152	North
0	South
16384	East
32768	West

6. Open the Properties window for the `LadderVolume` and go to the LadderVolume category. Set the `WallDir` property's Yaw to 49152 (North).

> **NOTE**
>
> For more information on how Unreal handles rotation, please refer to Chapter 8, "Creating Materials in Unreal."

7. Rebuild and run the map. The ladder should now be working properly. When you're done, save the map.

END TUTORIAL 6.8

After rebuilding the map, you might have noticed something rather interesting. You now have two AutoLadder Actors in your map: one at the top of the ladder and one at the bottom. These Actors are navigation points created so that bots can use the ladders. If you prefer to create these points manually, you must set the bAutoPath property of the LadderVolume to False so that it doesn't automatically generate the AutoLadder Actors. Then you would have to place Ladder Actors (Actor > NavigationPoint > SmallNavigationPoint > Ladder in the Actor Classes browser) at the top and bottom of the ladder and make sure they pointed toward the wall, just like the LadderVolume. Bots would then be able to use the ladder.

You can set two other useful properties for a LadderVolume: ClimbingAnimation and TopAnimation. ClimbingAnimation specifies which animation to use when a player is climbing up the ladder. TopAnimation specifies the animation to use when a player reaches the top of the ladder.

Summary

At this point, you should have a thorough understanding of the properties and uses for a variety of volume types. Volumes can be used to add more character and playability to your levels. However, as a level designer, you should be careful not to overuse them. As a general rule, volumes should be added only when they enhance gameplay or improve your level's look and feel. In Chapter 7, "Lighting in Unreal," you see how to create and control lights in your Unreal levels.

Chapter 7

Lighting in Unreal

In this chapter, you look at the lights available in Unreal and how you can use them in your projects. This chapter discusses how the Unreal Engine uses light and creates dark and light areas in your maps. The properties available to control the look and behavior of lights are covered as well as special effects that can be applied to your lights. From there, lighting workflow and the importance of rebuilding lights are explained.

Also, you learn how light affects a variety of surfaces in Unreal, including world geometry (constructive solid geometry; CSG), static meshes, Movers, terrain, and more. Advanced lighting effects are also covered, such as using ambient lighting, how other Actors can emit light, and how to use a TriggerLight, which is a dynamic light that can be animated to create a variety of effects. In addition, this chapter discusses projectors and how to use them in your maps. The chapter closes with a discussion of some common lighting pitfalls for beginners.

Light Concepts

This section covers the fundamental concepts behind Unreal's lighting system. You'll begin by taking a look at light maps and how they are created, and then learn the importance of light placement in your levels and how light location influences the look of your light maps.

Light Maps

One of the key factors in Unreal lighting is the creation of your level's light maps. Essentially, a *light map* is a texture placed over all world geometry in your level, which is then blended with the existing level texture. This blending between your light maps and level texture can create some areas that are completely black and other areas that are so intensely lit that the texture is washed out. Whenever you rebuild the lighting in your level, the light maps are recalculated and regenerated.

When creating light maps, you must remember that they are static, meaning they don't move. You can use light maps to create very realistic shadows in your levels, but you cannot make those shadows move as you play. The benefit of this architecture is that all your level's shadows are precalculated, instead of having to be constantly updated at runtime. This precalculation allows for beautiful lighting and shadow effects that remain steadfast while you play the game. Throughout this chapter, you'll see a variety of ways you can control the clarity of shadows created with your light maps and the overall look of the light maps. In **FIGURE 7.1**, you can see the result of light maps, with shadows created on the level's wall.

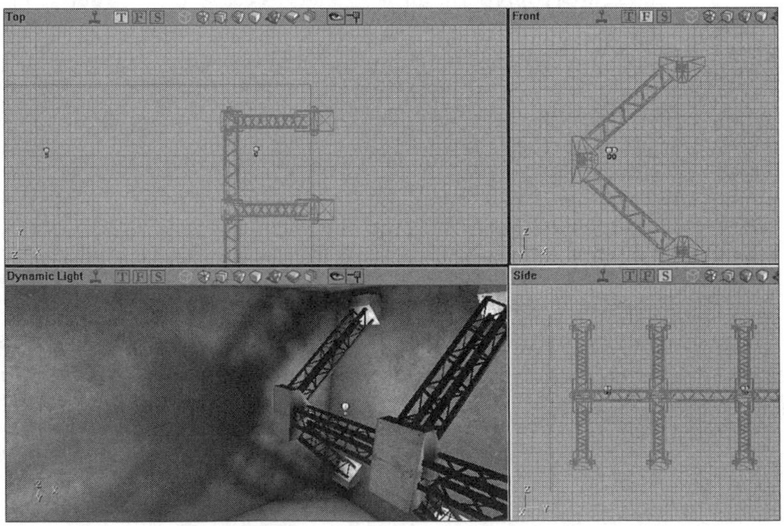

FIGURE 7.1 The shadows in this image are precalculated, meaning they are static and never change.

Light Placement

Light maps are created based on a series of factors; one of the most important is the placement of lights in your level. As you position lights in your worlds, you must take many things into account. You must consider the look you're trying to achieve, the textures on the surfaces you're lighting, the position of surrounding geometry, and what the shadows from that geometry will look like. If your lights are too close to the surface being lit, the light will have an unrealistic dimness; if they are too far away, the surface might also be too dim. Make sure you pay special attention to the kinds of lights you're using and how you're adjusting their properties. For example, if you're trying to create a room with dramatic shadows, you must make sure your lights are placed at an interesting angle in relation to the scene's geometry. You must also make sure you don't use too many lights, as this can wash shadows out. At the end of this chapter, in "Common Lighting Pitfalls," is a series of common problems many beginning lighters make.

Light Classification

Two main kinds of lights are available in Unreal: *static lights* and *dynamic lights*. The fundamental difference is that dynamic lights can be animated, and static lights cannot. The following subsections examine both lights, describe how they are used, and explain some rules you must keep in mind when placing them in your levels.

Static Lights

Static lights, also called normal lights, are the main light type used to light your levels in Unreal. Only static lights can be used to create light maps, so all cast shadows in your level must be created by static lights. As their name implies, static lights are intended to be stationary. Even if you could move a static light's Actor in the game, the visual effect of its emitted light would remain unchanged. Even if you forced a static light to animate, its subsequent shadows would stay still because areas of light and shadow in your levels are created with light maps. This behavior makes it possible to have beautifully realistic shadows (see **FIGURE 7.2**) without constantly updating them during gameplay, but also means you should never force a static light to animate.

FIGURE 7.2 Detailed shadows in DM-Gael, created by static lights.

Dynamic Lights

Dynamic lights are intended to be mobile. In Unreal, dynamic lights are often used when a light source must be in motion, such as the light emitted from firing weapons or explosions. When using dynamic lights, keep in mind that they are far more processor intensive than static lights. For this reason, they should always be used in moderation, not as a primary source of illumination.

A major consideration when using dynamic lights is how the graphics engine displays them. Behaviorally, dynamic lights function similarly to static lights. However, dynamic lights don't create cast shadows. Instead, they offer a more general kind of surface lighting, in which any polygons facing the light source receive light and polygons facing away do not. Furthermore, dynamic lights can be animated, which means you can use them for special effects, such as flickering and pulsing lights, or lights that move throughout your level. You'll look at creating and using dynamic lights later in this chapter in "Using a TriggerLight."

Light Properties

> **NOTE**
>
> **Some properties available in a light's Properties window are no longer functional because of changes in the Unreal Engine through its evolution from the original Unreal to Unreal Tournament 2004.**

A variety of properties control the look of your lights (see **FIGURE 7.3**). They include color and brightness, whether a corona is used, and whether the light is static or dynamic. In the following subsections, you explore several light properties and see what they do.

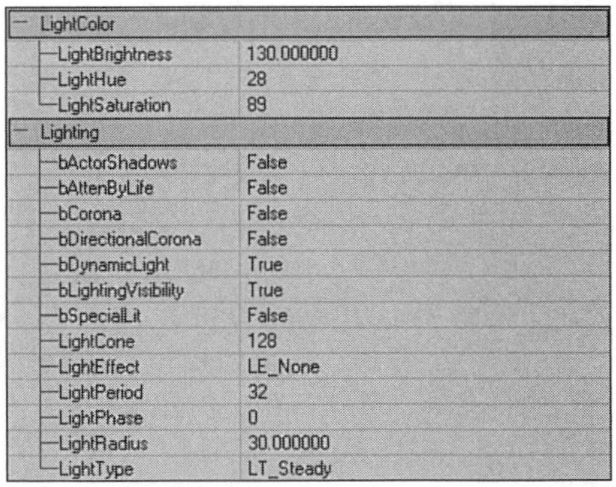

FIGURE 7.3 **Light properties with light-related sections expanded.**

Light Color

As the name of the property suggests, `LightColor` is used to control the color of your light. The color is controlled through three settings: `LightBrightness`, `LightHue`, and `LightSaturation`. These settings are similar to the hue, saturation, and brightness values available in graphics programs, such as Photoshop. Hue typically refers to the actual color being used, such as red, blue, purple, or any color of the rainbow. Saturation controls how intense that color appears, and brightness adds levels of white or black to the color to create a variety of shades or tints. `LightHue` and `LightSaturation` values are limited to ranges of 0 to 255, reflecting the RGB (red, green, and blue) values assigned to the property. `LightBrightness`, on the other hand, has no maximum value. You must use this property with care, however, as setting it too high can make your textures look overbright. Typically, you should stick with values of 255 or lower to keep the light's falloff (the amount at which it fades at a given distance) from looking unrealistic.

Light Radius

Every light in Unreal has an area of effect, which is determined by the `LightRadius` property. Within the radius set by this property is at least some amount of light. Outside a light's radius, no light exists. This property gives you a useful way to increase a light's intensity. Using this property, you can control the distance that light travels from its source. In **FIGURES 7.4** and **7.5**, you can see the effects of small and large `LightRadius` settings.

FIGURE 7.4 A single light with a small radius.

Light Type and Light Effects

The `LightType` property has been made obsolete in recent versions of the Unreal Engine. In the past, this property enabled you to create lights that pulsed, flickered, or behaved like strobe lights. You can still create these effects, but you must use a new kind of Actor called a *Projector*. Projectors and some of the remaining LightEffects are discussed later in this chapter.

FIGURE 7.5 A single light with a large radius.

Directional Lights

A *directional light* can be aimed in a specific direction, like a flashlight. Technically, a directional light is any light with its `bDirectional` property set to True. You can set it yourself, or you can create Actors that have the property already set. There are two such Actors: Sunlight and Spotlight. In the following subsections, you see how these Actors can be used in your scenes.

Sunlight

A *Sunlight* is a special kind of Actor that enables you to simulate a light source that's infinitely far away, such as the sun. It's especially useful for outdoor levels or any environment where you can see outdoors. Because the light appears to be infinitely far away, all cast shadows created from this light are parallel (see **FIGURE 7.6**), instead of fanning out from a single point as they do with a standard light (see **FIGURE 7.7**).

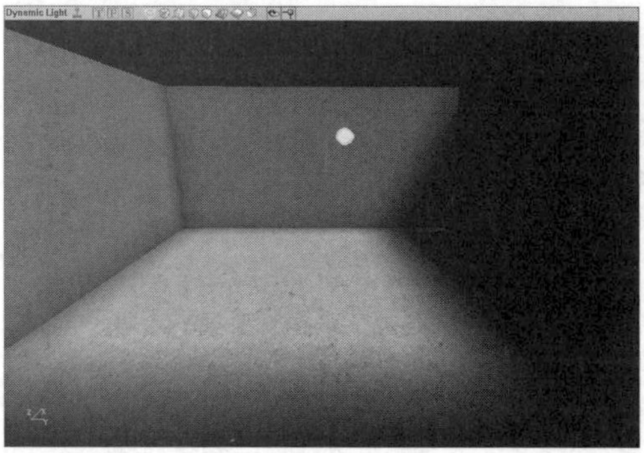

FIGURE 7.6 Sunlight scene.

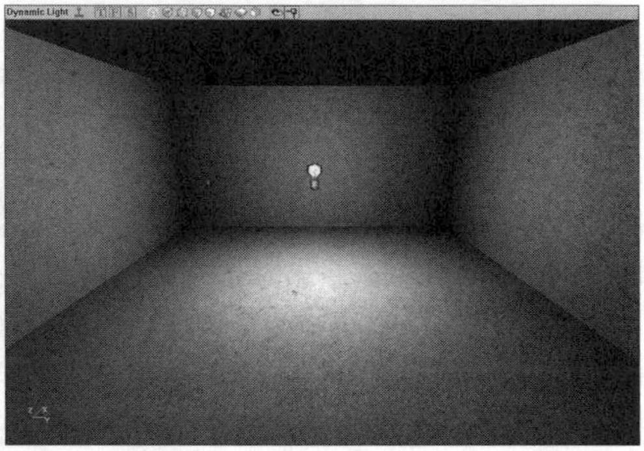

FIGURE 7.7 Normal light scene.

The most important thing to remember when working with a Sunlight is that the Actor itself emits no light. Instead, you designate a surface to be used to emit light. This surface, called a *fake backdrop*, is usually textured with some sort of skylike material. In **TUTORIAL 7.1**, you see how to create a skybox and use it to make your level appear to have a sky. This skybox serves as the basis for your Sunlight.

TUTORIAL 7.1: Creating a Simple Skybox

1. Open the `Sunlight_Start.ut2` file. This large room has two crossbeams set midway down the walls (see **FIGURE 7.8**). Notice that the room is composed of two subtracted cubes.

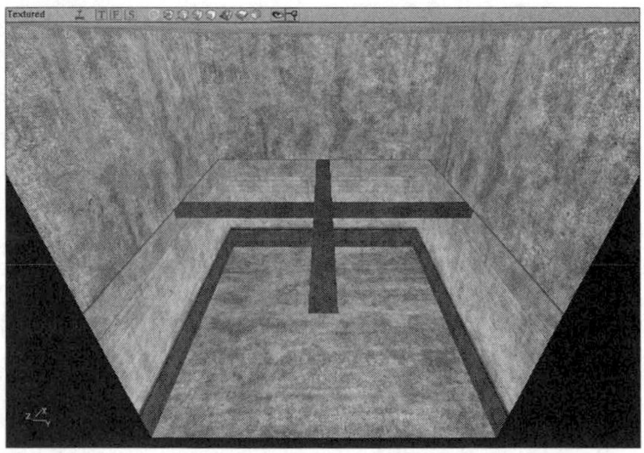

FIGURE 7.8 This is what you should see when you open the *`Sunlight_Start.ut2`* level.

2. In the Texture browser, open the Chapter7 package, and select the `panningClouds` texture.

3. To produce a convincing sky, you need to create a skybox. Do this by creating a 64×1024×1024 cube somewhere away from your level. Its position doesn't matter because this cube is used as a sample for the fake backdrop of the Sunlight.

4. Add two lights about 128 units away from the center of the new skybox (see **FIGURE 7.9**).
5. Double-click one of the lights, and in the Properties window, open the LightColor tab. Set the following properties:

   LightHue: 25

   LightSaturation: 100

6. Open the Actor Class browser, expand Info > ZoneInfo, and click SkyZoneInfo. Right-click the floor of the skybox, and choose Add SkyZoneInfo Here. Move the new Actor close to the floor of the Skybox.

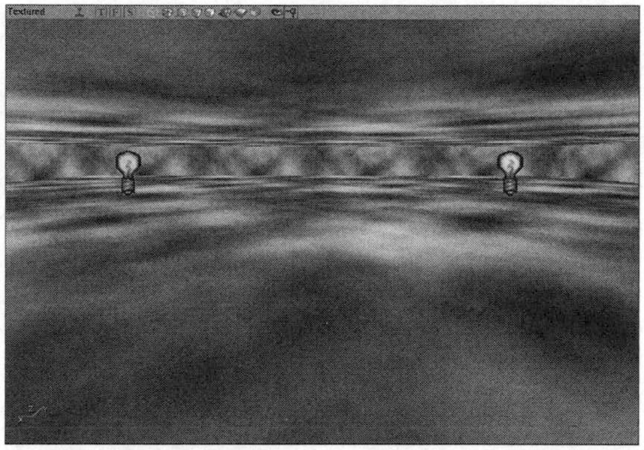

FIGURE 7.9 Lights added to the skybox.

7. In the main room, select all the faces of the top cube—the surfaces above the crossbeams. Right-click one of the selected surfaces, and choose Surface Properties.
8. Under the Flags tab, click the Fake Backdrop check box, and close the window. Rebuild the level's lighting, and activate Textured view in the 3D viewport. You can now press K to activate the skybox preview. Notice that the upper part of the main room appears to open into a cloudy sky and that the clouds don't move in relation to the camera.
9. Deactivate the preview by pressing K again. Save the level when finished.

END TUTORIAL 7.1

In **TUTORIAL 7.2**, you place a Sunlight in the level, which emits light from the fake backdrop of the level's upper surfaces. You then position and aim this light and use it to cast parallel shadows onto the level's floor.

TUTORIAL 7.2: Creating a Sunlight

1. Continue from **TUTORIAL 7.1**, or open the file saved at the end of that tutorial. In the Actor Class browser, select Light > Sunlight. Right-click and place this Actor anywhere in the main room. Its position is irrelevant, but for this example, place it in one of the room's upper corners (see **FIGURE 7.10**).
2. On the 3D viewport toolbar, click the Lock to Selected Actor icon, and then click the Sunlight Actor. The camera jumps to the exact location and orientation of the Sunlight.
3. As long as Lock to Selected Actor is active, when you rotate the camera, the Sunlight rotates as well. In a sense, you're using the camera to aim the light. Rotate the camera so that the crosshairs point at the center of the crossbeams, as shown in **FIGURE 7.11**.

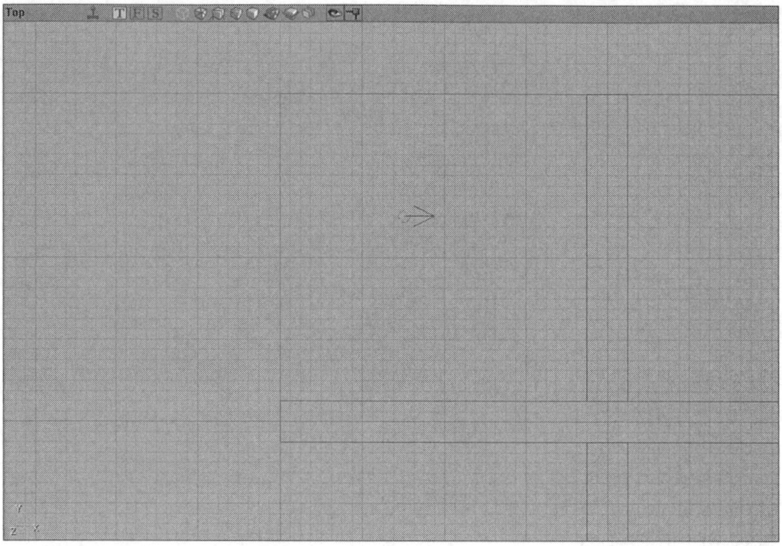

FIGURE 7.10 Sunlight added to main room.

4. Deactivate the Lock to Selected Actor option, and move the camera away from the Sunlight.

5. Double-click the Sunlight to open its Properties window, and then expand the Light Color tab. Set the following properties:

   LightHue: 31

   LightSaturation: 143

FIGURE 7.11 Sunlight aligned by using Lock to Selected Actor.

6. Next, you need to create a "filler" light to soften the shadows in the main room. Holding down the L key, click on the center of the main room's floor.

7. Double-click the new light to open its Properties window, and open the Lighting tab. Set the `LightEffect` property to `LE_NonIncidence`.

8. Rebuild and switch to Dynamic Light mode in the 3D viewport. Notice that the shadows on the ground are a bit blurry.

9. Select all five surfaces of the bottom half of the room. The easiest way to do this is to select one wall and press Shift+B.
10. Right-click any of the selected walls, and choose Surface Properties from the context menu.
11. Under the Pan/Rot/Scale tab, set Light Map to 8, and rebuild the lights. The final result should look something like **FIGURE 7.12**.

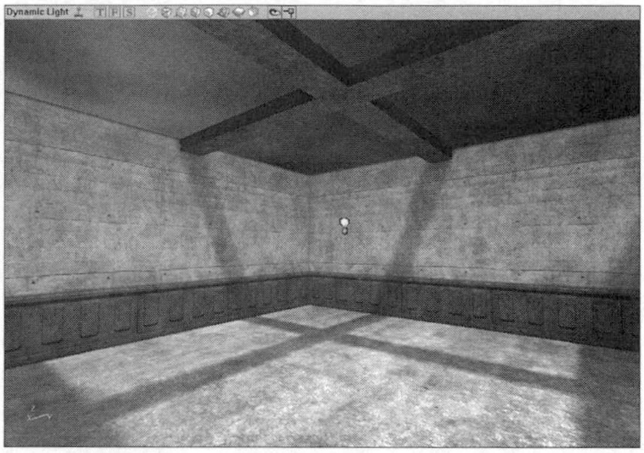

FIGURE 7.12 Clean shadows from an adjusted Light Map value.

END TUTORIAL 7.2

Spotlights

Spotlights are special Actors that create a directional light you can aim around your level, much like their real-world counterparts. Spotlights are a useful way to create realistic lighting in your levels, such as lamps, searchlights, and more. In **TUTORIAL 7.3**, you learn how to create and aim Spotlights to control the look of lights in your levels.

TUTORIAL 7.3: Using Spotlights

1. Open the `Spotlight_start.ut2` file, which contains a large room with a tall stone pedestal in the center (see **FIGURE 7.13**).
2. To create a Spotlight, in the Actor Class browser, expand Light, and select Spotlight.
3. Right-click in one of the upper corners of the room, and choose Add Spotlight Here. If you look at this new Actor in the Top viewport, you can see an arrow pointing out of it (see **FIGURE 7.14**). This arrow means that it's a directional light.

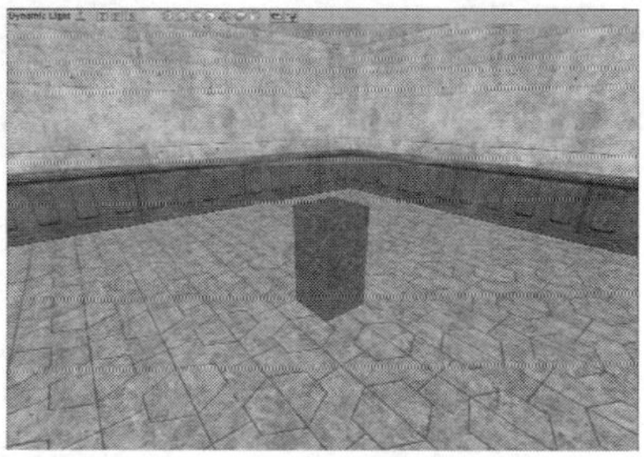

FIGURE 7.13 A view of the *`Spotlight_start.ut2`* level.

4. Using the skills you learned in **TUTORIAL 7.2**, click the Lock to Selected Actor icon to aim the light at the stone pedestal in the middle of the room (see **FIGURE 7.15**).

5. Deactivate the Lock to Selected Actor option, and set the following properties for the light:

   In the LightColor tab

   LightBrightness: 128

   LightHue: 170

   LightSaturation: 178

   In the Lighting tab

   LightRadius: 128

6. Rebuild lighting, and test the level. A Player Start has already been created for you. Notice that the light is staying within a cone shape (see **FIGURE 7.16**). You can change the size of this cone to suit your needs. Exit Unreal when finished, and go back to UnrealEd.

7. In the Spotlight's Properties window, open the Lighting tab, and set `LightCone` to 64. Notice in the 3D viewport that the cone of light gets smaller.

8. You now have less light in your level. The light was fairly dim already, so counteract the smaller light cone by setting `LightBrightness` to 200.

9. Rebuild your level. The effect should be similar to bright moonlight (see **FIGURE 7.17**). Test your level and see what it looks like.

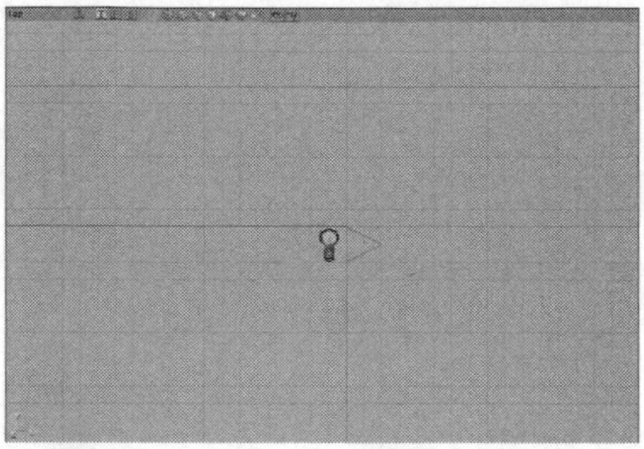

FIGURE 7.14 Spotlight added to the corner of the room.

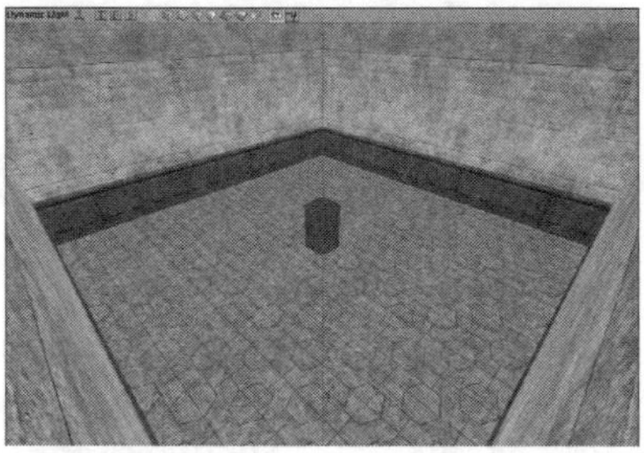

FIGURE 7.15 Spotlight aligned using Lock to Selected Actor.

FIGURE 7.16 Current lighting result after setting color and radius properties.

FIGURE 7.17 Final result.

END TUTORIAL 7.3

Lighting Workflow

When you first begin working with lights and trying to light your levels, you must first think about the appropriate light types for different situations, such as a Sunlight for outdoor effects or a Spotlight for theatrically focused light effects. You have to be able to control how you see lights in the viewports, how to fine-tune properties such as light falloff, and how and when to rebuild your light maps. At times you might also need to export your light maps from UnrealEd so that you can edit them in another program. In the following sections, you learn how to approach these aspects of lighting.

Light Creation

You have already seen basic light creation in UnrealEd through several chapters of this book. There are, however, a few workflow aspects of light creation that still need to be discussed. This section covers some new methods for creating lights in UnrealEd.

The first way to create lights has already been explained: Simply right-click on a surface, and choose Add Light Here. This method is most easily done in the 3D viewport, as you have more precise control over exactly where the light is placed. You can do this in orthographic views if you like, but you'll find that the light might not always be placed exactly where you want it. For example, if you place a light in a room using the Top viewport, the light might not be positioned correctly in the Z-axis (vertically), especially if your level had several floors. For this reason, creating your lights by right-clicking a surface in the 3D viewport is usually easier and more accurate.

The second method for creating lights is much faster than using the right-click method. You can automatically create a light by holding down the L key and clicking. This method is similar to using the right-click menu, in that you have more precise placement by using the 3D viewport rather than orthographic views, but you don't have to worry about navigating the context menu.

Another important method for creating your lights is simple duplication. This method becomes important when you need a light with the same settings as one already placed in your level. Say, for example, that you have set up a certain light with just the right color and brightness, and you need to create one just like it. Simply duplicating the one you have already is much faster than building one from scratch and adjusting all its properties.

Viewing Lights

When working with lights in your levels, being able to control how you see them is important. In UnrealEd, you can alter the way lights appear based on the type of lighting task you're doing. This section describes some viewport settings that control how you see lights in your levels.

The first mode—the default mode for the Perspective viewport—is the Dynamic Light mode. You'll probably use this viewport mode most often when working with lights in UnrealEd. This mode enables you to see all light maps and cast shadows created when you rebuild your lights and gives you the closest possible approximation of what the level will look like during play (see **FIGURE 7.18**). When you first create a light, the viewport gets brighter while you're in this mode. However, this preview is only an estimate of your light maps and doesn't include shadows. You must rebuild your lights to see the effect of any light changes.

FIGURE 7.18 Map with viewport in Dynamic Light mode.

Textured mode enables you to see your level without lighting being a factor. All lighting in the level is equal, with no shadows of any kind (see **FIGURE 7.19**). The effect is much like turning on a single master light for your level. This mode can be handy when you're working on a dark or dimly lit level and need to see your workspace. However, you must remember to switch back to Dynamic Light mode if you want to see the effects of your lights. For this reason, typically you don't use Textured mode much when creating or placing lights.

FIGURE 7.19 Map with viewport in Textured mode.

Lighting Only mode deactivates all textures in your level, leaving only the light maps on a clean white surface (see **FIGURE 7.20**). This mode is perfect for viewing your level's shadows without having to work around any textures you might have. For example, say you've created a level with dark textures. Controlling the exact location of all your shadows could be difficult if they were placed on top of these textures. With Lighting Only mode, seeing where all your shadows are falling is much easier.

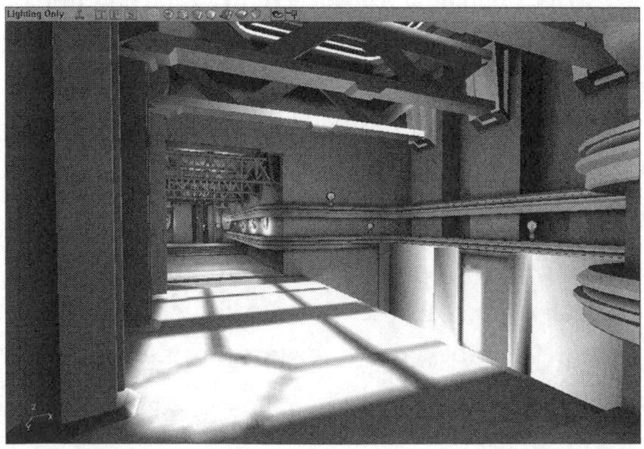

FIGURE 7.20 Map with viewport in Lighting Only mode.

Radii view is a special setting that can be used in any viewport. To access this view, right-click on a blank area of the viewport, and choose Actor > Radii View. This view enables you to see any Actor's area of effect. For lights, it's based on the `LightRadius` property found under the Lighting tab of the Properties window. A light's radius can be thought of as the maximum distance that light travels from its source. In the viewport, a radius is seen as a large red circle (see **FIGURE 7.21**). No light falls outside this circle. Therefore, you can use the Radii view to make certain the light's radius actually encloses your level. You want to keep all surfaces requiring light from a single source to be within that source's radius.

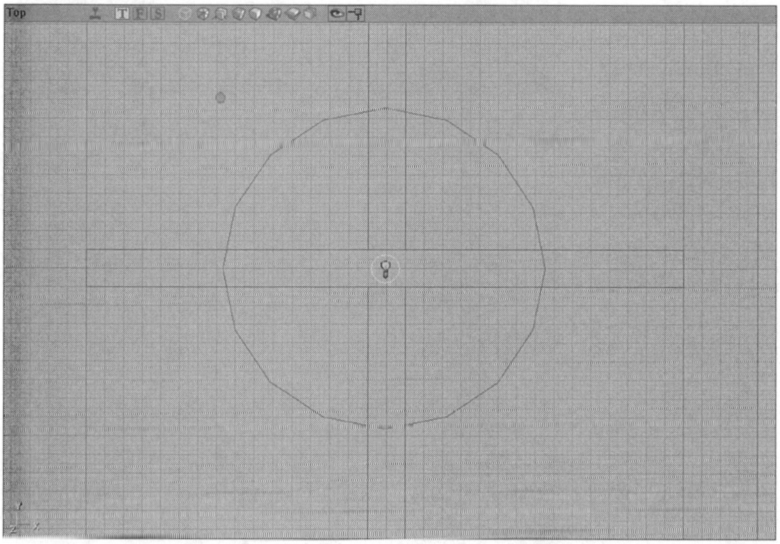

FIGURE 7.21 An orthographic view with light radius.

Working with Light Effects

Now that you know each light has a radius, and you've seen how to view that radius, you can learn how light changes inside the radius. *Falloff* is the degradation of light as it gets farther from its source. For example, the farther an object is from a light, the less light it receives.

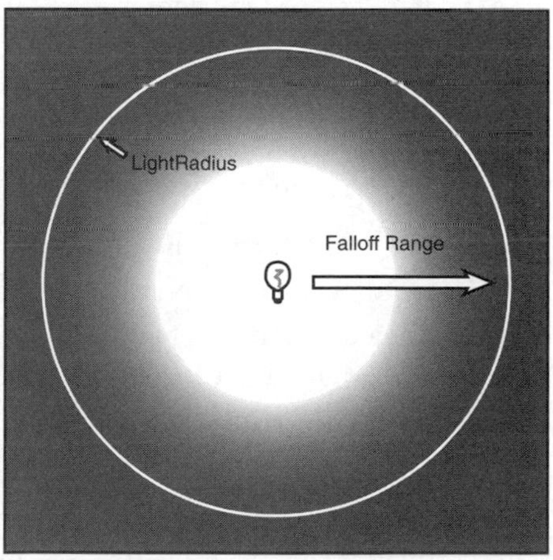

FIGURE 7.22 The falloff range is determined by the *`LightRadius`*.

You can think of falloff as a gradient that moves from the light source to the edge of the radius, going from light to dark (see **FIGURE 7.22**). By changing the falloff, you can greatly alter the look of your lights. In Unreal, several LightEffect settings, discussed in the following sections, control falloff. You can find them under the `LightEffect` property in the Lighting tab of the Properties window.

`LE_None`

`LE_None` is the default setting for the `LightEffect` property. It generates a constant rate of falloff from the source of the light to the radius. For example, as soon as an object is moved away from the light, it begins to receive less light from the source. The location of the light Actor receives 100% illumination, and objects past the edge of the radius receive no light at all. Between those points is a constant decrease in light intensity (see **FIGURE 7.23**).

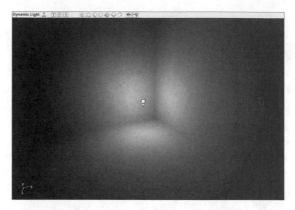

FIGURE 7.23 A light in the corner set to *LE_NONE*.

`LE_NonIncidence`

The `LE_NonIncidence` setting changes the falloff so that the light stays bright closer to its source, and then falls off quickly as it approaches the radius (see **FIGURE 7.24**). This setting is handy when you're trying to create brighter lights that don't fade as much as standard lights.

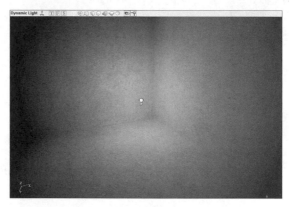

FIGURE 7.24 A light in the corner set to *LE_NonIncidence*.

`LE_QuadraticNonIncidence`

A Quadratic Non-Incidence light behaves similarly to a regular Non-Incidence light, but with even less light decay. This means the light stays bright much farther from the source, and then falls off rapidly near the edge of the radius (see **FIGURE 7.25**). This setting can be useful if you're trying to simulate the hot spot or light cone of a spotlight.

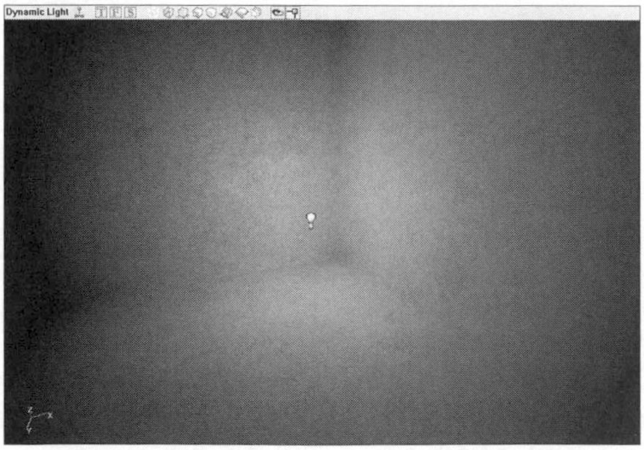

FIGURE 7.25 Room with a Quadratic Non-Incidence light in the corner.

Animated Light Effects

Animated light effects are also available, such as `LE_Disco`, `LE_Rotor`, and `LE_Warp`. These effects are animated only within UnrealEd, however, and move only until you rebuild your lights. The effect is then baked into the light maps and is no longer animated inside the level. You can use animated light effects to create interesting static effects for your lights; however, keep in mind that each time you rebuild, the effect is slightly different.

Rebuilding Lights

Whenever you add or change lights in your level, you need to rebuild those lights to see how your changes affect your light maps. For example, when you change your lights' color or brightness, the 3D viewport gets brighter as soon as you alter a property. This preview, however, is not an exact representation of the lights in your level. In **TUTORIAL 7.4**, you see the importance of rebuilding your lights when you edit their placement or quantity.

TUTORIAL 7.4: Rebuilding Lighting

1. Open the `Rebuilding1.ut2` file, which contains a room similar to the one you have used in previous tutorials.
2. Using the skills you have learned, place a light somewhere in the level to create an interesting shadow from the pedestal in the middle of the room.
3. Rebuild your lighting to see what the shadows look like. Compare your results with **FIGURE 7.26**.
4. Create a second light in the room, using any means you choose. Notice that as soon as the new light is created, your shadows look different. Rebuild your lights to see the new shadows (see **FIGURE 7.27**).

FIGURE 7.26 Light placed next to a wall.

FIGURE 7.27 Second light added to the level.

5. Now select either light, and move it to a new location. As soon as you do this, the shadows associated with that light cease to exist. The engine is trying to give you an approximation of the light based on where you move it (see **FIGURE 7.28**). The effect is similar to the look of dynamic lights moved in-game.

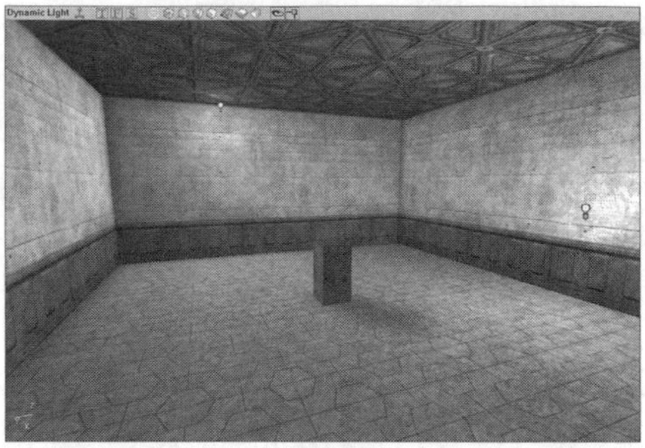

FIGURE 7.28 Approximated lighting after moving the light.

6. Now rebuild the lights, and see the new shadows you have created (see **FIGURE 7.29**). Whenever you move or change a light, you must rebuild your light map to get a clear picture of what the new position or settings create in your level.

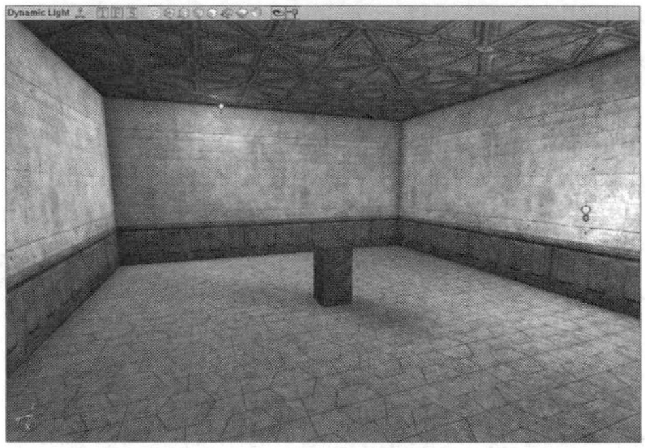

FIGURE 7.29 Final lighting after rebuilding.

END TUTORIAL 7.4

When working with lighting, remember that you might not always need to rebuild every single light in your level. Although running a full rebuild before you play-test or finalize a level is a good idea, you can save a great deal of time by using the Build Changed Lights Only button on the toolbar. In **TUTORIAL 7.5**, you see how this tool works and how you can use it to speed up your lighting workflow.

TUTORIAL 7.5: Rebuilding Changed Lights

1. Open the `Rebuilding2.ut2` file. You'll see the hangar and control room level created in Chapter 3, "Creating Your First Level with UnrealEd."

2. Navigate into the hangar area, where you'll see a series of girders with a pair of lights behind them (see **FIGURE 7.30**).

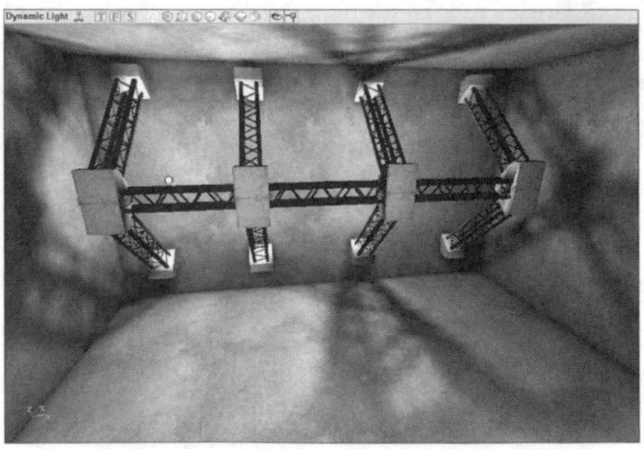

FIGURE 7.30 Backlit girders.

3. This scene would look better with one light behind each girder. Using the skills you have learned, move the two existing lights, and place one behind each girder, but don't rebuild the lighting yet.

4. Because this level is already large and detailed, rebuilding all the lights would take some time. Instead, you can tell UnrealEd to rebuild only the lights you have changed. Click the Build Changed Lights icon on the toolbar.

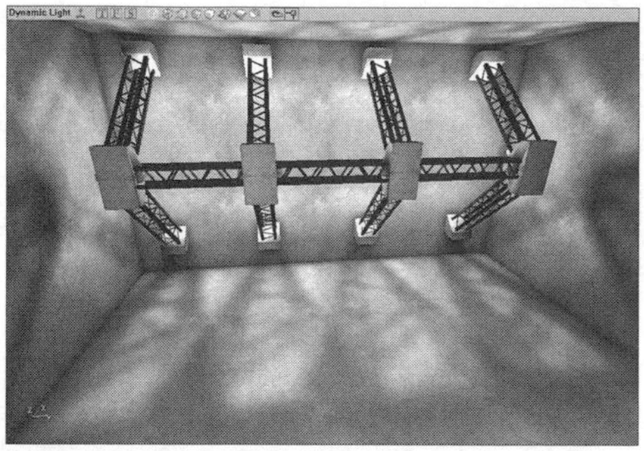

FIGURE 7.31 Final result.

5. This method is much faster than rebuilding every light in your level. If you like, you can try rebuilding all lights, just to make a comparison. When finished, you should have something like **FIGURE 7.31**.

END TUTORIAL 7.5

Light Map Size

You can control the accuracy of your light maps with the Light Map setting in the Surface Properties window. This property controls the resolution of your light maps to change their detail. The higher you set this value, the less accurate your shadows look on the surface. If the number is lower, your shadows are much more crisp. However, because you're increasing the light map's resolution, in effect, you're creating a larger calculation. This doesn't mean you always slow down gameplay if you use lower Light Map size settings. Rather, it's just a reminder that your shadows don't always need to be perfectly sharp. In fact, lower resolution shadows often create a soft shadow effect, such as when an object is lit by multiple light sources from the same general direction. In **TUTORIAL 7.6**, you learn how to adjust the Light Map setting to control the look of your shadows.

TUTORIAL 7.6: Adjusting Light Map Size

1. Open the `LightMap_start.ut2` file. You'll see a cylindrical room with a girder hovering in the middle and a light behind it. Notice that the girder's shadow crosses over five surfaces on the wall.

2. Select the leftmost surface that's receiving a shadow from the girder (see **FIGURE 7.32**). Right-click on the surface, and choose Surface Properties.

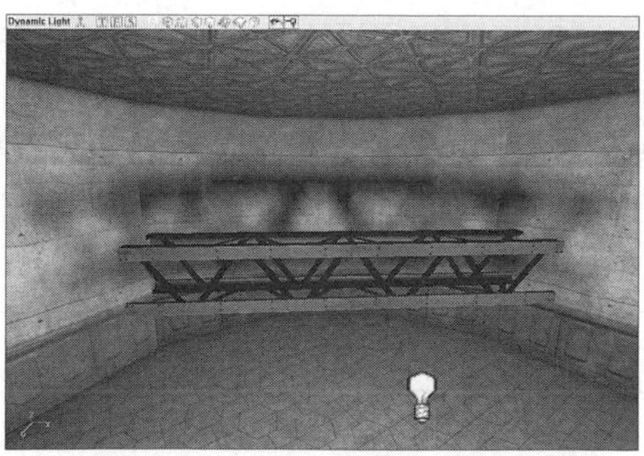

FIGURE 7.32 Leftmost surface selected.

3. In the Pan/Rot/Scale tab, change the Light Map value to 1.0 (see **FIGURE 7.33**), the sharpest setting you can achieve.
4. Select the next surface to the right, and repeat step 3, setting Light Map to 4.
5. Using these techniques, set the Light Map value for the next face to the right to 16. Set the next surface's Light Map to 64 and the last surface to 256.
6. Rebuild your lighting, and notice the differences in shadow clarity. On the left, you have very sharp shadows. As you move to the right, the shadows become more vague until they're barely distinguishable (see **FIGURE 7.34**).

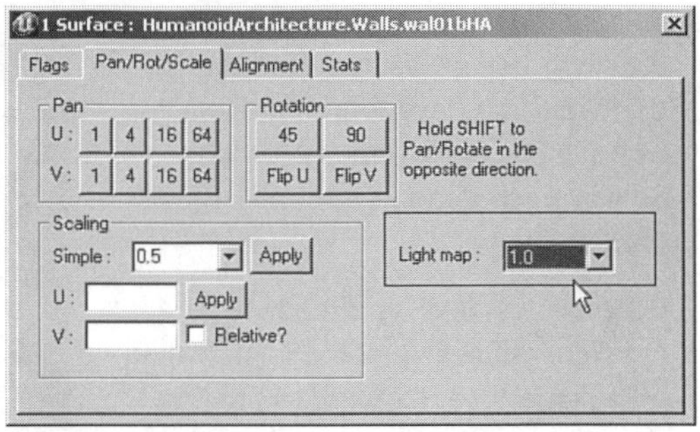

FIGURE 7.33 Light map value set to 1.

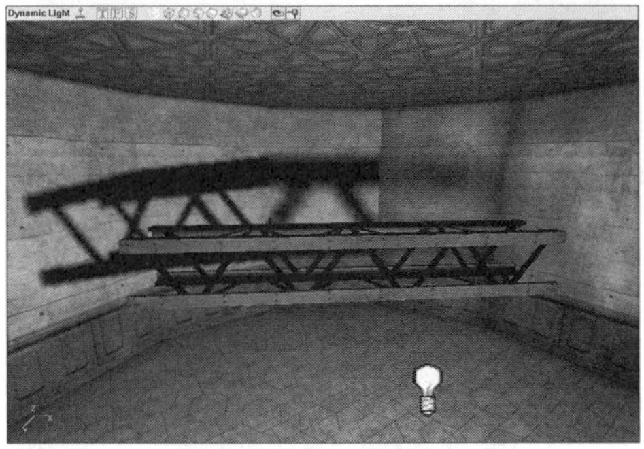

FIGURE 7.34 Final result.

END TUTORIAL 7.6

You can use these settings to control the level of detail for your shadows, but be careful not to use the sharpest setting too often, as it could slow down your level.

Lighting Surfaces

When lighting your levels, you'll notice that light behaves differently based on what kind of surface is being lit. The following sections explain how light affects a variety of surfaces in Unreal and some factors you need to be aware of when lighting such surfaces. World geometry, static meshes, Movers, terrain, meshes, and particles are also discussed.

World Geometry

The world geometry of your levels receives the most accurate representation of lights, largely because lights create light maps for world geometry during rebuilding. As mentioned previously, the clarity of these light maps depends on the light map size you set for each surface in the level. You get most of your level's shadows on the surface of world geometry, as shown in **FIGURE 7.35**.

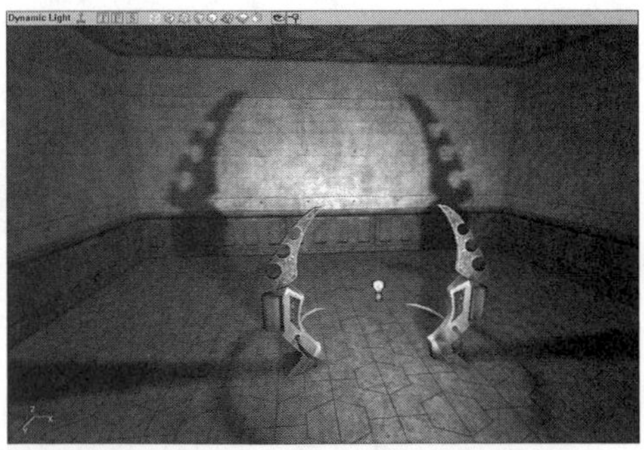

FIGURE 7.35 Room with lights casting shadows on world geometry.

Static Meshes, Meshes, and Movers

Static meshes receive shadows differently than world geometry does. They don't receive shadow maps in UnrealEd, but they cast shadows onto world geometry or terrain. Therefore, precise shadows can't fall across static meshes, but static meshes can cause those shadows. Static meshes receive a more basic lighting, in that surfaces of the static mesh facing a light source appear illuminated, and surfaces facing away from the light source receive no lighting. This means that static mesh surfaces that are opposite a light source receive no light from that source. However, this effect is usually adequate for your levels.

FIGURE 7.36 Light seems to come through the door, even though it's closed.

Meshes, such as animated characters, receive light similarly to static meshes. They can't receive shadows, nor can they self-shadow. They are lit in such a way that surfaces facing the light source receive light, and surfaces facing away receive none.

FIGURE 7.37 This is what it should look like if the door did block light.

Because a Mover is simply a static mesh that has been set into motion, it receives light in exactly the same way as a standard static mesh. It can't receive shadows, but it can cast them on world geometry. However, this poses a problem because light maps are static, not animated. So while a Mover is in motion, its light map shadow remains stationary. In **FIGURES 7.36** and **7.37**, notice how light is passing "through" the door, even though it's closed.

Terrain

Terrain receives light maps similarly to world geometry, but the light maps are stored in a slightly different fashion. When you create light maps on world geometry, the light and shadow areas are stored in a file with a layout that includes all surfaces of your level, as though every surface were laid out flat and side by side. When dealing with terrain, on the other hand, your light map is a bird's-eye view of the entire terrain surface, with all the light and shadow areas in place as though you were looking at the terrain from high above. You can view this combination of light map and color texture in the Texture browser, as shown in **FIGURE 7.38**.

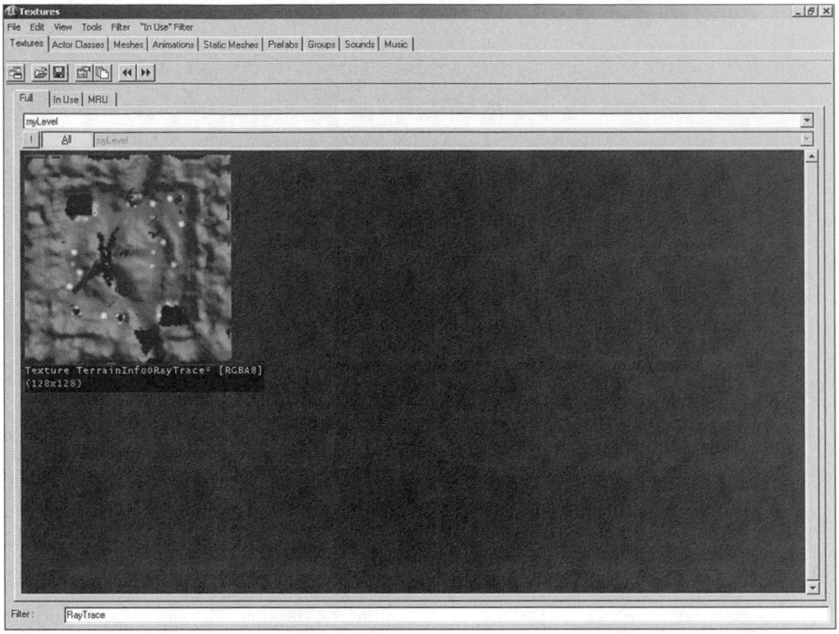

FIGURE 7.38 Light map from terrain.

Particles

Most particles don't receive light at all. An exception is particles from a mesh emitter, which actually emits instances of static meshes. These static meshes receive very general lighting, the same as any other static mesh (see **FIGURE 7.39**). For more information on particles and how to create them in UnrealEd, refer to Chapter 10, "Creating Particle Effects."

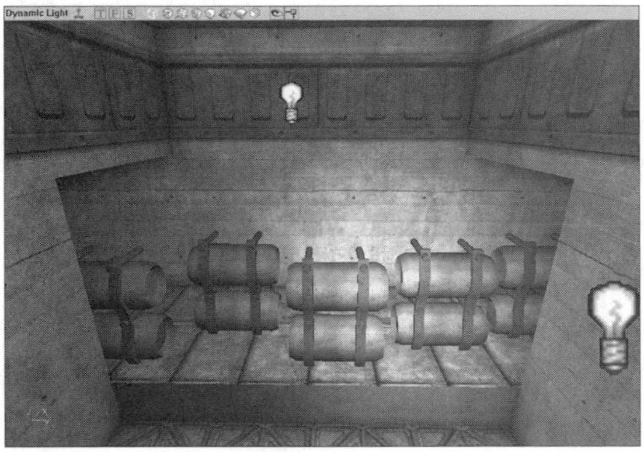

FIGURE 7.39 Mesh emitter objects under the Spotlight appear brighter.

Advanced Lighting Effects

This section explains several lighting techniques reserved for special situations: using the `SpecialLit` property to control which surfaces receive light, using ambient lighting, emitting light from other Actors, creating light coronas, and using TriggerLights.

Scaling Lights

The Scale Lights tool enables you to control the light brightness of several or all lights in your level simultaneously. This tool can be a tremendous time saver when you need to adjust multiple light sources but don't want to go through each one's Properties window. In **TUTORIAL 7.7**, you see how to access this tool and use it to control several different lights at the same time.

TUTORIAL 7.7: Scaling Lights in a Level

1. Open the `scaleLights.ut2` file, which contains a large room.
2. Using the skills you have learned, place three lights along the ceiling, evenly spaced from left to right (see **FIGURE 7.40**).
3. Set the lights' properties as follows (see the results in **FIGURE 7.41**):

   Leftmost light

   Light Brightness: 100

   Center light

   Light Brightness: 50

   Rightmost light

   Light Brightness: 10

4. Select all three lights, and choose Tools > Scale Lights from the main menu to open the Scale Lights dialog box, shown in **FIGURE 7.42**.
5. The window has two settings: Literal Value and Percentage. Select the Literal Value option, and enter `10` in the Value text box. Click OK, and rebuild your lights. If you don't notice the change, check the `LightBrightness` properties of your lights. They are now 110, 60, and 20, respectively, because Literal Value mode adds the value you enter to all selected lights. You can also add negative numbers to take brightness away.

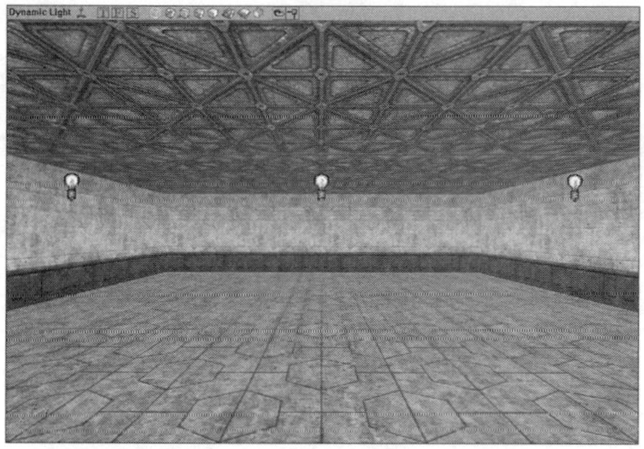

FIGURE 7.40 Three lights spaced evenly across the ceiling.

FIGURE 7.41 Current lighting with brightness properties set.

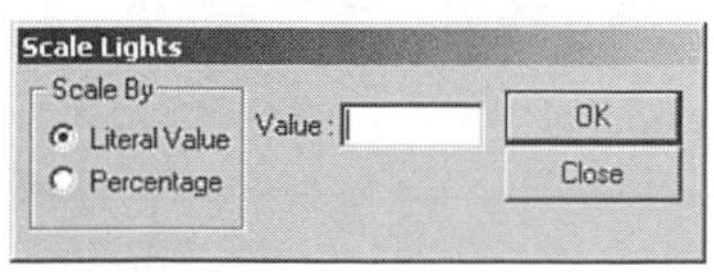

FIGURE 7.42 The Scale Lights dialog box.

6. Now switch to the Percentage option. Enter a value of 50, click OK, and rebuild your lights. Your level is now much brighter. If you check your `LightBrightness` values, you'll find they are now 165, 90, and 30 because the Percentage mode adds the percentage specified in the Value text box. You entered 50, so UnrealEd increased each light's current brightness by 50%. If you had input 100 instead of 50, it would have added 100% to each light, effectively doubling its `LightBrightness` value. In **FIGURE 7.43**, you can see the effect this setting has on lights in the level.

FIGURE 7.43 Final result after scaling the lights.

END TUTORIAL 7.7

Using `SpecialLit`

The `SpecialLit` property enables you to control which lights are illuminating a specific surface. For example, you can make your lights illuminate only a single surface or a series of surfaces. Conversely, you could make your lights illuminate all but a specific selection of surfaces.

The `SpecialLit` property is available in the Properties windows for lights and world geometry surfaces. The property works like this: If you have set a light's `SpecialLit` property to True, it illuminates only surfaces with their `SpecialLit` property also set to True. In **TUTORIAL 7.8**, you see how this works.

TUTORIAL 7.8: Using the *`SpecialLit`* Property

1. Open the `SpecialLit_start.ut2` file, which contains the room you've been working on, with no lights in it.

2. Create two lights, one on each side of the pyramid, about midway between the floor and ceiling. Give the lights the following settings:

Left light	Right light
LightBrightness: 150	LightBrightness: 150
LightHue: 170	LightHue: 0
LightSaturation: 0	LightSaturation: 0

These settings give you two bold lights: one blue and one red (see **FIGURE 7.44**).

3. Rebuild the lighting if you want to see the shadows. Then select the red light and open its Properties window. In the Lighting tab, set the `bSpecialLit` property to True, and rebuild the lighting. Now only the blue light is lighting the room (see **FIGURE 7.45**).

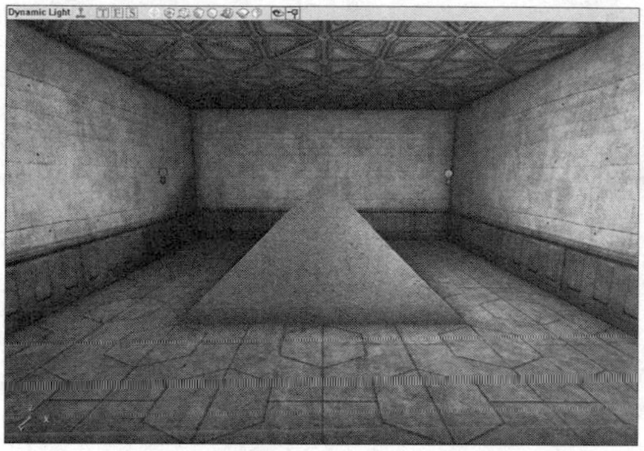

FIGURE 7.44 Red and blue lights blending across the pyramid.

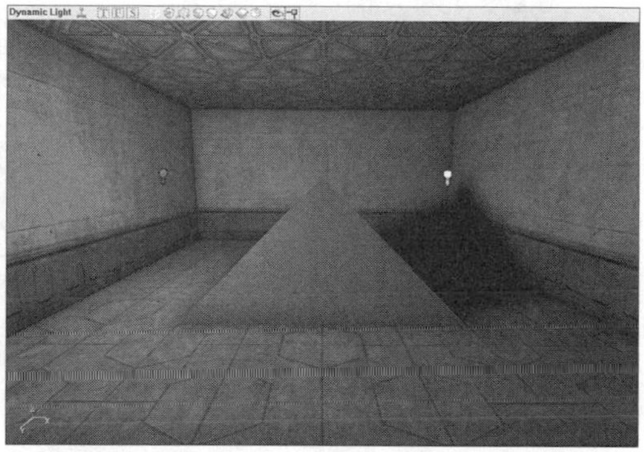

FIGURE 7.45 With the red light set to *SpecialLit*, the room becomes completely blue.

4. Select the nearest surface on the pyramid in the middle of the room. Right-click on it, and open its Properties window. In the Flags tab, select the Special Lit check box.

5. Rebuild your lighting. Notice that the pyramid's selected face is now receiving red light instead of blue (see **FIGURE 7.46**). Surfaces with the Special Lit flag selected receive light only from lights with the `bSpecialLit` property set to True.

FIGURE 7.46 Only the pyramid receives red light.

END TUTORIAL 7.8

Ambient Lighting

Setting your level's ambient light is a good way to control the overall lighting. This setting applies constant light to every surface of your level, be it in light or in shadow. It's a good way to lighten your level if it's too dark in some areas. In **TUTORIAL 7.9**, you see how to adjust the ambient lighting of your levels.

TUTORIAL 7.9: Using Ambient Lighting

1. Open the `Ambient_start.ut2` file, which contains a moodily lit room that's mostly black.
2. You need to increase the brightness of the black areas so that the room isn't so hard to see. To do this, first choose View > Level Properties from the main menu.
3. Expand the ZoneLight tab, and set the `AmbientBrightness` property to about 8. Rebuild the lights in your level.
4. Play-test the level. Notice that although the areas outside the spotlight are still dark, you can now see them faintly (see **FIGURE 7.47**). Using this setting is a good idea when you don't want the player's vision going to pure black.

FIGURE 7.47 The final result.

> **NOTE**
>
> By default, the hotkey for the Level Properties window (F6) also opens the Net Statistics heads-up display.

END TUTORIAL 7.9

Emitting Light from Other Actors

7

Light Actors are not the only objects that can emit light in Unreal. You can make almost any Actor emit light, as long as its LightColor and Lighting tabs are available in the Properties window. For example, you can make a static mesh emit light into your level. In **TUTORIAL 7.10**, you learn how to make a static mesh illuminate a level.

TUTORIAL 7.10: Emitting Light from an Actor

1. Open the `SMemit.ut2` file. You'll see the light test chamber with an interesting static mesh floating in the middle of it, above the pedestal.
2. Select this static mesh, and move it off to one side or in a corner to help you create more interesting shadows later.
3. Double-click the static mesh to open its Properties window. Notice that it has both a LightColor and a Lighting tab.

4. Set the following properties for the static mesh:

In the LightColor tab	In the Lighting tab
LightBrightness: 150	LightRadius: 128
LightHue: 42	LightType: LT_Steady
LightSaturation: 140	

5. You can see the light's effect as a preview. Rebuild the light, and notice that the light has disappeared. The problem is that the static mesh's pivot is being used as the light's origin. Because the pivot is inside the mesh, no light is escaping. Essentially, the rest of the light is in shadow, as shown in **FIGURE 7.48**.

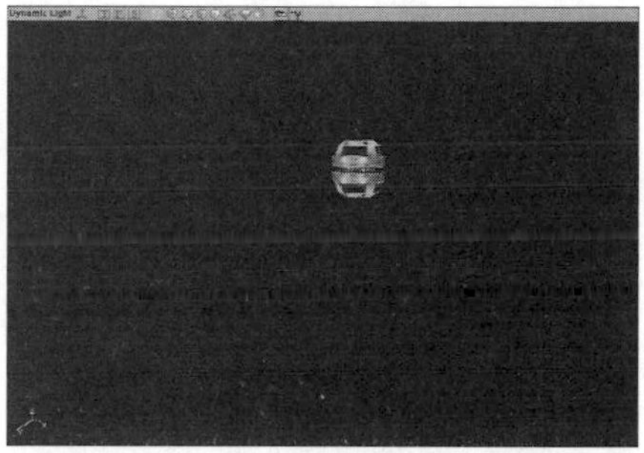

FIGURE 7.48 Initially the static mesh blocks all the light it emits.

6. In the static mesh's Properties window, expand the Display tab, and set the `bShadowCast` property to False. Rebuild the light now. Your mesh should be emitting light just like a static light (see **FIGURE 7.49**).

FIGURE 7.49 With *`bShadowCast`* set to False, the mesh emits light correctly.

7. There's still a problem, however. If you deselect the static mesh, it's completely black because the light is *inside* the mesh, so its outside is in shadow. In the Properties window for the static mesh, go back to the Display tab, and set the `bUnlit` property to False. This setting causes the mesh to stop receiving light, effectively making it visible again (see **FIGURE 7.50**). Test your level to see the effect.

FIGURE 7.50 The *`bUnlit`* property of the static mesh is set to True.

END TUTORIAL 7.10

Coronas

Coronas are a special light effect that creates a ringlike effect around a light, similar to the lens flare created when a camera looks at a bright light source. The effect is actually a texture, which is placed on a plane that always faces the camera. A corona is visible only at a certain distance and looks larger the farther you get from the light. However, this is a simple optical illusion. The corona's size never changes. As you move away from objects in 3D, they seem to get smaller. Because a corona's size is constant, it seems to be larger compared to the scenery around it, which looks like it's shrinking. The effect is similar to the effect the moon creates when it approaches the horizon. Even though the moon's size never changes, it appears larger when it's close to the ground. In **TUTORIAL 7.11**, you learn how to apply a corona to a light in your level.

TUTORIAL 7.11: Using Coronas

1. Open the `Corona_start.ut2` file, which contains a spooky (and familiar) scene. You'll be placing a corona on the Spotlight's Actor.
2. Double-click the spotlight, and in its Properties window, expand the Lighting tab. Set the `bCorona` property to True.
3. In the Texture browser, open the `Chapter7_tex.utx` package, and open the Coronas group. Select the Corona1 texture (see **FIGURE 7.51**).

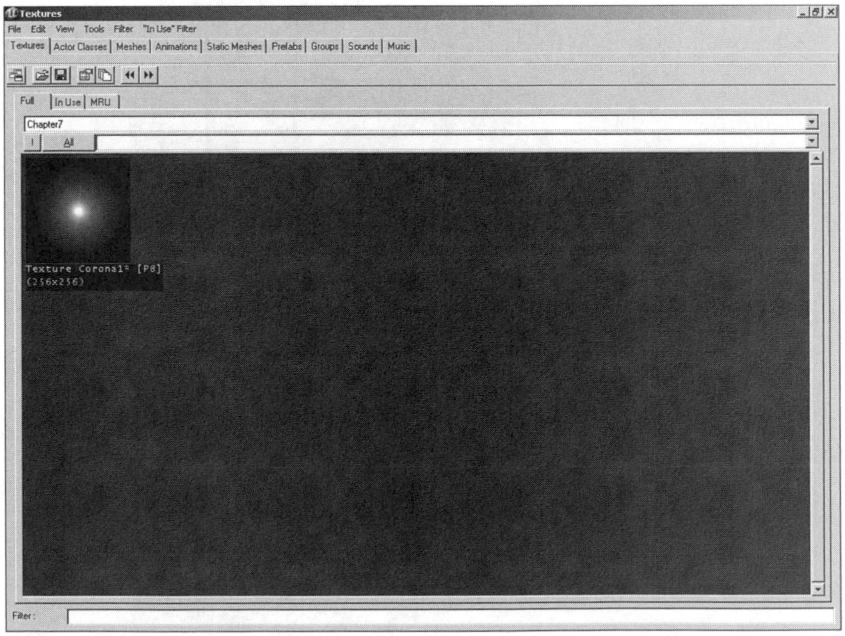

FIGURE 7.51 Selecting a texture for the corona.

4. Back in the light's Properties window, expand the Display tab. Under the `Skins` property, click the Add button.

5. In the new [0] index, click None, and then click the Use button to insert `Corona1` as the texture (see **FIGURE 7.52**). You should immediately see the corona in the viewport.

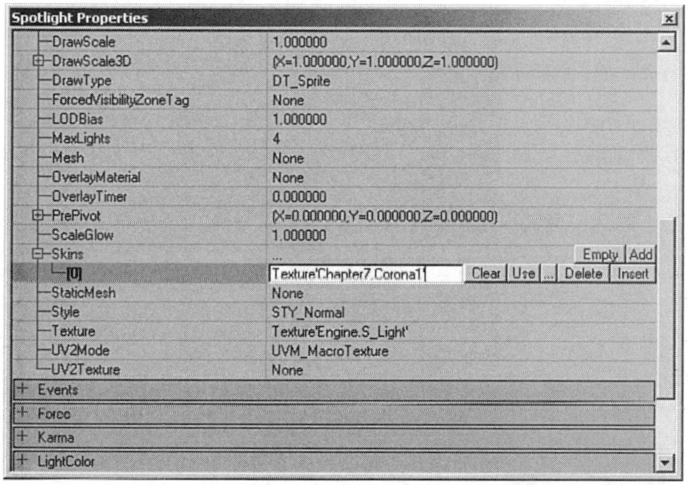

FIGURE 7.52 Using the texture as a skin for the light to use as a corona.

6. Test your level, and notice that the corona fades in and out of existence when it comes into view. The corona is too big, however. Exit Unreal, and go back to UnrealEd.

7. Select your light, and in the DrawScale3D section in the console bar, set the X and Y values to 0.5 to make the corona smaller, as shown in **FIGURE 7.53**.

FIGURE 7.53 The corona scaled down.

END TUTORIAL 7.11

Using a TriggerLight

When you need to use dynamic lighting, the TriggerLight is your tool of choice. This light has already been designated as dynamic through UnrealScript with properties unavailable in the Properties window. This light responds to events in your level, allowing you to trigger it on or off with the UseTrigger and ScriptedTrigger Actors. In **TUTORIAL 7.12**, you create a TriggerLight and use events to control its behavior. For an in-depth look at triggers and how they work, see Chapter 9, "Interactive Elements."

NOTE

Dynamic lights can't be created by adjusting properties. Only certain Actors, such as the TriggerLight, can act as dynamic lights.

TUTORIAL 7.12: Creating a TriggerLight

1. Open the `TriggerLight_start.ut2` file, which contains two rooms connected by a small hallway. You'll make one room lit and the other dark.

2. In the Top viewport, consider the room on the right to be the lit room and the room on the left to be the dark room (see **FIGURE 7.54**).

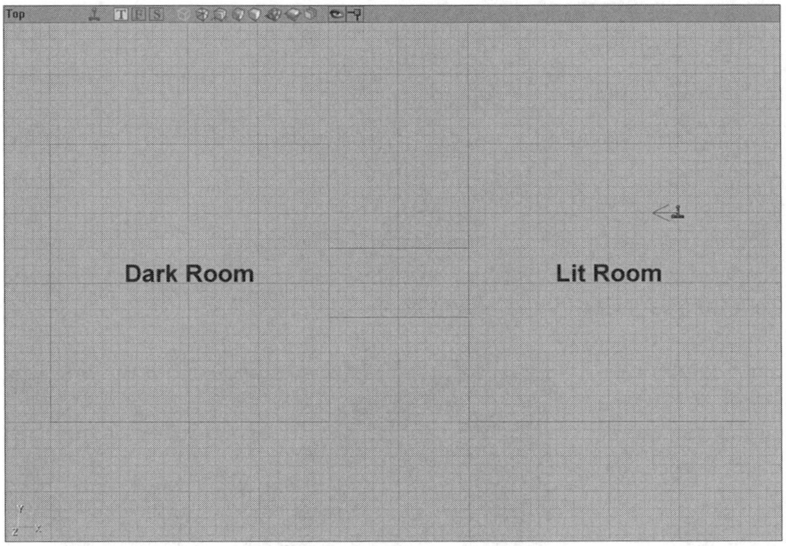

FIGURE 7.54 **Top-down view of the base level.**

3. In the lit room, create a light near the ceiling with the following properties (see the results in **FIGURE 7.55**):

   LightBrightness: 100

   LightRadius: 30

4. In the dark room, create a light in the center of the room with the following properties:

   LightBrightness: 32

   LightEffect: NonIncidence

   LightRadius: 20

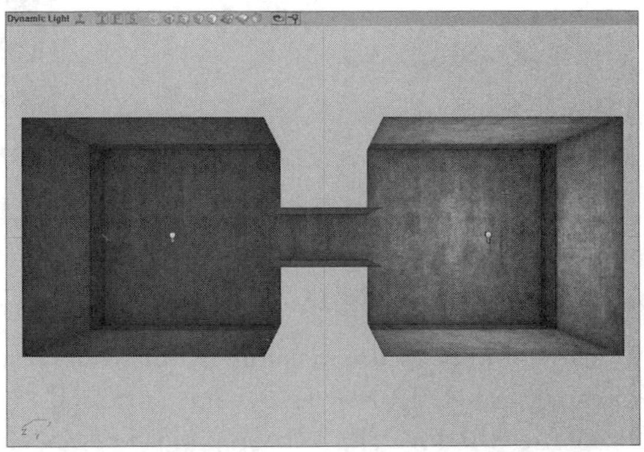

FIGURE 7.55 **Bright and dim lights added to the rooms.**

5. In the Actor Class browser, expand Triggers, and click UseTrigger. Right-click in the hallway, near the entrance to the dark room, and choose Add UseTrigger Here. This trigger acts as the switch for your light.

6. You learn how triggers and events work in Chapter 9. For now, set the following properties in the UseTrigger's Properties window:

   In the Advanced tab

   bHidden: False—This setting makes the trigger visible when you play the level.

   In the Events tab

   Event: TLight1—You need to type this entry in. This setting causes the UseTrigger to send out a signal named TLight1. You'll make the light listen for this signal.

7. You have your switch set up, so now you can create the TriggerLight. Open the Actor Class browser, expand Lights, and select TriggerLight (see **FIGURE 7.56**). Do not expand TriggerLight.

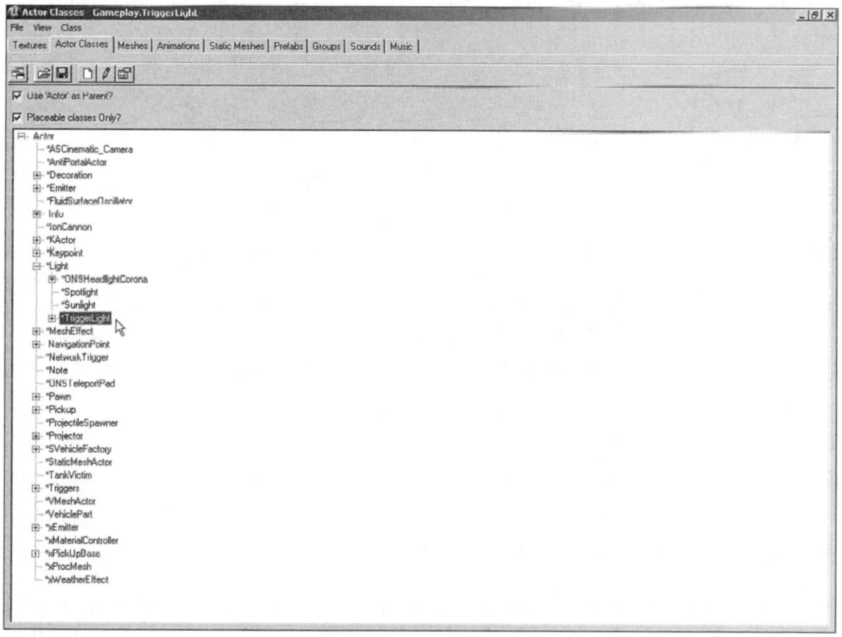

FIGURE 7.56 Selecting a TriggerLight in the Actor Class browser.

8. Right-click in the dark room, and place the TriggerLight. Move it to the center of the room, both horizontally and vertically.

9. To set up some controls for the TriggerLight's behavior, open its Properties window, and enter the following settings:

In the TriggerLight tab

ChangeTime: 0.1—This setting controls the amount of time in seconds that the light changes from unlit to lit and vice versa.

In the Lighting tab

LightRadius: 20—This setting is the light's radius, the same as other lights you have used.

In the Events tab

Tag: TLight1—This setting must be typed in. It makes the TriggerLight listen for the TLight1 signal before it activates or deactivates.

In the Object tab

InitialState: TriggerToggle—This setting determines the light's initial state (what the light is doing when the level is launched). The TriggerToggle setting causes the light to be off, awaiting a signal from the trigger.

10. Rebuild your lighting, and test the level. In the level, walk up to the eagle's head icon (the UseTrigger) and press the E key. Watch the lights come on!

END TUTORIAL 7.12

Projectors

A *Projector* is a special Actor that has replaced the functionality of many of the `LightEffect` property settings available in UnrealEd. In the past, LightEffects such as Disco or SlowWave were used to create animated effects. With the advent of static lights and precalculated shadows, this method became inefficient because these effects require dynamic lights, which are far more processor intensive than static lights. With Projectors, you now have animated light functionality that's not only faster, but also produces much cleaner results.

A Projector is not a light; it's an Actor that transmits a texture onto a surface. This texture is blended in such a way that dark areas appear to darken the surface, and lighter areas seem to illuminate it. Technically, the values of the surface texture are multiplied by the values of the texture coming from the Projector.

This behavior allows a Projector to work much like its real-world counterpart. You can place a texture into a Projector and aim it at any surface you like. Projectors can be used for a variety of purposes, including animated light passing through fan blades, a moving spotlight, or even an intricate colored shadow from a stained-glass window. The best feature of Projectors is that their effect also falls across animated meshes, meaning you can see the projected texture fall on your character as you play.

Using Projectors

To use a Projector, you place an image in it (in this chapter's example, a texture), and then aim it at a surface. The image is then projected onto that surface. In **TUTORIAL 7.13**, you see how to create and use Projectors in your levels. You begin by adding a Projector to your level, and then selecting a texture for it. You then adjust some settings to make it work correctly and alter its rotation.

TUTORIAL 7.13: Creating a Simple Projector

1. Open the `ProjectorLevel.ut2` file, which contains a simple room with a stained-glass window on one side. To begin, you add a simple Projector in the room to give the illusion that the stained-glass window is projecting light onto the floor.

2. First, open the Actor Class browser, and click Projector. Next, right-click in the middle of the window within the level, and choose Add Projector Here.

3. Just like a Spotlight, the Projector Actor is directional, with an arrow indicating its current direction. Currently, the arrow points out of the room, through the window. To fix this, click the Lock to Selected Actor icon, and position the Projector so that it's in front of the window, pointing at the floor (see **FIGURE 7.57**).

FIGURE 7.57 Projector after being pointed at the floor.

4. In the Texture browser, select the `StainedGlass` texture, found in the `Chapter7_tex.utx` package. In the Projector's Properties window, open the Projector category, click the `ProjTexture` property, and click the Use button. Notice that the texture now covers the entire floor of the map.

   Also notice the large boxes visible in the viewport around the Projector (see **FIGURE 7.58**). These boxes serve two purposes. The cyan box shows the area within which the texture is projected. The yellow box is a bounding box for the Projector's entire effect.

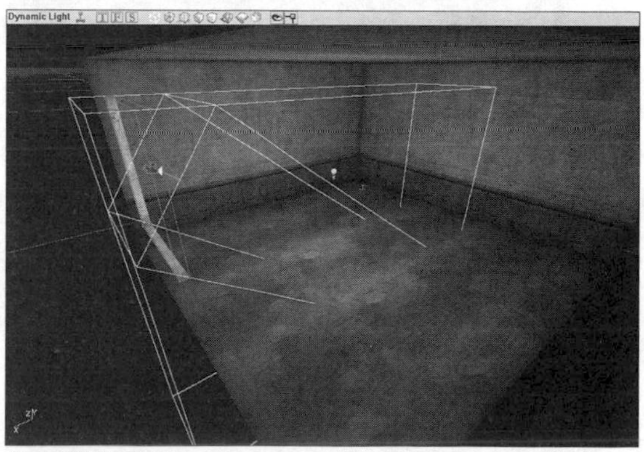

FIGURE 7.58 `StainedGlass` texture applied to the Projector.

5. To fix the tiling issue, you need to change two of the Projector's properties. Open the Properties window for the Projector and under the Projector category, set the `bClipBSP` property to True. Next, set the `FOV` property to 5. The texture is now contained within the cyan box's area, as shown in **FIGURE 7.59**.

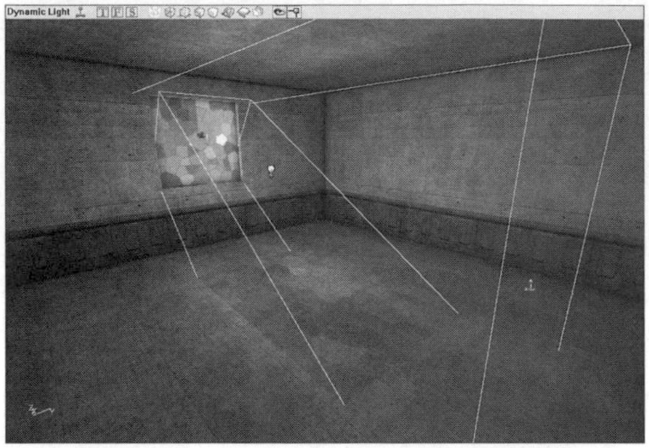

FIGURE 7.59 *bClipBSP* **set to True to avoid tiling.**

6. Save your work, and test the map. You now have a fully functional Projector. Notice when you play the map that the texture falls not only on the floor, but also on your character's gun. Keep in mind, however, that objects in the Projector's path don't cast shadows. For example, if you were to place a static mesh in the middle of the room, the stained-glass projection would fall on the surface of the mesh, but would also fall on the floor, completely without a shadow.

TUTORIAL 7.14 assumes that you're using Adobe Photoshop. If you don't have a copy of Photoshop, please skip to Step 7.

END TUTORIAL 7.13

TUTORIAL 7.14: Creating Non-square Projectors

7

1. Open the `ProjectorLevel2.ut2` file. You'll see a room similar to the one in **TUTORIAL 7.13**, but the stained-glass window is circular rather than square. For circular shapes, you need an irregularly shaped Projector texture.

2. To create the texture needed for a Projector, you need to edit a preexisting texture in Photoshop. Start Photoshop and then open the `StainedGlass.tga` file, found in the Chapter 7 folder on the CD.

3. Using the Elliptical Marquee tool, hold down the Shift key and make a circular selection in the middle of the texture. Make sure to keep your selection away from the edges, as shown in **FIGURE 7.60**.

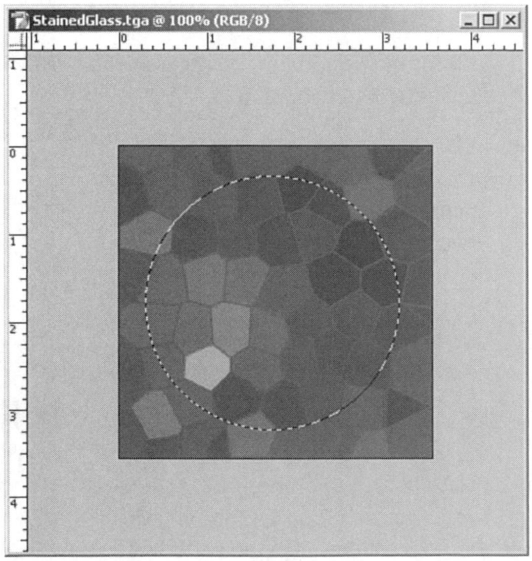

FIGURE 7.60 **Texture with circular area in the middle selected.**

4. Next, press Ctrl+Shift+I to invert your current selection. Set your color to a neutral gray (RGB values of 128, 128, 128). Choose Edit > Fill from the main menu, and in the dialog box that opens, make sure you're using the Foreground color and your mode is set to Normal at 100% opacity. The end result should be a stained-glass circle surrounded by gray (see **FIGURE 7.61**).

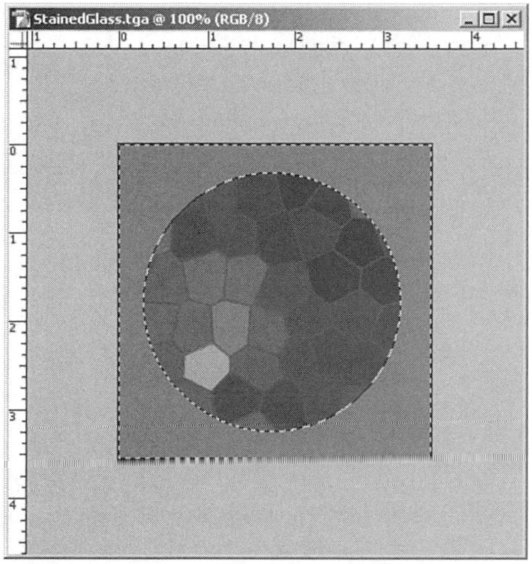

FIGURE 7.61 Area around the circle filled with gray.

> **NOTE**
>
> The image's gray border is important because the gray pixels have no effect on the surface at which the Projector is aimed. In effect, this makes the Projector look circular rather than rectangular.

5. Choose Select > Feather from the menu, and set the value in the dialog box to 40 to create a softened area around the selection. Next, choose Filter > Blur > Lens Blur from the main menu. Make sure the radius of the blur is set to 20 to blur the edges of the circular texture (see **FIGURE 7.62**).

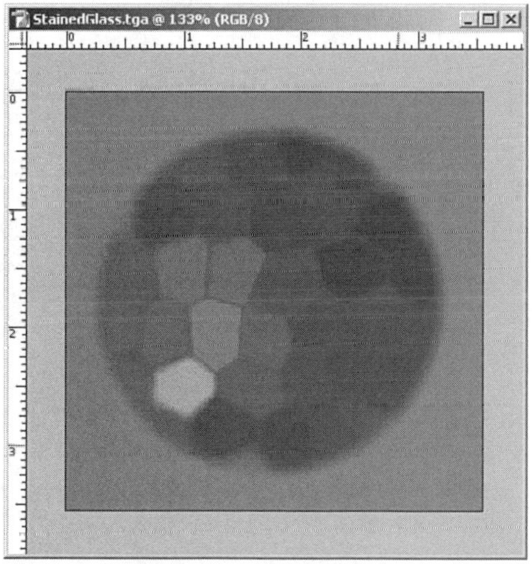

FIGURE 7.62 Edges of the circle blurred for a blending effect.

6. Now you're ready to export the texture in a format that UnrealEd can understand. Choose File > Save As from the Photoshop menu. Name the file `NewWindow`, and set its file type to Targa (TGA). In the Targa Options dialog box, set Resolution to 24 bits/pixel, and click OK.

7. Back in UnrealEd, open the Texture browser, and choose File > Import from the browser menu. Navigate to the `NewWindow.tga` texture you just created.

> **NOTE**
>
> If you have skipped to this step, you can find this texture in the Chapter 7 folder on the CD.

8. Click Open, and then use the following settings in the Import Texture dialog box (see **FIGURE 7.63**):

   Package: myLevel

   Group: none (Delete any entry in this area.)

   Name: NewWindow

9. Use the skills you learned in **TUTORIAL 7.13** to create and position a Projector in the level. This time, use the `NewWindow` texture you just created. As before, the texture tiles across the floor (see **FIGURE 7.64**). You could fix this problem by setting `bClipBSP` to True, but instead, you'll adjust a setting within the texture.

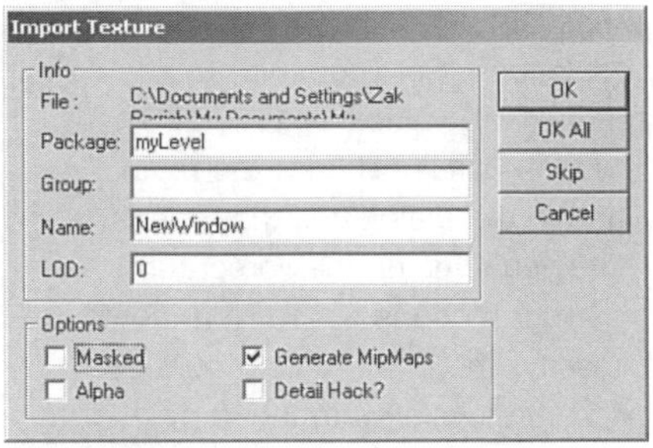

FIGURE 7.63 Importing the texture into UnrealEd.

10. Return to the Texture browser. Right-click on the `NewWindow` texture, and choose Properties to open the Texture Properties window, which is discussed in more detail in Chapter 8, "Creating Materials in Unreal." For now, open the Texture category, and set the `UClampMode` and `VClampMode` properties to `TC_Clamp`. Close the Texture Properties window when finished. The results are shown in **FIGURE 7.65**.

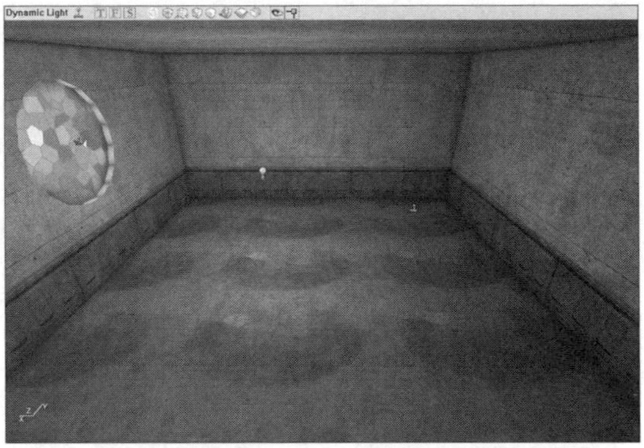

FIGURE 7.64 Texture assigned to the Projector.

11. Finally, tweak some of the Projector's properties to make it look more realistic. Open the Projector's Properties window, and set the following:

    FOV: 30

    bGradient: True

    MaxTraceDistance: 1500

    The `FOV` property expands the Projector's field of view, enlarging the texture. The `bGradient` property causes the projected texture to be more intense near the Projector Actor and fade off with distance. The `MaxTraceDistance` property enables you to adjust how far the Projector can project. In this example, the 50% increase prevents the texture from looking washed out.

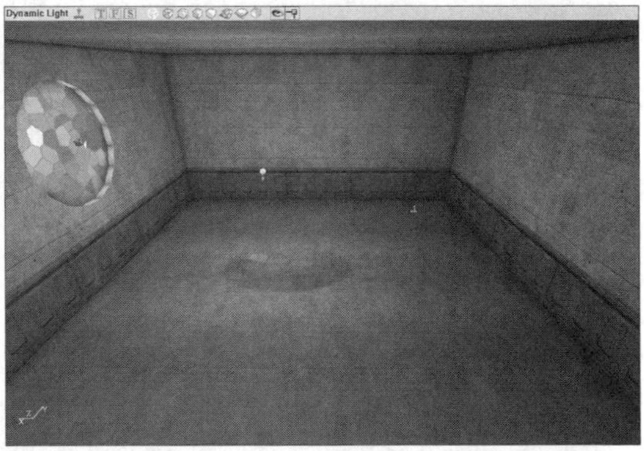

FIGURE 7.65 The Projector's result with the texture's *`UClampMode`* and *`VClampMode`* properties set to *`TC_Clamp`*.

12. Save and test your level. Notice that the Projector's effect is now circular and much more subtle.

END TUTORIAL 7.14

Common Lighting Pitfalls

This section describes some common problems that first-time lighters experience so that you know to look out for them. By knowing about these simple problems, you can avoid them in your own projects and be far more effective at lighting your levels:

- **Always have a light source.** Whether it's a static mesh or just a simple open window, make sure your light appears to originate from some object. A room lit by an invisible light source looks unrealistic and makes your levels look fake. For example, if you're lighting a dungeon level, you want your light to seem to come from torches, not from some unknown source. In **FIGURES 7.66** and **7.67**, you can see how much more realistic your lighting looks if you create a physical light source for it.
- **Avoid using too much ambient light.** Ambient light, or Zone light, is a good way to make your levels appear to have general illumination. It is good to use ambient light when you don't want your shadows to look perfectly black. However, you must be careful not to overuse this lighting, as it can make your level look washed out and remove the dramatic feel of your shadows (see **FIGURE 7.68**).
- **Keep an eye on your contrast.** The shadows of your level should be dramatic, but not overly so. Be careful that you don't have both brightly lit areas and pure black shadows, as shown in **FIGURE 7.69**. This look

FIGURE 7.66 Simple lighting with no visible light source.

FIGURE 7.67 Same lighting as **FIGURE 7.66** but with a light fixture.

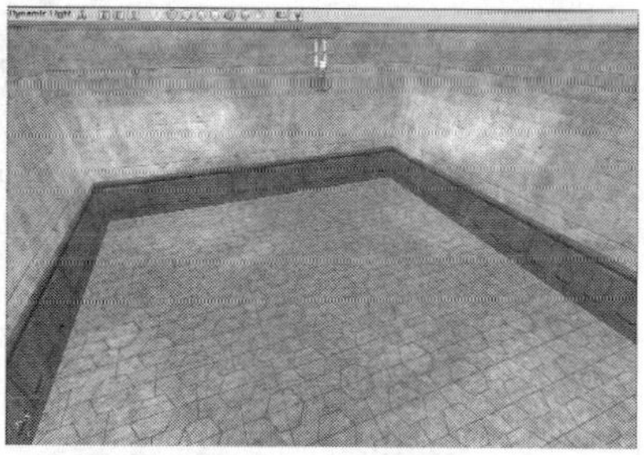

FIGURE 7.68 The shadows are washed out even though there's only one light.

FIGURE 7.69 Room with bright light and perfect black shadows.

rarely happens in the real world and should be avoided in your levels. Remember that bright light tends to reflect off surrounding surfaces, which typically lightens the shadows in your room.

- **Avoid using too many lights.** Often you need to use multiple lights in one area, but don't go too far. Remember to make the most of the properties you have available for your lights. When lighting large areas, be sure you don't place many lights when you could simply increase the `LightRadius` property of a single central light source. Compare **FIGURE 7.70** with **FIGURE 7.71** to see the difference. The results don't necessarily speed up gameplay, but they do make light map rebuilding much faster.
- **Don't overuse sharp shadows.** When adjusting your level's shadows, remember that changing the size of your light maps is, in fact, changing their resolution. The finer, or smaller, you set your Light Map size, the more high-resolution your shadows are. This setup can become a problem if used too much. The higher your light map resolution, the more texture data must be stored on your video card during gameplay, on top of the textures already in your level. This can result in level slowdown and should be avoided. In **FIGURES 7.72** and **7.73**, you can see the effect of having large and small Light Map sizes.

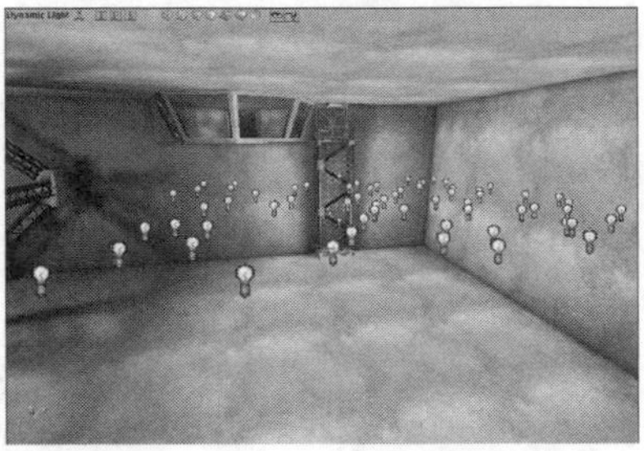

FIGURE 7.70 Large room filled with lights.

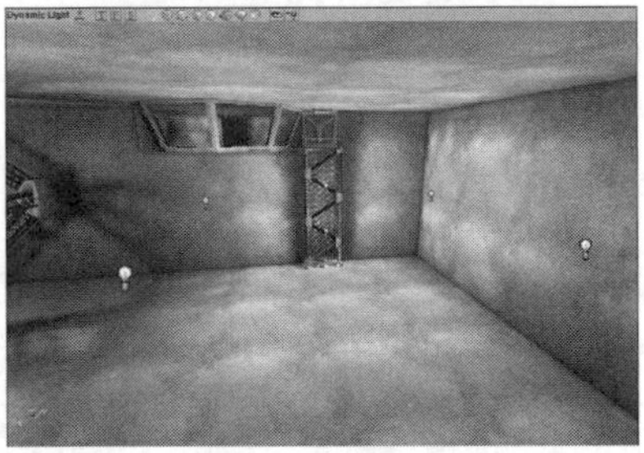

FIGURE 7.71 Only a few lights with larger radii.

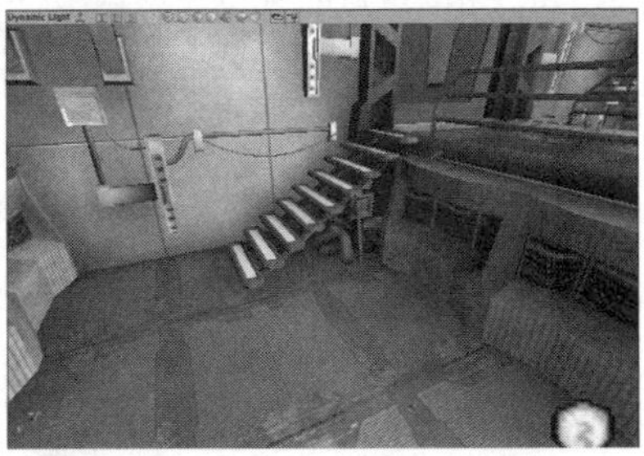

FIGURE 7.72 Room full of static meshes with Light Map size at about 32.

FIGURE 7.73 Same as **FIGURE 7.72** but with a Light Map size of 1. In this example, sharp shadows might not be necessary.

- **Keep dynamic light use to a minimum.** Static lights were designed to create beautiful and realistic lighting scenarios without a lot of overhead on the computer. Dynamic lights, on the other hand, are very processor intensive because they are updated every frame. If used too much in your levels, dynamic lights can drastically diminish your level's performance. Try not to use dynamic lights unless absolutely necessary. In **FIGURES 7.74** and **7.75**, you can see the difference between using static lights and dynamic lights.

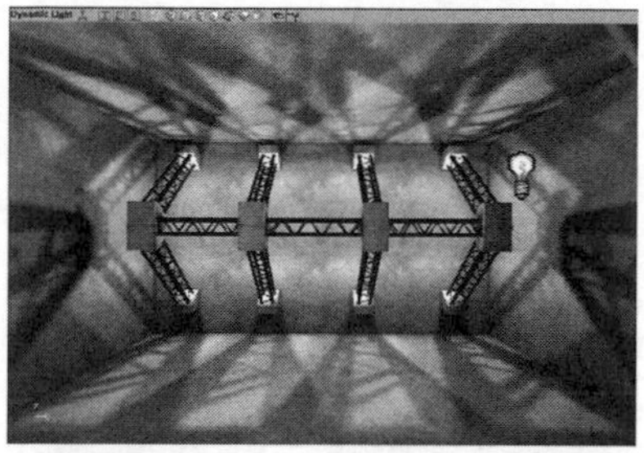

FIGURE 7.74 Room lit with static lights.

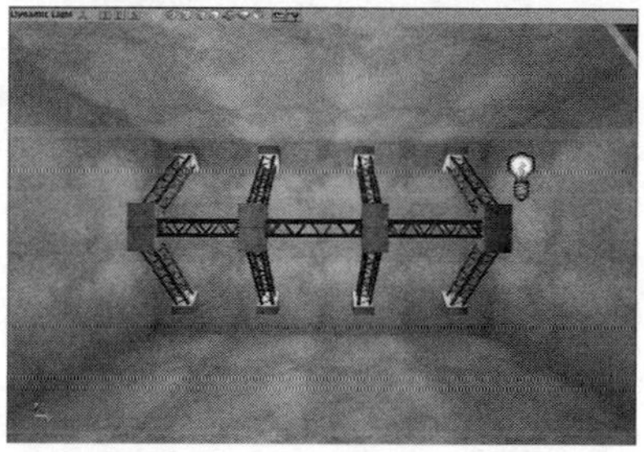

FIGURE 7.75 Room lit with TriggerLights. Notice that dynamic lights don't cast shadows.

Summary

This chapter has covered many aspects of lighting in Unreal. You should now have a solid understanding of the concepts behind creating light in your levels. Practicing your lighting skills is recommended so that you become accustomed to lighting workflow and methods of creating realistic light. The Unreal Engine is capable of fantastic light handling, but only through experience will you be able to take advantage of its full capabilities. In the next chapter, you take your first look at terrain creation and see how terrain can be used to generate outdoor areas for your levels.

Chapter 8

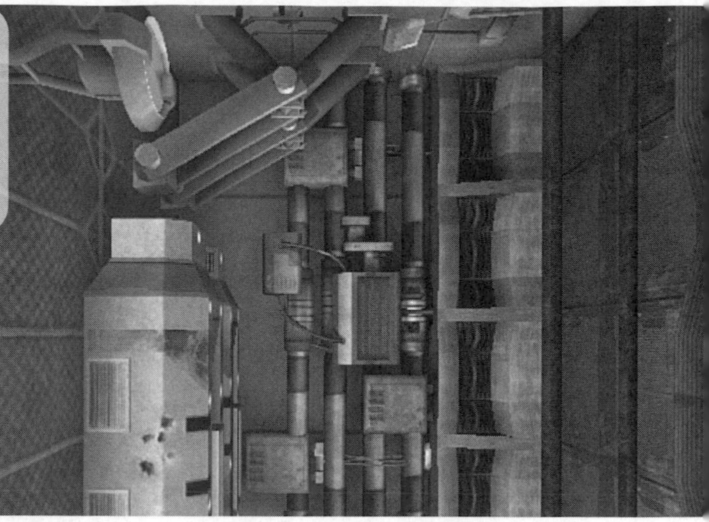

Creating Materials in Unreal

Materials can be thought of as coatings of paint applied to the surfaces of objects in your levels. Materials provide a specific look for your surfaces, whether they are made of wood, plastic, steel, or concrete. Materials can be divided into three separate categories: textures, shaders, and modifiers. A *texture* supplies the color for your object, like applying an image across the surface. A *shader* uses textures to create a kind of surface effect, such as reflectivity or specularity, which is how light creates highlights on the surface. A *modifier* is a component that applies some sort of action or process to a texture, such as a TexPanner, which pans the texture in a specific direction, or a TexRotator, which rotates the texture.

In this chapter, you take an in-depth look at materials and how they are made. You learn how textures can be imported into Unreal, how to create shaders, and how to apply modifiers to create powerful materials for your levels. The chapter begins with a discussion of textures and explains some considerations for generating your own textures.

Textures

A texture is technically nothing more than an image placed on a surface in your level. In this section, you take an in-depth look at textures, how they work, and how they are created. Textures are the material component that provides color and a tactile look. Keep in mind that textures are static—they don't animate on their own. To achieve motion or animated effects, you need to incorporate other components that are engineered to drive such effects. These components are discussed later in the "Modifiers" section.

Textures are created in external applications, such as Adobe Photoshop or Corel Painter. You can import images created in these applications into UnrealEd simply by saving them to the proper file format. UnrealEd supports five file formats: BMP, PCX, TGA, UPT, and DDS. The following list describes these formats and what kind of results you can expect from them:

- *BMP*—The Windows bitmap format is supported by many different 2D paint applications. This format is *lossless*, meaning it doesn't decrease or remove any information from your original image. As such, BMP files tend to be very large compared to other formats. This format does, however, support a few simple compression algorithms to help decrease file size.
- *PCX*—This image format was popular in the early days of MS-DOS and Windows. It is a lossless format, but its compression algorithm is inefficient by today's standards. It has been widely replaced by formats that support better compression, such as JPG.
- *TGA*—This is a lossless image format, commonly called a Targa file. It supports up to 32 bits per pixel and supports an alpha channel. It has become the preferred format for image importing when working with UnrealEd.

  An *alpha channel* is a separate grayscale image embedded in some image files that allows you to create transparent areas in your texture. Black areas on the texture, which have an RGB value of 0, are transparent, and white areas, having an RGB value of 255, are opaque. Shades of gray appear as varying levels of transparency. For example, if you want to create a texture of a wire mesh or a chain-link fence, you could create an alpha channel that was white where the wires or fencing exists and black in all the holes. The result would be that you could see through the texture in all the areas that are black on the alpha channel. Alpha channels are important in Unreal because they make it possible to create areas in your surfaces that are semitransparent or even fully transparent and provide a way to keep transparent areas independent of the rest of the texture.
- *UPT*—This format is created by UPaint, a 3D texture painting application by Right Hemisphere. UPaint is included with Unreal Tournament 2003 and Unreal Tournament 2004. The program allows you to paint textures directly on the surface of your models.

- *DDS*—This is the Direct Draw Surface format created by Microsoft and originally introduced for DirectX 7. The format allows saving compressed and uncompressed images. More important, it enables you to save multiple *mipmaps* of your texture.

  The word "MIP" is an acronym for *multum in parvo*, or "much in little." A mipmap is a series of textures that begin at high resolutions and move to lower resolutions. This allows for a "level of detail" effect when playing a game, so players see the higher resolution texture when they're close to a surface and lower resolution textures as they move away from that surface. The lower resolution textures are always smaller than their predecessor by a power of two. For example, if your initial texture has a resolution of 512×512, its next mipmap is 256×256. The next is 128×128, then 64×64, and so on, depending on the number of mipmaps created for your texture. Mipmaps use more memory than a standard texture but are far less processor intensive, allowing for much faster gameplay, especially on computers with large amounts of memory.

  DDS images also make it possible to store *cubic environment maps* and *volume textures*. A cubic environment map is a way to represent an object's surrounding environment from a specific point in space. In effect, it enables you to make an object seem to be reflecting its surrounding environment, similar to real-world materials such as stainless steel. Cubic environment maps, or Cubemaps, are discussed later in the "Creating Reflective Surfaces with Cubemaps and TexEnvMaps" section. Volume textures are three-dimensional textures used to simulate real-world effects such as fog, flame, and explosions. Although the DDS format supports volume textures, they haven't been implemented in the Unreal Engine.

  You can create DDS files by using several methods. UnrealEd provides some functionality for creating DDS files, including the creation of mipmaps. You can use other tools as well, including the Microsoft DXTex tool and the DDS Photoshop Plug-in available from Nvidia.

Creating a Texture

When creating a texture, you must keep a few things in mind. The size of your texture controls how detailed it appears in-game, and its file format controls how much data (if any) is lost when you create it. In **TUTORIAL 8.1**, you look at creating a texture completely from scratch in Adobe Photoshop. This tutorial assumes a basic understanding of Photoshop and does not include comprehensive instructions for every nuance of the program.

TUTORIAL 8.1: Creating a Texture in Photoshop

1. Start Photoshop, and choose File > New from the menu to create a new image. In the New dialog box (shown in **FIGURE 8.1**), enter the following settings, and click OK when finished:

   Name: tile

   Width: 512 pixels

   Height: 512 pixels

   Resolution: 72 pixels/inch

   Mode: RGB Color/8 bit

   Background Contents: White

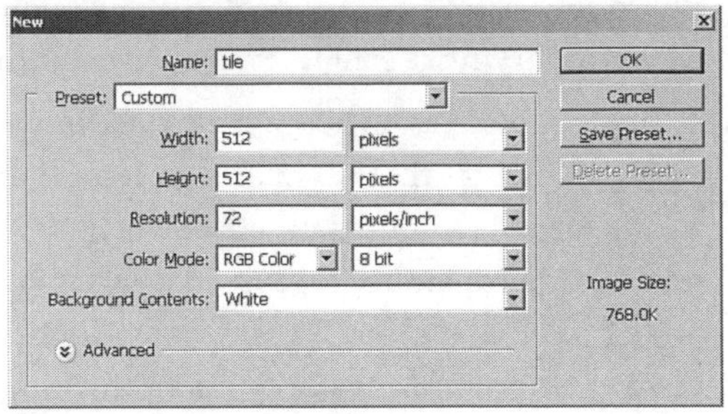

FIGURE 8.1 The New dialog box in Photoshop.

2. Choose Filter > Render > Clouds from the menu to cover your canvas with a basic cloud effect (see **FIGURE 8.2**).

FIGURE 8.2 Rendered cloud.

3. From the Layer menu, choose New Adjustment Layer > Curves. Click OK in the New Layer dialog box to use the default settings.

   In the Curves dialog box (shown in **FIGURE 8.3**), move the leftmost point down to about midway on the graph. This removes the primary dark areas on the image, resulting in something similar to **FIGURE 8.4**.

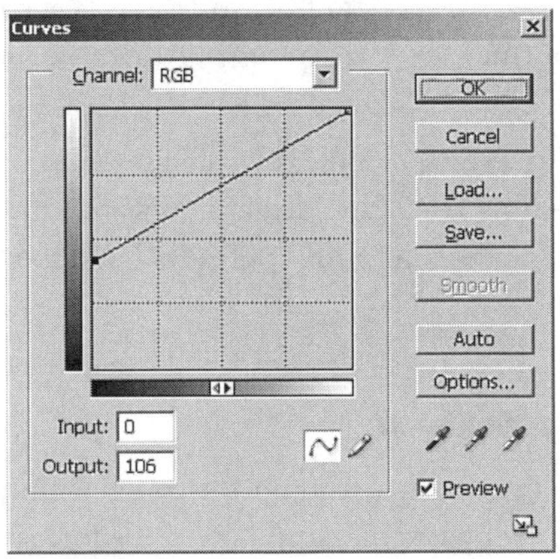

FIGURE 8.3 The Curves dialog box.

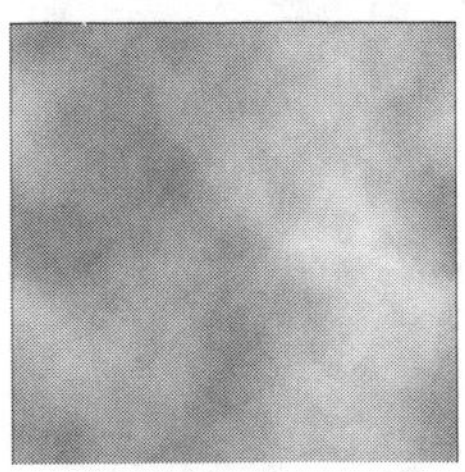

FIGURE 8.4 Clouds after brightening.

4. Choose Layer > New Adjustment Layer > Color Balance, and click OK in the New Layer dialog box. Set the following properties in the Color Balance dialog box (see **FIGURE 8.5**):

Cyan: -100

Magenta: 0

Yellow: 50

Tone Balance: Midtones

Preserve Luminosity: Select this check box

Click OK when done. Your result should be similar to **FIGURE 8.6**.

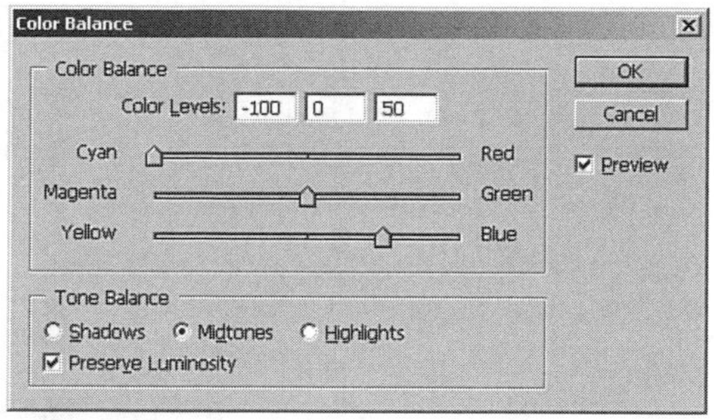

FIGURE 8.5 The Color Balance dialog box.

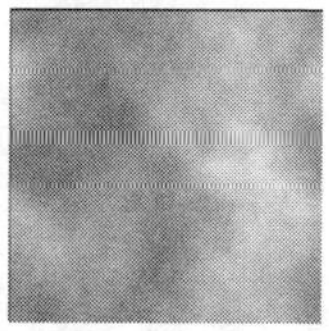

FIGURE 8.6 Clouds after adjusting the color balance.

5. Add a new layer by clicking the New Layer button, located at the bottom of the Layers palette. With this layer selected, choose Filters > Render > Clouds from the menu to add clouds to your new layer (see **FIGURE 8.7**).

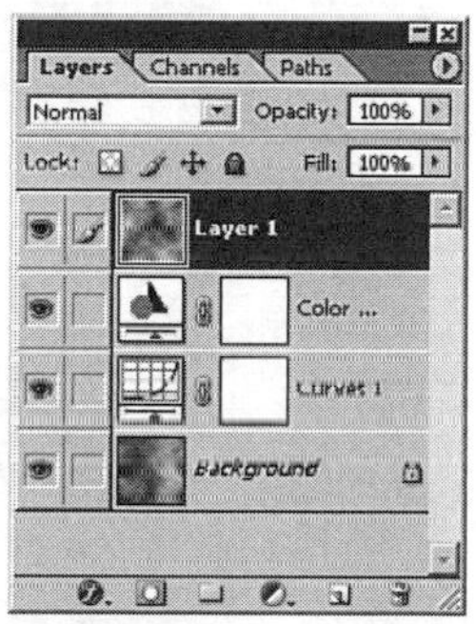

FIGURE 8.7 The Layers palette showing the cloud layer.

6. Edit the curves of this new layer by choosing Image > Adjustments > Curves from the menu. Move the first curve point to the top of the graph, and then create three points in the middle of the curve, moving the center point down to the bottom of the graph, as shown in **FIGURE 8.8**. The results should look similar to **FIGURE 8.9**.

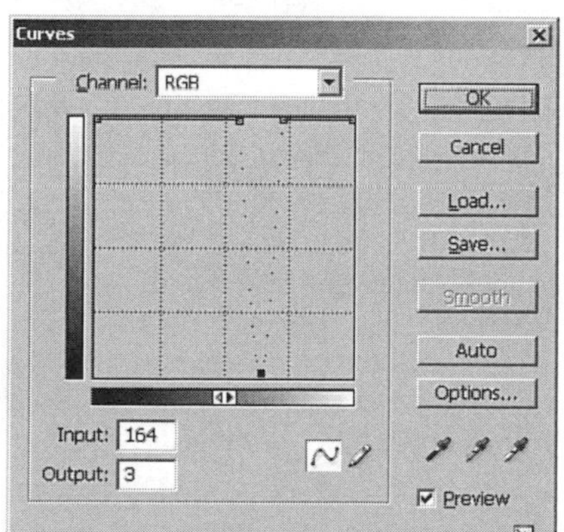

FIGURE 8.8 The edited curve used for the desired effect.

NOTE

To add new edit points to the curve, simply click on a section of the curve away from the existing points.

7. In the Layers palette's blending options, set the new layer's mode to Multiply and lower its opacity to 30%, as shown in **FIGURE 8.10**. You can see the results of these changes in **FIGURE 8.11**.

8. Select the Background layer and choose Filter > Distort > Ocean Ripple from the menu. In the Ocean Ripple dialog box, set the following properties (see the results in **FIGURE 8.12**):

   Ripple Size: 12

   Ripple Magnitude: 9

9. Next, you'll add an alpha channel to the tile image. Select the new Clouds layer (if it's not already). Press Ctrl+A to select the entire layer, and then press Ctrl+C to copy it to the Clipboard.

10. Click the Channels tab, and then click the New Channel button at the bottom of the palette to create a blank alpha channel (see **FIGURE 8.13**).

11. Select the new alpha channel, and press Ctrl+V to paste in the information from the layer (see **FIGURE 8.14**).

12. Choose File > Save As from the menu. Set the file format to Targa (`.tga` extension), and name the image `tile`. Click Save, and in the targa options dialog box that opens, choose 32-bits/pixel, and click OK.

END TUTORIAL 8.1

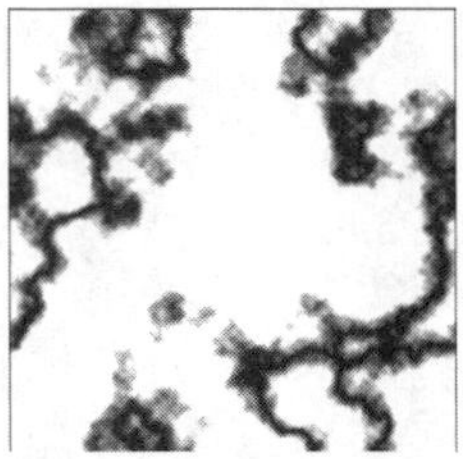

FIGURE 8.9 Cloud layer after the curve adjustment.

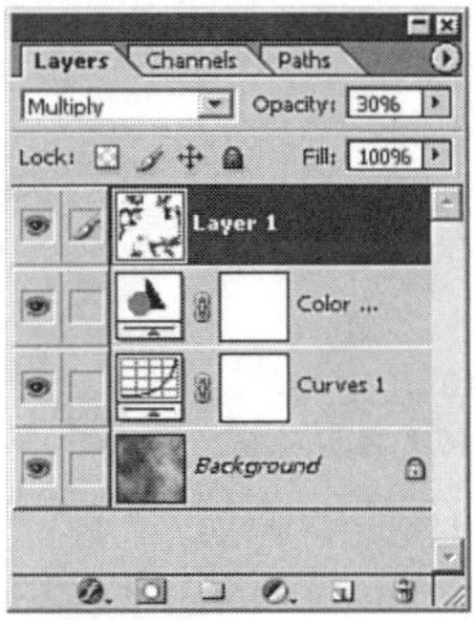

FIGURE 8.10 The Layers palette showing changes to the blending options.

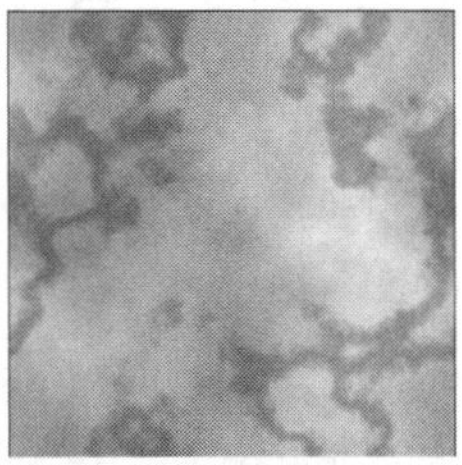

FIGURE 8.11 The tile image after changes to the blending options.

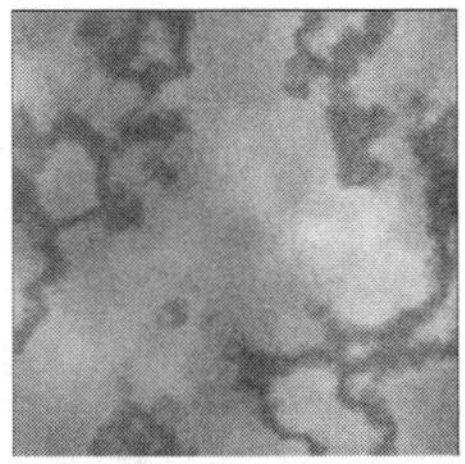

FIGURE 8.12 The tile image after applying the Ocean Ripple filter.

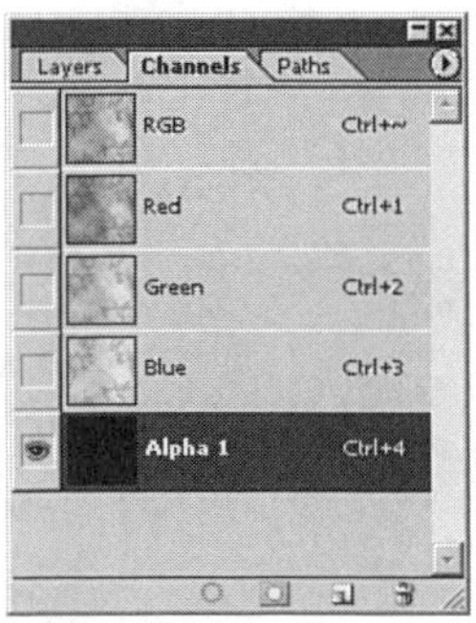

FIGURE 8.13 The Channels palette with a blank alpha channel.

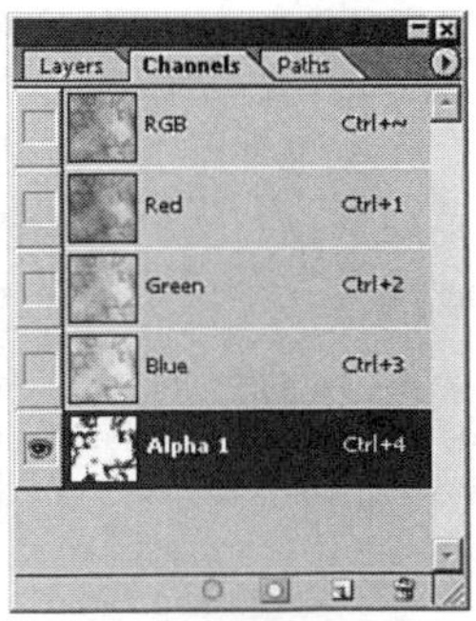

FIGURE 8.14 The Channels palette with an alpha channel from the cloud layer.

You have now created a new TGA file containing an alpha channel, which can be imported into Unreal.

Using 8-bit Textures

As an alternative to using a 32-bit texture with an alpha channel, you can use 8-bit textures. An 8-bit texture has no more than 256 colors, all of which are stored in a palette. This palette can hold no more than 256 entries, and each pixel of the image references a value in the palette. These textures are called 8-bit textures because in a computer's memory, 8 bits can hold up to 256 unique values. This means the name "8-bit" refers to the amount of memory used for each pixel of the image.

In Unreal, 8-bit textures are useful for two reasons: They save space, and you can mask out an entire color or, more precisely, an entry in the palette. In **TUTORIAL 8.2**, you see how to set up this texture.

TUTORIAL 8.2: Creating an 8-bit Texture

1. Start Photoshop and open the texture you created in **TUTORIAL 8.1**.
2. Choose Image > Mode > Indexed Color to open the Indexed Color dialog box (see **FIGURE 8.15**), where you can specify how to convert your image to a 256-color image. Obviously, this conversion decreases your image's detail because you're removing data.
3. Next, choose Image > Mode > Color Table from the menu. You can use the Color Table dialog box, shown in **FIGURE 8.16**, to view and set the colors in your palette. You can set a specific color for the first entry and force Unreal to read every instance of that color as transparent.
4. To set the transparency color, click the first entry of the color table, the square in the upper-left corner. The Color Picker opens, where you can select the color that becomes transparent after the texture is in Unreal. However, if you move the mouse over your original image, you see the Eyedropper tool, which you can use to select a color directly from your image.

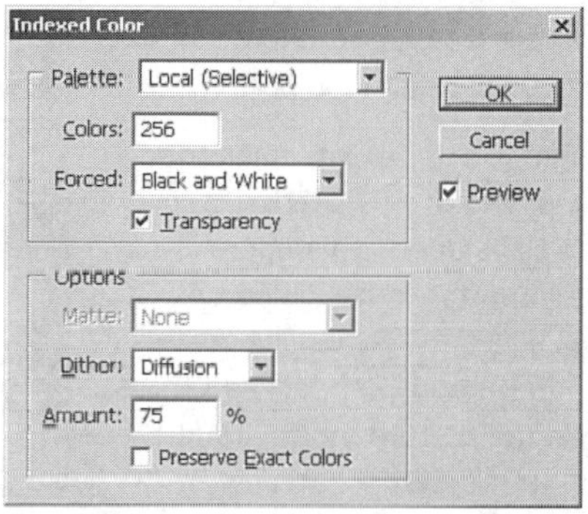

FIGURE 8.15 The Indexed Color dialog box.

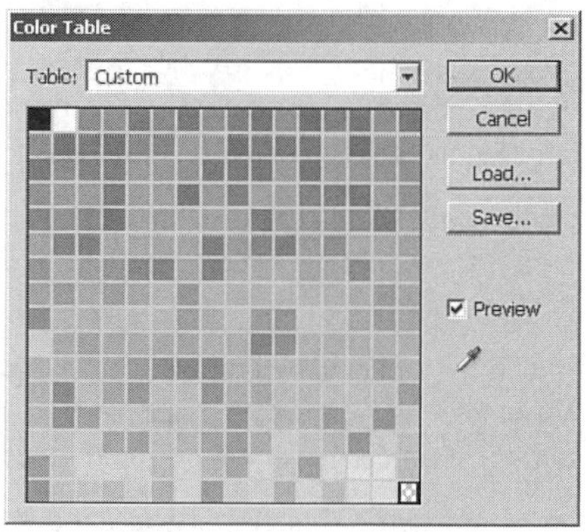

FIGURE 8.16 The Color Table dialog box.

END TUTORIAL 8.2

Importing a Texture

In this section, you learn how to get the texture you created in the previous section into UnrealEd so that you can use it to texture your surfaces. Before you begin, however, there's an important rule you need to keep in mind: Although your textures don't need to be perfectly square, they must have pixel dimensions that are powers of two, such as 2, 4, 8, 16, 32, 64, 128, and so on. For example, a texture that's 128×256 pixels is acceptable, but you can't have a texture that's 137×231 pixels. With that rule in mind, try importing a texture into a level by following **TUTORIAL 8.3**.

TUTORIAL 8.3: Importing and Using a Simple Texture

1. Start UnrealEd, and open the Textures browser, shown in **FIGURE 8.17**.

2. Next, choose File > Import from the menu to open the Import Textures dialog box, where you can select a file to import.

3. Select the `Tile.tga` image you saved in **TUTORIAL 8.1** and click Open. This opens the Import Texture dialog box (see **FIGURE 8.18**), where you can set which package to save the texture in, its group, and the name for the new texture.

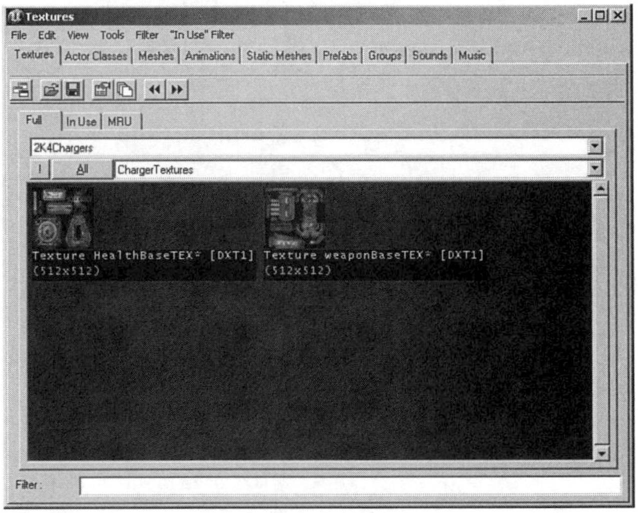

FIGURE 8.17 The Textures browser.

4. Change the package to **`MaterialTest`** to create a new package of the same name. Clear the Group text box, as you won't be creating any groups in this package. Finally, set the name to **`tileTex`**.

> **TIP**
>
> Remember that groups are used to organize multiple objects within a package.

5. Underneath the Name text box is the `LOD` attribute, which stands for Level of Detail. Make sure it's set to zero, which produces the highest quality setting. Anything higher than 0 decreases the quality.

6. Notice the Options section beneath the main Info section. Select the Alpha and Generate MipMaps check boxes. The options in this section can be changed after the texture is created, but it's more convenient to set them now. The following list explains the available options:

   - *Masked*—This property is used if your texture doesn't have an alpha channel. It takes a single color of your texture and makes it transparent. You could, for example, mask out the color green in your texture. The effect is similar to the green screen used in movie making: Anywhere the color green exists in your texture, you can see through to the surface behind.

- *Alpha*—This option specifies whether your image's alpha channel is used, provided you're using an image format that supports alpha channels, such as TGA. The file you're using in this tutorial is a TGA with an alpha channel. To use the alpha channel, you must make sure the Alpha check box is selected.

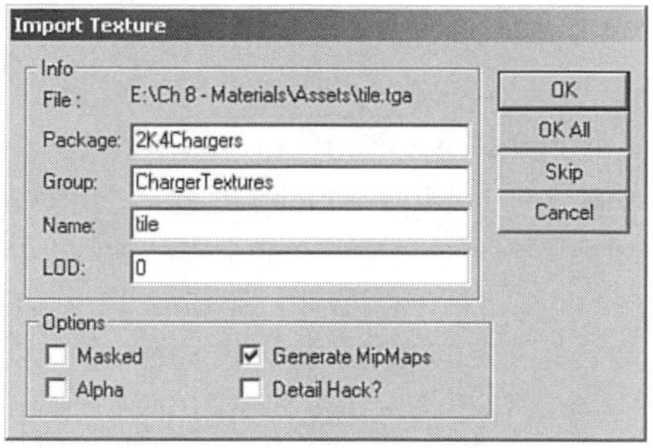

FIGURE 8.18 The Import Texture dialog box.

- *Generate MipMaps*—This option tells UnrealEd to generate a series of lower-resolution versions of your original image. They are displayed if players are positioned at a distance from the texture and don't need to see a high-resolution texture. It also prevents a moiré (pixel distortion) effect that happens when you view a high-resolution texture at a long distance.

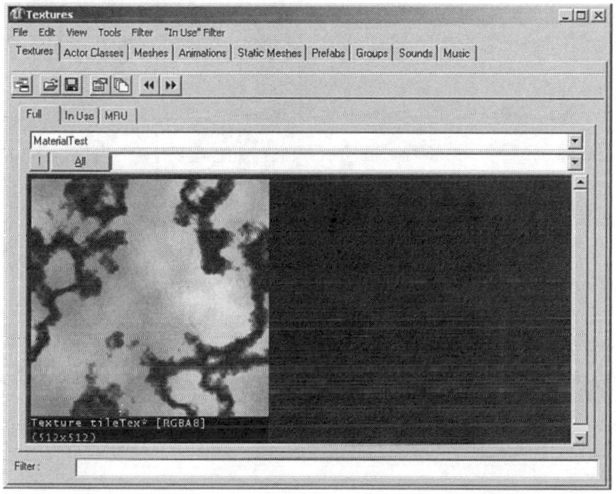

FIGURE 8.19 The Textures browser with the imported texture.

7. Click the OK button in the Import Texture dialog box to create your texture, which then shows up in the Textures browser (see **FIGURE 8.19**). You can place this texture on any surface in your level, just like any other texture.

8. Currently, this texture package has not been saved. You must save it if you want to be able to see the texture in the game. After making sure you're viewing the MaterialTest package, save your new texture by choosing File > Save from the Textures browser menu.

9. Leave the name as MaterialTest and click Save. Now you can use this package in any of your levels.

END TUTORIAL 8.3

The Texture Properties Window

At this point, you have created a fully functional texture that can be used in your Unreal levels. You can now make changes to this texture by altering its properties. To do this, you use the Texture Properties window, which has a few differences from the Properties windows you've been using for other objects. To help you better understand how this window works and how to use it, this section introduces you to the Texture Properties window interface and functionality. To get started, you can access the Texture Properties window by right-clicking your new texture in the Textures browser, and choosing Properties from the context menu (see **FIGURE 8.20**).

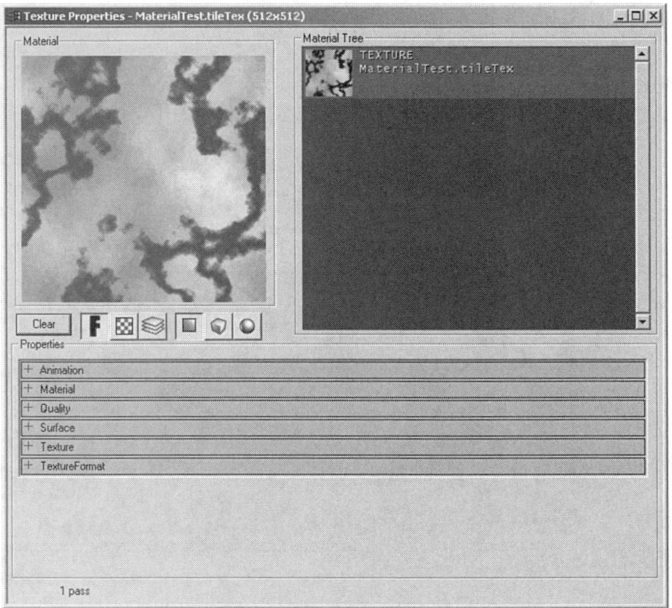

FIGURE 8.20 The Texture Properties window for your tileTex texture.

At the top left is the Material display window that gives you a preview of what your material will look like. You can use it to reference your material on a flat plane, a cube, or a sphere, as explained later in this section.

To the right of the Material display window is the Material Tree, which shows a hierarchical view of all the components of your current material. Here you can select and change the properties of any texture, shader, or modifier in your material's hierarchy.

Directly beneath the Material display window, you see the Material Display buttons for controlling what you see in the display window:

- *Clear*—At the time of this writing, the Clear button is nonfunctional.
- *Show Fallback Material*—You use this button to create a *fallback material*, which is a basic material that Unreal uses if your computer's hardware is incapable of displaying an

advanced material. When distributing your work, creating a fallback material is a good idea in case someone playing your level is using an older video card.

- The *Material Backdrop*—This button shows a multicolored checkered background in your display window. This view is especially useful for testing transparency.
- The *Layer-Looking*—When this button is activated, you always see the result of the components in the Material Tree or the effect produced at the top of the hierarchy. No matter which component in the tree you select, you always see the final result as long as this button is activated. If this button is not activated, you see only the result of the currently selected component in the Material Tree.

The three buttons on the right determine the type of geometry used in the Material display window. By default, the geometry is set to plane. You can also switch to cube and sphere, which show you what the material looks like if applied to those types of geometry. When using a cube or sphere, you can rotate the object in the Material display window by dragging on the object with the left or right mouse buttons. The left mouse button allows you to rotate only on the Z-axis by moving the mouse left and right. When using the right mouse button, you can likewise rotate on the Z-axis, but you can also rotate on the X-axis by moving the mouse up and down.

Texture Properties

This section describes the categories available in the Texture Properties window—Animation, Material, Quality, Surface, and Texture—and explains some properties available in each category. At the end of this chapter, you should have a broad understanding of the properties available in the Texture Properties window. For a complete listing of all properties found in this window, please refer to Appendix A, "The UnrealEd Manual."

Animation Category

The Animation category holds information for creating frame-by-frame animation in your textures (see **FIGURE 8.21**). The `AnimNext` property, for example, tells Unreal which texture is the next frame of an animation. This allows you to show one frame after the other to display an entire animation. Say you have a 10-frame animation of a character walking. The frames are named Character01, Character02, Character03, and so on. The frames are set up in such a way that you can follow the tenth frame with the first, creating a constant cycle. You could import all these frames as textures into UnrealEd, and in the Animation category, set Character01's `AnimNext` property to Character02. You then set Character02's `AnimNext` to Character03, and follow this pattern all the way through to the 10th image. The 10th image is set back to Character01, which causes the frames to loop back and cycle indefinitely.

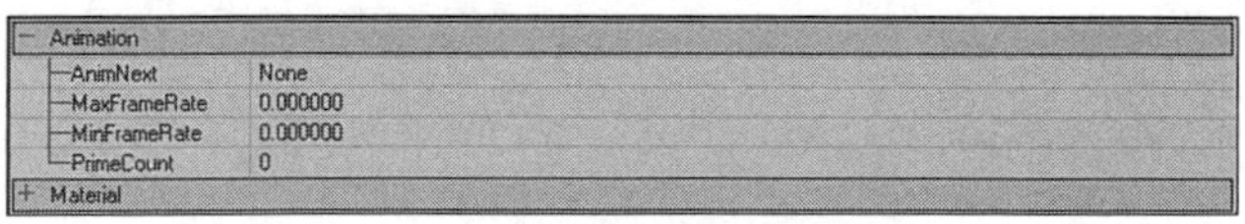

FIGURE 8.21 The Animation category.

In addition, this category contains the `MaxFrameRate` and `MinFrameRate` properties. If both properties are set to zero, Unreal loops through the frames of your texture as fast as the computer's hardware capabilities allow. Different computers play the animation at different speeds, so older machines might run the animation very slowly, and newer machines might run it so quickly you can't see what's going on. To force the animation to play at a constant speed from machine to machine, you must set these properties to a reasonable value. The value is measured in frames per second. Therefore, if you want your animation to cycle through 30 frames in a second, you need to set `MinFramerate` to 30. To set a playback speed limit for faster computers, you could set `MaxFramerate` as well, perhaps to 60.

Material Category

The Material category, shown in **FIGURE 8.22**, is where you can set the fallback material discussed earlier, in the `FallbackMaterial` property. This category also contains the `SurfaceType` property, which gives other Actors a way of determining the type of surface you're creating. For example, if you set the `SurfaceType` property to `EST_Snow`, other Actors look to that property to know what to do when they come in contact with that surface. A character, for instance, would make soft crunching sounds as its feet fall on the surface. A hovercraft would see the property and throw snowlike particles into the air.

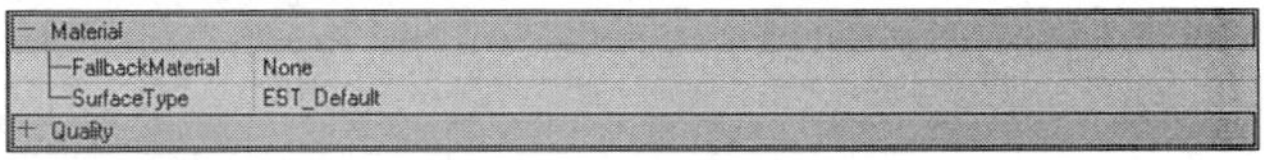

FIGURE 8.22 The Material category.

Surface Category

In the Surface category, shown in **FIGURE 8.23**, you have access to the properties available in the Import Texture dialog box when the texture is first imported. For example, if you create a 32-bit TGA file that includes an alpha channel, but didn't select the Alpha check box in the Options section, you could simply come to this category and set the `bAlphaTexture` property to True. The `bMasked` property corresponds to the Masked check box in the Import Texture dialog box. You also find the `bTwoSided` property in this category, which makes a texture visible from both sides. As you might recall from Chapter 4, "Advanced Brush Techniques," by default the Unreal Engine doesn't render the back faces of polygons. If you set this property to True, the texture can be seen from both sides, effectively making the polygon's back face visible in-game. This setting is especially useful when using Sheet brushes in your levels, which, by default, can be seen from only one side.

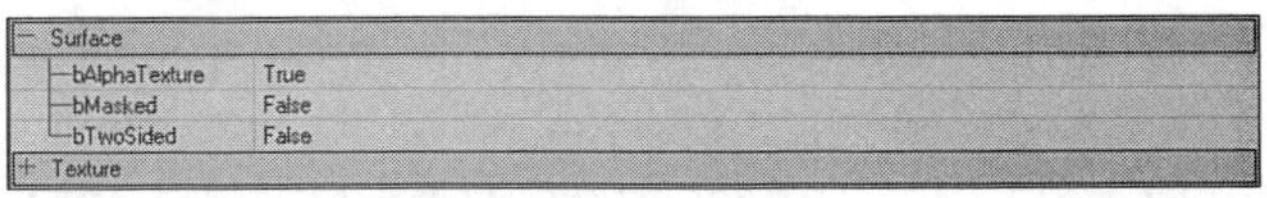

FIGURE 8.23 The Surface category.

Texture Category

In the Texture category (see **FIGURE 8.24**), you find the `Detail` property, which is used to add more levels of detail to your texture. The property enables you to overlay a grayscale image onto

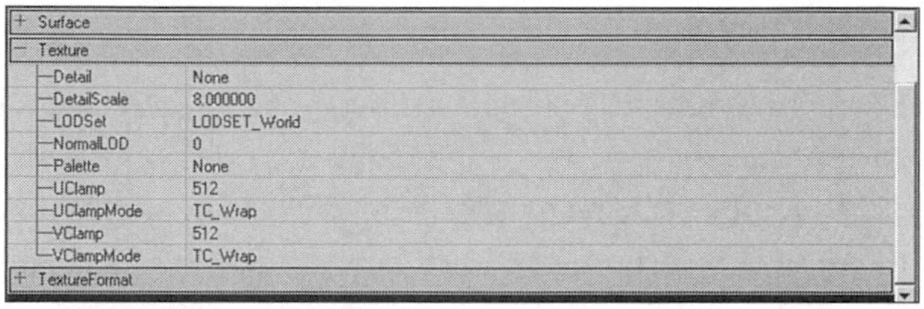

FIGURE 8.24 The Texture category.

your texture to give the appearance of minuscule cracks, crevices, and any other kinds of tactile detail you can imagine. The brightness or darkness of this grayscale image affects the final blend that occurs with your texture. You want to keep this image's overall value near 127, or perfect gray, so that you're neither increasing nor decreasing the original texture's brightness. You also want to keep these images fairly small and extremely tileable. The `DetailScale` property controls the number of times this image is tiled across your texture.

Up to this point, you have been dealing with textures of a fixed size, such as 256×256 or 512×512. In more advanced materials, such as a ScriptedTexture, Unreal creates the material on the fly during gameplay, and the size of the material isn't predetermined by a texture. The `UClamp` and `VClamp` properties are used to define the size of these materials. On most textures that have actual sizes, these properties are useless. ScriptedTextures are discussed later in this chapter in "Using a ScriptedTexture."

You can use the `UClampMode` and `VClampMode` properties to control whether the texture tiles (repeats) on a specific surface, such as a static mesh, in the U or V direction. The default setting, `TC_Wrap`, causes a texture to tile indefinitely in that direction. A setting of `TC_Clamp` restricts the tiling to one copy in the given direction. The remaining area in that direction is filled by stretching the line of pixels at the edge of that texture. This means if you have a nontransparent color at the edge of your texture, it's stretched across the surface from end to end. **FIGURE 8.25** shows the result of both settings.

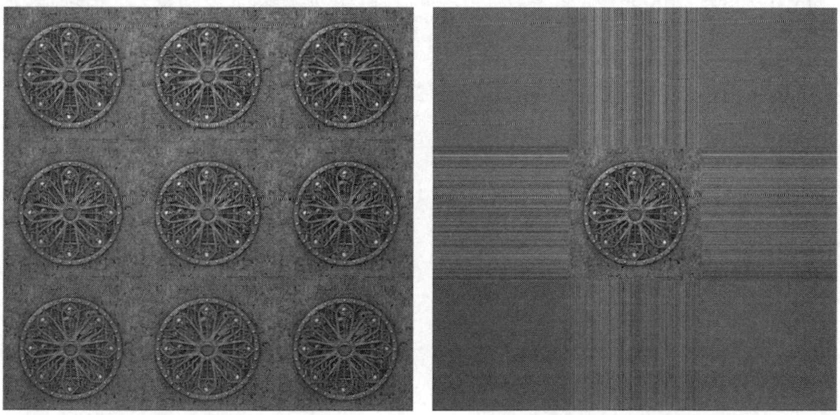

3x3 tiled texture (TC_Wrap) 3x3 tiled texture (TC_Clamp)

FIGURE 8.25 The difference between *`TC_Wrap`* and *`TC_Clamp`*.

Shaders

Shaders are material components that apply certain effects to your material, such as transparency and *specularity*—the way a highlight is created on a material when light reflects off its surface. These components help make your object look like it's made of glass, metal, polished wood, and more. In this section, you learn how to create shaders and see how they can add a new level of realism to your materials.

Shaders acquire the data they need from a series of "maps." This term is not to be confused with levels, which are also sometimes called maps. You use these maps to designate which parts of a shader are glossy, matte, transparent, opaque, and much more. You can create maps for these shaders directly in UnrealEd. **TUTORIAL 8.4** shows the steps for creating a shader in UnrealEd.

TUTORIAL 8.4: Creating a Shader

1. With the Texture browser open, choose File > New from the menu.
2. Make sure the package is set to MaterialTest. Leave the Group entry empty, and set the name to **`tileShader`**. Leave the Class setting as Raw Material for now (see **FIGURE 8.26**).
3. In the Properties section, you can select the type of `MaterialClass` to create. The `MaterialClass` property is easily the most important setting in this dialog box, as it defines what type of material you're creating. In this tutorial, you'll use `Engine.Shader`. You'll look at many other options in later sections.
4. Click the New button to create the shader and open its Properties window (see **FIGURE 8.27**).

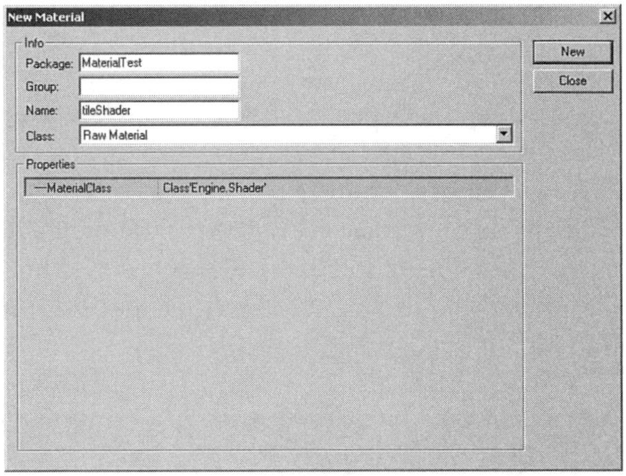

FIGURE 8.26 The New Material dialog box.

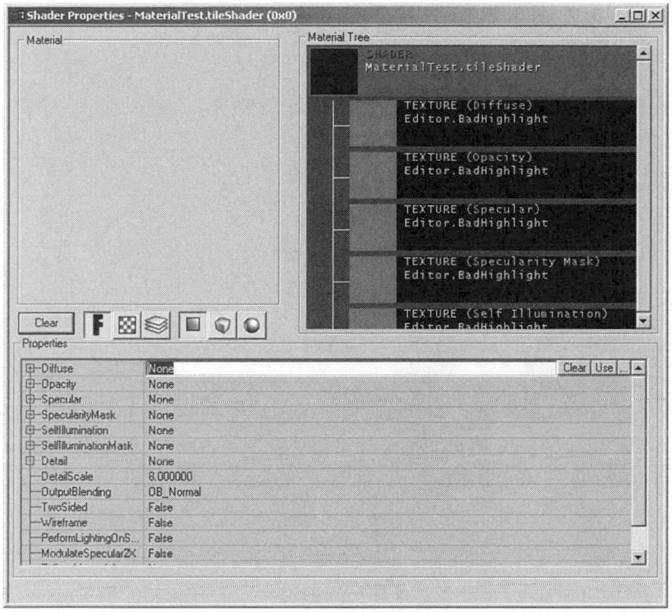

FIGURE 8.27 The Properties window for the new material.

END TUTORIAL 8.4

The Shader Properties window is similar to the Texture Properties window. In **FIGURE 8.27**, the Material Tree section has been filled with a new hierarchy of textures leading into the shader. The item at the top of the tree is the final material. It combines the information from all its child materials (that is, Diffuse, Opacity, Specularity, and so on) to form the material. This list is not static; it's adjusted and updated depending on which properties you use in your shader. Each child material holds a texture, a shader, or another type of material. The child materials of your shader are red by default to indicate that they have been assigned a default texture. In the following subsections, you see how to set up these maps to form your shader.

Diffuse and Specularity Maps

The Diffuse map determines the overall color for your material. In **TUTORIAL 8.5**, you establish your Diffuse map with a texture.

TUTORIAL 8.5: Setting Up the Diffuse Map

1. Open the Shader Properties window, if it's not open already. In the Textures browser, select the `tileTex` texture you created in **TUTORIAL 8.1**.
2. Back in the Shader Properties window, click `None` next to the `Diffuse` property, and then click the Use button. In the Material Tree network view, you see the red texture of Diffuse change to the blue texture you imported. You'll also notice that the icon for your top shader has changed (see **FIGURE 8.28**).

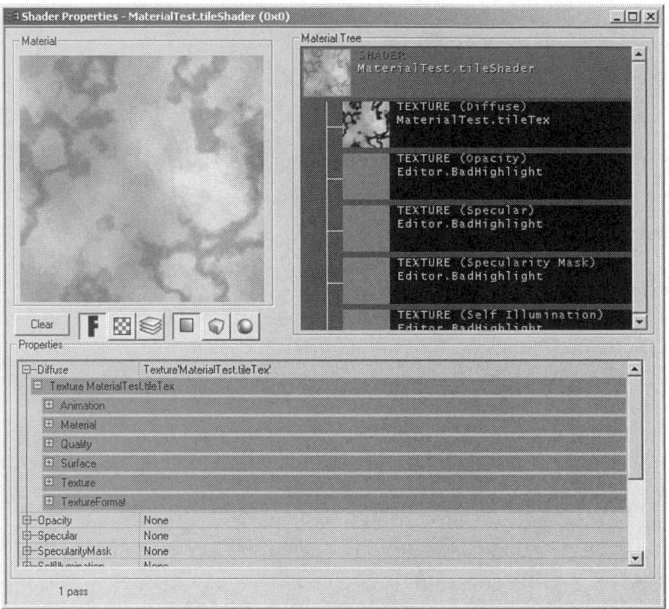

FIGURE 8.28 The Shader Properties window with the Diffuse property set.

3. The properties for your texture have also expanded. Keep in mind, however, that currently the Diffuse map and the texture in the Textures browser are one and the same, meaning that any changes you make to this texture for the Diffuse map affect the texture itself. If you select the Diffuse map in the Material Tree network view, you see only the texture's properties. This view can be useful if the other properties get in the way, and you want to focus on just one specific map.

END TUTORIAL 8.5

8

You now have a working shader that you can apply to any surface in your levels. Currently, however, this shader is no different from the texture that makes up its Diffuse map. In **TUTORIAL 8.6**, you make this shader more interesting by adding some specularity for a shiny look. For the Specular map, you'll create a texture environment map, which is discussed in detail later in the "Creating Reflective Surfaces with Cubemaps and TexEnvMaps" section.

TUTORIAL 8.6: Adding the Specular Map

1. You still haven't learned how to create environment maps, so you'll use one that's been created for you. In the Textures browser, open `Chapter8.utx` from the CD.

2. Next, you need to set the Specular map of your new shader to the `Chapter8.utx` environment map. First, make sure the tileShader's Properties window is displayed. Now switch to the Chapter8 package in the Textures browser and select EnvironmentMap.

3. In the tileShader's Properties window, select the `Specular` property and click the Use button. Switch your display window geometry to a cube, and look at the results. The cube now looks glossy (see **FIGURE 8.29**).

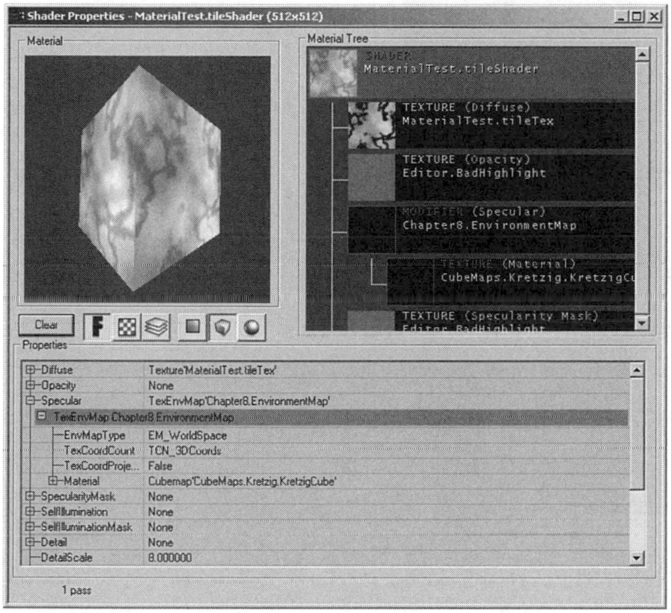

FIGURE 8.29 The glossy cube inside the tileShader's Properties window.

END TUTORIAL 8.6

Although this shader is looking far more interesting than it did previously, it would look even better if you removed the specularity from the darker, corroded areas of the tile. You do this with a `SpecularityMask`, which allows you to control which parts of the material appear to have specularity and which ones do not. A *mask* is a texture that can be used to hide or control aspects of other textures. However, the `SpecularityMask` property reads data only from a texture's alpha channel. In this case, the texture you originally imported included an alpha channel, but you need to remember to create one yourself when making your own textures. Because the `tileTex` texture you used for the Diffuse map includes an alpha channel, you can use that same texture in **TUTORIAL 8.7** for the `SpecularityMask`.

TUTORIAL 8.7: Taking Advantage of the *SpecularityMask* Property

1. You have already seen how to use the Use button, so this time you take a different approach to placing a texture into a property. Select the Diffuse property, select the text of the texture's name, and press Ctrl+C to copy it to your computer's Clipboard.

2. Select the `SpecularityMask` property, press Ctrl+V to paste the Clipboard contents into the field (see **FIGURE 8.30**), and then press Enter.

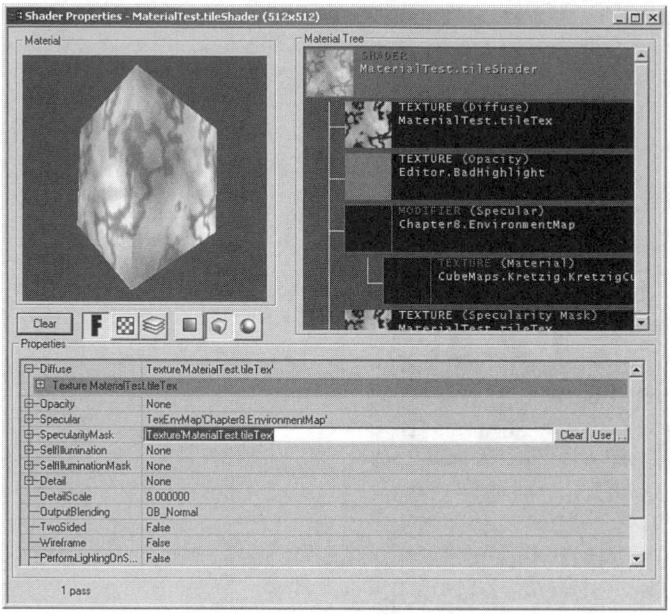

FIGURE 8.30 *`SpecularityMask`* **in operation.**

3. Make sure the `OutputBlending` property is set to `OB_Normal`. This setting ensures that all channels operate without adding any extra blending effects. You'll be looking at these options shortly.

END TUTORIAL 8.7

At this point, the darker spots of the material should no longer have any specularity. **FIGURE 8.31** shows the image and alpha channel side by side.

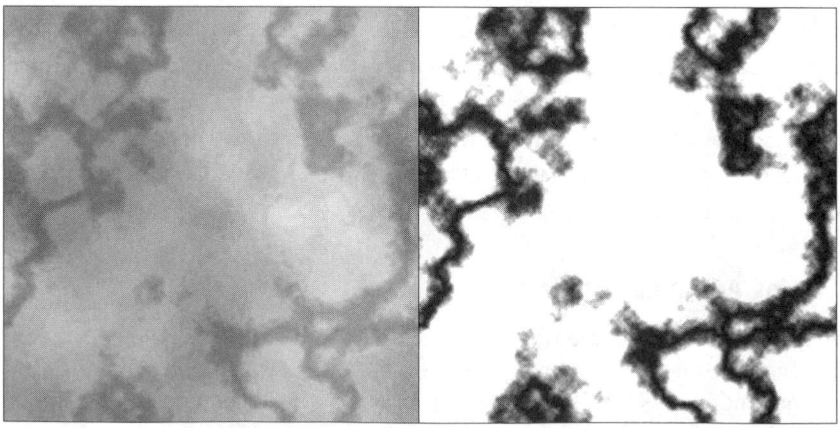

FIGURE 8.31 **On the left is the image, and on the right is the alpha channel.**

As you can see, the darker areas of the alpha channel are the areas that have less specularity, and the white parts have full specularity.

Opacity Maps

The Opacity map of a shader works the same way as the Specularity map. It reads the alpha channel of its assigned texture and uses it to designate which parts of a material are transparent, opaque, or some level in between. For the Opacity map, white areas of the texture are opaque (solid), and black areas be transparent. Shades of gray produce varying levels of transparency in relation to the brightness of the gray.

Self-Illumination Maps

You can use a Self Illumination map to brighten certain areas of your material. By default, however, a Self-Illumination map overlaps the entire Diffuse map. This causes the material to be unlit, or no longer responsive to lights, and hides the Diffuse map. To counteract this effect, you can use a Self-Illumination mask to determine which areas of your material show the Self-Illumination map and which parts show the Diffuse map.

The Self-Illumination mask works the same way as the Specularity mask, in that it reads your texture's alpha channel and uses that information to control where the Self-Illumination map is visible and where it is not. The white areas of the mask cause the Self-Illumination map to show on top; the black areas show the Diffuse map. The shades of gray in between allow for partial transparency of the Self-Illumination map, causing the Diffuse map to shine through partially. In addition, white areas of the mask designate areas that aren't affected by lights in the level. Black areas receive illumination regularly, and shades of gray create areas where light has only a partial effect. The Self-Illumination mask is especially useful for areas of a material that need to be glowing.

Other Properties

Shaders also include a Detail map, which functions in the same way as a texture's `Detail` property. You need to specify a texture to use as a Detail map and then set the `DetailScale` property, and you'll add a new layer of detail to your material.

If the `Wireframe` property is set to True, your material is rendered in-game as a wireframe. The `TwoSided` property determines whether the negative side of a polygon renders when the material is applied to it. This property is especially useful with a Sheet brush, which by default is visible from only one side. The `TwoSided` property also proves useful when you're creating a transparent or semitransparent material. If, for example, you apply a glass-like material to a cube, you expect to see all of the cube's surfaces when you look through it. If `TwoSided` is not selected, however, you can't see the back of the polygons that form the cube.

The `OutputBlending` property allows you to apply a variety of effects on your shader to control how it blends with other materials. Several modes are available for this property, described in the following list:

- `OB_Normal`—This mode causes no extra blending effects to be applied.
- `OB_Masked`—This mode uses an alpha channel to make certain areas of your shader visible or invisible. It doesn't produce any variation of transparency. If no alpha channel is specified, the transparency is calculated with the Diffuse map instead. If the map has an alpha channel, all areas with an alpha value less than 128 are invisible. If the image has no alpha channel and is not an 8-bit image with a palette, this property has no effect. Finally, if it's an 8-bit image, all colors located in the first entry of the palette are invisible.
- `OB_Modulate`—Areas that are white (RGB value of 255) become invisible, and black areas (RGB value of 0) become opaque. Every shade of gray in between creates a faded effect based on its value.
- `OB_Translucent`—This mode causes the dark areas of your material to be more transparent and the brighter areas more opaque.
- `OB_Invisible`—This mode hides your material based on your Opacity map, but leaves your environment map visible. If, for example, your material has a Reflectivity map, only the reflective areas remain visible; the rest of the material is hidden.
- `OB_Brighten`—This mode creates a general brightening of your entire material.
- `OB_Darken`—This mode creates a general darkening of your entire material.

Modifiers

8

A *modifier* is a type of material that alters or changes the look of an existing material. A wide variety of changes are possible, from a simple change of color to making the texture animate in some way. In this section, you learn about the most frequently used modifiers and how they can be used to manipulate your materials.

The Color Modifier

The Color modifier allows you to change a material's tint to a particular color. To use it, you simply need to choose a color and select the material you want to modify. In **TUTORIAL 8.8**, you see how to create this modifier and apply it to your material.

TUTORIAL 8.8: Creating and Using the Color Modifier

1. Create a material by choosing File > New from the Textures browser menu. Use the following properties:

   Package: MaterialTest
   Group: (Leave this setting empty)
   Name: ColorModifier
   Class: Raw Material
   MaterialClass: Engine.ColorModifier

2. Click the New button and take a look at the properties for this new material.

3. Only four properties are available for this modifier, described in the following list:

   - `Color`—This property allows you to choose a color for tinting your material.
   - `RenderTwoSided`—This property functions the same as the `bTwoSided` property for textures, discussed earlier. It enables you to see a material on the backface, or negative side, of a surface.
   - `AlphaBlend`—This property behaves the same as a texture's `bAlphaTexture` property. It checks the alpha channel you have applied to a material and uses it to control transparency for your material.
   - `Material`—This property determines which material is affected by this modifier.

   Set the `Color` property to some shade of green, and set the `Material` property to `tileTex`. The results are shown in **FIGURE 8.32**.

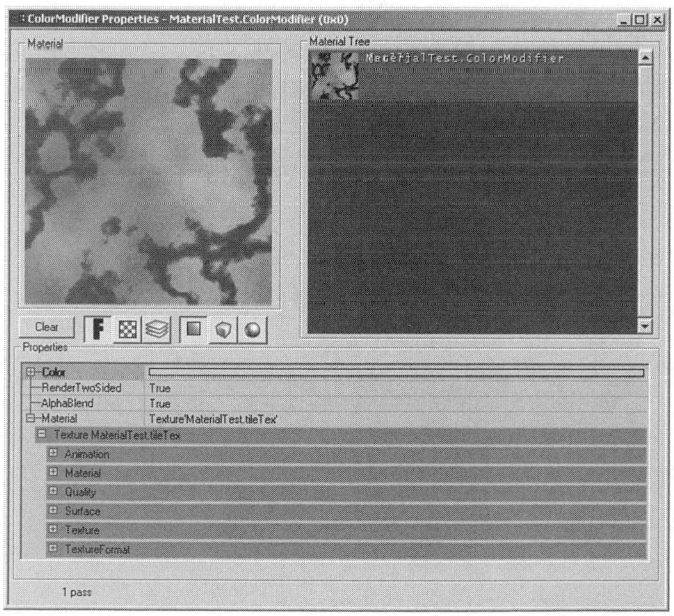

FIGURE 8.32 **The *`tileTex`* texture modified to have a green tint.**

END TUTORIAL 8.8

The TexOscillator Modifier

You can use the TexOscillator modifier to add repeating motion to your textures. It's created in the New Material dialog box in the same manner as the Color modifier. However, the effect of the TexOscillator changes over time. You can use it to make your textures move in a specific direction or to stretch them. The key aspect of the TexOscillator is that its animation oscillates, or moves back and forth in a cycling fashion. This means the animation starts at a certain point, goes to its extent, and then moves back to its original position. If you graph the motion, it would look like a sine wave (discussed in more depth later in this section).

The `UOscillationRate` and `VOscillationRate` properties control the speed at which the texture moves in the U or V direction. The speed is measured in complete revolutions per second. If, for example, you set it to 2, there would be two revolutions per second or one revolution every 0.5 seconds. You can set it to a negative number if you like, which causes the animation to begin by moving backward, and then oscillating forward.

The `UOscillationPhase` and `VOscillationPhase` properties control the point at which the animation begins in the U or V direction. The properties are set to a 0 to 1 scale: 0 is the beginning of the animation, and 1 is the end, which could also be considered the start of the second cycle. If you set `UOscillationPhase` to 0.5, for example, your animation would begin at the middle in the U direction.

The `UOscillationAmplitude` and `VOscillationAmplitude` properties control the distance traveled during animation. They are set to a value of 1 by default, meaning that if the texture is panning, it moves the length of its texture size from left to right, and then back to its original position. It then moves the length of its texture size from right to left, and then back to its original position. It repeats this cycle indefinitely as a constant, smooth motion. If you bump the size up to 2, the texture moves twice as far (two texture sizes) in each direction.

The motion can be represented by graphing a sine wave, as shown in **FIGURE 8.33**.

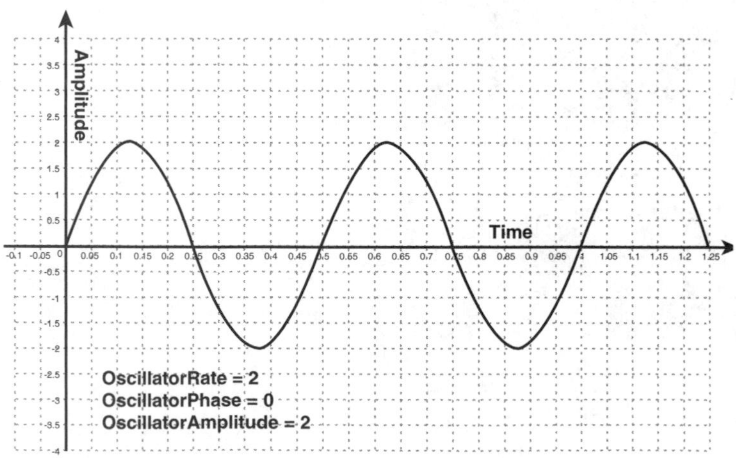

FIGURE 8.33 A sine wave representing the movement of a TexOscillator.

The final properties for a TexOscillator are `UOscillationType` and `VOscillationType`. These properties control the type of animation in your material. These are the four types available:

- `OT_Pan`—This type causes the texture to pan, or move in a sliding motion. You can set the distance it moves by adjusting the `VOscillationAmplitude` or `UOscillationAmplitude` property. The pan moves the texture in one direction, then back in the other direction, and finally back to its original position to complete one oscillation.
- `OT_Stretch`—This type scales your texture by the amount set for the amplitude. It then shrinks the texture back to its original size, completing one oscillation.
- `OT_StretchRepeat`—This type functions similarly to `OT_Stretch`, but does not smoothly shrink the texture back to its original size. Instead, the texture snaps back to its original size to complete one oscillation.
- `OT_Jitter`—This type moves the texture around randomly at the speed specified in the `OscillatorRate` property and by an amount no higher than the `OscillatorAmplitude` property specifies.

Remember that you can set separate oscillator types, oscillator rates, and oscillator amplitudes for both the U and V directions. If you mix and match these settings, you can create some interesting effects.

The TexPanner Modifier

The TexPanner modifier also animates your texture, but unlike the TexOscillator, the animation does not go back and forth. It simply pans your texture in a given direction at a constant rate. By default, the texture moves to the left. The `PanDirection` property controls the direction in which the texture moves. However, the settings for the `PanDirection` property are fairly unique. Although it includes `Yaw`, `Pitch`, and `Roll` settings, all the control you need to change the texture's pan direction is available by adjusting the `Yaw` setting. You can adjust it in Unreal rotation units to control the direction in which your texture moves.

Unreal's rotation units are quite different from standard rotation degrees or even radians. A 360-degree rotation is equal to 65,535 Unreal rotation units. The reason has to do with how a computer's memory functions internally. A computer's memory is divided into various compartments, and each compartment can hold only a certain amount of data. The largest number one of these compartments can hold is 65,535. So if you try to place the number 65,536 in one of these compartments, the computer stores a value of 0 instead.

When incrementing numbers in a computer, the computer internally counts up to only 65,535 and then starts at zero again. This is similar to degree-based rotations, in that if you rotate a texture 360 degrees, you could then start at 0 again and continue rotating. In Unreal rotation units, the same rule applies. Because a computer's memory compartments don't automatically reset to zero when they reach 360, an extra calculation is needed to tell the memory unit to restart at zero.

That calculation would take time. If a full rotation were set to 65,535, however, the reset would be automatic. Therefore, the rotation system has been converted to a number system that *automatically* restarts at zero when a full rotation has been reached, without the computer needing to create any extra computations.

You can easily convert from degrees to Unreal rotation units with the following formula:

(65535 × degrees) / 360 = Unreal rotation units

Using this formula, 90 degrees would be 16,383 units, and 180 degrees would be 32,768 units. You can use this system to control the direction in which the TexPanner moves your texture. A value of 0, which is the default setting, moves your texture to the left. To move the texture to the right, you need to rotate the direction 180 degrees, or 32,768 units. You can use **TABLE 8.1** to control the exact direction of the pan. The nature of Unreal's rotation units is discussed in more detail in the next section.

TABLE 8.1 Controlling the Direction of the Pan

Direction	`Yaw` Setting
Up	16384
Down	-16383
Left	0
Right	32768

The `Roll` setting has no affect on the `PanDirection` property. The `Pitch` setting influences the motion, but using only `Yaw` is recommended, as it gives you direct control over the texture's direction.

8

The `PanRate` property controls the speed of the pan, calculated in texture sizes per second. This means that if you set `PanRate` to 2, your texture moves two texture sizes in the given direction every second.

CAUTION

The `PanRate` property's result can become unpredictable if its `Yaw` value is set to a number other than what's listed in TABLE 8.1.

The TexRotator Modifier

The TexRotator modifier allows you to rotate your textures two-dimensionally to the right or left and three-dimensionally by flipping them in a horizontal or vertical direction. This modifier is immensely useful for controlling special textures, such as a rotating fan. You can create the modifier in the New Material dialog box, the same way as the other modifiers discussed previously.

The first property available in the TexRotator modifier is `TexRotationType`, which controls the kind of rotation you receive from the modifier. You can use these three types of rotation:

- `TR_FixedRotation`—This setting doesn't animate the texture at all. Instead, it simply rotates the texture to a specified angle. The `Yaw` setting allows you to rotate the texture to the left or right. `Pitch` allows you to flip the texture horizontally, and `Roll` flips it vertically.
- `TR_ConstantlyRotating`—As the name suggests, this setting causes your texture to rotate constantly in a given direction. The `Rotation` properties control not only the rotation's direction, but also its rate.
- `TR_OscillatingRotation`—This setting is similar to the effect of the TexOscillator, in that it rotates the texture a certain amount in one direction, and then the same amount in the opposite direction. It repeats this cycle indefinitely. The `OscillationRate`, `OscillationAmplitude`, and `OscillationPhase` properties apply only when this setting is active and function the same as their TexOscillator counterparts, discussed previously.

The `UOffset` and `VOffset` properties control the location of the center of rotation, also called the origin of rotation. By default, it's set to zero, which is the pixel at the texture's upper-right corner. To accurately place the origin, you need to know the size of your texture. For example, if you want to place the origin of rotation at the center of a 128×128 texture, you need a `UOffset` and `VOffset` value of 64.

The TexScaler Modifier

The TexScaler modifier does not animate your texture, so it scales your material only once. If you want to animate a scale, you use the TexOscillator modifier with an oscillation type of `Stretch` or `StretchRepeat`. The TexScaler modifier has four properties:

- `UScale` and `VScale`—These properties control the amount that the material is scaled in the U and V directions. For example, setting both to 2 would make the texture twice as large.
- `UOffset` and `VOffset`—These properties control the location of the origin of scaling, calculated in pixels. This setting is similar to the origin of rotation used in the TexRotator modifier. Bc default, it's set to 0, which is the pixel at the texture's upper-left corner. Therefore, the scale either shrinks the texture toward that point or expands the texture away from it. To place the origin of scaling at the center of a 128×128 texture, you need a `UOffset` and `VOffset` value of 64. **FIGURE 8.34** illustrates how an object scales with its origin in these two locations.

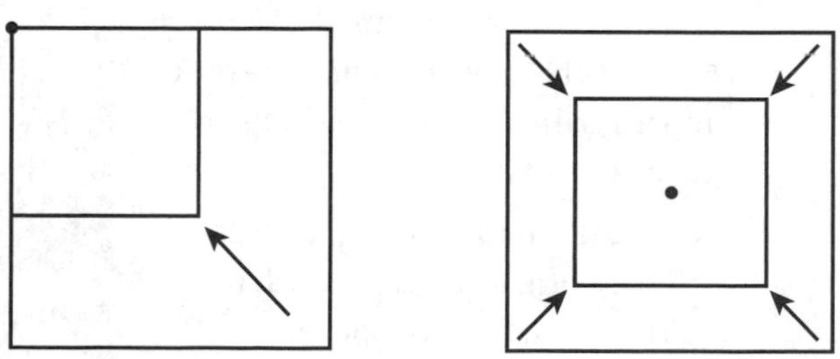

FIGURE 8.34 On the left, *`UOffset`* and *`VOffset`* are at the default of 0. On the right, *`UOffset`* and *`VOffset`* are adjusted so that the origin is in the center of the texture.

The Combiner Modifier

The Combiner modifier enables you to bring two materials together as one. This modifier has several different settings that control the manner in which the materials are blended. To use it, you need to designate the first material called Material1, a second material called Material2, and sometimes a mask, with an alpha channel used to control how the two materials are combined. A mask is not always necessary, as illustrated in some of the Combiner's properties.

The `CombineOperation` property determines how the materials interact with each other and specifies how or if they make use of the mask texture's alpha channel. The following list describes the available modes, with figures to illustrate. For these illustrations, the materials shown in **FIGURE 8.35** are used.

FIGURE 8.35 From left to right: Mat1, Mat2, and Mask.

- The `CO_Use_Color_From_Material1` and `CO_Use_Color_From_Material2` modes simply show Material1 or Material2 without adding any special blending processes.

NOTE

You can try these examples yourself, or open the `combinerTest.utx` package included with this book.

- `CO_Multiply` multiplies Material1 and Material2 together to produce a final output. **FIGURE 8.36** shows the result. When using this mode, Unreal considers the `Module2X` and `Module4X` properties. In any other mode, these properties are ignored.

  If `Module2X` is set to true, the final material's brightness is doubled. If `Module4X` is set to true, the material's brightness is quadrupled. Keep in

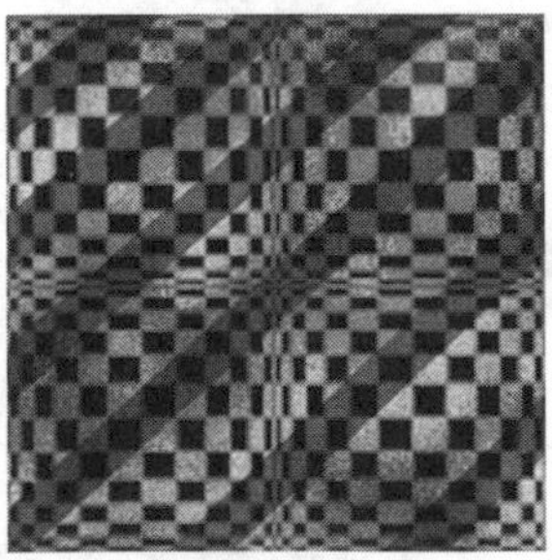

FIGURE 8.36 Using *`CO_Multiply`* for the *`CombineOperation`* property.

mind that the `Module4X` property has priority over `Module2X`. Therefore, if `Module4X` is set to True, the `Module2X` property is ignored.

- The `CO_Add` mode adds the values of the two materials together to produce the final material. In most cases, it considerably brightens your new material, as shown in **FIGURE 8.37**.
- `CO_Subtract` causes the values of Material2 to be subtracted from Material1 to produce the final output (see **FIGURE 8.38**).
- `CO_AlphaBlend_With_Mask` draws Material1 over Material2 and uses the mask to determine where you can see through to Material2 (see **FIGURE 8.39**). The white areas of the mask show Material1, and the black areas show Material2. If you need to reverse the result of the mask, you can use the `InvertMask` property. When set to True, it inverts your map.
- When using `CO_Add_With_Mask_Modulation`, the `Mask` property is ignored and the alpha channel of Material2 is used instead. Where the alpha channel of Material2 is white, Material1 and Material2 are added together. For example, say that Material2 has the alpha channel shown in **FIGURE 8.40**.

Then the Combiner modifier would output what's shown in **FIGURE 8.41**.

You can see that the black areas simply show Material2, and the white areas add the values of Material1 and Material2 together. If your Material2 didn't have an alpha channel, the two

FIGURE 8.37 Using *CO_Add* for the *CombineOperation* property.

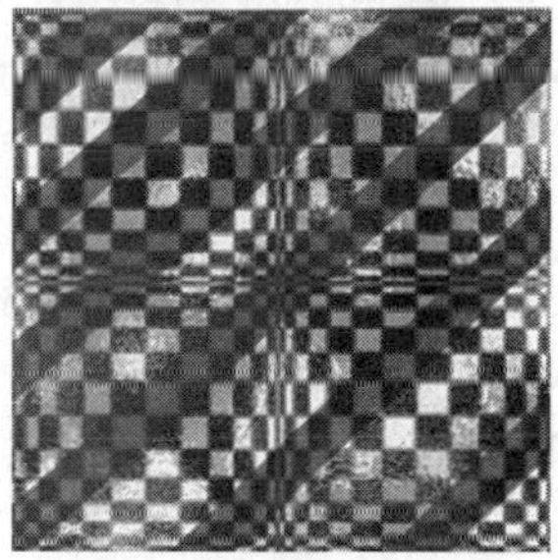

FIGURE 8.38 Using *CO_Subtract* for the *CombineOperation* property.

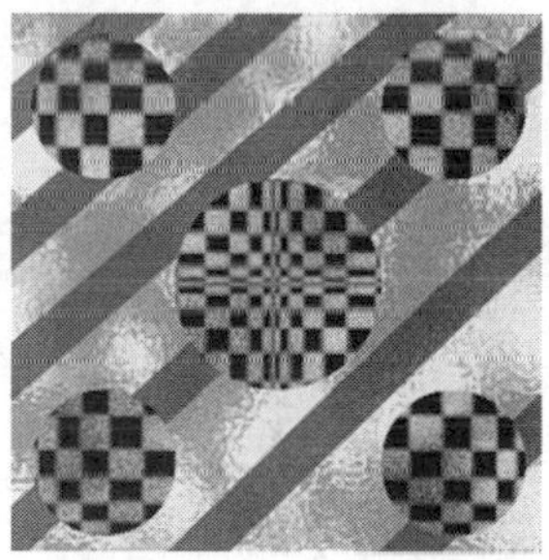

FIGURE 8.39 Using *CO_AlphaBlend_With_Mask* for the *CombineOperation* property.

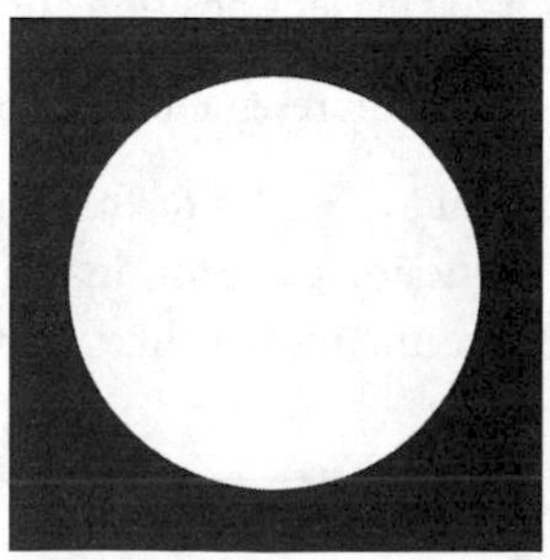

FIGURE 8.40 An alpha channel.

materials would be added together in their entirety, just like using the CO_Add mode.

- CO_Use_Color_From_Mask provides results that are the same as CO_Use_Color_From_Material1.

FIGURE 8.41 White circle with a black background used as the alpha channel.

The AlphaOperation property controls what the Combiner uses as the final alpha channel. By default, AO_Use_Mask is selected, causing the alpha channel to be the alpha channel of the mask. This mode also requires setting the Mask property to Material1, Material2, or nothing at all.

When using AO_Multiply, the alpha channels of Material1 and Material2 are multiplied together and the resulting alpha channel is used. AO_Add adds the two materials' alpha channels together to generate the final alpha. AO_Use_Alpha_From_Material1 and AO_Use_Alpha_From_Material2 simply allow you to use the alpha channel of the respective material. This mode also requires setting the Mask property to Material1, Material2, or nothing at all.

Creating Reflective Surfaces with Cubemaps and TexEnvMaps

To create a surface that appears to be reflecting its surrounding environment, you implement an *environment map* into your material. An environment map is a panoramic representation of your level's environment, sampled from a specific reference point in the level. To create this map, you acquire six images of your level, all taken from a single location and each pointing in one of six directions: up, down, north, south, east, and west. The Cubemap stores these images and compiles them together. However, this alone doesn't produce an environment map. The TexEnvMap converts the Cubemap into an environment map, based on the reference point used to create the Cubemap's images and the player's position and orientation.

The Cubemap's textures are represented internally in the configuration shown in **FIGURE 8.42**.

Notice that you could fold the sides of this image together and get a cube. If you were to do this, and then look at the images from inside the cube, you would have a representation of your surrounding environment, just like painting a panoramic landscape on the walls of a room.

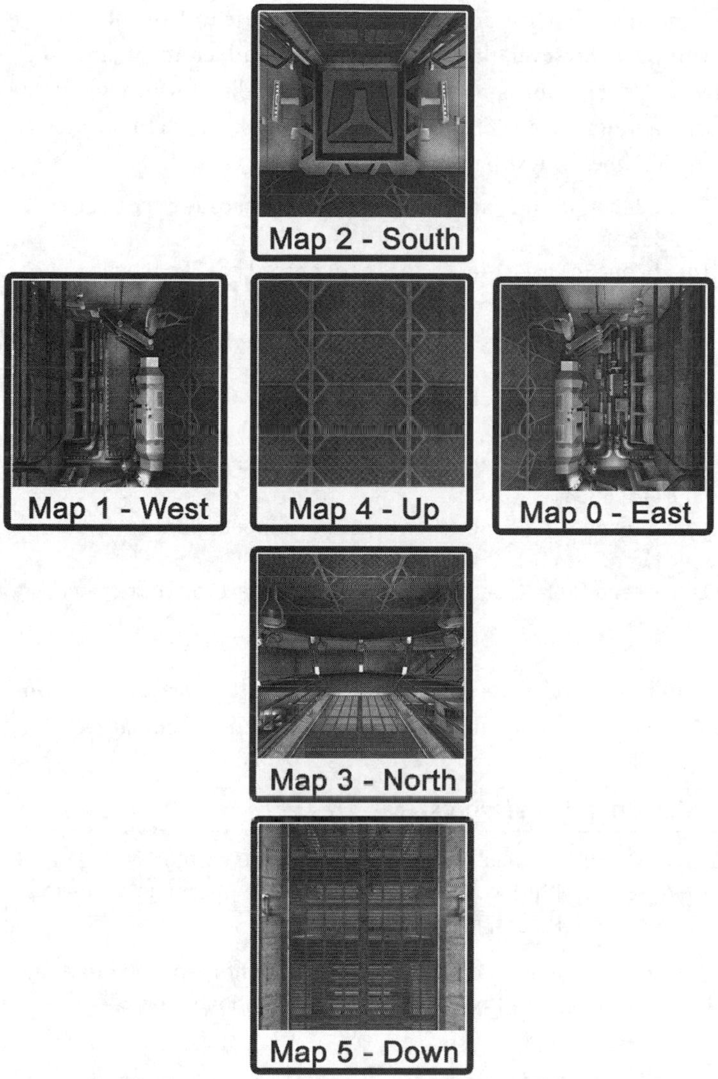

FIGURE 8.42 A Cubemap's internal representation.

When acquiring the images that become your environment map, precisely rotating the camera manually would be extremely difficult. To alleviate this problem, UnrealEd has a series of hotkeys that rotate your camera in the necessary directions. You can use the diagram in **FIGURE 8.42**, or you can use the following list:

- Number pad 0: East
- Number pad 1: West
- Number pad 2: South
- Number pad 3: North
- Number pad 4: Up
- Number pad 5: Down

If you're using the Runtime Engine, these hotkeys are already set up for use in UnrealEd. In the retail build of Unreal Tournament 2004, however, these hotkeys must be added manually. To do this, go to the System folder of your Unreal Tournament 2004 installation directory and open the `User.ini` file. Using whatever search function is available in your text editor, search for `NumLock=`. When you find it, place the following lines of text beneath that line:

```
NumPad0=set playercontroller bZeroRoll False ¦ set playercontroller rotation
       (pitch=0,yaw=0,roll=16384)
NumPad1=set playercontroller bZeroRoll False ¦ set playercontroller rotation
       (pitch=0,yaw=32768,roll=-16384)
NumPad2=set playercontroller bZeroRoll False ¦ set playercontroller rotation
       (pitch=0,yaw=16384,roll=32768)
NumPad3=set playercontroller bZeroRoll False ¦ set playercontroller rotation
       (pitch=0,yaw=16384,roll=0)
NumPad4=set playercontroller bZeroRoll False ¦ set playercontroller rotation
       (pitch=16384,yaw=0,roll=16384)
NumPad5=set playercontroller bZeroRoll False ¦ set playercontroller rotation
       (pitch=16384,yaw=0,roll=16384)
NumPad6=set playercontroller bZeroRoll True ¦ set playercontroller rotation
       (pitch=0,yaw=0,roll=0)
```

These lines simply assign the number pad keys to point the camera in the correct directions. **TUTORIALS 8.9** through **8.12** walk you through the creation of a working Cubemap.

TUTORIAL 8.9: Taking the Cubemap Screenshots

1. Open the `Tutorial8_09_Start.ut2` file, which is the same level you created in Chapter 3, "Creating Your First Level with UnrealEd." The goal of this tutorial is to make a Cubemap so that objects in the control room, such as the glass wall, can be reflective.

2. Before you make the six textures you need to create your environment map, you need to adjust some settings in UnrealEd. From the UnrealEd main menu, choose View > Viewports > Fixed.

3. Choose View > Advanced Options. In the Advanced Options dialog box, expand Editor > Advanced, and set `UseAxisIndicator` to False to hide the small axis indicator in the corner of the 3D viewport.

4. Because you want the Cubemaps to be a reflection of the room, you don't want the light icons, or any other icons, to interfere. To hide them, you're going to create a group, add all the Actors with icons to the group, and then hide the group temporarily. Open the Group browser by clicking the Group browser icon on the toolbar.

5. By default, there's only one group labeled None. This group holds every Actor that isn't in some other group, and because there's no other group at the moment, the None group contains every Actor in the level. You want a group to hold all miscellaneous icons in the control room. Before you can create the group, however, you need to have at least one Actor selected that you plan to put in the group. Therefore, select the eight lights that are immediately visible from the center of the control room, and then select the Player Start (see **FIGURE 8.43**).

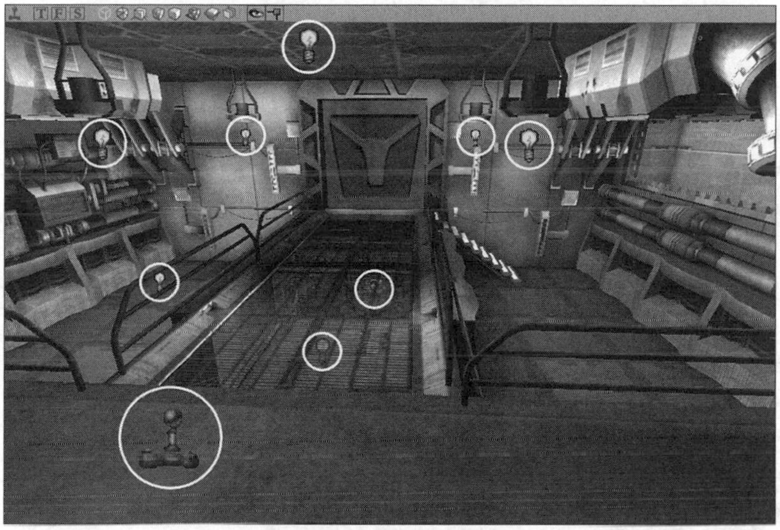

FIGURE 8.43 Icons that need to be selected.

6. From the Group browser's menu, choose Edit > New Group. In the New Group dialog box, type in the group name **Icons** and click OK.

7. To hide these icons, simple clear the check box next to the Icons group. If not all the icons disappear, that means you simply didn't place them in that group. To add other Actors to the group, select those Actors, make sure the Icons group is selected in the Group browser, and choose Edit > Add Selected Actors to Group. After that, you might need to choose View > Refresh so that everything is updated.

8. Because the final resolution you'll be using for these Cubemaps is 256×256, you're going to change the viewports into a configuration that more closely reflects that ratio. From the main menu, choose View > Viewports > Configure. Select the third button (large Perspective view on the right, with three stacked orthographic views on the left) and click OK.

9. Navigate the 3D viewport's camera into the center of the control room (see **FIGURE 8.44**). **FIGURE 8.45** shows the camera's position in the Perspective viewport.

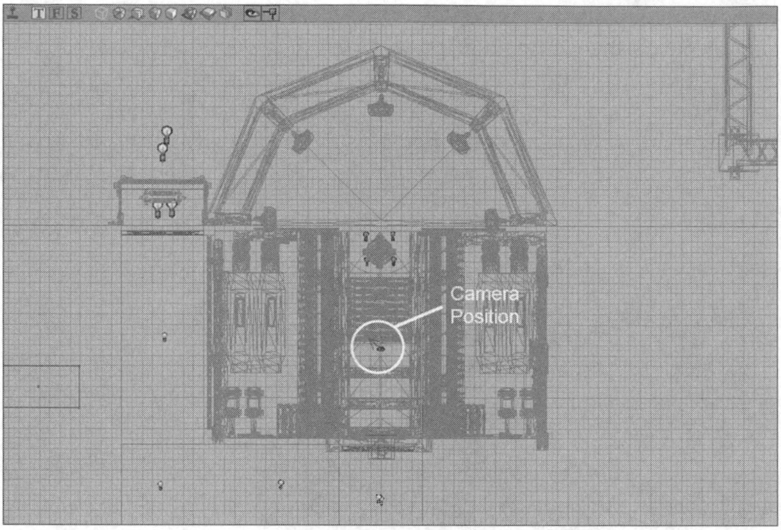

FIGURE 8.44 Top view of the camera position.

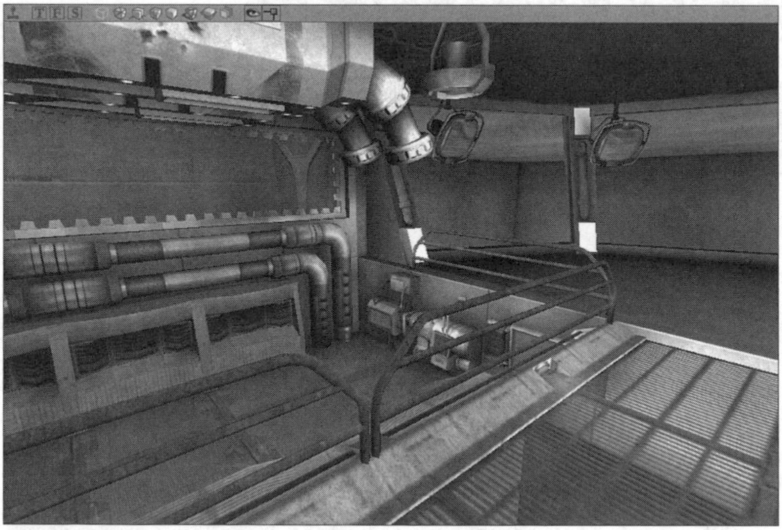

FIGURE 8.45 3D view of the camera position.

10. Now press 0 on the number pad to rotate the camera into position for your East shot. Press F9 to take a screenshot of this scene (see **FIGURE 8.46**).

11. Now press 1 on the number pad, and press F9 to take another screenshot. Press 2 on the number pad, and press F9 again. Continue until you've pressed 5 on the number pad for a total of six screenshots. However, before you use them in your Cubemap, you must change their size to something acceptable to Unreal.

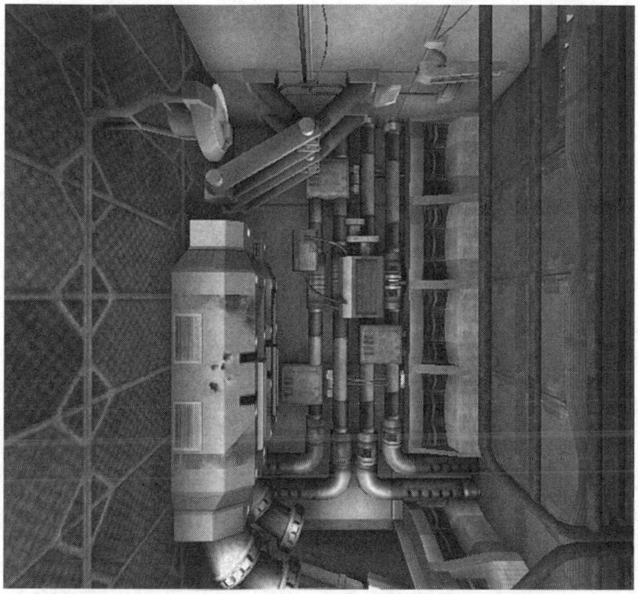

FIGURE 8.46 Image taken of the East position (number pad 0).

END TUTORIAL 8.9

In **TUTORIAL 8.10**, you resize the series of screenshots you just created to 512×512 in Adobe Photoshop. You'll be doing this with an Action, which automates the task, turning the entire process into just a few clicks and key presses. If you don't have Photoshop, you need to resize the images to 512×512 with the 2D image application of your choice.

TUTORIAL 8.10: Resizing Screenshots

1. Start Photoshop, and open your six screenshots. You can find them in the ScreenShots folder, located within the Installation folder of UT2004 or Unreal Runtime, depending on which program you're using. You can open all six by holding down Ctrl and clicking each file individually.

2. Notice that the images aren't 256×256. You'll fix the size manually for the first image, but then set up an Action that automates resizing the other images. Begin by clicking the Actions palette or choosing View > Actions from the menu (see **FIGURE 8.47**).

FIGURE 8.47 The Actions palette.

3. Click the Create New Action icon at the bottom of the Actions palette.
4. In the New Action dialog box, set the following properties, and click the Record button when you're finished:

   Name: EnvMap Resize

   Function Key: F2 (select the check box next to Shift)

   Color: None

5. All your Actions are now being recorded for future use. From the menu, choose Image > Image Size. Set the following properties (see **FIGURE 8.48**), and click OK when finished:

   Constrain Proportions: Clear this check box (do this first!)

   Width: 512 pixels

   Height: 512 pixels

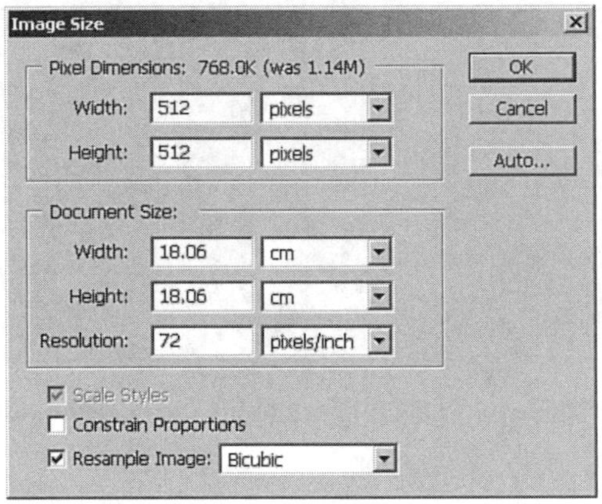

FIGURE 8.48 The Image Size dialog box.

6. Save the image and close it.
7. Click the Stop button at the bottom of the Actions palette.
8. The Action has now been recorded, and you can repeat the Action whenever you like by pressing Shift+F2. Try it by selecting the next image, and pressing the hotkey combination. Repeat until all six images have been resized.
9. Rename each image so that the first screenshot is named `cube0`, the second named `cube1`, and so on. If you're unsure as to the order, look at the number of the screenshot. The lowest number is cube0, the next is cube1, and so on up to cube5, which is the highest number.
10. You're finished with Photoshop for now, so go ahead and close it.

> **NOTE**
>
> **Make sure you save the images in one of the formats compatible with Unreal, as mentioned at the beginning of the chapter. In this case, BMP works fine.**

END TUTORIAL 8.10

Your images are now scaled to a size that's a power of two, so they are ready to be imported into Unreal. In **TUTORIAL 8.11**, you see how to get the textures into Unreal and use them to create a Cubemap.

TUTURIAL 8.11: Creating the Cubemap

1. In UnrealEd, open the Textures browser, and choose File > Import from the menu. Navigate to the six resized images you just saved, select all six, and click Open.
2. Change the package to controlRoom and make sure the Group entry is blank, as you're not adding a group to the package (see **FIGURE 8.49**). Click the OK All button.
3. With the new textures imported, you're ready to create your Cubemap. Choose File > New from the menu, set the following properties in the New Material dialog box, and click New when you're finished:

   Package: controlRoom

   Group: (Leave this entry empty)

   Name: controlRoomCube

   MaterialClass: Engine.Cubemap

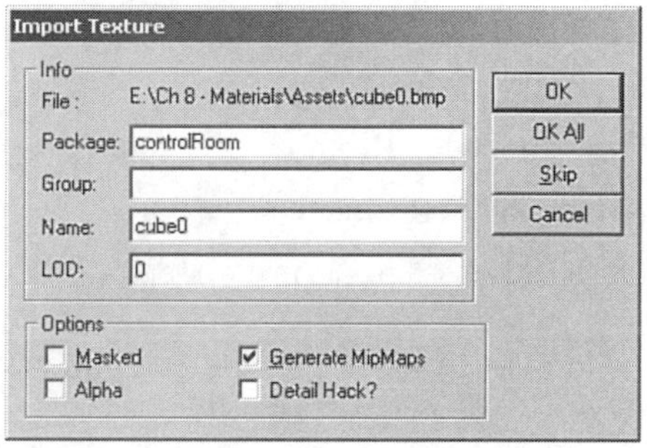

FIGURE 8.49 The Import Texture dialog box.

4. In the Properties window for the Cubemap, expand the Cubemap category. Select the Faces property, and click the Add button six times. This creates six new index entries, labeled [0] through [5]. Set index [0] to the cube0 texture by selecting the texture in the browser, and clicking the Use button next to index [0]. Repeat this process to set index [1] to the cube1 texture, index [2] to the cube2 texture, and so on. See **FIGURE 8.50** if you need help.

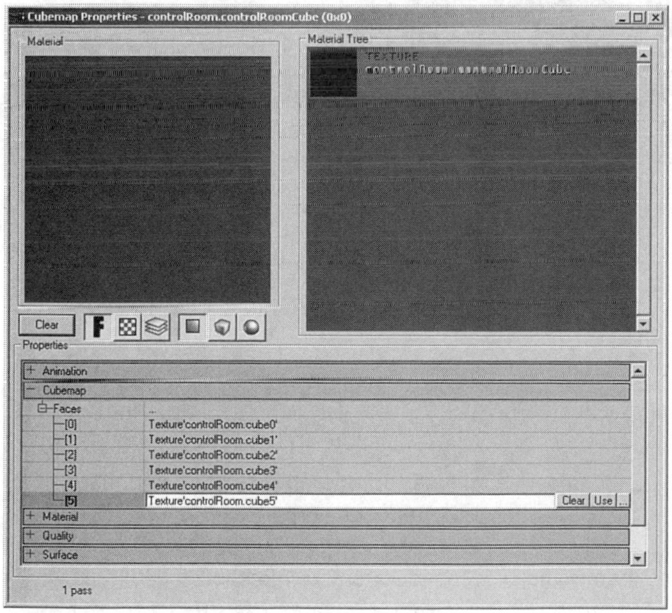

FIGURE 8.50 Cubemap properties.

END TUTORIAL 8.11

Your Cubemap has been created. As you'll recall from earlier in the chapter, however, it isn't enough to create the effect you want. In **TUTORIAL 8.12**, you create a TexEnvMap to convert the Cubemap into an environment map.

TUTORIAL 8.12: Creating the TexEnvMap

1. In the Textures browser, choose File > New, set the following properties, and click New when you're finished:

   Package: controlRoom

   Name: controlRoomEnv

   MaterialClass: Engine.TexEnvMap

2. In the Properties window for the TexEnvMap, change the `Material` property to `controlRoomCube` (see **FIGURE 8.51**).

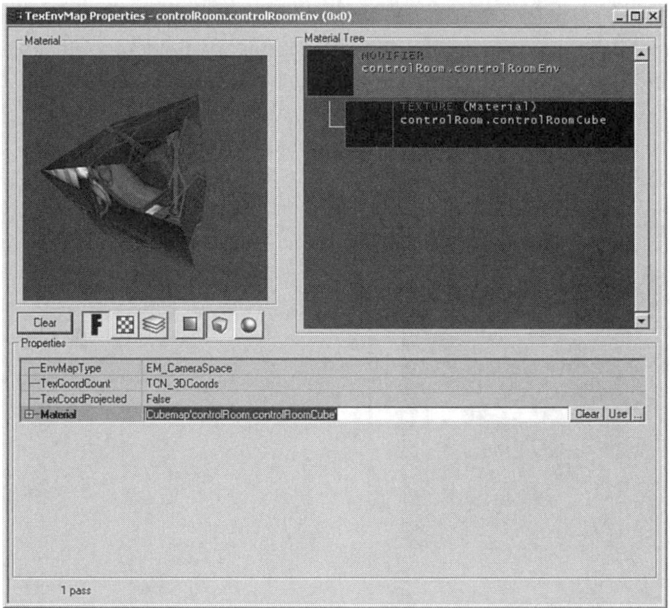

FIGURE 8.51 TexEnvMap properties.

3. Set the `EnvMapType` property to `EM_CameraSpace` so that the environment map takes the player's position and orientation into account when rendering. The result is that the reflection appears to be moving like a reflective surface. If you set the `EnvMapType` property to `EM_WorldSpace`, the reflection map would be dependent on the direction the surface was facing and would appear static, instead of moving with the player. **FIGURE 8.52** shows the final result.

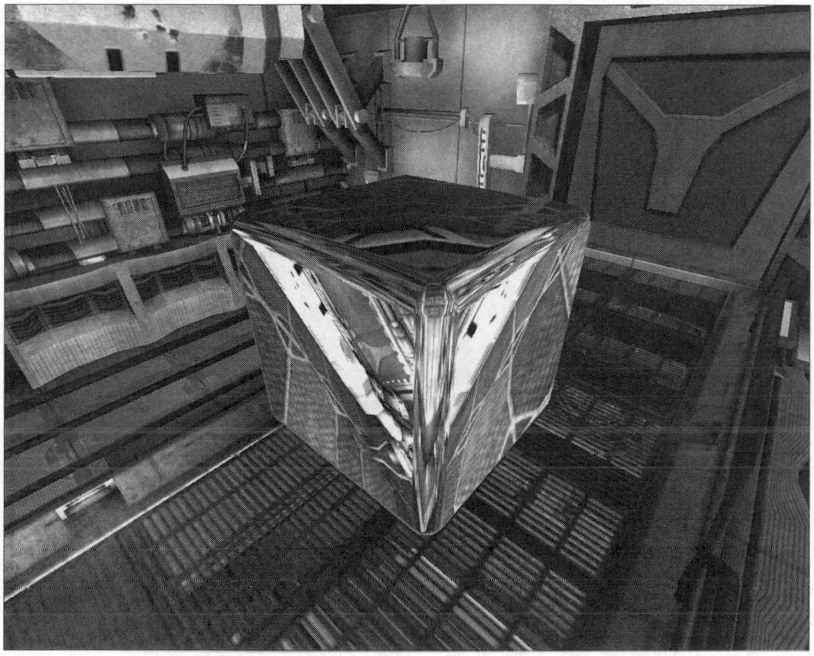

FIGURE 8.52 A cube placed inside the control room with the environment map applied to it.

END TUTORIAL 8.12

Now that you have successfully created an environment map, you can make any object in the control room reflective by placing this environment map on it. Iif you want more control, however, you could apply it to the Specular channel of a shader.

Final Blend Material

You can use the Final Blend material to add another layer of blending to your materials. It's similar to the Combiner modifier, but uses only a texture and its alpha channel (if it has one), instead of operating from two textures and a mask. You can create the Final Blend material by choosing it in the `MaterialClass` property when creating a new material. To illustrate how this material works, the same texture used as an example for the Combiner modifier is used (see **FIGURE 8.53**). The texture on the right is used as the alpha channel. The following properties are available for the Final Blend material:

- `AlphaTest`—This property activates the texture's alpha channel, allowing you to use it for blending. The `AlphaRef` property enables you to adjust the range of your alpha channel. As you know, an alpha channel is a grayscale image, and its values range from 0 (black) to 255 (white). All alpha channel values lower than the number placed in the `AlphaRef` property are treated as zero.

- FrameBufferBlending—This property specifies the way in which the blending of the material occurs. By default, it's set to FB_Overwrite, which has no effect on the texture. The following list describes the other available settings for this property and ilustrates their effects with figures:
  - FB_Modulate darkens all alpha channel values lower than 127 and brightens all others (see **FIGURE 8.54**). The material's transparency is affected as well. The color white is completely transparent, and black is completely opaque.
  - FB_AlphaBlend used on any material or texture is identical to setting the material's bAlphaTexture property to True. This setting blends the material's alpha channel for opacity. Therefore, the black areas of the channel become completely transparent, and the white areas become opaque (see **FIGURE 8.55**).
  - FB_AlphaModulate_MightNotFogCorrectly modulates all areas where the alpha channel is black. Therefore, the white parts of the alpha channel are not influenced (see **FIGURE 8.56**).
  - FB_Translucent makes the black areas of the material completely transparent and the white areas completely opaque. Every other color is partially transparent, based on its value (see **FIGURE 8.57**).

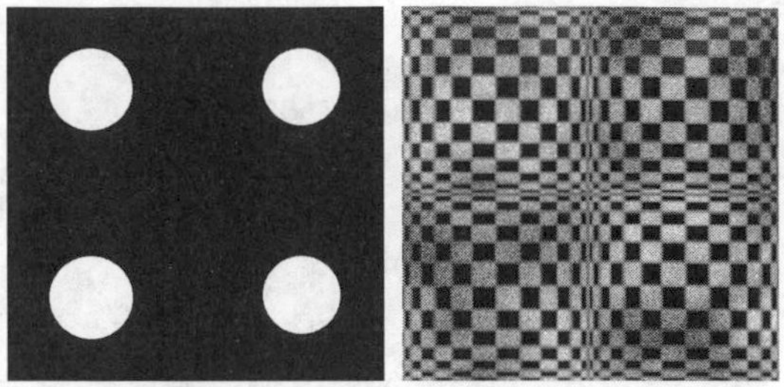

FIGURE 8.53 On the left is the image, and on the right is the alpha channel.

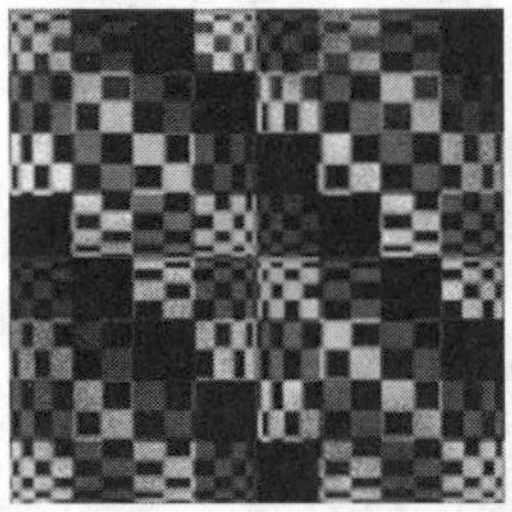

FIGURE 8.54 Effects of the *FB_Modulate* setting.

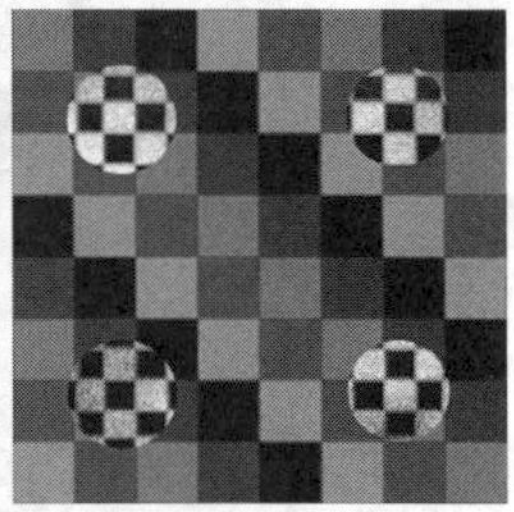

FIGURE 8.55 Effects of the *FB_AlphaBlend* setting.

FIGURE 8.56 Effects of the *FB_AlphaModulate* setting.

FIGURE 8.57 Effects of the *FB_Translucent* setting.

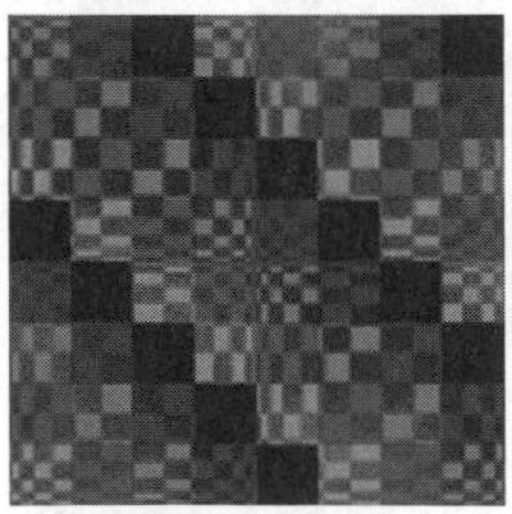

FIGURE 8.58 Effects of the *FB_Darken* setting.

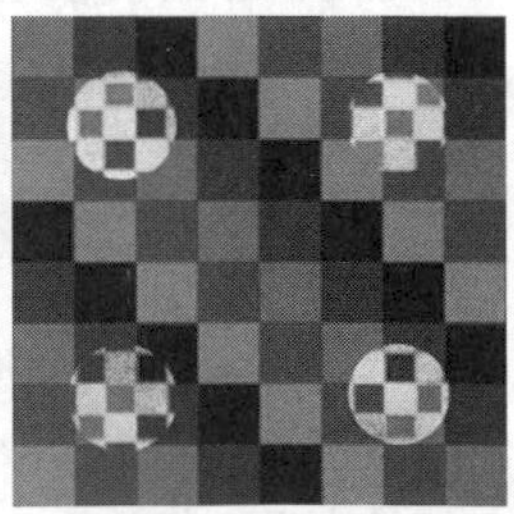

FIGURE 8.59 Effects of the *FB_Brighten* setting.

- FB_Darken darkens the texture so that it appears darker on the background. This makes the texture's colors look inverted (see **FIGURE 8.58**).
- FB_Brighten makes all black areas of the material completely transparent, and all others are blended according to the intensity of the alpha. The visible areas are then brightened (see **FIGURE 8.59**).
- FB_Invisible causes the texture to be completely hidden (see **FIGURE 8.60**). This setting is useful only when dealing with Zone Portals.

FIGURE 8.60 Effects of the *FB_Invisible* setting.

The last two properties for the Final Blend material are used to control the order in which the texture is drawn:

- ZTest—This property works with the ZWrite property (explained next) to control the order in which the texture is drawn. When the ZTest property is set to True, the position of the texture is tested to ensure that the rearmost texture is not drawn last—that is, on top of the texture above it. However, this property is useful only when two textures overlap, as in **FIGURE 8.61**, where ZTest is set to False. Notice that the smaller circles at the back of the cube are actually being drawn after (on top of) the circles on the front of the cube. To fix this, set ZTest to True.
- ZWrite—The Z information tested by the ZTest property is not saved unless the ZWrite property is set to True. After setting ZTest and ZWrite to True, the error is fixed, as shown in **FIGURE 8.62**.

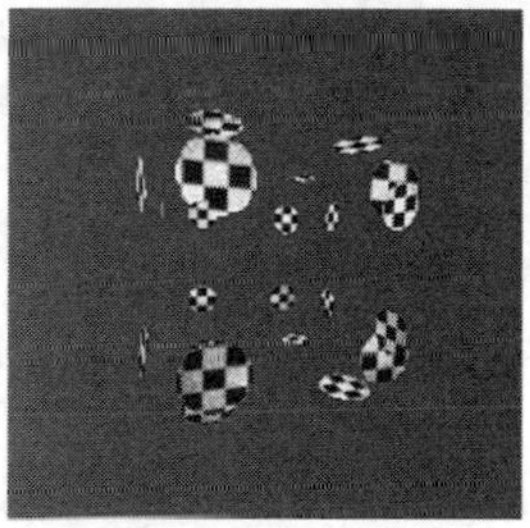

FIGURE 8.61 *ZTest* set to False.

FIGURE 8.62 *ZTest* and ZWrite set to True.

Using a ScriptedTexture

A ScriptedTexture material allows the Runtime Engine to create and alter the material during gameplay based on dynamic elements in the game, such as a player's score or walking in front of a security camera. When you first create this texture, the Material display window is blank because you're no longer basing the material on a pre-existing texture. All the information for creating the texture is produced during runtime, so you need to create an Actor that sends data to the ScriptedTexture while the game is playing.

Two types of Actors can be used for this purpose: the CameraTextureClient and the MessageTextureClient. The CameraTextureClient sends the pixel information it reads from a specific point in space and direction to the ScriptedTexture, resulting in a security camera effect. The MessageTextureClient sends text to the ScriptedTexture, allowing it to draw custom text onto the surfaces of your levels, such as a constantly updating scoreboard, making it possible to automatically display a character's name on a license plate when he or she enters a vehicle, for example.

In **TUTORIAL 8.13**, you use a ScriptedTexture to create a security camera effect.

TUTORIAL 8.13: Creating a Security Camera

1. Open the `Tutorial8_13_Start.ut2` file. You'll place a camera pointing down into the base of the elevator and have that camera feed into the middle monitor in the control room.
2. From the Textures browser menu, choose File > New. Create your ScriptedTexture with the following settings:

   Package: securityCamera

   Group: (Leave this entry empty)

   Name: cameraData

   MaterialClass: ScriptedTexture

3. As mentioned earlier, you won't see anything in the Material display window at this point because the texture has no pixel data. In addition, you haven't set the texture's size yet. You can do this with the `UClamp` and `VClamp` properties. In the ScriptedTexture Properties window, set both properties to 256 (see **FIGURE 8.63**). The other properties listed in this window should be familiar to you by now.
4. Next, you need to create the Actor that serves as your camera. It can be almost any Actor in your level. To designate a camera, you need a position and a direction, which all Actors can provide. In this case, you'll use an emitter, as it doesn't have a lot of excess functionality.

   In the Actor Class browser, select Emitter. Right-click somewhere near the base of the elevator, and add it to the level.

5. By default, however, an emitter doesn't specify a direction, which is necessary for the Actor to serve as a camera. Open the Properties window for the emitter, and under the Advanced category, set the `bDirectional` property to True. A red arrow points out of the Actor, showing its direction (see **FIGURE 8.64**).

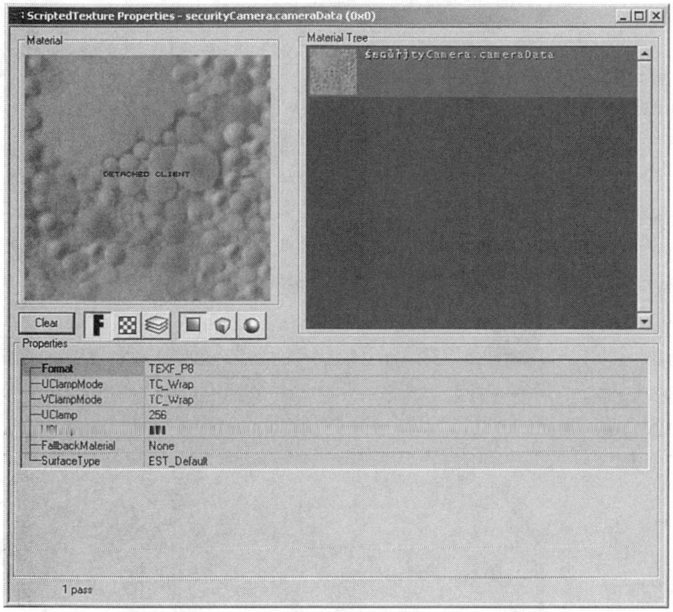

FIGURE 8.63 The ScriptedTexture Properties window.

6. Now move the emitter to the corner away from the wall and door, and rotate it until its red arrow is pointing toward the entrance to the elevator. Alternatively, you could click the Lock to Selected Actor icon above the 3D viewport and then click the emitter. Now as you move and rotate the camera around, you are, in fact, moving the emitter (see **FIGURE 8.65**). When it's in a good position, click the Lock to Selected Actor icon again, and the emitter stops moving around.

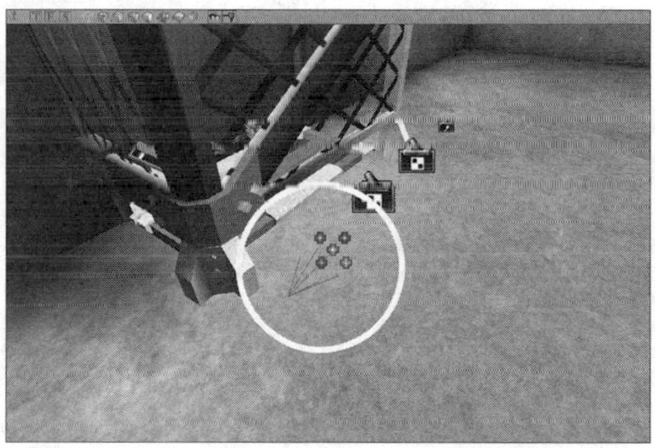

FIGURE 8.64 Emitter with a directional red arrow.

Also, set the Tag property of this emitter to `securityCamera`. The CameraTextureClient uses this information later.

7. Next, you need to create your CameraTextureClient. You can find it in the Actor Class browser under Info > CameraTextureClient. Although the position of this Actor has no effect, place it near the emitter for clarity (see **FIGURE 8.66**).

Open the Properties window for the CameraTextureClient by double-clicking the Actor. Under the CameraTextureClient category, you have four properties (see **FIGURE 8.67**):

- `CameraTag`—This property looks for the `Tag` property of the camera you'll be using. Set it to `securityCamera`.
- `DestTexture`—This property allows you to designate a destination texture, or the texture you'll be sending the data to, which must be a ScriptedTexture. With the `cameraData` texture selected in the Texture browser, click the Use button next to the `DestTexture` property.
- `FOV`—This property sets the field of view for your camera. Leave this setting at its default value.
- `RefreshRate`—This property specifies how often the camera updates (sends information back to your texture). It's calculated in frames per second. Leave this setting at its default value.

8. To make the ScriptedTexture appear on the screen of the control room's monitor, open the Properties window for the monitor and go to the Display category.

FIGURE 8.65 Looking through the emitter toward the entrance of the elevator.

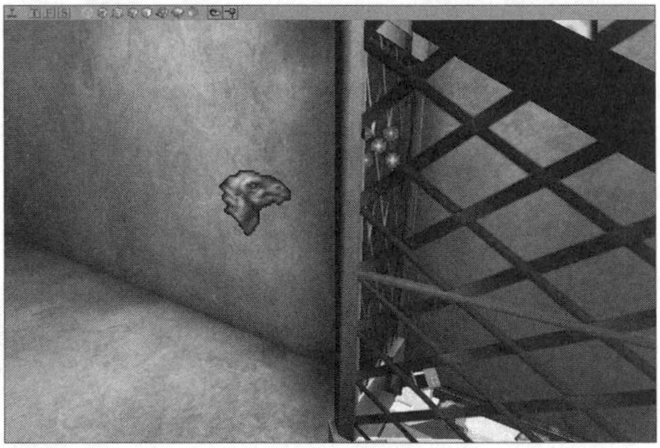

FIGURE 8.66 The CameraTextureClient placed near the emitter.

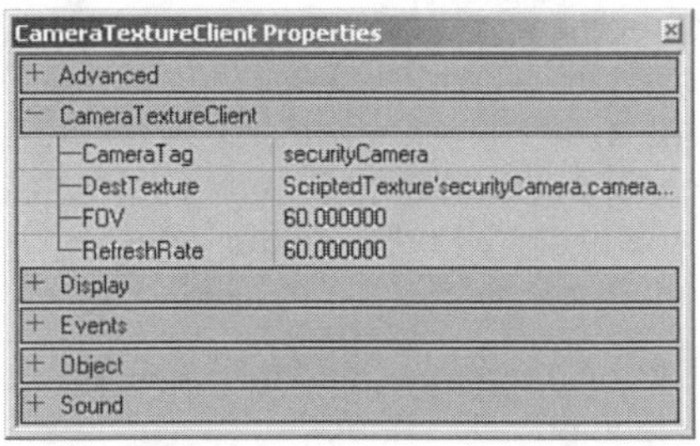

FIGURE 8.67 CameraTextureClient properties.

The `Skins` property is used to override some of the materials on your static mesh. You'll use it to change the first material to your ScriptedTexture. With the ScriptedTexture selected in the Texture browser, click Use for index [0] of the `Skins` property. You can now rebuild and test your new security camera in the game (see **FIGURE 8.68**).

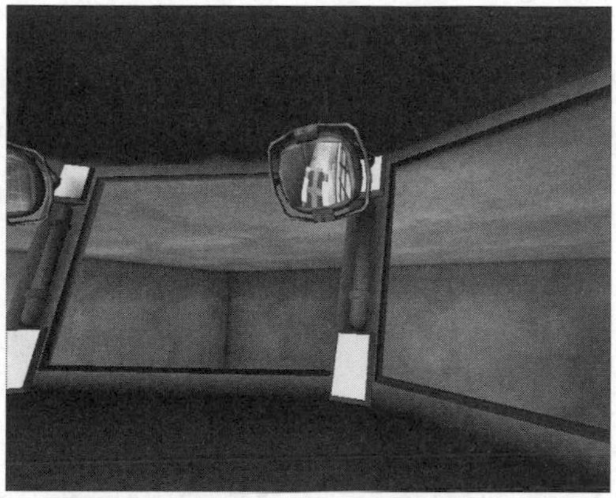

FIGURE 8.68 The security camera working in-game.

END TUTORIAL 8.13

Although the effect is interesting, it could look a little more realistic. In **TUTORIAL 8.14**, you use some of the skills you have acquired throughout this chapter to add video static and scanlines to the ScriptedTexture.

TUTORIAL 8.14: Improving the Security Camera

1. Within the securityCamera texture package is a texture named `screen1`, which contains a stagnant texture similar to television static. You'll use it to create more realistic static by adding a TexPanner to pan the texture at a very high rate. Using the skills you have learned so far in this chapter, create a new TexPanner and name it `static` (see **FIGURE 8.69**).

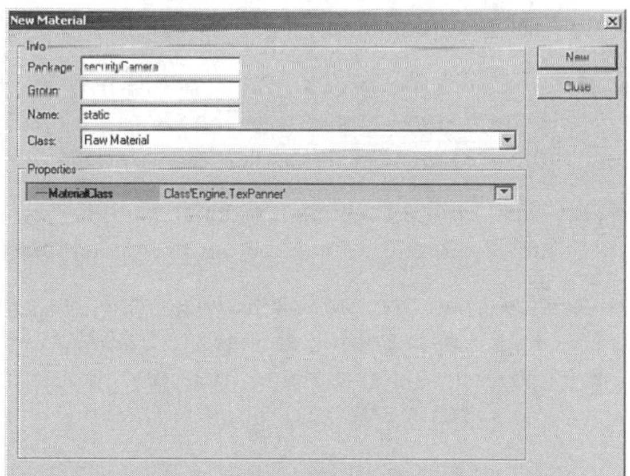

FIGURE 8.69 The New Material dialog box for the TexPanner.

2. In the Properties window for the TexPanner, change the `Material` property to `screen1`, set `PanRate` to about 125, and change `Yaw` to 20000 (see **FIGURE 8.70**). These settings cause your material to pan in both the U and V directions.

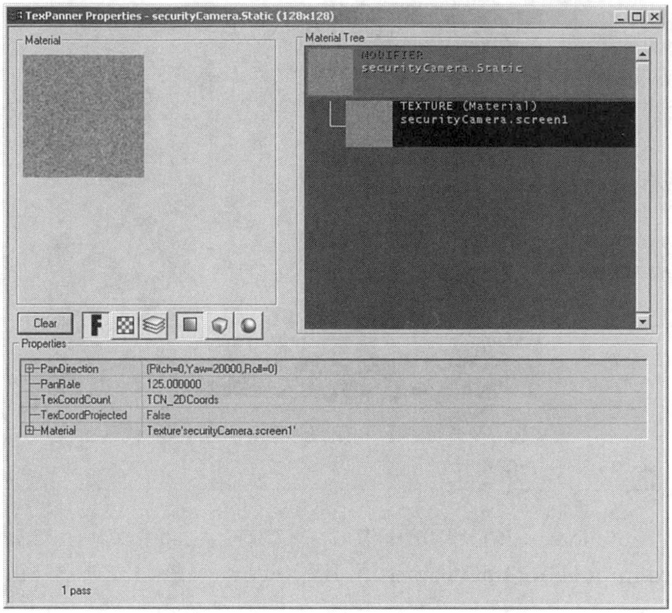

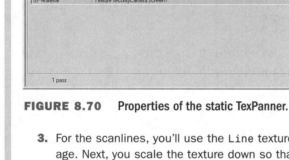

FIGURE 8.70 Properties of the static TexPanner.

3. For the scanlines, you'll use the `Line` texture, which is also in the securityCamera package. Next, you scale the texture down so that it repeats multiple times, and then pan it in an upward direction. First, create a TexScaler modifier and set its name to **`scanlines`**.

4. Open the Properties window of this new TexScaler, change its `Material` property to the `Line` texture, and change the `VScale` property to 0.01 (see **FIGURE 8.71**). Refer back to the section "The TexScaler Modifier" earlier in this chapter if you need to.

5. Next, create another TexPanner so that you can move the scanlines vertically. The name of this TexPanner should be set to **`movingScanlines`**.

6. Now open the new TexPanner's Properties window and change the `Material` property to `scanlines`. Set the `PanRate` to 0.05. You won't see any difference, however, because the movement is in U, not V. Therefore, change the `Yaw` value for `PanDirection` to 16383 (see **FIGURE 8.72**). Your scanlines now have an upward movement.

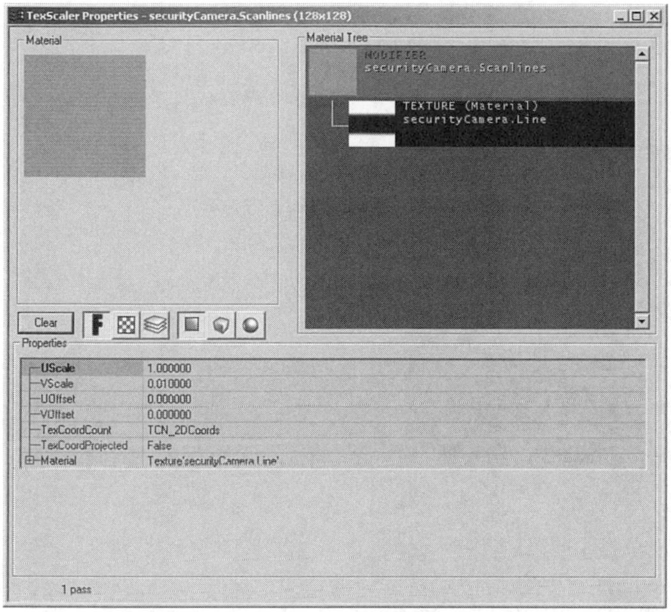

FIGURE 8.71 Properties of the scanlines TexScaler.

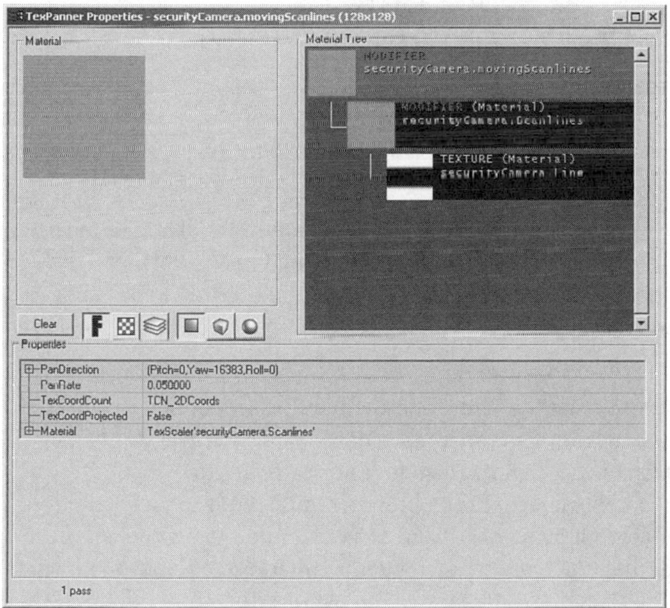

FIGURE 8.72 Properties of the movingScanlines TexPanner.

7. To combine the moving scanlines and static, create a Combiner modifier with the name **scanStatic**. Set Material1 to `movingScanlines` and Material2 to `Static` (see **FIGURE 8.73**).

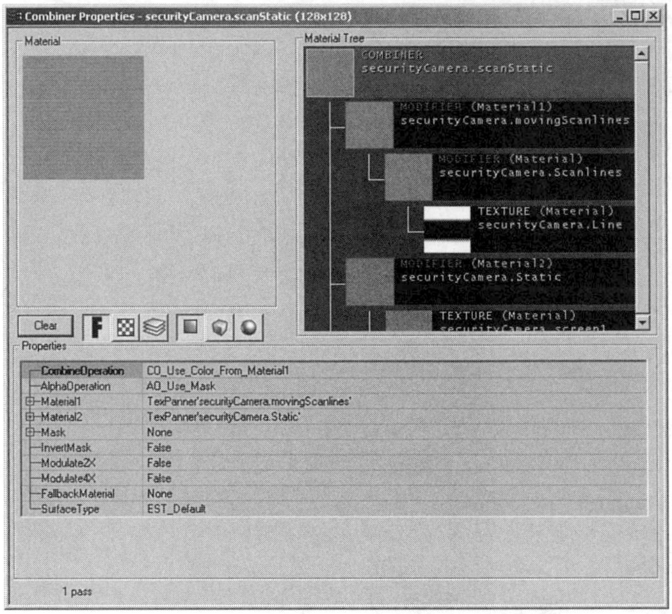

FIGURE 8.73 Properties of the scanStatic Combiner.

8. Change the `CombineOperation` property to `CO_Multiply` to combine your static and scanlines.

9. You'll use another texture in your securityCamera package called `MonitorFade` to fade the outside rim of the screen. Again, you'll use a Combiner. Name this new Combiner **fadedScanStatic**. Set Material1 to `scanStatic` and Material2 to `MonitorFade`. Change the `CombineOperation` property to `CO_Multiply`. The scanline/static effect is now blurred at the edges.

10. Now you need a final Combiner to bring the effect and ScriptedTexture together. Create a Combiner and name it **finalOutput**. In its Properties window (see **FIGURE 8.74**), set Material1 to `cameraData`, which is your ScriptedTexture, and Material2 to `fadedScanStatic`. Change the `CombineOperation` property to `CO_Multiply`. Finally, the material is a little dark, so brighten it by setting `Modulate4X` to True. As mentioned previously, this setting makes your material four times brighter. **FIGURE 8.75** shows the final result.

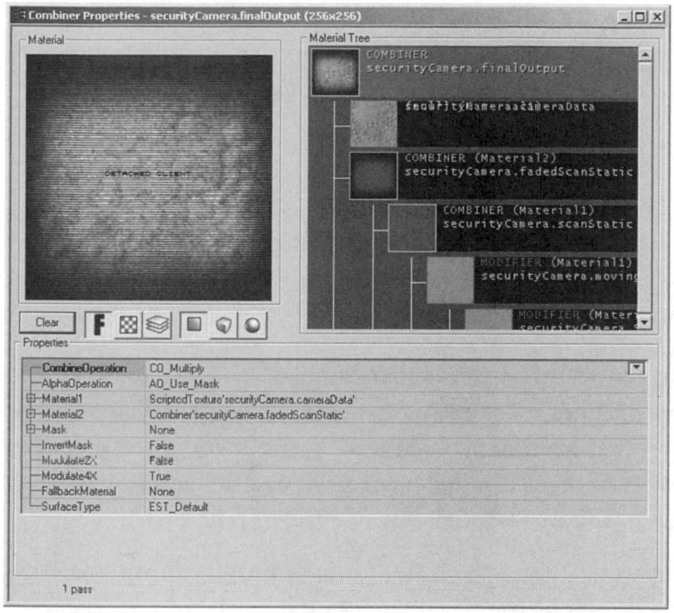

FIGURE 8.74 Properties of the finalOutput Combiner.

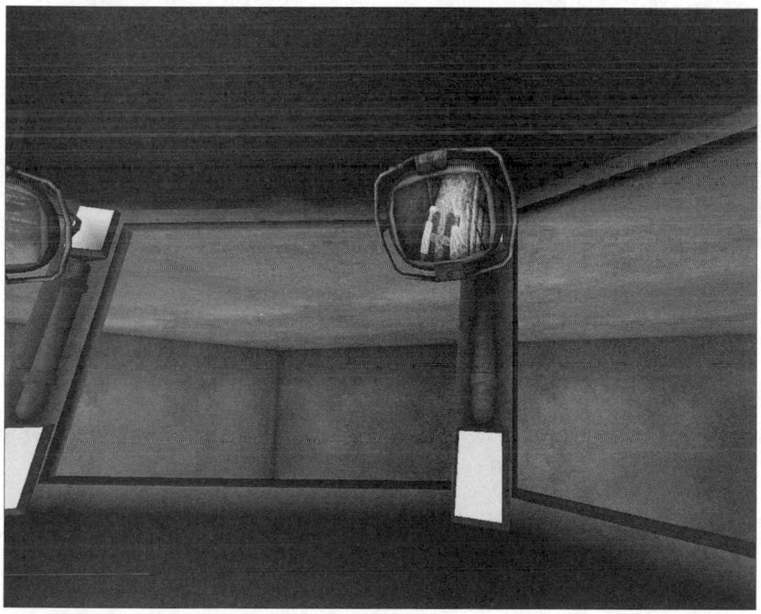

FIGURE 8.75 Final effect of your security camera.

END TUTORIAL 8.14

Your security camera effect is finished! You can use this technique to create security cameras that update in real-time in your single-player levels. Keep in mind, however, that Unreal's architecture currently doesn't allow such an effect to update during a multiplayer game session.

Summary

This chapter has covered many different materials and explained how they are created, the properties associated with them, and how they can be used in your levels. You started by creating a simple texture in Photoshop, and then imported it into UnrealEd.

You also learned that shaders give you real-time effects that combine materials together, and modifiers can be used to alter your textures over time or statically. In addition, you saw how Combiners are used to bring two textures together by using a mask, and environment maps can make your materials seem to be reflecting their surroundings. You learned about the Final Blend material and used a ScriptedTexture to add an advanced camera effect to your level.

By now, you should have a thorough understanding of the workflow associated with materials and how the different types of material can be combined to create extremely interesting effects. Remember that material creation, although highly technical, can be an art form, allowing you to create and express a variety of looks for your levels.

Chapter 9

Interactive Elements

In this chapter, you will expand on the level you created in Chapter 3, "Creating Your First Level with UnrealEd," by adding elements that players can interact with, including elevators, jump pads, and teleporters. The chapter begins with a simple overview of each element, and then goes into more detail on the parameters for controlling them. Next is a discussion of how to create a complex elevator with custom doors, camera vibration upon activation, and a texture that displays the elevator's current position. Finally, you learn how to create jump pads and teleporters to send your players to new locations on the map. These game elements are simple to incorporate into your level and can add realism and excitement to your levels.

Movers

In Unreal, a *Mover* is simply a special type of static mesh that's animated in the level. They are used to create practical level elements, such as moving doors and elevators, lifts, or any solid aspect of the level that requires motion. A Mover's motion can be activated in a variety of different ways. Each Mover has eight individual *keys*, which are recordings of an object's position and rotation during different points of animation. For example, you can set the first key of a door Mover to have an initial position and rotation for when it's closed.

Then you can then add a second key that stores the position and the rotation for the door when it's open. When the Mover is activated, it moves to its next key, which effectively opens the door.

By default, you can have only up to eight keys on any given Mover. After it's activated, a Mover smoothly cycles through any keys that have been recorded for it and doesn't stop until it reaches the last key. There are several ways to activate a Mover, depending on its settings. They can be activated by characters bumping into them or by shooting them with a weapon. More advanced Movers can be activated through a separate triggering system, which sends an event to the engine's message queue. Appendix A, "The UnrealEd Manual," contains a comprehensive list of all Mover-triggering methods.

In this section, you see how to implement Movers in your hangar level from Chapter 3. You begin with a simple door that leads into the control room and then learn how to make the door functional so that it opens when a player bumps into it and closes shortly thereafter.

> **NOTE**
>
> **The tutorials in this chapter assume that you have completed Chapter 3 or at least have a basic understanding of UnrealEd workflow. Make sure you know how to place static meshes, including adjusting their scale with `DrawScale3D`.**

Creating the First Door

Doors are one of the most common applications of Movers. In fact, many properties inherent to Movers are named after door functions, such as `StayOpenTime`. One of the greatest benefits of their architecture is that you can create many different kinds of doors, such as swinging or sliding doors, by using the same set of attributes. In the next few subsections, you examine the process of door creation one step at a time. This process has been divided into three major steps: placing the door, adding animation to the door, and controlling the door's behavior.

Placing the Door

Now that you know what Movers are, you can learn how to actually place one in your level. In **TUTORIAL 9.1**, you place an automatic door that leads into the control room, beginning with getting the Mover in place.

TUTORIAL 9.1 Placing the Door

1. Open the map you completed in Chapter 3, or open `Tutorial9_01_Start.ut2` from the book's CD.
2. Open the Static Mesh browser, and open the `XceptOneObjH.usx` package. In the Doors group, select Flux2DoorH (see **FIGURE 9.1**).

3. Move the Builder brush to the location of the door into the control room, and click the Add Mover icon . Notice that the mesh is purple in the viewport to indicate that it's a Mover rather than a standard static mesh, which is teal.

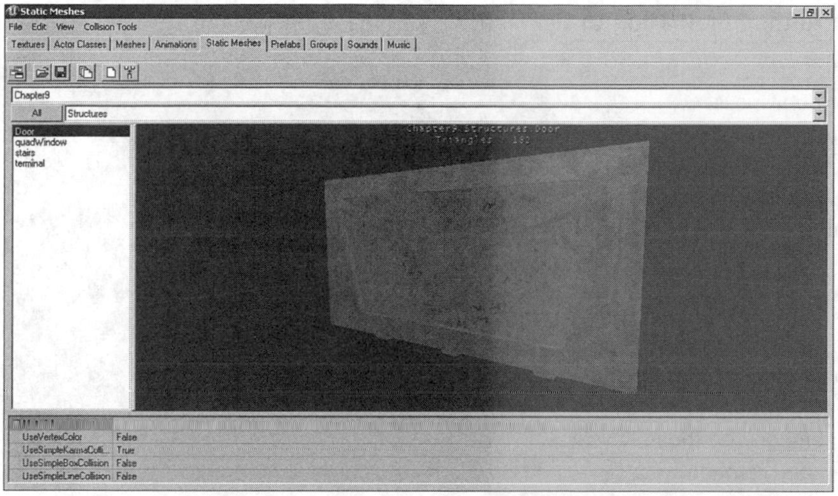

FIGURE 9.1 Static Mesh browser with Door selected.

4. Move the door into a closed position, and adjust the scale of the mesh accordingly. For this tutorial, the following values are recommended: 0.9, 0.45, and 1.85.

5. The texture applied to this static mesh is far too bright, so you need to replace it with a darker UV2 texture. In the Properties window for the Mover, go to the Display category and change the `UV2Texture` property to `Texture'XceptTwo.Flux2Stuff.FluxDoorB512'`. The result is shown in **FIGURE 9.2**.

FIGURE 9.2 Mover in position.

END TUTORIAL 9.1

You now have your Mover in place, and it's ready to be animated. In **TUTORIAL 9.2**, you see how to make this Mover respond in your level.

Adding Animation to the Door

Movers are animated by using keys containing positional and rotational values. When a Mover is activated, it goes down the list of keys, smoothly adjusting its position and rotation until it reaches the last key. In **TUTORIAL 9.2**, you place the required keys to make your door open and close.

TUTORIAL 9.2: Adding Animation to the Door

1. In the following steps, you'll set keys to make your door move. Fortunately, the first key has already been set for you. The position in which you initially place a Mover denotes its first key, called Key 0 (Base).

2. Right-click on the door, and choose Mover > Key 1 from the context menu. The next place you move the door will be its location for the second key. Remember that these keys store position and rotation.

FIGURE 9.3 Mover in open position.

3. In the 3D viewport, move the door upward until it's almost out of sight, as shown in **FIGURE 9.3**. This will be the open position.

4. Right-click on the door, and choose Mover > Key 0 (Base). Notice that the door jumps back to its original position. This means the animation data has been stored correctly, and the door is almost ready for use.

END TUTORIAL 9.2

Controlling the Door's Behavior

Your Mover is in place, and it's almost ready to test in the level. Before you do that, however, you need to see some properties you can set for the Mover to control its behavior when animated. In **TUTORIAL 9.3**, you're going to set the Mover up so that it opens when bumped by a player, remains open for a while, and then closes. You then look at a few other important properties for controlling a Mover's behavior. For a full list and explanation of these properties, be sure to check Appendix A.

TUTORIAL 9.3: Controlling Your Animation

1. Double-click the door to open the Mover Properties window, and open the Object category.

2. Click the `InitialState` property, and set it to `BumpOpenTimed` (see **FIGURE 9.4**). This state causes the door to open when it's bumped, stay open for a period of time, and then close.

3. Open the Mover tab. Scroll down until you see the `NumKeys` property. Because you have set up two keys, the value should be set to 2 (see **FIGURE 9.5**).

4. Below `NumKeys` is the `StayOpenTime` property. This property controls how long (in seconds) the door stays open or, to be more specific, how long the Mover sits at its last keyframe. Set this property to a value of 2, which causes the door to stay open for two seconds before it closes.

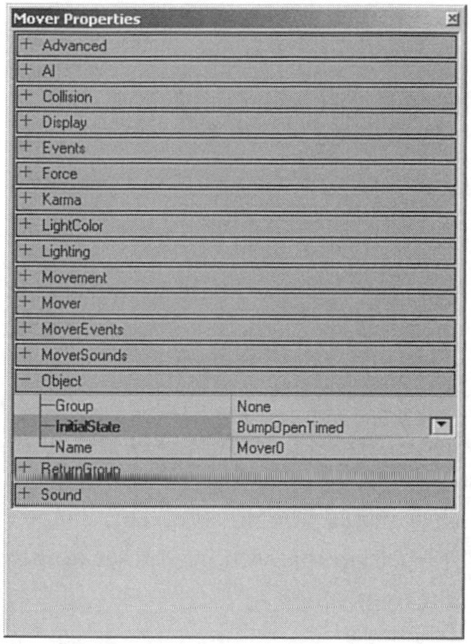

FIGURE 9.4 *InitialState* property set to *BumpOpenTimed*.

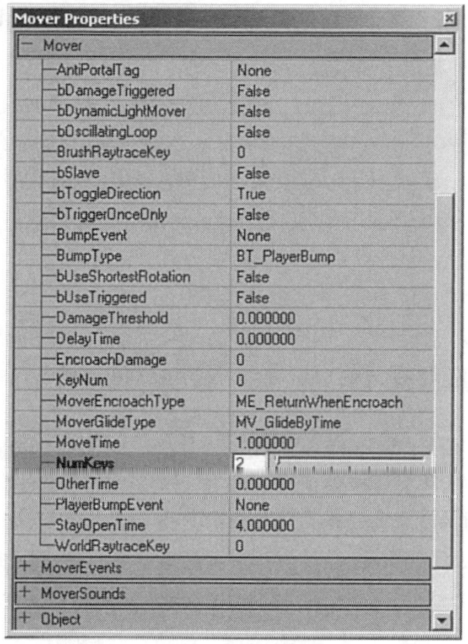

FIGURE 9.5 *NumKeys* property set to 2.

5. Scroll up until you find the `DelayTime` property. Set it to 0, if it isn't already. This setting means the door opens as soon as it's bumped.
6. Finally, make sure `KeyNum` is set to 0. This property controls the key that the Mover begins with.
7. Rebuild for good measure, and test your level. Your door should open when you bump into it, and stay open for two seconds.
8. Save your map.

END TUTORIAL 9.3

Using Encroachment

Before you go any further, take a look at some other ways you can control your door's behavior. One of the most important factors of a Mover's functionality is what it does when a player gets in its way when it closes or returns to its first key. You can set a Mover to stop when a player gets in its path, have the Mover go back to its open position, or just simply crush the player. You control this behavior with the `MoverEncroachType` property, available in the Mover Properties window under the Mover tab. The following is a list of the settings available for this property:

- `ME_StopWhenEncroach`—When an Actor gets in the way, the Mover stops dead in its tracks.
- `ME_ReturnWhenEncroach`—The Mover retreats to its previous position when it hits an Actor.

- `ME_CrushWhenEncroach`—This setting causes the Mover to kill any Actor in its path.
- `ME_IgnoreWhenEncroach`—The Mover goes right through the Actor, but still causes damage to the Actor. You can control the amount of damage with the `EncroachDamage` property.

Feel free to experiment with these settings, and see which behavior works best for you. The next section introduces you to triggers and explains how to use them to add new dimensions to Mover functionality.

Introduction to Triggers

Triggers are Actors that can be placed anywhere in your level. When they are activated, they initiate a uniquely named event. Any Actor that has been set to respond to that trigger then performs a function of its own. Many different types of triggers are available in UnrealEd. This chapter includes tutorials on how to use a variety of triggers in your levels. In this section, you see how to add a MessageTrigger to your level to make a message appear onscreen.

You can activate a trigger in different ways, depending on what kind of trigger you're using. Some are activated by the player via the `UseTrigger` property, some are activated by touching or shooting, and some are activated by scripting, which is discussed later in "Complex Elevator I: The ScriptedTrigger." When the trigger is activated, it creates an event. The user specifies the name of this event. If any other Actors have their `Tag` property set to the same name as the event, those Actors perform a certain function, called the Trigger function. The following section explains how this works.

Creating a MessageTrigger

In **TUTORIAL 9.4**, you create a MessageTrigger that flashes text onscreen when the door opens. Adding this trigger is easy because Movers trigger an event when they reach their *zenith*, or last keyframe. All you need to do is create a MessageTrigger Actor and make it respond to the event sent by the Mover.

TUTORIAL 9.4: Establishing a MessageTrigger

1. Open the Actor Class browser by clicking its icon on the toolbar.
2. Scroll down to Triggers, click the + sign next to it to expand it, and select MessageTrigger (see **FIGURE 9.6**).
3. Right-click near the door, and choose Add Message Trigger Here from the context menu.

> **NOTE**
>
> **The placement of this trigger is irrelevant because the player doesn't interact with it directly.**

4. Double-click the new trigger to open its Properties window, and scroll down to the MessageTrigger tab. You'll see three properties: The `Message` property controls the message that's displayed. `Messagetype` controls how the message is displayed. (**TABLE 9.1** lists the possible `Messagetypes`.) The `Team` property determines which team can see the message in team-based gametypes.

5. For the `Message` property, enter **`The Control Room Door Has Been Opened!`** You can add another message, if you like. The text in this field is what appears onscreen when the door is opened.

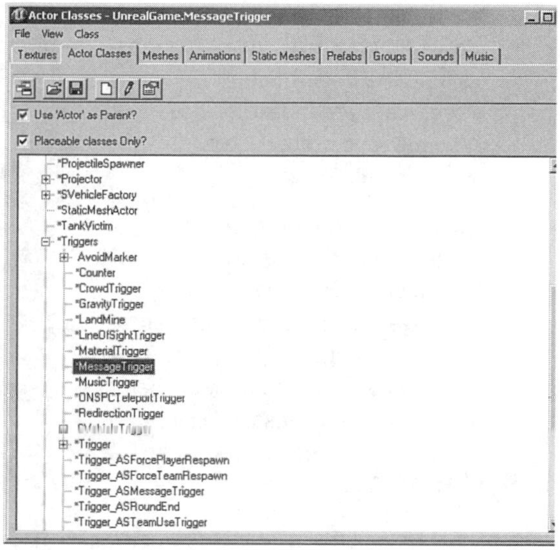

FIGURE 9.6 MessageTrigger selected in the Actor Class browser.

TABLE 9.1 *`Messagetype`*

`Messagetype`	Description
`EMT_Default`	This setting shows the message in the default font in the lower-left corner of the screen. The message appears in a similar manner to player join messages.
`EMT_CriticalEvent`	The message appears as large blue text in the middle of the screen to denote a critical event, such as a player going on a killing spree. This is the default setting.
`EMT_DeathMessage`	The message appears as text in the console bar.
`EMT_Say`	The message is displayed as though you had said it, even if some other player in a multiplayer game triggered it.
`EMT_TeamSay`	Same as `EMT_Say`, except that the result appears as though the message had been sent using `TeamSay`.

6. Make sure `Messagetype` is set to `EMT_CriticalEvent`, the default, so that the message is displayed as an in-game notification.

7. If you were to test the trigger now, you still wouldn't get any response. You have established the MessageTrigger, but you haven't yet set up the system to activate it. You need to set the MessageTrigger's `Tag` property to the same name as the event generated by the Mover. Expand the MessageTrigger's Event tab, and set the `Tag` property to `DoorOpened` (see **FIGURE 9.7**).

8. You're almost there. Go back to the Mover Properties window by double-clicking the door. Under the MoverEvents tab, next to the `OpenedEvent` property, type **`DoorOpened`**.

   The name of the event generated when the door opens is now called `DoorOpened`. By setting the MessageTrigger's `Tag` to the same name, the trigger "listens" for the `DoorOpened` event to be launched. When it is, the MessageTrigger displays its message, as shown in **FIGURE 9.8**.

9. Save your map.

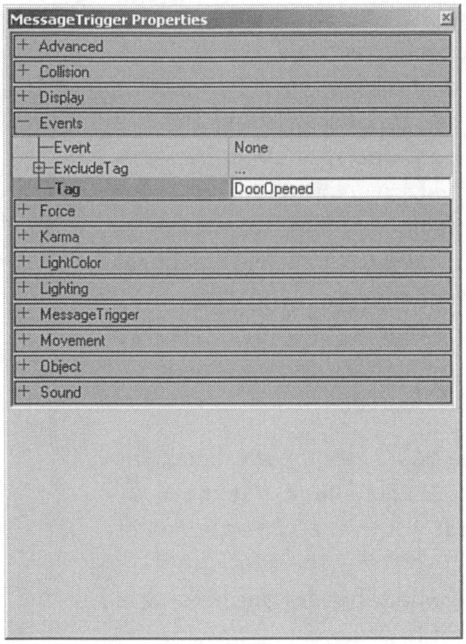

FIGURE 9.7 The *Tag* property of the MessageTrigger.

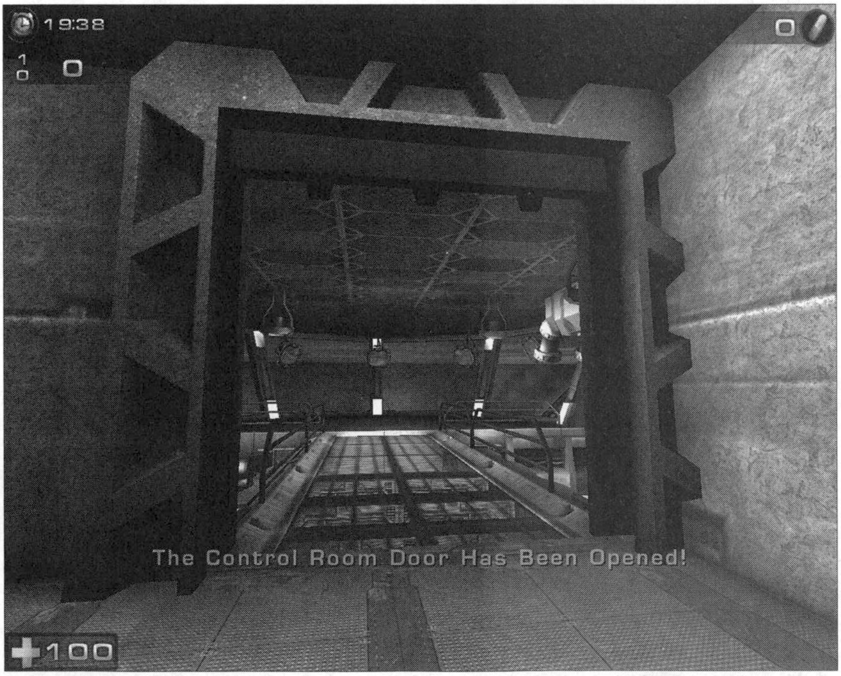

FIGURE 9.8 The MessageTrigger in operation.

END TUTORIAL 9.4

Launch the game, and test out your new door. When you open the door, the message you entered is displayed onscreen. MessageTriggers are a great way to keep players informed about events going on in the game and an excellent way to learn how triggers work in general.

Elevators

In essence, an elevator functions exactly like an automated door. It has a start position, usually the bottommost floor, and an end position, the extent of the elevator. In this section, you use a Mover to place an elevator in your level. You'll begin with a simple elevator controlled by the UseTrigger function. Later, you'll change it to a ScriptedTrigger to accommodate a wider range of functionality, including camera shake, automated doors, and animated textures. You'll also create a progress bar that allows players to see the elevator's progress while it's in use. **FIGURE 9.9** shows what the final elevator looks like.

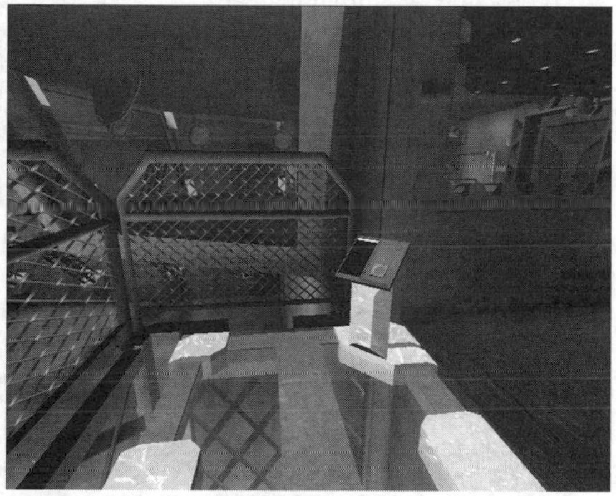

FIGURE 9.9 The final working elevator.

A Simple Elevator: UseTrigger

In this section, you create a simple elevator by using the UseTrigger Actor. Instead of bumping into the Mover, as in the door example, you set up a system by which players can activate the elevator with a UseTrigger. This means the elevator is set into motion in the game when a player stands within the UseTrigger's radius and presses the Use key (E, by default). In the next two sections, you place the necessary static meshes and a Mover for your simple elevator and establish the UseTrigger's functionality. These tutorials will further your knowledge of how events are generated and how they can be used to control the behavior of many aspects of your levels.

Placing the Elevator Geometry

In **TUTORIAL 9.5**, you place your static meshes and the Mover required for your elevator. This stage requires bringing some new static meshes into your level and duplicating a few that are already in the control room. After everything is in place, you can set up your UseTrigger so that players can have more direct control over the elevator's behavior.

TUTORIAL 9.5: Building the Elevator

1. Open your map from **TUTORIAL 9.4**, or open `Tutorial9_05_Start.ut2`.

2. In the Static Mesh browser, open the `newHangar2.usx` package. Select elevatorFrame from the Package0 group, and place it in the hangar. It should straddle the indentation in the wall and align with the floor. Use **FIGURE 9.10** if you need help.

3. At the top of the frame, you need to place some protective railings. Duplicate a railing from the control room, scale it accordingly, and place it along the top of the frame. Repeat this step two more times to place one rail on each of the frame's three sides (see **FIGURE 9.11**).

4. Now you need to place the elevator to serve as the Mover. In the Static Mesh browser, select elevatorLift from the Elevator group. Make sure the Builder brush is near the small indentation in the floor of the hangar. Click the Add Mover button in the toolbox. Align the elevator with all sides of the indentation. Rotate the elevator so that in the Top viewport, its control panel is in the lower-left corner. Use **FIGURE 9.12** as a guide.

5. Place some lights in and around the elevator shaft until you're satisfied with the result. Refer to **FIGURE 9.13**, if needed.

6. The original placement of the elevatorLift automatically set the first key, so you need to set the second. Right-click on the elevatorLift, choose Mover > Key 1, and move the elevatorLift up in the Z-axis so that the top surface aligns with the bottom of the hallway (see **FIGURE 9.14**).

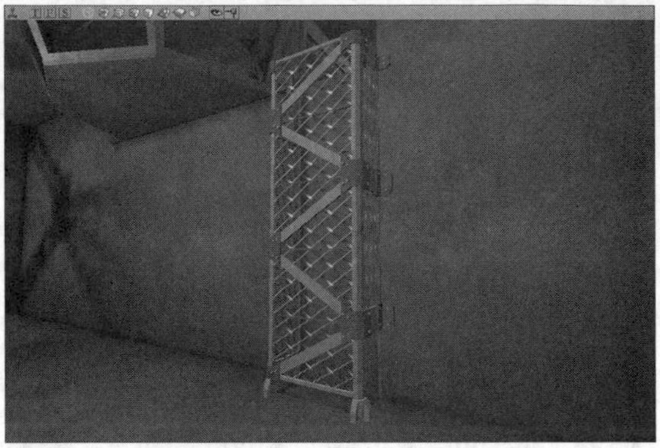

FIGURE 9.10 Use elevatorFrame as a protective barrier for the elevator.

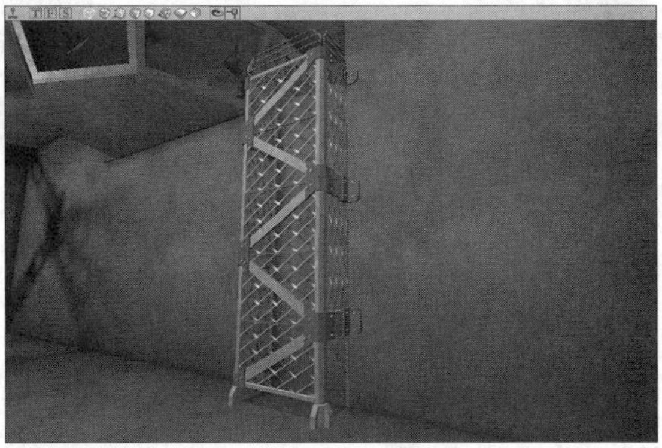

FIGURE 9.11 Three railings placed on top of the barrier.

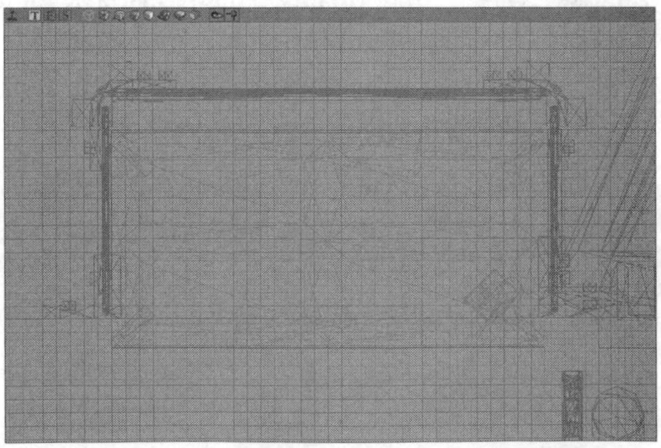

FIGURE 9.12 Top view of the elevatorLift Mover.

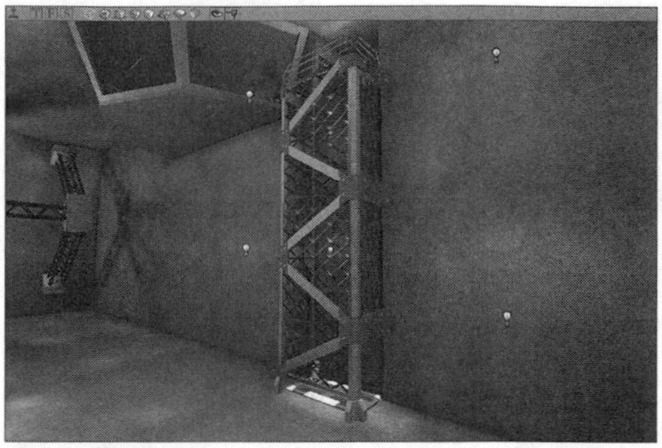

FIGURE 9.13 3D View of the elevator shaft.

FIGURE 9.14 3D View of the elevator at the top.

7. Set the key back to Key 0 (Base). The elevator should jump back down to the bottom of the elevator shaft.

8. Save your work.

END TUTORIAL 9.5

Implementing the UseTrigger

The elevator has been placed in your level, so now you can use some of the techniques you learned in the previous section to make it functional. This time, however, you expand on what you already know by making the elevator respond to a player's direct command. To do this, you implement a UseTrigger, which allows a player to make the elevator move by pressing the Use key rather than simply bumping into it.

TUTORIAL 9.6: Setting Up the UseTrigger

1. Because a player has to be within a certain distance from the UseTrigger to actually use it, the placement of this UseTrigger is an important factor. Also, because the trigger doesn't follow the elevator, you need to place two UseTriggers: one at the bottom of the lift's range and the other at the top. In the Actor Class browser, expand Triggers, and select UseTrigger, as shown in **FIGURE 9.15**.

2. Right-click in your 3D viewport on the elevator's control panel, and choose Place UseTrigger Here. Position the trigger so that it's right in front of the elevator's control panel (see **FIGURE 9.16**).

3. Double-click the trigger to open its Properties window. In the Advanced tab, set `bHidden` to False so that you can see the trigger while you're in the game, which is helpful during the creation process. After everything is finalized, you can switch this property back to True.

4. The UseTrigger generates an event whenever a player presses the Use key while within a certain radius of the trigger. This action perfectly simulates a player pushing a button. In the UseTrigger Properties window, go to the Events tab. Next to the `Event` property, type **`frontLift`**.
5. Double-click the elevator to access the Mover Properties window. In the Events tab, set the `Tag` property to `frontLift` as well to make the Mover respond whenever the `frontLift` event is generated.
6. In the Mover Properties window, go to the Object tab. Set the `InitialState` property to `TriggerToggle`. Next, in the Mover tab, set `MoveTime` to 5. With this setting, the elevator takes five seconds to move from its first to its last key.
7. Right-click the Mover, and choose Mover > Key 1. The elevator snaps to the top of the shaft. In the 3D view, select the UseTrigger at the base of the elevator shaft, and duplicate it by pressing Ctrl+W. Move the duplicated trigger up in the Z-axis so that it's in front of the control panel when the elevator is at the top of the shaft, as shown in **FIGURE 9.17**.
8. Save your work.

FIGURE 9.15 UseTrigger selected in the Actor Class browser.

FIGURE 9.16 Position the UseTrigger in front of the elevator's control panel.

FIGURE 9.17 A second UseTrigger at the top of the shaft.

END TUTORIAL 9.6

Your elevator is now fully functional, so you can rebuild and test your level. When you walk up to the elevator, press the Use key (the *E* key, by default). The elevator moves to the top of the shaft and waits for you to retrigger it.

Another Mover property can help control your elevator's motion. Under the Mover tab in the Mover Properties window is the `MoverGlideType` property, which controls how the Mover animates from its first key to its last. By default, it's set to `MV_GlideByTime`. This setting causes the Mover to accelerate as it leaves its first key and decelerate as it approaches its last. If you set this property to `MV_MoveByTime`, the Mover animates at a constant rate. For a full list of all the properties available for Movers, please see Appendix A.

Complex Elevator Overview

In this section and its subsequent tutorials, you enhance your simple elevator to add a series of advanced functionality. You'll begin by adding a ScriptedTrigger to the elevator's control panel that acts as a router, sending out several different events to other triggers. The final result will be an elevator that behaves according to the following list of features:

- Character activates the elevator by activating a control panel located on the lift mechanism.
- After a one-second pause, the player's view shakes violently as the elevator begins to move.
- An automated door at the top of the elevator opens only when the lift mechanism is at the top of the elevator shaft.

- There's a second control panel at the top of the elevator shaft so that the player can call the elevator.
- Both control panels have an activation button. While the elevator is in motion, the activation buttons on each control panel change from red to green. The buttons shift back to red when the elevator stops moving.
- Each control panel exhibits a progress bar that constantly displays the elevator's current position in the elevator shaft.

All this functionality is established through the use of a ScriptedTrigger, which sends events out to several other triggers.

Complex Elevator I: The ScriptedTrigger

In this section, you expand on the simple elevator created in the previous section by adding a ScriptedTrigger to your elevator's control panel. This trigger makes your system more powerful by allowing you to generate multiple events from one trigger. ScriptedTriggers can generate events based on user-defined conditions, cycle through loops, and much more. For this chapter's example, you'll rework your triggers so that the UseTrigger sends an event to the ScriptedTrigger, which then moves the elevator.

When using a ScriptedTrigger, you rarely use the properties in the Events tab. Instead, you set most of your functionality in the AIScript tab, where you'll find the `Actions` property. You can add as many Actions within this property as you like. They are stored in an array and completed in a linear fashion from top to bottom. Some Actions halt the process until certain conditions are met or even skip other Actions. In this way, you can stack as many Actions as you like into the trigger.

TUTORIAL 9.7: Implementing a ScriptedTrigger

1. Open the Actor Class browser, and expand Actor > Keypoint > AIScript > Scripted Sequence. Click ScriptedTrigger.
2. Right-click anywhere in your 3D viewport, and choose Add ScriptedTrigger Here. The trigger's placement is irrelevant, so just place it somewhere that you can easily access (see **FIGURE 9.18**).

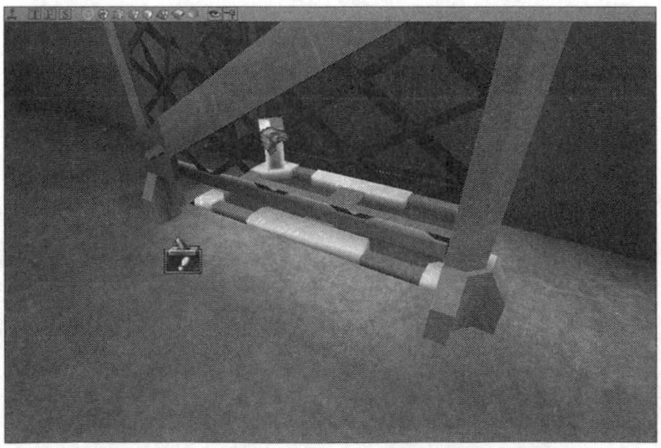

FIGURE 9.18 ScriptedTrigger in place.

3. Each Action added into the ScriptedTrigger has different properties. Open the AIScript tab, click the Actions tab, and click the Add button to add an Action. This allows a new Action to take place but doesn't designate what type of Action it is. Your new Action is indexed with a zero **(SEE FIGURE 9.19)**.

4. Next to the New tab, open the drop-down list and select `Action_WAITFOREVENT`. Then click the New button. This sets Action [0] to `Action_WAITFOREVENT` (see **FIGURE 9.20**). The `WAITFOREVENT` Action listens for a specific event, and then responds when that event is genterated.

5. The `WAITFOREVENT` Action has a unique property called `ExternalEvent`. You can see it listed underneath the Action in the AIScript tab. Click the word `None` next to `ExternalEvent`, and enter **`frontLift`** (see **FIGURE 9.21**). This means the trigger won't progress to the next Action until the `frontLift` event is generated.

6. Now that you have told the trigger when to progress, you need to tell it what to do. Click the Actions heading under the AIScript tab, and click the New button again. You get a new Action indexed with a [1].

7. Using the drop-down list next to the New entry in Action [1], set the Action to `Action_TRIGGEREVENT` (see **FIGURE 9.22**), and click the New button. This Action generates an event when the ScriptedTrigger reaches it. Remember that the ScriptedTrigger completes its Actions from top to bottom.

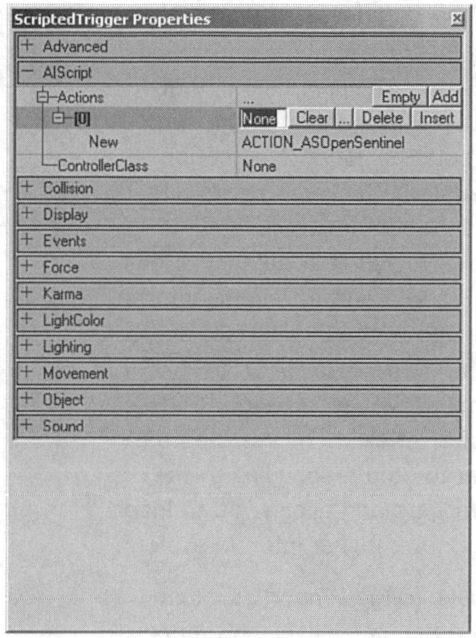

FIGURE 9.19 A new Action for the ScriptedTrigger.

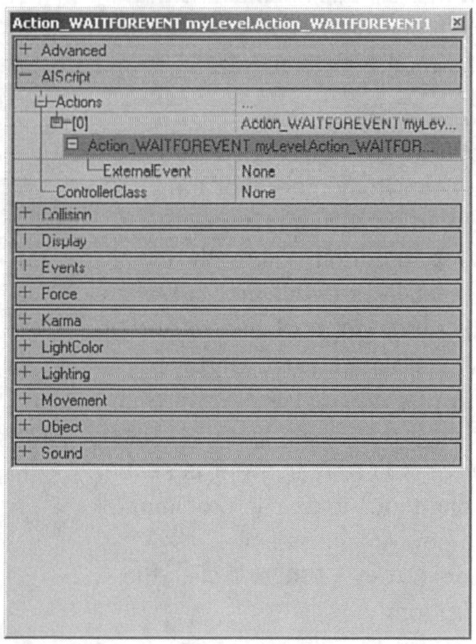

FIGURE 9.20 The *`WAITFOREVENT`* Action of the ScriptedTrigger.

8. Your UseTriggers are already generating the `frontLift` event. When the ScriptedTrigger "hears" that event, it then generates the event that sets the elevator in motion. Because the Mover is set to already respond to `frontLift`, the ScriptedTrigger is currently useless. Open the Properties window for the Mover, go to the Events tab, and set its `Tag` property to `frontLiftMover`, an event that doesn't yet exist. This causes the Mover to stop responding to the UseTriggers and allows you to insert the ScriptedTrigger into the system.

9. Go back to the Properties window for the ScriptedTrigger, and reopen the AIScript tab. Under the Actions tab, go to Action [1], and expand the Action_TRIGGEREVENT tab underneath the [1] index number. Set the `Event` property to `frontLiftMover`, as shown in **FIGURE 9.23**.

10. If you were to test the ScriptedTrigger now, you would have a problem. Remember that the Actions in the ScriptedTrigger move from top to bottom. Currently, the trigger receives the `frontLift` event, sends out the `frontLiftMover` event, and then stops. This means the elevator will work once and never again because the `frontLiftMover` event is sent only one time. To fix this problem, add a new Action, select `Action_GOTOACTION`, and click the New button.

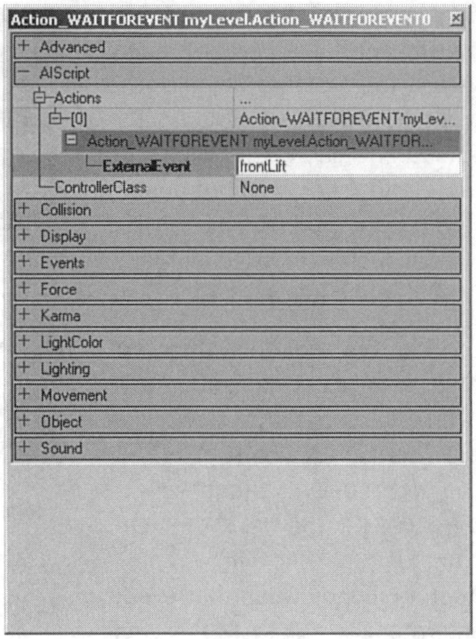

FIGURE 9.21 *ExternalEvent* property of the ScriptedTrigger set to *frontLift*.

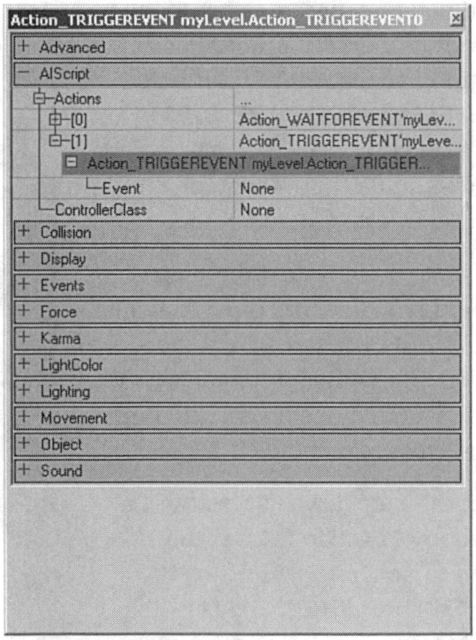

FIGURE 9.22 The *TRIGGEREVENT* Action of the ScriptedTrigger.

11. Expand the properties of your new Action, and make sure `ActionNumber` is set to 0, which is the default. This causes the ScriptedTrigger to jump back to the first Action after it sends out the `frontLiftMover` event so that it goes back to listening for the `frontLift` event. This setting allows the ScriptedTrigger to be used repeatedly.

12. Save your work.

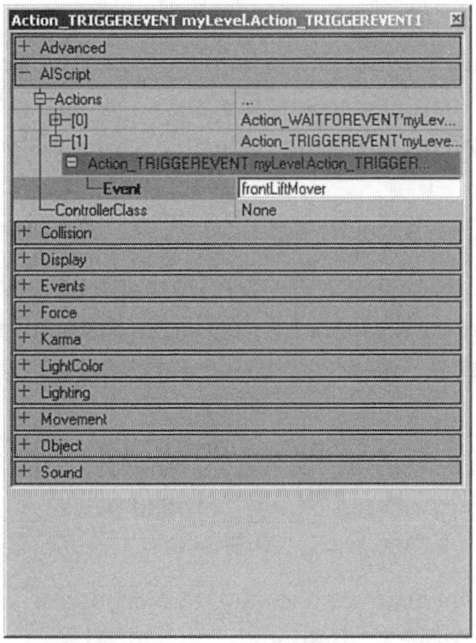

FIGURE 9.23 *`Event`* **property of the ScriptedTrigger set to** *`frontLiftMover`*.

END TUTORIAL 9.7

You have now placed the ScriptedTrigger into your elevator system. To recap, the Method 1 diagram in **FIGURE 9.24** shows how the original system flowed, when it was just the UseTriggers and the Mover. The Method 2 diagram shows the new flow using the ScriptedTrigger.

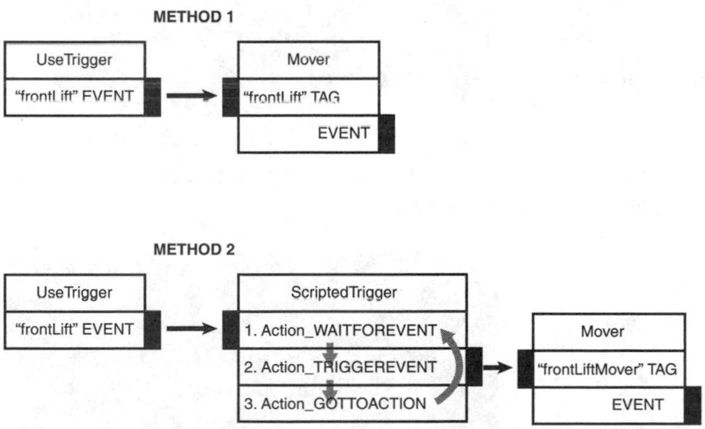

FIGURE 9.24 **This diagram demonstrates the flow of the ScriptedTrigger.**

FIGURE 9.24 shows how you created the ScriptedTrigger and then established a new Action that told the trigger to wait for the `frontLift` event. You then broke the connection between the UseTriggers and the Mover by setting the Mover's `Tag` property to `frontLiftMover`. You then placed a new Action that sent out the `frontLiftMover` event, causing the elevator to move.

It might look like you broke your system just to put it back together. However, using a ScriptedTrigger enables you to launch several different Actions simultaneously. In **TUTORIAL 9.8**, you add the ViewShaker, which derives its behavior from the ScriptedTrigger. Later, you use it to drive animated textures with the help of MaterialTriggers.

Complex Elevator II: Adding a ViewShaker

In this section, you add a ViewShaker trigger to your elevator. When a player activates the elevator, there's a short pause, then the view shakes left and right, as though the elevator jerked suddenly. In **TUTORIAL 9.8**, you see how to use the ViewShaker trigger and insert actions in the ScriptedTrigger.

TUTORIAL 9.8: Adding a ViewShaker

1. In the Actor Class browser, expand Actor > Triggers, and click ViewShaker.
2. Right-click near the elevator, and choose Add ViewShaker Here from the context menu. The placement of this trigger is important, as it has a radius of effect. Only players within the radius can see their views shake. Place it near the UseTrigger.
3. Double-click the ViewShaker to open its Properties window. In the ViewShaker tab, set the `ShakeRadius` property to 128.
4. You use three major properties to make the camera shake: `OffsetMag`, `OffsetRate`, and `OffsetTime`. `OffsetMag` determines the amount of shake in the three axial directions. Set all three values (X, Y, and Z) of `OffsetMag` to 3, as shown in **FIGURE 9.25**.
5. `OffsetRate` controls how fast the view will shake. Set each axial value to 100.
6. `OffsetTime` determines how long (set in hundredths of a second) the view shakes. Set this value to 15.
7. You have now established the ViewShaker's functionality, but you haven't determined *when* it functions. You still need to tell it which event brings

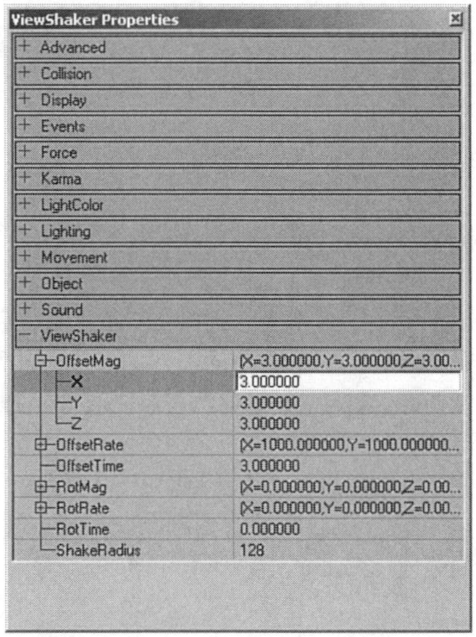

FIGURE 9.25 *OffsetMag* **property of the ViewShaker.**

FIGURE 9.26 **The ViewShaker trigger at the top of the elevator shaft.**

it to life. In the ViewShaker Properties window, open the Events tab and set the Tag property to `liftShaker`.

8. Duplicate the ViewShaker trigger, and place the duplicate near the top of the elevator shaft close to the second UseTrigger (see **FIGURE 9.26**).

9. You need the ScriptedTrigger to send out a `liftShaker` event to the ViewShaker. To do this, double-click the ScriptedTrigger, and open the AIScript tab in the Properties window. Expand the Actions list.

10. Select Action [1], which should be `Action_TRIGGEREVENT`. Click the Insert button next to it to insert a new Action directly above Action [1].

11. Set the new Action to another `Action_TRIGGEREVENT`, and click the New button. Set the event of this new Action to `liftShaker` (see **FIGURE 9.27**). The ScriptedTrigger is now sending out two separate events: one to shake the view and another to move the lift.

12. Next, you'll set up a delay so that when you push the button on the elevator's control panel, there's a slight pause before the elevator actually moves. Using the skills you just learned, insert a new Action before Action [1]. Set this new Action to `Action_WAITFORTIMER`, click New, and set the `PauseTime` property to 1 (see **FIGURE 9.28**). This causes the elevator to pause for one second before shaking and rising.

13. Test your level, and save your work.

END TUTORIAL 9.8

NOTE

This radius is measured in Unreal units.

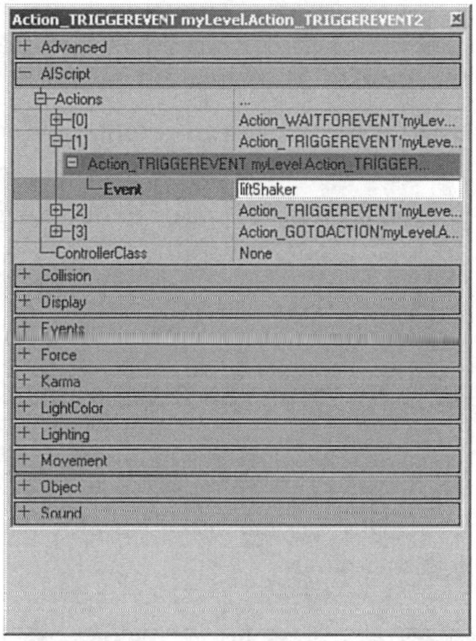

FIGURE 9.27 *TRIGGEREVENT* **action with the event set to** *liftShaker*.

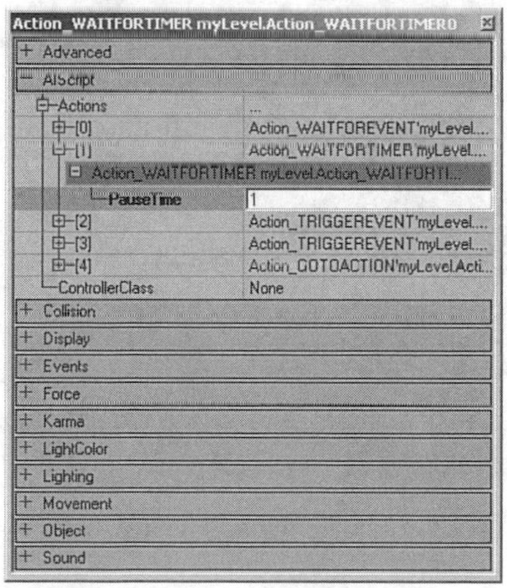

FIGURE 9.28 *WAITFORTIMER* **Action with the** *PauseTime* **property set to 1.**

You have established a solid system that enables you to activate the elevator, wait a moment, see the view shake, and then have the elevator rise. The elevator also waits at the top for a player to activate it again. In the next section, you add a new door to the top of the elevator shaft and a trigger to set it in motion when the elevator reaches the top.

Complex Elevator III: Elevator Door

In **TUTORIAL 9.9**, you place an automated door at the top of the elevator shaft and set it up so that it opens only when the elevator is on the top floor. This automated door adds a bit more realism to your level because it appears to be a safety feature. This addition also serves as a lesson to demonstrate how to activate multiple Movers from a single ScriptedTrigger and how to adjust the timing of that activation.

TUTORIAL 9.9: Setting up the Elevator Door

1. For continuity, use the same kind of door that you used earlier in the control room's entrance. The easiest method is to simply duplicate that door, and move the duplicate to the opening at the top of the elevator shaft (see **FIGURE 9.29**). Adjust the `DrawScale` setting accordingly.

FIGURE 9.29 The elevator door moved and scaled into position.

2. Make sure that Key 0 is the door's closed position and Key 1 contains the door's open position. The door will be sliding up, just like the control room door.

3. Double-click the elevator door. In the Properties window, open the Object tab, and set the `InitialState` property to `TriggerToggle`. As with the elevator, this setting enables you to trigger the door's up and down movement.

9

4. In the Events tab, set the `Tag` property to `liftDoor`.

5. Now you can use the events the elevator generates to open and close the door. Open the Properties window for the elevator. In the MoverEvents tab, set both the `ClosingEvent` and `OpenedEvent` properties to `liftDoor` (see **FIGURE 9.30**). This makes the elevator lift trigger the door once when it reaches the top of the shaft and again as it starts to go back down.

6. Save your map.

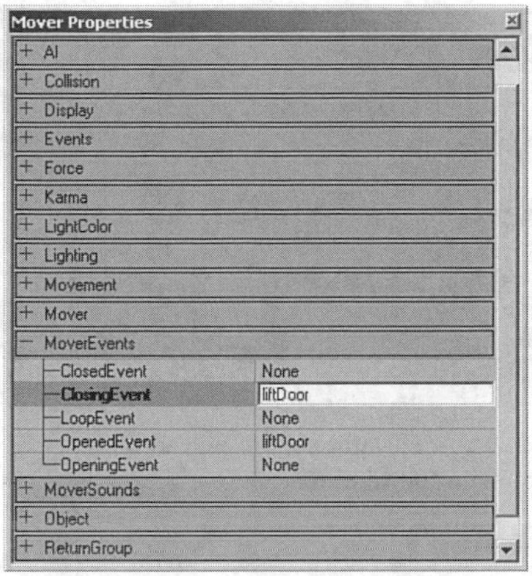

FIGURE 9.30 The elevator door's *Tag* property is set to *liftDoor*.

END TUTORIAL 9.9

Complex Elevator IV: Second Control Panel

You have the door in place and have established its animation, but there's still a problem: What if you're in the hallway, and the elevator is at the bottom? The door would be closed, and you'd have no way to call the elevator up! In **TUTORIAL 9.10**, you place a trigger and control panel into the hallway so that players can access the lift from the top or bottom.

TUTORIAL 9.10: Placing the New Elevator Control Panel

1. In the Static Mesh browser, open the Elevator group, and select the elevatorControl static mesh.

2. Navigate to the top of the elevator shaft, and place the mesh near the door, on the wall opposite the window, as shown in **FIGURE 9.31**. Don't worry about the lack of texture.

3. Duplicate one of the UseTriggers that have been placed in the level, and position the duplicate in front of the new control panel (see **FIGURE 9.32**). This UseTrigger provides a way to call the elevator if the door is currently closed.

4. Save your work, and test your level.

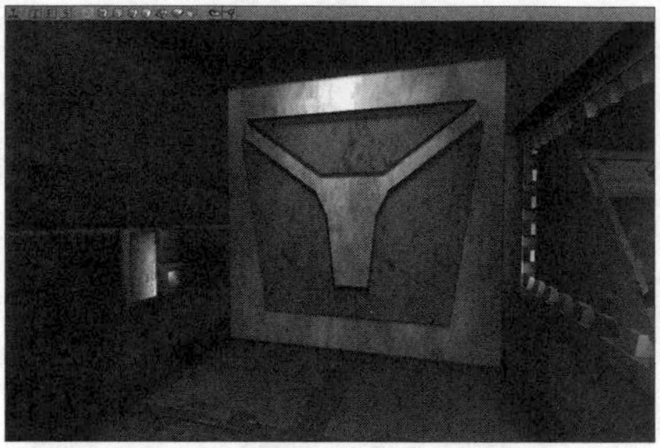

FIGURE 9.31 Elevator control placed on the wall opposite the window.

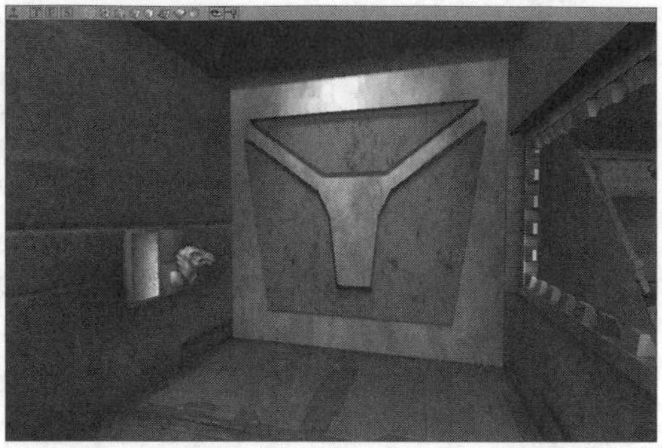

FIGURE 9.32 UseTrigger placed in front of the control panel.

END TUTORIAL 9.10

You now have a complete elevator system that allows you to call the elevator from the upper hallway or the floor of the hangar. You also have a door in the hallway to keep players from accidentally stepping out and falling to their doom. In the next section, you add a MaterialTrigger and set up some animated textures.

Complex Elevator V: MaterialTrigger

In this section, you see how a MaterialTrigger can be used to create animated textures. A *material* is a combination of a texture and a shader, which controls how light reacts on the texture's surface. First, you set up a texture for a button on the elevator's control panels. This button will be red when the lift is stationary and turn green while the lift is in motion. Next, you create a progress bar texture that displays the elevator's current location in the elevator shaft. Both systems take advantage of the MaterialTrigger and the MaterialSwitch, a type of material available in Unreal. For more information on materials, refer back to Chapter 8, "Creating Materials in Unreal."

In **TUTORIAL 9.11**, you set up the animated texture for the elevator control panel button. As mentioned previously, you want the button to be red when the elevator is not moving and green while the elevator is in motion.

9

TUTORIAL 9.11: Establishing the `MaterialTrigger` and `MaterialSwitch`

1. First you create the MaterialTrigger. In the Actor Class browser, expand Actor > Triggers, and click MaterialTrigger. This trigger's position is irrelevant, so place it somewhere that you can access easily.

2. Open the Texture browser, open the `Chapter9.utx` package, and select the MatTrigger group. This group has three textures: Green, Red, and LiftProgressTex. You'll use them shortly. For now, choose File > New from the Texture browser's menu to open the New Material dialog box.

3. Change the package to Chapter9, which saves your new material into the Chapter9 package. Set the Group entry to MatTrigger, and change the Name entry to StartStop. Finally, change the MaterialClass to MaterialSwitch.

4. Click New, and the properties for the newly created material appear in a new window (see **FIGURE 9.33**).

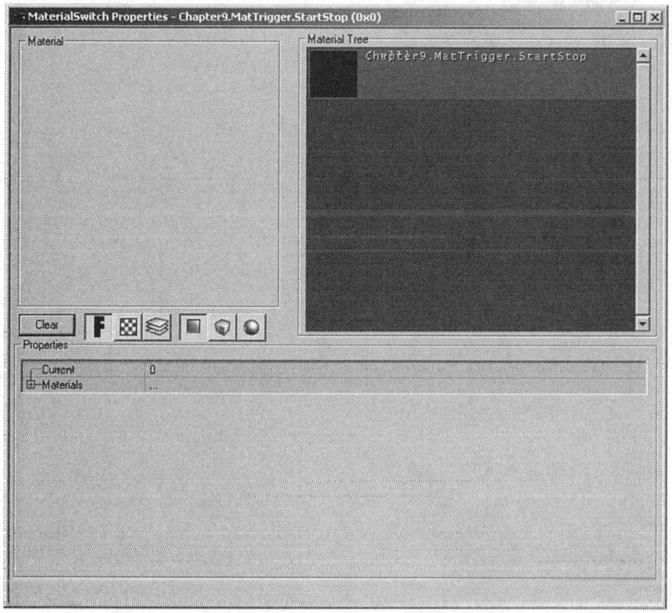

FIGURE 9.33 **The MaterialSwitch Properties window for the** `StartStop` **material.**

5. This material allows you to store other materials much like the ScriptedTrigger stores actions. Because you want to switch between a start material and a stop material, select the Materials entry, and click the Add button twice. **FIGURE 9.34** shows the two new materials added.

6. The first slot, entry [0], will be the Red texture. Back in the Texture browser, select the Red texture. Return to the MaterialSwitch Properties window, click entry [0], and click the Use button (see **FIGURE 9.35**).

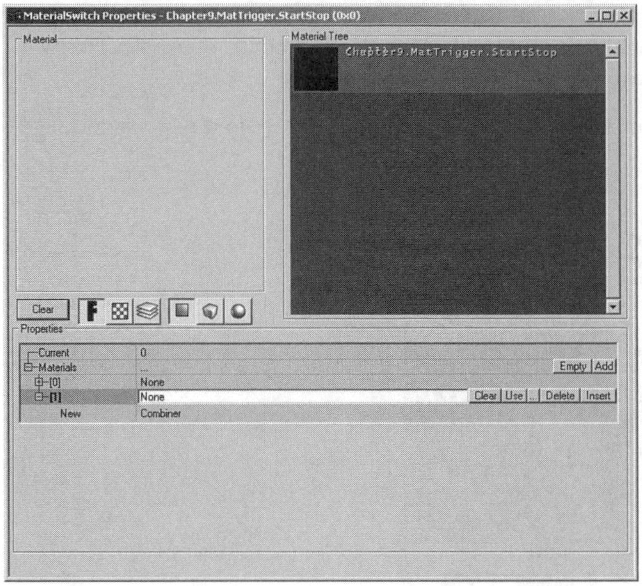

FIGURE 9.34 Two materials added to the `Materials` property.

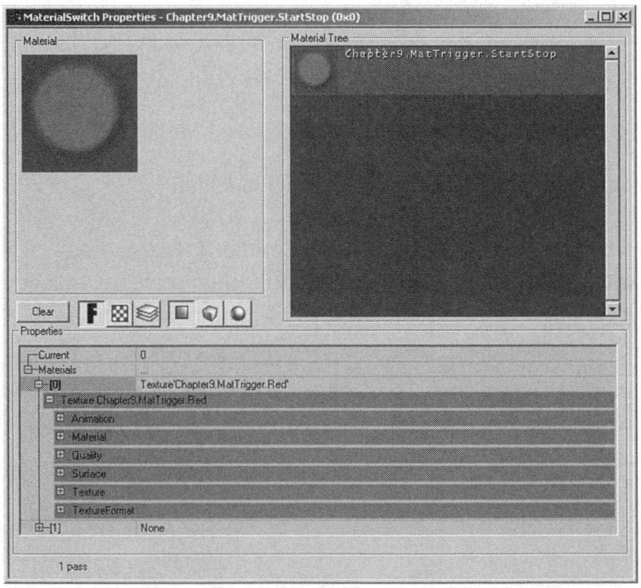

FIGURE 9.35 Entry [0] of the `Materials` property set to use the Red texture.

7. Repeat the process for entry [1], using the Green texture instead of Red (see **FIGURE 9.36**).

9

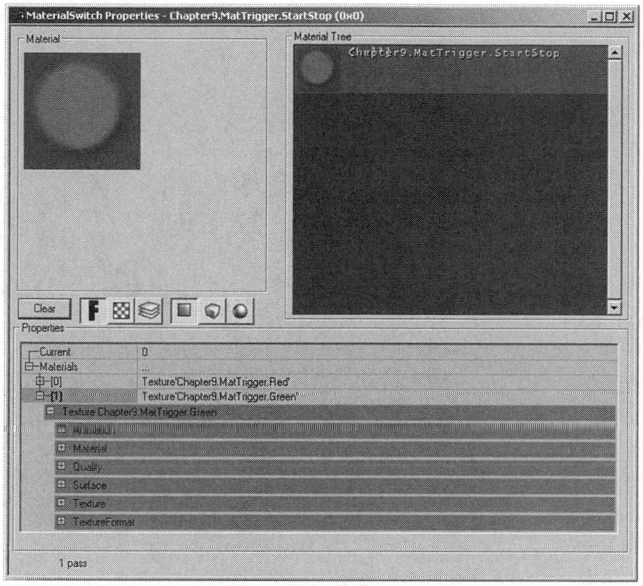

FIGURE 9.36 Entry [1] of the `Materials` property set to use the Green texture.

8. Save your work.

END TUTORIAL 9.11

In **TUTORIAL 9.12**, you set up the control system that drives your MaterialSwitch. To do this, you place a series of events into your MaterialTrigger, and then slightly modify some current settings for your ScriptedTrigger and lift Mover.

TUTORIAL 9.12: Controlling the MaterialSwitch

1. Double-click your MaterialTrigger to open its Properties window. Under the MaterialTrigger tab, click MaterialsToTrigger, and then click the Add button.
2. In the Material Editor, select the `StartStop` material you made in **TUTORIAL 9.11** (see **FIGURE 9.37**).
3. Back in the MaterialTrigger Properties window, click entry [0] under MaterialsToTrigger, and click the Use button.
4. Now you need to control when the switch takes place. First, go to the Events tab, and set the `Tag` property to `onOffTrigger` (see **FIGURE 9.38**). You haven't created this event yet, but you'll remedy that in the next step.

5. Open the ScriptedTrigger's Properties window. Expand the AIScript tab, and select Action entry [1]. It should currently be the `WAITFORTIMER` Action. Insert a new `Action_TRIGGEREVENT`, which becomes entry [1], pushing `WAITFORTIMER` to entry [2] (see **FIGURE 9.39**).

6. Set the `Event` property for the new `TRIGGEREVENT` to `onOffTrigger` (see **FIGURE 9.40**). This causes the material to be triggered as soon as a player activates the UseTrigger, but there's a problem. Currently, the button changes to green and stays green. You need to create another event that triggers the material a second time to switch it back to red.

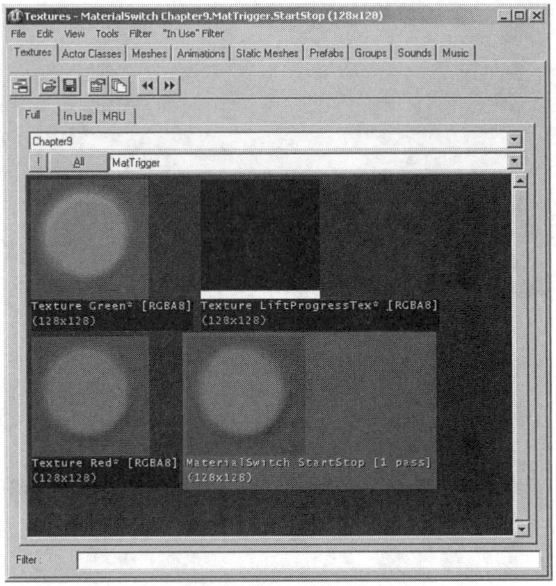

FIGURE 9.37 Select the *StartStop* material.

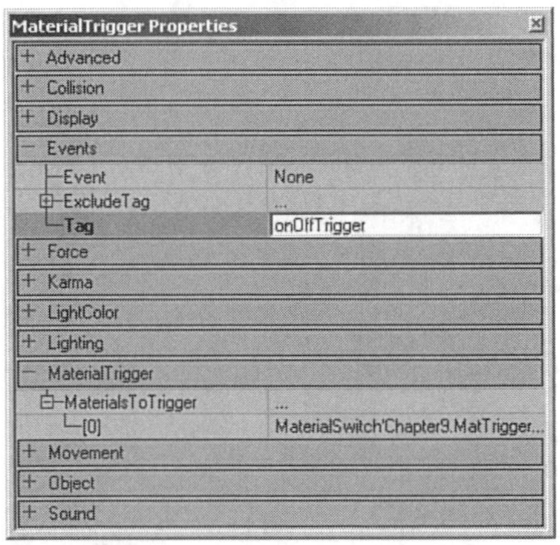

FIGURE 9.38 Properties of the MaterialTrigger.

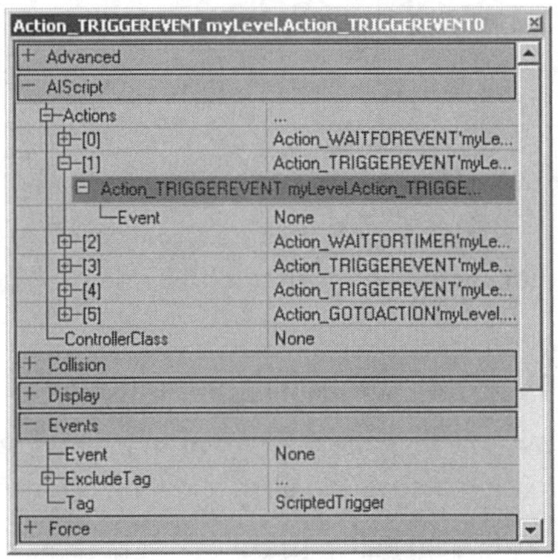

FIGURE 9.39 Action list for the ScriptedTrigger.

7. Open the lift Mover's properties. Open the MoverEvents tab, and set `ClosedEvent` to `onOffTrigger`. This setting triggers the material to switch when the elevator reaches the bottom, but you also need it to switch when it reaches the top. You can't switch the `OpenedEvent` because it's currently being used to open the door.

8. Instead of changing the lift's `OpenedEvent`, double-click the elevator door Mover. In its Properties window, expand the MoverEvents tab, if it isn't open already. Notice the `OpeningEvent` property, which generates an event as the door is opening. Logically, that means it generates an event at the same time as the lift Mover's `OpenedEvent`. Set the elevator door Mover's `OpeningEvent` property to `onOffTrigger`.

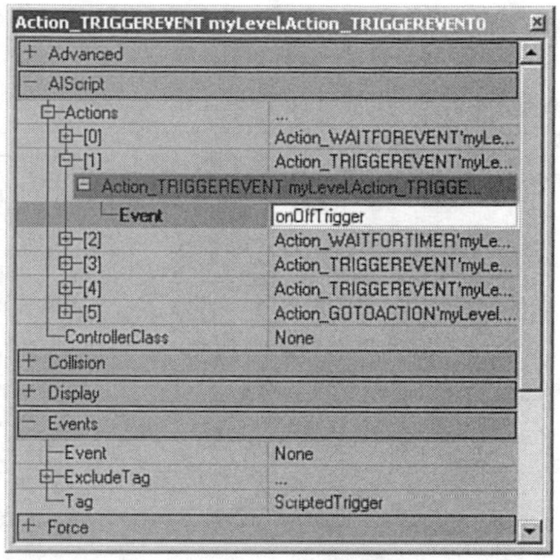

FIGURE 9.40 *TRIGGEREVENT* **Action with the** *Event* **property set to** *onOffTrigger*.

9. Open the Texture browser, and select the `StartStop` material. Switch to the Static Mesh browser, and locate the elevatorControl mesh. Select Material [1], and click the Use button (see **FIGURE 9.41**).

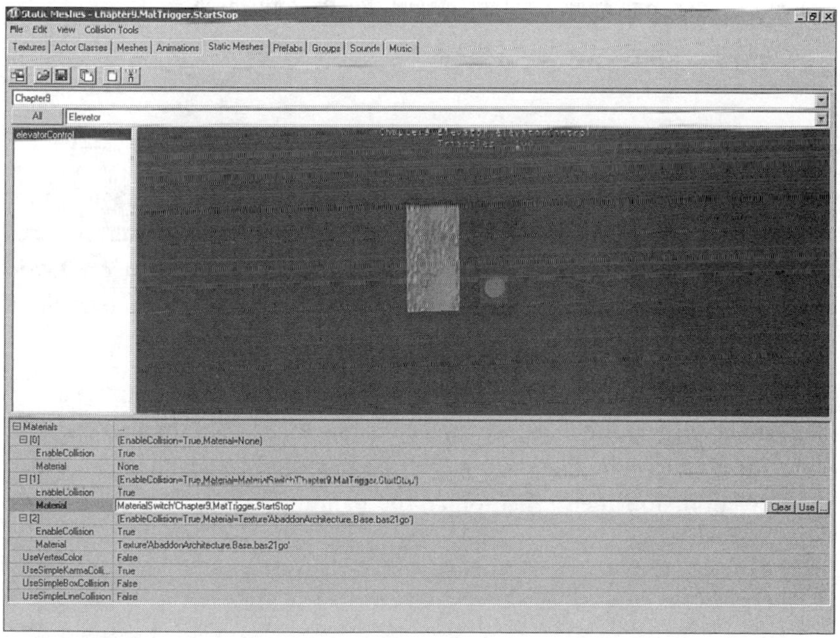

FIGURE 9.41 *StartStop* **material used on the elevatorControl static mesh.**

10. Locate the elevatorLift mesh, select Material [2], and click the Use button (see **FIGURE 9.42**).

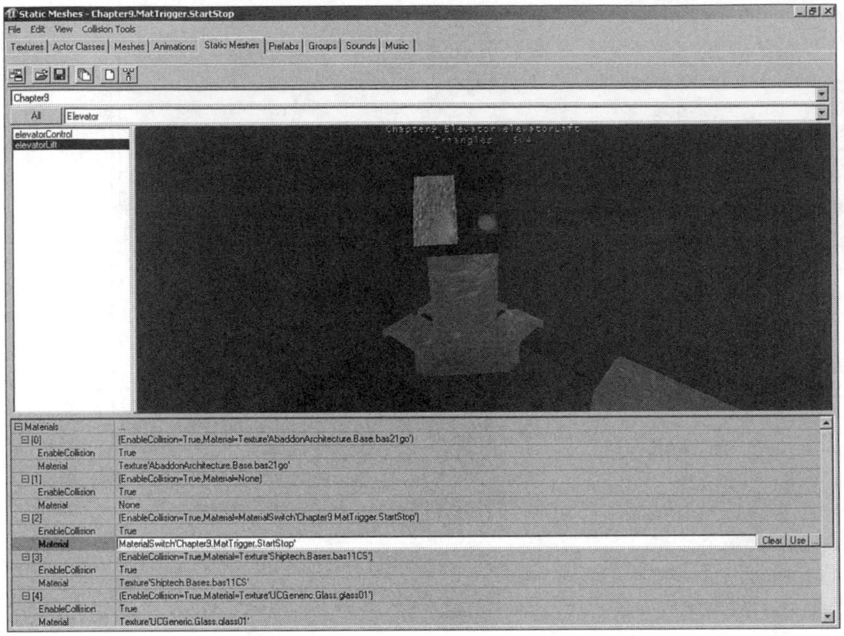

FIGURE 9.42 **Another *StartStop* material used on the elevatorLift static mesh.**

11. Save your work!

END TUTORIAL 9.12

You have just completed the button's texture as well as the system that allows it to switch from green to red. You can now rebuild your level and play-test the map. Notice that the button turns green while the elevator is in motion and red when the elevator stops. In **TUTORIAL 9.13**, you set up a progress bar texture that displays the current location of the elevator lift as it moves along the elevator shaft.

The progress bar requires creating another MaterialTrigger. This time, however, you use a new kind of material: a TexPannerTriggered. This material pans, or moves, in a certain direction and a certain distance each time it's triggered. The texture itself is a black bar on a white field, which you pan in a vertical direction. You then synchronize the panning action to the elevator's motion.

TUTORIAL 9.13: The Progress Bar

1. In the Texture browser, create a new material with the following settings:

   Package: Chapter9

   Group: MatTrigger

   Name: progressBar

   MaterialClass: MaterialSwitch

2. When the MaterialSwitch Properties window opens, expand the Materials tab (see **FIGURE 9.43**). Click the Add button to create a new material. Next to the New entry, change the material type to `TexPannerTriggered`, and click New.

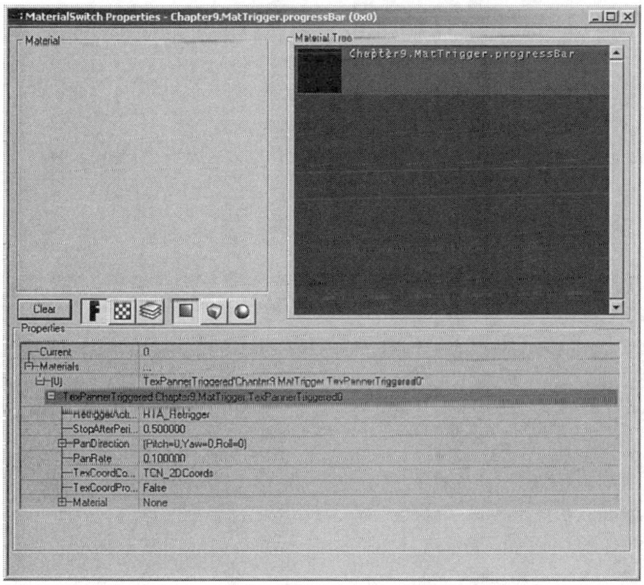

FIGURE 9.43 *`TexPannerTriggered`* **created as the first material for the** *`progressBar`* **material.**

3. A new `TexPannerTriggered` material has been created. To adjust its properties, select the LiftProgressTex texture from the Texture browser. Select the Materials entry in the TexPannerTriggered properties list, and click the Use button (see **FIGURE 9.44**).

4. The texture in the Properties window has changed, but it's not moving. Expand the `PanDirection` property, and set `Yaw` to 16000 (see **FIGURE 9.45**). This number controls the direction of the pan but also influences the pan's speed.

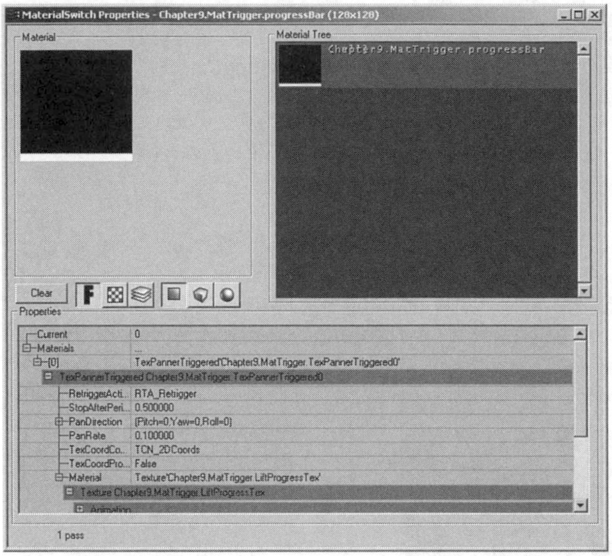

FIGURE 9.44 LiftProgressTex texture set for the `Materials` property of *`TexPannerTriggered`*.

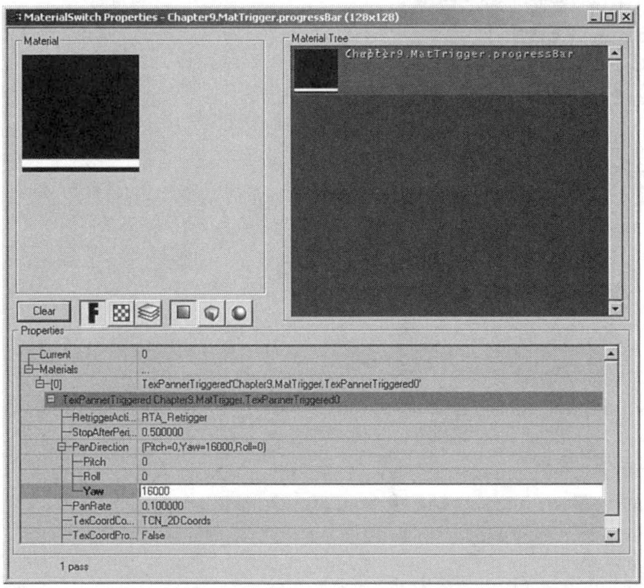

FIGURE 9.45 For *`PanDirection`*, set *`Yaw`* to 16000.

5. The `PanRate` property also controls the pan's speed. This property works similarly to a multiplier. If `PanDirection` is set to 16000 and `PanRate` is set to 1, the result is about one full cycle of the texture every second. You already know that the lift takes five seconds to go from the bottom of the shaft to the top, and vice versa. Therefore, you need the `PanRate` set to one fifth that amount, so give it a value of 0.2 (see **FIGURE 9.46**).

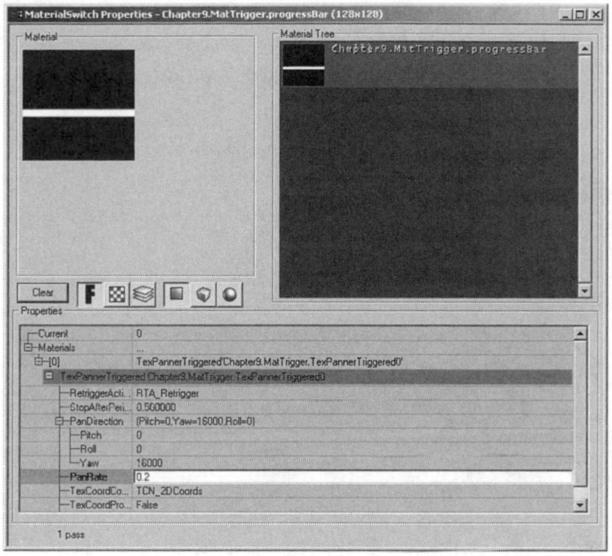

FIGURE 9.46 *PanRate* set to 0.2.

6. The `StopAfterPeriod` controls how many complete cycles will be performed. A `StopAfterPeriod` of 1 results in a full cycle of your texture, meaning your progress bar will wrap back around to the bottom of the display. You need to stop the texture panning before it wraps around. Therefore, the `StopAfterPeriod` needs a value slightly less than 1. Enter a value of 0.93 (see **FIGURE 9.47**).

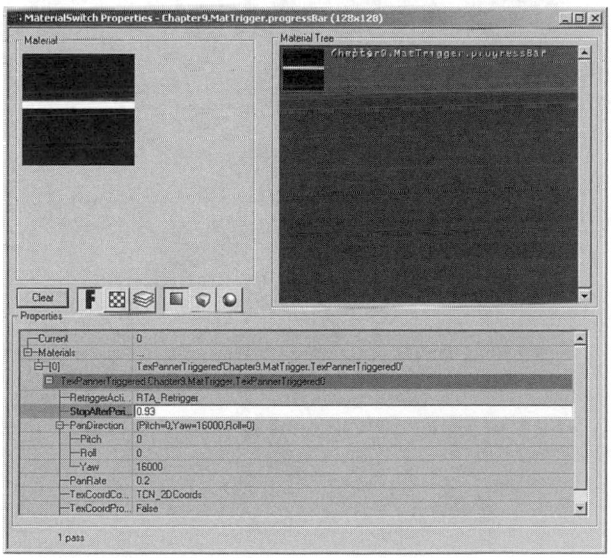

FIGURE 9.47 *StopAfterPeriod* set to 0.93.

7. Set the `ReTriggerAction` property to `RTA_Reverse` (see **FIGURE 9.48**). This setting causes the texture to move upward the first time it's triggered, down the second time, up the third, and so on. Because your elevator lift begins on the hangar floor, the texture now moves in tandem with the lift.

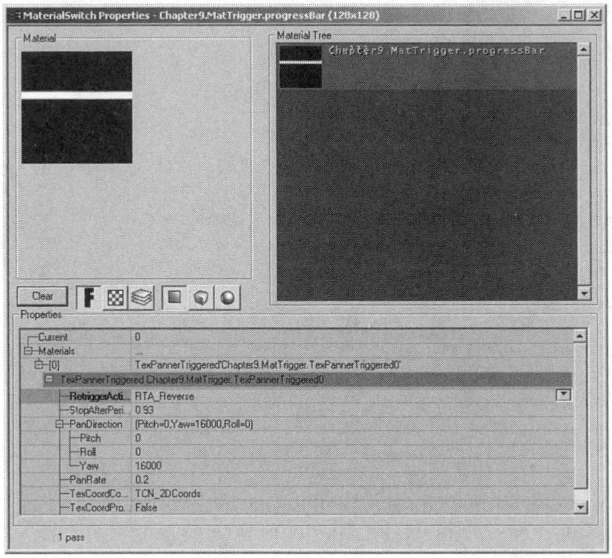

FIGURE 9.48 *ReTriggerAction* **changed to** *RTA_Reverse*.

8. Now you need to set up the events to handle when the material's animation is triggered. Duplicate the existing MaterialTrigger, and open its properties. Change its `MaterialsToTrigger` property to `progressBar` (see **FIGURE 9.49**).

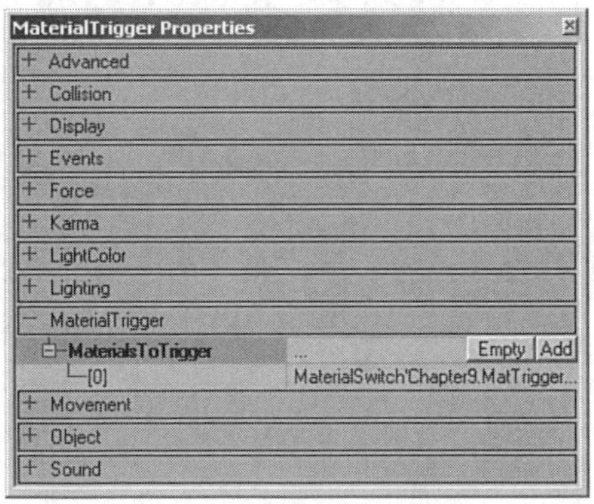

FIGURE 9.49 *MaterialToTrigger* **property set to the** *progressBar* **material.**

9. You already have an event in place that causes the lift to move, and you can use that event to trigger the texture as well. Open the MaterialTrigger's Events tab, and set the `Tag` property to `frontLiftMover` (see **FIGURE 9.50**).

9

10. In the Static Mesh browser, set Material [0] of elevatorControl and Material [1] of elevatorLift to the new `progressBar` material. Unless you have selected another texture in the Texture browser, you should be able to just click the Use key.

11. Save your texture package to record the new materials as well as the Chapter9 static mesh package. Save your map, and you're ready to test your new elevator!

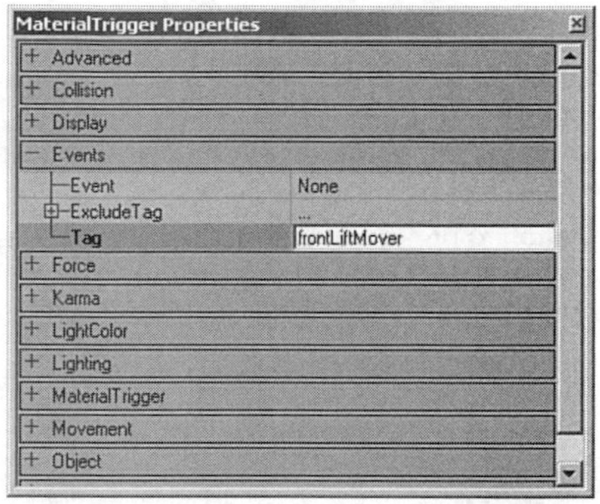

FIGURE 9.50 *Tag* property set to `frontLiftMover`.

END TUTORIAL 9.13

You have completed a complex elevator system complete with camera shake, automated doors, and animated textures. You should now have a thorough understanding of how Unreal uses events and tags to control your triggers' behavior. In the next section, you learn how to create jump pads in your levels to propel players across your map.

Jump Pads

Jump pads are Actors that launch players over great distances. The effect is similar to stepping into a catapult. Jump pads can be used to enhance the action and fun factors of your levels. They can also be used to allow players to cross over areas where a simple jump isn't enough. In **TUTORIAL 9.14**, you see how to place jump pads in your levels and control their trajectories. In this way, you have precise control over exactly where a jump pad sends your players.

TUTORIAL 9.14: Adding a Jump Pad to the Hangar

1. To begin, you need a small alcove near the top of the hangar's right wall to test your jumping pad. Create a 256×256×256 cube, subtract it from the wall, and put a light in the room. Use the Top and Side views to gauge alignment (see **FIGURE 9.51**).

2. Move the Player Start from the hallway into this new recession, and rotate it to point out into the room (see **FIGURE 9.52**).

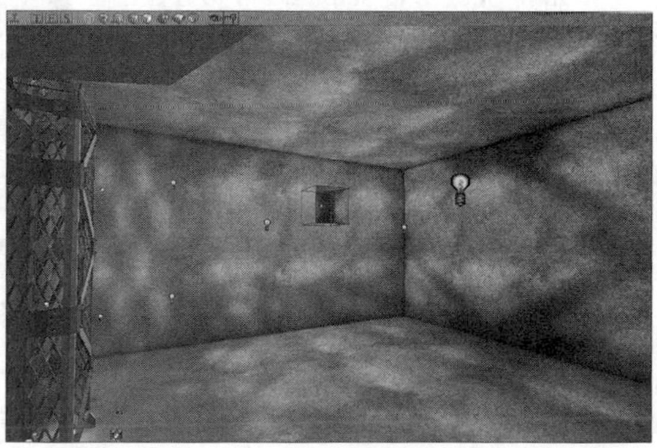

FIGURE 9.51 Subtracted area for the jump pad.

3. A functional jump pad actually requires two Actors: UTJumpPad is the launch point, and JumpSpot is the destination. Open the Actor Class browser and expand Actor > NavigationPoint > JumpPad. Click the UTJumpPad Actor. Note that you didn't select the JumpPad Actor, which is non-placeable.

> **TIP**
>
> **In the Actor Class browser, a star next to an Actor's name signifies that the Actor is placeable.**

FIGURE 9.52 A Player Start placed in the room.

4. Right-click on the floor of the new room, and choose Add UTJumpPad Here from the context menu to give you a launch point (see **FIGURE 9.53**).

5. Now you need to add the destination. Back in the Actor Class browser, expand Actor > NavigationPoint > JumpDest, and click the JumpSpot Actor. Right-click near the base of the elevator, and place the Actor there, as shown in **FIGURE 9.54**.

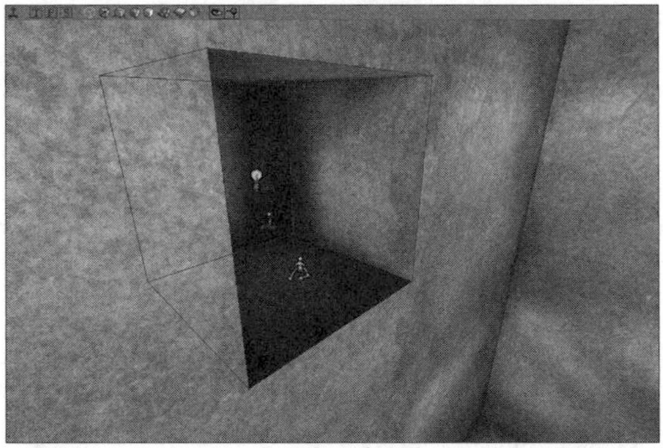

FIGURE 9.53 A UTJumpPad Actor placed in the room.

6. Next, you need to establish the connection between these two Actors. Open the Properties window for the JumpSpot, and scroll down to the Object tab. In this tab is the `Name` property, which is read-only and cannot be changed. Take note of this name (usually JumpSpot0), as you use it in the next step (see **FIGURE 9.55**).

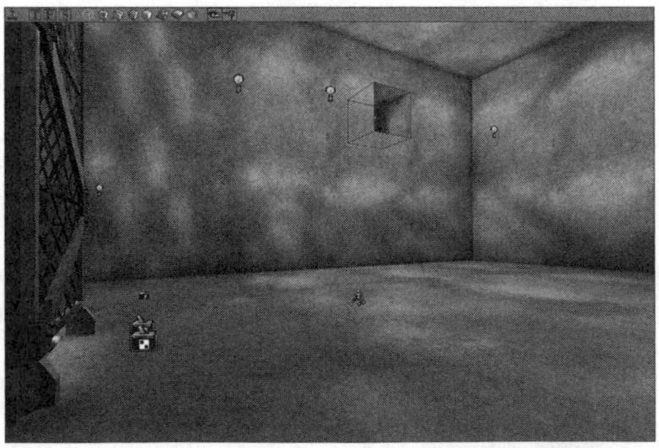

FIGURE 9.54 JumpSpot Actor placed near the base of the elevator.

7. Select the UTJumpPad, and in its Properties window, scroll down to the NavigationPoint tab. Expand the `ForcedPaths` property, and set the value of entry [0] to `JumpSpot0`, or whatever name appeared in your JumpSpot's `Name` property (see **FIGURE 9.56**). Also, expand the Advanced tab and set `bHidden` to False so that you can see the jump pad icon in the game.
8. Click the Build Paths icon on the toolbar, and select the JumpPad. Now you can see the arc that players travel if they pass through the jump pad (see **FIGURE 9.57**).
9. In the Properties window of the UTJumpPad, expand the JumpPad tab. You can edit the jump pad's arc of the jump pad by using the `JumpZModifier` property. Try setting it to 0.5, as shown in **FIGURE 9.58**. You must rebuild your paths, however, to see the change.
10. If you would like to see the area of effect for your jump pad, you can right-click on the top bar of the 3D viewport, and choose Actors > Radii View from the context menu. The result is shown in **FIGURE 9.59**.
11. Save your map, rebuild for good measure, and test your level.

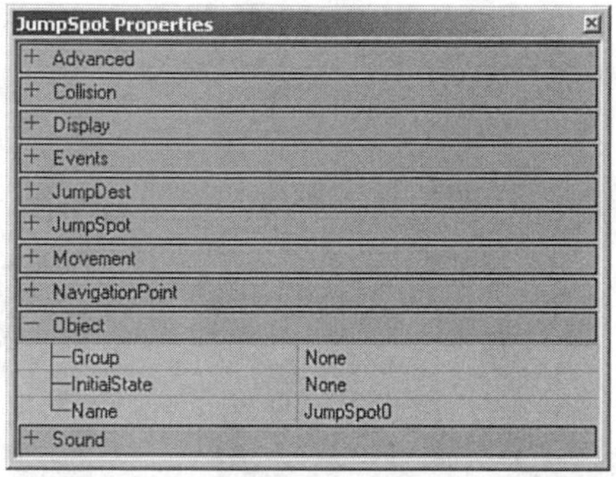

FIGURE 9.55 *Name* **property of the JumpSpot Actor.**

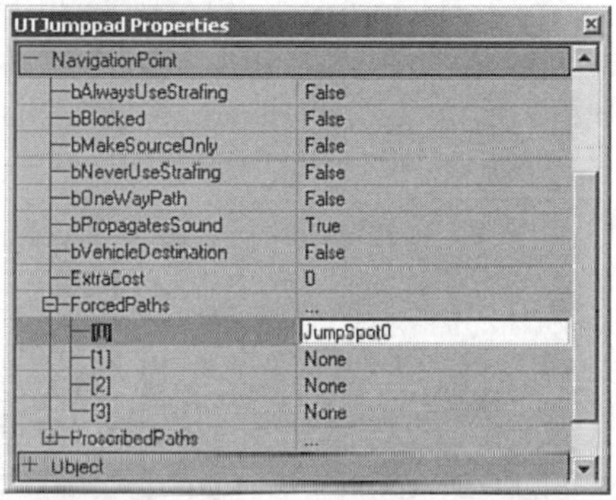

FIGURE 9.56 *ForcedPaths* **[0] property set to JumpSpot0.**

FIGURE 9.57 **Arc from JumpPad to JumpSpot.**

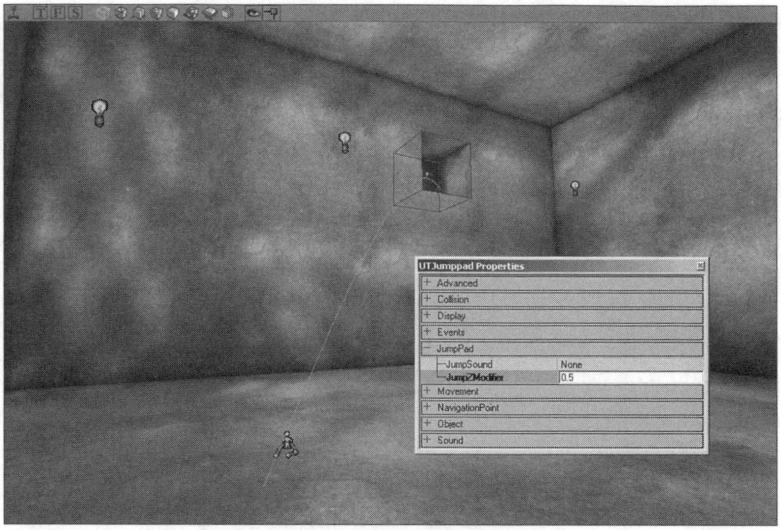

FIGURE 9.58 *JumpZModifier* property set to 0.5 and the newly generated arc.

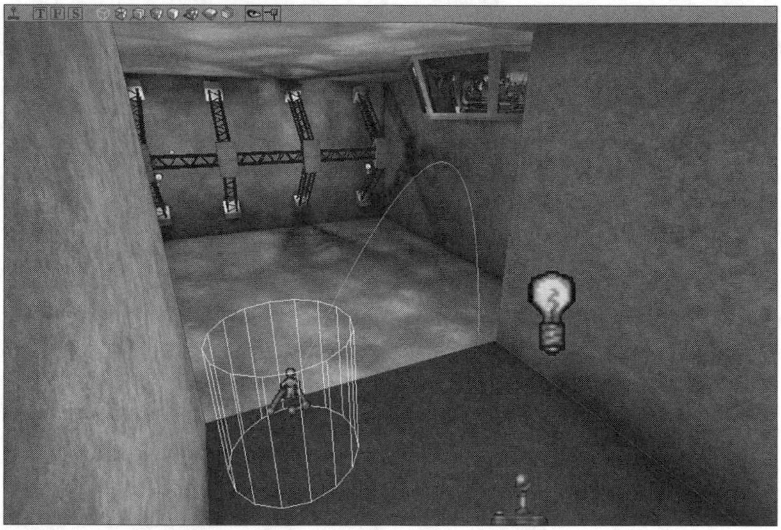

FIGURE 9.59 The radius of effect for the jump pad.

END TUTORIAL 9.14

You have now added a jump pad to your hangar that launches players across the level, based on the arc you established with the `JumpZModifier` property. Jump pads can add more gameplay depth by providing access to unreachable areas of a map. In the next section, you see how you can create teleporters to instantly send your players from one point on the map to another.

Teleporters

Teleporters, like jump pads, can be used to transport a player from one point on the map to another. Unlike jump pads, however, teleporters send players to the destination instantaneously, regardless of the obstacles between the origin and the destination. Teleporters can be set to send a player to a series of random locations or even to teleport the player to a new level! In **TUTORIAL 9.15**, you see how to set up a simple teleporter to send a player from one spot on the map to another.

TUTORIAL 9.15: Setting Up a Simple Teleporter

FIGURE 9.60 A teleporter Actor placed in the alcove.

1. In the Actor Class browser, expand Actor > NavigationPoint > SmallNavigationPoint, and click Teleporter.
2. Place the teleporter in the alcove near your jump pad (see **FIGURE 9.60**). If necessary, adjust the jump pad's position to make room. Place a second teleporter somewhere in the control room.
3. Now you need to establish the connection between these teleporters. Select the teleporter in the control room, and open its Properties window. In the Events tab, set the `Tag` property to `ControlRoom`. This setting functions as the teleporter's name, or designation.
4. Now select the teleporter you placed near the jump pad. In its Properties window, expand the Teleporter tab, and set the `URL` property to `ControlRoom`.
5. When you select a teleporter, you see a red arrow pointing out of it, similar to the Player Start icon. This arrow shows the player's orientation when teleporting to that destination, in relation to the direction the player was facing when entering the original teleporter. Adjust the rotation of the teleporters in the Top view so that they're facing in the correct directions (see **FIGURE 9.61**).
6. If you test the level now, you would find that the teleporter near the jump pad sends you to the control room, but not the other way around. Select the teleporter near the jump pad, and set its `Tag` property to `TopTeleporter`.
7. Select the control room teleporter, expand the Teleporter tab, and set the `URL` property to `ControlRoom`.
8. In the Advanced tab of both teleporters, set the `bHidden` property to False so that you can see the icons in the game.
9. Save your map, and test your level.

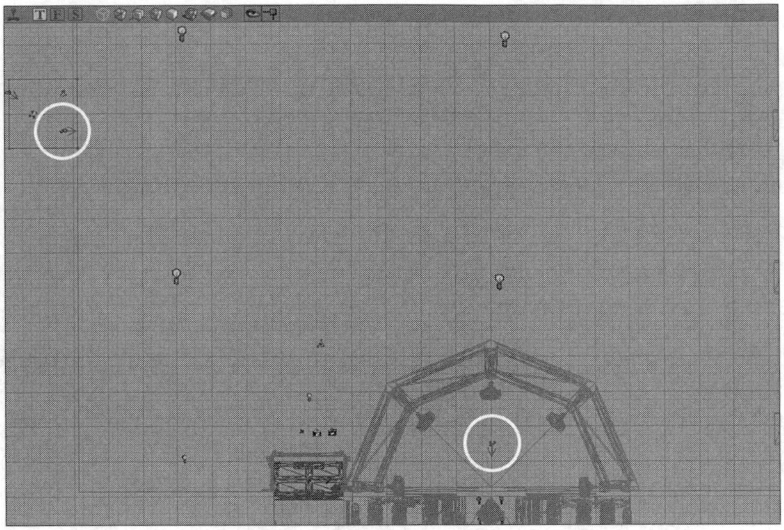

FIGURE 9.61 Top view showing the rotations of the two teleporters.

END TUTORIAL 9.15

You now have a teleporting system that sends players from the alcove in the wall to the control room, and back again. In **TUTORIAL 9.16**, you see how to expand on this technique by adding a random factor. You'll place a series of teleporters that send players to a random point each time they enter a teleporter.

TUTORIAL 9.16: Creating a Random Teleporter

1. Creating a series of random teleporters is simple. To begin, open the Properties window for the control room teleporter, and set *both* its `Tag` and `URL` properties to `Random` (see **FIGURE 9.62**).

> **NOTE**
>
> You can use any name you like, as long as it's the same name for both the `Tag` and `URL` properties.

2. Repeat this process for the teleporter in the hangar alcove.

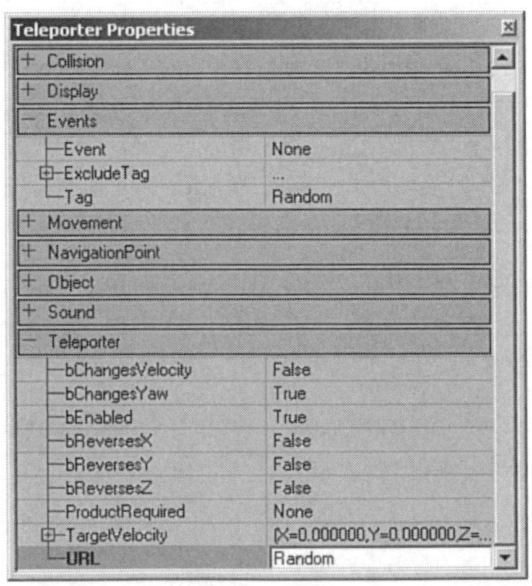

FIGURE 9.62 The *URL* and *Tag* properties of the control room teleporter are both set to *Random*.

3. Duplicate either teleporter three more times, and place the duplicates at random locations throughout the level, as shown in **FIGURE 9.63**.

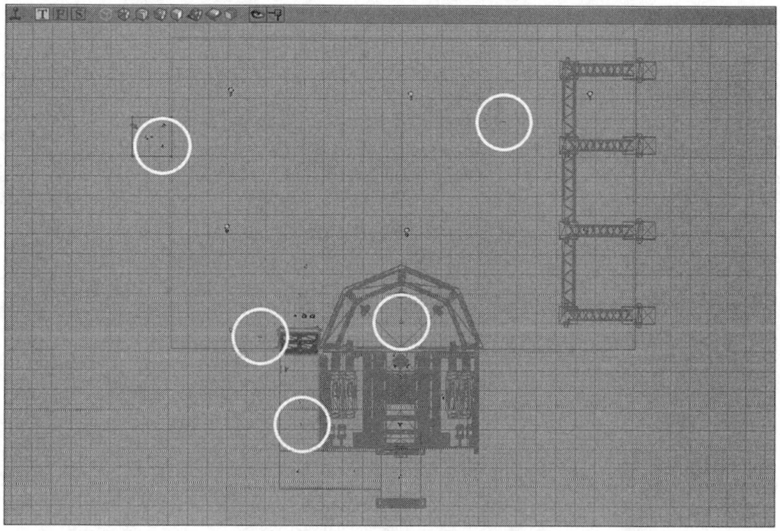

FIGURE 9.63 Five teleporters with random destinations.

4. Test the level, and enjoy your random teleporting experience.

END TUTORIAL 9.16

Challenge: If you test the level, you'll find that it is possible to ride the elevator to the top and teleport back into the hangar. However, from the hangar floor, there's no way to call the elevator back down. Using the skills you have learned in this chapter, place a new control panel for the elevator near the elevator shaft. Be sure to include the trigger needed to make the panel function properly.

Summary

In this chapter, you learned how triggers can be used to dramatically alter the way your game is played. By now, you should have a thorough understanding of how events are generated, how tags can be set, and how triggers can control multiple aspects of your level. Using these skills, you can create complex systems that turn your levels into living environments with multiple levels of interactivity.

Part II

Advanced Design Techniques

Chapter 10

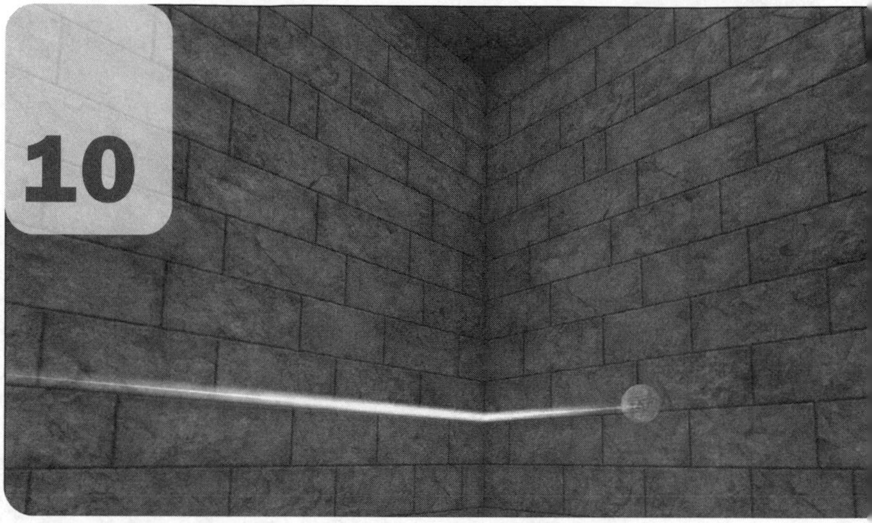

Creating Particle Effects

Nearly every game tries to replicate a real-world effect from a natural environment. Fire, smoke, rain, waterfalls, and a myriad other effects are all elements that can be used to enhance realism during gameplay. In many games, you also find special effects that go outside the realm of reality, such as teleportation effects, magical sparks, and more. To achieve these effects, you use what are known as *particles*.

Particles are added into Unreal levels through Emitter Actors. In this chapter, you learn about the practical use of particles and the emitter types used to create particle effects in Unreal. Keep in mind, however, that rather than cover all the available properties of particles and the Emitter Actor at once, the properties are discussed as they become relevant during the chapter. The properties specific to each emitter type, however, are discussed in the section corresponding to each type.

Particle Theory

In their simplest form, particles are nothing more than points in space with a certain look designated to make them resemble part of a specific effect, such as a single flame, a puff of smoke, or a sci-fi sparkle. The points are then assigned a specific behavior that controls their movement, scale, rotation, and much more. In **FIGURE 10.1**, you can see a particle effect from a level in Unreal Tournament 2004.

FIGURE 10.1 A cool particle effect in CTF-Chrome, a map included with Unreal Tournament 2004.

To be more technically correct, particles are a series of data blocks that hold information such as position, lifespan, velocity, scale, and many more. This data is then changed and updated over time based on the existing data. For example, a raindrop starts off somewhere in the sky, and then begins descending faster and faster because of gravity. Eventually, the drop hits the ground and dies. A particle can have a similar existence.

Taking that example a bit further, you could track a raindrop's activity as it falls. Say that the raindrop starts out with position <0, 5> (2D coordinates are used here for simplicity), and it's accelerating toward the ground in the Y-axis. You want the particle to accelerate in such a way that its speed doubles as each second goes by. To do this, you need to assign an acceleration of <0,-1>. **FIGURE 10.2** illustrates this simple raindrop moving for three seconds.

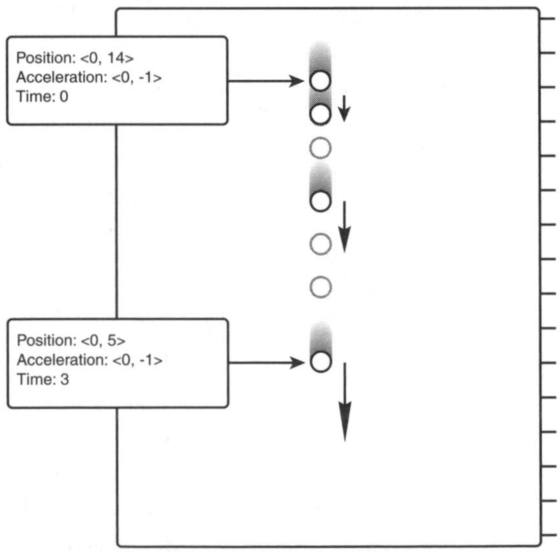

FIGURE 10.2 A particle in motion.

In Unreal, particles work in the same manner, in that you can assign a series of values that control various aspects of their behavior. However, using only a single particle rarely produces the effect you want. Most effects, such as fire, smoke, and steam, require creating hundreds, if not thousands, of particles. To handle the creation of vast quantities of particles, Unreal uses what's known as *emitters*. Emitters are Actors that simply pump out particles from a specific location.

They control how many particles are created, at what speed they start out, how long they live, and much more. Emitters give you enough control over your particles that you rarely, if ever, need to resort to programming to achieve the effect you want.

Emitter Types

Unreal has five different types of emitters, each designed to provide a specific type of effect: Sprite, Spark, Mesh, Beam, and Trail emitters (see **FIGURE 10.3**). These emitter types share a set of common properties, but each one also has individual properties unique to that type. For example, you can use the MeshEmitter to display your particles as static meshes, a feature that none of the other emitters is capable of. Some emitters are meant for effects such as snow or rain (SpriteEmitter), lightning effects (BeamEmitter), and electric sparks (SparkEmitter). The sheer number of properties might seem overwhelming at first, but most of the properties are fairly self explanatory.

The Emitter Actor is the container for the various emitter types. Within this Emitter Actor, you can have as many particle emitters as you want, and they can be of any type and in any combination you want. Although this design might sound confusing at first, it comes in handy when you're trying to create more complex effects that require multiple emitter types. Say, for example, that you want to create a fire effect. You could have three SpriteEmitters inside the Emitter Actor—one to simulate the fire, one to simulate the smoke, and a third to emit sparks (see **FIGURE 10.4**). This design means you don't have to place three separate Actors in your map to produce a single effect.

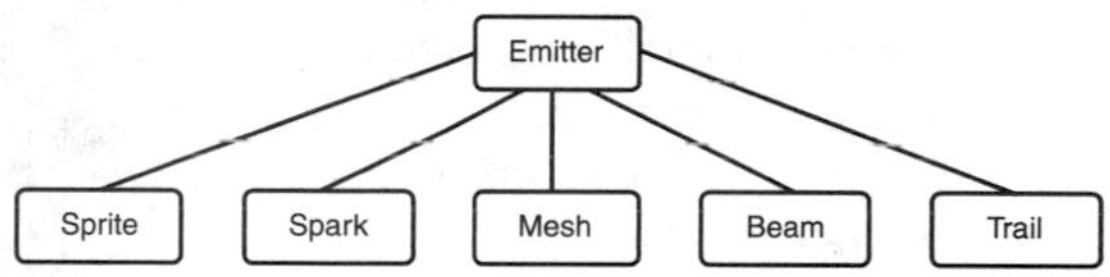

FIGURE 10.3 The relationship between the different emitter types.

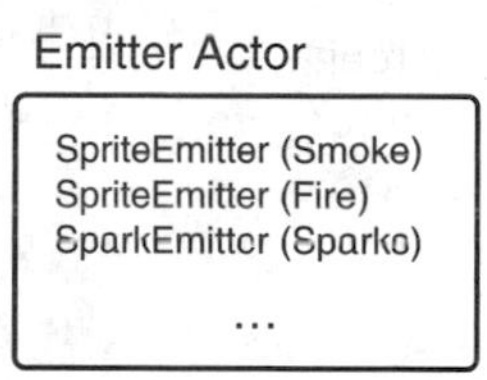

FIGURE 10.4 A single emitter Actor can hold many emitters.

SpriteEmitter

The SpriteEmitter, the most popular and most commonly used emitter, is used to create common effects such as waterfalls, fire, smoke, and much more. When using a SpriteEmitter, each particle onscreen is represented by a *sprite* (see **FIGURE 10.5**). A sprite is simply a rectangular 2D plane on which an image is placed. This plane always faces toward the camera. To be precise, this means sprites are always perpendicular to the camera. Because the images used for each sprite can have a mask or an alpha channel, the outer edge 2D planes can be transparent, effectively allowing you to make the sprite appear to be any shape you want.

In **TUTORIALS 10.1** through **10.3**, you simulate steam coming from a pipe by using a SpriteEmitter.

FIGURE 10.5 A simple smoke sprite.

TUTORIAL 10.1: Creating and Setting Up Your Emitter

1. Open the `Tutorial10_01_Start.ut2` file. This map contains a large air pipe with a smaller pipe connected to it that you'll use as the exit point for some steam (see **FIGURE 10.6**).

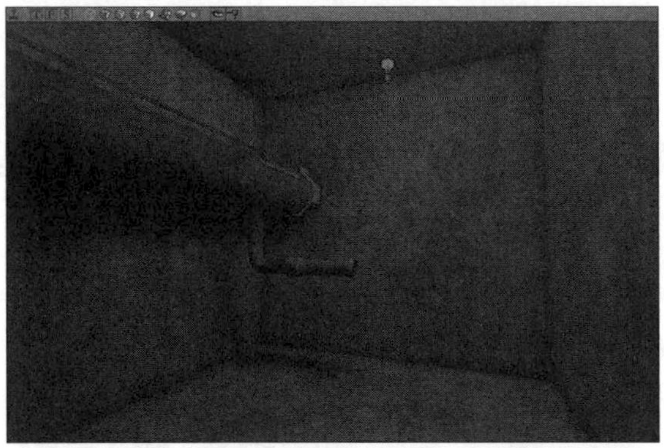

FIGURE 10.6 Room without any particle effects.

2. First, you need to create the Emitter Actor. Open the Actor Class browser and select Actor > Emitter. Underneath this Actor is a series of other emitters, mostly specialized for use within the game through UnrealScript. Place the Emitter Actor at the end of the pipe, as shown in **FIGURE 10.7**.

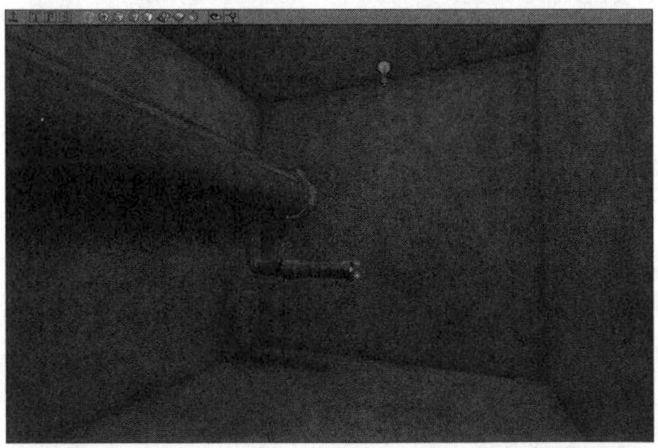

FIGURE 10.7 Emitter Actor placed at the end of the pipe.

3. You now have an Emitter Actor, in which you can start placing other emitter types. For this tutorial, you need only one simple SpriteEmitter. Open the Properties window for the Emitter Actor. Under the Emitter category is one `Emitters` property. This array starts out empty, so add one to it by clicking the Add button (see **FIGURE 10.8**).

4. Now you need to specify what kind of emitter type to add. Select SpriteEmitter from the drop-down list next to the New entry, and click the New button, which gives you access to a wide variety of new options, shown in **FIGURE 10.9**.

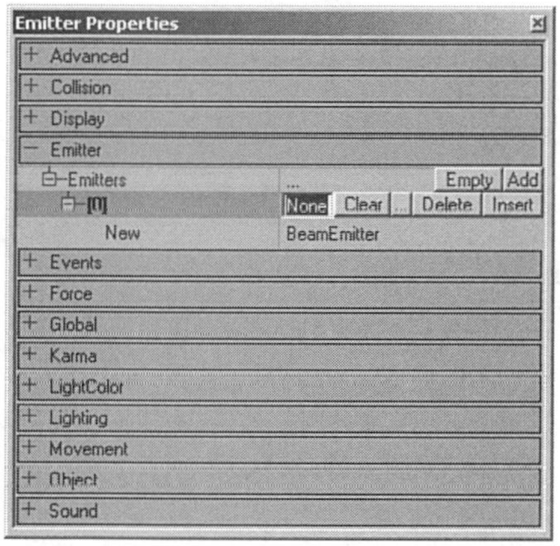

FIGURE 10.8 `Emitters` **property with one item in it.**

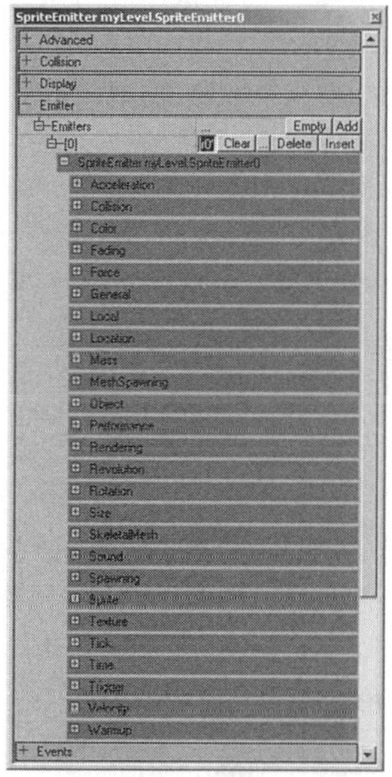

FIGURE 10.9 **Properties of the SpriteEmitter.**

5. At this point, you should already see some feedback in the main viewport. If not, make sure that Realtime Preview is enabled by clicking the joystick icon  in the viewport's upper-left corner or pressing the P key. Notice a few things you'll need to change (see **FIGURE 10.10**). First, the sprite is the same as the icon used for the Emitter Actor. Also, you need to change the sprites' size and add some movement to them. You'll do this in **TUTORIAL 10.2**.

6. Save the map.

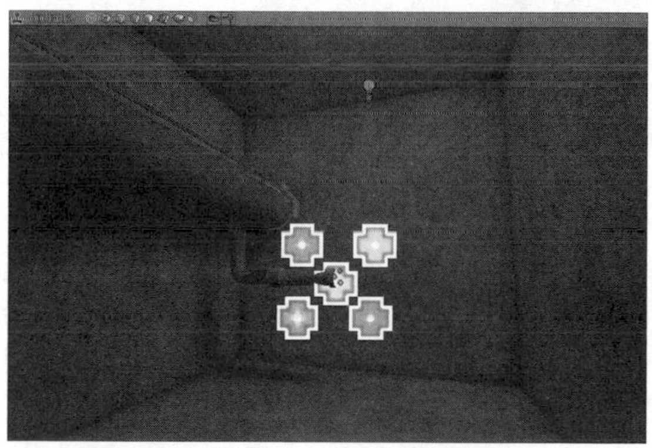

FIGURE 10.10 **The beginning of your particle effect.**

END TUTORIAL 10.1

In the Emitter Actors Properties window, the Texture category provides all the necessary properties for controlling your sprite textures. Only two of these properties are important at the moment: Texture and DrawStyle. Texture is used simply to specify the texture you want to use for your sprite. DrawStyle determines how the texture data is interpreted and drawn onscreen, much like the material properties discussed in Chapter 8, "Creating Materials in Unreal." For demonstration purposes, the texture shown in **FIGURE 10.11** is used.

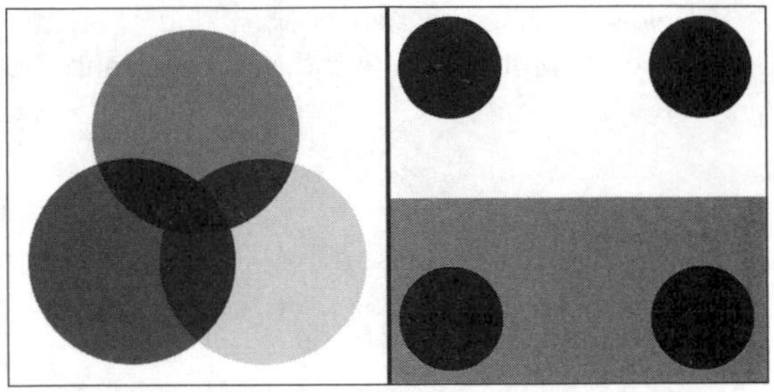

FIGURE 10.11 On the left is the texture's color data and on the right is the alpha channel.

TABLE 10.1 shows the `DrawStyles` available for use with particles. The right column contains a description of each `DrawStyle`, and the image in the left column shows what the texture in **FIGURE 10.11** would look like using that particular `DrawStyle`.

TABLE 10.1 Texture *`DrawStyle`*

Texture	Description
	`PTDS_Regular` makes the texture opaque. However, the alpha channel is still taken into account, making all black areas of the alpha channel completely transparent and all other parts opaque.
	`PTDS_AlphaBlend` makes the darker parts of the RGBA texture's A-channel more transparent than the bright parts. Black becomes completely transparent, and the white parts are completely opaque.
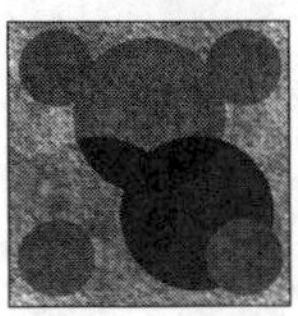	`PTDS_Modulated` makes the brightest colors of the texture more transparent than the darkest colors, so black becomes opaque, and white becomes completely transparent. However, the brighter colors still brighten the background.
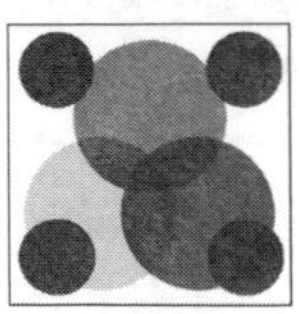	`PTDS_Translucent` makes the texture's darkest colors more transparent than the brightest colors, so white becomes opaque, and black becomes completely invisible. All other colors are partially transparent.

TABLE 10.1 Continued

Texture	Description
	`PTDS_AlphaModulate` makes the darker areas more transparent if the actual alpha channel is something other than white.
	`PTDS_Darken` makes the texture's colors negative and translucent.
	`PTDS_Brighten` makes the texture brighten the background, so the texture becomes translucent and brighter than its original version.

As you can see, the alpha channel is used in all the draw types. However, only in `PTDS_AlphaBlend` and `PTDS_AlphaModulate` are the alpha channel's gray areas used. The rest of the draw types make all black areas transparent and all other colors opaque. In **TUTORIAL 10.2**, you use the `DrawStyle` property with a SpriteEmitter to create a steam effect.

TUTORIAL 10.2: Creating the Steam

1. Open `Tutorial10_02_Start.ut2`, or continue with the file from **TUTORIAL 10.1**.
2. Open the Texture browser and load the `Chapter10.utx` package. Select the Smoke texture. In **FIGURE 10.12**, you can see this texture's RGB and alpha channels. Notice that the RGB information for the texture is completely white.
3. In the Properties window for the SpriteEmitter, open the Texture category. For the `Texture` property, click the Use button.
4. Your texture is now in use. However, your sprite looks like **FIGURE 10.13**.

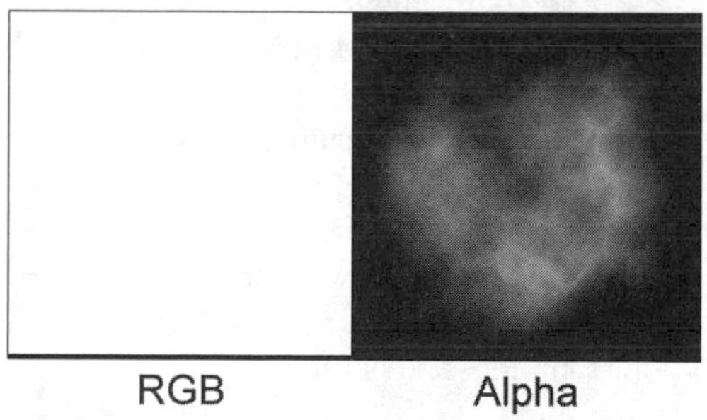

FIGURE 10.12 On the left is the texture's color data and on the right is the alpha channel.

Notice that your texture is completely white, except for the alpha channel, which actually holds the smoke formation. Because your current `DrawStyle`, found under the Texture category, is set to `PTDS_Regular`, the alpha information is used as a mask, making the texture either completely opaque or transparent and nothing in between. Change the `DrawStyle` property to `PTDS_AlphaBlend`, and notice that the alpha information is now read incorrectly. **FIGURE 10.14** shows what you should get.

FIGURE 10.13 The sprite information is being used incorrectly.

5. Your texture is correct now, but the size is still far too big. In the SpriteEmitter Properties window, open the Size category, where all adjustments to sprite size are made. The property `StartSizeRange` specifies a range from `Min` to `Max` in X, Y, and Z. The size is a random value within that range. Because the three axes are independent of each other, you do get considerable control over the texture's size. However, the `UniformSize` property is set to False by default and can't be set to True unless `UseDirectionAs` (under the Sprite category) is set to something other than `PTDU_None`. For your purposes, set the `Min` and `Max` values of X to 5 and 15, respectively. Because `UniformSize` is True, the sprite will always be a perfect square ranging in size from 5 to 15 units in width and height.

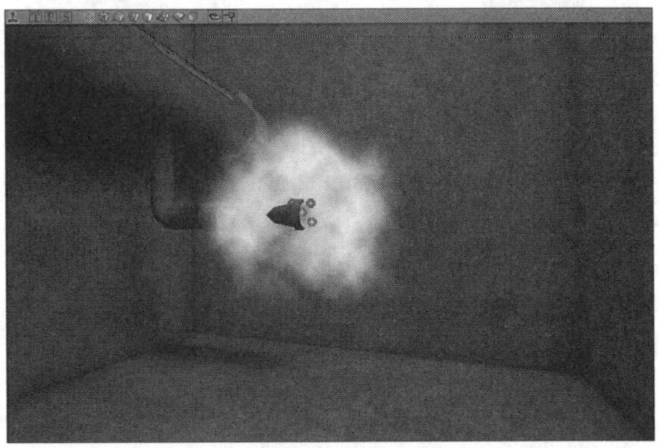

FIGURE 10.14 Setting *`DrawStyle`* to *`PTDS_AlphaBlend`* fixes the ugly sprite problem.

6. Now you need to give the steam some locomotion. Under the Velocity category is another set of properties specifically meant for setting the speed of particle motion. The `StartVelocityRange` property, measured in Unreal units per second, sets the range of possible velocities that a particle can have when it

FIGURE 10.15 The current progress of your steam.

begins its life. It works just like the `StartSizeRange` property except that you aren't hindered by a property such as `UniformSize`, meaning you can set the velocity range in any axis without restriction. For the `Y` property of the `StartVelocityRange`, set the `Min` and `Max` values to 50 and 80, respectively, to make your particles move anywhere from 50 to 80 units every second. To give the steam a little dispersion, set the `Min` and `Max` values of the X and Z components to -5 and 5, respectively. **FIGURE 10.15** shows what the steam should look like.

7. The steam should also rise slowly, so add some acceleration to it. In the Acceleration category is but one property: `Acceleration`. Because the Z-axis is pointing upward, set the Z component of the `Acceleration` property to 15 to make the velocity in the Z-axis increase over time. This setting causes the steam to rise into the air, as shown in **FIGURE 10.16**.

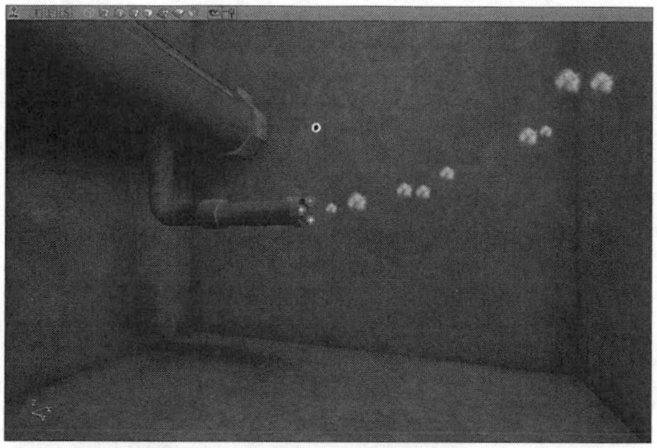

FIGURE 10.16 Steam rising into the air.

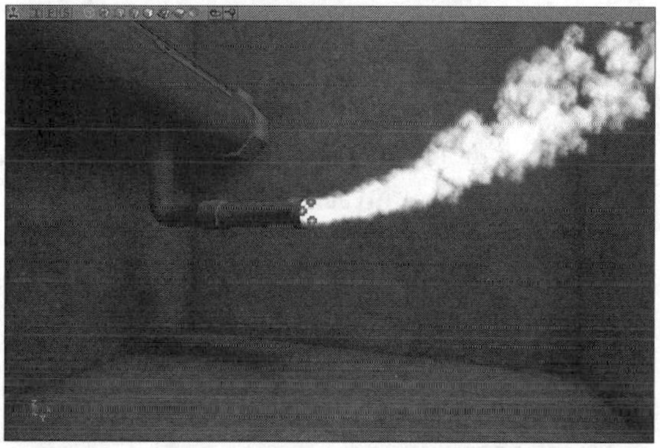

FIGURE 10.17 Thick steam rising into the air.

8. Now you need to fix the main problem that keeps your steam from looking like real steam: the lack of particles. Under the General category is the `MaxParticles` property, which tells Unreal the maximum number of particles this emitter can have at any given moment. By default, it's set to 10, which means you have only 10 particles onscreen at one time. Set this property to 400 to make the steam look much thicker (see **FIGURE 10.17**).
9. Save the map.

END TUTORIAL 10.2

Up to this point, the life of your particles hasn't been discussed. Every particle lives for only a certain amount of time, and then disappears into oblivion. Under the Time category, you have access to three useful properties: `InitialDelayRange`, `InitialTimeRange`, and `LifetimeRange`. **TABLE 10.2** describes their functionality.

TABLE 10.2 Time Category Properties

Property	Description
`InitialDelayRange`	This property sets the amount of time before the Emitter Actor actually begins emitting particles. For example, if the Min and Max values are both set to 5, the emitter waits five seconds before it begins emitting particles.
`InitialTimeRange`	This property sets the initial age of particles (their age at creation time). Therefore, if a particle's life is 5 and the initial time is set to 3, the particle lives for only two seconds.
`LifetimeRange`	The Min and Max values set a range, and each particle is given a lifetime, measured in seconds, somewhere within that range that determines how long it lives. By default, each particle lives for exactly four seconds. However, it's far more realistic if each particle doesn't live the same amount of time. To do this, use the `Min` and `Max` values to supply a range for this property.

Although your steam is looking fairly good, having the particles come into and out of existence instantly is rather unrealistic. This is where the Fading category of properties comes into play. These properties enable you to have your sprites fade into and out of existence smoothly by slowly increasing and decreasing the sprites' opacity, as illustrated in **FIGURE 10.18**.

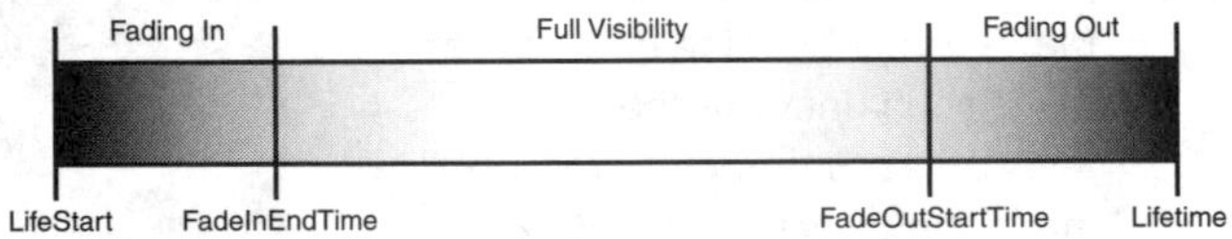

FIGURE 10.18 The visibility cycle of a particle.

If you set `FadeIn` to True, each sprite fades into existence from complete transparency to full visibility. `FadeInEndTime` specifies the amount of time in seconds that it takes for particles to fade in. If you set `FadeOut` to True, each sprite fades out of existence from full visibility to complete invisibility. `FadeOutStartTime` determines when a particle starts to fade out. By the end of its lifetime, the particle is completely invisible. If `FadeOut` is set to True and `Lifetime` is greater than `FadeOutStartTime`, the particles are completely invisible the moment they die.

`FadeInFactor` and `FadeOutFactor` are two other properties that come into play with fading. They control the amount of fading, either in or out, in the different channels: Red (X), Green (Y), Blue (Z), and Alpha (W). The lower the number, the faster each channel fades in or out. By default, all channels are set to 1, meaning that all components fade in or out at regular speed. If you set a channel to 0, that channel fades instantly and, hence, is completely visible at all times. Therefore, if you have a completely white texture fade in with the Red component set to 0, the texture starts out red because only that component is completely visible. In **TUTORIAL 10.3**, you use these properties to finish your steam effect.

TUTORIAL 10.3: Adding the Final Touches to the Steam

1. Open `Tutorial10_03_Start.ut2`, or use the file you saved in **TUTORIAL 10.2**.
2. In the Properties window for the SpriteEmitter, expand the Time category. Change the `LifetimeRange`'s `Min` and `Max` values to 3 and 3.5, respectively. This setting causes your particles to live anywhere from 3 to 3.5 seconds and helps prevent any particles from going through the adjacent wall.
3. In the Fading category, set `FadeIn` to True and `FadeInEndTime` to 1. Now set `FadeOut` to True and `FadeOutStartTime` to 2. Your particles will fade to visibility in one second, stay completely visible for one second, and then start to fade out until death. **FIGURE 10.19** shows the current progress of the steam.

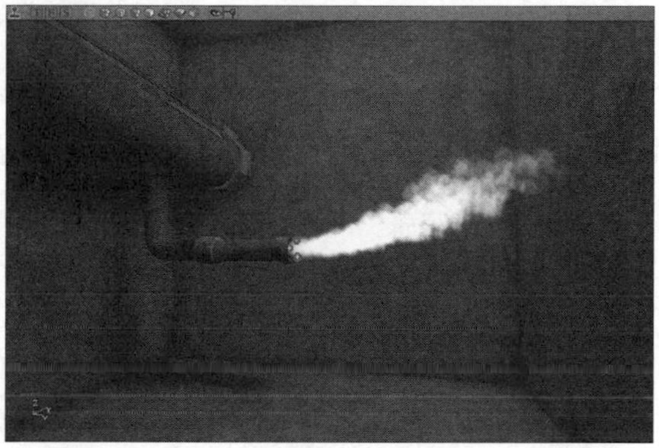

FIGURE 10.19 Current progress of your steam.

4. Although it's starting to resemble steam, it currently looks more like gravity-defying milk. To fix this, you need to make all the particles more transparent. In the Color category, the `Opacity` property controls the particles' overall opacity. Setting this property to 0 would make all your particles completely invisible. Set it to 0.1 to produce something that looks more like steam (see **FIGURE 10.20**).

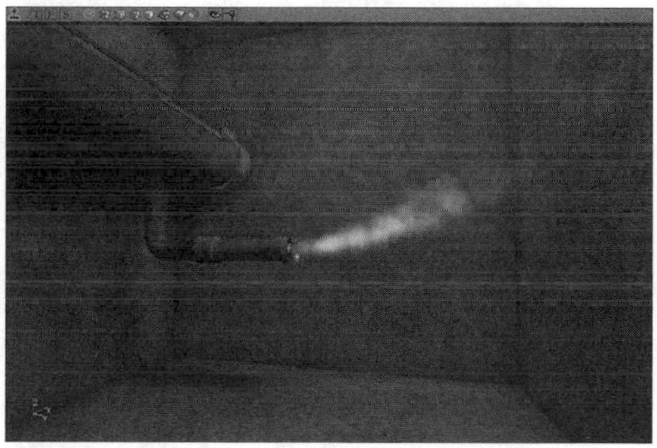

FIGURE 10.20 Steam after turning the opacity down.

5. Save the map.

END TUTORIAL 10.3

As you can see from this steam example, creating an effect is only a matter of understanding the effect you want to create and tweaking a series of parameters. A thorough understanding of the available properties and their uses simplifies your job.

As another example, take a look at **TUTORIAL 10.4**, which shows you how to create a generic teleporter effect.

TUTORIAL 10.4: Creating a Teleporter Effect

1. Open Tutorial10_04_Start.ut2. This map has a teleporter in the center of the room that you'll use as the basis of your effect—creating a spiraling group of particles that rise from the teleporter base (see **FIGURE 10.21**).

FIGURE 10.21 Final teleporter effect.

2. Using the skills you have learned, create an Emitter right on top of the base (see **FIGURE 10.22**), and then add a ParticleEmitter to the Emitter.

FIGURE 10.22 Emitter on top of the teleporter.

3. In the Texture browser, open the Chapter10 texture package and select the Flare texture. In the Properties window of the ParticleEmitter, go to the Texture category. Click Use for the Texture property. Also, make sure the DrawStyle property is set to PTDS_Translucent. You can see the result in **FIGURE 10.23**.

FIGURE 10.23 The new texture is now being used for the emitter.

4. Now you need to decrease the particle size. Under the Size category, change the StartSizeRange property's Min and Max values in X to 10 and 15, respectively. Also, change MaxParticles in the General category to 200. **FIGURE 10.24** shows the result.

FIGURE 10.24 Smaller particles with more being emitted.

5. Save the map. You now have the start of an emitter effect, but you need to make the emitter spawn particles over the base's entire area.

END TUTORIAL 10.4

By default, an emitter always emits particles from the location of the parent Emitter Actor. This is fine in many cases, but often you need particles to be emitted from an entire area or volume. For this purpose, you have the properties in the Location category.

You can use the `StartLocationOffset` property to control where particles begin their life. By default, it's set to (0, 0, 0), which means particles start out at the Emitter Actor's location. However, this setting depends on the coordinate system you have set up. Under the General category, you have the `CoordinateSystem` property. **TABLE 10.3** describes the available options for this property.

TABLE 10.3 *CoordinateSystem* **Settings**

Option	Description
`PTCS_Relative`	If this option is set, the particle's position is always in relation to the Emitter Actor's location. Therefore, a particle at position (0, 0, 0) is in the same location as the emitter.
`PTCS_Absolute`	If this option is set, the particle's position is based on the coordinate system of the world. Therefore, a particle at position (0, 0, 0) is at the center of the world.
`PTCS_Independent`	This mode functions almost exactly the same as `PTCS_Relative`. Particles are spawned at the Emitter Actor's location. However, after they've spawned, their location is absolute and no longer relative to the emitter's position. This difference becomes apparent only when the emitter is moved.

You'll find the `StartLocationOffset` property immensely useful when combining multiple emitter types into one parent Emitter Actor because often you need to give the emitter types a slight offset from each other.

In addition, you can cause particles to emit anywhere inside a particular volume. You start by setting the `StartLocationShape` property to the shape you want to emit from, and then adjust the corresponding property to match the dimensions of the shape you want. **TABLE 10.4** describes each shape and the corresponding properties.

TABLE 10.4 *StartLocationShape* **Settings**

Shape	Properties
`PTLS_Box`	This setting causes particles to be emitted from a box. `StartLocationRange` specifies the locations of the six sides of the box: `X(Min)`, `X(Max)`, `Y(Min)`, `Y(Max)`, `Z(Min)`, and `Z(Max)`. For example, if you set the `Min` value of X, Y, and Z to -50 and the `Max` value of X, Y, and Z to 50, you would get a perfect 100×100×100 cube.

TABLE 10.4 Continued

Shape	Properties
`PTLS_Sphere`	This setting causes particles to be emitted from a sphere. `SphereRadiusRange` specifies the `Min` and `Max` radius of this volume. If you set `Min` to 0 and `Max` to 60, particles are emitted from anywhere inside a sphere with a radius of 60. However, if you set both `Min` and `Max` to 60, particles are emitted only on the sphere's surface.
`PTLS_Polar`	This setting enables you to specify a polar region for particles to be emitted from. X, Y, and Z correlate to theta, phi, and radius, respectively. In Unreal, this means X controls the amount of rotation around the Z-axis, Y controls the amount of rotation around the Y-axis, and Z controls the radius. When Y is 0, you're at the very top of your hypothetical sphere. When Y is 32767 (180 degrees), you're at the very bottom of the sphere. You could use this setting to cause your particles to emit from a circular plane, for example (see **FIGURE 10.25**).

You'll use these new properties to adjust the teleporter's particle effect. In **TUTORIAL 10.4**, you continue from **TUTORIAL 10.3** to enhance the look and behavior of the current particle system.

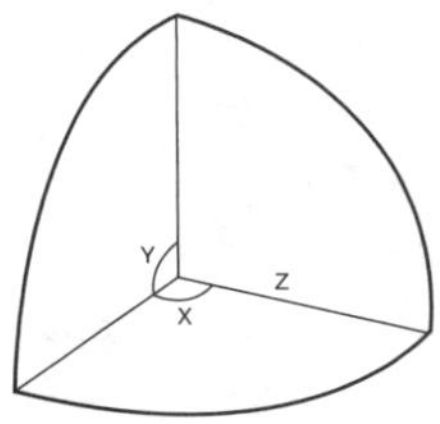

FIGURE 10.25 The X, Y, and Z values for *PTLS_Polar*.

TUTORIAL 10.4: Creating a Teleporter Effect (Continued)

1. Open the Properties window for the ParticleEmitter, and go to the Location category. Because the teleporter base is round, set the `StartLocationShape` property to `PTLS_Polar`. The radius of the base is about 35 units; therefore, set the `Max` value of the Z component in the `StartLocationPolarRange` to 35. Because you want particles to emit from anywhere inside this radius, set the `Min` value of the Z component to 0. The X component needs to go in one complete circle, so set `Min` to 0 and `Max` to 65535 (360 degrees). Finally, Y needs to be parallel to the teleporter base, so set Y's `Min` and `Max` to 16384 (90 degrees) to create a flat, circular area that's parallel to the ground (see **FIGURE 10.26**).

FIGURE 10.26 Particles covering the base of the teleporter.

2. To add some upward movement to the particles, in the Properties window for the SpriteEmitter, go to the Acceleration category and set the Z component of the `Acceleration` property to 50. **FIGURE 10.27** shows the results of this setting.

3. Some fading would improve the effect. To do this, set `FadeIn` under the Fading category to True and change `FadeInEndTime` to 0.5. Now set `FadeOut` to True and change the `FadeOutStartTime` to 1.5. Finally, under the Time category, set the `LifetimeRange` property's `Min` and `Max` values to 2 and 3, respectively. See **FIGURE 10.28** for the results.

4. Save the map. The effect is now close to being done, but you still need to change the particles' color over time and add some revolving action in **TUTORIAL 10.5**.

FIGURE 10.27 Particles rising from the teleporter.

FIGURE 10.28 Particles fading in and out from life to death.

END TUTORIAL 10.4

To change the color, you have the Color category. In this category, the most useful property is `ColorScale`, which enables you to change particle color over time. Basically, it's an array that holds the times at which the color changes and the color to which each particle changes. Each array element has two data items: `Color` and `RelativeTime`. The `RelativeTime` property specifies a point in the particle's life. If set to 0, you're referring to the beginning of the particle's life. When set to 1, you're referring to the end of the particle's life, regardless of the particle's lifetime. Say you added two elements to the `ColorScale` property. The first element's `Color` is set to black and `RelativeTime` is set to 0. The second element's `Color` is set to white and `RelativeTime` is set to 1. To make this setup work, however, you need to set `UseColorScale` to True or nothing will happen. With that setup, particles fade from black to white over their lifespan. **FIGURE 10.29** shows a simple example and a more complex example.

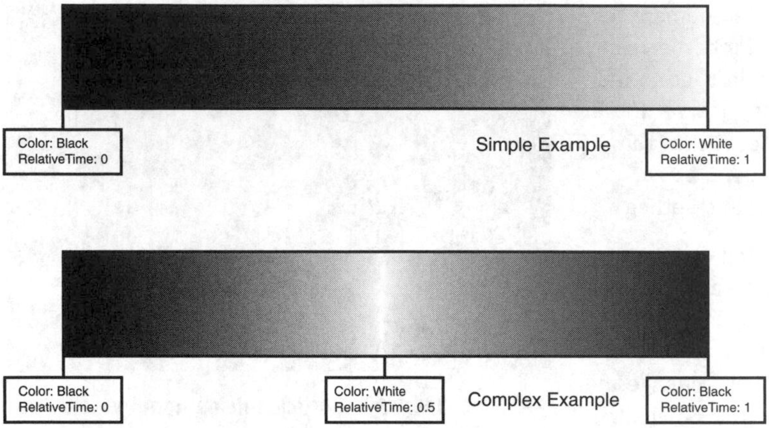

FIGURE 10.29 Examples of color scales.

You can also use the ColorScaleRepeats property to make the ColorScale repeat the number of times specified. If you set ColorScaleRepeats to 1, the simple example in **FIGURE 10.29** would go from black to white at the halfway point of the particle's lifespan and then from black to white again.

If you just want to give your particles a certain tint or apply random colors to each particle, you could do so with ColorMultiplierRange. This property enables you to specify a range for each component: X (Red), Y (Green), and Z (Blue). For example, if you specify a range from 0 to 1 for each component, each particle gets a random color.

To add some revolving motion to your particles, you can set the properties in the Revolution category. Before any revolution occurs, you must set UseRevolution to True. By default, particles revolve around the Emitter Actor, but if the CoordinateSystem property is set to PTCS_Absolute, they revolve around the center of the world. To change the point the particles revolve around, you can change RevolutionCenterOffsetRange.

For controlling the speed of revolution, you must set RevolutionsPerSecondRange. With a value of 1, each particle makes one complete revolution every second. Because you are given ranges for each axis, each particle can have a varying amount of revolution speed. You can also use the RevolutionScale and UseRevolutionScale properties to control the amount of revolution over time, much like the ColorScale property. In **TUTORIAL 10.5**, you finish off the teleporter particle system by using these settings.

TUTORIAL 10.5: Adding the Final Touches to the Teleporter Effect

1. Open `Tutorial10_05_Start.ut2`, or use the file you saved in **TUTORIAL 10.4**.

2. In the Properties window for the SpriteEmitter, open the Color category. Set `UseColorScale` to True and add two elements to `ColorScale`. You want the particles to go from yellow to blue over their lifetime. Therefore, set the first element's `Color` to yellow and `RelativeTime` to 0. Then set the second element's `Color` to blue and `RelativeTime` to 1 (see **FIGURE 10.30**). These settings produce the effect shown in **FIGURE 10.31**.

3. To make your particles revolve, in the Revolution category, set `UseRevolution` to True. You want the particles to revolve slowly around the Z-axis, so set the `RevolutionPerSecondRange` property's Z component `Min` and `Max` to 0.3 and 0.5, respectively. See the results in **FIGURE 10.32**.

4. You now have a convincing teleporter effect! Save the map.

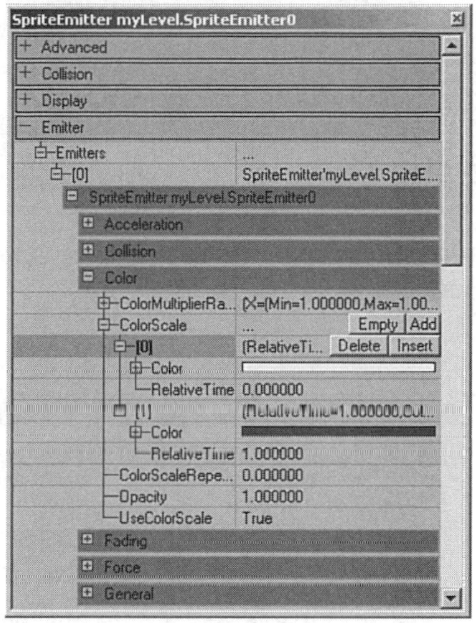

FIGURE 10.30 *UseColorScale* and *ColorScale* properties set up so that particles fade from yellow to blue.

FIGURE 10.31 Particles that fade from yellow to blue.

FIGURE 10.32 Particles that revolve around the Z-axis.

END TUTORIAL 10.5

You've learned about several important particle properties. There is, however, another important concept that hasn't been covered yet: subdivisions on textures. These subdivisions enable you to have an animated sprite. At this point, all your particles have only a single texture applied. By using subdivisions, you can divide a texture into sections and cycle through these sections. Under the Texture category are eight properties dealing with subdivisions. **TABLE 10.5** describes these properties. To demonstrate these properties, the texture shown in **FIGURE 10.33** is used.

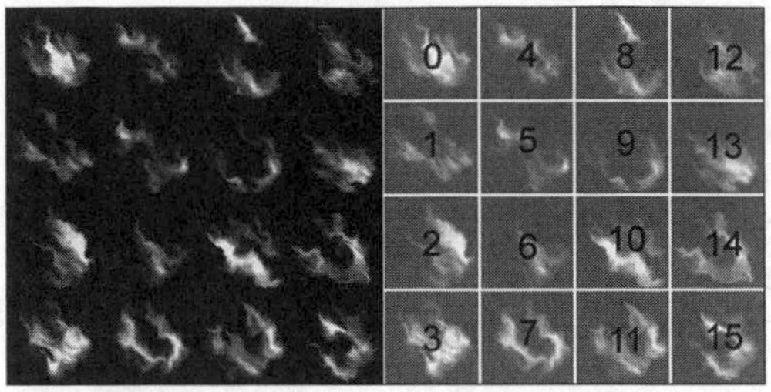

FIGURE 10.33 On the left is the texture, and on the right is the same texture with the indices for each tile.

TABLE 10.5 Texture Subdivision Properties

Property	Description
`TextureUSubdivisions`	This property specifies the number of tiles that make up the selected texture, from left to right. For the sample texture, this property should be set to 4.
`TextureVSubdivisions`	This property specifies the number of tiles that make up the selected texture, from top to bottom. For the sample texture, this property should be set to 4.
`SubdivisionStart`	This property specifies the first tile of the texture you want to use. The tiles' indices are shown on the right in **FIGURE 10.33**.
`SubdivisionEnd`	This property specifies the last tile of the texture you want to use. By default, each particle cycles through each available tile once in its lifetime. If `SubdivisionStart` is 3 and `SubdivisionEnd` is 6, tiles 3, 4, and 5 are used. If start and end are both 0, all tiles are used.
`SubdivisionScale`	Using this property enables you to control at what speed the tiles change from one to the other. Usually, the amount of time between tile changes is equal for all tiles, but you might not always want this setting. Each element in the array specifies when, in relative time, the tile changes. If you add only one item to the array and set the value to 1, the first tile is used for the particle's entire life. If you set it to 0, the first tile changes over to the second tile right when the particle's life begins. With only one item in the array, you have access to only two tiles. If you have two items in the array, you have access to three tiles, and so on. **FIGURE 10.34** shows how array indices and settings are used to control tile changes.
`UseSubdivisionScale`	This property must be set to True before `SubdivisionScale` can be used.

TABLE 10.5 Continued

Property	Description
`BlendBetweenSubdivisions`	When set to True, the tiles don't change instantly. Instead, they change smoothly from one to the next.
`UseRandomSubdivision`	When set to True, each particle randomly selects a tile between `SubdivisionStart` and `SubdivisionEnd`, and it uses that one tile throughout the particle's lifespan. When this property is set to True, `SubdivisionScale` is ignored entirely.

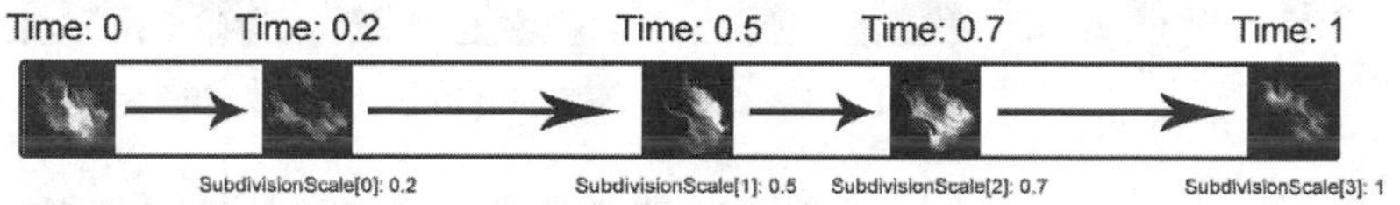

FIGURE 10.34 **The sprite changes at given index values when using the** ***`SubdivisionScale`*** **property.**

> **NOTE**
>
> **When using `SubdivisionScale`, `SubdivisionStart` and `SubdivisionEnd` are ignored.**

In **TUTORIAL 10.6**, you take advantage of texture subdivisions to create some fire.

TUTORIAL 10.6: Creating Fire

1. Your goal is to get the fire effect shown in **FIGURE 10.35**.

   Besides the fire, you also have dark smoke rising from the fire, so you'll be using two SpriteEmitters. Start by opening `Tutorial10_06_Start.ut2`, which contains only a torch in an otherwise empty room (see **FIGURE 10.36**).

FIGURE 10.35 **The final fire effect.**

2. Create an Emitter Actor on top of the torch, and add a SpriteEmitter to it (see **FIGURE 10.37**).
3. You're going to use the same fire texture with 16 tiles that was demonstrated previously. Open the Texture browser and load the `Chapter10.utx` texture package. Select the Fire texture. In the Properties window for the SpriteEmitter, go to the Texture category and click the Use button for the `Texture` property. Because you have four tiles in U and V, set `TextureUSubdivisions` and `TextureVSubdivisions` to 4. By having a texture with so many tiles, the sprites will be animated and hence look more random for the fire. To

prevent this animation from "popping" from one tile to the next, set `BlendBetweenSubdivisions` to True. Finally, ensure that the `DrawStyle` property is set to `PTDS_Translucent`.

4. Obviously, the size is far too big for the effect you want. Under the Size category, set the `Min` and `Max` values of the X component of `StartSizeRange` to 15 and 20, respectively. When fire rises, it tends to get smaller—or at least that's the way it appears. You can simulate this by taking advantage of the `SizeScale` property, which enables you to change the particles' size over time and works much like the other scale type properties you've already used. Add one item to the `SizeScale` property. Set `RelativeTime` to 1 and `RelativeSize` to 0.2. With this setup, the particles start out at their regular size and shrink to 20% of their original size by the end of their lifespan. In effect, the fire rises to a cone shape. Also, set `UseSizeScale` to True so that the `SizeScale` property is actually used.

5. To make particles emit from a larger area, under the Location category, set `StartLocationShape` to `PTLS_Sphere`. Set the `Min` and `Max` values of `SphereRadiusRange` to 0 and 15, respectively. **FIGURE 10.38** shows the current progress of the fire effect.

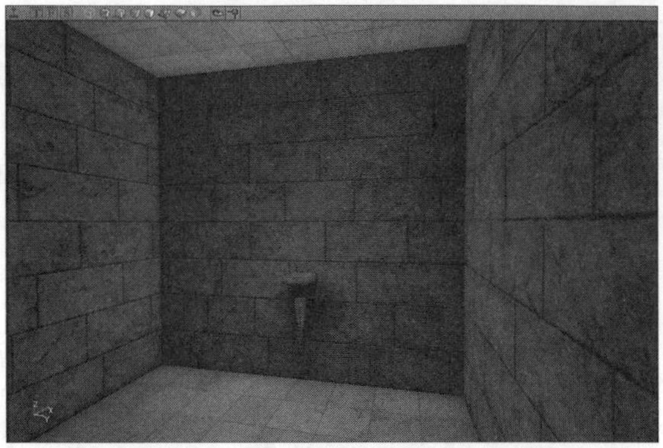

FIGURE 10.36 Empty room with an unlit torch.

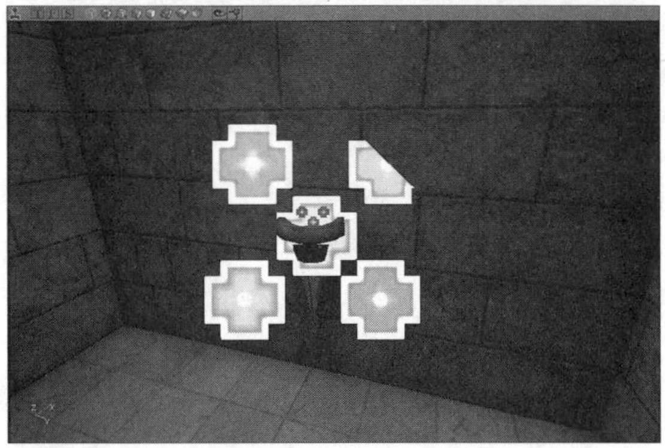

FIGURE 10.37 A SpriteEmitter added to the torch.

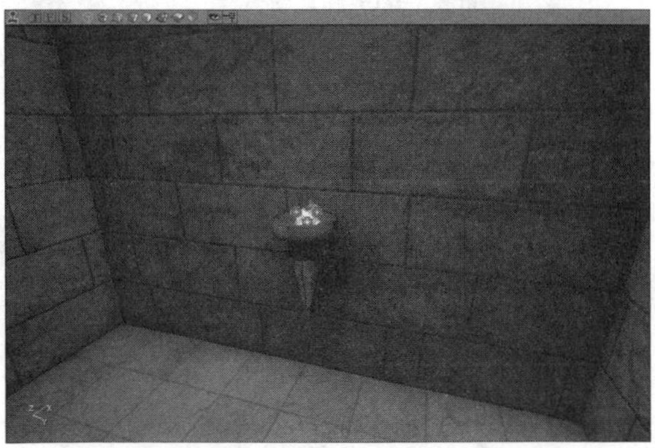

FIGURE 10.38 Fire effect up to this point.

6. The motion needed for the fire is simple. All you want is for the flames to move up. So in the Velocity category, set `Min` and `Max` of the Z component of `StartVelocityRange` to 20 and 60, respectively. **FIGURE 10.39** shows the results.

FIGURE 10.39 Upward-moving flame.

7. To increase the number of particles, go to the General category and set `MaxParticles` to 300. To decrease the lifespan of your particles, under the Time category, set the `Min` and `Max` values of `LifetimeRange` to 2 and 3, respectively. Finally, to add some fading to your particles, under the Fading category, set `FadeIn` to True. Now change `FadeInEndTime` to 0.1, set `FadeOut` to True, and set `FadeOutStartTime` to 1.5 (see **FIGURE 10.40**).

FIGURE 10.40 The flame effect with more particles, fading, and a shorter lifetime.

8. Although the fire is starting to look more like fire, it still needs to look a bit more random. To this end, you're going to use some of the properties in the Rotation category. With these properties, you can make individual particles rotate. **TABLE 10.6** outlines the three properties useful for your fire.

> **NOTE**
>
> If the flames penetrate the underside of the torch, simply move the emitter up.

TABLE 10.6 Particle Spin Properties

Property	Description
`SpinParticles`	When set to True, your particles spin at the speed specified in `SpinsPerSecondRange`.
`SpinsPerSecondRange`	This property specifies a range of speeds at which your particles spin in each specific axis. It's measured in number of 360-degree spins per second. Therefore, if it's set to 1, particles spin, in the specified axis, 360 degrees every second. If you're using a simple 2D sprite that's set up to face the camera at all times, the X component is the only one that needs to be adjusted.

TABLE 10.6 Continued

Property	Description
`SpinCCWorCW`	This property specifies whether the particle is going to spin clockwise or counterclockwise. By default, it's set to 0.5 for each axis, which means there's a 50-50 chance of the particle spinning clockwise or counterclockwise. If you set it to 1, all particles rotate clockwise. A setting of 0 causes all particles to rotate counterclockwise. A setting of 0.6 means there's a 60% chance the particles rotate clockwise.

Therefore, set `SpinParticles` to True and set the `Min` and `Max` of the X component of `SpinsPerSecondRange` to 0.5 and 1, respectively. This way, all particles will always be rotating.

9. Finally, under the Color category, set `Opacity` to 0.3. You now have a convincing flame, as shown in **FIGURE 10.41**. Save the map. In the next tutorial, you add smoke to the effect.

FIGURE 10.41 The flame effect without smoke.

END TUTORIAL 10.6

Another addition you can make to the fire is black smoke. **IN TUTORIAL 10.7**, you'll do that by adding another SpriteEmitter to your Emitter Actor and setting its properties to simulate smoke.

TUTORIAL 10.7: Adding Smoke to the Fire

1. Open `Tutorial10_07_Start.ut2`, or use the file you saved in **TUTORIAL 10.6**.
2. In the Properties window for your Emitter, add another SpriteEmitter. For the rest of this tutorial, you'll be working with the properties of this new SpriteEmitter that's located at index 1 (see **FIGURE 10.42**).
3. In the Texture browser, open the `Chapter10.utx` texture package and select SmokeTiles. In the Texture category, click Use next to the `Texture` property. This texture has four tiles across and four tiles down, so set `TextureUSubdivisions` and `TextureVSubdivisions` to 4. Also, set `BlendBetweenSubdivisions` to True. Finally, ensure that `DrawStyle` is set to `PTDS_Darken` so that the smoke is some shade of black (see **FIGURE 10.43**).

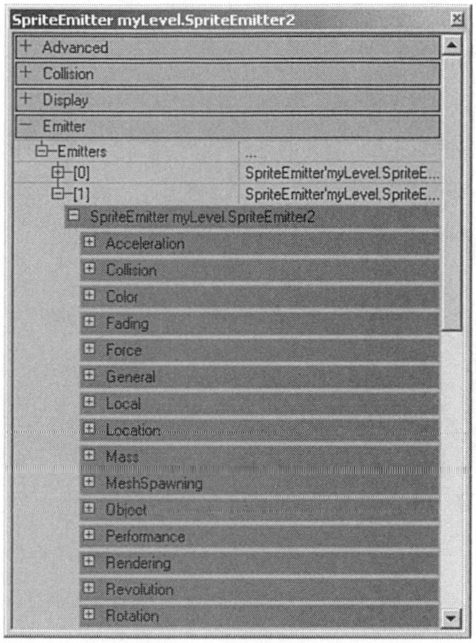

FIGURE 10.42 New SpriteEmitter located at index 1.

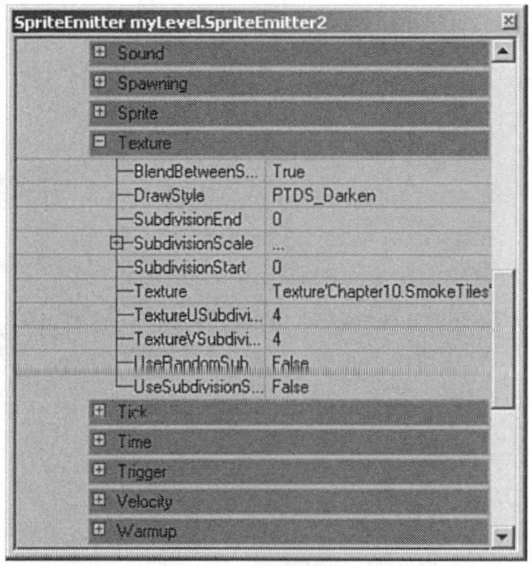

FIGURE 10.43 Texture category of the SpriteEmitter.

4. Under the Size category, set the `Min` and `Max` values of the X component of `StartSizeRange` to 10 and 20, respectively. Under the Velocity category, set the `Min` and `Max` values of the Z component of the `StartVelocityRange` to 20 and 60, respectively. These settings produce the smoke shown in **FIGURE 10.44**.

FIGURE 10.44 Smoke rising from the fire.

5. Under the Location category, set `StartLocationShape` to `PTLS_Sphere` and set the `Min` and `Max` values of `SphereRadiusRange` to 0 and 15, respectively. Also, you want the smoke to start slightly above the base of the fire, so set the Z component of `StartLocationOffset` to 40.

FIGURE 10.45 Smoke effect with more particles.

6. To produce more particles, go to the General category and set `MaxParticles` to 50. You're starting to get the smoke look you want (see **FIGURE 10.45**).
7. To help your smoke blend into the fire slightly better, go to the Color category and set `Opacity` to 0.6. Also, go to the Fading category and set `FadeIn` to True and `FadeInEndTime` to 0.5. Then set `FadeOut` to True and `FadeOutStartTime` to 3. Finally, under the Time category, set the `Min` value of `LifetimeRange` to 3.5, which creates a more random lifetime for the particles. You now have a complete fire effect, shown in **FIGURE 10.46**.

FIGURE 10.46 The final fire effect.

8. Save the map.

END TUTORIAL 10.7

By now, you should realize that working with particles is simply a matter of tweaking properties until you get the look you're going for. The following sections describe the other available emitters and how to use them in your maps.

SparkEmitter

As its name suggests, the SparkEmitter is used to create sparklike effects, such as the sparks from a welding torch, sparks from a short circuit, or even fireworks.

This emitter spawns particles that are represented as 1-pixel-thick lines that follow the direction of the particles. Because its whole purpose is to generate sparks, the single-pixel lines are all it needs. Consequently, the SparkEmitter has a lack of flexibility that makes many of the properties non-functional. The Size category, for instance, is completely unusable.

However, you have access to three new properties under the Spark category, described in **TABLE 10.7**.

TABLE 10.7 Spark Category Properties

Property	Description
`LineSegmentsRange`	This property controls the length of the spark segments. Setting a range with the `Min` and `Max` components means the lengths of the sparks can be random. If the lengths are too long, you can see the individual straight segments. You must be careful, however, not to make the lengths too long or too short or the SparkEmitter won't work.

10

TABLE 10.7 Continued

Property	Description
`TimeBeforeVisibleRange`	This property is not currently implemented.
`TimeBetweenSegmentsRange`	This property controls the detail of your lines. Setting this value to a lower number increases the segments on your lines. This increase is most obvious when the particles are on a curved path. If your particles' path is very curved, you'll want to set this property to something quite low, such as 0.2. When setting it to a low value, however, you might need to increase the `MaxParticles` property. Because each segment is considered another particle, the number of particles can increase rapidly.

When you're working with a SparkEmitter, the `Texture` property influences the line color. Therefore, all other properties under the Texture category, other than `Texture`, are no longer useful.

As an example of the SparkEmitter, **TUTORIAL 10.8** walks you through creating a fireworks system.

TUTORIAL 10.8: Creating Fireworks

1. Open `Tutorial10_08_Start.ut2`. In the middle of the room is a static mesh that you'll use as the firework launcher. On top of this launcher is an Emitter Actor that currently has a SpriteEmitter in it. This SpriteEmitter's only job is to shoot particles into the air. Your goal is to get the particles to explode into a dazzling display of multicolored fireworks, as shown in **FIGURE 10.47**.

   The fireworks are created with the SparkEmitter. Every time a particle collides with the world geometry in the sky, the fireworks from your SparkEmitter are spawned.

FIGURE 10.47 Final fireworks effect.

2. In the Properties window for the Emitter, add a SparkEmitter (see **FIGURE 10.48**).

3. First you need to get the fireworks effect to work correctly, and then you'll have it react only when sprites from the SpriteEmitter hit the ceiling. In the Properties window for the SparkEmitter, go to the Spark category and set the `Min` and `Max` values of `LineSegmentsRange` to 2. You want fairly good detail on your fireworks, so set both the `Min` and `Max` values of `TimeBetweenSegmentsRange` to 0.2.

4. Because you want the lines to start out white so that you can change them more easily, you need to use a white texture. In the Texture browser, open the `Chapter10.utx` texture package and select the Flare texture. Under the Texture category of your SparkEmitter, click the Use button for the Texture property.

5. Under the Velocity category, set the `Min` and `Max` values of the X, Y, and Z components of `StartVelocityRange` to -100 and 100, respectively. You should see some sparks be emitted from the Emitter Actor. However, there are far too few particles, so under the General category, set `MaxParticles` to 2000. **FIGURE 10.49** shows the results.

6. To apply some gravity to the sparks, go to the Acceleration category and set the Z component of the `Acceleration` property to -50 (see **FIGURE 10.50**).

7. Under the Time category, set the `Min` and `Max` values of `LifetimeRange` to 1 and 1.5, respectively. After setting these properties, you'll notice a dramatic increase in the number of particles

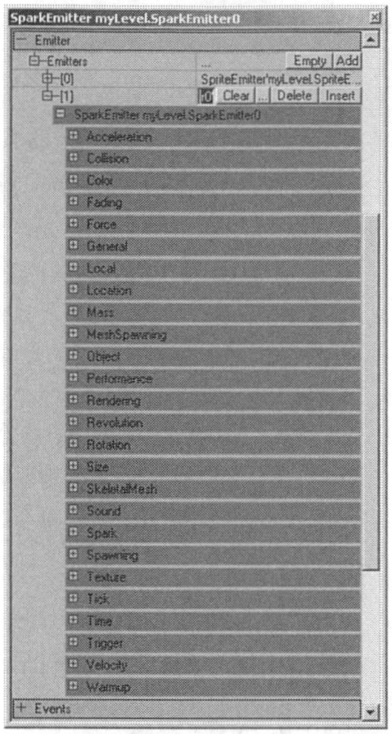

FIGURE 10.48 Properties for the new SparkEmitter.

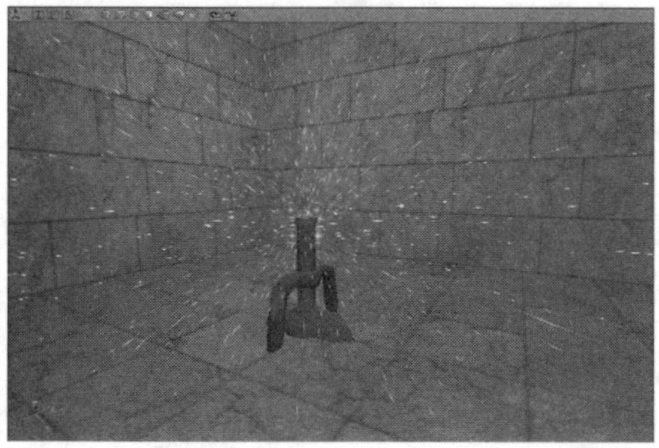

FIGURE 10.49 The SparkEmitter shooting out sparks.

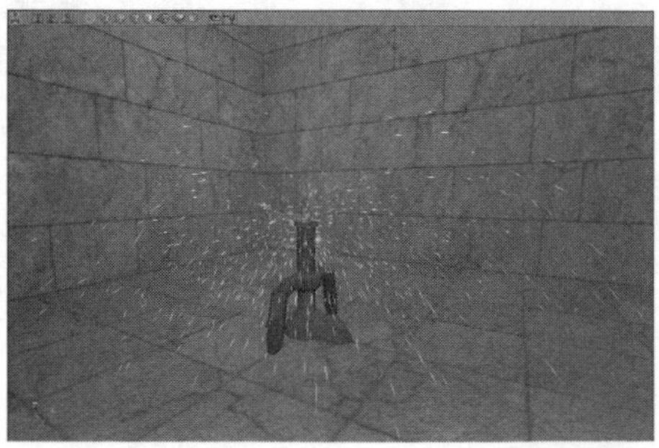

FIGURE 10.50 Sparks are now influenced by "gravity."

being emitted (see **FIGURE 10.51**). By default, the emission speed is determined by the number of `MaxParticles`, so you always have that number of particles emitted.

8. You want your particles to have completely random colors. Therefore, go to the Color category and set the `ColorMultiplierRange` property's `Min` and `Max` values of the X, Y, and Z components to 0 and 1, respectively (see **FIGURE 10.52**).

> **NOTE**
>
> Step 8 involves changing a total of six properties.

9. Right now the particles are snapping out of existence abruptly. To fix this problem, go to the Fading category and set `FadeOut` to True and `FadeOutStartTime` to 0.8. To give the particles a bit more randomness, go to the Location category and set `StartLocationShape` to `PTLS_Sphere`. Now set the `Min` and `Max` values of `SphereRadiusRange` to 0 and 15, respectively. **FIGURE 10.53** shows the results of these settings.

10. Now that the effect is looking the way you want it, you can attach it to the SpriteEmitter. Save the map.

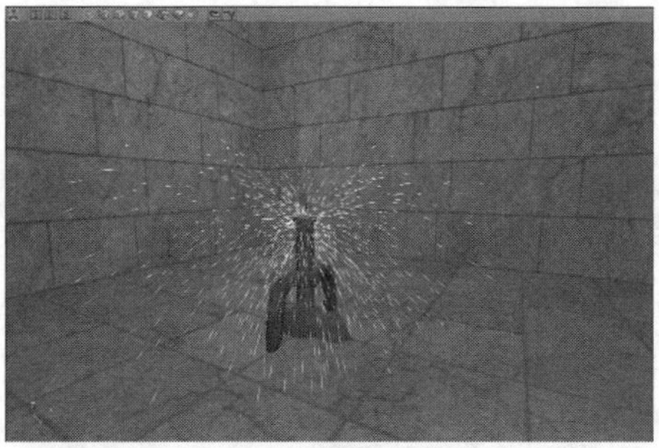

FIGURE 10.51 Decreasing the lifetime increased the density of sparks.

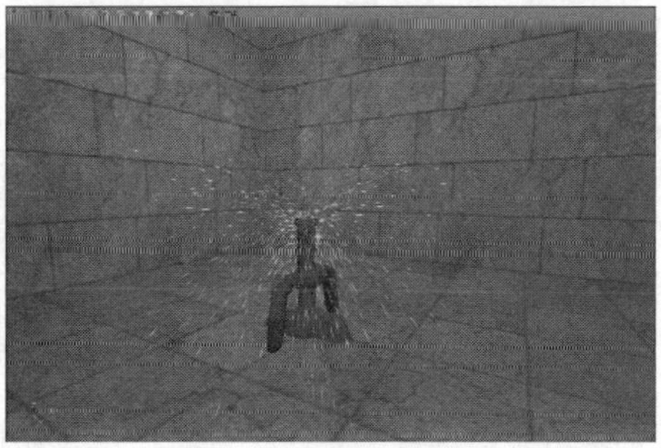

FIGURE 10.52 Randomly colored sparks.

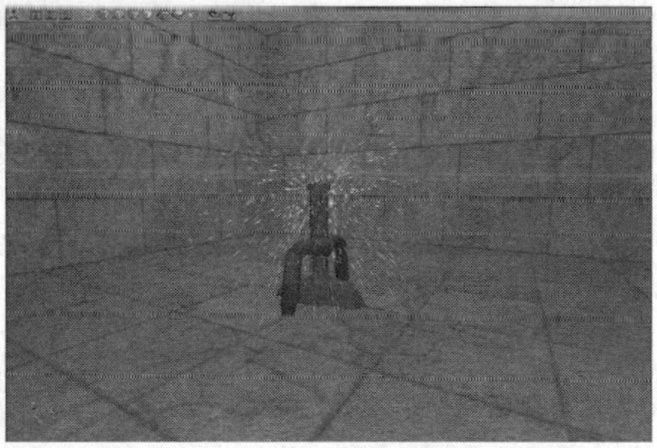

FIGURE 10.53 Changing the location shape helps make the spark positions more random.

END TUTORIAL 10.8

Under the Collision category of every emitter type, you have access to a variety of properties for controlling how your particles collide with other objects and how they react when a collision occurs. If you set `UseCollision` to True, your particles start to collide with objects in your map. However, the properties of most interest are the ones that enable you to spawn particles upon collision with another object. By setting `SpawnFromOtherEmitter`, you can specify an emitter type within your Emitter Actor that's called on to spawn particles every time a collision occurs. The number specified is an index to the current emitter. The `SpawnAmount` property specifies the number of particles to emit when a collision happens. Also, if you want to prevent the possibility of too many collisions, you can use the `MaxCollisions` property and set a range of the maximum number of collisions. If you set the `Min` and `Max` values of this property to 1, each particle can collide with something only one time.

The emitter that's called on does, however, need to have a few properties set correctly. First, the `AutomaticInitialSpawning` property under the Spawning category must be set to False. This setting prevents the emitter from emitting particles before a collision happens. Second, the `RespawnDeadParticles` property under the Local category must be set to False so that particles that are emitted aren't forced to respawn. In **TUTORIAL 10.9**, you take a look at colliding particles.

TUTORIAL 10.9: Making the Particles Respond to Collisions

1. Open Tutorial10_`09_Start.ut2`, or use the file you saved in **TUTORIAL 10.8**.
2. In the Properties window for the ParticleEmitter, go to the Collision category and set `SpawnFromOtherEmitter` to 1, which is your SparkEmitter. Set `SpawnAmount` to 500. Also, set both the `Min` and `Max` values of `MaxCollisions` to 1 so that only one collision is allowed for each particle. Finally, set `UseMaxCollisions` and `UseCollision` to True. At this point, you can already see the particles responding to the collisions. However, particles are still being emitted from the top of the launcher (see **FIGURE 10.54**).
3. Under the properties for the SparkEmitter, go to the Spawning category and set `AutomaticInitialSpawning` to False. Under the Local category, set `RespawnDeadParticles` to False.
4. That's it—you now have a fully functional firework effect! **FIGURE 10.55** shows the final result. Save the map.

FIGURE 10.54 Sparks emitted from collision points and from the launcher.

FIGURE 10.55 The final fireworks effect.

END TUTORIAL 10.9

MeshEmitter

The MeshEmitter is just an emitter that emits static meshes. The properties you've learned about for other emitter types work the same way for the MeshEmitter, except that properties with three dimensions can be used to their full potential with the MeshEmitter. Under the Mesh category, you have access to all the MeshEmitter-specific properties, described in **TABLE 10.8**.

TABLE 10.8 Mesh Category Properties

Property	Description
`StaticMesh`	This property specifies the static mesh to be emitted.
`RenderTwoSided`	This property causes Unreal to render both sides of a static mesh. As you learned in Chatper 8, "Creating Materials in Unreal," rendering both sides is useful when dealing with partially transparent objects in which both sides are visible. However, this property is useful only if `UseMeshBlendMode` is set to False.
`UseMeshBlendMode`	If set to True (the default), the static mesh looks like it does when you simply place it in your map. If set to False, the static mesh's look depends on the `DrawStyle` property under the Texture category.
`UseParticleColor`	When this property is set to True, the properties set in the Color category influence the color of the static meshes. However, this property is useful only if the `UseMeshBlendMode` property is set to True.

In **TUTORIAL 10.10**, you create a MeshEmitter and use these properties to control the meshes you're emitting.

TUTORIAL 10.10: Creating a Conveyor Belt with Barrels

1. Open `Tutorial10_10_Start.ut2` (see **FIGURE 10.56**).

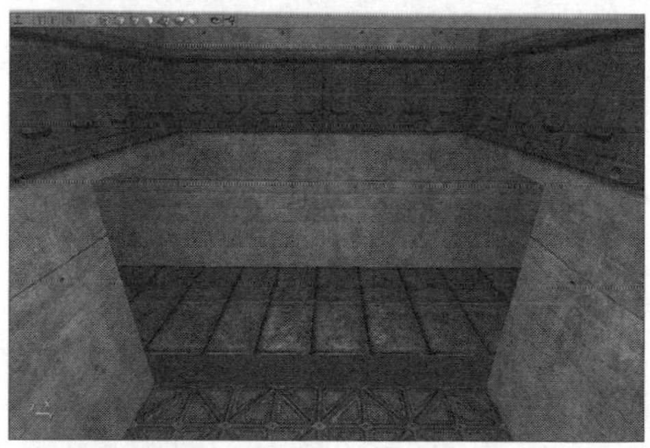

FIGURE 10.56 A room with a conveyor belt.

2. The goal is to create an emitter behind the gates that emits barrels moving along the conveyor belt. First, create an Emitter Actor and add a MeshEmitter to it, and then place the MeshEmitter at one end of the conveyer belt (see **FIGURE 10.57**).
3. With the Static Mesh browser open, load the `Chapter10_sm.usx` package and select Barrel. In the Properties window for the MeshEmitter, go to the Mesh category. Click the Use button for the `StaticMesh` property. The default size is a bit small, so under the Size category, change the `UniformSize` property to True to make sure you can scale the static meshes uniformly. Next, change the `Min` and `Max` values of the X component of `StartSizeRange` to 2. Changing this setting doubles the size of your static meshes.

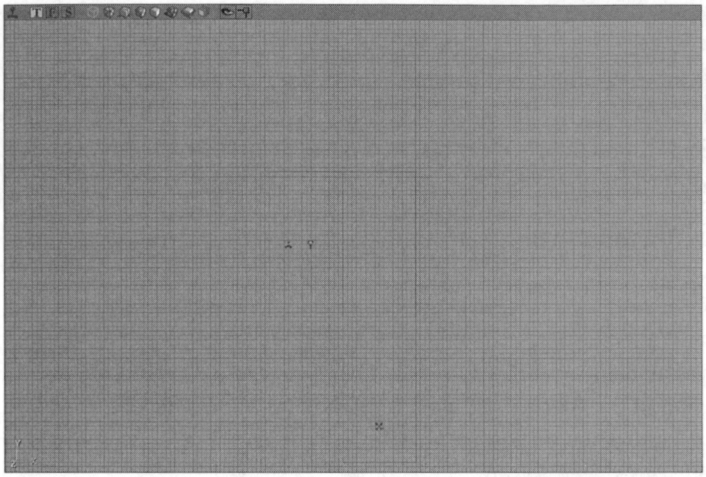

FIGURE 10.57 Top view showing where to place the emitter.

4. Under the Velocity category, set the `Min` and `Max` values of the Y component of `StartVelocityRange` to -51. This value should ensure that the barrels move at approximately the same speed as the conveyor belt texture. Now's a good time to make sure the barrels are resting right on the surface of the conveyor belt.

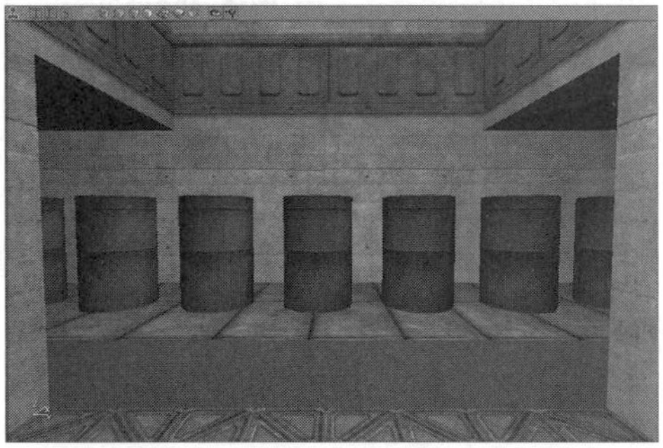

FIGURE 10.58 Barrels moving all the way to the end of the conveyor belt in a straight line.

5. Now you need to make the barrels live longer. Under the Time category, change both the `Min` and `Max` values of `LifetimeRange` to 25. **FIGURE 10.58** shows the results.

6. To give the barrels some variation in position, go to the Location category, and make sure `StartLocationShape` is set to `PTLS_Box`. Now set the `Min` and `Max` values of the X component of `StartLocationRange` to -70 and 70, respectively. **FIGURE 10.59** shows the results of these settings.

FIGURE 10.59 Barrels moving along the conveyor belt.

7. That's it! Save the map.

END TUTORIAL 10.10

BeamEmitter

With the BeamEmitter, you can create such effects as lightning. This emitter works by stretching a texture from one point to another. Most of the discussion about this emitter type centers on determining these two points. However, you can also divide your texture into multiple segments so that you can apply some noise to its overall shape. This technique can be immensely useful when you're trying to create a realistic lightning bolt that zigzags through the air. You can also make your lightning bolt have multiple branches that shoot from the main branch, which can make the lightning look more realistic.

Under the Beam category, you have access to all the properties you need to set to make your BeamEmitter function properly. **TABLE 10.9** explains the uses of these properties.

TABLE 10.9 Beam Category Properties

Property	Description
`DetermineEndPointBy`	This property controls how the end points are determined.
`BeamTextureUScale`	Use this property to determine how many times the texture is replicated in the U, or horizontal, direction. The default setting is 1.
`BeamTextureVScale`	Use this property to determine how many times the texture is replicated in the V, or vertical, direction. The default setting is 1.
`RotatingSheets`	This property determines how many 2D sprites (planes) are used to represent each beam. Values 0, 1, and 2 all have the same effect of using only one plane to represent a beam. Anything greater than 2 is translated as the number of planes. Therefore, if you set this property to 3, every beam is represented with three planes. **FIGURE 10.60** shows how the rotated sheets work in-game.
`TriggerEndpoint`	When this property is set to True and `DetermineEndPointBy` is set to `PTEP_Actor`, every time a beam hits an Actor, that Actor's trigger function is called. This property is often used to trigger emitters.

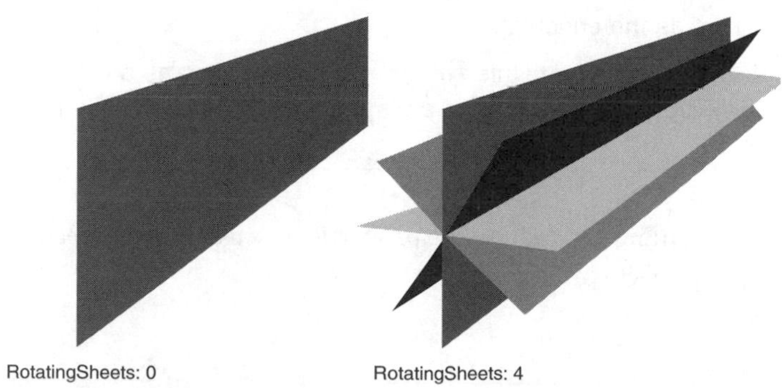

FIGURE 10.60 This figure shows two sets of rotated sheets to illustrate how the *`RotatedSheet`* property works.

TABLE 10.10 describes the different options available for DetermineEndPointBy.

TABLE 10.10 *DetermineEndPointBy* **Settings**

Setting	Description
PTEP_Velocity	The endpoint is determined by taking the particle's velocity and lifetime and calculating the direction and distance from the emitter. This means StartRangeVelocity and Acceleration are going to influence the endpoint's direction and distance.
PTEP_Distance	The endpoint is calculated by using the particle's velocity to determine the direction. The distance from the emitter is specified by the BeamDistanceRange property.
PTEP_Offset	This setting allows you to define an offset from the beam's start point. To define this offset, you must populate BeamEndPoints with at least one element. The Offset property in each element defines the distance from the start point. You can even define a range for the offset if you want a random offset. However, the Weight property of this element must be greater than 0. Furthermore, you can have multiple elements in BeamEndPoints if you want to have varying offsets to jump between. The Weight property is then used to define the possibility of this offset being used to calculate the endpoint. The possibility increases as the number in Weight is increased.
PTEP_Actor	The endpoint is calculated based on the position of certain Actors. The elements of BeamEndPoints have the ActorTag property, which allows you to specify the tags of Actors you want to use as targets. The Weight property has the same effect as PTEP_Offset.
PTEP_TraceOffset	This setting works much the same as PTEP_Offset except that instead of blindly going to the specified offset, it checks to see whether it hits a solid surface. If it does, it uses the point of impact as the endpoint.
PTEP_OffsetAsObsolute	Unlike PTEP_Offset, this setting uses the Offset as an absolute position instead of a distance from the beam's start point.

In **TUTORIAL 10.11**, you create a BeamEmitter and use the properties discussed in this section to create a randomly striking lightning effect.

TUTORIAL 10.11: Creating Electric Bolts

1. Open `Tutorial10_11_Start.ut2`. Your goal is to create lightning that goes from the large glass orb on the ceiling to the four surrounding posts containing smaller orbs, which are referred to as "conductors" in this tutorial. This magical lightning, however, doesn't strike all four posts at the same time; instead, it randomly strikes each one (see **FIGURE 10.61**).

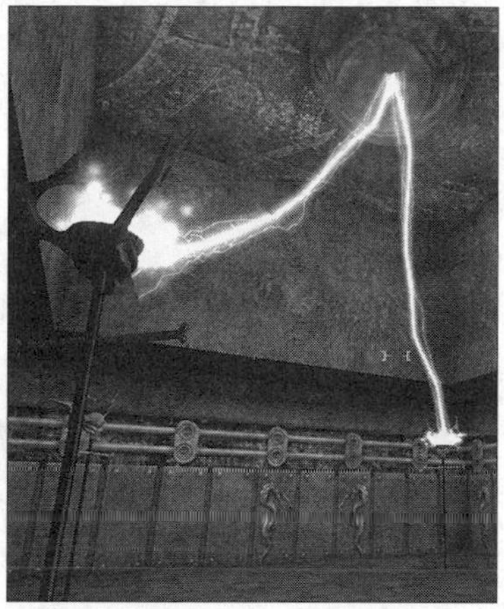

FIGURE 10.61 Lightning bolts randomly striking the four posts.

2. You're going to need a total of five Emitter Actors: one on the ceiling inside the orb and one at each conductor. Start by creating one Emitter Actor on the ceiling and then create another on *one* of the conductors (see **FIGURE 10.62**). After the emitter on the conductor is set up properly, you'll duplicate it over to the other three conductors.

FIGURE 10.62 Two emitters created and put in position.

3. In the ceiling emitter, add one BeamEmitter. Under the Beam category, change `DetermineEndPointBy` to `PTEP_Actor`. Now you need to populate `BeamEndPoints`, so add one element into it.

4. You need the tag for your destination Emitter Actor, so open the Properties window for your conductor emitter, and go to the Events category. Change the `Tag` property to `Conductor1`.

5. Back in the Properties window for the ceiling emitter, go to the Beam category. Change the `ActorTag` of the first element in `BeamEndPoints` to `Conductor1`. After ensuring that Realtime Preview is enabled, you should see a beam from the ceiling to the conductor (see **FIGURE 10.63**).

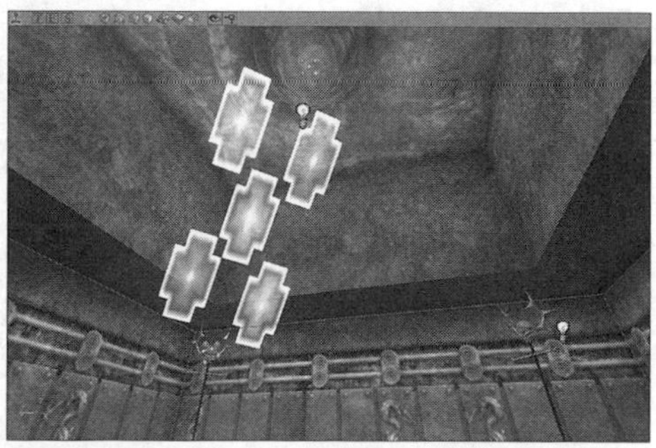

FIGURE 10.63 Texture stretched from one emitter to the other.

6. Open the Texture browser so that you can choose a more appropriate texture for your lightning bolts. Open the `Chapter10.utx` package and select the Lightning texture. Back in the BeamEmitter Properties window, go to the Texture category and click the Use button next to the `Texture` property. See the results in **FIGURE 10.64**.
7. In the Size category, change both the `Min` and `Max` values of `StartSizeRange` to 50 (see **FIGURE 10.65**).
8. Under the General category, change `MaxParticles` to 3 so that you have only the bolts of lightning at any one time. Change the `Min` and `Max` values of `LifetimeRange` under the Time category to 0.1 and 0.2, respectively. Because lightning bolts strike quickly, they should have very short lives.

FIGURE 10.64 Lightning bolt stretched from one emitter to the other.

9. The final area you need to fix is the lack of variation in the lightning bolts. Right now, each bolt of lightning is perfectly straight, but you can easily fix this by adding beam noise. You can add two kinds of noise: high frequency and low frequency. They work together to create the final effect. High frequency noise creates the little details and bends in the beam's curve, and low frequency noise changes the beam's overall flow more subtly. For each noise, specify the number of divisions or frequency points.

   Under the BeamNoise category, change `HighFrequencyPoints` to 6. Set the `Min` and `Max` values of the X, Y, and Z components of `HighFrequencyNoiseRange` to -10 and 10, respectively. Now change `LowFrequencyPoints` to 3. Finally, set the `Min` and `Max` values of all components of `LowFrequencyNoiseRange` to -50 and 50, respectively. **FIGURE 10.66** shows the final effect.

FIGURE 10.65 Thinner lightning bolt.

FIGURE 10.66 Each lightning bolt has noise applied to it.

10. Save the map.

END TUTORIAL 10.11

Under the Local category is the `RespawnDeadParticles` property. When this property is set to True, a particle dies and is then spawned again. However, if this property is set to False, particles are spawned until `MaxParticles` is reached, and after those particles die, they aren't spawned again. Therefore, the emitter is dead until a reset occurs.

By default, particles aren't reset. However, if you set `AutoReset` to True, the emitter resets after it dies. This causes particles to spawn until reaching `MaxParticles`; then they die, and the emitter is reset. This cycle repeats indefinitely. If you want to add a delay between resets, you can use `AutoResetTimeRange`. You can even set a range for this property if you want a random delay before resets. In **TUTORIAL 10.12**, you use these properties to finalize your lightning effect.

TUTORIAL 10.12: Finishing the Lightning

1. Open `Tutorial10_12_Start.ut2`, or use the file you saved in **TUTORIAL 10.11**.
2. In the Properties window for the BeamEmitter, go to the Local category. Set `RespawnDeadParticles` to False and `AutoReset` to True. Next, change the `Min` and `Max` values of `AutoResetTimeRange` to 0.5 and 3, respectively, to produce the delay between strikes that you're looking for.
3. Every time a lightning bolt strikes a conductor, you want some sparks emitted from the conductors. To do this, you have the `TriggerEndpoint` property. However, you have to run the map to see an emitter get triggered. Therefore, you'll create the effect first, and then set the properties for it to be triggered. In the Properties window for the conductor emitter, add a SpriteEmitter.
4. In the Texture browser, select the Flare texture from the `Chapter10.utx` texture package. Under the Texture category for the SpriteEmitter, click the Use button on the `Texture` property.
5. Under the Velocity category, set the `Min` and `Max` values in the X and Y components of `StartVelocityRange` to -150 and 150, respectively. Then set the `Min` and `Max` values in Z of `StartVelocityRange` to 50 and 100, respectively. These settings cause your particles to be scattered out and up (see **FIGURE 10.67**).
6. In the Size category, set the `Min` and `Max` values of the X component of the `StartSizeRange` property to 10 and 20, respectively (see **FIGURE 10.68**).

FIGURE 10.67 Large flares shooting out of the conductor.

7. To add some gravity, go to the Acceleration category and set the Z component of `Acceleration` to -300.

8. Under the General category, increase `MaxParticles` to 100. Also, in the Time category, change the `Min` and `Max` values of `LifetimeRange` to 1 and 1.2, respectively. **FIGURE 10.69** shows the results of these settings.

9. Next, under the Fading category, set `FadeIn` to True, change `FadeInEndTime` to 0.2, set `FadeOut` to True, and change `FadeOutStartTime` to 0.7 (see **FIGURE 10.70**).

10. The effect now looks the way you want it, so you just need to set the properties to make it react to the lightning. To this end, you have the Trigger category. Set the `TriggerDisabled` property to False to effectively make this emitter triggerable, and change `ResetOnTrigger` to True. To prevent the emitter from emitting particles initially, change `AutomaticInitialSpawning` under the Spawning category to False. Also, set `InitialParticlesPerSecond` to 1000. Because you have `MaxParticles` set to 100, it will take 0.1 seconds for all particles to be emitted. Finally, set `RespawnDeadParticles` under the Local category to False. With these settings, the particles will no longer emit constantly, so to test it, you have to change some property of the SpriteEmitter for the emitter to reset.

11. To make this work, go to the BeamEmitter's properties and set `TriggerEndpoint` under the Beam category to True. However, as mentioned before, you can see this work only if you run the map.

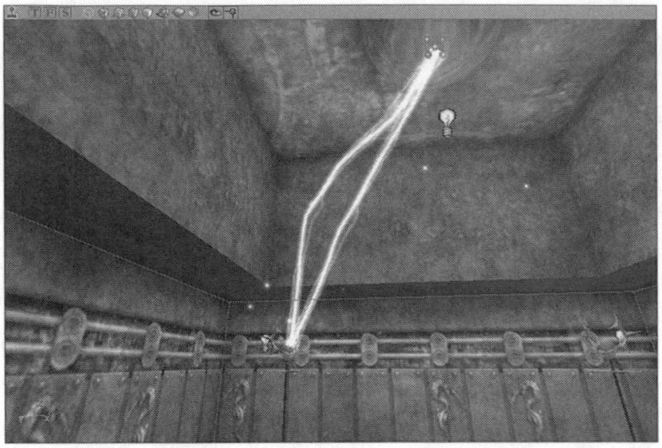

FIGURE 10.68 Small flares shooting from the conductor.

FIGURE 10.69 Large number of flares shooting from a conductor.

FIGURE 10.70 Flares fade in and out smoothly.

12. Finally, duplicate the conductor emitter to the other three conductors. However, you need to change the `Tag` properties of the other three emitters to `Conductor2`, `Conductor3`, and `Conductor4`. Also, add three more elements to `BeamEndPoints` and change the `ActorTag` of each element to one of the conductors. Finally, set the `Weight` property of the elements to `1` so that each conductor has an equal opportunity to receive a lightning strike (see **FIGURE 10.71**). You can see the final effect in **FIGURE 10.72**.

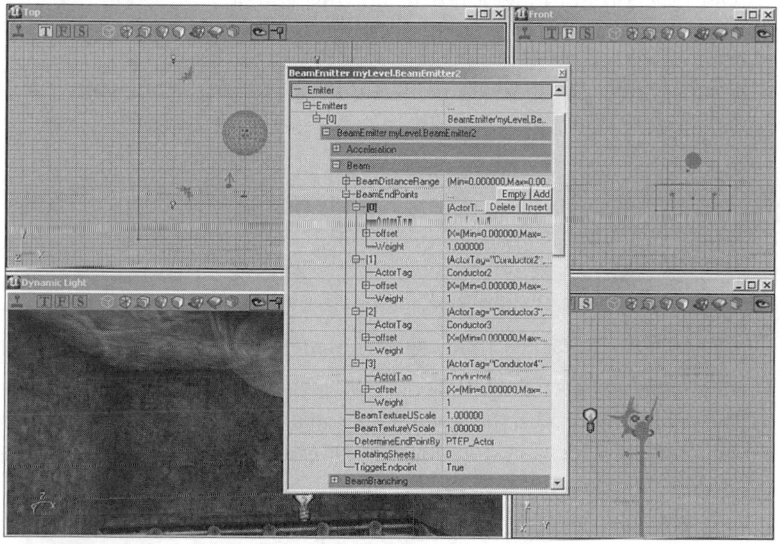

FIGURE 10.71 The *BeamEndPoints* property of the BeamEmitter.

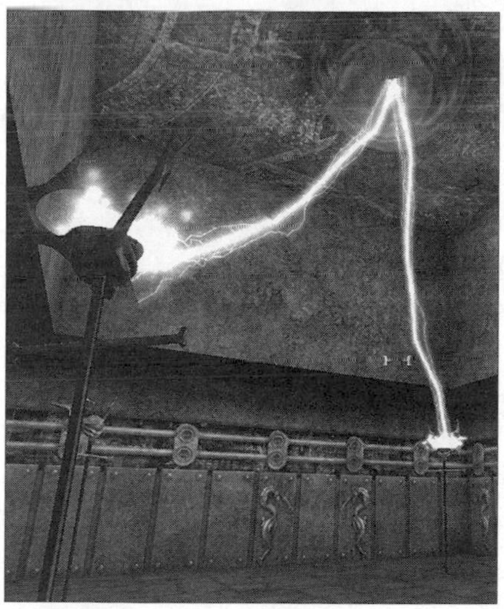

FIGURE 10.72 The final lightning effect.

END TUTORIAL 10.12

TrailEmitter

The TrailEmitter is a handy tool when you're trying to create such effects as laser trails for a sci-fi proton torpedo. TrailEmitters are used more commonly in UnrealScript than directly implemented in maps. The trail's length is primarily influenced by the speed at which the Emitter Actor is moving. For the TrailEmitter to work correctly, it must be attached to something that moves. Otherwise, you won't be able to see a trail of any kind. To do this, you attach the emitter to a Mover.

Under the Trail category of the emitter, you have access to a number of important properties, described in **TABLE 10.11**.

TABLE 10.11 Trail Category Properties

Property	Description
`DistanceThreshold`	This property determines the distance between each trail segment.
`MaxPointsPerTrail`	The property specifies the maximum number of points on a trail.
`MaxTrailTwistAngle`	This property determines how the trail faces the camera. If it's set to the default of 16535, the trail points more toward the camera. As values start to deviate from this default value, the trail starts to point away from the camera.
`PointLifeTime`	This property determines how long the points live. It's used only when `TrailShadeType` is set to `PTTST_PointLife`.
`TrailLocation`	This property determines how the trail is calculated. However, only the `PTTL_FollowEmitter` option is currently functional, so always use this setting for the `TrailLocation` property.
`TrailShadeType`	This property determines how the trail is going to fade out. These are the settings you can use: `PTTST_None`—No fading `PTTST_RandomStatic`—Not Implemented `PTTST_RandomDynamic`—Randomly fade in and out `PTTST_Linear`—Fade out based on number of points in existence and total number of points. `PTTST_PointLife`—Fade out is based on `PointLifeTime`.
`UseCrossedSheets`	If this property is set to True, the trail is composed of two perpendicularly intersecting planes instead of the default single plane.

TUTORIAL 10.13: Using the Trail Emitter

1. Open Tutorial10_12_Start.ut2, which is a simple room with a Mover that moves around the four corners.
2. Create an Emitter Actor and place it at the Mover's location. Because you want the Emitter to move with this Mover, you need to change the AttachTag property of the Emitter Actor to the Mover's Tag property. In the Properties window for the Emitter, go to the Movement category. Change AttachTag to trailMover, which is the tag of the Mover.
3. Add a TrailEmitter to the Emitter Actor. Open the Texture browser, load the Chapter10.utx texture package, and select the SoftFlare texture. Back in the Properties window for the TrailEmitter, go to the Texture category and click the Use button for the Texture property.
4. Under the Trail category for the TrailEmitter, set TrailLocation to PTTL_FollowEmitter to ensure that the trail is generated in relation to the emitter's speed and location. Set UseCrossedSheets to True so that the trails are composed of two planes. Also, change MaxPointsPerTrail to 500 so that the trails have a high amount of detail. To make the trails fade off, set TrailShadeType under the Trail category to PTTST_PointLife. Now set PointLifeTime to 2, which gives each point a lifetime of two seconds.
5. Under the Size category, set both the Min and Max values in the X component of StartSizeRange to 5. At this point, you should be able to see some fairly good results when you run the level. To test the emitter in UnrealEd, make sure Realtime Preview is enabled, and start moving the Emitter Actor in the Perspective view (see **FIGURE 10.74**).

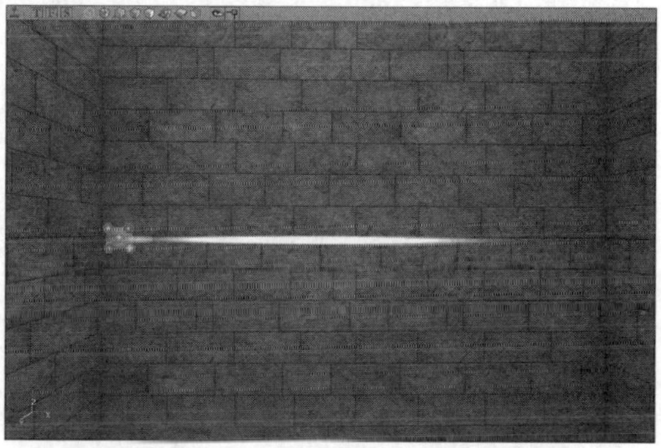

FIGURE 10.74 Moving the emitter in the Perspective view.

6. To make the trail fade from blue to yellow over its lifetime, in the Color category, set UseColorScale to True. Add two items to ColorScale. Set the first item's Color to blue and its RelativeTime to 0. Set the second item's Color to yellow and its RelativeTime to 1 (see **FIGURE 10.75**).
7. You now have a working TrailEmitter, shown in **FIGURE 10.76**. Save the map.

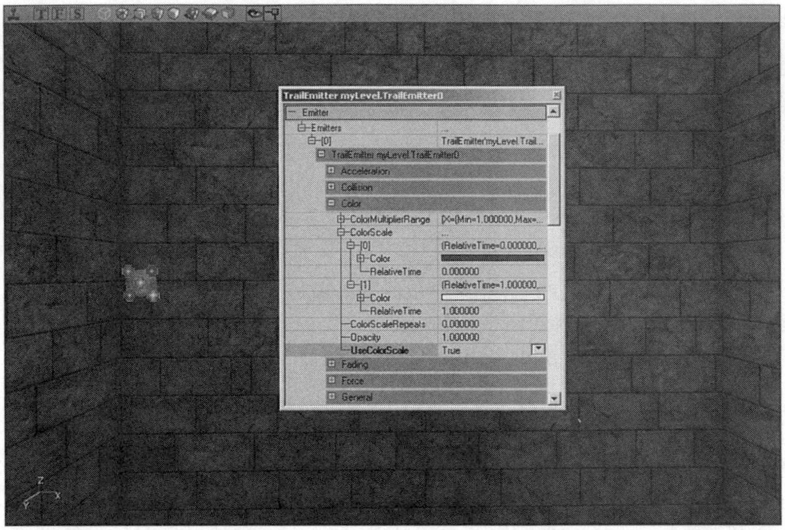

FIGURE 10.75 The Color category of the TrailEmitter.

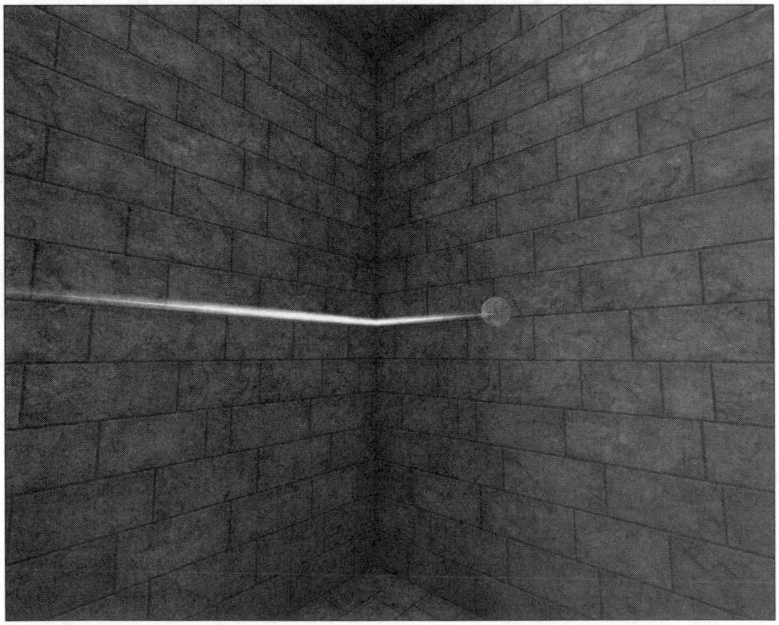

FIGURE 10.76 The TrailEmitter in action.

END TUTORIAL 10.13

Summary

At this point, you should have a good grasp of how to create a variety of particle effects in your levels. These concepts also extend into the realm of UnrealScript programming and can be used for such effects as projectile trails for your weapons. Also, with these fundamental rules, you should now be able to create your own new and interesting effects to add a heightened level of realism to your levels. Chapter 11, "The Karma Physics Engine," introduces you to the Karma physics engine and how it can be used to push your level's realism even further by including reactions and animations based on the real laws of physics.

Chapter 11

The Karma Physics Engine

In this chapter, you learn how to create animations in Unreal that are based on the laws of physics. Such animations are often called *dynamic simulations*, meaning that they're driven by outside forces such as gravity, wind, or the force of an explosion. Apart from the many other features of the Unreal engine discussed in previous chapters, the Unreal engine also contains a powerful physics engine that makes it possible for animations such as bouncing objects or complex collisions to be calculated in real time.

Instead of creating a physics engine from scratch, however, Epic Games utilizes a third-party physics solution known as Karma. The now defunct MathEngine company created this versatile engine, which was implemented into the existing Unreal engine. Aside from the basic real-world physics of collisions with objects, it also implements *Ragdolls*, which make realistic death sequences possible. Ragdolls are characters whose animation is driven entirely by the physics engine, allowing their joints to flex realistically as they fall, tumble, and so on. Ragdolls alone were a huge step in the evolution of game engines because they made unrealistic and repetitive animated death sequences a thing of the past.

The uses of the Karma engine extend to weapon projectiles and objects in your scene that react to physical forces, such as gravity, explosions, and collisions with other Karma objects. However, many aspects of the Karma engine are useful only when you delve into the programming world of UnrealScript. Because this book doesn't venture into the programming side of the Unreal Engine, you'll learn ways you can take advantage of the Karma engine without programming. First, you'll explore using simple Karma objects in UnrealEd and how to create these objects with external 3D packages, such as Maya. Then you see how to set up a character to work effectively as a Ragdoll. This topic leads to the introduction of the Karma Authoring Tool, commonly known as KAT, and how to use it to tweak a Ragdoll's effects.

First, however, you need a brief discussion on precisely where you can use these Karma effects. The Karma effects mentioned thus far would work perfectly well in a single-player game. However, if you were to create, say, a rope bridge that Karma controls, it wouldn't act as you would expect in a multiplayer game. On the server, all the Karma effects would act normally, but the clients wouldn't receive information about how the bridge should react to explosions, projectiles, and so forth. When playing on a client computer, the bridge wouldn't move at all. Ragdoll effects, however, such as death animations, work fine because they are calculated separately on each client machine, meaning the same death sequence varies on each client. The process of sending information from the server to the client is known as *replication*. It's possible for the rope bridge to work on a multiplayer map; however, it would require significant changes to the replication code in the Unreal engine. Because that topic goes far beyond the scope of this book, it's not covered here. When applying the information in this chapter to your own levels, be wary of where Karma effects can and cannot be used effectively.

Karma Theory

This section explores the basic ways to take advantage of the Karma engine from within UnrealEd. The key to accessing the Karma engine in UnrealEd is a special type of Actor: the *KActor*. This Actor and its subclasses are used to make objects react dynamically with the environment. The fundamental difference between this Actor and the other Actors you've used previously is that under the Movement category of its properties, the `Physics` property is set to `PHYS_Karma`. This setting passes control of the object's movement to the Karma physics engine.

How the object reacts, however, is determined by the `KParams` property found under the Karma category in the object's Properties window. Physical properties such as mass, buoyancy, and friction can be adjusted. Because of the many properties available, this entire section has been dedicated to discussing them.

So how does a Karma Actor know which parts of the environment it can interact with? The `bBlockKarma` property, which is inherent to all placeable Actors, enables level designers to control the surfaces that can affect a Karma Actor. Many Actors, such as static meshes and `BlockingVolumes`, have this property set to True by default, meaning that Karma Actors collide with their surfaces.

To begin, **TUTORIAL 11.1** leads you through constructing a level that shows how to create a simple Karma Actor.

TUTORIAL 11.1: Creating a Simple Karma Actor

1. Open `Tutorial11_01_Start.ut2`.
2. In the Static Mesh browser, open the `Chapter11.usx` package. Under the Karma group, select Barrel.

   In the Properties window under the static mesh viewport, the only property influencing Karma is `UseSimpleKarmaCollision`. This property determines the behavior of non-Karma objects that come into contact with Karma Actors. To be more precise, this property allows Karma to use a static mesh's collision model to calculate collisions. If set to True and the static mesh has a collision model, that collision model is converted and used to calculate the collision of Karma objects against this static mesh. If this property is True and the static mesh doesn't have a collision model, Karma objects don't collide with this static mesh at all. Finally, if this property is set to False, Karma objects collide directly with the static mesh's triangles. Be careful to use this option only if the static mesh consists of large triangles. If the mesh is composed of many small triangles, it's much harder (and, therefore, slower) for the computer to calculate collisions with the surface.

FIGURE 11.1 Karma barrel added into the level.

3. Right-click in the level, and choose Add Karma Actor from the context menu to place the Karma barrel in the level (see **FIGURE 11.1**).

> **NOTE**
>
> If you need access to the Rocket Launcher, bring down the console with the ~ (tilde) key, and enter **`loaded`**. This cheat code gives you all weapons and full adrenaline.

4. When you run the map, notice that the barrel hangs in the air. By default, Karma Actors are disabled at the start of a level. To enable them, you must apply a dynamic force to the object. A simple solution is just shooting the barrel with some sort of weapon. Unfortunately, the Assault Rifle doesn't have enough power to activate the Karma Actor on its own, so you need to use a more powerful gun, such as the Rocket Launcher. When you hit the barrel with enough force, it comes alive and falls to the ground realistically.

5. If you want the barrel to fall the moment the level starts, go to the object's Properties window. Under the Karma category, expand the `KParams` property, and expand `KarmaParams myLevel.KarmaParams9`. Under `KarmaParams` is the `KStartEnabled` property. As the name suggests, this property determines whether the Karma Actor is enabled the moment the level starts. By default, this property is set to False, which means you have to shoot the Actor to enable it. Set this property to True, as shown in **FIGURE 11.2**.

6. Save and test the map. Notice that the Karma barrel starts reacting before you even begin playing the level.

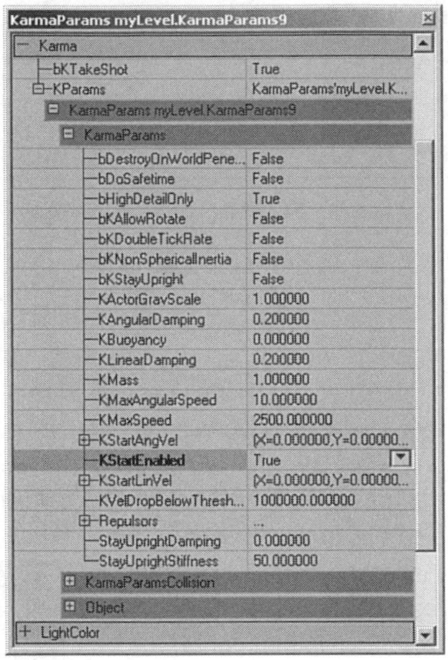

FIGURE 11.2 *`KStartEnabled`* **property of the Karma barrel.**

END TUTORIAL 11.1

General Karma Properties

Now that you know how to go about creating Karma Actors, you need to know what properties are available to control them. The `KParams` property can be set to one of these four property groups: `KarmaParams`, `KarmaParamsCollision`, `KarmaParamsSkel`, and `KarmaParamsRBFull`. **TABLE 11.1** lists the properties available in each group and describes what each property does.

TABLE 11.1 Karma Properties

Property	Description	Default
KarmaParams		
`bDestroyOnWorldPenetrate`	When this property is set to True, if the center of the Karma object passes through the world, the object is destroyed.	False
`bDoSafetime`	If this property is True, the Karma engine does extra checks to avoid objects passing through the world.	False

TABLE 11.1 Continued

Property	Description	Default
`bHighDetailOnly`	When this property is set to True, the Karma Actor doesn't react with anything in the level unless the game settings are set to a high detail level.	False
`bKAllowRotate`	This property, when set to True, allows the Karma Actor to rotate around the Z-axis. This property is relevant only when `KStayUpright` is set to True.	False
`bKDoubleTickRate`	When this property is set to True, the Karma Actor is updated twice as many times, which improves the simulation's accuracy. However, two objects with different tick rates might not collide because of the differences in accuracy.	False
`bKNonSphericalInertia`	By default, a Karma Actor uses a spherical *inertia tensor*, which is simply an approximation of an object's mass distribution. (For a description of an inertia tensor, see the explanation of the `KInertiaTensor` property at the end of this table.) If this property is set to True, the Karma Actor uses a non-spherical inertia tensor that more accurately simulates an object's inertia. Consequently, however, the calculation is slower. When using `KarmaParamsRBFull`, the values in `KInertiaTensor` are used. If not, the object's collision hulls are used to calculate an inertia tensor. A *collision hull* is an invisible shell of simple geometry that surrounds an object and is used for collision detection.	False
`bKStayUpright`	When this property is set to True, the Karma Actor tries to maintain its upright orientation. The `StayUprightStiffness` and `StayUprightDamping` properties (see their entries later in this table) contribute to how this property is calculated.	False

TABLE 11.1 Continued

Property	Description	Default
KActorGravScale	This property is a gravity multiplier for the Karma Actor. It can be used, for example, if you want to make certain objects fall faster than others. Be careful, however, because a value higher than 1 might cause the Karma Actor to fall through the world geometry.	1.0
KAngularDamping	This property sets the amount of force that's applied to decrease the Karma Actor's angular motion, which results in rotational drag. The higher the value, the more the Actor resists rotation.	0.2
KBuoyancy	With this property, you can determine how well the Karma Actor floats in a WaterVolume. The default value of 0 means that the object completely ignores the existence of water. A value of 1 causes the Actor to float in the water until it comes to rest. If you want the object to actually float toward the water's surface, you need to set this property to a value higher than 1. However, the value doesn't need to be much higher than 1 for noticeable differences.	0.0
KLinearDamping	Much like KAngularDamping, this property determines the force causing translational drag, or a resistance to linear movement. The higher the number, the more drag is applied to the movement (not rotation) of the Karma Actor.	0.0
KMass	This property is used as a multiplier for the mass of a Karma Actor. This mass is relative to the volume of an object's Karma Primitives. Just keep in mind, however, that this property does *not* determine a Karma Actor's absolute mass.	1.0
KMaxAngularSpeed	This property sets the maximum amount of angular, or rotational, speed that a Karma Actor can achieve.	10.0

TABLE 11.1 Continued

Property	Description	Default
`KMaxSpeed`	This property sets the maximum amount of linear (translational) speed that a Karma Actor can achieve.	2500.0
`KStartAngVel`	When the Karma Actor is first triggered, it rotates in the direction specified in these three fields, which indicate rotation in the X-, Y-, and Z-axes.	<0, 0, 0>
`KStartEnabled`	When this property is set to True, the Karma Actor starts simulating as soon as it spawns into the level.	False
`KStartLinVel`	As with `KStartAngVel`, this property determines the amount of linear translation that's applied to the object after it is triggered.	<0, 0, 0>
`KVelDropBelowThreshold`	When the Karma Actor drops below the specified speed, a function (that a programmer writes) is called. Because this function requires the use of programming, it's not discussed in this book.	1000000
`Repulsors`	Because this property can be set only in code, you can safely ignore it.	none
`StayUprightStiffness`	This property, which is relevant only when `bKStayUpright` is set to True, determines how a Karma Actor maintains its upright orientation. Basically, this property determines how quickly an Actor returns to the upright position. It works much the same way as a spring, and the spring's stiffness correlates quite well to the `StayUprightStiffness` property. Therefore, the higher `StayUprightStiffness` is, the faster the Karma object returns to the upright orientation.	50

TABLE 11.1 Continued

Property	Description	Default
`StayUprightDamping`	As with `StayUprightStiffness`, this property is useful only for Karma Actors that have `bKStayUpright` set to True. `StayUprightDamping` works directly with the `StayUprightStiffness` property. This property slows down the speed at which an object returns to the upright orientation. The higher the damping, the less the object wobbles back and forth before coming to rest in the center.	0
KarmaParamsCollision		
`KFriction`	This property sets the amount of resistance on the surface caused by friction. Any value between 0 and 1 yields realistic results. However, values outside that range might mean the object never reaches a state of rest or is always at rest. Therefore, a value of 1 means full friction, and 0 means no friction.	0.0
`KImpactThreshold`	When a Karma Actor is affected by a value higher than the value specified, a function (that a programmer writes) is called. Because this function requires programming, it's not discussed in this book.	1000000
`KRestitution`	This property determines a Karma Actor's amount of bounciness. A setting of 0 means no bounce whatsoever. When set to 1, the velocity after impact is the same as the moment of impact, meaning the object loses no energy when ricocheting off other surfaces and could potentially bounce forever.	0.0

TABLE 11.1 Continued

Property	Description	Default
`StayUprightDamping`	As with `StayUprightStiffness`, this property is useful only for Karma Actors that have `bKStayUpright` set to True. `StayUprightDamping` works directly with the `StayUprightStiffness` property. This property slows down the speed at which an object returns to the upright orientation. The higher the damping, the less the object wobbles back and forth before coming to rest in the center.	0
KarmaParamsSkel		
`bKDoConvulsions`	If this property is set to true, the Ragdoll convulses at the interval set in `KConvulseSpacing`.	0.0
`bRubbery`	This property causes the Ragdoll to bend and flex at very extreme angles, as though it were made of a rubbery material.	1000000
`KConvulseSpacing`	This property specifies a range, in seconds, between `Min` and `Max` during which the Ragdoll convulses. Using the default, the Ragdoll convulses every .5 to 1.5 seconds.	<0.5, 1.5>
`KSkeleton`	This property specifies the `KSkeleton` to use when simulating a Ragdoll. This property is discussed in more detail in "Ragdolls," later in this chapter.	
KarmaParamsRBFull		
`KCOMOffset`	This property is used as an offset to the Karma object's center of mass.	<0, 0, 0>
`KInertiaTensor`	The inertia tensor describes how an object's mass is distributed. Therefore, modifying the values of this property affects how a Karma object rotates in response to an external force. Six values are associated with this property. However, only three are crucial: index [0], index [3], and index [5]. All the other fields (index [1], index [2], and index [4]) can be set to 0 and can usually be ignored.	[0.4] [0.0] [0.0] [0.4] [0.0] [0.4]

11

TABLE 11.1 Continued

Property	Description	Default
	Index [0] controls how easy it is for the object to roll. The higher the number, the more the object resists rolling. This number, however, doesn't completely govern how an object resists rotation. The `KMass` and `DrawScale` properties directly influence how an object resists motion of any kind, including rotation. This calculation is done behind the scenes, but it's still important to keep in mind when tweaking the inertia tensor. In the same fashion as index [0] controls roll, index [3] controls pitch, and index [5] controls yaw.	

Karma Collision Primitives

The Karma Collision Primitives are much the same as normal collision geometry except they deal strictly with Karma. In other words, Karma collision geometry and the regular collision geometry that blocks characters and projectiles are two completely separate entities and must be treated as such. Also, if a static mesh contains no Karma Collision Primitives, it can't be placed into the level as a Karma Actor.

Typically, Karma Collision Primitives are imported along with the file containing the static mesh. To do this, simply create a new object or a series of objects in your favorite 3D package, and add one of the prefixes shown in **TABLE 11.2** to the beginning of the object's name to specify the Karma Collision Primitive type.

TABLE 11.2 Karma Collision Primitive Prefixes

Prefix	Primitive Type
MCDBX	Box Primitive
MCDSP	Sphere Primitive
MCDCY	Cylinder Primitive
MCDCX	Convex Mesh Primitive

When a static mesh is imported into UnrealEd, all objects that have any of the prefixes shown in **TABLE 11.2** at the beginning of the name are converted into a Karma Collision Primitive of the specified type.

After a static mesh is imported, you have several commands you can use to modify the Karma Collision Primitives in the Static Mesh browser. Under the Collision Tools menu is the Fit Karma Primitive category. The first command, Sphere, simply places a Sphere primitive around the existing object. If the object already has Karma collision geometry, you're asked if you want to replace it. The Cylinder X/Y/Z commands place a cylinder primitive around the current static mesh that points in the specified axis. If you use the Cylinder Z command, for example, the cylinder stands upright.

The Refresh Karma Primitives command converts the existing regular collision geometry to Karma collision geometry. The Karma Collision Primitives, however, remain intact. The final command available in the Static Mesh browser is Clear Karma Primitives, which removes all Karma Collision Primitives.

Constraints

Sometimes creating simple Karma objects that interact with the level isn't enough to generate the effect you want. To better control the behavior of Karma objects, you can use *constraints*, which effectively restrict the effects of your Karma objects. For example, if you want to create a lamp connected to the ceiling by a series of chain links, you would have to constrain each chain link to its neighboring link and then constrain the lamp to the bottommost chain link. Or perhaps you want to create a door that's hinged on one side. You simply need to constrain the door object to a specified hinge.

To this end, you have three constraint Actors: KBSJoint, KConeLimit, and KHinge. They are all subclasses of the aforementioned KActor and are used with Karma objects for extra control. You can access them in the Actor Class browser under Actor > KActor > KConstraint. The following sections cover these constraints and explain how to use them in your levels.

KBSJoint

The KSBJoint constraint is used to connect two Karma objects in much the same way that your shoulder connects your arm to the rest of your body. Therefore, it's known as the ball-and-socket joint—hence the name KBSJoint (Karma Ball Socket Joint). To use it, simply place the KBSJoint between two Karma objects, and then set its properties to point to the two Karma objects. The distance between the two Karma objects is maintained throughout the game. Also noteworthy is that Karma objects don't need to actually touch the KBSJoint Actor. In **TUTORIAL 11.2**, you use the KBSJoint Actor to create a dynamically swinging lamp.

TUTORIAL 11.2: Creating a Lamp

1. Open Tutorial11_02_Start.ut2. The goal of this tutorial is to create a lamp that's connected to the ceiling via a series of chain links.

2. In the Static Mesh browser, open the Chapter11 package. Under the LightSystem group, select ShortChain. You'll be using this static mesh as the chain links. In the top view, navigate to the southernmost room, where you'll be creating the lamp (see **FIGURE 11.3**). Right-click in the middle of this room, and choose Add Karma Actor. Move the chain so that the top of it rests on the ceiling, as shown in **FIGURE 11.4**.

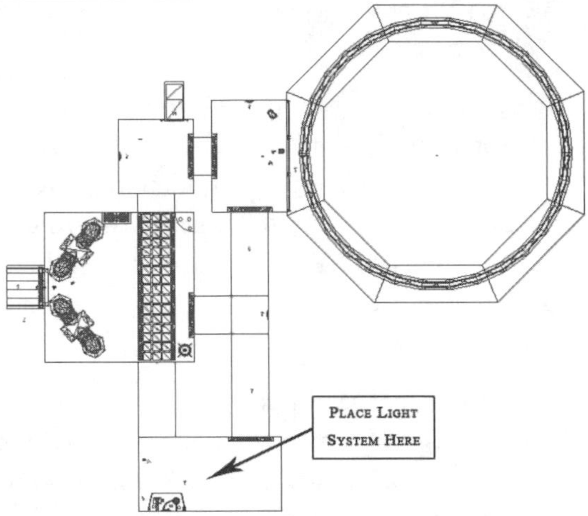

FIGURE 11.3 Top view of where you'll put the light system.

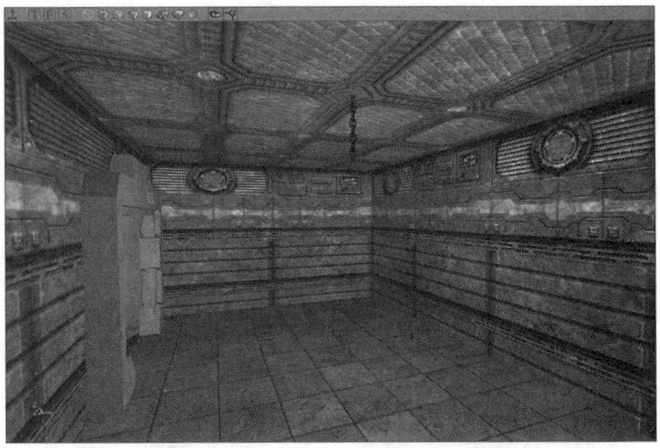

FIGURE 11.4 Perspective view of the newly placed chain.

3. With the chain still selected, press Ctrl+W or choose Edit > Duplicate from the menu. Now move this new chain below the previous one so that the two chains create a straight line (see **FIGURE 11.5**).

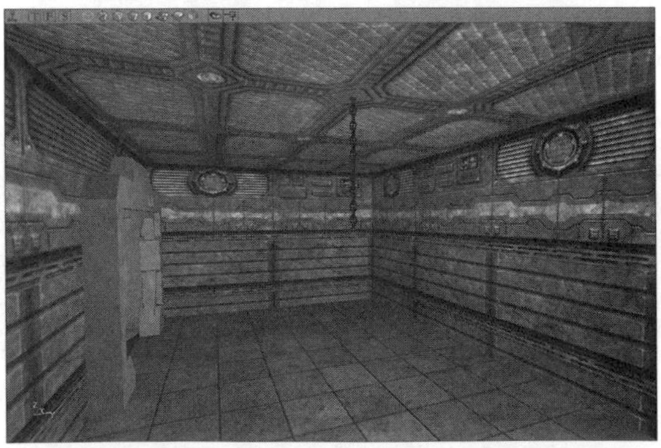

FIGURE 11.5 Both chains in position.

4. All you need now for Karma objects is the lamp. In the Static Mesh browser, open the Chapter11 package. Under the LightSystem group, select Light. Again, right-click in the viewport, and choose Add Karma Actor. Move this newly created lamp to the bottom of the chain (see **FIGURE 11.6**).

   If you run the level now, the lamp system would hang in midair until you shot it with enough force to start the simulation. When it did start reacting, however, it would just fall to the ground. This is where constraints come into play. You'll need a KBSJoint at each point where the Karma objects meet. You'll also need one between the ceiling and the first chain so that the entire lamp system stays attached to the ceiling. **FIGURE 11.7** shows you where each KBSJoint should be placed.

5. First, open the Actor Class browser. Expand Actor > KActor > KConstraint, and click KBSJoint. Now close the Actor Class browser, right-click near the lamp, and choose Add KBSJoint Here. Move it so that it connects the top chain to the ceiling (see **FIGURE 11.8**).
6. Duplicate the KBSJoint and move it down so that it connects the two chains, as shown in **FIGURE 11.9**.
7. Finally, duplicate the KBSJoint again and move it so that it connects the lamp to the bottom chain (see **FIGURE 11.10**).
8. At this point, you have everything you need to get the dynamic lamp system working properly. All you have to do now is set a few simple properties. Open the Properties window for the KBSJoint on the ceiling, and expand the KarmaConstraint category. The only two properties you need to be concerned with are `KConstraintActor1` and `KConstraintActor2`. `KConstraintActor1` is connected (constrained) to `KConstraintActor2`. Because you want the chain to be connected to the ceiling, or world, you simply set `KConstraintActor1` to the chain attached to the ceiling and leave `KConstraintActor2` set to None. **FIGURE 11.11** illustrates the constraint relationships.

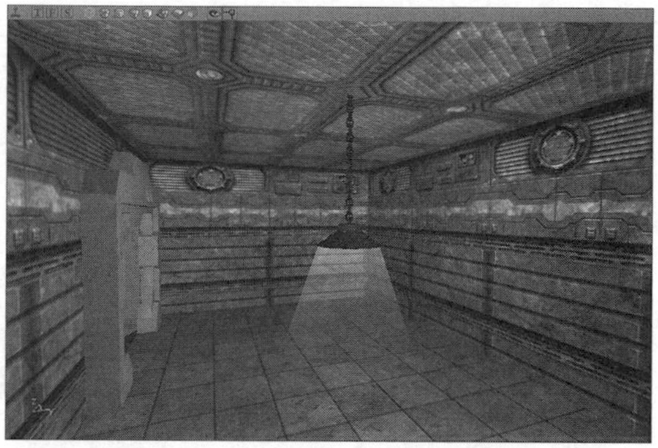

FIGURE 11.6 Light added at the end of the chain.

FIGURE 11.7 The placement of KBSJoint Actors.

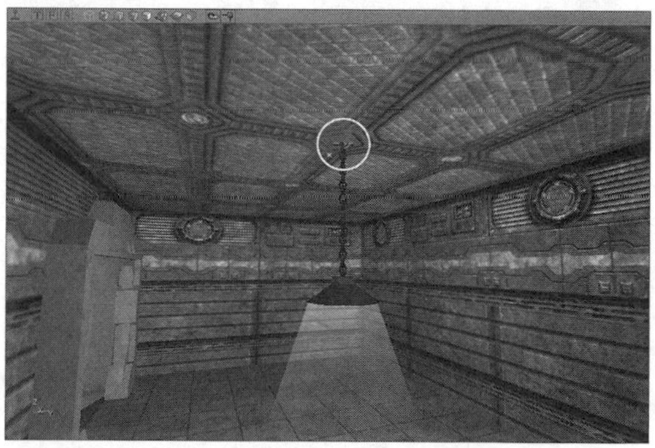

FIGURE 11.8 Position of the topmost KBSJoint.

9. To set `KConstraintActor1` to the chain, select the `KConstraintActor1` property and click Find. Doing this changes the mouse pointer to a crosshair and question mark. In the Perspective viewport, zoom in on the chain and click it.

> **NOTE**
>
> **If your first click catches an object that isn't right, simply zoom in closer to the object and try again. When you've done it correctly, the property should contain the name of the chain link. (This name varies depending on how you created the chain links.)**

10. Open the Properties window for the next KBSJoint. Under the KarmaConstraint category, set the `KConstraintActor1` property to the chain above the KBSJoint. Set `KConstraintActor2` to the chain right below the KBSJoint.

11. Finally, select the final KBSJoint that connects the lamp to the chain and open its Properties window. Again, under the KarmaConstraint category, set the `KConstraintActor1` property to the chain above the KBSJoint. Now set `KConstraintActor2` to the lamp.

12. That's it! If everything was done correctly, you should now have a fully working lamp system. Save the map as `LightSystem_Complete.ut2`.

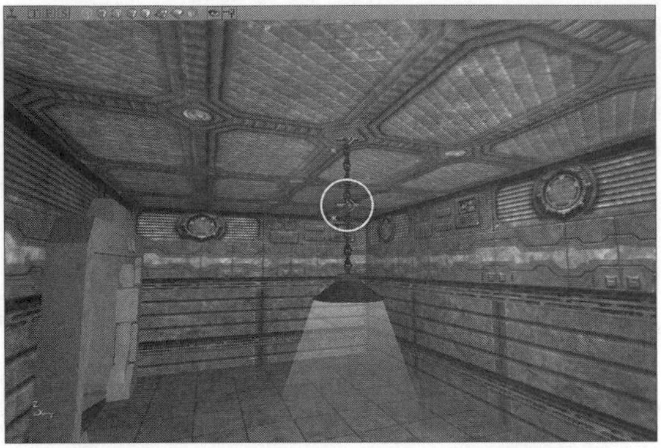

FIGURE 11.9 Position of the middle KBSJoint.

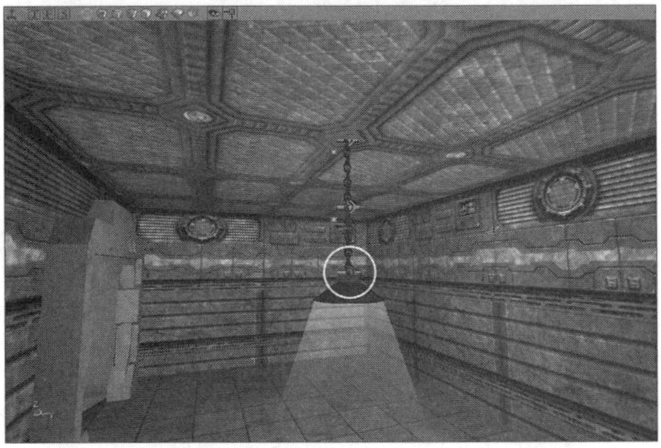

FIGURE 11.10 Position of the bottom KBSJoint.

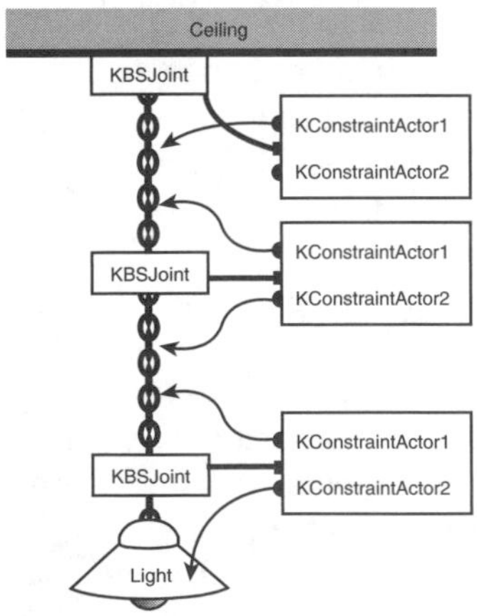

FIGURE 11.11 The relationship between the KBSJoints and chains.

END TUTORIAL 11.2

Besides the `KConstraintActor1` and `KConstraintActor2` properties already discussed, you have a few other less used, but still helpful, properties. **TABLE 11.3** describes each of them.

> **NOTE**
>
> **If you play the game and the lamp system stays completely stagnant, you might need to go into the properties of the three Karma Actors and set `bHighDetailOnly` to False.**

TABLE 11.3 KBSJoint Properties

Property	Description	Default
`bKDisableCollision`	When this property is set to True, collision between the two connected Karma objects is disabled.	True
`KConstraintBone1`	This property specifies the exact skeletal mesh bone in `KConstraintActor1` to constrain to.	None
`KConstraintBone2`	This property specifies the exact skeletal mesh bone in `KConstraintActor2` to constrain to.	None
`KForceThreshold`	When the force within the constraint joint reaches the amount specified by this property, the KForceExceed UnrealScript function is called. This function is unused with the current tools and is in place so that programmers can create constraints with new behavior.	0.0

KConeLimit

KConeLimit is an Actor that complements existing joints. It allows you to limit the amount of rotation between two Actors in a cone shape. For example, say you wanted to make the swinging light you created in **TUTORIAL 11.2** unable to swing high enough to touch the ceiling. The KConeLimit Actor makes this entirely possible. In **TUTORIAL 11.3**, you adjust the lamp system by implementing this Actor.

TUTORIAL 11.3: Modifying the Lamp System

1. Open `LightSystem_Complete.ut2` that you saved in **TUTORIAL 11.2**, or open `Tutorial11_03_Start.ut2` from the Chapter 11 folder on the CD.
2. In the Actor Class browser, navigate to Actor > KActor > KConstraint, and click KConeLimit.

3. Right-click in the level near the lamp, and choose Add KConeLimit Here. The exact location of this Actor isn't particularly important because only its rotation is used. However, moving it near the Actors it will be affecting, as shown in **FIGURE 11.12**, is a good practice.

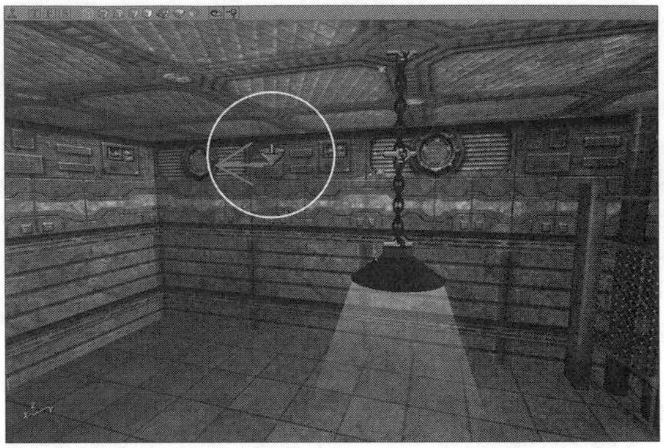

FIGURE 11.12 KConeLimit placed next to the light system.

4. The red arrow extending out of the KConeLimit Actor points down the X-axis. This arrow determines around which axis rotation is limited. In this case, all rotation revolves around the Z-axis. Therefore, you need to rotate the KConeLimit so that it points down the Z-axis. With the KConeLimit Actor still selected, hold down the Ctrl key, right-click, and drag in the Front viewport until the arrow points down the Z-axis (see **FIGURE 11.13**).

FIGURE 11.13 KConeLimit pointing down the Z-axis.

5. Now it's simply a matter of choosing which Actors you want to limit. As with KBSJoint, you have the `KConstraintActor1` and `KConstraintActor2` properties. If you specified the top chain as `KConstraintActor1` and left `KConstraintActor2` blank, KConeLimit would simply be limited in relation to the world by the amount specified in `KHalfAngle`. If you set `KHalfAngle` to 0, the chain would always try to stay perfectly straight. **FIGURE 11.14** illustrates the relationship between KConeLimit and the chain.

6. If, however, you specified the top chain as `KConstraintActor1` and the second chain as `KConstraintActor2`, the second chain is limited so that the angle between `KConstraintActor1` and `KConstraintActor2` conforms to the angle specified in `KHalfAngle` (see **FIGURE 11.15**).

7. You can experiment with these settings and see a variety of results. Keep in mind that `KHalfAngle` is measured in Unreal angles, so 65535 is equal to 360 degrees.

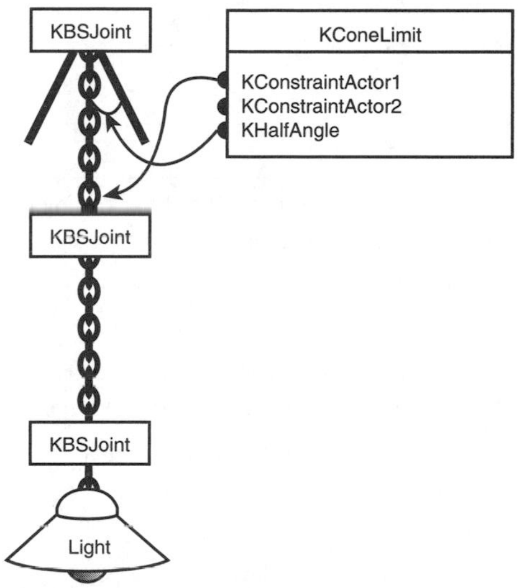

FIGURE 11.14 The relationship between KConeLimit and the chain.

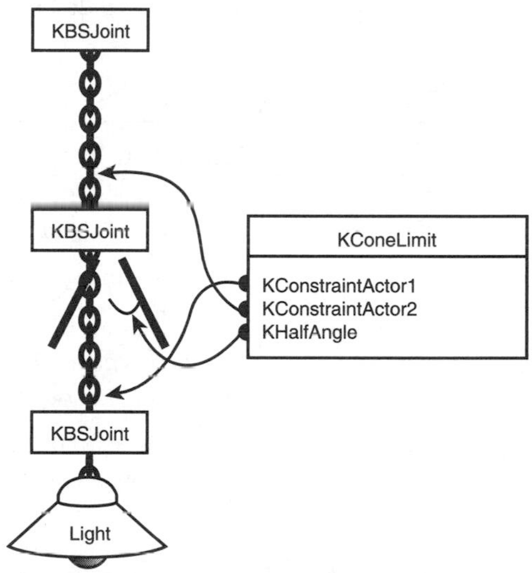

FIGURE 11.15 How to make both chains constrained to each other.

END TUTORIAL 11.3

Aside from the `KHalfAngle` property, you also have `KStiffness` and `KDamping`. **TABLE 11.4** describes these properties and their default values.

TABLE 11.4 *KStiffness* and *KDamping* Properties

Property	Description	Default
`KStiffness`	This property determines how firmly the limit is enforced. As the number gets higher, the force that resists the motion of the KBSJoint becomes stiffer. This property can be thought of as similar to the stiffness of a spring.	50.0
`KDamping`	This property slows the speed at which the limit is enforced.	0.0

KHinge

The KHinge constraint is much the same as the KBSJoint constraint, except it works more like a door hinge, constraining rotation to only one axis. As with KBSJoint, you have the option of specifying two Karma Actors to constrain; if you specify only one Karma Actor, that one Actor is going to be constrained to the world. Unlike the KBSJoint, however, the KHinge has four different modes (KHingeTypes) that alter its behavior. Depending on the mode you select, the other properties behave differently. **TABLE 11.5** describes the four modes.

TABLE 11.5 KHingeType Modes

KHingeType	Description
`HT_Normal`	This mode causes the constraint to act like a basic hinge, constraining the object to the world or to the specified Karma Actor.
`HT_Springy`	In this mode, the hinge acts like a spring while trying to achieve a given angle.
`HT_Motor`	This mode causes the hinge to act like a motor. Therefore, the constrained object rotates around the specified axis at the specified speed.
`HT_Controlled`	This mode acts much like `HT_Motor` except that it tries to achieve the specified angle and then stops when it does.

You can also trigger KHinges much as you do Movers. Under the Object category of the KHinge properties is the `InitialState` property, which gives you access to four different modes. **TABLE 11.6** describes each of them.

TABLE 11.6 *`InitialState`* Modes

`InitialState` Mode	Description
`ToggleMotor`	If the KHingeType is not already `HT_Motor`, the trigger changes it to `HT_Motor`. Otherwise, the trigger changes the KHingeType to `HT_Controlled` and changes `KDesiredAngle` to the current angle. This causes the motor to come to a stop.
`ControlMotor`	A trigger turns the motor on, and an untrigger turns the motor off. An "untrigger" can be thought of as an automatic off switch for particular triggers. Some triggers, such as simple proximity-based triggers, can be said to be "triggered" when a player enters their defined proximity, and then "untriggered" when the character leaves that proximity. The `ControlMotor` mode works the same as `ToggleMotor` except that it responds to trigger and untrigger events instead of simply inverting the state.

TABLE 11.6 Continued

InitialState Mode	Description
ToggleDesired	This mode toggles the hinge between using KDesiredAngle and KAltDesiredAngle. Because it doesn't change the hinge type, this mode is useful only when dealing with HT_Controlled and HT_Springy.
ControlDesired	A trigger causes the hinge to use KAltDesiredAngle, and an untrigger causes the hinge to use KDesiredAngle. As with the ToggleDesired mode, this mode is relevant only when the type is HT_Controlled or HT_Springy.

Because the HT_Normal hinge type works as a basic hinge, you'll use it in **TUTORIAL 11.4** to see how to create a dynamic bridge.

TUTORIAL 11.4: Creating a Dynamic Bridge

1. Open Tutorial11_04_Start.ut2.
2. Go into the large room with the fan, where you'll notice that you already have a bridge in place (see **FIGURE 11.16**).
3. At this point, running the level and shooting the bridge would cause the bridge to simply collapse. Instead, you want the parts of the bridge to be connected by using a series of KHinge constraints. In the Actor Class browser, expand Actor > KActor > KConstraint and click KHinge.
4. Right-click in the level, and choose Add KHinge Here. Move the KHinge to the place where the bridge and wall connect. Also, be sure that the arrow for the KHinge is pointing toward the pipes against the corner of the wall (see **FIGURE 11.17**).
5. With the KHinge selected, duplicate it and move it to the point where the next two Karma Actors meet. Continue duplicating until you reach

FIGURE 11.16 Room with the bridge.

FIGURE 11.17 First KHinge Actor in place.

the other side of the bridge. **FIGURE 11.18** show the final result.

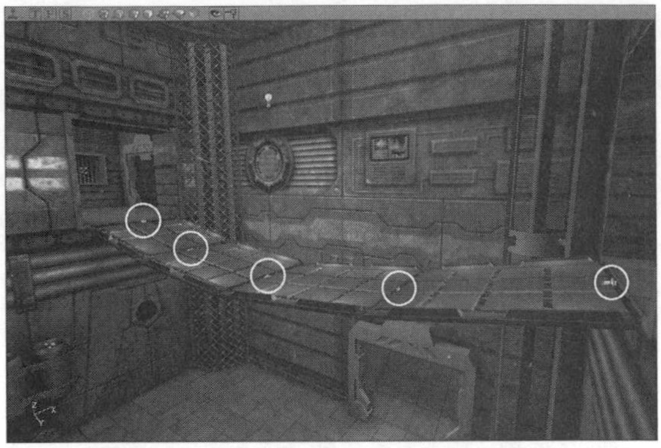

FIGURE 11.18 All the KHinge Actors in place.

6. Now you just need to set the relationship between the constraints and the bridge pieces. Open the Properties window for the first constraint created. Under the KarmaConstraint category, select the `KConstraintActor1` property. Click the Find button and select the bridge segment nearest the KConstraint Actor. For the second KHinge, set `KConstraintActor1` to the first bridge piece and `KConstraintActor2` to the second bridge piece. Continue in this manner, with `KConstraintActor1` being the Karma Actor to the left of the constraint and `KConstraintActor2` being the Karma Actor to the right of the constraint. For the last KHinge, set `KConstraintActor1` to the last bridge piece. Use **FIGURE 11.19** as a guide.

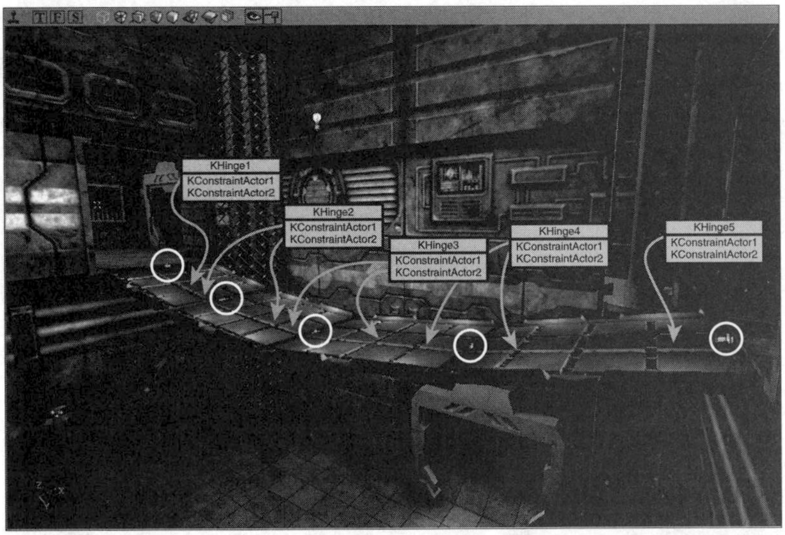

FIGURE 11.19 The relationship between the pieces of the bridge.

7. You should now have a completely functional bridge that reacts to outside forces such as projectiles. Save and run the map.

END TUTORIAL 11.4

As you can see, the KHinge constraint can be extremely useful. However, this tutorial showed only one of the types available for the KHinge. In **TUTORIAL 11.5**, you see how to use the `HT_Motor` type to create a constantly rotating fan.

TUTORIAL 11.5: Creating a Fan

1. Open `Tutorial11_05_Start.ut2`.
2. Across from the previously created bridge is a fan at the entrance of a cylindrical hole. At the moment, the fan just sits there until you shoot it, at which point it simply falls to the ground. First, you need to create the actual KHinge constraint. In the Actor Class browser, expand Actor > KActor > KConstraint, and click KHinge. Right-click near the fan, and choose Add KHinge Here. Move the KHinge to the center of the fan and ensure that it's rotated in the same direction as the fan (see **FIGURE 11.20**).

FIGURE 11.20 Move KHinge to the middle of the fan.

3. In the Properties window for the KHinge, go to the KarmaConstraint category and select the `KConstraintActor1` property. Click the Find button and select the fan.
4. Next, change the `KHingeType` to `HT_Motor` so that you can get a constant rotation for the fan. Now change `KDesiredAngVel` to 16384, which sets the speed of rotation. Because it's measured in Unreal angular units, the fan spins 45 degrees a second. Before you can get any movement out of this fan, however, you need to give the fan a maximum torque. Because torque is a measurement of how much a force applied to an object causes that object to rotate, you want to ensure that the maximum torque is large enough that the fan can rotate the amount specified in `KDesiredAngVel`. To this end, set `KMaxTorque` to 100.
5. You now have a fully working fan. Save and run the map.

END TUTORIAL 11.5

The `HT_Controlled` type is very similar to the `HT_Motor`, but it takes advantage of the `KDesiredAng` and `KAltDesiredAng` properties to specify the angle to achieve. In this way, the motor starts spinning at the specified speed and stops when it reaches the specified angle. You also have the `HT_Springy` type for the KHinge. With this type, you can simulate a spring that has two angular goals. In **TUTORIAL 11.6**, you see how to use this type to create a catapult.

TUTORIAL 11.6: Creating a Catapult

1. Open `Tutorial11_06_Start.ut2`. The goal of this tutorial is to use the catapult in front of the fan (shown in **FIGURE 11.21**) to propel a barrel onto the bridge.

FIGURE 11.21 Catapult in front of the fan.

2. In the Actor Class browser, select Actor > KActor > KConstraint > KHinge. Right-click in the level, and choose Add KHinge Here. Place it on the side of the catapult closer to the bridge and ensure that it's in the center of the catapult in the Y-axis. Finally, rotate the KHinge so that it points down the Y-axis (see **FIGURE 11.22**).

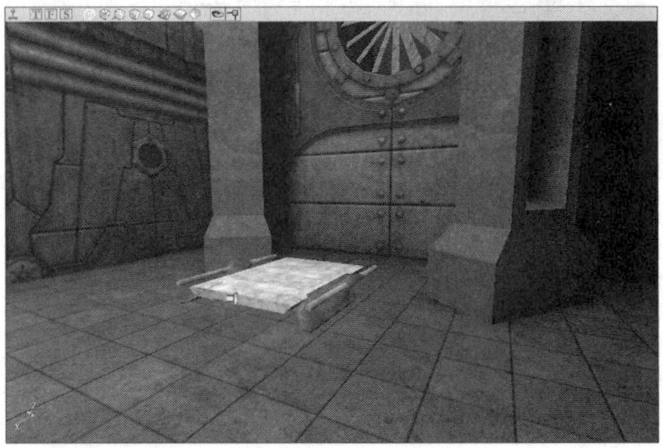

FIGURE 11.22 KHinge Actor on the side of the catapult.

3. In the Properties window for the KHinge, select the `KConstraintActor1` property. Click the Find button and select the catapult.
4. Now change the `KHingeType` to `HT_Springy`, and change `KStiffness` to 5000 so that the spring is relatively strong. Also, set `KDamping` to 250 so that the catapult doesn't swing back and forth too much.
5. At this point, the catapult acts like a spring. However, currently you can't trigger the catapult to swing into action. To do this, you need a trigger. In the Actor Class browser, select Actor > Triggers > UseTrigger. Right-click in the level, and choose Add UseTrigger Here. Move it next to the catapult, as shown in **FIGURE 11.23**.
6. In the Properties window for the UseTrigger, go to the Advanced category and set `bHidden` to False so that you can see the UseTrigger in the game. Under the Events category, set the `Event` property to `TriggerCatapult`.
7. Now you just need the catapult to actually respond to this event. In the Properties window for the KHinge, go to the Object category. Change `InitialState` to `ToggleDesired`. Under the KarmaConstraint category, set `KAltDesiredAngle` to 16384 (90 degrees). This setting results in a hefty plunge for whatever objects are innocently resting on the catapult's surface. To associate the UseTrigger with the KHinge, go to the Events category of the KHinge, and set the `Tag` property to `TriggerCatapult`.

8. Finally, to test this catapult, place a barrel on top of it. In the Static Mesh browser, open the `Chapter11.usx` package, and under the Karma group, select Barrel. Right-click in the level, and choose Add Karma Actor. Place this barrel on top of the catapult. In the Karma properties for the barrel, set `bHighDetailOnly` to False and `bKStartEnabled` to True, as you did with the catapult. Also, change `KMass` to 0.5 so that the barrel is slightly lighter. Run the level, use the trigger, and the barrel will be propelled into the air!

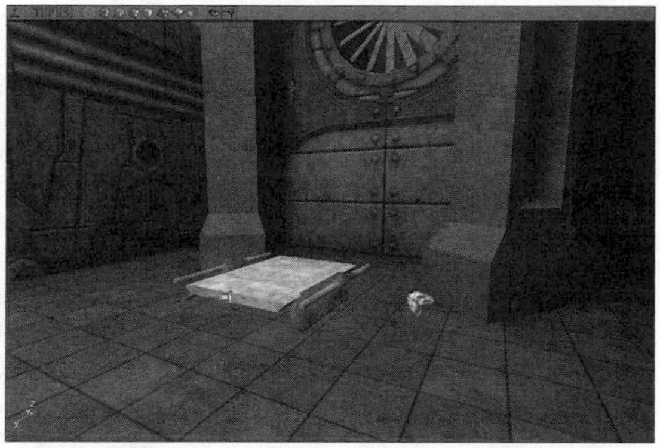

FIGURE 11.23 Move the UseTrigger next to the catapult.

9. Save the map.

END TUTORIAL 11.6

Ragdolls

As discussed briefly a earlier in this chapter, Ragdolls are the simulation of characters controlled entirely by Karma. Usually, you see the effects of Ragdolls only when a character dies. At that point, the Ragdoll simulation takes over, and a death sequence is generated.

For a character model to be used as a Ragdoll, you must have *skeletons*. These skeletons, or Karma Assets, hold information that tells Karma how to simulate a Ragdoll. Usually, if you create a simple bipedal character, the existing skeletons can be used. However, if your character is oddly shaped, you need to create a custom skeleton by using the *Karma Authoring Tool* (*KAT*). The information this tool generates is saved in files with a `.ka` extension and later used by Unreal. This tool is discussed in more depth in the next section, "The Karma Authoring Tool."

First, however, you'll see how to take advantage of Ragdolls in UnrealEd. **TUTORIAL 11.7** shows you how to take a simple Karma Actor and convert it into a fully working Ragdoll.

TUTORIAL 11.7: Creating Ragdolls

1. Open `Tutorial11_07_Start.ut2`. The goal of this tutorial is to create a Ragdoll that attaches to the chain that swings around the cylindrical room in the level's northeast corner. Notice a button right next to the room you spawn from (see **FIGURE 11.24**). Activating this button causes the chain to start revolving around the room.

2. First, you must create the Actor to act as your Ragdoll. As a template, any KActor will work. For this example, however, select the barrel static mesh you used earlier in the Static Mesh browser, and place it in the level (see **FIGURE 11.25**). The exact location isn't particularly important until you start using the correct model.

3. In the Properties window for the newly created Karma Actor, go to the Display category. Change the `DrawType` property to `DT_Mesh`. Next, to set the `Mesh` property, open the Animation browser. Open the `HumanMaleA` package and select the MercMaleA mesh. Select the `Mesh` property, and click Use. **FIGURE 11.26** shows the results.

4. Now that the correct mesh is being displayed, move the model so that the Ragdoll's right hand is inside the bottom KBSJoint. This constrains the right hand to the KBSJoint. Remember that when you're using this technique, the KBSJoint automatically attaches to the nearest bone in the skeleton. In the Properties window for this KBSJoint, go to the KarmaConstraint category and select the `KConstraintActor2` property. Click the Find button, and select the MercMaleA mesh.

5. At this point, the correct mesh is displayed, but it isn't being controlled by Karma's Ragdoll. To do this, open the MercMaleA Properties window, and go to the Movement category. Change the `Physics` property to `PHYS_KarmaRagDoll`.

FIGURE 11.24 Where the Ragdoll creation will take place.

FIGURE 11.25 Barrel soon to be converted into a Ragdoll.

FIGURE 11.26 Barrel transformed into MercMaleA.

6. Finally, you need to access the Karma properties dealing with Ragdolls. To do this, go to the Karma category and select the `KParams` property. Click the Clear button. For the `New` property, select `KarmaParamsSkel` and click the New button. Within the `KParams` property, expand KarmaParamsSkel myLevel.KarmaParamsSkel0 > KarmaParamsSkel, and set the `KSkeleton` property to `Male` (see **FIGURE 11.27**). This setting specifies which skeleton to use for this Ragdoll and varies depending on which mesh you use. Also, if you don't have your in-game detail settings very high, expand KarmaParamsSkel myLevel.KarmaParamsSkel0 > KarmaParams, and set the `bHighDetailOnly` property to False.

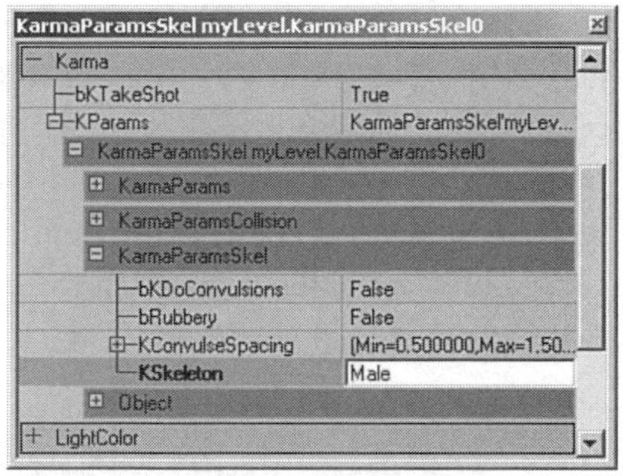

FIGURE 11.27 Karma category of the Ragdoll.

7. You now have a fully working Ragdoll. Save and test the level.

END TUTORIAL 11.7

The Karma Authoring Tool (KAT)

You've already seen how to place Karma-controlled Actors into your levels and how to use constraints to control their behavior, but what if you want to create a more complex system with multiple joints? That's where the Karma Authoring Tool (KAT) comes into play. With this tool, you can set up a skeletal mesh created in an external 3D package to work as a Ragdoll. You can also create and adjust physical properties, such as mass and inertia tensor, and adjust joints to be ball-and-socket joints, hinge joints, skeletal joints, and more.

After you have everything set up the way you want, you export the data to a `.ka` file and reference it from within Unreal. The following sections introduce you to the steps required to turn a model created in Maya into a fully working Ragdoll in Unreal. First, you'll take a look at the basic interface of KAT and how to go about using it.

The KAT Interface

FIGURE 11.28 shows the KAT interface. The four viewports that take up the majority of the interface are used to display the Karma objects you'll be setting up for simulation. On the right is the main panel, where you have access to the tool's main features. The first tab, File, deals with file and workspace management, which is discussed in the next section, "Workspaces." You use the second tab, Utilities, to manage plug-ins and basic properties that influence performance and display. The last tab, Edit, gives you access to all the tools you'll be using to modify imported skeletal meshes. The control bar contains a series of properties related to transformations, some view options, and play controls for simulations. These controls look and function much like what you find on a VCR, allowing you to play the simulation, pause the simulation, and so forth. Finally, you use the status line to see the frames per second (fps) rate and run scripts. You'll see what you can do in other parts of the interface as you work through the following tutorials.

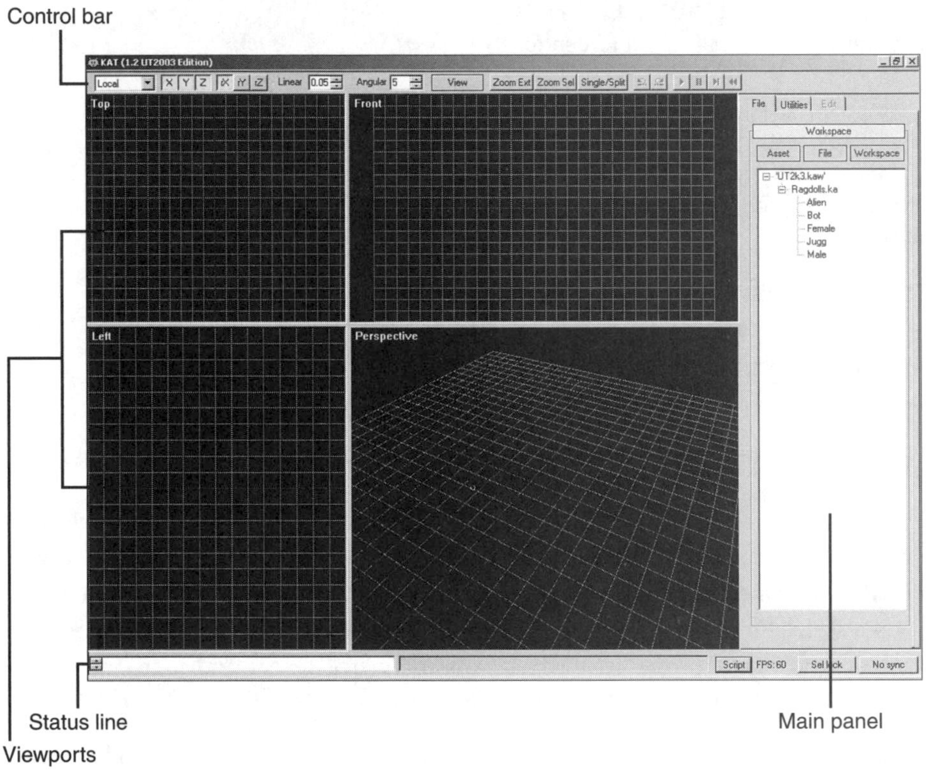

FIGURE 11.28 The KAT interface.

Workspaces

In KAT, you manage your files with *workspaces*. Each workspace manages a file or group of files. These files contain one or more assets. An *asset* is a collection of geometry, parts, and joints (constraints). These assets, which you can think of as "game objects," are designed to work as individual entities that can be placed multiple times in a level. An example of a good asset is a character Ragdoll or rope. An asset that contains all the physics objects in one level, on the other hand, is a poor asset.

To create a new workspace, switch to the File tab of the main panel, and click the Workspace button. From the context menu, choose New. Specify a name for the workspace, and click Save. The workspace area is cleared, and you have a file saved with the extension `.kaw`.

Now you can start placing new Karma asset (`.ka`) files into the workspace. To do this, click the File button, and then select New from the menu. As with creating a new workspace, specify a name and click Save. A new file with the specified name is created, and your workspace is updated with the new file.

After you've created both a workspace and a file, you can then start placing assets in the files. To do this, click the Asset button, and select New from the menu. The Create New Asset dialog box (shown in **FIGURE 11.29**) opens, where you have a variety of options.

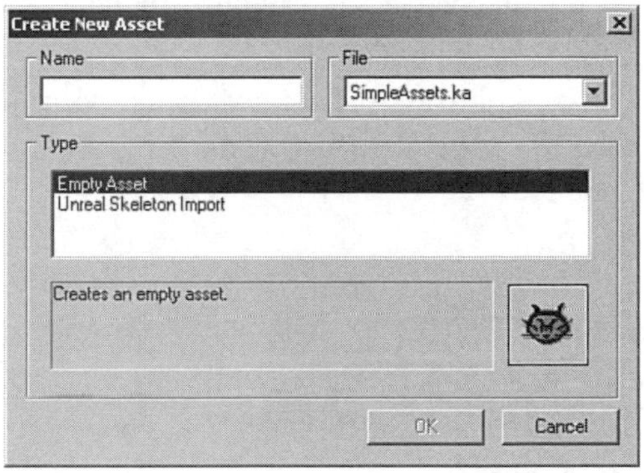

FIGURE 11.29 The Create New Asset dialog box.

In this dialog box, you can specify the asset name and the file where you want to place the asset. For the asset type, you can create an empty asset, or you can import an Unreal skeleton. Typically, you import an Unreal skeleton, so you would select Unreal Skeleton Import in this Type list box.

Viewports

Because you'll be using the viewports often, you need to know how to go about navigating them. **TABLE 11.7** describes the basic navigation hotkeys.

TABLE 11.7 KAT Navigation Hotkeys

Hotkey	Navigation Task
RMB	In the perspective viewport, you tumble around the view. If you're in an orthographic viewport, you pan around the view.
Shift+RMB	This key combination works only in the Perspective viewport. It allows you to pan around the scene.
Ctrl+RMB	This key combination allows you to dolly in and out. It works the same in both perspective and orthographic views.

Right-clicking in any viewport opens a context menu for performing a variety of operations. The Single Viewport menu item sets the currently selected viewport to full screen. The other viewport options are discussed as you use them in the following tutorials. In **TUTORIAL 11.8**, you use KAT to create a simple Karma Asset.

TUTORIAL 11.8: Creating a Simple Karma Asset (Part I)

1. The goal of this tutorial is to create a rope in Maya, bring it into KAT, and see it working within Unreal. To begin, start Maya. If you need help navigating Maya's interface, be sure to check out Chapter 17, "Overview of Maya." Please note that you need the ActorX plug-in to complete this tutorial. For more information on installing this plug-in, go to http://udn.epicgames.com.

2. Choose Create > Polygon Primitives > Cylinder from the main menu, and click the options box. In the Polygon Cylinder Options dialog box that opens, change the following properties:

   Radius: 5

   Height: 200

   Subdivision Around Axis: 10

   Subdivision Along Height: 12

   Axis: Z

3. This cylinder is going to act as the rope. You do, however, need to triangulate it. With the rope selected, press F3 to go to the Modeling menu set, and choose Polygons > Triangulate from the menu.
4. Before you add any joints, you need to adjust their display size so that you can see them in the viewport. To do this, choose Display > Joint Size > Custom from the main menu. In the Joint Display Scale dialog box, enter **5** in the text box to make the joints large enough to see when created.
5. Press F2 to go to the Animation menu set, and choose Skeleton > Joint Tool from the menu.
6. Tap the spacebar in the viewport to switch to Four View mode. Notice the viewport labels under each view panel. In the Side view, create a joint on the far left of the cylinder. While holding down the Shift key, create a joint at every other segment of the cylinder until you reach the end. Create a total of seven joints, as shown in **FIGURE 11.30**.
7. Now you need to create a connection between the joint chain and the rope. Select the root of the chain (the first joint you placed). Then hold down the Shift key, and select the cylinder. Choose Skin > Bind Skin > Smooth Bind from the main menu to attach the cylinder to the joints.
8. The last thing you need to do in Maya is to export this rope as a `.psk` file. With the root of the joint chain selected, type **`axmain`** into the Command Line at the bottom of the screen, and click Enter.
9. In the Skeletal Exporter dialog box, change the output folder to an eligible path, and enter **`RopeSkeletal`** for the mesh file name (see **FIGURE 11.31**). Click the Save Mesh/Refpose button. You should get a message box displaying information about the unsmooth groups processed. Simply click OK. That completes everything you need to do in Maya.

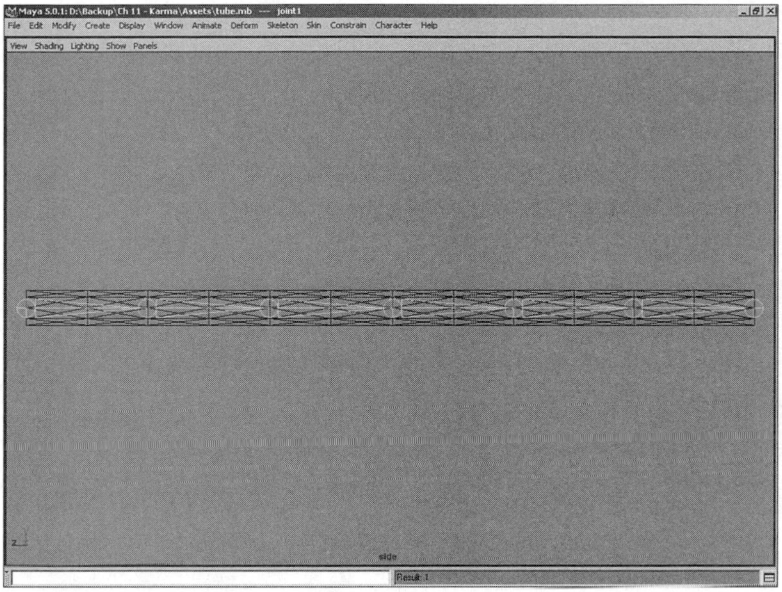

FIGURE 11.30 Joints placed in the cylinder.

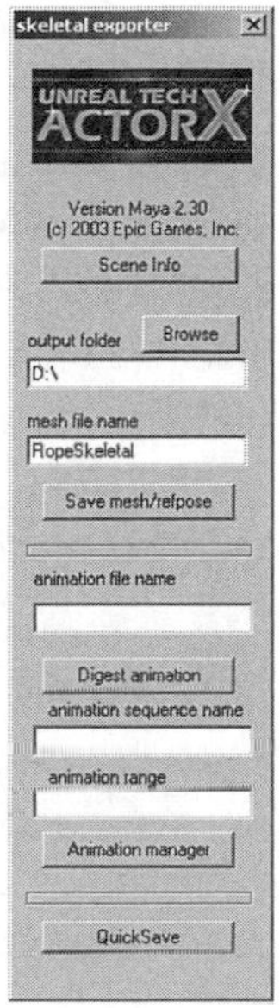

FIGURE 11.31 The Skeletal Exporter dialog box.

END TUTORIAL 11.8

Now that the rope has been created in Maya and exported, you need to bring it into KAT so that it can be properly set up as a Karma Asset. **TUTORIAL 11.9** demonstrates how to import and adjust your new Karma Asset.

TUTORIAL 11.9: Creating a Simple Karma Asset (Part II)

1. Open KAT. Using the techniques discussed thus far, create a new workspace named **`KarmaTests`**.
2. Create a new file and name it **`SimpleAssets`**.
3. Next, select `SimpleAssets.ka` from the workspace and choose Asset > New from the menu. Set the name to **`Rope`**, change the type to Unreal Skeleton Import (see **FIGURE 11.32**), and click OK. In the Select PSK to Import dialog box, locate and select the `RopeSkeletal.psk` file exported earlier, and click Open.

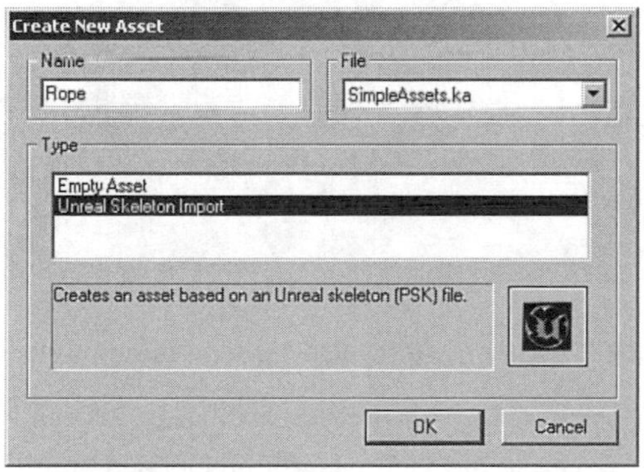

FIGURE 11.32 The necessary setup for importing the rope object that was exported from Maya.

4. Leave the settings in the PSK Import Options dialog box at the defaults, and click OK. You should see a message box saying that you have successfully imported seven parts.

5. In the workspace view, double-click the Rope, which puts you into Edit mode. The Edit tab then comes alive with options and settings, and you'll be able to see the rope in the viewports (see **FIGURE 11.33**).

6. There are three different asset components to deal with in the Edit tab (see **FIGURE 11.34**): Parts, Joints, and Geometry:

   - Parts hold the dynamic properties associated with each joint. Parts also hold information about whether the joint reacts dynamically, has geometry, or both.
   - Joints hold information about what kind of joint is being used. Depending on the type, the available properties change.
   - Geometry is just that: geometric data used as collision data. This data can be created and edited within KAT. When the PSK file is first imported into KAT, a cylinder is created between each joint. Therefore, the necessary collision geometry is already in place.

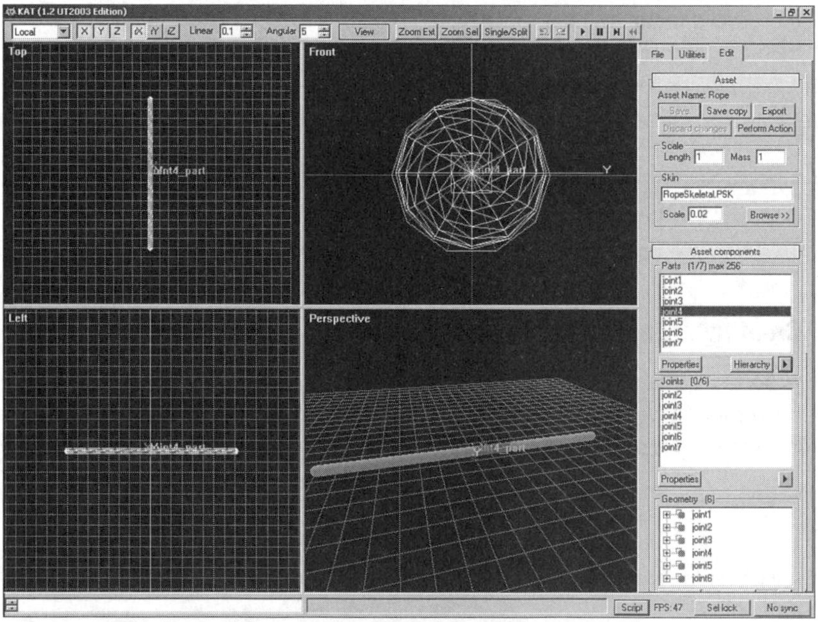

FIGURE 11.33 Rope displayed in the viewports.

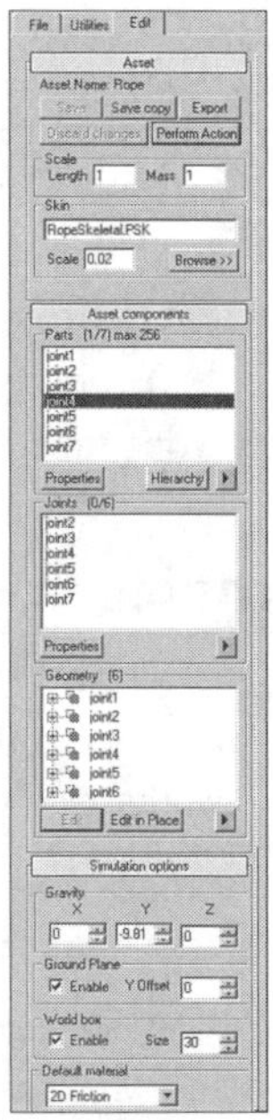

FIGURE 11.34 The Edit tab.

Because the joint type for all joints is set to ball and socket, there are no limits for how the joints can rotate. The rope would look far more realistic, however, if its joints had some limits. Also, a ball and socket allows joints to twist, which is something you don't want your rope to do. Therefore, select all the joints in the Joints list box in the Edit tab, as shown in **FIGURE 11.35**, and click the Properties button.

7. In the Type list box at the top of the Multiple Joints Selected dialog box, change the setting from Ball and Socket to Skeletal (see **FIGURE 11.36**).

8. Although this setup works fine, you can make it more efficient by deleting joint7 from the Parts list. Joint7 was placed just so that the collision geometry could be generated properly. Because the collision geometry has already been created, you can delete joint7 without damaging the simulation. To do this, select joint7 in the Parts list of the Edit tab, and press Delete.

9. Now click the Play button, located at the far right of the control bar. While the simulation is playing, you can LMB-drag the rope around and see it react dynamically (see **FIGURE 11.37**).

10. Finally, save the asset by clicking Save at the top of the Edit tab. Now you're ready to load this asset into UnrealEd.

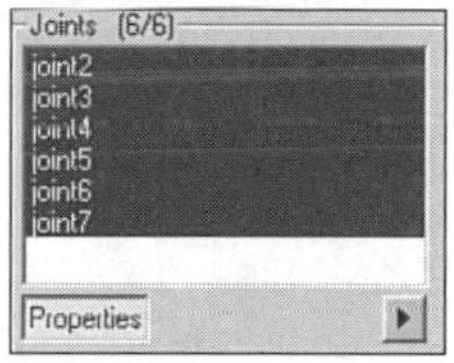

FIGURE 11.35 Select all joints in the Joints list.

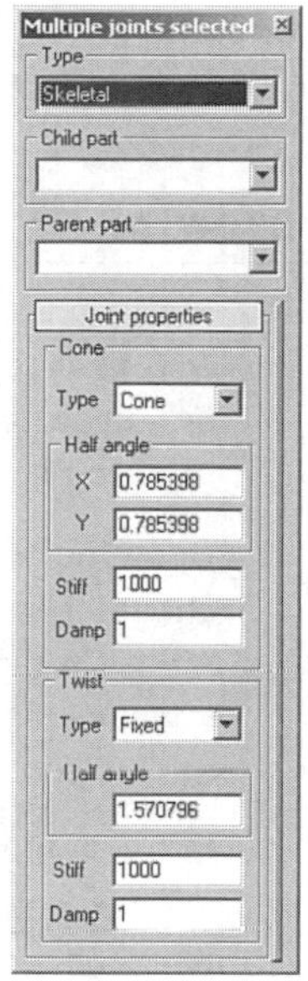

FIGURE 11.36 Select a new type for the joints.

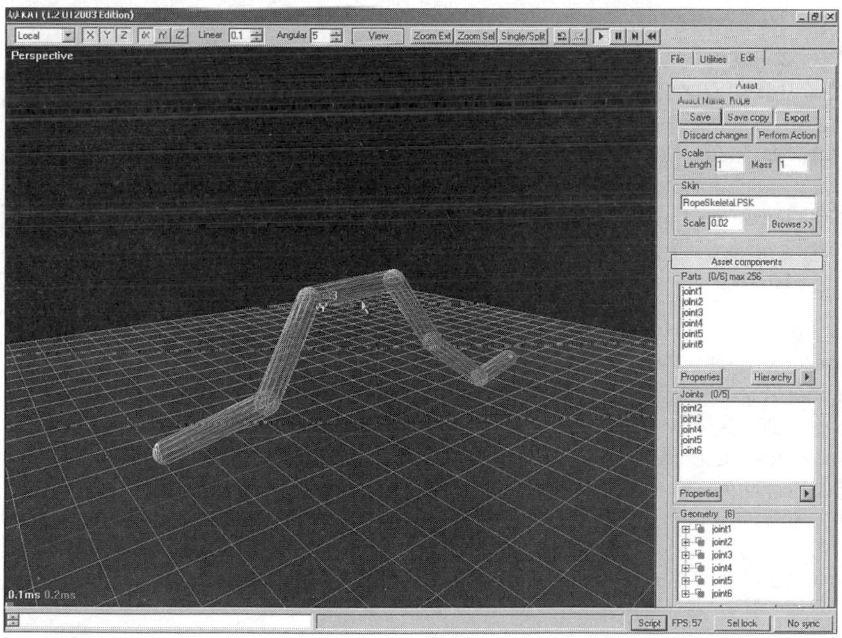

FIGURE 11.37 Moving the rope around in the Perspective viewport.

END TUTORIAL 11.9

The Karma Asset has now been fully established in KAT and is ready for import into UnrealEd. In **TUTORIAL 11.10**, you do this by using UnrealEd's Animation browser.

TUTORIAL 11.10: Creating a Simple Karma Asset (Part III)

1. Start UnrealEd, and open `Tutorial11_10_Start.ut2`. You'll be replacing the Ragdoll with the rope you created.
2. Open the Animation browser, and choose File > Mesh Import from the menu. In the file browser, select the `RopeSkeletal.psk` file you saved earlier, and click Open.
3. In the Import Mesh/Animation dialog box, change the package to `KarmaObjects` and the name to `Rope`. Also, enable the Assume Maya Coordinates check box (see **FIGURE 11.38**). Click the OK button, and save the package as `KarmaObjects`.

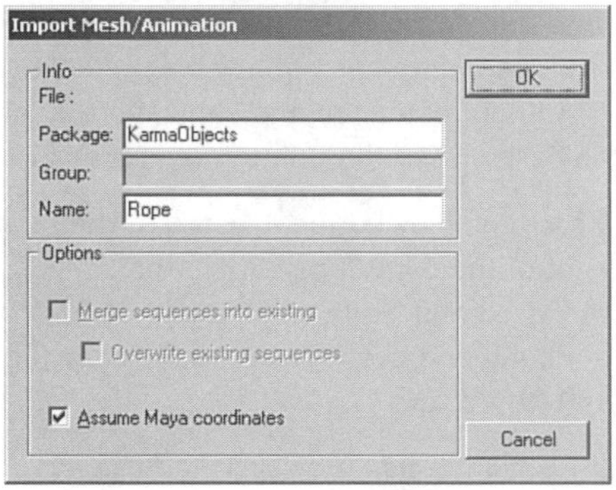

FIGURE 11.38 The Import Mesh/Animation dialog box.

4. Make sure the rope is selected in the Animation browser. Open the Properties window for the Ragdoll you created earlier. Under the Display category, select the `Mesh` property and click Use to display the rope. Rotate and move the rope into position, using **FIGURE 11.39** as a reference.

FIGURE 11.39 Rope moved and rotated into position.

5. Finally, you need to change the KSkeleton of your Ragdoll, which is currently set to Male. Change it to Rope, which is the KSkeleton you created in KAT. The information for this KSkeleton is stored in `SimpleAssets.ka`, which you saved earlier. To get Unreal to see this information, copy `SimpleAssets.ka` into the Unreal directory in the KarmaData folder. That's it! Run the map, and you'll find that the rope is completely dynamic.

END TUTORIAL 11.10

You should now have a good idea of how to use KAT to set up a working Karma Actor for Unreal. However, you typically use KAT for setting up a character to work as a Ragdoll. In theory, there isn't much difference between setting up a character and the simple rope you used in the previous tutorials, but in practice you must take a few important steps. **TUTORIAL 11.11** walks you through the steps required to set up an Unreal character's PSK file within KAT.

TUTORIAL 11.11: Setting Up a Character in KAT

1. Start KAT. Use the KarmaTests workspace you created earlier, and create a new asset. Set the asset name to **`Character`** and select Unreal Skeleton Import in the Type list box. Click OK, select `Character.psk` from the file browser dialog box, and click Open. Leave the settings in the PSK Import Options dialog box at the defaults, and click OK. Double-click the character in the workspace view, and you should see the character in the viewports (see **FIGURE 11.40**).

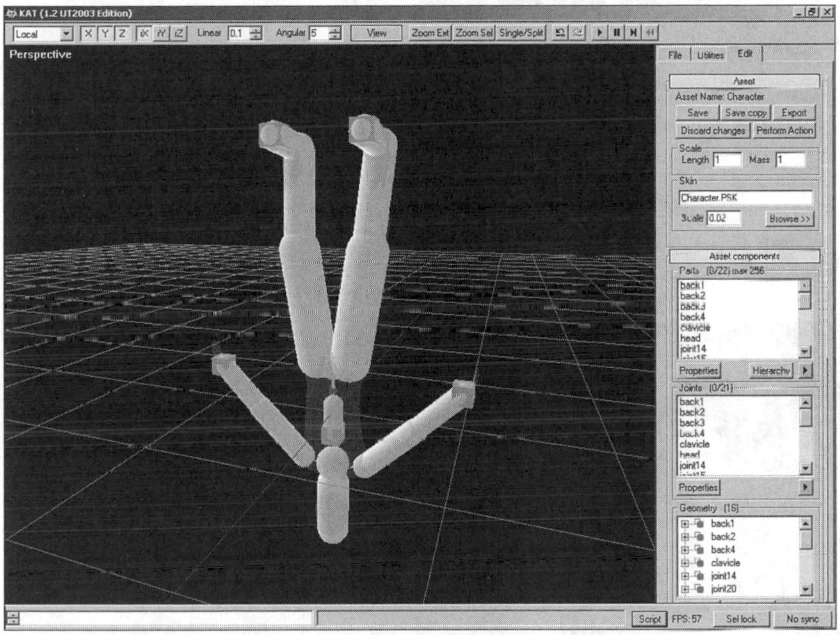

FIGURE 11.40 Character imported into KAT.

2. The first problem is that the character is upside down. Under the Parts list of the Edit tab, click the Hierarchy button to display a hierarchy of the character's bones. Select the topmost bone, named "root," in the hierarchy (see **FIGURE 11.41**).

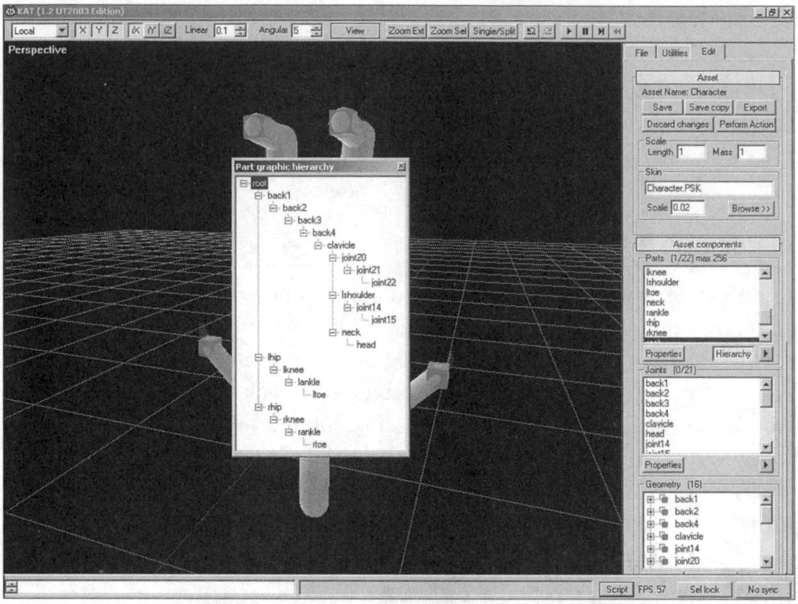

FIGURE 11.41 Root selected in the Part Graphic Hierarchy dialog box.

3. On the control bar, ensure that the rotation constraint is set to rX, and enter **90** in the Angular text box to make the character rotate in 90-degree increments. In the Perspective viewport, hold down the Alt key and drag with the middle mouse button (MMB) to rotate the character upright, as shown in **FIGURE 11.42**.

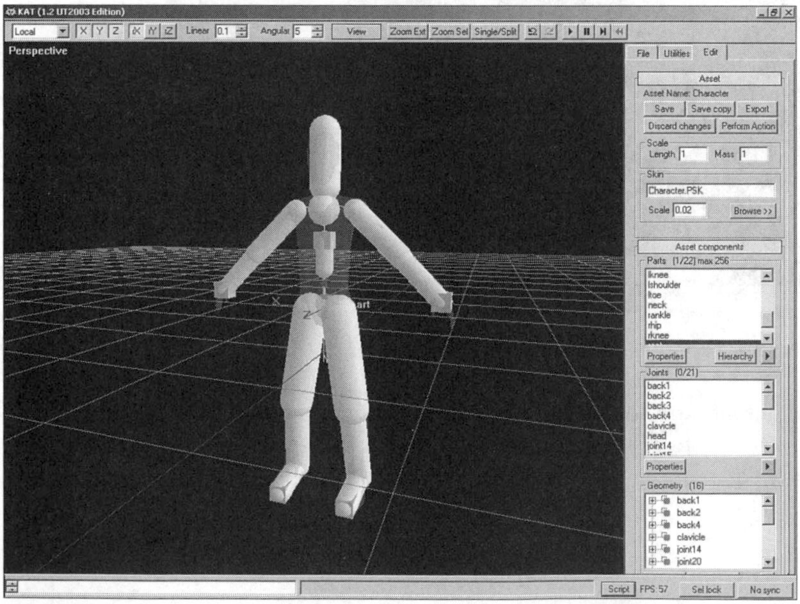

FIGURE 11.42 Character rotated right-side up.

4. Now you need to move the character above the grid. On the control bar, set the translational constraint to the Y-axis by deactivating the X and Z axes. MMB-drag up until the character is above the grid (see **FIGURE 11.43**).

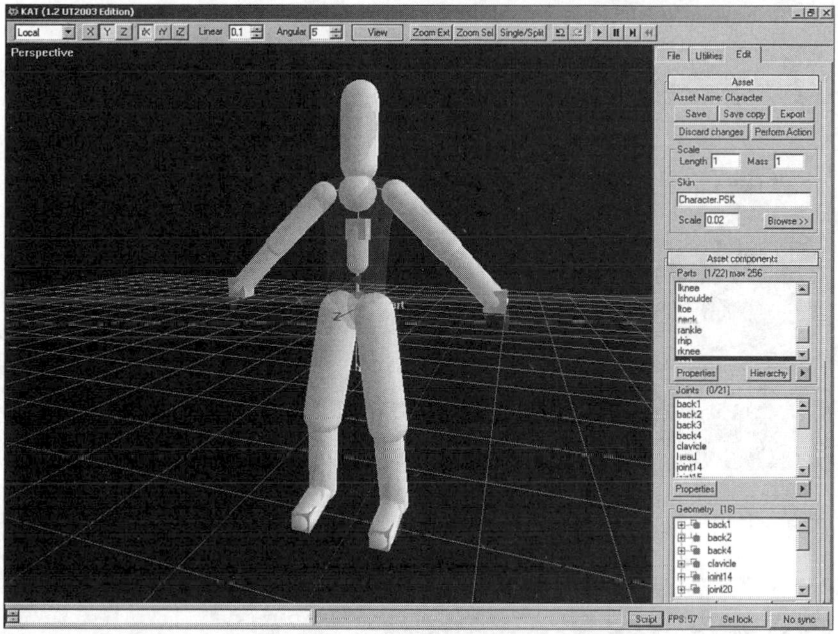

FIGURE 11.43 Character moved above the grid.

5. Now the cleaning begins. First, you don't need the joints at the ends of the arms. Click anywhere in a viewport to deselect everything. Now right-click in a viewport, and choose Mode > Part Hierarchy (with skin) from the menu. **FIGURE 11.44** shows the results. As with the rope, deleting unnecessary parts speeds up calculation.

6. LMB-drag in the Perspective viewport to draw a marquee selection around the areas highlighted in **FIGURE 11.45**. Hold down the Ctrl key to add to the selection. After all areas are selected, press the Delete key.

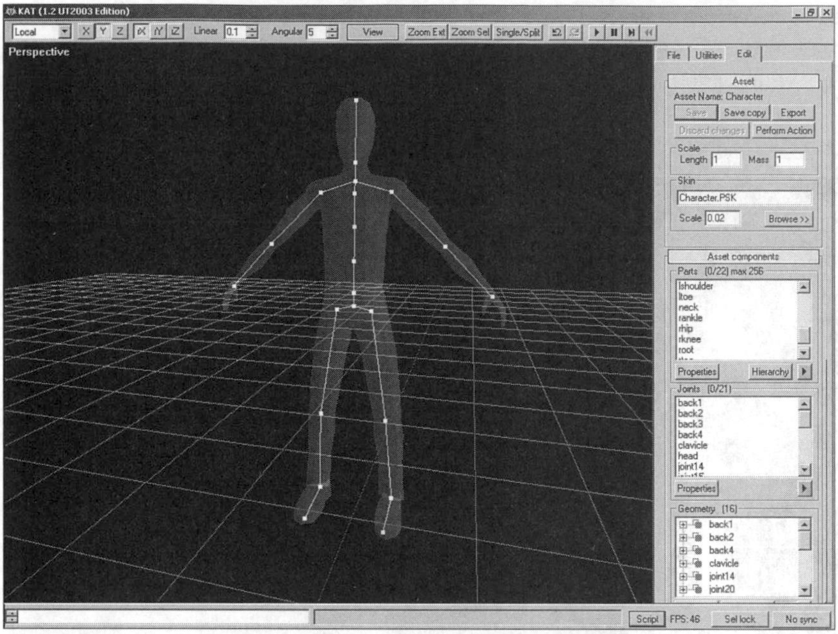

FIGURE 11.44 Character shown in part hierarchy.

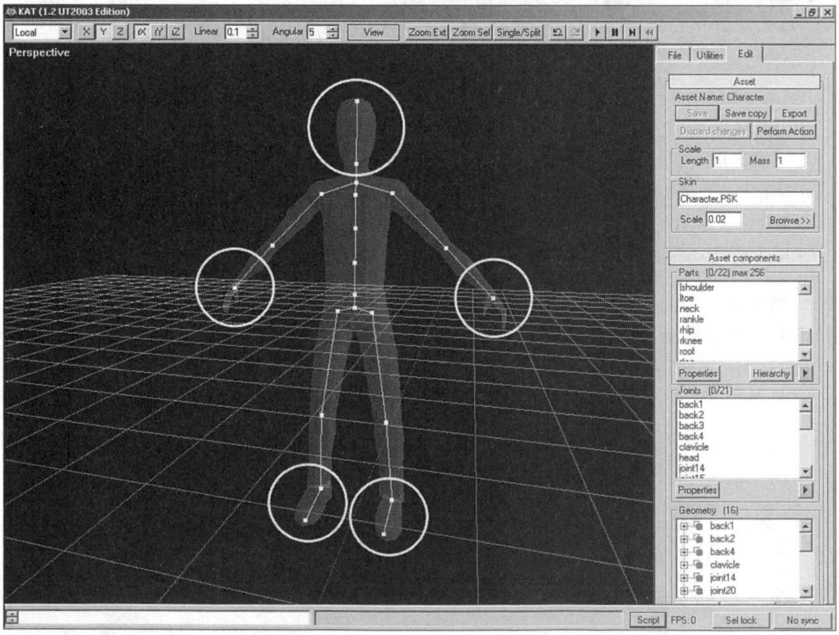

FIGURE 11.45 Highlighted parts to be selected and deleted.

7. Now you need to change some of the character's joints so that it reacts more like a human. Right-click in a viewport, and choose Mode > Joint Editing. Under the Joints list of the Edit tab, click the Properties button. **FIGURES 11.46** and **11.47** show the joint types of each joint.

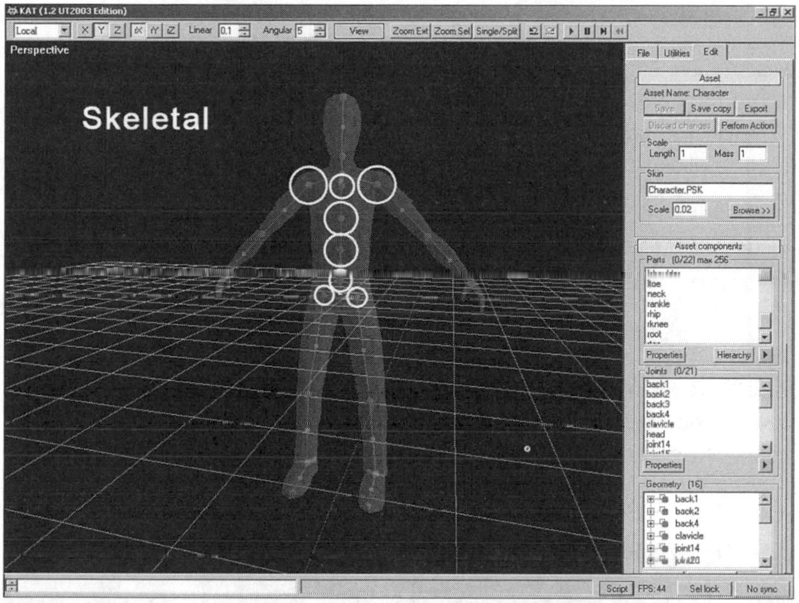

FIGURE 11.46 Skeletal joints.

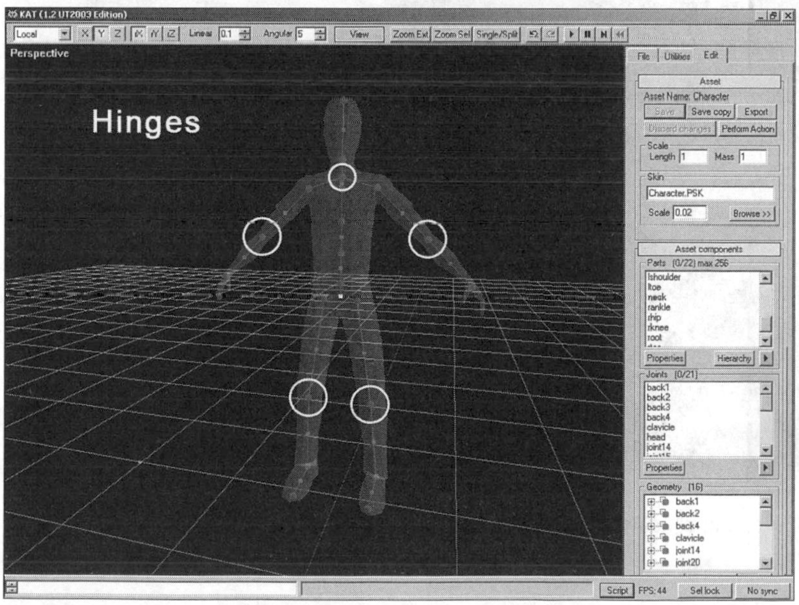

FIGURE 11.47 Hinge joints.

8. For the hinges, enable the Limit Active check box, located under the Properties dialog box opened in step 7, so that you can set the range of motion for that joint. After enabling limits and selecting the joint, an arc is displayed that shows the range of motion. To adjust it, simply click and drag on the red squares at either side of the arc. The Y-axis line (INIT) should always point down the bone. You'll probably need to rotate the joints so that the arcs arch in the correct direction.

9. The skeletal joints also have limits. As with the hinges, you can adjust them by clicking and dragging on the red squares. Because the limit is in the shape of a cone, you can deform the cone however you see fit. If you want to scale the cone down uniformly, hold down the Shift key while clicking and dragging on either red square.

10. Now you need to edit all the collision geometry so that it covers the character well. To do this, right-click in a viewport, and switch to Wireframe Collision mode. At this point, you can select any piece of geometry on the character, right-click, and choose Edit Geometry *name*.

11. This action puts you into another form of Edit mode, in which the Edit tab changes into the Geometry Editor (see **FIGURE 11.48**). In this mode, you can create new geometry, edit old geometry, or delete existing geometry. After you're done, you can click the Finish button to save your changes and exit Edit mode, or you can click the Cancel button to just exit.

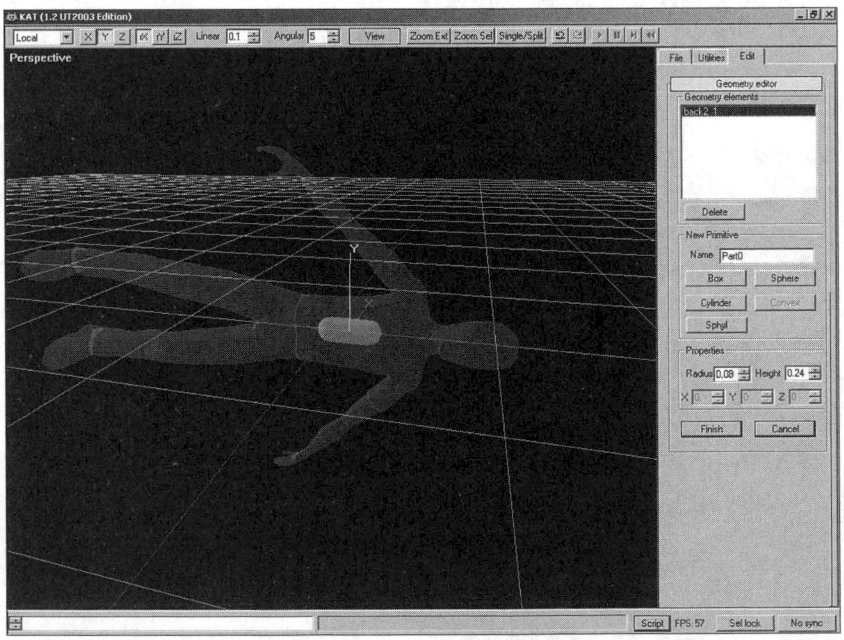

FIGURE 11.48 Edit mode in which you can edit the collision geometry.

12. Edit any collision geometry that doesn't fit correctly to the source geometry. You can have collision geometry penetrate other collision geometry. However, if it does, select the pieces that penetrate each other, right-click, and then choose Disable Collisions from the context menu. Some parts, however, need to collide with other parts for the simulation to work correctly. For instance, the leg should collide with the chest and arms. Therefore, select the parts that should collide with each other, right-click, and choose Enable Collisions from the context menu.

13. The final operation you need to complete is calculating your character's mass. As discussed previously, each part has a mass associated with it. When you first import your character, a mass is automatically calculated for each part. However, because you've made changes to the collision geometry, the mass needs to be recalculated.

At the top of the Edit tab, click the Perform Action button to aooooo a list box containing a variety of actions you can perform. At the bottom is a box describing the currently selected action. To calculate the mass, select Auto-Calculate Mass Distribution in the list box, and click OK. In the Auto-Calculate Mass Properties dialog box, make sure the All Parts option button is selected. Select the Total Mass option button (clear the Density option button), and make sure that 1 is entered in the text box (see **FIGURE 11.49**).

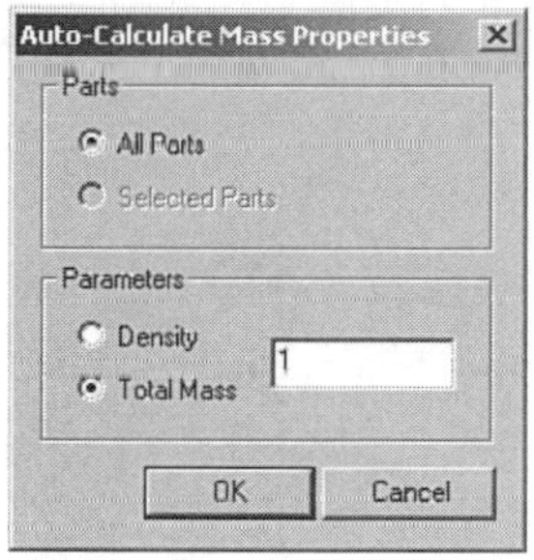

FIGURE 11.49 The Auto-Calculate Mass Properties dialog box.

14. Click the OK button. The mass is then evenly distrubted thoroughout the character's parts. However, there's one small problem. If you run the simulation now, you might see Karma simulation errors because some parts have a mass that's too low. To alleviate this problem, click the Perform Action button again in the Edit tab. This time, select Mass and Inertia Clamping in the list, and click OK. In the Mass Clamping Options dialog box, select the Clamp Mass and Clamp Inertia check boxes. Change Min Clamp Mass to `0.01` and Min Inertia Clamp to `0.001`, as shown in **FIGURE 11.50**.

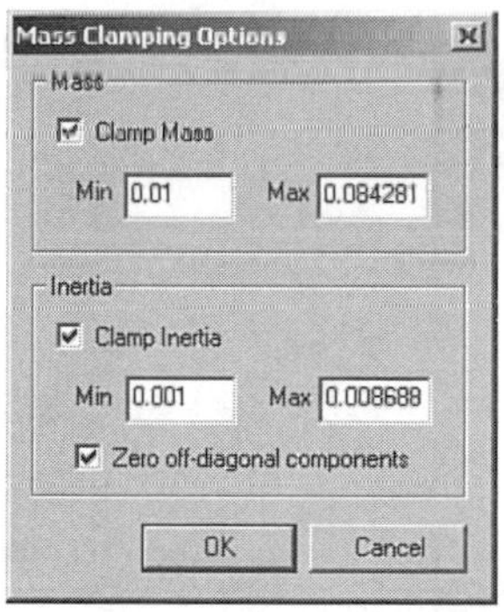

FIGURE 11.50 The Mass Clamping Options dialog box.

15. Click OK. That's it! Your character is now ready to be imported into UnrealEd.

END TUTORIAL 11.11

Summary

In this chapter, you have had a solid grounding in how to create physics-driven assets in your Unreal worlds. You have learned about the theory, creation, and use of Karma Actors and how to create dynamic assets in external packages, including Maya and KAT. Using the techniques covered in this chapter, you can add new layers of dynamic realism to your levels, along with a heightened sense of player interactivity in your level's environment. In the next chapter, you see how to control the "artificially intelligent," computer-controlled players (known as "bots") in your level.

Chapter 12

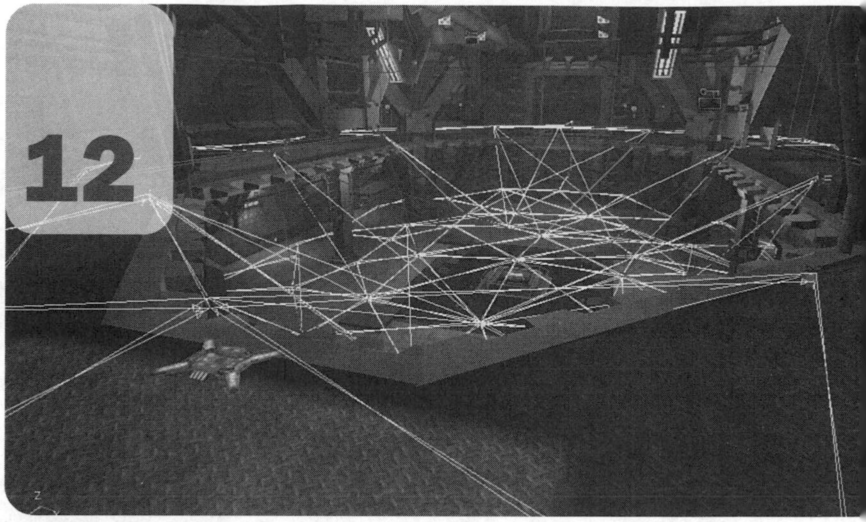

Advanced Bot/ AI Navigation

After creating your map, you'll probably want to play against artificial intelligence (AI) controlled bots. Unfortunately, this process isn't automatic. Bots don't automatically know how to navigate your map or find secretly placed power-ups. To help the bots, you designate points in your map that the bots can follow. If some places can be accessed only by jumping or double jumping, you need to further specify these points so that the bots know how to access those areas as well. After specifying these points throughout the level, UnrealEd uses the points to calculate the best way for bots to navigate between them. In the end, you'll have an interlocking network of lines connecting the various points, as shown in **FIGURE 12.1**. Essentially, this network specifies where a bot can navigate. The goal, of course, is to create enough points so that the entire map is accessible to the bots. Although this task can be tedious for large maps, seeing a bot navigate intelligently through your map is an extremely rewarding experience. This chapter demonstrates how these networks are created, along with some important considerations a level designer must remember when creating navigation points for a level.

FIGURE 12.1 The web of paths generated for bots to navigate.

Basics of Bot Navigation

Making a map in which bots can navigate efficiently requires two steps:

1. Placing the navigation points.
2. Letting UnrealEd generate paths between these points to create the interlocking network on which your bots travel.

> **NOTE**
>
> Because the Unreal Runtime Engine does not come equipped with any sort of bot AI, this chapter is useful only for those who own Unreal Tournament 2003 or Unreal Tournament 2004.

A variety of Actors are used as these navigation points, most of which are a subset of the NavigationPoint Actor. This Actor holds all the information about a certain point on the map: the next point connected to the current point, how to get to this point, and so on. The other Actors you'll be using expand on this foundation to cause bots to perform more specific actions, such as using a jump pad, using the Translocator, and so on.

For basic navigation, the only Actor you need is *PathNode*. If you had an extremely simple, mostly flat map, you would simply need to distribute these Actors throughout the level while making sure each PathNode is roughly 1000 Unreal units apart. Because PlayerStarts are also navigation points, a path is automatically generated to them. Also, every pickup in the level, such as weapons, ammunition, and health pickups, has an associated InventorySpot Actor, which is also a navigation point. Although you don't see InventorySpot Actors, a path is generated between them and other NavigationPoint Actors, nonetheless.

If you have a more complicated level, however, such as one that includes lifts and doors, you need to use special Actors designed to have bots handle these obstacles. Each subsection in this chapter covers the series of Actors associated with helping your bots make decisions about completing certain tasks. **FIGURE 12.2** shows all the Actors you'll be using in this chapter.

After placing all the required Actors to make bots do what you want them to do, you must build the paths. You can do this in UnrealEd by choosing Build > Rebuild AI Paths or by clicking the *Build Paths* button on the toolbar. This process generates paths between all the navigation points in your level. After this process is completed, you can view the paths by right-clicking on a Perspective view's title bar and choosing View > Show Paths from the context menu. After turning this option on, you see lines traveling from navigation point to navigation point. Because these lines are color-coded, you can use the colors as a debugging tool. **TABLE 12.1** describes the meaning of each color.

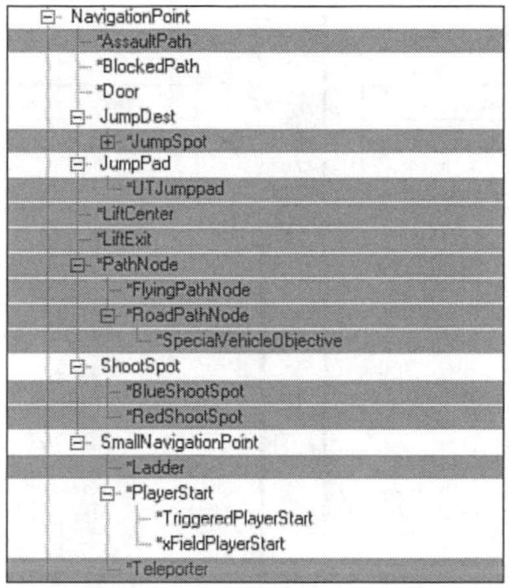

FIGURE 12.2 Hierarchy of Actors used in this chapter.

TABLE 12.1 Bot Path Color-Coding

Color	Meaning
White	This path is very wide and can be traversed by large non-player characters (NPCs). If a path is a main route used by vehicles, the color should be white. Bots prefer these paths because they have lots of room to dodge and strafe.
Green	This path is relatively wide and can be used by large NPCs. For medium-size maps, you want most paths to be green.
Blue	This path is quite narrow and traversable only by smaller NPCs. From a design standpoint, these small, cramped areas usually decrease game flow, so try to avoid them or ensure that wider alternate paths are available.
Purple	This path indicates a lift, teleporter, or jump pad.
Light Purple	This path indicates a ladder.
Yellow	This is a forced path. If you want a path between two navigation points but one isn't generated automatically, you can force a connection by entering the destination navigation point's name in the ForcedPaths array of the source navigation point. You can find this property under the NavigationPoint category. **FIGURE 12.3** shows a forced path.
Red	This is a *proscribed path*. It does exactly the opposite of a forced path: allows you to break the connection between two navigation points. To do this, enter the destination navigation point's name in the `ProscribedPaths` array of the source navigation point. **FIGURE 12.4** shows a proscribed path.

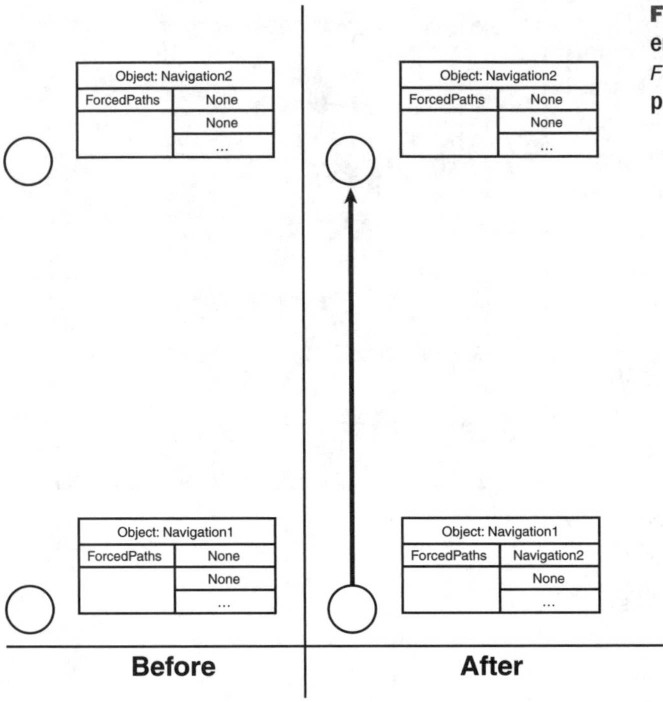

FIGURE 12.3 A forced path. After entering the name Navigation2 in the *ForcedPaths* array of Navigation1, a path is forced between them.

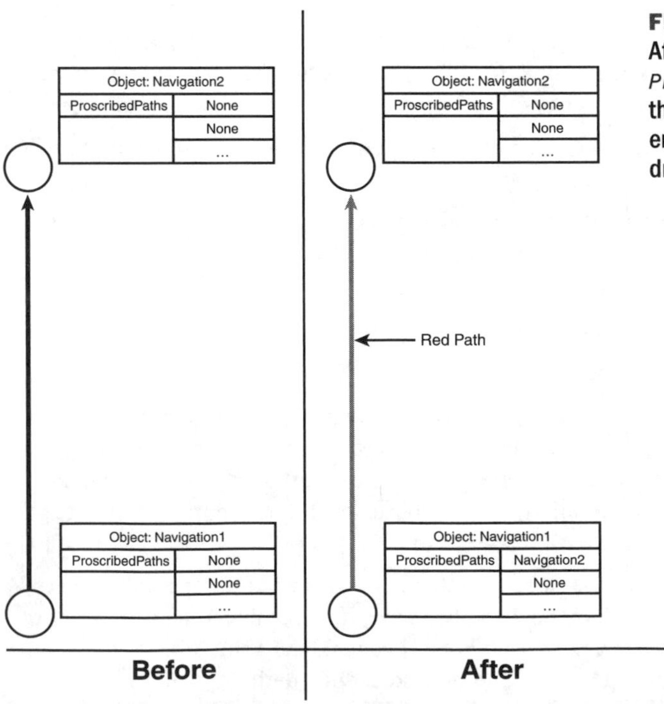

FIGURE 12.4 A proscribed path. After entering Navigation2 in the *ProscribedPaths* array of Navigation1, the original path between them is severed and is replaced with a red path drawn between the nodes.

While creating navigation points for your level, keep in mind that bots prefer white paths and take them if available. If a white path isn't available, the bot chooses green paths, and if all else fails, it chooses blue paths. This isn't *always* the case, however, because many other variables come into play when a bot chooses a path. In **TUTORIAL 12.1**, you see how to create a basic PathNode system to help your bots navigate a simple level.

TUTORIAL 12.1: Basic PathNodes

1. Open `Tutorial12_01_Start.ut2`. This level simply contains a room with a Player Start, a weapon base, and a Super Shield Charger (see **FIGURE 12.5**). If you start the level now and spawn a bot, it would do nothing after spawning, much like a hypnotized monkey. To make this bot actually navigate the level effectively, you must place PathNodes.

FIGURE 12.5 The unpathed map.

2. Right-click between the Player Start and the weapon base, and choose Add Path Node Here from the context menu. **FIGURE 12.6** shows the placement of the PathNode.

FIGURE 12.6 First PathNode placed in the map.

3. Now click the Build Paths button on the toolbar. You won't see anything at this point. However, behind the scenes, UnrealEd has generated paths between the PlayerStart, the PathNode, and the weapon base. To view these paths, right-click on the Perspective viewport toolbar, and choose View > Show Paths. In the Perspective viewport, you then see paths between the three Actors, as shown in **FIGURE 12.7**. If you placed the PathNode in a good position, the path colors are some shade of green. If not, adjust the PathNode by moving it farther away from obstructions, centered between the column and the wall. You have to rebuild paths every time a navigation point's position changes. For slight modifications, you can use the Build Changed Paths button, located next to the Build Paths button on the toolbar.

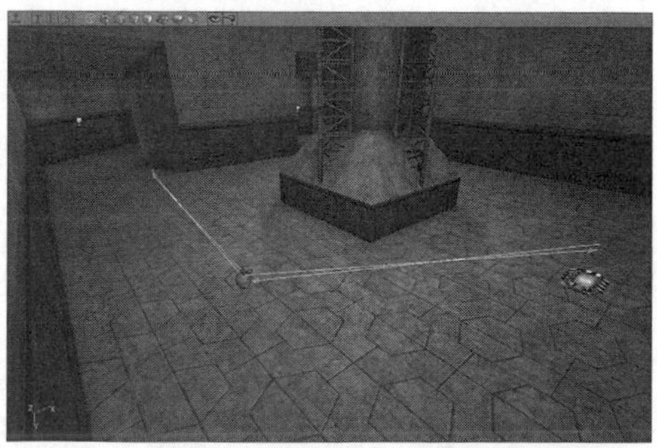

FIGURE 12.7 After rebuilding, paths are drawn between the navigation points.

4. Although the bot reaches the weapon base, it still doesn't have access to the entire map or the Super Shield Charger. You can easily solve this problem by placing a few more PathNodes. The general guideline is to add enough PathNodes so that bots can easily access all playable parts of the level. To avoid adding unnecessary PathNodes, place just enough so that most paths are green, as shown in **FIGURE 12.8**. **FIGURE 12.9** shows all the PathNodes you have added circled in white.

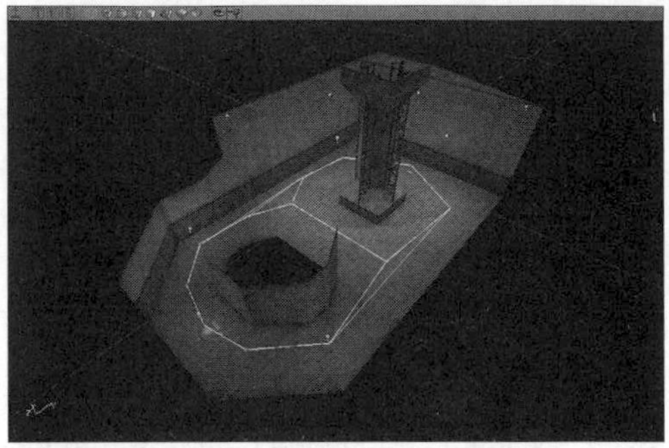

FIGURE 12.8 Fully pathed map.

5. Rebuild the paths and run the map. Bring down the console with the tilde (~) key. Type **ghost** and then press Enter. Put away the console, and move above the level so that you have a good view. Now go to the console and type in **addbots 1**. Put away the console again, and enjoy the fluid motion of the AI-controlled bot. If, however, your bots don't move effectively, it's a clear sign you need to modify the PathNodes' positions or add more if the bots don't reach certain areas of the level.

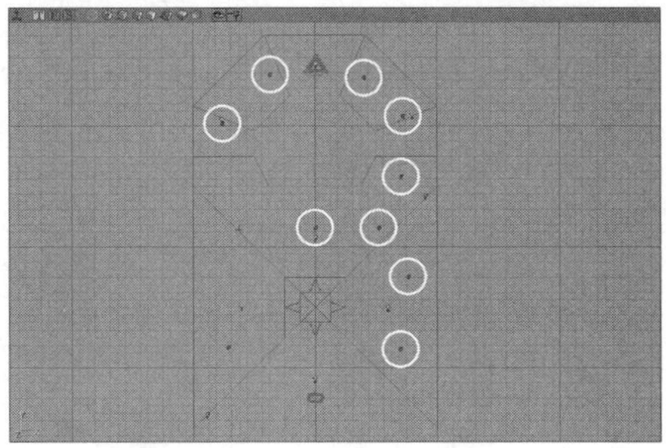

FIGURE 12.9 PathNodes circled in white.

END TUTORIAL 12.1

Aside from placing PathNodes, you can also tweak a variety of properties to make the bots react the way you want them to. **TABLE 12.2** describes these properties and lists their default values.

TABLE 12.2 NavigationPoint Properties

Property	Description	Default
`bAlwaysUseStrafing`	Setting this property to True ensures that bots strafe to this navigation point.	False
`bBlocked`	Setting this property to True makes all paths to this navigation point unusable.	False
`bMakeSourceOnly`	By setting this property to True, paths leave the navigation point, but no paths lead to the navigation point.	False
`bNeverUseStrafing`	Setting this property to True causes the bots to navigate directly to this navigation point without strafing back and forth.	False

TABLE 12.2 Continued

Property	Description	Default
bOneWayPath	This property takes into account the navigation point's rotation. Therefore, to use this property, you must set bDirectional to True in the Advanced category of the Properties window. Setting bOneWayPath to True causes bots to go only in the direction this Actor points. Therefore, after a bot reaches this navigation point, it can continue only in the navigation point's direction.	False
bPropagatesSound	When this property is set to True, this navigation point can be used to carry sound.	True
bVehicleDestination	If this property is set to True, forced paths to this navigation point have maximum width to accommodate vehicles.	False
ExtraCost	This property adds an extra cost to the navigation point. The higher the cost, the less likely it is that a bot uses this navigation point.	0
ForcedPaths	A path is forced from this navigation point to every navigation point specified in this array.	N/A
ProscribedPaths	All paths to navigation points specified in this array are broken.	N/A

Design Considerations

When placing navigation points in your level, you need to understand what bots are "thinking." One of their primary concerns is finding goodies: weapons, power-ups, health packs, and so forth. Therefore, you don't want to place all the goodies in one part of the level, as the bots would simply congregate in that area of the map the entire time. A bot rarely goes down a path unless there's some reason to do so. To alleviate this problem, you need to spread the goodies evenly around the entire level so that bots have a reason to explore the level. If a certain part of your level has no objectives, strategic advantage, or worthy pickups, you might want to remove that part from the level.

Another important consideration is placing less powerful weapons and ammo in the level's main paths. Doing this keeps your bots more focused on the objective and prevents them from spending a lot of time searching for weapons. Conversely, more powerful weapons, such as the Redeemer, should be placed in harder-to-reach areas so that bots don't try to grab the most powerful weapons on a whim. You want to keep bots from hoarding certain items by placing them in out-of-the-way areas. Because a bot attaches a cost to every action it takes, the product of the action has to justify the cost. For example, translocating has an extra cost, so unless translocating provides a much shorter path to the bot's goal or allows access to a valuable item, such as a Super Shield, a bot isn't likely to go that route.

Tools for Debugging

Now that you have a general idea of how to get bots to navigate your levels, it's time to introduce some debugging tools that can help when your bots are misbehaving. The first place to investigate is the Map Check dialog box, which automatically shows you problems with your map. This dialog box pops up just after rebuilding only if there's a serious problem with your path setup. You also have access to a variety of console commands that help you in-game with problems that aren't quite as obvious and take closer examination to solve and remedy.

Diagnosing Problems with the Map Check Dialog Box

Because the Map Check dialog box displays a variety of possible errors that might not be self-explanatory, understanding what each error means and how you can fix it is important. If you double-click on an error, the Perspective viewport snaps to the Actor in question. The following list shows possible errors, their descriptions, and how to fix them.

- *No navigation point associated with this mover!*—This error indicates that a Mover doesn't have a navigation point associated with it. If the Mover is *not* a lift or door, go to its AI category and set the `bNoAIRelevance` property to True. This setting effectively makes bots ignore the Mover. However, if it *is* a lift or door, see the "Lifts" section later in this chapter for how to make bots recognize the Mover and use it properly.
- *Cannot reach [specific point] from this node!*—If the Actor generating the error is too far from the specified point, this error message is generated. Typically, the point is some sort of objective, such as a flag, weapon base, and so on. To fix this problem, simply place a few PathNode Actors between the objective and the complaining Actor.
- *Should be JumpDest for PathNode X!*—This error is usually generated if you can go from PointA to PointB but not from PointB to PointA. For example, PointA might be on a higher plane than PointB, so you have to jump to get to it. To fix this problem, place a JumpSpot at the complaining Actor's location and remember the `Name` property under the Object category. In the properties of PathNodeX, enter the JumpSpot's name in the `ForcedPaths` array. Finally, just delete the originally complaining Actor.
- *Only X PlayerStarts in this level*—If your map is set to play with more than *X* number of players, increase the number of PlayerStarts in the level. You should *always* have more PlayerStarts than the number of bots intended for the level.
- *Path to PathNodeX is very long—add a PathNode in between*—This error message tells you not only the error, but also the solution. Basically, the path between the complaining Actor and PathNodeX is longer than desirable; therefore, just place a PathNode between the two Actors. Make sure the distance between two navigation points isn't too far because a bot won't make certain decisions while traveling down a path. Of course, this delays the bot's reaction. For example, if the distance is too far, a bot continues along the path instead of chasing an opponent going in the opposite direction with his team's flag.

- *JumpDest has no forced paths to it*—This error occurs if a JumpDest doesn't have a PathNode associated with it. As you'll see in the "JumpSpots" section later in this chapter, for every JumpDest, there must be a PathNode with a `ForcedPaths` array containing the JumpDest's name.
- *No forced destination for this jumppad!*—As you'll see in the "Jump Pads and Teleporters" section later in this chapter, a JumpPad Actor must have a destination. The JumpPad's `ForcedPaths` array must contain the name of a PathNode. If it doesn't, you'll get this error message.
- *Navigation point not on valid base, or too close to steep slope*—Every NavigationPoint Actor, except for FlyingPathNode, must be placed on the ground and not too close to a sharp drop-off.
- *No paths from [specific point]*—This error indicates that no paths lead to a specific point. Either delete the navigation point if it's completely unnecessary, or create some PathNodes that lead existing paths to this lonely navigation point.

Console Commands

While in-game, you can type the commands shown in **TABLE 12.3** into the console to debug bot pathing in your level. If you're using the default key bindings, use the tilde key to bring down the console.

TABLE 12.3 Console Commands for Bot Navigation Debugging

Console Command	Description
`ShowDebug`	This console command displays information that varies depending on the current state you're in.
`Viewclass` *class*	This command snaps your view to a certain Actor of the specified class in the level. Repeating the command cycles you through other Actors in the level. For example, if you want to cycle through lights in the level, type `Viewclass light`.
`ReviewJumpSpots`	This command spawns a bot and makes that bot attempt various jump types on every jump spot in your level. Later in this chapter when you learn about jump spots, this command becomes a crucial debugging tool. `ReviewJumpSpots` also takes an optional parameter that enables you to limit the type of jump tested. This parameter can be `Transloc`, `Combo`, `Jump`, or `LowGrav`.
`ShowAI`	This command is similar to `ShowDebug` but shows only information that relates to AI debugging.
`ViewBot`	This command cycles your view through the bots in the level.
`ViewFlag`	This command sets your view to the current flag carrier.

TABLE 12.3 Continued

Console Command	Description
`SoakBots`	This command causes bots to report any errors they encounter. If an error occurs, the game pauses and shows you information about the error. To continue, simply press any key bound to a command.
`RememberSpot`	This command records your current location. Later, you can type `ShowDebug`, and two paths are displayed: a white line drawn directly to the spot you remembered and, if a route can be traced through the navigation points to the remembered spot, green lines representing that route.

Pathing

As mentioned previously, you can use a variety of Actors other than PathNode to give specific orders to bots. These orders can include telling bots to translocate, use an elevator, defend a flag, and so on. The following sections discuss each action and which Actors you can use to direct bots.

Jump Pads and Teleporters

In Chapter 9, "Interactive Elements," you learned how to use jump pads and teleporters in your levels. Because the UTJumpPad and Teleporter Actors are child objects of the NavigationPoint Actor, bots automatically respond accurately to both of them. If an element such as a jump pad or teleporter works for human players, it will work just as well for bots. Therefore, when a bot is trying to calculate the shortest distance between two points in the path network, it takes the paths generated by jump pads and teleporters into account.

Jump Spots

A *jump spot* specifies a location to which a bot can jump. Usually, bots automatically decide the kind of jump to make, whether it's a double jump, translocation, dodge jump, or just a regular jump. As with the PathNode, you simply place a JumpSpot Actor at the location to which you want the bot to jump. If, however, you want the bot to jump back, you have to place another JumpSpot Actor at the other end of the path (see **FIGURE 12.10**).

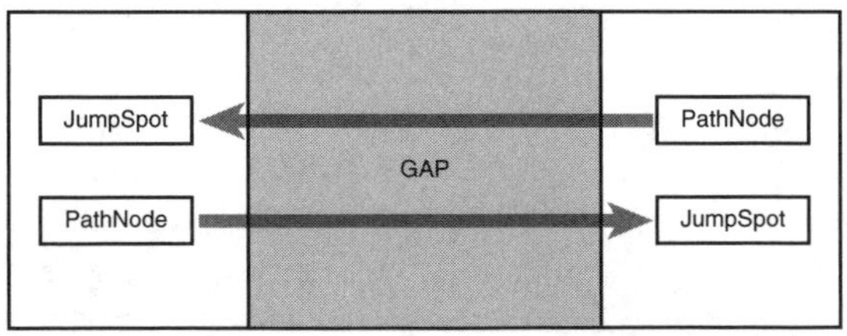

FIGURE 12.10 How you jump from a PathNode to a jump spot and create the same setup to get back.

No more than eight paths can lead to one jump spot. Also, keep in mind that because jump spots are probably hard-to-reach areas, you might need to force a path to the jump spot. To do this, place the JumpSpot Actor's `Name` property in the `ForcePaths` array of any PathNode you want to be the source to the jump spot.

Although bots do decide which kind of jump to make, in special cases you might want them to use other means, such as the Translocator. The properties shown in **TABLE 12.4**, found under the Actor's JumpSpot and JumpDest categories, help tremendously for these special cases.

TABLE 12.4 JumpDest and JumpSpot Properties

Property	Description
JumpDest	
`bForceDoubleJump`	This property causes the bot to double jump no matter what the circumstance.
JumpSpot	
`bDodgeUp`	If you want a bot to dodge jump against a steep incline in order to climb it, you must set this property to True.
`bForceAllowDoubleJumping`	If a bot decides to double jump, this property simply tells the bot to go ahead and double jump instead of performing a final check to see whether the jump will succeed or fail.
`bNeverImpactJump`	If you set this property to True, bots don't try to use the ShieldGun to boost themselves to the jump spot.
`bNoLowGrav`	If this property is set to True, bots don't attempt to get to the jump spot while playing in low gravity.
`bOnlyTranslocator`	Setting this property to True causes bots to translocate only to this jump spot.
`TranslocTargetTag`	If the jump spot is hard to reach, you can specify the tag of some target object in this property, and the bot aims at this target when translocating.
`TranslocZOffset`	If a bot is aiming too high or too low, you can offset its aim with this property. It should be used only to handle minor translocation problems, so adjust with care.

TUTORIAL 12.2 shows how to effectively make a bot jump onto a steep ledge.

TUTORIAL 12.2: Jumping onto a Steep Ledge

1. Open `Tutorial12_02_Start.ut2`. This map has a lower level containing a Player Start and two weapon bases, with PathNodes scattered throughout so that a bot can easily navigate among them. However, the upper level is totally inaccessible to a bot, as shown in **FIGURE 12.11**. If you ran the level now and added a bot, the bot would simply run back and forth on the lower level. To fix this problem, you'll add a JumpSpot Actor near the ledge of the upper level and tell a PathNode to make a path to it.

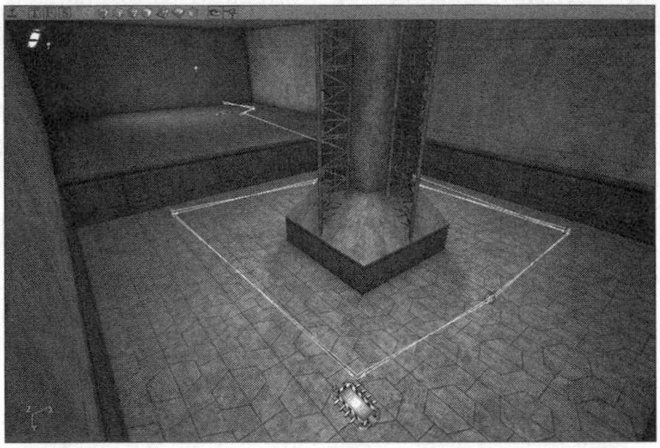

FIGURE 12.11 Initial paths without a way to get to the upper level.

2. Open the Actor Class browser, expand NavigationPoint > JumpDest, and click JumpSpot (see **FIGURE 12.12**).

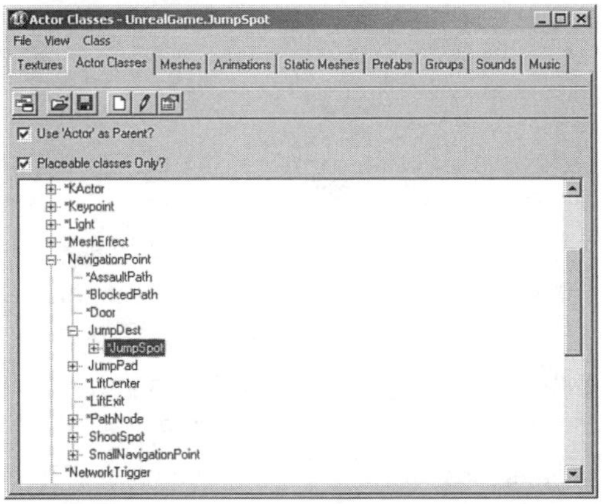

FIGURE 12.12 JumpSpot selected in the Actor Class browser.

3. Right-click near the middle edge of the upper level, and choose Add JumpSpot Here. **FIGURE 12.13** shows the placement of the JumpSpot Actor.

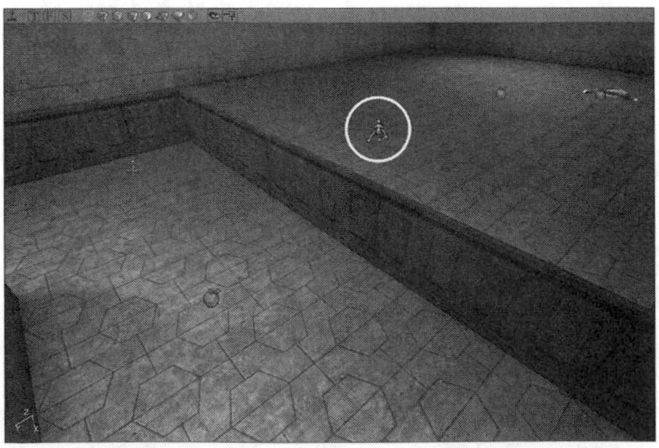

FIGURE 12.13 The JumpSpot Actor (circled in white) has been added to the upper level.

4. Rebuild the paths now. Depending on exactly where you placed the JumpSpot, you'll probably notice that no path is generated from the PathNode to the JumpSpot (see **FIGURE 12.14**). There's a return path from the JumpSpot to the PathNode, but if the bot can't get up to the JumpSpot, the return path is useless.

5. To fix this problem, you force a path from the PathNode to the JumpSpot. In the Properties window for the PathNode, go to the NavigationPoint category. In index [0] of the `ForcedPaths` array, type in the name of the JumpSpot Actor (see **FIGURE 12.15**). You can find this name in the Properties window of the JumpSpot Actor under the Object category.

6. Now if you rebuild the paths, you see a path that goes from the PathNode to the JumpSpot, as shown in **FIGURE 12.16**.

7. If you run the map now, however, the bots rarely, if ever, jump to the JumpSpot; they get there only via the Translocator, if it's available. To fix this problem, open the Properties window for the JumpSpot Actor. Under the JumpSpot category, set the `bForceAllowDoubleJumping` property to True. Run the map again, and notice that the bots are now intelligent enough to jump onto the upper level.

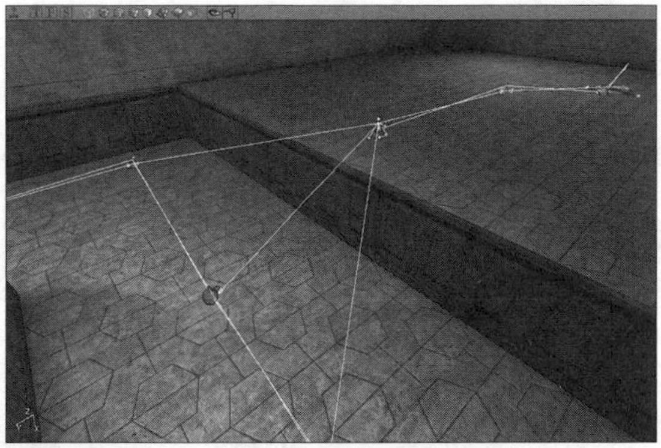

FIGURE 12.14 A path from the JumpSpot to the PathNode, but not one from the PathNode to the JumpSpot.

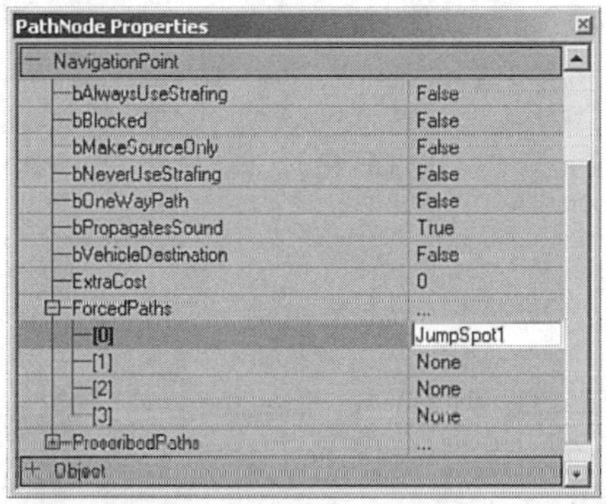

FIGURE 12.15 JumpSpot1 in the *ForcedPaths* array of the PathNode.

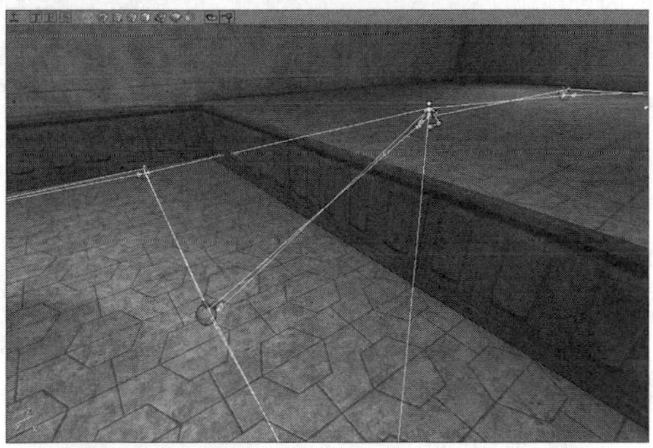

FIGURE 12.16 A path now goes from the PathNode to the JumpSpot.

END TUTORIAL 12.2

TUTORIAL 12.3 shows how you can force a bot to get into areas that are accessible only via the Translocator.

12

TUTORIAL 12.3: Translocating Through a Small Hole

1. Open `Tutorial12_03_Start.ut2`. This map consists of two rooms with a small window that connects them (see **FIGURE 12.17**), so the only way to get into the room is with the Translocator. The bots, of course, have absolutely no way of knowing how to do this, without supreme direction from the level designer. To use the Translocator, you're going to need a target along with a jump spot. However, because you need to provide a way to get out of the room as well, you'll need another jump spot on the other side.

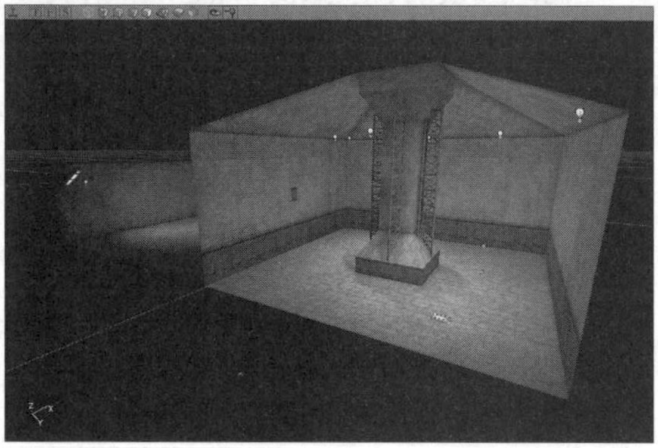

FIGURE 12.17 Map for testing bots with translocators.

2. First, place a JumpSpot Actor next to the wall in the room with the Super Shield Charger. You don't want to place it too far from the wall because it won't work well (see **FIGURE 12.18**).

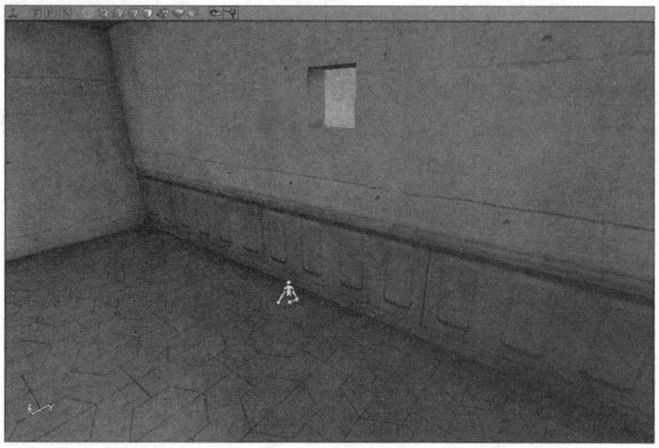

FIGURE 12.18 JumpSpot Actor placed at the base of the window.

3. Open the Actor Class browser, expand Keypoint, and then click LookTarget. Place it in the level so that it rests on the base of the window (see **FIGURE 12.19**). In its Properties window, go to the Events category and set the `Tag` property to `WindowTarget`.
4. In the Properties window for the PathNode nearest the window, go to the NavigationPoint category. Add the JumpSpot Actor's name in the `ForcedPaths` array. Again, you can find the name in the Object category of the JumpSpot Actor.
5. Now you need to tell the bots to aim at the target when using the Translocator. To do this, open the Properties window for the JumpSpot Actor and go to the JumpSpot category. Set the `TranslocTargetTag` property to `WindowTarget`, which you specified earlier in the `Tag` property of the LookTarget. Finally, set the `bOnlyTranslocator` property to True so that bots use the Translocator only to reach that JumpSpot.

6. After rebuilding the paths, run the level. If you don't have Translocators enabled in deathmatch, you can temporarily enable them by typing the following into the console: **open autoplay?translocator=1**. The bot should then translocate into the room. If the bot aims too high or low when shooting the Translocator into the room, simply raise or lower the LookTarget.

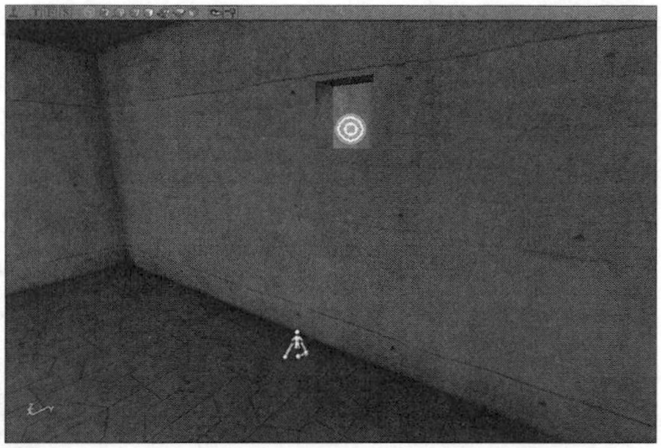

FIGURE 12.19 LookTarget placed at the base of the window

7. You do, however, have one final task. When a bot does get into the room, he's stuck. To fix this problem, you need a jump spot next to the PathNode in the main room and a PathNode next to the originally placed jump spot. Select the JumpSpot Actor and duplicate it. Because the name changes when you duplicate, select the original JumpSpot Actor and move it to the main room next to the PathNode.

8. Now select the PathNode in the main room and duplicate it. Move this new PathNode into the shield room next to the jump spot. All that's left to do is make the new PathNode generate a path to the new jump spot.

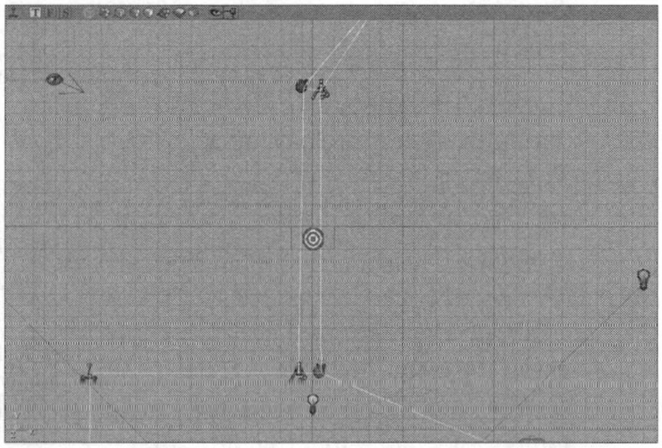

FIGURE 12.20 Final setup for the bots to translocate back and forth through the window.

9. Open the Properties window for the PathNode in the shield room and go to the NavigationPoint category. Change index [0] of the `ForcedPaths` array to the name of the JumpSpot Actor in the main room.

10. Rebuild paths and run the map. Your bots should now jump from room to room intelligently with the Translocator. See **FIGURE 12.20** for the final setup.

END TUTORIAL 12.3

Doors

Doors are Movers that respond to a player's presence and open accordingly. Although these navigation types are easy for human players to use, they require some setup before bots can use them. The main problem you have when working with doors is that a Mover blocks paths much like a static mesh. In this section, you explore various ways around this problem and see some capabilities of the Door navigation type. In **TUTORIAL 12.4**, you see how to have a bot navigate through a door without the use of any special Actors.

TUTORIAL 12.4: Simple Door Setup Without Door Actor

1. Open `Tutorial12_04_Start.ut2`. This map has a simple door in it that responds to player interaction. However, a Mover is blocking the paths (see **FIGURE 12.21**), so bots don't realize they can navigate through the door.
2. Open the Properties window for the door. Under the Collision category, set `bPathColliding` to False.
3. Rebuild the paths, and you'll notice a path generated through the door (see **FIGURE 12.22**). This path, in effect, causes the bot to use the door properly. This fix is a simple one because the door opens fast enough for players to simply walk through. If it took any amount of time to open the door, the current setup would cause the bot to repeatedly knock itself against the door until it finally opened. **TUTORIAL 12.6** examines this special-case scenario.

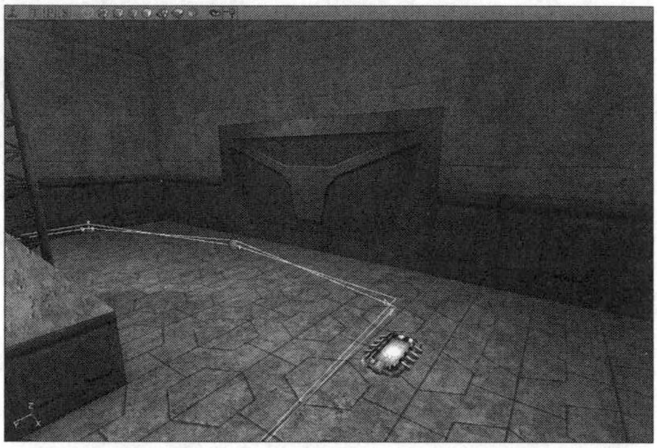

FIGURE 12.21 Door without a path through it.

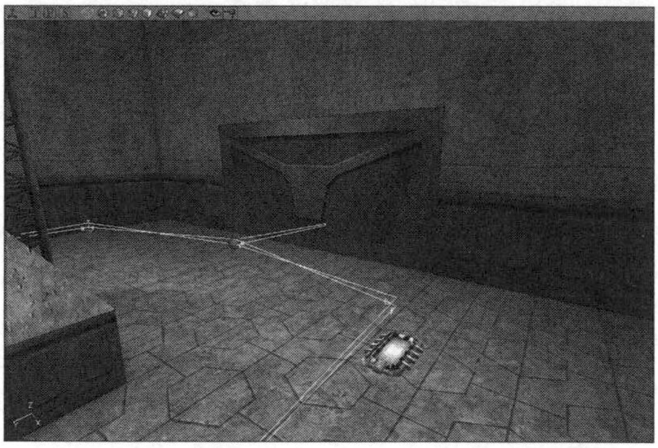

FIGURE 12.22 Door with a path through it.

END TUTORIAL 12.4

Although **TUTORIAL 12.4** shows a viable way of making bots navigate through doors, you can get more control by using the Door Actor. This Actor is a control system that makes sure paths continue through doors without needing to modify the Mover. It also tells the bot what to trigger to open the door. This way, if a button or switch isn't directly next to the door, the bot can still find it and understand that it must hit the button or switch before it can pass through the door. The Door Actor can also completely block the path running through the door when the door is closed. This way, if you have a secret area that's unlocked later during gameplay, the bots don't try to navigate to that secret area until the door is opened.

The bAutoDoor property found under the AI category of a Mover automatically generates a Door Actor when rebuilding paths. This Door Actor is automatically associated with the Mover. However, this automatic association may or may not work depending on your setup. If the automatic setup doesn't function properly, you can tweak it or create the entire setup manually. **TABLE 12.5** describes the pertinent properties of the Door Actor.

TABLE 12.5 Door Actor Properties

Property	Description	Default
bBlockWhenClosed	Setting this property to True causes the door to block any paths running through it while the door is closed. While the door is closed, bots don't attempt to open or navigate through the door. Therefore, if this property is True, the door must be opened via some other trigger or event that happens in-game.	False
bInitiallyClosed	This property should be set to reflect whether or not the Door Mover is open or closed before being triggered. A value of True means the door begins closed; False means it begins with the door open.	True
DoorTag	This property should be set to the Door Mover's Tag property.	None
DoorTrigger	This property should be set to the Tag property of the Actor that triggers the door.	None

You have now seen how to set up an AI-navigable door system by simply adjusting the properties of a Mover. In **TUTORIAL 12.5**, you create a similar setup using the Door Actor.

TUTORIAL 12.5: Simple Door Setup with a Door Actor

1. Open Tutorial12_05_Start.ut2. This map is exactly the same as the one in **TUTORIAL 12.4**, but instead of tinkering with the Mover's collision, you'll add a type of navigation point that handles pathing through the door.
2. Open the Actor Class browser. Under NavigationPoint, select Door. Add a Door Actor in the level and center it on the Mover.
3. Open the Door Properties window, and navigate to the Door category. Set the DoorTag property to BlastDoor, which is the Mover's Tag property. Now set the DoorTrigger property to BlastDoorTrigger, which is the trigger's Tag property.

12

4. Rebuild the paths, and notice that even though the mover's `bPathColliding` property is set to True, paths are generated though the door (see **FIGURE 12.23**). Bots now respond properly to the door.

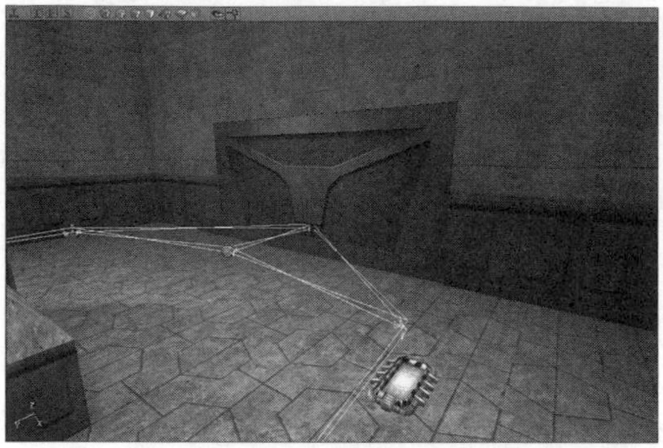

FIGURE 12.23 Using the Door Actor to generate paths through the door.

END TUTORIAL 12.5

TUTORIAL 12.5 demonstrated a simple setup for the Door Actor. In **TUTORIAL 12.6**, you see how to use the Door Actor to drive the behavior of your bots so that they can also use more complex door systems, such as a door that's opened through the use of a separate trigger.

TUTORIAL 12.6: Complex Bot-Door Interaction

1. Open `Tutorial12_06_Start.ut2`. In this map, you must access a trigger, which is away from the door, and then wait for the door to finish opening before walking through it. As in **TUTORIAL 12.5**, you'll use a Door Actor to accomplish this feat.
2. Add a Door Actor into the center of the Mover. In the Properties window for the Door, set the `DoorTag` property to `BlastDoor` and the `DoorTrigger` property to `BlastDoorTrigger`. Although the setup is the same as in **TUTORIAL 12.5**, this map demonstrates the power of the Door Actor in enabling bots to deal with more complicated situations.
3. Finally, rebuild the paths, verify that the paths do, in fact, run through the door, and then test the map. You'll notice that the bots act intelligently by going to the trigger, waiting for the door to open, and then traveling through it.

END TUTORIAL 12.6

Lifts

As with most interactive elements, to get bots to work with lifts, you must create a few extra Actors and set a few properties. The two Actors specific to lifts are LiftCenter and LiftExit. LiftCenter is used to specify where bots should stand while on the lift. **TABLES 12.6** and **12.7** show the pertinent properties for these Actors.

TABLE 12.6 LiftCenter Properties

Property	Description
`LiftTag`	Set this property to the `Tag` of the Mover being used as the lift.
`LiftTrigger`	Set this property to the `Tag` of the trigger that triggers the lift. This is, of course, necessary only when a trigger is controlling the lift.

LiftExits should be placed at every location where the bot can get on or off the lift.

TABLE 12.7 LiftExit Properties

Property	Description
`LiftTag`	Set this property to the Tag property of the Mover being used as the lift.
`SuggestedKeyFrame`	This property associates a certain keyframe with a keyframe of the Mover. Therefore, the bot uses this LiftExit when the Mover is at the specified keyframe. However, this property is merely suggestive and isn't always necessary.

When creating the actual Mover for the lift, often setting the Mover's `InitialState` to `StandOpenTimed` is a good practice. This setting ensures that the Mover waits until the player is actually on the lift before advancing to another keyframe. With `BumpOpenTimed`, the Mover starts moving as soon as the player touches it, even though the player might not be completely on the lift. Also, setting `InitialState` to `BumpOpenTimed` is required to make non-triggered lifts usable by bots. In **TUTORIAL 12.7**, you create a lift that can be used by bots in your level.

TUTORIAL 12.7: Creating a Bot-Navigable Lift

1. Open `Tutorial12_07_Start.ut2`. This map has one lift that gets you from the lower level to the upper level.

2. Open the Actor Class browser, expand NavigationPoint, and click LiftCenter.

3. Somewhere on the lower level, right-click near the lift and choose Add LiftCenter Here. Move this Actor to the center of the lift, as shown in **FIGURE 12.24**.

FIGURE 12.24 LiftCenter placed on the base of the lift.

4. In the Properties window for the LiftCenter, go to the LiftCenter category. Change the `LiftTag` property to `LiftMover`, which is the `Tag` property of the Lift Mover.
5. Open the Actor Class browser, expand NavigationPoint, and click LiftExit.
6. Right-click in front of the lift, and choose Add LiftExit Here. At the exit from the lift on the upper level, right-click and choose Add LiftExit Here. **FIGURE 12.25** shows the placement of these LiftExits.

FIGURE 12.25 LiftExits placed on the upper and lower levels.

7. In the Properties window for the LiftExit on the lower level, go to the LiftExit category. Change the `LiftTag` property to `LiftMover` and the `SuggestedKeyFrame` property to 0. Please note, however, that with such a simple two-keyframe lift, this property isn't crucial, but it's always a good practice to associate the correct keyframe with the correct exit.
8. In the Properties window for the LiftExit on the upper level, go to the LiftExit category and set `LiftTag` to `LiftMover` and change `SuggestedKeyFrame` to 1.

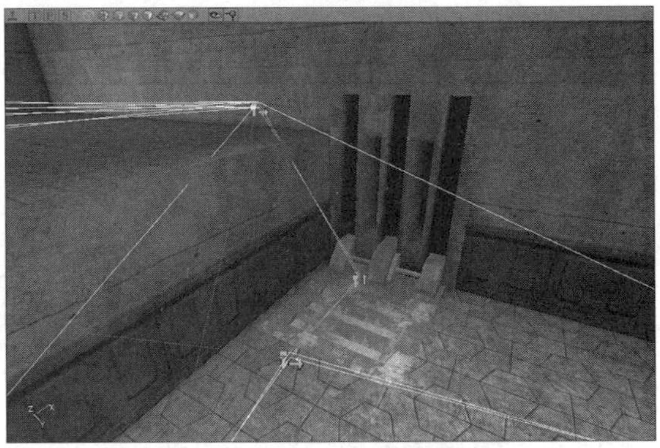

FIGURE 12.26 The bot paths are now running between the upper and lower levels.

9. Rebuild paths and run the map. If the bots are ignoring the lift, you might need to increase their difficulty level. Generally, skill levels of Adept or higher work. **FIGURE 12.26** shows the bot paths in place.

END TUTORIAL 12.7

Ladders

As discussed in Chapter 9, "Interactive Elements," ladders are created with a `LadderVolume`. This volume, in and of itself, is enough for a player to climb up a ladder. For bots, however, you need navigation points. The `LadderVolume` has the `bAutoPath` property, which by default is set to True. When you rebuild paths with this setting, one AutoLadder Actor is placed on the top of the `LadderVolume` and one AutoLadder Actor approximately 40 units from the bottom. You must, however, rotate these two Actors to point in the opposite direction as the `LadderVolume`.

Because the one AutoLadder Actor is placed at the top of the `LadderVolume`, you should make sure the `LadderVolume` extends about 40 units above the ledge you're trying to reach with the ladder.

If you're having trouble with the automatically generated navigation points, simply set `bAutoPath` to False and manually place Ladder Actors at the top and bottom of the `LadderVolume`. This Actor, which works much like any other navigation point, can be found under NavigationPoint > SmallNavigationPoint in the Actor Class browser.

Advanced Pathing

Using everything discussed to this point, you can make bots navigate everywhere in a level. They can grab power-ups, weapons, and everything else you've placed in a level. However, in Capture the Flag (CTF) or Bombing Run gametypes, you might want the bots to act more intelligently when it comes to choosing a path. For example, you might have multiple paths to a flag or other objective, and you want bots to favor one path over the other. And what if you want to specify certain points as defense points and others as sniping points? You couldn't do all this with the basic navigation points; you need to introduce a few new Actors, covered in detail in the following sections.

AssaultPaths

An *AssaultPath*, or a series of AssaultPaths, defines a path to an objective. Each path you create can be assigned a priority so that bots can choose one path more often than another. You can even define paths as attacking paths or returning paths so that bots use one path for attacking and another for returning to their own base when completing an objective. See the diagram in **FIGURE 12.27** as an example.

There are two paths to get from the Red base to the Blue base: Path A, which is on the lower level, and Path B, which is on the upper level. By simply placing one AssaultPath Actor on each path, you can control how you want those paths to be used. For example, you could make the bot attack via Path B and return via Path A. To do this, you would set `bReturnOnly` of AssaultPath 1 to True and `bNoReturn` of AssaultPath 2 to True. **TUTORIAL 12.8** shows how to set these paths up.

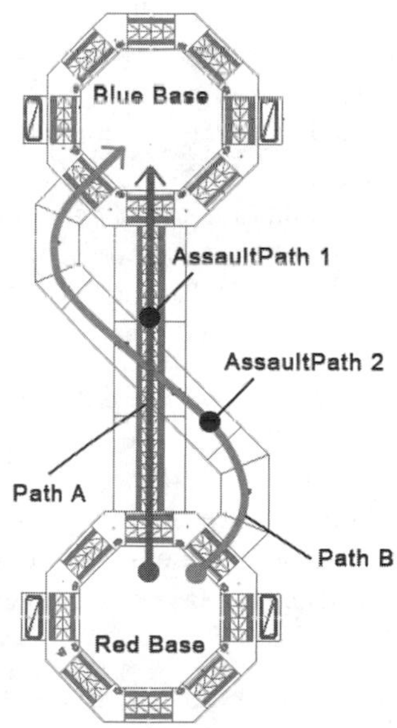

FIGURE 12.27 A simple AssaultPath diagram.

TUTORIAL 12.8: Using AssaultPaths

1. Open Tutorial12_08_Start.ut2. This map is a CTF map with two separate pathways leading to each base (see **FIGURE 12.28**). The goal is to make Red team bots attack from the upper hallway and return through the lower hallway.

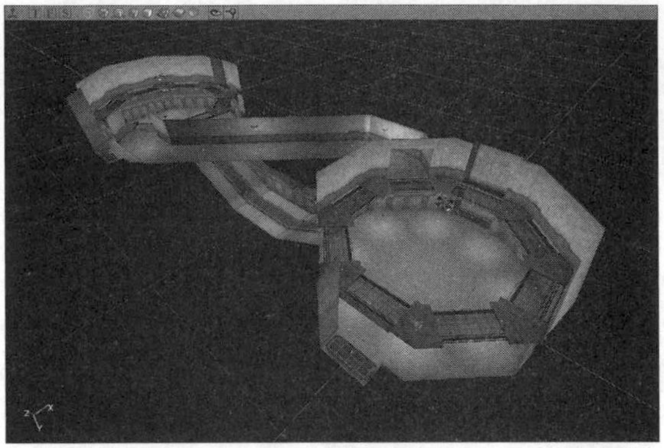

FIGURE 12.28 The map used for this tutorial.

2. Open the Actor Class browser, expand NavigationPoint, and click AssaultPath.
3. Place this AssaultPath along the upper hallway near the Shield Charger (see **FIGURE 12.29**).

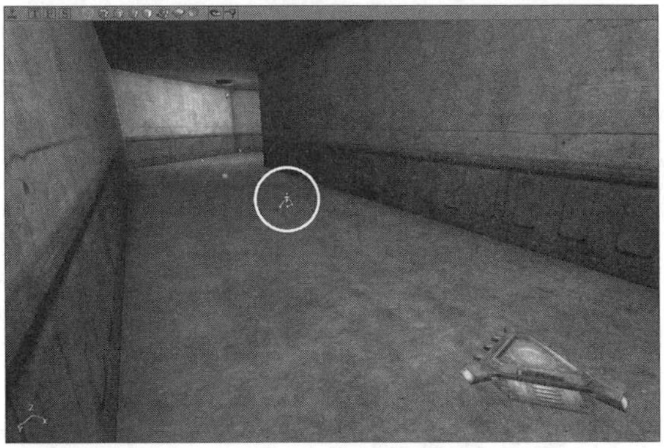

FIGURE 12.29 AssaultPath placed after the Shield Charger in the upper hallway.

4. Place another AssaultPath along the lower walkway, as shown in **FIGURE 12.30**.

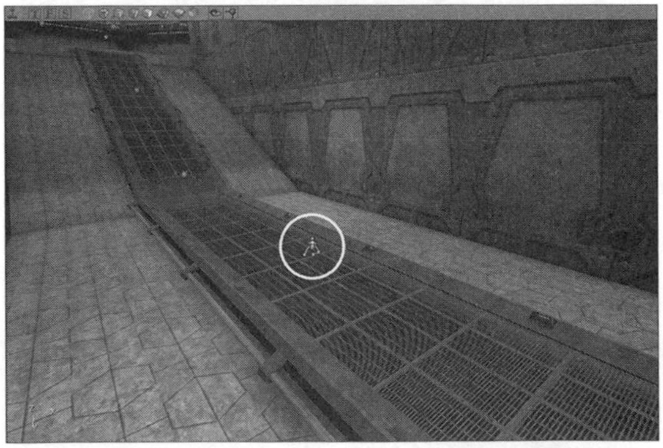

FIGURE 12.30 AssaultPath placed along the lower walkway.

5. In the Properties window for the AssaultPath in the upper hallway, set `PathTag` index [0] to `AttackPath`. Although setting the `PathTag` property isn't entirely necessary, using `PathTag` to describe what the assault points are for is a good practice. So that Red bots use this AssaultPath, set `ObjectiveTag` to `xBlueFlagBase`, which is the `Tag` property of the flag base. Also, set `bNoReturn` to True.
6. In the Properties window for the AssaultPath in the lower walkway, set `PathTag` index [0] to `ReturnPath`. As with the previous AssaultPath, set `ObjectiveTag` to `xBlueFlagBase` and `bReturnOnly` to True.
7. Rebuild the paths, and test your map. The bots should now attack according to your AssaultPaths.

END TUTORIAL 12.8

You can also set up your level so that after a bot reaches the end of one AssaultPath, he has to go on to another one. This setup is specified in the `Position` property. In the example shown previously in **FIGURE 12.27**, you could set AssaultPath 1's `Position` to 0 and AssaultPath 2's `Position` to 1. This setup causes a bot to go to AssaultPath 1 and then AssaultPath 2 before finally going to the Blue base.

When creating more complicated scenarios, however, you must also use the `PathTag` property. Until now, the `PathTag` property has been used only to give a certain path a name. Consider the diagram shown in **FIGURE 12.31** as an example.

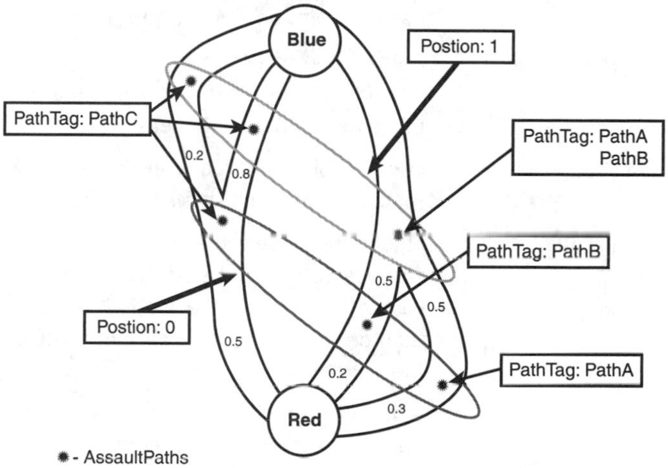

FIGURE 12.31 A more complicated AssaultPath example.

To get from the Red base to the Blue base, the bot can choose from three separate paths. You want a 50% chance the bot will take the left route, so simply give the AssaultPath on the left a priority of 0.5. The same idea goes for the center and right paths: Set them to 0.3 and 0.2 so that the total adds up to 1. After the bot chooses one of the paths and arrives at the AssaultPath, he has to choose which AssaultPath he goes to next. The first criteria is which AssaultPaths accept him. All other AssaultPaths that have the current AssaultPath's `PathTag` property in their `PathTag` array will accept the bot. If this criteria were not in place, nothing would stop a bot from going down the left path, reaching the AssaultPath, and then going all the way back to the AssaultPath on the rightmost side. This is why the AssaultPath on the rightmost intersection has both PathA and PathB in its `PathTag` property. After that criteria is met, the bot decides which AssaultPath to go down based on the priority. Just be sure the priorities for each set of paths add up to 1. **TABLE 12.8** shows the pertinent properties for the AssaultPath Actor.

TABLE 12.8 AssaultPath Actor Properties

Property	Description	Default
`bEnabled`	Setting this property to False causes bots to ignore the AssaultPath. You can, however, toggle this property by triggering it.	True
`bNoGrouping`	When this property is set to True, bots gather reinforcements before moving on.	False

TABLE 12.8 Continued

Property	Description	Default
`bNoReturn`	When this property is set to True, bots use this AssaultPath only when attacking.	False
`bReturnOnly`	When this property is set to True, bots use this assault point only when returning.	False
`ObjectiveTag`	Bots whose objective is the same as this property use this AssaultPath. The setting is usually `FlagBase` or `BombDelivery`.	None
`PathTag`	The four slots available are used to specify which routes run through this AssaultPath.	N/A
`Position`	This property sets the position of the AssaultPath. The position should start from 0 and increase as you get closer to the objective. When there's more than one path, the next path is selected based on the priority.	0
`Priority`	When using multiple paths, this property is used to specify the probability of going down certain paths. Divide the positions that go along the same path so that the priorities add up to 1.	1.0

Defense Points and Sniping Points

In the Deathmatch gametype, a *defense point* simply specifies a good place for bots to stay to get a good view of other players. These points can also be used as *sniping points*—positions where a bot is likely to try to attack at long range using a sniper rifle. In objective-based games, however, a defense point tells bots where to camp to protect an objective from the opposing team. The Actor that defines defense points is the UnrealScriptedSequence Actor found under Keypoint > AIScript > ScriptedSequence. Because this Actor is not a child object of the NavigationPoint Actor, paths aren't directly connected to this Actor. This means you'll need to place the UnrealScriptedSequence Actor within view of a path. To associate this Actor with an objective, the UnrealScriptedSequence Actor's `Tag` property must be the same as the `DefenseScriptTags` property, found under the GameObjective category of the objective.

Because the UnrealScriptedSequence Actor is such a multipurpose Actor, you need to set only a few properties when using it as a defense or sniping point. **TABLE 12.9** is a list of the important properties under the UnrealScriptedSequence category.

TABLE 12.9 Defense Point Properties of the UnrealScriptedSequence Actor

Property	Description	Default
`bNotInVehicle`	If this property is set to True, bots ignore this defense point if they're in a vehicle.	False
`bRoamingScript`	If this property is set to True, after a bot reaches this point, it's free to roam around the point while it's defending.	False
`bSniping`	When this property is set to True, bots use this point as a sniping point.	False
`Priority`	If multiple defense points are associated with an objective, this property enables you to set weighting for a certain point so that bots use one more often than another.	0
`WeaponPreference`	This property specifies the weapon the bot should use while defending at this point. Most commonly used to ensure that bots are using the sniper rifle when `bSniping` is set to True.	None

In **TUTORIAL 12.9**, you see how to place an UnrealScriptedSequence Actor in your level and use it as a way to designate defense points for objectives. The bots in your level use these points as prime locations for objective defense.

TUTORIAL 12.9: Creating Defense Points

1. Open `Tutorial12_09_Start.ut2`. In this map, which is the same as Tutorial 12.8's map with only slight modifications, you'll create a sniping point in the Blue base.
2. Open the Actor Class browser, and select UnrealScriptedSequence.
3. Add an UnrealScriptedSequence Actor to the Blue base just in front of the weapon base that spawns the sniper rifle. Now rotate the Actor to point toward the area being defended.

> **NOTE**
>
> This is the only weapon base in the level.

4. Open the Properties window of the UnrealScriptedSequence Actor, go to the Events category, and set the `Tag` property to `DefendBlueFlag`, the `bSniping` property to True, and the `WeaponPreference` property to `SniperRifle`.
5. Run the map.

END TUTORIAL 12.9

Vehicle Navigation

To get vehicles to navigate throughout a level, you need to add HoverPathNodes, RoadPathNodes, or FlyingPathNodes. You place RoadPathNodes in your map much like regular PathNodes; however, unlike regular PathNodes, you must space them out more and make sure that all paths are white. Also unlike PathNodes, you don't want to create a web of road paths. Instead, you want to ensure that each road follows a single line and branches only when necessary, depending on the terrain. If paths start to connect roads that are separate, you can slowly lower the value of the `MaxRoadDist` property of the offending RoadPathNode until it connects only to the nodes you want.

When only a hovering vehicle, such as the Manta, can navigate over a certain area, place a HoverPathNode in that location instead of a RoadPathNode. This way, only hovering vehicles try to use these navigation points.

FlyingPathNodes define the area and routes that bots can use when using flying vehicles such as the Raptor. Paths are generated not only between FlyingPathNodes, but also to any navigation points on the ground. With this in mind, you should always have some FlyingPathNodes that have a view of nearby objectives. Because flying vehicles should be able to navigate most of the level freely, use the same web technique as with normal PathNodes, in which every FlyingPathNode connects to all FlyingPathNodes around it. The area that a FlyingPathNode controls is defined by its `CollisionHeight` and `CollisionRadius` properties. Therefore, when debugging FlyingPathNodes, activating the Radii view in the viewport you're working in is helpful.

Summary

In this chapter, you have learned a variety of methods for making your computer-controlled opponents more intelligent in your levels. This chapter has covered basic bot pathing as well as how to make your bots navigate specific obstacles, including areas that can be reached only by jumping, double jumping, and translocating. You have also learned how to make your bots use interactive elements, such as lifts and triggerable doors, in your levels. In addition, you have seen how to use and control AssaultPaths and how to set them up so that your bots make more combat-conscious decisions on your level's battlefield. This chapter has also covered points you must consider when implementing vehicles in your level. At this point, you should be able to confidently control bots' actions in almost any situation within your level. Remember that bot pathing, although not exactly difficult, is another aspect of proper game design that requires careful planning and consideration to achieve the best results. Make sure you practice these skills so that you become accustomed to how artificially intelligent characters interact in your levels.

Chapter 13

Matinee: Creating Custom Cinematics

This chapter introduces you to Matinee, an UnrealEd tool that enables you to easily create in-game cinematic sequences and fly-throughs or even animate Actors in your levels (see the interface in **FIGURE 13.1**). The chapter begins with a discussion of *machinima*, a new generic term used to describe the creation of real-time movies with a gaming engine. From there, you take a close look at how to create Matinee sequences and explore the Scene Manager Actor and the components it manages: Actions and Sub Actions. Next, you'll set up a simple Matinee sequence of your own in which your viewport camera is instructed to move from point to point. With this in place, you can view the sequence in action through the built-in Matinee Preview window. When you're satisfied with the camera movement, you can move on to learn how to trigger this sequence within the game.

With a general understanding of how Matinee works, you then move into a series of more complex examples that involve such things as creating camera cuts, manipulating camera orientation, moving Actors along paths, and adding text into your movies. By the end of this chapter, you'll have a solid foundation for the methods required to develop your own Matinee cutscenes or complete machinima films.

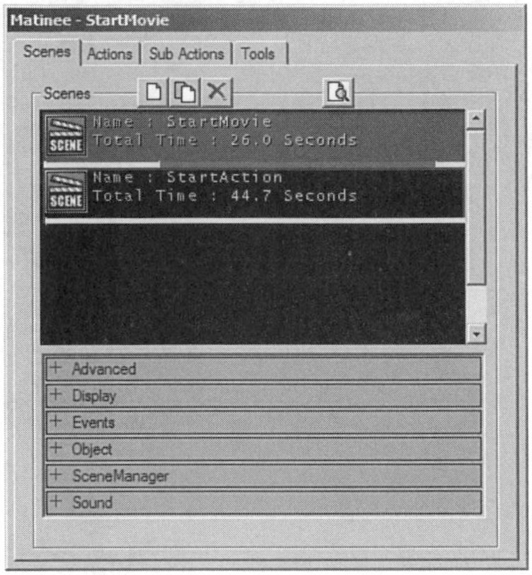

FIGURE 13.1 The Matinee interface.

Introduction to the World of Machinima

In today's gaming world, in-game animated movies have become very popular. You can find them in many games. They can further a game's plot, enhance the action, or teach you more about the characters in a game. In fact, many games begin by playing some sort of movie designed to give players pertinent information. This information can be a history of the game's story line, a preview of the gameplay, an introduction to the main character, or anything that would promote the game or inform the player.

Until only a few years ago, these movies, often referred to as *cutscenes*, were created in external 3D animation applications, such as 3ds max or Maya. The final animation was then rendered into a movie, and the game was set to play these movies at specific points throughout gameplay.

As gaming engines evolved and their graphical capabilities were enhanced, real-time cutscenes became possible. Game studios were finally able to develop their movies with the game engine itself, instead of having to render them from another application. Level designers could develop the "set" (the level), add in the "actors" (characters), and script a series of events to take place. These events could be anything—dialogue between characters, moving objects, sound effects or music, explosions, or any other cinematic component or effect needed for the movie.

As the ability to use the game engine for cinematic cutscenes continued to improve, tools were created to ease the process of developing real-time movies. These tools became more robust and easier to use, allowing more people to get involved in the process of creating their own mini-movies. From this came the birth of *machinima*, the process of filmmaking within a computer-generated, real-time 3D environment. Today, machinima is quickly becoming a popular method for creating animated movies and shorts. There's even an annual Machinima Film Festival where filmmakers compete for awards in several film-related categories.

With the Runtime Engine or Unreal Tournament 2004, machinima movie development has been made easy by creating Matinee sequences. The Matinee tool has been developed and implemented into UnrealEd to make the process of creating these sequences fast, efficient, and simple. The next section covers the Matinee system and discusses how it can be used to create these sequences.

Overview of the Matinee System

Before you begin looking at the Matinee interface in more depth, take a minute to read about the elements involved in a Matinee sequence. At the heart of the system lies the Scene Manager Actor. This Actor is necessary for creating a Matinee sequence. Although the Actor can be created through the Actor Class browser, generating it in the Matinee interface is notably easier. Finding multiple Scene Managers used throughout a scene is not uncommon. One manager might be responsible for controlling the whereabouts of the viewport camera (the camera through which you play the game), and the other manager might handle moving an Actor.

As its name implies, the Scene Manager is a management system. It manages a series of Actions and gives you control over how the sequence is carried out. Depending on the Scene Manager's configuration, these Actions enable you to control the movement of the viewport camera or another Actor in the level. If you need to control both, you need two Scene Managers in your map.

Actions define where a camera or Actor needs to be at a specific time. Location and orientation are determined by *interpolation points,* which are associated with each Action. The time between two Actions is the amount of time the system takes to move the Actor from one interpolation point to another or the amount of time an Actor pauses at a given point.

Each Action can have a list of *Sub Actions*, which give you additional control over what's going on in the scene, such as controlling the camera's orientation, fading in or out of Actions, controlling game speed, or triggering other Actors. Although a simple Matinee sequence doesn't require Sub Actions for every Action, generally Sub Actions are necessary to achieve the look you want.

FIGURE 13.2 illustrates a simple Matinee sequence in which a camera moves along a path. The sequence is composed of a single Scene Manager that governs three Actions. In this scenario, after the Scene Manager is activated, viewport camera control is handed off to the Scene Manager and can no longer be influenced by the player. The Scene Manager moves the camera from Action to Action, its location determined by associated interpolation points. As the first and third Actions are initiated, Sub Actions *within* the Actions are launched, providing control over the camera's orientation and producing fade-ins and fade-outs. When the last Action is reached, camera control is handed back to the player, and the Scene Manager goes into an idle state waiting to be triggered again.

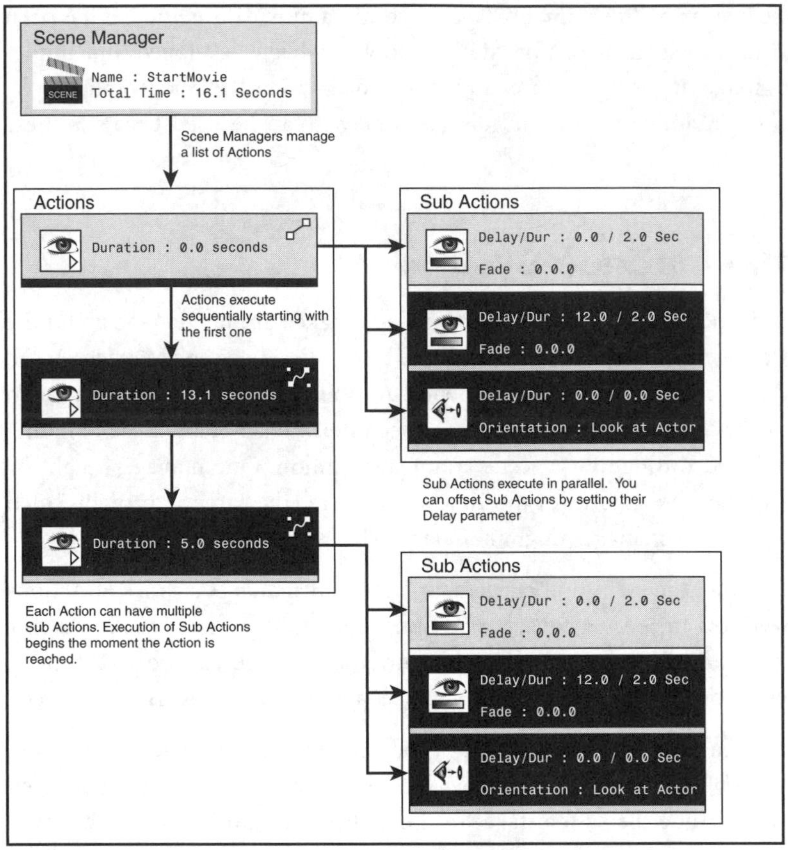

FIGURE 13.2 Overview of the Matinee system.

One of the key elements in this example is the camera, which is moving along a path. A camera path is generated after you have created at least two Actions associated with interpolation points. Interpolation points are special Actors that level designers place in a scene. They are used to specify the position and orientation of the camera or Actor the Scene Manager is controlling.

During setup, level designers create a series of interpolation points defining a camera or Actor's location. Next, Actions are created, and the interpolation points are then associated with their respective Actions. In this way, the Scene Manager is instructed where the camera should be located when that Action is performed. The Scene Manager also interpolates between the points of two sequential Actions, creating a path of animation. By setting the `Duration` property of each Action, you can control the timing of the sequence, or how long it takes the Actor to traverse the path from one interpolation point to the next. **FIGURE 13.3** demonstrates the relationship between Actions, interpolation points, and the resulting camera and Actor paths that are generated.

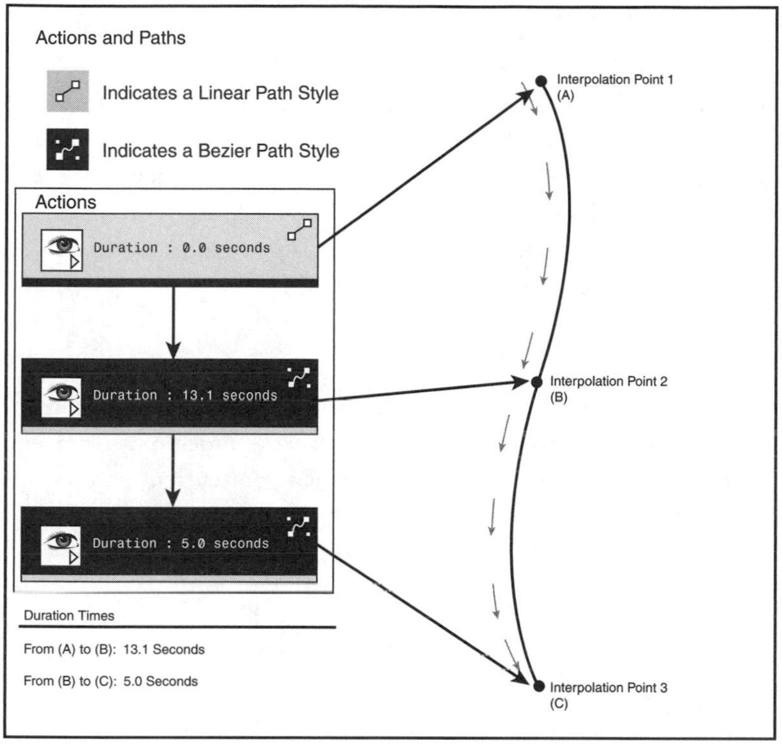

FIGURE 13.3 How Actions create paths.

Two of the Actions in **FIGURE 13.3** contain Sub Actions. Actions are carried out linearly—one after the other. Sub Actions, on the other hand, are performed in parallel, meaning they are all launched at the same time when their corresponding Action takes place. The Scene Manager processes each Action in order, from the top of the list to the bottom. As an Action is reached, all its Sub Actions are performed simultaneously. Even though the Sub Actions for an Action occur in parallel, you do have fine-tuned control over their timing through each Sub Action's `Delay` parameter, which offsets the time at which they take place.

A Scene Manager isn't automatically activated when a level begins. It must be triggered before it begins processing Actions. This triggering is caused by an event that occurs within the game, such as a player walking into a specific area, or by a scripted sequence. Until the manager is triggered, it controls nothing.

The Matinee Interface

Now that you have a basic understanding of how the Matinee system works, you can take a closer look at the Matinee tool. At its core, Matinee is an interface designed to ease the process of setting up and managing Scene Managers, Actions, and Sub Actions. Everything you do in Matinee can be done without this interface, but this approach to developing a Matinee sequence would be far more tedious.

To open Matinee, simply click the Matinee icon in the toolbox. The Matinee interface is divided into four sections, each accessible through its own tab at the top of the interface: Scenes, Actions, Sub Actions, and Tools. The first three sections are basic management systems for creating and controlling Scene Managers, Actions, and Sub Actions. The final tab, Tools, gives you access to three different tools for developing controlling animation paths within a sequence. The following three subsections provide an overview of these tabs.

The Scenes Tab

In the Scenes tab, you can create new Scene Managers to add to your level as well as remove them. You can set and adjust Scene Managers' properties and organize the order of your Scene Managers. The tab also provides access to a Preview window to view your current progress on your sequence. **FIGURE 13.4** illustrates the functionality of the Scene tab.

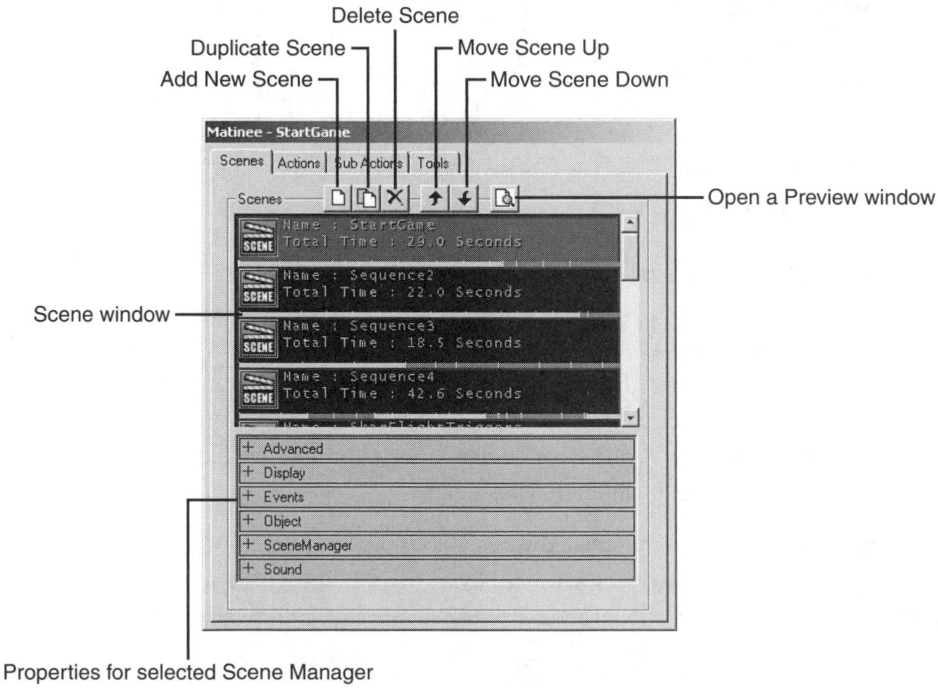

FIGURE 13.4 **Overview of the Scenes tab.**

Notice that each Scene Manager in the Scenes tab has a teal bar across the bottom, designed to show you important events along that scene's timeline. Actions in your scene are represented as small yellow tick marks on this bar. Areas of the timeline alternate between bright and dark teal to differentiate from one Action to the next.

The Actions Tab

In the Actions tab, you can add new Actions to the selected Scene Manager. You can also copy an Action and delete Actions from the Scene Manager. You can also adjust the order of your Actions, and this tab also includes a Preview window to check out your current progress. **FIGURE 13.5** shows the interface of the Actions tab. The buttons for this tab perform the same functions as those for the Scenes tab. The Actions appear in the Actions window, with the properties for the selected Action appearing below that.

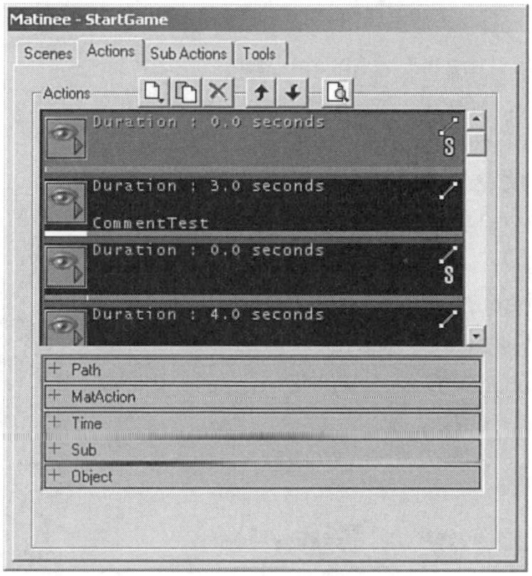

FIGURE 13.5 Overview of the Actions tab.

At the bottom of each Action is a small white bar that indicates at what point along the timeline Actions take place and the duration of these Actions.

The Sub Actions Tab

In the Sub Actions tab (see **FIGURE 13.6**), you can create new Sub Actions for the currently selected Action. You can also clone a specific Sub Action, delete a Sub Action, or change the order of Sub Actions in the list. This tab also provides access to the Preview window. The buttons for this tab perform the same functions as those for the Scenes and Actions tabs. The Sub Actions appear in the Sub Actions window, with the properties for the selected Sub Action appearing below that.

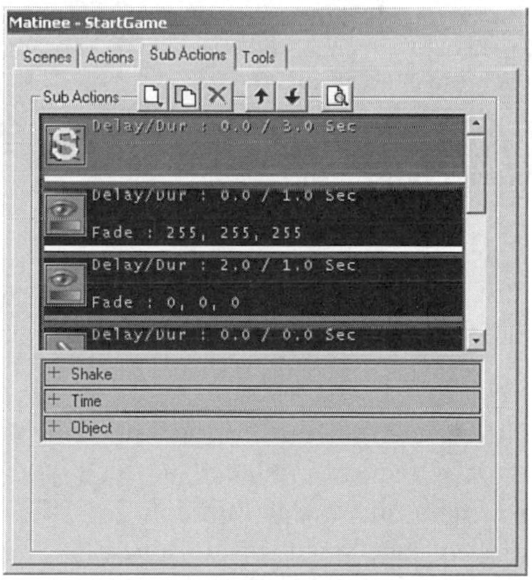

FIGURE 13.6 Overview of the Sub Actions tab.

Notice that the white bar underneath each Sub Action doesn't behave the same as in the Action tab because all Sub Actions of a given Action are launched simultaneously. Therefore, they aren't really using a percentage of the total timeline.

The Tools Tab

The Tools tab provides a small interface for creating the Actors needed for a Matinee sequence. You can create new interpolation points or LookTargets (see **FIGURE 13.7**). If you're using UT2003 or UT2004, you can also create both a new interpolation point *and* a new Action (see **FIGURE 13.8**). When the pair is created together in this fashion, the Action is automatically associated with the interpolation point.

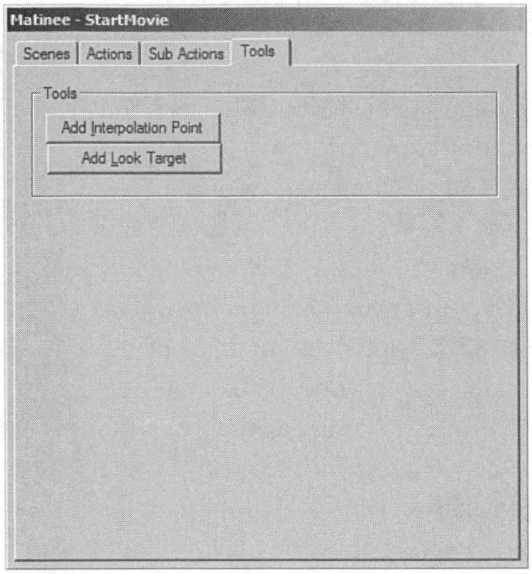

FIGURE 13.7 Overview of the Tools tab in Unreal runtime.

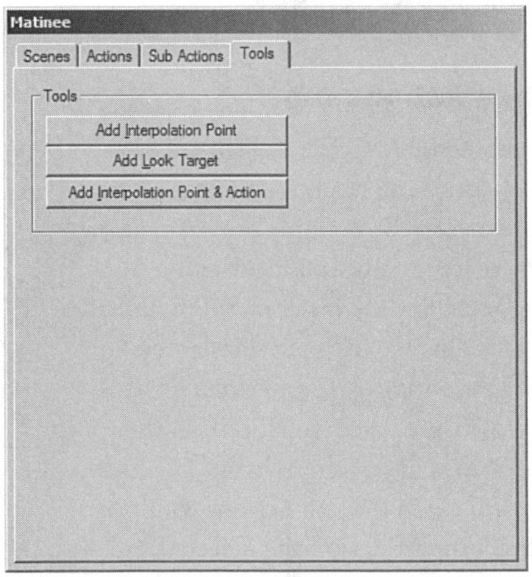

FIGURE 13.8 Overview of the Tools tab in UT2003 and UT2004.

Creating a Simple Matinee Sequence

This section explains how to generate a basic Matinee sequence, as shown in the following list:

- Create a Scene Manager.
- Create two Actions (setting durations and so forth).
- Create two interpolation points.
- Preview the sequence.

This section covers the steps in the preceding list and provides tutorials so that you can learn the techniques behind each step.

In **TUTORIAL 13.1**, you construct your first Matinee sequence. Note that this tutorial is done in Unreal2 Runtime. To begin the sequence, you'll move a camera from one point to another (referred to as Points A and B) over a specified amount of time.

TUTORIAL 13.1: A Basic Matinee Sequence

1. In UnrealEd, open the map `Tutorial13_01_Start.urt`. Take a moment to become familiar with the level's layout. Most of the action will take place near the stable. Navigate your Perspective viewport somewhere close to the stable, as shown in **FIGURE 13.9**. Position and orientation aren't important at this time.

FIGURE 13.9 The scene in which you'll create a Matinee movie.

2. Click the Matinee button in the toolbox to open the Matinee interface.

3. In the Scenes tab, click the Add New Scene icon to add a Scene Manager Actor to your scene (see **FIGURE 13.10**). The Scene Manager is then listed in the Scene window.

FIGURE 13.10 When you add the Scene Manager, its icon appears in the Perspective viewport.

4. At this point, the Scene Manager has a total time of 0.0 seconds because it currently has no Actions. Select your new Scene Manager in the Scene window. Click the Actions tab, and click the Add New Action button. From the menu that opens, select ActionMoveCamera.

> **NOTE**
>
> To see the Scene Manager Actor in your Perspective viewport, simply dolly your camera back from where it currently is.

An Action is added to the Action window (see **FIGURE 13.11**). Repeat step 4 to add another Action.

One of the most important functions of Actions is defining the time at which the camera or Actor will be at the associated interpolation point. This time is set through the `Duration` property, which establishes the time needed to move from one Actor to the next.

Currently, you can see that the `Duration` property of both Actions is 0.0 seconds. Previewing the scene in this state can cause UnrealEd to crash because it's essentially like instructing the camera to be two places at once. Camera cuts typically use `Duration` settings of zero, but they don't crash Unreal. Camera cuts are discussed in more detail shortly.

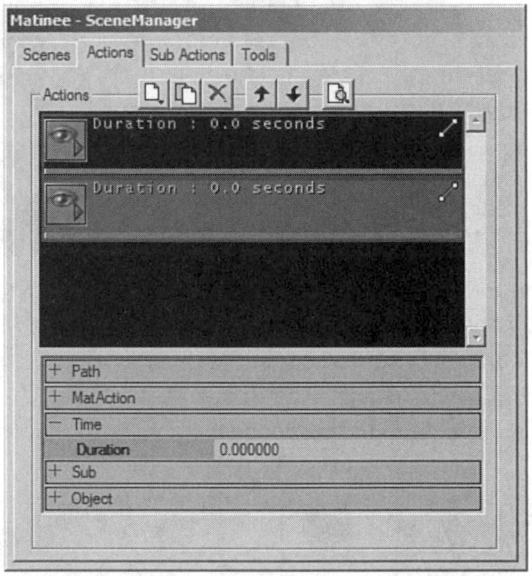

FIGURE 13.11 The Actions seen in the Action window.

5. Make sure the second Action is selected (it will be highlighted); if not, click it. In the Properties section, expand the Time category and set `Duration` to 6. This setting tells the Scene Manager that it takes six seconds to go from the first Action to the second Action. However, where is the first point actually located? You need to define the location and orientation of both Point A and Point B so that you can associate the interpolation points with their corresponding Actions.

6. In the Perspective viewport, position your view exactly where you would like your camera to start. Keep in mind that both position and orientation of the camera are important, as they are used in the interpolation point you're about to create (see **FIGURE 13.12**).

FIGURE 13.12 This image shows what the camera should see when you create the first interpolation point, which you'll do in the next step.

7. In the Matinee dialog box, click the Tools tab, and click Add Interpolation Point. You'll see red crosshairs within a white box (see **FIGURE 13.13**).

   If you navigate your 3D viewport so that you can see the icon, you'll find that the crosshairs are really an arrow pointing in the direction your camera was looking (see **FIGURE 13.14**).

8. Now that you have an interpolation point, you need to specify that it will be associated with Point A. All you need to do is tell the first Action to use this point. Back in the Matinee dialog box, go to the Actions tab, and select the first Action.

9. In the Properties section, expand the MatAction category. Select the interpolation point in the viewport (if it isn't already). Click the word `None` in the `IntPoint` property and then click Use (see **FIGURE 13.15**).

FIGURE 13.13 Looking through the interpolation point.

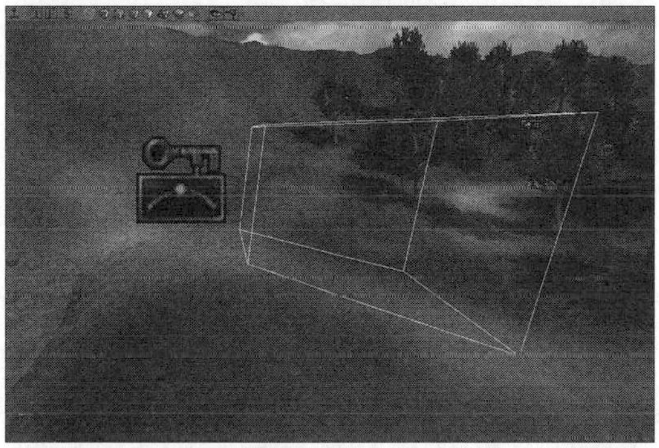

FIGURE 13.14 A Side view of the interpolation point.

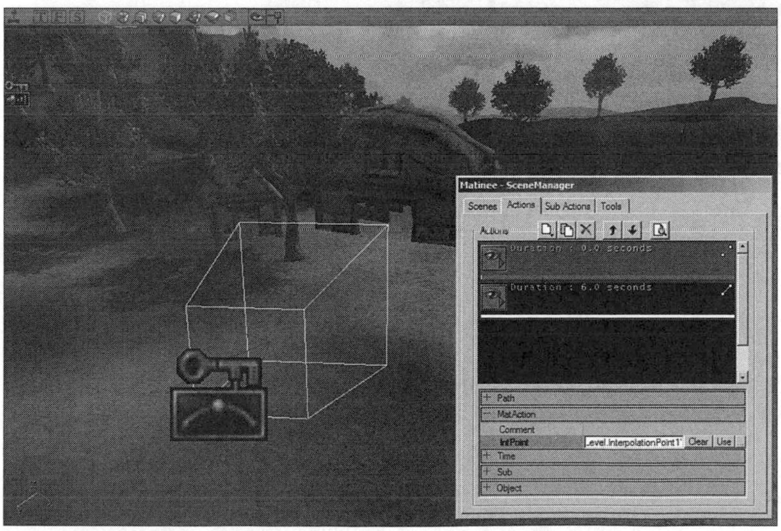

FIGURE 13.15 Assigning interpolation points to Actions.

10. Now you need to set up Point B. Again, you need to use an interpolation point to specify where Point B is. Complete the following steps:

- Navigate the Perspective viewport as though you were the camera moving in a straight line from the first interpolation point to where you would like to place the second one. For this tutorial, move forward so that you're looking into the opening of the stable (see **FIGURE 13.16**).
- Add another interpolation point.
- Set this new interpolation point as the `IntPoint` parameter in the second Action by clicking the Use button (see **FIGURE 13.17**).

FIGURE 13.16 **Navigate to the point where the camera needs to stop.**

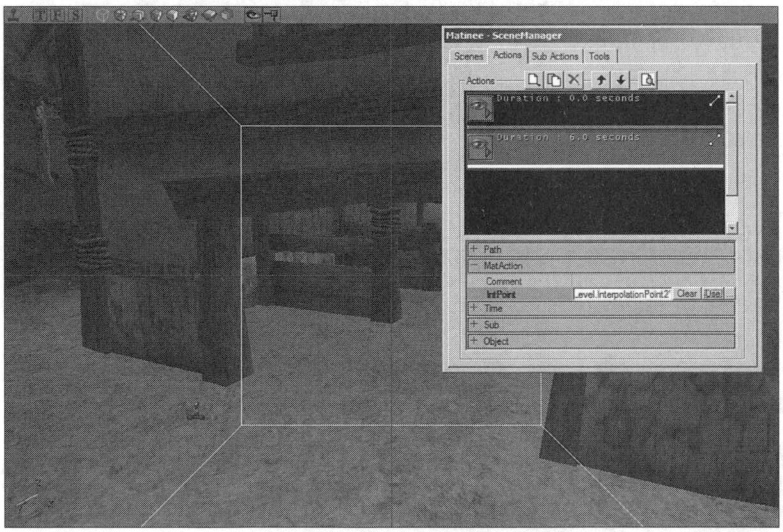

FIGURE 13.17 **Adding another interpolation point and linking it to the second Action.**

In any viewport, you can see that a line now connects the two interpolation points. The viewport camera will follow this path.

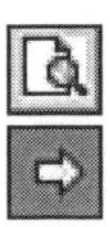

11. You can preview the sequence through the Preview window. In the Matinee dialog box, click the Preview window icon. In the Preview window, click the Play button. You can now watch your viewport camera move from Point A to Point B (see **FIGURE 13.18**).

FIGURE 13.18 Using the Preview window to watch the camera travel between the two points.

12. Save your work.

END TUTORIAL 13.1

Congratulations on completing your first Matinee sequence! In the following sections of this chapter, you'll improve and enhance this sequence to understand the tools and effects available in Matinee.

Working with the Scene Manager

Although the Scene Manager's primary function is carrying out its list of Actions, it includes several important properties with which you should become familiar. You can find these properties in the Scenes tab under the SceneManager category. **TABLE 13.1** describes each of these properties.

TABLE 13.1 Scene Manager Properties

Property	Description
`Affect`	This property is one of the most important for the Scene Manager. Its setting determines whether the sequence affects the viewport's camera or a specific Actor. The two settings are `AFFECT_ViewportCamera` and `AFFECT_Actor`.
`AffectedActor`	If you're using this Scene Manager to control an Actor, you need to set this property so that the manager knows which Actor to control. Assigning an Actor is easy; simply select the Actor in any viewport and then click the Use button in the `AffectedActor` field. If the `Affect` property is set to `AFFECT_ViewportCamera`, this property is useless because you don't need to specify an Actor to affect.

TABLE 13.1 Continued

Property	Description
bCinematicView	This property applies only if the Affect property is set to AFFECT_ViewportCamera. When bCinematicView is set to True, the camera viewport is displayed in letterbox format.
bHideHUD	As of this writing, the bHideHUD property appears to have no effect. The goal is allowing the designer to display or hide the heads-up display during playback of the Matinee sequence. The HUD automatically vanishes at the start of a Matinee sequence.
bLooping	When set to True, this property causes the Actions to continue looping. In other words, after the last Action is reached, the Scene Manager starts over at the first Action and continues processing.
EventEnd	This property enables you to trigger an event after the Scene Manager has completed its Action list.
EventStart (UT2003 and UT2004)	This property enables you to trigger an event at the same moment the Scene Manager is triggered.
NextSceneTag (UT2003 and UT2004)	This property triggers another Scene Manager as soon as the current Scene Manager's Actions are completed.

Triggering the Matinee Sequence

The Matinee sequence you've created works great when previewed through the Matinee Preview window, but currently, it doesn't play within the game. This is because the sequence hasn't been told to play. In this next tutorial, you're going to see how to trigger the sequence to begin playing it in-game.

Scene Managers lie dormant until they receive a broadcasted event that they're listening for. By default, that event is `SceneManager`. However, this name isn't very descriptive and can become confusing, especially if the scene contains multiple Scene Managers. Therefore, changing your Scene Manager's `Tag` property to something more descriptive is always a good idea.

In **TUTORIAL 13.2**, you see how to launch your Matinee sequence during gameplay by using a standard trigger.

TUTORIAL 13.2: Establishing a Trigger

1. Continue from **TUTORIAL 13.1**, or open `Tutorial13_02_Start.urt`. In the Scenes tab of Matinee, select the SceneManager entry in the Scene window (see **FIGURE 13.19**).

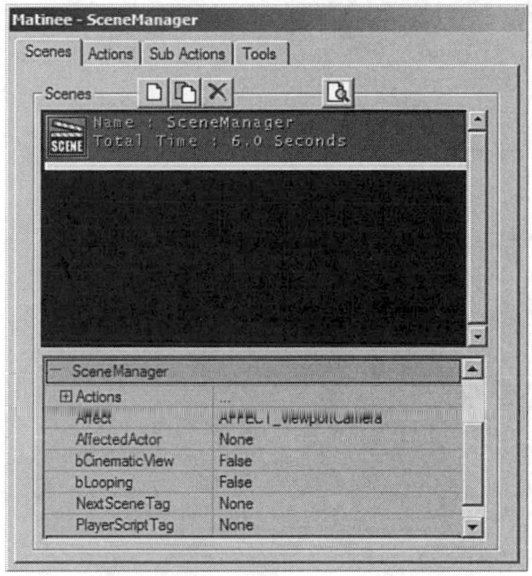

FIGURE 13.19 Select the Scene Manager.

2. Expand the Events category and set the `Tag` property to `StartMovie`. Now the Scene Manager is listening for the `StartMovie` event to be sent through the level.

3. Open the Actor Class browser, expand Actor > Triggers, and click Trigger.

4. Right-click on the ground under the first interpolation point, and choose Add Trigger Here from the menu. A trigger is placed above the ground (see **FIGURE 13.21**).

> **NOTE**
>
> The name of the SceneManager has now changed to `StartMovie`, as shown in **FIGURE 13.20**. Also, notice that the Total Time setting is now 6.0 seconds.

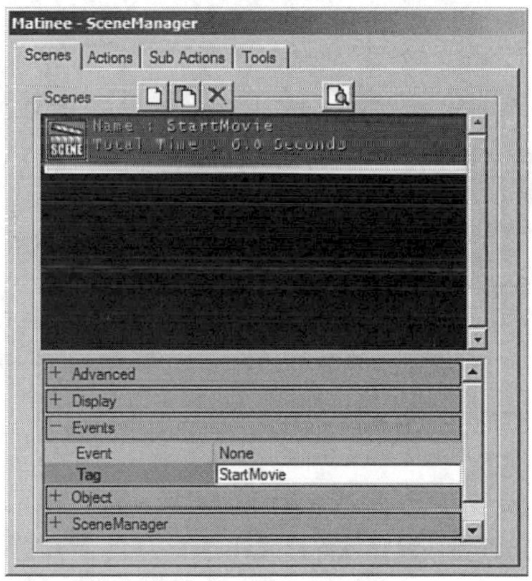

FIGURE 13.20 Set the *Tag* property to *`StartMovie`*.

5. To see this trigger during runtime, double-click the trigger icon to open its Properties window, expand the Advanced category, and set the `bHidden` parameter to False.

6. To set the event, expand the Events section and set the `Event` property to StartMovie. This event will be used to trigger the Scene Manager.

7. You're now ready to test your sequence in the game. No compiling is necessary because you haven't affected geometry, lights, or bot paths. Simply run the level by clicking the Play Map icon. **FIGURE 13.22** shows the result.

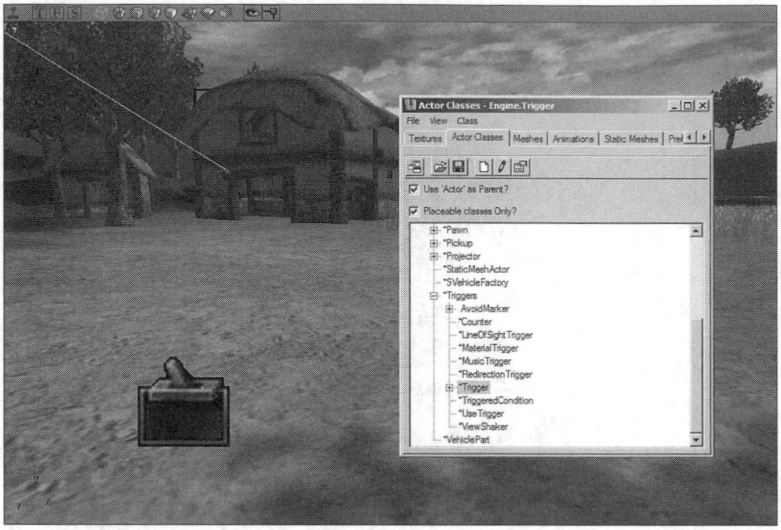

FIGURE 13.21 Add a trigger into your scene.

When you run over the trigger Actor, the `StartMovie` event is broadcast. The Scene Manager hears the broadcast and takes control of the camera's viewport. The camera then begins at Point A and interpolates to Point B over six seconds. After the camera reaches Point B, control is handed back to the player.

9. Save your work.

FIGURE 13.22 You can see the trigger in-game.

END TUTORIAL 13.2

Controlling the Camera Path

So far, you have created a simple path for the camera to move on. This path is defined by two points, A and B, making it a straight line (referred to as a *Linear path*). A straight line can be limiting when you want to have a flythrough in which the camera moves along a curvy path, for example. To help resolve this limitation, you can set interpolation points to a *Bezier path*, allowing you to adjust their shape with Bezier weight handles.

In **TUTORIAL 13.3**, you see how to change the path style, how to add interpolation points, and how to use the `bSmoothCorner` property.

TUTORIAL 13.3: Camera Path Enhancement

1. Continue from **TUTORIAL 13.2** or open `Tutorial13_03_Start.urt`. The path between two interpolation points can be one of two types: Linear or Bezier. The Bezier path provides two Bezier handles for adjusting the line's curvature. In the Actions tab, select the second Action. Expand the Path category and set the `PathStyle` parameter to `PATH-STYLE_Bezier`. Notice that your path suddenly becomes a wild arc (see **FIGURE 13.23**). Actually, whenever you convert a path style from Linear to Bezier, the section of the curve in question changes to an S shape.

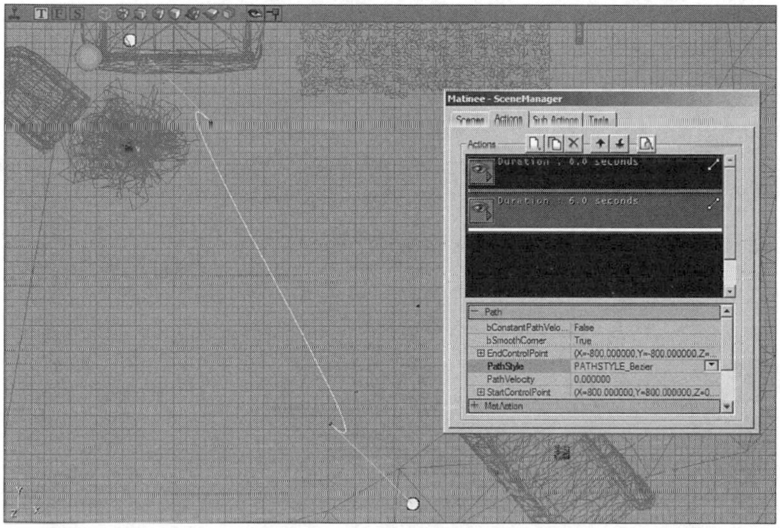

FIGURE 13.23 Top view showing the path.

2. To adjust the curve, simply drag one of the Bezier handles around (see **FIGURE 13.24**). This handle can be freely moved in 3D space, so you can move it in any viewport.

3. Continue to experiment with the shape of the curve by using the Bezier handles, while watching the results in the Preview window (see **FIGURE 13.25**).

TIP

In UT2003 and UT2004, you can right-click on the line and choose Straighten Curve to quickly straighten a curve.

TIP

If you deselect the Actions in the Actions tab of the Matinee dialog box, the curve vanishes. Reselect an Action to make it reappear.

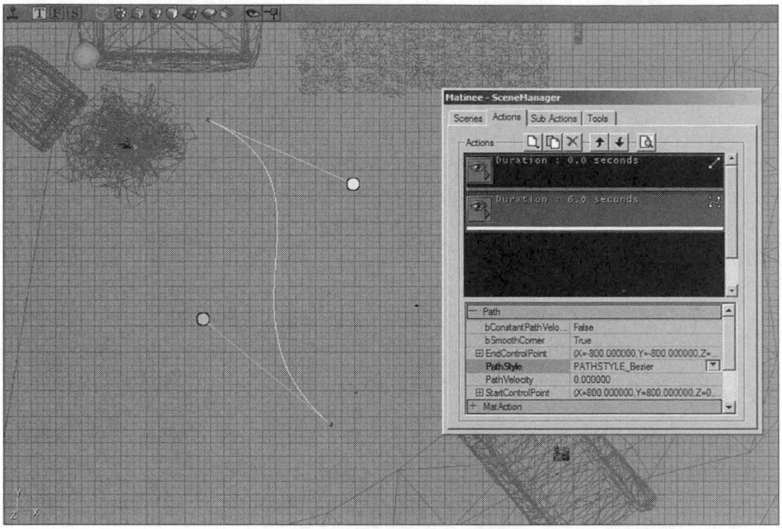

FIGURE 13.24 Using the Bezier handles to adjust the path.

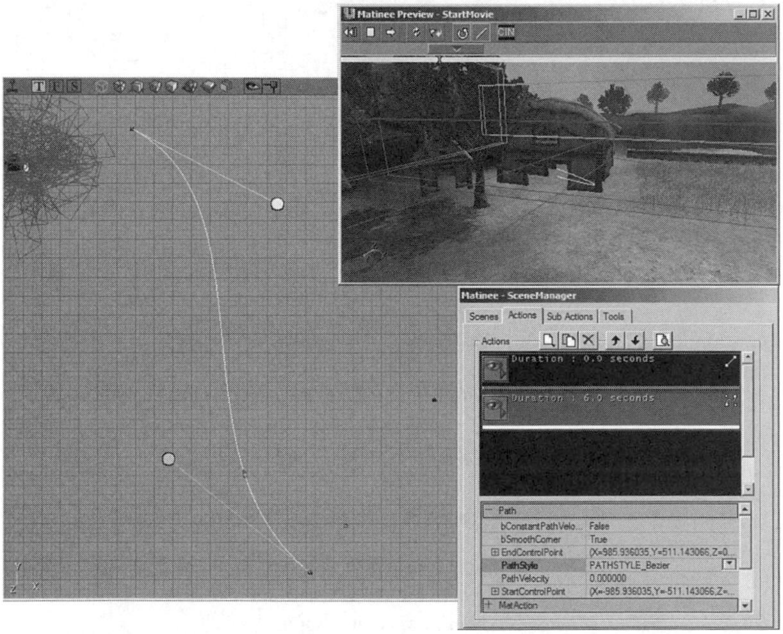

FIGURE 13.25 It helps to preview the scene while making adjustments to the path.

4. Now try adding another Action into the mix. Make sure the last Action is selected, or you'll insert an Action between the two Actions. Add another ActionMoveCamera and set its `Duration` to 4 (see **FIGURE 13.26**). You can call this new Action Point C. It now takes a total of six seconds to go from Point A to Point B and an additional four seconds to go from Point B to Point C.

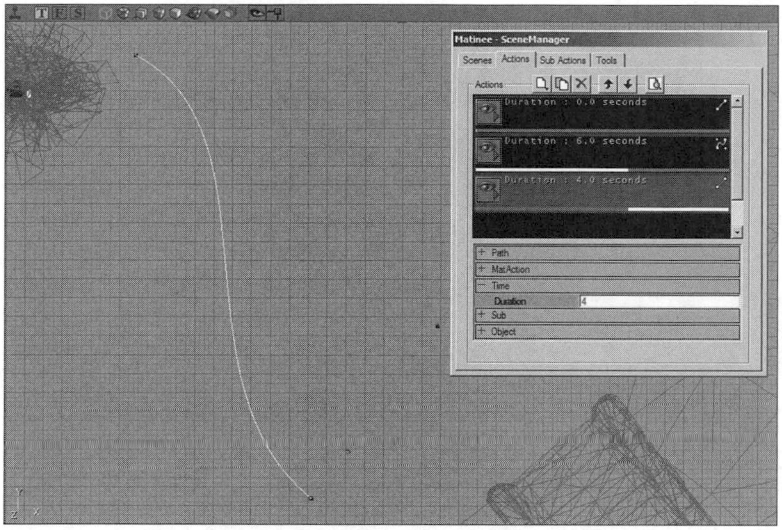

FIGURE 13.26 **Adding a third Action to the Action window.**

You can start to see how the timeline is being displayed in the window. Look at the bright white lines at the bottom of Actions 2 and 3. These lines indicate when a specific Action is active.

> **NOTE**
>
> **If you don't see the lines, reselect the third Action.**

5. Open the Tools tab, and click Add Interpolation Point to create a new interpolation point inside the stable. Keep in mind that the camera needs to continue pointing in the same general direction if you're going to get good results from the interpolation. Back in the Matinee dialog box, click the Actions tab, and select the third Action.

6. Expand the MatAction category, and set `IntPoint` to the new interpolation point by clicking the Use button (see **FIGURE 13.27**). If this doesn't work, make sure the interpolation point is selected in the viewport.

   Currently, this new section of the path is linear. Play back the sequence, and see what it looks like. You'll notice a "hiccup" when the camera passes over the second interpolation point because you are going from a smooth to a linear interpolation.

7. To keep the path smooth, you need to convert the last Action's path to Bezier. Do that now by selecting the third Action in the Actions tab, and expanding the Path category. Set the `PathStyle` property to `PATHSTYLE_Bezier` (see **FIGURE 13.28**). Play back the sequence again, and notice that the transition through the second interpolation point is smoother now.

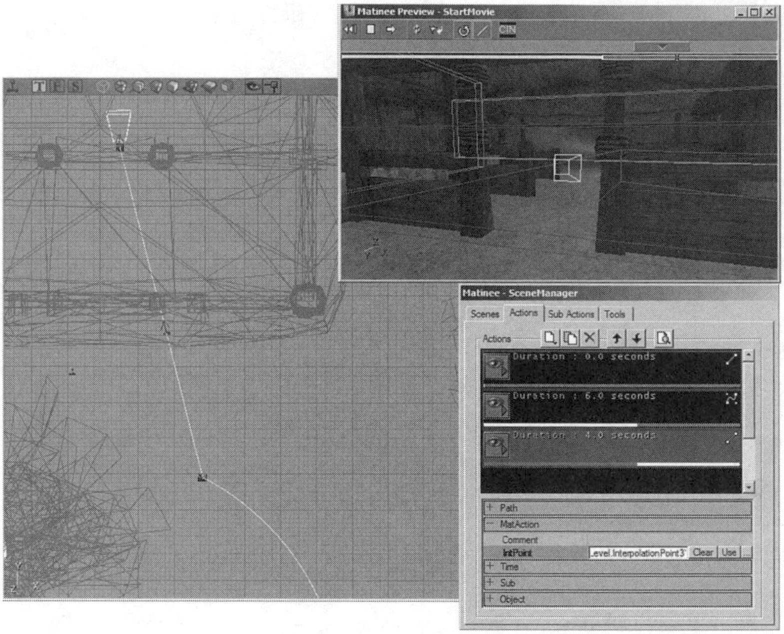

FIGURE 13.27 Assigning the new interpolation point to the second Action.

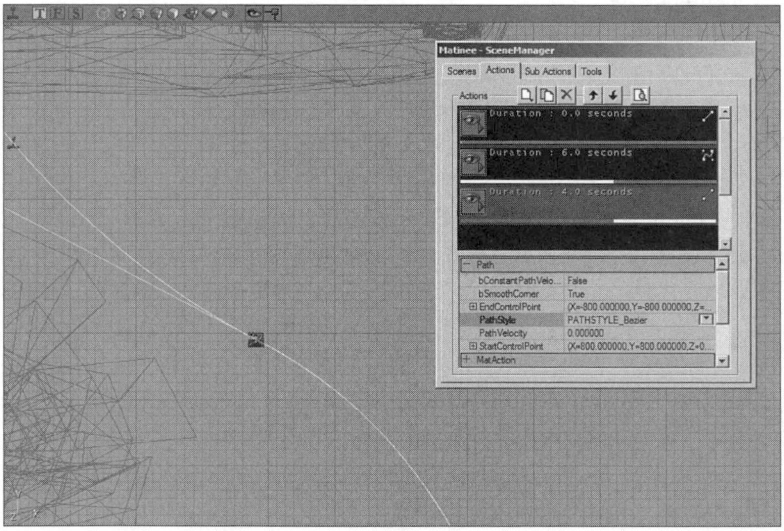

FIGURE 13.28 `PathStyle` set to Bezier for the last Action to keep the camera movement smooth.

As you select each Action, you see that segment of the path highlighted in yellow. If the `PathStyle` property is set to Bezier, you'll see two Bezier handles, but what happens when two segments joined by an interpolation point are both Bezier? To better understand how having multiple Bezier sections can affect your path, try the following:

- Verify that the last Action is still selected.
- Select and move the Bezier handle at the second interpolation point (Point B). You can see that it's affecting the segment between the first and second interpolation points (see **FIGURE 13.29**).

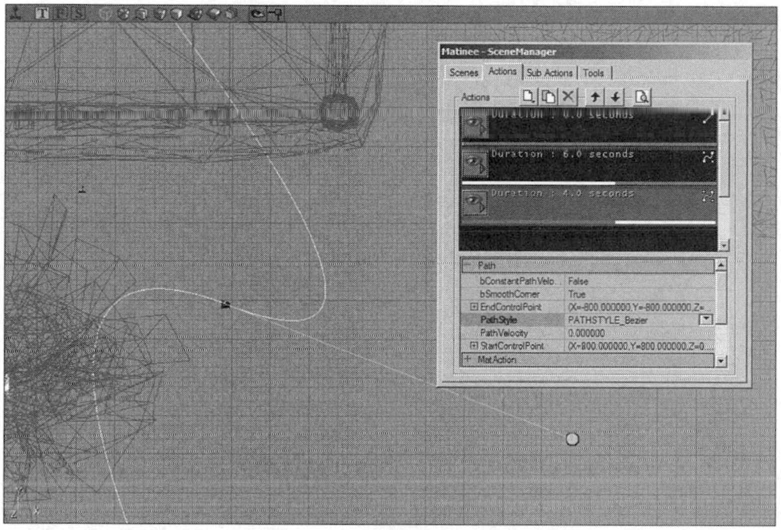

FIGURE 13.29 Adjusting the Bezier handles at Point B.

- The two Bezier handles are moving in tandem because of a parameter setting. In the Path category, set `bSmoothCorner` to False (see **FIGURE 13.30**).
- Try moving the Bezier handle again. Same thing: Both handles continue to move together. Now select the second Action and change `bSmoothCorner` to False. Try moving the handles again for both Actions. Notice that the Bezier handles are now "broken," meaning you can point them in two separate directions. You now have complete control over the handles' positioning.

8. Having total control over the Bezier tangents might not necessarily be beneficial, however. Play back the scene in the Preview window, and watch what the camera does when it transitions from the first path segment to the second. Notice the sharp change in direction—typically an undesirable effect.

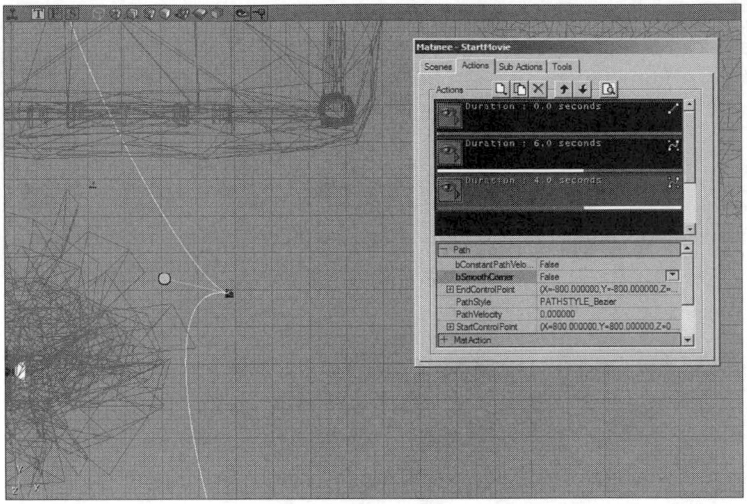

FIGURE 13.30 **Setting *bSmoothCorner* to False allows the Bezier handles to be moved independently of one another.**

9. If you didn't intend for this sharp change to happen, don't worry; it's easy to correct. Set the `bSmoothCorner` parameters for both Actions back to True, and then try to move one of the handles. The curve will become smooth again.
10. Adjust the curve back so that a smooth path is established for the camera to move from outside to inside the stable.
11. Save your work.

END TUTORIAL 13.3

Creating Camera Pauses and Camera Cuts

So far, you have learned how to make a camera move along a path. The movie would be more interesting, however, if you could create pauses in the camera's movement as well as cuts from camera to camera. **TUTORIAL 13.4** introduces you to the techniques for accomplishing these tasks.

You'll begin by having the camera pause at the last interpolation point you added (Point C) for a total of three seconds. After the pause is over, you'll do a camera cut to the other side of the stable.

TUTORIAL 13.4: Pausing and Cutting

1. Continue from **TUTORIAL 13.3** or open `Tutorial13_04_Start.urt`. Add an ActionPause Action to the end of your Action window, and set its `Duration` property to 3.
2. Even though this Action represents a pause, you still need to associate it with an interpolation point. Use the last interpolation point (Point C) you added for this Action. You want the camera to pause rather than move from its current location.

3. Play back the preview. You'll find that you have a problem. When the pause Action is reached, the camera snaps to the orientation of the associated interpolation point. So what happened? By default, a camera always looks down the path it's traveling. It doesn't interpolate its orientation between the first interpolation point and the second one. In this case, however, you need direct control over the camera's orientation. You learn how to do this in **TUTORIAL 13.5** by using a Sub Action. For now, leave it as it is and continue with creating the camera cut.

4. To have the camera instantly cut to a new location after the 3-second pause is over, follow these steps (see **FIGURE 13.31** for the results):

   - First, add two new ActionMoveCamera Actions to the end of the Action window.
   - Leave the `Duration` property of the first new Action set to 0.
   - Set the `Duration` property of the last Action to 4. This setting should give you an instant camera cut after the pause, and at the cut, the camera will begin moving again.
   - Create two new interpolation points: one on the opposite side of the stable and the other inside the stable.
   - Associate the new interpolation points with their respective Actions. You should have the camera cut to the outside of the stable and then let it move inside.

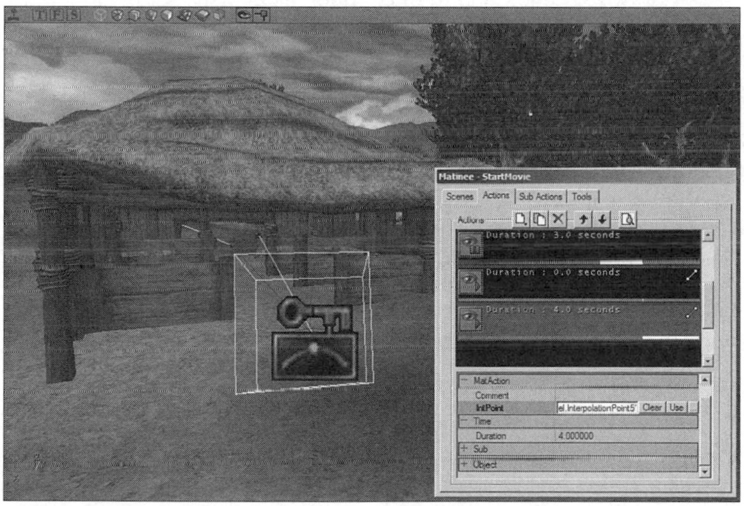

FIGURE 13.31 The camera cut is now in place.

5. Play back the preview. The camera does perform a camera cut, but its motion is a bit jerky. You'll fix this problem in **TUTORIAL 13.5** by using Sub Actions.

6. Save your work.

END TUTORIAL 13.4

A Closer Look at Sub Actions

With Sub Actions, designers can stage a range of effects or events at specific times. You could say that Actions "own" their Sub Actions. This doesn't mean that Sub Actions are required; they are optional, but they can produce more advanced results than using Actions alone. This section focuses primarily on two Sub Actions: Orientation and Fade.

TABLE 13.2 describes the eight available Sub Actions and what they do.

TABLE 13.2 The Available Sub Actions

Sub Action	Description
Scene Speed	The Scene Speed Sub Action enables you to control the speed of the current Scene Manager. This Sub Action doesn't affect overall game speed or any other Scene Manager, for that matter. All Actions and Sub Actions belonging to this manager are affected. The key properties are `Max` (the speed exiting this Sub Action) and `Min` (the speed coming into this Sub Action). For example, if you enter a Sub Action with a `Min` value of 1, that represents normal speed. If the Sub Action's `Duration` property is set to 2 and the `Max` value is .5, the Scene Manager's speed would slow by half over a period of two seconds and then continue at this speed. If you need the Scene Manager to speed back up, you need to add a second Scene Speed Sub Action with settings such as `Max` = 1 and `Min` = .5 so that you enter at half speed and then increase to normal speed again.
Game Speed	The Game Speed Sub Action gives you control over the entire game's speed. The method of operations is the same as the Scene Speed Sub Action. The entire game speed changes over the duration period you set from the `Min` value to the `Max` value. Again, a value of 1 is standard speed.
Orientation	The Orientation Sub Action enables you to control the viewport camera's orientation. Several methods can be used in this Sub Action for controlling orientation. These methods are covered in **TABLE 13.3**.
Camera Shake	The Camera Shake Sub Action enables you to perform a camera shake operation on the viewport camera.
FOV	The FOV Sub Action enables you to set the field of view for the viewport camera.
Trigger	With this Sub Action, you can broadcast an event.
Fade	The Fade Sub Action enables fade-ins and fade-outs to occur.
Camera Effect	Camera Effect can be used to overlay textures over the HUD or apply Motion Blur to the scene.

Setting Camera Orientation

Now that you have the camera pausing and cutting, you need to fix the abrupt snap the pause caused. Controlling camera orientation is a task you need to deal with in nearly every Matinee sequence. To do this in **TUTORIAL 13.5**, you'll use the Orientation Sub Action.

TUTORIAL 13.5: Inserting Sub Actions

1. Continue from **TUTORIAL 13.4** or open `Tutorial13_05_Start.urt`. In the Matinee dialog box, click the Actions tab, and select the first Action.
2. In the Sub Actions tab, click the Add New Sub Action button . From the menu, select SubActionOrientation.

3. The Orientation Sub Action has four methods for controlling the camera, as shown in **TABLE 13.3**.

   In this tutorial, you're going to use the `LookAtActor` method, which requires designating an Actor to serve as the camera's target.

TABLE 13.3 Camera Orientation Methods

Orientation Method	Description
`None`	The camera doesn't change from its current direction.
`LookAtActor`	The camera looks at the Actor specified in the `LookAt` property. Generally, using the LookTarget Actor is a good idea, as it stands out in the level.
`FacePath`	The camera looks in the direction it is moving.
`Interpolate`	When traveling between two points, the camera starts with its orientation matching the orientation of the starting interpolation point. Over the time required to get from the first point to the second, the camera interpolates its orientation to match that of the interpolation point it's coming into. When using the `Interpolate` method, making use of the `EaseInTime` property is important. This property is the time it takes for the camera to change to its new orientation. If this property isn't set, the camera simply snaps to the new orientation when it reaches that point. Using `EaseInTime` gives you a way of smoothly interpolating the camera over the time of the two Actions.
`Dolly`	If you want to have the camera perform a simple dolly (a push), you can use this method of orientation. The camera inherits the orientation of the starting Action's associated interpolation point and maintains that orientation as it travels to the next Action.

4. In the Matinee dialog box, click the Tools tab. Position your camera in the Perspective view where you want the LookTarget to appear—use a location in one of the stables. After the camera is positioned, click the Add Look Target button. If you back your camera up, you can see the newly created Actor (see **FIGURE 13.32**).

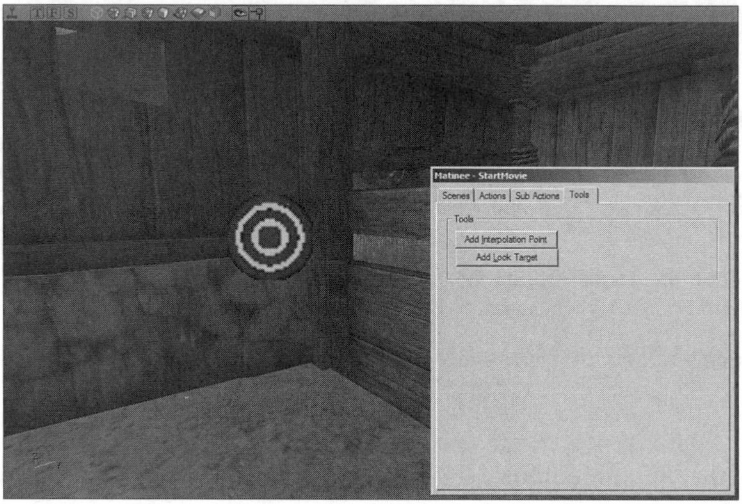

FIGURE 13.32 **The LookTarget icon.**

5. The Actor is selected by default. While it's still selected, click the Sub Actions tab, click the `LookAt` property, and click the Use button to add the selected Actor's name to the field (see **FIGURE 13.33**). Make sure to change `CamOrientation` to `CAMORIENT_LookAtActor`.

6. Play back the sequence through the Preview window. Notice that the camera stays fixed on the new target throughout the sequence. Furthermore, you might notice that after the pause, the camera continues to look at the target. After you set a camera Orientation Sub Action, the camera continues to use the set method of orientation until another camera Orientation Sub Action is reached.

7. Save your work.

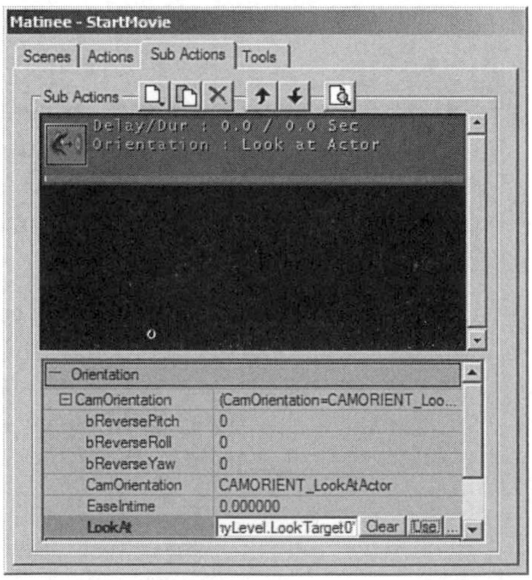

FIGURE 13.33 **Setting the *LookAt* property.**

END TUTORIAL 13.5

Introducing Fades

Fade-ins and fade-outs are an effective method of creating cinematic-style Matinee sequences. They keep your movie from popping in or out too quickly and can be used to create dramatic effects at the beginning and end of your sequences.

In **TUTORIAL 13.6**, you see how to add camera fades to your sequences to make them resemble a "real" movie even more.

TUTORIAL 13.6: Fading In and Out

1. Continue from **TUTORIAL 13.5** or open `Tutorial13_06_Start.urt`. To create a fade-in, open the Matinee dialog box, click the Sub Actions tab, select the first Action in your Action window, and then add the SubActionFade Sub Action.
2. By default, the fade is set to fade-out, which would be a strange way to start a movie. In the Fade properties, set the `bFadeOut` property to False to make the movie fade in. You can see that the `FadeColor` property is black by default. Changing this color enables you to fade into or out of a specific color. For this tutorial, leave it set to black.
3. In the Time category, set `Duration` to 3 (see **FIGURE 13.34**). This setting means the fade in from black will take a total of three seconds. Test the effect by playing the scene in the Preview window.
4. To make your fades a little more advanced, you'll have the sequence fade out by the end of the pause and then fade back in at the camera cut. Add another Fade Sub Action to the first Action. This step might seem a bit strange at first, but it enables you to make use of the `Delay` property.
5. If you add the `Duration` settings of the first four Actions, you'll find they total 13 seconds. To make the scene fade out over the last two seconds of the pause Action, set the `Delay` property to 11 and `Duration` to 2.
6. Now you need to fade back in on the camera cut. Select the MoveCamera Action that immediately follows the ActionPause Action. It's the second Action with a `Duration` setting of 0.

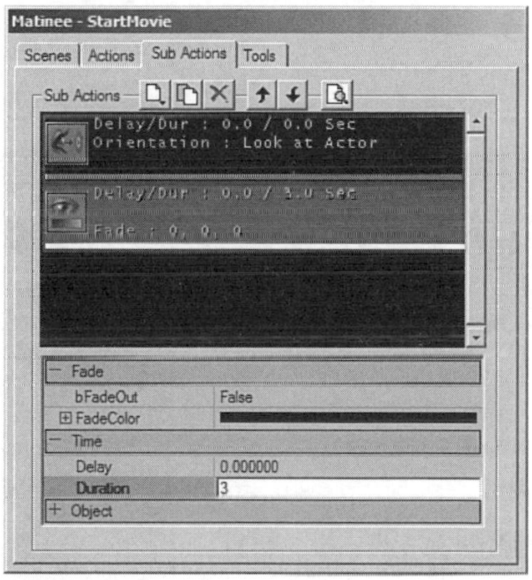

FIGURE 13.34 Setting the fade's *`Duration`* property to three seconds.

7. Add a Fade Sub Action and set its bFadeOut property to False and Duration to 2. Play back the sequence. You should see the camera fade out at the end of the pause and then fade back in after the camera cut.

8. Save your work.

END TUTORIAL 13.6

13

Using Matinee to Control Actors

Up to this point, you've been using the Scene Manager to control your viewport's cameras. However, as mentioned previously, you can have Scene Managers control Actors as well. The concept is the same; you still have interpolation points associated with Actions, which specify the time required to move from point to point. The resulting path can be adjusted the same way as the camera's path. The only real difference is that you must tell the Scene Manager to control an Actor and specify the Actor to be controlled.

In **TUTORIAL 13.7**, you create a new Scene Manager that controls the location of your LookAt Actor. By moving the LookAt Actor while Matinee is in progress, you can produce more dynamic camera movements.

TUTORIAL 13.7: Moving Actors with Matinee

1. Continue from Tutorial 13.6 or open Tutorial13_07_Start.urt. In the Matinee dialog box, add a new Scene Manager.

2. Set the new Scene Manager's Tag property to MoveTarget (see **FIGURE 13.35**).

   The idea is for this Scene Manager to begin at the same time the other one does. You could easily do this by setting the Tag property to StartMovie, the same name used for the other scene. However, this method isn't generally considered good workflow because it makes it more difficult to quickly decipher which Scene Manager is doing what. To solve this problem, you'll make use of another Sub Action, the SubActionTrigger.

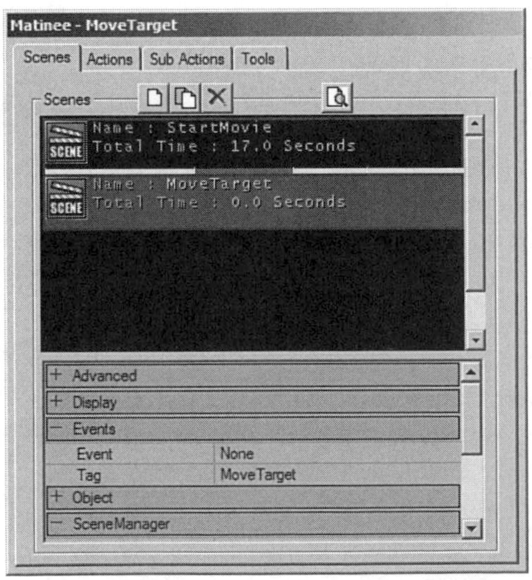

FIGURE 13.35 Setting the new Scene Manager's *Tag* property to *MoveTarget*.

3. Select the first Scene Manager, and add the SubActionTrigger Sub Action to the first Action in the list.

4. Under the Trigger properties, set the `EventName` property to `MoveTarget`.

   The Sub Action creates the `MoveTarget` event, which triggers the second Scene Manager because that Scene Manager's `Tag` property is set to `MoveTarget`. In this way, both Scene Managers begin at the same time.

5. Now you need to create a path along which your LookAt target can travel. The method you use is up to you, but don't forget you need two new interpolation points and two new Actions. These Actions need to be under the MoveTarget Scene Manager. Set the `Duration` property of the second Action to 12. **FIGURE 13.36** shows an example of a path created by two new Actions.

6. Return to the properties of the new Scene Manager. Under the SceneManager section, set the following parameters (see **FIGURE 13.37**):

   Affect: AFFECT_Actor

   AffectedActor: Select the LookTarget and click Use

NOTE

If you're using UT2003 or UT2004, you can use the `EventStart` property of the first Scene Manager to trigger.

FIGURE 13.36 **The path generated from the new Actions.**

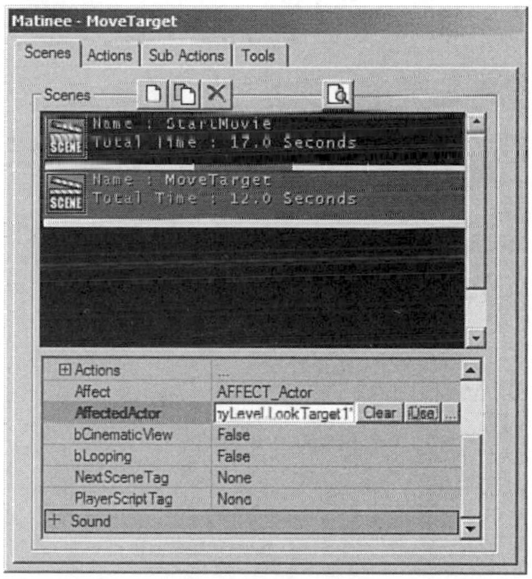

FIGURE 13.37 **Setting the new Scene Manager to affect Actors instead of the player's view.**

7. Play back the preview. What went wrong? If you play the preview back with the second Scene Manager selected, you see the viewport move along the path, as though you were controlling the camera again. If you preview the first Scene Manager instead, it appears that nothing has changed. (You need to close the Preview window, select the first Scene Manager, and then reopen the Preview window to see its playback using the correct Action's path.) This happens because the SubActionTrigger's event broadcast never occurred. You need to actually run your map to test it out. Run the map now.

8. After testing the map, you might need to tweak the location of the new interpolation points or the `Duration` setting of the second Action. If your LookTarget seems to be standing still for the first part of the sequence, simply lower its `Duration` setting.

> **TIP**
>
> To make it easier to see the LookTarget in-game, you can make it visible by opening its properties and setting `bHidden` (found in the Advanced category) to False.

END TUTORIAL 13.7

Adding Text to Your Cutscenes

Another cinematic-style effect you can add to your movies is text, especially if you're creating an intro movie for your game. This text can be the game's name, opening credits, or any other kind of message you want players to read. At this point, you should be getting the hang of Matinee and how to use it to set up your own scenes.

In this two-part tutorial, you use the Camera Effect Sub Action to add custom text to your movie. In **TUTORIAL 13.8**, you create a custom texture in Photoshop and import it into the `myLevel` package in UnrealEd.

TUTORIAL 13.8: Text Creation, Part I—Creating and Importing

1. Continue from **TUTORIAL 13.7** or open `Tutorial13_08_Start.urt`. Open Photoshop and create a new image with the following options:

   Width: 1024

   Height: 1024

   Mode: RGB Color

   Contents: Transparent

2. Set the foreground color to red and the font size to 174 pt. Select any font.

3. Use the Text tool to create some text. For this example, the text `A Matinee Production` was used (see **FIGURE 13.38**).

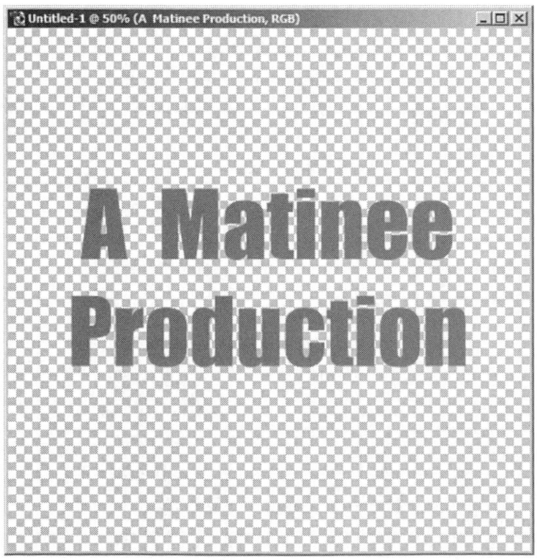

FIGURE 13.38 Adding text to the document.

4. Save the file to your hard drive as `Matinee_Text.tga`. Be sure to set your options to 32 bits/pixel.
5. In UnrealEd, open the Texture browser and import the `Matinee_Text.tga` file.
6. In the Import Texture dialog box, set the following:

   Package: myLevel

   Group: Matinee

   Name: Matinee_Text

> **NOTE**
>
> **If you didn't set `bAlphaTexture` to True, you won't be able to see anything but this graphic when you display the text. The alpha property is used to cut away everything except the text.**

7. When you import the texture, the image might not look like what you expected, as shown in **FIGURE 13.39**. Don't worry. You can fix this by adjusting a single property. Select the newly imported texture, right-click the texture, and choose Properties.

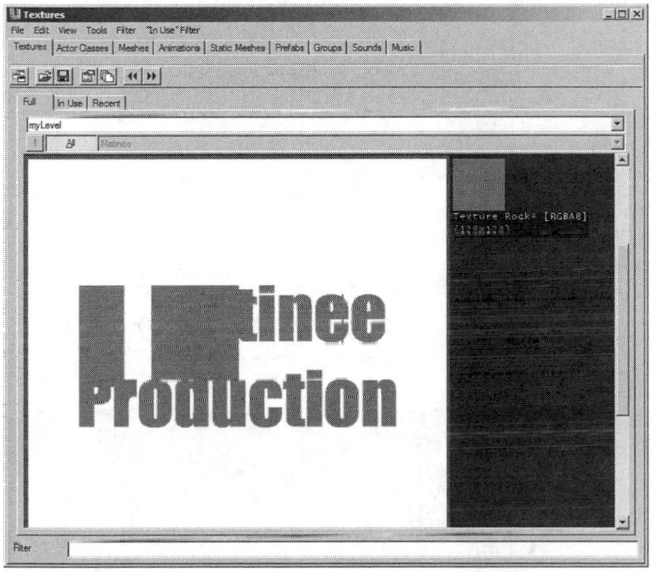

FIGURE 13.39 The text might look a little scary at first!

8. In the Texture Properties dialog box, expand the Surface category and set `bAlphaTexture` to True to correct the problem. Close the dialog box.

END TUTORIAL 13.8

Now that you have added the texture to the scene, you can use it in your Matinee sequence in **TUTORIAL 13.9**. For this example, the text should fade in three seconds after the movie begins.

TUTORIAL 13.9: Text Creation, Part II—Fading Text

1. Continue from **TUTORIAL 13.8** or open `Tutorial13_09_Start.urt`. Make sure the Matinee dialog box is open. Select the StartMovie Scene Manager.
2. Verify that the first Action is highlighted, and add the SubActionCameraEffect Sub Action.
3. Expand the `CameraEffect` property and click CameraOverlay (see **FIGURE 13.40**). Click the New button to see several new properties.
4. In the Texture browser, verify that the `Matinee_Text` texture is selected.
5. Back in the CameraOverlay Sub Action, click the `OverlayMaterial` property and then click the Use button to assign the selected material as the overlay.
6. Set the `DisableAfterDuration` property in the CameraEffect section to True. If you don't do this, the text remains in your viewport for as long as the game runs, even after the Matinee sequence has finished and control is handed back to the player.
7. Set three final properties:

   StartAlpha: 1

   Delay: 3

   Duration: 2

8. If you play back the scene in the Preview window, you won't see any text. To see the CameraOverlay Sub Action work, you need to actually launch the map and trigger the sequence. Test it now. **FIGURE 13.41** shows the results.

   At this point, the text is being displayed during the movie as you've instructed it to do. There are a few ways you can display the text. In this example, the text pops in and pops out, but in the next few steps, you'll make it fade in and fade out.

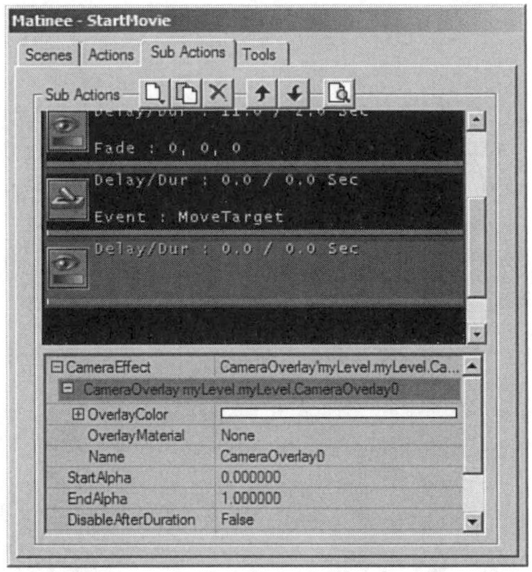

FIGURE 13.40 Adding the CameraOverlay effect.

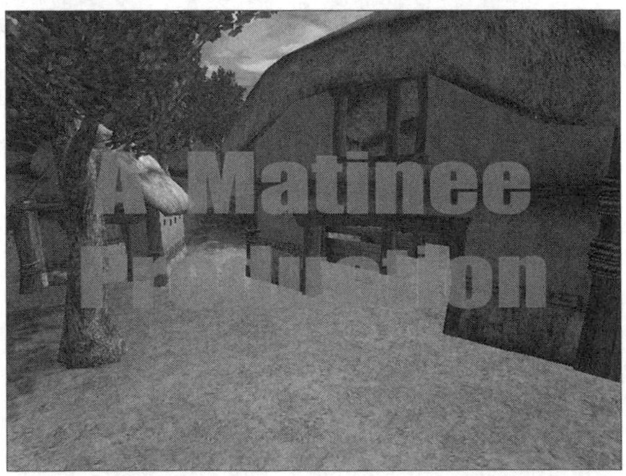

FIGURE 13.41 The text is now visible in-game when the Matinee sequence is triggered.

9. Set `StartAlpha` to 0 and `EndAlpha` to 1. These settings tell the Sub Action to start by not drawing the overlay at all. The image slowly fades in (from 0 to 1) over the specified duration. In this case, it takes two seconds for the text to fade all the way in.

10. To get the text to fade out, add another SubActionCameraEffect Sub Action.

11. As before, create the CameraOverlay Sub Action and assign `Material_Text` to the `OverlayMaterial` property.

12. Set the following properties (see **FIGURE 13.42**):

    StartAlpha: 1

    EndAlpha: 0

    DisableAfterDuration: False

    Delay: 5

    Duration: 2

    Now take a look at what you've done. By reversing the `StartAlpha` and `EndAlpha` settings, you have instructed the overlay to draw at 100% and fade out over a duration of two seconds. You have delayed this Sub Action from processing for five seconds. Think about it: You have already used the first five seconds of the movie for the first text overlay (three-second delay and a two-second duration), so if you delay this Sub Action by five seconds, everything should work out perfectly.

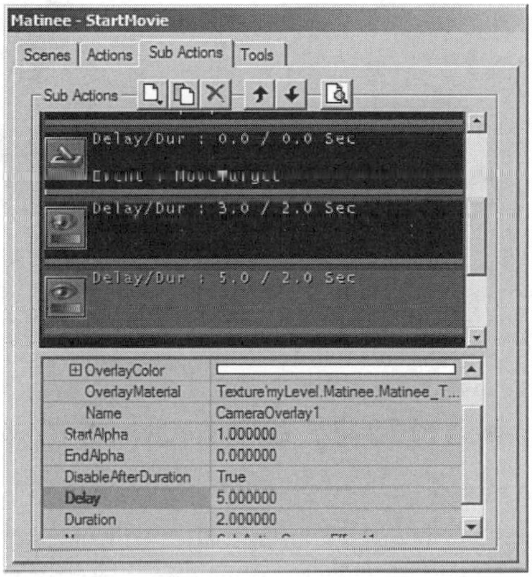

FIGURE 13.42 Setting the text to fade out over a two-second duration.

13. Play-test the level in-game one final time. Verify that the text now fades in and out.

14. Save your work.

END TUTORIAL 13.9

Adding a More Cinematic Feel

Your sequence is nearly complete. However, you can give it a more movielike feel by adding a letterbox effect at the top and bottom of the screen. In **TUTORIAL 13.10**, you see how to do this by adjusting the `bCinematicView` property.

13

TUTORIAL 13.10: Creating Letterboxes

1. Continue from **TUTORIAL 13.9** or open `Tutorial13_10_Start.urt`. Open the Matinee dialog box.
2. In the Scenes tab, select the StartMovie Scene Manager.
3. In the SceneManager category of the Properties window, set `bCinematicView` to True.
4. Play your map. When you trigger your movie, notice that it's now in widescreen letterbox format.

FIGURE 13.43 The final effect with *bCinematicView* set to True.

END TUTORIAL 13.10

Automatically Launching the Movie

You have come a long way! Your movie is finished, and you can view it at any time by activating its trigger in the level. To make your sequence seem even more like an intro movie, you'll use a ScriptedTrigger to make the movie automatically start when the level begins. For more information on ScriptedTriggers and their workflow, please refer to Chapter 9, "Interactive Elements."

TUTORIAL 13.11: Launching the Movie as the Level Begins

1. Continue from **TUTORIAL 13.10** or open `Tutorial13_11_Start.urt`. To launch the movie when the level starts, you need to make a change to your triggering system. For starters, delete the old trigger you had originally placed in the level, but remember its name (`StartMovie`). To replace it with a ScriptedTrigger, in the Actor Class browser, expand Actor > Keypoint > AIScript > ScriptedSequence, and click ScriptedTrigger.
2. Right-click in the viewport and choose Add ScriptedTrigger Here to add this new Actor anywhere in the level (see **FIGURE 13.44**); its placement is irrelevant.
3. Double-click the new trigger to open its Properties window.
4. Under the AIScript category, select the `Actions` property. Click the Add button located next to it.
5. Underneath this property, select index [0], and choose `ACTION_TriggerEvent` from the drop-down list (see **FIGURE 13.45**). Click the New button to add this Action to your ScriptedTrigger. This step also gives you access to this Action's properties.

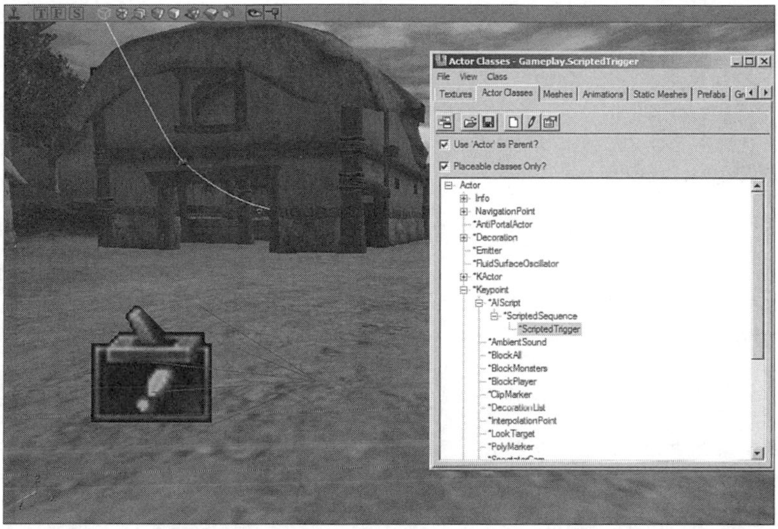

FIGURE 13.44 You can place the ScriptedTrigger anywhere in the level.

6. Beneath the new `ACTION_TriggerEvent` you just created is the `Event` property. Set it to `StartMovie`, the same event your original trigger used.

7. Launch your map. Because there are no latent Actions before the `ACTION_TriggerEvent`, the Action takes place immediately, without any input from the player. This triggers the Scene Manager, which begins to play the movie as soon as you enter the map.

8. Save your work.

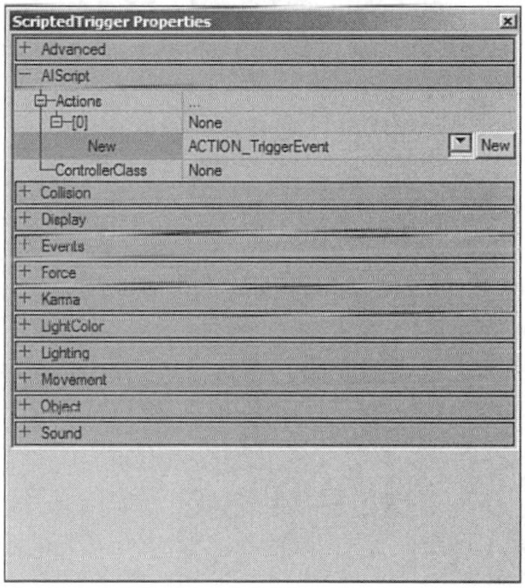

FIGURE 13.45 Clicking the New button is required to commit the Action to the list.

END TUTORIAL 13.11

Changing Levels with Matinee

As your scenes become increasingly complex, you might wish you could divide them into different levels. Chaining levels together with Matinee is actually quite easy and allows you to play a transitional movie or sequence as your players move from one level to the next. In **TUTORIAL 13.12**, two simple levels named Level1 and Level2 are used, each one containing a Player Start, a light, and two interpolation points. You'll set up a simple Matinee sequence that begins in Level1, and when you complete the sequence, Level2 is automatically loaded and its Matinee sequence begins playing.

TUTORIAL 13.12: Setting up Level1

1. In UnrealEd, open the map `Level1.urt`, which is a simple room.
2. Open Matinee and create a new Scene Manager. Set its `Tag` property to `StartMovie` (see **FIGURE 13.46**).
3. In the Actions tab, create an ActionMoveCamera Action, and associate it with the upper interpolation point in the map.
4. Create another ActionMoveCamera. Set its `Duration` to 5, and associate it with the other interpolation point (see **FIGURE 13.47**).
5. Select the first Action, and click the Sub Actions tab.
6. Create a SubActionTrigger Sub Action and set the following properties (see **FIGURE 13.48**):

   Delay: 4.99

   EventName: LaunchLevel2

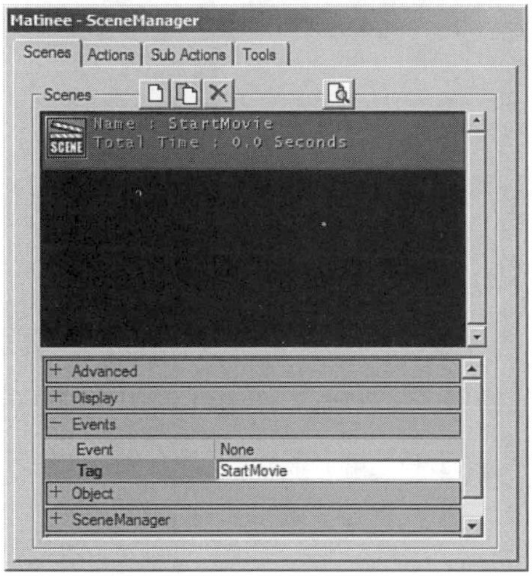

FIGURE 13.46 Create a new Scene Manager and set the *Tag* property.

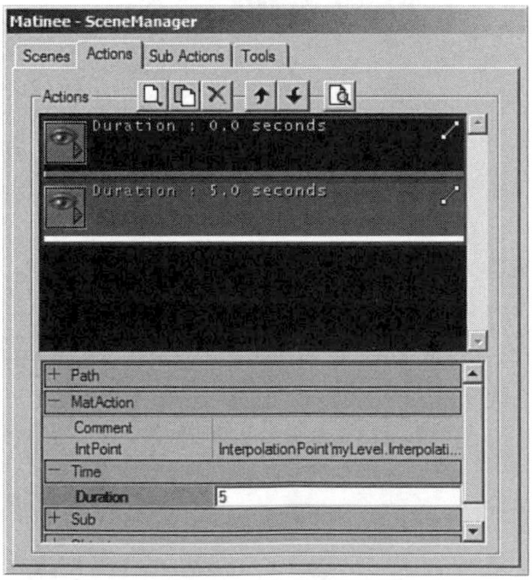

FIGURE 13.47 Two Actions should be in the list.

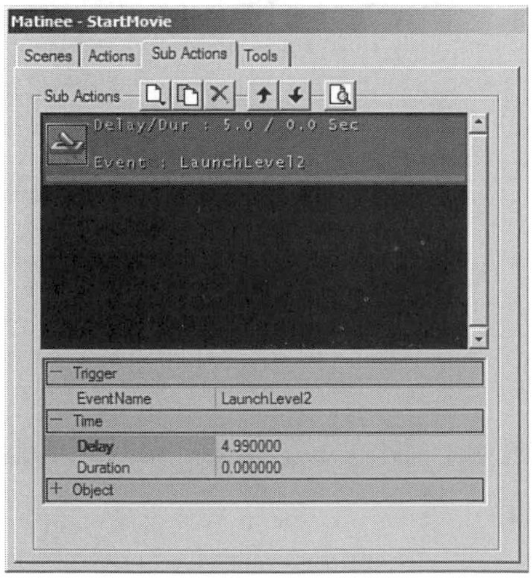

FIGURE 13.48 Set the *`Delay`* and *`EventName`* properties.

7. In the Actor Class browser, expand Actor > Keypoint > AIScript > ScriptedSequence and click ScriptedTrigger. Place this trigger anywhere in your level.
8. Set up the following Action list for the ScriptedTrigger (see **FIGURE 13.49**):

   ACTION_TriggerEvent

   Event: StartMovie

   ACTION_WaitForEvent

   ExternalEvent: LaunchLevel2

   ACTION_ChangeLevel

   URL: Level2
9. Save the map.

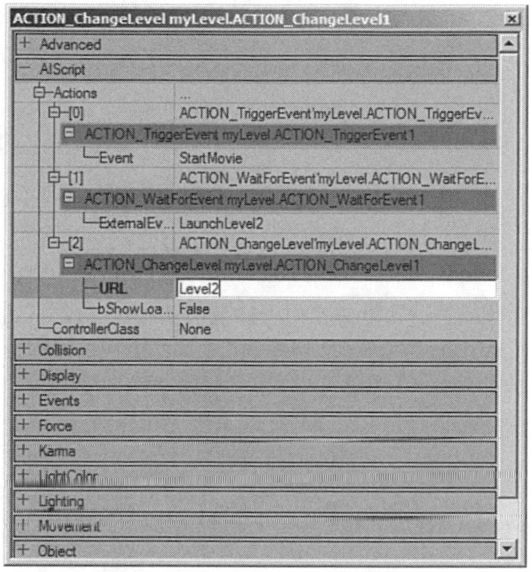

FIGURE 13.49 The Action list for the ScriptedTrigger.

END TUTORIAL 13.12

In **TUTORIAL 13.13**, you set up your system in the second level so that your Matinee sequence jumps from one level to the other.

TUTORIAL 13.13: Setting up Level2

1. Open the map `Level2.urt`, shown in **FIGURE 13.50**.
2. Open Matinee and create a new Scene Manager. Set its `Tag` property to `StartMovie`, just as you did before.
3. In the Actions tab, create an Action and associate it with one of the interpolation points in the map.
4. Create another Action. Set its `Duration` to 5, and associate it with the other interpolation point.
5. Using the techniques you have learned, create a ScriptedTrigger Actor somewhere in the level.

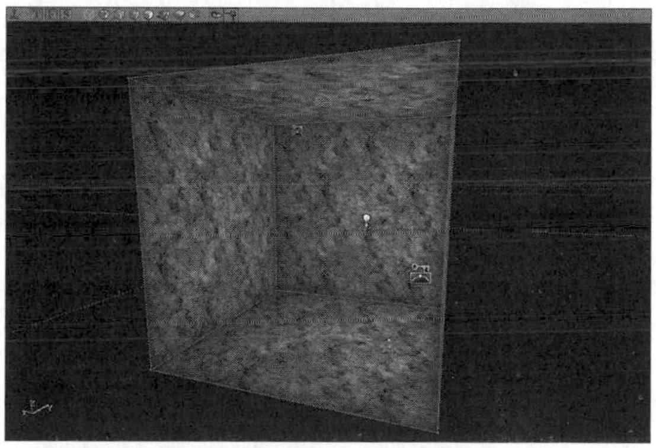

FIGURE 13.50 This is what you should see when you open *`Level2.urt`*.

6. Set up the following Action list for the ScriptedTrigger:

   ACTION_TriggerEvent

   Event: StartMovie

7. Save the map.

END TUTORIAL 13.13

You can now test the sequence by opening the `Level1.urt` map and running it. Verify that as soon as the level loads, the simple Matinee sequence launches, propelling the camera forward. When the camera reaches the end of its path, Level2 should load. Using this technique, you could easily establish a system by which players could finish a level, view a congratulatory movie of some kind, and then see a preview of the next level. **FIGURE 13.51** demonstrates how this system works.

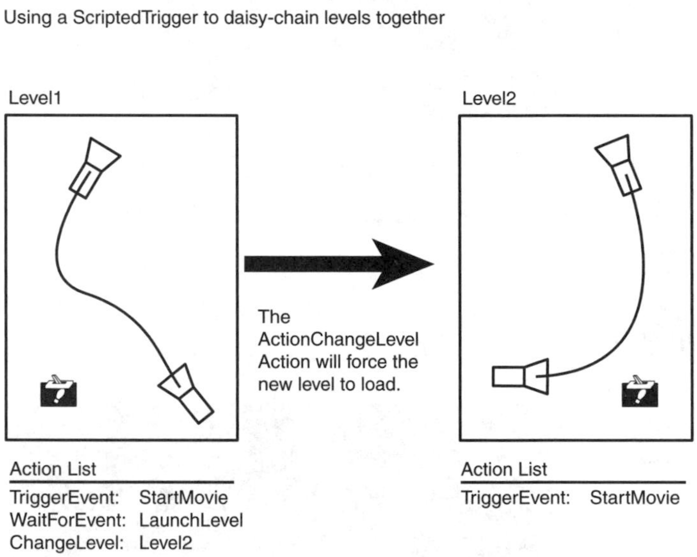

FIGURE 13.51 Overview of using a ScriptedTrigger to daisy-chain levels together.

Summary

This introductory chapter to Matinee has covered a wide variety of topics, from a simple overview of the Matinee interface to creating your own basic sequences, including fades and camera cuts, and adding an aim for the camera. You've also learned how to create cinematic effects, such as movie titles and letterbox formatting, and learned how to develop intro movies to levels and use a Matinee sequence when jumping from one level to another. By now, you should have a basic understanding of how Matinee works and how to create sequences for your levels. You can use these sequences to animate the camera or Actors within the level. You should also understand how all these components are related and how they can be used to create interesting Matinee sequences.

Chapter 14

Creating Scripted Sequences

In many games, you find that the player character is not the only element involved with the environment. Often the game drives many actions and events to enhance the overall experience. For example, you might be playing a game in which you're moving through a science laboratory and see scientists going about their duties, assistants moving equipment, secretaries carrying important items, and so forth. Within Unreal, these elements must be added into a level as scripted sequences. This chapter covers how you can use the ScriptedSequence Actor to create a variety of custom events within your Unreal levels.

Adding interactive or reactive game elements, making non-player characters (NPCs) perform actions, and other such events add an incredible amount of gameplay value to your levels. For example, say your character is behind a closed door, and you want a scientist NPC on the other side to open the door for you. With scripted sequences, you can tell a bot, or NPC, to move to the button that opens the door, start a door-pressing animation, and then open the door.

To create these scripted sequences, you have the ScriptedSequence Actor, located under Keypoint > AIScript in the Actor Class browser. This Actor contains all the main functions for controlling NPCs, or xPawns, and controlling how events are processed. Subsets of this Actor are the ScriptedTrigger and UnrealScriptedSequence Actors. The ScriptedTrigger should be used when handling events, as when you used it in Chapter 9, "Interactive Elements," to create an advanced elevator. UnrealScriptedSequence Actors are used when you want to control the behavior of bots, as you did in Chapter 12, "Advanced Bot/AI Navigation."

This chapter starts with a general discussion of how to create Actions, the backbone of scripted sequences. From there, you learn how to control the timing of events and see that certain Actions are latent, meaning they must be finished before moving on, and some are not. Then you learn how to use logical conditions to control whether certain Actions should occur.

Using an Actions List

Scripted sequences have an `Actions` property located under their AIScript category. This property can hold a series of Actions that are performed from the top to the bottom of the list. This series of Actions is known as the *Actions list*. An Action can perform a variety of tasks: trigger an event, play a sound, spawn an Actor, control artifical intelligence (AI), and much more. When a level starts, the first Action is performed, followed by the second, and continuing until reaching the final Action in the list. Unless there's an Action that alters the sequence, such as an `Action_GOTOACTION`, the ScriptedSequence carries out the last Action and then stops.

Using Latent and Non-latent Actions

Actions are categorized into two main types, depending on how they are performed: latent and non-latent. *Latent* actions cause Actions in the list to pause until the current Action is finished before they're carried out. *Non-latent* actions cause some effect or event and then immediately proceed to the next Action without waiting until the first Action is completed. For example, if you use an `Action_PLAYANIM` to play an animation of a character waving, and then immediately follow it with an `Action_PLAYSOUND`, both Actions would seem to happen simultaneously.

TABLES 14.1 and **14.2** describe the available non-latent and latent actions.

TABLE 14.1 Non-latent Actions

Action	Description	Notes
`ACTION_ASSetPlayerSpawnArea`	Enables or disables `PlayerSpawnManagers`.	Used in Assault gametype
`ACTION_ASTeleportToSpawnArea`	Causes players to spawn at points controlled by the specified `Player SpawnManager`.	Used in Assault gametype

TABLE 14.1 Continued

Action	Description	Notes
ACTION_ChangeLevel	Loads another map. Useful for creating Matinee sequences that span multiple maps.	
Action_ChangeObjectiveTeam	Updates the specified objective so that it belongs to the specified team.	
ACTION_ChangeScript	Leaves the current script and starts running the specified script.	AI control only
ACTION_ChangeWeapon	Causes the controlled pawn to switch to the specified weapon. The pawn must already have the weapon in its inventory.	AI control only
Action_ConsoleCommand	Performs a console command.	
Action_CROUCH	Causes the controlled pawn to crouch until an ACTION_Run or ACTION_Walk is used.	AI control only
ACTION_DamageActor	Causes all Actors with the specified Tag to receive damage of a certain type and amount.	
ACTION_DamageInstigator	Damages the player or NPC that caused the current script to run.	
ACTION_DestroyActor	Removes all Actors of the specified Tag from the level.	
ACTION_DestroyPawn	Removes the controlled pawn from the level.	AI control only
ACTION_DisableObjective	Allows an objective to be bypassed and counted as complete.	Used in Assault gametype
ACTION_DisableThisScript	When performed, causes the in-game (bot) AI to ignore this script. Applies only to UnrealScriptedSequence Actors.	
ACTION_DisplayMessage	Displays or broadcasts a message to one or all players in the game.	

TABLE 14.1 Continued

Action	Description	Notes
ACTION_EndSection	Used to mark the end of a group of Actions controlled by an Action_IFCONDITION or Action_IFRANDOMPCT.	
ACTION_FireWeapon	Causes the controlled pawn to start or stop firing its current weapon.	AI control only
ACTION_FireWeaponAt	Causes the controlled pawn to shoot at an Actor, designated by a Tag.	AI control only
Action_FORCEMOVETOPOINT	Snaps the controlled pawn to the specified point.	AI control only
ACTION_FreezeOnAnimEnd	Freezes the controlled pawn's animation and physical movement after its current animation finishes.	AI control only
Action_GOTOACTION	Jumps the script to the specified Action. Useful for making scripted sequences repeatable.	
ACTION_GotoMenu	Displays the game's main menu. A custom menu class can be specified with the MenuName property.	
Action_IFCONDITION	If the associated TriggeredCondition's bEnabled property is False, it causes the script to skip to the Action after the next Action_ENDSECTION.	
Action_IFRANDOMPCT	Based on the given probability, the script may or may not j ump to the Action after the next Action_ENDSECTION.	
ACTION_Jump	Causes the controlled pawn to jump. The type of jump can be controlled with the JumpAction property.	AI control only
Action_KILLINSTIGATOR	Kills the player that caused the script to run. Should be used only with ScriptedTriggers.	

14

TABLE 14.1 Continued

Action	Description	Notes
Action_LEAVESEQUENCE	Exits the current script and ignores any further Actions.	
ACTION_LocalizedMessage	Broadcasts a localized message.	
Action_PLAYAMBIENTSOUND	Causes the ScriptedSequence's AmbientSound properties to be set according to this action.	
Action_PLAYANIM	Causes the controlled pawn to play an animation.	AI control only
Action_PLAYANNOUNCEMENT	Plays an announcement sound in the game's currently selected announcer voice. The specified sound must be a valid announcer sound.	
ACTION_PlayerViewShake	Causes the instigator's view to shake as though hit by a weapon. Occurs only when the instigator is within a specified radius from the ScriptedSequence Actor.	
Action_PLAYLOCALSOUND	Causes all players to hear a sound. This sound is not location based.	
Action_PLAYMUSIC	Sets the current music to the specified song. This Action can set the music for just the instigator or for all players in the level. The song must be a file from the Music directory under the folder where you installed Unreal, without the .ogg extension. For example, if you want to play KR-DM1.ogg, you would set the Song property to KR-DM1.	
Action_PLAYSOUND	Plays a sound that originates from the ScriptedSequence Actor.	
Action_RUN	Causes the controlled pawn to run when moving. (Disables the effect of Action_CROUCH and Action_WALK.)	AI control only

TABLE 14.1 Continued

Action	Description	Notes
`Action_SETALERTNESS`	Sets the alertness of the controlled pawn.	AI control only
`ACTION_SetHidden`	Hides all Actors with the specified `Tag`.	
`ACTION_SetObjectiveActiveStatus`	Determines whether the specified objective is active.	Used in Assault gametype
`ACTION_SetPhysics`	Sets the instigator's current physics type.	
`Action_SETVIEWTARGET`	Sets the location that the controlled pawn tries to look toward. Because this Action is non-latent, you need more time to pass after this Action to see the effect.	AI control only
`ACTION_ShootTarget`	Causes the controlled pawn to shoot at its current target.	AI control only
`ACTION_SpawnActor`	Spawns an Actor of the specified class. The Actor can be spawned from the location of the ScriptedSequence Actor or from a controlled pawn's location. Additional location and rotation offset can also be set.	
`Action_STOPANIMATION`	Causes the controlled pawn to stop playing its current animation.	AI control only
`ACTION_StopShooting`	Aborts the effect of `ACTION_ShootTarget`.	AI control only
`ACTION_SubTitles`	Causes the heads-up display's (HUD's) current subtitles to advance.	Used in assault
`ACTION_ThrowWeapon`	Causes the controlled pawn to throw its current weapon in the direction specified by the `WeaponVelocity` property.	AI control only

TABLE 14.1 Continued

Action	Description	Notes
`Action_TRIGGEREVENT`	Causes the specified event to be broadcast.	
`Action_USE`	Causes the controlled pawn to use the player.	
`Action_WALK`	Causes the controlled pawn to walk when moving.	AI control only

TABLE 14.2 Latent Actions

Action	Description	Notes
`Action_DrawHUDMaterial`	Renders the specified material as an overlay onto the HUD. You can specify the width, height, and size the material is displayed at. Also, you can set the amount of time the material is displayed.	
`ACTION_FinishRotation`	Waits until the instigator or controlled pawn is facing its goal.	
`ACTION_Freeze`	Freezes the controlled pawn's animation and physical movement.	AI control only
`Action_MOVETOPLAYER`	Causes the controlled pawn to navigate to the instigating player. Script running continues when the pawn reaches the player.	AI control only
`Action_MOVETOPOINT`	Causes the controlled pawn to navigate to the specified point. Script running continues when the pawn reaches that point.	AI control only
`ACTION_PlayExplosionSound`	Plays a random explosion sound. With the `SoundEmitterActorTag` property, you can specify a location for the sound to be emitted from. (Default location is the scripted sequence itself.)	
`Action_TELEPORTTOPOINT`	Teleports the instigator to the specified point. The audiovisual teleportation effect can be enabled or disabled.	

TABLE 14.2 Continued

Action	Description	Notes
Action_TURNTOWARDPLAYER	Causes the controlled pawn to face the player.	AI control only
Action_WAITFORANIMEND	Causes script running to pause until the controlled pawn's current animation finishes.	AI control only
Action_WAITFOREVENT	Causes script running to pause until the specified event is broadcast.	
Action_WAITFORPLAYER	Causes script running to pause until the player is within the specified distance of the controlled pawn.	AI control only
Action_WAITFORTIMER	Causes script running to pause for the time specified. Note that the time is in seconds.	

TUTORIAL 14.1 shows how to create a simple ScriptedTrigger that uses both latent and non-latent Actions to open a door in a complex manner.

TUTORIAL 14.1: Using a ScriptedTrigger

1. Open `Tutorial14_01_Start.ut2`. In this map, you'll create a UseTrigger that plays a sound, opens a door, and turns on a "caution" light.
2. In the Actor Class browser, navigate to Triggers, and click UseTrigger.
3. Add the UseTrigger in front of the door (see **FIGURE 14.1**). To make the UseTrigger visible in-game, open the Properties window for the UseTrigger, go to the Advanced category, and set the `bHidden` property to False.

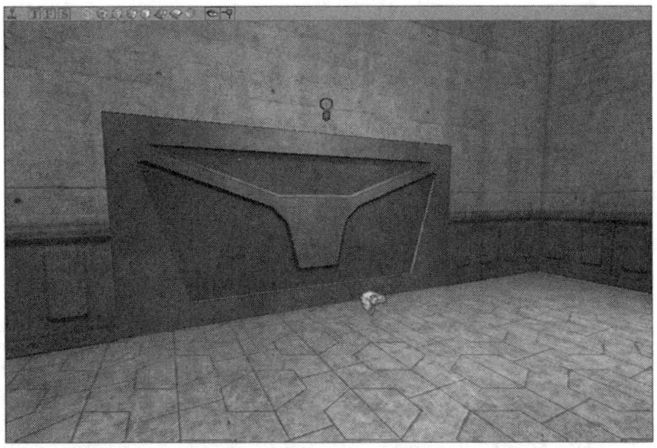

FIGURE 14.1 The UseTrigger placed in front of the door.

4. Because you have three separate Actions to perform, this is a great place for a ScriptedTrigger. Open the Actor Class browser, expand Keypoint > AIScript > ScriptedSequence, and click ScriptedTrigger.

5. Place the ScriptedTrigger next to the UseTrigger (see **FIGURE 14.2**). Although the location of a ScriptedTrigger is irrelevant, place it near the UseTrigger because the two triggers will be working with one another.

FIGURE 14.2 The ScriptedTrigger placed next to the UseTrigger.

6. Open the Properties window for the UseTrigger. Under the Events category, type `MultiTrigger` as the setting for the `Event` property. This event will be the one that triggers the chain of events.

7. Open the Properties window for the ScriptedTrigger. Under the AIScript category, select the `Actions` property, and click the Add button. By default, the Actions in the Actions list begin evaluating as soon as the level starts. In this case, however, you don't want anything to happen until you activate the UseTrigger. This means you need to wait for the `MultiTrigger` event to be triggered before any Actions take place. To do this, select `Action_WAITFOREVENT` and click the New button. Set the `ExternalEvent` property to `MultiTrigger` (see **FIGURE 14.3**). Until this event is triggered, the next Action is not performed.

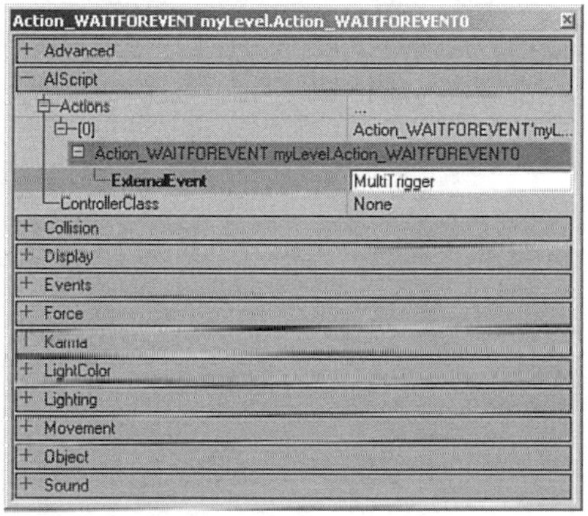

FIGURE 14.3 One Action created for the ScriptedTrigger.

8. Now you need to add three Actions to the list: one to play the sound, one to open the door, and one to turn on the light. Select the `Actions` property and click the Add button three times. For index [1], select `Action_PLAYSOUND` and click New. Open the Sound browser. If you're using Unreal Tournament 2004, open the `IndoorAmbience` package and select `door10`. If you're using the Unreal Runtime Engine, open the `EM_Runtime_A` package and select `door12`. Back in the Properties window for `Action_PLAYSOUND`, select the `Sound` property, and click the Use button.

> **NOTE**
>
> **You need to manually enter `MultiTrigger` for the `Event` property.**

9. For index [2], select `Action_TRIGGEREVENT` and click New. Because the `Tag` property for the door is `BlastDoor`, set the `Event` property of the `Action_TRIGGEREVENT` to `BlastDoor`.

10. For index [3], select `Action_TRIGGEREVENT` and click New. The `Tag` property for the light is `CautionLight`, so set the `Event` property of the `Action_TRIGGEREVENT` to `CautionLight`. This setting activates a dynamic light that's already in the scene.

11. Save the map, and give it a test spin. Note that the door opens, the sounds plays, and the light switches on after you hit the trigger. Also, notice that although the Actions are taking place in a specific order, they all appear to be happening at the same time.

END TUTORIAL 14.1

Controlling xPawns

Now that you have an idea of how to control events, you're ready to take it one step further and control actual non-player characters (NPCs). This brings another property of ScriptedSequences into the spotlight: `ControllerClass`. By default, it's set to None. For controlling an xPawn, you must set it to `ScriptedController`. Basically, this setting overrides the `ControllerClass` for the xPawn, allowing the ScriptedSequence Actor to take control of the xPawn and alter its behavior. If you didn't use this setting, it would default to a bot-style AI, which would, in effect, spawn an additional player into the game.

To associate the xPawn with the ScriptedSequence Actor, set the xPawn's `AIScriptTag` property, found under the AI category, to the `Tag` property of the ScriptedSequence. **TUTORIAL 14.2** demonstrates how to set up a simple scenario in which a ScriptedSequence controls an xPawn.

TUTORIAL 14.2: Controlling a Pawn

1. Open `Tutorial14_02_Start.ut2`. In this tutorial, you're going to create an NPC that runs to the player, beckons for the player to follow, and then opens the door. You already have a series of PathNodes set up for the NPC to follow; you just need to give the NPC the proper commands. For more information on creating bot paths, please refer to Chapter 12, "Advanced Bot/AI Navigation."

2. First, you need to create the NPC. Open the Actor Class browser, navigate to Pawn > UnrealPawn, and click xPawn. In the Top view, move the xPawn to the lower right of the level, near the PathNode. Rotate the xPawn to point toward the PathNode (see **FIGURE 14.4**).

3. Open the Actor Class browser, navigate to Keypoint > AIScript, and click ScriptedSequence Actor. Place this Actor next to the xPawn.

4. In the Properties window for the ScriptedSequence Actor, go to the Events category and change the `Tag` property to `PawnController`. Also, under the AIScript Category, set the `ControllerClass` property to `ScriptedController`.

5. Now open the Properties window for the xPawn and go to the AI category. Set the `AIScriptTag` to `PawnController`, which forces the xPawn to listen for behavior commands from the ScriptedSequence Actor. After doing this, you'll see a line connecting the ScriptedSequence icon to the xPawn (see **FIGURE 14.5**).

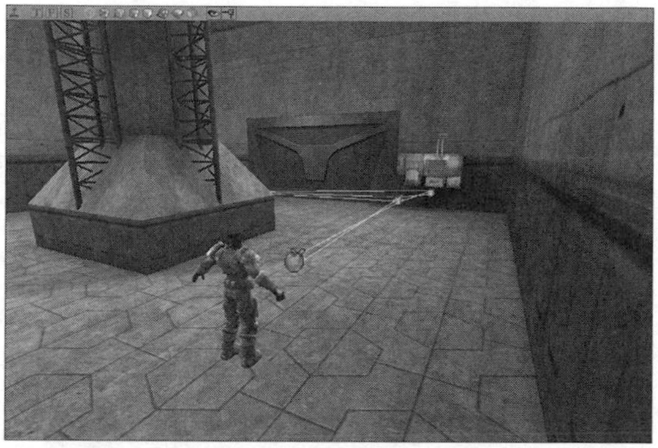

FIGURE 14.4 xPawn ready for action.

6. Now that everything is set up properly, you can create the Actions for the xPawn to follow. Open the Properties window for the ScriptedSequence. First, you need to wait for the player to hit the UseTrigger, which sends the `CallNPC` event, so add an `Action_WAITFOREVENT` and set the `ExternalEvent` to `CallNPC`.

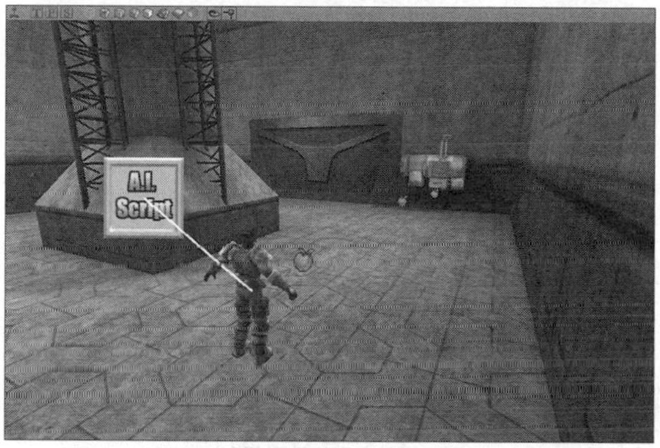

FIGURE 14.5 ScriptedSequence connected to the xPawn.

7. Second, the xPawn needs to move to the player. To do this, add an `Action_MOVETOPOINT` and set the `DestinationTag` to `CallPoint`, which is the `Tag` property of the PathNode next to the UseTrigger. Because you have PathNodes leading to the `DestinationTag`, the xPawn moves correctly from PathNode to PathNode until reaching the destination.
8. At this point, you need the xPawn to look at the player. To do this, add an `Action_TURNTOWARDPLAYER`.
9. With the xPawn now facing the character, you must make sure the xPawn is stationary and not playing any animations. For this, add an `Action_WAITFORTIMER` and set the `PauseTime` to 0.5. Now add an `Action_PLAYANIM` and set the `BaseAnim` to `gesture_beckon`. Because `Action_PLAYANIM` is non-latent, you need to make sure the animation ends before moving to the next Action; therefore, add an `Action_WAITFORANIMEND` and leave `Channel` set to 0.
10. To make the xPawn turn toward the console as he moves toward it, add an `Action_SETVIEWTARGET` and change the `ViewTargetTag` property to `ConsoleTag`. As before, add an `Action_MOVETOPOINT` and set the `DestinationTag` to `ConsolePoint`, which is the `Tag` property of the PathNode in front of the console.

11. As before, you need to ensure that the xPawn is stationary and isn't playing any other animations. So add an `Action_WAITFORTIMER` and set the `PauseTime` to 0.2, which is lower than before because the previous `Action_SETVIEWTARGET` should already have the xPawn facing in the right direction. Now add an `Action_PLAYANIM` and set the `BaseAnim` to `gesture_halt`. To ensure that the animation ends, add an `Action_WAITFORANIMEND`.

12. Finally, you need the door to open. Add an `Action_TRIGGEREVENT` and set `Event` to `BlastDoor`, the `Tag` property of the door Mover.

13. Save the map and run it. When you're in-game, go over to the UseTrigger and press the Use key (the E key, by default). If it doesn't work correctly, use **TABLE 14.3** as a reference for the Actions in this tutorial.

TABLE 14.3 Actions for the ScriptedSequence

Index	Action	Properties to Set
[0]	Action_WAITFOREVENT	ExternalEvent = CallNPC
[1]	Action_MOVETOPOINT	DestinationTag = CallPoint
[2]	Action_TURNTOWARDPLAYER	N/A
[3]	Action_WAITFORTIMER	PauseTime = 0.5
[4]	Action_PLAYANIM	BaseAnim = gesture_beckon
[5]	Action_WAITFORANIMEND	N/A
[6]	Action_SETVIEWTARGET	ViewTargetTag = ConsoleTarget
[7]	Action_MOVETOPOINT	DestinationTag = ConsolePoint
[8]	Action_WAITFORTIMER	PauseTime = 0.2
[9]	Action_PLAYANIM	BaseAnim = gesture_halt
[10]	Action_WAITFORANIMEND	N/A
[11]	Action_TRIGGEREVENT	Event = BlastDoor

END TUTORIAL 14.2

You can also use ScriptedSequences when you're creating intro movies with Matinee and custom animations. **TUTORIAL 14.3** shows you how to use a custom character with custom animation to create a movie sequence. For more information on using Matinee, see Chapter 13, "Matinee: Creating Custom Cinematics."

TUTORIAL 14.3: Using Matinee with ScriptedSequences

FIGURE 14.6 xPawn placed in the level.

FIGURE 14.7 Custom character rotated and moved into position.

1. Open `Tutorial14_03_Start.ut2`. In this level, you have a Matinee sequence where the camera flies around the level and circles around the inside of a room. Inside this room, you're going to place a custom character and cause it to play some of the custom animation included with it.

2. To start off, place an xPawn in the center of the room, which is located in the center of the level (see **FIGURE 14.6**). Change `ControllerClass` to `ScriptedController`. Also, under the UnrealPawn category, set the `bNoDefaultInventory` property to `True` so that the character isn't holding a gun.

3. Because you want to use your own custom character, not the default, open the Animation browser so that you can load the correct character. Open the `Chapter14_Anim.ukx` package. With this character visible in the browser, open the Properties window for the xPawn. Under the Display category, select the `Mesh` property and click Use. Also, select the `Skins` property and click Empty. Rotate the xPawn so that it points between the two interpolation points. Also, move the xPawn so that it rests on the floor (see **FIGURE 14.7**). Because you need to control this pawn with a ScriptedSequence, go to the AI category and set the `AIScriptTag` property to `LFController`.

4. Next, create a ScriptedSequence near the xPawn. Under the Events category, change the `Tag` property to `LFController`. If you ran the level now, you would notice that the xPawn is in the wrong pose. Playing an animation at this point would cause the character to snap from this pose to the first frame of the animation you want. To correct this, you have a single-frame animation (KickStart) that leaves the character at the correct pose for starting the animation. From there, you need to start the Matinee sequence, which can be triggered with the `StartMovie` event. **TABLE 14.4** shows the Actions needed for the ScriptedSequence Actor.

TABLE 14.4 Actions for the ScriptedSequence

Index	Action	Properties to Set
[0]	`Action_PLAYANIM`	`BaseAnim = KickStart`
[1]	`Action_TRIGGEREVENT`	`Event = StartMovie`

5. Because you want the animation to start when the camera enters the room, you need to have the Matinee sequence trigger an event. To do this, open the Matinee dialog box. Select the StartMovie scene and switch to the Actions tab. Then select the second Action from the bottom. Now switch to the Sub Actions tab, and select the third Sub Action from the top. Add a SubActionTrigger. Under the Trigger category, set the `EventName` property to `StartAction`.

6. With that set up, reopen the `ScriptedSequence` property and add the final Actions that will wait for the event, as shown in **TABLE 14.5**, and then play the animation. At the very end, quit to the main menu.

TABLE 14.5 Actions for the ScriptedSequence

Index	Action	Properties to Set
[2]	`Action_WAITFOREVENT`	`ExternalEvent = StartAction`
[3]	`Action_PLAYANIM`	`BaseAnim = Kick`
[4]	`Action_WAITFORANIMEND`	N/A
[5]	`Action_GotoMenu`	N/A

7. That's it! Save and run the map. The character's animation won't begin until the Matinee sequence tells it to. **FIGURE 14.8** shows a screenshot of the custom animation.

FIGURE 14.8 The character playing the custom animation.

END TUTORIAL 14.3

Logical Conditions

Although the simple Actions you've seen so far can handle most situations you run into, at times you want the result or running of a script to differ depending on external conditions. To this end, you have the following three Actions (described previously in **TABLE 14.1**): `Action_IFCONDITION`, `Action_ENDSECTION`, and `Action_IFRANDOMPCT`. To use the `Action_IFCONDITION`, you must also have a TriggeredCondition Actor, which is located under the Triggers section of the Actor Class browser. When this Actor is triggered, an internal value toggles between True and False. To use it, you create a section of Actions that are blocked off by an `Action_IFCONDITION` and `Action_ENDSECTION`. If the internal value is True, the Actions within the block are carried out, and those outside it are disregarded.

TUTORIAL 14.4: Using If Conditions

1. Open `Tutorial14_04_Start.ut2`. In this tutorial, you create a system in which a pawn must activate a control unit before the player can open the door.
2. First, you'll set up the ScriptedSequence to make the pawn run over to a PathNode and send the `IC_DoorControl` event to the `TriggeredCondition`. Add a ScriptedSequence Actor next to the existing Trigger. In the Properties window for the ScriptedSequence, first set the `ControllerClass` to `ScriptedController`. Next, the xPawn must be associated with the ScriptedSequence. The xPawn's `AIScriptTag` is currently set to `NPCScript`, so set the ScriptedSequence's `Tag` property to `NPCScript`. Now add the Actions shown in **TABLE 14.6** to the ScriptedSequence.

TABLE 14.6 Actions for the ScriptedSequence

Index	Action	Properties to Set
[0]	`Action_WAITFOREVENT`	`ExternalEvent = CallBot`
[1]	`Action_WALK`	N/A
[2]	`Action_SETVIEWTARGET`	`ViewTargetTag=BotPanel`
[3]	`Action_MOVETOPOINT`	`DestinationTag= SwitchPoint`
[4]	`Action_WAITFORTIMER`	`PauseTime=0.2`
[5]	`Action_PLAYANIM`	`BaseAnim=gesture_halt`
[6]	`Action_WAITFORANIMEND`	N/A
[7]	`Action_TRIGGEREVENT`	`Event=IC_DoorControl`

3. Now you need to actually create the TriggeredCondition. In the Actor Class browser, go the Triggers section and click TriggeredCondition. Place this Actor next to the trigger.

4. In the Properties window for the TriggeredCondition, go to the TriggeredCondition category, and set `bTriggerControlled` to True so that the TriggeredCondition can be externally controlled by a trigger. Also, set the `Tag` property under the Events category to `IC_DoorControl`.

5. The UseTrigger in front of the second PathNode sends the `TestConsole` event. Therefore, open the ScriptedTrigger Properties window and create the set of Actions shown in **TABLE 14.7**.

TABLE 14.7 Actions for the ScriptedTrigger

Index	Action	Properties to Set
[0]	`Action_WAITFOREVENT`	`ExternalEvent = TestConsole`
[1]	`Action_IFCONDITION`	`TriggeredConditionTag = IC_DoorControl`
[2]	`Action_PLAYSOUND`	`Sound = MenuSounds.J_MouseOver`
[3]	`Action_TRIGGEREVENT`	`Event= OpenDoor`
[4]	`Action_ENDSECTION`	N/A
[5]	`Action_GOTOACTION`	`ActionNumber= 0`

As you can see, what's between `Action_IFCONDITION` and `Action_ENDSECTION` isn't performed unless the TriggeredCondition is toggled to True by the ScriptedSequence.

6. Save the map and test the level. Run over to the trigger and watch the xPawn run to the first PathNode. Now you should be able to open the door.

END TUTORIAL 14.4

14

`Action_IFRANDOMPCT` is used when you want some group of Actions to happen randomly. As with `Action_IFCONDITION`, you must also have an `Action_ENDSECTION` to signify the end of the block. The one property available in this Action is `Probability`. Setting this property to 1 causes the Actions inside the block to always be performed. A value of 0, however, means the Actions are never carried out. Finally, setting it to 0.5 means there's a 50% chance of the Actions being performed.

TUTORIAL 14.5 shows how to create a flickering dynamic light by using `Action_IFRANDOMPCT`. This method gives you more control over how the light flickers and is an excellent demonstration of how useful this Action can be.

TUTORIAL 14.5: Using Random Conditions

1. Open Tutorial14_05_Start.ut2. This level is nothing but a simple cube with a light fixture where you'll be placing the flickering light.

FIGURE 14.9 TriggerLight placed next to the static mesh.

2. In the Actor Class browser, select Light > TriggerLight. Place this light next to the static mesh (see **FIGURE 4.9**). In the Properties window for the TriggerLight, go to the LightColor category and set LightBrightness to 200, LightHue to 150, and LightSaturation to 150. Also, under the Lighting category, set LightRadius to 10. Under the Events category, change the Tag property to FlickerLight. Finally, under the Object category, set InitialState to TriggerToggle so that the light responds to external events.

3. Now add a ScriptedTrigger near the TriggerLight, and then add the Actions shown in **TABLE 14.8**.

TABLE 14.8 Actions for the ScriptedTrigger

Index	Action	Properties to Set
[0]	Action_WAITFORTIMER	PauseTime = 0.10
[1]	Action_IFRANDOMPCT	Probability = 0.50
[2]	Action_TRIGGEREVENT	Event = FlickerLight
[3]	Action_ENDSECTION	N/A
[4]	Action_GOTOACTION	ActionNumber= 0

When the level starts, you wait for 0.1 seconds, and then a random condition says that there's a 50% chance you switch the light on or off. After that, you just jump back to the top, wait another 0.1 seconds, and so on.

4. Save the map and test the level. You should now have a flickering light.

END TUTORIAL 14.5

Summary

In this chapter, you've learned everything you need to create more interactive levels and intro movies. You started with a look at how to use scripted sequences, and then learned how to use Actions to control what takes place in your sequences, along with a list of the primary Actions available and the differences between latent and non-latent Actions. Finally, you learned how to use logical conditions with your scripted sequences to create conditional actions. With these simple foundations, you should be able to create a massive variety of scripted sequences to enhance the look and feel of your levels.

Chapter 15

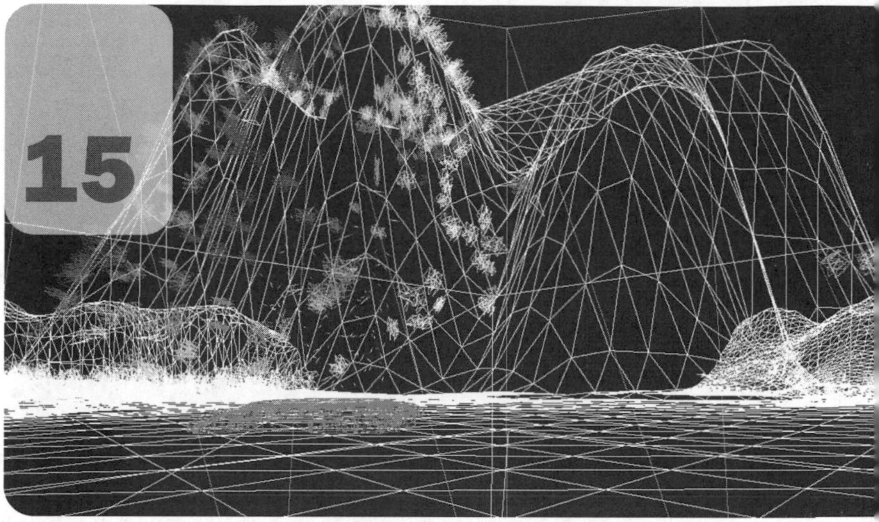

Level Optimization (Zoning) and Distribution

Introduction to Level Optimization

Each level you create is a collection of triangles that are sent to your video card to be "rendered." Why is this important? Well, video cards can draw, or "crunch," only a limited number of these triangles per frame. Therefore, if the video card had to render an entire level, the frame rate is slowed down drastically unless it's a very small level. Obviously, if the graphics engine is crunching data for areas that are invisible to the player, it's doing unnecessary work, which can lead to a drop in game performance. To optimize a level, level designers must use a series of techniques that allow video cards to render only what players can see.

Although many optimization techniques are controlled by level designers, one important technique is automatically controlled by the rendering engine. This chapter focuses on optimizations that must be actively created, but understanding this automatic optimization technique, called *frustum culling*, can be helpful. This optimization ensures that only what's in the player's field of view is rendered, as shown in **FIGURE 15.1**. The graphics engine ignores everything to either side or behind the character. This form of optimization is simple and automatic.

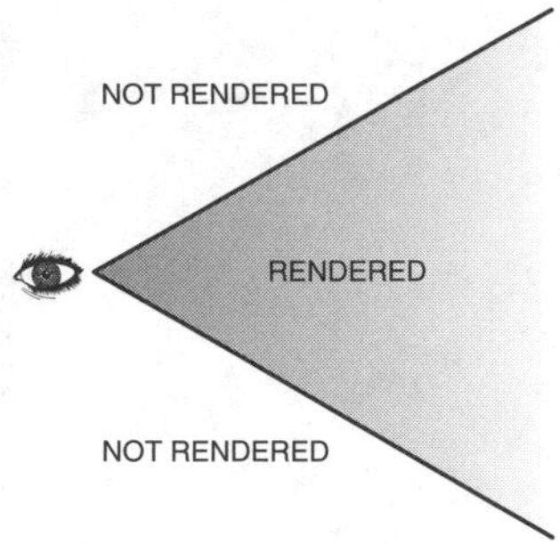

FIGURE 15.1 Frustum culling.

Zoning

Zoning is the primary method of level optimization. It requires level designers to "zone" a level, which is the process of separating the level into different sections. These sections are defined by sealing off your levels with brushes called Zone Portals, which are typically placed in areas such as doorways or at corners of a hallway. The zones are actually calculated when rebuilding your level's geometry. After these zones have been defined, the rendering engine uses them when deciding what can and cannot be seen. If the Zone Portal that seals off a specific zone isn't within the player's field of view, the zone behind the portal is not rendered. This technique can prevent entire sections of the level from being calculated if the player isn't within visual range of them. Furthermore, Zone Portals make it possible to render objects only as they come into view. For this reason, zoning is by far the most efficient way for level designers to optimize a level. Of course, this is true only when a level can be cleanly divided at narrow interconnections, such as doors or windows.

The Zone Portals between each zone are created with a BSP sheet. This surface must be created as a special brush specified as a Zone Portal prefab. When placing this BSP sheet, be sure that it seals off the entire opening between the two zones; otherwise, the zones might not be separated. After rebuilding the geometry, you'll notice that the zones have different colors when viewed in Zone/Portal mode, a special viewport setting in UnrealEd. In **FIGURE 15.2**, you can see a Zone Portal separating two rooms in a simple zoning scenario.

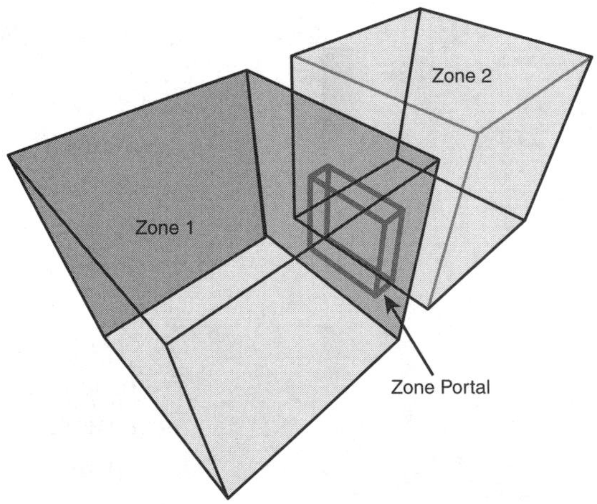

FIGURE 15.2 A Zone Portal placed between two rooms, causing two zones to be created.

TUTORIAL 15.1: Zoning a Level

1. Open Tutorial15_01_Start.ut2. You'll use this unzoned level and follow the steps in this tutorial to zone it. **FIGURE 15.3** shows where you'll be creating Zone Portals.

2. First, you need to change the Builder brush into a sheet. Right-click the Sheet button in the toolbox. The first Zone Portal you're creating is for the hallway on the lower level. Therefore, enter the following values in the SheetBuilder dialog box:

Height	512
Width	768
Axis	AX_YAxis

3. Move the brush to the entrance of one of the hallways (see **FIGURE 15.4**).

4. Before creating the Zone Portal, you should select a texture for the surface. Open the Texture browser and load the wm_textures.utx package. From the editor group, select the ZonePortal texture (see **FIGURE 15.5**). Although you don't *have* to use this texture, it's good to have a texture that clearly distinguishes the surface as a Zone Portal, so as not to confuse it with the rest of the level.

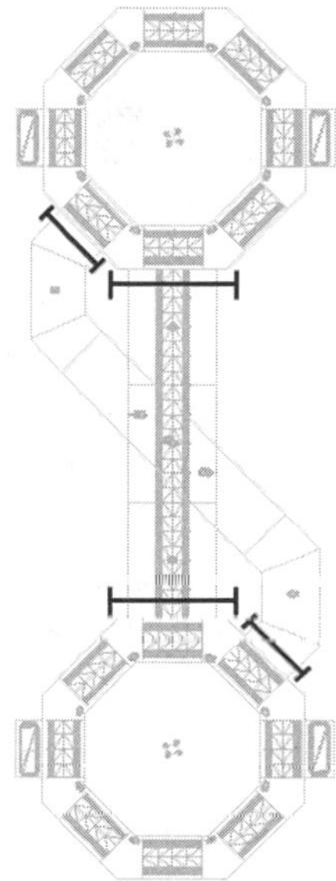

FIGURE 15.3 This top view of the level shows where you'll be placing Zone Portals.

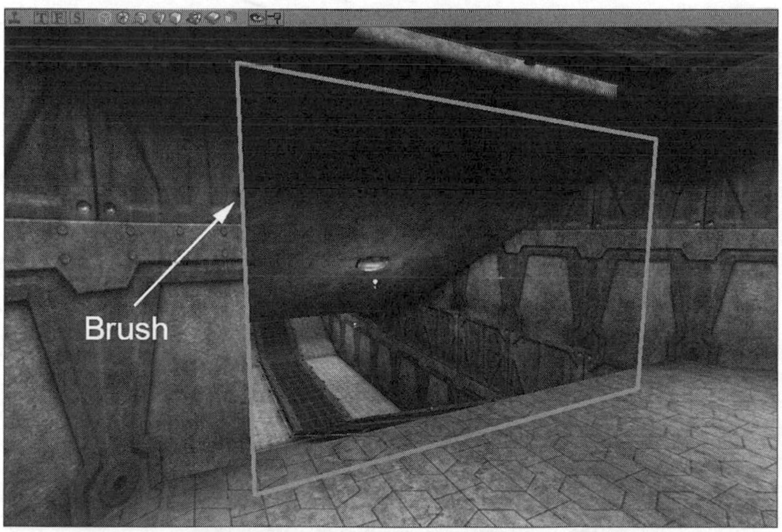

FIGURE 15.4 The brush fits perfectly in the hallway.

5. Click the Add Special Brush button  in the toolbox.
6. In the Add Special dialog box, select Zone Portal in the Prefabs list box (see **FIGURE 15.6**). This option sets the solidity to Non-Solid so that players can run through the Zone Portal. Also, the Invisible check box is selected so that the player can't see the Zone Portal in-game. Click OK and then Close.
7. Select the newly created Zone Portal and duplicate it. Move it to the other entrance to the hallway. Rebuild the geometry and switch to Zone/Portal view mode. You'll notice that the hallway is now a different color because the hallway is one zone, and the rest of the level is another zone. In **FIGURE 15.7**, you can get an idea of the change in coloration from one zone to the next.

FIGURE 15.5 Static Mesh browser with the ZonePortal texture selected.

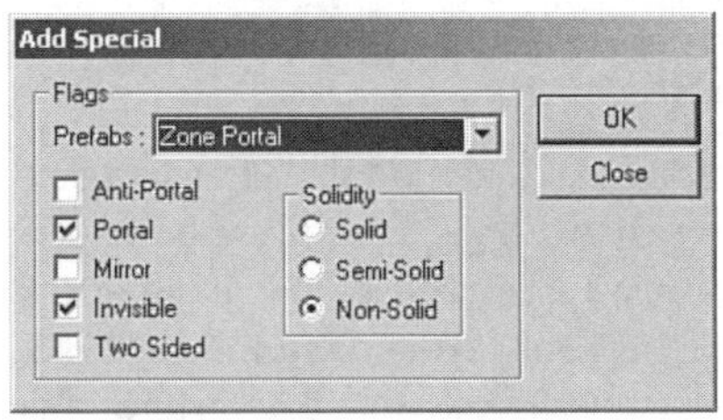

FIGURE 15.6 Set Prefabs to Zone Portal in the Add Special dialog box.

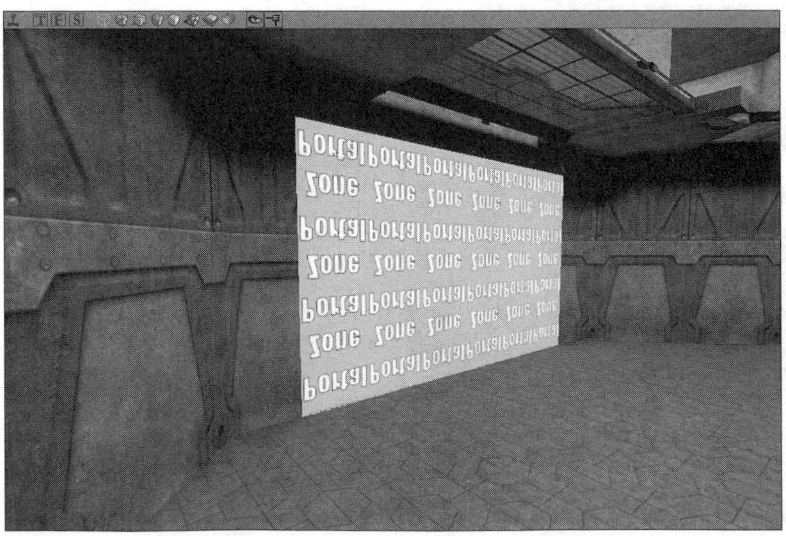

FIGURE 15.7 Perspective view of one Zone Portal.

8. For the entrances to the upper hallway, create a Sheet brush with the following dimensions:

   Height: 384

   Width: 528

   Axis: AX_YAxis

   Move the brush to the upper level at one of the entrances to the hallway. You need to rotate the brush in Top view to align it with the entrance (see **FIGURE 15.8**). Also, make sure it aligns in the Z-axis.

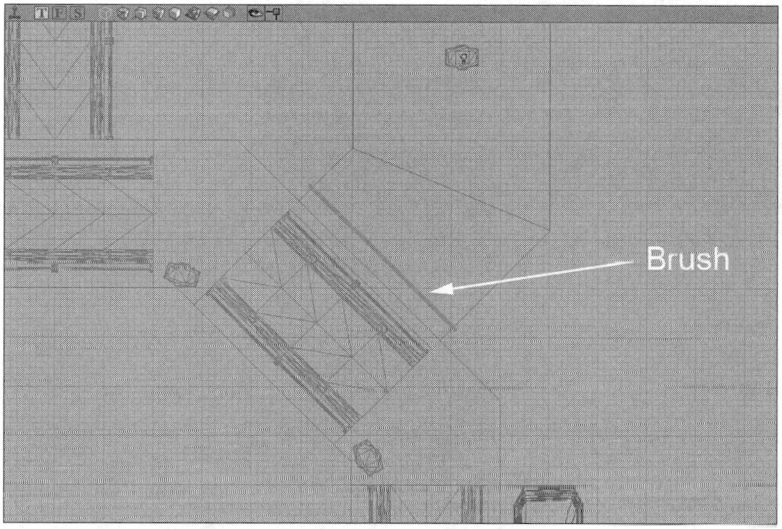

FIGURE 15.8 **Brush rotated and moved into place.**

9. Add a Zone Portal. Now duplicate the Zone Portal and move it to the other entrance. After rebuilding the geometry, you should have a total of four different zones, as shown in **FIGURE 15.9**.

10. Rebuild your level's geometry. Switch to Zone/Portal mode in the Perspective view by clicking its icon. Save and test your level. Right now, you won't notice any change as far as gameplay is concerned. Later in this chapter, you learn how to debug, diagnose, and view your optimization results.

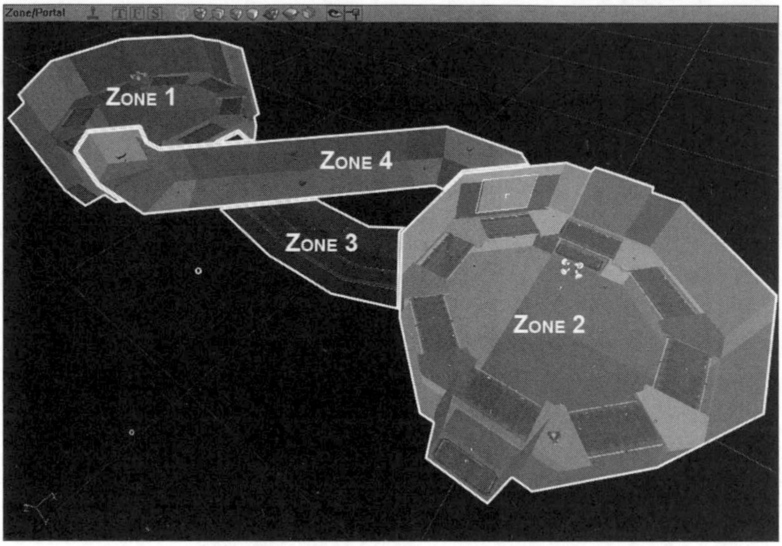

FIGURE 15.9 A Zone/Portal view of the final zoned map. Each zone is surrounded with a white border.

END TUTORIAL 15.1

Antiportals

Consider a large outdoor level in which you have two bases with a large mountain between them. This mountain prevents players at either base from seeing their enemy's base. Unfortunately, the graphics engine still calculates and draws the polygons for each base, not to mention the players as well. This means that although players on each base don't necessarily see each other, each time they look in the direction of the enemy base, that base and all the players in it are being calculated. Naturally, this leads to a slowdown in gameplay, as excessive graphics calculations must be made.

The problem is that you can't use a simple Zone Portal to fix the problem. The Zone Portal would have to be massive to divide the terrain, so it would be useless; as long as a Zone Portal is within a player's field of view, the zone on the opposite side of the portal is visible. You need some way to tell Unreal that as long as the player is on one side of the mountain, the information on the opposite side of the mountain no longer needs to be rendered. To accomplish this, you could fit an *Antiportal* inside the mountain. Antiportals are convex volumes that prevent objects hidden behind them from being rendered. They are useful in large, open areas where zoning would be inefficient. Placing an Antiportal within the mountain prevents the graphics engine from rendering anything the mountain occludes.

Because Antiportals must be convex, you need to know how to differentiate between a convex and a concave object (see **FIGURE 15.10**). With convex objects, such as a cube, sphere, or cylinder, you can draw a line from one point to every other point in that object, and the line would never leave the object's boundaries. However, with a concave object, such as a torus, at some point the line would leave the object's boundaries.

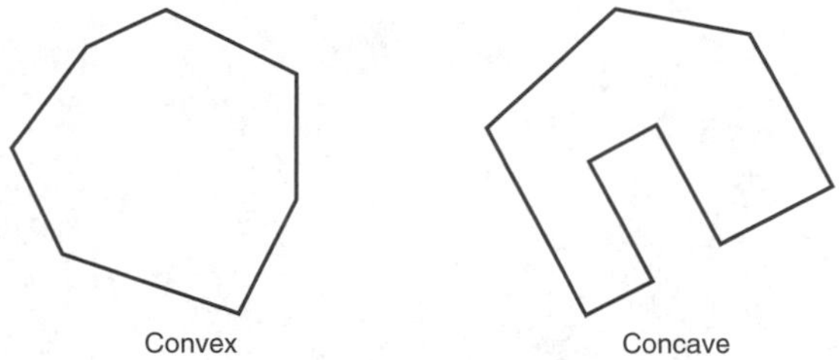

FIGURE 15.10 A concave versus a convex object.

TUTORIAL 15.2: Using Antiportals

1. Open `Tutorial15_02_Start.ut2`. This onslaught level is an outdoor level with two bases separated by mountains: a perfect target for Antiportals. As **FIGURE 15.11** shows, you can see the blue base while standing in the red base. This is precisely what you don't want. Therefore, you're going to place some Antiportals in the mountains to occlude the blue base (see **FIGURE 15.12**).

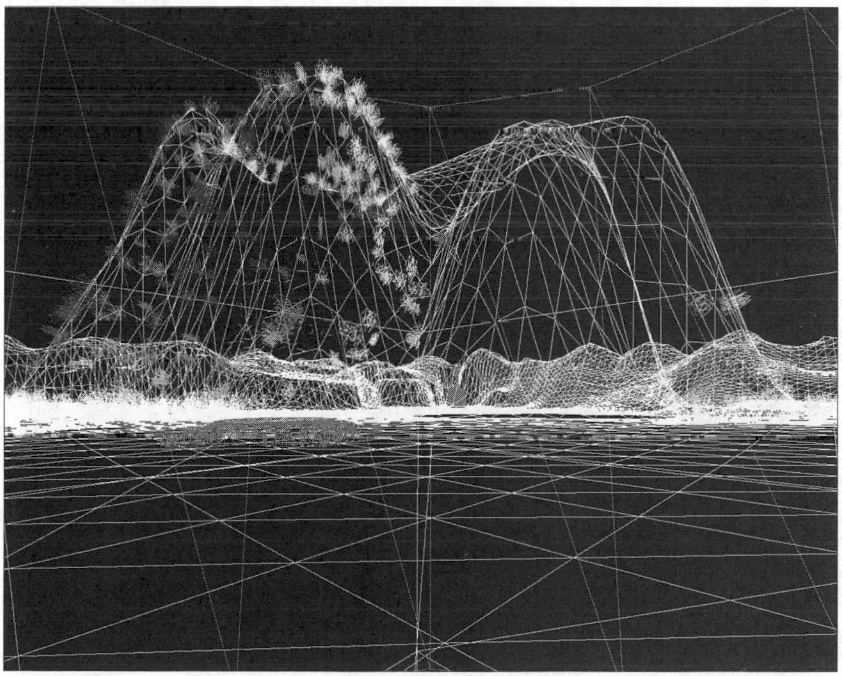

FIGURE 15.11 Before creating Antiportals. Note the blue base's static mesh in the center of the figure.

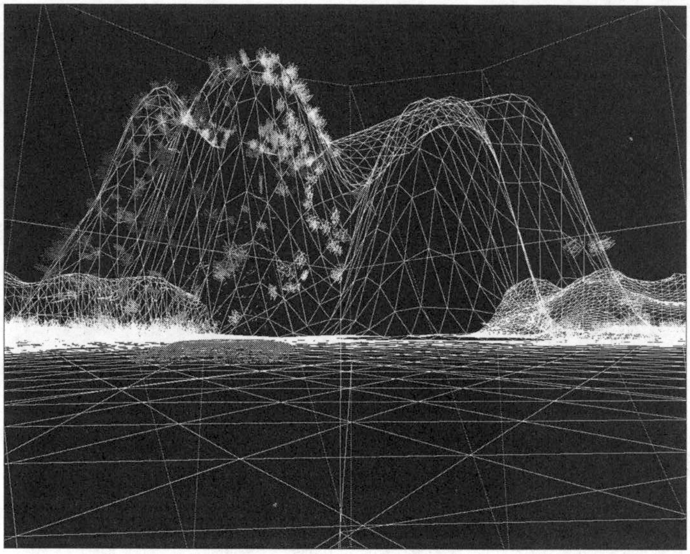

FIGURE 15.12 After creating Antiportals, the blue base's static mesh is no longer rendered.

2. Right-click the Cylinder button on the toolbar. Use the following values for the cylinder:

    Height: 1024

    OuterRadius: 768

> **NOTE**
>
> To view similar results in UnrealEd, make sure you switch to Wireframe mode in the Perspective viewport.

3. Center this brush on the terrain, as shown in **FIGURE 15.13**. Also, make sure the bottom of the cylinder is below the terrain.

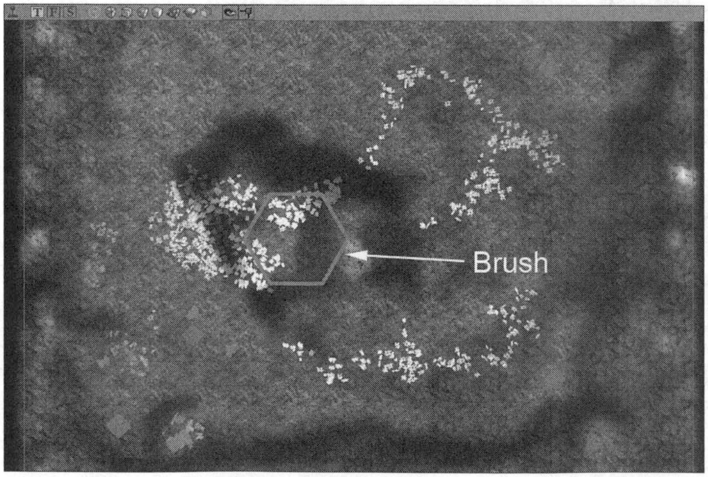

FIGURE 15.13 Cylinder brush centered on the terrain.

2. Using the Vertex Editing tool, move the brush's vertices so that the brush more accurately approximates the shape of the terrain (see Figure **15.14**).

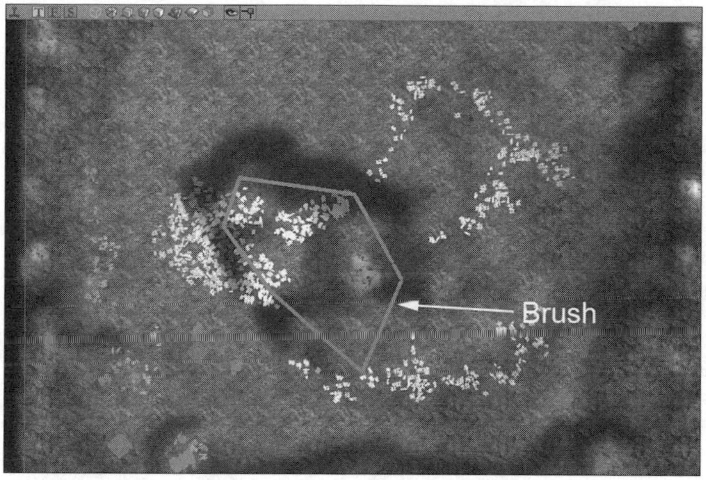

FIGURE 15.14 Brush after editing the vertices.

3. In the Perspective view, make sure the brush is completely inside the mountain. If a player somehow gets inside the Antiportal, the result will be a Hall of Mirrors effect because the rendering engine stops everything from being rendered.

> **NOTE**
>
> If you want to edit the Antiportal, you *cannot* modify the Antiportal's vertices. You must delete it, then modify the Builder brush, and then create another Antiportal.

4. Click the Add Antiportal button in the toolbox.
5. That's it! You should have a working Antiportal.

END TUTORIAL 15.2

Aside from working in outdoor areas to optimize rendering, you can also use Antiportals when zoning isn't sufficient. Take a moving door, for example. When a player is looking at a closed door, whatever is behind the door shouldn't be rendered, although it is by default. However, just zoning the two rooms won't alleviate this problem because a Mover wouldn't keep the player from "seeing" the Zone Portal. In this case, you would combine the use of Zone Portals and Antiportals.

If you set the door Mover's `AntiPortalTag` property to the `Tag` property of one or more Antiportals that cover the door, the Antiportal occludes everything behind the door when it's closed and lets everything render when it's open. **TUTORIAL 15.3** demonstrates how to set up this scenario.

TUTORIAL 15.3: The Antiportal Tag

1. Open `Tutorial15_03_Start.ut2`.
2. To create an Antiportal that covers the door, first create a Sheet with the following dimensions:

   Height: 244

   Width: 496

   Axis: AX_YAxis
3. Move the brush to the center of the doorway.
4. Click the Add Antiportal button in the toolbox.
5. In the Properties window for the newly created Antiportal, go to the Events category. Set the `Tag` property to `DoorAP`.
6. Open the Properties window for the Mover. In the Mover category, set the `AntiPortalTag` property to `DoorAP`.
7. Save and run the map. After loading the map, bring down the console with the tilde (~) key and type **`rmode 1`**, which puts the view into Wireframe mode. Notice that the door occludes everything behind it when closed, but when it's open, everything is rendered properly.

END TUTORIAL 15.3

An Antiportal can be activated and deactivated by using a trigger. To enable this behavior, simply set the Antiportal's `InitialState` to `TriggerToggle` or `TriggerControl`. For more information on using triggers in Unreal, please refer to Chapter 9, "Interactive Elements."

Antiportals can also be attached to other objects, such as Movers. Simply set the Antiportal's `AttachTag` to the Mover's `Tag` property, and it will follow the Mover. You could have done this in Tutorial 15.3 by setting the Antiportal's `AttachTag` to `BlastDoor`, the Mover's `Tag` property. If you did this, you could safely ignore the `AntiPortalTag` property. With this setup, the objects on the other side of the door would come into view as the door opened.

Distance Fog

As you learned in Chapter 5, "Terrain," fog is useful for creating moody atmospheric effects, such as murky fog. However, it's also useful for optimization. Everything after the `DistanceFogEnd` property is no longer rendered, meaning that the graphics engine ignores any objects that are completely hidden by fog. For outdoor levels with a single-colored sky, fog is easy to set up; however, when there's a sky texture, it can be quite tricky. In **TUTORIAL 15.4**, you see how this works by adding fog to the playable area of an outdoor map.

TUTORIAL 15.4: Using Distance Fog

1. Open Tutorial15_04_Start.ut2. Currently, the level doesn't have fog enabled inside the playable area. For optimization purposes, you're going to enable fog, and then finalize the effect by making the skybox and fog blend together.
2. Open the Properties window of the ZoneInfo located in the center of the map.
3. Under the ZoneInfo category, set bDistanceFog to True.
4. Although the map now has fog, you need to tweak the fog's color and density. Under the ZoneLight category, set the DistanceFogColor property to [B:150, G:155, R:147]. Now set DistanceFogEnd to 2000 and DistanceFogStart to 1000.
5. Fog is now set up for the level's playable area. You can save and run the map if you want to test it at this point. Notice that everything beyond the DistanceFogEnd stops rendering, which is precisely what you want. However, the skybox doesn't blend with the fog color at eye level. One possible fix is setting the skybox's fog to a matching color. Doing this, however, would make the sky texture in the skybox disappear. Instead, you'll use a cylindrical static mesh that surrounds the SkyZoneInfo.
6. Go to the skybox and delete the TerrainInfo because you won't be able to see it anyway with the cylinder surrounding the SkyZoneInfo.
7. Open the Static Mesh browser and load the Chapter15_SM.usx package. From the Fog group, select the FogRing static mesh (see **FIGURE 15.15**).

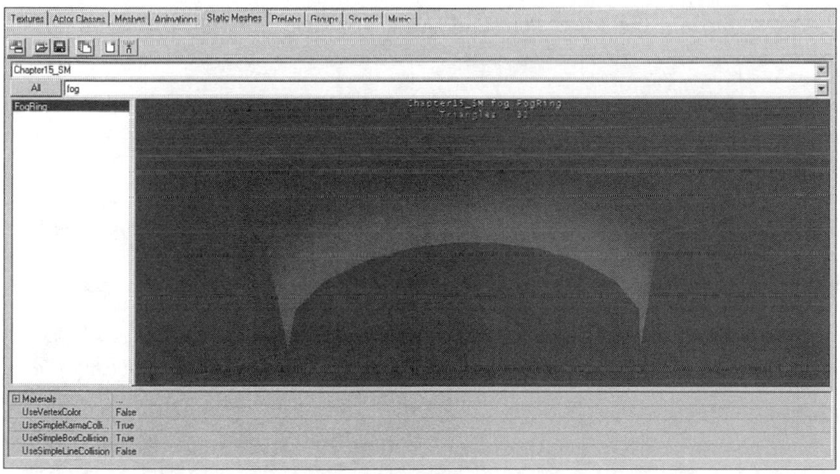

FIGURE 15.15 Static Mesh browser with the FogRing static mesh selected.

8. Add the FogRing to the skybox and set DrawScale3D to (2, 2, 4). Center it on the SkyZoneInfo, and in the Side view, move the FogRing so that it's sticking out of the skybox by approximately 16 units (see **FIGURE 15.16**).

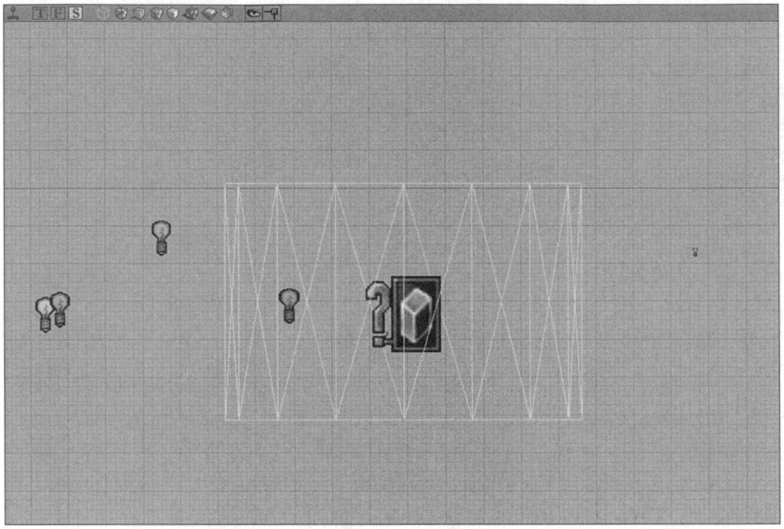

FIGURE 15.16 Side view of the fog ring in position.

9. Open the Texture browser and load the `Chapter15_tex.utx` package. Select the `fog_fade` texture.
10. In the Properties window of the FogRing, go to the Display category. Add an element to the `Skins` property and set it to the selected `fog_fade` texture.
11. Set `bUnlit` to True to prevent the lights surrounding the FogRing from influencing its color. Also, set `bShadowCast` to False so that it doesn't cast shadows on the sky's visible area.
12. Save and play the map. The fog should now blend seamlessly with the skybox.

END TUTORIAL 15.4

Terrain Optimization

Optimizing the rendering of terrain focuses primarily on one property: `TerrainSectorSize`. Essentially, this property divides your terrain into sectors so that when a portion of that sector is visible and should be rendered, the entire sector is rendered. As your terrain disappears, entire sectors disappear in blocks. In **FIGURE 15.17**, you can see the result of setting `TerrainSectorSize` to 16.

FIGURE 15.17 `TerrainSectorSize` of 16.

When `TerrainSectorSize` is set to a smaller value, the graphics engine takes longer to process which sectors to render. On the other hand, setting this property to a higher value often causes more of the terrain to be rendered, but less time is spent calculating what should be calculated, or rendered. Therefore, you'll have to play with this value to see what works best for your level. In a large map where a lot of the terrain can be hidden at a given time, such as an area with dramatic mountains, it makes sense to set a large `TerrainSectorSize` value.

Tweaking this value in-game can be immensely useful. To do this, you use the `editactor` command. Type the following into the console to open the Properties window for the TerrainInfo Actor:

```
editactor class=TerrainInfo
```

If you have multiple TerrainInfo Actors, check the name under the Object category before playing the map, and then use the following console command:

```
editobj TerrainInfo0
```

In this command, `TerrainInfo0` is the name of the TerrainInfo Actor you want to edit. After the Properties window opens, simply modify the `TerrainSectorSize` property located under the TerrainInfo category. Finally, observe the effect this setting has on the terrain by using the `rmode 1` console command, as demonstrated earlier in **TUTORIAL 15.3**.

Profiling and Debugging

Often you can use all the optimization techniques in a single level, but some optimization techniques don't work well in certain levels or situations. Therefore, after using zones, Antiportals, or any other optimization technique in your level, it's wise to check whether there was an actual gain in level efficiency, usually marked as an increase in speed. This section covers the different ways to check the speed of rendering and describes debugging techniques to ensure that your optimizations have been implemented properly and are working correctly.

Viewport Display Modes

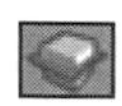

As you have no doubt noticed while using UnrealEd, the Perspective viewport has many settings to aid you in constructing your levels. One useful display mode for viewing how your zones have been divided is Zone/Portal view. In this mode, each zone is displayed with a different color (see **FIGURE 15.18**). Also, different shades of the same color within a particular zone indicate BSP cuts. Therefore, you can use this mode to view where your zones exist and the extent of the BSP cuts within them. Remember that the fewer BSP cuts you have, the faster your level can be calculated. You can access this mode by clicking the Zone/Portal icon (second icon from the right)  in the toolbox.

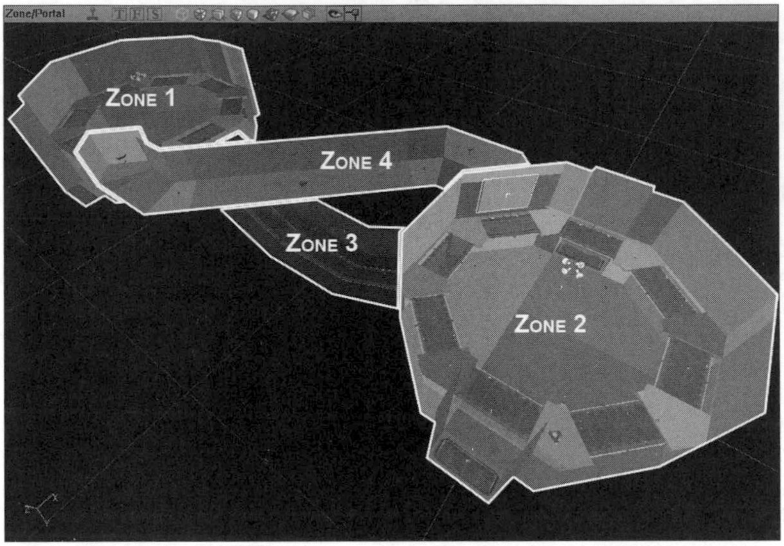

FIGURE 15.18 **A Zone/Portal view of a zoned map. Each zone is surrounded with a white border.**

When using Depth Complexity mode, you see how many textures are being drawn over a given part of the screen. This mode is useful when determining where terrain layers, deco layers, particles, and so forth have become too dense and could slow your game down on certain machines. After switching over to this mode, a bar appears on the right side of the viewport with a gradient from green to red (see **FIGURE 15.19**). Green areas of the viewport represent areas that have but one texture. When an area is covered with more textures, the gradient shifts toward red. If the area goes beyond red, it simply loops back through the gradient to start again (see **FIGURE 15.20**). If this happens, you might want to consider decreasing the number of textures covering that area. You can access this mode by clicking the Texture Usage icon. Seeing the behavior of this mode in **FIGURE 15.20** might be difficult. If necessary, open any Unreal level and switch to this mode to see the effect of the texture complexity.

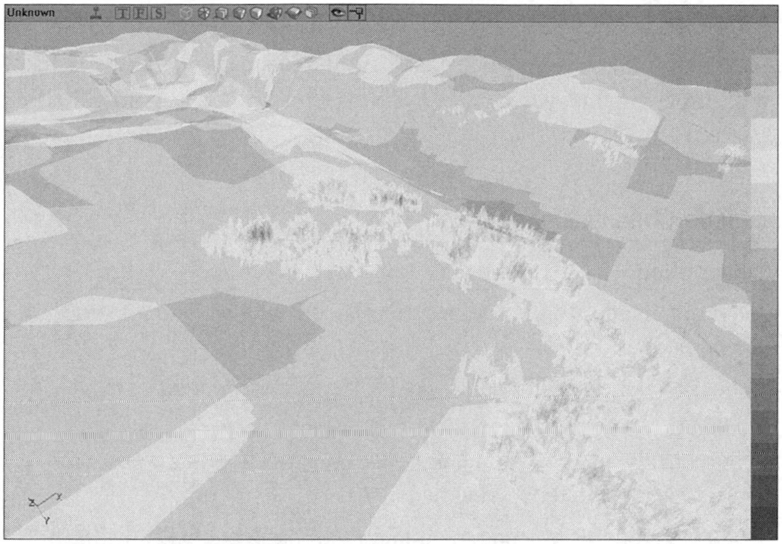

FIGURE 15.19 Texture depth complexity on terrain and deco layers.

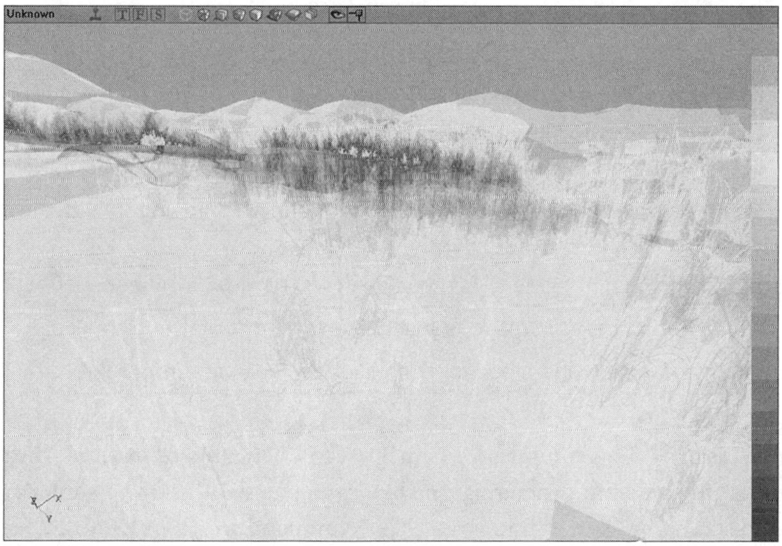

FIGURE 15.20 Texture depth complexity going beyond the green-to-red scale and looping back to green.

Console Commands

The first command you'll be looking at is `rmode`, which enables you to change the "render mode." By specifying an argument to this command, you can choose between 11 different render modes, described in **TABLE 15.1**.

TABLE 15.1 Render Mode Console Commands

Console Command	Description
`rmode 1`	Wireframe mode. This mode is extremely useful if your zones are working properly.
`rmode 2`	Zone/Portal mode. This works exactly like the same mode available in UnrealEd.
`rmode 3`	Texture usage mode. This mode color-codes every BSP surface to indicate what texture is being used.
`rmode 4`	BSP cuts mode. This mode is no longer fully operational. To view BSP cuts, use `rmode 2`, as explained previously in the "Viewport Display Modes" section.
`rmode 5`	Dynamic Light mode. This is the default mode when playing the game.
`rmode 6`	Textured mode. This mode is the same as `rmode 5` except that no lighting is applied to surfaces or objects in-game.
`rmode 7`	Lighting Only mode. In this mode, all textures appear white, but have both light maps and vertex lighting applied.
`rmode 8`	Depth Complexity mode. Unlike it's counterpart in UnrealEd, this mode doesn't work properly in-game.
`rmode 13`	Top view mode. This mode is much like the Top view in UnrealEd.
`rmode 14`	Front view mode. This mode is much like the Front view in UnrealEd.
`rmode 15`	Side view mode. This mode is much like the Side view in UnrealEd.

The second useful command is `stat`. This command, whether used in UnrealEd or in-game, displays a huge array of useful information, depending on the argument supplied. The simplest usage is `stat fps`, which displays the current frame rate. This command works in UnrealEd as well, but the frame rate is capped at 30. Also note that in UnrealEd, the stats are updated only if you update the viewport or enable real-time preview. **TABLE 15.2** describes the rest of the arguments.

TABLE 15.2 Statistics Console Commands

Console Command	Description
`stat all`	This command displays all information relevant to the game, such as the number of polygons, animated meshes, terrain sectors, particles, and many other items visible in the current view. Much of the information is related to optimization; however, the next commands in this table narrow down the amount of visible information onscreen, instead of showing all statistics.
`stat hardware`	This command shows you technical information about what's being rendered. `NumPrimitives`, located at the top, shows the total number of primitives currently being rendered. `NumTextures` shows the number of textures currently in view. For those with a technical background, the rest of the information this command displays can be quite useful. However, an in-depth discussion of this additional information goes far beyond the scope of this book and requires an understanding of programming concepts.
`stat render`	This immensely useful command shows render statistics. Each section has information about the different elements that make up the current frame. Furthermore, every section of information shows how long an element takes to render in milliseconds. The Frame section shows information about how long it takes to render an entire frame, for example. When optimizing your level, check the sections of information to see which element takes the most time; using optimization techniques, if possible, reduces the amount of time rendering takes.
`stat none`	This command removes all the information from the view.

Summary

In this chapter, you have learned a variety of techniques for optimizing your levels: zoning for areas that can be divided, Antiportals for open areas or dynamic occlusion of objects (as in the door example), and using distance fog to your advantage. For terrain, you can use the `TerrainSectorSize` property to more accurately control what parts of terrain should be rendered. You should now have an understanding of why optimization is so important when working with levels in Unreal, and you should be comfortable establishing your own systems of optimization for your own levels. Doing so keeps your levels fast and highly playable across a wide variety of computer types and allows more players to use your level simultaneously without as much risk of performance drop.

Chapter 16

Gametypes

This chapter discusses the technical details of how to take an existing map you've created and make it playable as a specific gametype. Eleven gametypes are available in Unreal Tournament 2004: Deathmatch, Team Deathmatch, Last Man Standing, Mutant, Invasion, Capture the Flag, Double Domination, Bombing Run, Onslaught, and Assault. With each gametype, you can play the maps you've created using different rules. However, nearly every gametype requires you to make certain changes to how your map is set up. For example, Capture the Flag maps require placing a pair of flags, Double Domination maps require domination points, and Onslaught maps require Power Nodes. In **FIGURE 16.1**, you see the map used for demonstrations in this chapter.

Each map you create should be designed with a specific gametype in mind. If, for instance, you design a map for Capture the Flag (CTF), you wouldn't use that same map to play Double Domination because a CTF map requires elements that aren't necessary in a Double Domination map, and vice versa. Although you can force Unreal to use a specific gametype on a map, this can lead to unpredictable results. Therefore, if you want to use the same map with multiple gametypes, you need to create a separate map file for each gametype.

The gametype used when you load a map depends on two things: the filename and the `DefaultGameType` property in the Level Properties window. In Unreal, the levels associated with each gametype are decided based on the filename. For example, when you launch Unreal Tournament 2004 and are looking for a level to play, the map named `CTF-Citadel.ut2` is always displayed under the CTF gametype, regardless of the `DefaultGameType` setting. **TABLE 16.1** specifies the abbreviation for each gametype.

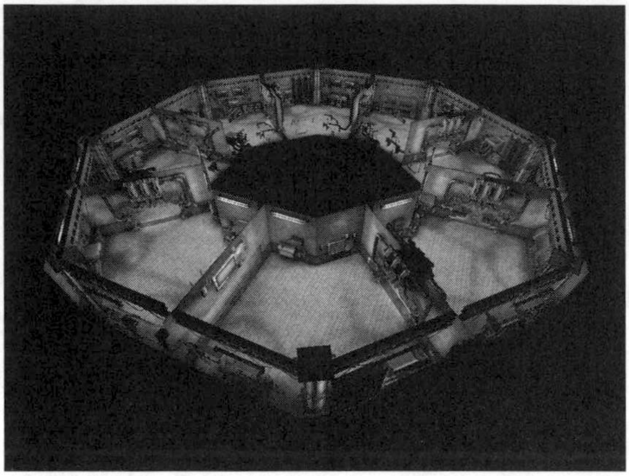

FIGURE 16.1 The demonstration map.

TABLE 16.1 Abbreviations for Gametypes

Abbreviation	Gametype
DM-	Deathmatch, Team Deathmatch, Last Man Standing, Mutant, Invasion
CTF-	Capture the Flag
DOM-	Double Domination
BR-	Bombing Run
ONS-	Onslaught
AS-	Assault

16

Setting Level Properties

Before you can play a map with a specific gametype, you need to set its `DefaultGameType` property. This step is a universal one for level creation, so it's covered here, at the beginning of the chapter.

The `DefaultGameType` property is the class that controls the game's operation. If you run your map from within UnrealEd, the gametype specified in this property is used. Also, when using the `open` *`<map>`* command in Unreal's console, the specified map is loaded and played with the gametype designated by that map's `DefaultGameType`.

To set this property, open your map in UnrealEd and choose View > Level Properties from the main menu or press the F6 key. Under the LevelInfo category, you must set the `DefaultGameType` to the class of the gametype you want to use. **TABLE 16.2** specifies the class for each gametype.

TABLE 16.2 Gametype Classes

Gametype	Class
Deathmatch	`xGame.xDeathMatch`
Team Deathmatch	`xGame.xTeamGame`
Capture the Flag	`xGame.xCTFGame`
Double Domination	`xGame.xDoubleDOM`
Bombing Run	`xGame.xBombingRun`
Onslaught	`Onslaught.ONSOnslaughtGame`
Assault	`UT2k4Assault.ASGameInfo`

The following sections cover all the different Actors you need to create and the properties that need to be set before these gametypes work properly. Important design tips and tricks are also given for each gametype.

> **NOTE**
>
> **You must type these classes in manually. There's no drop-down list in the Level Properties window for this particular property.**

Deathmatch-Style Gametypes

Deathmatch is the simplest gametype. The rules are simple: Kill or be killed. Players relentlessly hunt and destroy each other in an "every player for themselves" fashion. Every kill awards the player with a "frag," and the first player that reaches the "frag limit" or the player with the most frags when the timer runs out wins the game.

With Team Deathmatch, an entire team of people work together to demolish the opposing team. The number of frags each team member acquires is added to the team's total frags. The first team to reach the maximum number of frags wins the game. There's absolutely no difference in the implementation of Deathmatch and Team Deathmatch.

Creating a Deathmatch map isn't difficult. The only requirements are placing PlayerStarts around the map and setting the level's `DefaultGameType` property to `xGame.xDeathMatch`. During a game, a player is randomly spawned from the PlayerStart Actors. In UnrealEd, however, you can add these PlayerStarts by simply right-clicking in a viewport and choosing Add Player Start Here from the context menu, as mentioned throughout this book.

Other gametypes are intended to be created in the same fashion as Deathmatch maps: Last Man Standing, Mutant, and Invasion. In the Last Man Standing gametype, each player

> **NOTE**
>
> **Should you need to access the PlayerStart Actor, you can find it in the Actor Class browser under NavigationPoint > SmallNavigationPoint.**

is given a certain number of lives. After players lose all their lives, they are out of the match. The last player remaining is the winner.

In the Mutant gametype, the first player to gain a frag is declared the "mutant." That player is then invisible, deals more damage, and gains a tremendous load of ammunition. The mutant's health also drains constantly and can be replenished only by killing other players. Naturally, the mutant is a coveted position. Any players who kill the mutant then become the mutant themselves. Also, nonmutant players are not allowed to kill each other, with one exception. The player with the lowest score is designated the "bottom-feeder" and is allowed to kill any other player, as compensation for his score deficit.

In the Invasion gametype, all players (whether they are human or bot) are on the same team. The team is then attacked by waves of computer-controlled monsters. Each subsequent wave gets more difficult. When players die, they must sit out and wait for the next wave. The game is over when all human players die in a single wave of attacking monsters.

Adding Weapons

For Deathmatch as well as the other gametypes listed in this section, the most)important items to populate your level with are weapons, ammunition, and other pickups, such as health, armor, and adrenaline. In **TUTORIAL 16.1**, you see how to bring these Actors into your level and get them positioned on the map.

TUTORIAL 16.1: Adding Weapons and Pickups

1. Start UnrealEd, and open the `Tutorial16_01_Start.ut2` file included in the Chapter 16 folder on the CD.
2. Although this level has been equipped with several PlayerStarts, it has no weapons. Open the Actor Class browser, and expand the xPickUpBase category. This category has seven separate pickup classes, described in **TABLE 16.3**. **FIGURE 16.2** illustrates these pickup bases.

   From the list, choose `xWeaponBase`. Right-click on the floor in the Perspective view, and choose Add xWeaponBase Here to place a weapon base on the floor.

TABLE 16.3 xPickupBase Pickup Classes

Class Name	Description
`HealthCharger`	This class creates a base that spawns simple Health Pack pickups, visible in-game as floating blue crosses.
`ShieldCharger`	This class creates a base that spawns simple Shield Pack pickups, which are displayed in-game as floating gold crests.
`SuperHealthCharger`	This class creates a base that spawns the "Big Keg O' Health" pickup.

TABLE 16.3 Continued

Class Name	Description
SuperShieldCharger	This class creates a base that spawns Super Shield Pack pickups.
UDamageCharger	This class spawns Double Damage pickups.
WildcardBase	This base randomly spawns items included in its list, which are discussed later in this section.
xWeaponBase	This base spawns a particular kind of weapon, which you can control via its properties.

FIGURE 16.2 The pickup bases, from left to right: HealthCharger, ShieldCharger, SuperHealthCharger, SuperShieldCharger, UDamageCharger, WildcardBase.

3. Double-click the weapon base mesh to open its Properties window. Under the xWeaponBase category, set the `WeaponType` property to the mighty Rocket Launcher (see **FIGURE 16.3**).

4. Now you need some ammunition pickups for your weapon. In the Actor Class browser, expand Pickup > Ammo > UTAmmoPickup. Various ammo types are listed, their names corresponding with their weapons.

   From the list, select RocketAmmoPickup. Right-click on the floor next to the weapon base you just created, and choose Add RocketAmmoPickup Here from the context menu (see **FIGURE 16.4**).

5. From these few steps, you should be able to equip your level with a veritable arsenal and enough pickups to keep the game's pace up. However, there are a couple of other important pickups that you have not yet discussed: the Health Vial and the Adrenaline pickup.

NOTE

You'll probably need to move the weapon base up a little so that it's sitting on the floor, not passing through it.

NOTE

You won't see the selected weapon type in the editor, but it's spawned when you play the game.

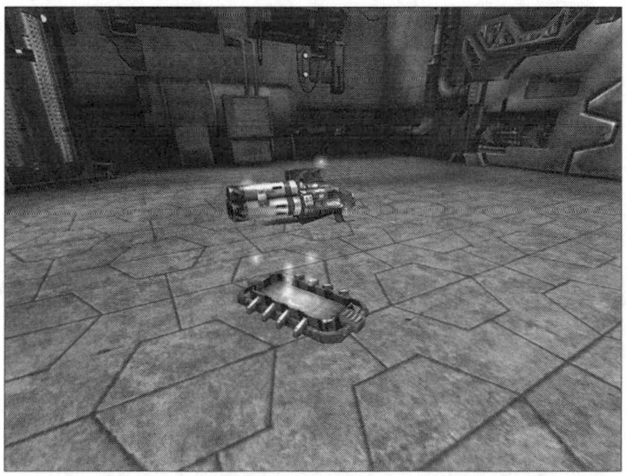

FIGURE 16.3 Rocket Launcher floating over the weapon base while in-game.

The Health Vial appears in-game as a small floating blue test tube (see **FIGURE 16.5**). When collected, it adds five health points to your character, even if it's already at 100% health. Collecting Health Vials allows you to increase your character's health to 199%.

The Adrenaline pickup (shown in **FIGURE 16.6**) adds three points of Adrenaline to your character. As you play the game, activities such as kills also increase your Adrenaline. When your Adrenaline reaches 100, you can perform Adrenaline Combos, which boost your character's abilities in some way.

FIGURE 16.4 Rocket ammo next to the floating Rocket Launcher.

Creating these Actors is easy: Simply navigate to them in the Actor Class browser, and then right-click in your level and place them. The following are the paths in the Actor Class browser for each pickup:

Health Vial: Pickup > TournamentHealth > MiniHealthPack

Adrenaline: Pickup > TournamentPickup > AdrenalinePickup

Add a few of these pickups around the level.

FIGURE 16.5 The Health Vial.

6. Using the skills discussed so far in this tutorial, populate your level with weapons, ammo, and other pickups until you're satisfied. Save your work and test the level.

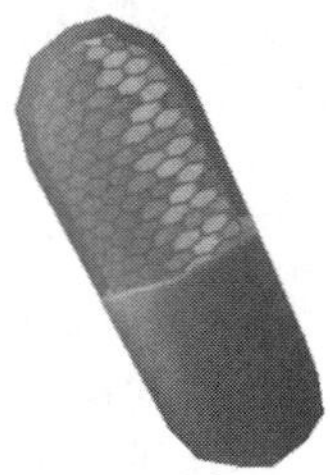

FIGURE 16.6 The Adrenaline pickup.

NOTE

If you have set up any bot paths in your level, you should at least rebuild your paths before you test and save. Flags and weapon bases create navigation points of their own, so make sure you have rebuilt so that bots can use these objects to navigate through the level as well as access any pickups or items.

END TUTORIAL 16.1

Now that you know how to add a variety of pickups to your level, you can have more control over how your level is played. In **TUTORIAL 16.2**, you expand on this knowledge by learning about the wildcard base, which can randomly spawn a variety of pickups.

TUTORIAL 16.2: Using the Wildcard Base

1. Continue from **TUTORIAL 16.1**, or open the file you saved at the end of that tutorial. You're going to add a wildcard pickup base to your level. As mentioned earlier, this base generates random pickups based on a list you set in its Properties window.

2. From the Actor Class browser, expand xPickupBase, and select WildcardBase. Right-click in the Perspective view, and place the base on the floor somewhere in your level. A point near the halfway mark of the level would be best for the sake of game balance.

3. Double-click the base to open its Properties window, where you see the WildcardBase category. When expanded, it reveals two properties. The first is `bSequential`, which forces the base to spawn items in the list sequentially, from highest to lowest. So the item in entry 5 would spawn just before entry 4, and so on. If this property is set to False, the items spawn in a random order.

   The second property is `PickupClasses`, which is the list where you store the items you can include in the wildcard base. Make sure you don't skip entries, as this can yield unpredictable results.

4. Set the list to any items you like, and then save and test your map. Find your wildcard base, and see how it spawns the pickups that were in your list. In **FIGURE 16.7**, you can see the wildcard base with a Double Damage pickup floating above.

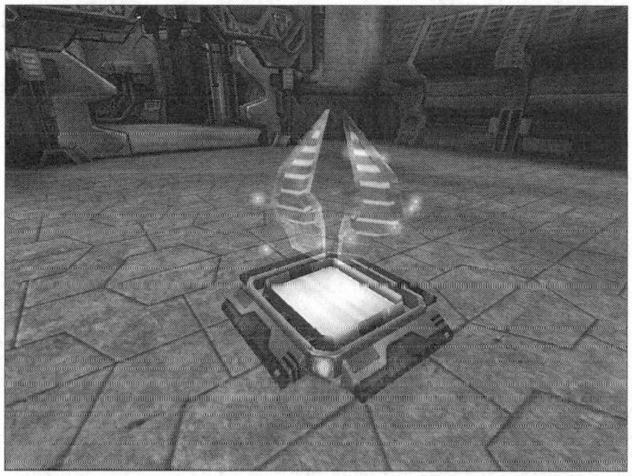

FIGURE 16.7 A wildcard base with a Double Damage pickup.

END TUTORIAL 16.2

Deathmatch Design Considerations

Although Deathmatch is the simplest gametype, making a good Deathmatch map requires careful planning. When your map is play-tested, bugs and design flaws become all too obvious. Therefore, keep the following tips in mind:

- If you have a huge map, make sure you can't see large portions of your map from any point or angle. This prevents a player from seeing an excessive number of players simultaneously, which can slow gameplay down by forcing too many calculations on the computer.
- When placing weapons inside your level, make sure that powerful weapons and pickups aren't placed too closely together. These items should be evenly spaced throughout the map.

- If you design a map that's more suited to a 1 on 1 Deathmatch, you should modify the filename to include `1on1` after the prefix (such as `DM-1on1-Albatross.ut2`). Modifying the map name to reflect the type of map you have is always a good idea.
- Place your PlayerStarts in locations that aren't completely obvious. For example, don't allow players to spawn from some sort of static mesh pod, or that area will likely become a target for other players. Nothing can take the fun out of a game quite like being fragged instantly when you enter a match!

Capture the Flag (CTF)

In the Capture the Flag gametype, players are divided into two teams. Each team has its own base and controls a flag. The goal of the game is to infiltrate the enemy's base, take its flag, and bring it back to your own base to get points. However, a team is awarded a capture only if it manages to take its opponent's flag while keeping its own flag at its base. The team that reaches a certain number of points, or captures, wins.

> **CAUTION**
>
> **Although you can place more than one blue and red flag, it's not recommended and doesn't work as expected, meaning you can't capture multiple flags of a single color.**

To make a map compatible with this gametype, a level designer has only two tasks: set the level's `DefaultGameType` to `xGame.xCTFGame`, and place two flags in the map. The two Actors for this task are xBlueFlagBase and xRedFlagBase. The Actor Class Browser path to find these two Actors is shown in **FIGURE 16.8**. Both Actors must be placed in your map for the level to work correctly. Keep in mind that only the flag appears in UnrealEd. Its base appears only when the map is run.

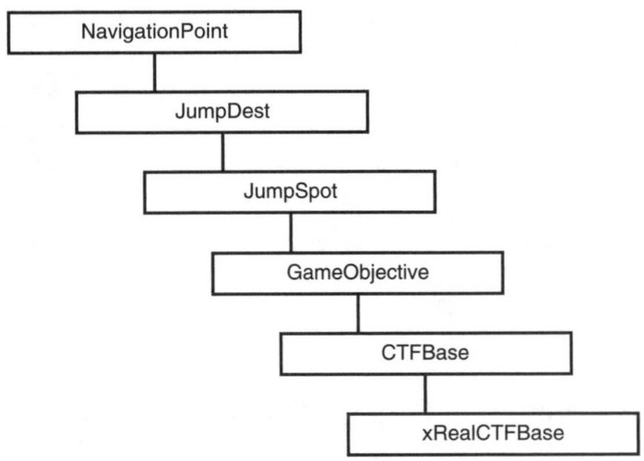

FIGURE 16.8 The Actor Class browser path to the red and blue flag bases.

16

TUTORIAL 16.3: Creating a CTF Map

1. Start UnrealEd, and open the `Tutorial16_03_Start.ut2` map found in the Chapter 16 directory on the CD. You'll be converting this map, shown in **FIGURE 16.9**, to a Capture the Flag map.

FIGURE 16.9 Map before being converted to a CTF map.

2. First, press F6 to open the Level Properties window. Open the LevelInfo category, and set the `DefaultGameType` property to `xGame.xCTFGame`. Remember that you must type this class name into the entry field.

3. At the southern end of the map is a wall with a window. On either side of that wall, you'll create the two flag bases. First, open the Actor Class browser and expand NavigationPoint > JumpDest > GameObjective > CTFBase > RealCTFBase, where you'll see the red and blue flags, which are listed as xBlueFlagBase and xRedFlagBase. Place the blue flag on the eastern side of the wall and the red flag on the western side (see **FIGURE 16.10**).

FIGURE 16.10 Map after being converted to a CTF map.

4. Save the map as `CTF-Ring13.ut2` and give it a test run. The flags and their bases are now in place, and you can take the flag and return it to your own base to score.

END TUTORIAL 16.3

Now that you have set up the necessary Actors to create a CTF map, you need to set up the PlayerStart Actors in a manner that coincides better with this gametype. For team-based gametypes, you don't want your players to spawn at random locations across the map. Instead, you have players spawn at their team's base. You learn how to set this up in **TUTORIAL 16.4**.

TUTORIAL 16.4: Adjusting PlayerStarts for CTF

1. Continue from **TUTORIAL 16.3**, or open the file you saved at the end of that tutorial.
2. Right-click any of the PlayerStarts, and choose Select > Select All PlayerStart. Press Delete to remove all PlayerStarts from the level.
3. Using the skills you have learned thus far, create a new PlayerStart next to the blue flag (see **FIGURE 16.11**).

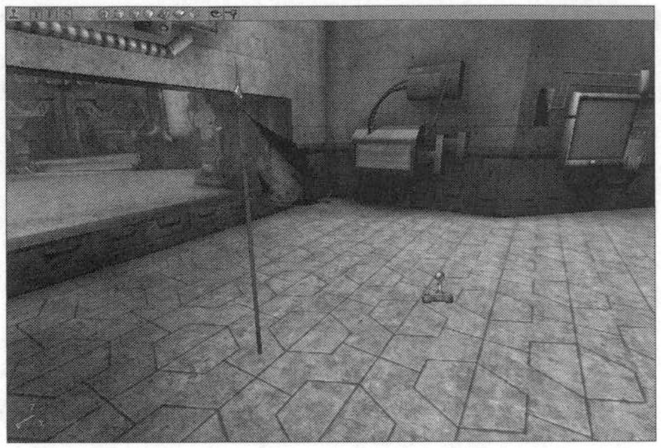

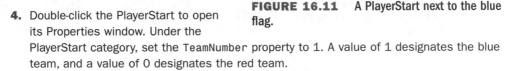

FIGURE 16.11 A PlayerStart next to the blue flag.

4. Double-click the PlayerStart to open its Properties window. Under the PlayerStart category, set the `TeamNumber` property to 1. A value of 1 designates the blue team, and a value of 0 designates the red team.
5. Duplicate this PlayerStart to several positions near the blue flag.
6. Repeat steps 2–5, placing the new PlayerStarts near the red flag, and verify that the `TeamNumber` property for each one is set to 0 instead of 1.
7. Save your work.

END TUTORIAL 16.4

You now have a functional CTF map. In many maps included with Unreal Tournament 2004, you see view screens at each base that display the team's color and insignia. In **TUTORIAL 16.5**, you see how to set these items up in your map.

TUTORIAL 16.5: Setting Up View Screens for CTF

1. Continue from **TUTORIAL 16.4**, or open the file you saved at the end of that tutorial. You're going to set up the monitor view screens in each base so that they display the team colors and team symbols.
2. Select and delete the monitors in each flag room (see **FIGURE 16.12**). They are currently static meshes, which you'll replace with special Actors designed specifically for this task.

FIGURE 16.12 Monitor deleted, leaving only the shadow.

3. In the Actor Class browser, expand Decoration > xMonitor to see a list of monitors to choose from. The one most similar to the monitor that was originally in the level is xMonitorC. Select it, and place it in the same location as the original monitor. You might need to use the `DrawScale3D` property to adjust its size.

4. Double-click the monitor to access its settings. Under the xMonitor category, adjust the `Team` property to correspond with the teams. Remember that 0 equals the red team, and 1 equals blue. **FIGURE 16.13** shows the monitor for the red team.

5. Save your work and test the map.

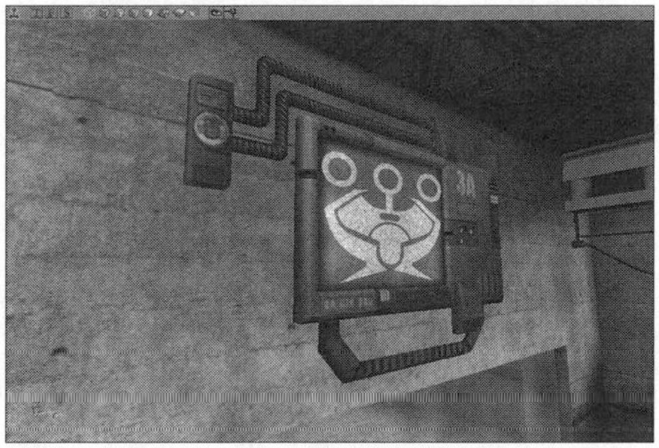

FIGURE 16.13 A monitor for the red team.

END TUTORIAL 16.5

CTF Design Considerations

Every CTF map should have two distinct sections: a red base and a blue base. Naturally, the red flag should be placed within the red base and the blue flag within the blue base. The area in and around each base should be designed and textured in such a way that players can easily identify which base they are in. For example, you might want to have red decorations in the red base, and vice versa.

Also, one team should not have any unfair advantages over the other because of the base's design. One way to prevent this is to simply create one base and mirror it on the other side of the map, but this duplication can make the maps look and feel stagnant. Structurally, mirroring is a good idea, but you should usually change the decorations in each base, along with any other artifacts that don't change gameplay. Therefore, try to make the two bases as different as possible while ensuring that neither team has an advantage over the other.

This guideline also applies to pickups and weapons. You don't want one base to be filled with powerful weapons while the other has practically nothing. Make sure you strive to keep your levels balanced for gameplay. This balance ensures that your players are satisfied with their experience and that the game moves at a decent speed.

Double Domination

In Double Domination, players are divided into two teams. The goal of each team is to take simultaneous control of two specific locations in the map. When a player runs over one of these domination points, that point becomes controlled by that player's team. One team has to control both domination points simultaneously for 10 seconds to get a point. After scoring, both domination points become neutral, and the process begins again.

Similar to CTF maps, a level designer's most important job is placing two domination points in the map. xDomPointA and xDomPointB are the two Actors that represent these domination points. **FIGURE 16.14** shows the Actor Class browser path to these Actors. You need to place only one of each Actor somewhere in your map to have a working Double Domination map. In **TUTORIAL 16.6**, you convert your Deathmatch map from earlier into a Double Domination map.

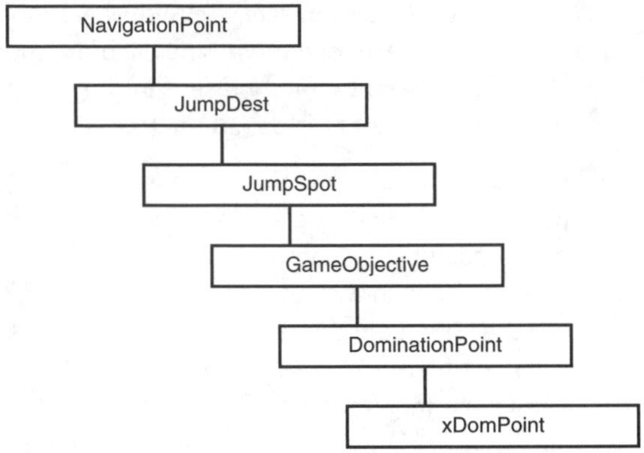

FIGURE 16.14 The Actor Class browser path leading to the Actors used in a Double Domination map.

TUTORIAL 16.6: Creating a Double Domination Map

1. Open the `Tutorial16_06_Start.ut2` file from the Chapter 16 folder on the CD. **FIGURE 16.15** shows the current map.

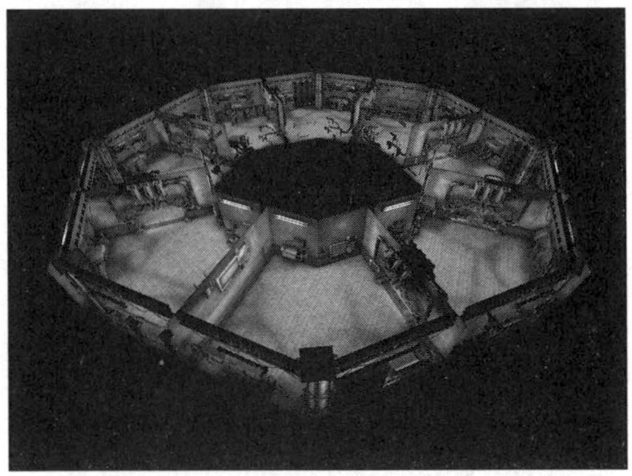

FIGURE 16.15 The map before being converted to Double Domination.

2. Press F6 to open the Level Properties window. Under the LevelInfo category, set the `DefaultGameType` property to `xGame.xDoubleDOM`. Remember that you must type this class name into the entry field.

3. In the Actor Class browser, expand NavigationPoint > JumpDest > GameObjective > DominationPoint > xDomPoint, where you see two Actors: xDomPointA, and xDomPointB. Obviously, these Actors are the domination points needed for your level.

As in **TUTORIAL 16.3**, you need to place one of each of the Domination Point Actors on the east and west sides of the southern wall (see **FIGURE 16.16**).

4. Using the skills you acquired in **TUTORIAL 16.4**, place two groups of PlayerStarts, each designated for a corresponding team.
5. Save the map as `DOM-Ring13.ut2`, and test it out.

FIGURE 16.16 Both domination points in the map.

END TUTORIAL 16.6

Your domination points are now in place. At this point, the map is playable for a Double Domination game. However, some screens that show the current status of each domination point would be useful for players. In **TUTORIAL 16.7**, you set these screens up.

TUTORIAL 16.7: Creating Monitor Screens for Double Domination

1. Continue from **TUTORIAL 16.6**, or open the file you saved at the end of that tutorial. You're going to populate your level with screens that display which team controls which domination point.
2. In the Actor Class browser, expand Decoration > xMonitor > xDOMMonitor, where you find xDOMMonitorA and xDOMMonitorB. These meshes automatically update to display which team has control of the A or B domination points.
3. Select xDOMMonitorA, and place a copy on the left side and slightly above one door in the level. Repeat with xDOMMonitorB, placing a copy on the right side (see **FIGURE 16.17**).
4. Select the pair of monitors and duplicate them, placing them on both sides of each doorway in the map. This way, players can always look at the doorways to see the current status of the domination points.
5. Save and test the map.

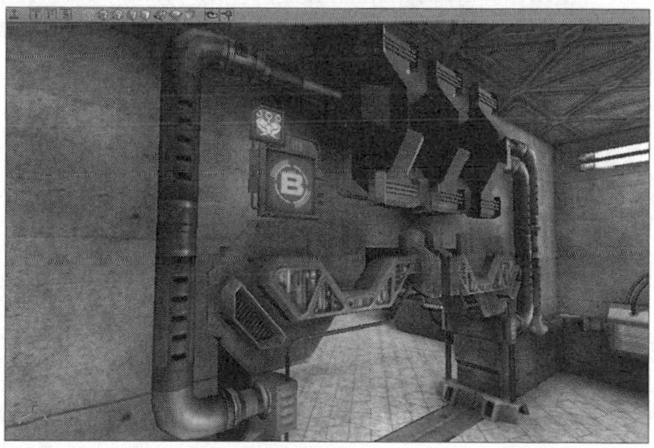

FIGURE 16.17 The domination point status screens are now in place.

END TUTORIAL 16.7

Design Considerations for Double Domination

As with the other gametypes, you need to keep a few guidelines in mind when creating a map for Double Domination. First, be sure to avoid placing spawn points too close to domination points. Placing spawn point too close makes domination points overly easy to control and results in a possible stalemate.

Second, avoid placing powerful weapons, ammo, or an excessive amount of health near domination points. To make domination point defense more challenging, defenders should not be given a large supply of ammo for their favorite weapon while covering a control point.

Bombing Run

Bombing Run is another team-based gametype, in which the object is to take a ball and throw it into the enemy team's hoop. If a player jumps through the hoop while holding the ball, his team scores seven points. Simply tossing the ball through the hoop gives the team only three points. The team with the most points wins the game.

A Bombing Run map must contain three things: a ball and two delivery points, which act as hoops. One xBombDelivery Actor (the hoop) should be placed in both bases. Only one xBombSpawn Actor (the ball) needs to be placed in the map. This ball should be placed at an equal distance from the xBombDelivery Actors so that no team has an unfair advantage. The Actor Class Browser path to locate these Actors is displayed in **FIGURE 16.18**.

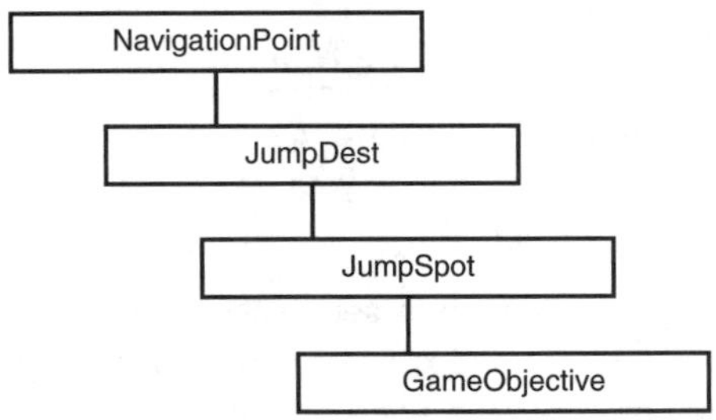

FIGURE 16.18 The Actor Class browser path to the necessary Actors for a Bombing Run map.

Under the xBombDelivery properties is the Team category with the `Team` property. One of the xBombDelivery Actors must have this property set to 0 (for the red team), and the other must have this property set to 1 (for the blue team). Obviously, these properties should correspond with their bases so that the blue delivery point is in the blue base, and vice versa.

Another important property when working with Bombing Run is `TouchDownDifficulty`, found under the xBombDelivery category in the xBombDelivery Actor's Properties window. This property determines the probability of a bot shooting the ball through the hoop instead of running through the hoop with ball in hand. A value of 1 means the bot will most likely shoot the ball through the hoop; a value of 0 means the bot will probably run through the hoop with the ball in hand.

Two other Actors that are important when working with Bombing Run are BlueShootSpot and RedShootSpot (see **FIGURE 16.19** for the Actor Class browser path). These two Actors specify a point at which bots attempt to shoot the ball into the hoop. Hitting these points doesn't mean the bots will *definitely* shoot, but if they do shoot, they shoot from these points. If you don't place these Actors in your map, bots never try to shoot the ball through the hoop.

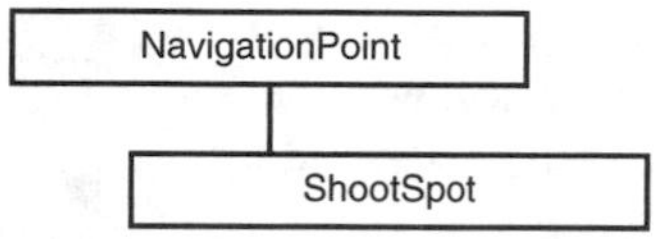

FIGURE 16.19 The Actor Class browser path leading to the ShootSpot navigation points used by bots in your level.

TUTORIAL 16.8: Setting Up a Bombing Run Map

1. Open the Deathmatch version of the map, `Tutorial16_08_Start.ut2`. You'll convert this map into a Bombing Run arena.
2. Press F6 to open the Level Properties window. Under the LevelInfo category, set the `DefaultGameType` property to `xGame.xBombingRun`. Remember that you must type this class name into the entry field.
3. In the Actor Class browser, expand NavigationPoint > JumpDest > JumpSpot > GameObjective. Within, you find the xBombDelivery and xBombSpawn Actors.

   To begin, you place the goals. Select xBombDelivery in the Actor Class browser, and right-click to place one on either side of the southern wall of the arena, much as you did for the CTF and Double Domination gametypes.
4. Now you need to specify which bomb delivery, or goal, corresponds with which team. Open the Properties window of the goal in the blue base. Under the Team category, set the `Team` property to `1`. Setting this property for the goal in the red base isn't necessary, as the Actor comes in with this value set to 0 (red) by default. **FIGURE 16.20** shows both goals set up.
5. Now you need to add the ball. The only problem is that the center point of your map has two doors on the north wall. These doors get in the way of the ball's spawn point, so select both Movers and delete them for the time being.

FIGURE 16.20 Both goals set up.

> **NOTE**
>
> In most levels, you want to set the goal up so that a player cannot get behind it. You can do this by adding pits, walls, and so forth.

6. Using the skills you acquired in **TUTORIAL 16.4**, place two groups of PlayerStarts, each designated for a corresponding team.

7. To add the ball, select the xBombSpawn Actor in the Actor Class browser. Right-click and place this Actor directly in the doorway on the north wall (see **FIGURE 16.21**). This position is in the center of the map, meaning that neither team has an advantage.

8. That's about it, as far as setup. Save your map as `BR-Ring13.ut2`. Play-test the map, and try to shoot a hoop or two!

FIGURE 16.21 Ball spawn base.

NOTE

When creating Bombing Run levels, often you want to place particle effects into the goals to create a visual effect. For more information on particle systems, refer to Chapter 10, "Creating Particle Effects."

END TUTORIAL 16.8

Design Considerations for Bombing Run

The main concern when working with the Bombing Run gametype is PlayerStarts. Don't put them too far away from the goal, such as several hundred units away; however, avoid putting them right on or next to the goal.

Also, preventing the goal from being visible from long distances is a good idea. This keeps players from being able to shoot the ball through the goal as soon as they get their hands on the ball.

Onslaught

Onslaught is another team-based gametype. The player's main task during an Onslaught game is to initialize Power Nodes in a connect-the-dots fashion to establish a link between the player's base and the enemy team's Power Core (see **FIGURE 16.22**). After that link is established, the enemy's Power Core is vulnerable to attack and can be damaged as long as the link from the Power Nodes remains in place. The object of Onslaught is to destroy the enemy team's Power Core.

An Onslaught map has four main components: Power Cores, Power Nodes, Vehicles, and Teleport Pads. The Weapon Racks found in most Epic maps could be considered a fifth component, but they aren't completely necessary, and you can easily use standard weapon bases.

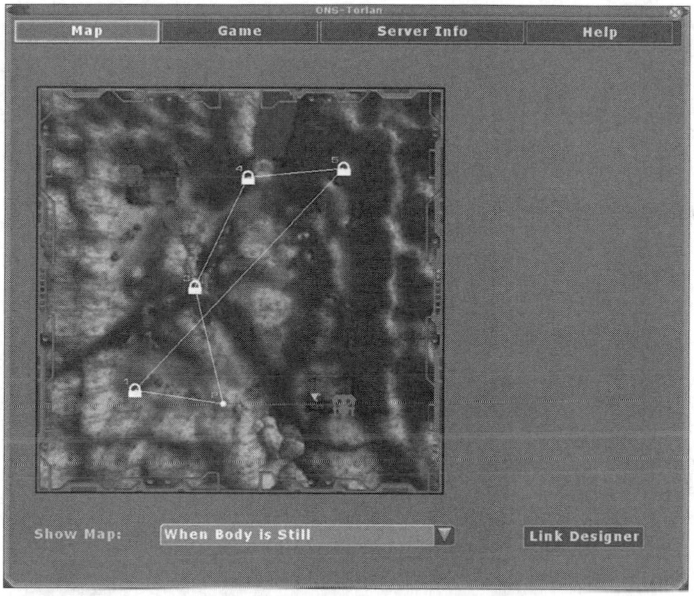

FIGURE 16.22 Onslaught map showing link setup.

The most vital components are the Power Cores and Power Nodes for each team, known as ONSPowerCoreBlue, ONSPowerCoreRed, which can be found in the Actor Class browser path shown in **FIGURE 16.23**. You also need the ONSPowerNodeNeutral Actor, found in the path shown in **FIGURE 16.24**.

In **TUTORIAL 16.9**, you see how to establish Power Cores and Power Nodes.

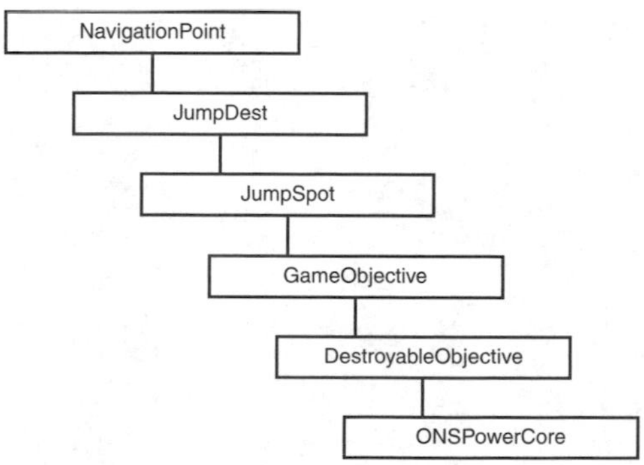

FIGURE 16.23 The Actor Class browser path to the Onslaught Power Cores.

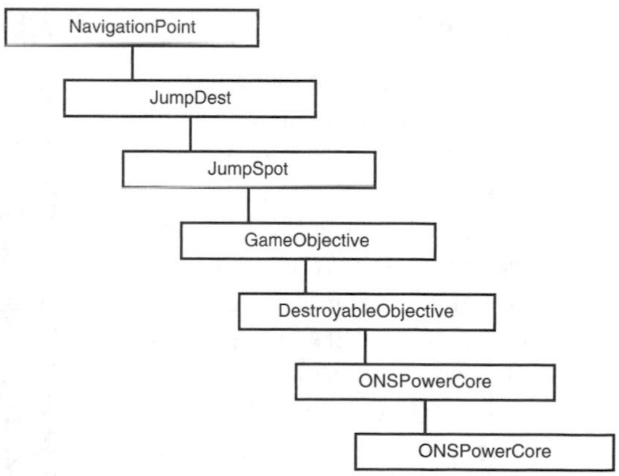

FIGURE 16.24 The Actor Class browser path to the ONSPowerNodeNeutral Actor.

TUTORIAL 16.9: Placing Power Cores and Power Nodes

1. Open the `Tutorial16_09_Start.ut2` map, which is an open landscape: prime area for an Onslaught map.

2. To place the two Power Cores, press F6 to open the Level Properties window. Under the LevelInfo category, set the `DefaultGameType` property to `xGame.xOnslaught`. Remember that you must type this class name into the entry field.

3. In the Actor Class browser, expand NavigationPoint > JumpDest > JumpSpot > GameObjective > DestroyableObjective > ONSPowerCore, where you find the red and blue Power Cores, listed as ONSPowerCoreRed and ONSPowerCoreBlue. Place the red core at the *southern* end of the map in an open area (see **FIGURE 16.25**).

3. Select and place the blue power core in a similar open area at the *northern* end of the map (see **FIGURE 16.26**).

4. Return to the Actor Class browser, and expand the ONSPowerNode category, located in the same path as the Power Cores. Select the ONSPowerNodeNeutral Actor, the Actor used to create Power Nodes. Place this Actor in a few choice locations (see **FIGURE 16.27**). Exact placement doesn't matter for this tutorial, but when creating your own maps, you should consider placement carefully.

FIGURE 16.25 Red Power Core in position.

FIGURE 16.26 Blue Power Core in position.

FIGURE 16.27 A Power Node in place.

5. Using the skills you acquired in **TUTORIAL 16.4**, place two groups of PlayerStarts, each designated for a corresponding team.
6. Save the map as `ONS-Ring13.ut2`. There's no point in testing now, as you have only a series of unlinked nodes.

END TUTORIAL 16.9

You have added the nodes needed for the map, but without links between them, the map is unplayable. In **TUTORIAL 16.10**, you bring this map to life by creating the links needed to make the nodes and cores functional for this gametype.

TUTORIAL 16.10: Linking Power Nodes

1. Continue from **TUTORIAL 16.9**, or open the file you saved at the end of that tutorial. You'll connect the Power Nodes you created previously to create the links needed for the map to function.
2. First, start the map from UnrealEd. To establish links between your Power Nodes and Power Cores, you use the Link Designer, which must be accessed from within the game. Notice that when the game starts, the Power Cores and Power Nodes are missing (see **FIGURE 16.28**).
3. When the game begins, press the Esc key. In the window that pops up, click the Map button in the upper-left corner. Next, click the Link Designer button in the lower-right corner. A window opens to show the location of all your Power Nodes and Power Cores, despite the fact that you don't see them in the game (see **FIGURE 16.29**).
4. Next, you click Power Nodes to create links. The pattern is simple: Click the Power Node or Core where you want the link to begin, and then click the Power Node or Core where you want the link to end. Repeat

FIGURE 16.28 The Power Cores and Power Nodes don't yet appear in-game.

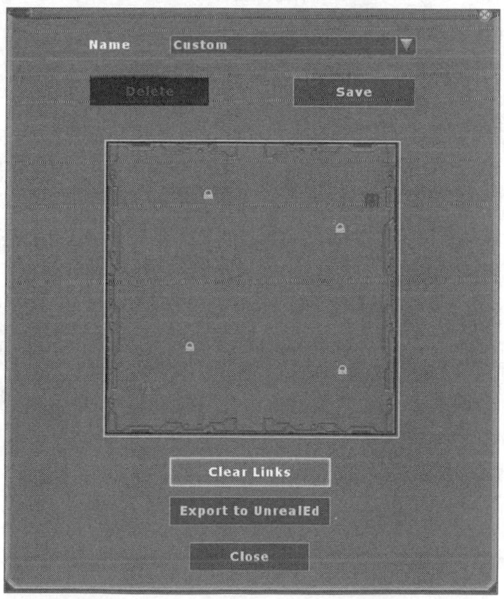

FIGURE 16.29 The Link Designer.

this process until all the Power Nodes have been linked, and the links eventually run back to the Power Cores (see **FIGURE 16.30**).

5. When you're finished, click the Export to UnrealEd button to place the links you created in the Clipboard for pasting into UnrealEd. Next, bring down the console with the tilde (~) key, and type **`exit`** to leave the game.

6. Back in UnrealEd, right-click anywhere in your level, and choose Edit > Paste > Here from the context menu. This places a small eagle head icon—the Link Setup icon—in your map (see **FIGURE 16.31**). Double-click this icon, and verify that its properties say `ONSPowerLinkOfficialSetup Properties`.

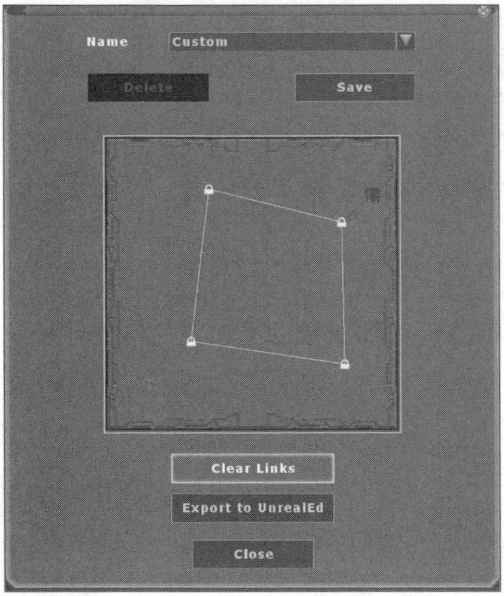

FIGURE 16.30 Link Designer with links in place.

7. Save your work. Retest the map, and notice that the Power Cores and Nodes are in place and fully functional (see **FIGURE 16.32**).

FIGURE 16.31 ONSPowerLinkOfficialSetup is displayed with the Link Setup icon in UnrealEd.

FIGURE 16.32 In-game shot of the now functional Power Core.

END TUTORIAL 16.10

Many of the Onslaught maps included with Unreal Tournament 2004 offer different setups for node links, which adds a tremendous variety of playability to all your favorite maps. In **TUTORIAL 16.11**, you create some alternative link setups to change how the level is played.

TUTORIAL 16.11: Creating Alternative Link Setups

1. Continue from **TUTORIAL 16.10**, or open the file you saved at the end of that tutorial. You're going to learn how to create alternative links for your map. This is a fast and easy way to make variations of your map to change its difficulty and game speed.

2. Open the map. When the game starts, press Esc, click the Map button in the upper-left corner of the window, and then click the Link Designer button in the lower-right corner.

3. Click the Clear Links button. Next, using the skills you learned in **TUTORIAL 16.10**, reestablish the links in a different pattern (see an example in **FIGURE 16.33**). When you're finished, click the Export to UnrealEd button and exit the map.

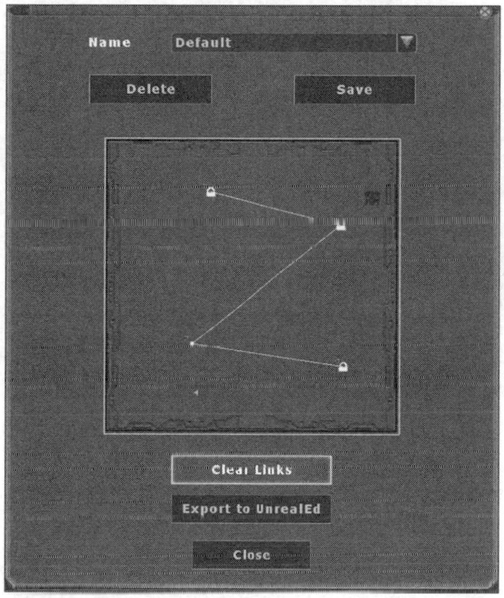

FIGURE 16.33 The Link Designer with a new pattern of links.

4. In UnrealEd, right-click next to the original Link Setup icon you created earlier, and paste the new Link Setup Actor next to it, just as you did in **TUTORIAL 16.10**.

5. Double-click this new Actor to open its Properties window. Under the LinkSetup category, change the `SetupName` property to `AlternateSetup1`. (When creating your own map, any name can be used.) Save your map when finished.

6. Instead of playing the map from UnrealEd, start Unreal Tournament 2004. Click the Instant Action link in the title screen, and choose Onslaught as your gametype. In the Map List, you'll see ONS-Ring13 (see **FIGURE 16.34**).

   In **FIGURE 16.34**, the small plus sign next to the map name has been expanded to display both the default link setup and the new AlternateSetup1. You can repeat these steps in this tutorial to create as many link setup variations as you like.

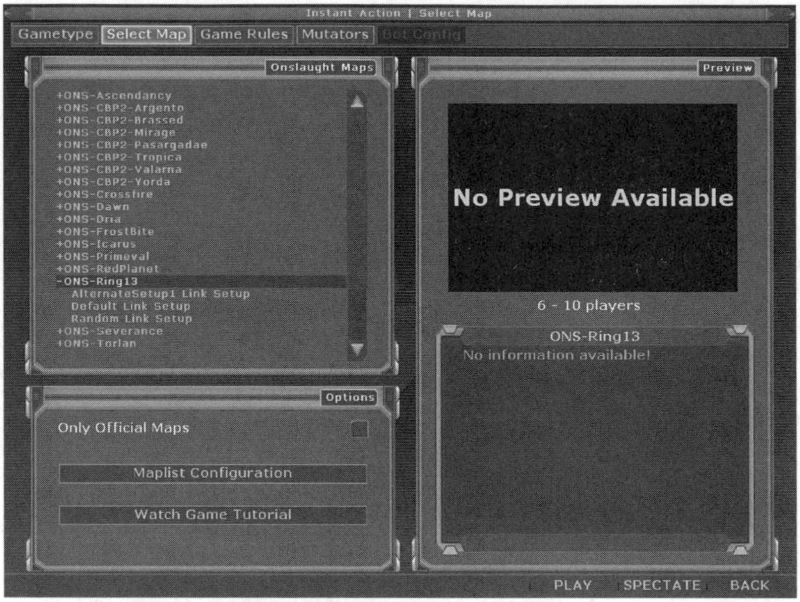

FIGURE 16.34 ONS-Ring13 in the map list with the link setups expanded.

END TUTORIAL 16.11

For all intents and purposes, you now have a functional Onslaught map. However, most Onslaught maps included with Unreal Tournament 2004 contain vehicles to help navigate the level. Vehicles add a new stage of playability to your levels. In **TUTORIAL 16.12**, you see how to place vehicles in your level.

TUTORIAL 16.12: Placing Vehicles

1. Continue from **TUTORIAL 16.11**, or open the file you saved at the end of that tutorial. You'll add some vehicles and weapon racks into the map.
2. In the Actor Class browser, expand SVehicleFActory > ONSVehicleFactory, where you see a list of Actors that correspond to the available vehicles for Onslaught. **TABLE 16.4** describes these Actor classes.

TABLE 16.4 Available Vehicles in Unreal Tournament 2004

Actor Class	Vehicle and Description
`ONSAttackCraftFactory`	Raptor: A fast-moving flying vehicle, good for air strikes and ground support.
`ONSBomberFactory`	A currently unused bomber aircraft.
`ONSHoverCraftFactory`	Manta: A single-occupancy attack vehicle that hovers just above the ground, allowing it to cross harsh terrain quickly.

TABLE 16.4 Continued

Actor Class	Vehicle and Description
ONSMASFactory	Leviathan: This massive "fortress on wheels" packs several plasma turrets and can transform to deploy an extremely powerful cannon.
ONSPRVFactory	Hellbender: This jeep-like vehicle can be driven by one player, but requires a second to occupy the cannon in its rear. A third passenger can also control a plasma cannon.
ONSSRVFactory	Scorpion: This one-player off-road vehicle has a plasma bola launcher in the rear and packs massive retractable blades, which can be deployed from the sides for quick decapitation.
ONSTankFactory	Goliath: This awesome tank has a main cannon turret as well as a heavy machine gun that can be controlled by a passenger.

3. The next part is simple: Select the vehicle you want to add, and then right-click next to a Power Node or Core to add the vehicle, as you would any other Actor. Unreal does the rest of the work for you. When you start the game, the vehicles are controlled by the team who controls the nearest Power Node or Core. Place as many vehicles as you like, referring to **FIGURE 16.35** for comparison.

FIGURE 16.35 Vehicles next to a Power Core and Nodes.

4. (Optional) If you have a Power Node near the center of the map, you might want the vehicles to spawn facing one direction for the red team or facing the opposite direction for the blue team. To do this, open the Properties window for the vehicle you want to reverse, and expand the ONSVehicleFactory category, where you find the `bReverseBlueTeamDirection` property. If set to true, the vehicles face the opposite direction when the blue team controls that Power Node (see **FIGURE 16.36**).

FIGURE 16.36 Vehicle faces the opposite direction when controlled by the blue team.

5. In the same category is the `RespawnTime` property, which enables you to control how quickly a vehicle respawns in a factory after it's

destroyed. Be careful that you don't use values lower than 5, which could result in the vehicle never respawning.

6. Save your work and test the map. Activate a few Power Nodes, and notice that vehicles spawn for your team after the node is constructed.

END TUTORIAL 16.12

Defending the Power Core is a major part of any Onslaught game. As such, it's a good idea to install turrets around Power Cores and Nodes to help fend off advancing enemies. In **TUTORIAL 16.13**, you see how to add turrets to your level.

TUTORIAL 16.13: Adding Turrets

1. Continue from **TUTORIAL 16.12**, or open the file you saved at the end of that tutorial. You're going to add player/bot-controlled turrets to help with Power Node and Core defense.

2. In the Actor Class browser, expand Pawn > Vehicle > ONSWeaponPawn > ONSStationaryWeaponPawn, where you see the ONSManualGunPawn Actor. This is the controllable turret found in many Epic maps for Onslaught. Select this Actor.

3. Right-click and place the turret near one of the Power Cores or Nodes (see **FIGURE 16.37**). Really, that's all there is to it. Unreal takes care of the rest, in that the turret becomes active only when that Power Node is online and accessible only to team members from the team who controls it.

FIGURE 16.37 Shot of the turret in place.

4. Continue placing turrets near the rest of your Power Cores and Nodes. Even if you don't place the turret right next to a Power Node, it automatically calculates which Power Node it's closest to.

5. Save your work and test the map. Give the turret a try!

END TUTORIAL 16.13

Another game element common to Onslaught maps is the weapon locker. In the game, it appears as a circular rack covered in a variety of weapons, and it's a great place to load up before marching forth to lay waste to the enemy. In **TUTORIAL 16.14**, you see how to place weapon lockers in your level.

TUTORIAL 16.14: Adding Weapon Lockers

1. Continue from **TUTORIAL 16.13**, or open the file you saved at the end of that tutorial. You'll add the weapon lockers, where players can load up on all the weapons they need to vanquish their enemies.

2. To begin, open the Actor Class browser, expand Pickup, and click WeaponLocker Actor. This Actor enables you to create "racks" of weapons in your map that players can use to load up before diving into the fray.

3. Right-click and place a weapon locker anywhere in your level (see **FIGURE 16.38**), and then double-click it to open its Properties window.

4. Under the WeaponLocker category is the `Weapons` property, which contains an array list. Simply click the Add button for as many weapons as you want, and then set the `WeaponClass` property for each entry. You can also add extra ammo to a specific weapon with the `ExtraAmmo` property, but that ammo boost applies only on the first pickup, not on subsequent locker contact. You can see what the weapon locker looks like in the game in **FIGURE 16.39**.

5. Test your level, and save your work.

FIGURE 16.38 Weapon locker added to the level.

FIGURE 16.39 Weapon locker stocked (in-game).

> **NOTE**
>
> You need only one of each weapon. Placing multiple copies is futile, as you can pick up each weapon only once.

END TUTORIAL 16.14

Getting around a larger Onslaught map can be tedious if you don't have a vehicle nearby, but you can solve this problem with the use of teleport pads. In **TUTORIAL 16.15**, you take a look at how to add teleport pads to the existing level.

TUTORIAL 16.15: Adding Teleport Pads

1. Continue from **TUTORIAL 16.14**, or open the file you saved at the end of that tutorial. You're going to add Teleport Pads to the game so that players can transport directly to Power Nodes or Cores under their control.

2. In the Actor Class browser, you'll see the ONSTeleportPad Actor. You don't need to expand anything (unless the Actor category has been closed). Right-click and place this Actor in your level (see **FIGURE 16.40**). Typically, placing it relatively close to a Power Node or Core is a good idea.

   This Actor follows similar rules as vehicles. It's automatically associated with the Power Node or Core it's closest to. If the red team controls that Power Node or Core, only the red team can access the teleporter, and vice versa.

> **NOTE**
>
> **Transporting is already inherent to Power Nodes and Cores. You're simply creating extra areas from which a player can teleport.**

FIGURE 16.40 A Teleport Pad added to the level.

3. Start the map. When you enter an activated teleporter, press the Use key (the E key, by default). A screen is displayed where you can choose to which Power Node or Core you'd like to teleport.

4. Save your work.

END TUTORIAL 16.15

Your level is almost finished. Now you need to create the bird's-eye view of the level that's shown in the Link Designer. In **TUTORIAL 16.16**, you see how to create this image.

TUTORIAL 16.16: Creating the Link Designer Picture for Your Level

1. Continue from **TUTORIAL 16.15**, or open the file you saved at the end of that tutorial. You're going to create an image of the level for the Link Designer screen.

2. Start your map. When the game begins, press Esc. Click the Game tab at the top of the window, and then click the Settings button. Adjust the following settings:

   - In the Player tab, change the Weapon Hand setting to Hidden. This means you won't be able to see your weapon in the view.

- In the Weapons tab, disable Custom Weapon Crosshairs, and set the Crosshair option to Hidden, which is at the bottom of the list.
- Finally, in the HUD tab, select the Hide HUD check box.

3. If you're currently running in full-screen mode, press Alt+Enter to go to a windowed mode.
4. Bring down the console, using the tilde (~) key. Type **setres 256x256** to set the window's resolution to 256×256, which is exactly the resolution you need for your image (see **FIGURE 16.41**).
5. Next, at the console, type **ghost** to make your character able to fly. Press the tilde (~) key again to put away the console, and fly yourself high above the level so that you can see it in a top-down view. Rotate yourself so that north is at the top of the window, as in the UnrealEd's Top viewport.

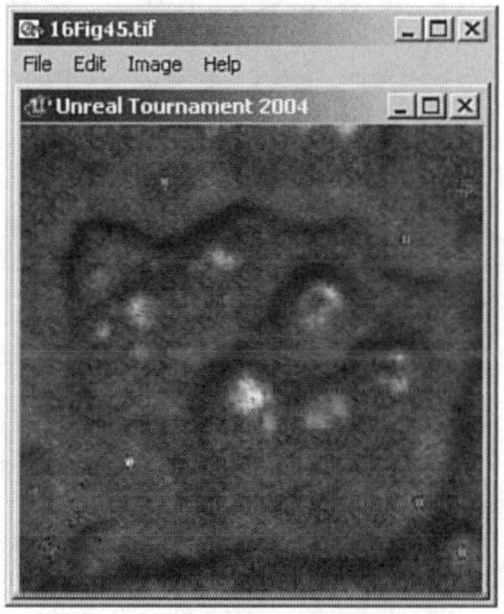

FIGURE 16.41 UT2004 as a 256×256 window.

6. Finally, notice that at this resolution, the field of view (FOV) seems too high. To correct this, go back to the console, and enter the command **FOV 20** to lower the field of view, alleviating the "fish-eye" distortion. After doing this, you'll likely need to position yourself higher above the map. If you're already looking down, simply use the Back button (S by default).
7. You should now see a bird's-eye view of the map. Make sure you position yourself so that the window outlines the playable area of your map perfectly.
8. Use the screenshot button (F9 by default) to create a new screenshot in your Screenshots folder, typically located in your UT2004 folder. The screenshot should be named something like `Shot00001.bmp`. Your screenshot number might be different, so sift through the images until you find the one you just took.

NOTE

If your texture's scale doesn't align to where the Power Nodes and Cores appear on the link map, there's a fix. Go to the Level Properties window, and in the RadarMap category, set the `bUseTerrainForRadarRange` property to False. Next, set the `CustomRadarRange` property. Use half the width of your map plus 100. So if your map is 4,096 units across, you'd use a value of 2,148 (4,096 / 2) + 100). Depending on your map size, small adjustments might be necessary, although this formula should get you very close in most cases.

NOTE

This is only one method of collecting this screenshot. You could use a variety of other methods, including taking a larger screenshot, and then altering it and adjusting its size in your favorite imaging software, such as Adobe Photoshop.

9. Go to the UnrealEd Texture browser, import the image using the name `RadarMap`, and store it in the myLevel package. Next, right-click the texture, and choose Compress > DXT1 to reduce the image's file size.

10. Make sure the new RadarMap texture is selected in the Texture browser. Next, go to the Level Properties window for your level, and under the RadarMap category, click the `RadarMapImage` property, and click the Use button.

11. Save and test your map. Notice that your new image appears in the game map as well as in the Link Designer (see **FIGURE 16.42**).

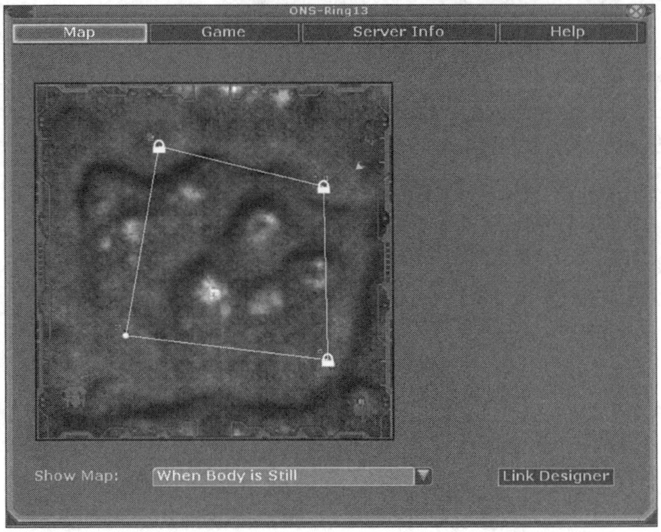

FIGURE 16.42 Link Designer with image in place.

END TUTORIAL 16.16

Design Considerations for Onslaught

When designing an Onslaught map, it's a good idea to plan your map carefully, especially placement of nodes and their links. You want the map to be challenging but not impossible, yet ensure that neither team has any geographical or equipment-based advantage. To avoid one team having an advantage, you should make certain both teams have the same number of each vehicle type, the same number of turrets, and so on.

Place your Power Cores in a well-defended location that's not visible from long distances. Few things are as frustrating as discovering that the enemy can pummel your Power Core into oblivion with a tank cannon while firing from a mile away.

Keep in mind that teams swap locations from one round to the next. Because of this, level symmetry is strongly advised to keep the game from becoming unbalanced.

Be aware of the kinds of vehicles you need for your map, and don't overdo it. For example, remember that the Manta is very fast and doesn't take steep inclines well, or the Leviathan is excessively large and might be out of place in a smaller map. If airborne attacks would make the map too easy or be out of place, avoid adding Raptors. If, however, your bases are divided by a massive chasm, you need flight-capable vehicles.

Make sure all weapon bases and weapon lockers are equipped with Link Guns. They are vital in an Onslaught map, as they allow you to repair vehicles, repair damaged Power Cores, and construct Power Nodes faster.

When creating your Onslaught map, you might want to keep in mind two special properties located in the Level Properties window. The first is `DustColor`, under the DustColor category. If left at the default (black), dust from tires and Manta fans is brown. You can use the Color Picker to change the color to anything you like, such as white for snowy levels.

The second is `StallZ`, under the LevelInfo category. This property, set in Unreal units, sets a limit on how high the Raptor can fly, but does so in a smooth manner so that if the Raptor goes beyond this limit, its vertical velocity slowly bleeds off, and the Raptor falls until it's back below this height. A horizontal blue line, visible in the Front and Side views, gives you a visual representation of the height limit.

Assault

Assault is another team-based gametype in which one team is attacking while the other is defending. The game is objective based, in that the attacking team is trying to complete a series of objectives, and the defending team opposes them. The objective types include destroying objects, holding objects, or activating switches.

The game also has a set time limit, dictating how long the attacking team has to complete its objectives. If it fails, the defending team is successful. If the attacking team completes each objective, it's successful.

After this, the two teams swap positions: The attackers become the defenders, and vice versa. If the new attackers complete all the objectives in less time than their opponents did, they win the match. If the new defenders manage to hold the objectives longer than their opponents did, they win instead. If neither team completes all objectives, the win goes to the team that scored the most objectives. To sum up, both teams attack. The team that attacks the most effectively is the winner.

Setting up an Assault map requires quite a bit of work, so you'll be going through it step by step. As an overview, the process requires the following:

- Setting up objectives
- Setting up player spawn management
- (Optional) Matinee intro and ending scenes

In this chapter, we will be discussing the first two of these: establishing the objectives and controlling player spawn locations. For more information on Matinee sequences, be sure to check out Chapter 13, "Matinee: Creating Custom Cinematics."

Before you begin, take a look at the map you're going to create. Planning your objectives before the level design is a good idea, so the following list explains the types of objectives you're going to create so that you have a good idea of where you're going before you get into the tutorials:

1. The first objective is to throw the switch to open the first set of doors, which requires walking up to a computer and pressing the Use key. After that's completed, the doors open and your team can proceed.
2. Next, you need to get through the second set of doors. This time, you have to hack the door's computer instead of pushing a button. Fortunately, there's an AutoHacker 9000 in your pocket. You simply need to stand near the computer long enough, and the doors slowly open as the system is compromised. If you die or get knocked aside, however, the doors begin closing slowly until they are completely closed again, or until you or a teammate gets back into position to hack the computer.
3. Finally, you need to get through the third door. At this point, subtle tactics must go out the window. You need to destroy the lock mechanism over the third door. After it's blown away, you can enter the final room.
4. In the final chamber, you need to access a computer in the room to stop its calculation cycle. Simply walking into it should do the trick. With that, you will have successfully completed all your objectives.

Now that you know what you're going to be doing in terms of play, the following list outlines these same objectives using UnrealEd terminology:

1. The first objective is a TriggeredObjective. In this case, you hook it up to a simple UseTrigger so that when a player activates the trigger, the objective is completed.
2. The second objective is called a HoldObjective, meaning that a player must hold a certain position for a set amount of time before the objective is considered complete. In this case, if the player moves away from that spot for any reason, the timer slowly counts back, meaning that the doors slowly close until someone holds the position again.
3. The third objective is considered a DestroyableObjective. This means some object must be destroyed before the objective is completed.
4. The final objective is a ProximityObjective. This objective is completed when players enter a specific radius from a set point.

You also have to carefully control how your player spawns react to objectives being taken. For example, when the match starts, the attacking team spawns and begins charging the first objective. If the defenders spawn near the back of the map, they could be too far away to defend that first objective. This means they need to spawn somewhere near the first objective to have a chance to protect it.

At the same time, if the defenders fail and that objective is taken, they need to be spawned closer to the second objective when they are killed. The same goes for the attackers. As soon as they complete the first objective, there's no reason for them to spawn all the way back at the beginning of the map. Instead, they need to spawn a little farther along in their progress, possibly at the first objective they just claimed.

Player spawn management can be complex and confusing. You might find yourself getting disoriented as to where players should spawn at different times. You have a few alternatives: You could create entirely new sets for both defenders and attackers as each objective is taken, or you could set up a system so that as attackers claim an objective, they use the same spawn points the defenders were using to try to hold that objective. You could follow this pattern all the way across the map so that you don't need two separate sets of spawn points. Which method you use simply depends on the design of your map. If it's convenient to reuse spawn points from one team to the other, by all means do so. If defenders and attackers are taking separate routes across the map, however, having two sets of points for defenders and attackers might make more sense.

Either way, planning your objectives on paper is probably best. Make a quick sketch of your map, and diagram where you want attackers and defenders to spawn for each objective. In **FIGURE 16.43**, you can see an example that you'll be using, in which the attackers simply reuse the defender's spawn points as the objectives are progressively claimed. Therefore, O points (defending spawn points) become attacking spawn points after that objective has been claimed. For example, the O^1 points become X^2 points after the first objective has been claimed, meaning that when attackers are working on objective 2, they spawn from the same place the defenders did on the first objective.

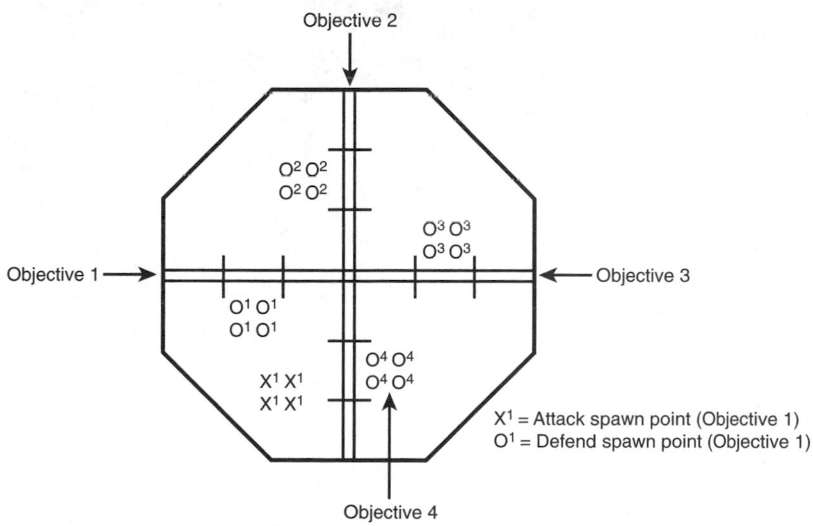

FIGURE 16.43 **Plan your objectives on paper first.**

In **TUTORIAL 16.17**, you establish your map as an Assault map and create your first objective.

TUTORIAL 16.17: Setting Up an Assault Map and Creating an Objective

1. Open the Deathmatch version of your map, `Tutorial16_17_Start.ut2`. You'll convert this map into an objective-based Assault map. Before you begin, open its Level Properties window, setting the `DefaultGameType` property to `UT2k4Assault.ASGameInfo`.
2. Locate the computer terminal just to the right of the first closed door. This is the position of your first objective. In the Actor Class browser, expand NavigationPoint > JumpDest > JumpSpot > GameObjective, and click TriggeredObjective. Place this Actor on the floor right in front of the monitor (see **FIGURE 16.44**).

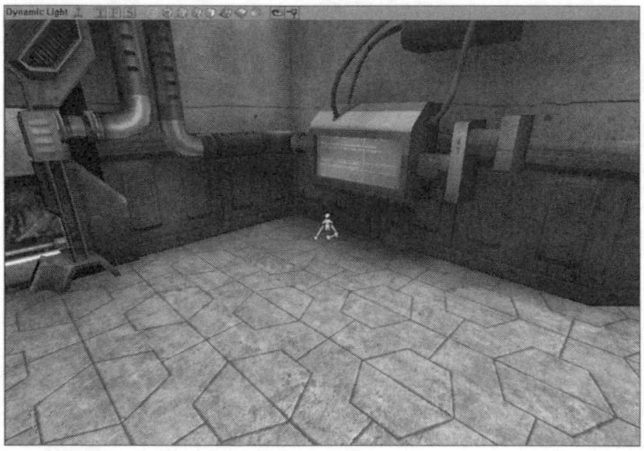

FIGURE 16.44 A monitor with a TriggeredObjective in front of it.

3. You need to set some properties for this objective. Open its Properties window, and under the Events category, set the `Tag` property to `OBJswitch`. This setting causes the Actor to "listen" for the `OBJswitch` event.
4. Next, set the `Event` property to `OBJswitch_complete`. This means that after the objective is complete, it "transmits" the `OBJswitch_complete` event, which you can use to cause other events to happen, such as doors opening.
5. Now you need to add a UseTrigger from the Actor Class browser under the Triggers category. Place it very close to the TriggeredObjective Actor (see **FIGURE 16.45**). Next, you need to set some properties for it. Under the Collision category, set the `CollisionRadius` property to 70, which means players need to be within 70 units of the trigger to activate it.

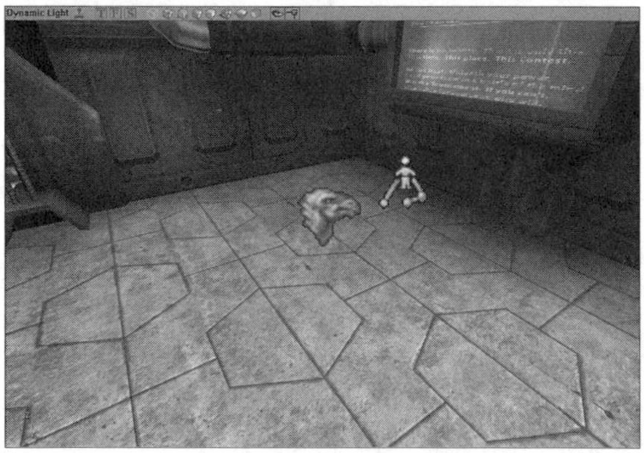

FIGURE 16.45 A UseTrigger added next to the TriggeredObjective.

6. Now you need to set up events for the UseTrigger. Under its Event category, set the `Event` property to `OBJswitch` so that the trigger transmits this event when it's activated.
7. Select the trigger located between the first two doors and delete it. Select both doors, and open the Properties window. Under the Events category, change the `Tag` property to

16

OBJswitch_complete, which causes the doors to open after the objective is completed.

8. (Optional) You can add a TriggerLight in front of the objective, mostly for visual effect but also to give you a better idea of where the objective is located. In the Actor Class browser, expand the Light category, and click TriggerLight Actor. Place this Actor near your TriggeredObjective and UseTrigger. Next, set the following properties (see **FIGURE 16.46** for the results):

FIGURE 16.46 A light added to indicate the location of the trigger.

Under the Light Color category

LightBrightness: 255

LightHue: 150

LightSaturation: 50

Under the Lighting category

LightRadius: 5

Under the Events category

Tag: OBJswitch_complete

Under the Object category

InitialState: TriggerTurnsOff

Under the TriggerLight category

bInitiallyOn: True

9. Save the map as AS-Ring13. Test it out, and try to complete the first objective.

NOTE

You might need to move the light closer to the floor to see an effect.

END TUTORIAL 16.17

You've now completed the first objective in your Assault map. Next, you set up a new type of objective, called a HoldObjective. **TUTORIAL 16.18** shows how to get this objective into the level.

TUTORIAL 16.18: Creating the HoldObjective

1. Continue from **TUTORIAL 16.17**, or open the file you saved at the end of that tutorial. Next, you add the second objective, the HoldObjective, to the level.

2. In the Actor Class browser, expand NavigationPoint > JumpDest > JumpSpot > GameObjective > ProximityObjective, and click HoldObjective Actor. Place this Actor on the computer at the left side of the second set of doors (see **FIGURE 16.47**).

3. In the HoldObjective's Properties window, expand the Events category, and set the `Tag` property to `OBJhold` and the `Event` property to `OBJhold_complete`.

4. In the HoldObjective category, set the `MoverTag` property to `Doors2` (which is the name of the doors, as you might recall).

5. Delete the trigger between the two doors. Select both doors and open the Properties window. Under the Events category, set the `Event` property to `OBJhold` so that the doors transmit this event when they are completely open. This, in turn, will complete the objective.

6. To slow the doors down a little, under the Mover category, set the `MoveTime` property to 5, meaning that a player needs to hold that position for five seconds to complete the objective.

7. Save and test the map. Your second objective should now work properly (see **FIGURE 16.48**).

> **NOTE**
>
> Under the Mover's Object category, the `InitialState` property is currently set to `TriggerControl`. This means that, behaviorally, the door opens only as long as someone is triggering it (that is, standing on the HoldObjective). If you change the `InitialState` property to `TriggerAdvance` instead, the door would continue to open until the player was killed or moved away from the spot. Then the door would simply stop and wait to be moved further.

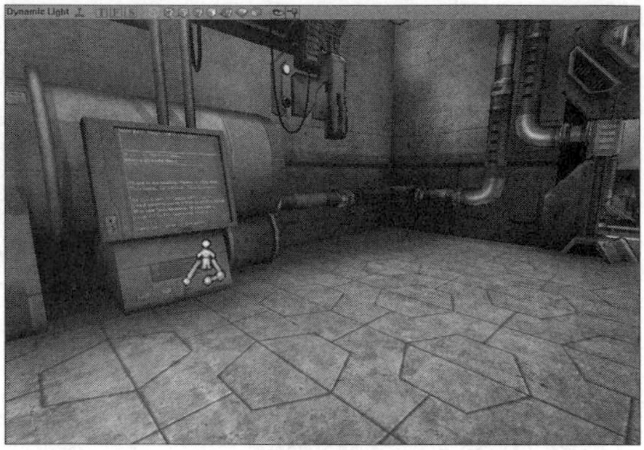

FIGURE 16.47 Second objective room with a HoldObjective added in front of the monitor.

FIGURE 16.48 The HoldObjective in-game with its graphical indicator for where you should stand.

END TUTORIAL 16.18

In Assault maps, often you find objectives that require you to destroy some type of object. **TUTORIAL 16.19** introduces you to the DestroyableObjective and shows how to set it up in your level.

TUTORIAL 16.19: Creating the DestroyableObjective

1. Continue from **TUTORIAL 16.18**, or open the file you saved at the end of that tutorial. You're going to add the third objective for your map, a DestroyableObjective.
2. Navigate the Perspective view to the third door. You see a static mesh centered over the door (see **FIGURE 16.49**). In the Properties window, expand the Display category. Click the `StaticMesh` property, and copy the line you see there to the Clipboard by pressing Ctrl+C. You'll be using this mesh in your next Actor, and copying this line keeps you from having to dig the Actor out of the Static Mesh browser. When you're finished, delete this static mesh.

FIGURE 16.49 **The mesh you'll be using for the DestroyableObjective.**

3. In the Actor Class browser, expand NavigationPoint > JumpDest > JumpSpot > GameObjective > DestroyableObjective, and click DestroyableObjective_SM Actor. Place this Actor in the level. When it comes in, it looks like a simple cube.
4. To fix this, you need to adjust one of this Actor's properties. Open the DestroyableObjective's Properties window, and expand the Display category. Click the `StaticMesh` property, and click Paste to paste in the line you copied from the static mesh previously. This line changes the cube into the static mesh shown in **FIGURE 16.48**. Rotate the mesh, and place it in its original position.
5. Under the Actor's Events category, set the `Event` property to `OBJdestroy_complete`. Now you need to specify how easily the object can be destroyed. For testing purposes, you'll leave this setting low, but you might want to set it higher when you finish the map. For now, set it to 100, which allows it to be destroyed by about two rockets.
6. Next, you'll set up a damage mesh for the door lock so that it has a separate model when it's destroyed. To do this, in the Static Mesh browser, open the `Chapter16_SM` package, and select the smashMesh model.

   Now open the Properties window for the DestroyableObjective. Expand its DestroyableObjective_SM category, and click the `DestroyedStaticMesh` property. Click the Use button next to this property to paste the smashMesh's path into the property. The mesh now converts to the new damage model after it's destroyed in the game. To set up an explosion effect, simply create an emitter that waits for the `OBJdestroy_complete` event. For more information on emitters, see Chapter 10, "Creating Particle Effects."

7. Finally, you need to adjust the doors to respond to the objective and slow down their motion a bit. If you haven't already, delete the existing trigger that was used to open them in the Deathmatch version of the level.

   Select the doors, and open their Properties window. Under the Events category, set the `Tag` property to `OBJdestroy_complete` to open the doors after the lock is destroyed. Under the Mover category, set the `MoveTime` property to 2 to make the doors run more slowly.

8. Save your work and test the level. Verify that all three objectives are working.

END TUTORIAL 16.19

Another type of objective is the ProximityObjective. This objective can be completed simply by coming within a specific range of the associated Actor. In **TUTORIAL 16.20**, you see how to create this objective.

TUTORIAL 16.20: Creating the ProximityObjective

1. Continue from **TUTORIAL 16.19**, or open the file you saved at the end of that tutorial. You're going to create the fourth and final objective, the ProximityObjective.

2. In the Actor Class browser, expand NavigationPoint > JumpDest > JumpSpot > GameObjective, and click ProximityObjective Actor. Place this Actor in your level, just in front of the computer along the north wall of the last room, near the window.

3. Open the Actor's Properties window. Under its Event category, set the `Event` property to `OBJfinal_complete`. This setting causes the Actor to send out this event when it's triggered. The event sent out is used to end the map. The Actor requires no tag, as its inherent nature is to trigger when a player reaches a certain proximity to it.

4. Under the Collision category, set the `CollisionRadius` property to 70. This setting causes the Actor to trigger when an attacking player gets within 70 Unreal units of it.

5. Back in the Actor Class browser, expand Triggers, and click Trigger_ASRoundEnd. This Actor's only function is to end an Assault round after all objectives have been completed. Place this Actor in the map; its location doesn't matter.

6. In the Properties window of this new Actor, expand the Events category, and set the `Tag` property to `OBJfinal_complete`, which as you might recall, is being sent out by the final objective.

7. Save and test the map. Make sure that all objectives are functioning correctly.

END TUTORIAL 16.20

Now that your objectives are in place, you need to be able to choose the order in which they need to be accomplished. Because the objectives have no order by default, your map would be unplayable if you had to complete an objective to which you hadn't yet been able to advance. In **TUTORIAL 16.21**, you see how to assign an order to the objectives in your level.

TUTORIAL 16.21: Setting Objective Order

1. Continue from **TUTORIAL 16.20**, or open the file you saved at the end of that tutorial. If you played through the map right now (with a cheat or two activated to move through walls), you would see that you can complete these objectives in any order. This won't do because sometimes drastic changes in the level take place after an objective is claimed. You always want objectives to be taken in a specific order, so you'll number them to make sure this happens.
2. For setting up objective order, each objective has a common category named GameObjective and a common property, `DefensePriority`. This is a zero-based property that you must use to give each objective a certain priority. Keep in mind, however, that this system must be numbered *in reverse*, meaning that the *final* objective is numbered zero, counting upward back to the first objective.
3. Open the Properties window of the final objective (the ProximityObjective), expand its GameObjective category, and set its `DefensePriority` property to zero.
4. Repeat this process with the remaining objectives, setting their `DefensePriority` properties as follows:
    - Objective 3 (DestroyableObjective) set to 1
    - Objective 2 (HoldObjective) set to 2
    - Objective 1 (TriggerObjective) set to 3
5. Save and test your map. The objectives can now be completed only in the proper order. You're ready for player spawn management now.

> **NOTE**
>
> **You can have multiple objects with the same priority. This allows you to set up alternate routes or create areas that players can access for special bonuses.**

END TUTORIAL 16.21

Your level is nearing completion. Now you need to control how players spawn as they play the level. This can sometimes be difficult, as your attacking and defending teams need to spawn from different points at different times during gameplay. In **TUTORIAL 16.22**, you see how to set up these spawn points.

TUTORIAL 16.22: Establishing Player Spawn Points

1. Continue from **TUTORIAL 16.21**, or open the file you saved at the end of that tutorial. You're going to set up your system of player spawns for the match. To avoid confusion, you begin by deleting all existing PlayerSstarts. Select a PlayerStart, right-click on it, choose Select > Select All PlayerStarts, and then press the Delete key.
2. Next, create a cluster of four PlayerStarts in the southwest corner of the first room. Select all four of these PlayerStarts, duplicate them, and move them to the defender's spawn location. They should be somewhere in front of the first door, where the computer can easily be defended.
3. Select all four of the defender's PlayerStarts. In the Properties window, expand the PlayerStarts category, and set the `TeamNumber` property to 1.
4. Duplicate the four defender PlayerStarts, and place them near the second door, just across from the HoldObjective. Set the `TeamNumber` property for this group to 2. Repeat to set another group in front of the third objective with a `TeamNumber` of 3, and again to place a final group in front of the last objective, with a `TeamNumber` of 4.

> **NOTE**
>
> **The `TeamNumber` properties don't necessarily indicate specific teams in this case. Rather, they are used to give each group of spawn points a specific ID number so that they can later be assigned to a PlayerSpawnManager Actor.**

5. Save your work. There's no point in testing just yet.

16

END TUTORIAL 16.22

Next, you need to control how the spawn points in your map are used. To this end, you can use the PlayerSpawnManager Actor, which gives you control over when particular spawn points become available for each team. In **TUTORIAL 16.23**, you see how to place these Actors and use them in the level.

TUTORIAL 16.23: Setting Up PlayerSpawnManagers

1. Continue from **TUTORIAL 16.22**, or open the file you saved at the end of that tutorial. You're going to place some special Actors in your level to control where attackers and defenders spawn at any time in the match.
2. In the Actor Class browser, expand Info, and click PlayerSpawnManager Actor. Place one of these Actors just outside the first group of four PlayerStarts (TeamNumber 0). You're using a specific pattern when placing these Actors: Attacker-based managers are placed *outside* the group, and defense-based managers are positioned *inside*. Because this first group is only attackers, you have only a manager outside the group.

3. Open the Properties window, expand the Events category, and set the `Tag` property to `PSM_Att1`. This setting designates the manager as affecting the first group of attacker spawn points.

4. Move the view to the second group of PlayerStarts (TeamNumber 1). Add a PlayerSpawnManager in the middle of the group. Remember that managers in the middle of the group are designated for defender spawn points. Set its `Tag` property to `PSM_Def1` to designate the manager as controlling the first defense spawn point.

   Expand the PlayerSpawnManager category. Set the `AssaultTeam` property to `EPSM_Defenders`. Next, set the `PlayerStartTeam` property to 1 to associate it with this particular set of PlayerStart Actors.

5. Add a new PlayerSpawnManager Actor outside the group for attackers. Set its `Tag` property to `PSM_Att2`. In the PlayerSpawnManager category, set `bEnabled` to False, so that the manager isn't active when the match begins. Set the `PlayerStartTeam` property to 1 to associate it with these spawn points.

6. Select the two managers at the TeamNumber 1 group of PlayerStarts. Duplicate the pair, and move the duplicates to the third set of spawn points, located in front of the HoldObjective. Position and rotate them so that the manager that was originally inside the cluster of spawn points is still within the new cluster.

7. Open the Properties window for the manager within the group (defender). Set its `Tag` property to `PSM_Def2`. Under the PlayerSpawnManager category, set `bEnabled` to False and `PlayerStartTeam` to 2.

8. Now open the Properties window for the other duplicated manager. Set its `Tag` property to `PSM_Att3`, and set the `PlayerStartTeam` to 2.

9. Duplicate the two current spawn managers, and move the duplicate to the next cluster (in front of the DestroyableObjective) of PlayerStarts, positioning them as you did before. The manager within the group needs its `Tag` property set to `PSM_Def3` and its `PlayerStartTeam` set to 3. The manager outside the group needs a `Tag` property of `PSM_Att4` and a `PlayerStartTeam` of 3.

10. Select only the central manager (defender) and duplicate it. Move the duplicate to the last group of PlayerStarts, and open its Properties window. Set its `Tag` property to `PSM_Def4` and its `PlayerStartTeam` to 4.

11. Save your work. You still can't test this map yet, but you're getting close.

END TUTORIAL 16.23

Now you need to create a system that controls the PlayerSpawnManagers, telling them when to switch team spawn locations from one point to another. To do this, you set up a ScriptedTrigger Actor in **TUTORIAL 16.24**.

TUTORIAL 16.24: Hooking It All Up

1. Continue from Tutorial 16.23, or open the file you saved at the end of that tutorial. You're going to establish a ScriptedTrigger that's controlled by the objectives and uses the events sent from those objectives to control and reroute player spawn locations.
2. In the Actor Class browser, expand Keypoint > AIScript > ScriptedSequence, and click the almighty ScriptedTrigger Actor. Place this Actor anywhere in your level.
3. In its Properties window, expand the AIScript category, where you'll be setting up an Action list. Click the `Actions` property, and then click the Add button to add a new blank Action. Click the New line, and in the drop-down list, choose `Action_WAITFOREVENT`. Click the New button to create this Action.
4. With the new Action added, you now have a new property named `ExternalEvent`. Set it to `OBJswitch_complete`, which causes the trigger to listen for the event sent when the first objective is completed.
5. Under the `Actions` property, click the Add button again. This gives you Action index [1]. In the New line, choose `ACTION_ASSetPlayerSpawnArea`. Click the New button next to the drop-down list.
6. This Action should now show two new properties: `PlayerSpawnManagerTag` and `bEnabled`. These properties are used to enable and disable PlayerSpawnManagers. Set `PlayerSpawnManagerTag` to `PSM_Att1`, and set `bEnabled` to False.
7. You might have noticed a pattern when using the ScriptedTrigger: You add an Action, specify the Action, and set the corresponding properties. You'll add several more Actions to this trigger, using **TABLE 16.5** to walk you through setting up the rest of the trigger. You can check your ScriptedTrigger against this table if you need help.

16

TABLE 16.5 Necessary Actions for ScriptedTrigger1

Index	Action	Properties
[0]	`Action_WAITFOREVENT`	`ExternalEvent` = `OBJswitch_complete`
[1]	`ACTION_ASSetPlayerSpawnArea`	`PlayerSpawnManagerTag` = `PSM_Att1` `bEnabled` = False
[2]	`ACTION_ASSetPlayerSpawnArea`	`PlayerSpawnManagerTag` = `PSM_Att2` `bEnabled` = True
[3]	`ACTION_ASSetPlayerSpawnArea`	`PlayerSpawnManagerTag` = `PSM_Def1` `bEnabled` = False
[4]	`ACTION_ASSetPlayerSpawnArea`	`PlayerSpawnManagerTag` = `PSM_Def2` `bEnabled` = True

Here's how this setup works, one Action at a time:

- Index [0]: During this Action, the ScriptedTrigger waits until it receives the `OBJswitch_complete` event when the first objective is completed. Then it continues to the next index.
- Index [1]: This Action disables the first group of attacking spawn points.
- Index [2]: This Action enables the second group of attacking spawn points.
- Index [3]: This Action disables the first group of defending spawn points.
- Index [4]: This Action enables the second group of defending spawn points.

In a nutshell, the first Action starts the trigger, indices [1] and [2] advance the attackers, and indices [3] and [4] advance the defenders.

8. Duplicate the ScriptedTrigger, and adjust your Action indices to match **TABLE 16.6**.

TABLE 16.6 Necessary Actions for ScriptedTrigger2

Index	Action	Properties
[0]	`Action_WAITFOREVENT`	`ExternalEvent` = `OBJhold_complete`
[1]	`ACTION_ASSetPlayerSpawnArea`	`PlayerSpawnManagerTag` = `PSM_Att2` `bEnabled` = False
[2]	`ACTION_ASSetPlayerSpawnArea`	`PlayerSpawnManagerTag` = `PSM_Att3` `bEnabled` = True
[3]	`ACTION_ASSetPlayerSpawnArea`	`PlayerSpawnManagerTag` = `PSM_Def2` `bEnabled` = False
[4]	`ACTION_ASSetPlayerSpawnArea`	`PlayerSpawnManagerTag` = `PSM_Def3` `bEnabled` = True

9. Next, duplicate the trigger again, and match the action indices with **TABLE 16.7**.

TABLE 16.7 Necessary Actions for ScriptedTrigger3

Index	Action	Properties
[0]	`Action_WAITFOREVENT`	`ExternalEvent` = `OBJdestroy_complete`
[1]	`ACTION_ASSetPlayerSpawnArea`	`PlayerSpawnManagerTag` = `PSM_Att3` `bEnabled` = False
[2]	`ACTION_ASSetPlayerSpawnArea`	`PlayerSpawnManagerTag` = `PSM_Att4` `bEnabled` = True
[3]	`ACTION_ASSetPlayerSpawnArea`	`PlayerSpawnManagerTag` = `PSM_Def3` `bEnabled` = False
[4]	`ACTION_ASSetPlayerSpawnArea`	`PlayerSpawnManagerTag` = `PSM_Def4` `bEnabled` = True

10. Make sure you rebuild paths at least once before starting the map. Save and test your work. Now you can progress through the map as you expect. As you complete each objective, test your respawning position by killing yourself. A fast way to do this is to type **`suicide`** in the console.

END TUTORIAL 16.24

Summary

In this chapter, you have taken an extensive look at necessary Actor setup for the available gametypes in Unreal. With this knowledge, you should be ready to experiment and create your own variations of any kind of map you like. Combine what you have learned in this chapter with the skills you find throughout this book, and you'll become a more versatile level designer.

Part III

External Design

Chapter 17

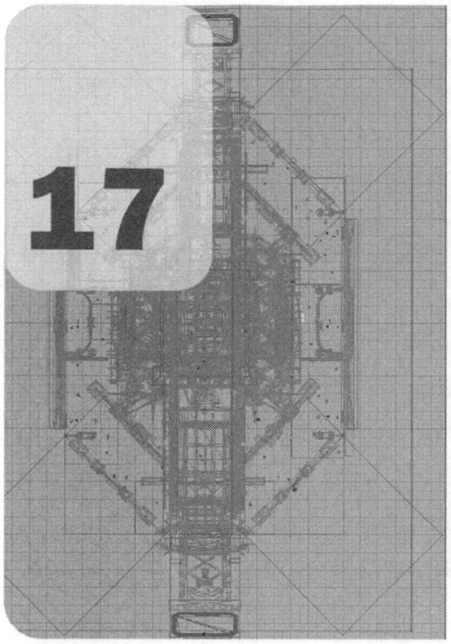

Overview of Maya

This chapter introduces you to Alias's powerful 3D content creation tool, Maya. For years, Maya has been an industry standard in the filmmaking industry and has recently been used in some of today's hottest games. The lessons covered in this chapter are used as the cornerstone for most of the remaining chapters in this book.

By now, you should already be accustomed to using UnrealEd, so you should be familiar with the basic concepts of working in 3D space. The chapter begins by covering some basic theory behind how Maya works and continues with a thorough discussion of Maya's user interface. You then move on to learn about Maya's powerful material creation tool, Hypershade, and a tool for seeing 3D scenes at their most fundamental level—Hypergraph.

> **NOTE**
>
> Please keep in mind that this chapter is intended to give you a basic overview of using Maya, not to teach you every nuance of the program.

Y-Up Versus Z-Up

When working in Maya, an important factor to keep in mind is the difference in coordinate systems among 3D applications. Some programs, such as UnrealEd, use a coordinate system in which the Z-axis points upward. Other programs, such as Maya, use a Y-up system, in which the Y-axis points upward. **FIGURE 17.1** shows the difference between the two coordinate systems. Both coordinate systems function on an equal level, and neither is technically better than the other. However, when you're switching from one program to the other, you must keep the differences in coordinate systems in mind. Fortunately, most exporting programs and plug-ins have settings to deal with the conversion so that you don't have to.

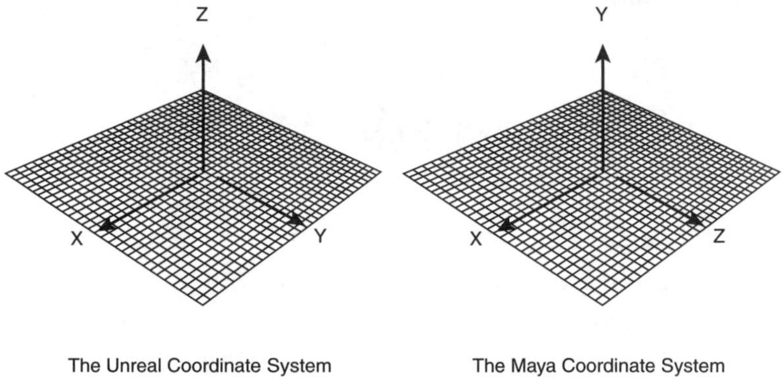

FIGURE 17.1 Unreal coordinates versus Maya coordinates.

Maya Theory

The following sections discuss the fundamental nature of Maya. You must understand some of this program's concepts before you can use it effectively. These concepts include nodes and connections as well as how construction history works. These concepts are discussed first to help you better understand how Maya works internally.

Nodes and Connections

At its heart, Maya is simply a system that creates nodes and connections between them. Even the simplest object is actually composed of a series of nodes. These nodes define the object you see in the viewport. In **FIGURE 17.2**, you can see a

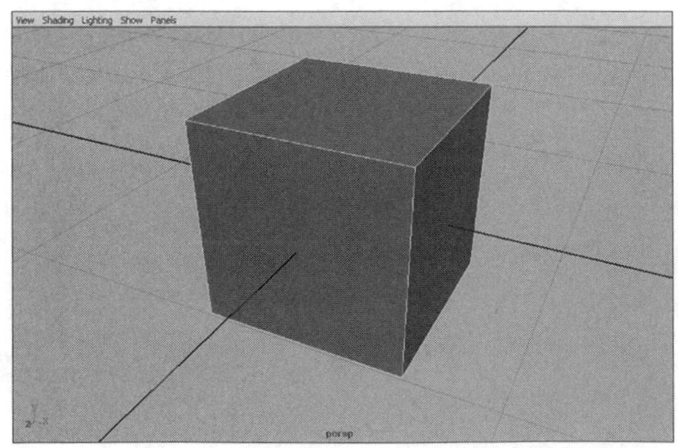

FIGURE 17.2 What you see onscreen.

simple cube in a Maya viewport, and **FIGURE 17.3** shows the series of nodes used to create it. **TABLE 17.1** lists the types of nodes and describes what sort of data each node provides to create the cube object you see.

> **NOTE**
>
> The node structure explained in **TABLE 17.1** is the same for any polygonal object, not just cubes.

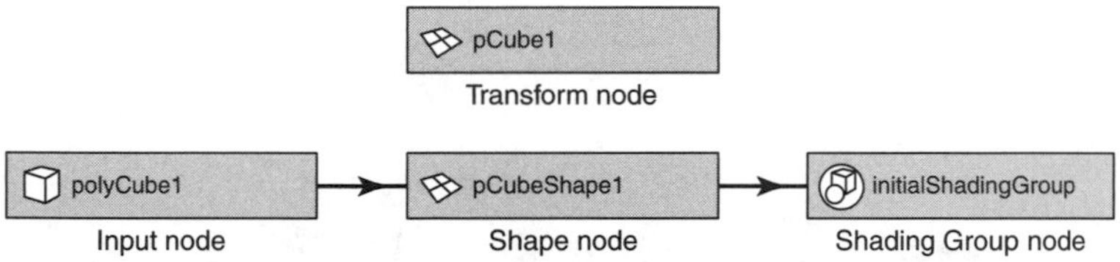

FIGURE 17.3 What goes on inside Maya.

TABLE 17.1 Polygonal Object Node Structure

Node	Description
Input node	This node contains all the geometric data for the object, including such attributes as width, height, depth, and the number of subdivisions (edges) in each direction. You can think of this node as the "blueprint" of your cube.
Shape node	This node receives data from the Input node and uses it to construct the cube. The attributes of the Shape node control the cube's internal behavior rather than its external appearance. You can think of this node as the "builder" of your cube.
Shading Group node	This node is used to control what your object looks like when rendered. It controls the behavior of the material applied to the object. This node can be thought of as the "painter" of your cube.
Transform node	This node contains all the transform data for your cube—its positional, rotational, and scale data. You can think of this node as the "mover" of your cube.

Therefore, as you can see in **FIGURE 17.3**, your blueprint (Input node) is sending data to the builder (Shape node) of your cube. After construction, the builder hands the cube off to the painter (Shading Group node) to determine what sort of paint job it should have. Finally, the finished work is sent to the mover (Transform node), which then decides where the cube is placed and what sort of scale (size) it should have.

> **NOTE**
>
> When you are looking at the nodes in the Hypergraph, the Transform node appears to be separate from the other nodes. Keep in mind that the Transform node is tied into the network, although you cannot see the connections.

Because the example discussed so far is only a single object, the node network is currently simple. The more actions you perform on objects, the more complex their node network becomes. These networks can eventually become quite massive. **FIGURE 17.4** shows a node network for defining an entire character, after it has been constructed and prepared for animation.

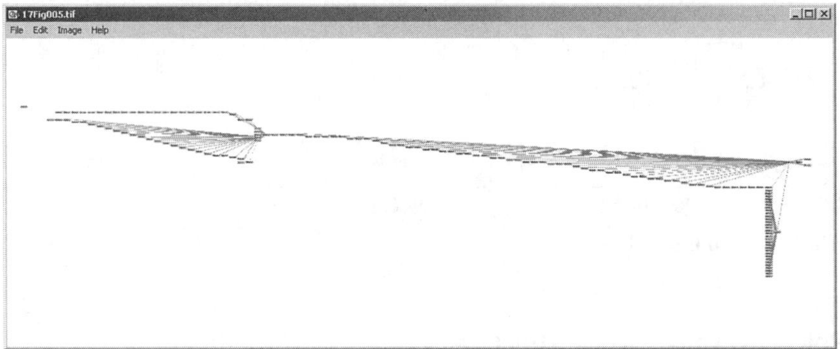

FIGURE 17.4 Maya's node network for a character.

There are so many nodes and connections that you can barely see the individual nodes. In fact, if each node icon in **FIGURE 17.4** were one inch long, the network would span over 10 feet!

Construction History

17

Now that you understand that all Maya scenes are constructed as a series of interconnected nodes, you can see how construction history works. As mentioned, the Input node feeds data to the Shape node, which then constructs the object you see in the viewport. However, as you perform actions on an object, more nodes are created that are connected into the Shape node. In **FIGURE 17.5**, you can see a simple cube, just like the example in the previous section. **FIGURE 17.6** shows the nodes to create this cube.

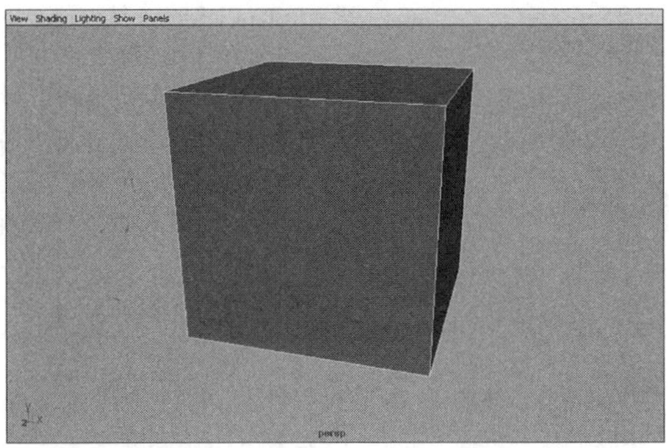

FIGURE 17.5 A cube in Maya.

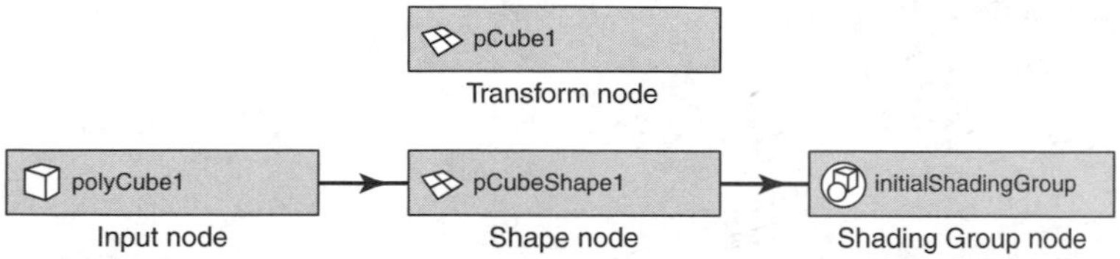

FIGURE 17.6 The nodes needed to create the cube in **FIGURE 17.5**.

To illustrate how construction history works, an extrusion has been performed on the cube. An extrusion is simply a way to pull out part of an object while adding more geometric detail. (This simple modeling operation is discussed in Chapter 18, "Polygonal Modeling Tools.") After the extrusion, the shape of the cube has changed as well as it subsequent node network (see **FIGURES 17.7** and **17.8**).

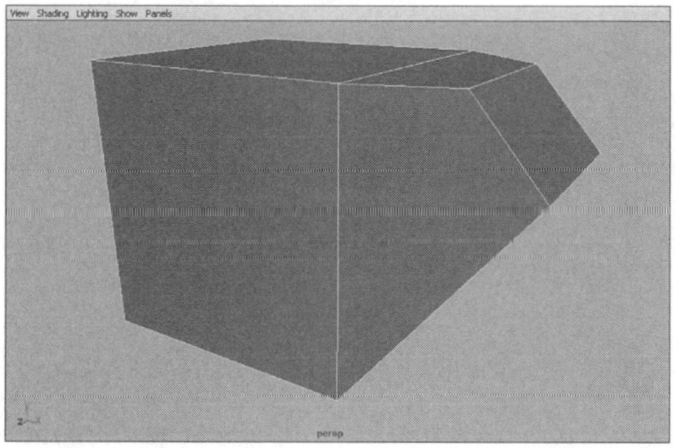

FIGURE 17.7 Cube's appearance after the extrusion.

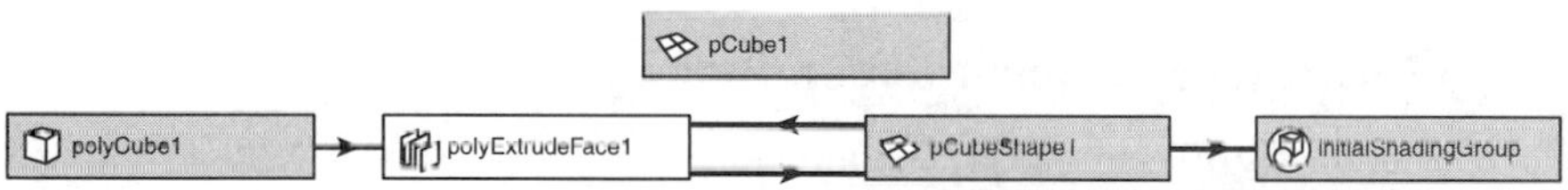

FIGURE 17.8 A new node, polyExtrudeFace1, is added behind the scenes.

A new node, polyExtrudeFace1, has been added to the network and is feeding information of its own into the Shape node. This means the Shape node must now consider data from two separate sources. The mass of nodes used as inputs is called *construction history*. In effect, it records every operation performed on an object as a separate node in the network. Currently, this network is still quite small. In **FIGURE 17.9**, the simple cube has been modeled into a basic spaceship. **FIGURE 17.10** shows the resulting network.

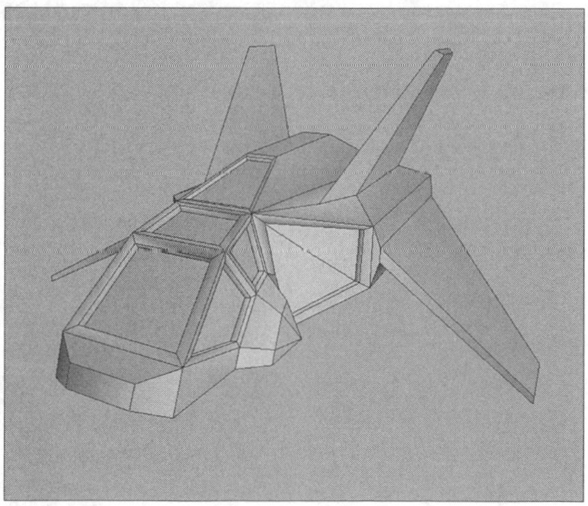

FIGURE 17.9 A spaceship model.

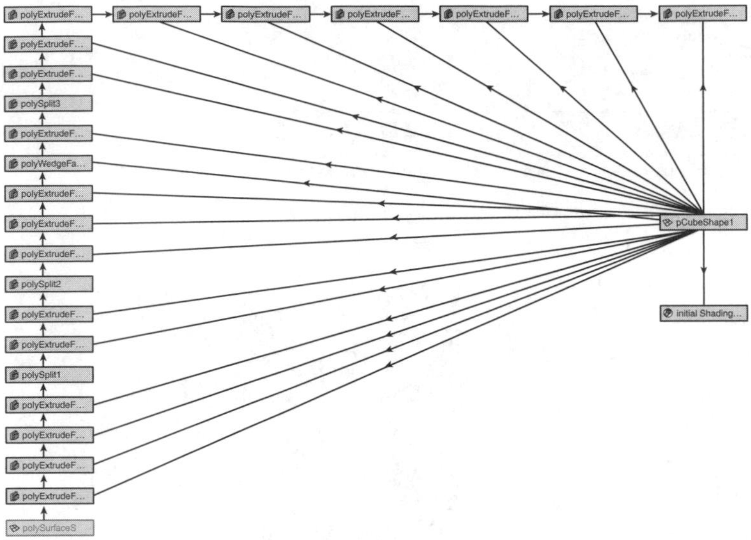

FIGURE 17.10 Maya's node network for this spaceship.

Every action performed to create the spaceship was stored in the network as a separate node. This model is relatively simple, yet the network is already quite large and complicated, even to the point that you can't see what the individual nodes are if you take in the network as a whole.

The Benefits and Drawbacks of Construction History

As you can see, construction history can quickly become quite large. Construction history can be a help in some cases and a hindrance in others. Because each operation you perform is stored as a node, you can access each node and change the attributes in it. These changes are sent back down the network, thereby changing your object's shape. In **FIGURE 17.11**, two operations have been performed on the cube. The first is a 90-degree wedge; the second is a polygonal face extrusion.

Using the object's construction history, you can access the settings of the wedge and change its angle from 90 to 45 degrees (see **FIGURE 17.12**). Notice the object's new shape in **FIGURE 17.13**. This method allows you to alter modeling operations that took place several actions ago. In a way, it allows you to go back in time and make changes to operations that have already taken place. The shape you see in **FIGURE 17.11** was achieved without having to undo the extrusion, even though the extrusion took place *after* the wedge.

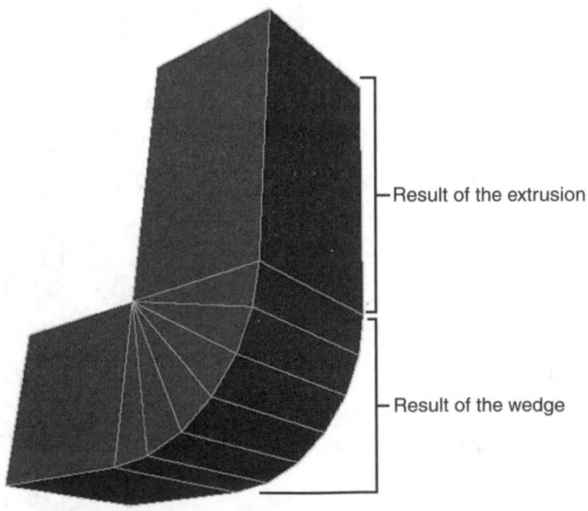

FIGURE 17.11 Shape after the two operations.

The drawbacks of construction history are twofold. First, although you can edit the attributes of actions performed at any point along the history, you must avoid changing attributes that alter the *topology*, or number of polygons in the object. For example, in the spaceship model created earlier, the original Input node for the cube still exists in the network. If you used it to change the number of subdivisions in length, height, and depth, you would see a drastic change in the object's shape (see **FIGURE 17.14**).

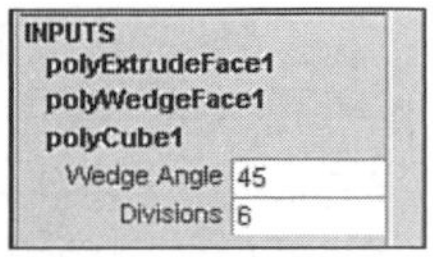

FIGURE 17.12 Changing the wedge angle to 45.

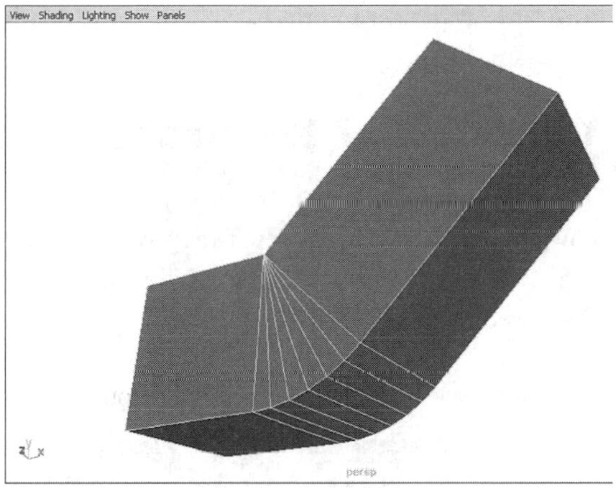

FIGURE 17.13 Result of changing the wedge angle.

As you can see, the shape has been changed to an indistinguishable mass of polygons. This happens because the number of polygons has changed, and new unaltered polygons have been added to the shape's polygons, resulting in the changed polygons moving to new positions. You must be careful, as changing the topology of highly complex models can cause Maya to crash.

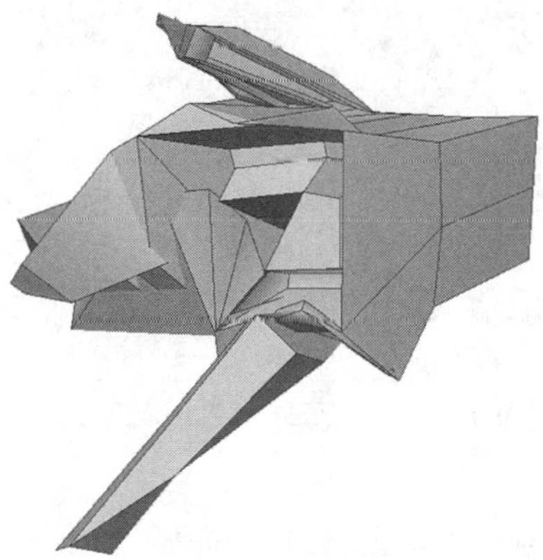

FIGURE 17.14 Spaceship after changing the construction history.

The second drawback of construction history is that each node of an object's history is calculated *separately* and, therefore, requires a lot of processing power. So the more operations you have performed on an object, the slower your computer is likely to run. Eventually, this increase in construction history can make your scene so dense that Maya becomes unstable. You can combat this problem by deleting your object's construction history periodically. Doing this takes all nodes that are sending information to the Shape node and records their information permanently into the node. **FIGURE 17.15** shows how greatly simplified the spaceship's network from **FIGURE 17.10** becomes after history deletion.

The huge network of nodes is gone. This means the computer runs faster, but you can no longer edit attributes of the individual nodes because their results have been permanently written to the Shape node. Now that you have a general idea of what's going on under Maya's hood, take a look at Maya's user interface.

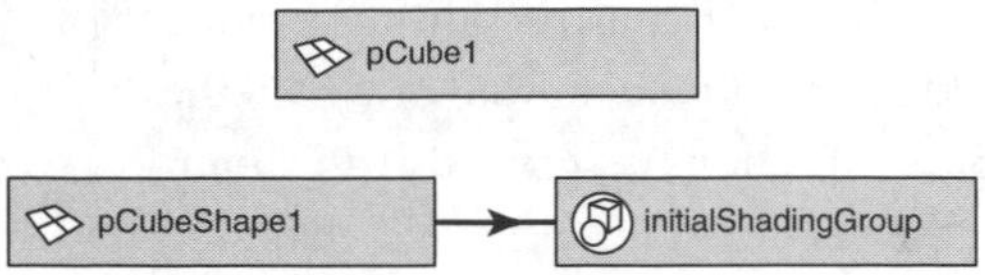

FIGURE 17.15 After history is deleted, the spaceship's network shrinks.

Overview of the User Interface

The following sections introduce you to the Maya user interface (see **FIGURE 17.16**) and cover the parts of the UI separately. As you read, it's a good idea to have your copy of Maya or Maya Personal Learning Edition (PLE) open to help you refer to each component as it's being discussed.

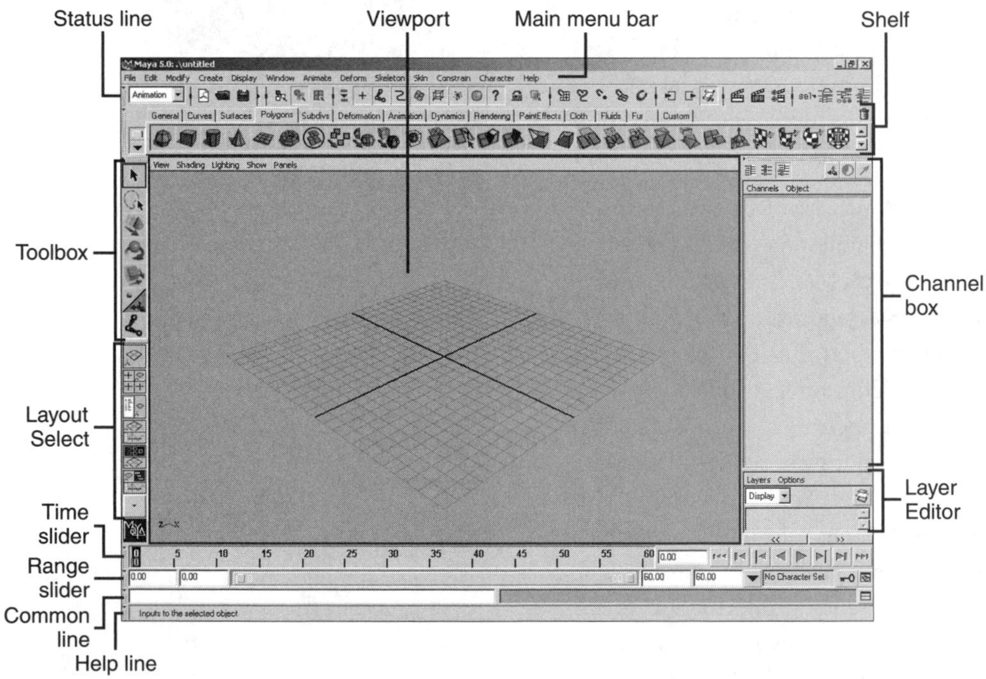

FIGURE 17.16 The Maya user interface.

The Viewports

The viewports are your windows into the three-dimensional world. They are very similar to the viewports in Unreal: You have one three-dimensional viewport, called the Perspective view, and three two-dimensional views known as the orthographic views (see **FIGURE 17.17**). The orthographic views consist of the Front camera, which looks down the Z-axis, the Side camera, which looks down the X-axis, and the Top camera, which looks down the Y-axis.

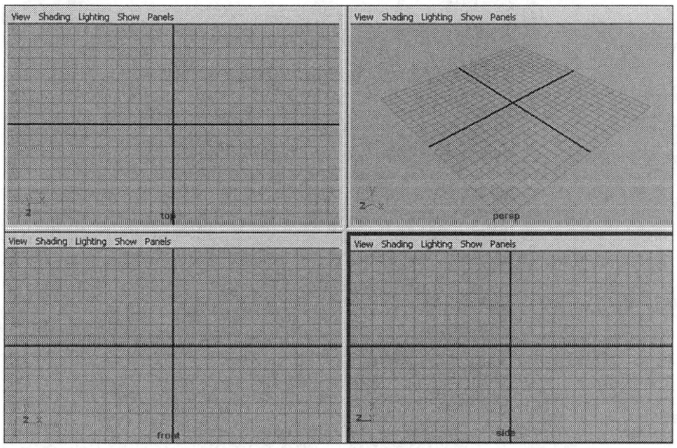

FIGURE 17.17 A four viewport layout.

Around one of the viewports (typically the Perspective when a new scene is opened) is a thick blue bar to designate that the viewport is active. By default, some actions, such as playing animation in the viewports, respond in real time only within the active viewport. Only one viewport can be active at a time, but you can change which viewport is active by clicking another view panel.

When you begin a new scene, you see only the Perspective viewport in full screen mode. You can toggle any viewport by tapping the spacebar to minimize the Perspective viewport so that you can also see the three orthographic views. You can use the same technique to expand viewports to full screen. When doing this, Maya reads the location of the mouse and expands the viewport that your cursor is over.

View Modes

The viewports have four separate view modes to adjust how you see your objects. The first mode, Wireframe, is the default setting. It allows you to see the edges of a polygonal object. You can also view objects with a smooth shaded surface or see how they would look with textures or lighting applied. **TABLE 17.2** shows the hotkeys for each view mode.

TABLE 17.2 View Mode Hotkeys

Mode	Hotkey	Mode	Hotkey
Wireframe	4	Textured	6
Smooth Shaded	5	Lighting	7

Viewport Navigation

Now that you know the general areas of the UI, you can see how to navigate the viewports. There are three major ways to move the view around while in the Perspective viewport: rotate, pan, and dolly (see **TABLE 17.3**). Pan and dolly are the navigation options for the orthographic views (see **TABLE 17.4**).

> **NOTE**
>
> **Textured and Lighting modes are useful only if you have textures or lights created in your scene.**

> **NOTE**
>
> **In TABLES 17.3 and 17.4, LMB stands for left mouse button, RMB stands for right mouse button, and MMB stands for middle mouse button.**

TABLE 17.3 Viewport Navigation for the Perspective View

Operation	Key Combination	Description
Rotate	Alt+LMB-drag	This operation rotates the camera around its focus in the direction defined by the mouse's movement.
Pan	Alt+MMB-drag	This operation pans the camera (moves without rotating) in the direction defined by the mouse's movement.
Dolly	Alt+RMB-drag or Alt+LMB-drag and MMB-drag	This operation is similar to zooming except that you move the camera instead of adjusting its focal length.

TABLE 17.4 Viewport Navigation for the Orthographic Views

Operation	Key Combination	Description
Pan	Alt+MMB-drag	This operation pans the camera (moves without rotating) in the direction defined by the mouse's movement.
Dolly	Alt+RMB-drag or Alt+LMB and MMB-drag	This operation is similar to zooming except that you physically move the camera instead of adjusting its focal length.

Practicing these navigation skills is highly recommended, until you become as accustomed to them as you are the UnrealEd navigation methods.

Camera Focus

When using the Perspective view, notice that the camera rotates around a specific point in space. This is called the camera's *focus*. You can center this focus on a selected object by pressing the F key or average it between all objects in the scene with the A key.

The Main Menu Bar and Menu Sets

Maya's main menu bar, shown in **FIGURE 17.18**, is located across the top of the window. This menu bar gives you access to nearly all the tools and commands needed to use the program. Certain commands are found in menus pertaining to those commands' functions. For example, you find the Create Polygon Tool command in the Polygons menu.

FIGURE 17.18 The Modeling menu set.

Maya has hundreds of commands, which are spread across nearly *30* separate menus. However, nowhere near this many menus are visible at the top of the screen because the menus have been organized into *menu sets*. These menu sets enable you to see only the menus you need and hide those that aren't needed for the task you're performing. Moreover, unless you're viewing at a very high resolution, you wouldn't be able to fit all the available menus on your screen.

> **NOTE**
>
> The File, Edit, Modify, Create, Display, Window, and Help menus are always visible, regardless of your current menu set.

You can switch between these menu sets by using two methods, which is typical of Maya's workflow: Usually several methods are available for performing a task. The two most common methods for switching between menu sets are using the Menu Set drop-down list or the hotkeys. The Menu Set drop-down list shown in **FIGURE 17.19** is located just beneath the main menu bar in the Status Line (discussed in "The Status Line" later in this chapter).

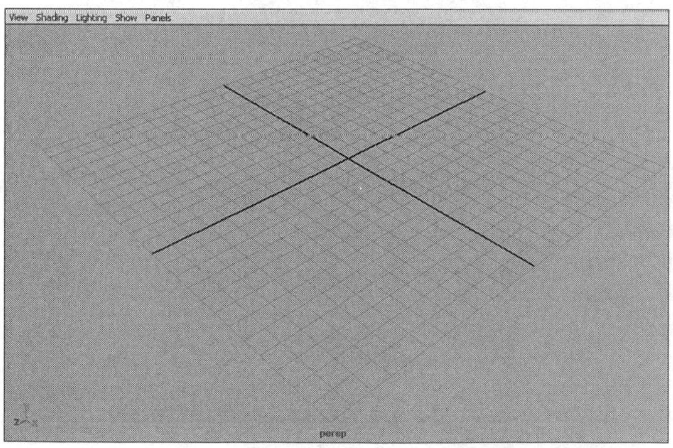

FIGURE 17.19 The Menu Set drop-down list is set to Animation.

The second method for changing menu sets is using hotkeys. **TABLE 17.5** lists the available menu sets, their associated hotkeys, and the menus items in each menu set.

TABLE 17.5 Menu Set Hotkeys

Menu Set	Hotkey	Menu Items
Animation	F2	Animate, Deform, Skeleton, Skin, Constrain, Character
Modeling	F3	Edit Curves, Surfaces, Edit NURBS, Polygons, Edit Polygons, Subdiv Surfaces
Dynamics	F4	Particles, Fluid Effects*, Fields, Soft/Rigid Bodies, Effects, Solvers
Rendering	F5	Lighting/Shading, Texturing, Render, Paint Effects, Fur*

**These menus are available only in Maya Unlimited, not in Maya PLE.*

Tear-Off Menus

One of the handiest features of the menu system in Maya is the ability to tear menus off and leave them floating in your window. In **TUTORIAL 17.1**, you see how to do this.

TUTORIAL 17.1: Using Tear-Off Menus

1. Start Maya if it's not already running.
2. From the main menu, click File.
3. In the menu that drops down, click the two horizontal bars running across the top, just above New Scene. This step tears the menu off, making it a floating window.
4. Notice that the menu has turned into a new floating window (see **FIGURE 17.20**). You can click any command in this tear-off menu as many times as you like, and it doesn't close until you use the close button in the upper-right corner. You can use this technique on any menu in Maya, even those in the viewport menus. You can move this floating window around the screen by dragging its title bar.

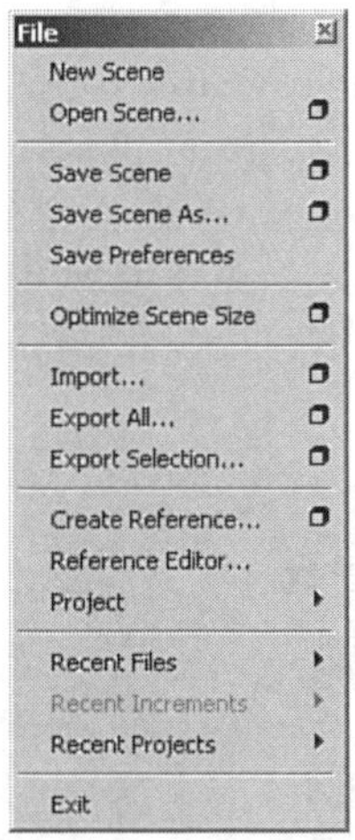

FIGURE 17.20 The floating File menu.

END TUTORIAL 17.1

The Status Line

The Status Line shown in **FIGURE 17.21** is located directly beneath the main menu bar. It contains a variety of commands for scene management and enables you to swap between different modes in Maya. **TABLE 17.6** describes the components of the Status Line.

FIGURE 17.21 The Status Line.

TABLE 17.6 Components of the Status Line

Name	Description
Menu Set drop-down list	You can use this drop-down list box to change between the different menu sets, as described previously.
File buttons	You can use these three buttons to start a new scene, open a saved scene, or save your current scene.
Selection Mask drop-down list	You can use this drop-down list to control what types of objects are selectable in your scene. Clicking the small black triangle opens a list box for choosing selectable objects.
Selection Mode	Here you can switch between Hierarchy, Object, and Component modes.
Selection Masks (Hierarchy, Object, and Component)	You can use this area to determine which objects or components are selectable in the viewport. It can appear in three different ways, depending on which selection mode you have chosen.
Snapping buttons	You can use these buttons to snap objects to the grid, to curves, to points, or to view planes or to make a selected object live.
Construction History options	You can use this area to access all input or output connections of an object or to switch off construction history.
Rendering options	You can use these buttons to render the current frame, open an Interactive Photorealistic Renderer (IPR) render, or access the Render Global Settings dialog box.
Input box	You can use this multifunction window to select objects by name, rename multiple selected objects, and edit numeric values in absolute or relative modes.
Sidebar buttons	These buttons switch your sidebar between the Attribute Editor, the Tool Options, and the Channel Box.

You can expand or collapse the sections of the Status Line to make more room. At the beginning of each section is a small black bar. If the shape in the middle of it is rectangular, the section is expanded. If the central shape is triangular, the area has been collapsed:

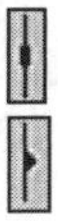

-  Expanded area
-  Collapsed area

The Shelf

The Shelf shown in **FIGURE 17.22** is the horizontal area just under the Status Line. You can use the Shelf to perform common Maya functions with a single click, instead of having to dig through menus or navigate deep into other parts of the UI. Best of all, you can even create your own Shelves.

FIGURE 17.22 **The Shelf for polygons.**

By default, the Shelf displays an array of tabs across the top, which give you quick access to the different available shelves.

Creating Your Own Shelves

If you like, you can even build your own Shelf to include the tools you use most. You can also add and remove items from existing Shelves. In **TUTORIAL 17.2**, you see how to create and edit Shelves.

TUTORIAL 17.2: Creating and Editing Shelves

1. Start Maya, if you haven't already.
2. To the left of the Shelf area is a small white square with a black triangle underneath (see **FIGURE 17.23**).

   The gray tab is a Shelf selector, which is practical only if you have hidden your Shelf tabs, which can be done from the list that opens when you click the black triangle below this tab.

FIGURE 17.23 **The Shelf selector.**

3. Click the black triangle. From the list that opens, select New Shelf.
4. The Create New Shelf dialog box opens, where you can enter the name for your new Shelf. Enter `myShelf`, and click OK.
5. You now see your new Shelf at the far right of the available shelf tabs. Click the new tab shown in **FIGURE 17.24**.

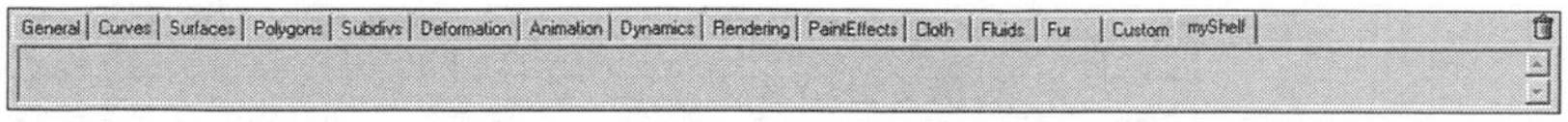

FIGURE 17.24 The myShelf tab.

6. The shelf is currently empty, so you need to add some commands to it. Hold down the Ctrl+Shift keys, and choose Create > Polygon Primitives > Cube. Instead of a cube being created in the viewports, a new icon appears in your Shelf.

7. You can also remove items from your Shelf. MMB-drag your new cube icon to the small trashcan icon on the Shelf's upper-right corner.

> **CAUTION**
>
> In step 6, be sure not to click the options box icon. Clicking it opens the Polygon Cube Options dialog box.

END TUTORIAL 17.2

The Channel Box and Layer Editor

The Channel Box, shown in **FIGURE 17.25**, is an easy way to access your object's attributes and place animation keyframes (discussed in Chapter 23, "Character Animation"). To be technical, the Channel Box displays the object attributes that can be animated, so everything you see in the Channel Box can be animated. By default, this includes the object's location in three-dimensional space, its rotation on all three axes, and its scale. You can also set the object's visibility and see a list of an object's construction history.

> **TIP**
>
> If you're not sure what a specific Shelf button does, hold your mouse cursor over it, and a tooltip is displayed to let you know.

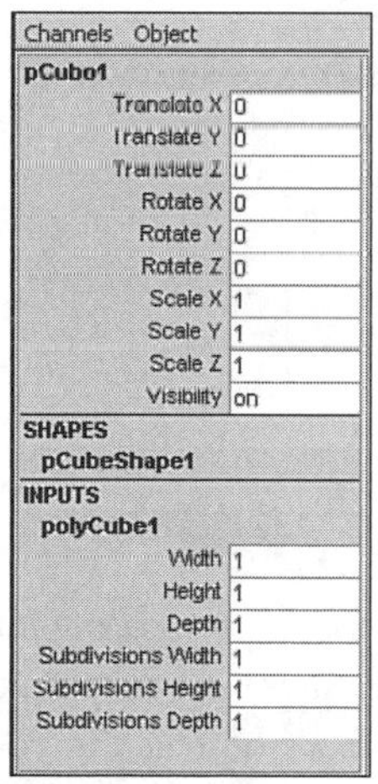

FIGURE 17.25 The Channel Box for a newly created cube.

Just above the Channel Box, you see three buttons for controlling whether the Channel Box, the Layer Editor, or both are visible (see **FIGURE 17.26**). By default, both are displayed.

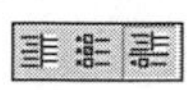

FIGURE 17.26 Channel Box and Layer Editor controls.

Channel Sliders

The Channel Box doesn't show any visible sliders or any other way to change values besides typing in numbers manually. This is because the Channel Box uses an invisible slider system called *channel sliders*. **TUTORIAL 17.3** introduces you to these tools and shows you how to control their behavior.

TUTORIAL 17.3: Using Channel Sliders

1. From the Maya main menu, choose Create > Polygon Primitives > Cube to create a polygon cube in the center of the viewport.
2. In the Channel Box, click Translate X.
3. Place your mouse cursor on the viewport, and MMB-drag to the left and right. Notice that the cube moves back and forth in the X-axis with your mouse motions.

END TUTORIAL 17.3

You can also control the slider's speed and configure whether it works at all. The three buttons above and to the right of the Channel Box control the modes and behavior of the channel sliders. **TABLE 17.7** describes them.

TABLE 17.7 Channel Slider Controls

Button	Image	Description
Channel slider/ manipulator switch		You use this button to switch between using manipulators and channel sliders, channel sliders only, or neither.
Channel slider speed		You use this button to adjust the speed of channel sliders to fast, medium, or slow.
Channel slider setting		You use this button to adjust between linear and hyperbolic slider motion. You can't use this button unless you've chosen to use channel sliders only.

The Layer Editor

At the lower-right area of the Maya interface is the Layer Editor (see **FIGURE 17.27**), which is used to separate objects in your scene into layers. Layers are a great way to organize complex scenes or hide geometry that's obstructing your work. One layer can have several objects in it, but each object can be in only one layer at a time.

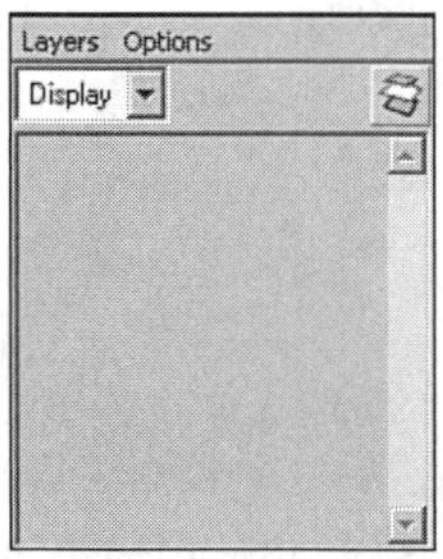

FIGURE 17.27 The Layer Editor.

In **TUTORIAL 17.4**, you see how to create a layer, how to add objects to it, how to adjust the layer's visibility, and how to remove the layer.

TUTORIAL 17.4: Using Layers

1. Click the New Scene button in the Status Line. If prompted to save, click No.
2. Click the Polygons Shelf tab. In the Polygons Shelf, click the Cube button to create a cube in your scene.
3. In the Layer Editor, click the New Layer button. A new layer named layer1 is displayed (see **FIGURE 17.28**).
4. Double-click this new layer in the Layer Editor to open the Edit Layer dialog box (see **FIGURE 17.29**). Change the name to **`myLayer`**, and set the color to red. Click Save when finished.

FIGURE 17.28 Layer1 is found at the top of the Layer Editor.

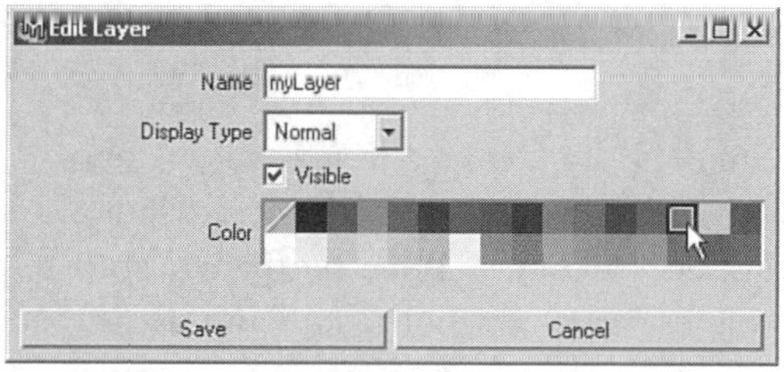

FIGURE 17.29 The Edit Layer dialog box.

5. Next, you'll add the cube to the layer. The cube should already be selected in your viewport and highlighted green. If not, click it. Next, right-click the layer in the Layer Editor and choose Add Selected Objects from the context menu.

   The cube is then added to the layer. You can verify this by looking at the Channel Box. Under the Inputs section, you should see myLayer (see **FIGURE 17.30**).

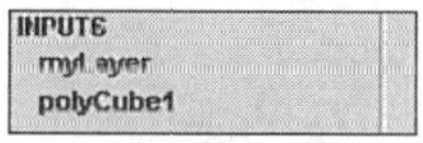

FIGURE 17.30 There are now two items in the Inputs section.

   If you deselect the cube by clicking in an open area of the viewport, notice that the cube's wireframe turns red.

6. In the Layer Editor, the small *V* to the left of the layer (see **FIGURE 17.31**) is a toggle for controlling the layer's visibility and the objects within it. Click the V, and notice the cube vanish.

FIGURE 17.31 When the V is visible, objects in the layer are also visible.

7. To delete the layer, right-click on it in the Layer Editor and choose Delete from the context menu. The layer is now gone, and the object returns in its original navy blue color.

> **NOTE**
>
> The box next to the Visibility toggle is used to select Template or Reference layers for your object. These options enable you to see your object, but not select it.

END TUTORIAL 17.4

The Attribute Editor

The Attribute Editor shown in **FIGURE 17.32** gives you access to all an object's attributes, whether they can be animated or not. The Attribute Editor shows all properties available on each node connected to an object.

At the top of the window is a menu that includes commands to help you sort through attributes, add or remove attributes, or get help on specific attributes. Below the menu are tabs representing the nodes that make up your object.

Below these tabs is an area where you can rename the currently selected object, and under that is the list of available attributes for the current object. You can expand or collapse these areas for more room and use the scrollbar on the right to navigate through the list.

In **TUTORIAL 17.5**, you use the Attribute Editor to adjust the width of a cube.

> **TIP**
>
> **Beneath the Layer Editor are two buttons for controlling the width of the sidebar containing the Channel Box and the Layer Editor.**

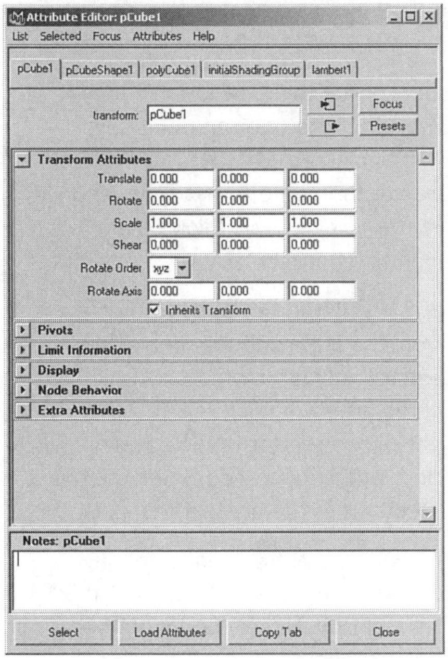

FIGURE 17.32 Attribute Editor for a cube.

17

TUTORIAL 17.5: Using the Attribute Editor

1. Using the skills you have learned so far, start a new scene and create a cube.
2. With the cube selected, press Ctrl+A to open the Attribute Editor, shown in **FIGURE 17.33**.
3. Click the polyCube1 tab to access the attributes of the cube's Transform node.
4. In the Poly Cube History area, you see the Width attribute, which has a numerical entry field as well as a slider (see **FIGURE 17.34**). Adjust the slider, and notice the cube's width change, as shown in **FIGURE 17.35**.

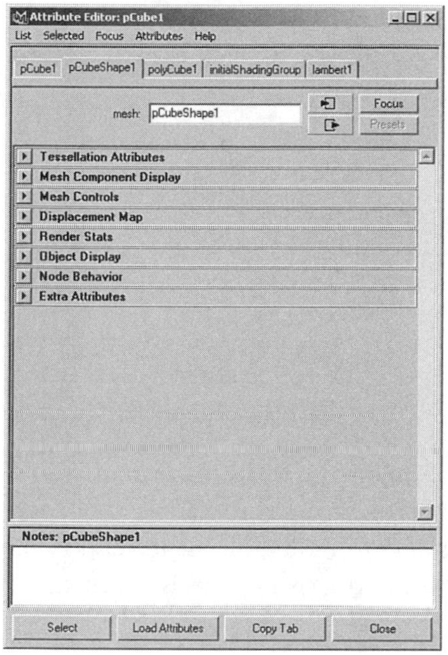

FIGURE 17.33 The Attribute Editor open to the pCubeShape1 tab.

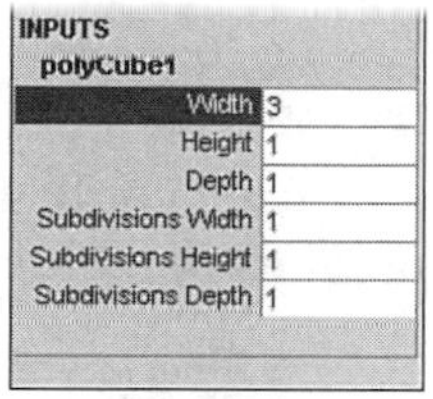

FIGURE 17.34 The Width attribute.

FIGURE 17.35 The width changes on the cube.

END TUTORIAL 17.5

The Attribute Editor gives you another way to access an object's attributes. However, you must remember that the Attribute Editor displays all attributes of an object, whether they can be animated or not.

The Time and Range Sliders

Near the bottom of the Maya interface, you see the Time Slider and Range Slider, which are used to control your animation timeline. The following sections give you an overview of these controls, but their use is discussed in depth later in Chapter 23.

Time Slider

You can use the Time Slider, shown in **FIGURE 17.36**, to switch between different frames, or moments in time, of your animation. You can think of it as a ruler that shows all the frames in the current time range. You can click anywhere on the Time Slider to jump immediately to that frame. You can also drag right or left to sample your animation forward or backward. This dragging is called *scrubbing* the timeline. A thick black line displayed on the Time Slider wherever you click is called the Current Time Indicator. As its name implies, it indicates the current frame.

At the end of the timeline is the Current Time Field, where you can type a specific frame into the timeline, instead of clicking on or dragging to a specific frame. This field can be extremely useful when you have thousands of frames visible in the Time Slider.

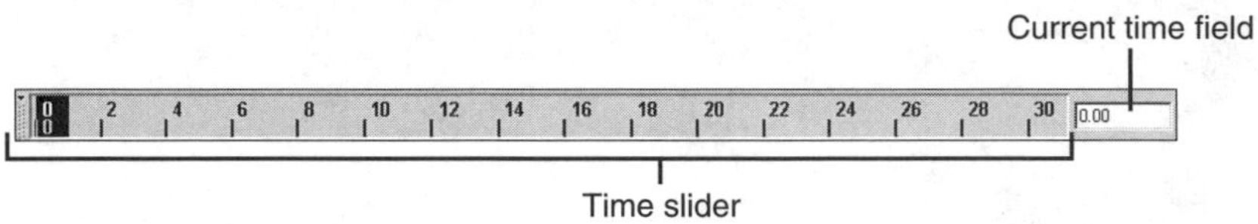

FIGURE 17.36 The Time Slider.

Transport Controls

To the right of the Time Slider are the Transport controls, similar to the controls on a VCR or DVD player (see **FIGURE 17.37**). You can use them to play your animation forward or backward, to jump forward or back by frames or keyframes, and to rewind or fast-forward to the beginning or end of the animation. **FIGURE 17.37** shows the Transport controls' functions.

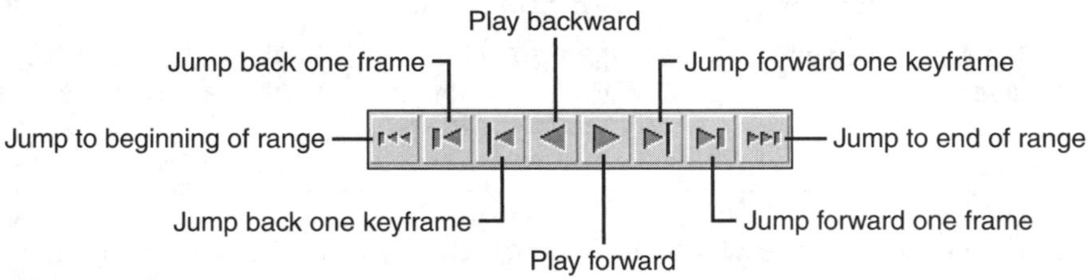

FIGURE 17.37 The Transport controls.

Range Slider

The Range Slider is used to control the length of your animation and the visible range of the timeline (see **FIGURE 17.38**). The entry fields on the outside of the Range Slider are used to determine the animation's total time, and the numbers inside control the visible range on the Time Slider. Between these entry fields is a slider for changing the visible range or moving the range back and forth along the total timeline. You can use this slider to "focus" the Time Slider on a certain area of your animation for tweaking purposes.

To the right of the Range Slider, you have access to Maya's character sets and two buttons. From left to right, they are the Auto Keyframe button and the Preferences button (which opens the Preferences dialog box). Much of the functionality in this area is discussed in detail in Chapter 22, "Importing Characters into UnrealEd."

FIGURE 17.38 The Range Slider.

The Toolbox and Layout Selection

On the left side of the Maya window are the Toolbox and the Layout Selection options (see **FIGURE 17.39**). The Toolbox at the top is where you access the manipulation tools, such as Move, Rotate, and Scale. You can click any of these icons to use the corresponding tool.

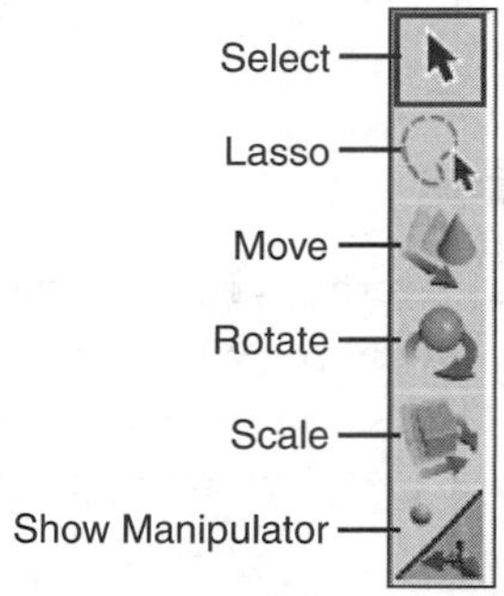

FIGURE 17.39 The Toolbox.

> **NOTE**
>
> The Show Manipulator tool displays the manipulator for many of the nodes in an object's construction history.

You can use the Layout Selection options to quickly switch between different layouts for your viewports (see **FIGURE 17.40**). Some layouts include different tools, such as the Outliner, which lists all objects in your scene, the Curve Editor, which enables you to tweak your animation, the Hypergraph, used to view network connections, and the Hypershade, for working with materials.

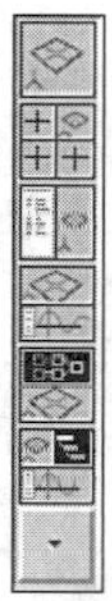

FIGURE 17.40 The Layout Selection options.

The Hotbox

If you have pressed the spacebar for any amount of time while using Maya, you might have already seen the Hotbox. The Hotbox is a large hidden menu that appears only when the spacebar is held down (see **FIGURE 17.41**). The top bar includes all the constant menus that are available regardless of menu set, and the bar just below includes the menus available in each viewport.

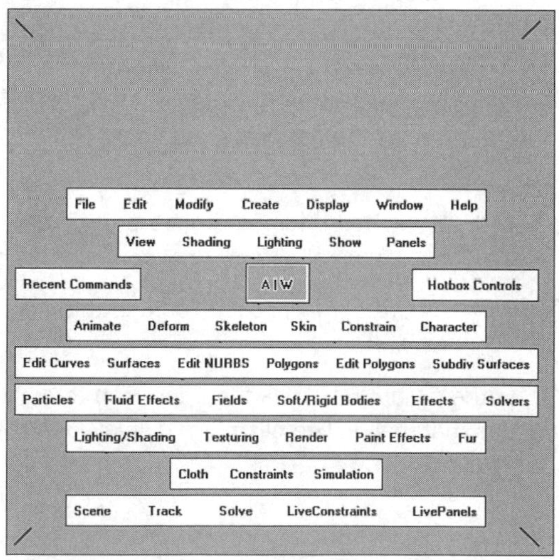

FIGURE 17.41 The Hotbox.

Along the bottom are the many menus available in the different menu sets. With the Hotbox, you can access any menu in

Maya without needing to switch menu sets. They are visible even if you have chosen to hide all menus.

The Hypershade

The Hypershade is Maya's powerful system for creating and applying materials and shader networks. This section gives you an overview of how to create and apply a simple material to an object by using the Hypershade. You work with the Hypershade in more depth in Chapter 19, "The Art of Texturing in Maya." In **TUTORIAL 17.6**, you create your first material using the Hypershade.

TUTORIAL 17.6: Creating a Basic Material and Texture

1. Using the skills you have learned so far, start a new scene and create a polygon sphere (see **FIGURE 17.42**).

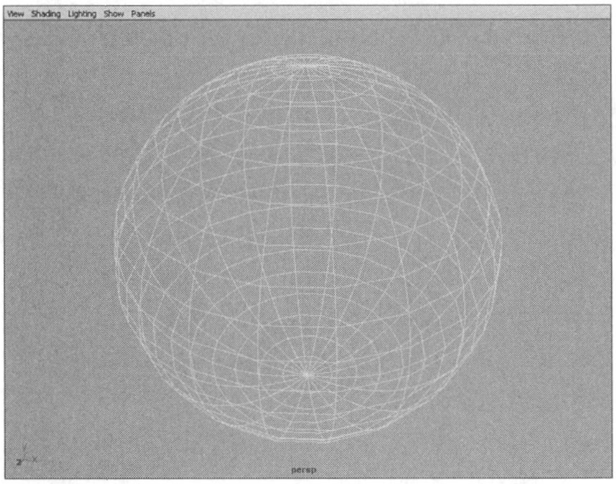

FIGURE 17.42 A wireframe sphere in the viewport.

2. Open the Hypershade from the main menu by selecting Window > Rendering Editors > Hypershade. (This might take a moment on some computers.) The Hypershade window is composed of three major areas (see **FIGURE 17.43**):

   - *Tab area*—This area can display a variety of things, depending on which tab you have selected. By default, it shows the materials you have created.
   - *Work Area*—You use this area to create your material's shader networks. You can have several different networks in this area, if needed.
   - *Create Bar*—Typically, you use this area to get new components for your shader network.

3. In the Create Bar, click the Blinn icon to create a new Blinn material. The new node for this material, called blinn1, is displayed in the tab area and the Work Area (see **FIGURE 17.44**).

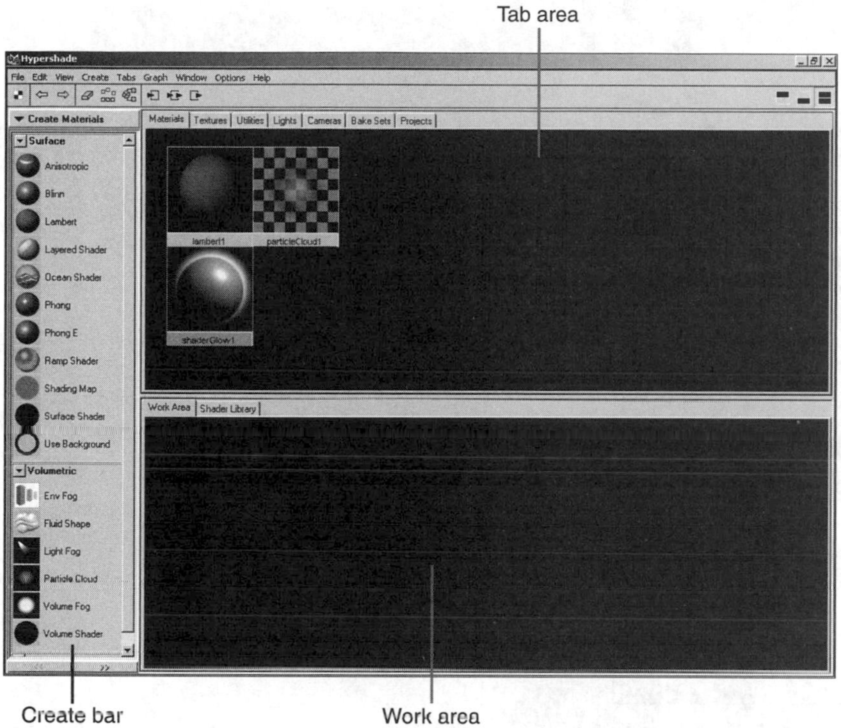

FIGURE 17.43 The Hypershade window.

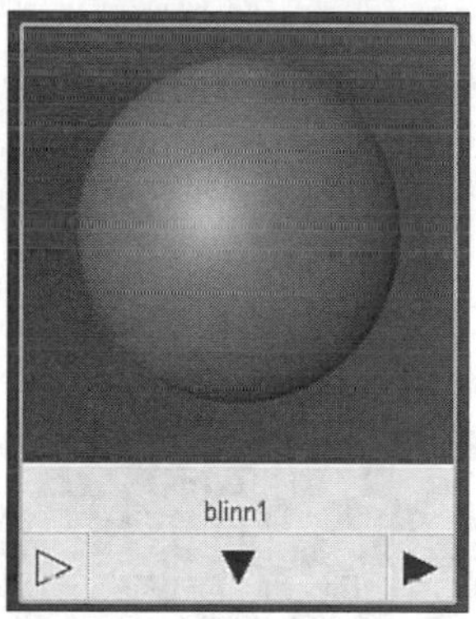

FIGURE 17.44 A new Blinn material.

4. Double-click the new Blinn node (in either area) to open the Attribute Editor (see Figure **17.45**).

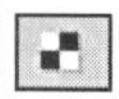

5. Next to the Color entry, click the small button with a checkered pattern to open the Create New Render Node dialog box (see **FIGURE 17.46**).

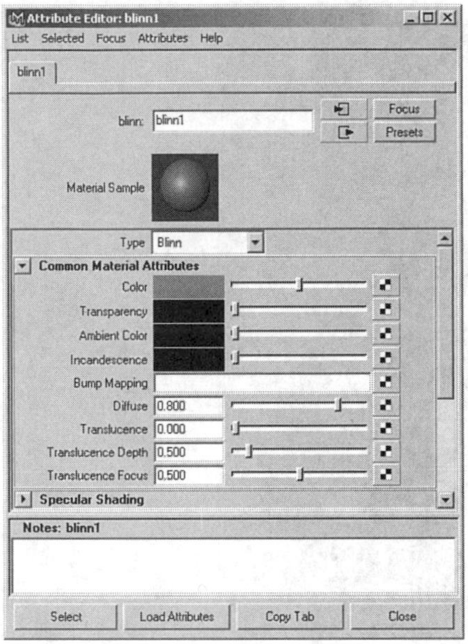

FIGURE 17.45 Attributes for the Blinn material.

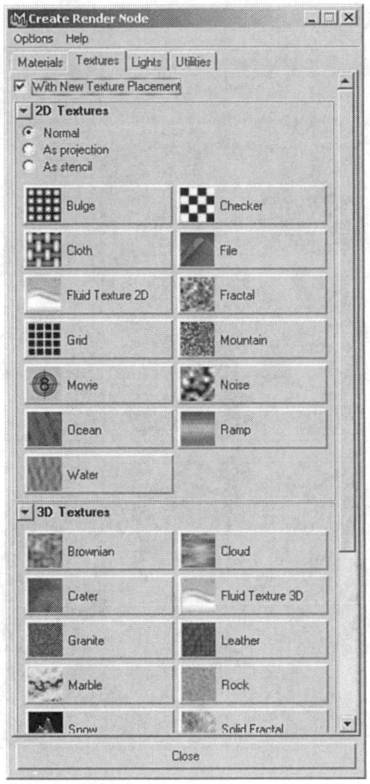

FIGURE 17.46 The Create Render Node dialog box.

6. Click the Checker button to create a new checker node, which is connected to the Blinn material's Color attribute. You see the material become covered with a checker texture. Also, you can see both nodes in the Work Area as well as how they are connected (see **FIGURE 17.47**).

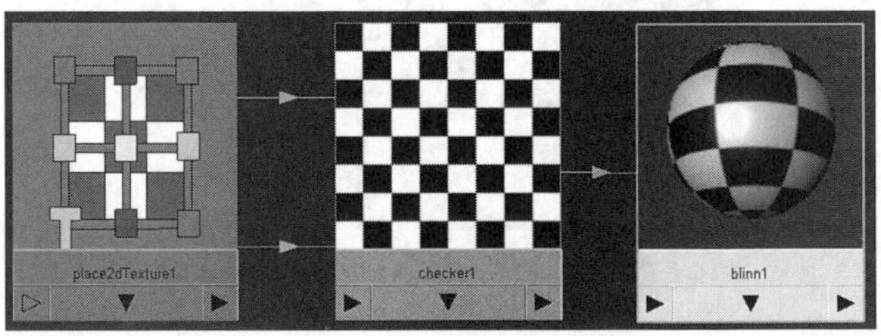

FIGURE 17.47 The nodes that make a checker material.

7. Move the Hypershade window so that you can also see the sphere in the viewport, and MMB-drag the blinn1 node onto the sphere.

> **NOTE**
>
> If you're viewing the sphere in Wireframe mode, you need to release the mouse button while your cursor is over one of the wires.

8. Press 5 to enter Smooth Shaded view, and then press 6 to enter Textured view. You can see the result of the texture on the surface (see **FIGURE 17.48**).

> **TIP**
>
> You can navigate the Hypershade window just as you do the orthographic viewports. You can pan with Alt+MMB and zoom with Alt+RMB.

FIGURE 17.48 Sphere with the new checker material.

END TUTORIAL 17.6

The Hypergraph

The Hypergraph enables you to see your scene's nodes and the connections between them. You can open it by choosing Window > Hypergraph from the main menu. In **TUTORIAL 17.7**, you take a look at how to use the Hypergraph.

TUTORIAL 17.7: Introduction to the Hypergraph

1. Start a new scene, and create a polygonal sphere (see **FIGURE 17.49**).
2. From the main menu, choose Window > Hypergraph to open the Hypergraph window (see **FIGURE 17.50**).
3. The Hypergraph can be displayed in two different modes: Scene Hierarchy and Dependency Graph. By default, you see the Scene Hierarchy mode, which shows all the objects in your scene as single nodes.

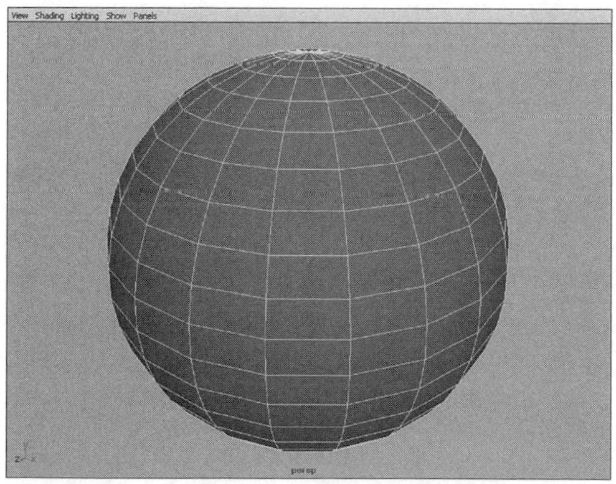

FIGURE 17.49 Sphere in viewport.

4. Select the polygonal object's node, if it isn't selected already (see **FIGURE 17.51**). Selected nodes are displayed as yellow.

5. Click the Input and Output Connections icon on the toolbar at the top to switch the window to the Dependency Graph mode (see **FIGURE 17.52**), which enables you to see the nodes that connect to form your object (as discussed at the beginning of the chapter). The more you use Maya, the more you'll find yourself using the Hypergraph to analyze and edit the connections between your scene's nodes.

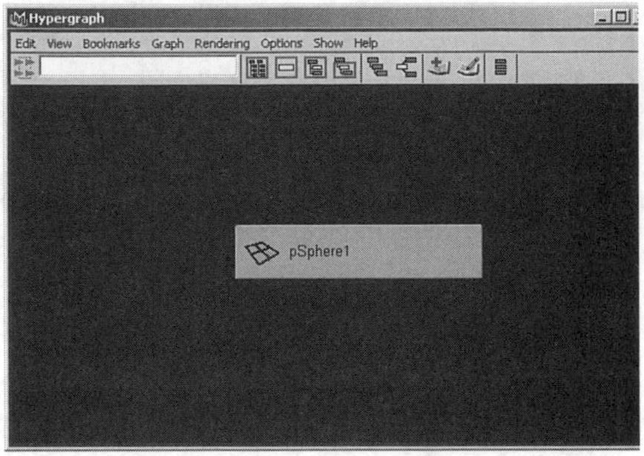

FIGURE 17.50 The Hypergraph window.

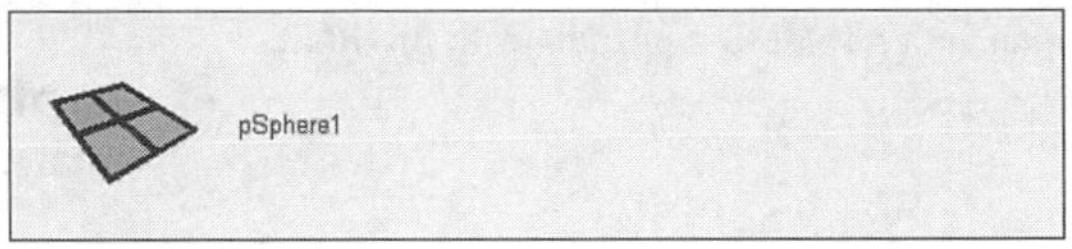

FIGURE 17.51 The polygon sphere node in the Hypergraph window.

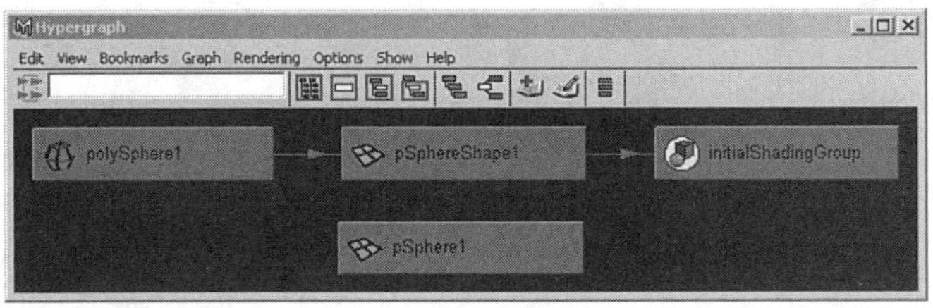

FIGURE 17.52 Dependency Graph mode shows the nodes needed when making a polygonal sphere.

END TUTORIAL 17.7

Object Manipulation

When working with objects in Maya, there are two ways to manipulate them: manipulating the object as a whole (Object mode) and manipulating the components that make up that object (Component mode). For polygons, "components" refers to the object's vertices, edges, and faces. The following sections discuss both methods and how to access them.

Object Mode

In Object mode, you're manipulating the entire object. You can move it, rotate it, and scale it, all while manipulating the object as a whole. You can do this with the Channel Box and the Attribute Editor, as mentioned earlier, or with Maya's set of transform tools. These tools have a manipulator that's visible in the viewport, allowing you to interactively adjust your objects' position, rotation, or scale. You can access these tools with the Toolbox, as mentioned earlier, or with hotkeys. In **TUTORIALS 17.8** through **17.10**, you see how to use these tools to manipulate an object in the viewport.

TUTORIAL 17.8: Moving Objects in Maya

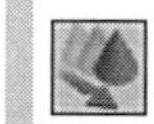

1. Using the skills you have learned so far, start a new scene and create a polygon cube (see **FIGURE 17.53**).
2. Select the cube, if it isn't already, and click the Move Tool icon in the Toolbox or press the W key. Make sure the Caps Lock key is not on, as Maya's hotkeys are case sensitive.
3. Notice the new manipulator that appears in the middle of the cube (see **FIGURE 17.54**). The Move manipulator (also called the Translate manipulator) can be used to move the object around in 3D space without having to adjust any attribute numbers. Do this now by dragging on any of the arrows.

   The manipulator's arrows are color-coded to correspond with three-dimensional axes. The code works as follows:

Color	Corresponding Axis
Red	X-axis
Green	Y-axis
Blue	Z-axis

   You can remember this code with the simple equation RGB = XYZ.

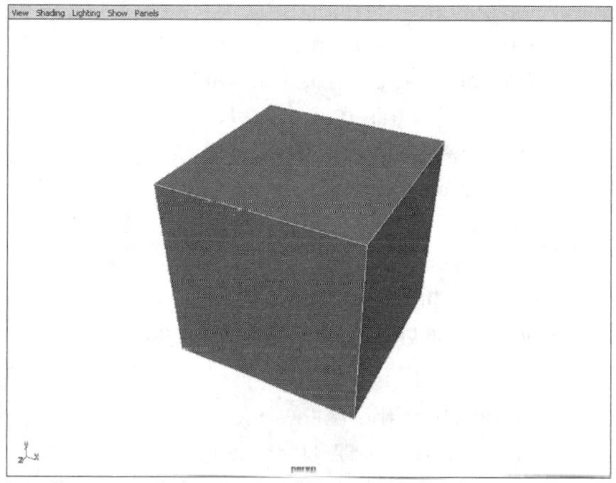

FIGURE 17.53 The polygon cube.

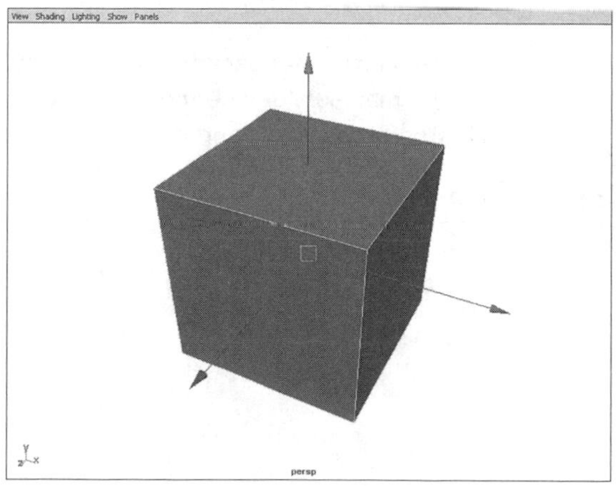

FIGURE 17.54 Cube showing the Move manipulator.

4. As you drag an arrow, you move the cube in the direction of the related axis. You can move in all three axes by dragging the yellow square in the center of the manipulator. Try this now.

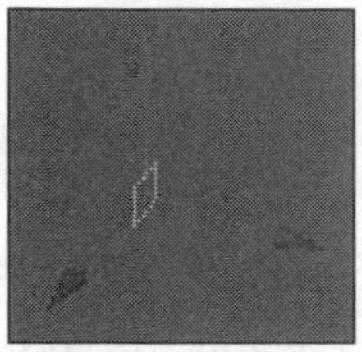

FIGURE 17.55 Center of the Move manipulator after canceling out the X-axis motion.

> **TIP**
>
> **You can expand and shrink any manipulator with the + and – keys.**

5. You can also move on two axes at a time or in a plane-like fashion in the Perspective viewport. You can cancel out motion on any axis by Ctrl+clicking the axis you want to cancel. Try this now by Ctrl-clicking on the X-axis (red). **FIGURE 17.55** shows the result.

> **NOTE**
>
> **Moving in all three axes actually moves the cube on a plane perpendicular to the camera.**

Notice that the yellow square is now parallel to the YZ plane, which means that when you move the object by using the square, you move on only the Y and Z axes. Try this now.

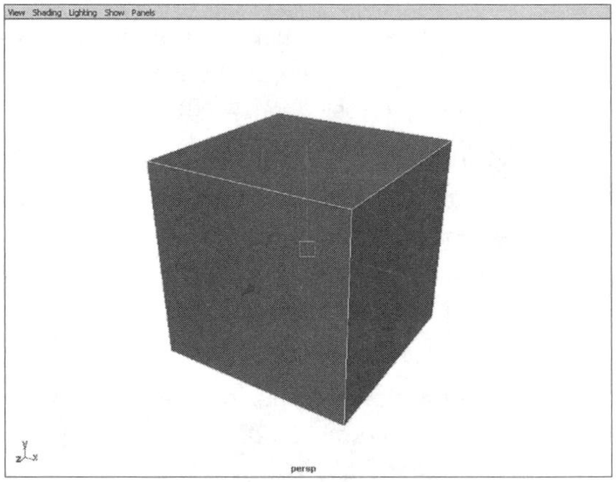

FIGURE 17.56 Manipulator back to normal.

6. To put the manipulator back to its normal state, Ctrl-click on the yellow square. This makes the manipulator face the camera again (see **FIGURE 17.56**), so you'll be moving on all three axes, on a plane perpendicular to the camera.

END TUTORIAL 17.8

TUTORIAL 17.9: Rotating Objects in Maya

1. Continue from **TUTORIAL 17.8**, or start a new scene and create a cube.
2. With the cube selected, click the Rotate Tool icon in the Toolbox or press the E key.
3. You'll see a new manipulator that looks like three orthogonal rings with a fourth yellow ring surrounding it. The Rotate manipulator uses the same color-coding system as the Move manipulator, with red being the X-axis, green the Y-axis, and blue the Z-axis. Try dragging on any of the rings. A small pie-wedge indicator appears to show you how far you have rotated (see **FIGURE 17.57**).
4. The yellow ring that surrounds the entire manipulator enables you to rotate perpendicularly to the camera (see **FIGURE 17.58**). Try this now.
5. You can also rotate freely on all three axes by clicking anywhere between the red, green, and blue axes (see **FIGURE 17.59**).

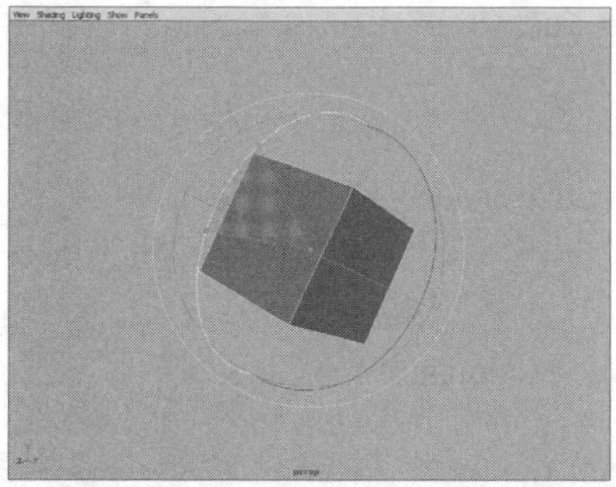

FIGURE 17.57 The farther you rotate, the larger the wedge.

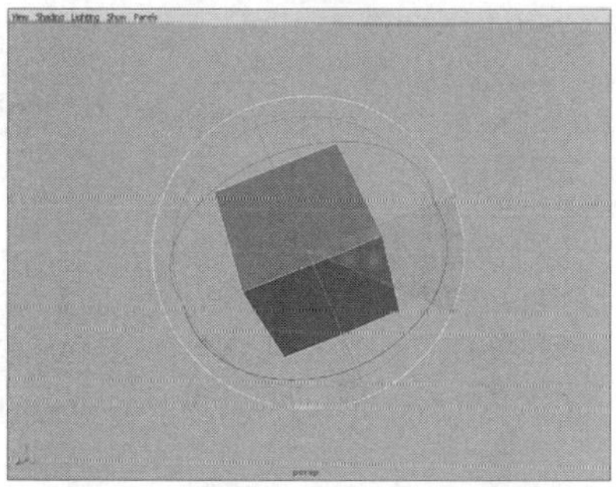

FIGURE 17.58 Rotating with the yellow ring.

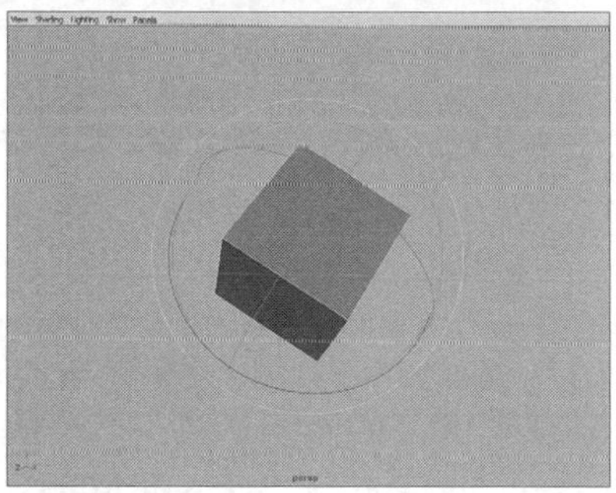

FIGURE 17.59 No wedge appears when rotating freely.

END TUTORIAL 17.9

TUTORIAL 17.10: Scaling Objects in Maya

1. Continue from **TUTORIAL 17.9**, or start a new scene and create a cube.

2. With the cube selected, click the Scale Tool icon  in the Toolbox or press the R key.
3. The Scale manipulator that appears is composed of four cubes: three colored for the main axes and a fourth yellow cube in the center (see **FIGURE 17.60**).
4. Click the red cube, and drag it toward the object. Note that it scales the cube in the X-axis (see **FIGURE 17.61**).
5. You can also scale uniformly on all three axes by dragging the yellow cube in the center of the manipulator (see **FIGURE 17.62**). Try this now.

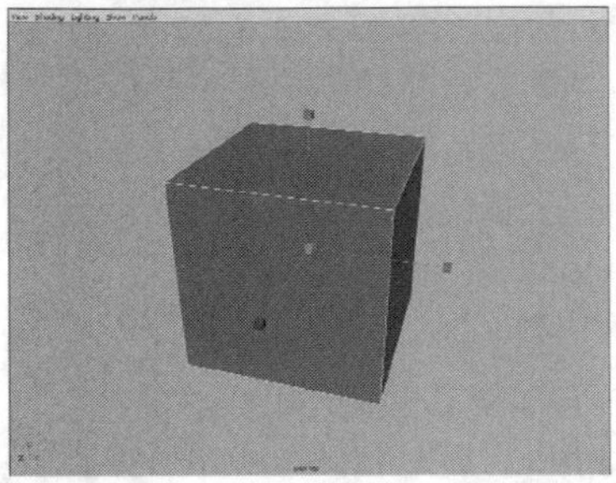

FIGURE 17.60 Cube showing the Scale manipulator.

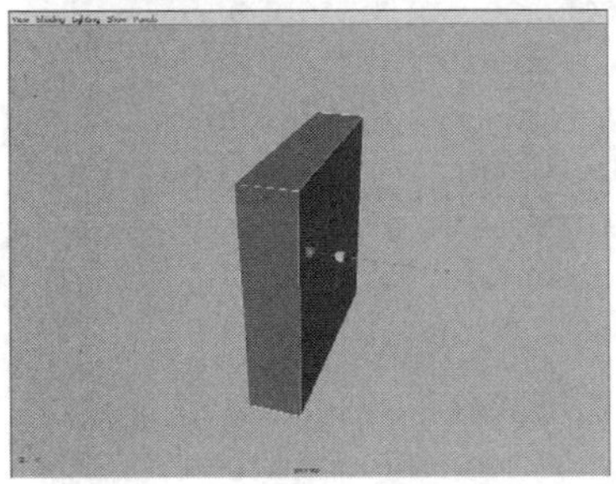

FIGURE 17.61 The other axes disappear when you're scaling in only one.

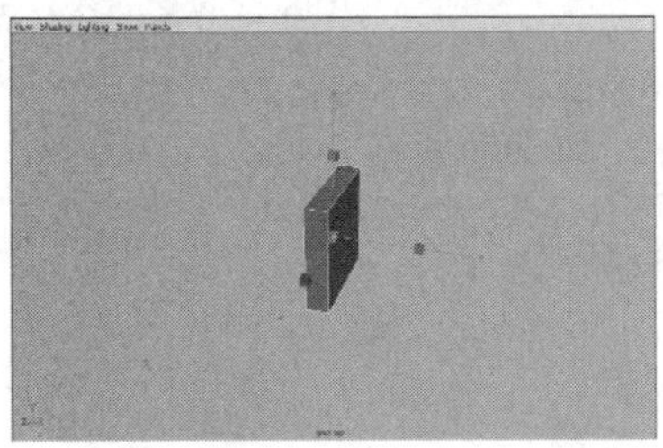

FIGURE 17.62 All the axes are visible when scaling uniformly.

END TUTORIAL 17.10

Now that you've seen how you can manipulate at the object level, you can take a look at component manipulation. But first, review the hotkeys for manipulating objects:

Tool	Hotkey	Tool	Hotkey
Select	q	Rotate	e
Move	w	Scale	r

All the hotkeys are listed in lowercase. If you have the Caps Lock key on when using hotkeys, you get different results.

Component Mode

Each object in Maya, polygonal or otherwise, is constructed of components. As mentioned earlier, polygons are composed of vertices, edges, and faces. After selecting a component, you can perform a wide variety of actions on it, including moving, rotating, or scaling. There are three main ways to switch between Object and Component mode. **TUTORIALS 17.11** and **17.12** introduce you to all three methods: using the Status Line, using hotkeys, and using marking menus.

TUTORIAL 17.11: Using the Status Line

1. Using the skills you have learned so far, start a new scene and create a polygon sphere (see **FIGURE 17.63**).

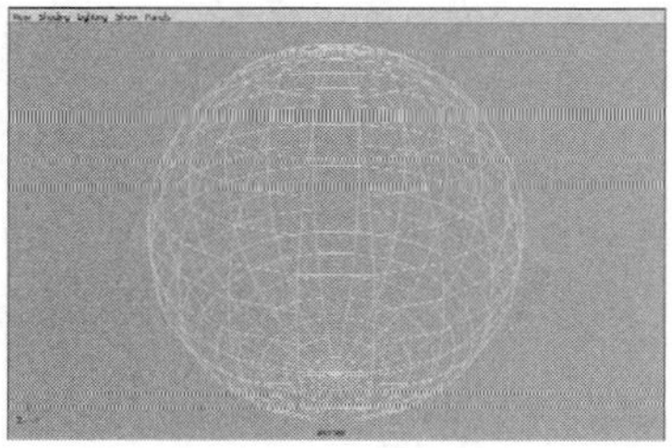

FIGURE 17.63 Polygon sphere in the viewport.

2. To make vertices selectable, you must be in Component mode. To enter Component mode, click the Select by Component Type icon in the Status Line, near the top of the screen. You should see small purple points appear across the sphere's surface (see **FIGURE 17.64**). If you don't, make sure the Select by Component Type: Points selection mask button is activated in the Status Line.

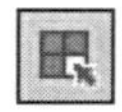

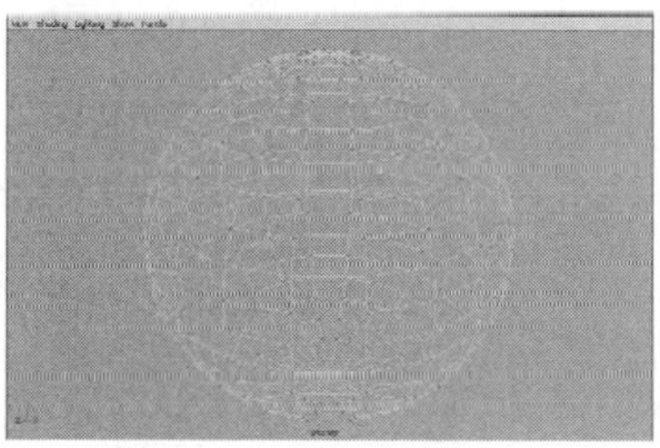

FIGURE 17.64 Polygon sphere in Component mode.

3. With the vertices visible, LMB-drag a marquee selection around several of the vertices or click the vertices individually. Notice that the selected vertices become yellow (see **FIGURE 17.65**). Make a few selections to get a feel for selecting vertices.

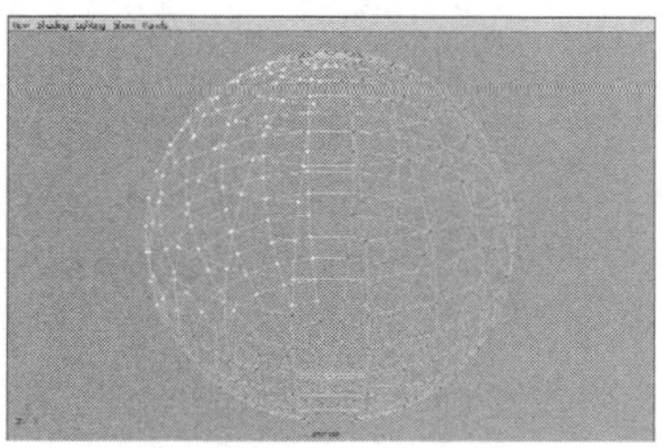

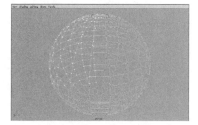

FIGURE 17.65 The selected vertices are yellow.

4. To select edges, you can click the Select by Component Type: Lines selection mask button in the Status Line. The purple spots on the surface disappear (see **FIGURE 17.66**), and you can select edges by drawing a marquee

or clicking on individual edges. Notice that selected edges are orange.

To select faces, click the Select by Component Type: Faces button, also in the Status Line. A blue dot appears in the center of each face, which is a handle you can use to select specific faces (see **FIGURE 17.67**). You can select faces by clicking on them or drawing a marquee selection over them. Selected faces turn orange.

5. When finished, you can switch back to Object mode by clicking the Select by Object Type icon.

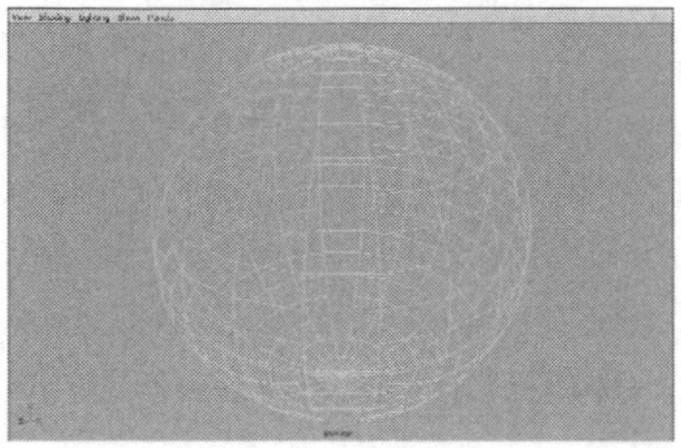

FIGURE 17.66 Each line is one edge.

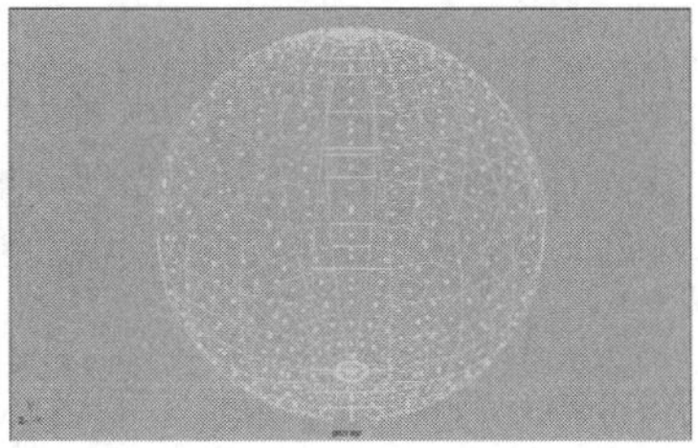

FIGURE 17.67 Each blue dot represents one face.

In **TUTORIAL 17.12**, you learn the other two methods of accessing components.

END TUTORIAL 17.11

TUTORIAL 17.12: Hotkeys and Marking Menus for Selection

1. Begin by selecting the sphere you created in **TUTORIAL 17.11** and pressing the F9 key to make vertices selectable. When finished, press the F8 key to toggle back to Object mode.

2. Now press the F10 key to make edges selectable, just as when using the Status Line. Press F8 when finished.

3. Press F11 and notice that the object's faces are now visible. Press F8 again when finished. For your reference, these are the selection hotkeys:

Hotkey	Function
F8	Toggles between Object and Component mode
F9	Makes vertices selectable
F10	Makes edges selectable
F11	Makes faces selectable

4. Now hold down the RMB while the cursor is on your object to display a floating marking menu. Surrounding the center of the marking menu are the names of all the components (see **FIGURE 17.68**).

5. While still holding the RMB, move the cursor over Vertex (see **FIGURE 17.69**), and release the mouse button.

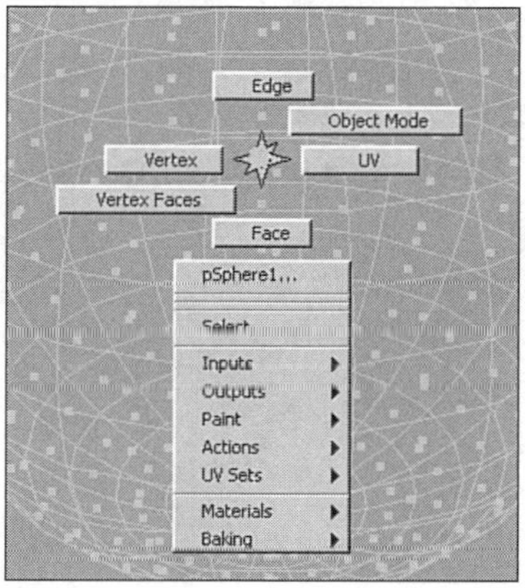

FIGURE 17.68 The marking menu.

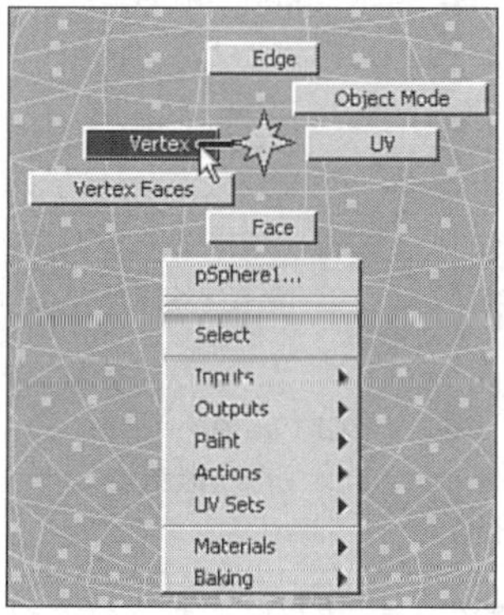

FIGURE 17.69 A line follows your cursor when using the marking menu.

Vertices are now selectable, as shown in **FIGURE 17.70**. You can use this method to make any of an object's components selectable.

6. When finished, hold down the RMB over the object to make the marking menu appear and choose Object Mode to go back to Object mode.

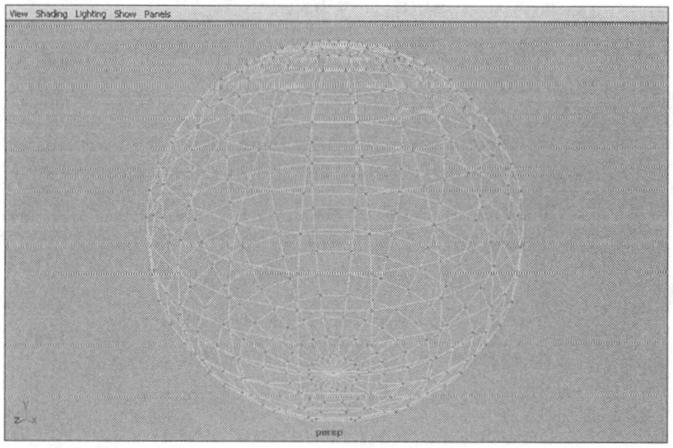

FIGURE 17.70 The sphere's vertices are now selectable.

END TUTORIAL 17.12

Now that you have seen the three methods for accessing an object's components, you can learn more about selecting them. You can make multiple selections in Maya, such as selecting several sets of components simultaneously, by using hotkeys. In **TUTORIAL 17.13**, you see how to use hotkeys for selection.

TUTORIAL 17.13: Making Selections

1. You'll be using the sphere you created in **TUTORIAL 17.12**. Begin by switching to Component mode and making vertices selectable. Review the previous tutorial, if necessary.

2. Tap the spacebar to open the Four View layout. Tap the spacebar again over the Side view to make it full screen (see **FIGURE 17.71**).

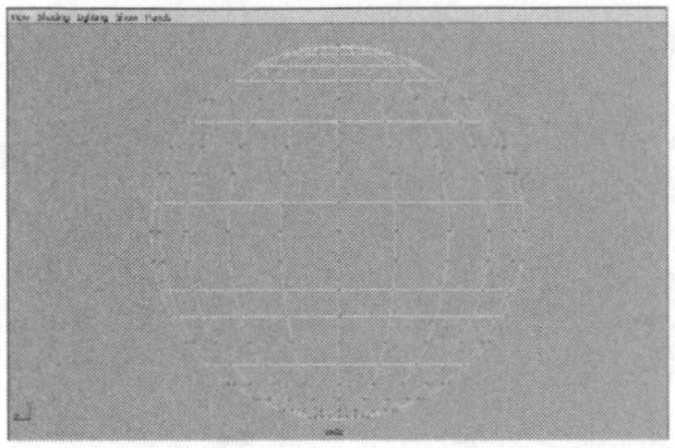

FIGURE 17.71 Side view of the sphere.

3. Draw a marquee selection box over the vertices of the sphere's upper half, as in **FIGURE 17.72**.

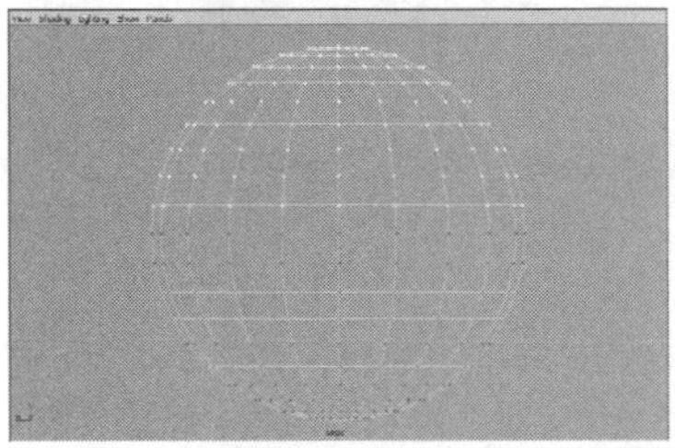

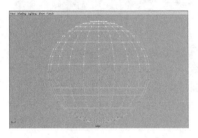

FIGURE 17.72 The top half of the sphere's vertices are selected.

4. Hold down the Shift key, and draw another selection box around the entire sphere (see **FIGURE 17.73**).

   Notice that the selection was inverted; the selected vertices were deselected, and the unselected vertices became selected. Holding down the Shift key inverts the selection status of any object or component.

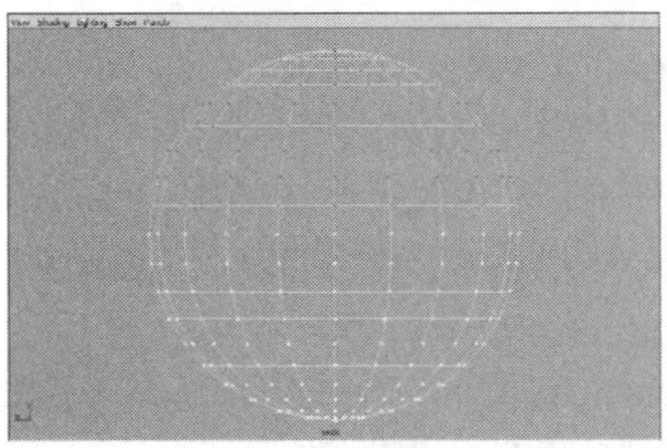

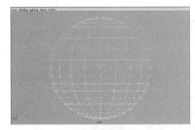

FIGURE 17.73 The bottom half of the sphere's vertices are selected.

5. Hold down the Ctrl key, and draw a selection box around the right half of the sphere (see **FIGURE 17.74**).

   Notice that the selected vertices become deselected, and the unselected vertices remain unselected. Holding down the Ctrl key subtracts from your current selection, not adds to it.

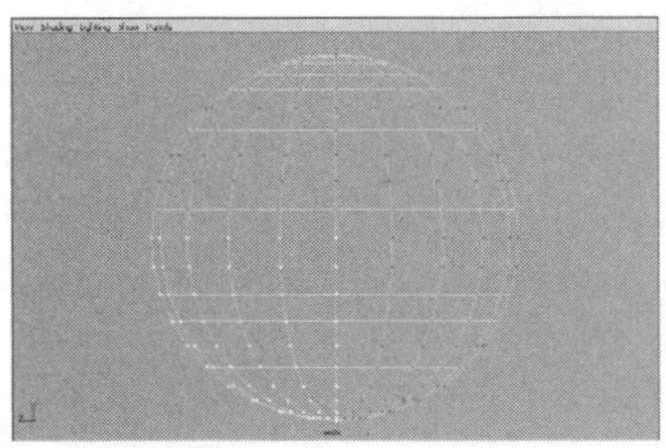

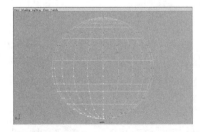

FIGURE 17.74 The bottom left half of the sphere's vertices are selected.

6. Hold down the Ctrl and Shift keys together, and draw a selection over the left half of the sphere (see **FIGURE 17.75**).

17

Notice that the selected vertices at the bottom remain selected, and the unselected vertices at the top become selected. The Shift+Ctrl keys only add to your selection.

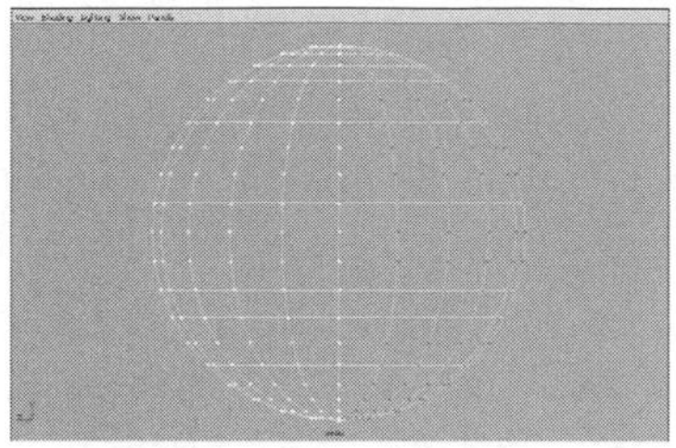

FIGURE 17.75 The left half of the sphere's vertices are selected.

END TUTORIAL 17.13

The three selection methods are valuable tools for making complex selections in your scenes. Keep in mind that all three work in Object mode as well as Component mode, so you can use them to select multiple objects onscreen. This list summarizes the selection hotkeys:

Hotkey(s)	Method
Shift	Invert selection
Ctrl	Subtractive selection (deselect)
Ctrl+Shift	Additive selection

Summary

Throughout this chapter, you have learned several fundamentals behind using Maya, from its node-based architecture to its user interface. You have also practiced several methods of object manipulation, including how to access components of your polygonal objects. By now, you should have a general familiarity with Maya's interface and understand how to create polygonal primitive objects. You should also have a basic understanding of how Maya's node-based architecture is used in the formation of construction history and how history can both help and harm you.

In the next chapter, you build in this knowledge by learning how to use the tools for polygonal modeling and begin constructing your own creations for placement in Unreal.

Chapter 18

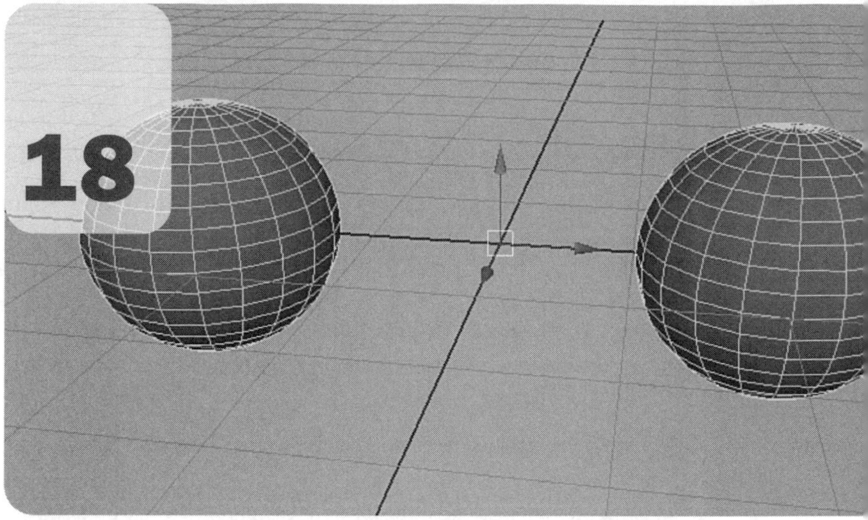

Polygonal Modeling Tools

This chapter discusses a variety of polygonal modeling tools available in Alias Maya 5. Chapter 17, "Overview of Maya," explained the difference between Object and Component modes in Maya as well as what you can do with an object's components. In this chapter, you'll move on to learn about many of the tools you need to construct your Unreal models in Maya. Please note, however, that not every available modeling tool is covered. Instead, this chapter concentrates on a wide variety of tools you'll likely use when creating low-polygon game content for Unreal.

Practicing with the tools and commands covered in this chapter to get the hang of how they are used is a good idea. The better you understand how each tool works, the more you'll be able to use a variety of tools instead of restricting yourself to merely a few. This can dramatically speed up your workflow and decrease your turnaround time for model completion.

NOTE

This chapter assumes that you have a reasonable understanding of navigation in Maya, especially using the menu and viewports. If you don't have a solid grasp of these topics, please refer back to Chapter 17.

Modeling Terminology

This section provides a list of common terms used in modeling that can be confusing to beginning modelers. These terms are used throughout this chapter, so getting familiar with them is a good idea:

- *Polygon*—Defined as a many-sided shape, a polygon is the basic unit of game modeling. A model is constructed by using many polygons. In game models, polygons are usually three-sided (triangular).
- *Triangles*—Three-sided polygons. All game models, including ones designed for Unreal, are constructed as a series of triangles. Triangles are used because, logically, they are the only surface that always exists on a single plane. Nonplanar faces are difficult for many programs (even some 3D applications) to calculate, so games engines don't support them. Triangular faces are often called *tris*, pronounced as "tries."
- *Quads*—Four-sided polygons are often called quads. When modeling, constructing your object primarily with quads is a good idea, and then you can simply run a Triangulate operation to convert the quads into triangles.
- *Vertex, vertices*—Vertices are one of the three key elements of a polygon. They are the points that form the model's shape. You can think of them as the dots in a massive 3D connect-the-dots game. These points are connected to form your final model.
- *Edge*—If vertices are the dots in a connect-the-dots game, edges are the lines connecting those dots. To be more technical, an edge is a line that connects two (and only two) vertices.
- *Face*—A face is the surface created across a series of vertices and edges, allowing you to see your model. In some programs, a face is always a triangle, and a polygon can be composed internally of many faces. This means a four-sided polygon is actually composed of two faces. In Maya, the term *face* and *polygon* are interchangeable.
- *Primitive*—A primitive object is a prefabricated 3D shape. In Maya, primitives consist of spheres, cubes, cylinders, cones, planes, and tori. You can often create complex models by building from a primitive object.
- *Extrude, extrusion*—An extrusion is essentially an extension of a single face or a selection of faces. For example, you can select a single face and extrude it from the model, which effectively moves the face away from the model while creating new faces that stretch from the extruded face back to the edges of that face's original position. For more information, please see the "Extrusions" section later in this chapter.
- *Split*—The term *splitting* usually refers to adding an edge to your model, such as with the Split Polygon Tool, which is covered later in "Splitting Polygons." It also refers to the action of dividing a single vertex into multiple vertices. Because of this dual definition, splits that create new edges are casually referred to as *cuts*.

- *Cut*—The addition of an edge to a model. Many tools in Maya can perform this operation.
- *Merge*—Merging in Maya is the conversion of two or more components into a single component, such as combining two vertices into a single vertex. You can use this technique to remove excess detail from your model or to "stitch" two separate models together into a single seamless model.
- *Backfaces*—Backfaces are the back (or negative) side of a polygon. In Maya, Unreal, and all other 3D programs, a polygon has a front and back side. By default, Maya shows polygonal backfaces in the viewport, although you can adjust the display settings so that they don't. In Unreal, backfaces aren't rendered at all.
- *Surface normals*—A surface normal is a line that designates the front of a polygon. You can use surface normals to verify that the positive side of your polygons are pointed outward. If they aren't, your model won't render in Unreal.
- *Vertex normals*—Unlike surface normals, which define a polygon's positive and negative sides, vertex normals control the shading across a model from one polygon to the other. They can be used to create hard and soft edges.
- *Hard and soft edges*—Using vertex normals, you can control how the surface of your model appears to be shaded when rendered in Unreal. The faces on each side of a soft edge appear to be blended together with no seam. The faces on each side of a hard edge appear to have a crease between them. The Unreal Engine reads hard and soft edges to create creases between certain areas of your model. In **FIGURE 18.1**, you can see a constant smooth sphere with softened edges, which appears to be only a single surface. **FIGURE 18.2** shows the same sphere with all its edges hardened.

FIGURE 18.1 A sphere with soft edges.

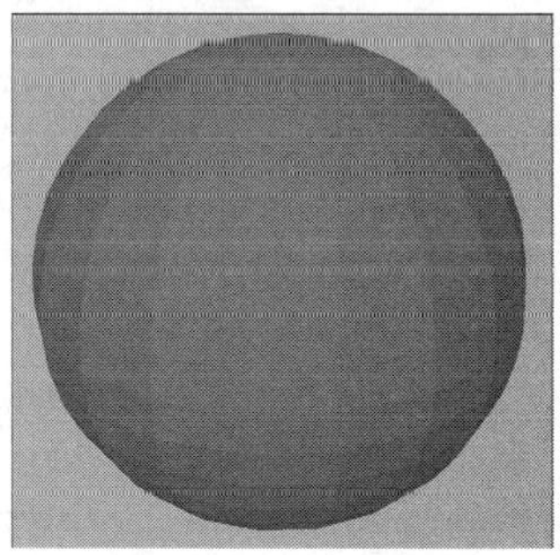

FIGURE 18.2 A sphere with hard edges.

Modeling Methods

There are many different ways to model an object in Maya. The following sections describe two major methods for polygonal modeling: box modeling and polygon creation.

Box Modeling

Box modeling is creating a model from a polygon primitive, usually a box or cube. Typically, new modelers like this method, as it's easy to see fast results. As a brief overview of this method, first you create a box. Then you scale the box to the general proportions of the object being modeled, and then you perform a series of modeling actions, such as polygonal splits, merges, and extrusions, to create the model's details.

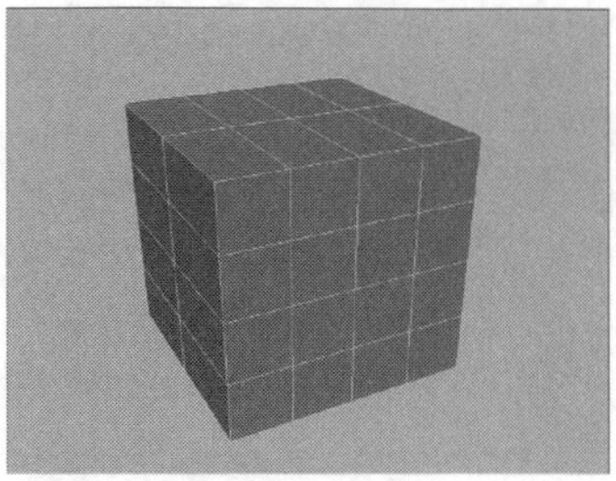

FIGURE 18.3 A.

For example, **FIGURES 18.3** through **18.5** illustrate the progression from a basic cube into a simple character, using only a few modeling tools:

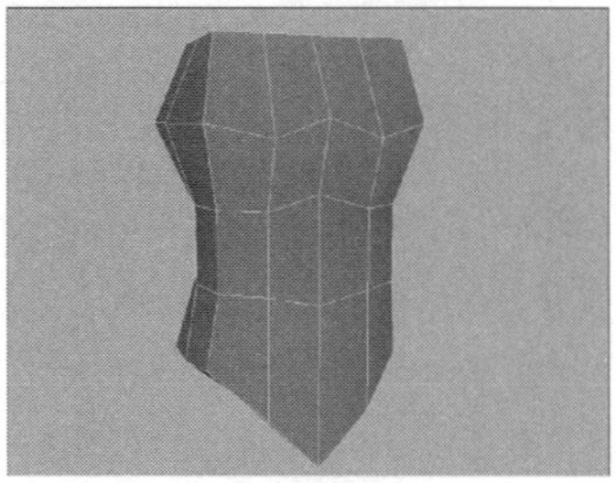

FIGURE 18.4 B.

- **A.** In this step, there's only a cube with a few divisions added to its width, height, and depth.
- **B.** The vertices of the box have been moved around to form a torso. No modeling tools have been used yet.
- **C.** Using only a handful of modeling tools, you can extrude and shape arms, legs, and a head for a character.

FIGURE 18.5 C.

Polygon Creation

Polygon creation is different from box modeling in that you don't begin by creating a polygonal object. Instead, you create a single polygon by using Maya's Create Polygon Tool, which is covered later in "Creating Polygons." After creating the first polygon, you append new polygons to it to create your overall shape. When these polygons are in place, you continue by using the polygon modeling tools.

18

In the example shown in **FIGURES 18.6** through **18.9**, you can see how to use this method by creating a simple four-sided polygon and then appending more polygons onto it to create an object:

- **A.** You begin with a simple four-sided polygon, constructed with the Create Polygon Tool (see **FIGURE 18.6**).

FIGURE 18.6 A.

B. In **FIGURE 18.7**, new polygons have been appended to the original and branch outward. Each time you create a new polygon, you adjust vertices to shape the model as you work.

C. In **FIGURE 18.8**, you can see the model taking shape, one polygon at a time.

D. The finished model, with the same result as in the previous example, is shown in **FIGURE 18.9**.

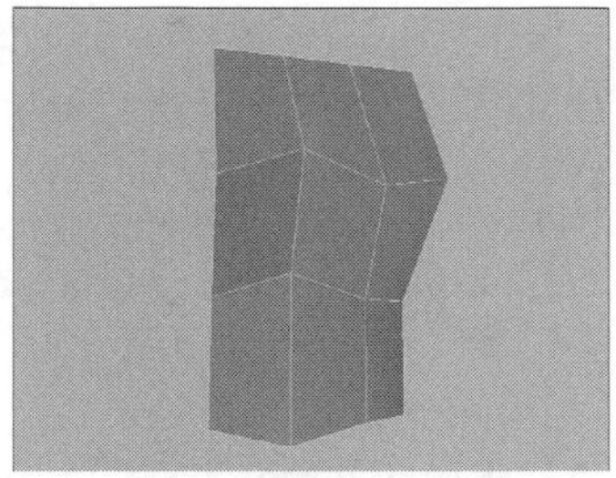

FIGURE 18.7 B.

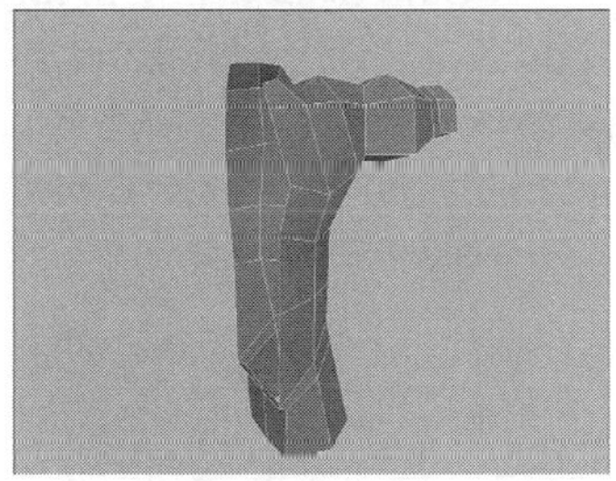

FIGURE 18.8 C.

FIGURE 18.9 D.

Understanding the Tool Options and Display Settings in Maya

This section covers some of the important settings and display modes you need when modeling in Maya. While you work, typically you switch these settings on and off repeatedly, so practicing until you're accustomed to their use is a good idea. To begin, the Polygons > Tool Options menu item contains two important options: Keep New Faces Planar and Keep Faces Together.

The Keep New Faces Planar option is used primarily with the Create Polygon tool and Append to Polygon tool. When this option is enabled, new polygons are forced to be planar—that is, to have all their vertices exist on the same plane—when they are created. If you try to create a nonplanar face with this option selected, you see an error message.

The Keep Faces Together option is one of the most important options for modeling with polygons. This option affects a variety of polygonal modeling tools, such as Extrude Face, Extract, and Duplicate Face. It works like so: When this option is enabled, new polygonal faces created with functions such as Extrude Face stay connected at their adjacent edges. When this option is disabled, the two faces are extruded individually. Compare the differences in **FIGURES 18.10** and **18.11**.

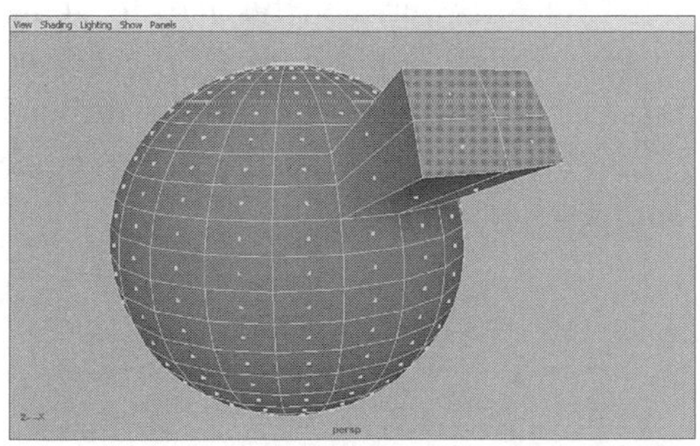

FIGURE 18.10 Four faces extruded with Keep Faces Together enabled.

Often you need to see different areas or aspects of your model at different points in the modeling process. Maya comes with several viewport features that enable you to easily switch through these aspects, making game modeling much easier. For example, often you need to see how many polygons your model contains to verify that it's staying under your polygon budget. To do this, choose Display > Heads Up Display > Poly Count from the main menu. When the Poly Count option is enabled, it displays a list in your viewport that gives you constant feedback about the polygon components visible in the viewport (see **FIGURE 18.12**).

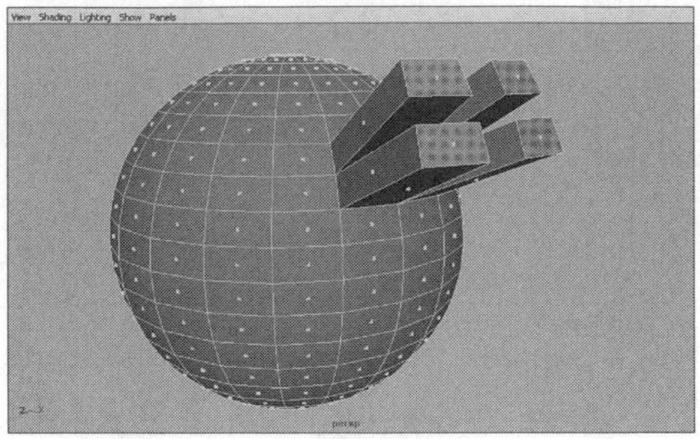

FIGURE 18.11 Same four faces with Keep Faces Together toggled off.

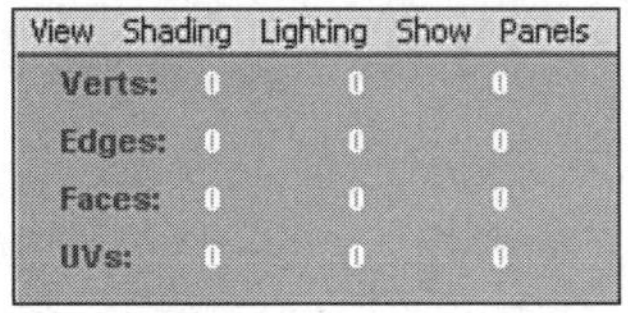

FIGURE 18.12 The Poly Count system.

The system is displayed as a series of rows and columns. The rows are fairly self-explanatory; they allow you to see the current number of total polygon components onscreen. The columns, however, need a little explanation:

- The first column gives the total count of polygon components for all polygonal objects in the viewport.
- The second column shows the number of polygon components for the selected polygon objects in the viewport.
- The third column shows all the selected components for objects partially visible in the viewport. So if you have selected a few vertices in Component mode, for example, this column shows how many you selected.

You might also need information about your model's surface normals so that you are aware which side of your model is actually going to render in Unreal. As you know, the backfaces (negative sides) of polygons aren't rendered in Unreal, so you must use the polygon's surface normals to determine which side of each polygon is displayed. There are a couple of ways to do this in Maya, and you can choose the method that best suits you. **TUTORIAL 18.1** shows you both methods.

TUTORIAL 18.1: Displaying Surface Normals in Maya

1. Open Maya, and start a new scene. Make sure you're in the Modeling menu set (if not, press F3).
2. Create a polygon sphere by choosing Create > Polygon Primitives > Sphere from the main menu. Then press the F key to focus the Perspective viewport camera on it (see **FIGURE 18.13**).
3. Next, choose Display > Polygon Components > Normals from the main menu to show the model's normals as a series of lines that point perpendicularly away from each face's surface. The lines point toward the positive side of the polygon, so your cube should look like it has spines sticking out of it (see **FIGURE 18.14**).
4. Press the G key to switch normals back off. From the main menu, choose Display > Custom Polygon Display > options box. This opens the Custom Polygon Display Options dialog box (see **FIGURE 18.15**), where you can choose a variety of display options designed to make polygon modeling easier. For the purposes of this tutorial, you'll use Backface Culling, at the bottom of the dialog box. Make sure your sphere is selected, and click On in the drop-down list box. You won't see any change in your model right now.
5. With the sphere selected, press F11 to make polygon faces selectable. Select about half the faces on the

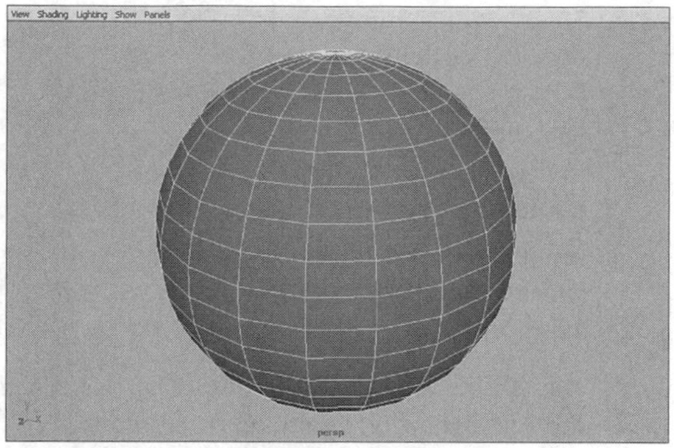

FIGURE 18.13 A polygon sphere.

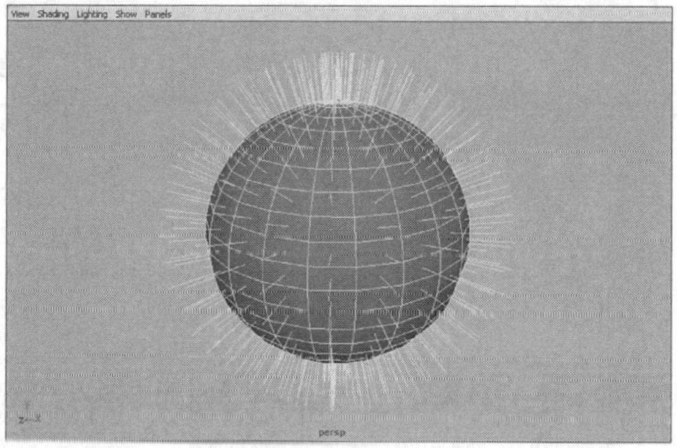

FIGURE 18.14 Normals visible on the sphere.

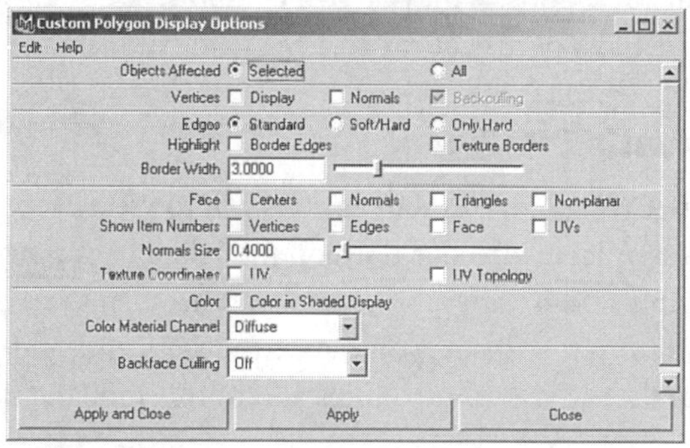

FIGURE 18.15 The Custom Polygon Display Options dialog box.

sphere with a marquee selection, and delete them with the Delete key. Rotate the camera so that you can see the inside of the sphere. Notice that you can't see the back side of the sphere, and your marquee selection ignored the faces on the back side of the object (see **FIGURE 18.16**).

This step shows the dual nature of the Backface Culling option. It hides all polygonal backfaces in the viewport and, as a result, prevents you from selecting polygonal components from behind. The upshot to all this is that polygonal objects appear in the viewport as they would in Unreal, meaning you can't see the reverse side of the polygon.

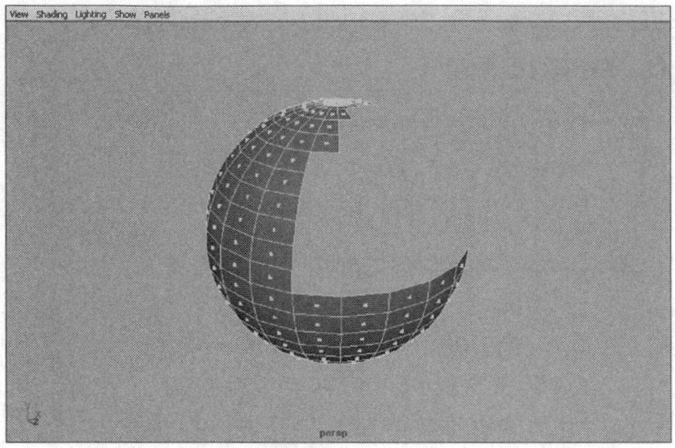

FIGURE 18.16 Backfaces of the sphere now appear to be invisible.

> **NOTE**
>
> You must return to the Custom Polygon Display Options dialog box whenever you want to toggle Backface Culling on and off.

END TUTORIAL 18.1

Polygon Modeling in Maya

This section lists the polygon modeling tools found under the Polygons menu on the main menu bar. This menu centers primarily on tools that affect entire polygonal objects rather than tools that focus mostly on polygon components. Not every tool in the menu is covered; instead, the tools most pertinent for creating game models are discussed.

Creating Polygons

The Create Polygon tool enables you to create your own custom polygons in 3D space. This tool is essential to effective polygon modeling because eventually you'll find that an existing primitive simply doesn't offer the control you need. In these cases, you can create your own polygon shape, and from that shape, you can extrude, append, and shape other components to form your model. **TUTORIAL 18.2** introduces you to this tool and demonstrates its use.

TUTORIAL 18.2: Using the Create Polygon Tool

1. Open Maya, and start a new scene. Make sure you're in the Modeling menu set (if not, press F3). Press the 5 key to use Smooth Shaded mode in the viewport.
2. Choose Polygons > Create Polygon Tool from the main menu.

3. Click once on the grid in the viewport. A square point appears on the grid, which is a reference showing you where the object's first vertex will be created.

4. Click a second time on the grid, away from the first point. A line appears between the two points, showing you where one of the polygon's edges will be located.

5. Click a third time to form a triangle. Notice that the triangle is filled in with pink to represent where the polygon's surface would be if you finalized the tool operation at this point (see **FIGURE 18.17**).

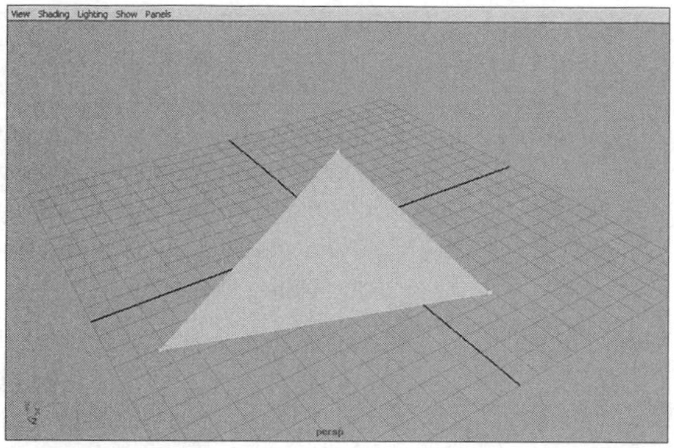

FIGURE 18.17 The Create Polygon tool before finalization

6. Click as many times as you like, creating any polygonal shape you desire. Notice, as in **FIGURE 18.18**, that the pink surface updates to show you what the object will look like when you finish.

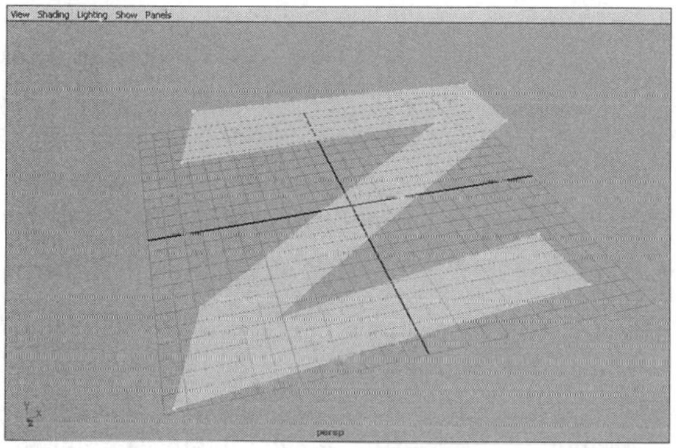

FIGURE 18.18 An interesting polygon.

7. Press Enter to complete the tool operation. This step finalizes the creation process, and you are rewarded with a complete polygon. Notice, however, that despite the number of times you click, you're creating only a single surface. This means you can potentially make single polygons that are composed of many sides. Polygons with several sides can be quite a problem, as Unreal displays only triangular polygons (those with only three sides).

> **NOTE**
>
> When creating a polygon, you can click with the middle mouse button (MMB-click) and relocate the last point you placed.

END TUTORIAL 18.2

If you click the options box icon for the Create Polygon tool, you see a variety of options for creating polygons. **TABLE 18.1** describes these options and explains how to use them.

TABLE 18.1 Create Polygon Tool Settings

Option	Description
Subdivisions	This option enables you to control the number of subdivisions along each edge of the polygon you create. It doesn't subdivide the actual surface, so don't use it in the hopes of creating a polygon grid. For those actions, you can use the Subdivide command, covered later in this chapter in "Subdividing Polygons."
Limit Points To	This option allows you to limit the number of vertices in your polygon. For example, if you set it to 3, you can create only triangles, and after the third click, the tool automatically completes its operation. A setting of -1 removes any limitation.
Texture	This area controls how UV texture coordinate information is stored for the new polygon. It has two main settings: Normalize and Unitize. Normalize scales the entire polygon's UVs uniformly so that they fit within the 0 to 1 texture space. Unitize arranges all the UVs for the object along the outer edge of the 0 to 1 texture space. This effectively shapes your polygon's UVs into a square. If your polygon has three vertices, they are placed at three of the 0 to 1 texture space corners. For more information on texturing and the nature of UVs in Maya, be sure to see Chapter 19, "The Art of Texturing in Maya."
Ensure Planarity	This option ensures that the polygon you create is entirely planar. The plane on which your polygon exists is determined by the location of the first three vertices. This option is directly linked to the Keep New Faces Planar option, located under Polygons > Tool Options.
Operation	This option effectively switches the tool between the Create Polygon and Append to Polygon tools.

Adding to Existing Polygons

18

As its name suggests, the Append to Polygon tool enables you to add to existing polygons. You should note, however, that this tool can be used only to add onto polygonal borders, meaning edges that are next to a hole or on the edge where the polygon object stops. You can use this tool to create new polygon faces that are simply attached to a single face or to fill in holes in areas of your model that are missing polygons. In **TUTORIAL 18.3**, you see how to use this tool to add polygons onto an existing face.

TUTORIAL 18.3: Using the Append to Polygon Tool

1. Open Maya, and start a new scene. Make sure you're in the Modeling menu set (if not, press F3). Using the skills you learned in **TUTORIAL 18.2**, select the Create Polygon Tool, and create a triangular polygon (see **FIGURE 18.19**).

2. Select the Append to Polygon tool from the Polygons menu. The edges of the triangle now look thicker. These thickened edges are used to designate edges where you can use the Append to Polygon tool. Click any edge of the triangle. Purple arrows indicating the direction of each edge are displayed (see **FIGURE 18.20**).

3. Click on the grid at some point directly away from the edge you clicked on. A new pink polygon appears to show you where the append will take place after you finalize the tool operation. Also, the new polygon has one solid green edge and one dashed edge. If you click on the side with the dashed edge, you can add as many points as you like to the new polygon without the polygon folding back over itself. Click once to turn the new polygon into a quad, as shown in **FIGURE 18.21**.

4. Press Enter to complete the tool operation. Feel free to make as many appends as you like. **FIGURE 18.22** shows an example after several appends. You can also edit the vertices' locations when you're done to close the shape. In this way, you can model polygons much as you'd fold bits of cut paper.

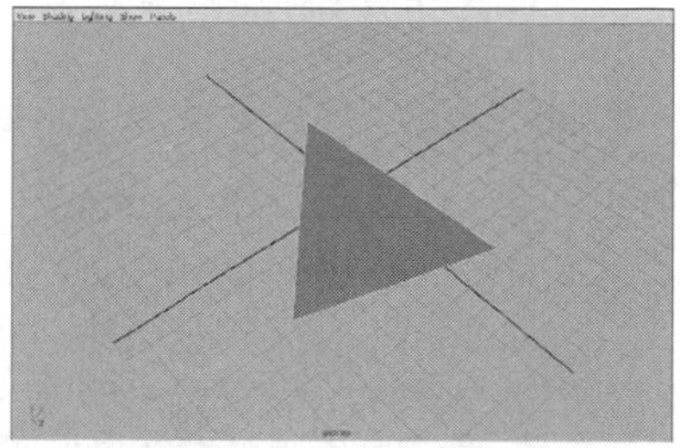

FIGURE 18.19 A triangular polygon.

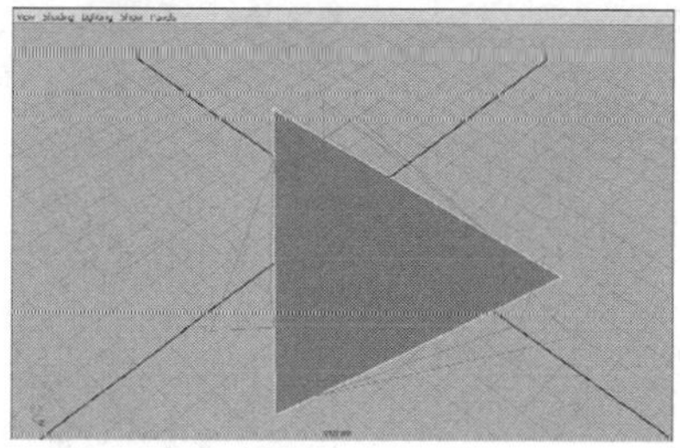

FIGURE 18.20 Edge direction arrows visible.

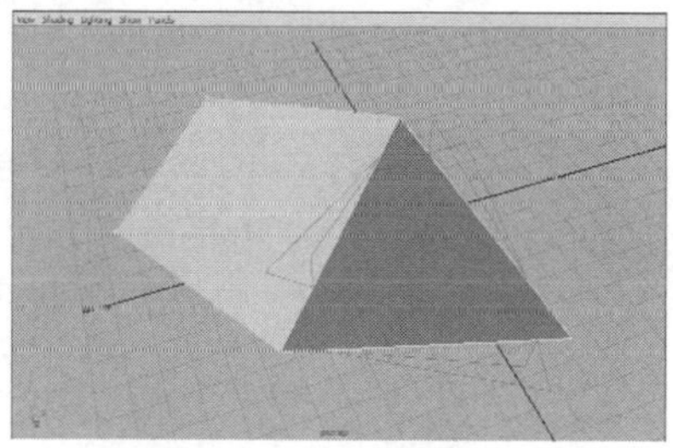

FIGURE 18.21 A quad appended to the triangle.

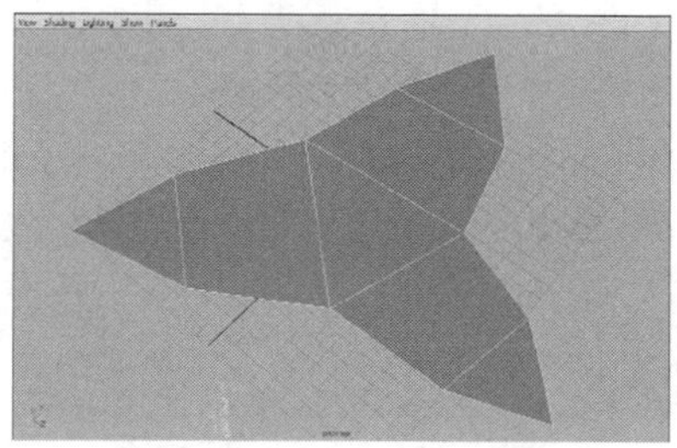

FIGURE 18.22 The original triangle, after several appends.

END TUTORIAL 18.3

As with the Create Polygon tool, you can use several options to change the Append to Polygon tool's behavior. **TABLE 18.2** lists these options and describes what they control.

TABLE 18.2 Append to Polygon Tool Settings

Option	Description
Subdivisions	This option allows you to control the number of subdivisions along each edge of the polygon you create. It doesn't subdivide the actual surface, so don't use it in the hopes of creating a polygon grid. For those actions, you can use the Subdivide command, covered later in "Subdividing Polygons."
Limit Points To	This option enables you to limit the number of vertices in your appended polygon. For example, if you set it to 3, you can append only triangles, and after the third click, the tool automatically completes its operation. A setting of -1 removes any limitation.
Rotation Angle	This option becomes available only while you're clicking to create an appended polygon. Use the slider to adjust the rotation of the appended polygon. This option is much like folding on the edge of the append.
Texture	This area controls how UV texture information is stored for the new polygon. It has two main settings: Normalize and Unitize. Normalize scales the entire polygon's UVs uniformly so that they fit within the 0 to 1 texture space. Unitize arranges all the object's UVs along the outer edge of the 0 to 1 texture space. This option effectively shapes your polygon's UVs into a square. If your polygon has three vertices, they are placed at three of the 0 to 1 texture space corners. For more information on texturing and the nature of UVs in Maya, be sure to see Chapter 19.
Ensure Planarity	This option ensures that the polygon you append is entirely planar. The plane on which your polygon exists is determined by the rotation of the polygon to which you're appending. This option is directly linked to the Keep New Faces Planar option, located under Polygons > Tool Options.
Operation	This option effectively switches the tool between the Create Polygon and Append to Polygon tools.

Combining Objects

When modeling for Unreal, especially characters, in some situations you might need polygonal meshes to behave as though they were one polygon object. For example, you might need a piece of armor, such as a shoulder plate, to follow your character's movement. In this case, simply combining the meshes is usually easier than adjusting the models so that the character and the shoulder plate are one seamless model. Also, modeling this kind of detail into your characters by making several adjustments to separate models results in a severe increase in your polygon count. Many professional game models, including those in Unreal Tournament 2004, use combining to avoid this problem. In **TUTORIAL 18.4**, you see how this tool works.

TUTORIAL 18.4: Using the Combine Command

1. Open Maya, and start a new scene. Make sure you're in the Modeling menu set (if not, press F3).

2. Create a polygon sphere, and move it a few units away from the center of the grid, as shown in **FIGURE 18.23**.

3. With the sphere selected, press Ctrl+D to duplicate the sphere. Move the duplicate to the other side of the grid's origin point (see **FIGURE 18.24**).

   The names of the spheres in the Channel Box are currently pSphere1 and pSphere2. These names will be important in a moment.

4. Draw a marquee selection box around both spheres to select them, and choose Polygons > Combine from the main menu.

5. The two spheres are now considered to be a new single object (see **FIGURE 18.25**). Notice that the pivot of the new object is located at the origin point, and that the name has been changed in the Channel Box to polySurface1. This is important to remember because if you combine and then separate objects, you lose their original pivot and naming information.

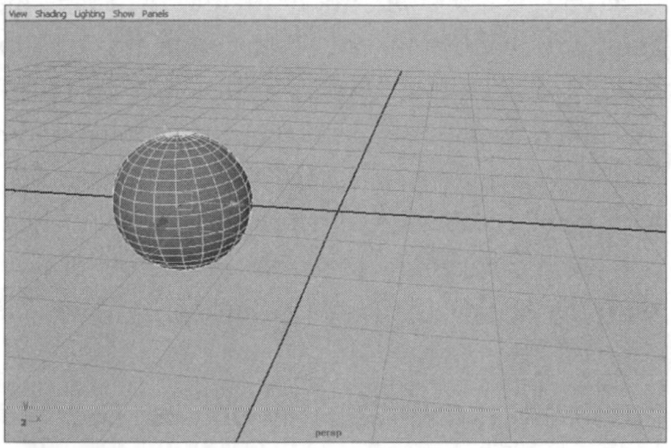

FIGURE 18.23 The first sphere created.

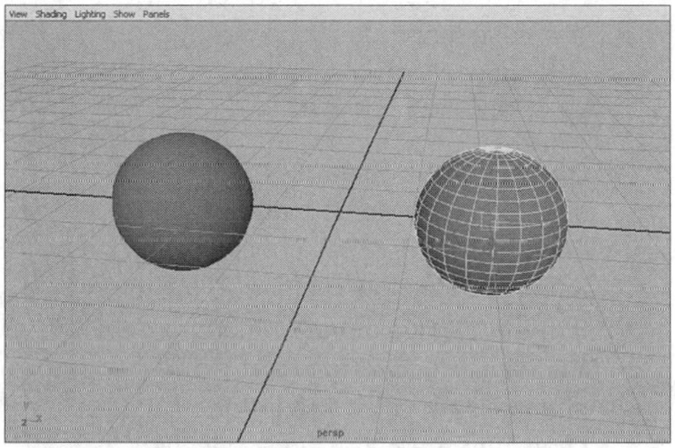

FIGURE 18.24 Two separate spheres.

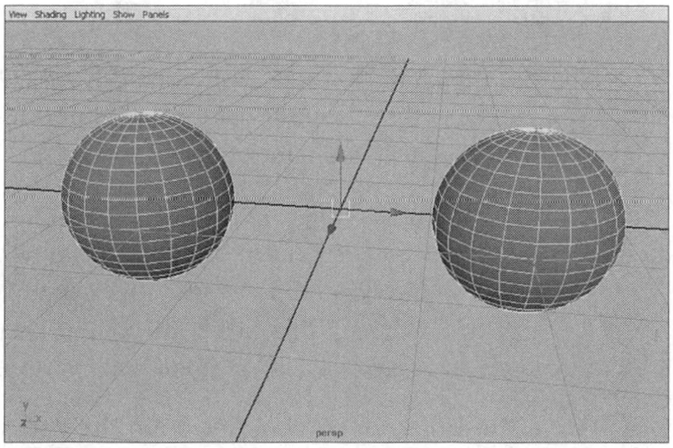

FIGURE 18.25 The two spheres combined.

> **NOTE**
>
> **The opposite of the Combine command, Separate, can be found under the Edit Polygons menu rather than the Polygons menu.**

END TUTORIAL 18.4

Using Booleans

Boolean operations are a way to alter the shape of one polygonal object based on the shape of another polygonal object. For example, if you subtract a cylindrical shape from a large cube, the result is a cube that appears to have a hole in it. Boolean operations are an easy way to create machined-looking shapes. These operations can be used for a wide variety of objects, from gun barrels to windows in walls. You must be careful when using Boolean operations, however, because all meshes imported into UnrealEd must be converted to triangles, and using a Boolean operation can significantly raise the number of polygons in your model. In **TUTORIAL 18.5**, you learn the Boolean operations available in Maya and see how to apply them to your model.

TUTORIAL 18.5: Applying Boolean Operations

1. Open Maya, and start a new scene. Make sure you're in the Modeling menu set (press F3 if not). Create two cubes, and position them so that they're intersecting each other, as in **FIGURE 18.26**.

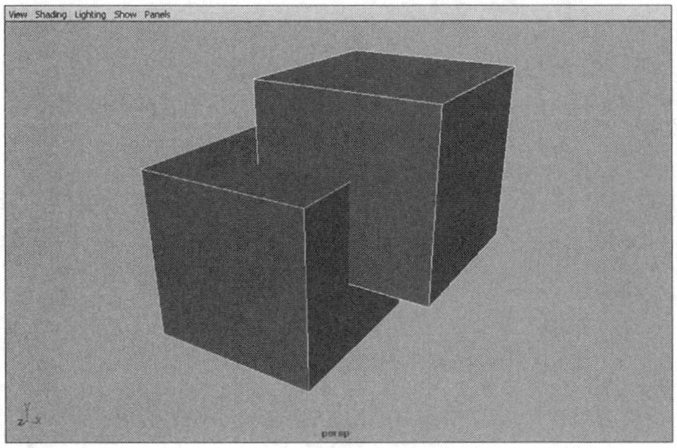

FIGURE 18.26 Two cubes for the Boolean demonstration.

2. For your first Boolean operation, selection order is no matter. Therefore, simply select both cubes using your favorite method. Choose Polygons > Booleans > Union from the main menu. If you're in a shaded view, you'll see little to no change in the cubes' look because the change is taking place where the two cubes pass through each other.

   If you press the 4 key to show the objects' wireframe, you can see that the edges where the two objects are intersecting have been removed. This Boolean operation has effectively turned the two cubes into one seamless model.

3. Rather than undo and reapply the command, you can simply use construction history to change the Boolean operation. With the new object still selected, go to the Channel Box and click the polyBoolOp1 node. This expands the Inputs list to display a new attribute: `Operation`. Clicking this attribute opens a drop-down list that you can use to switch between the three available Boolean operations.

   Click the Union operation, and from the pop-up menu, choose Difference. **FIGURE 18.27** shows the result—it looks as though the second cube's area was removed from the first cube.

4. Repeat step 3, setting the `Operation` attribute to Intersect. This operation leaves only the area where the two cubes intersected one another.
5. As a point of interest, open the Outliner by choosing Window > Outliner from the main menu. Sift through the list until you find the pCube1 and pCube2 entries. They are the remaining transform nodes of the original cubes. You can select either one, and move, rotate, or scale it in the viewport to affect the shape of your Boolean object in real time.

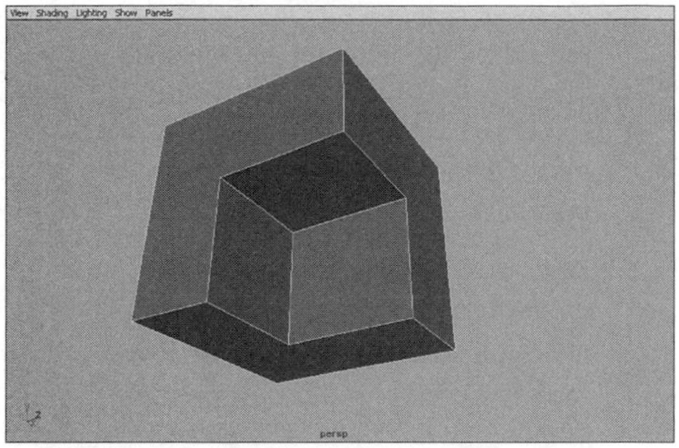

FIGURE 18.27 The result of using the Difference operation on the cubes.

END TUTORIAL 18.5

Mirroring

One of the easiest ways to speed up a modeling project is to model only half of your object. In Maya, you can use the Mirror Geometry command to make a mirrored duplicate of half an object and merge the two objects together. Obviously, this technique can dramatically speed up modeling time on symmetrical objects. In **TUTORIAL 18.6**, you see how to use this command to duplicate and mirror half a model.

TUTORIAL 18.6: Mirroring Geometry

1. Open Maya, and start a new scene. Make sure you're in the Modeling menu set (press F3).
2. Create a polygon cube. In the Channel Box, set its Subdivisions Height, Subdivisions Width, and Subdivisions Depth to 4. **FIGURE 18.28** shows the result of these settings.
3. Right-click over the object, and choose Face from the marking menu to make faces selectable on the object.

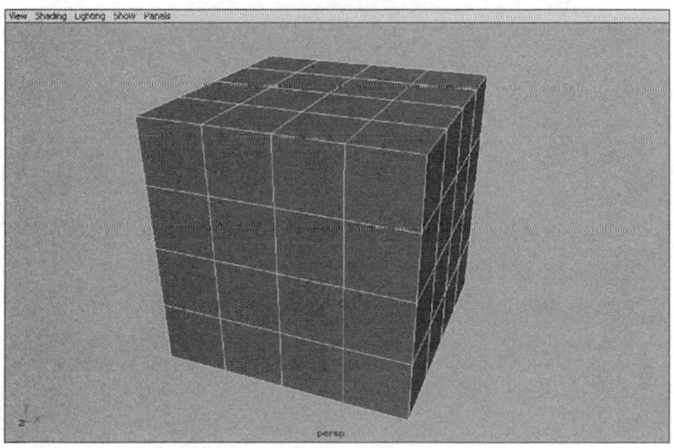

FIGURE 18.28 A polygon cube.

4. Select and delete half the faces on the cube that are in the negative X direction (see **FIGURE 18.29**). If you haven't rotated the camera much, these faces are on the left side of the cube.

5. Next, try selecting some faces on the remaining side of the cube and moving them around. Use **FIGURE 18.30** as a reference, or just make an interesting shape. Don't move any of the faces that are on the seam.

6. Return to Object mode by pressing the F8 key. Choose Polygons > Mirror Geometry > options box from the menu. In the Mirror Geometry Options dialog box, set the following options:

   Mirror Direction: -X

   Merge With Original: Select this check box

   Connect Border Edges: Active

7. Click Mirror, and you can see that the model has been copied, mirrored, and welded together (see **FIGURE 18.31**).

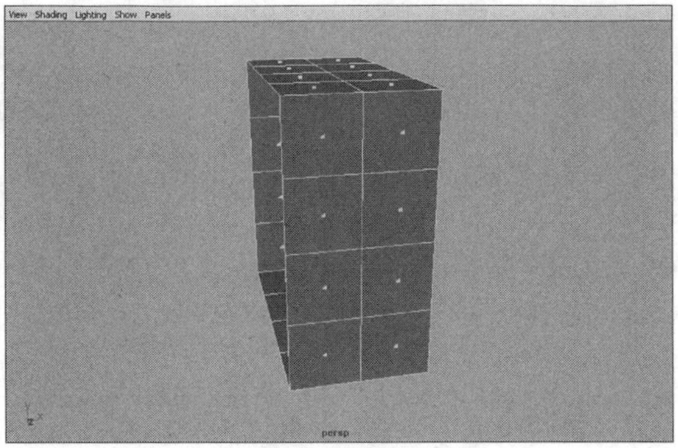

FIGURE 18.29 Half the cube has been removed.

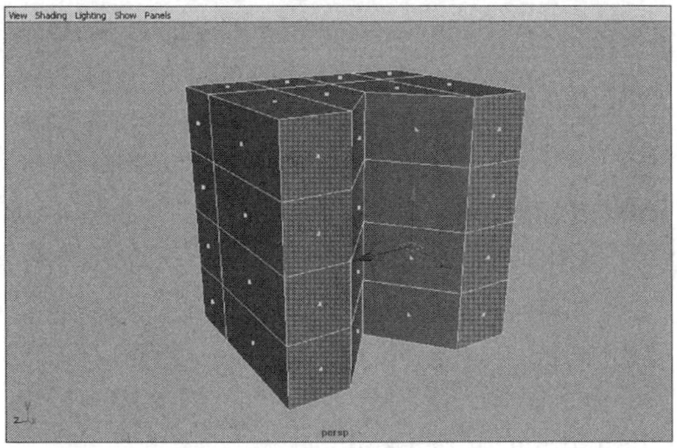

FIGURE 18.30 The cube reshaped after faces are moved.

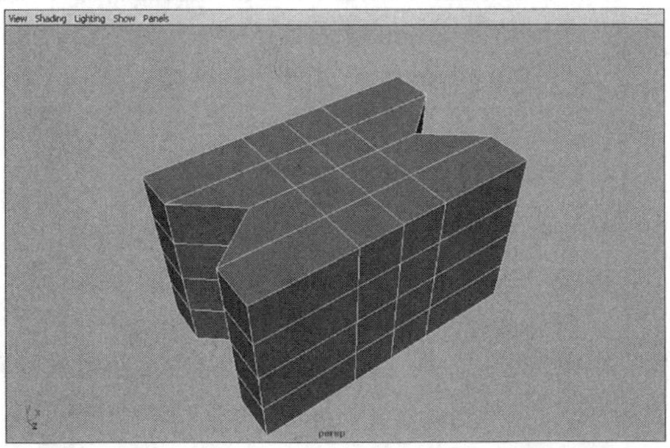

FIGURE 18.31 Your model, fully mirrored.

> **NOTE**
>
> **If you don't toggle off Backface Culling in the Custom Polygon Display Options dialog box, selecting and removing these faces in step 4 can be more difficult.**

END TUTORIAL 18.6

Smoothing Versus Averaging Vertices

When modeling, sometimes you need a model that's relatively smooth, such as an organic or a rounded surface. Unfortunately, the inherent polygon limit of most game engines, including Unreal, makes these types of surfaces difficult to achieve without creating an excessive number of polygonal faces. You can, however, use a couple of commands in Maya should the need for smooth rounded objects be impossible to avoid.

Smoothing

The Smooth command, located under the Polygons menu, offers a pair of algorithms (methods) called Exponential and Linear that tessellate your model to a higher number of polygons, and then adjust those polygons' position to create a smoothed result. The problem is that this command results in objects with a very high number of polygons. The Exponential and Linear methods offer different options for controlling polygon count in the resulting model. Both methods can be accessed in the Smooth Options dialog box or in the Inputs area of the Channel Box after the Smooth command is applied. In **FIGURES 18.32** and **18.33**, you can see before and after images of the effects of smoothing.

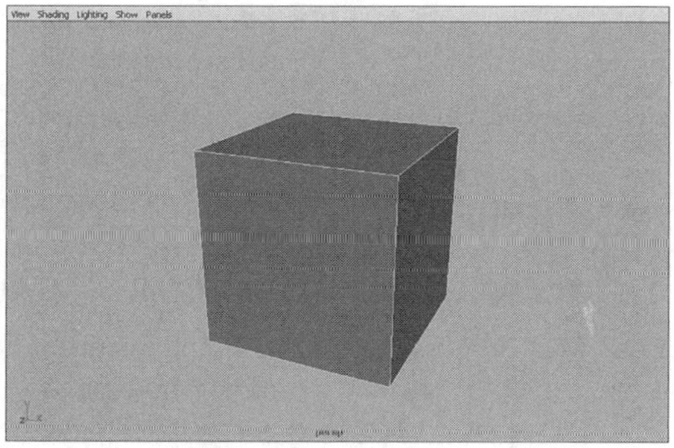

FIGURE 18.32 Polygon cube before being smoothed.

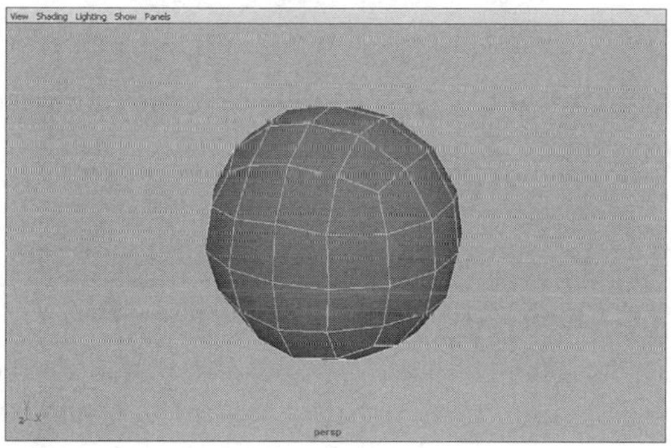

FIGURE 18.33 Polygon cube after being smoothed.

The Exponential method gives you a much smoother result at the cost of a high face count. **TABLE 18.3** lists its options.

TABLE 18.3 Smooth Command Options (Exponential)

Option Name	Description
Subdivision Levels	This option controls how many faces are in the resulting mesh. Each time you increase this value, the number of faces increases exponentially.
Continuity	This attribute controls how smoothly the new faces blend together to create a complete model. It has two settings: 0 is no smoothing, and 1 results in full smoothing.

TABLE 18.3 Continued

Option Name	Description
Smooth UVs	This option determines whether the Smooth operation affects UVs as well.
Keep Geometry Borders	This option prevents border edges from being smoothed.
Keep Selection Borders	If you have selected only specific faces for smoothing, this option stops the Smooth operation at the edge between the selected and nonselected faces.
Keep Hard Edges	If you have specified any hard edges, a technique covered later in "Adjusting Surfaces and Hard Edges," those edges aren't smoothed.
Keep Tessellation	This option prevents the Smooth operation from adding new vertices, should you make any construction history adjustments after smoothing.
Keep Map Borders	This option controls how UV borders are smoothed and is active only if the Smooth UVs check box is selected. The None setting doesn't affect the borders (outer edges) of the object's UVs. The Internal setting smoothes only internal borders, and All smoothes all borders.

The Linear method doesn't typically produce as smooth a result as the Exponential method, but it gives you far more control over the resulting number of faces. **TABLE 18.4** lists and describes the options for this method.

TABLE 18.4 Smooth Command Options (Linear)

Option Name	Description
Subdivision Levels	Similar to the Subdivision Levels option for the Exponential method, this option controls the number of faces in the final mesh.
Divisions Per Face	This option is also used to control the number of final polygons by controlling the number of times each face is subdivided. You can think of it as a fine-tuning for the final number of polygons.
Push Strength	This option determines the final object's volume. A setting above 0 pushes the resulting faces outward. This option can help solve the problem of smoothed objects looking much smaller than the original presmoothed model.
Roundness	This option scales vertices from the center of the model, resulting in a rounder look. It has an effect only if Push Strength is set higher than 0.

Averaging Vertices

Because smoothing typically creates a high number of polygons, you can use the alternative method of averaging the location of preexisting vertices in your model. The result is a smoother-looking model, without the need to add more detail. To do this, you use the Polygons > Average Vertices command. This command is useful only if you want to smooth your object's shape without adding any more vertices. Compare the differences in **FIGURES 18.34** and **18.35**.

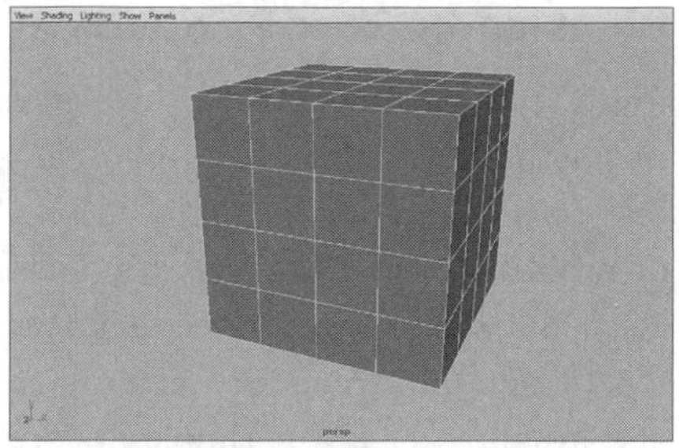

FIGURE 18.34 Polygon cube before averaging its vertices.

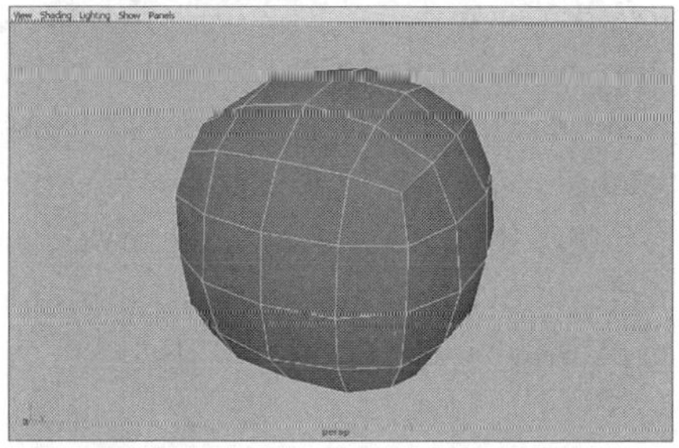

FIGURE 18.35 Polygon cube after averaging its vertices several times.

The number of vertices in the cube hasn't changed. Be aware that when you're using the Average Vertices command, the selected vertices become much smaller each time the command is applied, so you'll likely need to scale them back up.

Triangulation

When working on projects for Unreal, your models must always be composed of triangles. There's no exception to this rule because a triangular face, logically, is always planar, and the rendering engine requires much more calculation to display nonplanar faces.

In Maya, you don't have to worry about this rule much. First, you can still view nonplanar faces in the viewport as you model, and second, you can convert every face in your entire model to a triangle with a single command. The Triangulate command is simple to use, and it doesn't have any options for you to worry about setting. **FIGURES 18.36** and **18.37** show the results of using Triangulate.

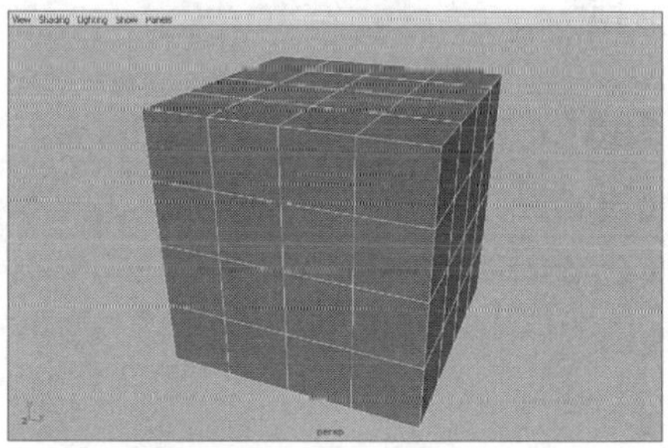

FIGURE 18.36 Polygon cube before triangulation.

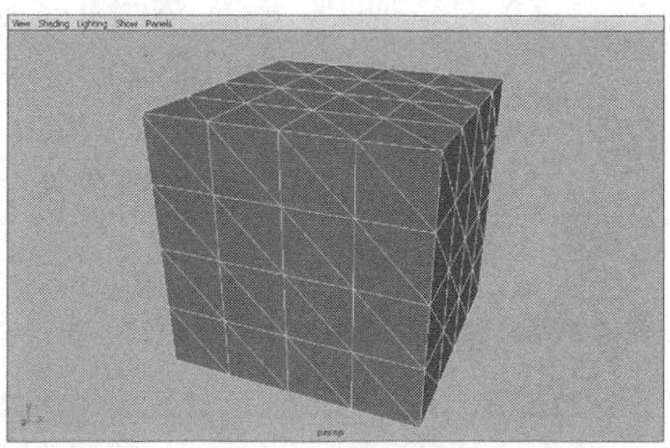

FIGURE 18.37 Polygon cube after triangulation.

> **NOTE**
>
> For many of the static meshes in Unreal Tournament 2004, you should try to keep the number of vertices down to just a few hundred.

> **TIP**
>
> The Average Vertices command doesn't work unless you are selecting vertices. If you're averaging an entire model, you must actively select all its vertices.

Cleaning Up Your Polygons

The Cleanup command in the Polygons menu is used to correct or point out errors in a polygonal mesh. It can find a long list of problems and offers a few options for correcting them. This command is a mainstay of beginning modelers, as it can easily and instantly repair the simple or careless mistakes made when still learning the toolset. The Polygon Cleanup Options dialog box (choose Polygons > Cleanup > options box to open it) is divided into four main sections: General Options, Tesselate Geometry, Other, and Remove Geometry (see **FIGURE 18.38**). The following sections describe this tool's features and explain what each option is used for.

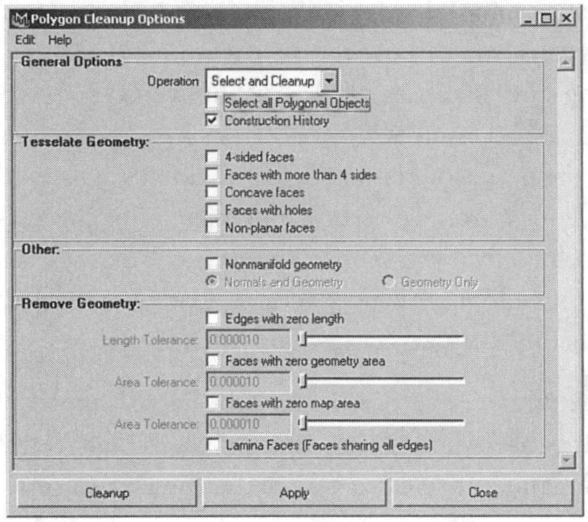

FIGURE 18.38 The Polygon Cleanup Options dialog box.

General Options

This section contains basic parameters that control how the Cleanup operation functions. The settings are all fairly straightforward, as shown in **TABLE 18.5**.

TABLE 18.5 General Options of the Cleanup Command

Option	Description
Operation	This option tells Maya what to do with any of the problems it finds. Your choices are Select Geometry, which more or less simply points out the problem areas, or Select and Cleanup, which locates and fixed your errors.
Select All Polygonal Objects	This option tells the Cleanup tool which objects to fix. If this check box is selected, the operation is performed on all polygonal objects in your scene. If it's not selected, the operation affects only the selected polygonal object.
Construction History	Select this check box if you want to keep the construction history of the repaired object.

Tessellate Geometry Options

You can use the options in this section to establish the areas of a model to be tessellated (divided into triangles). Selecting all these check boxes is the same as running the Triangulate function on your entire model. **TABLE 18.6** lists the settings for this section.

TABLE 18.6 Tessellate Geometry Options of the Cleanup Command

Option	Description
4-Sided Faces	This option tells the Cleanup operation to triangulate all faces that are four-sided (quads).
Faces with More Than 4 Sides	This option triangulates all faces that have more than four sides.
Concave Faces	This option triangulates all concave faces on your object. You can imagine concave faces as any face on which a straight line could enter the face, exit it, and leave it again. For example, a single face shaped to look like the letter *C* would be concave; a face that's a simple square would not. Concave faces can be difficult for a variety of calculations, such as dynamic simulations. This option breaks a concave face into a series of triangles, which can never be concave.
Faces with Holes	This option triangulates any face that has an opening in it, such as a single face in the shape of the letter *O*.
Non-planar Faces	This option triangulates all faces that don't exist on a single plane. For example, a quad (four-sided face) could have three vertices that are all coplanar and a fourth vertex raised above the rest. The result would be a nonplanar face. This option divides nonplanar faces into a series of planar triangles.

Other Options

The options in this section specialize in the selection of nonmanifold geometry, which is essentially, geometry that can't be unfolded into a single, flat piece. Certain tools in Maya, such as Boolean operations, can't use nonmanifold geometry. **TABLE 18.7** lists the settings for this section.

TABLE 18.7 Other Options of the Cleanup Command

Option	Description
Nonmanifold Geometry	This option tells the Cleanup operation whether it deals with nonmanifold geometry. If this check box is selected, the operation selects and attempts to repair geometry. If it's not selected, nonmanifold geometry is ignored.
Normals and Geometry	If selected, this option causes the Cleanup operation to repair the nonmanifold geometry and fix any problems with the surface normals.
Geometry Only	This option repairs the model's geometry without affecting the normals.

Remove Geometry Options

This section includes a variety of settings to help you remove excess geometry from your model. It's perhaps one of the most useful areas for beginning modelers, as it's easy to create unnecessary detail when you first begin exploring the toolset. **TABLE 18.8** lists the settings for this section.

TABLE 18.8 Remove Geometry Options of the Cleanup Command

Option	Description
Edges with Zero Length	This option removes edges that exist between two vertices sharing the same location. The Length Tolerance setting for this option enables you to control how short the edge must be before it's removed. Be careful not to set it too high.
Faces with Zero Geometry Area	This option removes faces that are almost infinitely small in area. They can be created in a variety of ways, especially when making careless extrusions. You can use the Area Tolerance setting to control how close to zero the face's size must be before it's deleted.
Faces with Zero Map Area	This option removes faces with zero area for UV coordinates. Again, the Area Tolerance setting provides a threshold so that you can control how close to zero the area can be before the face is removed.
Lamina Faces	These faces rest one on top of the other, with normals facing in opposite directions. An example is merging two cubes without deleting the faces that are touching.

Editing Polygons

The Edit Polygons menu is dedicated to actual modeling tools—tools that are intended to manipulate the components of polygonal objects. The following sections explain the most important tools for you to know as a beginning modeler. Keep in mind that many tools in this menu work only when a particular type of component is selected. In this case, Maya typically issues a warning to tell you which component you need to select.

Subdividing Polygons

The Subdivide tool simply adds more topology to selected faces or edges. This tool is great to use when you simply need more detail on which to model. Its use is fairly simple: It can tessellate your model into quads or triangles. In **TUTORIAL 18.7**, you take a look at using this tool.

TUTORIAL 18.7: Using The Subdivide Tool

1. Start a new scene and go to the Modeling menu set.
2. Create a polygon cube, and press F11 so that you can select its faces.
3. From the Edit Polygons menu, choose Subdivide > options box. Set the mode to Triangles, and click the Subdivide button.
4. Your polygon has been divided into triangles, as shown in **FIGURE 18.39**. You could move the new vertex in the middle of the face to create a different shape that would have been impossible a moment ago.

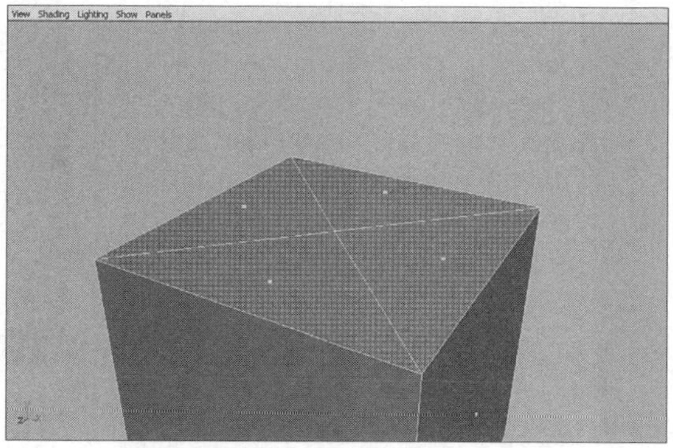

FIGURE 18.39 The face at the top of the cube has been subdivided.

5. Feel free to apply the tool several times and view the results. You can also set the mode to Quads, which divides the faces into more four-sided faces.

END TUTORIAL 18.7

Splitting Polygons

The Split Polygon tool is quite possibly the most important tool in polygon modeling. You can use this tool to add edges to your model and control where they are located, how detailed they are, and much more. **TUTORIAL 18.8** introduces you to this vital tool.

TUTORIAL 18.8: Splitting Polygons

1. Start a new scene and go to the Modeling menu set. Create a polygon cube to be used as your test object.
2. From the Edit Polygons menu, choose Split Polygon Tool. Notice the cursor turn into a *V*-shaped arrow.
3. Click any edge of the cube, and then click another edge directly across from the first one you clicked. Notice the green line that connects the two points you clicked. Next, click the next parallel edge around the cube. A new split appears, connecting the points to the third edge (see **FIGURE 18.40**).

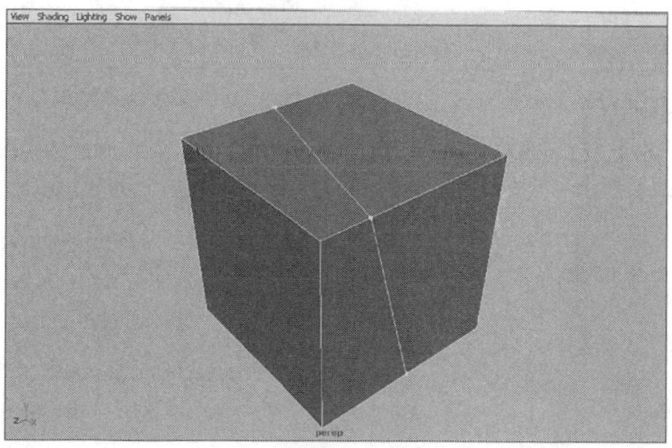

FIGURE 18.40 A split across three edges of the cube.

4. Press the Y key, which completes the split, finalizes the new edges you just made, and then restarts the tool for you to make a new split. Feel free to make another split. Repeat as much as you like, and press Enter after the last split. **FIGURE 18.41** shows a cube with several splits.

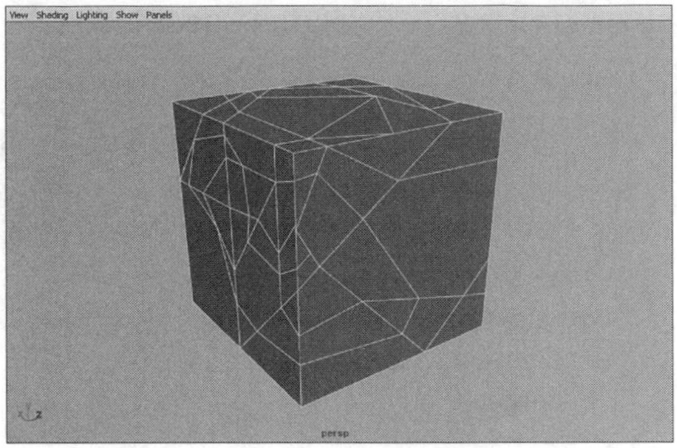

FIGURE 18.41 An excessively split cube.

END TUTORIAL 18.8

When using the Split Polygon tool, you should keep the following rules in mind:

- A split must begin and end on an edge. When splitting, you can create points in the middle of a face, but keep in mind that the first and last points must be on edges.
- A split cannot end on the same edge from which it began. If you need to make such a split, you need to make it from two separate split operations.
- You cannot "jump" edges. This means you must click on each individual edge as you split across an object. This process can be quite confusing for beginners, especially when creating splits in corners. Be sure you know from which edge you begin your splits.
- You can relocate the last split point you create by MMB-clicking it.

The Split Polygon tool also has several options you can use to adjust or fine-tune the splitting process. **TABLE 18.9** describes each of these options.

TABLE 18.9 Split Polygon Tool Options

Option	Description
Subdivisions	This option controls the number of vertices to be spread across your new splits.
Snap To Edge	This option allows split points to be placed only on existing polygon edges. Switch it off if you want to add points to the middle of a face.
Snap To Magnets	This option activates snapping magnets, invisible markers that allow you to mark off percentages of edges for precise splitting. When this option is selected, split points tend to "pop" to these invisible magnets as you drag across an edge.
Number Of Magnets	This option controls the number of snapping magnets on each edge. Setting it to an odd number enables you to make splits down the center of an object.
Magnet Tolerance	This option controls the strength of snapping magnets. The higher this value, the farther away the snapping point jumps to the magnet.

Extrusions

Extrusions are one of the most common modeling functions. You can extrude almost every polygon component except UVs. For your purposes, this chapter focuses mainly on face extrusions, although you can easily apply the knowledge to edge extrusions, which function exactly the same. Extruding vertices is a little different, so this technique is covered separately in "Extruding Vertices."

In essence, an *extrusion* moves an existing component away in its local space. It then connects that component back to its original position with new geometry. This process can sound a little confusing at first, so take a look at this tool first hand in **TUTORIAL 18.9**.

TUTORIAL 18.9: Making Face Extrusions

1. Start a new scene, and enter the Modeling menu set. Create a (you guessed it) polygon cube.
2. Press F11, and select the face on top of the cube. From the Edit Polygons menu, choose Extrude Face.
3. A new manipulator appears that's a hybrid of the Move, Rotate, and Scale manupulators (see **FIGURE 18.42**). Clicking one of the arrows enables Move mode. Clicking one of the rings around the manipulator enables Rotate mode, and clicking one of the small cubes enables Scale mode.

   Notice that the manipulator's blue-Z axis is pointing straight up, even though in world coordinates the Y-axis points upward. By default, the Extrude manipulator works in local coordinates, in which Z always points in the direction of the surface normal.

   To fix this, you can click on the small pale blue circle above and to the right of the manipulator. This allows you to move your extrusion in world rather than local coordinates.

   Move the extrusion upward, and notice that the face is connected back to its original location with four new faces (see **FIGURE 18.43**). This step

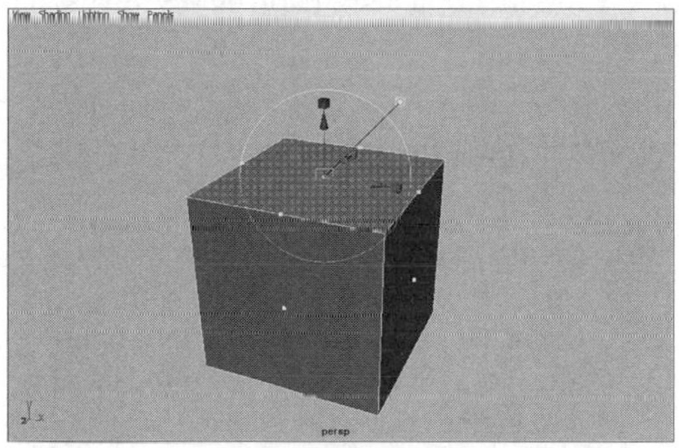

FIGURE 18.42 The Extrude manipulator.

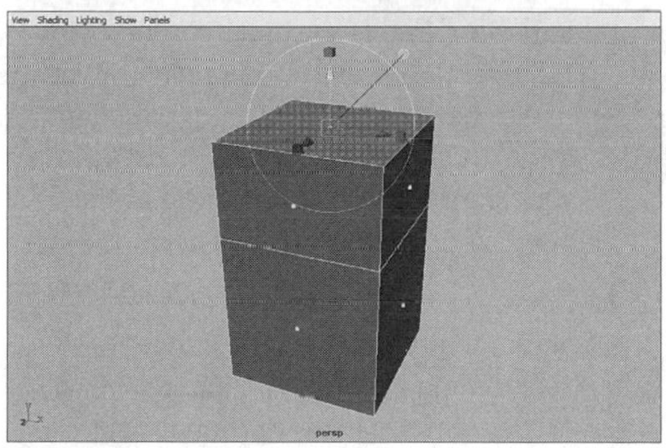

FIGURE 18.43 The extrusion has been moved up.

> **NOTE**
>
> If you like the Move/Rotate/Scale manipulator, you can use it for normal object transformations. To use it, choose Modify > Transformation Tools > Move/Rotate/Scale Tool from the main menu.

demonstrates how powerful the extrusion function can be, as it enables you to create a lot of detail on your object quickly.

4. Select other faces and make more extrusions. Try extruding more than one face at a time (see an example in **FIGURE 18.44**). Make adjustments using the manipulator's Rotate, Scale, and Move modes. Also, experiment with toggling the Keep Faces Together option, as explained in "Understanding the Tool Options and Display Settings in Maya" earlier in this chapter.

5. When finished, go back to Object mode, and move the object you created out of the way.

6. Create a new cube. Switch to the Side viewport, and choose Create > CV Curve Tool from the main menu. Create a curve from the top of the cube into an interesting shape, as shown in **FIGURE 18.45**.

   The starting point of the curve is *very* important in this case, as it's the point from which the extrusion begins. If you make the curve in the wrong direction, the extrusion runs backward. Be certain you begin the curve at the top of the cube.

7. Return to the Perspective view, and select the top face of the cube. Right-click on the curve, and choose Object Mode from the marking menu. This command enables you to select the curve in Object mode, even though you might be in Component mode. Do this now by Shift-clicking the curve.

   When you're finished, you should have the face at the top of the cube (indicated in orange) and the curve (indicated in green) selected, as shown in **FIGURE 18.46**.

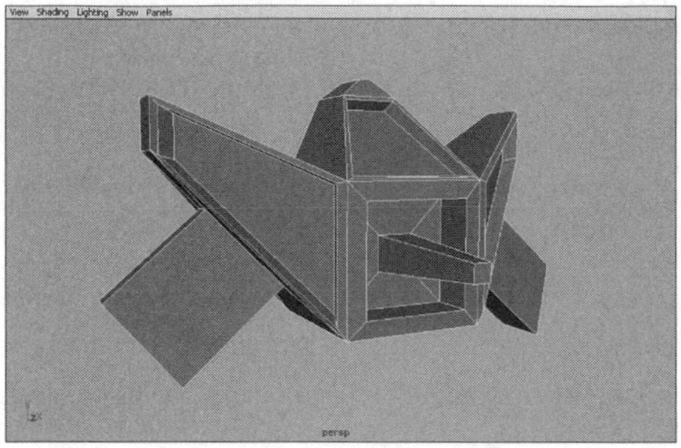

FIGURE 18.44 A simple abstract shape, made completely of extrusions.

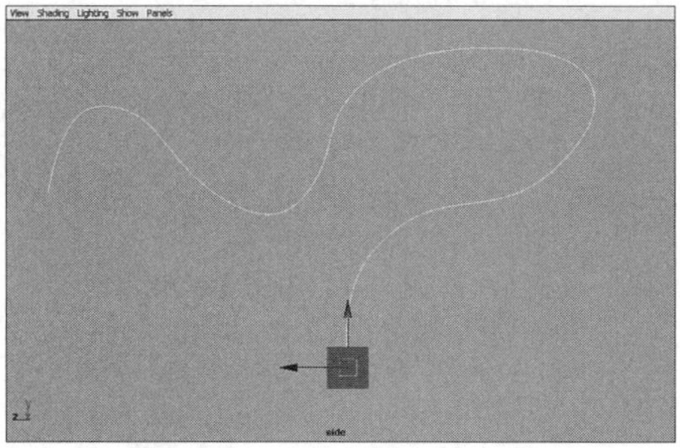

FIGURE 18.45 A curve that starts from the top of the cube.

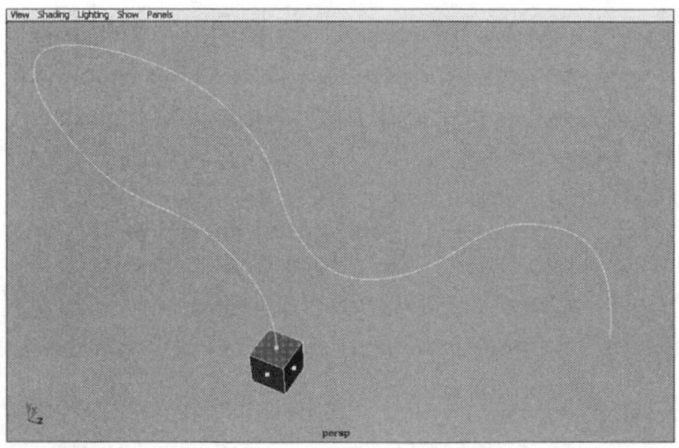

FIGURE 18.46 Both the face and curve are selected.

8. From the Edit Polygons menu, choose Extrude Face. Notice that the face snaps to the end of the curve (see **FIGURE 18.47**).

9. In the Channel Box, find the ExtrudeFace node. (There should be only one.) Click on it to see a list of attributes. Scroll to the bottom of this list, find and click the `Divisions` attribute, and then MMB-drag to the right in the viewport to use the virtual slider. This operation increases the extrusion's divisions. Notice that the more divisions you add, the more the extrusion conforms to the shape of the curve (see **FIGURE 18.48**).

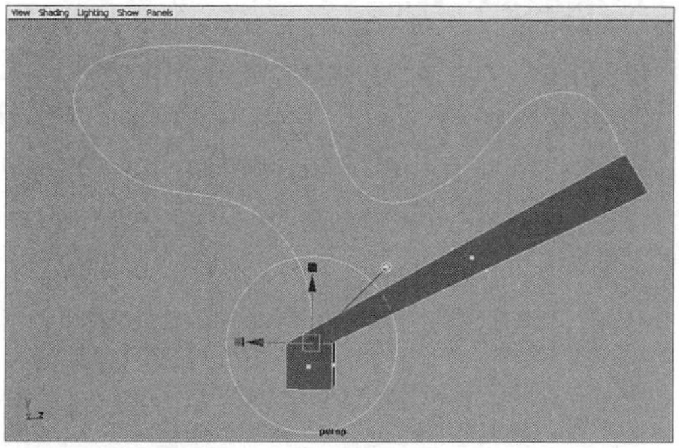

FIGURE 18.47 The initial result isn't quite what you expected.

> **TIP**
>
> **With the virtual slider, you can raise the `Divisions` value up to a limit of 25, but you're free to type in whatever value you like.**

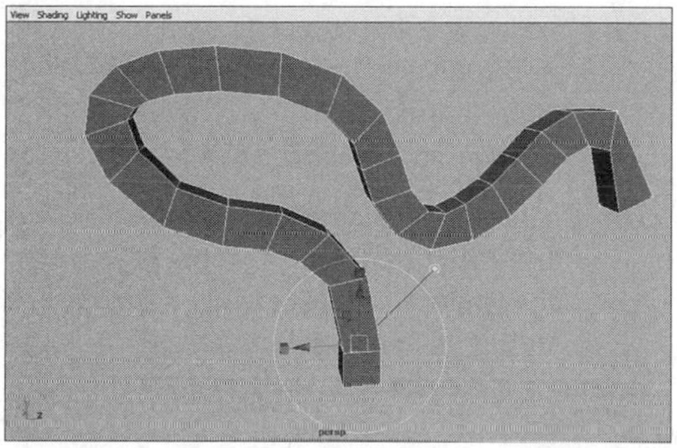

FIGURE 18.48 The extrusion is now following the curve.

10. Experiment with the `Twist` and `Taper` attributes, and see what results you can come up with. **FIGURE 18.49** shows an example of the result of modifying these attributes.

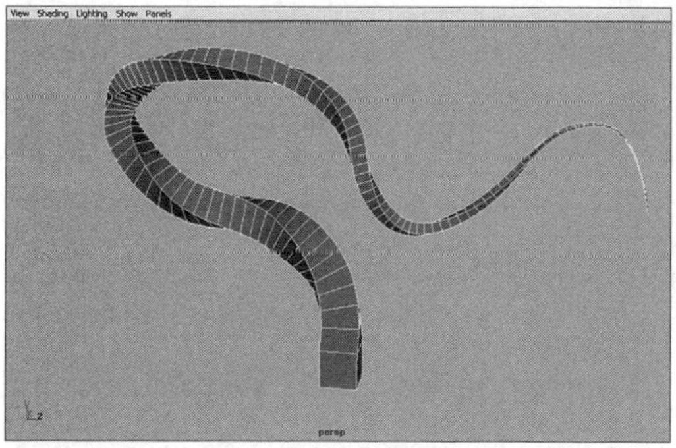

FIGURE 18.49 Extrusion after modifying the *`Divisions`*, *`Twist`*, and *`Taper`* attributes.

END TUTORIAL 18.9

Extruding Vertices

Extruding an edge is virtually identical to extruding a face, but extruding vertices is quite a bit different because there's no manipulator for vertex extrusions. Extruding a vertex isn't the most commonly used function, but it's good for pulling points, spikes, and other similar shapes out of geometry. **TUTORIAL 18.10** gives you a look at using this command.

TUTORIAL 18.10: Vertex Extrusions

1. Start a new scene, enter the Modeling menu set, and create a cube.
2. Press F9, and select a single vertex from the object's surface.
3. Choose the Extrude Vertex command from the Edit Polygons menu. Notice that no manipulator appears, as shown in **FIGURE 18.50**.
4. Go to the Channel Box, and click the polyExtrudeVertex1 node. Make adjustments to the `Length`, `Width`, and `Divisions` attributes to see how the manipulation process works without a manipulator. **FIGURE 18.51** shows an example of the results of adjusting these attributes.

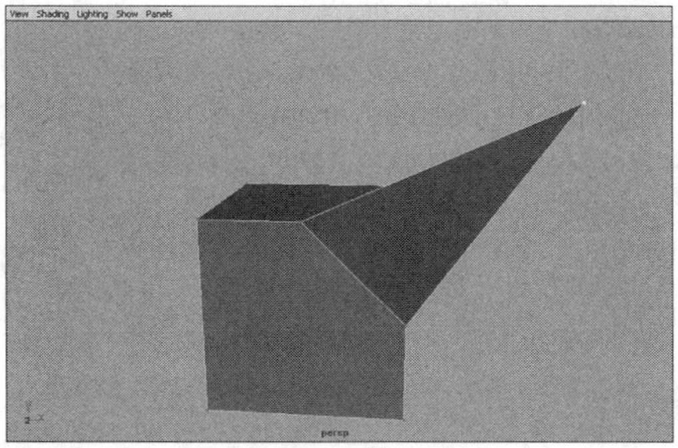

FIGURE 18.50 A vertex extrusion.

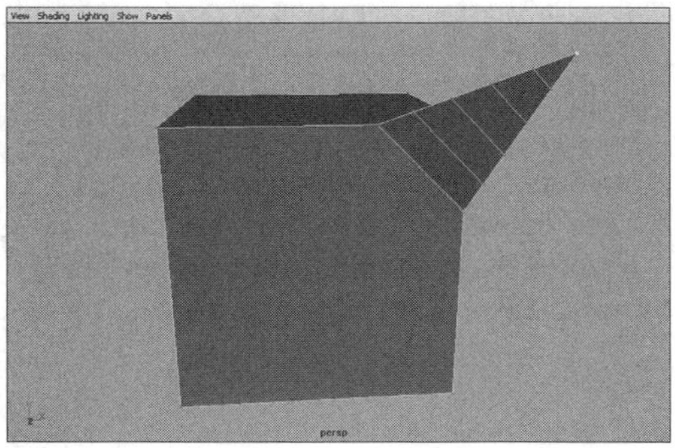

FIGURE 18.51 Several alterations made to the vertex extrusion.

> **TIP**
>
> You can manually enter values between 0 and 1 for the `Width` attribute, although the virtual slider allows values only between 0 and 0.5.

END TUTORIAL 18.10

Chamfering Vertices and Beveling Edges

Even though you should try to avoid excessive polygon counts when creating game models, sometimes you need to create objects with rounded edges. Adding slightly rounded edges always makes your models look more realistic than creating razor-sharp 90-degree angles. Two commands are available for creating slightly rounded edges: Bevel (for edges) and Chamfer Vertex. These two functions add new detail to the shape to make it look less sharp. **TUTORIAL 18.11** demonstrates how to use these tools to round off the edges and corners of shapes.

TUTORIAL 18.11: Chamfering and Beveling

1. Start a new scene and go to the Modeling menu set. Create two polygon cubes, and move them apart from each other.

2. Choose one of the cubes and select all its vertices. Choose Chamfer Vertex from the Edit Polygons menu (see the result in **FIGURE 18.52**).

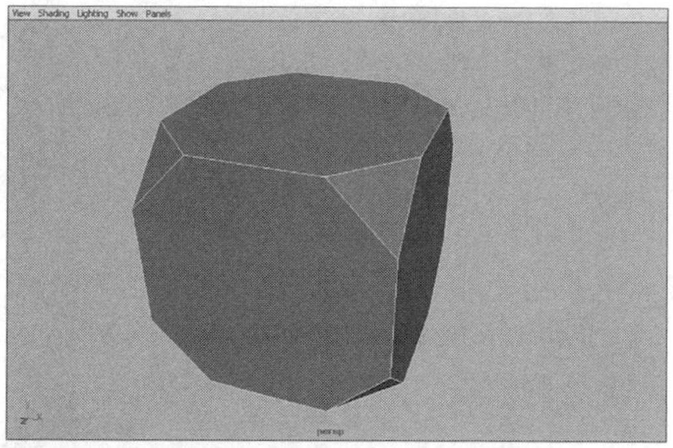

FIGURE 18.52 A cube with all vertices chamfered.

Each vertex is divided into three vertices, and a surface is stretched across each group of three. This is how chamfering works. In essence, it splits a single vertex so that there's one new vertex for each edge that was leading into the original, and a surface is stretched between these new vertices. In effect, this command rounds off the corners of objects.

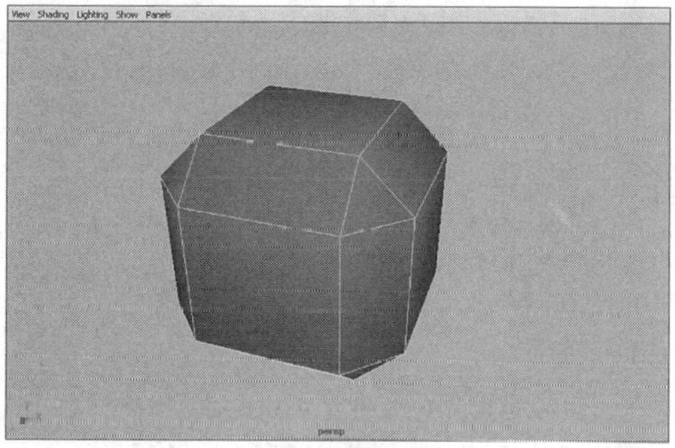

FIGURE 18.53 A beveled cube.

3. Now select the second cube, and choose the Edit Polygons > Bevel command to round off all the edges and corners. In the Channel Box, click the polyBevel1 node to see four options for controlling the bevel. The most important option is the `Offset` attribute, which controls how far the edges are beveled. Play with the settings and see what kind of shapes you can create. **FIGURE 18.53** shows an example.

When you're modeling photorealistic objects, keep in mind that beveling is a major factor because no objects in the real world have perfectly sharp edges. In game engines such as Unreal, however, beveling is typically seen as extra faces. If you don't need beveling for a specific shape, you should consider avoiding it.

END TUTORIAL 18.11

Cutting Faces

You can think of the Cut Faces Tool as a massive cutting laser. You can quickly cut all the way through a model, if you're in Object mode, or cut through a specific selection of faces. **TUTORIAL 18.12** demonstrates how to use this tool to add detail right where you need it in your model.

TUTORIAL 18.12: Using the Cut Faces Tool

1. Start a new scene, and go to the Modeling menu set. Although you could create any polygonal object you like, for this example, create a cube so that you can easily see the results.

2. From the Edit Polygons menu, choose Cut Faces Tool. Your cursor turns into a triangular arrow. Click on the center of your object and drag away. A thick black line that crosses the viewport appears to indicate where the new cut will be placed (see **FIGURE 18.54**). Release the mouse button at the angle you like.

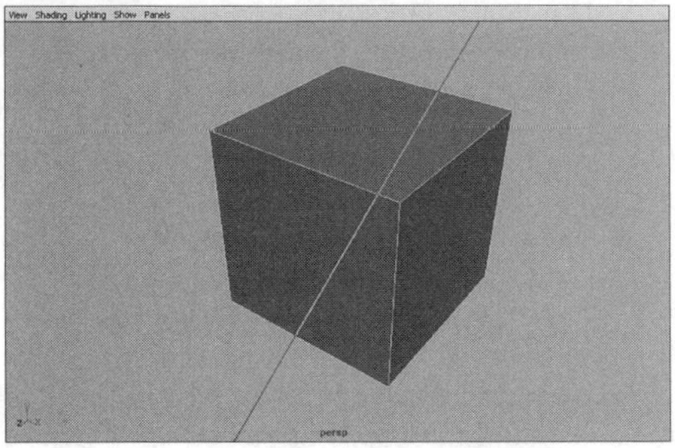

FIGURE 18.54 The Cut Faces tool indicator.

3. Use the tool again, but hold down the Shift key as you do to make the cut line snap to 45-degree increments. Make a cut or two using this method.

4. Now open the Options dialog box for the tool (choose Edit Polygons > Cut Faces Tool > options box from the menu). In the Cut Direction drop-down list, select Custom Cut, and click the Cut button. A plane manipulator that can be moved, rotated, and scaled is displayed (see **FIGURE 18.55**). This manipulator gives you precise control over where to locate the cut.

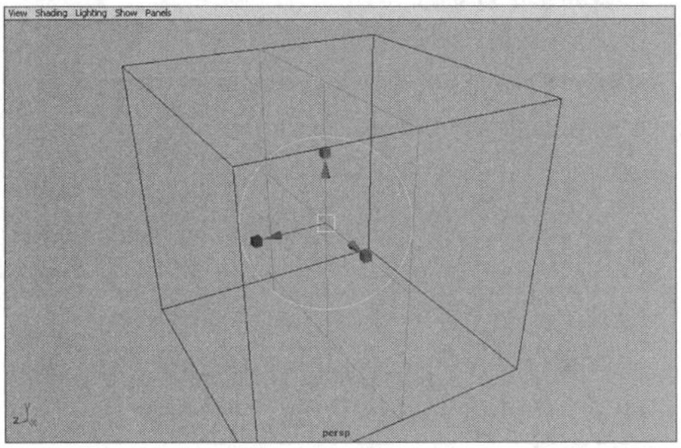

FIGURE 18.55 The Custom Cut manipulator.

> **NOTE**
>
> Using these settings, you can also make cuts that are perfectly aligned to specific axes.

END TUTORIAL 18.12

Wedging Faces

The Wedge Faces command is a powerful weapon for a polygon modeler's arsenal. Basically, it allows you to hinge an extrusion from a single edge. Its uses are practically limitless, from creating folded plates and pipe works to even making intersections in catwalks. In **TUTORIAL 18.13**, you see how this tool is used.

TUTORIAL 18.13: Using the Wedge Face Command

1. Start a new scene and enter the Modeling menu set. Create a polygon cylinder, and in the Channel Box, set its `Subdivisions Caps` to 0.
2. Select the face on top of the cylinder, as shown in **FIGURE 18.56**.
3. Right-click over the object, and choose Edge from the marking menu. With the face still selected, hold down the Shift key and select one edge on the side of the selected face.
4. From the Edit Polygons menu, choose Wedge Faces. The face pops up from its original location, as though it were hinged from the selected edge (see **FIGURE 18.57**).
5. With the object selected, click the polyWedgeFace1 node in the Channel Box to access the wedge's angle and divisions.
6. Practice using this tool a few times. Combine it with Face Extrusions, and see what kind of shapes you can come up with. **FIGURE 18.58** shows an example.

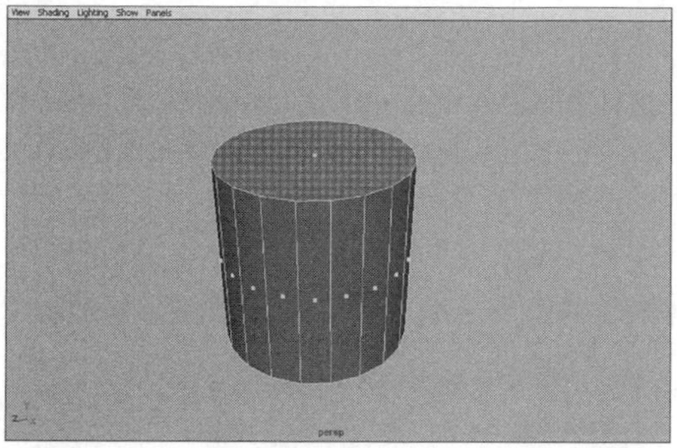

FIGURE 18.56 The first step in creating the wedge is to select a face.

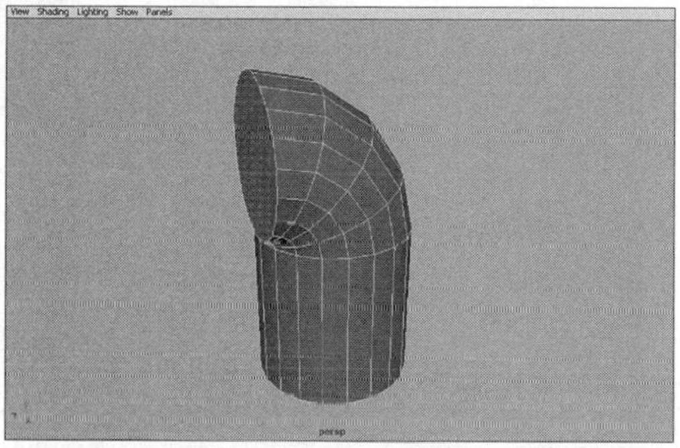

FIGURE 18.57 The initial result of the wedge operation.

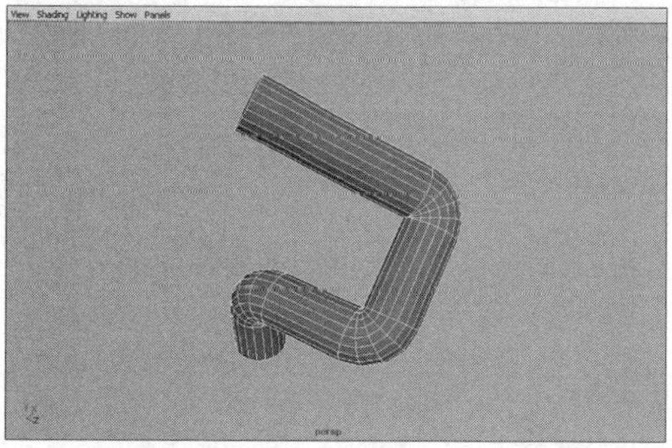

FIGURE 18.58 The result of a few wedges and face extrusions.

END TUTORIAL 18.13

Merging Vertices

The Merge Vertices command is a vital tool for polygon modeling. It enables you to convert two models into one solid, seamless mesh. To use it, simply select a group of vertices, run the command, and specify a threshold distance. If the vertices are within the specified distance of each other, they snap together and merge to become one vertex. **TUTORIAL 18.14** introduces you to this concept.

TUTORIAL 18.14: Using the Merge Vertex Command

1. Start a new scene and enter the Modeling menu set. Create two cubes, and move them slightly apart from each other on a single axis, as shown in **FIGURE 18.59**.

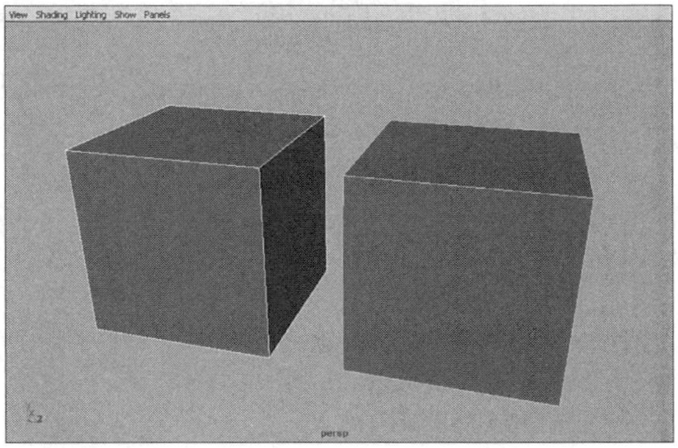

FIGURE 18.59 Your two subjects.

2. On each cube, delete the faces that are facing each other. If you were to skip this step and merge the vertices anyway, the result would be a Lamina face.
3. Select both cubes in Object mode and choose Polygons > Combine from the menu. This step is crucial, as you can merge only vertices that are on the same model.
4. Select two vertices directly across from each other. From the Edit Polygons menu, choose Merge Vertices Tool > options box. In the Tool Settings dialog box, set `Threshold` to 0.5. **FIGURE 18.60** shows the results.

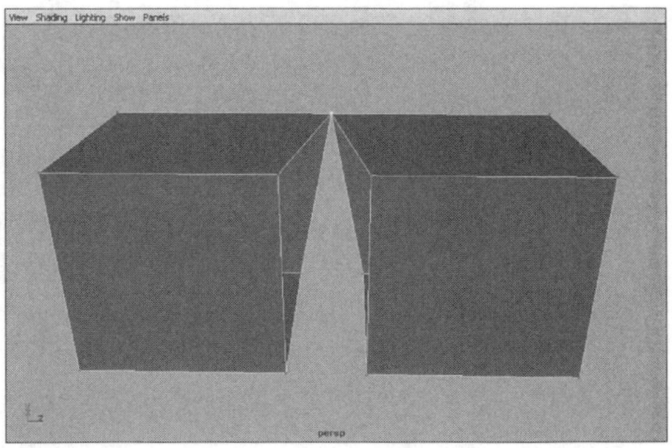

FIGURE 18.60 A pair of vertices merged to a single vertex.

5. Repeat step 4 for the other three vertices, or you can select them all at once and adjust the `Threshold` setting until they merge properly (see **FIGURE 18.61**). This process can be tricky, however, especially if the distance between the two cubes is actually larger than their width, height, and depth.

18

The result is a rectangular object that is a fully merged, seamless model. This tool is a valuable one, and you should practice using it to help prevent excess geometry in your model.

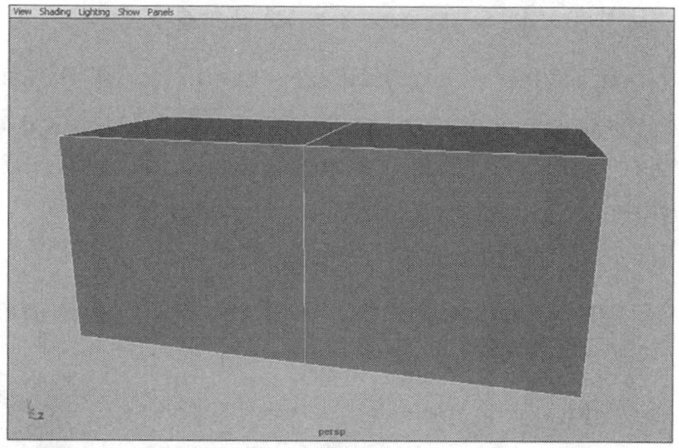

FIGURE 18.61 The cubes are merged into one model.

> **NOTE**
>
> If the vertices don't merge at this point, you can adjust the `Threshold` setting in the Channel Box by clicking the polyMergeVert1 node.

END TUTORIAL 18.14

Flipping Triangle Edges

As mentioned earlier, all game models intended for use in Unreal need to be triangulated. For this reason, modelers need a great deal of control over how those triangles behave. Often, particularly with character models, a triangle can be facing the wrong direction, resulting in poor deformation when the model is animated. You can improve it by changing the direction of the triangular edge. Instead of having to delete the edge and replace it in a new direction, in Maya you can flip these edges over quickly with the Flip Triangle Edge tool.

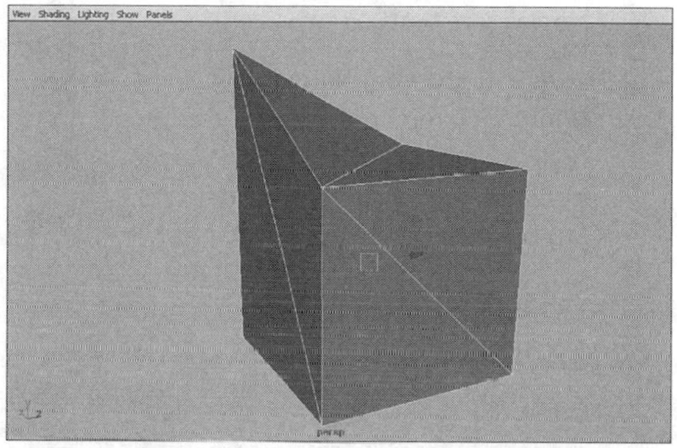

FIGURE 18.62 With the triangle edge pointed at the camera, the face folds as shown here.

The tool's use is simple: Just select the edge in question, and run the command. In **FIGURES 18.62** and **18.63**, notice the dramatic changes in the shape of the model just because of the placement of this edge.

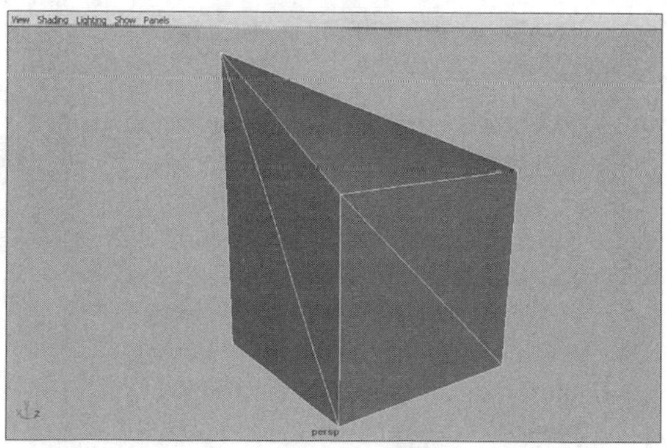

FIGURE 18.63 After the triangle is flipped, however, the face folds in the other direction, completely changing the model's look.

Adjusting Surfaces and Hard Edges

Normals are an essential aspect to be aware of when modeling an object for Unreal because a polygon's negative side isn't rendered, as stated earlier. Controlling the direction of your normals is easy, but does deserve some discussion. In **TUTORIAL 18.15**, you see how to change the direction of surface normals of a polygonal object.

TUTORIAL 18.15: Controlling Surface Normals

1. Start a new scene, and go in the Modeling menu set. Create a polygon sphere, and using Component mode, delete the upper half of its faces. Using the skills you learned in **TUTORIAL 18.1**, display the normals. Your example should be similar to **FIGURE 18.64**.

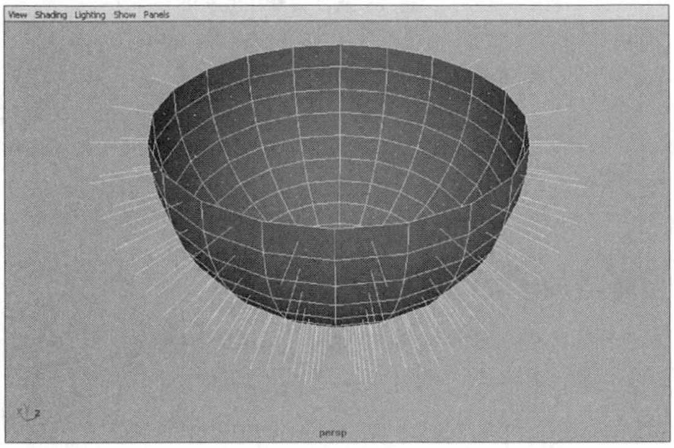

FIGURE 18.64 A half sphere with visible normals.

2. Open the Custom Polygon Display Options dialog box. For the Backface Culling option at the bottom, select Keep Wire so that you see only the wireframe when looking at the backface of polygons (see **FIGURE 18.65**). This option makes reversed normals even easier to see.

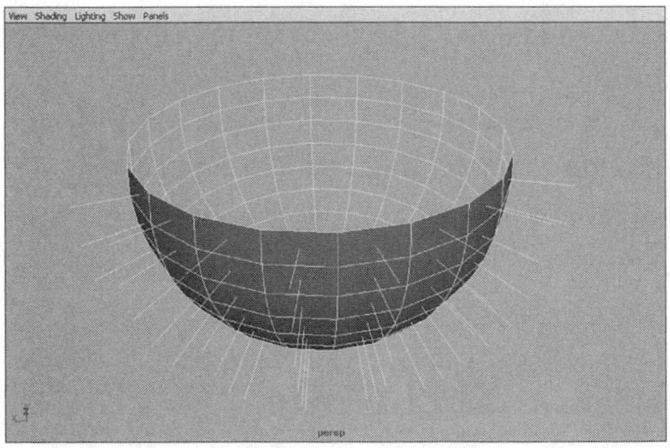

FIGURE 18.65 Backface Culling set to Keep Wire.

3. Often the tools you use cause your model's surface normals to run in two separate directions. Although you don't currently have this situation, knowing how to reverse the direction of a polygon"s normals is helpful.

   To do this, select a few faces of the half-sphere, and from the Edit Polygons menu, choose Normals > Reverse > options box. In the Reverse Options dialog box, set the mode to Reverse to simply change the direction of the normals. Notice that you can see the faces with reversed normals on the inside of the sphere (see **FIGURE 18.66**).

18

The second mode in this dialog box is Reverse and Propagate, which effectively flips all normals in a model, even if you selected only one. The third mode is Reverse and Extract, which reverses the normal and completely separates it from the model, making it a free-standing polygon face.

You can use the Edit Polygons > Normals > Reverse command whenever you see that a normal is pointed the wrong direction on your model. Normals should always point in the direction of the surface you need to display. For example, if you were modeling a crate and the normals were pointed inward, the crate would not render in-game.

Another handy tool for controlling surface normals is the Conform command, located under Edit Polygons > Normals. This command hunts for stray normals and makes sure they point in the same direction as the majority of the faces. This command is a one-click fix when you have just a few normals pointed in the wrong direction.

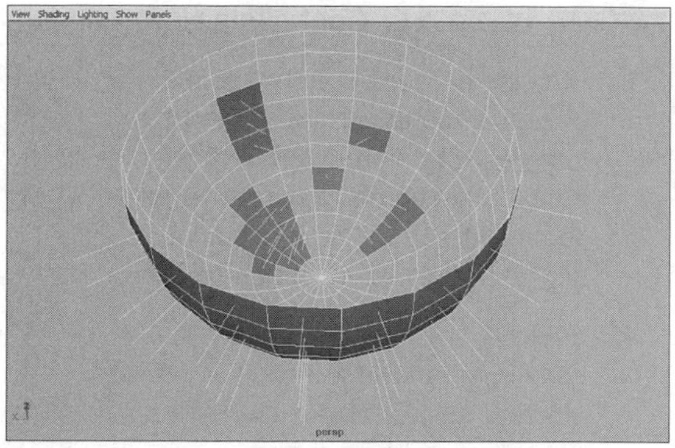

FIGURE 18.66 The same sphere with a few normals flipped.

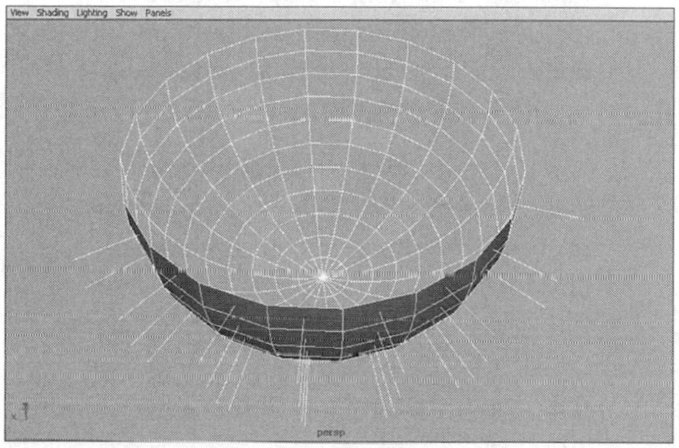

FIGURE 18.67 Conform has reversed the normals you flipped a moment ago.

4. Apply the Conform command to your model now to make all the normals face in the same direction (see **FIGURE 18.67**). If, after you use Conform, all the normals face in the wrong direction, you can then use the Reverse command to flip them.

   You can apply these few techniques to make sure your models' normals face in the proper direction. This step is a vital one after your model is finished and just before you import it into Unreal.

END TUTORIAL 18.15

Another way to have normals control the look of polygon models is by using hard edges. Hard edges allow you to create the appearance of creases or seams along the edges of a model. The advantage of hard edges is that they can be transferred into Unreal, allowing you to control when an edge should look smooth or sharp. In **TUTORIAL 18.16**, you work with a simple example to see how to use hard edges to control your model's look.

TUTORIAL 18.16: Controlling Hard Edges

1. Start a new scene, and go to the Modeling menu set. Create a polygon sphere. Rotate around it a bit, and notice that you don't see any edges. You might see a hint of shading that suggests the edges, but no creases.

2. Select a ring of edges around the sphere, as shown in **FIGURE 18.68**. Any ring will do, so don't worry if it's not exactly at the equator.

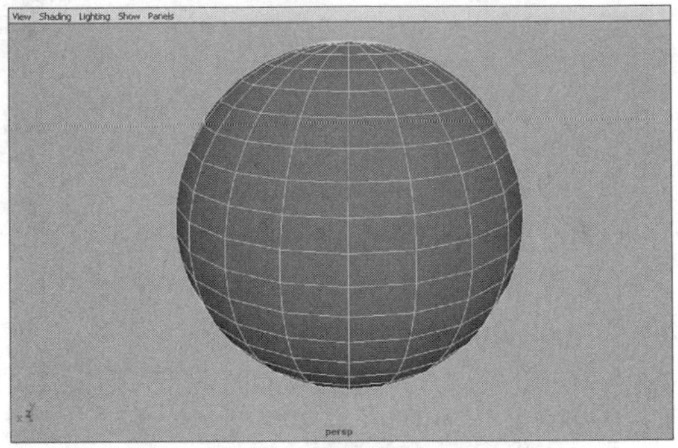

FIGURE 18.68 A ring of selected edges around the sphere.

3. From the Edit Polygons menu, choose Normals > Soften/Harden > options box. In the Soften/Harden Options dialog box is a slider with two buttons underneath for moving the slider fully to one side or the other.

   The number in the slider is an angle value that controls when a hard edge occurs. If two faces meet at an angle greater than this value, the edge where the faces meet is considered hard. If the angle where they meet is less than this value, that edge is soft.

4. Set this angle value to 0, and click the Soft/Hard button.

5. Deselect the sphere entirely, and then rotate the camera around the sphere. Notice the crease-like edge around it (see **FIGURE 18.69**). This edge is a result of the object's normals being modified to simulate a crease. No extra topology has been added.

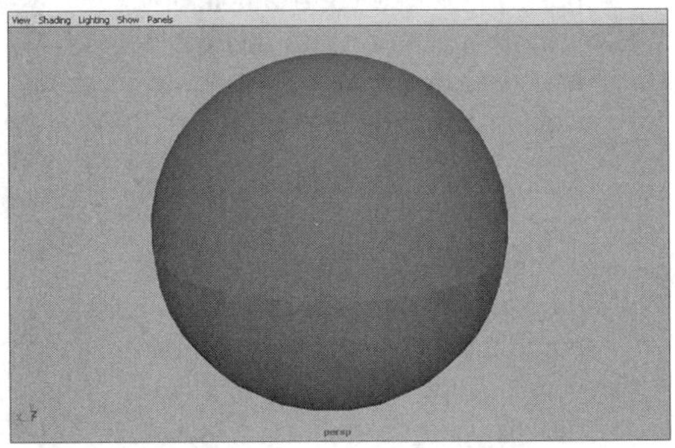

FIGURE 18.69 You can see the crease around the middle of the sphere indicating the location of the new hard edge.

> **TIP**
>
> A fast way to select a ring of edges is to select a single horizontal edge and choose Edit Polygons > Selection > Select Contiguous Edges.

END TUTORIAL 18.16

18

Summary

This chapter has covered a wide variety of polygon modeling tools. You have been introduced to many of the fundamental skills needed to shape polygon objects. At this point, you need to practice with many of these until you're comfortable with how they function.

Chapter 19

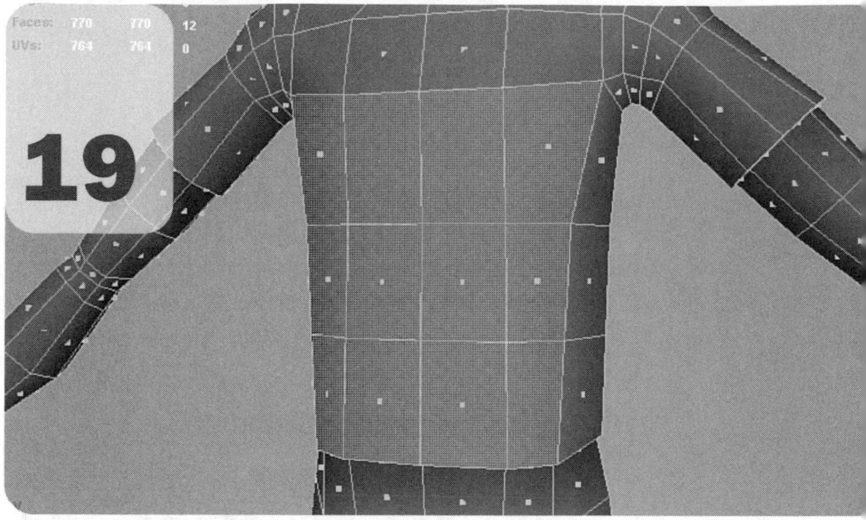

The Art of Texturing in Maya

In this chapter, you examine how to prepare your polygonal model to receive a custom texture in Photoshop. This process requires understanding the concepts behind UVs and UV layouts for polygons in Maya. You learn how to create these UV layouts, import them into Photoshop, and use them as a template to create a texture for your objects.

UVs and the UV Coordinate System

Every polygonal object in Maya has UVs. They are a vertex-like polygon component used strictly for texturing purposes. UVs enable you to take a three-dimensional surface and lay it out flat so that you can paint a texture on it in a program such as Photoshop. As an analogy, consider having to print a design on a beach ball using a computer printer. To do this, the beach ball's surface needs to be completely flat and laid out in a configuration that fits completely within a standard sheet of paper. Unfortunately, laying the surface out in this manner means you would have to completely destroy the beach ball. This is where UVs come into play. UVs are an entirely separate coordinate system, fully independent of the location of a model's vertices. They are almost like a "second surface" that you can use to flatten the object out without destroying the model's shape.

All the polygonal primitives in Maya are created with a default set of UVs that can be viewed with the UV Texture Editor, located under the Window menu in Maya. In **TUTORIAL 19.1**, you use this editor to get an idea of what a UV layout looks like on a primitive cube.

TUTORIAL 19.1: Examining UV Layouts

1. Open Maya and start a new scene.
2. From the Create menu, choose Polygon Primitives > Cube.
3. Choose Window > UV Texture Editor. This window shows you the UV layout on selected objects (see **FIGURE 19.1**). Keep in mind that if you have nothing selected, this window is blank.

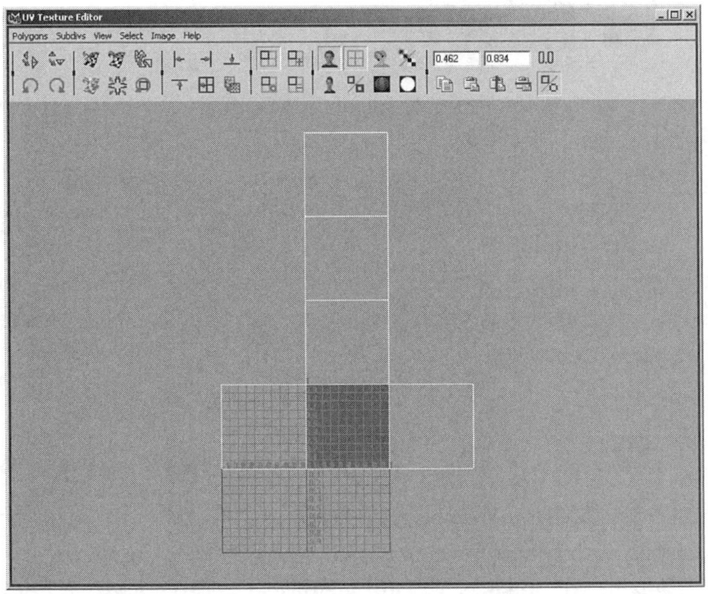

FIGURE 19.1 The default UV layout of a cube.

Notice that the UVs for the cube are arranged as though it were unfolded and laid out flat. At the same time, however, the cube retains its original shape because the actual vertex locations in 3D space are separate from the UV coordinates.

END TUTORIAL 19.1

Because UVs exist in a coordinate system separate from a model's vertices, their position has no effect on the final model. UV coordinate space is a two-dimensional system rather than a three-dimensional one. Its two dimensions, U and V, are surface dependent, meaning they exist only along an object's surface. For example, pretend that your stomach has UV coordinates. The U direction runs horizontally, and the V direction runs vertically. If you draw a line across your stomach from left to right, that line moves only in the U direction of the UV coordinate space. No matter how far you continue the line, even around to your back, you are still moving only in the U direction along the surface. The UV coordinate system, therefore, is a two-dimensional system that "wraps around" a three-dimensional one.

The UV Texture Editor

The UV Texture Editor is the primary tool for creating UV layouts in Maya. UVs can be edited, manipulated, and controlled by using the UV Texture Editor, which you viewed in **TUTORIAL 19.1**. In this section, you examine this editor briefly to see how it's used to control your object's UVs. The editor is divided into three main areas: the menu bar, the toolbar, and the view.

The Menu Bar

The menu bar contains all the relevant commands to control your UVs. The following list describes the menu items:

- *Polygons*—This menu contains all the commands needed to lay out the UVs of a polygon model. Instead of explaining each one now, you learn about these commands as you use them in the following tutorials.
- *Subdivs*—This menu contains a few commands necessary for adjusting UVs on a subdivision surface. This menu isn't covered in this book.
- *View*—This menu contains many commands for controlling what you see in the viewport. Sometimes it can be difficult to tell what UVs are doing, especially when your layout consists of several overlapping pieces. Using this menu, you can show or hide specific groups of UVs to help make the arrangement process easier.
- *Select*—This menu has a variety of useful commands to help with selection of your object's components. You can use these commands to select all UVs within a contiguous piece, or shell, and to convert a specific selection into vertices, edges, faces, or UVs.
- *Image*—This menu provides controls for how the texture is displayed in the UV Texture Editor.
- *Help*—This menu gives you access to Maya's help system.

The Toolbar

Across the toolbar are a series of icons and entry fields that can be used for many commands (see **TABLE 19.1**); these commands are also available from the main menu. Also, notice that the toolbar is divided into six collapsible groups to save space.

TABLE 19.1 UV Texture Editor Toolbar

Icon	Name	Description
	Flip UVs (U direction)	Flips the selected UVs horizontally in the UV Texture Editor.
	Flip UVs (V direction)	Flips the selected UVs vertically in the UV Texture Editor.
	Rotate UVs Counterclockwise	Rotates all selected UVs 45 degrees in a counterclockwise direction.
	Rotate UVs Clockwise	Rotates all selected UVs 45 degrees in a clockwise direction.
	Cut UVs	Divides a piece of the UV layout along selected edges. Although selecting edges is the most efficient way to use this tool, you can also use it with selections of UVs.
	Sew UVs	Attaches two edges together in UV space. It doesn't affect the shape of the actual model, even though you're working with polygonal edges. Note that when selecting one edge in the UV Texture Editor, the corresponding edge shared on the model is also selected.
	Layout UVs	Automatically generates a layout for the UVs of your model based on a set of criteria you enter in the options dialog box. Using this command from the Polygons menu to open the Options dialog box is usually easier.
	Move and Sew UVs	Moves and attaches selections of edges to one another. The difference between this command and Sew UVs is that Move and Sew UVs tries to move the pieces of the layout, instead of just the edges.
	Split Selected UV	Breaks a single UV up so that there's one UV for each edge that was leading into that UV. For example, if you have four edges leading into a single UV, this command would break that UV into four separate UVs.

TABLE 19.1 Continued

Icon	Name	Description
	Cycle UVs	Cycles through all the UVs within the face that contains the selected UV, and then selects all the edges of that face. This command can be useful when you're having a difficult time seeing what a particular face is shaped like in the UV Texture Editor.
	Align UVs (minimum U)	Aligns a selection of two or more UVs in the U direction so that they line up with the UV that was farthest to the left in the UV Texture Editor.
	Align UVs (maximum U)	The same as the previous command, except that the UVs are aligned in the U direction to the UV that was farthest to the right in the UV Texture Editor.
	Align UVs (minimum V)	Aligns a selection of two or more UVs in the V direction so that they line up with the UV that was the closest to the bottom of the UV Texture Editor.
	Align UVs (maximum V)	The same as the previous command, except that the UVs are aligned in the V direction to the UV that was closest to the top of the UV Texture Editor.
	Grid UVs	Moves the selected UVs to the nearest grid intersection based on the settings created for the command. Using this command's Options dialog box from the Polygons menu is easier.
	Relax UVs	More evenly distributes the selected piece of the UV layout to make more efficient use of texture space. The result is not unlike taking an average location for all the UVs of a selected piece.
	Toggle Isolate Select Mode	Hides all UVs that aren't currently selected, which can make manipulating the UVs much easier.
	Add Selected	Adds the current selection to the current isolated selection, making it visible.
	Remove All	Clears the current isolated selection, essentially hiding all objects visible while the isolated select is active.
	Remove Selected	Removes any selected UVs from the current isolated selection.

TABLE 19.1 Continued

Icon	Name	Description
	Show Background Image (toggle on/off)	Shows or hides the texture you're applying to your objects in the UV Texture Editor. The texture tile outside the 0 – 1 texture space, which you discuss in a moment.
	Show Grid (toggle on/off)	Toggles the display of the grid in the UV Texture Editor.
	Snap to Pixels (toggle on/off)	Controls whether you can snap UVs to pixel borders. This option is useful when you're trying to be precise about which texture pixels are included in your UV layout.
	Filtered Display Mode (toggle on/off)	Specifies whether the texture is rendered with hardware filtering in the UV Texture Editor or is drawn with sharply defined pixels.
	Image Ratio (toggle on/off)	Controls whether the texture space is square or matches the size ratio of the selected texture. Because all Unreal textures must be square, you don't need to use this option for game models.
	Texture Borders (toggle on/off)	Controls whether UV borders are drawn with a thick line instead of the single pixel line.
	Display RGB Channels	Displays the color information of the texture in the UV Texture Editor.
	Display Alpha Channel	Displays the alpha information for the texture in the UV Texture Editor.
0.308 0.361	U and V coordinate entry fields	Used to type in an exact location in UV space, moving the selected UV to that location.
0.0	Refresh the Current UV Values	Refreshes the UV coordinate entry fields to display the correct number for the selected UV.
	Copy UVs	Copies the selected vertex colors, UVs, or shaders to the Clipboard so that you can paste them onto other UV sets.
	Paste UVs	Pastes any vertex colors, UVs, or shaders that are stored in the Clipboard.
	Paste U Value to Selected UVs	Pastes the U value that has been stored in the Clipboard onto the selected UVs.
	Paste V Value to Selected UVs	Pastes the V value that has been stored in the Clipboard onto the selected UVs.
	Copy/Paste for UVs/Faces (toggle)	Determines whether copy and paste work for UVs or faces.

The Viewport

You navigate the UV Texture Editor viewport exactly the same way as the orthographic views in Maya. Alt+MMB pans the view, and Alt+LMB and MMB zoom the view. You can also use Alt+LMB to pan the camera, something you can't do in an orthographic viewport.

The UV Texture Editor viewport has a unique grid that's divided into four quadrants, with the upper-right quadrant darker than the rest. This quadrant is darker to indicate that your entire texture fits into this quadrant. Outside the upper-right quadrant, the texture simply repeats, or tiles. In most cases, therefore, you want your entire UV layout to exist within this grid's upper-right quadrant, which is also known as the 0–1 texture space because all the coordinates for this quadrant exist within 0 and 1.

Mapping UVs

Before you can start laying out an object's UVs, you must understand how to map UVs in the UV Texture Editor. UV mapping is a way to take a selection of faces and lay out their corresponding UVs in the UV Texture Editor. Several types of UV mapping are available in Maya, but this book focuses on three: automatic mapping, planar mapping, and cylindrical mapping.

Mapping Methods

With *automatic mapping*, Maya automatically lays out your model's UVs based on a series of criteria (see **FIGURE 19.2**). You can control the method used in automatic mapping in the tool's Options dialog box, which you can access by choosing Edit Polygons > Texture > Automatic Mapping from the main menu. You'll find several options for controlling the way the automatic mapping takes place. Unfortunately, this command rarely yields usable results for your game models because the UVs are usually laid out in a pattern that's practically impossible to follow. However, you can use this method as a "quick fix" to achieve a simple UV layout, especially when you intend to use the textures already included in Unreal.

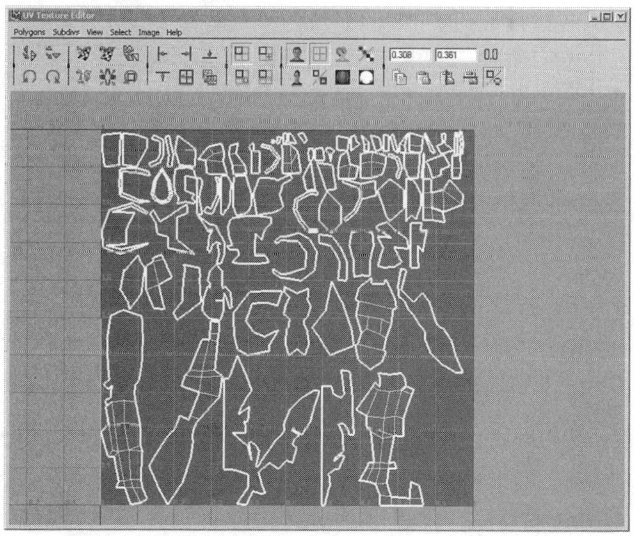

FIGURE 19.2 A character model with UVs laid out with automatic mapping.

In *planar mapping*, the UVs of selected faces are laid out as though they had been pulled off the model and laid out flat onto a single plane. You can choose a specific axis on which the plane is projected, or you can let Maya act to interpolate one based on the angle of all the selected faces. You'll be using this mapping method a bit later. **FIGURE 19.3** shows a planar mapped sphere, in which the plane is projected down the Z-axis.

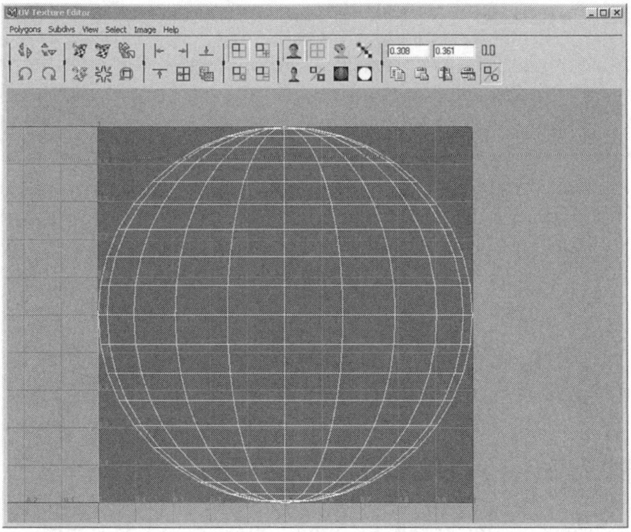

FIGURE 19.3 A planar projected sphere.

In *cylindrical mapping*, the UVs are laid out as though they had been projected onto a cylinder. This mapping method is especially useful for character faces and for any object that's roughly cylindrical in form, such as an arm or leg. For example, if you cut the leg off a pair of pants, the leg would be a cylindrical form. If you make a cut that runs all the way along the inseam, you could then lay the fabric out flat. This is exactly how cylindrical mapping works. **FIGURE 19.4** shows a character's leg that has been mapped cylindrically.

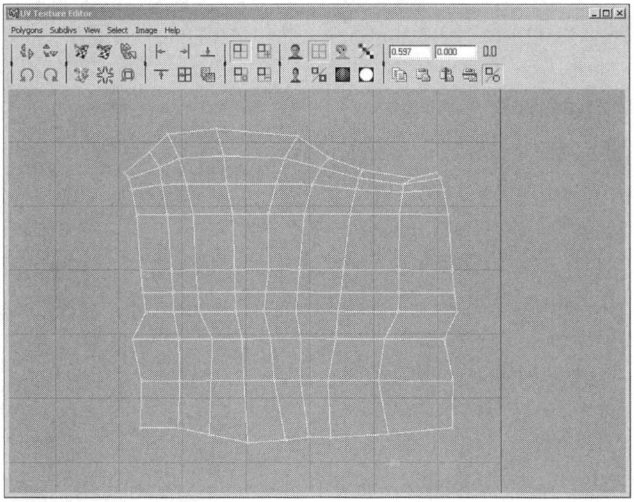

FIGURE 19.4 A cylindrically mapped leg.

Creating UV Layouts

Mapping is only the first step in creating a proper layout for your UVs. On an actual model, you map each part of the model, a piece at a time, using the mapping method best suited to that specific area of the model. When finished, you have a series of pieces representing your model that are laid out flat. At that point, all you need to do is move, rotate, and scale each piece in the UV Texture Editor so that they all fit in the 0–1 texture space.

This process might seem easy, and in concept, it *is* quite easy; in practice, however, laying out an object's UVs can be time consuming. Also, many beginners wonder what's the *right* or *correct* way to lay out an object's UVs. Unfortunately, this is where many users run into the fine line between a skill and an art form. The truth is that there is no single "correct" way to create a UV layout—only the method that works best for you or your texture artist. Before you get too far into that, however, try creating your own UV layout for a simple object in **TUTORIAL 19.2**. Over the next few tutorials, you create a static mesh of a dice; later, using the skills you learn in Chapter 20, "Static Meshes," you can import it into Unreal with a complete texture.

TUTORIAL 19.2: Creating a Mesh and Preparing for UV Layout

1. Start a new scene in Maya. Verify that you're in the Modeling menu set (if not, press F3).

2. Create a polygon cube with a length, width, and height of 64 (see **FIGURE 19.5**). Name the cube `Dice`.

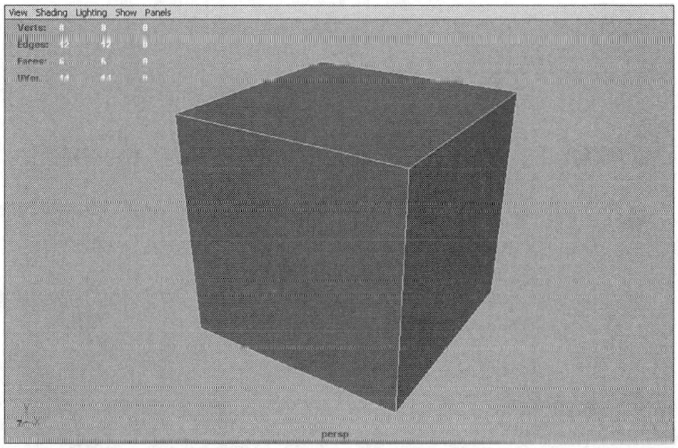

FIGURE 19.5 The cube that will become your `Dice`.

3. With the cube selected, choose Edit Polygons > Bevel > options box from the menu. In the Bevel Options dialog box, set the Offset value to 6, and click Bevel. This creates an extra set of faces at the corners of the cube, which round it out without adding too much detail (see **FIGURE 19.6**).

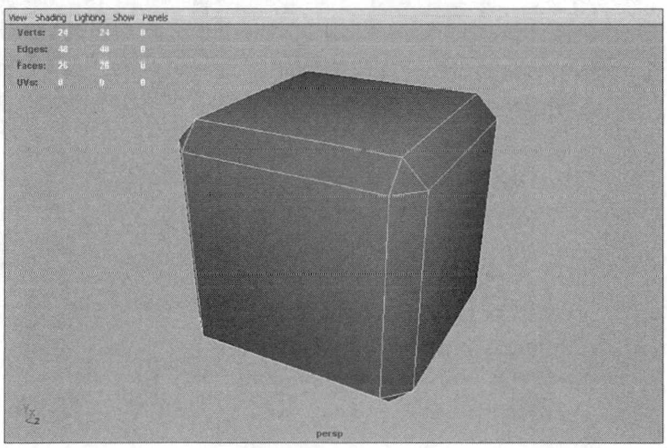

FIGURE 19.6 The edges of the cube have been beveled to create a simple rounding.

4. The bevel action has caused the cube to lose its UVs, so you need to create them from scratch. You can verify this by selecting the `Dice` and opening the UV Texture Editor from the Window menu.

   For now, you'll just create a simple mapping to use as a reference so that you can tell what has been laid out and what has not. To do this, select the `Dice` and choose Edit Polygons > Texture > Planar Map > options box from the menu. Make sure the Fit to Best Plane option is enabled, and click Project. This creates a single map that includes all the faces.

5. Select the `Dice` in Object mode, and open the UV Texture Editor. You see the UV layout for the object, which looks similar to an orthographic view.
6. Press F12 to make UVs selectable, and then draw a marquee selection across all the UVs in the UV Texture Editor. Try the Move, Rotate, and Scale tools to see how they work on the UV selection. When you're finished, move the UVs to the side, outside the 0–1 texture space. You'll be using these UVs only as a starting point for your layout. With that, your `Dice` is ready to create the UV layout. Save the file as `UnrealDice`.

END TUTORIAL 19.2

As mentioned earlier, there's no right or wrong way to lay out an object's UVs. There are some fundamental guidelines to consider, however, and they are explained as you come across them in subsequent tutorials. In **TUTORIAL 19.3**, you create a simple UV layout for the static mesh created in **TUTORIAL 19.2**.

TUTORIAL 19.3: Creating a UV Layout for the Static Mesh

1. Continue from **TUTORIAL 19.2**, or open the file you saved at the end of that tutorial. You're going to create a UV layout that you can paint in Photoshop.
2. In the Perspective viewport, press F11 to make faces selectable. Select the face at the top of the `Dice`. From the Edit Polygons menu, choose Texture > Planar Map.
3. Open the UV Texture Editor. Notice the interesting manipulator visible on the mapped UVs (see **FIGURE 19.7**). It's a combination of the Move, Rotate, and Scale tools. You can use the arrows or the small blue ring in the center to move. The arc in the middle is for rotation. The three squares are

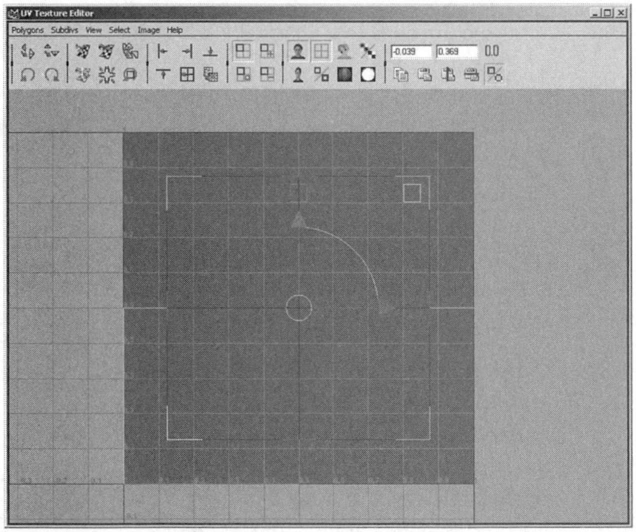

FIGURE 19.7 This manipulator becomes available when you create mappings.

used for scaling in U, V, or U and V simultaneously. Areas on the border of the manipulator, such as at the corners, are pale blue, red, or green. They are used for a special type of scaling that enables you to expand the manipulator without affecting the other sides.

4. Move and scale the selected face so that its lower-left corner is at the UV coordinates 0.4, 0.7. Place the upper-right corner at the coordinates 0.6, 0.9. You can use the numeric entry fields in the toolbar, or simply use the Move tool with grid snapping activated to help. Make sure the piece remains a perfect square, as in **FIGURE 19.8**.
5. Now, select the bottommost face of the `Dice` and apply planar mapping to it. Adjust the face so that it's aligned with the grid, exactly one grid space to the right of the first face you mapped (see **FIGURE 19.9**).

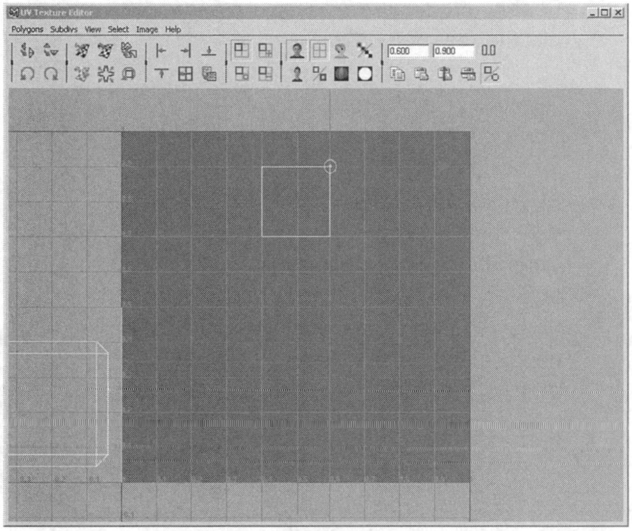

FIGURE 19.8 The first face of the `Dice` is now laid out.

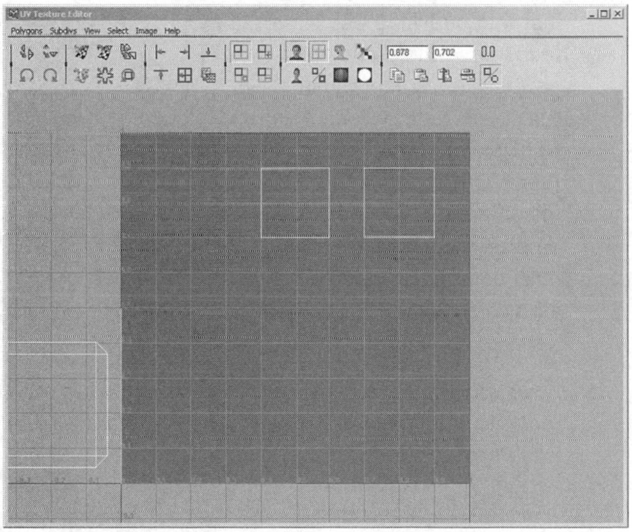

FIGURE 19.9 Two faces are now laid out.

6. Continue this pattern to lay out the rest of the `Dice` object's major faces. After you map a face, always place the face on the opposite side next to it. For example, place the left and right faces next to each other and the front and back faces next to each other. When finished, you should have something similar to **FIGURE 19.10**.

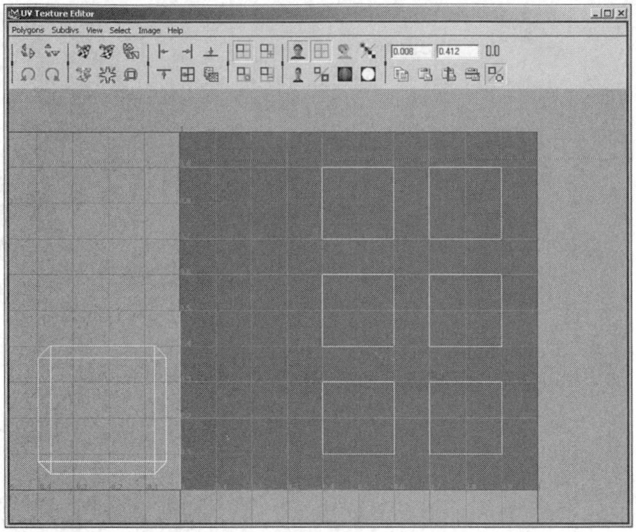

FIGURE 19.10 The major faces of the `Dice` object are now laid out.

7. In the UV Texture Editor, move and scale the remaining UVs that are still outside the UV Texture Editor so that they fit in the area to the right of the major faces you just laid out. All these corner faces have the same color, so their placement is not that important. In fact, if you want to, you could scale them down so that they fit inside a single pixel. Whatever color that single pixel contains is spread across all the UV faces that were scaled into the area.

8. Save your work. Now you're ready to take this UV layout into Photoshop.

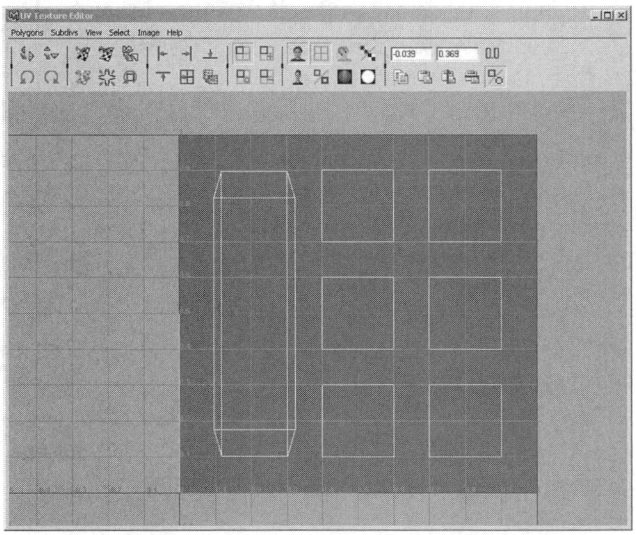

FIGURE 19.11 All the faces of the `Dice` are completely laid out.

END TUTORIAL 19.3

Creating Textures from UV Layouts

Now that you have seen how to create a UV layout for your object, you need to learn how this layout can be used to create a texture in an external paint application, such as Photoshop. You won't, however, import the texture into Unreal, as the methods for this process have already been covered in Chapter 9, "Interactive Elements." In **TUTORIAL 19.4**, you import the UV layout created in Maya into Photoshop to create a texture.

TUTORIAL 19.4: Exporting Your UVs into Photoshop

1. Continue from **TUTORIAL 19.3**, or open the file you saved at the end of that tutorial. You're going to import the UV layout you created into Photoshop so that you can create a texture with it.

2. With the `Dice` selected, go to the UV Texture Editor. From the Polygons menu, choose UV Snapshot. Set the File Name text box to a path and name you can easily locate. Set the size in X and Y to 512. The Color Value setting controls what color the lines of the UV layout are. Because the background is always black, stick with white for the UV layout lines. Also, make sure the image format is set to Targa (see **FIGURE 19.12**). Click OK when done.

3. Open Photoshop, and open the Targa file you just created from the same path used in the UV Snapshot dialog box. You see the same thing you saw in the 0–1 texture space in Maya's UV Texture Editor, except that the image is white UVs on a black background.

4. As a rule, you should never paint on your UV snapshot, so create a new layer over the background layer. Name this layer `DiceColor`.

5. With the new layer selected, use the Paint Bucket tool and fill the layer with white. Bring the layer's opacity down to about 90% so that you can barely see where the UVs exist.

6. Remember how you mapped first one side of the `Dice` object and then the opposite side? On real dice, numbers on opposite sides always add up to seven. With that in mind, make a series of dots in the laid out UVs that coincide with the dots on an actual set of dice. Use **FIGURE 19.13** if you need help.

7. Set the opacity for the DiceColor layer back to 100%. Save your work as a new Targa file with the name `DiceTextureComplete`. Choose 32-bit when prompted how to save the Targa file.

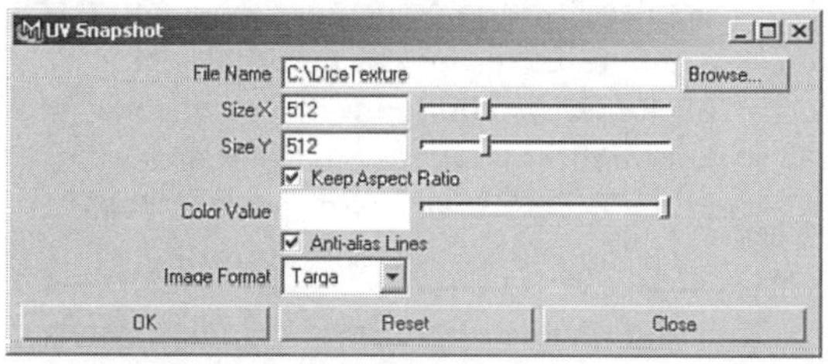

FIGURE 19.12 These are the settings you need in the UV Snapshot dialog box.

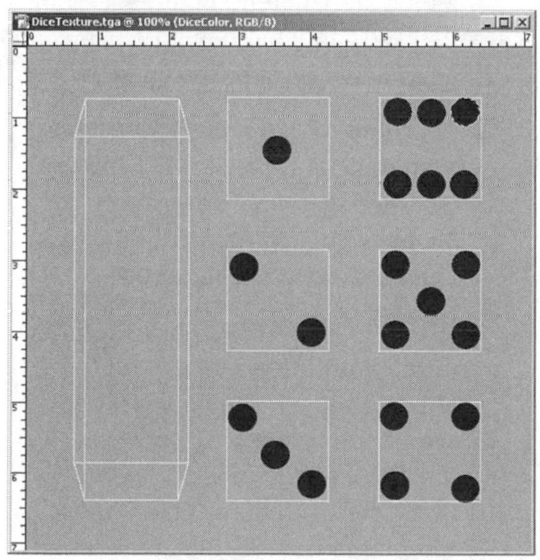

FIGURE 19.13 Here is the dot pattern for your layout. Note that the DiceColor layer has been lightened a bit for clarity.

END TUTORIAL 19.4

Because you already know how to create new textures for materials (covered in Chapter 8, "Creating Materials in Unreal") and because you have yet to learn how to get Maya models into Unreal as static meshes, in **TUTORIAL 19.5**, you simply add the texture to the object in Maya. After you read Chapter 20, "Static Meshes," you'll know everything you need to know to create static meshes and import a custom texture based on UV layouts.

TUTORIAL 19.5: Applying the New Texture

1. Return to Maya. Open the Maya file you saved in **TUTORIAL 19.3**, if it's not open already.

2. Right-click on the object, and from the marking menu, choose Material > Assign New Material > Lambert. This creates a new Lambert material, applies it to the object, and opens the Attribute Editor for the new material. Click the Map button (with the checkered pattern) next to the Color slider. In the Create Render Node dialog box, click the File texture button.

> **NOTE**
>
> **You can also disconnect the nodes by typing the following Maya Embedded Language (MELScript) line into the command line at the bottom of the interface:**
>
> ```
> disconnectAttr file1.outTransparency lambert2.transparency;
> ```
>
> **This line performs the same function as removing the wire between the two nodes.**

> **NOTE**
>
> **Because the texture's placement now depends on the UVs, you can delete the Place2DTexture node from the Lambert2 network. It has no effect on the final object.**

3. In the Attribute Editor, next to Image Name, is a small button with a folder icon. Click this button, and navigate to the `DiceTextureComplete.tga` texture you finished in **TUTORIAL 19.4**.

4. If you press 6 on the keyboard, you'll notice that the object seems to be almost completely transparent, but this is nothing to worry about. The reason it looks transparent is that the Targa file has an alpha channel to control its transparency. Maya noticed the alpha channel and took the liberty of assigning its data to the Transparency attribute.

5. You need to break the connection from the File texture to the material's Transparency. Open the Hypershade window. Right-click on Lambert2, and choose Graph Network.

6. In the Work Area of the Hypershade, you see the network from the shader. Note that between the File1 and Lambert2 nodes, there are two connections: The top one is feeding the color, and the bottom is feeding the transparency (see **FIGURE 19.14**).

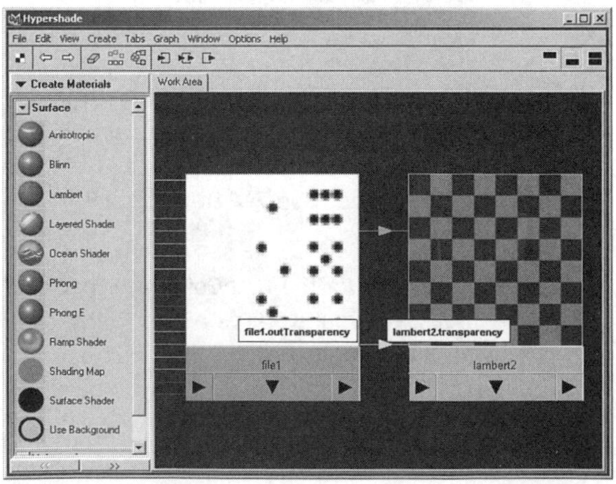

FIGURE 19.14 **The two nodes of the shader, with two connections between.**

Click on the bottom connection wire. The tooltip should say it connects from file1.outTransparency to lambert2.transparency. With the wire selected, press the Backspace or Delete key to break the connection between the nodes, allowing you to see the `Dice` clearly in the viewport (see **FIGURE 19.15**).

7. Save your work. After Chapter 20, "Static Meshes," you'll be able to bring this Dice into Unreal and use it as a new decoration in your levels.

FIGURE 19.15 The `Dice`'s texture can now be seen because the connection from the alpha channel to the transparency has been broken.

END TUTORIAL 19.5

One of the most important things to remember about UVs is that they can be overlapped to repeat a texture on a surface. This process can be a little difficult to picture at first, so in **TUTORIAL 19.6**, you see how it works.

TUTORIAL 19.6: Overlapping UVs

1. Continue from **TUTORIAL 19.5**, or open the file you saved at the end of that tutorial.
2. Select the `Dice` object, and open the UV Texture Editor. You see the texture you created in Photoshop in the background. If necessary, switch off the background image to make it easier to see the UVs.
3. You have six squares of UVs that make up the sides of the `Dice`. For this tutorial, you place each square on top of the square that's in the upper left, which is the side with one dot. One at a time, place the other five squares on top of the first square. You can snap the vertices if you like, but for this example, precision is not vital. In **FIGURES 19.16** and **19.17**,

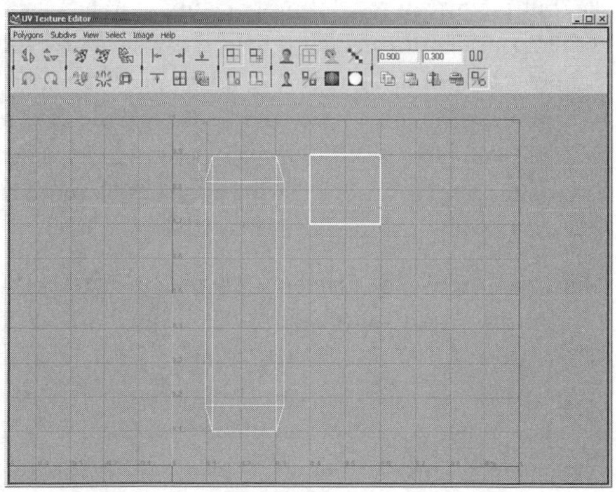

FIGURE 19.16 All six squares have been "stacked" onto the area with the one dot.

you can see what this looks like in the UV Texture Editor and the viewport.

4. Save your work. Remember that you can think of UVs in the UV Texture Editor as points that sample areas of the texture. Moving the UVs around causes your object to sample different parts of the texture at the locations those UVs have on the surface.

FIGURE 19.17 The result of overlapping these UVs is that the texture repeats on the surface.

> **NOTE**
>
> If you can, watch the viewport as you move the UV squares. You see the texture shift along the surface of the `Dice` until each side contains a single dot.

END TUTORIAL 19.6

UV Layouts for Characters

At this point, you have created a basic UV layout for a static mesh. Character UV layouts are similar, but often require a lot more planning. When creating a UV layout for your character, you should consider three major points. First, you'll probably have an easier time if you begin the layout process by drafting your layout on a piece of paper. This gives you a map that you can follow as to where certain pieces should be. Second, develop a standard layout for your characters. For example, you place faces for a character's right leg in generally the same location for the UV layouts of all your characters. Having a standard layout makes it easier for you or your texture artist when it's time to paint a texture.

Third, you should consider how you plan to use the textures on your character. All the characters available in Unreal Tournament 2004 include two textures: one for the main body, which is usually at a resolution of 1024×1024, and a separate texture just for the head, also at 1024×1024. Having these two textures serves two purposes. First, it allows for highly detailed faces and heads because all the texture's resolution is used to color only the head. Second, it makes it possible to create several different characters by using the same model and body textures. The end result is as though you had several different characters wearing the same uniform or one character wearing different uniforms.

In **TUTORIALS 19.7** and **19.8**, you take a look at how to lay out some of a character's UVs. The entire character layout process isn't covered, however, as it's typically a slow process involving repeating many of the same techniques.

TUTORIAL 19.7: Laying Out the UVs of a Character's Shirt

1. In Maya, open the `CharacterComplete.mb` file, which contains a completed character model. If you check the UV Texture Editor, you can see that the character's UVs are completely haywire right now.

2. Select the character, and choose Edit Polygons > Texture > Planar Mapping > options box from the main menu. In the Polygon Planar Projection Options dialog box, enable the Fit to Bounding Box option and select Z Axis to create a planar projection of the entire character (see **FIGURE 19.18**). Click the Project button when you're done.

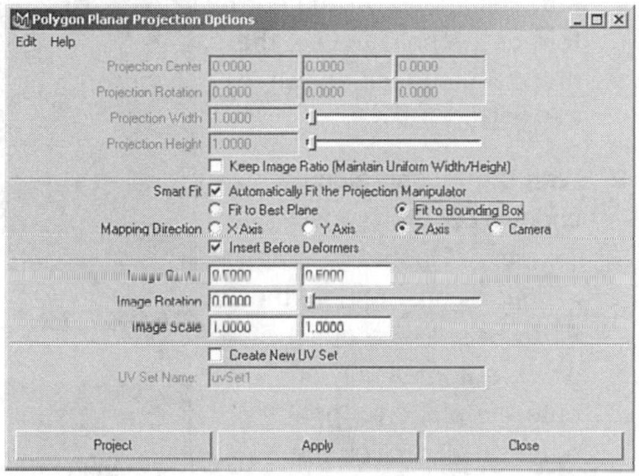

FIGURE 19.18 You can use these settings for your initial planar projection.

> **NOTE**
>
> At this point, you could use the Polygons > Layout UVs command from the UV Texture Editor's menu, and you would get a basic but relatively usable layout. This method is sometimes useful when you need to quickly texture a character or object that isn't seen often or not up close.

3. Open the UV Texture Editor, and take a look at what you've done. The character's UVs are very similar to what the character would look like in the Front orthographic view. Using an initial mapping of this type gives you a guide for what parts have been mapped and what parts have not.

   Move and scale the UVs a bit, and place them outside the 0–1 texture space, as shown in **FIGURE 19.19**.

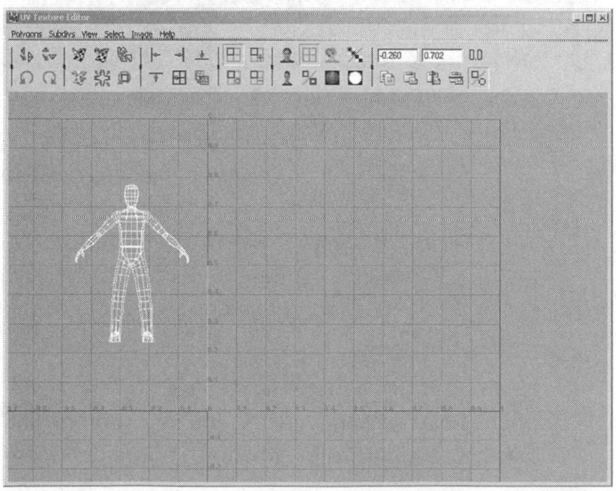

FIGURE 19.19 This initial planar map is just a reminder of which parts have yet to be laid out.

4. Back in the viewport, switch to Face component mode by pressing F11. Select the faces on the front of the character's shirt. Make sure you select only faces

that are relatively planar to each other, meaning that the faces should meet each other at a very slight angle whenever possible. This helps avoid texture stretching later. At the bottom of the shirt, select the first 16 faces, as shown in **FIGURE 19.20**.

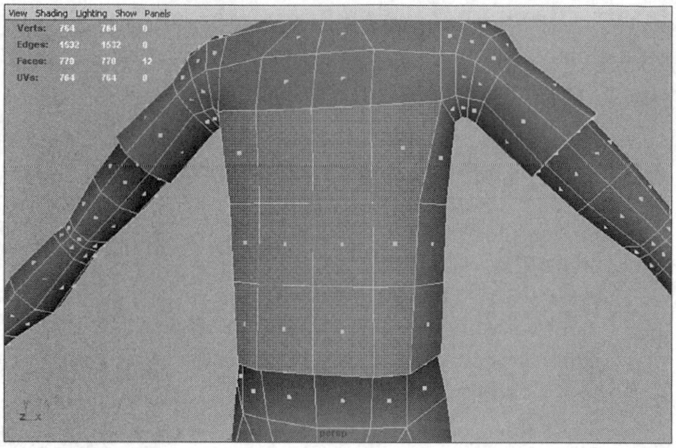

FIGURE 19.20 Faces selected for the next mapping.

5. With the faces selected, choose Edit Polygons > Texture > Planar Mapping > options box. Enable the Fit to Best Plane option, which automatically orients the plane for optimum results. Click the Project button when finished.

6. Back in the UV Texture Editor, move, rotate, and scale the newly mapped faces so that they're somewhere within the 0–1 texture space (see **FIGURE 19.21**). The placement doesn't really matter now; you can always move them around later. Notice that the faces you just mapped have been moved off the original planar map.

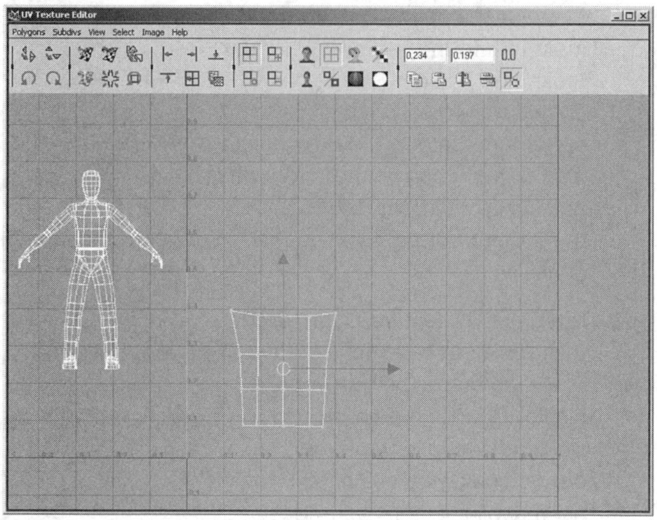

FIGURE 19.21 The first faces of the shirt have been mapped and positioned.

7. In the viewport, select the next row of faces on the shirt, and make another planar map. In the UV Texture Editor, rotate and scale these newly mapped faces so that they're directly above the last set you mapped. Be sure to scale them to a size relative to the faces you mapped earlier.

   When you first map the new faces, you can't see the last mapping you created because when you're selecting faces, you can see only the faces that are selected. Right-click over the new mapping, and choose UVs from the marking menu. Some of these new UVs are probably overlapping some of your older mappings, as in **FIGURE 19.22**.

8. In this situation, you can use a special selection operation for UVs: selecting a separate piece, or shell. Select a single UV vertex of the four faces you just mapped, and choose Select > Select Shell from the UV Texture Editor menu. This command automatically selects all the UVs in that piece, which makes selecting overlapping UV pieces easy. With the piece selected, move and scale it into position over the first 12 faces you mapped earlier (see **FIGURE 19.23**).

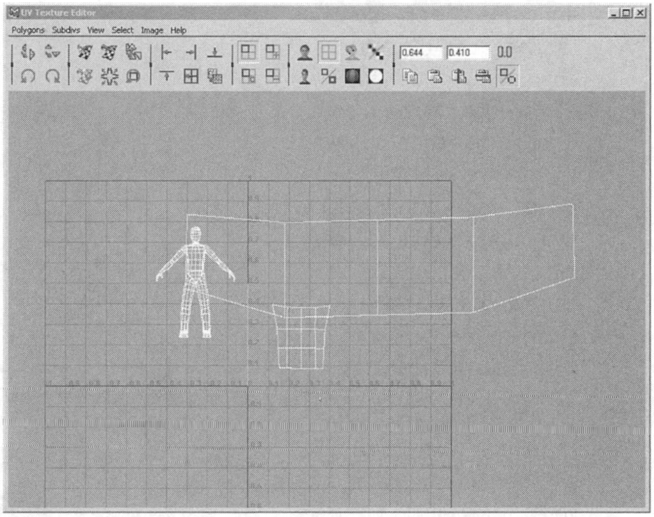

FIGURE 19.22 The new mapping for the four faces of the chest overlaps the other UVs, making it difficult to select specific UVs.

9. You now have a gap between these two pieces. Gaps between UV pieces can lead to seams in the texture, so you should go ahead and remove them. Keep in mind that you can't always remove every gap between your UV pieces. Inevitably, you'll have gaps somewhere. Just do your best to have them fall in places where a seam would be less likely to be noticed, such as on the shirt's sides and under the arms.

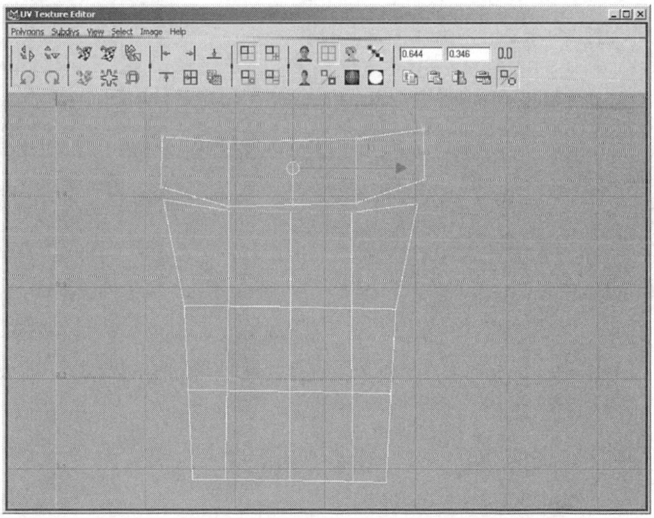

FIGURE 19.23 The next set of UVs has been moved above the first.

To close the gap between these two pieces, you use the Sew UVs command. Press F9 to make edges selectable. Select one edge at the bottom of the most recent mapping. Notice how the corresponding edge beneath it is automatically selected, too, because these two edges are, in fact, the same edge on the model. Choose Polygons > Sew UVs from the UV Texture Editor menu. You'll see the two edges merge together into one. Repeat this step to sew up the seam between the two pieces (see **FIGURE 19.24**).

10. Repeat the steps for making planar maps and sewing them together until you have a single piece that represents the front of the shirt (see **FIGURE 19.25**). You can then make a separate piece that forms the back of the shirt, or if you prefer, make a single piece that's the whole shirt. This piece would be like making a cut on either side of the shirt, from the bottom, through the armpit, and to the bottom of the end of the sleeve. You could then open the shirt up and lay it flat.

11. Save your work. You could use these methods to move around the entire character, laying out all the UVs you find.

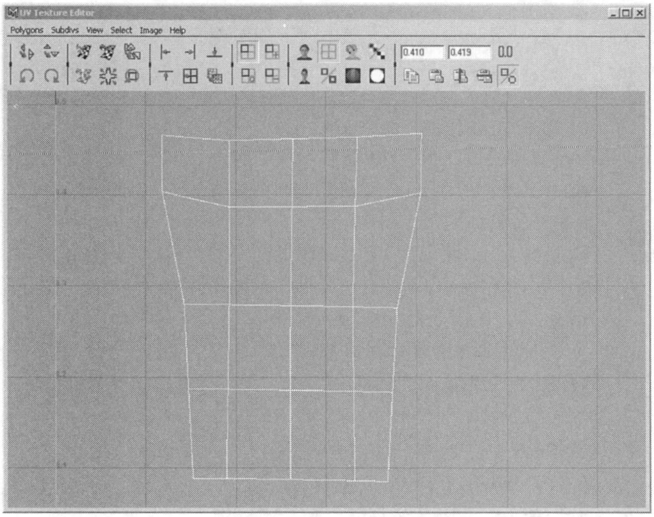

FIGURE 19.24 The two pieces of the shirt have been sewn together.

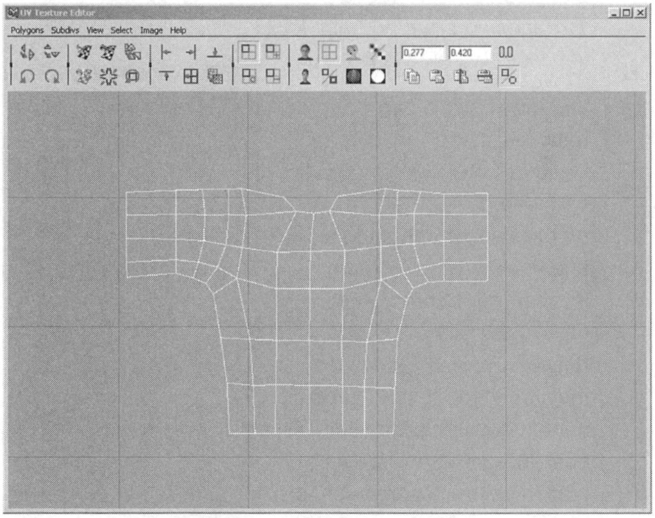

FIGURE 19.25 The UVs of the front of the shirt have been laid out.

You can try the other mapping methods discussed earlier. In **TUTORIAL 19.8**, you'll try using a cylindrical map around the faces of the character's leg.

NOTE

Remember when making your planar maps to select faces that are already close to being planar to each other. This technique helps avoid texture distortions later.

END TUTORIAL 19.7

TUTORIAL 19.8: Using a Cylindrical Map for a UV Layout

1. Continue from **TUTORIAL 19.7**. You're going to lay out the UVs for one of the character's legs.

2. First, select all the faces around the character's left leg (see **FIGURE 19.26**). You can make several marquee selections while holding the Shift and Ctrl keys, or you can use the Paint Selection tool, found under the Edit menu. This tool enables you to select components in a paintbrush fashion across your model.

3. With the faces selected, choose Edit Polygons > Texture > Cylindrical Mapping to create a wireframe cylinder to be used for the map. To begin using it, MMB-drag one of the red handles midway along the cylinder. This enables you to close the cylinder's sweep (circumference).

4. At the middle of the cylinder, MMB-drag the red ring to rotate the cylinder so that its seam runs along the inside of the character's leg (see **FIGURE 19.27**). If possible, watch the UV Texture Editor while you're doing this to help prevent obvious texture seams on the leg.

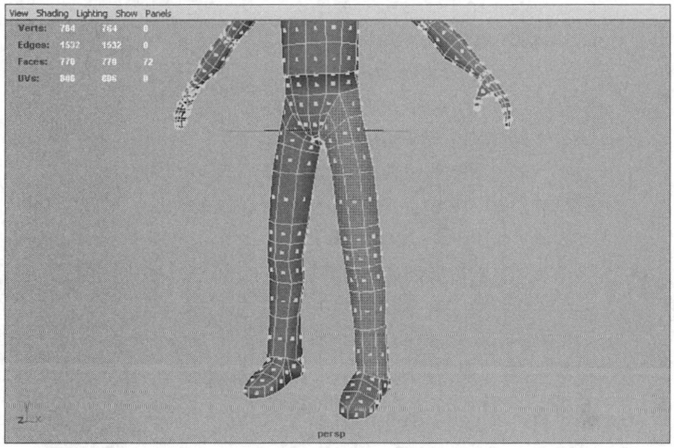

FIGURE 19.26 All faces of the leg have been selected.

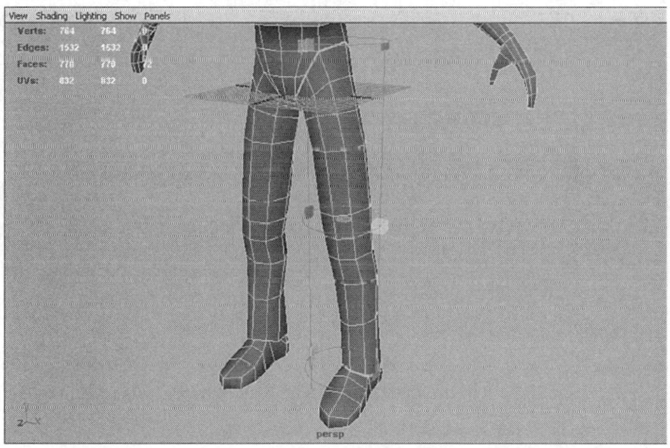

FIGURE 19.27 The Cylindrical Mapping manipulator is surrounding the leg.

5. At the bottom of the Cylindrical Mapping manipulator is a small red cross. MMB-click it to activate a new manipulator that's similar to the Move/Rotate/Scale tool. Use it to rotate the entire cylinder in the X-axis so that it's aligned more with the angle of the leg. A rotation of about -5 degrees should do. Look at your results in the UV Texture Editor (see **FIGURE 19.28**).

6. You can repeat this process with the right leg and both arms. Combining the skills you learned in **TUTORIAL 19.7**, you could then create your own UV layout.

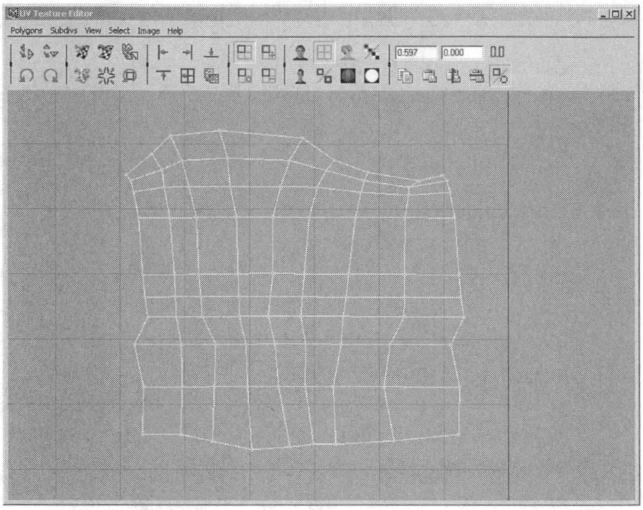

FIGURE 19.28 The UVs of the leg have been cylindrically mapped and are ready to be laid out.

END TUTORIAL 19.8

Considerations for UV Layouts

Remember that laying out UVs for a character isn't the kind of process you're going to finish in a matter of minutes or even hours. Creating an efficient UV layout is a skill that comes with practice and effort. The following list offers a few pointers, however, that should help you as you get started:

- Go slow. Don't rush by mapping several faces at the same time and just fitting them in wherever you can.
- Be organized. Don't just sling your mappings into the texture space. Have a plan when you begin, and try to follow it.
- Use as much of the texture space as you can. Typically, your texture is 1024×1024. Any gaps in your pieces are a waste of precious pixels. Try to keep everything as tight as possible.

- Keep UV face sizes in relation to their polygonal counterparts. This guideline can be confusing, but think about it: If a single face of your model is very small, you don't want that face to take up half your available texture space. Keeping the sizes of polygon faces and faces relative in the UV Texture Editor prevents your texture from becoming distorted.
- You can place the UVs of your character's head so that they stretch across the entire 0–1 texture space, even though they overlap other UVs. This is because you're usually placing a separate face texture on the head anyway.
- Practice and use as many of the tools in the UV Texture Editor as you can, especially those in the View menu. Hiding what you're not working on makes your life far easier when working on UV layouts.
- Don't be hard on yourself. UV layouts are an art form that no one just knows spontaneously. Becoming skilled at UV layouts takes a lot of time and effort.

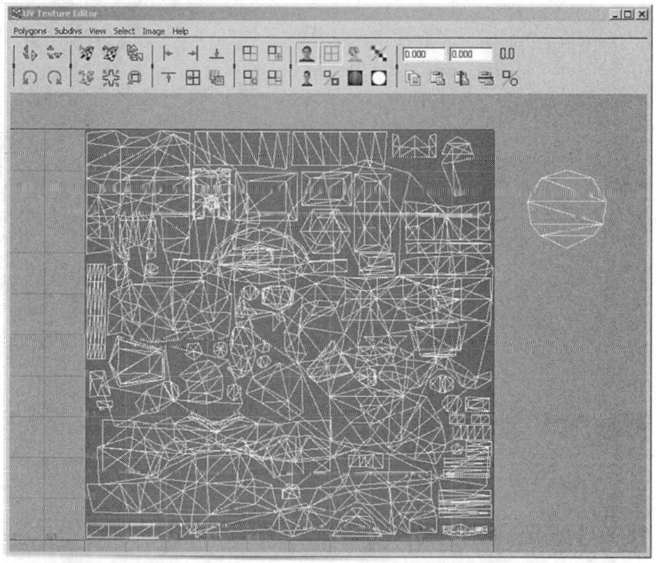

FIGURE 19.29 The UV layout for an official Unreal Tournament 2004 character.

As an example, **FIGURE 19.29** shows the UV layout for the Jugg character in Unreal Tournament 2004, such as Gorge. Notice that it's broken up into many pieces—so many pieces, in fact, that differentiating one piece from the next is hard. On the other hand, you can also see that it uses almost every pixel of the texture area, so the character can be covered with as much texture as

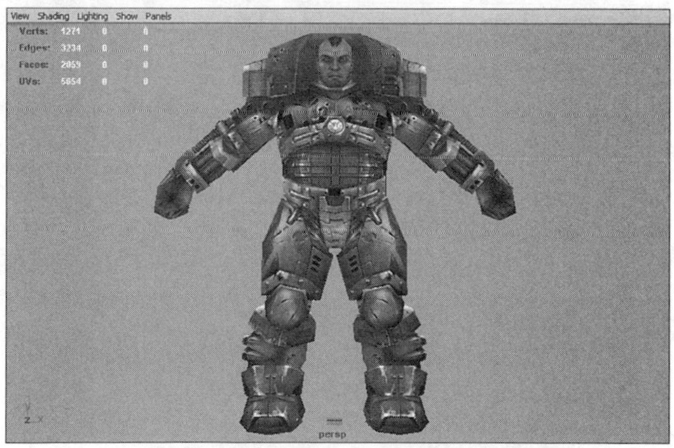

FIGURE 19.30 The same Unreal Tournament 2004 character whose UV layout is shown in **FIGURE 19.29**.

possible. Obviously, this layout required a lot of planning and work to ensure that the texture artist knows which pieces of the UV layout correspond with what parts of the character. Also, notice a piece that sits outside the 0–1 texture space. This piece is making use of the fact that textures repeat as you go outside the 0–1 texture space. **FIGURES 19.30** and **19.31** show the character with his texture applied and what the texture looks like in the UV Texture Editor.

FIGURE 19.31 The texture used on the character, as seen in the UV Texture Editor.

Summary

In this chapter, you've taken a look at several aspects of creating a UV layout for your character. You learned how to use the UV Texture Editor, a variety of mapping methods, and several tools you can use to lay your UVs out in the 0–1 texture space. Remember that no one can tell you the "right" way to lay out the UVs of your characters or objects. The best way is always the way that's easiest for you to understand and follow.

Chapter 20

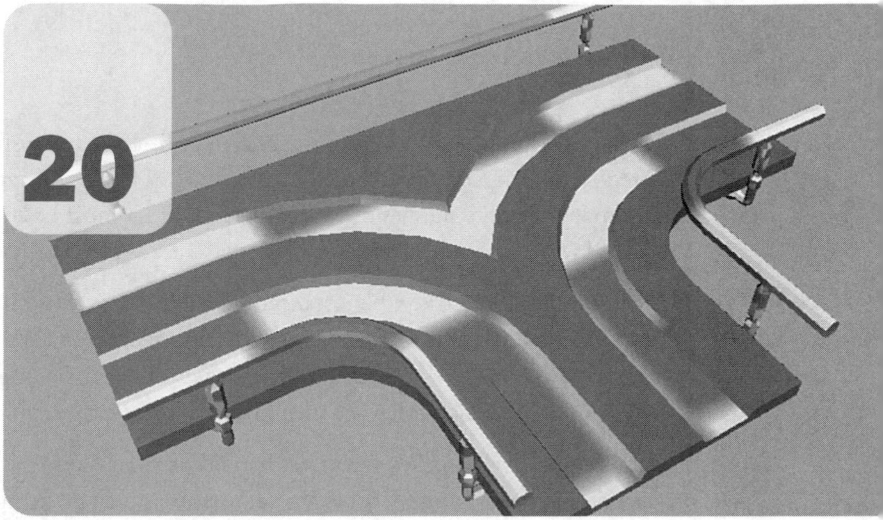

Static Meshes

In this chapter, you learn about static meshes in Unreal and how to create them with Alias Maya. When you finish this chapter, you should have a good understanding of the procedure for creating your own static meshes for your Unreal levels. The bulk of this chapter is dedicated to creating static meshes and getting them into Unreal. Therefore, it's mainly tutorial-based. You begin by reviewing the use of static meshes in Unreal, and then work through a variety of tutorials to construct a series of catwalks that can be used to create continuous walkway networks in Unreal. You also learn about creating collision models to simplify the calculation of player collisions with static meshes. Finally, you learn how to get these meshes into Unreal and use them to create a level.

The Importance of Static Meshes

When playing an Unreal level, static meshes are what provide the bulk of the geometric detail. A *static mesh* is an optimized polygonal model, meant to be instanced (duplicated) throughout your level. The vertex locations of a static mesh are stored in your video card, allowing multiple copies of a single mesh to exist in a level, with virtually no more overhead than the original mesh.

Although the architecture of a static mesh enables you to create multiple instances of a single mesh, you must be aware that loading too many *different* meshes negates their advantage. When you bring in a single mesh, all its geometric data is stored in your video card. All subsequent copies of that mesh can be stored as location data. If you have many separate meshes in your level, each mesh must be stored in your video card's memory, which is why newer, more powerful video cards are so important for gaming with the Unreal Engine.

Because a static mesh can be instanced multiple times, you can fill your levels with tremendous amounts of rich detail. Computationally, meshes carry far less overhead than the world geometry of your levels. In fact, many levels made with the Unreal Engine are mostly composed of massive, open BSP shells, which are then filled with static meshes to create the actual physical detail.

Static meshes are also used for more than decoration. Many static meshes are designed with more practical purposes in mind. For example, you can make a static mesh to generate walkways or lifts to help players move throughout your levels. Later in this chapter, you see how to create a series of catwalks that can be snapped together to create an intricate series of walkways throughout your levels.

Preparing to Model

As mentioned in Chapter 3, "Creating Your First Level with UnrealEd," the grid is important when working in UnrealEd. Your BSP brushes and static meshes look much better if they are accurately snapped and aligned to the grid, so you should make sure your Maya models are created on a similar grid. In the following sections, you see how to set up Maya's grid for easy transfer of models from Maya to Unreal. You also learn how to create a new Maya project to help organize how your files are saved.

Adjusting the Grid

As a reminder, one Maya unit is equal to one Unreal unit. As you have seen in Unreal, the grid is always divided into multiples or factors of 16. You can establish the same setup in Maya by adjusting the default grid. In **TUTORIAL 20.1**, you change Maya's grid to match the UnrealEd grid exactly. By doing this, you can create meshes that snap exactly from end to end so that you can create a seamless series of catwalks.

TUTORIAL 20.1: Setting Up the Grid

1. When you open Maya, you see the default grid. You *could* use this grid to construct your static meshes, but you would probably need to scale them up after you import them into Unreal. Instead, you'll make the grid larger.
2. From the main menu, choose Display > Grid > options box to open the Grid Options dialog box.
3. Using the formula discussed earlier, you need to set the grid to give you one major line every 16 units. In the Grid Lines Every text box, enter **16**. You also need to enlarge the grid as a whole. In the Length and Width text box, enter **1024** (see **FIGURE 20.1**). You can also adjust

the grid line colors and the number of subdivisions to whatever you're comfortable working with.

4. Click the Apply and Close button at the bottom, and you'll see your new grid. There is, however, a problem: If you try to zoom out far enough to see the entire grid, you'll notice that it chops off in the distance (see **FIGURE 20.2**).

   This cut-off view is caused by the camera's clipping plane. A *clipping plane* is a two-dimensional plane that hides everything behind it. To see the entire grid, you need to push this clipping plane back farther.

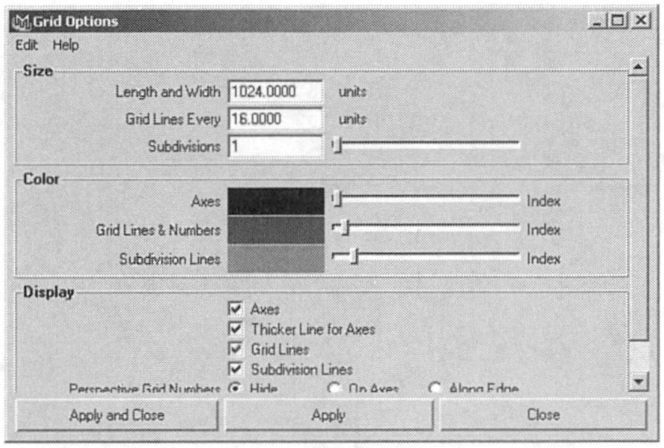

FIGURE 20.1 Updated settings in the Grid Options dialog box.

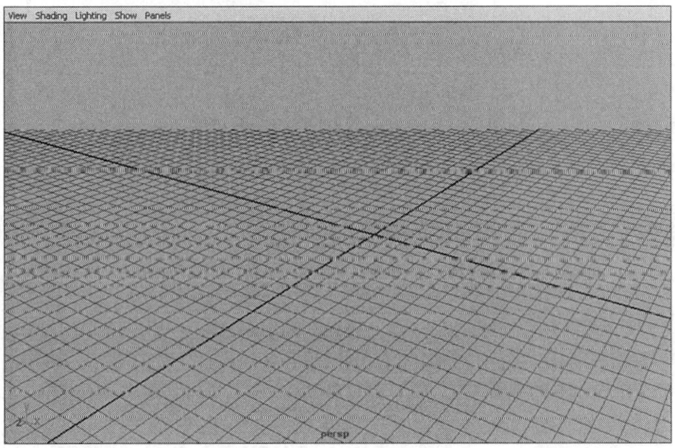

FIGURE 20.2 Viewport showing the newly resized grid.

5. From the Perspective viewport's menu, choose View > Camera Attribute Editor.

6. Under the Camera Attributes category, set the Far Clip Plane attribute to **`4000`** (see **FIGURE 20.3**).

   You can immediately see the entire grid surface, as shown in **FIGURE 20.4**.

7. Repeat steps 6 and 7 for each orthographic view.

8. Save this scene as **`UnrealModeling.mb`**.

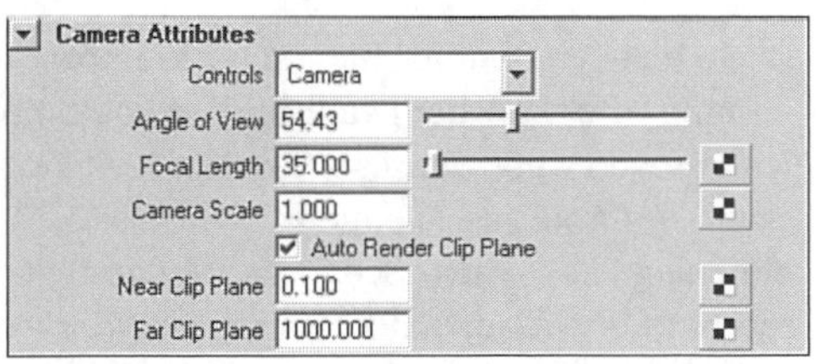

FIGURE 20.3 Far Clip Plane attribute.

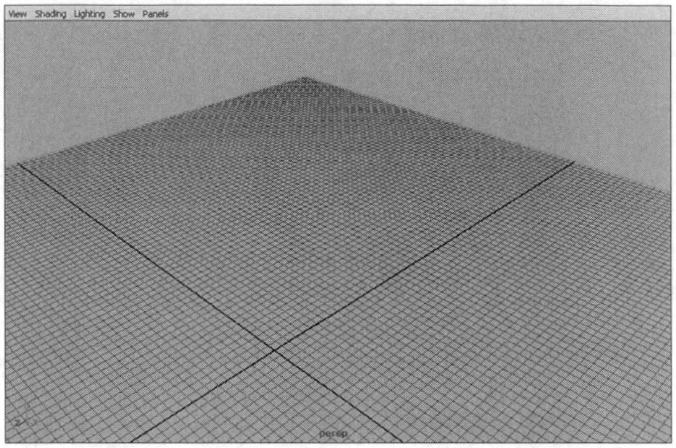

FIGURE 20.4 Viewport with the proper falloff.

END TUTORIAL 20.1

Creating a Project

When using Maya, creating a project is the easiest way to control how and where your files are saved as you work. If you don't create a project, all files are stored in a default folder, making it difficult to discern which files are associated with your current work. In **TUTORIAL 20.2**, you learn how to establish a project in Maya to store files for your static mesh models.

TUTORIAL 20.2: Setting Up Your Project

1. Continue from **TUTORIAL 20.1**, or open the `UnrealModeling.mb` file you saved.

2. You begin by setting your project. A project in Maya is simply a way to keep track of where your files are saved when working on a particular scene or a variety of scenes. From the main menu, choose File >Project > New.

3. In the Name text box of the New Project dialog box, enter **`UnrealCatwalkSM`** (see **FIGURE 20.5**). For the location, enter any path you like.

4. Click Accept when finished. You have now created a folder where your files are automatically saved when you use Save or Save Scene As from the File menu. Test this by choosing File > Save Scene As. Notice that the path is already set to your new folder. Save the file as **`GridSetUp.mb`**, and You're ready to begin modeling!

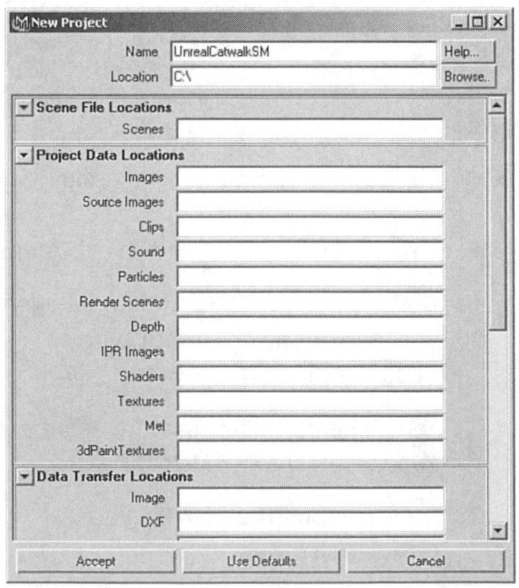

FIGURE 20.5 The New Project dialog box.

END TUTORIAL 20.2

Modeling the Catwalks

Now that you have set up your project and adjusted Maya's default grid, you're ready to begin modeling. In **TUTORIALS 20.3** through **20.19**, you see how to create a series of five different catwalk types. After you import them as static meshes, you can instance them numerous times to create a variety of different catwalk networks. The following subsections focus on the tutorials for creating each different model.

Creating the Base Catwalk

The base catwalk is strictly a Maya model and won't be exported into Unreal. Instead, it's used as a foundation from which to create the other models for your catwalks. In **TUTORIALS 20.3** through **20.9**, you see how to set up this base model.

You also create the placeholder textures for your model. Materials created in Maya cannot be simply transferred to Unreal. However, placing textures on the geometry of your models enables you to control how many material slots are available for your model and which polygons those material slots affect. You'll begin in **TUTORIAL 20.3** by creating the floor of the base catwalk.

TUTORIAL 20.3: Modeling the Floor of the Catwalk

1. Continue from **TUTORIAL 20.2**, or open the `GridSetUp.mb` file you saved earlier.
2. Press F3 to enter the Modeling menu set, and from the main menu, choose Create > Polygon Primitives > Cube > options box. In the Polygon Cube Options dialog box, set the following attributes, and click Create when finished:

   Width: 256

   Height: 16

   Depth: 256

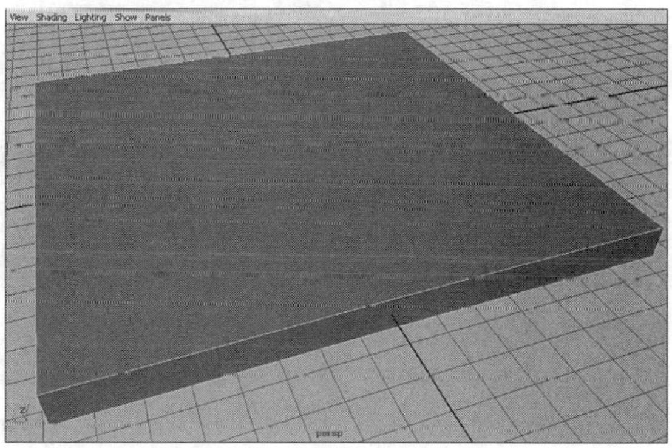

FIGURE 20.6 A polygon cube placed on the grid.

3. The new cube has been created in your viewport. Press 5 to use Shaded mode in the viewport (see **FIGURE 20.6**). Also, in the Channel Box, click the name pCube1, and change it to **`Walkway`**.
4. You'll be adding some physical detail to the walkway. For this, assume that the Z-axis points forward. With the cube selected, press F11 to make faces selectable. Select the face on top of the cube. In the Polygons Shelf, click the Extrude Faces icon. **FIGURE 20.7** shows the Extrude manipulator displayed on the cube.

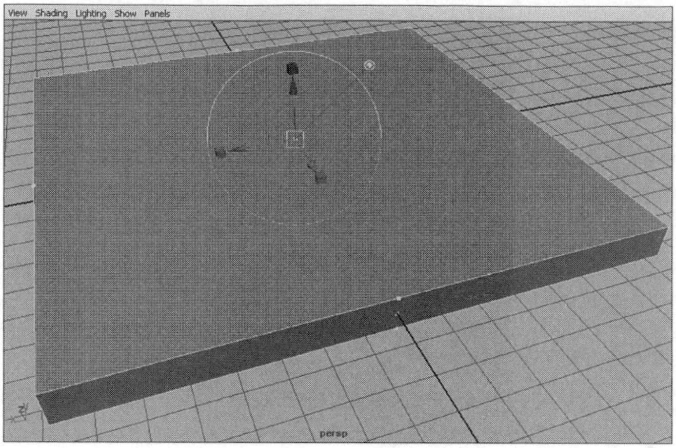

FIGURE 20.7 Polygonal face ready for extrusion.

5. Click the red scale handle on the Extrude manipulator, and scale the face up about 50% (see **FIGURE 20.8**).

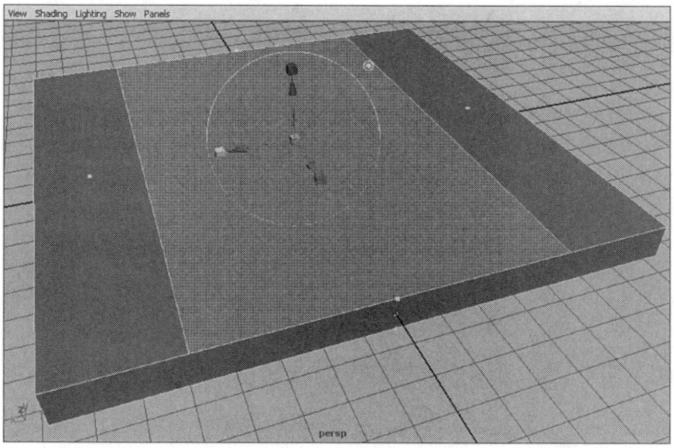

FIGURE 20.8 Polygonal face after first extrusion.

6. Press the G key to repeat the Extrude command. Scale the face down in X, as shown in **FIGURE 20.9**.

7. You should now have five faces across the top of the cube. Select the two faces that straddle the center face (see **FIGURE 20.10**), and press the G key again.

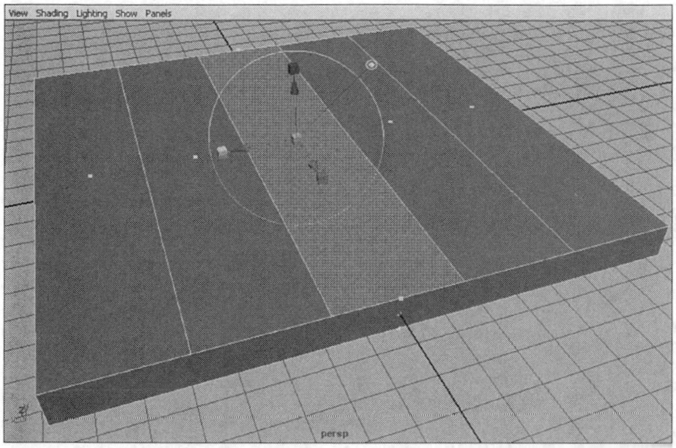

FIGURE 20.9 Polygonal face after second extrusion.

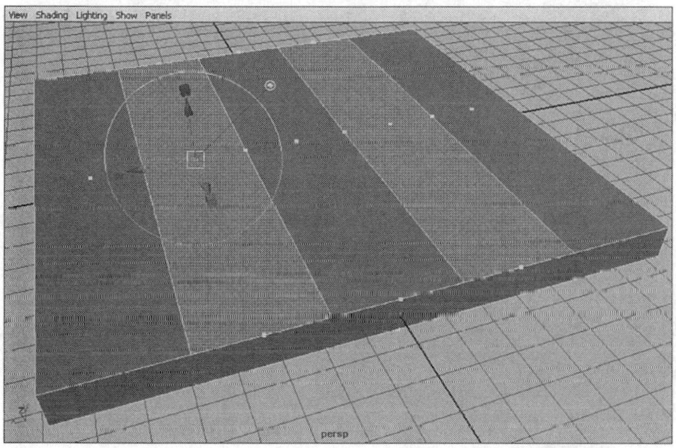

FIGURE 20.10 Two faces selected with the Extrude manipulator showing.

8. Because both faces were selected, using the manipulator changes both faces. Scale the faces down in X slightly, and use the blue arrow to move them both down about 50% into the cube, as shown in **FIGURE 20.11**. This should create two depressions similar to tire tracks.

9. The cube now has several extra faces on its front and back. You need to delete them and replace them with a single face. To do this, switch to the Top view, and select the topmost and bottommost faces in the viewport (see **FIGURE 20.12**). You can do this easily holding down the Shift key and making two marquee selections. After you have the faces selected, press the Delete or Backspace key to remove them.

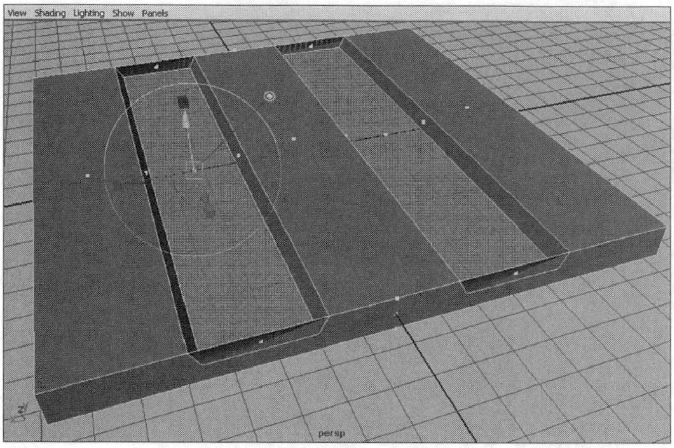

FIGURE 20.11 Cube shape after depressions have been added.

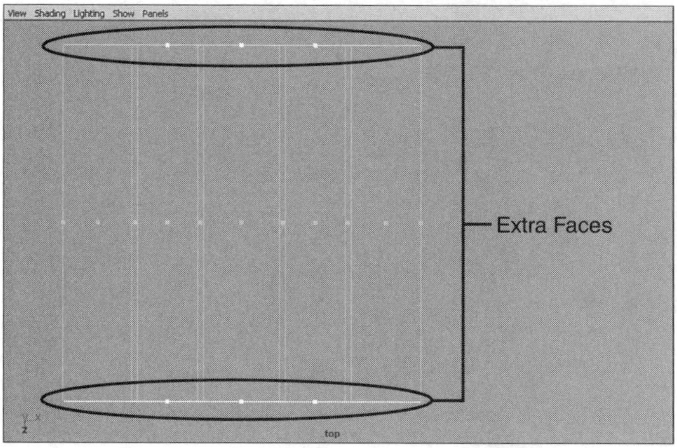

FIGURE 20.12 Faces that need to be deleted.

10. The shape now has a hole on each end. To fill in these holes so that the object looks solid again, press F10 to select edges, and select one edge at each open end (see **FIGURE 20.13**).

From the main menu, choose Edit Polygons > Fill Hole. A single face replaces the holes at the ends of the shape.

11. Delete your shape's construction history by choosing Edit > Delete by Type > History from the main menu. In the Channel Box, set Translate Y to **-8** to place the top of the Walkway at the center of the grid (0,0,0), which is also called the origin (see **FIGURE 20.14**).Finally, save your scene as **`BaseCatwalk.mb`**.

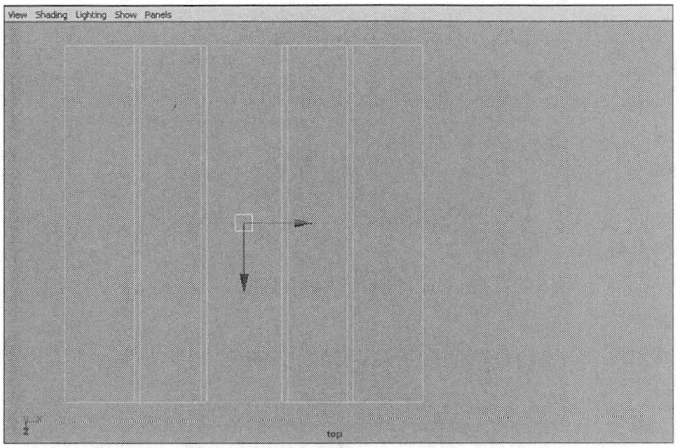

FIGURE 20.13 Two edges have been selected.

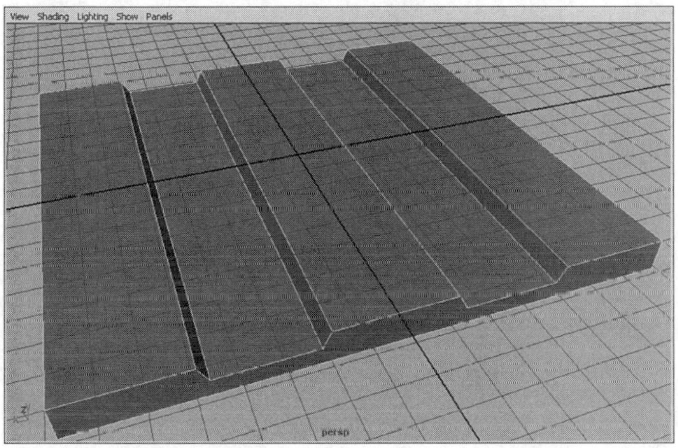

FIGURE 20.14 The floor for your catwalk is now complete.

END TUTORIAL 20.3

Now that the floor for the catwalk is in place, it would be nice to have some handrails. In **TUTORIAL 20.4**, you see how to place cylinder primitives to act as handrails for your model.

TUTORIAL 20.4: Building the Handrails

1. Continue from **TUTORIAL 20.3**, or open the `BaseCatwalk.mb` file you saved. You're going to create two rails to go on either side of the walkway.

2. From the main menu, choose Create > Polygon Primitives > Cylinder > options box. In the Polygon Cylinder Options dialog box, set the following options, and click Create when you're finished:

   Radius: 8

   Height: 256

   Subdivisions Around Axis: 8

   Subdivisions on Caps: 0

   Axis: Z

3. Move the cylinder up in the Y-axis a bit so that it's easier to see (see **FIGURE 20.15**). You need to make some more adjustments to the cylinder in the following steps so that it works properly for some of the functions you'll be doing later.

4. First, the edges on either side of the rail need to be vertical. To do this, you'll rotate the cylinder. With the cylinder selected, switch to the Front view and press the F key to focus on the cylinder (see **FIGURE 20.16**).

5. In the Channel Box, click in the Rotate Z text box, and enter a value of **22.5** (see **FIGURE 20.17**).

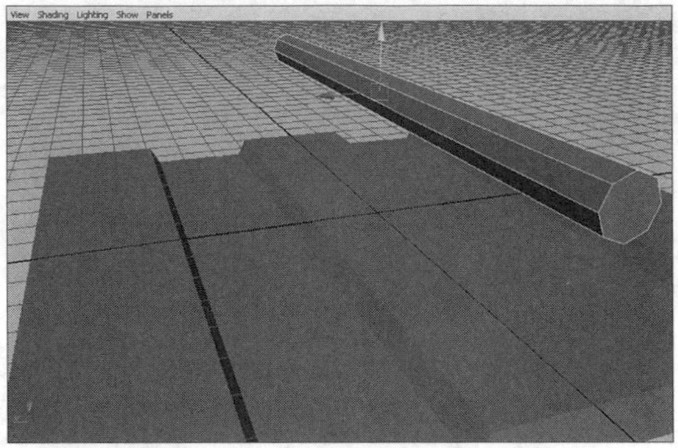

FIGURE 20.15 The cylinder is above the catwalk's base.

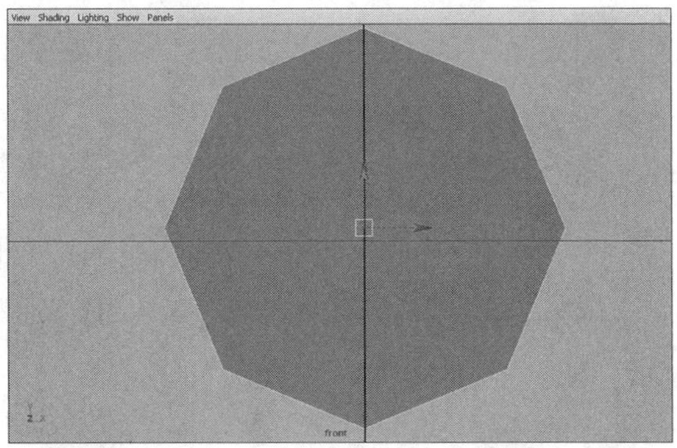

FIGURE 20.16 Focusing on the cylinder.

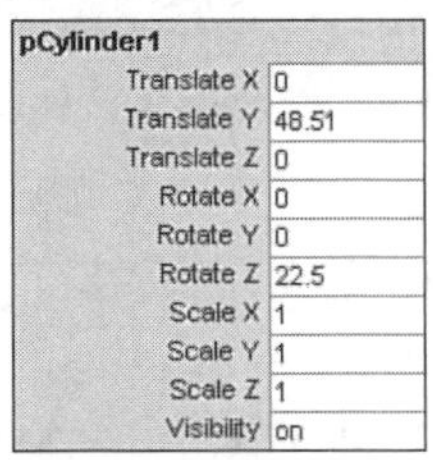

FIGURE 20.17 Channel Box with the new Rotate Z value.

This setting rotates the cylinder so that the faces on the left and right sides are perfectly vertical (see **FIGURE 20.18**), which will help tremendously when you make the 90-degree turn later in this chapter.

6. You need to move the rail into position. However, you need to make sure the rail's upper and outer edges are snapped to the grid. To ensure this, you'll relocate the object's pivot point—the center of its transformation. With the cylinder selected, press the Insert key.

   Notice that the manipulator for the object's pivot point changes into a series of simple lines (see **FIGURE 20.19**). As you move this manipulator, you're relocating the pivot.

7. To move the pivot into position, you'll use snapping—curve snapping, in this example. In the Front view, click the red X-axis of the pivot manipulator, and the axis then turns yellow (see **FIGURE 20.20**).

   With the axis selected, hold down the C key and move the cursor over the leftmost edge of the cylinder. MMB-drag slightly, and the pivot should snap to the left edge (see **FIGURE 20.21**).

8. Now click the vertical green (Y) axis. It should turn yellow, as in step 7. Again, hold down the C key, but place the cursor over the horizontal edge at the top of the cylinder. MMB-drag slightly, and the pivot snaps straight up so that it's even with the top edge (see **FIGURE 20.22**).

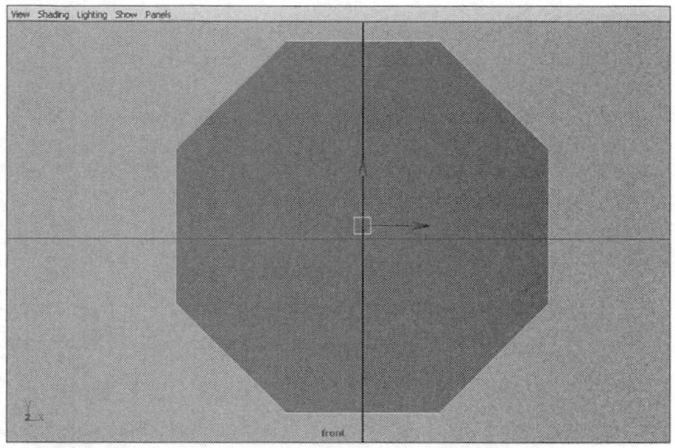

FIGURE 20.18 The cylinder rotated 22.5 degrees in the Z-axis.

FIGURE 20.19 The manipulator's appearance in Pivot Editing mode.

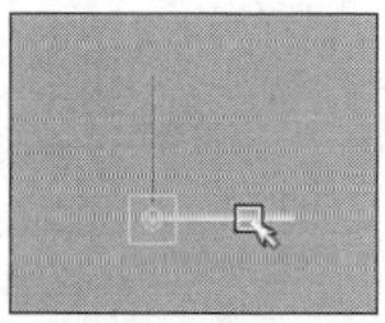

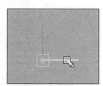

FIGURE 20.20 The manipulator's axis becomes yellow when clicked.

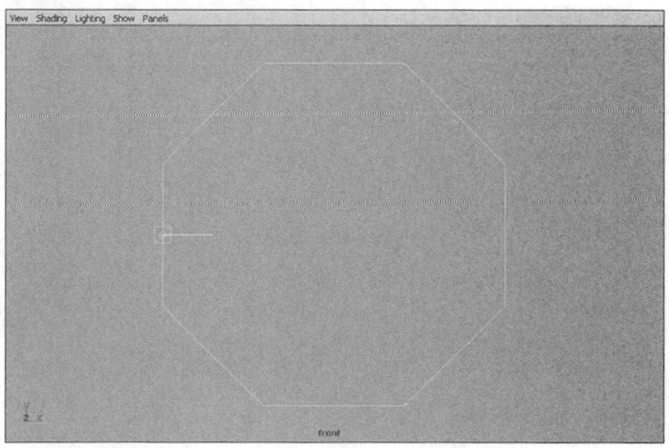

FIGURE 20.21 Manipulator snapped to the cylinder's left edge.

The pivot is now aligned with both the left and top edges. Press the Insert key again so that you can no longer move the pivot.

9. You want the top of the rail to be about 64 units from the top of the Walkway. In the Front view, select the rail. Holding down the X key, place the cursor over the grid intersection that's four grid spaces up and one grid space to the left of the Walkway's edge, as shown in **FIGURE 20.23**.

10. Next, you need to duplicate the rail and place a copy on the other side. With the cylinder selected, press Ctrl+G to place the cylinder in a group with its pivot at the coordinates 0,0,0 (see **FIGURE 20.24**).

11. With the group (named Group1) selected, press Ctrl+D to duplicate the entire group. You should now have Group2 selected. In the Channel Box, set Scale X to **-1** to place the copy exactly on the other side.

12. Change the name of the two cylinders to **Rail1** and **Rail2**. Save your work.

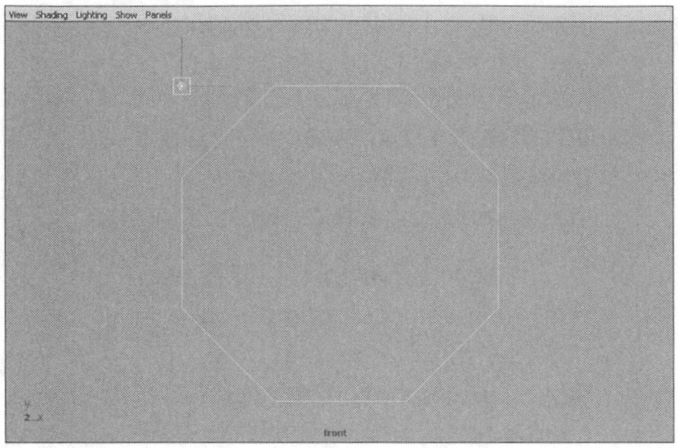

FIGURE 20.22 Manipulator aligned with left and top edges.

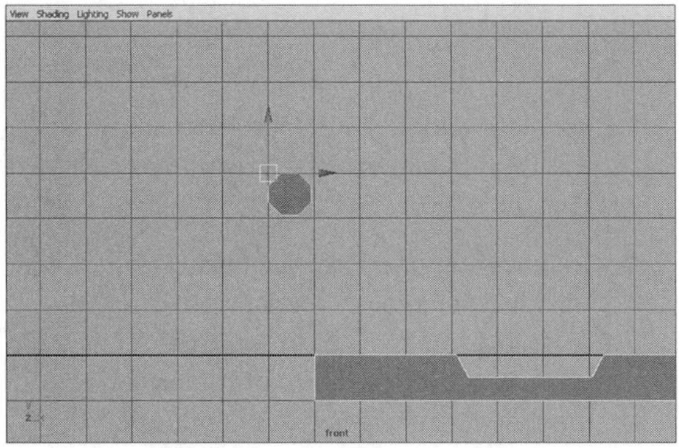

FIGURE 20.23 Rail moved into position.

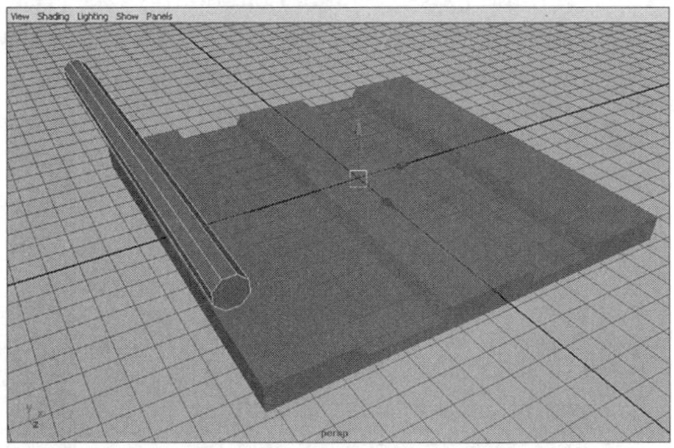

FIGURE 20.24 Cylinder after being added to a group.

END TUTORIAL 20.4

20

You have now created the rails for your catwalk. Logically, you need some sort of support system to hold the rails in place. In **TUTORIAL 20.5**, you begin creating these supports by modeling the anchor for the rail supports.

TUTORIAL 20.5: Building the Support Anchor

1. Continue from **TUTORIAL 20.4**, or open the `BaseCatwalk.mb` file you saved earlier. You'll be creating the anchor that holds the rail supports in place. **FIGURE 20.25** shows your progress so far.

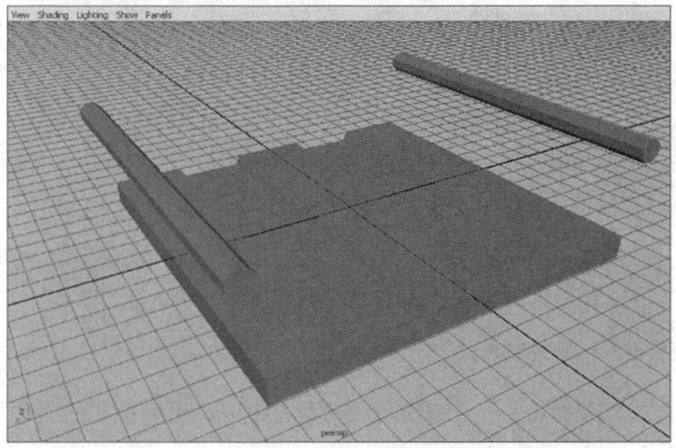

FIGURE 20.25 Your catwalk's progression to this point.

2. Using the skills you have learned, create a cube with the following settings:

   Width: 64

   Height: 32

   Depth: 32

   Subdivisions Height: 3

3. In the Channel Box, set Translate Y to **-32** to position the cube on the bottom of the walkway.

4. With the cube selected, press F11 to make faces selectable. Assuming that the X-axis runs left to right, select the bottommost face on the left and right side of the cube. **FIGURE 20.26** shows the bottom-right face selected.

   With both faces selected, press the R key to select the Scale tool. Scale the faces down slightly in the Z-axis to produce the results shown in **FIGURE 20.27**.

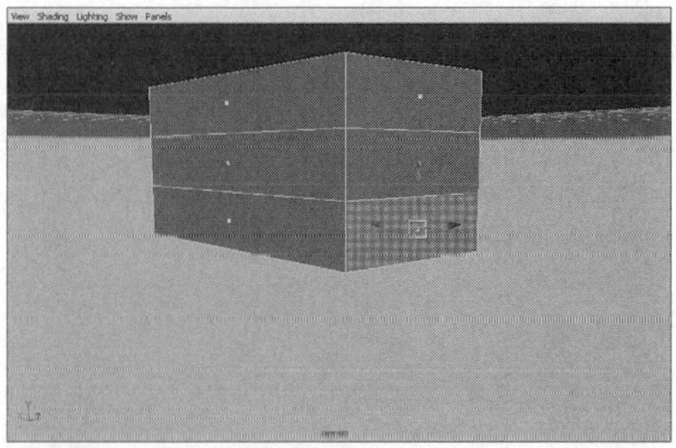

FIGURE 20.26 Bottom-right face selected.

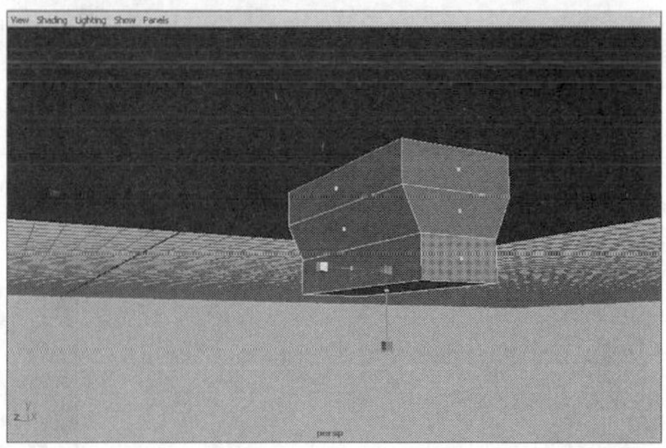

FIGURE 20.27 Cube after faces have been scaled down in Z.

5. Select the face on the underside of the cube, and scale it down in Z even farther (see **FIGURE 20.28**). Then use the Move tool (W key) to move it up along the Y-axis a bit so that the bottom of the cube looks rounded (see **FIGURE 20.29**).

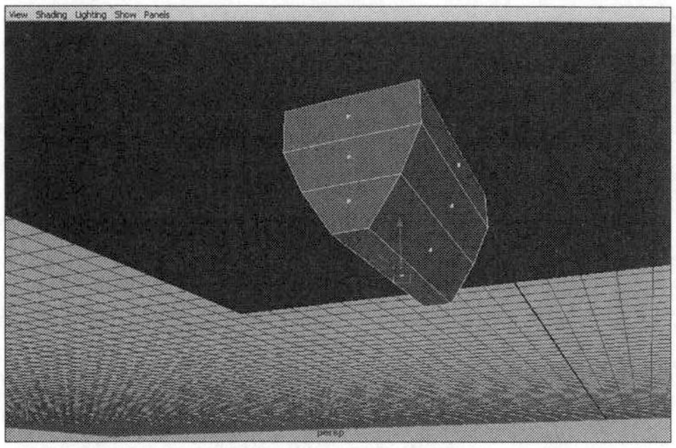

FIGURE 20.28 Bottom face after being scaled down in Z.

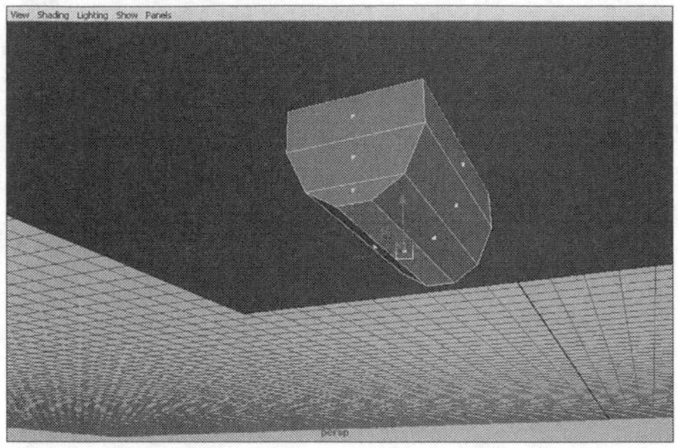

FIGURE 20.29 Bottom face after being moved up in Y.

6. Select the face at the top of the cube. You might need to go into Wireframe mode (4 key) to see it. Scale the face out slightly in X. **FIGURE 20.30** shows the results.
7. Change the name of the cube to **Anchor**, and save your work.

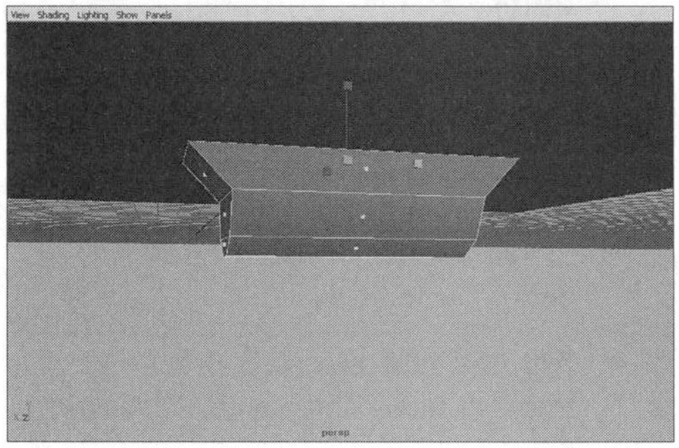

FIGURE 20.30 The anchor for the rail supports is now complete.

END TUTORIAL 20.5

Now that the anchors are in place, you can add some brace pieces to them to make the structure look more stable. **TUTORIAL 20.6** shows how you can make these pieces using the Create Polygons tool.

TUTORIAL 20.6: Adding Braces to the Anchor

1. Next, you add some small braces to either side of the Anchor. Continue from **TUTORIAL 20.5**, or open your saved file. Switch to the Side view, and use Shaded mode in the viewport (5 key). Zoom in on the Anchor, as shown in **FIGURE 20.31**.
2. From the Polygons menu, choose Create Polygon. Click three times to create a triangle that runs from the underside of the Walkway to the Anchor, as shown in **FIGURE 20.32**.

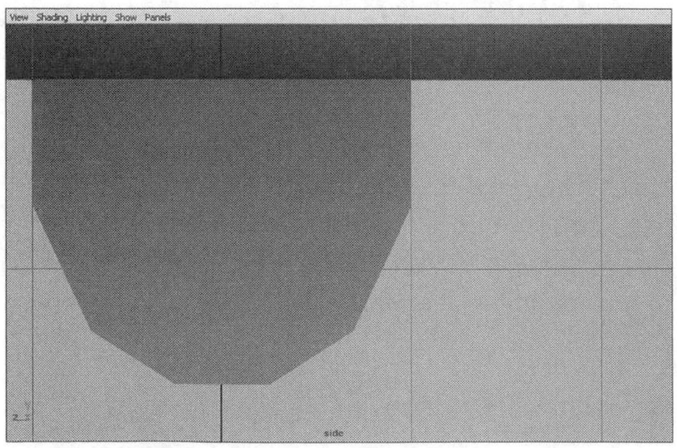

FIGURE 20.31 Zoomed Side view of the Anchor.

It doesn't matter where you start, but be sure to move in a counterclockwise direction. You don't need to click a fourth time to close the triangle; instead, simply press Enter to complete the creation process.

> **NOTE**
>
> **It doesn't matter if your polygon passes into the floor or the anchor objects.**

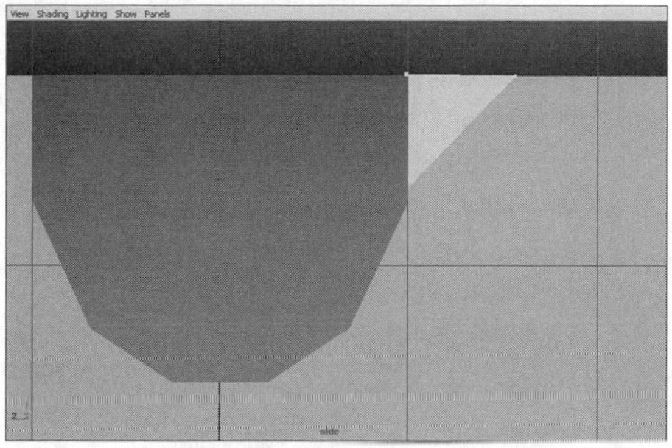

FIGURE 20.32 **Polygon creation process after three clicks.**

3. Switch back to the Perspective view. With the new polygon selected, click the Extrude Faces icon in the Polygon Shelf. Extrude the shape out in local Z to add thickness to the triangle (see **FIGURE 20.33**).

4. From the main menu, choose Modify > Center Pivot to place the object's pivot at its center.

5. Select the shape, and then Shift-select the Anchor. From the main menu, choose Modify > Snap Align Objects > Align Objects > options box. Use the following settings, and click Align when finished to center the new triangle shape on the anchor:

   Align in: World X (make sure it's the only check box selected)

   Align to: Last Selected Object

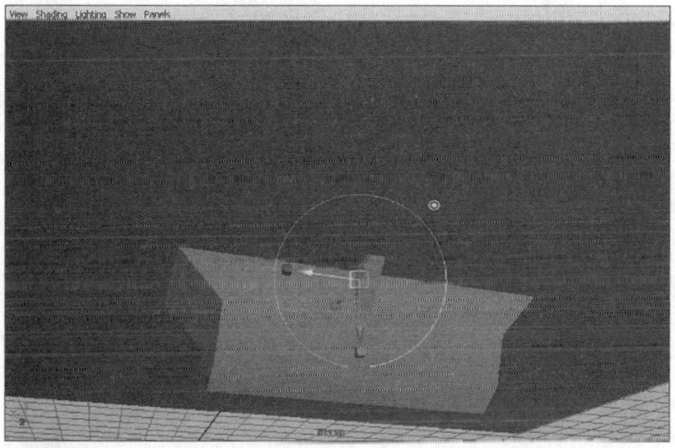

FIGURE 20.33 **The extruded shape now has thickness.**

6. Next, you copy the triangular brace, using the Numeric Input field at the far right of the Status Line. First, click the small black down arrow next to the field, and set the mode to Relative. Recall from Chapter 17, "Overview of Maya," that you can collapse icon sets in the Status Line to access other sets.

7. Select the triangular brace, and press W to enable the Move tool. Don't move the manipulator! Instead, type **20** in the Numeric Input field, and press Enter. The triangle jumps 20 units in the positive X direction (see **FIGURE 20.34**).

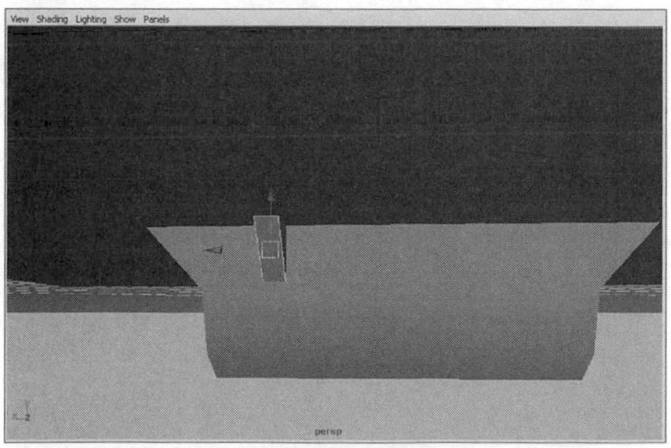

FIGURE 20.34 **The triangle should snap 20 units farther in the X direction.**

8. With the triangular brace selected, press Shift+D to duplicate the object and record its next transform. In the Numeric Input field, type **-20**, and press Enter. The duplicate jumps 20 units in the negative X direction, or back to the brace's original location (see **FIGURE 20.35**).

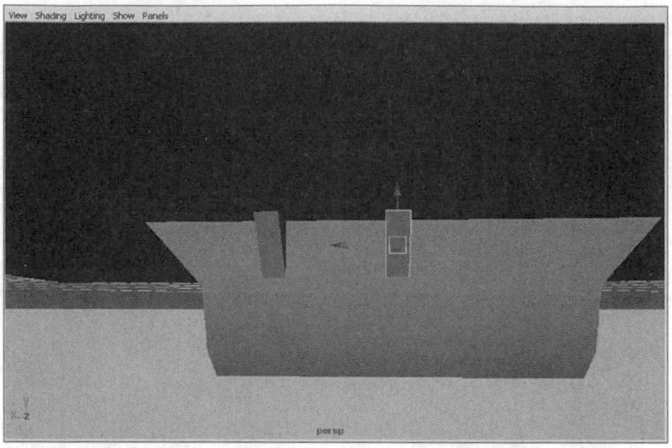

FIGURE 20.35 Two triangular bases 20 units apart in X.

9. Now for a cool trick: Press Shift+D again, and a new duplicate appears, already moved 20 units in the same direction (see **FIGURE 20.36**).

   The benefit of using Shift+D to duplicate is that you can make a transformation, and it's applied to all subsequent duplicates. You can use this technique to create arrays of objects—that is, long successions of a single shape.

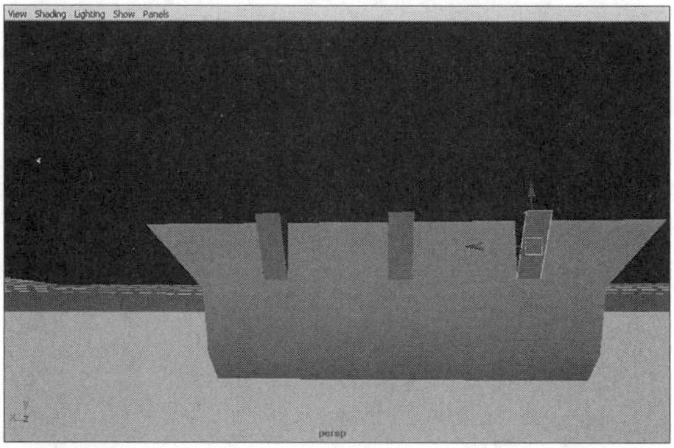

FIGURE 20.36 Three triangular bases 20 units apart in X.

10. Select all three braces, and press Ctrl+G to group the braces together. With the group selected, press Ctrl+D to duplicate the group. Use the Channel Box to set the Scale Z for the new group to **-1**. This setting makes braces appear on the other side of the anchor as well (see **FIGURE 20.37**).

11. Rename the braces as **brace0** through **brace5**. Save your work.

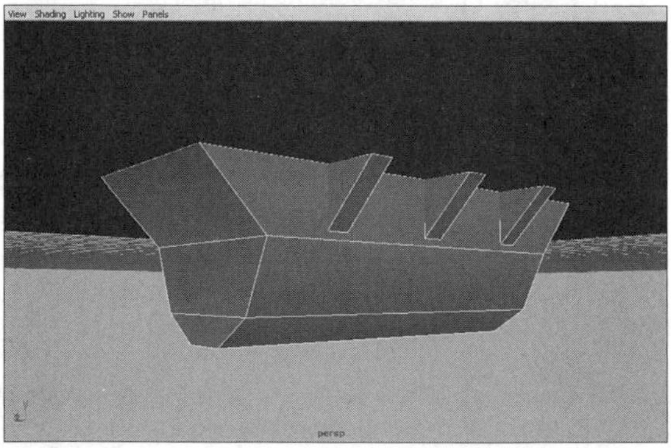

FIGURE 20.37 The completed braces for the Anchor.

END TUTORIAL 20.6

The anchors are fully modeled, and it's time to create the rail supports. In **TUTORIAL 20.7**, you create these supports by making several extrusions from a polygon cylinder primitive.

20

TUTORIAL 20.7: Creating the Rail Supports, Part I

1. Continue from **TUTORIAL 20.6**, or open the `BaseCatwalk.mb` file you saved earlier. **FIGURE 20.38** shows your progress to this point.

2. Using the skills you have learned, create a polygon cylinder with the following settings, and click Create when you're finished:

   Radius: 8

   Height: 96

   Subdivisions Around Axis: 6

   Axis: X

3. Move the cylinder down about -30 units in the Y-axis to center it on the Anchor (see **FIGURE 20.39**). Also, use the Channel Box to rotate the cylinder 30 degrees in X. This places a perfectly horizontal edge on the top of the object.

4. Select the face at either end of the cylinder. Switch to the Front view, and click the Extrude button in the Shelf. Extrude the faces out in local Z just a few units, and scale them down uniformly. You can do this by clicking on any of the manipulator's cube-shaped ends, and then dragging the pale blue cube that appears at the center of the manipulator. Your result should be similar to **FIGURE 20.40**.

> **NOTE**
>
> **Because you selected both faces, using one manipulator affects both sides of the cylinder.**

5. Press G, and pull the extrusion out about one grid unit in local Z (see **FIGURE 20.41**).

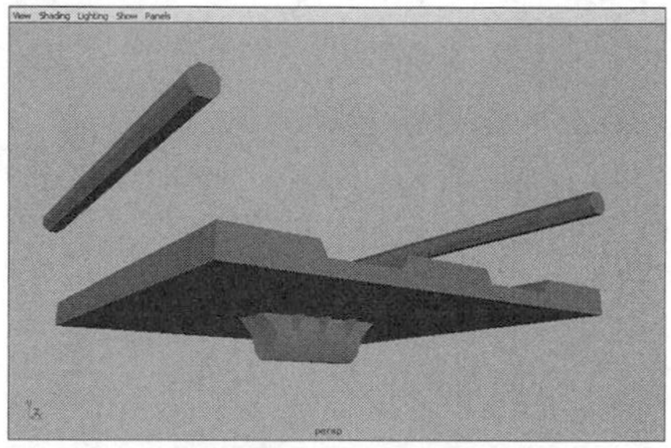

FIGURE 20.38 Your catwalk's progression to this point.

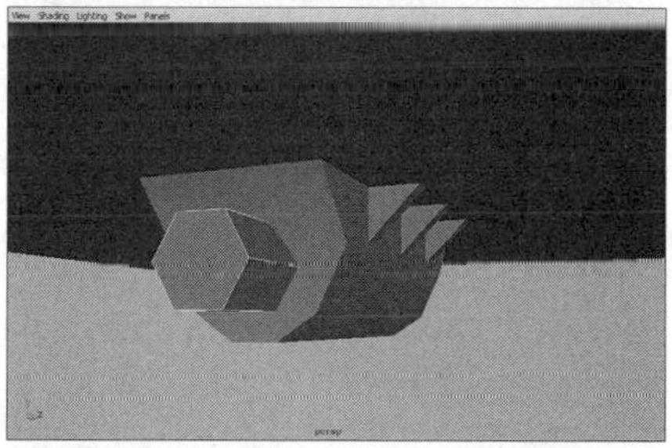

FIGURE 20.39 The cylinder passes through the Anchor.

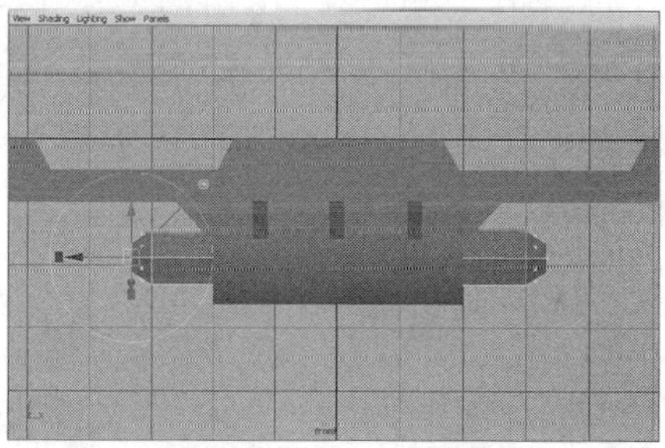

FIGURE 20.40 The cylinder after the first extrusion.

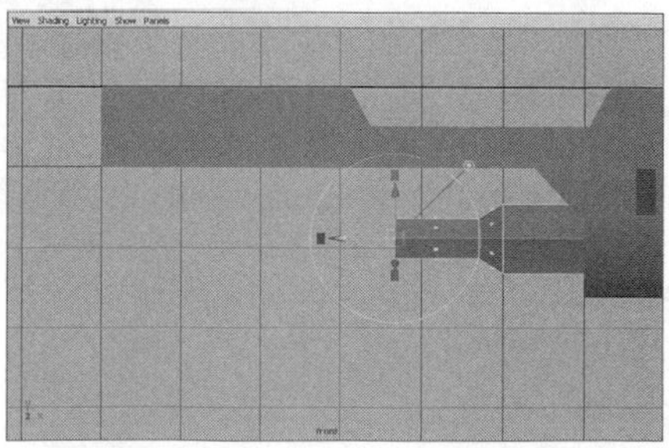

FIGURE 20.41 The cylinder after a second extrusion.

6. Press G again, scale the extrusion up uniformly, and move it out in local Z a bit (see **FIGURE 20.42**).
7. Press G again to create another extrusion. Move this one out in local Z to within about one grid unit from the edge of the Walkway. Then use the skills you have learned to create a shape similar to **FIGURE 20.43**.

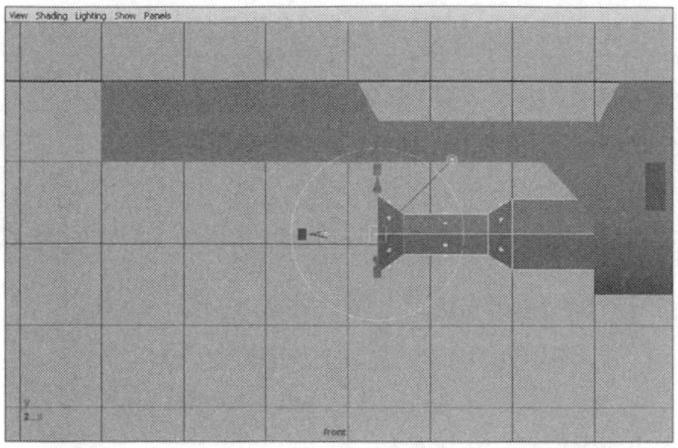

FIGURE 20.42 The cylinder after a third extrusion.

> **NOTE**
>
> In step 7, try to make sure your shape ends about one third of a grid unit past the edge of the Walkway.

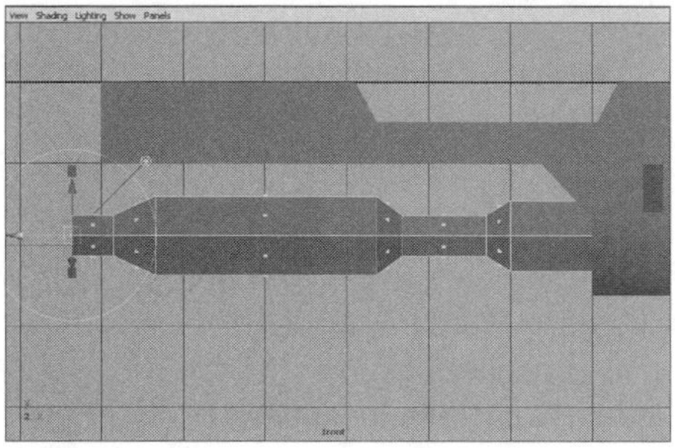

FIGURE 20.43 The completed base of the catwalk's cylindrical supports.

8. Change the name of the cylinder to `Support`. Save your work.

END TUTORIAL 20.7

Now that the initial shape for the rail supports is complete, you need to "bend" the geometry up so that it can connect with the rails. **TUTORIAL 20.8** walks you through this process using the Wedge Faces tool.

TUTORIAL 20.8: Creating the Rail Supports, Part II

1. Continue from **TUTORIAL 20.7**, or open the `BaseCatwalk.mb` file you saved earlier. **FIGURE 20.44** shows your progress so far.
2. Select the face at one end of the Support shape (see **FIGURE 20.45**). It doesn't matter which end you choose because you'll be repeating steps 2 through 4 on the other side in a moment.

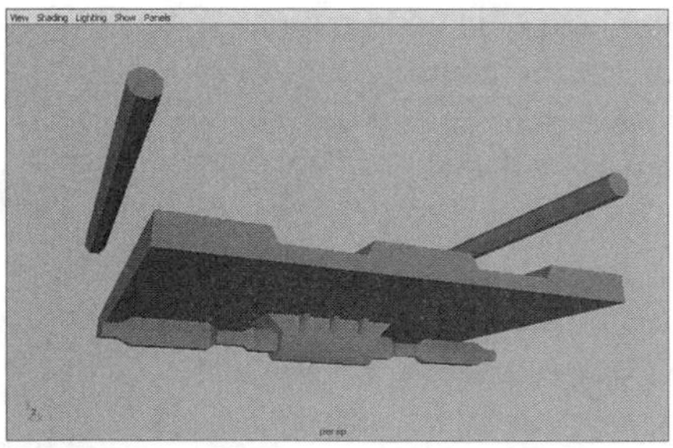

FIGURE 20.44 Your catwalk's progress to this point.

3. Hold down the RMB over the object, and select Edges from the marking menu. Then Shift-select the edge at the top of the selected face (see **FIGURE 20.46**).
4. From the Edit Polygons menu, choose Wedge Faces > options box. In the Wedge Faces Options dialog box, enter the following settings to create a low-polygon 90-degree bend in the support, and click Apply when you're finished:

   Wedge Angle: 90

   Wedge Divisions: 3
5. Repeat steps 2 to 4 for the face at the other end of the Support. This should give you two 90-degree bends, one on each end (see **FIGURE 20.47**).
6. Select the new horizontal faces at both ends of the Support shape, and use the skills you have learned to extrude them upward and into the rails, as shown in **FIGURE 20.48**.

NOTE

Remember to select both new faces so that you don't have to do the series of extrusions twice. Also, if the Supports don't run perfectly into the bottom of the Rails, don't worry: You'll see how to fix that next.

7. Save your work.

END TUTORIAL 20.8

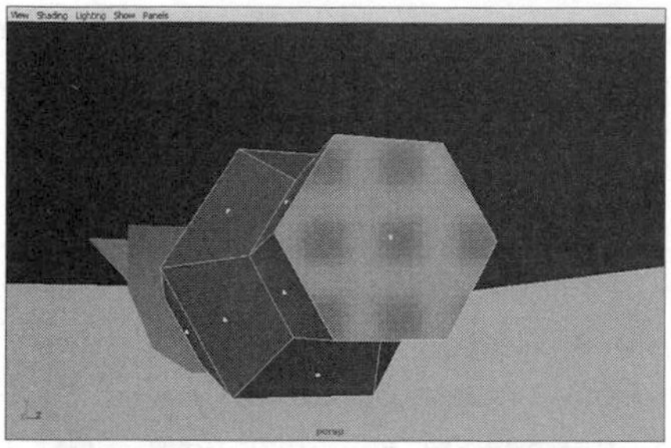

FIGURE 20.45 Choose either face on the Support.

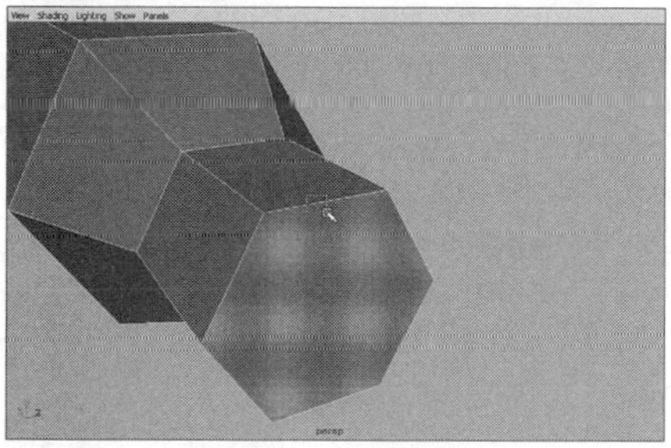

FIGURE 20.46 Edge at the top of the selected face.

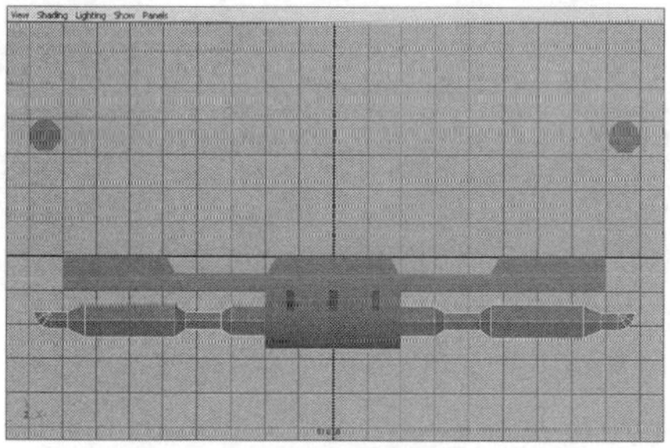

FIGURE 20.47 After applying the wedge to both sides, the result should look like this figure.

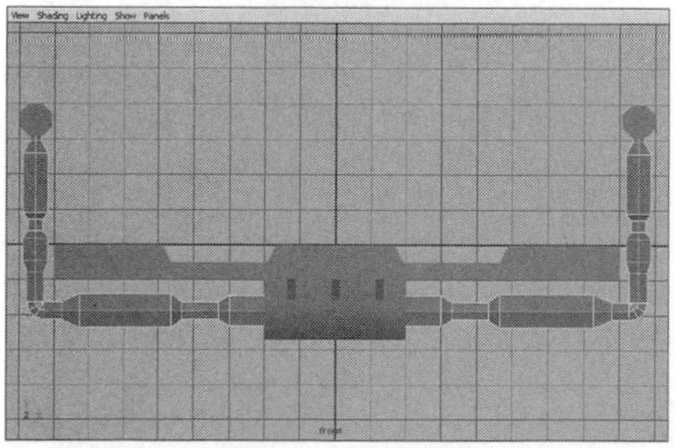

FIGURE 20.48 Extrude upward to connect the Supports and Rails.

The next step is editing the shape of the rail supports by using the construction history from the earlier extrusions. This process is covered in **TUTORIAL 20.9**.

TUTORIAL 20.9: Using Construction History to Fix the Supports

1. Continue from **TUTORIAL 20.8**, or open the `BaseCatwalk.mb` file you saved earlier. Depending on how you created the Support, you might have results that go too far out, as shown in **FIGURE 20.49**, or not far enough to meet up with the Rails, as shown in **FIGURE 20.50**.

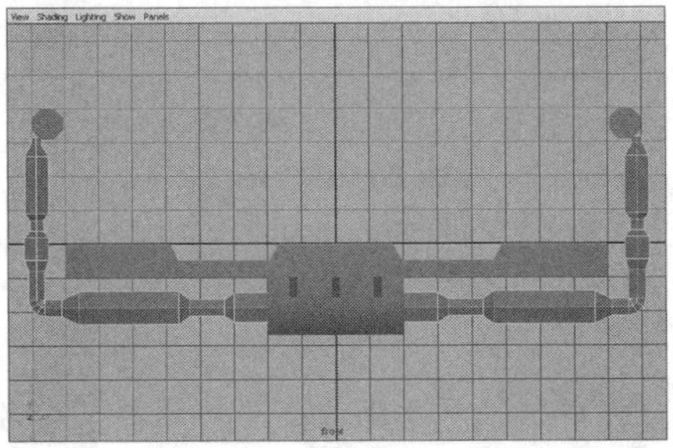

FIGURE 20.49 Maybe the Supports go too far.

2. You can fix either problem through the use of construction history. Select the Support shape in the Front view, and activate the Show Manipulator tool by clicking its icon  in the Toolbox or pressing the T key.

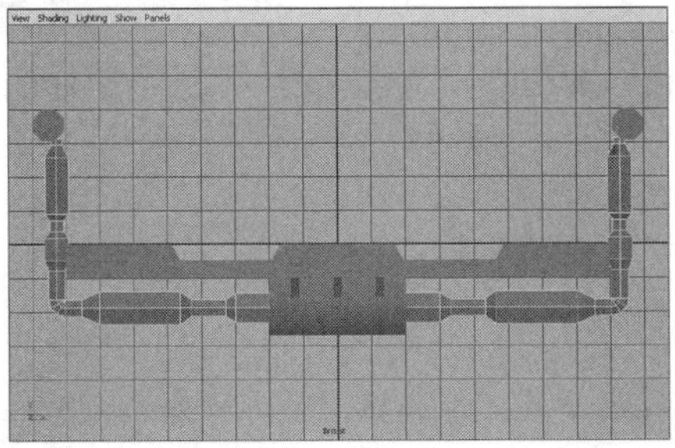

FIGURE 20.50 Maybe the Supports don't go far enough.

3. Next, go to the Channel Box, and scroll down under the Inputs section. Find polyExtrudeFace5 and click it. The Extrude manipulator for that particular extrusion reappears (see **FIGURE 20.51**).

4. Use the local Z move handle to adjust the Support until it goes cleanly into the Rail without passing through the edge of the Walkway, as shown in **FIGURE 20.52**.

> **NOTE**
>
> Because you had selected both sides of the Support when creating this extrusion, you'll see both sides being fixed. However, keep in mind that construction history can occasionally make your system unstable, so use this technique in moderation.

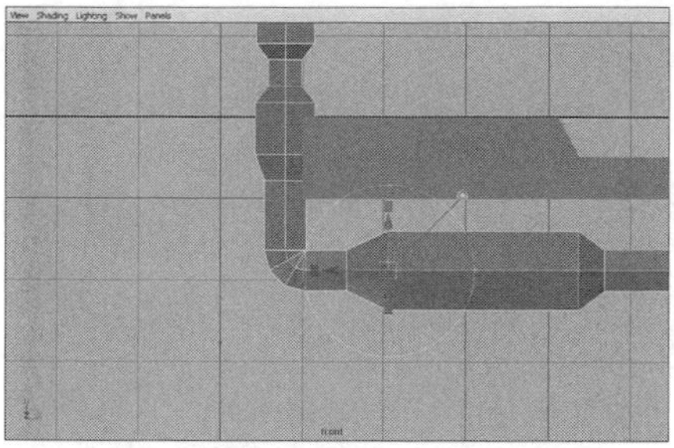

FIGURE 20.51 Make sure the manipulator appears at this location on the extrusion.

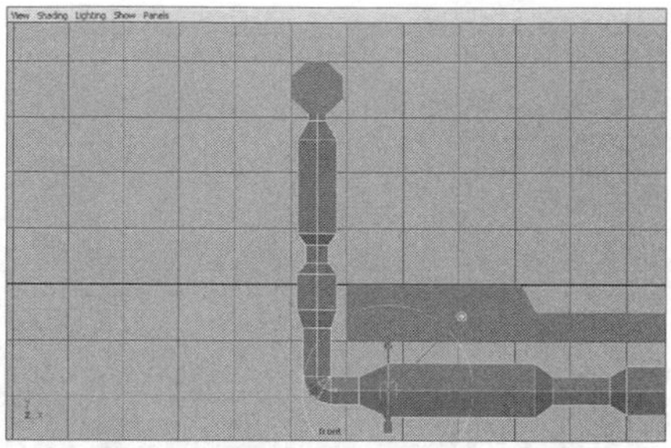

FIGURE 20.52 The Supports should line up perfectly with the Rails.

5. Select the Support, the Anchor, and all six Braces, and press Ctrl+G to group them (see **FIGURE 20.53**). Rename this group **`RailSupport`**.

6. Draw a marquee selection around the entire catwalk, and choose Edit > Delete by Type > History from the main menu to delete the objects' construction history.

7. Save your work.

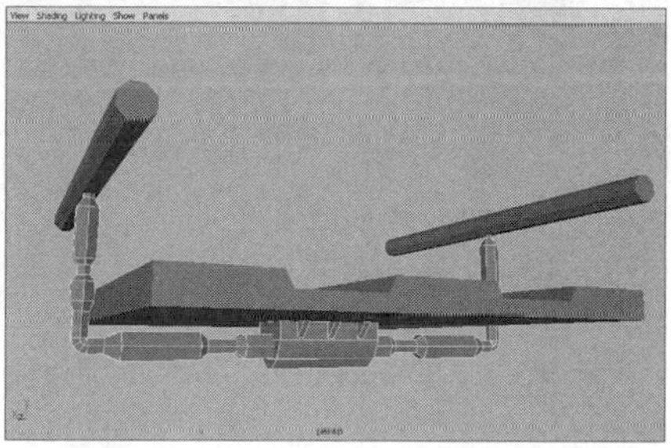

FIGURE 20.53 The RailSupport group selected.

END TUTORIAL 20.9

The BaseCatwalk is now complete. From here, you'll use it to construct all the static mesh types covered in this chapter. In **TUTORIAL 20.10**, you create some basic textures for your mesh. These textures serve a dual purpose: They give you an idea of what the UV layout looks like, and they provide material slots in UnrealEd where you can place materials.

TUTORIAL 20.10: Creating the Placeholder Textures

1. Continue from **TUTORIAL 20.9**, or open the `BaseCatwalk.mb` file you saved earlier (see **FIGURE 20.54**). In this tutorial, you establish the placeholder textures used to designate how many materials can be applied to the static mesh and where those materials appear on the surface. You're not applying the textures now, just getting them in place for later use. For simplicity, you'll create only two materials.

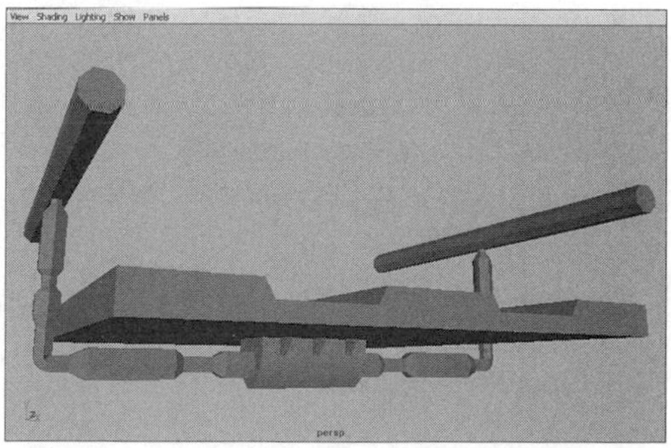

FIGURE 20.54 The BaseCatwalk is finished.

2. From the main menu, choose Window > Rendering Editors > Hypershade.
3. From the Create Bar, MMB-drag two new Lambert shaders into the bottom Work Area (see **FIGURE 20.55**). One is named Lambert2, and the other, Lambert3.

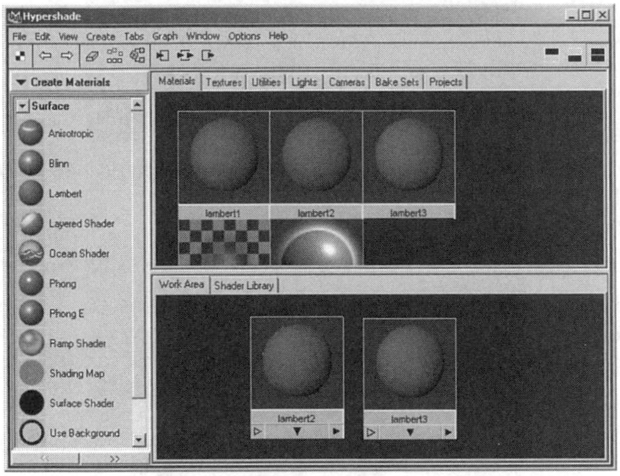

FIGURE 20.55 Lambert2 and Lambert3 in the Hypershade window.

4. Double-click Lambert2 to open its Attribute Editor. Next to the Color field, click the checkered button. In the Create Render Node dialog box, click Checker.
5. The Attribute Editor changes to show the attributes of the Checker node. Click the black field next to Color2, and set the color to some shade of blue (see **FIGURE 20.56**).
6. Repeat steps 4 and 5 for Lambert3, but this time set the Color2 attribute to a shade of red. When finished, you should have two new materials: one blue checker and one red checker.
7. Save your work. These materials are used later to designate areas for materials in Unreal.

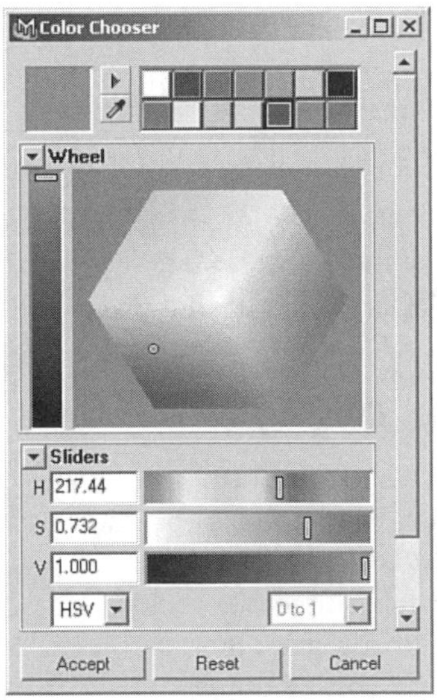

FIGURE 20.56 Pick your favorite blue from the Color Chooser.

END TUTORIAL 20.10

You have now completed the base model for your catwalk systems. In the following subsections, you learn how to create the actual models to be sent to Unreal as static meshes.

Constructing the Straight Catwalk

In this section, you learn how to create your first model for the static mesh network: a simple straight section of catwalk. In **TUTORIAL 20.11**, you'll use the pieces you made for your base model to set it up. In **TUTORIAL 20.12**, you apply the placeholder textures you created earlier.

TUTORIAL 20.11: Creating the StraightCatwalk

1. Continue from **TUTORIAL 20.10**, or open the `BaseCatwalk.mb` file you saved earlier.
2. From the main menu, choose File > Save Scene As, and rename the file as **`StraightCatwalk`**. Resaving now prevents you from accidentally saving over the BaseCatwalk later.
3. In the Status Line at the top of the Maya window, click the Select by Hierarchy and Combinations icon. Then click any of the RailSupport group's pieces. The whole group becomes selected (see **FIGURE 20.57**).

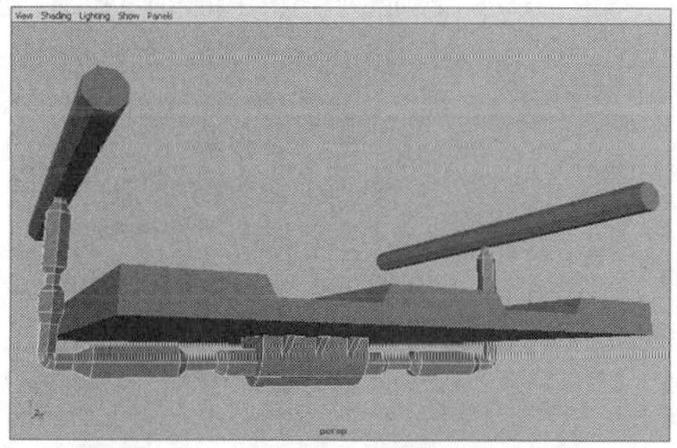

FIGURE 20.57 Both the Rails and the Anchor get selected with only one click.

> **TIP**
>
> **Alternatively, you can select any piece of the group, and press the up arrow key until you have the RailSupport group selected.**

4. With the RailSupport group selected, go to the Channel Box and enter **64** in the Translate Z text box. The RailSupport group jumps to the new location (see **FIGURE 20.58**).

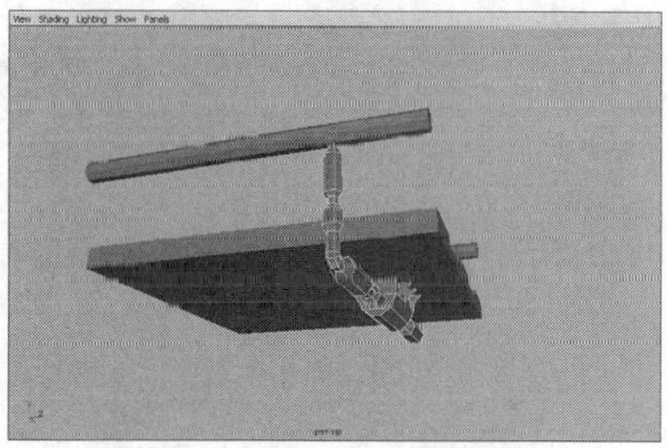

FIGURE 20.58 The RailSupport group snaps in your viewport.

5. Next, press Ctrl+D to duplicate the RailSupport group. In the Channel Box, set the Translate Z of the newly duplicated group to **-64**. You now have two Rail Supports forming a section of the catwalk (see **FIGURE 20.59**).
6. Save your work. You have the geometry in place for your StraightCatwalk.

FIGURE 20.59 The two supports for the catwalk.

END TUTORIAL 20.11

The geometry for the StraightCatwalk has been established. All that needs to be done now is to add the placeholder textures for use as material slots in UnrealEd. **TUTORIAL 20.12** shows how this is done.

TUTORIAL 20.12: Applying Placeholder Textures to the StraightCatwalk

1. Continue from **TUTORIAL 20.11**, or open the `StraightCatwalk.mb` file you saved earlier. You'll be applying placeholder textures onto your catwalk.

2. You need to clean up the texture coordinates for your object. To save time, you do this by applying an automatic texture mapping to the catwalk. Marquee-select the entire catwalk, and from the main menu, choose Edit Polygons > Texture > Automatic Mapping.

3. As you place materials in Maya, you're simply designating which faces receive a specific material in Unreal. The checkered textures you created don't appear in Unreal at all. They are simply a way to indicate which materials are placed where.

In the Toolbox, click the Hypershade/Persp icon to open the Hypershade window with the Perspective viewport directly beneath it (see **FIGURE 20.60**).

> **NOTE**
>
> **Step 2 doesn't create perfectly efficient texture coordinates (called UVs), but it keeps your textures from becoming too stretched.**

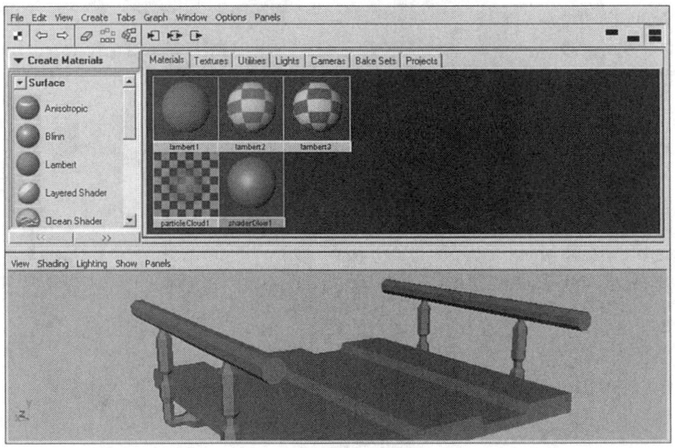

FIGURE 20.60 **The Hypershade and Perspective view layout.**

4. Any material applied to your object is considered a placeholder, which means the default material (Lambert1) already allows you to place one material when you get the mesh into UnrealEd. Therefore, you'll use the other two materials to add decoration. Begin by selecting the two Support objects (not the groups), as shown in **FIGURE 20.61**.

5. Hold down the RMB over the Lambert2 node in the Hypershade window, and choose Apply Material to Selection. Press 6 on the keyboard to see the result (see **FIGURE 20.62**).

6. Use the same technique to apply Lambert3 to both Rail objects (see **FIGURE 20.63**).

7. You can also apply materials on individual faces. Select the Walkway object, and make faces selectable by pressing F11. Then select the faces at the bottom of the recessed tracks (see **FIGURE 20.64**).

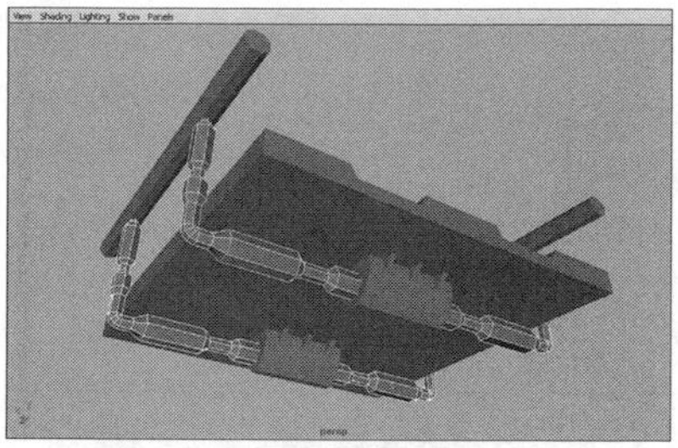

FIGURE 20.61 Avoid selecting the Anchors.

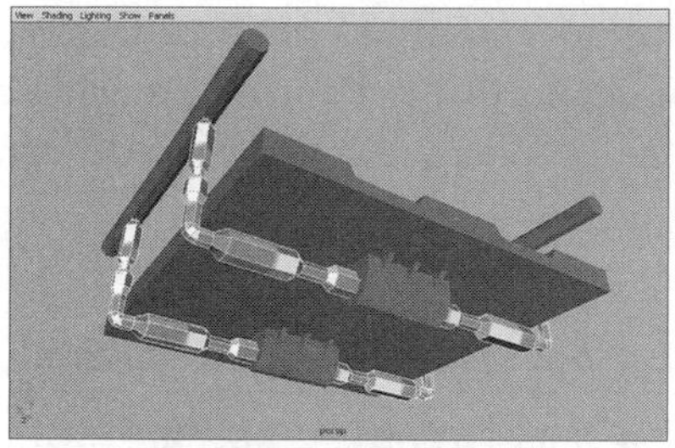

FIGURE 20.62 You can see all the materials on your objects in the viewport.

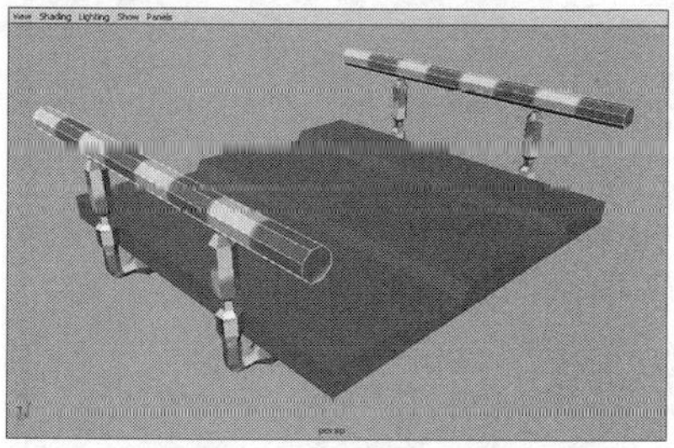

FIGURE 20.63 You now have one material on the Rails and another on the Supports.

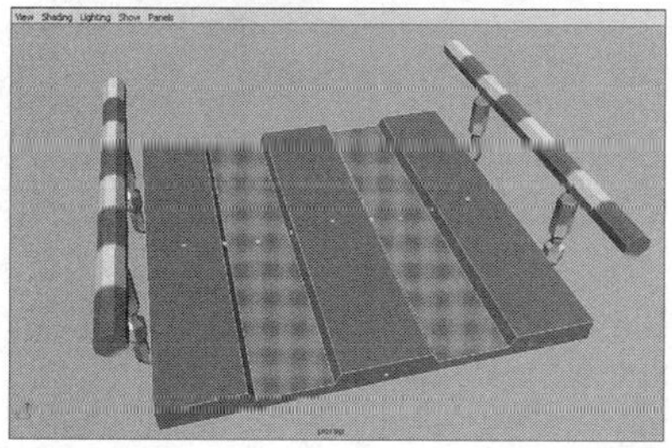

FIGURE 20.64 The two faces have been selected.

Again, right-click on Lambert3 and apply it to the selection. The red checkered material appears only on the selected faces (see **FIGURE 20.65**).

8. Use this method to apply the Lambert3 (red checkered) material to bands of polygonal faces on the Supports. Also, apply the blue checkered material to the thin strips along the tracks of the Walkway and to the Braces on the bottom of the Walkway. **FIGURE 20.66** shows the results.

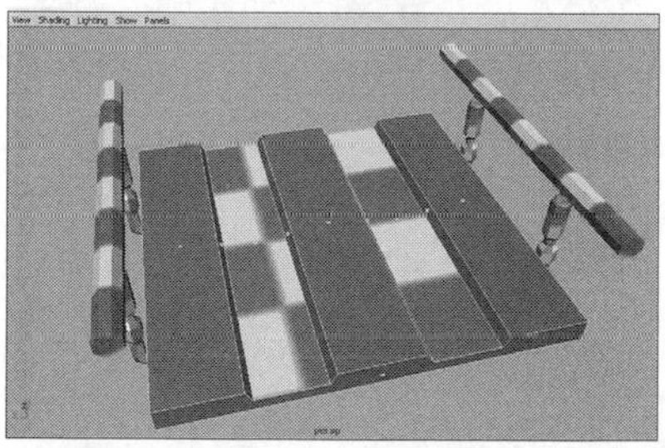

FIGURE 20.65 The two faces now have a checkered material applied.

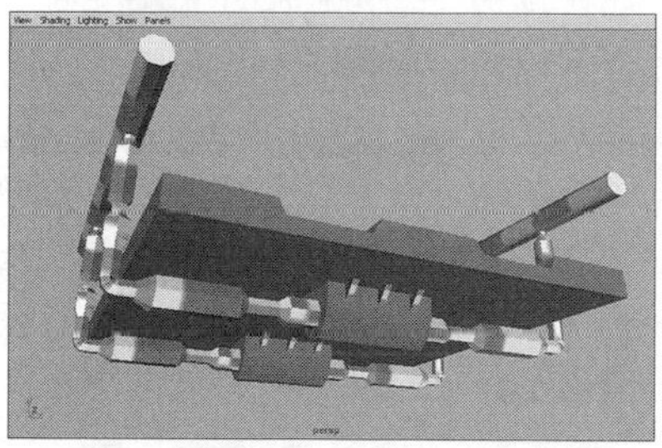

FIGURE 20.66 The StraightCatwalk with all the materials applied.

The placeholder textures are now applied to the object. Take note of the pattern you used for placing these textures so that you can place them on other static meshes in a similar manner.

9. Save your work.

END TUTORIAL 20.12

Now that the StraightCatwalk has been textured, it's almost ready to send into UnrealEd. First, however, the objects that make up the StraightCatwalk need to be combined to a single mesh, and the model as a whole needs to be converted to triangular polygons. **TUTORIAL 20.13** covers these tasks.

TUTORIAL 20.13: Preparing the StraightCatwalk for Export

1. Continue from **TUTORIAL 20.12**, or open the `StraightCatwalk.mb` file you saved earlier. You're going to make the StraightCatwalk ready to export in **TUTORIAL 20.21**.
2. To begin, you need the entire catwalk to be a single object. To do this, marquee-select the entire object, and choose Polygons > Combine from the main menu. Maya now considers the catwalk to be a single object.
3. In the Channel Box, rename the object as **`StraightCatwalk`**.
4. Next, you need to convert the mesh into triangles because UnrealEd doesn't accept four-sided polygons. To do this, choose Polygons > Triangulate from the main menu. **FIGURE 20.67** shows the results.

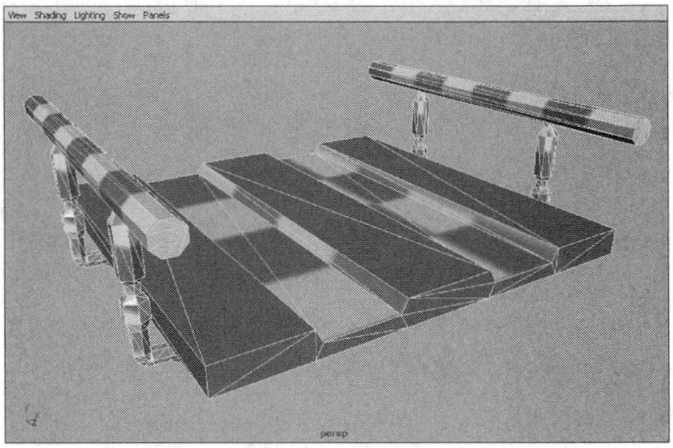

FIGURE 20.67 Your triangulated StraightCatwalk.

> **NOTE**
>
> The Exporter plug-in has an option for automatically triangulating an object. However, triangulating in Maya is far more efficient, especially for concave objects.

5. Finally, delete the object's construction history by choosing Edit > Delete By Type > History.
6. Save your work. The StraightCatwalk is now ready for export.

END TUTORIAL 20.13

Making a Ramp

In **TUTORIAL 20.14**, you use a quick modeling trick to turn your straight section of catwalk into a ramp. You do this with a lattice, which, when applied to a model, enables you to manipulate many vertices of the model as a single unit. You also take advantage of the Numeric Input field in Maya's Status Line.

20

TUTORIAL 20.14: Creating the RampCatwalk

1. Continue from **TUTORIAL 20.13**, or open the `StraightCatwalk.mb` file you saved earlier (see **FIGURE 20.68**). You'll use the StraightCatwalk to create the ramp.

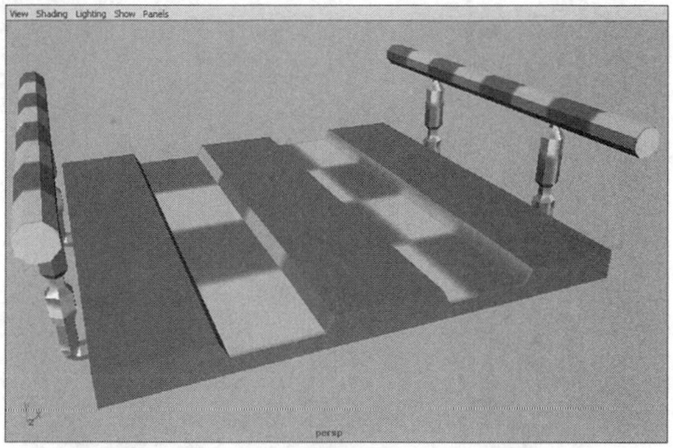

FIGURE 20.68 The progress so far on the StraightCatwalk.

2. From the main menu, choose File > Save Scene As, and rename the file as **`RampCatwalk.mb`**.
3. You'll be turning the StraightCatwalk into a ramp by using a lattice—a new technique. First, select the catwalk, and switch to the Animation menu set by pressing the F2 key.
4. With the catwalk still selected, choose Deform > Create Lattice > options box. In the Lattice Options dialog box, set Divisions to **2, 2, 2** and select the Autoparent to Selection check box. Click Create when finished.
5. A green box representing the lattice appears around the catwalk. As you edit the vertices of the lattice, you also change the shape of the catwalk. Hold down the RMB over one of the lattice's lines, and choose Lattice Point from the marking menu (see **FIGURE 20.69**).

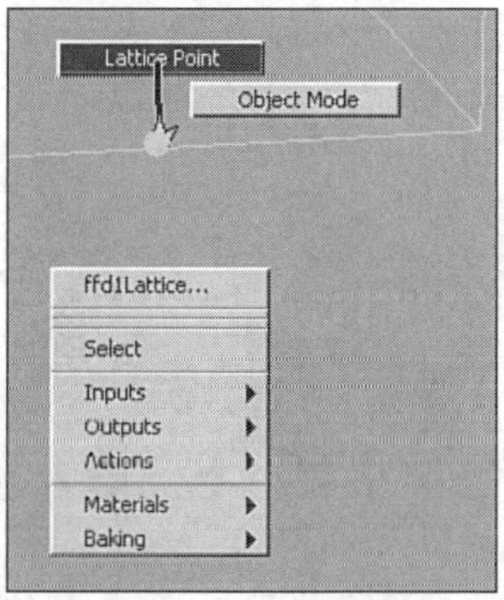

FIGURE 20.69 Select Lattice Point from the marking menu.

6. You can now select the four lattice points at the front of the catwalk (see **FIGURE 20.70**), which is designated by the positive Z direction.
7. Activate the Move tool with the W key. Then set the Numeric Input field in the Status Line to Relative, and enter **`0 64 0`**. Note that you should enter spaces between each number.
8. The catwalk changes into a ramp because the lattice points at one end have been moved up (see **FIGURE 20.71**). Remember that lattices can be used to reshape entire models, saving you tremendous amounts of work.

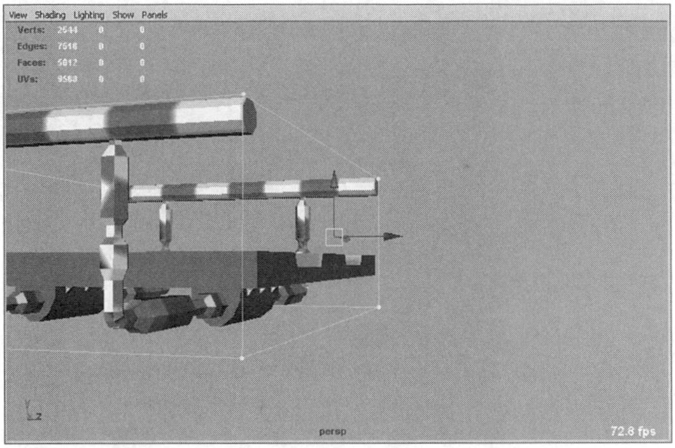

FIGURE 20.70 As you select lattice points, they turn yellow.

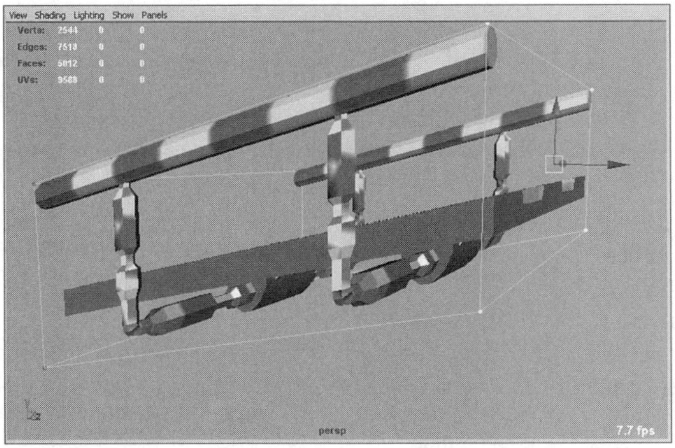

FIGURE 20.71 Your second catwalk is this RampCatwalk.

Delete the catwalk's construction history to remove the lattice. Also, be sure to rename the catwalk in the Channel Box as **RampCatwalk**.

9. Save your work.

END TUTORIAL 20.14

Making a Turn

20

In this section, you learn how to create a 90-degree turn section for your catwalks. This section fits perfectly to the end of the straight or ramp parts you created earlier. In **TUTORIALS 20.15** through **20.17**, you use the base mesh you saved at the beginning of this chapter to create the turn section.

TUTORIAL 20.15: Modeling the 90-Degree Turn, Part I

1. In this tutorial, you'll be creating the 90-degree turn section's static mesh. As you do this, you'll notice that some of the extra work you did on the BaseCatwalk saves you time and effort now. To start, open the `BaseCatwalk.mb` file you saved earlier (see **FIGURE 20.72**).

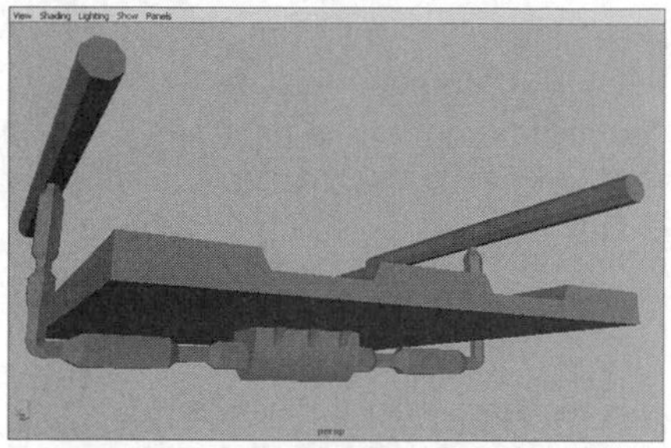

FIGURE 20.72 The BaseCatwalk.

2. From the main menu, choose File > Save Scene As. Save the file as **`90DegreeCatwalk`**.

3. Select the RailSupport group by selecting the Rail or Anchor pieces and pressing the up arrow key. In the Channel Box, enter **`-64`** for the group's Translate Z attribute.

4. Press the F3 key to enter the Modeling menu set. Select the Walkway and both Rail objects. Choose Polygons > Combine from the main menu to make the three pieces a single object (see **FIGURE 20.73**).

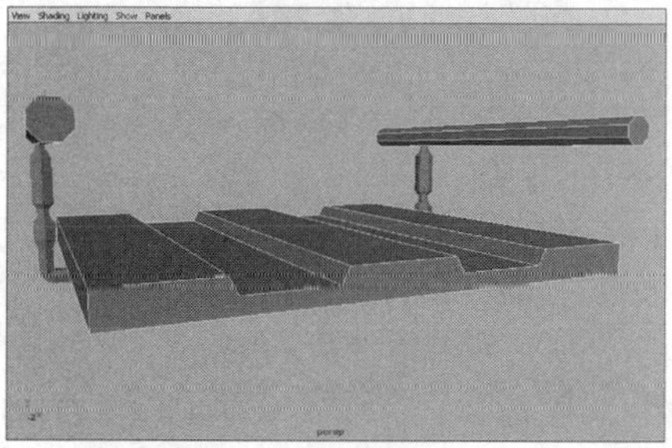

FIGURE 20.73 The Walkway and Rails have merged.

5. Switch to the Top view. Select the new combined object, and press the F key to frame it in the viewport. Press the F9 key to make vertices selectable, and select the row of vertices at the bottom of the view (see **FIGURE 20.74**).

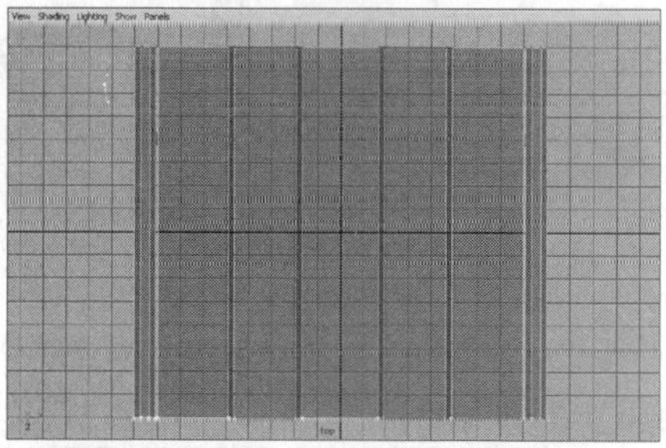

FIGURE 20.74 Use a marquee to select all the vertices at once.

6. With the vertices selected, activate the Move tool with the W key. Click the blue Z-axis arrow to highlight it. (If you don't select the Z-axis before you snap, all the vertices snap to a single point.) Next, hold down the X key to enable grid snapping. Place the cursor over the center of the grid and MMB-drag very slightly to snap all the vertices back to the X-axis. **FIGURE 20.75** shows the results.

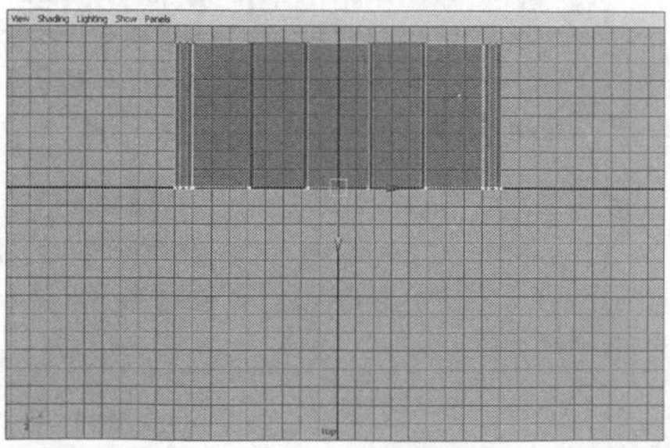

FIGURE 20.75 You just truncated half the object.

7. Go back to the Perspective view. As a reminder, you're assuming that the Z-axis is pointing forward. With this in mind, select the outermost vertical edge at the front of the right-hand Rail (see **FIGURE 20.76**).

8. Click the Extrude Edge icon  in the Polygons Shelf. This tool works the same way as Extrude Face. In the Channel Box, under the Inputs section, click the PolyExtrudeEdge1 entry. Set Translate X to **-64**. Scroll down and set Divisions to **2** to place an extra face on the new extrusion. **FIGURE 20.77** shows the results of these settings.

9. Of the two faces on the edge extrusion, select the face closest to the railing, and press the Delete key to remove it (see **FIGURE 20.78**).

10. Save your work.

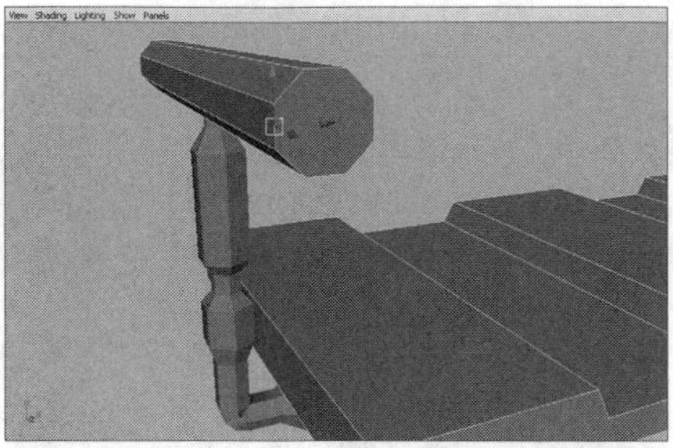

FIGURE 20.76 The edge should be on the XY plane.

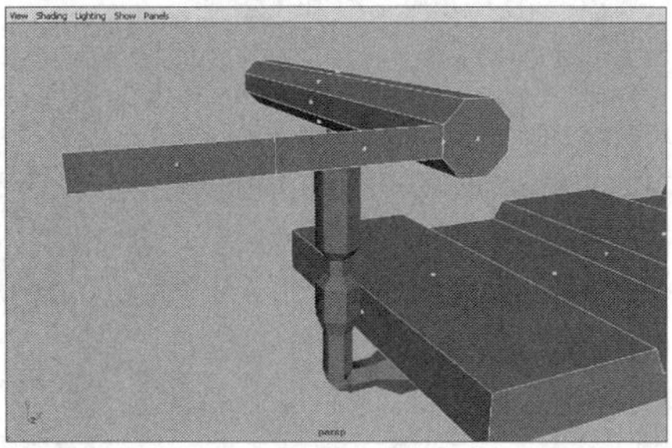

FIGURE 20.77 The result of extruding an edge.

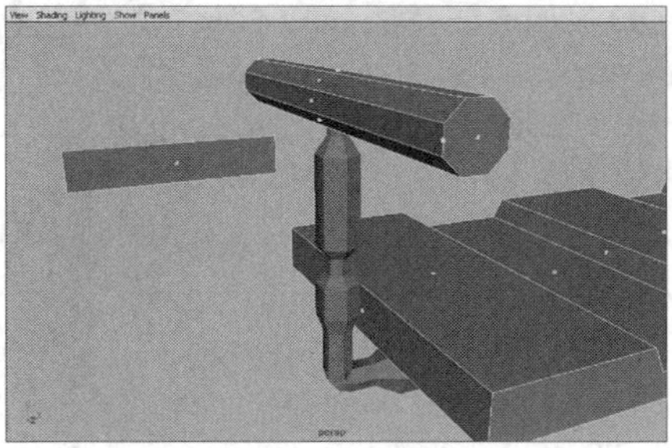

FIGURE 20.78 Deleting the face leaves a gap between the extrusion and the railing.

END TUTORIAL 20.15

TUTORIAL 20.16: Modeling the 90-Degree Turn, Part II

1. Continue **TUTORIAL 20.15**, or open the `90DegreeCatwalk.mb` file you saved earlier. **FIGURE 20.79** shows your progress so far.

2. Now you're going to create the 90-degree bend in the catwalk. Select the floating face created from the edge extrusion at the end of **TUTORIAL 20.15**. Also, Shift-select the face at the front of the Walkway and both faces at the front of the Rail shapes (see **FIGURE 20.80**).

Next, hold down the RMB over the object, and choose Edges from the marking menu. Shift-select the edge on the outside of the floating face (see **FIGURE 20.81**).

3. With the edge and all the faces selected, go to the main menu, and choose Edit Polygons > Wedge Faces > options box. Use the following settings, and click the Wedge Face button when finished:

   Wedge Angle: 0

   Wedge Divisions: 6

> **NOTE**
>
> In step 3, you're actually going to use a negative wedge angle, but the Options dialog box doesn't allow negative entries.

4. In the Channel Box, click the PolyWedgeFace1 entry. Set Wedge Angle to **-90**. **FIGURE 20.82** shows the results.

> **NOTE**
>
> Depending on which side of the catwalk you have been working on, you might need to set the Wedge Angle to 90 instead of -90.

5. With the faces still selected, click the Extrude Faces icon in the Polygons Shelf. Don't move the manipulator! Instead, go to the Channel Box, click the PolyExtrudeFace1 entry, and set Translate X to **-128**. **FIGURE 20.83** shows the results of this extrusion.

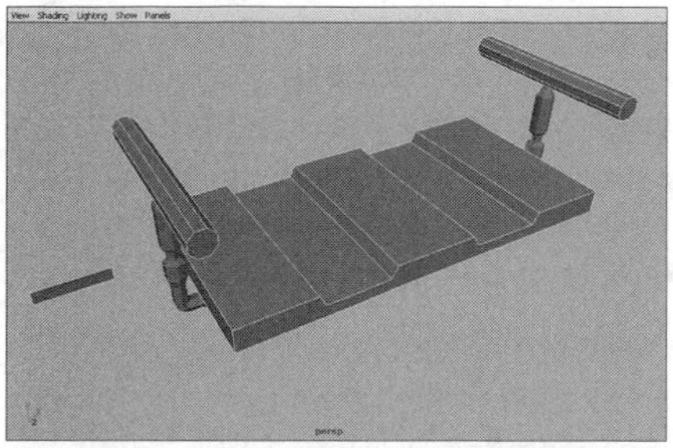

FIGURE 20.79 Your 90DegreeCatwalk's progression to this point.

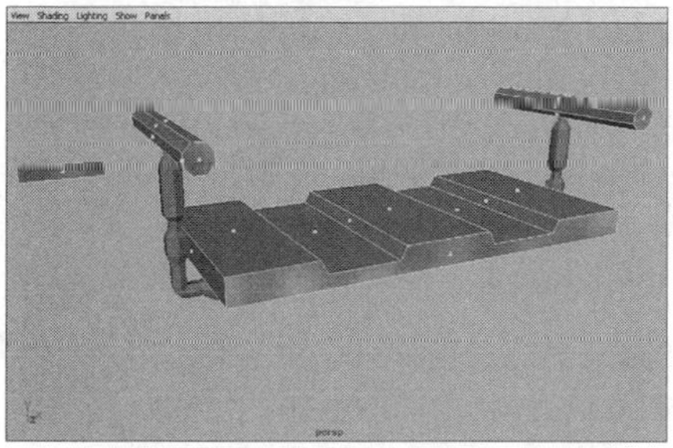

FIGURE 20.80 Four faces selected.

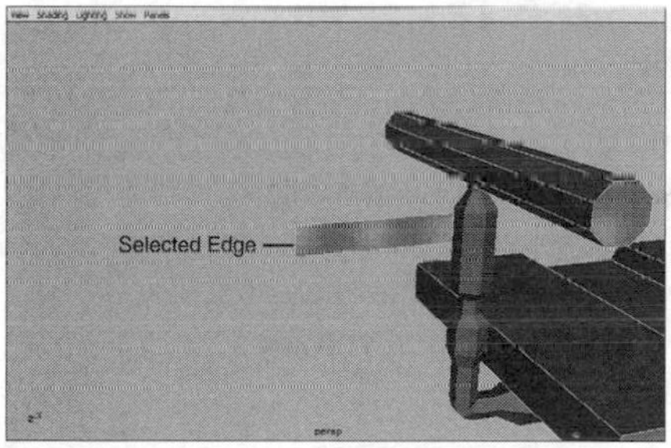

FIGURE 20.81 The selected edge.

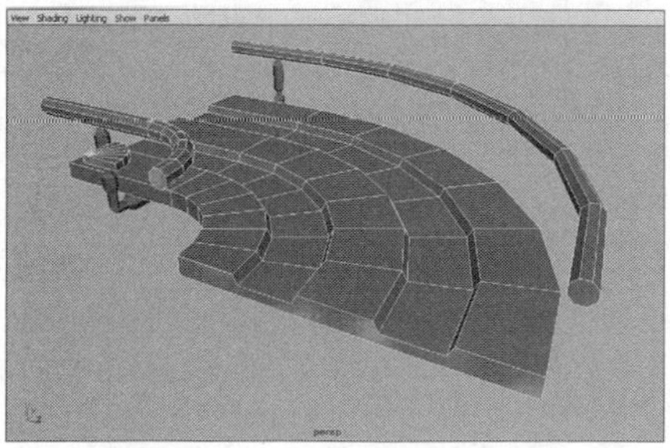

FIGURE 20.82 You've just added the 90-degree turn to your catwalk.

6. As you rotate around the model, you might notice some hard edges on the Walkway or Rails. These hard edges look darker than the rest of the catwalk. **FIGURE 20.84** shows an example of this phenomenon.

   To fix the hard edges, select the combined object. From the main menu, choose Edit Polygons > Normals > Soften/Harden > options box. In the Soften/Harden Options dialog box, set the Angle attribute to **30**. This setting smoothes the edge between all faces that meet at a 30-degree angle or less. Incidentally, it also removes the darkened areas from the catwalk.

7. Make faces selectable by pressing F11, and delete the faces that make up the extra floating piece created from the edge extrusion earlier, as shown in **FIGURES 20.85** and **20.86**.

8. Select the RailSupport group, and press Ctrl+D to duplicate it. In the Channel Box, enter the following values to place the new copy on the other side of the bend (see **FIGURE 20.87**):

   Translate X: -272

   Translate Z: 208

   Rotate Y: 90

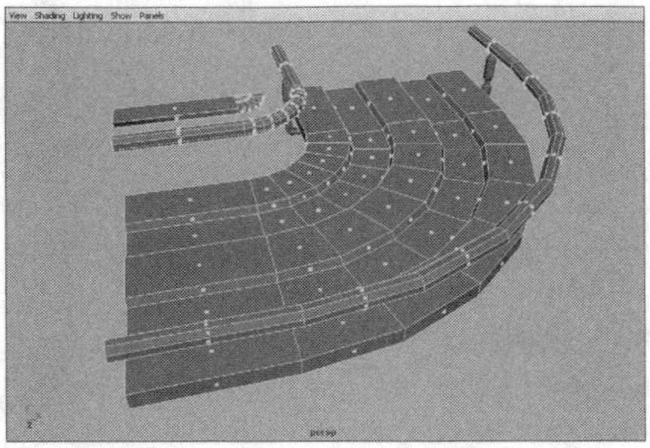

FIGURE 20.83 Your 90DegreeCatwalk's Walkway and Rails are now complete.

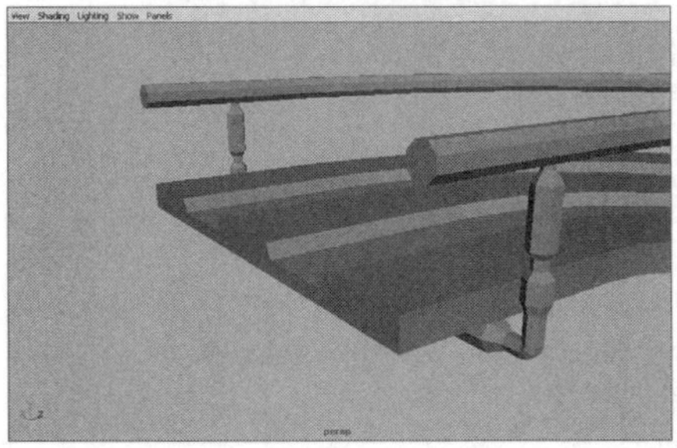

FIGURE 20.84 A model with hard edges.

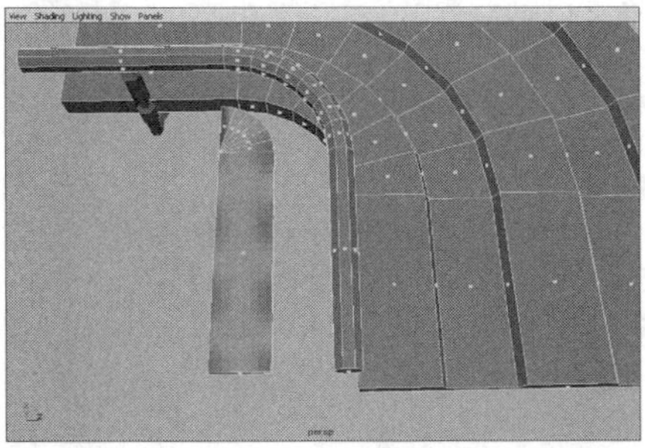

FIGURE 20.85 Select the floating face.

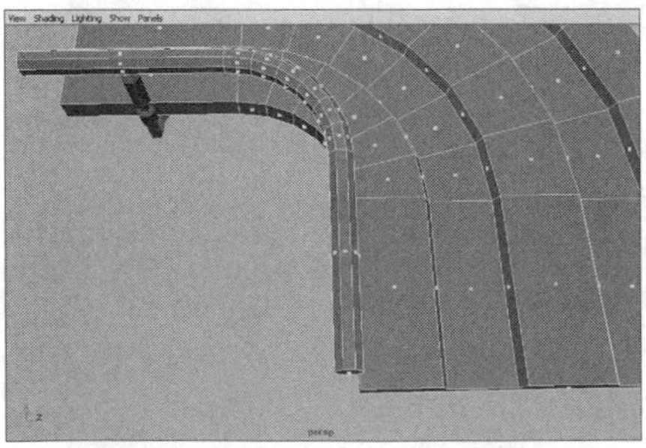

FIGURE 20.86 Press the Delete key to remove the floating face.

9. Create another duplicate of the RailSupport group, and enter the following values in the Channel Box to place a RailSupport in the middle of the bend (see **FIGURE 20.88**):

   Translate X: -61.5

   Translate Z: 146.5

   Rotate Y: -45

10. Save your work.

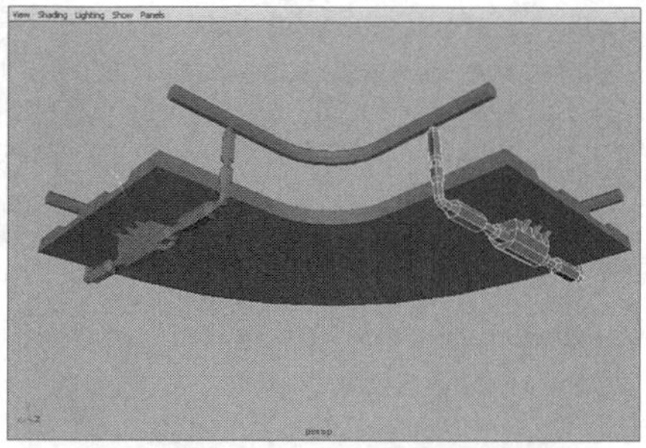

FIGURE 20.87 Your 90-degree turn now has two RailSupports.

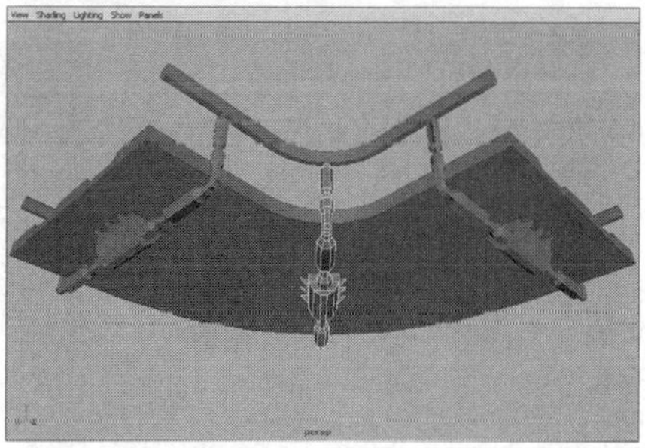

FIGURE 20.88 Your 90-degree turn now has three RailSupports.

END TUTORIAL 20.16

TUTORIAL 20.17: Modeling the 90-Degree Turn, Part III

1. Continue from **TUTORIAL 20.16**, or open the `90DegreeCatwalk.mb` file you saved earlier. **FIGURE 20.89** shows your progress so far.

2. First, draw a marquee selection around the entire catwalk. From the Polygons menu, choose Edit Polygons > Texture > Automatic Mapping.

3. Take a few minutes to apply the placeholder textures in the same pattern as you did for the StraightCatwalk (see **FIGURE 20.90**). Refer back to **TUTORIALS 20.12** and **20.13** if you need help.

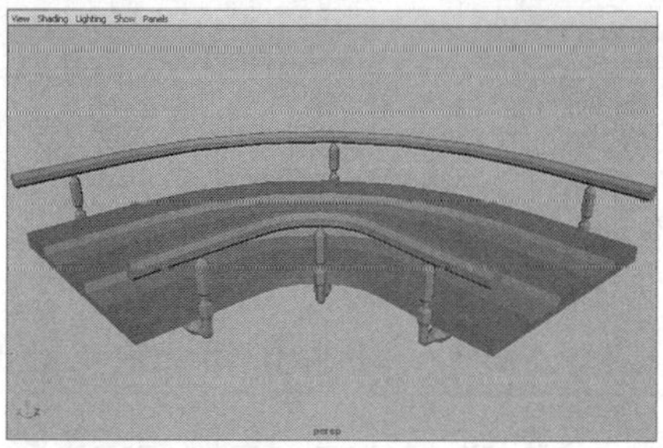

FIGURE 20.89 Your 90DegreeCatwalk's progression to this point.

4. Before you go any further, be sure to save your scene. Then choose File > Save Scene As, and save a copy of the file. Name the copy **`T_Intersection.mb`**. You'll use this file later to create the intersection.
5. Marquee-select all pieces of the catwalk, and choose Polygons > Combine from the main menu. Delete the new object's construction history, and rename it **`NinetyDegree`**.

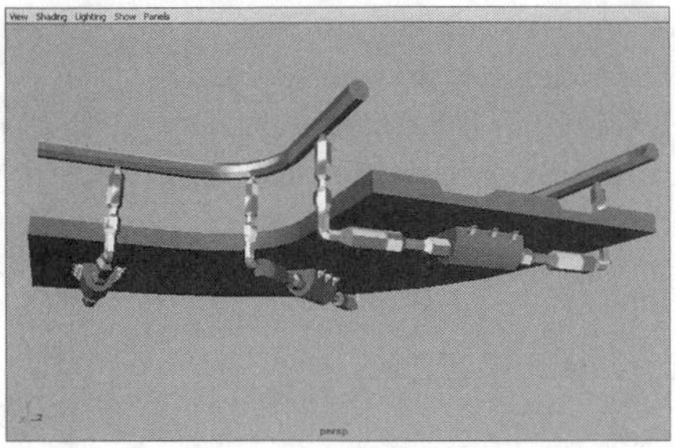

FIGURE 20.90 The 90DegreeCatwalk should look like this with placeholder textures.

> **NOTE**
>
> Object names in Maya cannot begin with a number, although scene names can.

6. Choose Polygons > Triangulate to triangulate the object (see **FIGURE 20.91**).
7. Choose File > Save Scene As. Set the name back to **`90DegreeCatwalk.mb`**, and click Save. When asked if you want to replace the existing file, click Yes.

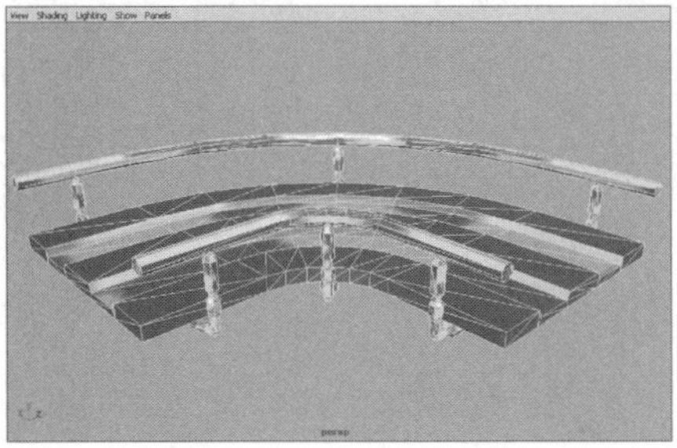

FIGURE 20.91 Your triangulated NinetyDegreeCatwalk.

END TUTORIAL 20.17

Building a T-Intersection

Now that you have created a 90-degree turn, creating the T-intersection is easy. In **TUTORIAL 20.18**, you see how to construct a fully snappable intersection model.

TUTORIAL 20.18: Creating the T-Intersection

1. Open the `T_Intersection.mb` file you saved earlier (see **FIGURE 20.92**). You'll use this file to create a T-intersection.
2. Select the RailSupport group that was placed at the catwalk's bend, and delete it (see **FIGURE 20.93**).

   Next, select the remaining pieces of the catwalk, and combine them with Polygons > Combine.

20

3. From the Edit Polygons menu, choose Cut Faces Tool > options box. In the Cut Faces Options dialog box, enter the following settings to remove the left half of the catwalk (see **FIGURE 20.94**), and click Cut when you're finished:

   Cut Direction: Custom Cut

   Cut Plane Rotation: 0 –90 0

   Delete the Cut Faces: Select this check box

4. Select the curving faces of the outermost rail, as shown in **FIGURE 20.95**, and delete them, as shown in **FIGURE 20.96**.

5. Next, you want to straighten out the curving edge of the Walkway. To do this, you use a MELScript command entered in the Command Line. (Maya Embedded Language is an internal programming language on which all of Maya's commands are structured.)

   First, switch to the Top view and select the six vertices that make up the curved edge of the walkway, as shown in **FIGURE 20.97**.

6. In the Command Line at the bottom, enter the following command:

   ```
   move -a -z 336
   ```

   This command tells Maya to move the selected components in absolute coordinates and place them at 336 in the Z-axis. The result should look like **FIGURE 20.98**.

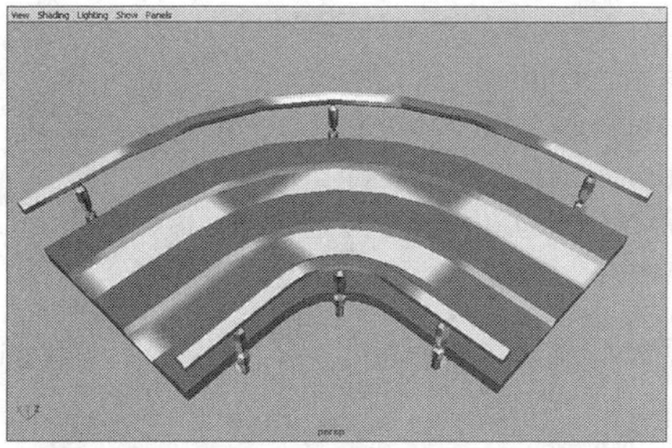

FIGURE 20.92 The NinetyDegreeCatwalk geometry is used to create the T-intersection.

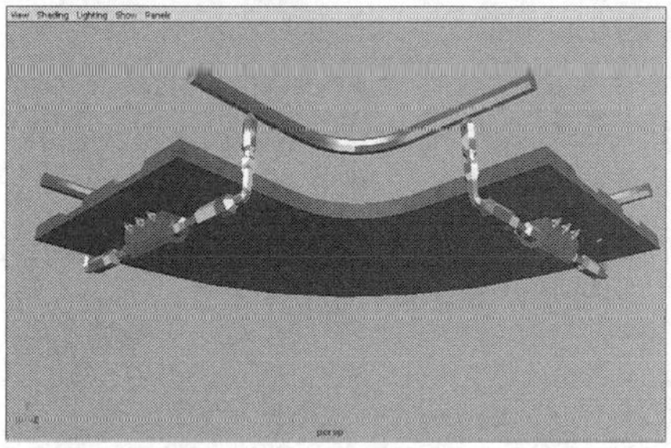

FIGURE 20.93 Now there are only two RailSupports on the catwalk.

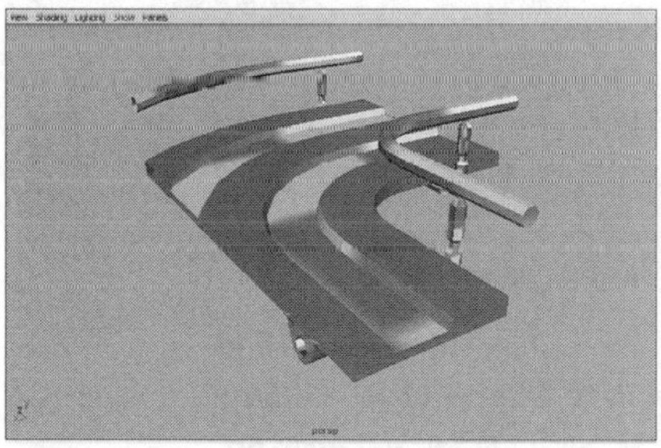

FIGURE 20.94 A piece of the catwalk has been truncated.

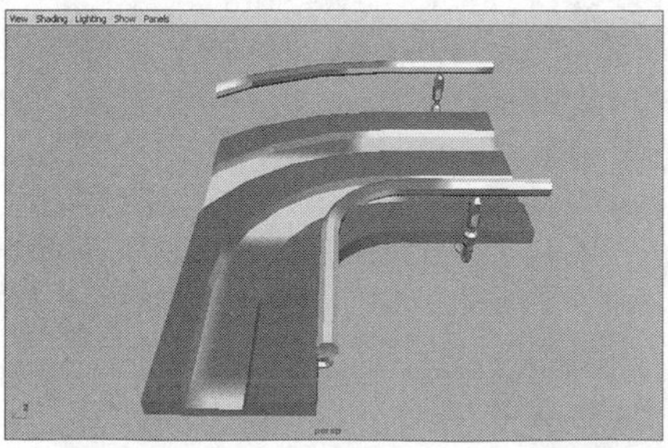

FIGURE 20.95 The rail before deleting faces.

7. Return to Object mode (F8 key). With the entire object selected, choose Polygons > Mirror Geometry > options box. In the Polygon Mirror Options dialog box, set the following:

   Mirror Direction: +X

   Merge with the Original: Select this check box

   Connect Border Edges: Select this option

   Click the Mirror button when finished. These settings mirror the object across the YZ plane in the positive direction and connect the mirrored object to your original.

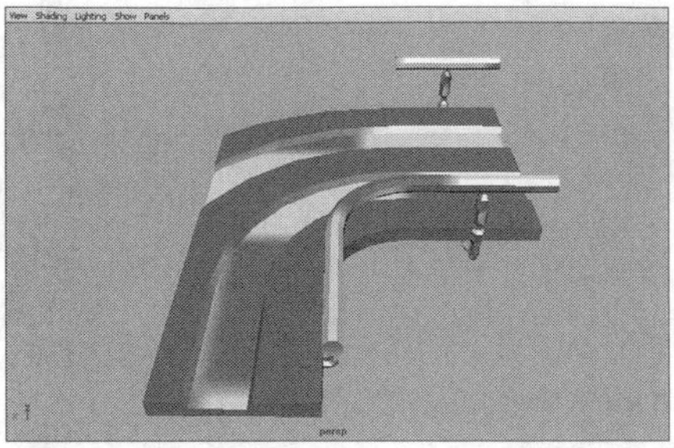

FIGURE 20.96 The rail after deleting faces.

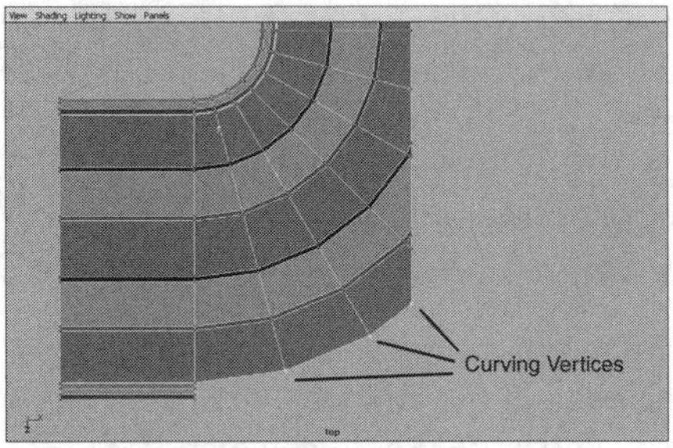

FIGURE 20.97 Select these vertices.

CAUTION

If you deleted the wrong half of the walkway, you might need to set Mirror Direction to –X.

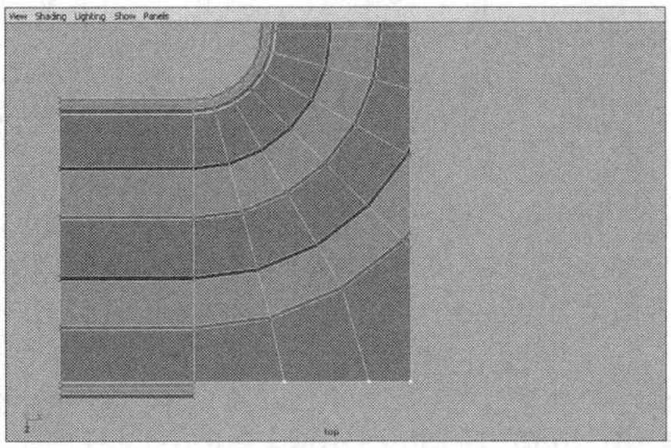

FIGURE 20.98 The edge has been straightened.

8. Delete the object's construction history. Then choose File > Save Scene As, and save a copy of the file. Name this new file **`FourWayCatwalk.mb`**.

9. Use the skills you have learned to triangulate the catwalk. Rename the object as **`T_Intersection`**. Finally, choose File > Save Scene As, and save the file as **`T_Intersection.mb`**. Overwrite the existing file. **FIGURE 20.99** shows the final results.

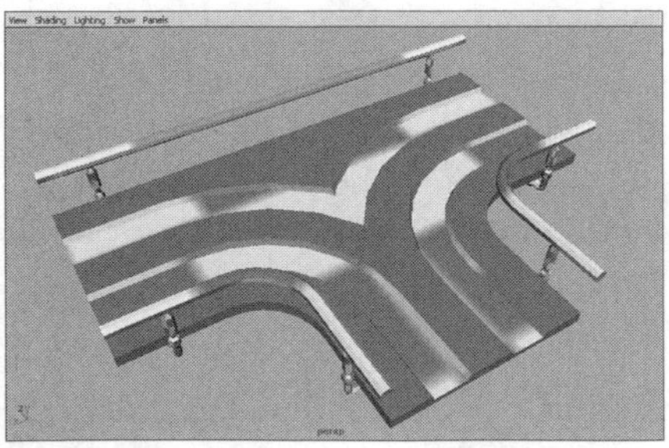

FIGURE 20.99 The T-intersection catwalk.

END TUTORIAL 20.18

Building a Four-Way Intersection

In this section, you create a four-way intersection model from the T-intersection. You use a technique similar to to the one for creating the 90-degree turn. With the completion of this model, you're nearly ready to export your models to Unreal.

In **TUTORIAL 20.19**, you see how to use the same geometry in the T-Intersection catwalk to create a four-way intersection.

TUTORIAL 20.19: Creating the Four-Way Intersection

1. Open the `FourWayCatwalk.mb` file you saved earlier. You'll use this file to create a four-way intersection. **FIGURE 20.100** shows your progress so far.

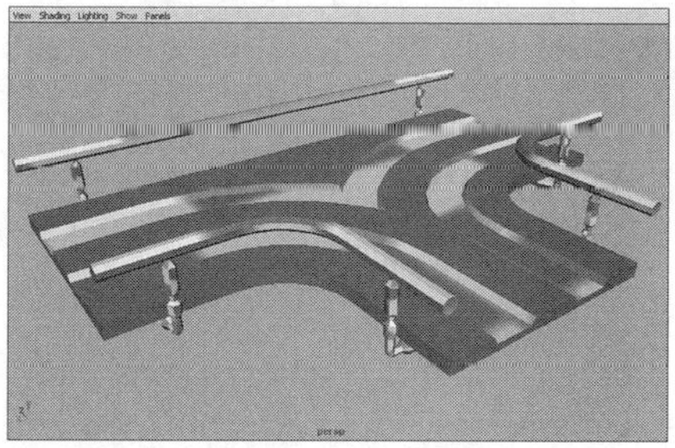

FIGURE 20.100 The T-intersection catwalk, saved just before triangulation at the end of **TUTORIAL 20.18**.

2. From the Edit Polygons menu, choose Cut Faces > options box. In the Cut Faces Options dialog box, enter the following settings to chop off the back Rail of the Walkway (see **FIGURE 20.101**), and click Cut when you're finished:

   Cut Direction: Custom Cut

   Cut Plane Center: 0 0 208

   Cut Plane Rotation: 0 180 0

   Delete the Cut Faces: Select this check box

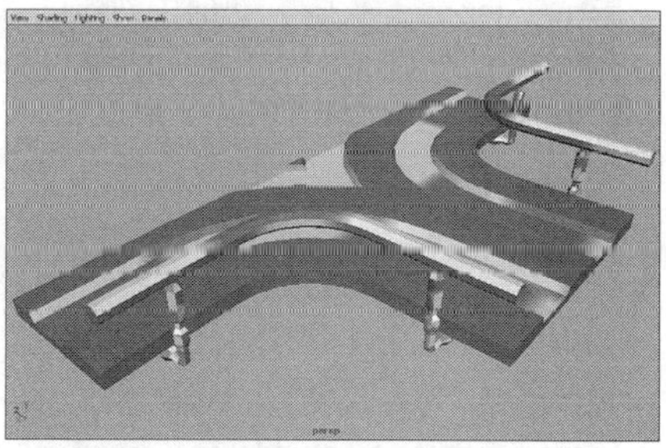

FIGURE 20.101 The back Rail of the catwalk has been truncated.

3. Select the object, and from the main menu, choose Polygons > Mirror Geometry > options box. Set the following options, and click Mirror when finished (see **FIGURE 20.102**):

   Mirror Direction: +Z

   Merge with the Original: Select this check box

   Connect Border Edges: Select this option

4. Triangulate the model, and rename it as **FourWay**. Delete its construction history, and save your work.

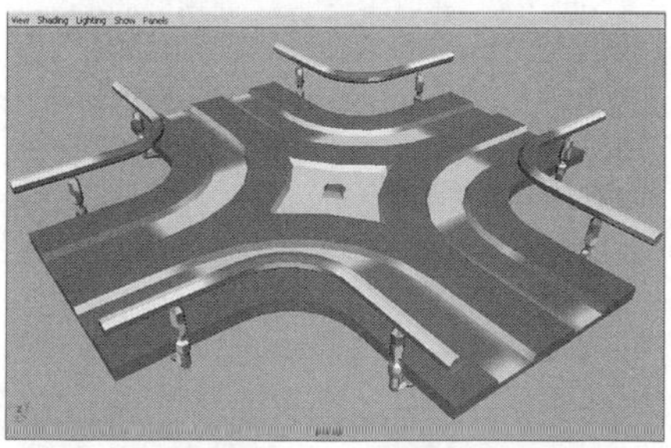

FIGURE 20.102 The four-way catwalk.

END TUTORIAL 20.19

Collision Models

When creating your static meshes, creating a custom collision model for your mesh is a good idea. If you don't, all collisions on your new static mesh are calculated on a per-polygon basis, which can slow down game speed drastically. Best of all, if created correctly, a collision model remains invisible by default, meaning that it simplifies your collisions without hiding or obstructing your existing geometry. In **TUTORIAL 20.20**, you learn how to create a collision model for the StraightCatwalk model you created earlier. From there, you use the skills you have learned to create collision models for the other catwalk models.

TUTORIAL 20.20: Creating a Collision Model for the StraightCatwalk

1. Open the `StraightCatwalk.mb` file (see **FIGURE 20.103**). In this tutorial, you'll be creating the collision model for the StraightCatwalk. You then use the skills you have learned throughout this chapter to construct collision models for the other catwalks.

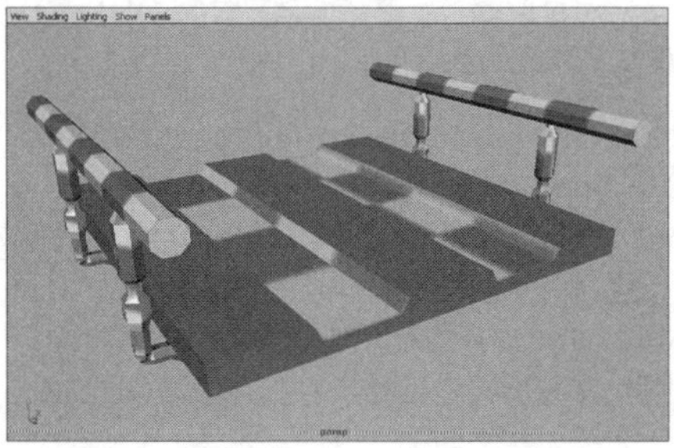

FIGURE 20.103 The StraightCatwalk.

2. The idea is to keep your collision models much simpler than your actual geometry. To do this, create a polygon cube with the following settings:

   Width: 256

   Height: 16

   Depth: 256

   Subdivisions Width: 1

   Subdivisions Height: 1

   Subdivisions Depth: 1

3. In the Channel Box, set Translate Y to **-8**. This cube serves as the collision model for the floor (see **FIGURE 20.104**).

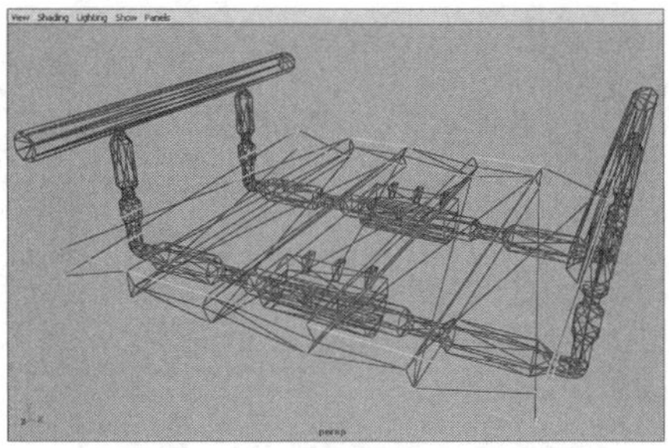

FIGURE 20.104 The collision model for the floor is ready.

4. To create collision models for the Rail objects, create a new cube with the following settings:

   Width: 16

   Height: 64

   Depth: 256

5. In the Channel Box, place the cube at the following coordinates:

   Translate X: 136

   Translate Y: 32

   Translate Z: 0

   Duplicate this cube, and set the duplicate's Translate X to **-136**. **FIGURE 20.105** shows the results.

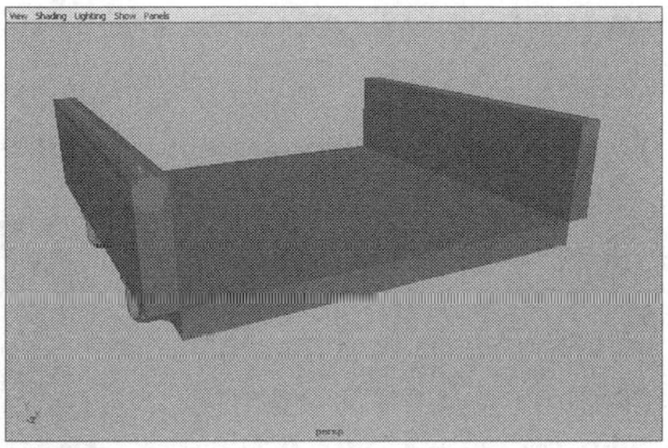

FIGURE 20.105 The collision models for the Rails are set up.

6. Create two cubes with the following dimensions:

   Width: 64

   Height: 25

   Depth: 32

   Place the cubes at the following coordinates to provide collisions for the Anchors under the Walkway:

First Cube	Second Cube
Translate X: 0	Translate X: 0
Translate Y: -30	Translate Y: -30
Translate Z: -64	Translate Z: 64

7. Select all five of the new cubes you have created. They are named pCube1 through pCube5. Use the skills you have learned to combine them into a single object. Rename the object as **MCDCX_Collision**, and triangulate it.

NOTE

The MCDCX prefix is important. It tells UnrealEd that this model is a collision hull and keeps it from being visible in the game.

8. With the new collision model selected, Shift-select the StraightCatwalk object. It might be easier to do this in Wireframe mode.
9. Next, press P to parent the collision model to the catwalk. This step is essential, as this collision model must be exported with your base model.
10. Use the skills you have learned in this chapter to create collision models for the rest of your catwalks. Remember to keep them as simple as possible, and always name them by using the `MCDCX` prefix. Parent each collision model to its respective base model when finished, and save your work. **FIGURES 20.106** and **20.107** show collision models for the other meshes.

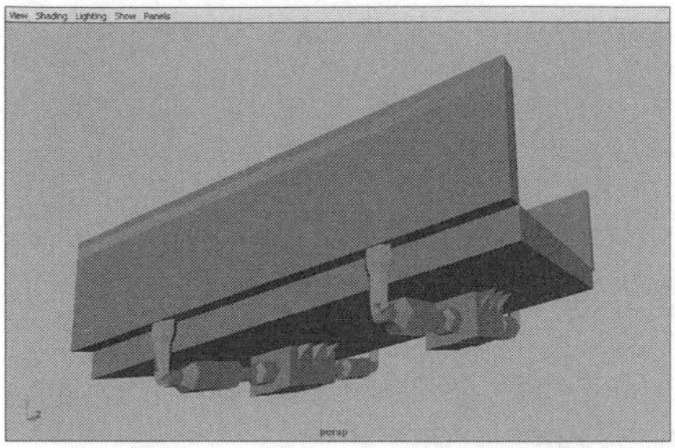

FIGURE 20.106 The collision model for the RampCatwalk.

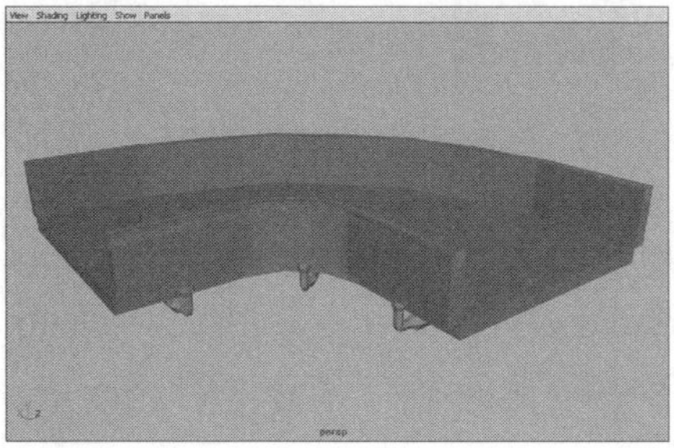

FIGURE 20.107 The collision model for the 90DegreeCatwalk.

END TUTORIAL 20.20

Exporting Models to UnrealEd

Now that you have completed all your models, you need to get them into UnrealEd so that you can actually place them in a level. To do this, you use the Unreal Tournament 2004 Exporter plug-in included with this book or with the UT2004 game. **TUTORIAL 20.21** introduces you to how this exporter program is used to send your meshes to UnrealEd.

TUTORIAL 20.21: Exporting Static Meshes from Maya into UnrealEd

1. Now that you have all the static meshes completed, you can export them to UnrealEd. To begin, open the `StraightCatwalk.mb` file you saved earlier (see **FIGURE 20.108**).
2. Using the aforementioned UnrealEd Exporter plug-in, select the UnrealEdExport tab in the Shelf.
3. Click the Connect to UnrealEd icon. If you don't already have UnrealEd running, the plug-in starts it for you.
4. Select the StraightCatwalk model, and click the Static Mesh Export button to open the Static Mesh Export dialog box.

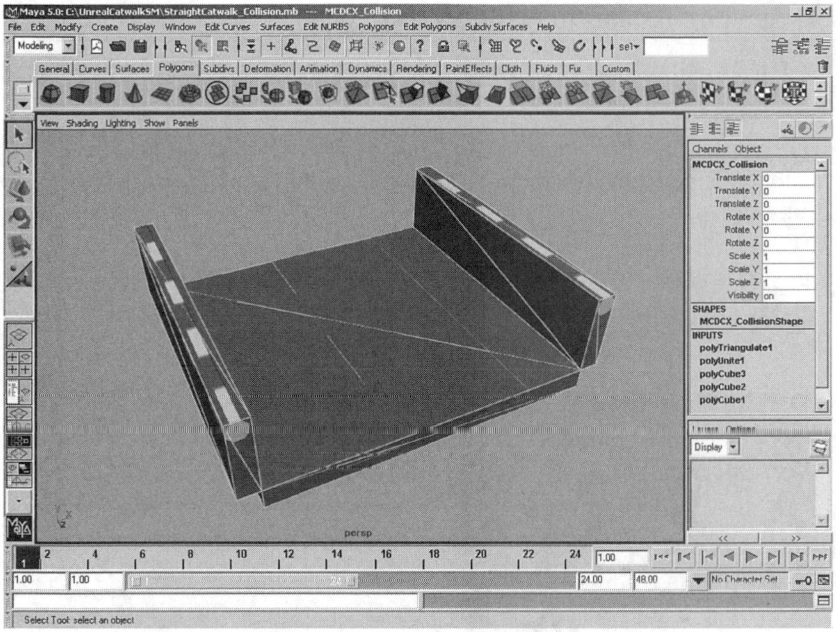

FIGURE 20.108 The StraightCatwalk with collision model.

5. In the Package drop-down list, select Create New Package. In the New Package dialog box that opens, enter **MyCatwalks**. Click OK when finished.

6. Select Create New Group, and enter **Catwalks1** in the New Group dialog box.

   Note that the name of the object, StraightCatwalk, has already been placed in the Name text box. Leave the Relative/World Space radio buttons set to Relative.

7. Click the Export button. You see a return message in the gray area of the Command Line at the bottom of the Maya window, which should say `Result: Export Complete`.

8. Repeat these steps for each mesh you have created. When you're finished, all the meshes will be in UnrealEd. In **TUTORIAL 20.22**, you see how to access these meshes and apply textures to them. You can close Maya now.

END TUTORIAL 20.21

Texturing Your Static Meshes in UnrealEd

After all your meshes are available in UnrealEd, you need to apply textures to them. This is where the placeholder textures you applied earlier come in handy. In **TUTORIAL 20.22**, you see how to use the Textures browser and the Static Mesh browser to select and apply textures to your new static meshes.

TUTORIAL 20.22: Applying Textures to Static Meshes

1. Continuing from **TUTORIAL 20.21**, open the Static Mesh browser, and use the Package drop-down list to switch to the myCatwalks package.
2. All your static meshes are listed on the left side. Click the StraightCatwalk mesh to select it. Notice that it is currently textured with the default green bubbly texture (see **FIGURE 20.109**).

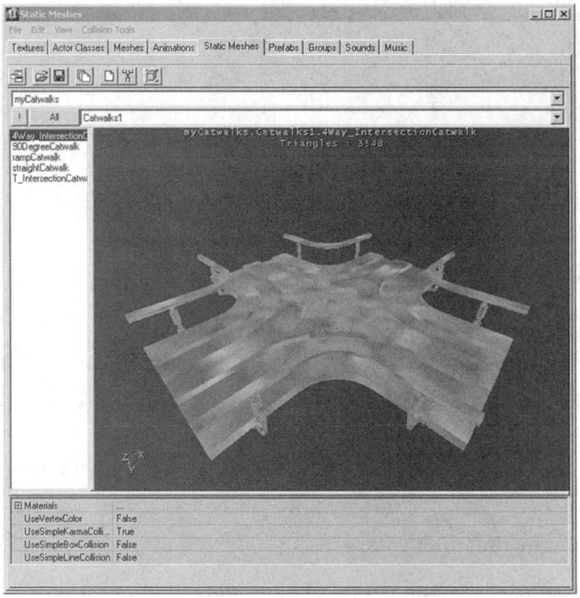

FIGURE 20.109 The meshes are now accessible in the Static Mesh browser.

3. Switch to the Textures browser. Open the `Chapter20.utx` package, and locate the Walkway texture. Back in the Static Mesh browser, expand the Materials category for the StraightCatwalk mesh, and then expand Material [0]. Click the `Texture` property, and click the Use button. If you don't see the result right away, move the browser's viewport to update it.
4. Repeat this procedure to place the Rail texture in the Material [1] Texture property and the Deco texture in the Material [2] Texture property. The StraightCatwalk is now textured (see **FIGURE 20.110**).
5. Next, use the same techniques to apply textures to the other meshes. Depending on the order in which you applied the placeholder textures, you might need to change the order in which you apply the textures. Just make sure they all appear to be textured in the same fashion.
6. Choose File > Save from the Static Mesh browser menu. Name the file **MyCatwalks**, and click Yes when asked to overwrite.

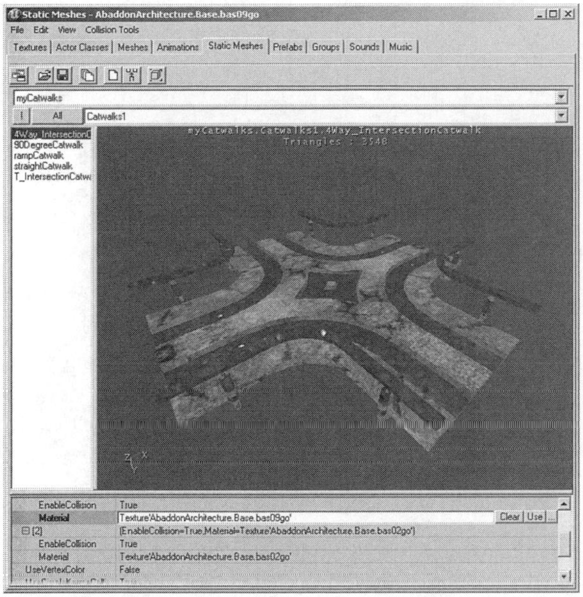

FIGURE 20.110 The first catwalk is now textured.

END TUTORIAL 20.22

Congratulations! Your static meshes are now ready to be placed in a level. Because you created each mesh by keeping it snapped to the grid, you'll find that you can place the meshes perfectly end to end while leaving UnrealEd's snap grid at a high setting, such as 32 or 64. You can use them in a level.

Summary

By now, you should be reasonably comfortable with the methods for creating a model in Maya and exporting it to UnrealEd. You have learned not only the modeling process, but also adding placeholder textures to your model and importing them into an Unreal level. In Chapter 21, "Character Modeling," you learn how you can model your own character in Maya to be used in Unreal Tournament 2004.

Chapter 21

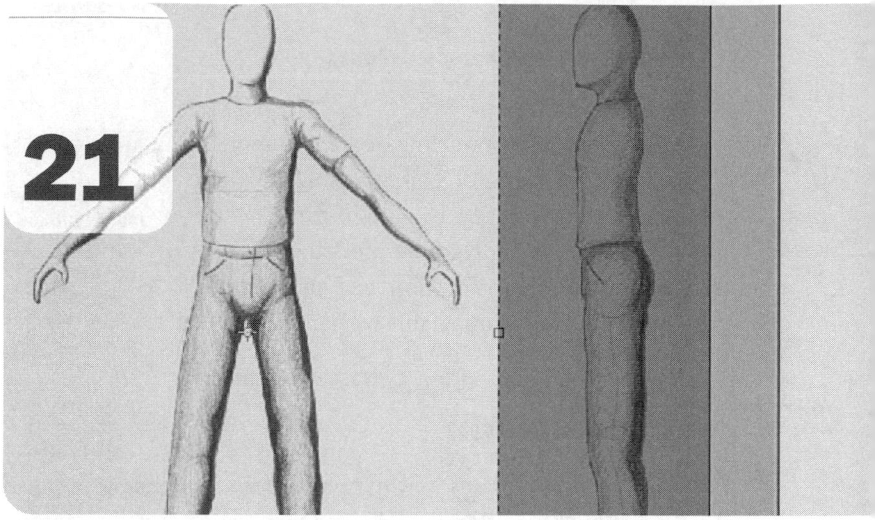

Character Modeling

This chapter discusses the steps for creating your own characters to be placed within the Unreal Engine. Throughout this chapter, you see how to model a complete game character. There are, however, a couple of things you should keep in mind. First, for the purpose of this chapter, the character you'll be working on is relatively simple, without complex armor, decorations, or even any facial detail. This has been done to keep tutorials straightforward so that you can create a character that's easy to visualize.

Second, this chapter covers modeling techniques in general terms. This means that step-by-step processes for the exact placement of each vertex of the model aren't demonstrated. To put it more bluntly, this chapter assumes that you already have a working knowledge of modeling tools. This has been done primarily to simplify the chapter and prevent it from becoming too excessive. Also, the steps for this chapter's tutorials progressively become less detailed, reflecting your increasing experience with the modeling process.

If you're new to modeling or are still uncomfortable with the polygon modeling tools and techniques in Maya, be sure to turn back to Chapter 18, "Polygonal Modeling Tools." Remember that only time and practice can make you feel comfortable with modeling.

NOTE

As this chapter is fairly straightforward, it becomes mainly tutorial based after you begin modeling.

Preparation

This section explains how to prepare for a modeling project. You should never simply dive into a modeling project without having planned what you're going to do. To help with this planning process, a few simple guidelines are offered in the following sections; you can follow these guidelines to help you get started modeling as soon as possible.

In Chapter 2, "The Process of Game Development," you learned how to develop the story for your game. During this phase, you also develop the stories and backgrounds behind each character. Because this topic has already been covered, this chapter and subsequent ones focus more on the actual creation process rather than on plot and character development.

Concept Art

Before you begin modeling, knowing what your character is going to look like is a good idea. You probably already have a general idea of the kind of character you want to make; however, you'll find it much easier to make important decisions about the character's design, posture, and even its texture and animation if you've already made plans in each of these areas. To this end, creating conceptual drawings of your character is a good idea. If you're not skilled at detailed drawing, these conceptual sketches can be anything: general sketches of the way your character looks, separate sketches of important pieces of the character's equipment, or anything else you deem important to the character's look.

If you're already comfortable with pencil and paper, however, you'll find it's helpful to expand your conceptual drawings to include dynamic action poses, stance and posture drawings, and anything else that helps you remember not only what the character looks like, but how the character is intended to move and behave.

Image Planes

After you've drawn exactly what the character should look like, you can use those drawings as a basis to create your 3D model. To accomplish this, you need to create a pair of schematic-style drawings of your character: one from an orthographic side view, and the other from an orthographic front view. You can then download these images into Maya and use them to derive the locations for each polygon of your model. In this section, you see how to create these image planes and make them visible in the Maya viewport. Again, however, this book isn't intended to instruct you on drawing techniques, so this chapter offers only a series of guidelines for creating your own image planes. **FIGURE 21.1** shows an example of the pair of image planes used to create the character in this chapter.

When creating your own image planes, first keep in mind that all parts of your character must be aligned in both the front and side views. With image planes, you'll constantly reference parts of the model from one view to the next. If, for example, your character's head is taller in one image than it is in the other, you could run into a severe problem: The model would line up with one image but not with the other. If you tried to adjust the model to match the other image, it would no longer match the first. This problem can lead to a nightmarish cycle of moving back and forth incessantly between images trying to make your model look correct.

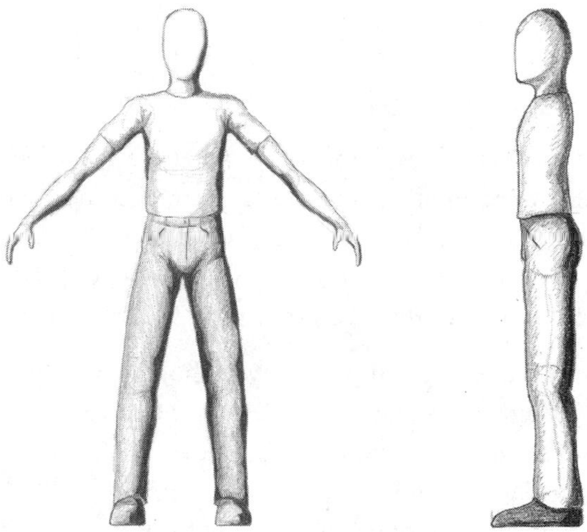

FIGURE 21.1 On the left, a side view; on the right, a front view.

To avoid this problem from the outset, make sure you create image planes so that all parts of the images line up. For example, you want the characters in both images to be exactly the same height. You also want their shoulders, knees, ankles, waistline, and so forth to be the same height from the ground. **FIGURE 21.2** is a diagram of the two image planes shown earlier, but this time with lines running between the two to demonstrate how each part of the two images aligns with each other.

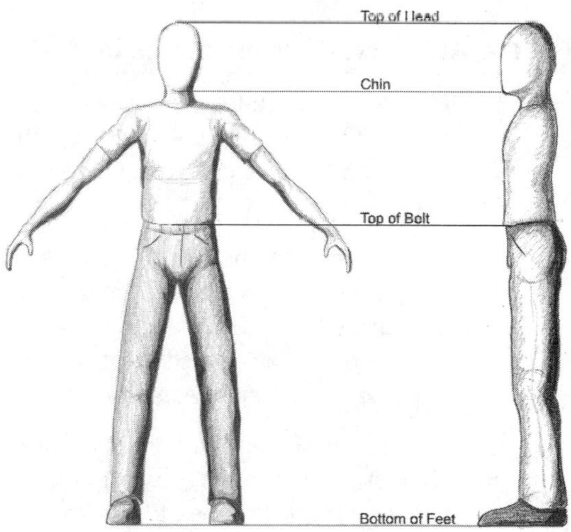

FIGURE 21.2 Image planes with lines connecting each major part.

Minor inconsistencies between the two images are acceptable and can be difficult to avoid if you're using hand-drawn image planes. Just remember to keep these inconsistencies to a minimum; this precaution makes your modeling experience faster and easier. For example, if your character's nose goes a tad further down the face in the front view than it does in the side view, you could compensate by simply averaging the distance between the two images. Don't let yourself get too hung up with small inconsistencies. As long as your major proportions are correct, the model should turn out just fine. Besides, you can always make corrections (commonly known as *tweaks*) later when your model is near completion.

Image Plane Set Up

If you have drawn your image planes so that everything is nicely lined up and proportional, setting them up in Maya is no problem. Your next job is scanning the drawings into your computer and verifying that everything is still aligned. Scanning can sometimes lead to small distortions in your images, depending on where on the scanner's glass you placed the object, whether the scanner automatically crops your images, and many other factors.

After scanning your images, you should open them in an application such as Photoshop and verify their alignment. In **TUTORIAL 21.1**, you see how to do this in Photoshop so that you can be sure you have accurate image planes. This tutorial is simply intended to demonstrate a technique, not to go into deep explanations of what each tool or command is doing.

> **NOTE**
>
> **If you don't have a copy of Photoshop, the final image planes have been supplied in JPEG format as `CharacterFront(IP).jpg` and `CharacterSide(IP).jpg`.**

TUTORIAL 21.1: Aligning Images in Photoshop

1. The images have already been scanned for you, but although the drawn proportions are correct, you'll see that they don't line up properly with one another. First, start Photoshop, and then open the files `OriginalScanFront.jpg` and `OrignalScanSide.jpg` (see **FIGURE 21.3**).

2. Because of scanning, the two images are slightly different sizes. To fix this problem, you need to get the two images into the same document. First, you need to make the front image's canvas larger to hold both images. Select the front image, and choose Image > Canvas Size from the Photoshop menu. Set the Width value to 10, and be sure to anchor the image on the left side, as shown in **FIGURE 21.4**.

3. Now that the canvas for the front image is larger, it can hold both the front and side images. Move the side image over to the same canvas by selecting the Move tool and dragging from the side image to the front image. This creates a duplicate of the side image as a new layer and places it in the same document as the front image.

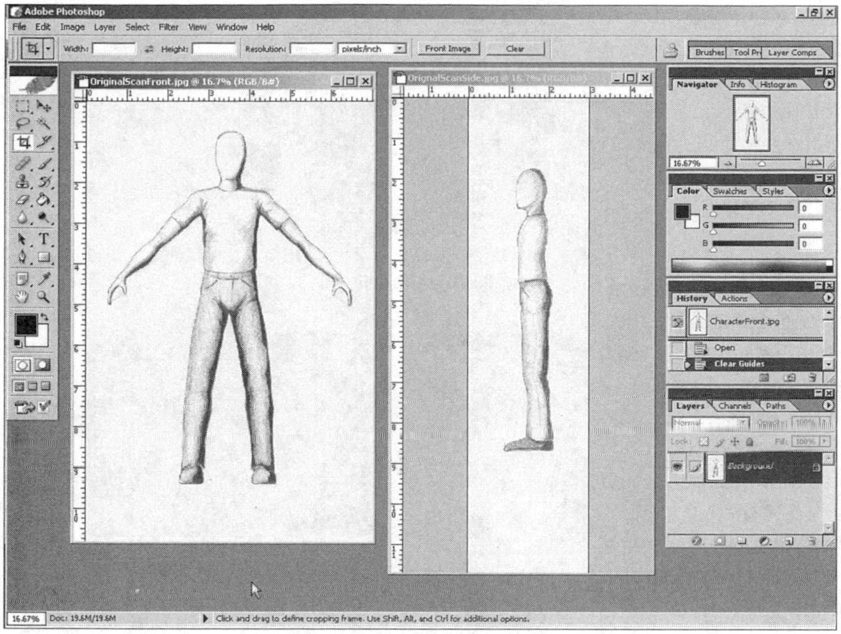

FIGURE 21.3 Both images open in Photoshop.

4. Even though both images are now in the same document, they are separate layers, meaning they can be altered and affected separately. If you look in the Layers palette, you can see that Layer 1 is actually the side view (see **FIGURE 21.5**). As long as it's selected, you can use the Move tool to move the side image around the canvas without affecting the front image.

5. You can use this layering to your advantage. Because you can't currently affect the front view, you can assume that it's correct and adjust the side view to match it. First, however, you need to set up some guides so that you know how to adjust the side image.

   Make sure rulers are visible on the document. If they aren't, simply

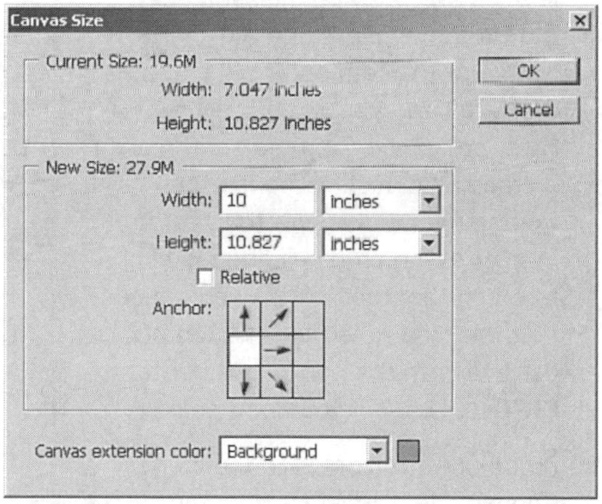

FIGURE 21.4 The Canvas Size dialog box.

> **NOTE**
>
> You can change the color of the guide lines by choosing Edit > Preferences > Guides, Grid & Slices from the Photoshop menu.

press Ctrl+R. Click and drag from the ruler at the top of the screen, and drag a blue guide down to the top of the front image's head. Repeat and place another guide at the bottom of the feet. Use **FIGURE 21.6** as a guide if you need help.

6. With Layer 1 still selected, choose Edit > Transform > Scale from the menu. While holding down the Shift key for uniform scaling, drag the selection's corner markers to scale the image up so that the top of the head and bottom of the feet match the guides (see **FIGURE 21.7**). You'll likely have to move the image as well. To do this, simply drag near the middle of the image.

7. Now you need to split the document apart so that you have two separate images again. To do this, you use the Crop tool. First, use the Navigator to zoom out a bit, just so that you can see the entire canvas. Next, select the Crop tool, and make a cropping selection around the front image. Make sure the center marker of the crop selection is centered on the front image, and notice that the crop runs from the top of the image to the bottom. (Refer to **FIGURE 21.7** if you need help.)

8. Press Enter to complete the crop. Choose File > Save As from the menu, and save the image as `FrontImage.jpg`.

9. Undo the crop by pressing Shift+Ctrl+Z. Make a new crop in the side view, and save it in the same fashion with the name `SideImage.jpg`.

END TUTORIAL 21.1

FIGURE 21.5 Notice that the Layer 1 image is actually the side view.

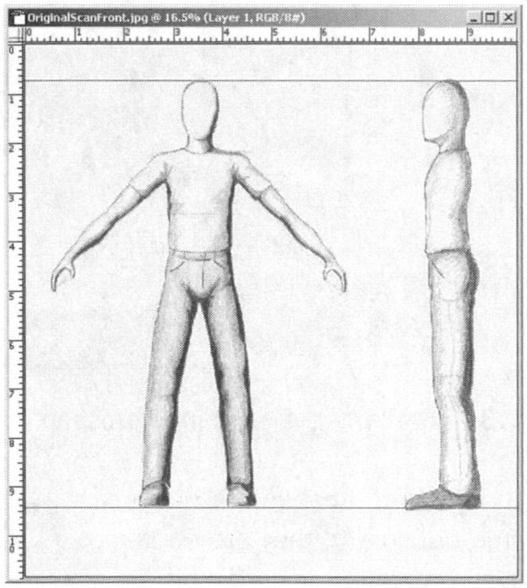

FIGURE 21.6 The top and bottom guides in place.

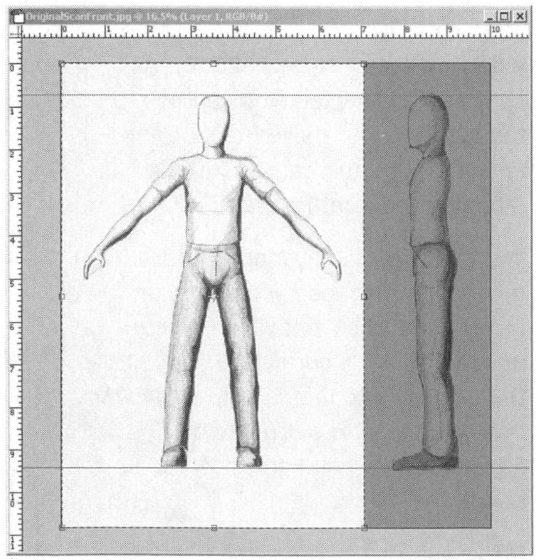

FIGURE 21.7 After using the Scale command, the side and front views match.

Darkening Image Planes

If you leave your image planes white, often you have a hard time seeing the green and pale-blue wireframe lines for your model. Instead of spending time changing your wireframe colors, simply darken the image planes to make the wireframe stand out. In **TUTORIAL 21.2**, you see how to use a single Photoshop command to make this happen.

TUTORIAL 21.2: Lowering the Image Plane Brightness

1. Continue from **TUTORIAL 21.1**, or open the two image planes you just saved.
2. With FrontImage.jpg selected, choose Image > Adjustments > Brightness/Contrast. Set the Brightness value to `-100` (see **FIGURE 21.8**).

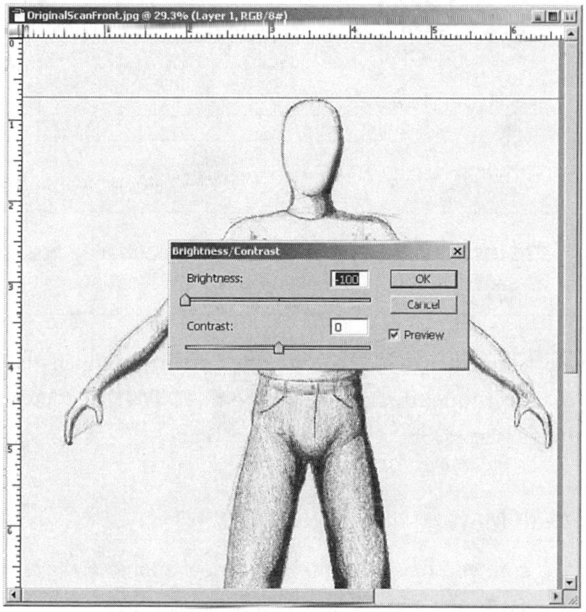

FIGURE 21.8 The Brightness/Contrast dialog box.

3. Repeat the process for the second image. Save the images as `FrontFinal.jpg` and `SideFinal.jpg`.

END TUTORIAL 21.2

Importing Image Planes into Maya

Now that your image planes are created, it's time to import them into Maya and use them to create a model. In the following tutorials, you see how this is done and learn how to make sure the image planes are properly aligned in the viewports. You'll also learn how to set up a Maya project to control where your files are being saved.

TUTORIAL 21.3: Creating a Project in Maya

1. Begin by starting Maya. Before you bring in the image planes, you need to create a new project by choosing File > Project > New from the main Maya menu.
2. Name the new project `UnrealCharacter`, and set an appropriate path location, such as C:\ (see **FIGURE 21.9**). Leave the rest of the lines blank, as you don't need to create a folder structure. Click Accept when done.
3. Next, choose File > New Scene from the menu to verify that your next save will be placed in your new project folder.

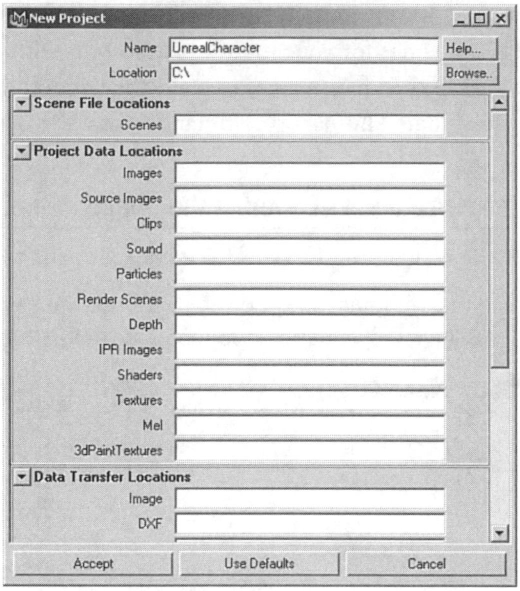

FIGURE 21.9 Fill in the New Project dialog box as shown in this figure, using any path location.

END TUTORIAL 21.3

Now that your project is set up, you're ready to begin working. You'll start by bringing in the images you altered in Photoshop so that you can model directly from them. **TUTORIAL 21.4** shows you how to do this by using Maya's image planes.

TUTORIAL 21.4: Loading Image Planes in Maya

1. Continuing from **TUTORIAL 21.3**, make sure you have just started a new scene in Maya.
2. Tap the spacebar while the mouse cursor is over the main viewport to switch to the Four View layout, as shown in **FIGURE 21.10**.
3. Choose View > Image Plane > Import Image from the Front viewport panel menu, and navigate to the `FrontFinal.jpg` file you saved earlier.
4. As soon as the image plane is visible (this might take a few minutes), set or verify the following attributes in the Channel Box on the right side of the screen, as shown in **FIGURE 21.11**: If an attribute is not specified in a step, leave it at its default value.

   Center X: 0

   Center Y: 0

   Center Z: -20

   Width: 30

   Height: 30

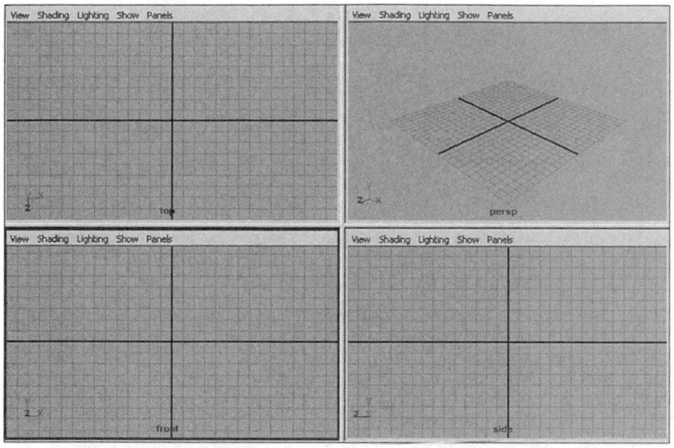

FIGURE 21.10 The Four View layout.

5. Switch to the Side viewport, and repeat step 3 to import the `SideFinal.jpg` image into the viewport. Then set the following attributes in the Channel Box:

   Center X: 0

   Center Y: 0

   Center Z: 0

   Width: 30

   Height: 30

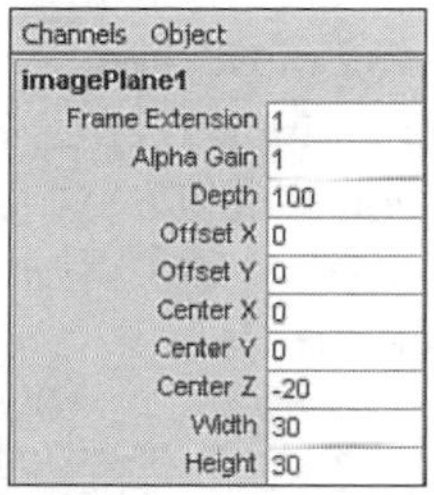

FIGURE 21.11 Set the attributes as shown in the image.

6. Switch to the Perspective viewport, and notice that you can now see both image planes clearly in the viewport (see **FIGURE 21.12**). Because you set the Center X and Center Z attributes on the image planes, the planes themselves are offset from the center of the grid. This means they won't be in your way if you work in the Perspective view. Best of all, because of the nature of orthographic viewports, there's no difference in the Front and Side views when the image planes are moved out in this manner.

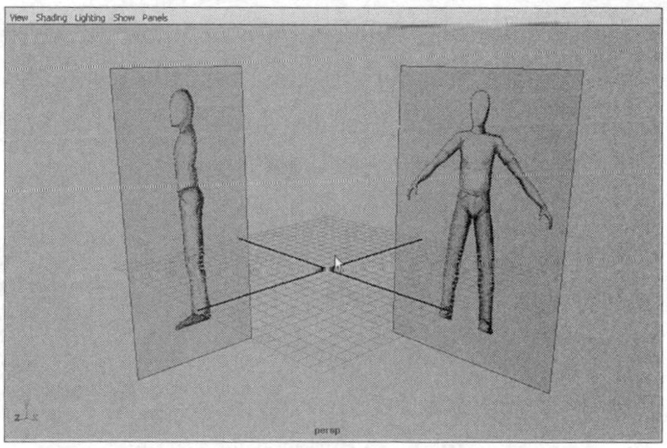

FIGURE 21.12 Both image planes are now visible in the viewport.

7. Save the file as `UnrealCharacter_Start.mb`.

END TUTORIAL 21.4

21

The Modeling Process

In this section and the following subsections, you'll be modeling your Unreal character. You can use many methods for polygon modeling, as described in Chapter 18. For this chapter, you'll model based on preexisting polygon shapes (primitives) to expedite the modeling process and make the steps easier for you to follow. Keep in mind, however, that the techniques demonstrated in the following sections are not hard-and-fast rules for character modeling. There are numerous ways to go about modeling characters, none of which is more or less correct than the next. After you have experienced modeling on your own, you'll develop your own workflow, which may or may not resemble the workflow used in this book. Before you begin the following tutorials, make sure you're relatively comfortable with manipulating polygon components, especially vertices, in Maya.

Before you start, read on for a discussion of how modeling from image planes actually works. You begin by bringing in a piece of geometry, whether it's a cube, a cylinder, or any other object. You then access the object's vertices and move them so that they appear to be in the same location on both images. For example, if you position a vertex so that it appears to be on the front of the character's chest in the Front view, you should make sure it seems to be in the same location in the Side view. If you follow this pattern with all vertices of your model, eventually you get a shape that strongly resembles your drawing.

Modeling and Animation

When creating a polygon model that will be animated, especially a character, it's important to know how much physical detail is needed to achieve the look you want and to allow for proper deformation of the model when animated. If you have too much detail, the model wastes precious polygons on the screen and is tedious to *skin* (attach the geometry to the joints). On the other hand, without enough detail, the geometry, such as arms, legs, shoulders, and hips, looks strange when bending or flexing. Consider the following example: Try to bend an ordinary drinking straw. You'll see that it creases and makes a sharp fold. On the other hand, if you do the same thing with a bendable straw, you get a smoother fold. The bendable straw has a series of edges around one section, allowing the shape to deform. The same thing is true of polygonal geometry.

In the example shown in **FIGURES 21.13** and **21.14**, a simple cylinder-style arm has been created. The first example has only two subdivisions along the length of the arm. The second has four subdivisions, mostly centered on the elbow area, as that's where most of the deformation would take place.

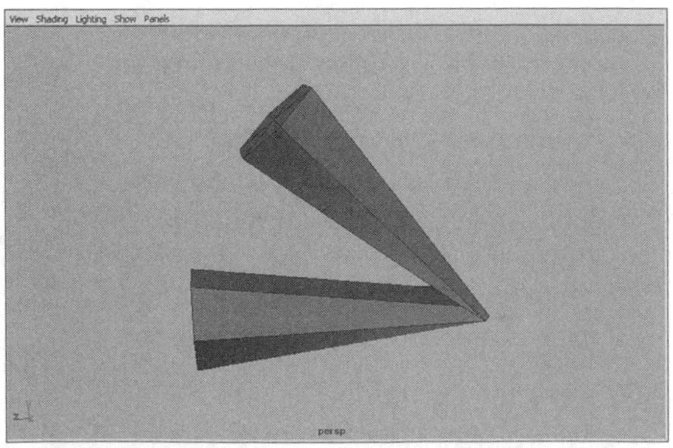

FIGURE 21.13 An arm with two subdivisions at the elbow.

When modeling characters, always keep in mind what they are intended to do. If a character is simply going to walk across your scene, you don't need a tremendous amount of detail for animation. If, on the other hand, the character performs a long series of acrobatic moves, you need more points of flexibility and more detail at areas of deformation.

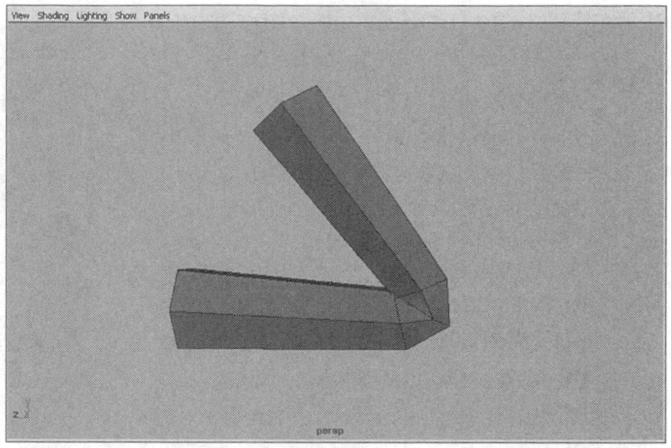

FIGURE 21.14 An arm with only two extra subdivisions added to the elbow. Notice how much better the arm keeps its volume at the bend.

The Character

For this model, you'll use the torso as the starting point for the modeling process. It doesn't particularly matter where you start when modeling; any point you're comfortable with works fine.

Modeling the Torso

In **TUTORIAL 21.5**, you bring in your original shape and rough it out so that it resembles your character's torso.

TUTORIAL 21.5: Beginning the Torso

1. Open the file `UnrealCharacter_Start.mb` that you saved earlier, or simply open the one from the CD.
2. Press F3 to enter the Modeling menu set, and choose Create > Polygon Primitives > Cube from the main Maya menu (see **FIGURE 21.15**). Press 5 to use Smooth Shaded mode in the Perspective viewport.
3. Switch to the Front view, and then move and scale the cube to fill the general proportions of the character's torso, from the base of the crotch to the top of the shoulder (see **FIGURE 21.16**). Keep in mind that you're scaling it only in the Front view at this time.

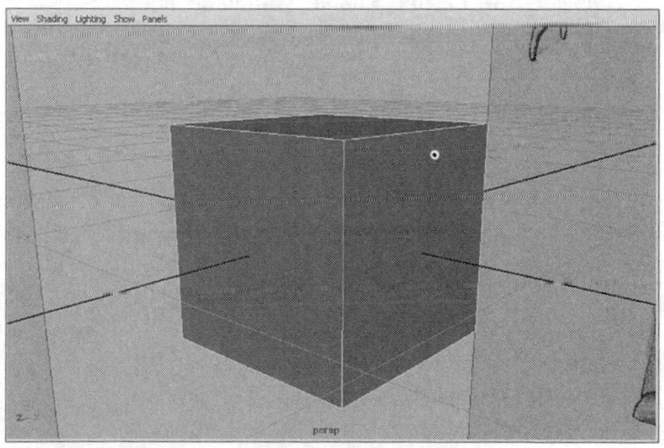

FIGURE 21.15 The initial cube.

> **TIP**
>
> You should move the cube only in the Y-axis.

4. Switch to the Side view, and then move and scale the cube to fill the torso volume from the side (see **FIGURE 21.17**). You should move and scale the cube only in the Z-axis.

5. Next you'll add more subdivisions to the cube so that you have more vertices with which to model. With the cube selected, click in the Channel Box, under the Inputs section, on the word `polyCube1`. This gives you access to the cube's Input node, allowing you to alter its construction history. Set the following attributes, as shown in **FIGURE 21.18**:

   Subdivisions Width: 4

   Subdivisions Height: 8

   Subdivisions Depth: 2

> **NOTE**
>
> **The number of subdivisions used in this model was calculated based on the amount of geometric detail needed for proper animation and to achieve the desired shape. With time and practice, you'll be able to gauge how many subdivisions to use on your own work.**

6. Just one thing left to do: deleting the faces on one side of the character. Because your character is almost perfectly symmetrical, after you model half of the character, you can simply mirror the other half, thereby shaving off 50% of your modeling time.

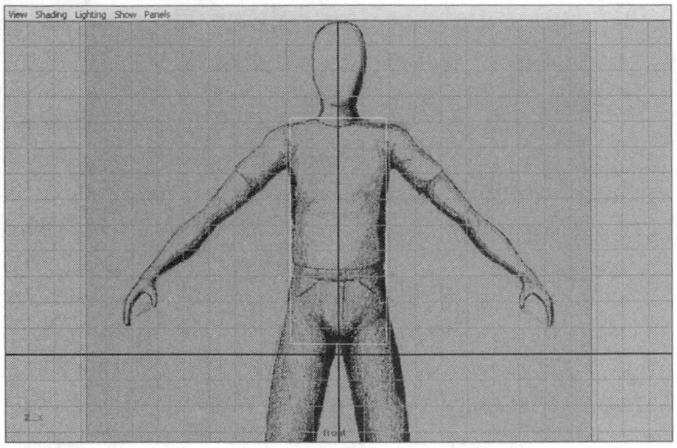

FIGURE 21.16 The cube filling the torso volume in the Front view.

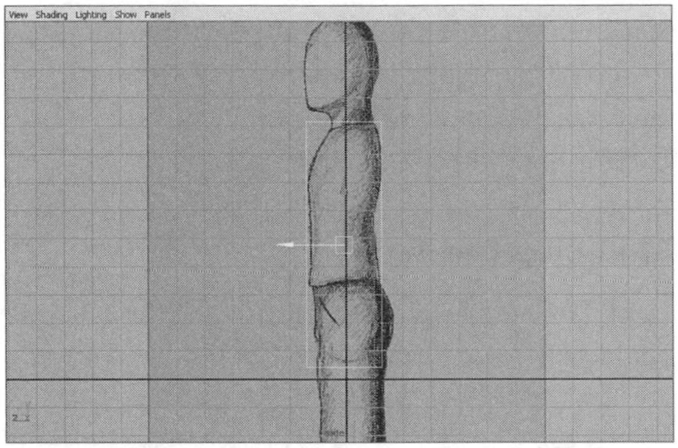

FIGURE 21.17 Cube adjusted to fit the Side view.

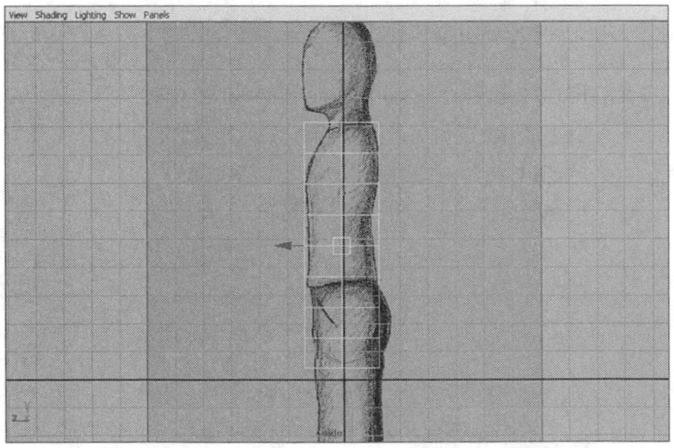

FIGURE 21.18 Increasing the number of subdivisions adds more detail to the cube.

To do this, make faces selectable by pressing F11. In the Front view, select the faces on the right side of the character (that would be the faces on the *left* side of the viewport) and delete them by pressing Backspace or Delete, as shown in **FIGURE 21.19**.

7. Click the cube's name in the Channel Box, and change it to `Torso`. Save your work.

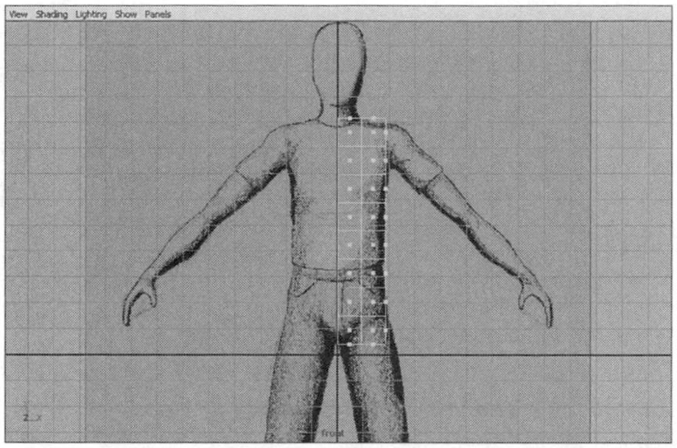

FIGURE 21.19 Half of the cube removed.

END TUTORIAL 21.5

Now that you have the basic geometry in place, it's time to begin modeling it into a torso. In **TUTORIAL 21.6**, you start to change this half-cube into a basic torso shape.

TUTORIAL 21.6: Roughing In the Torso

1. Continue from **TUTORIAL 21.5**, or open the file you saved at the end of that tutorial.

2. You need to move the cube's vertices around so that they line up with the drawing in the Front view. Make sure that you marquee-select the vertices so that you're also selecting the vertices on the back of the cube. You'll start at the bottom and work your way up. Arrange the first two rows of vertices at the crotch so that they're similar to the image in **FIGURE 21.20**. Note that the vertices at the bottom of the cube are close, but not on top of one another.

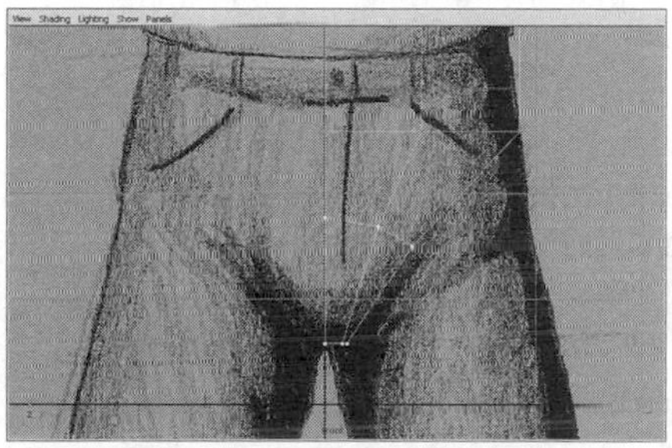

FIGURE 21.20 Try to follow the contour of the drawing whenever possible.

3. Continue up the torso, one row at a time. Adjust the vertices to line up with the drawing and to follow the contours and flow of the character's shape. Use **FIGURE 21.21** to help.

   Take a closer look to see where certain vertices were moved. First, look at the vertex on the outside edge of the

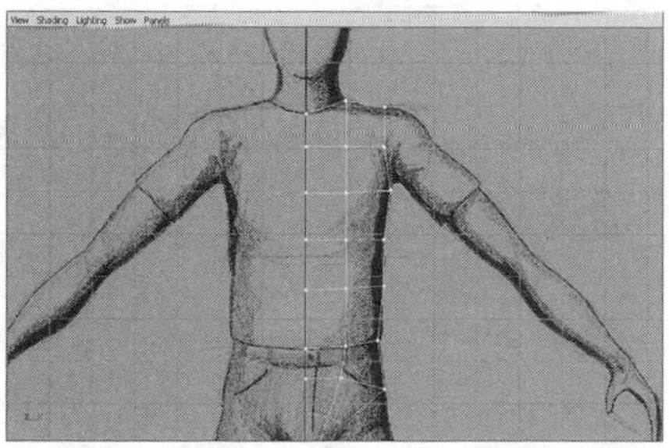

FIGURE 21.21 The rest of the vertices lined up in the Front view.

waistline (see **FIGURE 21.22**). Notice that it's aligned with the pants rather than the shirt. Later, you'll add a new edge around the waist to differentiate the pants and the shirt.

> **TIP**
>
> **If you're moving vertices that happen to be on the seam, be sure not to move them in the X-axis because this causes problems with the character's seam when the geometry is mirrored to the other side.**

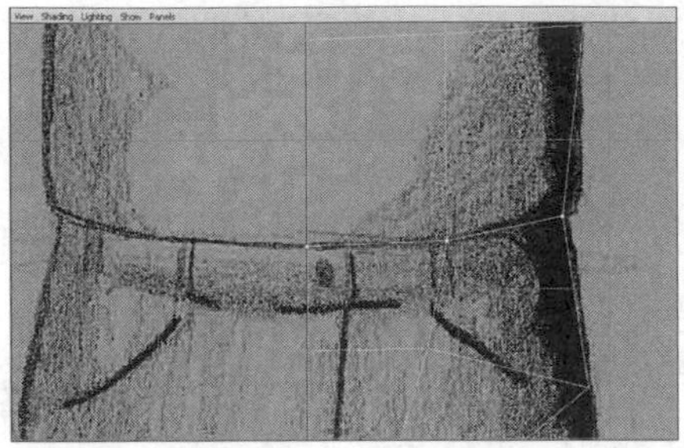

FIGURE 21.22 The vertices at the waistline.

Also notice the vertices at the neckline (see **FIGURE 21.23**). The shirt is being used as the guide for where the torso ends and the neck begins.

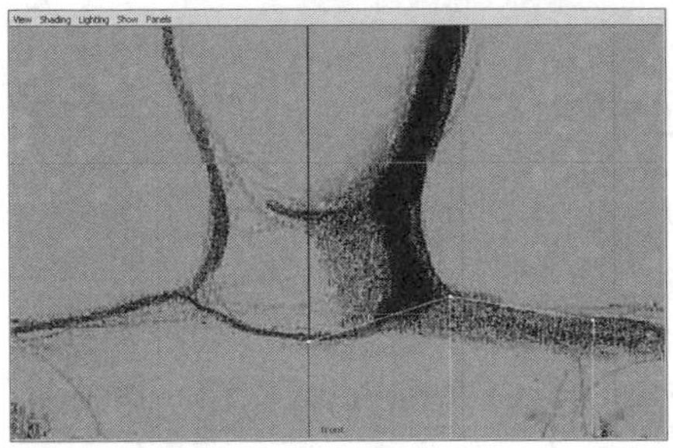

FIGURE 21.23 The vertices at the neck.

4. Next, you need to adjust the vertices in the Side view so that they line up with the side drawing. Keep in mind that you should move or scale these vertices only in the Z-axis because you have already established their locations in the X- and Y-axes. **FIGURE 21.24** shows how you simply go row by row, moving and scaling the vertices to match the drawing's outline.

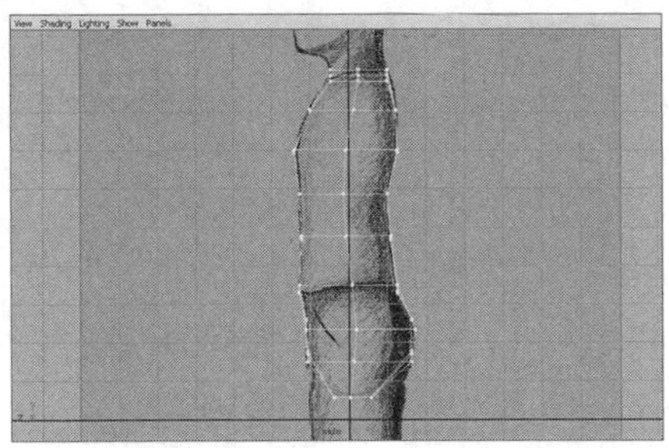

FIGURE 21.24 The vertices at the bottom of the crotch have been scaled toward each other in the Z-axis.

> **NOTE**
>
> **Keep in mind that in the Side view, not all rows of vertices will be in a straight line, depending on whether you moved some vertices in that row up or down in the Y-axis.**

5. Go to the Perspective view, and take a look at what you've done so far. The shape is already starting to look a bit like a torso (see **FIGURE 21.25**). Save your work.
6. To see a completed version of this tutorial, open the `UC_TorsoRough.mb` file included on the CD.

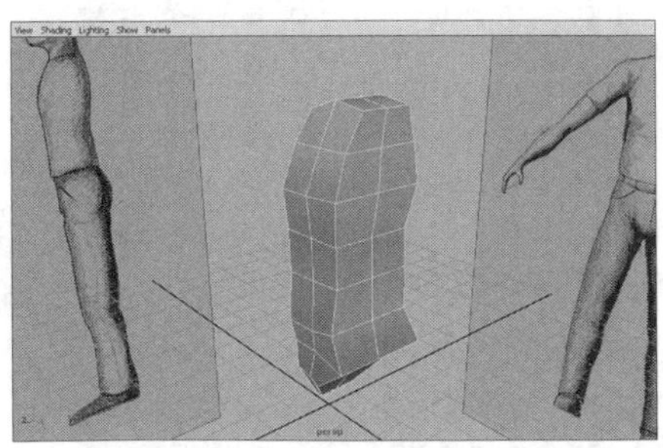

FIGURE 21.25 The torso completely roughed in.

END TUTORIAL 21.6

Now that you have the torso's basic form, it's time to add more detail and continue modeling the shape to make it match the drawing more closely. In **TUTORIAL 21.7**, you clean up the shape of the character's torso.

TUTORIAL 21.7: Refining the Torso

1. Continue from **TUTORIAL 21.6**, or open the file you saved at the end of that tutorial.
2. You'll begin by moving the vertices at the character's outer edges (corners) to round out the character's shape, making more efficient use of the detail you have at hand. Beginning with the vertices on the torso's outside front edge, move them one at a time back in the Z-axis and inward in the X-axis. You'll see the torso start to take shape as you do this (see **FIGURE 21.26**). Again, use the drawing as a guide.
3. Repeat step 2 for the column of vertices at the torso's back outer edge (see **FIGURE 21.27**). Because you don't have a drawing to follow, you'll likely need to work in the Perspective view. For now, use your judgment to round out the character.
4. Next, use the vertices at the collarbone area and at the back of the shoulders to round out the top of the torso. You might want to follow the drawing in the Side view. Use **FIGURE 21.28** for help.

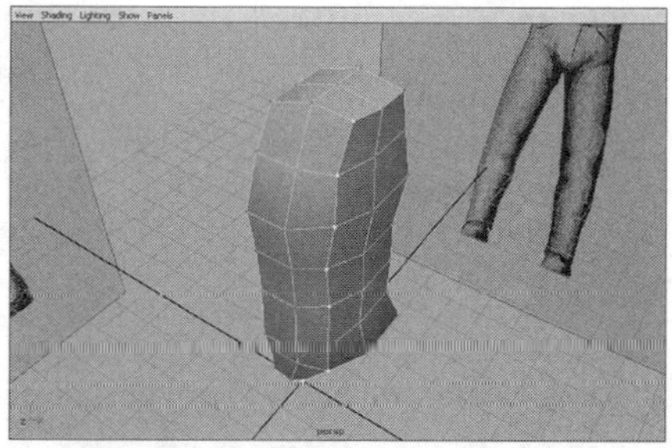

FIGURE 21.26 The front outer column of vertices has been used to round out the torso.

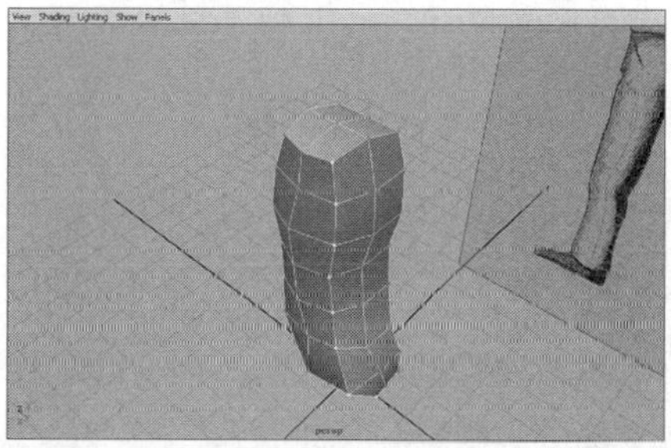

FIGURE 21.27 The vertices at the back have been used to round out the outer edge.

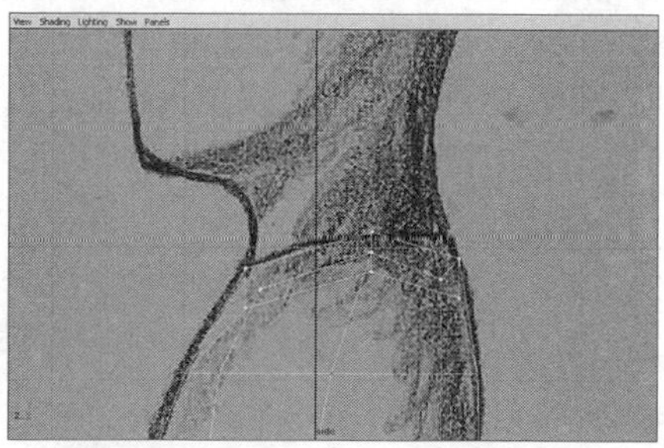

FIGURE 21.28 The shoulder vertices used to round the shoulder.

5. Using a similar technique, round out the vertices at the base of the crotch in the Side view, as in **FIGURE 21.29**.
6. Take a look at your work in the Perspective view, and tweak as you deem necessary. Save your work.
7. To see a completed version of this tutorial, open the `UC_TorsoRefine.mb` file included on the CD.

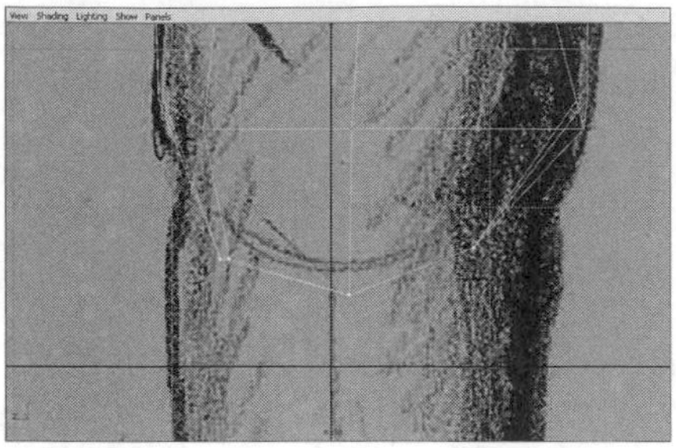

FIGURE 21.29 The rounded vertices at the base of the crotch.

END TUTORIAL 21.7

In **TUTORIAL 21.8**, you make a few more adjustments to the object you have been modeleding to finalize the shape of the character's torso.

TUTORIAL 21.8: Completing the Torso

1. Continue from **TUTORIAL 21.7**, or open the file you saved at the end of that tutorial. Note that some steps of this tutorial simply guide you to position vertices so that the character's shape looks natural, instead of giving you detailed instructions.

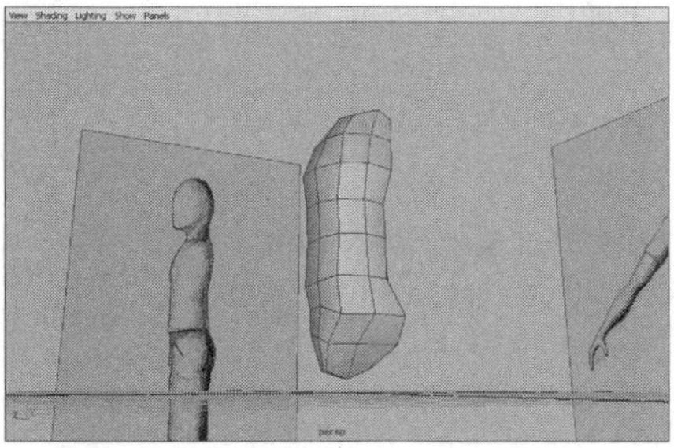

FIGURE 21.30 The faces that need to be removed.

2. Along the side of the character are two sets of four faces that need to be removed to create holes for the character's arms and legs. If you're in a Perspective view, they should be rather obvious; in case you need help seeing them, however, they're highlighted in **FIGURE 21.30**. Select these faces and press Backspace to remove them.
3. You should now have two holes in your geometry. Using the vertices at the borders of the holes, round out the shape of the holes so that they aren't quite as square. Use **FIGURE 21.31** for help, and remember to keep using the drawings for reference.

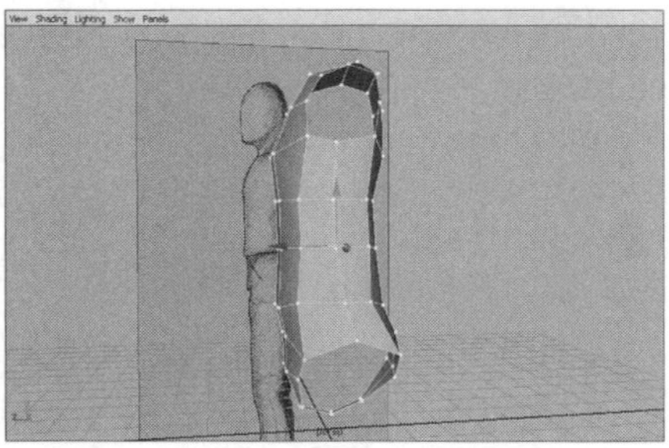

FIGURE 21.31 Holes rounded out for the arm and leg.

4. In the Side view, you should see an edge near the hem of the shirt. Align it with the line where the shirt ends and the pants begin, as shown in **FIGURE 21.32**.

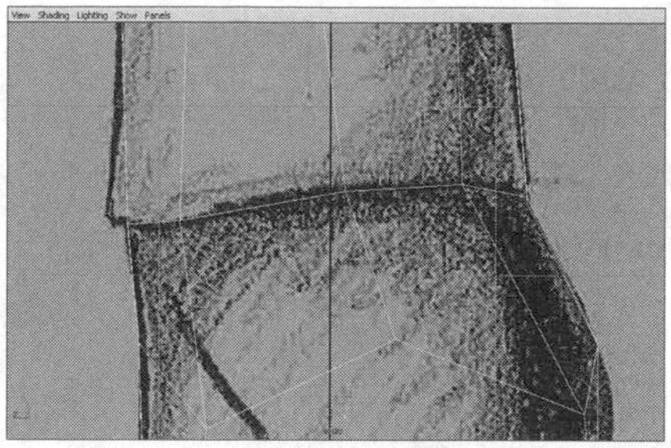

FIGURE 21.32 The shirt edge adjusted.

5. Use the Split Polygon tool to create a new edge just above the shirt's hem. Move around in the Perspective view and pull this edge out slightly, one vertex at a time, to create a more noticeable difference between the shirt and the pants (see **FIGURE 21.33**).

   Your torso should now be complete. Feel free to go back over the model in the Front, Side, and Perspective viewports to double-check everything.

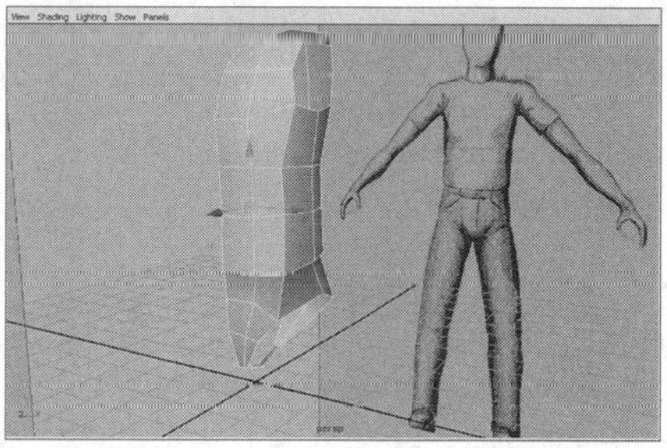

FIGURE 21.33 Splitting polygons creates a ridge between the pants and shirt.

6. Choose Edit > Delete by Type > History from the menu to delete your model's construction history. From now on, this step is simply referred to as deleting history. Save your work.

END TUTORIAL 21.8

Modeling the Legs

Because your character is symmetrical, you can get away with modeling one leg. For the purposes of this model, this process in **TUTORIAL 21.9** is fairly simple.

TUTORIAL 21.9: Modeling the Legs

1. Continue from **TUTORIAL 21.8**, or open the file you saved at the end of that tutorial.
2. To create a leg for your character, first create a polygon cylinder with the following settings:

   Radius: 1

   Height: 9.5

   Subdivisions Axis: 8

   Subdivisions Height 8:

   Subdivisions Caps: 0

3. Move and rotate the cylinder so that it aligns with the character's left leg in the Front viewport, as shown in **FIGURE 21.34**.

4. Stay in the Front view, and select one row of vertices at a time. Rotate and scale the vertices to make them line up with the image. Your end result should be similar to **FIGURE 21.35**.

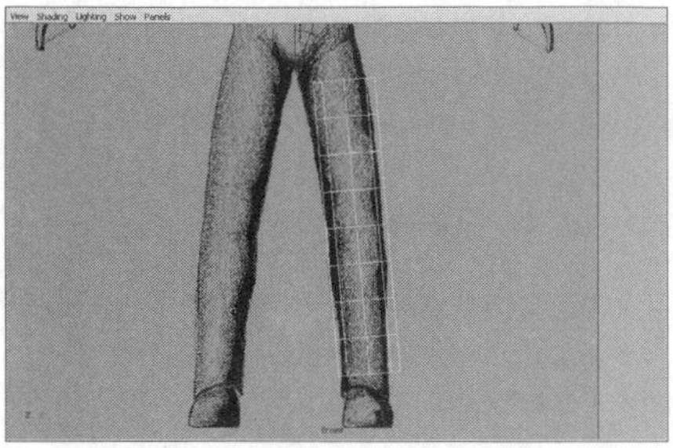

FIGURE 21.34 The leg cylinder created and moved into place.

> **TIP**
>
> **For now, leave the row of vertices at the bottom of the leg completely flat. Don't worry about making the vertices follow the contour of the pants cuff. You'll take care of that after you construct the foot.**

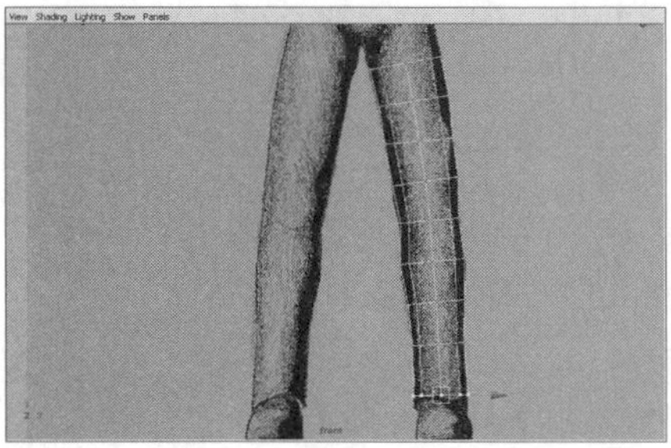

FIGURE 21.35 The leg vertices adjusted in the Front view.

5. Switch to the Side view, and move and scale the rows of vertices in the Z-axis only. Make them follow the contour of the leg as closely as you can (see **FIGURE 21.36**). Again, for the time being, ignore the shape of the pant cuff.

6. Create a split that goes all the way around the knee to add some detail so that the knee is more flexible when animated (see **FIGURE 21.37**). Reshape these vertices if necessary.

7. Delete the faces that form the caps (the closed cylinder ends) for the leg. Select the border edges around the top of the leg. From the Polygons menu, verify under Tool Options that the Keep Faces Together option is set to On.

8. From the Edit Polygons menu, choose Extrude Edge. Move the extruded edges in world space about halfway to the edge of the hole in the torso (see **FIGURE 21.38**).

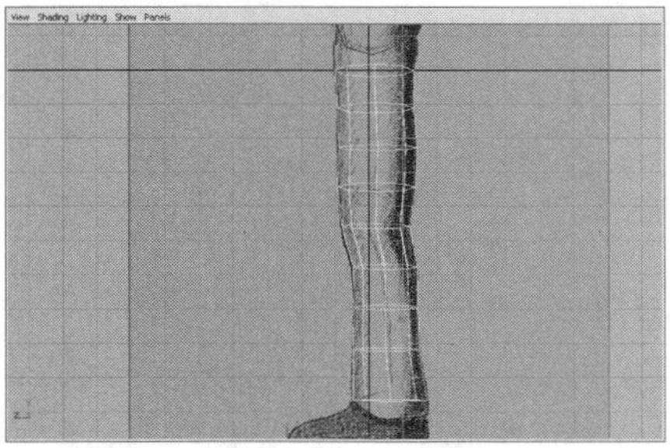

FIGURE 21.36 Leg vertices adjusted in the Side view.

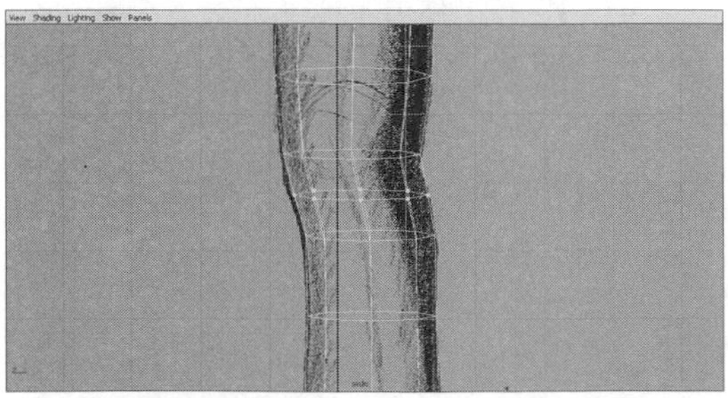

FIGURE 21.37 The Split Polygon tool used to create another row of vertices.

9. Extrude the edge again, and this time, point-snap each vertex to the corresponding vertex on the torso (see **FIGURE 21.39**). There should be eight vertices around each hole. Keep in mind that this step will probably require quite a bit of camera rotation in the Perspective view.

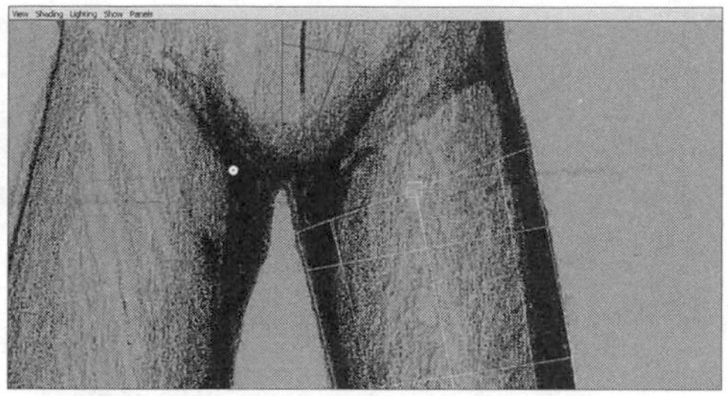

FIGURE 21.38 An edge extrusion of the leg vertices.

> **NOTE**
>
> Remember that the protocol for point-snapping is to select a vertex, hold down the V key, move the cursor over the destination point, press the middle mouse button, and move the mouse slightly. If this doesn't seem to be working, verify in your Move tool settings that you're moving in world coordinates.

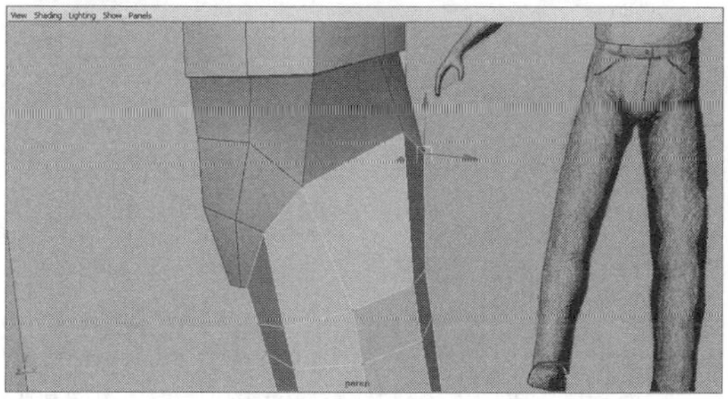

FIGURE 21.39 The vertices at the top of the leg are snapped to the vertices around the leg hole. It currently looks like you have a single piece of geometry, but you don't just yet.

10. Select both the leg and torso in Object mode, and choose Combine from the Polygons menu. Go into Component mode, and select the 16 vertices at the edge where the leg meets the torso. It should look like you have only eight vertices, but remember that you snapped the leg vertices on top of the torso vertices.

> **TIP**
>
> You can use the F8 key to toggle between Object and Component modes.

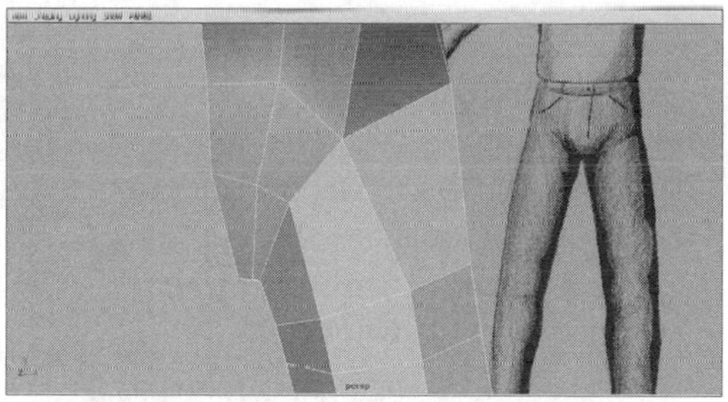

FIGURE 21.40 The objects have been combined, and the vertices around the leg have been merged.

11. From the Edit Polygons menu, choose Merge Vertices > options box. In the Merge Vertex Options dialog box, choose Edit > Reset Settings to set Distance back to its default value of 0.0001. Click the Merge Vertex button when done. The result is shown in **FIGURE 21.40**.

> **NOTE**
>
> At the bottom of the crotch, notice that three other vertices split through the crotch area (see **FIGURE 21.41**). You can save some polygons by merging them into the leg vertices, as shown in **FIGURE 21.42**.

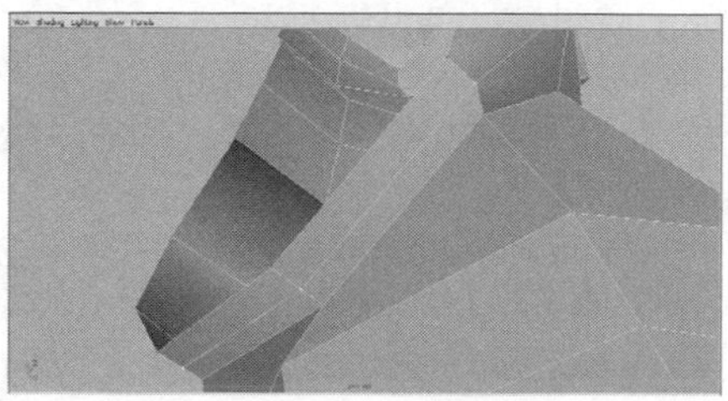

FIGURE 21.41 Three vertices underneath the crotch.

12. Tweak the vertices at the hip to create a smoother blend into the crotch. When you're satisfied, delete your history and save your work.

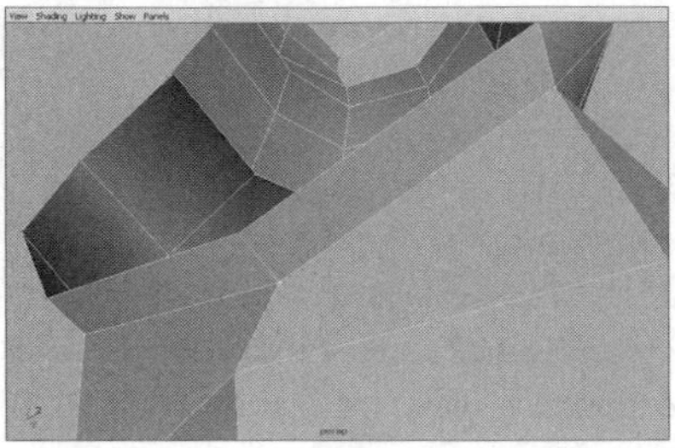

FIGURE 21.42 The vertices now merged into the leg.

END TUTORIAL 21.9

Modeling the Arms

Now it's time to create your model's arms. The method you'll be using in **TUTORIAL 21.10** is similar to the way you constructed the leg, so this time you'll move a little faster.

TUTORIAL 21.10: Modeling the Arms

1. Continue from **TUTORIAL 21.9**, or open the file you saved at the end of that tutorial.
2. To add an arm to your model, first create a polygon cylinder with the following settings:

   Radius: 0.5

   Height: 6.5

   Subdivisions Axis: 8

   Subdivisions Height: 7

   Subdivisions Caps: 0

3. Move and rotate the new cylinder into the position of the arm, as shown in **FIGURE 21.43**.

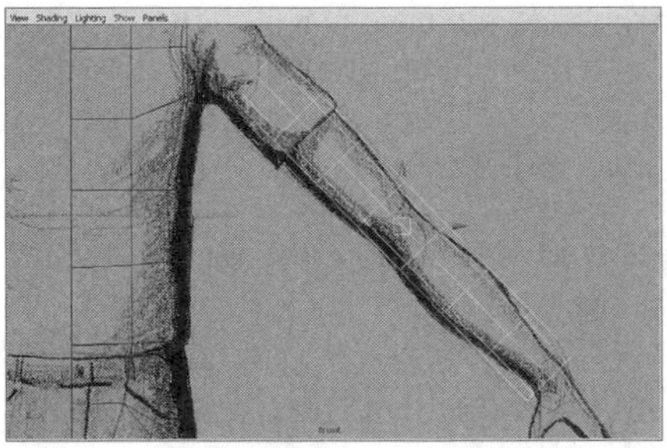

FIGURE 21.43 The arm cylinder in position.

4. Adjust the vertices of the arm, again one row at a time. You should move one row to line up with the end of the shirt sleeve, and two other edges should straddle the elbow (see **FIGURE 21.44**).
5. Add a new edge around the middle of the elbow and another just above the wrist. Also, with the same technique you used on the

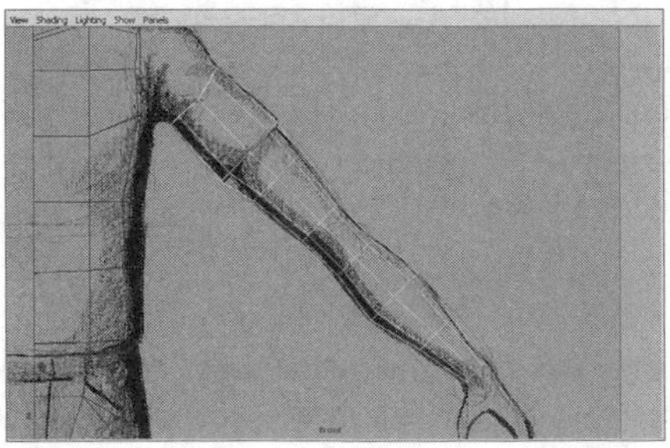

FIGURE 21.44 The vertices of the arm cylinder adjusted in the Front viewport.

torso to create a separation at the end of the shirt sleeve, delete the face at the top of the cylinder, but leave the face at the bottom.

6. Next, you need to adjust the vertices in the Side view. Unfortunately, you don't have a side view of the arm available. You'll have to adjust the vertices based on what you think the arm should look like. Add some subtle contours to the bicep, tricep, and elbow. Use **FIGURE 21.45** as a reference.

7. Select the edge around the top of the arm. Extrude it out, and then snap all the vertices to the corresponding vertices on the torso.

8. Add two edges around the shoulder, and use the resulting vertices to round out the shoulder. Your results should look similar to **FIGURE 21.46**.

9. Now, using the skills you learned in **TUTORIAL 21.9**, attach the arm to the leg by combining and merging vertices (see **FIGURE 21.47**). Do any necessary tweaks, delete the history, and save your file.

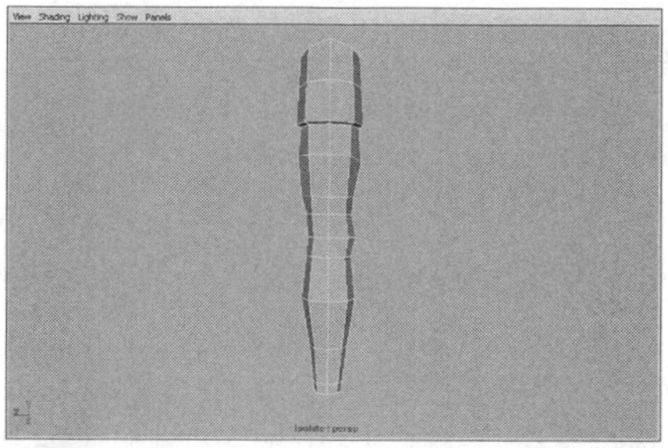

FIGURE 21.45 A Side view of the modeled arm.

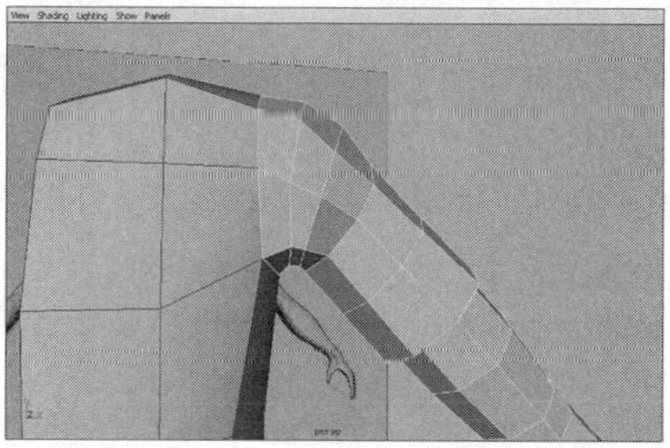

FIGURE 21.46 The shoulder has been adjusted.

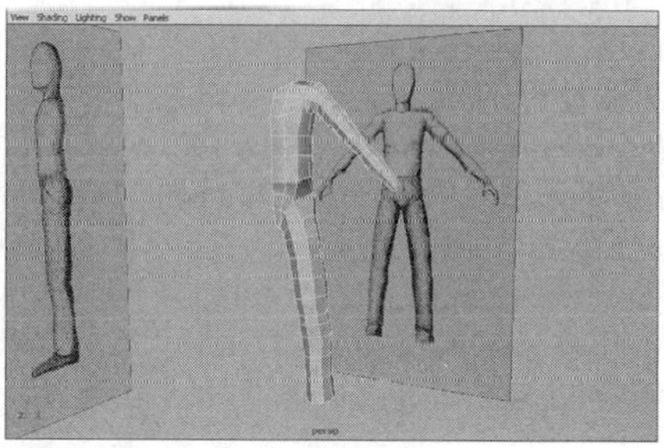

FIGURE 21.47 The arm is now complete.

END TUTORIAL 21.10

Modeling the Feet

Now that the arms and legs are in place, you're ready to model the character's feet. In **TUTORIAL 21.11**, you see how to do this.

TUTORIAL 21.11: Modeling the Feet

1. Continue from **TUTORIAL 21.10**, or open the file you saved at the end of that tutorial.
2. To add a foot to your character, first create a polygon cube with the following dimensions:

   Width: 1.5

   Height: 1.2

   Depth: 1.7

   Subdivision Width: 2

   Subdivision Height: 1

   Subdivision Depth: 1
3. Move the cube into position so that it surrounds the foot in the Front viewport, and set it slightly forward from the heel in the Side view (see **FIGURE 21.48**).
4. Select the two faces at the front of the cube, and extrude them out in local Z. Change the Divisions setting for the extrusion to **3**. Reshape the vertices into a more foot-like shape. Follow the Side view for the profile, and use your best guess for the view from above, referring to **FIGURE 21.49** for guidance.
5. Select the large square face on each side of the foot. Use the Polygons > Triangulate command to tessellate them. The triangle edge needs to slant downward toward the front of the foot, as in **FIGURE 21.50**. Use the Flip Triangle Edge command, if necessary.
6. Create a split that runs from the middle of the edge at the ankle, around the back of the heel, to the middle of the edge on the opposite side (see **FIGURE 21.51**).

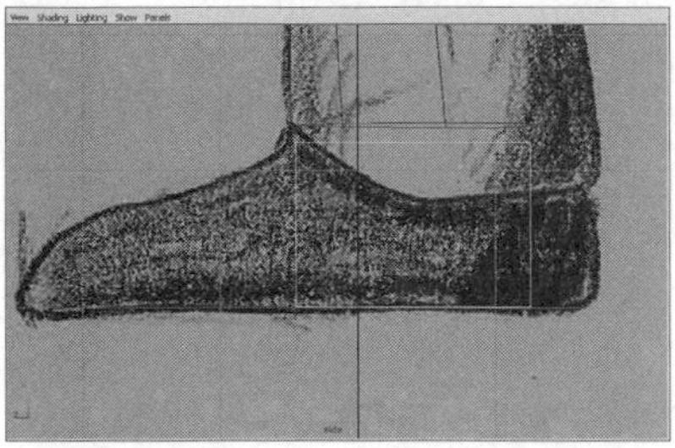

FIGURE 21.48 The cube's position in the Side view.

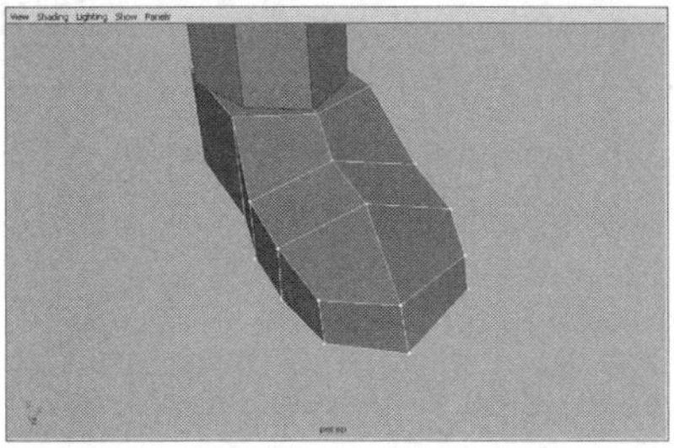

FIGURE 21.49 The extruded vertices shaped into a foot.

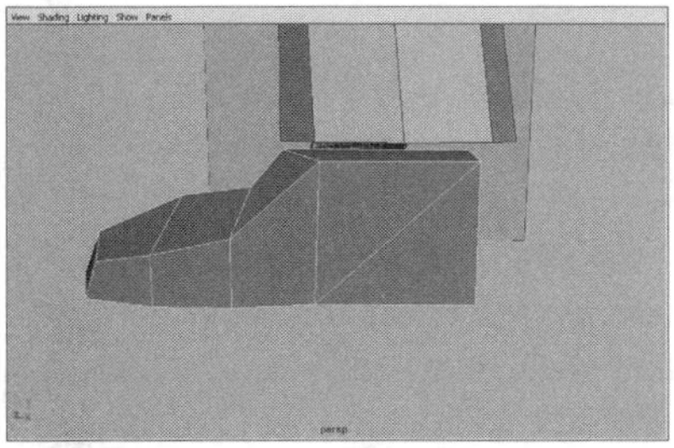

FIGURE 21.50 The side of the foot triangulated. Make sure the face on the opposite side of the foot is triangulated in the same fashion, with the triangle edge slanting down toward the toe.

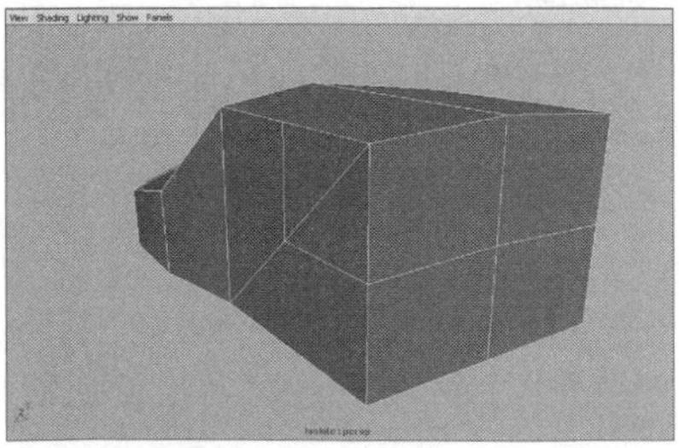

FIGURE 21.51 Notice that the split runs all the way around the heel.

7. Using the vertices you just created, reshape the heel to align with the image. When finished, delete the two faces at the top of the foot, and adjust the eight vertices to form a more rounded hole (see **FIGURE 21.52**).

8. Extrude the edge around the top of the foot up once. Next, select the edges around the end of the pant leg, and move them straight up to get them out of your way (see **FIGURE 21.53**). When finished, go ahead and choose Combine from the Polygons menu to combine the two models.

9. Now use the Append to Polygon tool to attach the models together into one seamless mesh, as shown in **FIGURE 21.54**. Simply activate the tool, click on one of the edges of the pants, and then click on a corresponding edge of the foot. Continue this procedure all the way around the foot.

10. Now select the vertices from the leg you moved up earlier. Use the Front and Side views to line them up with the pant cuff in the image, as shown in **FIGURE 21.55**. Delete history and save your work.

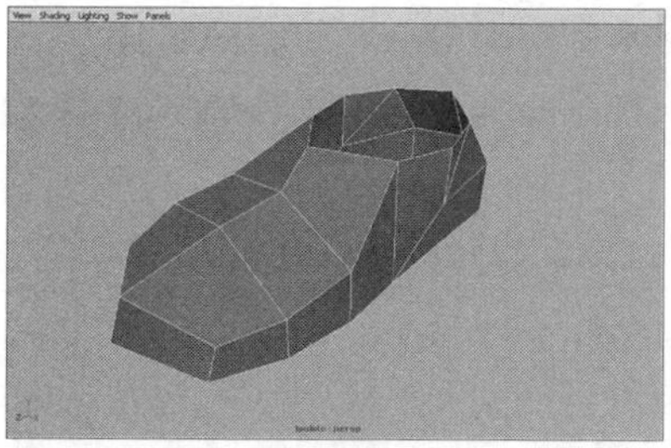

FIGURE 21.52 The foot, fully shaped. Note that the rest of the body is hidden in this image.

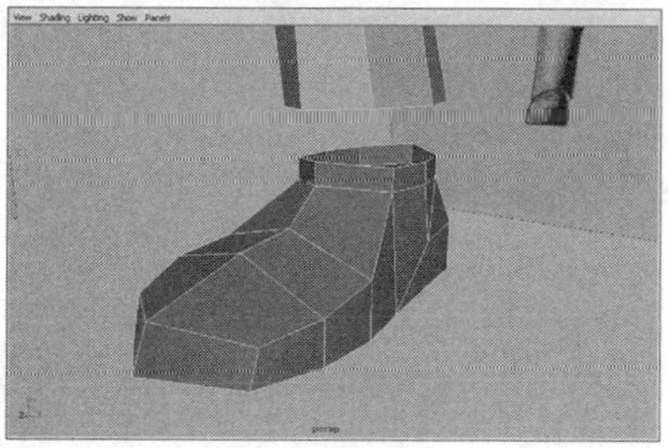

FIGURE 21.53 The foot and body are now attached.

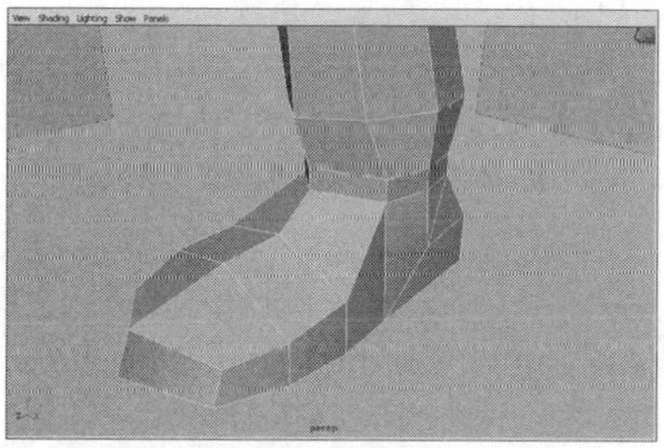

FIGURE 21.54 The foot and leg have now been attached with faces, forming a single mesh.

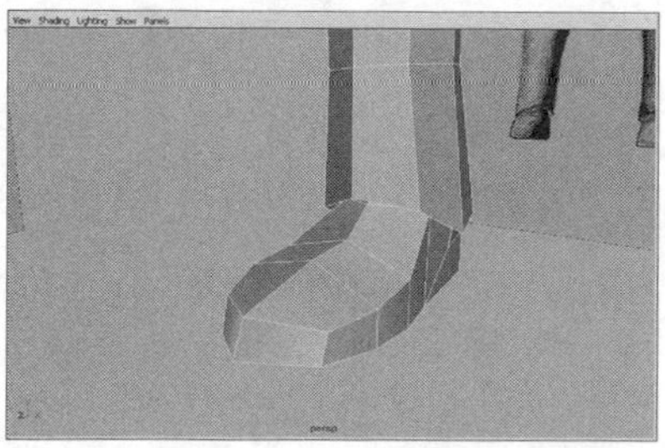

FIGURE 21.55 The foot is now complete.

END TUTORIAL 21.11

21

Modeling the Hand

Your character is taking shape nicely. In **TUTORIAL 21.12**, you see how to model the character's hand.

TUTORIAL 21.12: Modeling the Hand

1. Continue from **TUTORIAL 21.11**, or open the file you saved at the end of that tutorial.
2. Extrude the two faces at the end of the wrist out four times to shape them into a palm and fingers. Use the image as a guide for the Front view. For the Side view, use your judgment and refer to **FIGURE 21.56** for guidance.
3. Select the two faces near the wrist, where the thumb should be. They've been highlighted in **FIGURE 21.57** for your convenience.
4. Extrude these faces out once. Select the two vertices of the extrusion that are toward the back of the hand, as shown in **FIGURE 21.58**. Merge them straight over with their corresponding vertices; the results are shown in **FIGURE 21.59**.
5. Extrude the remaining face out three more times, and shape the vertices to form a thumb (see **FIGURE 21.60**).
6. Make any tweaks you deem necessary. Delete your history and save. The hand is complete.

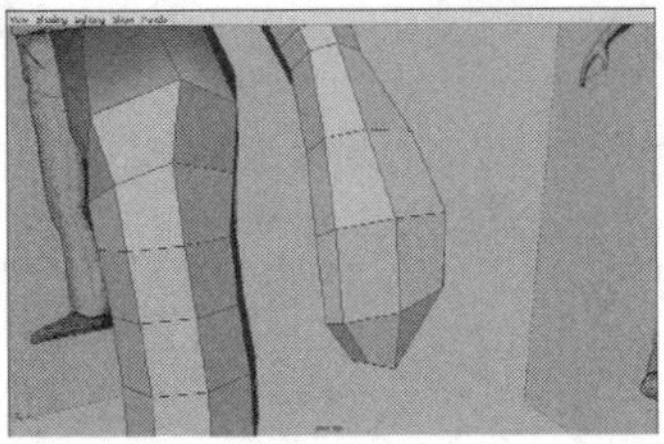

FIGURE 21.56 The four extrusions of the hand reshaped.

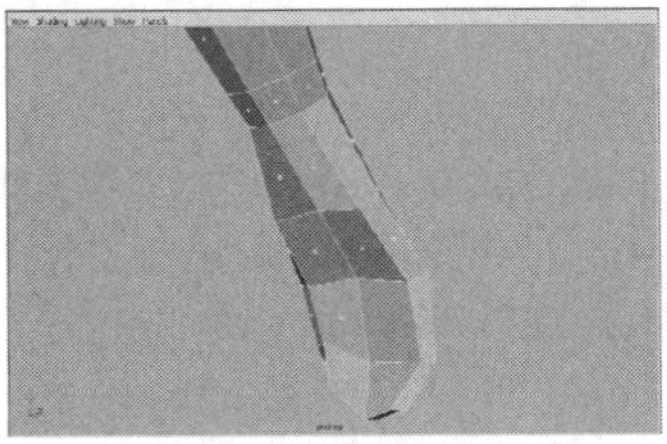

FIGURE 21.57 The faces you use to extrude the thumb.

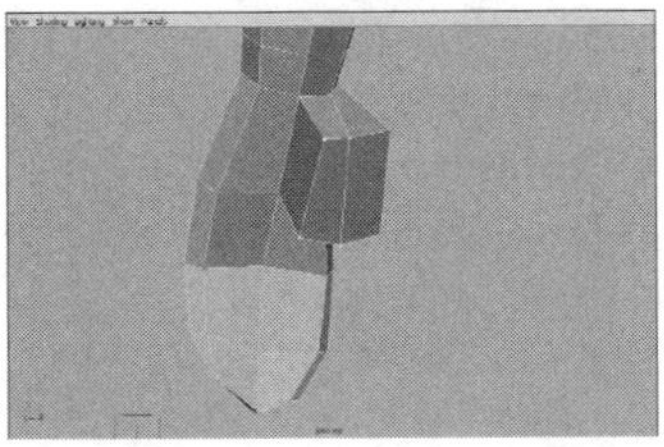

FIGURE 21.58 The vertices of the thumb before merging.

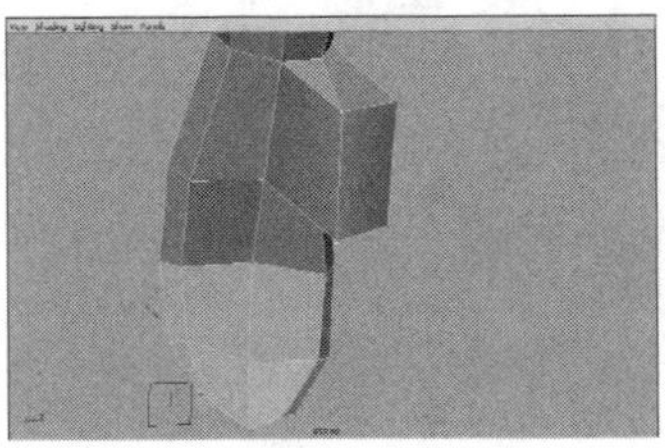

FIGURE 21.59 The vertices of the thumb after merging.

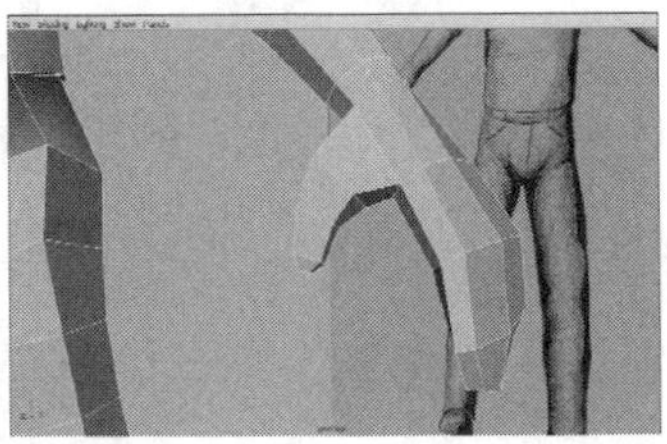

FIGURE 21.60 The thumb created.

END TUTORIAL 21.12

Modeling the Head

At this point, the character is looking great, except for one small problem: He has no head! In **TUTORIAL 21.13**, you complete this character by adding a head to the model.

TUTORIAL 21.13: Modeling the Head

1. Continue from **TUTORIAL 21.13**, or open the file you saved at the end of that tutorial. You'll finish your model by creating a head. For the purposes of this tutorial, the head has been kept very simple, without any facial details.

2. Create a polygon cube with the following dimensions:

   Width: 2

   Height: 3.3

   Depth: 2.5

   Subdivisions Width: 4

   Subdivisions Height: 5

   Subdivisions Depth: 2

3. Move the cube up in the Y-axis so that it aligns with the head (see **FIGURE 21.61**). Don't worry if the fit isn't perfect, as you'll be adjusting the vertices in a second. Delete the faces that fall on the right side of the character.

4. Adjust the vertices in the Front view to make them align with the image, as shown in **FIGURE 21.62**.

5. Next, you need to adjust the vertices from the side, which will likely require a lot of switching between the Side and Perspective views (shown in **FIGURES 21.63** and **21.64**, respectively). Keep in mind that your intention should be to round out the shape with the vertices on hand. No other detail has been added to the cube yet.

6. Create a split that runs under the chin, as shown in **FIGURE 21.65**. Use it to help define the chin area.

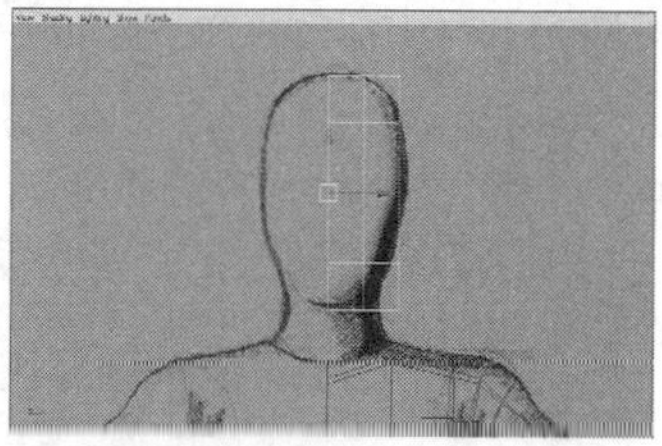

FIGURE 21.61 The half-cube that will become the head.

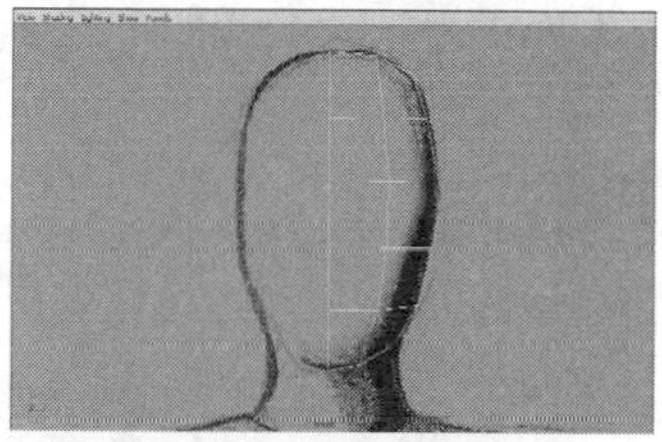

FIGURE 21.62 The vertices adjusted in the Front view.

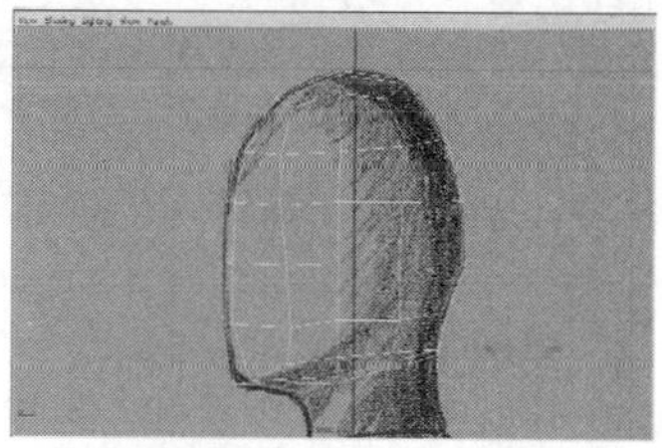

FIGURE 21.63 The head vertices in the Side viewport.

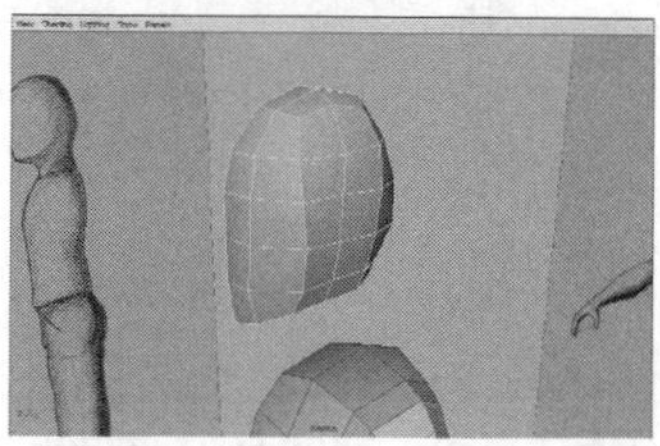

FIGURE 21.64 The head in the Perspective viewport.

7. Select the two faces on the underside of the chin, toward the back of the head. They've been highlighted in **FIGURE 21.66** for your convenience. Delete them, and then use the vertices to resize and round out the hole.
8. Back on the torso, delete the two faces at the top of the shoulder, right next to the seam.
9. You should now have a five-edged hole at the bottom of the head and a four-edged hole at the top of the torso. Even this up by creating a split from the neck hole to the shoulder, as shown in **FIGURE 21.67**.
10. Reshape the hole to round it out, and combine the two meshes. Then, using the Append to Polygon tool, create a series of faces that connect the head and the torso (see **FIGURE 21.68**).
11. Create two splits on the neck faces, and use them to reshape the neck, as shown in **FIGURE 21.69**.
12. Time for the last step. From the Polygons menu, choose Mirror Geometry > options box. In the settings, make sure you're using the –X-axis, and that the Merge with the Original option is enabled and set to Connect Border Edges. The results are shown in **FIGURE 21.70**.
13. Make any necessary tweaks. When satisfied, use the Triangulate command on the model, delete history, and save. Congratulations! You have completed an entire game model.

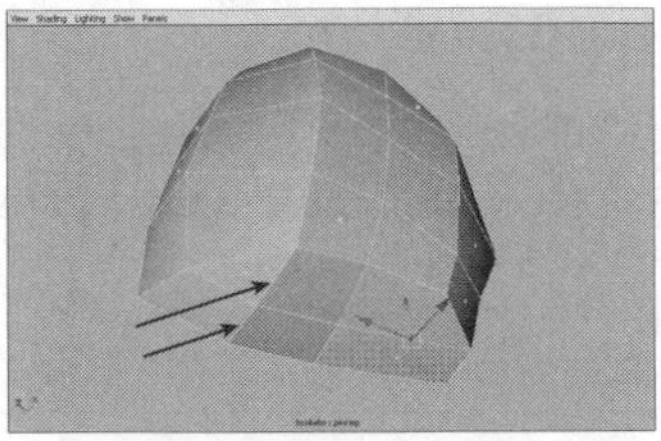

FIGURE 21.65 The split needed for the chin.

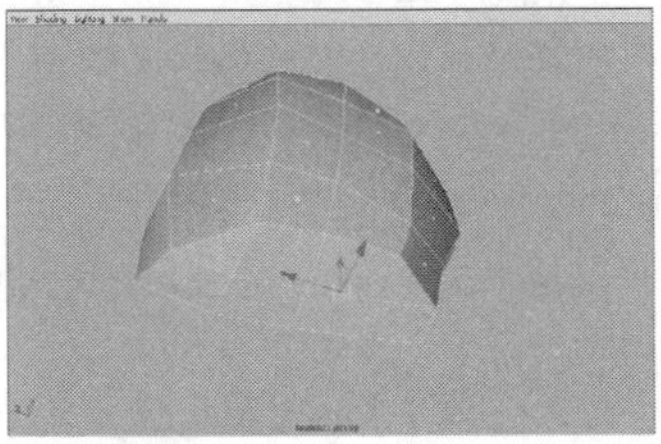

FIGURE 21.66 You need to remove these faces.

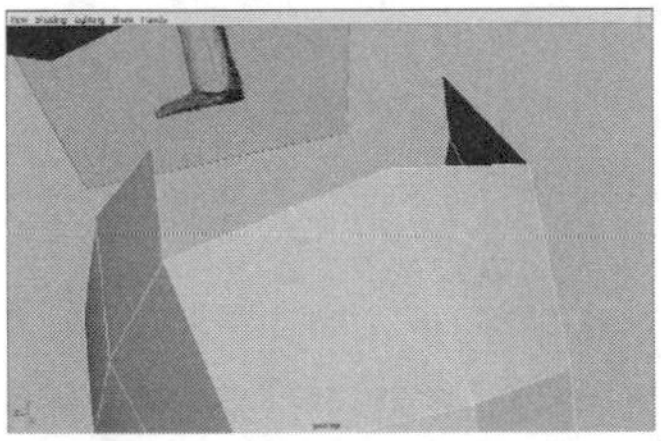

FIGURE 21.67 This split enables you to have five edges around the neck hole.

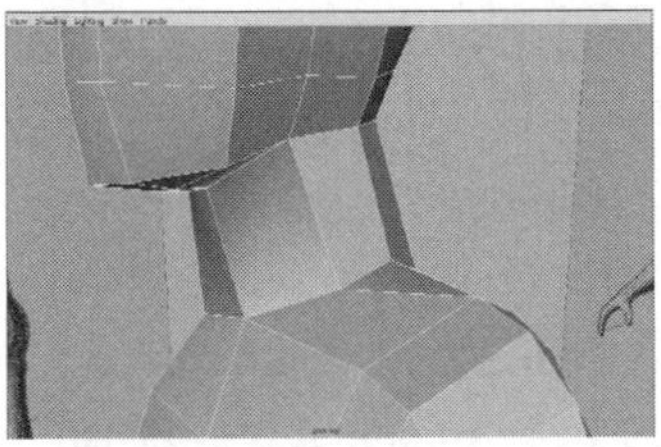

FIGURE 21.68 The new faces attach the head and torso.

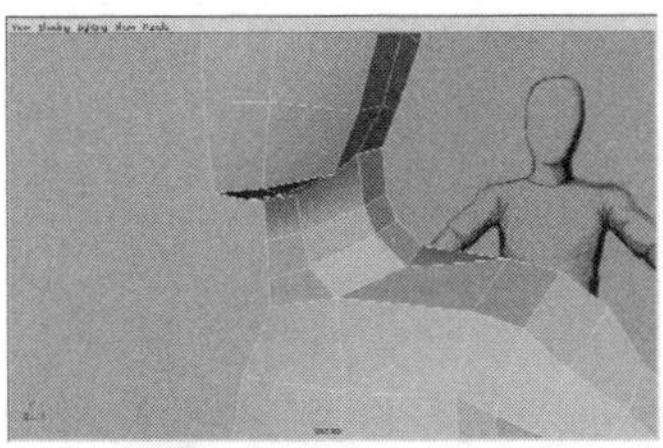

FIGURE 21.69 The neck completed.

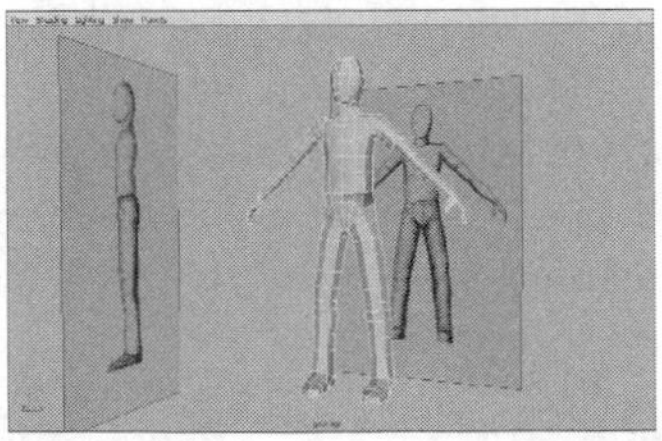

FIGURE 21.70 The completed model.

END TUTORIAL 21.13

Summary

In this chapter, you have walked through the completion of an entire character. Given that this character design was fairly simple, if you were able to follow all the way through this project, you're more than ready to venture out and create your own characters. You should be pleased with yourself, as this is no small accomplishment. In the following chapters, you'll be animating, texturing, and getting this model into Unreal as a playable character.

Chapter 22

Importing Characters into UnrealEd

So far, you have fully modeled a character and covered it with a texture. Now you breathe life into the character by giving it motion. In this chapter, you're introduced to the concepts of animation in Maya and learn how to create digital skeletons for your character, how to attach your character's geometry to that skeleton, how to create a control system by which to move that skeleton, and finally, how to create a series of animations to make the character mimic human movement. You also see how to export your own character animations into Unreal or use the animations included with the Unreal Tournament 2004 characters.

What Are Skeletons?

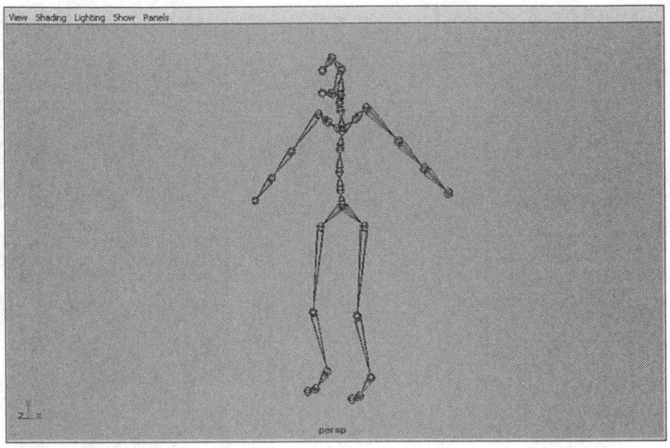

FIGURE 22.1 A character skeleton in Maya.

To animate game characters, you need to construct a skeleton for them. For a digital character, however, the term *skeleton* takes on an entirely different meaning from the bone framework that holds you up. A digital skeleton is actually nothing more than a hierarchical series of rotation points. To be technical, they are a hierarchy of Transform nodes to which joint clusters are attached. **FIGURE 22.1** shows a character skeleton in Maya.

FIGURE 22.2 Skeletons in action.

A character skeleton is necessary because a game character is nothing more than a series of polygons. It might form the shape of a person and look like it has features such as elbows, knees, a head, and so on, but of course, it actually has none of these features. Polygons have no way of knowing where they should bend or how they should flex. The joints of a skeleton supply this information, allowing you to control the points at which the character's body parts rotate. The geometry of the model is then attached to these joints in a process known as *skinning*, which is discussed in detail later in this chapter in "Binding a Character to a Skeleton: Skinning." After the connection is complete, your character can bend, reach, and take on a variety of different poses, as shown in **FIGURE 22.2**.

Introduction to Maya Joints

When working in Maya, the fundamental component of a skeleton is the *joint*, which is a location in space that designates a point of rotation. To construct a skeleton, you create networks of these joints and parent them to one another in a logical fashion. For instance, if you picture joints that form an arm, such as a shoulder, an elbow, and a wrist, you could imagine this parenting hierarchy as follows:

- As the elbow rotates, the wrist moves with it. Therefore, the wrist is parented to the elbow.
- As the shoulder rotates, both the elbow and wrist move, meaning that the elbow is parented to the shoulder.

Parenting

Because *parenting* is such an important part of a skeletal system, this section discusses its nature in more depth. Say that you're sitting in a chair, holding this book as you read. If you move your hands, the book follows, meaning that the book's current position depends on where your hands go. If someone comes up behind you and moves the chair you're sitting in, you move as well because your position depends directly on the chair's position. The chair, however, is resting on the surface of the earth. As the earth revolves around the aun, it brings the chair, you, and the book along for the ride. In this way, you could say the book is parented to you, as your motions directly influence it. You are parented to the chair, which is parented to the earth, which is in turn parented to the sun. You could represent this example by using objects in a Maya scene (see **FIGURE 22.3**).

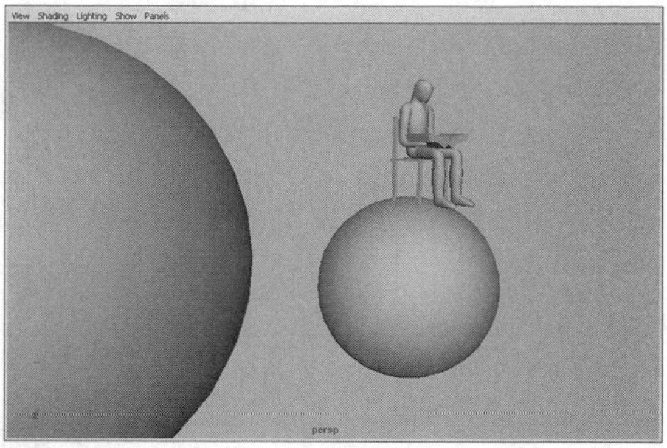

FIGURE 22.3 A Maya scene depicting the parenting hierarchy.

Although this relationship can be seen as you move objects around the screen, it's also represented in Maya's Hypergraph. If you opened the Hypergraph for this scene, you would see a hierarchy such as the one shown in **FIGURE 22.4**.

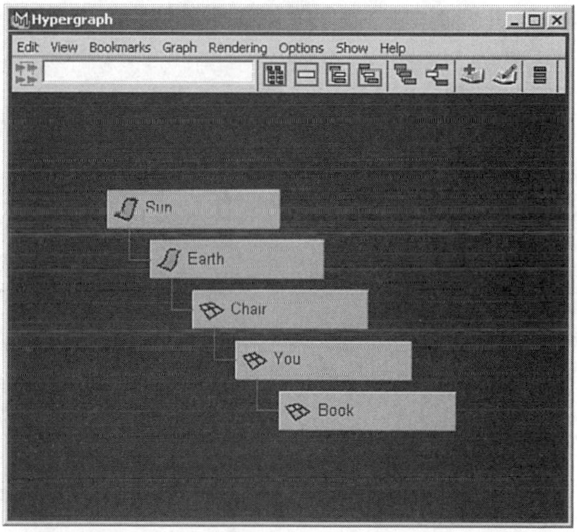

FIGURE 22.4 The Hypergraph's interpretation of the hierarchy.

This hierarchy is straightforward, as each object has only one child. To make this analogy a little more complicated, what if you were holding this book in one hand and a cup of coffee in the other? In the hierarchy you have created, this means you now have two descendants (child objects): the book and the coffee. As you move, both objects move with you. At this point, your hierarchy would look something like **FIGURE 22.5**.

Because of the nature of Maya's parenting system, however, an object can have any number of child objects but can have only one parent. Think about it: If a parent *directly* influences its child's location, having two parents would mean it's possible for the child to be influenced to be in two places at once.

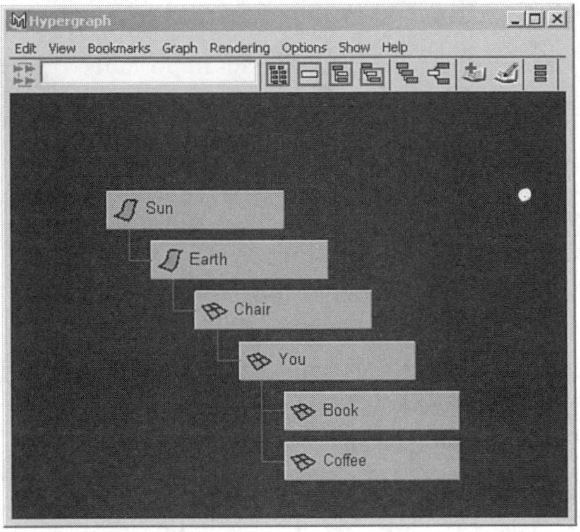

FIGURE 22.5 The new hierarchy, with a cup of coffee added into the mix.

The most interesting aspect of this system is that a parent's influence doesn't affect the values in child Transform nodes. For example, if a parent object moves along the X-axis, its child objects are completely unaware of the motion, regardless of the fact that they come along. This system is very similar to how hierarchies respond in the real world. Think about it: Hold yourself as still as you can. Do you feel any motion? You don't—or shouldn't, anyway—even though earth is hurtling through space at about 67,000 miles per hour.

Joints and Parenting

Joints use the parenting system to create the hierarchy that becomes the skeleton. Each joint has a parent joint, eventually leading to the highest level parent of the hierarchy, known as the *root joint*. The root joint is important in Maya because as it's moved, rotated, or scaled, the rest of the skeleton is moved, rotated, and scaled with it. Also, several functions necessary to working with skeletons can be performed only if the root joint is selected, such as returning the skeleton to its original pose.

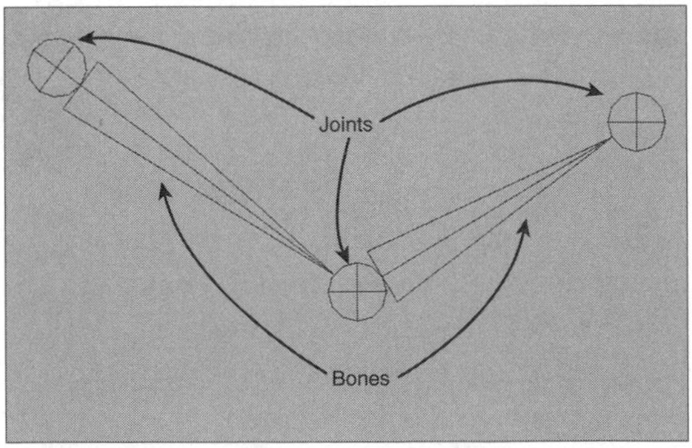

FIGURE 22.6 The bones and joints of a skeleton.

Joints are unique in Maya's hierarchies, as their parenting system is visually represented in the viewport. You can always tell which joints are parented to which by looking at the *bones* between each pair. A bone appears as a wireframe triangular shape that points from parent to child. An example of bones and joints can be seen in **FIGURE 22.6**.

The bone itself, however, is little more than a visual reference and an aid in joint selection. A bone, in and of itself, serves no purpose independent of joints. A bone is created automatically wherever two joints are created. So if you have two separate joint chains and you parent the root of one chain to the last child in the other, you see a bone instantly created that turns the two chains into one continuous strand of joints. You can see this reflected in the Hypergraph as well (see **FIGURE 22.7**).

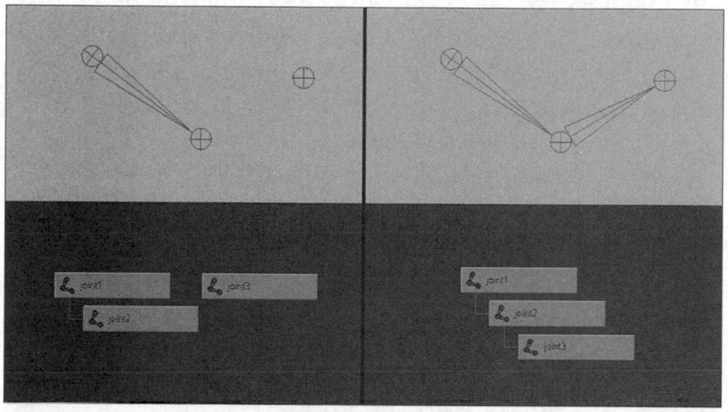

FIGURE 22.7 On the left, before joint3 is parented; on the right, after joint3 is parented.

Joints and Rotation

After joints are added to a character, they typically serve only one function: rotation. Joints have little or no need to move or scale, unless the artist is trying to achieve a cartoon-like effect, such as the character's bones seeming to stretch.

All objects in Maya have a *local rotation axis*, which is a coordinate system that's individual to the object and doesn't necessarily coincide with the world coordinate system. To make this system a bit clearer, pretend you have your own local rotation axis centered in the middle of your torso, near your heart. If you were an object in Maya, this spot would be your pivot point.

First, to establish the directions of the world coordinates, say that Y always points up, Z always points to the north, and X always points toward the west. For your local rotation axis, the Y-axis always points toward your head, the Z-axis always points out of your chest, and the X-axis always points out of your side, toward your left hip.

If you were to stand on your head, your local Y-axis would point downward, although the world coordinate's Y-axis actually points up. Your local rotation axis would rotate with you, which illustrates how the local rotation axis works in Maya.

Working with Local Rotation Axes

Although the local rotation axis rotates with the object, it can also be adjusted independently of that object through Maya's Component mode. Occasionally, you run into situations in which you would like to rotate an object in a single axis to create rotation in a specific direction. The axis you choose and the direction in which you want the object to rotate might be completely different from one another.

For example, say you're animating a car wheel spinning, and you want that spin to occur along the Y-axis. Unfortunately, the wheel spins properly only when it's rotated about the Z-axis. The solution to this problem is simple: Adjust the wheel's local rotation axis so that its Y-axis points in the correct direction.

This same technique applies to joints. All joints have their own local rotation axis. The orientation of this axis is controlled by a setting established before the joint is created. If, however, you should discover after creating a joint that the orientation of the local rotation axis is incorrect, you can always adjust it to give you the proper rotation. The techniques for adjusting this setting are explained later in this chapter in "Joints and Local Rotation Axes."

Using the Joint Tool

Most of the time, you don't create joints as separate objects in the same way you create primitive geometry. Most often, you use the Joint tool to create your skeleton's joint networks. With this tool, you can create joints in the viewport in a point-and-click fashion and automatically parent the joints as you click. The first joint you place is the highest level parent in the hierarchy. The second click is that joint's child, the third click creates the second joint's child, and so on. As you click, you see not only the joints being created, but also the bones between them. In **TUTORIAL 22.1**, you use this tool to create a simple joint chain.

TUTORIAL 22.1: Creating Joints with the Joint Tool

1. Open Maya, and start a new scene. Make sure you're in the Animation menu set, or press F2 to go there.
2. Switch to the Side viewport, and choose Skeleton > Joint Tool from the main menu.
3. Click three times in the viewport. You'll see joints created at each click and bones connecting each joint hierarchically (see **FIGURE 22.8**). You can click as many times as you like, but remember that as long as the tool is active, each click creates a new joint.
4. Press Enter to complete the tool's operation and finalize the joint chain you just created.

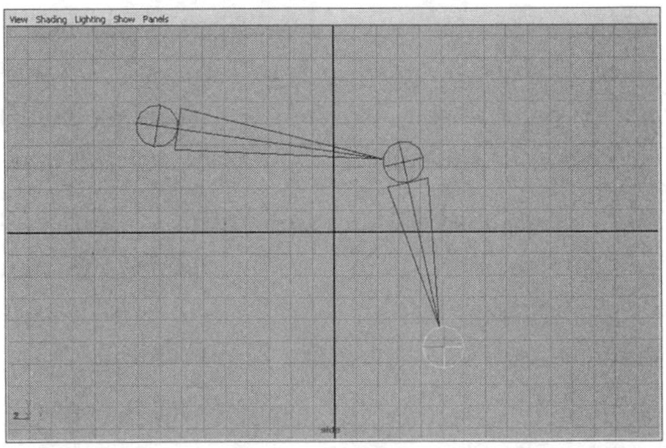

FIGURE 22.8 Three joints created with the Joint tool.

> **NOTE**
>
> If you MMB-click the last joint you placed, you can relocate it by MMB-dragging. Relocating affects the joint's local rotation axis, however, as outlined later in "Moving Joints."

5. Aside from creating freestanding joint chains, you can also branch off existing joint chains to make more complex skeletons. To do this, begin by clicking on any of the joints in the chain you just created. Notice that the joint is highlighted.

6. Now click a second time, and notice that a new bone is created along with the joint. The bone points from the location of the joint you clicked to the one you just created. Press Enter to complete the joint chain (see **FIGURE 22.9**). Feel free to experiment by branching off as many times as you like.

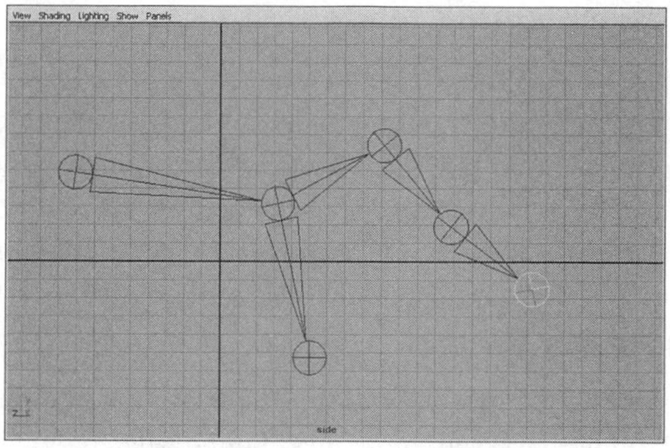

FIGURE 22.9 A branching joint chain has been added.

END TUTORIAL 22.1

Joints and Local Rotation Axes

Because joints are mainly used for rotation, the local rotation axis becomes vitally important. Eventually you'll run into situations in which a joint is pointing in one direction, but needs to rotate in a direction that doesn't fall on one if its local rotation axes. Take your thumb, for instance: Place your hand flat, palm facing down. Relax your hand, and move your thumb up and down. Try to imagine the axis of rotation for that movement. It should run roughly parallel to your index finger, although your thumb points out of your hand at a completely different angle.

This situation is common when creating skeletons for characters, and you need to rotate a joint in a direction that doesn't coincide with any single axis. Of course, because a joint can rotate in all three axes, it can theoretically achieve any rotation. The problem comes in when you try to edit the animated channels for that object. For example, what if, to rotate the knee, you needed to rotate the joint on all three axes? It might look fine onscreen, but if you edit that animation, you would find three separate animation curves that need to be adjusted, one for each axis. Instead, you could simply adjust the knee joint's local rotation axis so that the rotation occurs only on a single axis, thereby simplifying any editing you need to do later.

You can set the local rotation axis for a joint at the time of its creation by adjusting the Auto Orient Joint setting of the Joint tool. By default, it's set to XYZ. Many combinations of the three axes are available, and each combination works as follows: The first axis listed points into a joint's bone. The third joint listed points sideways, and the second joint is at a right angle to the other two. So in the case of XYZ orientation, the X-axis would point down the bone toward the first child of the joint. The Z-axis would point sideways into the joint, and the Y-axis would point into the joint perpendicularly to the plane created by the X and Z axes.

Manipulating Joints

Now that you see how to create a few joints, you need to know how to adjust them. You won't always be able to create joints exactly where you need them, so it's often necessary to create several joints and then position them accordingly. You can manipulate joints in three ways: moving, rotating, and scaling. Each method has its repercussions. The following sections explain these three methods of joint manipulation and explore the consequences of each one.

Moving Joints

One of the most obvious methods of joint manipulation is to simply move the joint. However, you need to keep some rules in mind when moving joints. First, by default, moving a joint causes all that joint's child joints to move as well. Second, moving joints also offsets the orientation of the joint's local rotation axis. In **TUTORIAL 22.2**, you see how to use the joint moving method.

TUTORIAL 22.2: Adjusting Joints Through Moving

1. Start a new scene and go to the Animation menu set. Using the Joint tool, create a series of six joints in an S-style pattern, as shown in **FIGURE 22.10**. Press Enter when finished to complete the joint chain.

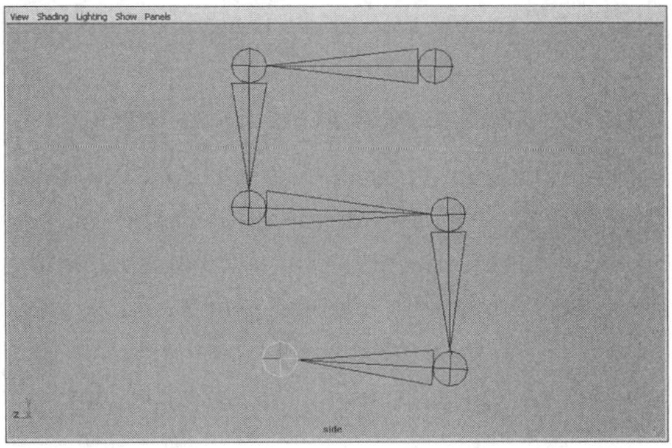

FIGURE 22.10 Joints created in an S-pattern.

2. Notice that each time you click, you can see the axis marker in the center of the joint orient itself so that the X-axis is pointed down the bone. This is the result of the Auto Joint Orient setting of the Joint tool.

   Select the Move tool, and then select and move the second joint of the chain you just created. Each of that joint's child joints follows the movement, as dictated by the nature of parenting. The rotation of the joint doesn't change, meaning that the X-axis no longer points down the bone. This could cause problems later when you're animating the joint.

3. What if you want to adjust the joint without changing the location of all its child joints? There's a way to do this, and it's much like adjusting an object's pivot point. With the second joint still selected, press the Insert key. Notice that the manipulator changes to a series of lines without arrows. Use this manipulator to move the joint around in the viewport, and notice that the child joints are unaffected.

4. But what about the problem of the local rotation axis? Most of the time, you want one of the axes to point down the bone, as this helps with animating. Unfortunately, now that you

have moved that second joint, at least two joints no longer follow this rule. You can fix this problem by using the Orient Joint command.

Select the root of the joint chain. From the Skeleton menu, choose Orient Joint > options box. In the Orient Joint Options dialog box, set the following:

Orientation: XYZ

Hierarchy: Select the Orient Child Joints check box

Click Orient when finished. Notice that the joints have been reoriented so that the X-axis again points down the bone.

END TUTORIAL 22.2

Rotating and Scaling Joints

Instead of moving joints, often rotating and scaling are far better alternatives because you can change a joint's position without disturbing its local rotation axis. You can also use the Scale tool to adjust the length of bones, thereby repositioning all joints in the hierarchy. Combining rotation and scaling is a far better method of reshaping joint chains, as you run no risk of offsetting the rotation information of the chain's joints.

Binding a Character to a Skeleton: Skinning

Right now, if your skeleton's joints bend, the model itself would stay behind. So now that you have completed a skeleton for your character, it's time to attach that skeleton to the geometry of your character model—a process known as *skinning*.

In Maya, there are two major methods of skinning: *Rigid Bind* and *Smooth Bind*. In a nutshell, the main difference is that with Rigid Bind, each vertex of the model is influenced by a single joint. With Smooth Bind, a vertex can be influenced by multiple joints simultaneously. Both methods have their pros and cons, but Unreal understands only skinning information that's created through the Smooth Bind process. For this reason, only smooth skinning is covered in this book.

Introduction to Smooth Bind

So how exactly does smooth skinning work? The process is simple: A model's vertices are influenced by the position, rotation, and scale of the skinned joints. As you move, bend, and flex the skeleton, the character model follows along. Because each vertex can be influenced by many joints at the same time, the effect of the character bending is averaged out, producing a smoother result.

So how do you specify the number of joints that can influence each vertex? When you use Smooth Bind on a character, you can set the Max Influences value in the command's options. This value is the number of possible joints that can affect each vertex of the model. In **TUTORIAL 22.3**, you learn how to set up a Smooth Bind skinning.

TUTORIAL 22.3: Smooth Binding a Simple Model

1. Start a new scene and go to the Animation menu set. You'll set up a simple system to understand the use of the Smooth Bind process.
2. Create a polygon cylinder by choosing Create > Polygon Primitives > Cylinder > options box from the main menu. In the Cylinder Options dialog box, set the following:

   Radius: 1

   Height: 10

   Subdivisions Around Axis: 20

   Subdivisions Along Height: 16

   Subdivisions on Caps: 1

   Axis: Z

3. Switch to the Side viewport, as shown in **FIGURE 22.11**. Using the Joint tool, create three joints within the cylinder: one at the beginning (for the shoulder), one at the middle (for the elbow), and one at the end (for the wrist). Press Enter when done.
4. Select the root joint, the one created at the shoulder. Shift-select the geometry of the cylinder. Choose Skin > Bind Skin > Smooth Bind > options box from the main menu. **TABLE 22.1** describes the settings in the Smooth Bind Options dialog box.

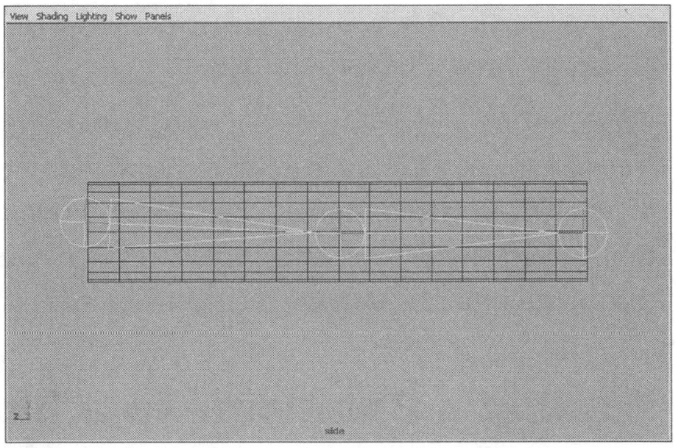

FIGURE 22.11 Joints within the cylinder.

TABLE 22.1 Smooth Skinning Options

Setting	Description
Bind To	This setting has two modes: Complete Skeleton and Selected Joints. The Complete Skeleton mode attaches the selected geometry to the entire joint hierarchy, regardless of which joints are currently selected. The Selected Joints mode skins the geometry only to the joints that are currently selected.
Bind Method	This setting also has two modes: Closest Joint attaches vertices to the joints while respecting the hierarchy. Closest Distance attaches the joints while ignoring the joint hierarchy; instead, this mode relies on the distance the geometry is from a given joint. The difference between the two modes can be seen most clearly when skinning areas such as the fingers. When Closest Joint is active, Maya makes sure to skin the vertices of each area of the finger to joints that are in the same hierarchy as the finger bone. Therefore, influence from the joint at the tip of the index finger is not likely to influence the vertices at the tip of the middle finger. The Closest Joint setting is most often used for character skinning.

TABLE 22.1 Continued

Setting	Description
	Closest Distance, on the other hand, ignores the hierarchy, meaning that a situation in which joints in the index finger are influencing vertices in other fingers of the hand is very possible. Because the influence doesn't respect the hierarchy's layout, you could easily get an influence that jumps from the tip of one finger to the tip of another. The result would be that when one finger rotates, other fingers near it seem to stretch toward it, as though they were made of gum or taffy.
Max Influences	As mentioned earlier, this setting controls the number of joints that influence each vertex of the model. This number is valid only at the moment skinning is applied. So even if Max Influences is set to 2, you can edit your influences to have vertices controlled by as many other joints as you like.
Dropoff Rate	This setting controls the rate at which Maya stops looking for joints to influence each point. The higher this number, the faster the influence drops off. The lower the number, the farther Maya looks to find joints to influence each vertex. The default is 4, which works great in most situations.

For now, leave the options at their default values, and click the Bind Skin button.

5. Select the Rotate tool. Click the elbow joint and rotate it up 90 degrees. Notice that the cylinder's geometry now flexes with the skeleton. However, the area of flex doesn't seem to be keeping its volume; instead, it's bending much like a wet noodle (see **FIGURE 22.12**). You can fix this in the next tutorial by adjusting how much influence each joint has on the object. Save the scene.

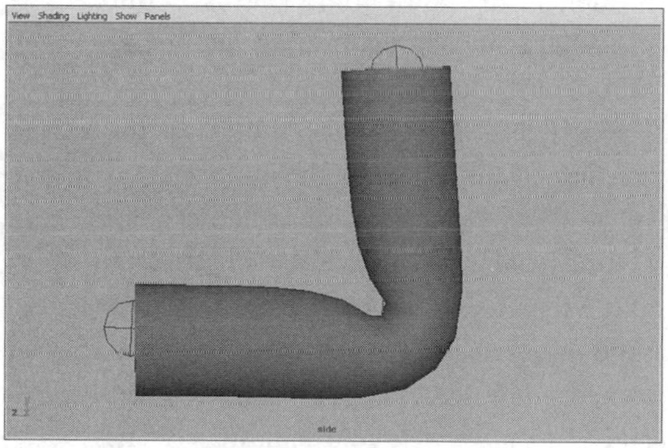

FIGURE 22.12 The skinned cylinder is deforming, although not as cleanly as you would like.

END TUTORIAL 22.3

Adjusting Joint Influence

Not only can you control how many joints influence each vertex of a particular model, but you can also change the percentage of influence each joint is using. The amount of influence each joint exerts is referred to as the joint's *weight*. You can adjust this weight to give more influence to some joints and to take it away from others.

The skin weighting system works as follows: Each vertex is controlled by a specific number of joints, and each of those joints controls a percentage of the influence sent to that particular joint. Because the value is a percentage, the combined value of all influences affecting each vertex must equal 100%, or in Maya, a value of 1. As an example, say that you have a single vertex being controlled by only two joints. Each joint controls 50% of the weighting, meaning they both have a value of 0.5. If you set one joint's weight to 75%, the weight from the other automatically adjusts to 25%. This automatic adjustment is always the case with smooth skinning.

So what happens when you have an entire character, composed of thousands of polygons, skinned to a skeleton with many joints and a relatively high Max Influences value? Naturally, the result would be literally thousands of influence values for the model's vertices. Going vertex by vertex and adjusting the weight values numerically takes far too much time. Fortunately, Maya comes equipped with a tool engineered specially for this problem: the Paint Skin Weights tool.

The idea of the Paint Skin Weights tool is relatively simple: Because all the values of skin weights are calculated on a 0 to 1 basis, you could represent them visually by using a grayscale image with 0 equal to black and 1 equal to white. When using the Paint Skin Weights tool, you would then see a visual representation of the weight being applied to your geometry from any joint.

The Paint Skin Weights Tool is a brush-based tool that enables you to adjust the influence of your joints across your model's geometry in a fast, interactive manner. It displays a grayscale texture across your model that indicates the amount of influence for the joint selected in the Influence section of the Tool Settings dialog box (see **FIGURE 22.13**). With this tool, you can "paint" weights onto different areas of the surface. As mentioned, white areas denote 100% influence, and black areas denote 0% influence. The varying levels of gray designate percentages between those values.

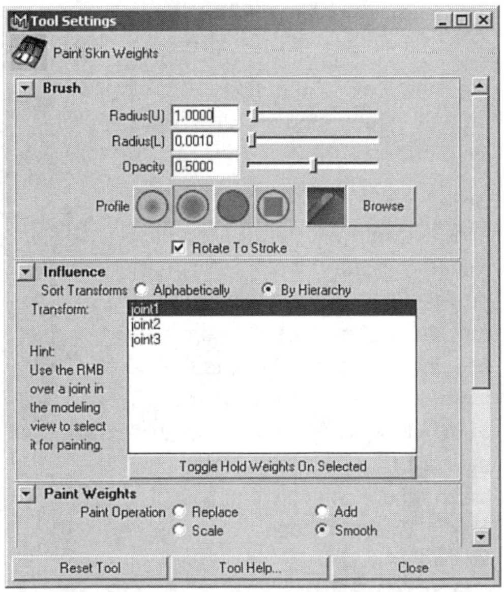

FIGURE 22.13 **The Paint Skin Weights Tool Settings dialog box.**

The key elements in the Tool Settings dialog box are in the Brush section, where you can control the size and profile of your brush. Note that the Radius(L) is valid only if you have a pressure-sensitive device attached to your computer, such as a digital pen. The Opacity value is one of the most important settings you use while adjusting skin weights with this tool. It controls how dramatic the effect of each stroke is as you paint. Leaving this value fairly low is always a good idea; then you can build strokes on top of one another to achieve your final solution.

The settings in the Influence section are used to designate the joint to which you're adding or subtracting weight. A list of all the joints skinned to the selected piece of geometry is displayed in this section. The list of joints can be sorted alphabetically by name or by position in the hierarchy. Keep in mind that sorting your joints by hierarchy can be quite tedious if you're working with an exceptionally complex skeleton.

You can use the settings in the Paint Weights section to control the function of the brush. For the Paint Operation setting, four options are available, described in the following list:

- *Replace*—This operation applies the brush's set value uniformly across the painted surface. For example, if you need to set the weight in a specific area to 0.5, you could set the Value slider (located just under the Paint Operation options) to that weight and paint on the surface with this operation. Wherever the brush stroke falls, the weight is set to 0.5.
- *Add*—This operation adds the number set in the Value slider to the existing value on the surface. This is a great tool to gently increase weight in a given area.
- *Scale*—This operation is used to reduce the amount of weighting applied by faraway joints.
- *Smooth*—This operation applies an average value from all the vertices that fall within the brush's radius. The end result is that skinning in the painted area is smoothed out.

The settings in the Display section control how you see the tool's feedback in the viewport. Two main options of interest are the Show Wireframe check box, which removes the wireframe from the selected model while painting weights, and the Color Feedback check box, which can be used to remove the grayscale color pattern across the surface of the skin. The color can be confusing sometimes, especially when a large complex area is only one color, such as white. In **TUTORIAL 22.4**, you use this tool to adjust the skin weights from **TUTORIAL 22.3**.

TUTORIAL 22.4: Using the Paint Skin Weights Tool

1. Continue **TUTORIAL 22.3**, or open the file you saved at the end of that tutorial (see **FIGURE 22.14**). You're going to adjust the weight influence across the surface of the cylinder to make the elbow area keep more of its volume. Before you begin, select the middle (elbow) joint, and rotate it upward in the Side view to about 90 degrees.

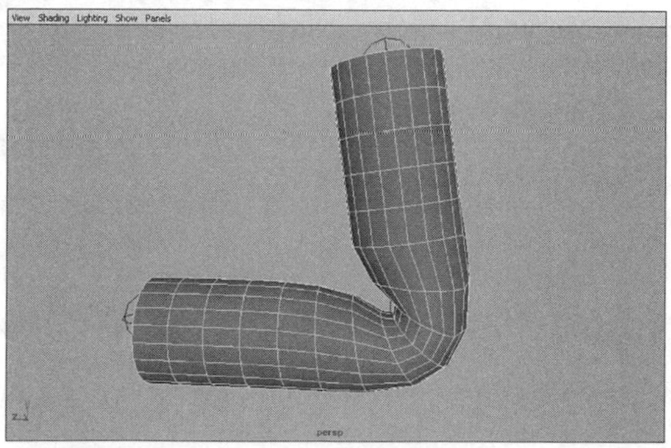

FIGURE 22.14 The example from **TUTORIAL 22.3**.

2. Select the cylinder geometry. Choose Skin > Edit Smooth Skin > Paint Skin Weights Tool > options

box from the main menu. This activates the Paint Skin Weights Tool and opens the Tool Settings dialog box. If you don't see a change in the viewport, make sure you're in Smooth Shaded mode by pressing the 5 key.

3. In the Influence section, select Joint2 to display the weight for that specific joint. In the Paint Weights section, set Paint Operation to Add, and set the Value slider to about 0.5. In the Brush section, set Radius(U) to 1 and Opacity to 0.5.

4. In the Perspective viewport, carefully paint around the bottom of the elbow and the inside of the bend's vertical side. As weight is added, you can see the elbow gaining more of its original volume back (see **FIGURE 22.15**). Be careful not to add too much. If necessary, adjust your Weight and Opacity settings in the Tool Settings dialog box.

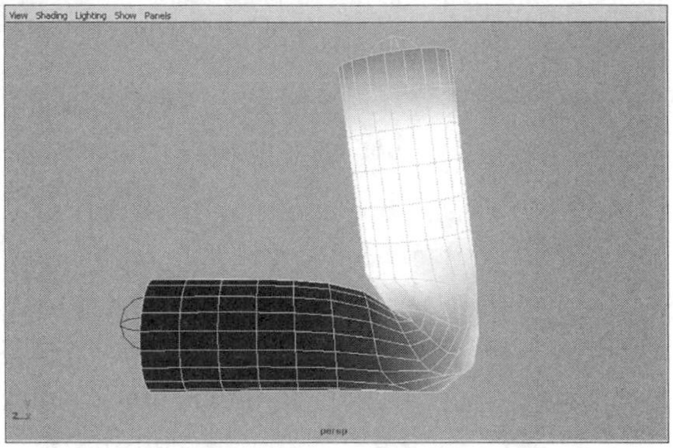

FIGURE 22.15 Weight added to Joint2.

5. In the Influence section, select Joint1 and repeat the process, adding weight to the outside of the elbow and the bicep area.

6. To clean up the results, set Paint Operation to Smooth, and carefully paint around the edited area of the elbow. Notice that the effect of the painting is adjusted to look smoothed (see **FIGURE 22.16**). Switch to different joints, and experiment with the tools until you achieve a result you like.

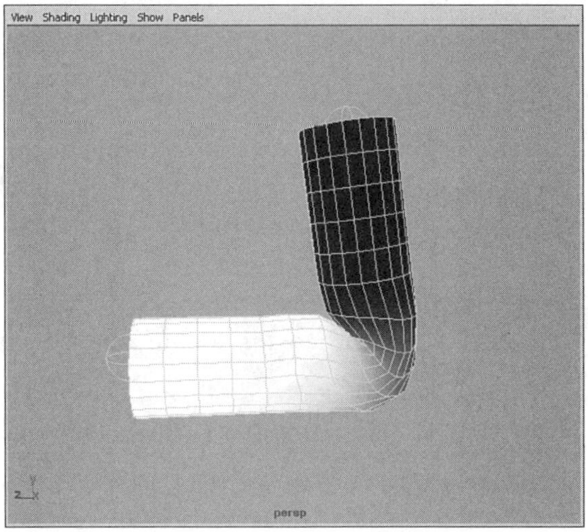

FIGURE 22.16 The weight is now adjusted. Notice that the elbow area is keeping more of its volume.

END TUTORIAL 22.4

Importing a Character Without Custom Animation

Now it's time to apply everything you've learned throughout this chapter to successfully import a character into UT. You begin by importing a skeleton provided by Epic Games. The character needs to be adjusted to fit the joints. After this is done, the character is smooth bound to the skeleton. When the weights have been properly adjusted and deformation looks good, you begin the process of preparing for export. When everything is ready, the character is exported directly into UnrealEd, where you can link the character to already existing animation and create an Unreal Player List (UPL) file to define the character in Unreal Tournament 2004. Then you're ready to play!

Importing a Skeleton

In **TUTORIAL 22.5**, you import a premade skeleton specifically designed for use with Unreal Tournament 2004 characters into Maya and set it up for use with your character.

TUTORIAL 22.5: Importing a Skeleton

1. Open the `UTCharacter_Model.mb` file from the DVD (see **FIGURE 22.17**) or use the character you modeled earlier in Chapter 21, "Character Modeling."
2. From the main menu, choose File > Import and select `Epic_Skeleton.mb` from the dialog box. The skeleton doesn't fit the geometry correctly because the geometry and the skeleton were modeled at different scales (see **FIGURE 22.18**). Select the root of the skeleton, and move it back in the Z-axis so that it's positioned within the character's geometry.
3. You need the skeleton to fit the character, but it's best not to disturb the joints' translation or scale, which could cause extreme deformation after the character is in Unreal linked with existing animation. Rotating the joints, on the other hand, is not a problem. The best way to do this so that you don't disturb the joints is to begin by scaling the geometry up to match the skeleton as closely as possible. Select the Scale tool and uniformly scale the geometry to match. Use the Front viewport to gauge just how much the character needs to be scaled up (see **FIGURE 22.19**). The joint arms and legs don't fit within the geometry arms and legs, but don't worry about this. Simply try to match up the

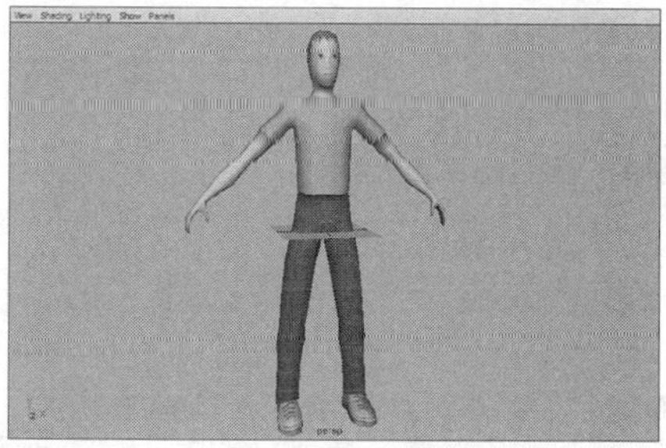

FIGURE 22.17 Preparing the character in Maya for export into Unreal Tournament.

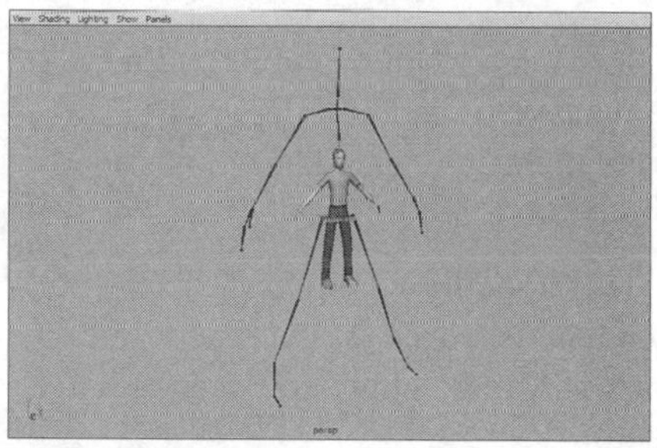

FIGURE 22.18 The imported skeleton is nearly three times larger than the geometry.

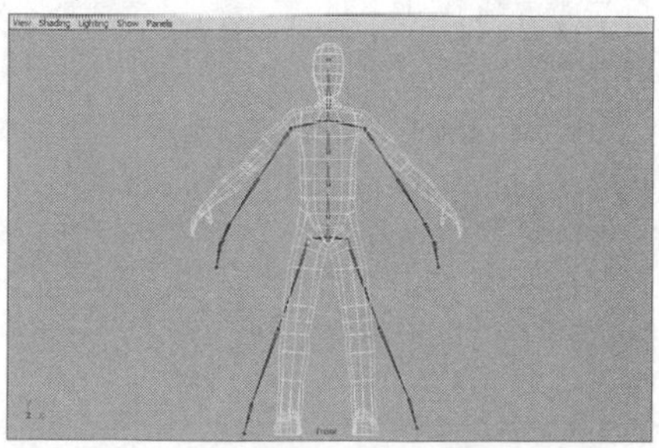

FIGURE 22.19 The character's geometry has been uniformly scaled to match the skeleton.

shoulders and hips. You'll rotate the joints in the next step to match the character more closely.

4. Rotate the shoulders, elbows, hips, and knee joints so that the arms and legs fit within the geometry (see **FIGURE 22.20**). Don't move or scale the joints, as this can cause several problems in Unreal after existing animation is linked to your character.

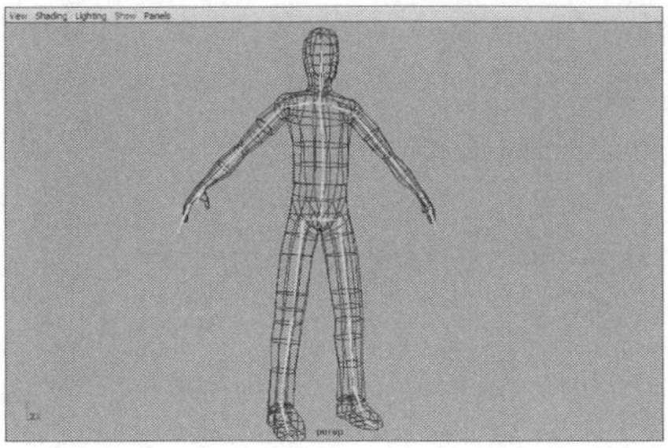

FIGURE 22.20 The joints have been rotated so that the skeleton fits perfectly within the geometry.

END TUTORIAL 22.5

Skinning a Character

Now that the bones are aligned to the character, you can attach the geometry to the skeleton, or "skin" the character. **TUTORIAL 22.6** walks you through this process.

TUTORIAL 22.6: Skinning a Character

1. Open the `UTCharacter_Skeleton.mb` file, or continue where you left off with **TUTORIAL 22.5**.

2. Select the root joint, and Shift-select the character geometry. From the main menu, choose Skin > Bind Skin > Smooth Bind > options box.

3. In the Smooth Bind Options dialog box (see **FIGURE 22.21**), use the following settings and then click Bind Skin:

   Bind To: Complete Skeleton
   Bind Method: Closest Joint
   Max Influences: 3
   Dropoff Rate: 6

4. To see the effects of the Smooth Bind, select and rotate several joints and watch the deformation caused to the geometry (see **FIGURE 22.22**). After you're finished testing the deformation, make sure you undo all rotations.

END TUTORIAL 22.6

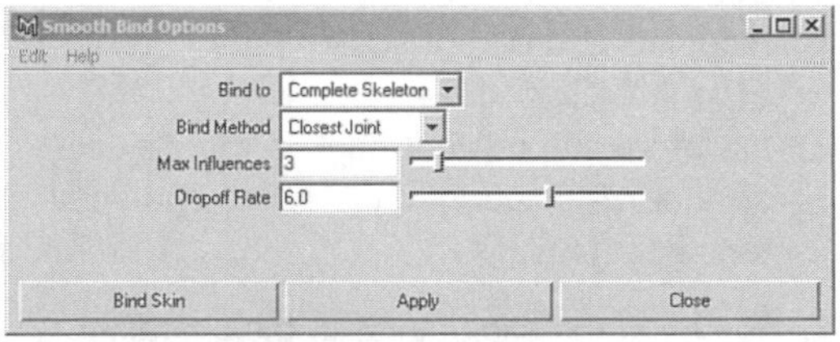

FIGURE 22.21 Setting the Smooth Bind options can produce better results in the default skin.

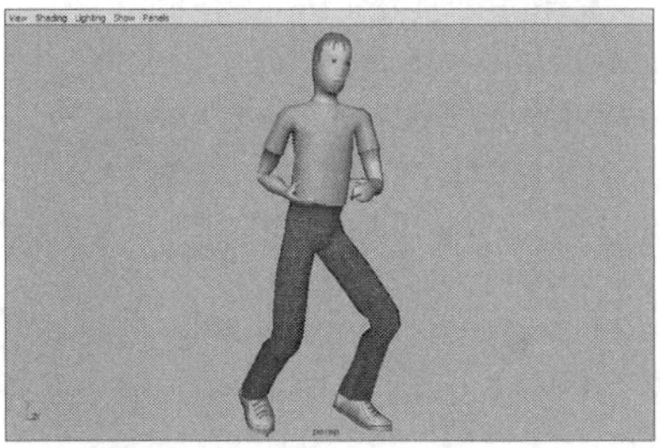

FIGURE 22.22 Test the geometry deformation by rotating the joints.

> **TIP**
>
> You can always return a character to its original bind pose quickly by selecting the root joint and then choosing Skin > Go To Bind Pose from the main menu.

Adjusting the Skin Weights

The character's geometry is now fully attached to the skeleton. Currently, however, he won't deform properly if you rotate his joints, so you need to modify and adjust his skin weights. **TUTORIAL 22.7** introduces you to this process.

TUTORIAL 22.7: Adjusting the Skin Weights

1. Continue from **TUTORIAL 22.6** or open the `UTCharacter_SkinWeights_Start.mb` file.
2. Rotate the joints so that the character appears to be sitting on an imaginary chair (see **FIGURE 22.23**). Rotate the arms down and add some rotation to bend the elbows. The idea is to pose the character into a position that shows off the deformation at major joint bends, such as shoulders, elbows, hips, and knees.

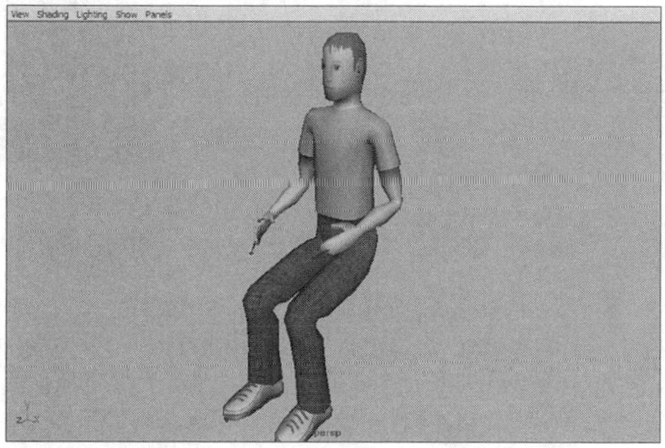

FIGURE 22.23 The character has been posed so that deformation problems can be easily identified.

3. Select the character. From the main menu, choose Skin > Edit Smooth Skin > Paint Skin Weights Tool > options box. Make sure you're viewing your character in Smooth Shaded mode in the Perspective view.
4. Take a close look at the shoulder region of the left arm. The chest has caved in a bit, making the arm look more like a noodle (see **FIGURE 22.24**).

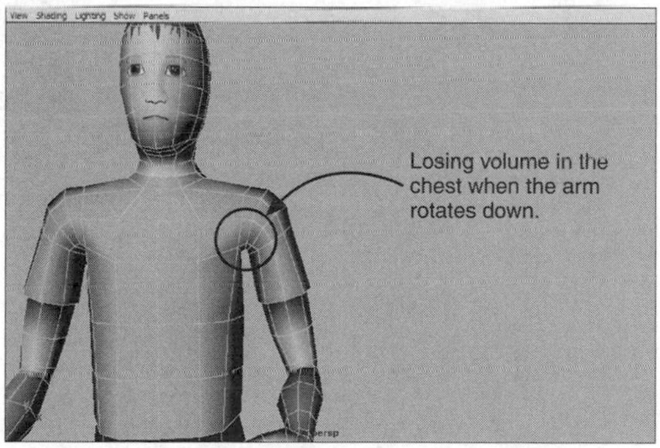
Losing volume in the chest when the arm rotates down.

FIGURE 22.24 When the arm is rotated down, you can see how some of the volume is lost in the chest.

   Use the following steps in the Tool Settings dialog box to correct this problem (see **FIGURE 22.25**):

   - Select `Bip01_L_UpperArm` in the Influence section.
   - Set Radius(U) to 2.5.
   - Set Opacity to 0.35.
   - Set Paint Operation to Replace.
   - Set the Value slider to 0.

Move the brush over the intersecting edges on the torso near the underarm area, and click to begin removing weights. As the weight is removed, notice that the volume begins to return. Continue painting under the arm to fill the chest back in (see **FIGURE 22.26**).

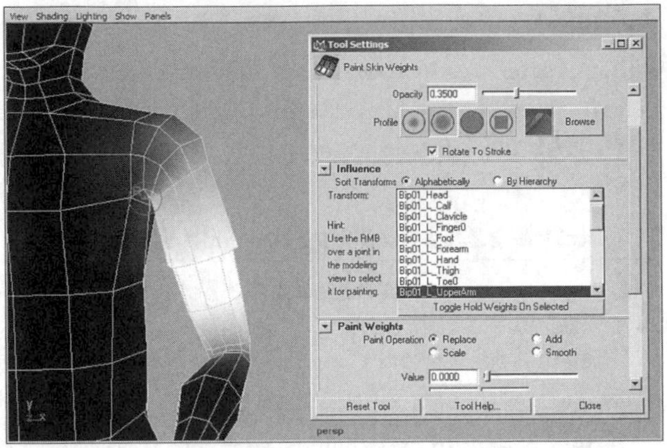

FIGURE 22.25 Removing weights from the underarm area help bring volume back into the chest.

5. Continue adjusting weights on the right side of the character until the character deforms properly in a series of action poses.

6. After the right side of the character has been weighted, you can mirror the weights to the left side. This works only if the character is symmetrical. To mirror the weights, use the following steps:

   - Select the skeleton root and choose Skin > Go To Bind Pose.
   - Select the character's geometry.
   - From the main menu, choose Skin > Edit Smooth Skin > Mirror Skin Weights > options box.
   - In the Mirror Skin Weights Options dialog box shown in **FIGURE 22.27**, set Mirror Across to YZ and verify that the Direction check box is selected so that you mirror the weights from positive X to negative X.
   - Click the Mirror button.

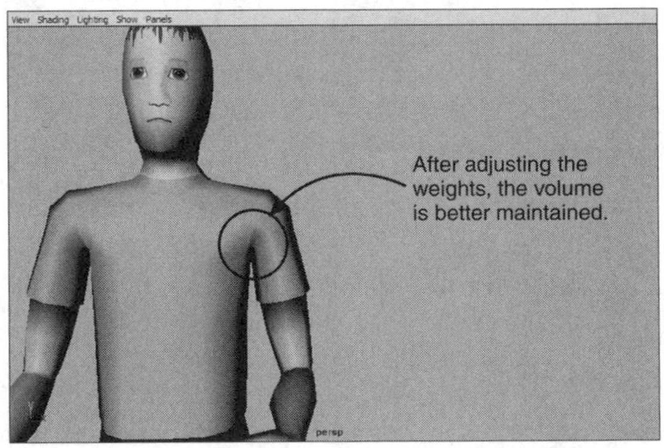

FIGURE 22.26 The underarm area has been corrected so that volume is maintained.

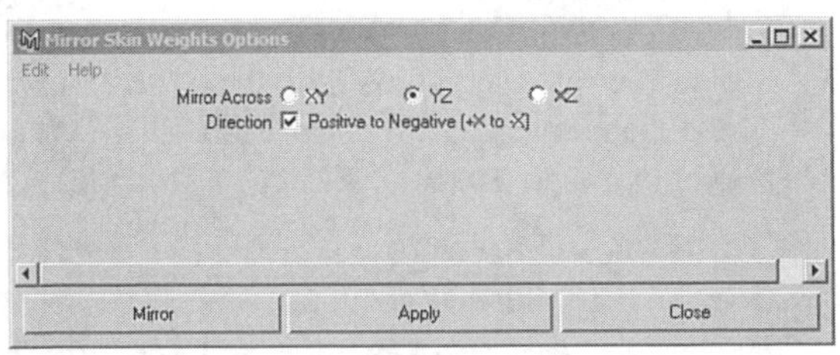

FIGURE 22.27 Use the Mirror Skin Weights action to mirror weights from the left side of the character to the right side.

END TUTORIAL 22.7

Exporting the Character

The character is now fully skinned and ready to be exported. **TUTORIAL 22.8** shows you how to get the character into UnrealEd so that you can link up his properties and animations, bringing him one step closer to being a fully playable game character.

TUTORIAL 22.8: Exporting the Character

1. Open the `UTCharacter_Export_Start` file.
2. Before the character is ready to be exported, you need to triangulate the skinned character by following these steps:
   - Select the character's geometry.
   - Go to the Modeling menu set (press F3), and choose Polygons > Triangulate from the main menu. **FIGURE 22.28** shows the result.
   - The Triangulate action causes all the faces for the geometry to be selected. Simply deselect them, and reselect the character.
3. From the Shelf, click the Connect to UnrealEd icon ( ).
4. Select the root joint.
5. From the main menu, choose Character > Create Character Set > options box.

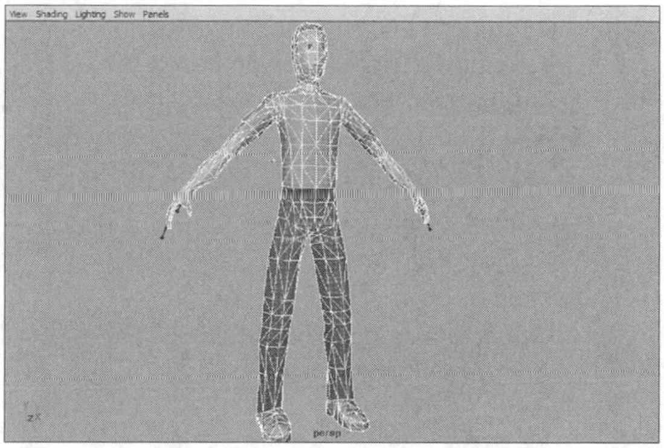

FIGURE 22.28 The character must be triangulated before exporting to UnrealEd.

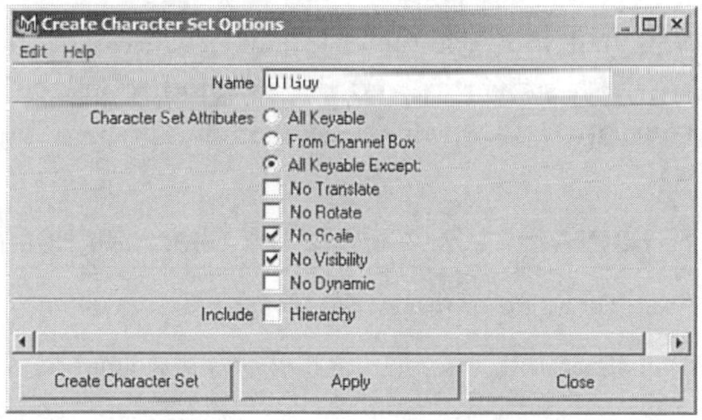

FIGURE 22.29 A character set must be created before you can export the character to Unreal.

6. In the Create Character Set Options dialog box shown in **FIGURE 22.29**, set the name to **UTGuy**. All other parameters should be at their default settings. Click Create Character Set.
7. Click the Skeletal Mesh Export Window button ( ) in the Shelf.
8. In the Skeletal Mesh UT2K4 Export dialog box shown in **FIGURE 22.30**, click the Package drop-down list and select Create New Package. In the New Package dialog box, set the package name to **UTGuyAnim**, and click OK.

22

9. Back in the Skeletal Mesh UT2K4 Export dialog box, select the Underscore to Space check box. Maya does not allow spaces in object names, but bone names require spaces in Unreal. Selecting this check box handles the conversion for you.

10. Click the Export button. The Command Feedback line (located at the bottom right of the Maya UI) shows `Result: Export complete`. At this point, the character has been exported to Unreal in the UTGuyAnim package. The package has not been saved, so you need to be careful not to close UnrealEd.

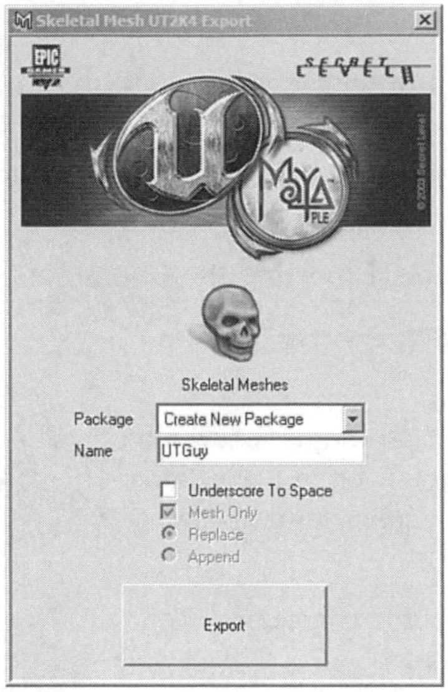

FIGURE 22.30 Creating the Unreal package that the character will be created in.

END TUTORIAL 22.8

Getting the Character Ready for Gameplay

Now that you have the character in UnrealEd, you need to configure several settings, such as his mesh properties and default animations, before you can use the character in-game. In **TUTORIAL 22.9**, you use UnrealEd to prepare your character for gameplay.

TUTORIAL 22.9: Getting the Character Ready for Gameplay

1. Continue from **TUTORIAL 22.8**.
2. Switch to UnrealEd and open the Animation browser.
3. Set the Package drop-down list to UTGuyAnim. You see the character that was exported from Maya (see **FIGURE 22.31**). The most noticeable thing is that he's missing his textures! You'll correct that in the next steps.
4. Before you can assign textures, you need to create the texture package. At the moment, the textures exist only as external files, so follow these steps:
    - Switch to the Texture browser.
    - From the menu, choose File > Import.
    - In the Import Texture dialog box shown in **FIGURE 22.32**, select both `Head.tga` and `Body.tga`, and click Open.

- In the Import Texture dialog box that opens, set the following options:

Package: UTGuyTextures

Group: (Clear any entries)

Leave everything else at the defaults and click OK All.

- On the toolbar, click the Save icon to save the package.

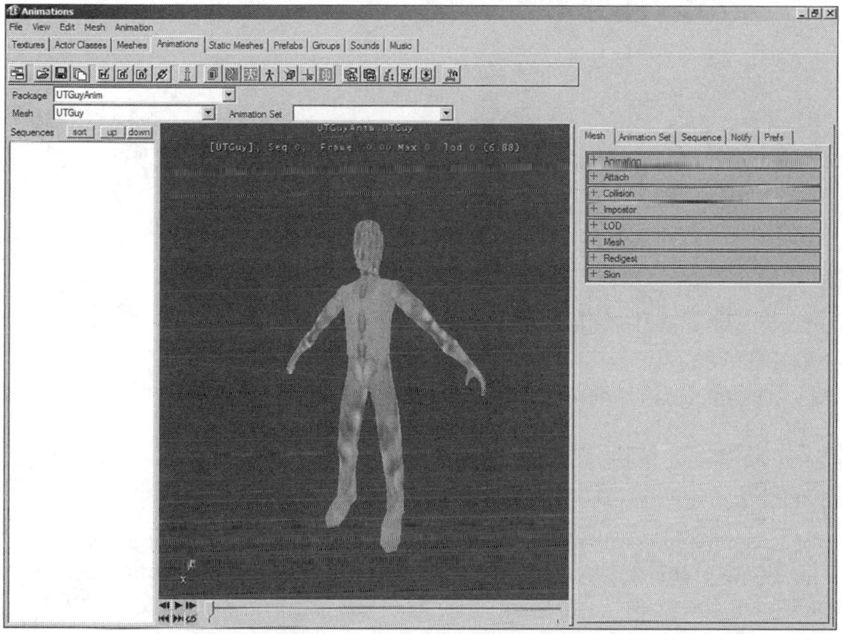

FIGURE 22.31 The character can be viewed in the Animation browser, but is seen without any textures.

5. In the Texture browser, select the Head texture.

6. Switch back to the Animation browser. In the properties section under the Mesh tab, expand Skin > Material and click the index [0] property (see **FIGURE 22.33**). Click the Use button.

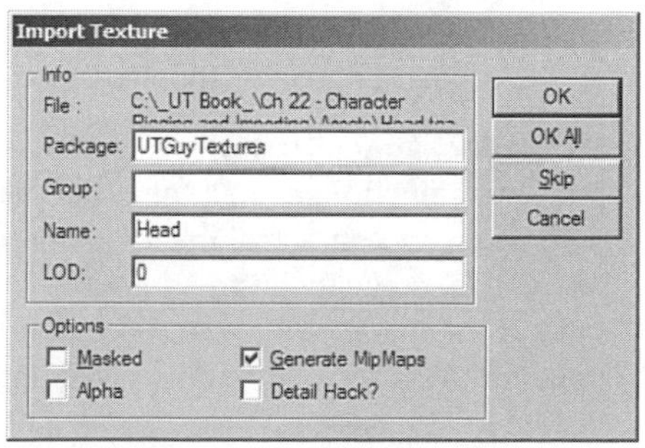

FIGURE 22.32 Importing the character's textures into a new package.

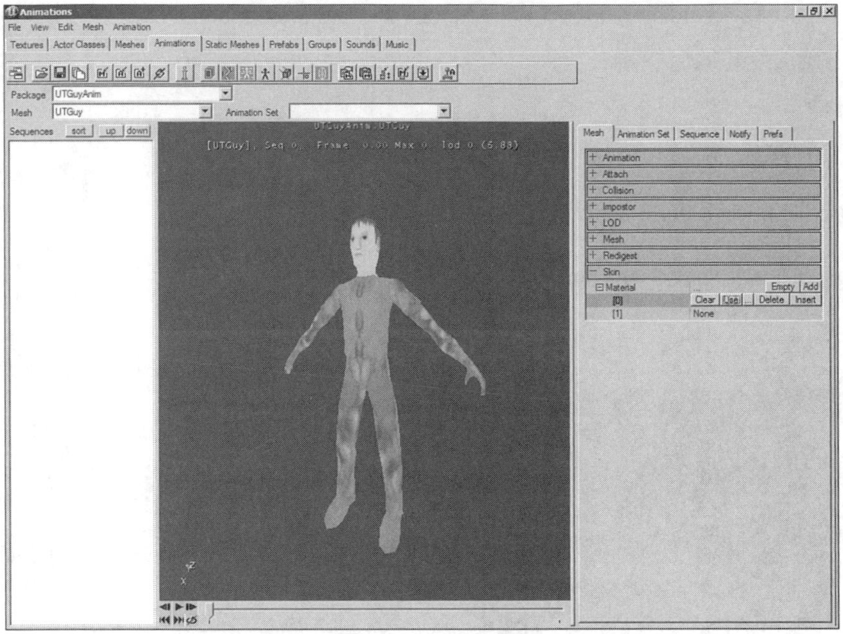

FIGURE 22.33 Assigning the Head texture to your character.

7. In the Texture browser, select the Body texture. Back in the Animation browser, assign the Body texture to index [1]. The character is now textured.

8. For the character to behave properly in the game, you need to set several properties. Instead of setting these properties by hand, however, you'll simply use a set of properties from an existing Unreal character:

   - In the Package drop-down list of the Animation browser, select the ThunderCrash package, where you'll see the JakobM character. Take note of how small the character looks.

   - Choose Mesh > Copy Mesh Properties from the Animation browser's menu to place all the properties for the ThunderCrash character in the Clipboard for later use.

   - Switch back to the UTGuyAnim package, and choose Mesh > Paste Mesh Properties from the menu to place all the properties used with the ThunderCrash character onto your new character. You'll see the character shrink in size significantly, but don't worry; this is supposed to happen. The character's scale has been reset to reflect the size of characters already in the game. Also, don't be alarmed that the character appears to be lying flat on his back, as shown in **FIGURE 22.34**. This happened because the original characters were created using a different coordinate system. The problem will be corrected when you apply animation to the character.

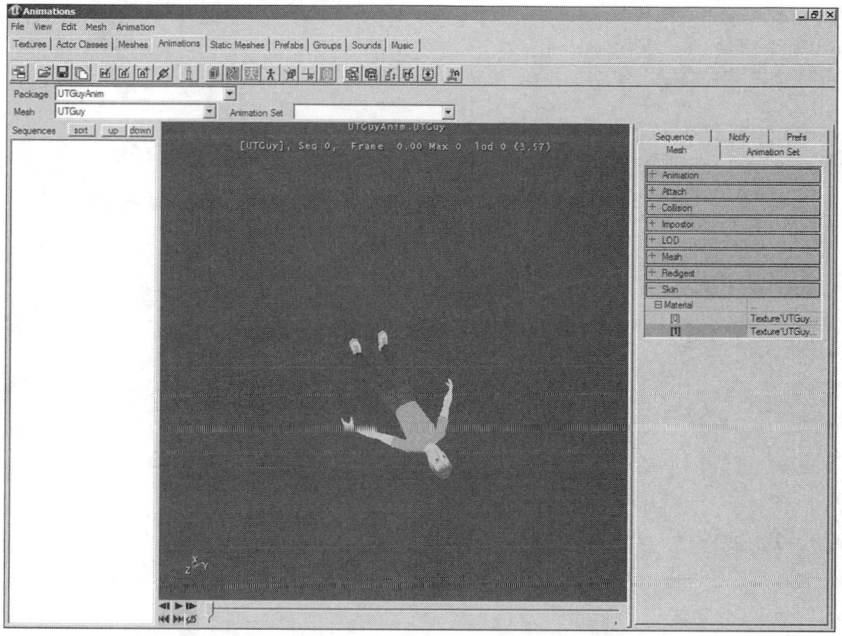

FIGURE 22.34 The character's rotation will change after the ThunderCrash mesh properties are pasted.

9. Along with using the mesh properties of an established character, you can also borrow the default animations for that character. To use another character's animation, follow these steps:

    - In the Package drop-down list, select ThunderCrash. You'll see a long list of animation sequences in the Sequences list on the left side of the browser. To apply these sequences to your character, simply go to the Mesh properties tab, and under the Animation category, highlight the DefaultAnimation entry. Press Ctrl+C to copy this information to the Clipboard.

    - In the Package drop-down list, select UTGuyAnim. Click in the `DefaultAnimation` property (it's currently empty) and press Ctrl+V to paste the information that was copied in the previous step. Press the Enter key to apply the change. Notice that the character stands back up at the correct orientation. Notice, too, that the Sequences list is empty, but this is a redraw issue. To see the sequences, simply click the Mesh drop-down list (at the upper left, under the Package drop-down list), and select UTGuy (see **FIGURE 22.35**).

    - Navigate around the character and test some of the animation sequences by highlighting a sequence and clicking the Play button (see **FIGURE 22.36**).

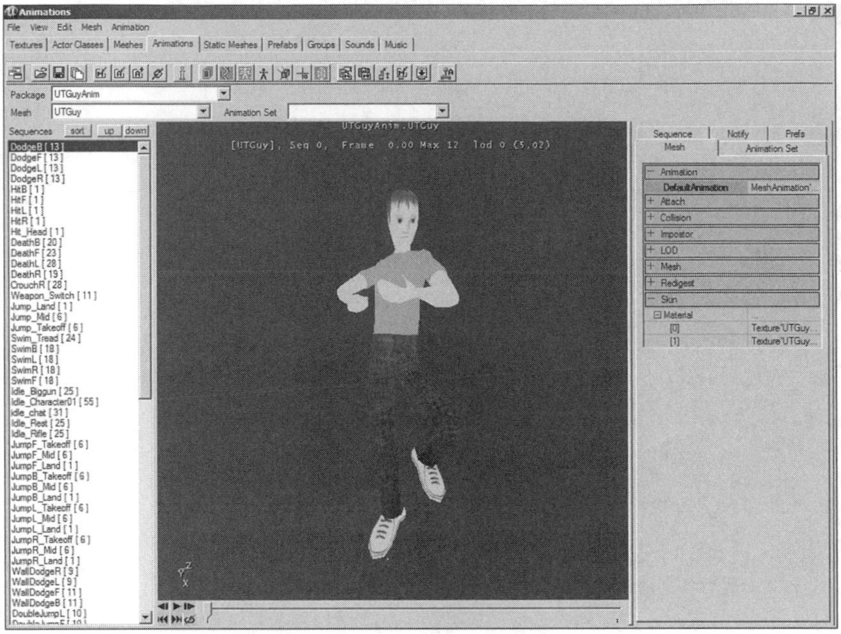

FIGURE 22.35 The Sequences list now populated with various sequences.

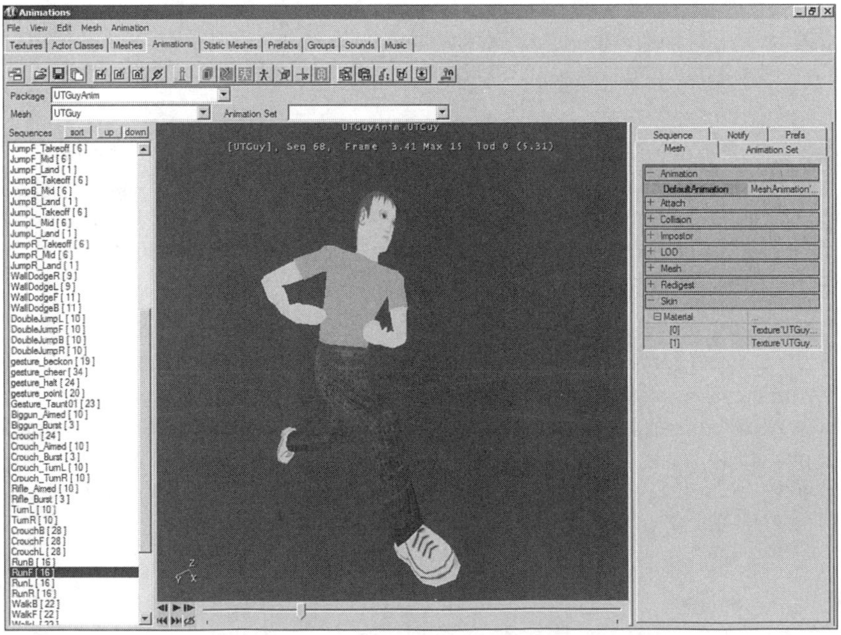

FIGURE 22.36 The character is shown using the RunF (run forward) animation sequence.

10. To control whether the character can hold a weapon or flag, you need to use *sockets*, which represent a dynamic array of aliases. These aliases are used to define specific bones that Unreal uses to attach items to the character. For your purposes, the two most important items are the weapon and the flag.

Because you copied mesh properties of ThunderCrash, you already have sockets established, but in this case, the name of one of your bones is different from the one ThunderCrash uses. To fix this, you need to update two of the sockets:

- In the properties area, under the Mesh tab, expand Sockets > [0] and [1]. In the `BoneName` properties for both [0] and [1], change the name from `Bone_weapon` to `BoneWeapon` (see **FIGURE 22.37**).
- To apply these changes, set the `ApplyNewSockets` property to True. It looks like the property value doesn't change, but that's not how this property works. The property "finalizes" the changes you have made to the sockets, but its value does not appear to change.

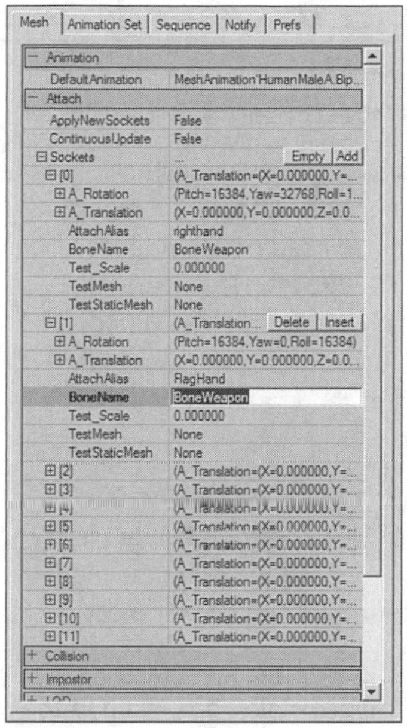

FIGURE 22.37 Setting the *BoneName* properties correctly allows the socket to work. If this error isn't corrected, the character can't hold a gun.

11. All the properties have been set, so save the package.

END TUTORIAL 22.9

Creating the Character's Portrait

The character portrait is another important file that you need to create. When Unreal players decide to change characters, they can browse a list of character portraits, so you want your character portrait to show in that list. In **TUTORIAL 22.10**, you take a look at one of many possible methods for generating a character portrait image. You use Maya, Photoshop, and UnrealEd in this tutorial.

TUTORIAL 22.10: Creating the Character's Portrait

1. In Maya, open the `UTCharacter_Export_Start` file.

2. Rotate the character's joints to pose his upper body into some sort of naturally relaxed position (see **FIGURE 22.38**). The character's pose is really up to you. Think about how you would like the character viewed in the character selection screen.

3. To make the image look better, try setting the background color to black. From the main menu, choose Window > Settings/Preferences > Colors.

4. In the Colors dialog box, expand the 3D Views category under the General tab. Set Background to black (see **FIGURE 22.39**). Click the Save button to save your changes.

5. Position the Perspective camera in a way that gives an interesting view of the character. Press Shift+Print Screen to take a snapshot of the screen.

6. Open Photoshop, create a new file, and click OK to accept the sizes automatically entered in the New dialog box. Press Ctrl+V to paste the image into the new document (see **FIGURE 22.40**).

7. Select the Crop tool and use the following settings:

   Width: 256 px

   Height: 512 px

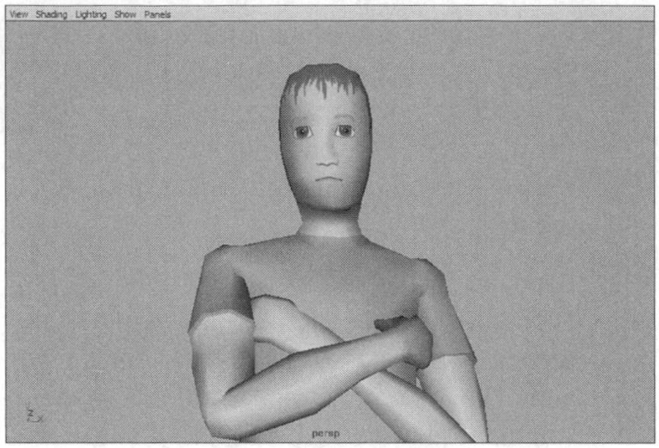

FIGURE 22.38 The character has been posed for the portrait shot.

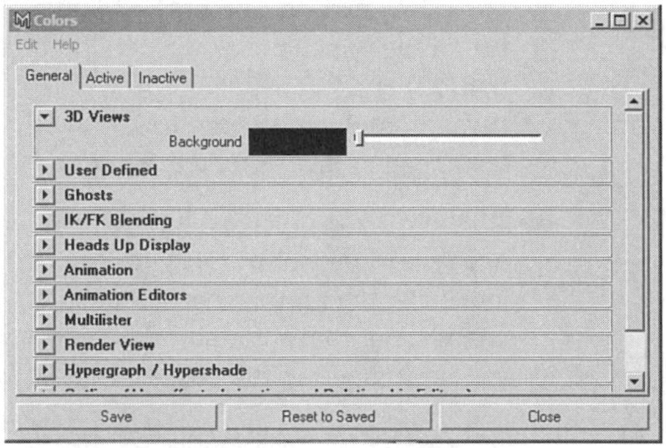

FIGURE 22.39 Changing the background color helps improve the final image.

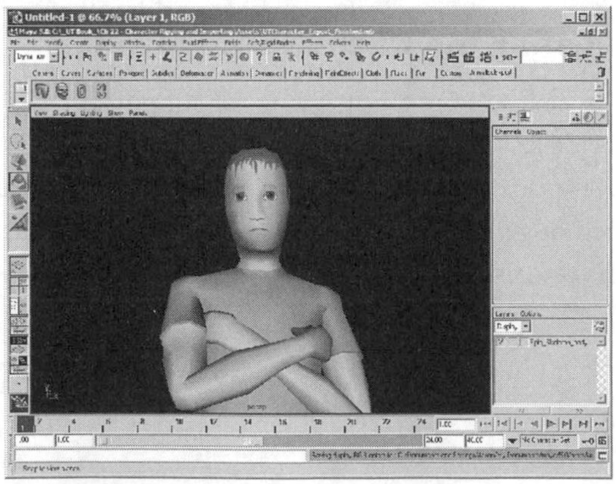

FIGURE 22.40 The character image in Photoshop where the final tweaks are applied.

8. Crop the area around the character, leaving the best possible results (see **FIGURE 22.41**).

9. Save the file as `UTGuyPortrait.tga`.

10. Switch back to UnrealEd. Open the Texture browser, and change to the UTGuyTexture package.

11. Import the new `UTGuyPortrait.tga` file into the UTGuyTexture package.

12. Save the package.

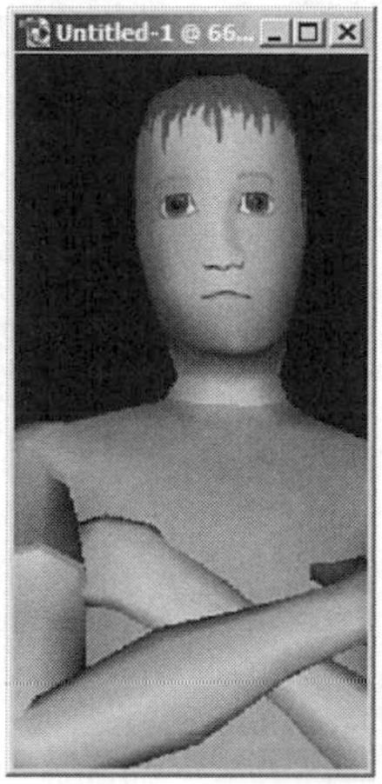

FIGURE 22.41 The cropped character image.

END TUTORIAL 22.10

The UPL File and Testing the Character In-game

Now that the character is complete and the packages have been saved, there's one final step before you can use this character in-game: You need to create a UPL file. A UPL file contains important information about characters. By default, Unreal Tournament 2004 contains two UPL files in the System folder: `XplayersL1.upl` and `XplayersL2.upl`. These two files contain all the characters used in UT.

When a new character is added to the game, creating its own UPL file is a good idea, instead of adding an entry to an existing file. You don't want to upload your character to the Internet and have to include instructions that force users to modify an original UT2004 file. Instead, it's better workflow to simply create a new file that can be dropped into the System folder.

Fortunately, you don't have to start the UPL file from scratch. Instead, you can "borrow" the line needed from an existing UPL file, add it to a new file, modify a few settings, and you'll be ready to go. **TUTORIAL 22.11** shows you the necessary steps.

TUTORIAL 22.11: The UPL File and Testing the Character In-game

1. Open Windows Explorer and navigate to the UT2004\System folder.
2. Open the `XplayersL1.upl` file in any text editor. (Notepad is fine.)
3. Find the character with the name JakobM (see **FIGURE 22.42**). Highlight the line and copy it to the Windows Clipboard by pressing Ctrl+C.
4. In Notepad, start a new file.
5. Type the following:

```
[Public]
```

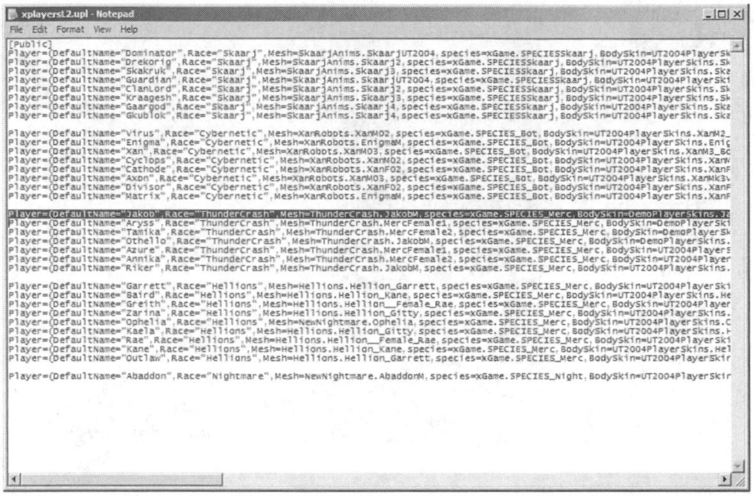

FIGURE 22.42 Copying a line from the `XplayersL1.upl` file can speed up the creation of a custom UPL file.

6. On the next line, press Ctrl+V to paste the line copied in step 3.

7. To make your character available in-game, locate and change the following properties in the Player line you copied:

   DefaultName: UTGuy

   Mesh=UTGuyAnim.UTGuy

   BodySkin=UTGuyTextures.Body

   FaceSkin=UTGuyTextures.Head

   Portrait=UTGuyTextures.UTGuyPortrait

   Text="Name: UTGuy|Age: 36|Race: Human||Data:|UTGuy is a custom character created through this book.||"

8. Save this file as `UTGuy.upl` in the UT2004\System folder. Time to test your character in-game!

9. Start Unreal Tournament 2004. From the main menu, choose Settings > Player. Click the Change Character button to see a listing of characters. If everything has been set up properly, you should see your character in the lineup, as shown in **FIGURE 22.43**. Select your character and click OK.

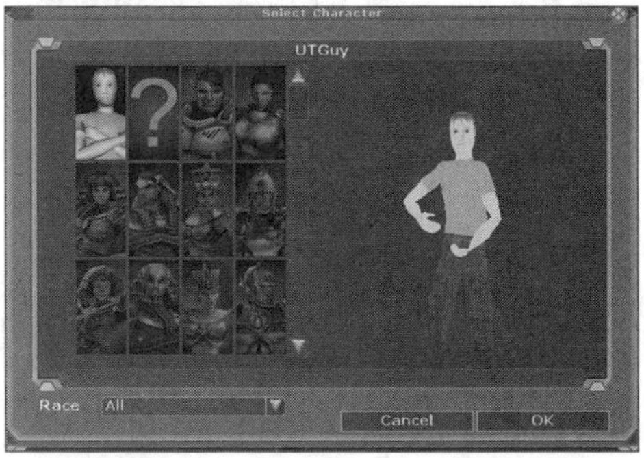

FIGURE 22.43 Your character is now playable in Unreal Tournament 2004.

FIGURE 22.44 UTGuy is now in the game and is holding his weapon.

10. From the main menu, choose Instant Action and start a game. Press F4 to adjust the camera behind your character. Another console command that's often helpful is `freecamera 1`, which allows players to rotate the camera around the character. In **FIGURES 22.44** and **22.45**, you can see the player in the game, behaving the same as any other default character.

FIGURE 22.45 UTGuy is able to play all the standard animations.

TABLE 22.2 Properties of the UPL File

Property	Description
`DefaultName`	This property is the name of the character shown in the Select Character dialog box.
`Race`	This organizational property enables you to sort the available characters in Unreal Tournament 2004. You can place anything in this line, and that race is then available in the Race drop-down list of Unreal's character selection screen.
`Mesh`	This property controls which polygonal model is used for your character.
`Species`	This property contains an Unreal class, such as `xGame.SPECIES_merc`. It controls such things as the character's blood color in-game.
`BodySkin`	This property allows you to specify which texture is used for the character's body.
`FaceSkin`	This property specifies the texture used for the character's head or face.
`Portrait`	This property specifies the portrait that's displayed in Unreal Tournament 2004's character selection screen.
`Text`	This property controls the text in the character's bio on the character selection screen.
`Sex`	This setting enables you to specify whether your character is male or female, which is important when Unreal designates a voice and creates death messages for your character, such as "UTGuy has blown himself up."
`CombatStyle`	This bot setting controls how a bot would behave in combat if controlling this character.
`FavoriteWeapon`	As its name suggests, this property allows you to specify which weapon this character favors. Naturally, it's valid only when a bot is controlling the character.
`BotUse`	This setting is a 0–255 value that controls the chance that a bot will use the character. A value of 0 disables the character for bot use; higher values increase the odds that the bot is added to your level.

END TUTORIAL 22.11

Summary

In this chapter, you have examined how to make a modeled and textured character playable in Unreal Tournament 2004 by using the default animations from the game. You have learned how to import skeletons, how to skin your character, and what steps you need to take to get the character into UnrealEd. You also learned how to add existing properties and animations to the character, set up his portrait, and finally create the UPL file so that the character can be selected just like the characters included in the game. From here, you should be ready to create your own army of playable characters for the Unreal universe.

Chapter 23

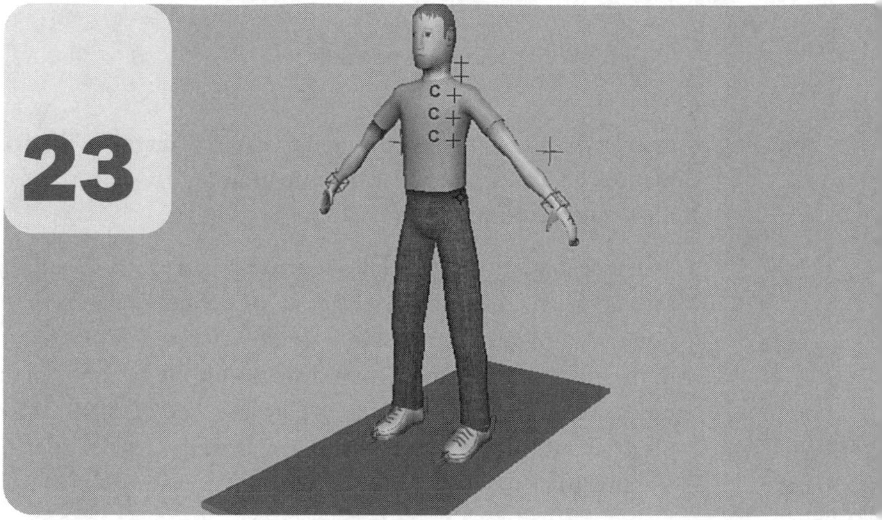

Character Animation

So far, you have modeled a character, and covered it with some sort of texture. You have also seen how to attach a character's geometry to a skeleton, and to import the character into Unreal so that it uses the prefabricated animations included with Unreal Tournament 2004. Now we will breathe life into the character by giving it motion. In this chapter, you will be introduced to the concepts of animation in Maya, in order to create a control system by which to move the character's skeleton, and finally to create a series of animations to make the character mimic human movement. We will also show you how to export your own character animations into Unreal, rather than using the animations that are included with the Unreal Tournament 2004 characters.

Introduction to Animation

Generally, when someone thinks about animation, one of the first things that comes to mind is physical motion. Although this is true, it does not accurately portray what animation *is*. In Maya, *animation* is defined as the change in an attribute value over time. There are thousands of attributes in Maya that can be animated. These parameters range from an object's location in world space, to light intensity, material parameters, and so on. A wide range of effects can be generated through animation. Of course, the world of animation in Maya as it relates to Unreal Technology is generally movement and rotation animation.

When dealing with animation, we are required to work with time. This means that animation in Maya typically refers to the change in an attribute value as time progresses. Time in Maya is represented through frames, so one could say that a frame is a division of time. The number of frames representing one second depends on the target media for which the animation is being produced. NTSC Television has a playback rate of 29.97 frames per second, whereas film has a playback rate of 24 frames/second. For Unreal-related games and simulations, 30 frames/second is standard.

Popular Animation Methods in Maya

When animating in Maya, the artist must first decide which method of animation to use. This is determined by the project at hand and the personal preferences of the animator. Maya offers many different animation approaches: keyframes, reactive animation, dynamic simulations, expressions, path animation, and more. In the world of game design, you will find that keyframes and reactive animation are most commonly used. The next two sections will focus on these methods.

Keyframes

Keyframe animation is by far the most common method of animation in nearly every 3D software package available. The animation process involves an animator recording an attribute value at a given frame; this recording is referred to as a *keyframe*. The keyframe stores both the frame and the current attribute values. The animator then advances to another frame, generally later in time, changes the attribute's value, and records another keyframe. With only two keyframes recorded, Maya can interpolate the change in the attribute's value between the two keyframes as time changes. The interpolation generated by Maya results in animation taking place between the two keyframes.

This interpolation is represented by what is called an *animation curve*. The animation curve defines the value of an attribute at any given point in time. The curve travels from keyframe to keyframe, passing through each one along the way. This curve is stored in an Animation Curve node. A separate Animation Curve node is generated for each attribute that is keyframed. If you were to look at any of these curve nodes in the Attribute Editor, you would find a table. The table stores all of the keys recorded for that given attribute. Additional keyframes created for that attribute are simply added to the table.

In **FIGURE 23.1**, an object's Translate X, Y and Z attributes have been keyframed. Three animation curve nodes have been created. Notice the table in the Attribute Editor on the right. This is where the keyframes for the selected Animation Curve node are stored.

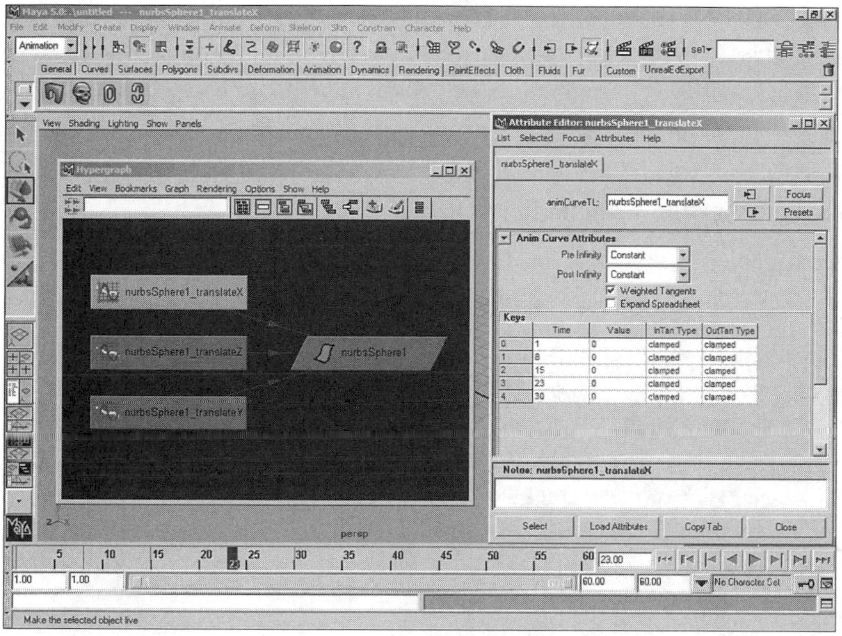

FIGURE 23.1 The three nodes form the animation curves, along with the table of keyframes in the Attribute Editor.

Although the animation curve is a representation of how Maya will interpolate a given attribute's value between keyframes, the animator does have the ability to edit its shape, which in turn directly affects the animation. Editing the curve is done through Maya's Graph Editor. The Graph Editor is a utility that allows an animator a way to visualize how the interpolation between keyframes will take place, edit keyframe timing and attribute values, and adjust the overall shape of the curve.

To understand how an animation curve can be edited, you must understand *tangents*. A tangent defines how an animation curve enters and exits a keyframe. This means that we have an in-tangent and an out-tangent for every keyframe created. There are five tangent types available in Maya:

- Spline—Generates a smooth interpolation into and/or out of a keyframe.
- Linear—Generates a constant interpolation into and/or out of a keyframe.
- Clamped—Generates a smooth interpolation into a keyframe and prevents overshoot from occurring if a value is to be held for a specific number of frames.
- Stepped—Keeps an attribute's value constant until the next keyframe is reached; the change is instant.
- Flat—All tangent handles will be horizontal. This generates an ease-in/ease-out condition for each keyframe.

Although the curve can be edited by assigning new tangent types to a keyframe, you can also use the tangent handles (visible when a keyframe is selected in the Graph Editor) to define custom tangents. **TUTORIAL 23.1** walks you through the basic steps of animating a bouncing ball, using keyframe animation and the Graph Editor.

TUTORIAL 23.1: Basic Keyframe Animation

1. Open Maya and begin a new scene.
2. Create a NURBS sphere. We will refer to this object as our ball.
3. Activate the Move tool. In the Perspective view, move the ball in the Z-axis so that it appears to be sitting on the edge of the grid. Then move the sphere up along the Y-axis so that it appears to be sitting on top of the grid (see **FIGURE 23.2**).

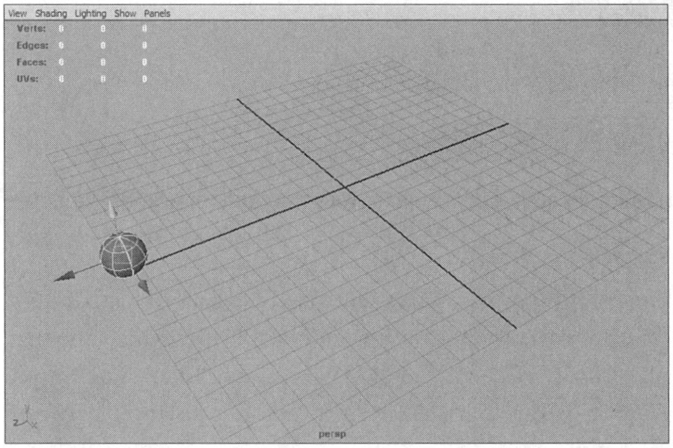

FIGURE 23.2 The sphere has been positioned so that it appears to be sitting on top of the grid.

4. Before we begin animating our ball, we need to define the length of our animation. In the Range Line at the bottom of the UI, set the Start Time to 1 and the End Time to 60. Set the Playback Start Time to 1 and the Playback End Time to 60. We have just blocked off 60 frames (2 seconds) for our animation (see **FIGURE 23.3**).

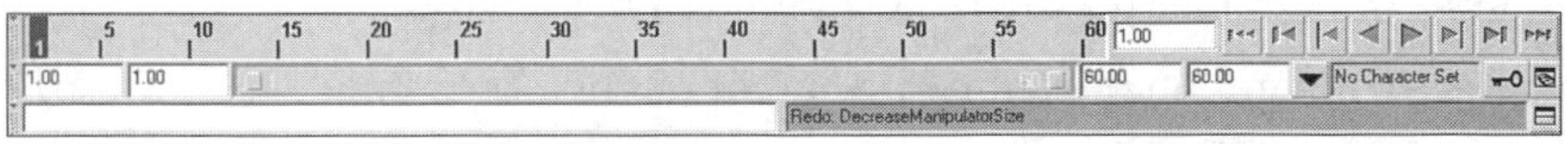

FIGURE 23.3 The range slider has been set to 60 frames.

5. Verify that the viewport has focus (you should see a dark blue border around it) and then press the S key. This is the hotkey for setting a keyframe. By default, every attribute that is visible in the Channel Box will receive a key. Note that all of the transform attributes have changed from white to an orangish color. This indicates that they have been keyed.

A total of ten keyframes have been created: three for the translate attributes, three for the rotate attributes, three for the scale attributes, and one for visibility. Now, not all of these keyframes are necessary. In our animation, the plan is to animate the ball bouncing along the Z-axis. To achieve this animation, all we'll need to do is animate the Translate Y and Z attributes. The Z-axis will supply our forward motion, although the Y-axis will allow the ball to bounce up and down. All of the remaining attributes that have been keyframed will become what are known as *static channels*, meaning that they represent no change over time. If you have enough of them, static channels can actually slow Maya's calculation down. We will address this issue shortly.

6. In the Timeline, drag the Time Slider to frame 60. This is where we will record our next set of keyframes. After moving the Time Slider, move the ball along the Z-axis so that it appears to be sitting on the other side of the grid. Press the S key. Another ten keys are recorded. If you look at the timeline, you will notice red tick marks, one at frame 1 and the other at frame 60. These marks represent keyframes (see **FIGURE 23.4**).

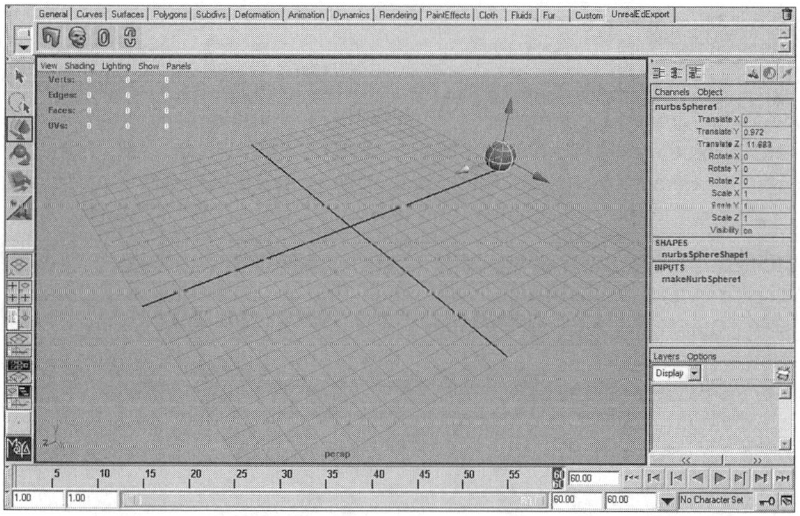

FIGURE 23.4 **The ball has now been animated, moving from one side of the grid to the other.**

If you drag the Time Slider back and forth, you'll find that the sphere moves from left to right. This is because only the Translate Z attribute has received a parameter value change, and Maya is interpolating that value between the keys. All of the other attributes are static, so no visible change will occur.

7. Now we will anchor the ball at frames 20 and 40. This will make it easy for us to add the bounce. Move the Time Slider to frame 20 and without moving the sphere, press S. Move the Time Slider to frame 40 and press S again. If you drag the Time Slider back and forth, you will notice that the animation has not changed.

8. Because we've recorded values of the ball on the ground at frames 20 and 40, adding the bounce will be easy. Drag the Time Slider to frame 10 and move the ball up in the Y-axis (see **FIGURE 23.5**). Press S to record keys.

23

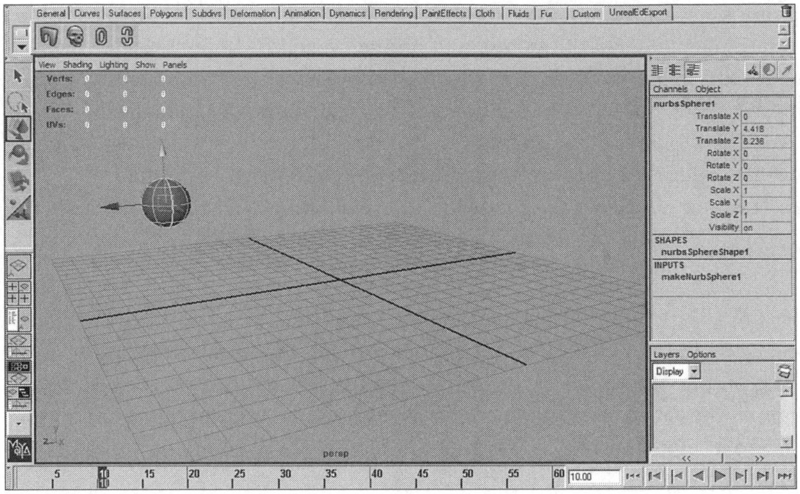

FIGURE 23.5 **The ball has been moved off the grid as we begin to animate the bounce.**

9. Move the Time Slider to frame 30 and watch what happens. You will notice that the ball will drop back down to the ground by frame 20. This is because of the keyframe that you set at frame 20 just a moment ago. It's pulling the ball back down to the ground. These keyframes were used to "anchor" the ball to the ground. When the Time Slider is at frame 30, move the ball up again and press S. Repeat this for frame 50 as well.

10. Click the Play button. You should have some sort of bouncing ball. Although it is not the most realistic-looking bounce, the ball is indeed moving up and down as it travels in the Z direction. If the ball is bouncing at a crazy speed, you probably have the Play Every Frame option activated in your preferences. For the most part, this setting is only required when working with dynamics. In our case, we will want to view the playback in real time.

11. To set the playback speed to real time you can open the Preferences dialog (Window > Settings/Preferences > Preferences), shown in **FIGURE 23.6**. In the Categories list, select Timeline, and set Playback Speed to Real-time (30 fps). Play the animation again.

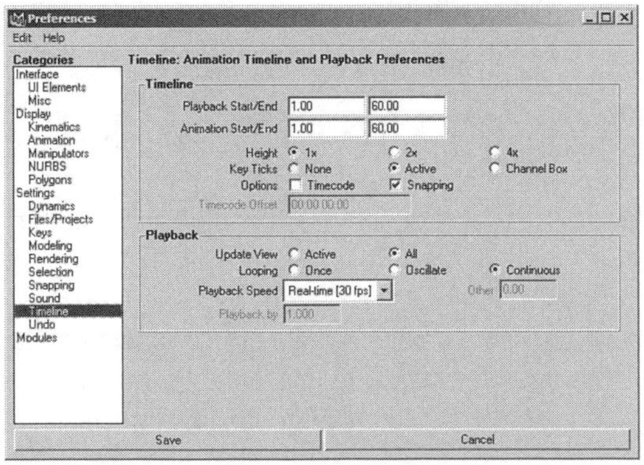

FIGURE 23.6 **The Preferences dialog for Maya.**

END TUTORIAL 23.1

Now that we have a bouncing ball (well, sort of), we need to refine the animation curves that Maya has produced. **TUTORIAL 23.2** will take a basic look at using the Graph Editor for editing the shape of the animation curves Maya has generated.

TUTORIAL 23.2: Using the Graph Editor

1. Continuing from **TUTORIAL 23.1**, open the Graph Editor: choose Window > Animation Editor > Graph Editor. (See **FIGURE 23.7**.)

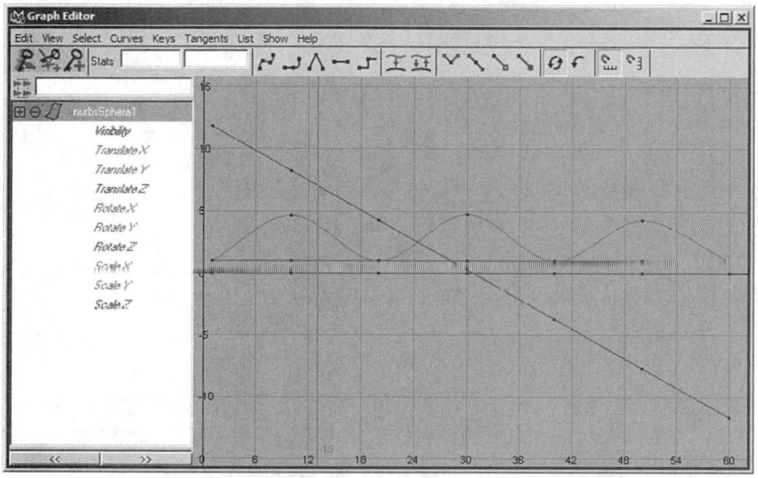

FIGURE 23.7 The animation curves generated from animating the ball.

The Graph Editor can be divided into four elements: the menu bar, the toolbar, the outliner (left), and the graph view (right). By default, the outliner will show selected objects and only their animated attributes. By highlighting an object within the outliner, you will see all of the animation curves in the graph view. If you select individual attributes in the outliner, you will only see those curves.

In our case, if the embedded outliner is empty, the ball has become deselected. Simply move the Graph Editor to the side and reselect the ball.

2. At this point, we have already added all of the keyframes necessary for our animation. In fact, we've added too many keyframes (don't forget all of those static channels mentioned earlier!). Before we begin editing our animation curves, let's get rid of all unnecessary animated channels.

   In the Graph Editor, highlight all attributes with the exception of the Translate Y and Translate Z.

3. From the Graph Editor's menu bar, choose Edit > Delete. All of the highlighted attributes are now deleted. Select the sphere in the Graph Editor's outline and you will see only two animation curves: the curves for Translate Y and Translate Z. From the menu bar, choose View > Frame All. This will position the graph view such that both animation curves fill the area (see **FIGURE 23.8**).

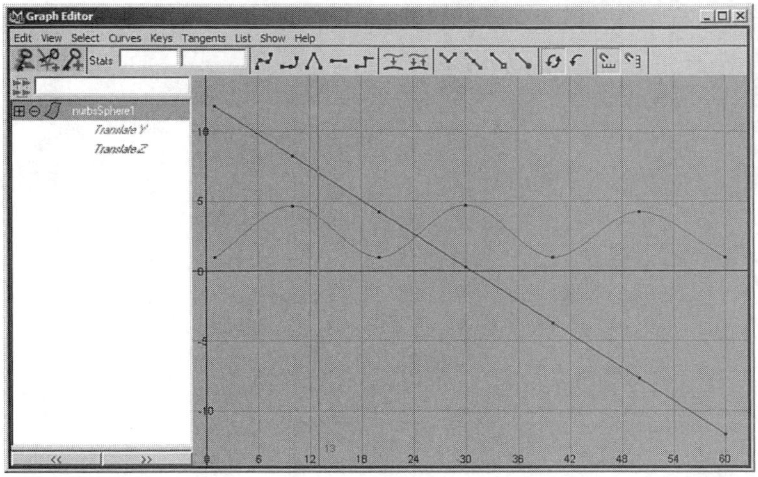

FIGURE 23.8 All of the static channels have been deleted.

With the static channels out of the way, we can now focus our efforts on making the animation look better. Because all of our keyframes have already been recorded and the information they contain is correct, we are left only with manipulating the way Maya interpolates between those keyframes. As mentioned earlier, this is done through the manipulation of keyframe tangent handles.

4. In the Graph Editor's outliner, select the Translate Y attribute so that we can focus only on this animation curve in the graph view.

5. In the Graph view, marquee-select the four keyframes at the bottom of the curve (see **FIGURE 23.9**).

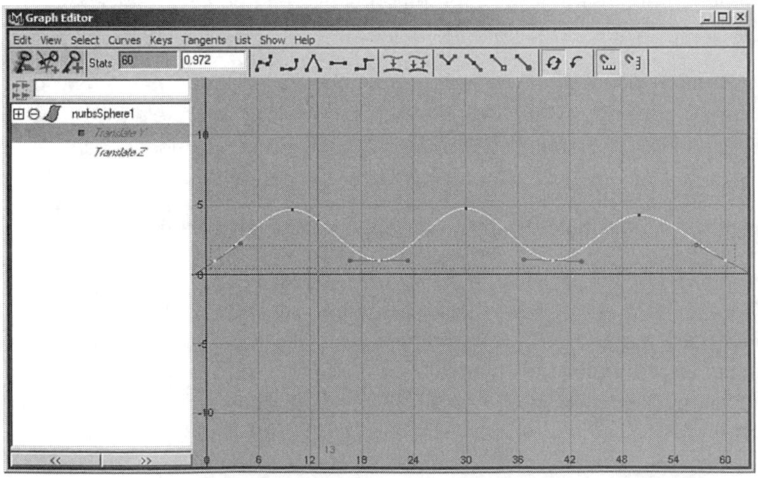

FIGURE 23.9 Select the four bottom keyframes.

6. In this step, we are going to change the in- and out-tangents of each keyframe to linear. Linear tangents provide a direct interpolation in and out of keyframes, depending on which tangent is set. By setting all of the tangents on the bottom keyframes to linear, we will create a distinct impact when the ball hits the ground.

   With the four keyframes selected, choose Tangents > Linear. Play back the animation. Although the motion is still not 100% perfect, it is starting to look better. The curve now produces a more direct change when the ball hits the ground.

7. We can fine-tune this curve even further by manipulating the keyframe tangents directly. As mentioned previously, you can see the tangent handles by simply selecting a keyframe. By default these handles are tied together so that if one is moved, the other would move in the opposite direction, in a see-saw fashion. In our case, we need to break this connection so that we can move each handle independently of the other.

   With the four keyframes still selected, choose Keys > Break Tangents. You will notice that all of the tangent handles on the left side of their associated keyframe (the in-tangents) have turned blue. The color change indicates that the tangent handles have been broken and can now be freely manipulated independently of one another.

8. Select all of the in-tangents (the tangent handles to the left of each key). You will need to hold down the Shift key while selecting the handles.

9. Activate the Move tool from the toolbox. Move the mouse over one of the selected tangent handles and drag with the middle mouse button to move the tangent handles upward (see **FIGURE 23.10**).

> **TIP**
>
> **It will be easier if you marquee-select each tangent handle that you are trying to add to the selection.**

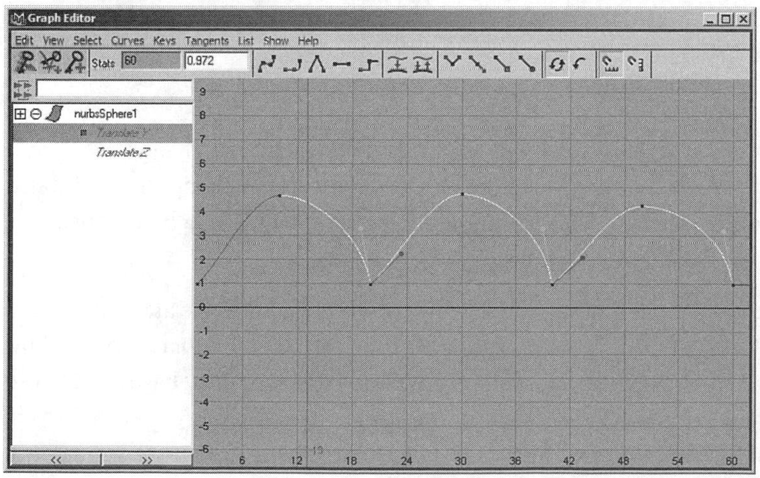

FIGURE 23.10 The in-tangent handles have been moved up.

10. Repeat step 9, but this time select and manipulate the out-tangents instead of the in-tangents (see **FIGURE 23.11**).

TIP

If you lose your selection, it is easy to find the tangent handles again. All you need to do is select the associated keyframe and the handles will again be visible.

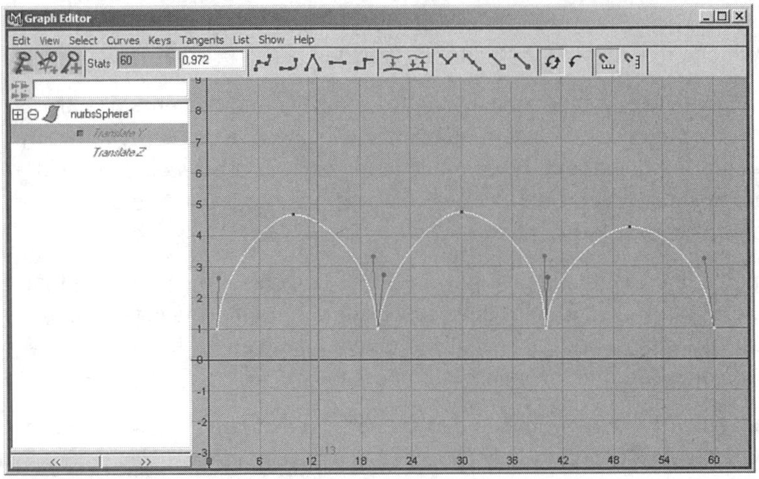

FIGURE 23.11 **The curve is starting to take shape.**

11. Play back the animation. You will notice that the ball slows down as it approaches the apex of each bounce. This is due to the way the animation curve has been edited. Take a minute to study the curve and its relationship to time versus change. With a little practice, editing curves to achieve the desired animation is very easy.

END TUTORIAL 23.2

Reactive Animation

Reactive animation is more of an indirect approach to achieving an attribute change over time. But in this case, instead of time being the driving factor of the attribute's change, the attribute responds in reaction to another attribute. This method of animation may seem a bit confusing at first, but when you've mastered the concept, its application is a breeze.

In a reactive animation scenario, there is always one *Driving* attribute. This is the attribute that is responsible for causing change to occur in some other attribute. The attribute that is changed by the driver is referred to as a *Driven* attribute. It is important to note that you may have one Driver attribute controlling several Driven attributes, even on multiple objects! However, each Driven attribute can only have one Driver attribute.

In Maya, reactive animation is defined through the *Set Driven Key (SDK)*, which is simply the recording of attribute relationships. The recordings are stored in keyframes, and as with regular keyframe animation, Maya will interpolate between them. But in the case of reactive animation, manipulating the Time Slider will not have an effect on the animated object. Instead, you would need to manipulate the Driver attribute, which will in turn alter the value of the Driven attribute.

In **TUTORIAL 23.3**, we are going to create a very simple reactive animation. Our goal is to have a sphere appear to shrink when another sphere is moved up in the Y-axis. We will name these two objects *sDriver* and *sDriven* to help better demonstrate the relationship between the two.

TUTORIAL 23.3: Using Maya's Set Driven Key (SDK)

1. Create two NURBS spheres. Name the first object sDriver and the second sDriven. Position them in the X-axis so that they are not on top of one another. Do not move them in the Y-axis. (See **FIGURE 23.12**.)

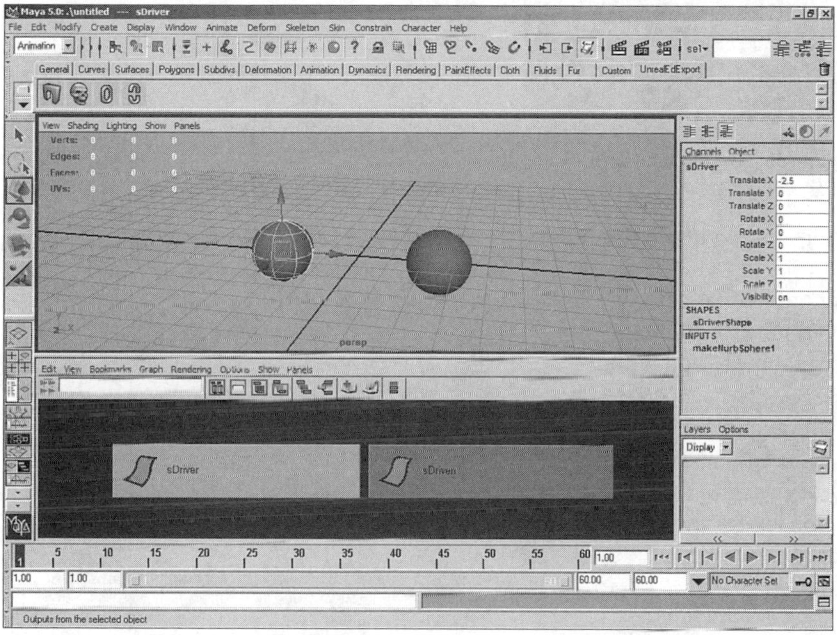

FIGURE 23.12 Two spheres will be used to demonstrate the Set Driven Key ability of Maya. The sphere on the left will "drive" the scale of the sphere on the right.

2. From the Animation menu, choose Animate > Set Driven Key > Set > Options Group ❐. The Set Driven Key dialog opens (see **FIGURE 23.13**).

   The Set Driven Key dialog is divided into four key areas: the menu bar, the Driver group, the Driven group, and then buttons at the bottom. When the dialog is first opened, the Driver group will be empty, but the Driven group will have information loaded if any object was selected before the dialog was open. If any of the boxes do contain data, do not worry about it; it's about to be overwritten anyway.

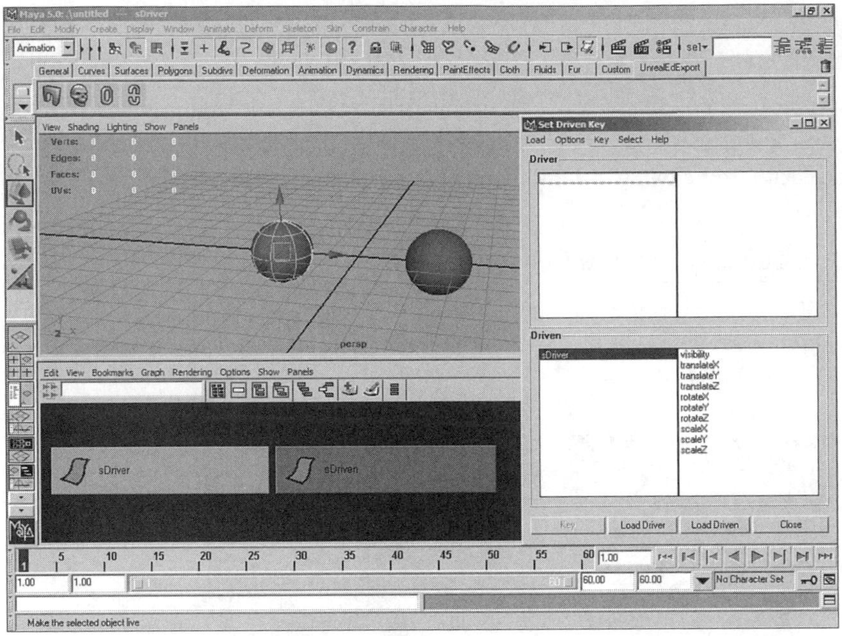

FIGURE 23.13 The Set Driven Key dialog.

3. Select the sphere named sDriver and click the Load Driver button in the SDK dialog. You will notice that sDriver appears in the left box in the Driver group section (see **FIGURE 23.14**). The right box will contain all of sDriver's properties. Repeat this process for the driven object: Select sDriven and click the Load Driven button.

4. Now that we have determined the driver and driven objects, it is time to specify which attributes will be involved in the relationship.

   In the Set Driven Key dialog, select Translate Y in the Driver group and Scale X, Y, and Z in the Driven group.

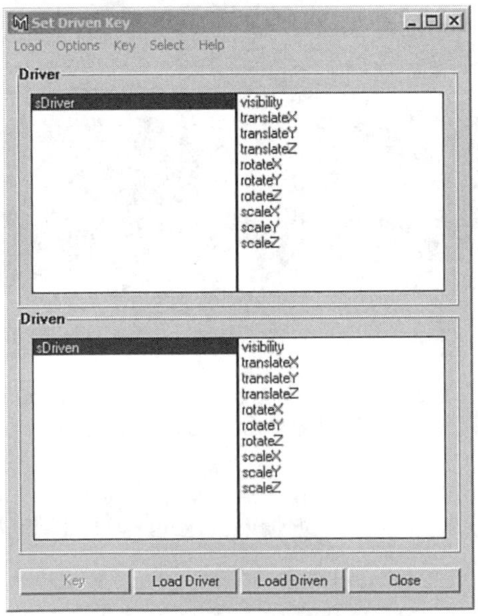

FIGURE 23.14 The sDriver and sDriven objects have been loaded into the SDK dialog.

5. You are now ready to start setting keys, or if you prefer, recording relationships between the two attributes. But before we begin, you should always have a clear understanding of what it is you are trying to achieve. In our case, we are looking to set up the following two relationships:

   - When sDriver's Translate Y attribute value is at 0, sDriven's Scale X, Y, and Z values will all be at 1.
   - When sDriver's Translate Y attribute value is 5, sDriven's Scale X, Y, and Z values are all at 0.25.

> **TIP**
>
> **You can hold the Ctrl key down while selecting multiple attributes, or you can click and drag with the mouse if the attributes are all stacked atop one another, as in this case.**

> **CAUTION**
>
> **You must be very careful when placing the keys of a reactive animation. It is sometimes easy to get confused as to which attribute should be doing what. Also you must remember that you have to change the value of the Driver object *first*, adjust the value of the Driven object, and then click the Key button. If this pattern is not followed, the animation will not work properly.**

The effect of this reactive animation would be as follows: As the driving sphere is moved up, the driven sphere will progressively get smaller. The driven sphere will continue to uniformly scale down until the driving sphere reaches 5 units. At this point the driven sphere will have a Scale X, Y, and Z value of 0.25. If the driving sphere is moved above 5 units, no further scaling action will occur to the driven sphere.

Let's begin by recording the first relationship. Currently, the driving sphere is still at a Translate Y value of 0 and the driven sphere has a Scale of 1 (we will be referring to Scale X, Y, and Z simply as Scale throughout the rest of this tutorial).

Click the Key button in the SDK dialog.

6. Move sDriver 5 units up in Y. Select sDriven and set its Scale to .25 (see **FIGURE 23.15**). Click the Key button to record the relationship.

7. Select sDriver and move it up and down. Watch what happens to the driven sphere. This is a reactive animation; as one attribute is changed, another attribute is directly changed.

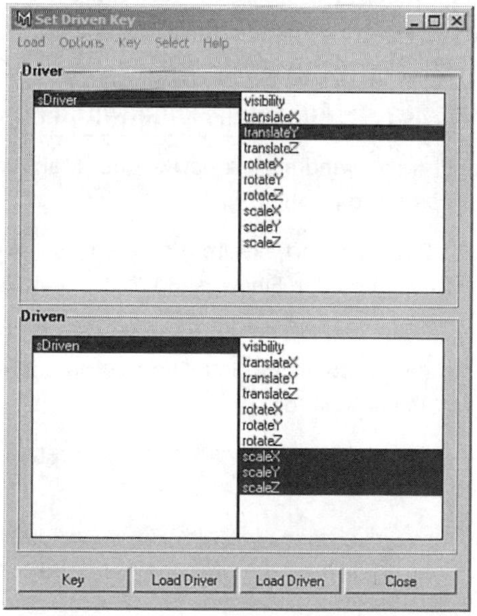

FIGURE 23.15 **Set up the second relationship and record the values with the Key button.**

END TUTORIAL 23.3

Animation Choices—FK Versus IK

Before a character can be animated, there is generally a great deal of preplanning involved. One of the most important decisions that an animator must make involves simply figuring out how the character will be animated. There are three main ways to animate the joints of a character. These are Forward Kinematics, Inverse Kinematics, or a combination of both.

23

Forward Kinematics, also known simply as *FK*, is the name given to the method of rotating a parent joint in a hierarchy. As the parent is rotated, the children revolve around the parent joint while maintaining their distance from one another. This can be both good and bad. FK allows complete freedom when animating because you are not hindered by the inability to rotate any specific joint. It's also easier to achieve fluid arcing motions, such as arms swinging. Conversely, however, this animation method can be rather slow, and it can be very tedious to achieve decent results this way.

Inverse Kinematics, called *IK* for short, is a method of joint animation in which the user does not directly rotate the joints. The term *inverse* comes from the fact that rather than rotating a parent joint, the animator indirectly moves the children with an IK handle, and the parent joints automatically rotate to accommodate the movement. As an example, consider grasping your friend's wrist and moving it about. You would see their shoulder and elbow rotate to allow for the movement of the wrist.

To be more technical, IK involves the use of an Inverse Kinematic Solver, which calculates a rotational solution for the involved joints, based on the position of an IK handle. This may sound very confusing at first, but after you use IK a few times, you will see that there's really nothing to it. In **TUTORIAL 23.4**, you will see how to animate a simple skeletal arm using both FK and IK.

TUTORIAL 23.4: Animating Joints with FK

1. Launch Maya, and start a new scene. Make sure that you are in the Animation menu set, or press F2 to go there.
2. In the Side viewport, create a series of three joints in the configuration of an arm. Name the joints Shoulder, Elbow, and Wrist.

   Now, create a cylinder, and place it a few units in front of the arm (see **FIGURE 23.16**). Name the cylinder Grip. Imagine this as a handhold that the character will grasp and use to pull itself forward.
3. In the Range Slider, set your animation range from Frame 1 to Frame 30. When finished, save the file as `FK_IKstart`.
4. Because we're animating with FK, we will be rotating each of the joints by hand. Therefore, we must place keyframes on the joints that require animation, in this case the Shoulder and Elbow joints.

   Set the Time Slider to Frame 1. Make sure that the Caps Lock key is not active. Select the Shoulder and the Elbow joints, and press Shift+E. This will place a keyframe on only the rotational attributes of the joints. This is a great way to help prevent creating a vast excess of static channels as we would with the S key.

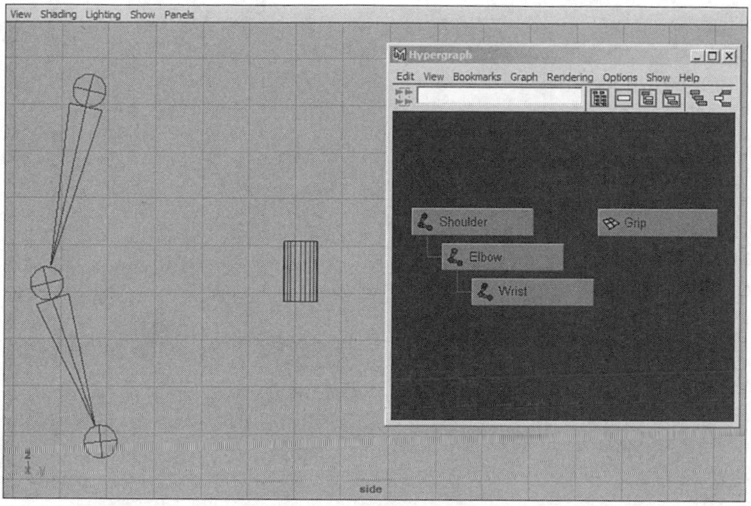

FIGURE 23.16 A simple joint chain for a basic arm.

5. Set the Time Slider to Frame 15. Rotate the Shoulder and Elbow so that the wrist joint is resting on the Grip cylinder, as shown in **FIGURE 23.17**. When finished, select the Shoulder and Elbow joints, and press Shift+E again, in order to place a new keyframe.

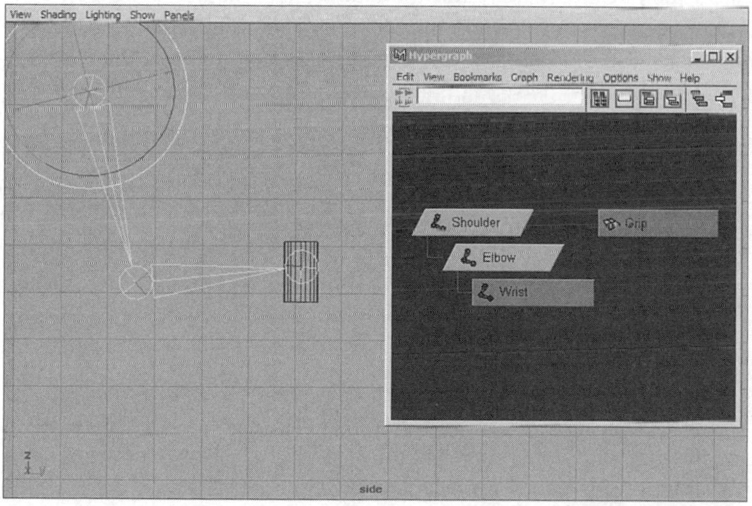

FIGURE 23.17 Arm is rotated so that wrist is grabbing the cylinder.

At this point, you can drag the Time Slider back and forth and you will see that the arm is now animated.

6. Now, between Frames 15 and 30, we want the Shoulder to move forward, but for the wrist to remain planted on the Grip, as if the character was pulling itself forward. This will be a little more difficult than it seems.

Select the Shoulder joint, and verify that you are still at Frame 15. Press Shift+W, which will place a keyframe on all of the translate attributes of the shoulder.

7. Drag the Time Slider to Frame 30, and use the Move tool to move the Shoulder joint forward. Move it about half the distance to the Grip cylinder. Notice the problem that occurs: The Wrist joint does not stay planted on the Grip cylinder (see **FIGURE 23.18**). Instead, it moves forward in tandem with the shoulder, due to the nature of parenting systems in Maya and animating with FK.

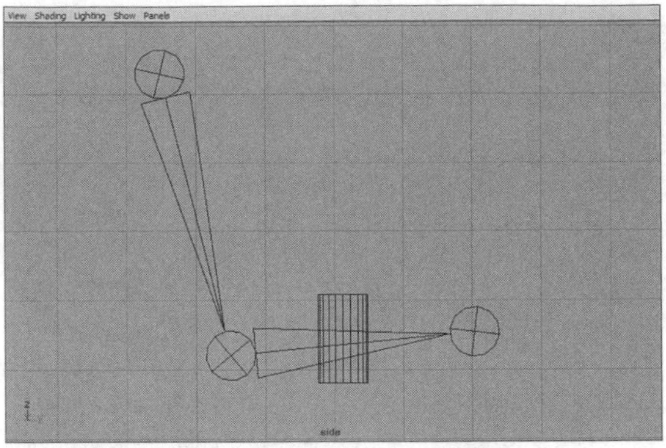

FIGURE 23.18 The forearm and wrist move through the cylinder.

Verify that the Shoulder joint is still selected and that you are at Frame 30, and press Shift+W. Drag the Time Slider back and forth between Frames 1 and 30. Notice that the rotation is nice between Frames 1 and 15, but the translation disrupts the effect between Frames 15 and 30.

8. Challenge: Using the skills you have learned, rotate the elbow and shoulder joints between Frames 15 and 30 so that the Wrist joint stays in the same location after Frame 15. This is not as easy as it may seem. You are only allowed to fix this through rotating the joints; you may not move them. When you are finished, make sure that you *do not* save over your existing file.

END TUTORIAL 23.4

You have now seen how to animate the joints using Forward Kinematics, along with the benefits and drawbacks to an FK system. In **TUTORIAL 23.5**, you will animate the same scenario using an Inverse Kinematic setup.

TUTORIAL 23.5: Animating Joints with IK

1. Reopen the `FK_IKstart` file that you saved earlier in the last tutorial. We will now attempt the same exercise using Inverse Kinematics rather than Forward Kinematics.

2. From the main menu, choose Skeleton > IK Handle Tool > Options Group. In the Tool Settings dialog, set the Current Solver to ikSCsolver. This will create a Single Chain IK Solver, which is the simplest of the available IK solvers in Maya. We will discuss the available solver types shortly.

3. We need to select the start joint for the IK Solver. In this case, we will use the Shoulder joint. Click on it to select it, and notice that the entire joint chain becomes highlighted in green.

   Now, click on the Wrist joint, and notice that a small green handle appears at the location of the wrist, and that this handle is automatically selected. Also, note that the joint chain has turned a shade of bright purple (see **FIGURE 23.19**). Often in Maya, this color is used to designate which objects are being influenced by the selected object. In our case, the joints of the chain are being influenced by the IK handle, and so they turn purple when the IK handle is selected.

   Move the IK handle around a bit, and see how the arm responds. Undo the movements with the *Z* key when finished.

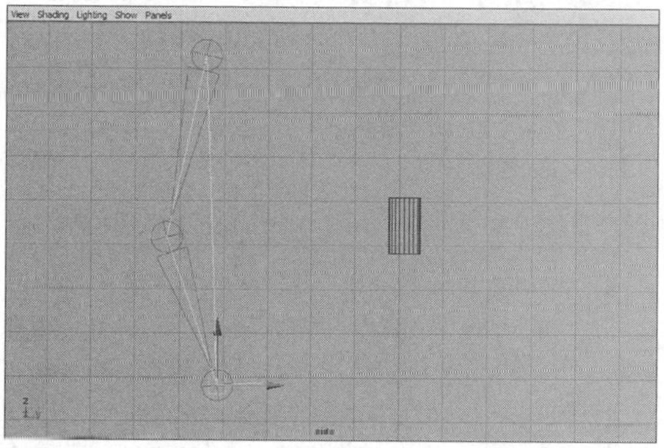

FIGURE 23.19 The IK Solver has now been created for the arm.

4. Make sure you are at Frame 1. With the IK handle selected, press Shift+W. Remember that animating with IK requires that you animate the *position* of an IK handle, rather than the *rotation* of selected joints, as in FK.

   Go to Frame 15, and move the IK handle so that the wrist is on the Grip cylinder. Press Shift+W again to set a second keyframe. If you drag the Time Slider back and forth now between Frames 1 and 15, you will see an animation in which the arm reaches for the Grip cylinder.

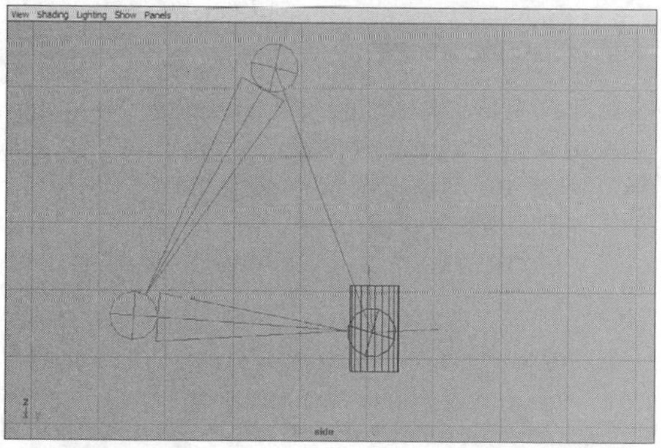

FIGURE 23.20 For this situation, the arm is much easier to animate using IK.

5. At Frame 15, select the Shoulder joint and press Shift+W. Advance the Time Slider to Frame 30, and move the shoulder forward, about half the distance to the Grip cylinder. Notice that the wrist stays in its exact same location throughout the movement. This is because the Wrist joint will always match the location of the IK handle, and the other joints of the chain must rotate to allow this to take place, as seen in **FIGURE 23.20**.

END TUTORIAL 23.5

23

IK Solvers

When animating in Maya, you have a choice of three different IK solvers. These are the Single Chain IK Solver, the Rotate Plane IK Solver, and the Spline IK Solver. Each of these solvers has its own individual functionality, and each can be applied in a variety of ways.

Single Chain IK Solvers

Single Chain IK is the simplest type of IK available by default in Maya. A Single Chain IK Solver will solve the rotation of at least two joints based on the location of its IK handle, and the preferred angle of the given joints. A joint's preferred angle is the angle that is used to tell the direction in which a joint should bend when affected by IK. Without this, the joint chain will fail to rotate properly, or may simply not rotate at all. In **TUTORIAL 23.6**, you will see how the preferred angle is used to control rotation in a simple Single Chain IK scenario.

TUTORIAL 23.6: Setting Preferred Angle on Joints

1. Start a new scene in Maya, and verify that you are in the Animation menu set. Switch to the Side view.

2. Activate the Joint tool. Then, holding down the Shift key, click three times to create three joints in a vertical configuration, starting at the top and moving down. Notice that the Shift key has caused the joints to be created in a perfectly straight line (see **FIGURE 23.21**).

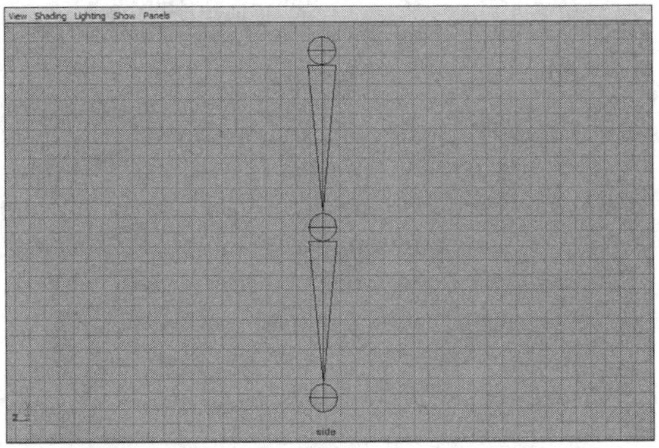

FIGURE 23.21 The Shift key allows you to constrain the creation of joints to a straight line.

3. Using the IK Handle tool, create a Single Chain IK Solver that runs from the first joint created to the last. As demonstrated earlier in **TUTORIAL 23.5**, this creates the IK Solver.

4. Try to move the solver's handle about, and notice that the joint chain does not bend. This is because the joints have no preferred angle. To fix this, first delete the IK Solver, and then in the Side view, select the second joint, and rotate it in the Z-axis. You may rotate it in either direction; just keep in mind

> **NOTE**
>
> For the sake of controlling the direction the arm bends when using the solver, you do not need to worry about how far you rotate the joint. Any rotation whatsoever in a given axis will determine how the IK Solver will rotate the joints.

that your choice will determine which way the joint chain will bend when you move the IK handle.

5. Hold down the right mouse button on the second joint. From the context menu, choose Set Preferred Angle. This will record the direction that you bent the joint, and with this, the IK Solver knows the direction to bend the chain. Set the Rotate Z attribute back to 0 to straighten the joint chain. Add the Single Chain IK Solver back in. **FIGURE 23.22** shows the setting of the preferred angle.

6. Now that you have set the preferred angle for the joint and added the IK Solver, select and move the IK handle again. Notice that you can now see the joints bending to accommodate this new angle, rather than staying perfectly straight.

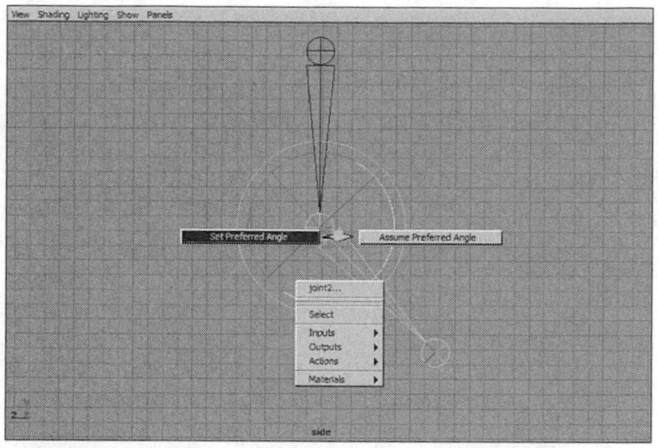

FIGURE 23.22 Setting the preferred angle is critical when joints have been created in a straight line.

> **NOTE**
>
> When creating a joint chain, any bend in the chain's direction will result in a preferred angle automatically being set. In most cases, you will only need to manually set the preferred angle when you create the joints in a perfectly straight line.

END TUTORIAL 23.6

Rotate Plane IK Solvers

The other main IK system available in Maya is the Rotate Plane IK Solver. It is different from the Single Chain IK Solver in one major respect: You can alter the rotation of the plane upon which the joints are solved. To fully grasp this concept, try to imagine all of the joints in an IK system rotating so that they always exist on the same plane. Take the joints at your shoulder, elbow, and wrist, for example. As you move your arm around, those three joints are always on the same plane. If you were to rotate that plane from your shoulder, you would, in effect, be wagging your elbow back and forth. This is exactly the same type of control available with the Rotate Plane IK Solver. In **TUTORIAL 23.7**, we will take a look at how we can apply and manipulate a Rotate Plane IK Solver.

23

TUTORIAL 23.7: Creating a Rotate Plane IK Solver

1. Start a new scene in Maya, and create a three-joint chain to represent an arm. Name the joints Shoulder, Elbow, and Wrist. For now, do this in one of the orthographic views. Make sure there is a slight bend at the elbow to accommodate an automatic preferred angle.

2. From the Skeleton menu, choose IK Handle Tool > Options Group. In the settings for the tool, set the Current Solver to ikRPsolver. Click on the Shoulder joint, and then on the Wrist. Just as with the SC Solver, an IK handle has now been created. You will notice, however, that it looks a bit different (see **FIGURE 23.23**). There is a ring at the top, with a white arrow. This shows the location of the current plane and is often referred to as the Joint Chain plane indicator.

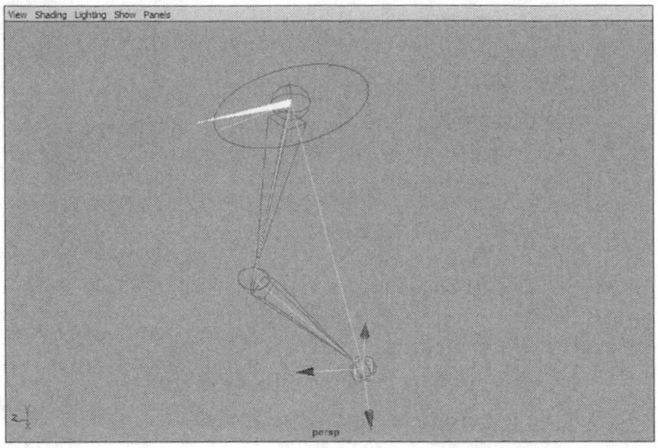

FIGURE 23.23 The Rotate Plane IK Solver looks a bit different than the Single Chain IK Solver because of the Joint Chain plane indicator located at the starting joint of the IK Solver.

3. To edit the location of the rotation plane, press the T key to invoke the Show Manipulator tool. You will see a new Move manipulator appear near the shoulder (see **FIGURE 23.24**). This is the Pole Vector handle. As you move the handle, notice that the joints rotate from the shoulder in such a way that the elbow always points to the pole vector manipulator. In this way, you can adjust the orientation of the solver's rotate plane.

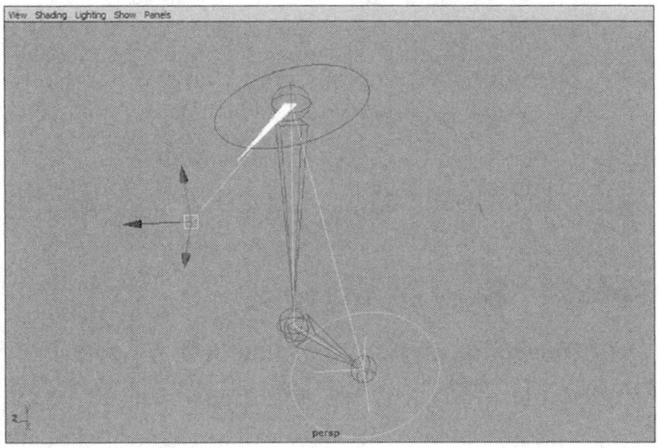

FIGURE 23.24 Moving the Pole Vector handle causes the plane that the IK Solver solves on to rotate.

4. At the bottom of the IK handle, near the wrist, you will see the Twist disc, a ring-like manipulator. This allows you to control the Twist of the solver, which acts like an offset from the plane rotation provided by the pole vector. It also provides you with a way to move the rotate plane while only animating a single value, rather than three, as you must with the pole vector.

This type of IK is perfectly suited for creating control systems for areas of a character such as arms and legs. The control it offers is very similar to wagging your elbow or knee.

END TUTORIAL 23.7

IK Spline Solvers

The third kind of solver available in Maya is the IK Spline Solver. Compared to the other two, this solver is unique in that rather than the joint rotations being calculated from the position of an IK handle, the joint chain for the solver is influenced by a NURBS curve. As the control vertices (CVs) of the curve are moved, the curve changes shape, which will cause the joints to try to follow the shape of the curve as best they can. This kind of IK is perfectly suited for character spines, tentacles, tails, whips, chains, and any other ropelike object. In **TUTORIAL 23.8**, we will demonstrate how to apply this kind of IK to a simple joint chain.

TUTORIAL 23.8: Using Spline IK

1. Start a new scene in Maya, and switch to a Side view.
2. Using the Joint tool, hold the Shift key and create a vertical column of about 8 to 10 joints. Start at the bottom and work your way up, and space them out as evenly as you can.
3. From the Skeleton menu, choose IK Spline Handle Tool. Click on the first joint you created, and then click on the end joint. You will see what appears to be an IK handle, though you will not be able to move the IK handle directly.

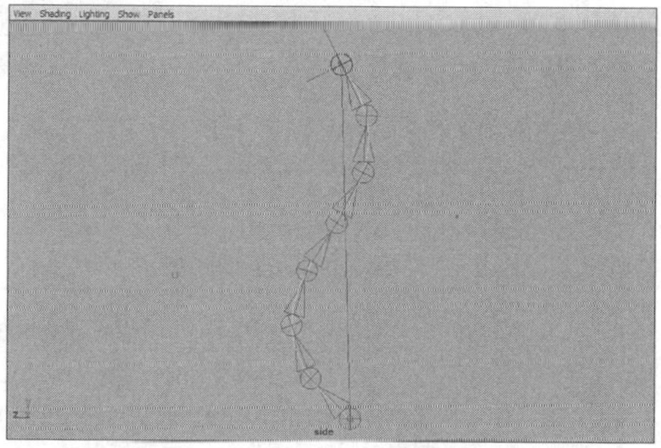

FIGURE 23.25 A curve is created when an IK Spline Solver is used. The joints will rotate in such a way that their chain matches the shape of the curve as best it can.

4. In the Status Line at the top of the UI, click on the Joints selection type so that joints are no longer selectable. Switch to Component mode, and make CVs selectable.
5. Marquee-select over some of the joints. You will see that a NURBS curve has been created within the joint chain. Select and move the CVs of the curve. You will notice that as the shape of the curve changes, the joints will rotate to approximate the curve's shape. Using a variety of different animation methods, you could animate the location of these CVs and thereby animate the joint chain. You can see an IK Spline Solver in **FIGURE 23.25**.

END TUTORIAL 23.8

Constraints

Constraints provide a way to bind the translation, rotation, or scale of one object to another. The relationship created is similar to parenting, but the differences become quite obvious when you begin working with them. As discussed previously, with a parenting relationship, the child object's Transform node is influenced by the parent's Transform node. When the parent is transformed, the child is transformed as well. Translations, rotations, and even scales will have an effect on all child objects. Also, although a child is affected by its parent, the child can still be moved, rotated, and scaled independently.

Constraining objects has a more direct effect on specific attributes. The child object is constrained so that it cannot be directly affected by the user without special operations. The Constraint node ensures that the constrained object will only receive data from the object it is constrained to.

Although Maya provides several types of constraints, six of them are very helpful when setting up a character control system, or rig. **TABLE 23.1** describes these constraints.

TABLE 23.1 Maya's Constraints

Point	Point constraints lock the translation of one object to another.
Aim	Aim constraints allow for an object to be constrained in such a way that it will always rotate to point toward the object it is constrained to.
Orient	Orient constraints will lock the orientation of one object to another.
Scale	Scale constraints will lock the scale of one object to another.
Parent	Parent constraints serve as a combination of both Point and Orient constraints mixed.
Pole Vector	A Pole Vector constraint is a special constraint used in conjunction with Rotate Plane IK Solvers. In essence, it provides the IK handle with a target that controls the orientation of the plane upon which the joints are rotating.

In **TUTORIAL 23.9**, you will see how you can apply constraints to objects in Maya to exert specific controls over objects as you animate them.

TUTORIAL 23.9: Applying Constraints to Objects

1. Start a new scene in Maya.
2. Create two objects:
   NURBS Cone (Name: Locked_Child)
   NURBS Sphere (Name: Parent)

   Position the objects so that they can be viewed in the Front viewport (see **FIGURE 23.26**).

3. When constraining one object to another, the object that is being constrained to is always selected first. In our case, we are constraining the cone to the sphere. Because the sphere will act similarly to the parent in a parenting scenario, it must be selected first. Select the sphere. Shift-select the cone. From the main menu, choose Constrain > Point. Notice the Translate attributes in the Channel Box. The color of the channels has changed from white to a light sky-blue. This indicates that translation data is being sent to the cone's translation channels. **FIGURE 23.27** shows the result of this constraint.

   After the constraint is applied, the cone snaps to the sphere. To be more precise, the cone's pivot snaps to the sphere's pivot.

4. Select the cone and move it. It appears to move without a problem, but see what happens when you move the sphere. When the sphere is moved, the cone snaps back to its constrained location and moves along with the sphere.

5. So what happens if we need to offset an object that has been constrained? This is not a problem, as all that needs to be done is adjust the pivot point of the constrained object. Select the cone. Press the Insert key and move the cone's pivot down in the Y-axis. Because the pivot of the cone is constrained to the pivot of the sphere, the pivot will not be seen moving. Instead, the cone will move in the opposite direction. Continue to move the pivot point until the cone is sitting on top of the sphere as if it were a hat. Press the Insert key again to exit pivot-modification mode (see **FIGURE 23.28**).

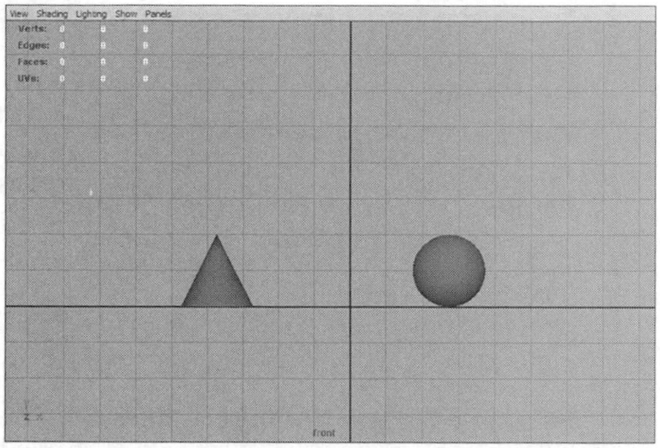

FIGURE 23.26 Using two objects to demonstrate Point and Orient constraints.

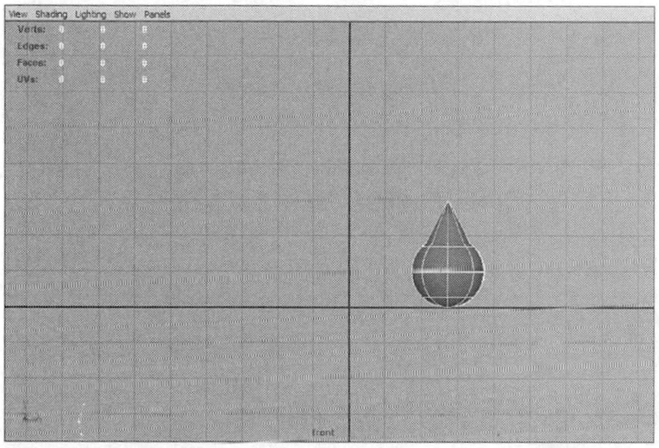

FIGURE 23.27 The results of the Point and Orient constraints.

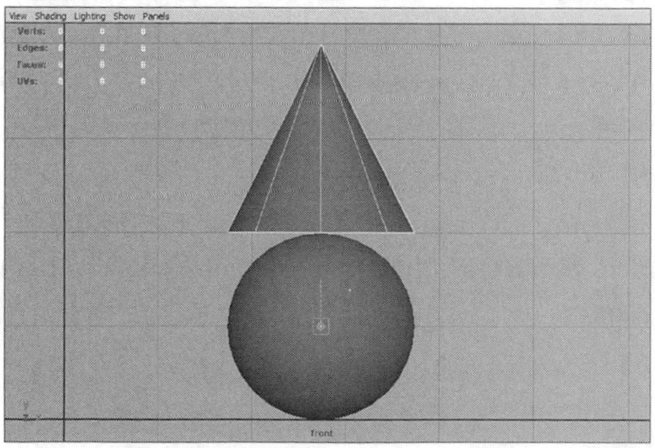

FIGURE 23.28 Manipulating the pivot point for the cone allows an offset to be created between the two objects.

6. As the sphere is moved, the cone will maintain its offset although moving along with it. Try rotating the sphere. Notice that the cone stays in place. This is because we are not sending any sort of rotation data to the cone. To have this happen, we need to orient-constrain the cone to the sphere.

   Select the Sphere. Shift-select the cone. From the main menu, choose Constrain > Orient. Notice the Rotation attributes in the Channel Box. The color has again changed to the light blue.

7. Rotate only the sphere and observe the cone. Notice the relationship between their rotations, as shown in **FIGURE 23.29**.

> **NOTE**
>
> **If you look in the Shapes area of the Channel Box, you can actually see the node created by the constraint. If you click this, three attributes will become visible: Offset X, Y, and Z. You can use these as a way to create an offset between two constrained objects without having to change their pivot points.**

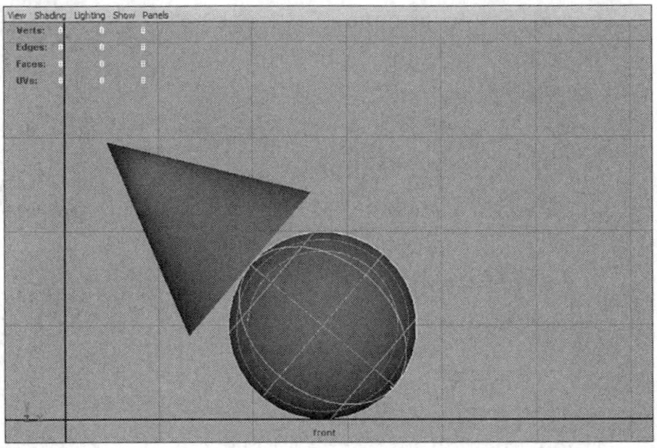

FIGURE 23.29 **With the cone oriented to the sphere, all rotations applied to the sphere will affect the cone.**

END TUTORIAL 23.9

Selection Handles

A *selection handle* is a transform component visible as an icon that can be used to simplify the process of selecting an object that may be hard to locate. For example, it can be difficult to select specific objects due to Maya's selection priority system when higher-priority objects are located in the same space, such as an IK handle in the same location as a joint. A selection handle is sort of an alias to an object. When the user clicks on a selection handle, the associated object is selected. Best of all, selection handles have the highest selection priority, making them the easiest thing to select in the viewport.

Every object in Maya has a selection handle. By default, however, these selection handles are hidden. **TUTORIAL 23.10** will demonstrate how to make selection handles visible as well as how to relocate them.

TUTORIAL 23.10: Using Selection Handles

1. Start a new scene in Maya.
2. Create a sphere.
3. With the sphere selected, from the main menu, choose Display > Component Display > Selection Handles. Look closely at the center of the sphere (this may require that you rotate the Perspective view so that the sphere's wireframe is not hiding the icon). You will see that a new icon is visible at the center of the sphere. The default location is at the object's pivot point and because the pivot point was at the center of the sphere, that's where the selection handle is. You can see the selection handle in **FIGURE 23.30**.
4. Now let's take a look at how you can move the selection handle. With the sphere selected, press F8 to switch to a Component mode. Click the Selection Handle filter icon and select the selection handle. The selection handle will turn yellow indicating that it has been selected.
5. Activate the Move tool and move the selection handle above the sphere (see **FIGURE 23.31**).
6. Press F8 to return to Object mode. Deselect the sphere. Marquee-select the selection handle and take note that it is the same thing as if you had selected the sphere directly. By strategically positioning selection handles, an animator can always select specific objects quickly.

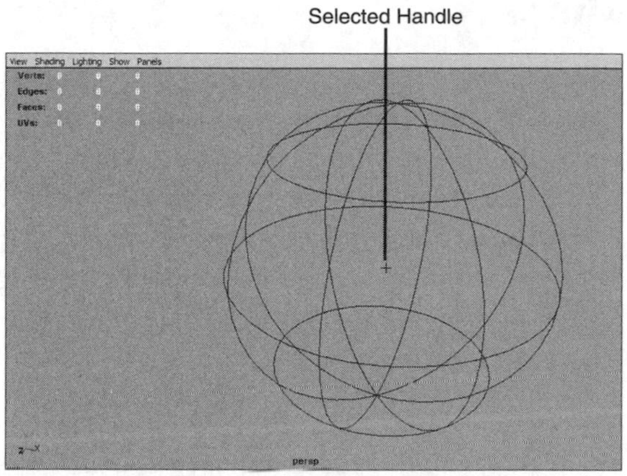

FIGURE 23.30 Selection handles ease the selection of objects that may be difficult to reach.

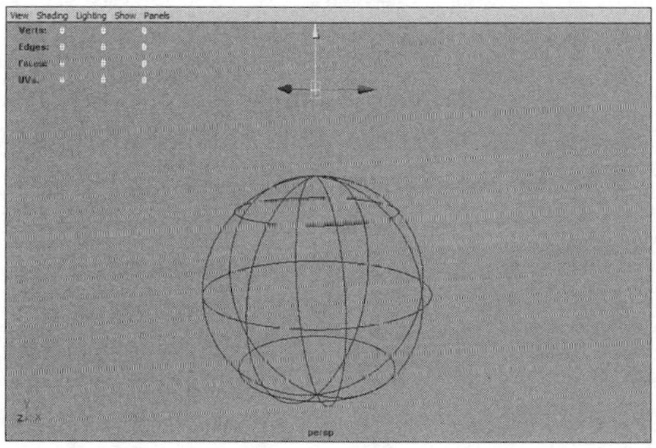

FIGURE 23.31 The Selection handle has been relocated above the sphere.

> **NOTE**
>
> Many beginners will confuse a selection handle and a pivot. Keep in mind that moving a selection handle does not alter the pivot information of an object whatsoever.

END TUTORIAL 23.10

Character Rigs: What They Are and Why We Need Them

Character rigs are special control systems that are set up throughout a character to ease the process of animation. Rigs range in complexity from simple to sophisticated depending on the animator's needs. For instance, a very simple rig might consist of a few custom attributes that control set-driven key scenarios, making it easier for an animator to manipulate hard-to-reach objects such a finger joints. A complex rig, on the other hand, might provide an animator with numerous controls for positioning limbs, driving various facial features, along with custom expressions used to automate elements of the character, such as breathing, pupil dilation, skin stretching, and so on.

To better understand the need for a rig, let's take a look at a real-world example. Picture a marionette puppet. This type of puppet has numerous strings connected to various parts of its body, which are used by the puppeteer in order to control the action it is performing. These strings make up a rig that eases the process of bringing the puppet to life. Now, try to imagine how difficult it would be to manipulate the puppet without this rig. In the 3D world, character rigs are equally important. Although it is possible to animate the character without such a rig, the time to do so will become significantly longer.

Character rigs require planning. You must first determine the type of animation required for the character. Is the character simply going to be walking forward, or will the character need to be able to perform a variety of nimble acrobatic moves as well? Next, the animator needs to decide which controls would be required to drive the necessary joints or IK handles, as well as which parts of the character should be automated to ease complex animation processes.

In **TUTORIALS 23.11** through **23.13**, we will explore various rig setups that will allow us to easily control our character for animating the cycles needed by Unreal. The rigs are divided into different categories: the legs, the arms, and the back. Keep in mind that there are many steps to creating character rigs, so each step of the tutorial will be centered on a specific goal, and will include several substeps.

Creating the Character Rig

To start, begin with creating the legs. The objective with the leg rig is to set up a central point of control for each leg. This control object will be used to position the leg as well as rotate the various articulated parts of the foot.

TUTORIAL 23.11: The Legs

1. Open the file `LegRig_Start.mb`.
2. The character rigging process generally begins after the character's model is complete. To prevent accidental geometry selection while developing the rig, it is good workflow to add the character to a layer and save it as a template:
    - Select the character.
    - In the Layer Editor, click the Create a New Layer icon.
    - Double-click on the new layer to open the Edit Layers dialog. Set the name to UTGuy_Geometry and click Save.
    - Right-click on the layer and select Add Selected Object from the menu.
    - Template the layer by clicking the second check box in the layer. The letter "T" should appear when the layer is templated.
    - Deselect the character and then try reselecting it. You will find that you are no longer able to select the character. You will further note that the character is being displayed as a light gray wireframe, even in a shaded view. This will make adding the joints easier to do as we are now able to see through the geometry.
3. Before the rig can exist, we will need to create the leg joints. Because we will be creating a reverse foot leg setup, we will need to set the Auto Joint Orient options of the Joint tool to None.
    - From the main menu, choose Skeleton > Joint Tool > Options Group.
    - Set Auto Joint Orient to None (see **FIGURE 23.32**).
    - Switch to a Side view and create the following joints: Hip, Knee, Ankle, Ball, and Toe. Make sure to name each of the joints as they are shown here. See **FIGURE 23.33** for placement.
    - When you have created the leg skeleton, press the Enter key to finalize the joint chain and close the Tool Settings dialog box.

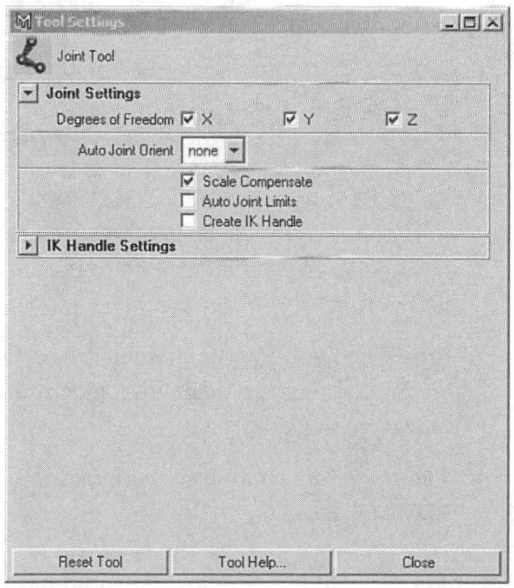

FIGURE 23.32 Setting Auto Joint Orient to None for this particular joint chain.

4. We will control this leg indirectly through three Single Chain IK Solvers:

    - From the main menu, choose Skeleton > IK Handle Tool > Options Group.
    - Set the Current Solver to ikSCsolver.
    - Create the following IK solvers (see **FIGURE 23.34**):

      IK from Hip to Ankle. IK handle name: ikAnkle

      IK from Ankle to Ball. IK handle name: ikBall

      IK from Ball to Toe. IK handle name: ikToe

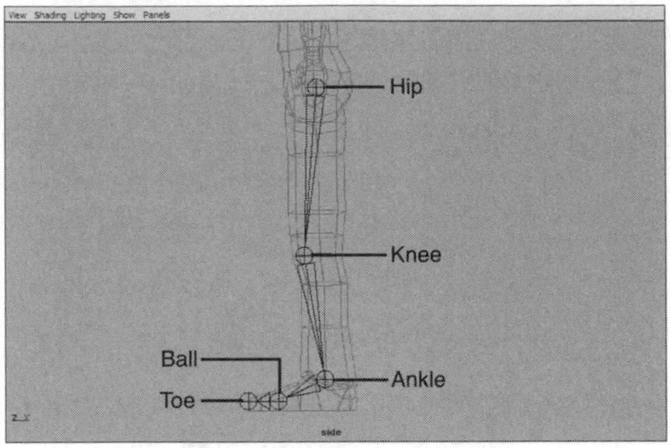

FIGURE 23.33 Creating the joints for the leg. Note the placement of the joints.

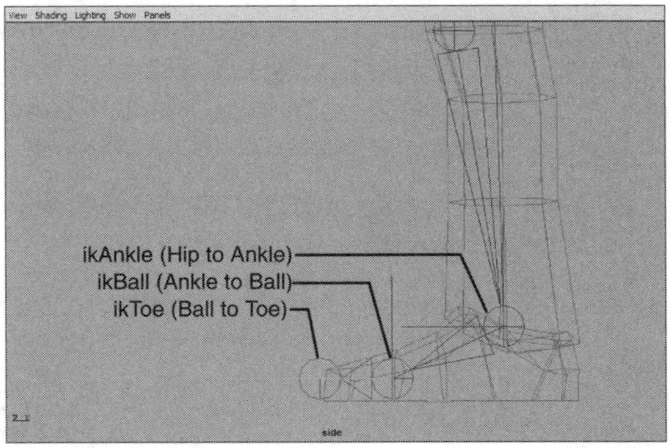

FIGURE 23.34 Creating the three IK handles.

5. Now that we have IK handles in our leg, we need a way of controlling them in such a way that their generated solutions will provide a useful result. We will use a second skeleton chain for this control:

    - Activate the Joint tool. Verify that the Auto Joint Orient option is still set to None.
    - Hold down the V key on your keyboard. This will temporarily toggle the point snap option on. Click *near* the Ankle joint you created earlier. Be very careful not to click on the Ankle joint as you do not want to branch off the old skeleton. Instead, you are creating a new hierarchy.
    - Create the next joint at the heel of the foot. Try to align this joint with the Ball and Toe joints. Continue creating three additional joints snapped to the following: Toe, Ball, and finally the Ankle.
    - Click the Enter button to complete the hierarchy. You can see the final result in **FIGURE 23.35**.

6. Now that the control hierarchy of joints has been created, we need to parent each of the IK handles to their respective inverse joint (see **FIGURE 23.36**):

    Parent ikAnkle to iAnkle joint

    Parent ikBall to iBall joint

    Parent ikToe to iToe joint

7. Although adding the inverse foot creates a way for us to be able to control the foot, it is not the most intuitive way. We would need to select iMain if we wanted to move the foot around, and we would need to select any of the remaining inverse joints if we wanted to rotate the foot joints in any way. In this step, we are going to simplify the process of controlling our foot by creating a foot controller:

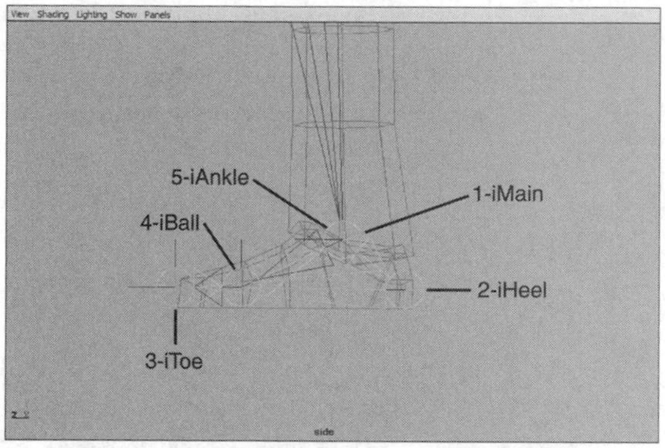

FIGURE 23.35 Creating the inverse foot skeleton chain. The order of creation for the joints is very important for this rig to function properly.

- From the main menu, choose Create > CV Curve Tool > Options Group.
- From the Tool Settings dialog, set the Curve Degree to 1 Linear.
- In the Side view, draw an L-shaped outline that appears to be connected to the bottom of the shoe. The actual shape is not that important; something that resembles a shoe works great. The idea is to create a control object that can be quickly identified as a foot control. Press Enter when you are done outlining the control. You can see an example curve in **FIGURE 23.37**.
- Rename the new curve: Foot_Control.
- With the Foot_Control curve selected, press the Insert key. This will allow you to move the pivot point of the curve. Hold down the V key, move the mouse over the Ankle joint, press the middle mouse button, gesture the mouse in any direction, and the pivot point will snap to the Ankle joint.
- Press the Insert key again to exit pivot-editing mode.
- With Foot_Control selected, Shift-select iMain joint.

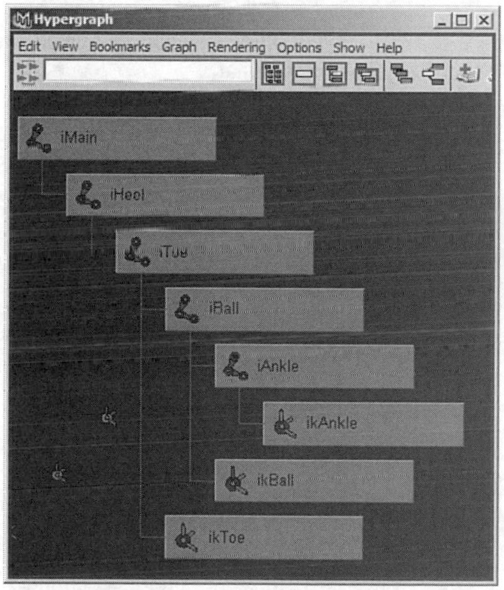

FIGURE 23.36 Parenting the IK handles to their respective joints. The Hypergraph shows the new relationships.

- From the main menu, choose Constrain > Parent.
- Select only Foot_Control and move it around to see how it affects the rest of the leg. Undo all movements when you have completed testing it.

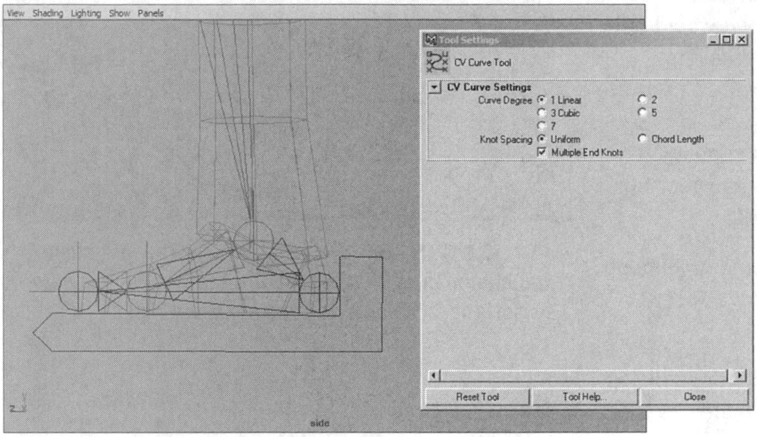

FIGURE 23.37 Using Curves as control objects makes it easier for an animator to determine what control object controls what.

8. In this step, we are going to create three attributes (HeelRX, BallRX, and ToeRX) that will make it easier to rotate the joints in the inverse skeleton:
   - Verify that only Foot_Control is selected.
   - From the main menu, choose Modify > Add Attribute.
   - From the Add Attribute dialog, add the following attributes (see **FIGURE 23.38**):

     HeelRX (Type: float)

     BallRX (Type: float)

     ToeRX (Type: float)
9. In this step, we will use the Connection Editor to make direct connections from the new attributes we added in the last step to the various joints in the inverse foot chain:
   - From the main menu, choose Window > General Editors > Connection Editor.
   - Verify that Foot_Control is still selected, and click the Reload Left button in the Connection Editor. You will see that the list box will become populated with many different parameters. You can verify that the Foot_Control object was loaded by looking at the bottom of the Connection Editor under the left-side properties box.
   - Select the iHeel joint and click the Reload Right button in the Connection Editor. You are now ready to make the connection.
   - Scroll down on the outputs side until you locate the `HeelRX` property. Click on it to select it as the origin of the connection.

- Scroll down on the inputs side until you see the `Rotate` property. Expand the `Rotate` property so that you can see the three subentries. Click Rotate X to complete the connection. This means that whatever data is input into `HeelRX` will be sent directly to the Rotate X of the iHeel joint, as shown in **FIGURE 23.39**.

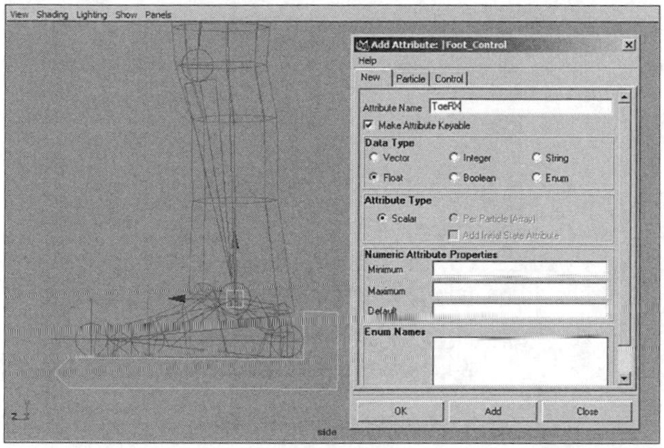

FIGURE 23.38 **Adding attributes to `Foot_Control` to make it easier to control the inverse hierarchy.**

NOTE

You will only need to reload the inputs side with the iBall and iToe joints.

- Make the remaining connections:

  BallRX > iBall.RotateX

  ToeRX > iToe.RotateX

  When you are done making the required connections, close the Connection Editor.

- Test the new attributes to make sure they work by selecting them one at a time in the Channel Box, and then using the virtual slider (middle mouse button in the view panel) to see the response, as shown in **FIGURE 23.40**.

- You will find that some values are simply not desirable; for instance, it is possible to rotate the joint too far. You can easily correct for this by editing the attributes. From the main menu, choose Modify > Edit Attributes.

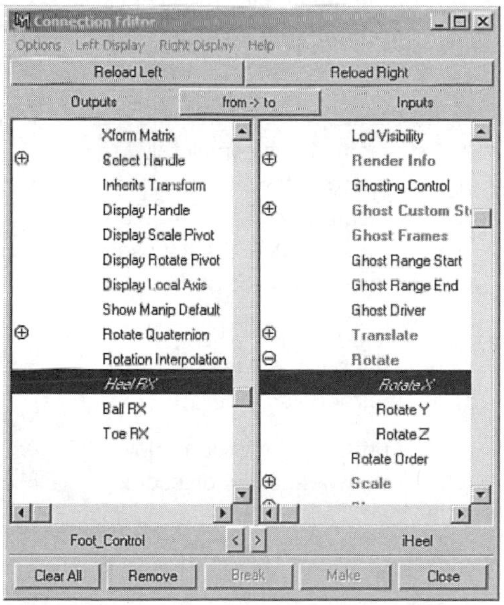

FIGURE 23.39 **Connecting `Foot_Control.HeelRX` to `iHeel.RotateX` in the Connection Editor.**

- Select `HeelRX` in the Edit Attribute dialog. Check the Has Maximum check box. We have done this because `HeelRX` will need to rotate in a negative direction. A positive number for `HeelRX` will give undesired results. By setting the Has Maximum check box and leaving the Max value at 0, we can prevent this attribute from ever going positive.

  Set the other attributes as follows (see **FIGURE 23.41**):

  BallRX: Has Minimum (checked)

  ToeRX: Has Minimum (checked)

- Retest the foot. If you like, set extreme limits for each of the attributes. Use the Edit Attributes dialog to accomplish this by adding a maximum value as well.

10. At this point, we have only one leg. Now that the leg is completely rigged, we can move it into place and duplicate it for the other side. We will need to align the leg skeleton inside our character's leg geometry:

- Select the Hip joint and the Foot_Control objects.
- In the Front viewport, move the two selected objects in the X-axis so that the Hip joint is aligned as in **FIGURE 23.42**.
- Select only the Foot_Control object and move it into place (see **FIGURE 23.43**).

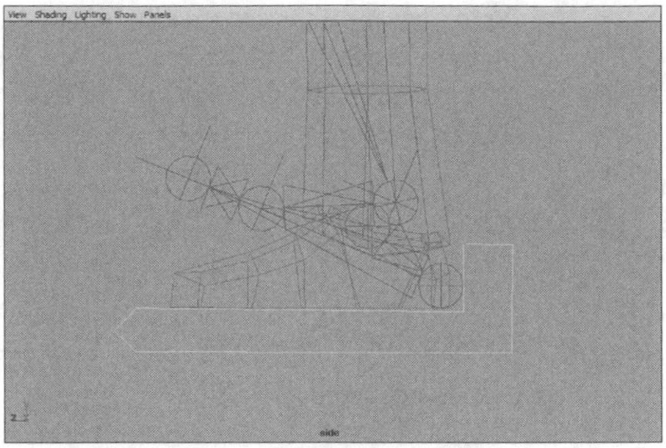

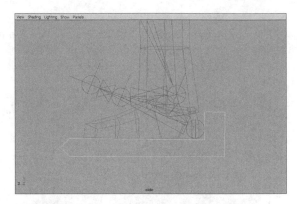

FIGURE 23.40 Testing the `HeelRX` property should reveal the rotation of the foot at the heel.

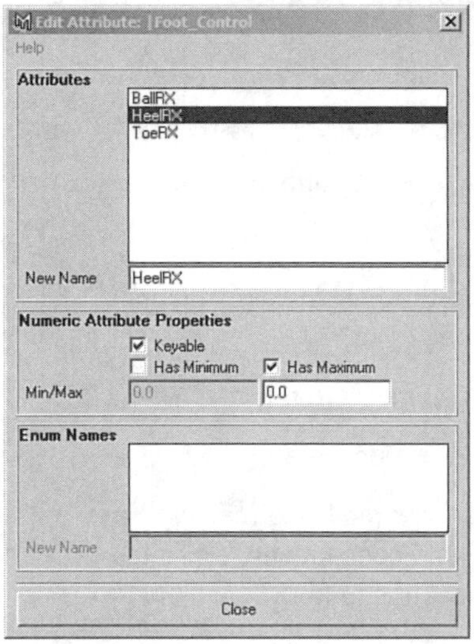

FIGURE 23.41 Editing the attributes to prevent undesired rotations.

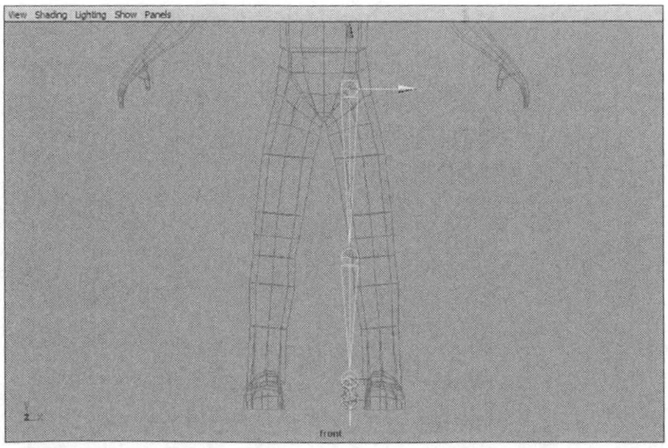

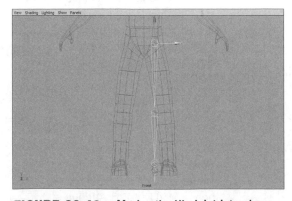

FIGURE 23.42 Moving the Hip joint into place.

11. Now you need to duplicate and position the leg:

- Open the Hypergraph.
- Select the three top-level nodes that make up the leg (Hip, iMain, and Foot_Control), as shown in **FIGURE 23.44**.
- From the main menu, choose Edit > Duplicate > Options Group.
- In the Duplicate Options dialog, check the Duplicate Input Graph check box and click Duplicate. This will create another leg rig that is completely independent of the first one.
- Select Hip1 and Foot_Control1 and position them on the character's opposite side. You will then have two separate legs, as shown in **FIGURE 23.45**.

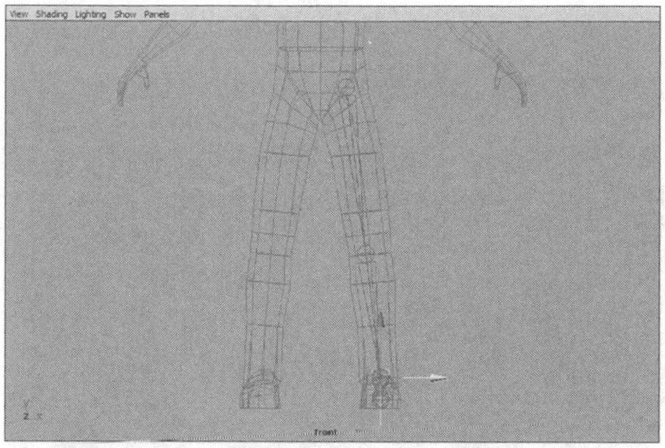

FIGURE 23.40 Move the `Foot_Control` object to complete the alignment.

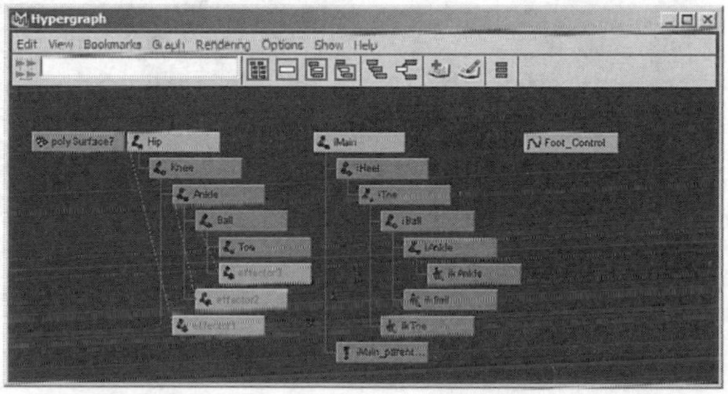

FIGURE 23.44 Select the root nodes involved in the leg rig.

12. There are now a series of things that can be done to "clean up" the rig. These things include renaming all of the objects to include a Left_ and Right_ naming convention, as well as locking and hiding attributes that will not be keyframed:

- Select the original Hip joint.
- From the main menu, choose Modify > Prefix Hierarchy Names.
- Enter **`Left`** in the Prefix Hierarchy dialog and click OK. Confirm that the names now have the word "Left_" appended to the beginning of each joint name.

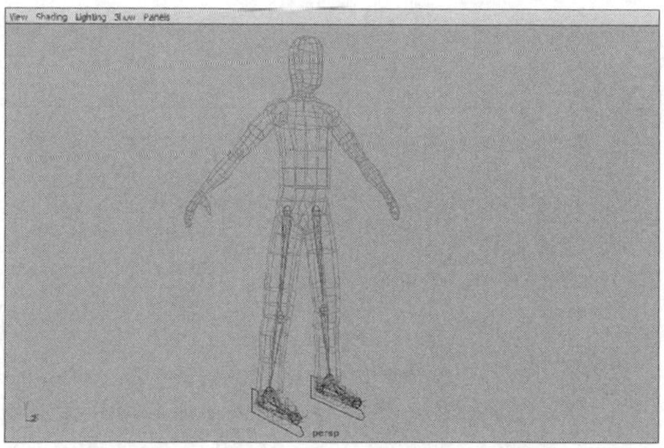

FIGURE 23.45 Two independently set up legs.

23

- Repeat this process for the right leg and each of the inverse foot hierarchies, as shown in **FIGURE 23.46**.

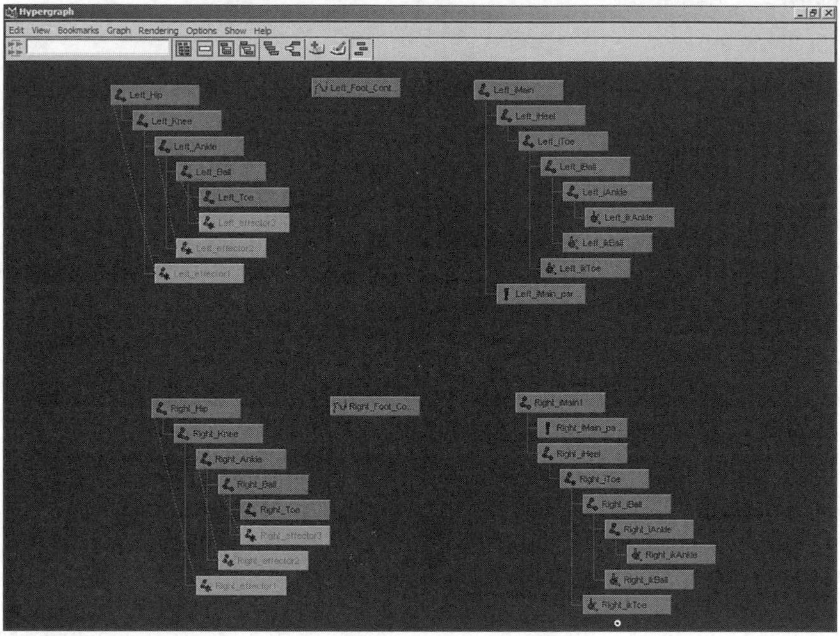

FIGURE 23.46 All of the naming has been corrected so that it is easy to identify each side of the character's rig.

END TUTORIAL 23.11

The rig for the arms does not need to be complex. The goal will be to apply a Rotate Plane IK Solver from shoulder to wrist. The solver will be constrained to a control object similar to the foot. We will use an additional control object for positioning the elbow.

TUTORIAL 23.12: The Arms

1. Open the file `ArmRig_Start.mb` or continue from **TUTORIAL 23.11**.
2. First you need to create and name the arm joints. There are numerous ways to set up the skeleton in the arm. In a game rig, there is no need for significant levels of control, so we are going to use a simpler setup. Open the Tools Settings dialog for the Joint tool by using the Options Box, and set Auto Joint Orient to XYZ.
3. In the Front viewport, create a total of six joints, outlining the Clavicle, Shoulder, Elbow, Wrist, Hand, and Finger. It is important to follow **FIGURE 23.47**. Note that the joints after the Clavicle are created in a straight horizontal line, rather than in the direction of the arm. After creating the Shoulder joint, hold down the Shift key as you click.

4. Select the Shoulder joint, and rotate it downward so that it is at the same angle as the arm geometry.

5. Scale the joints in their local X-axis, in order to make them fit properly into the arm. Use **FIGURE 23.48** for help.

6. Set the Preferred Angle for the joint. Select the Elbow joint, and rotate it forward on the Y-axis. Hold the right mouse button over the joint, and choose Set Preferred Angle from the Marking menu, as in **FIGURE 23.49**.

7. In the Channel Box, set Rotate Y back to 0.

8. Now you need to add IK to the arm. From the main menu, choose Skeleton > IK Handle Tool > Options Group, and set the Current Solver to ikRPsolver.

9. Click on the Shoulder for the start point of the IK chain, and then click on the Wrist joint as the end point. A new IK handle is created, as shown in the **FIGURE 23.50**. Name this handle ikArm.

10. Now create the Pole Vector locator to control the elbow. From the main menu, choose Create > Locator. A new locator is created at the center of the scene. Name this locator pvArm.

11. Press Ctrl+G to group the locator unto itself. Name this group pvArmBuffer.

12. With the pvArmBuffer group still selected, use the techniques you have learned thus far to point-snap the locator to the elbow joint, and then move the group straight back in the Z-axis.

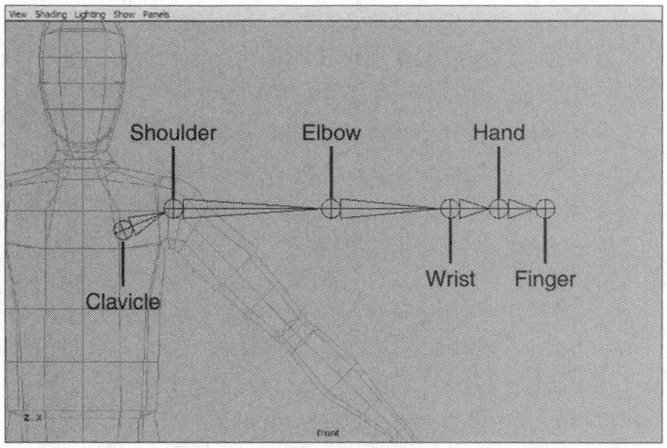

FIGURE 23.47 The joints of the arm have been created, but are still straight out from the shoulder.

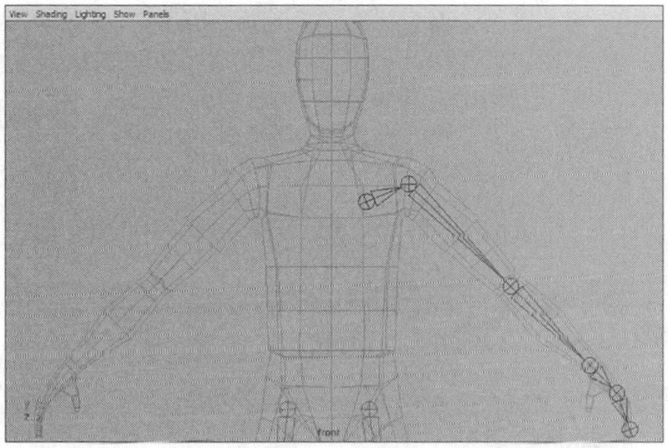

FIGURE 23.48 The joints of the arm have now been rotated and scaled to fit into the arm's geometry.

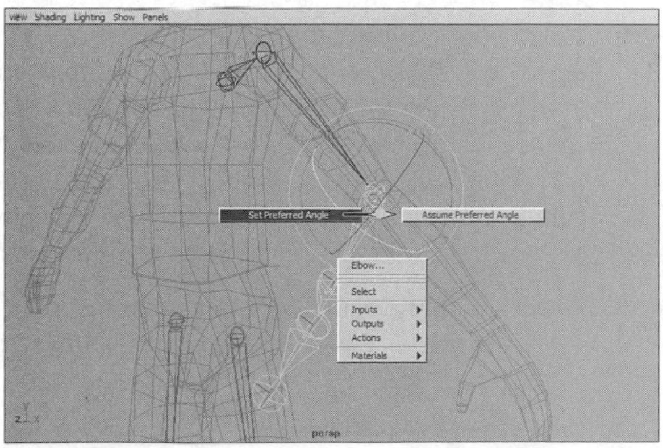

FIGURE 23.49 Setting the preferred angle of the Elbow joint.

13. Marquee-select over the locator, and notice that you now have the pvArm locator selected, rather than the group itself. You can also press the down-arrow key to step down the hierarchy from pvArmBuffer to pvArm.

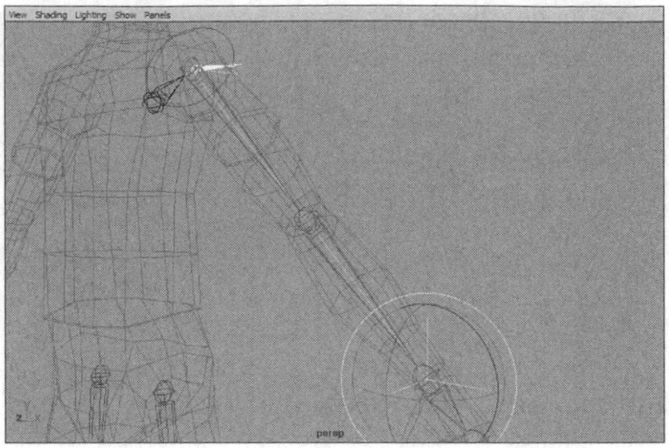

FIGURE 23.50 IK has been added to the arm system.

14. Shift-select the ikArm IK handle, and from the main menu, choose Constrain > Pole Vector. You can see the result in **FIGURE 23.51**.

    The purpose of the buffer group we added is to prevent undesired rotation from occurring to the pole vector when it is parented back into the skeleton later. It also allows us to select the pvArm locator at any time and return it to its original position by setting its translation in X, Y, and Z back to 0.

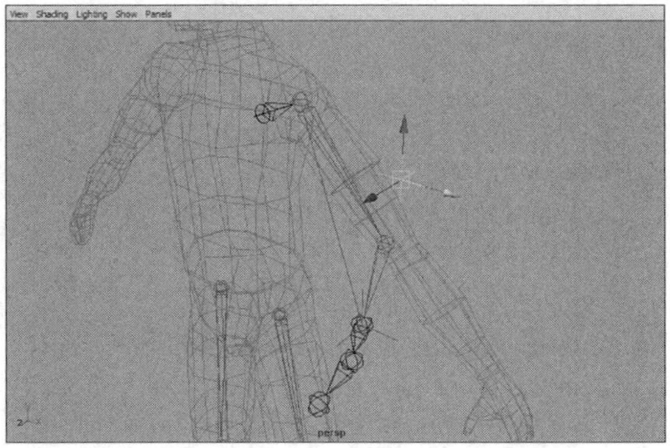

FIGURE 23.51 The arm's elbow joint can now be adjusted with the pole vector locator.

15. Now set up the Wrist control. From the main menu, choose Create > Polygon Primitives > Cube. Name the cube Arm_Control.
16. Point-snap the cube to the Wrist joint.
17. Scale up to an appropriate size to encompass the joint at the wrist without being inordinately large.
18. We do not want the cube to be shaded in the viewport. To fix this, open the Hypershade by selecting Window > Hypershade from the main menu. Make sure the cube is selected, and from the Hypershade's menu choose Graph > Input and Output Connections. Select the connection between the Arm_ControlShape and the initialShadingGroup nodes. The line will highlight yellow when properly selected. Press the Delete key to remove the connection. Ignore any warnings you may get at the bottom of the screen. This will force the cube to always show in wireframe. Close the Hypershade when done.
19. Select the Arm_Control cube, and from the main menu choose Modify > Freeze Transformations. This will force all of the translations, rotations, and scales to 0 at the current location.
20. Select Arm_Control, and then Shift-select the ikArm IK handle. From the main menu, choose Constrain > Point. This will point-constrain the IK handle to the cube so that as the cube moves, the IK handle will move with it.

21. Select the Wrist joint and then Shift-select the Arm_Control cube. From the main menu, choose Constrain > Orient. This will force the cube's rotation to match the rotation of the wrist joint. Test this out by selecting and moving the cube. Feel free to test out the pole vector as well, as shown in **FIGURE 23.52**.

    Now that you have moved the two controllers around, you can put both the pole vector and the arm-controlling cube back into their original positions by selecting them and setting their translations back to 0 in all three axes.

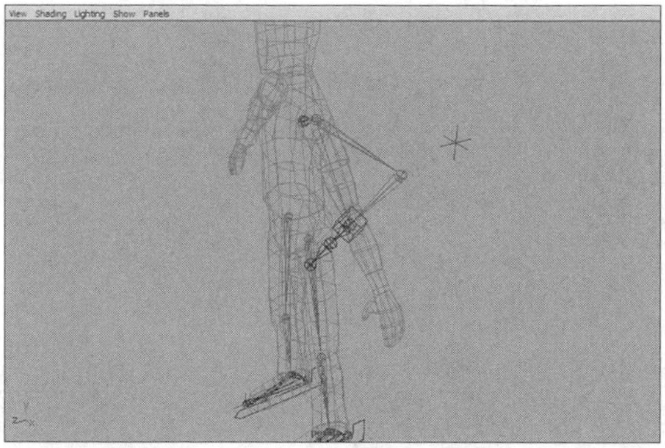

FIGURE 23.52 The arm in motion. Notice the use of the `Arm_Control` and the pole vector.

22. Controlling the wrist rotation is as important as controlling the location of the arm. Select the Arm_Control cube, and from the main menu, choose Modify > Add Attribute. In the Add Attribute dialog, enter the attribute name **`WristTwist`** and click OK (see **FIGURE 23.53**).

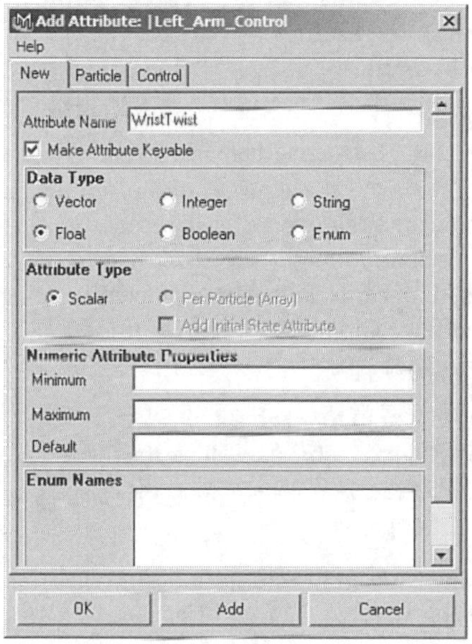

FIGURE 23.53 Adding custom attributes can make it easier to control various parts of the character.

23. From the main menu, choose Window > General Editor > Connection Editor. Verify that Arm_Control is still selected and from the Connection Editor dialog, click Reload Left. You will see the left side of the dialog become populated with attributes from the Arm_Control. Scroll down to the bottom of the list and select WristTwist, as shown in **FIGURE 23.54**.

24. In the Perspective view, select the Left_Wrist joint and then click the Reload Right button in the Connection Editor. The right side of the dialog becomes populated with the Left_Wrist's attributes. In the attribute list on the right side, locate the Rotate attribute and click the plus symbol next to it. Select the `Rotate X` property. You will see the attributes become highlighted, as shown in **FIGURE 23.55**.

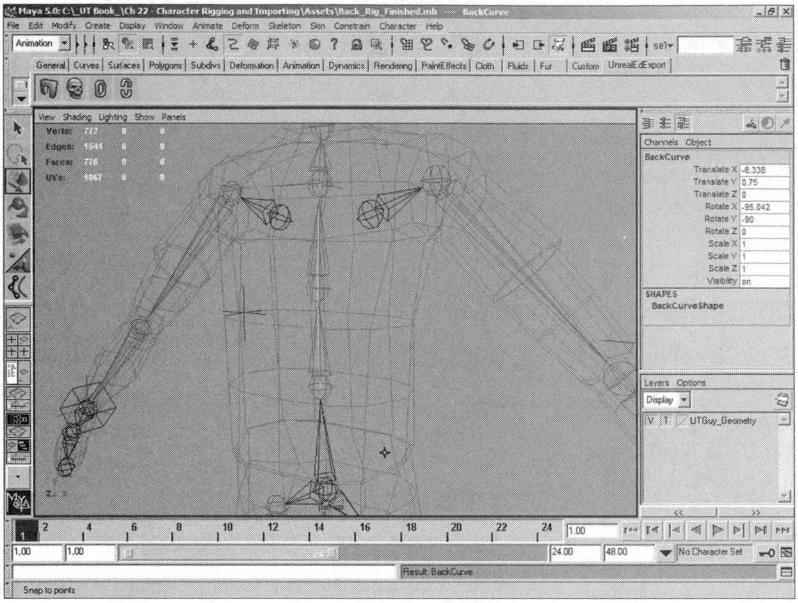

FIGURE 23.54 The Connection Editor is used to make direct attribute connections between nodes.

25. Select the Clavicle, and from the main menu, choose Modify > Prefix Hierarchy Names. Enter the prefix **`Left_`** (include the underscore), and click the OK button when finished.

26. Repeat this step to add the prefix Left_ to the Arm_Control cube, as well as the ikArm IK handle, the pvArm locator, and the pvArmBuffer group.

27. Now duplicate and re-create the arm rig. Select the Clavicle joint and from the main menu, choose Skeleton > Mirror Joint > Options Group. Set the Mirror Across setting to *YZ*. Click the Mirror button when finished. You can see the result in **FIGURE 23.56**.

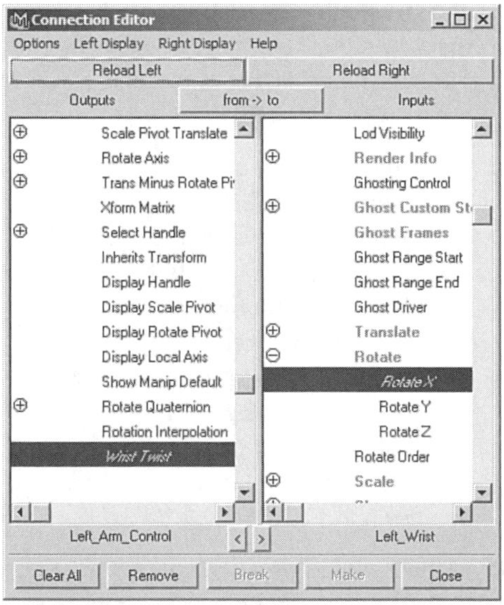

FIGURE 23.55 When the attributes on both the left and right sides are highlighted, there is a connection between these two attributes and data will flow from one side to the other.

28. Create a new layer in the Layer Editor. Don't worry about the name, as this is only a temporary layer and will be removed momentarily. Select the mirrored Clavicle1 joint, and add the mirrored joint chain to the layer. Click the square next to the V icon in the layer until the letter *R* appears. This indicates that the layer has been referenced, meaning that we can snap to it, but not select it.

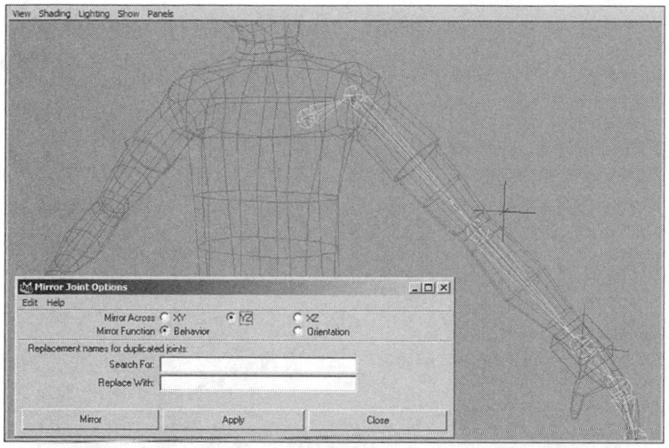

FIGURE 23.56 A new joint chain has been mirrored over to the other side.

29. Switch to the Front viewport. Activate the Joint tool. Holding down the V key, click on each of the mirrored joints, starting at the Clavicle and moving down to the Wrist. This will create a new joint chain at the exact same location as the mirrored original. You can see the new joint chain in **FIGURE 23.57**.

This is done so that the local rotation axes of the right arm will not be disrupted. If you were to look closely at the rotations of the mirrored arm joints, you would notice that their rotation axis information was not correct.

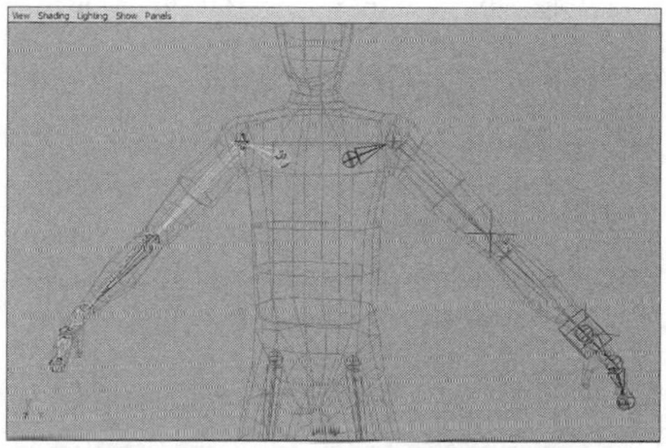

FIGURE 23.57 A new joint chain has been created with the Joint tool by snapping to the referenced mirrored joint chain.

30. Under the Layer Editor, right-click on the new layer you just created and choose Select Objects. Press the Delete key to remove the mirrored joints. Right-click the layer again and choose Delete to remove the layer entirely.

31. Rename these joints Clavicle, Shoulder, Elbow, Wrist, Hand, and Finger.

32. Repeat the steps used earlier to add an IK handle, pole vector locator and buffer group, and a new arm control cube to the right arm. When finished, use the Prefix Hierarchy Names command to add the prefix Right_ (underscore included) to all relevant objects in the right arm, just as you did for the left. The completed arms can be seen in **FIGURE 23.58**.

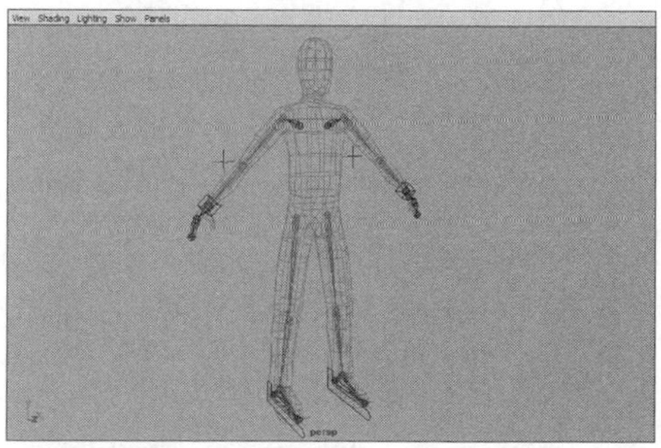

FIGURE 23.58 Both of the arms are now completed.

END TUTORIAL 23.12

With the arms and legs done, we are now ready to create the spinal joints for our character, as well as attach the arms and hips to the spine.

TUTORIAL 23.13: Creating the Spine and Finishing the Rig

1. To begin, switch to the Side viewport, and create a series of seven joints for the spine, neck, and head. Use **FIGURE 23.59** to assist in joint placement. Name these joints Character_Root, Spine_1, Spine_2, Spine_3, Neck_1, Neck_2, and Head.

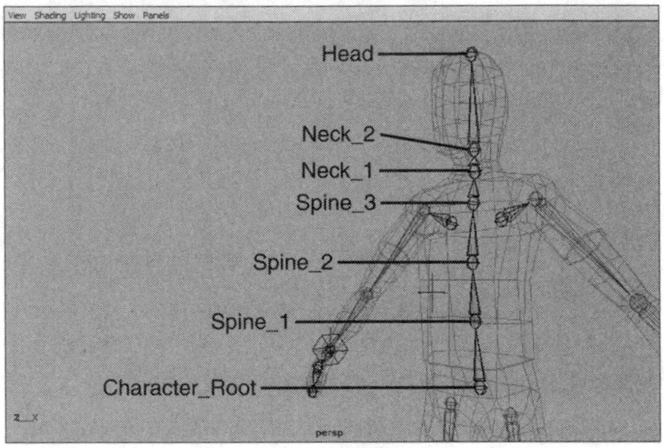

FIGURE 23.59 The joints of the spine have now been created.

2. From the main menu, choose Skeleton > IK Spline Handle Tool. Click Spline_1 to start the IK chain. Click Spline_3 to end the chain. We did not start the IK chain at the character's root joint because of the possibility of undesired effects due to the root branching to the hips. In many cases, a joint is created close to the root to serve as the starting point of the IK Spline Solver. This allows the solver to mimic starting at the root. In our particular case, we have a very simple setup that does not require this action. In **FIGURE 23.60**, you can see the IK Spline Solver setup we will be using.

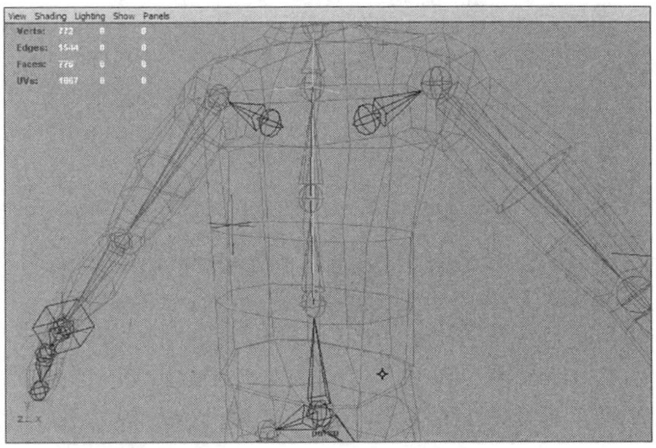

FIGURE 23.60 An IK Spline Solver has been added from `Spine_1` to `Spine_2`.

3. From the Status Line, set the Pick Mask option to All Objects Off. Turn the Curves pick mask on. Marquee-select over Spine_2. You have now selected the new curve that was created by the IK Spline Solver, as shown in **FIGURE 23.61**. Name this curve BackCurve.

4. With the BackCurve still selected, press F8 to switch to Component mode. Make sure the Component mode pick mask only has Points active. Select the CV at the top of the curve. From the main menu, choose Deform > Create Cluster > Options Group. In the Cluster Options dialog, check the Relative check box. Click Create. The result is shown in **FIGURE 23.62**.

5. Select the BackCurve again and then marquee-select the next CV down. Press G to create another Cluster. Repeat this operation for the next CV down as well. You should have now created a total of three clusters, starting at the topmost CV and the two beneath it.

6. Press F8 to toggle back to Object mode. Set the pick masks so that only the Deformations icon is active. Select each cluster one at a time from the bottom and name them: BackControl_1, BackControl_2, and BackControl_3 respectively.

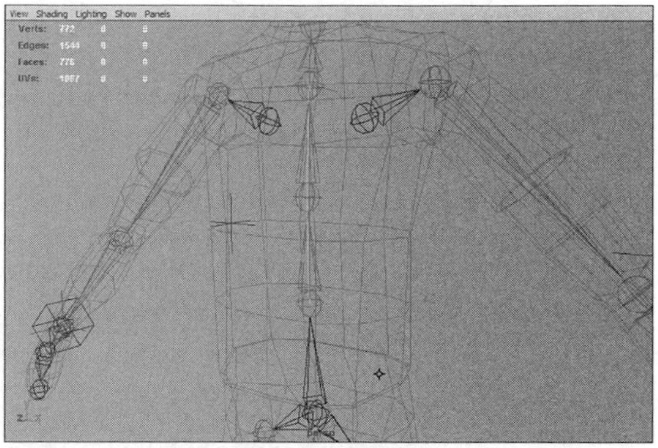

FIGURE 23.61 **The curve created by the IK Spline Solver has been selected. In the Status Line, the Curve pick mask is hte only object type active.**

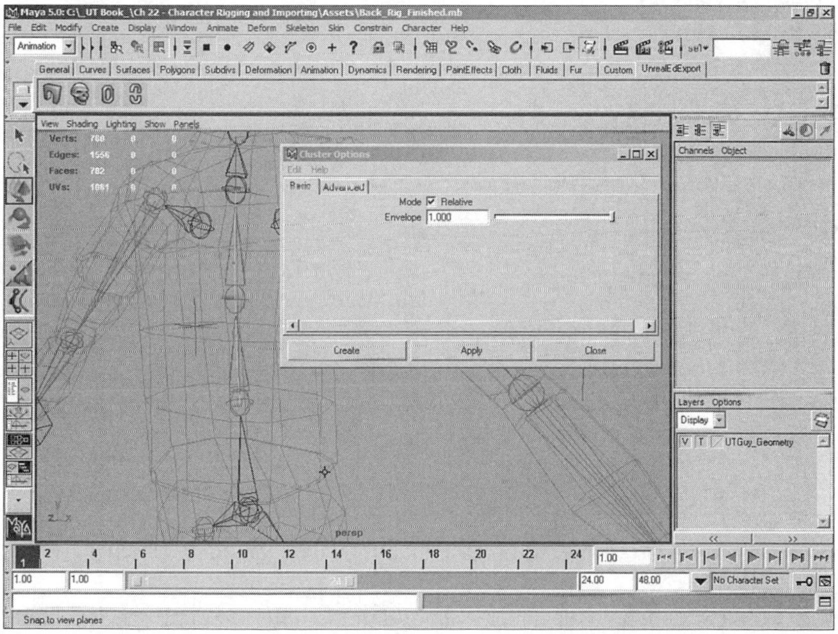

FIGURE 23.62 **Creating a cluster with relative mode active for the top three CVs of the curve.**

7. To make it easier to select the clusters, we will make their selection handles visible and move them behind the character. Select all three clusters. From the main menu, choose Display > Component Display > Selection Handles. Switch to Component mode. From the pick masks, right-click on the plus sign icon and choose Selection Handles. Select and move the three selection handles straight back in the Z Axis, as shown in **FIGURE 23.63**. Switch back to Object mode.

8. All three clusters should still be selected. From the Object pick masks, activate the Curve icon. Shift-select the BackCurve and press P to parent the clusters to the BackCurve.

9. Make the Selection Handles for the neck and Character_Root joints visible and move them directly behind the character the same as you did for the clusters.

10. Finally, select the Character_Root joint and add a BackTwist custom attribute. No minimum or maximum values are required. Open the Connection Editor and load the Character_Root on the Left side and the Back_IK handle on the Right side. Connect BackTwist to Twist (see **FIGURE 23.64**).

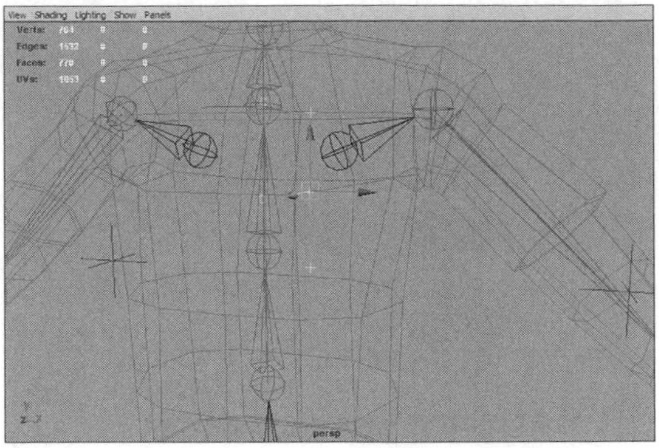

FIGURE 23.63 Moving the selection handles behind the character and making them visible will make manipulating the BackCurve much easier.

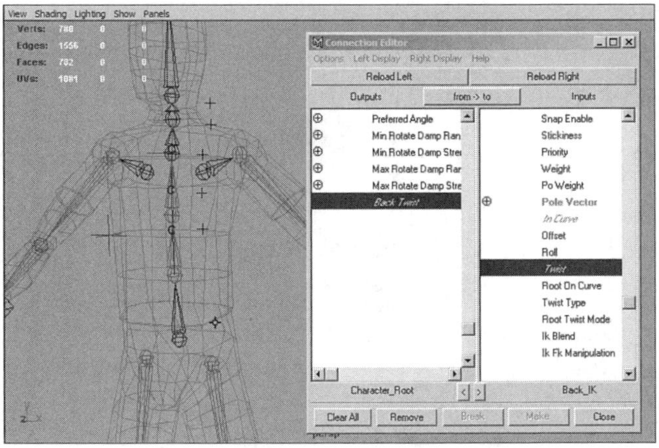

FIGURE 23.64 BackTwist has been connected to the Twist attribute on the `Back_IK` handle.

11. Now you need to connect the hierarchies. Select Left_Hip, then Shift-select Right_Hip, and finally Character_Root. Press the P key, and notice that bones now connect the Character_Root to the two hips.

12. In this order, select Left_Clavicle, Right_Clavicle, and Spine_3, and press P. This will create bones in between these joints, as shown in **FIGURE 23.65**.

13. Select the Left_pvArmBuffer group and the Right_pvArmBuffer group. Shift-select Spine_3, and press P to parent.

14. Save your work. Your rig is now complete, and you are ready to skin your character.

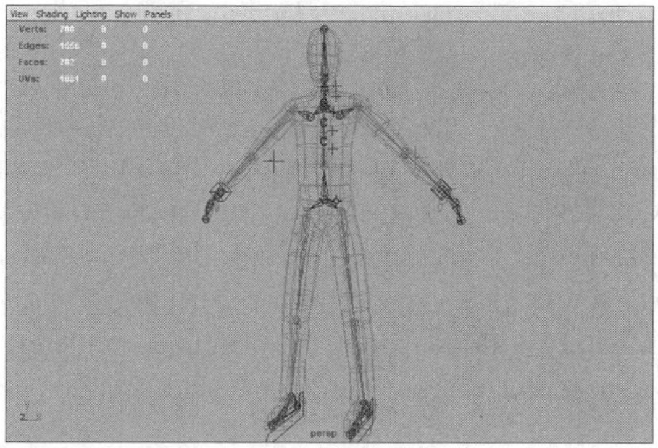

FIGURE 23.65 The hips and clavicles have now been added to the skeleton.

END TUTORIAL 23.13

Skinning the Character

As mentioned in the preceding chapter, we now need to attach the character's geometry to the rig we just finished. This requires the process of skinning. Regardless of whether you are attaching the geometry to a simple skeleton or a completed character rig, the techniques for this process are identical. Refer back to the preceding chapter, and follow the techniques outlined there in order to attach the character's polygons to our new rig. This will finalize the process of turning our character into a digital puppet that we can animate in our scene. Be sure to adjust your weighting properly so that the character's joint areas, such as the elbows and knees, maintain their appropriate volume as the skeleton bends and flexes. Of special concern will be the area at the wrist. As the wrist joint rotates, you will want the skin of the entire forearm to rotate as well. Because of this, you will want the weighting from the wrist to smoothly bleed back into the forearm.

Animating the Character

When creating custom animations for a character in Unreal, we have quite a bit of freedom in how we animate and the animations we create. There are, however, some rules that need to be followed. First, you must understand how Unreal handles character animation in the game. When the character is performing various tasks, Unreal will attempt to play specific animations. These animations are identified by hard-coded names. For example, when a character is running forward, the Unreal Engine looks for an animation cycle named RunF. If the cycle is found, it is played over and over until the character performs some other action, such as jumping, stopping, and so on. At that point, the animation is blended from the RunF cycle to the new cycle that must be played. The end result is a smooth animation from one cycle to another. If an animation cycle is not found, the character will continue to use that last cycle and an error will be generated in the log explaining that the specific cycle that the engine was looking for could not be found.

Because the animation cycles within the game are called by specific names, we will need to make sure that our custom animations use the same names; otherwise, the animation would not be used.

In this section, we are going to take a look at creating two specific cycles: the RunF and the Idle_Rest. Both of these cycles are used heavily in-game. Please keep in mind that the focus of this book is not solely on Maya and the many techniques associated with it. Entire books have been dedicated to both Maya and the world of animation. Instead, we will focus on the generation of very simple cycles, so that we can quickly get our character with a custom rig and animation into the game. With the knowledge acquired from creating these two cycles, you will have everything you need to create the numerous cycles required for a fully functional character inside Unreal.

Pose-to-Pose Animation

There are many techniques that you can use when animating a character. It is important to understand that there is no right or wrong way to do it. In the end, it really comes down to the animator's preference for animation. If you are new to animation, it is recommended that you try a few different techniques so that you can find what works best for getting the job done.

In this chapter, we will be using a technique known as *pose-to-pose animation*. This animation method is straightforward and quite popular among animators. We will be creating key poses for a character at specific frames. By doing this, we will be able to block in our animation quickly. This technique provides quick results, which in return allows us to get a feel for the overall timing. Because of this, it is easier to adjust the timing without having to deal with so many keyframes.

From there, we can quickly achieve our desired animation through adding additional keys and adjusting the animation curves generated by Maya.

Creating Custom Animation Cycles

In **TUTORIALS 23.14** through **23.17**, we will demonstrate how you can create two basic character animations. One of these will be a simple run cycle, and the other will be a basic standing/breathing cycle that the character will use when not in motion.

Keep in mind that animation is more of an art form than a technical skill. Creating convincing animation requires a strong understanding of several key elements. The animator must have a strong feel for timing, weight, skeletal movement, and more. If you are a beginner, do not become discouraged if you are unable to create the animations you visualize—a good animator is one who has spent countless hours practicing.

In the preceding chapter, we had to use a Character Set so that the Unreal Exporter plug-in would recognize our character. Although we still need the Character Set for the exporting process to work, creating our own animation allows us to use Character Sets for what they were originally intended for in Maya—capturing poses with a single Set Key operation.

As previously explained, a *Character Set* is a collection of attributes. This in itself is not that big of a deal. Character Sets become powerful when they are activated during the animation process and an animator sets a key. Instead of a single keyframe being added to the currently selected object, every attribute found within a Character Set receives keys. This saves the animator a tremendous amount of time as he or she no longer has to select each and every control to set keyframes.

Character Sets are best used to block animation quickly. In **TUTORIAL 23.14**, we will create a single character set for creating our animation.

TUTORIAL 23.14: Preparing for Animation

1. Begin creating the Character Set by selecting all of the control objects and selection handles for our character.
2. From the main menu, choose Character > Create Character Set > Options Group.
3. From the Create Character Set Options dialog, set the Name to UTCharacter.
4. Click Create Character Set.
5. Now create a floor for the character. Create a polygon cube. Scale and position the cube so that it resembles a floor for our character to stand on. We won't actually send this object into Unreal. Rather, it is merely a reference object that will help make animation easier as we will not be guessing where the ground will be.
6. In **TUTORIAL 23.11**, you created a UTGuy_Geometry layer for our character's geometry. We then saved this layer as a template so that the character could not be accidentally selected although working with the skeleton or rig. We will take a similar approach with the floor as you would not want to select it while animating the character.

   Create a new Layer and name it Floor. Set the layer's mode to Reference (click the third box twice so that the letter R appears in it.) This is similar to the Template mode we used with the character with the exception of being able to see the floor shaded instead of in a wireframe mode (see **FIGURE 23.66**).

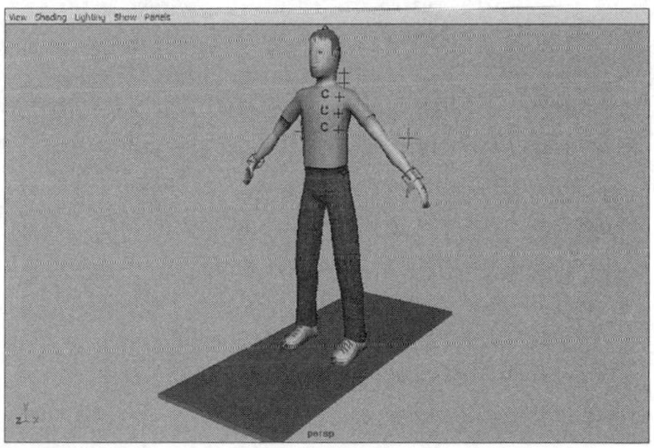

FIGURE 23.66 A floor will help in the animation process as it takes the guesswork out of figuring out where the feet need to contact the ground.

7. Now set the animation ranges. Many of the animation cycles that need to be created for Unreal will have different animation ranges. In the end, the length of an animation cycle is up to the animator. We will begin with only the range required to animate a run cycle:

   Set the Start Time to 1.

   Set the End Time to 16.

   Verify that the Start Range is at frame 1 and that the End Range is at frame 16.

8. To make it easier to select the character's control system, turn all pick masks off and then activate only Selection Handles (requires right-clicking on the Handles pick mask) and NURBS curves.

END TUTORIAL 23.14

In **TUTORIAL 23.15**, we will be creating a very basic run cycle in order to acquaint you with the various methods employed to animate a character in Maya. Later, you can edit this cycle, improve it, and add more cycles to your characters so that they will have access to all available animations in Unreal.

TUTORIAL 23.15: Creating a Run Cycle

1. Set the Time Slider to Frame 1.
2. Verify that the UTCharacter Character Set is active.
3. Select the Left_Foot_Control and move it forward along the Z-axis.
4. Rotate the Left_Foot_Control around the X-axis. Set it so that the character is landing on the heel of the left foot.
5. Move the Right_Foot_Control back along the Z-axis and move it up in the Y-axis.
6. Rotate the Right_Root_Control around the X-axis.
7. Select the Character_Root and move it down slightly. Rotate it around X so that the hips are turned into the forward left leg.
8. Adjust the BackTwist attribute on the Character_Root so that the character's shoulder is leaning a bit more into the left hip. We are doing this because the character is holding a heavy gun.
9. Position the hands so that the left hand is supporting the bottom side of a gun and the right hand is holding the gun's handle. Add a polygonal cylinder into the scene as a stand-in object for the gun. Do not forget to move the pole vector locators to help make the positioning look natural and to adjust the left hand's WristTwist attribute so that the hand is rotated properly for supporting the bottom of the gun.
10. Rotate the Neck joints so that the head is looking forward.
11. Press S to keyframe. The pose can be seen from two angles in **FIGURES 23.67** and **23.68**.

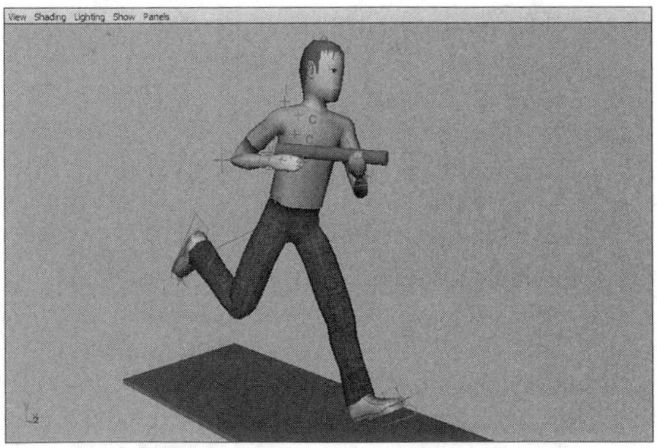

FIGURE 23.67 The pose as seen in the Perspective viewport.

12. Copy this pose to frame 16 so that our character will cycle properly. Hold down the middle mouse button and drag the time slider to frame 16. Manipulating the time slider like this allows us to change our current frame without evaluating time. This is an easy approach to copying poses or keyframes in general.

13. Press S to record the pose.

14. Now set the opposite pose—right leg forward. First, set the active Character Set to None.

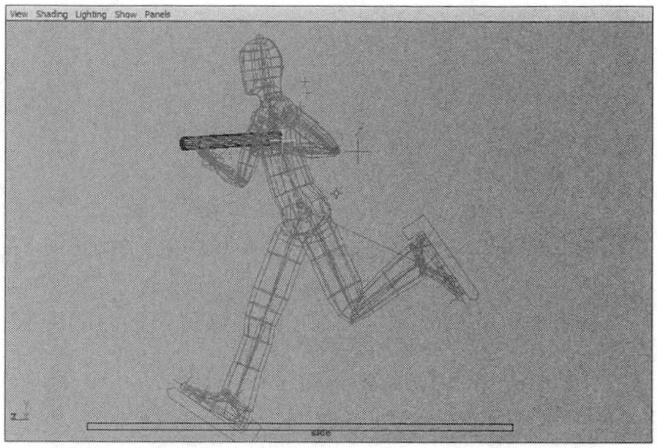

FIGURE 23.68 The pose as seen in the Side viewport.

15. Hold down the middle mouse button and drag the time slider to frame 8.

16. Select the Left_Foot_Control and in the Side viewport, position it so that the left leg matches the right leg. You will need to rotate the Left_Foot_Control as well (see **FIGURE 23.69**).

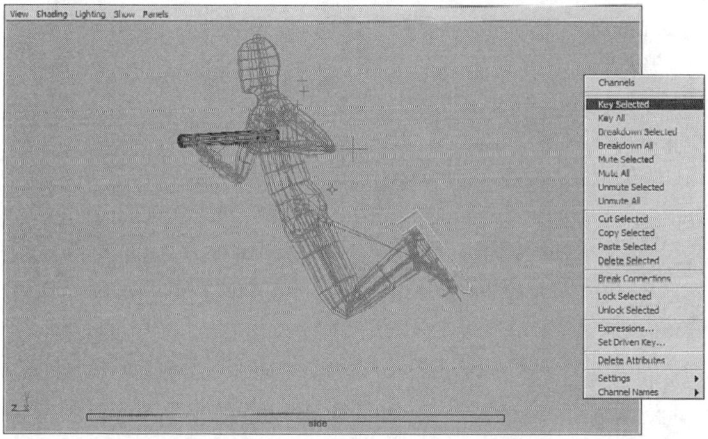

FIGURE 23.69 Matching the left leg to the right leg.

17. In the Channel Box, click and drag over all of the translate and rotate channels. Ctrl+click and add Heel RX, Ball RX, and Toe RX to the channel selection. Right-click and choose Key Selected.

18. Click Frame 1 on the time slider.

19. Hold down the middle mouse button and drag the time slider to frame 8.

20. Select the Right_Foot_Control and match its position to the forward left foot. As before, manually key all of the translate, rotate, and custom attributes on this foot control (see **FIGURE 23.70**).

21. Fix the hip rotation at frame 8 by selecting the Character_Root. Make sure the time slider is at frame 8. In the Channel Box, remove the negative sign in the Rotate X Attribute. Right-click on that attribute and choose Key Selected.

22. Rotate and keyframe the Neck joints so that the head continues to look straight at frame 8, as shown in **FIGURE 23.71**.

23. If you play back the animation, you can see the cycle starting to take shape. But although the animation is cycling, it does not look much like a run. The main reason is that our feet never really plant. Now you will fix that here. Go to frame 4.

24. Select the Left_Foot_Control and move it so that it is directly under the character. Rotate the control so that the foot is flat.

25. Activate the UTCharacter character set.

26. Set a keyframe. You can see the pose in **FIGURE 23.72**.

27. Move the time slider to frame 12. Now repeat these steps for the right leg.

28. Play back the animation. Things are starting to look a bit better, but there are still issues with the legs/feet. Set the Character Set to None.

29. Go to frame 2 and select the Left_Foot_Control.

30. Rotate the foot control around the X-axis so that the foot is flat, as shown in **FIGURE 23.73**.

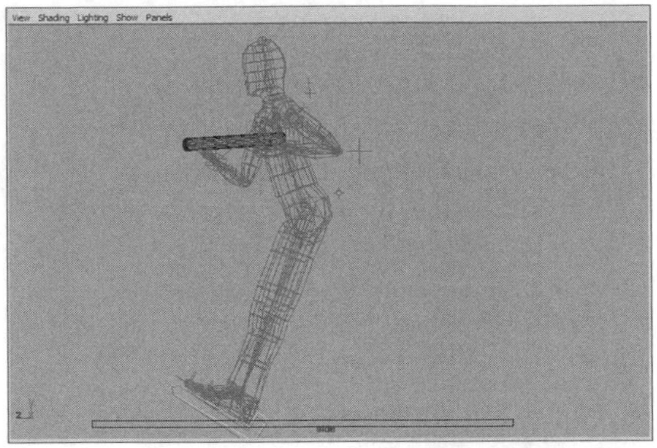

FIGURE 23.70 Matching the right leg to the left leg.

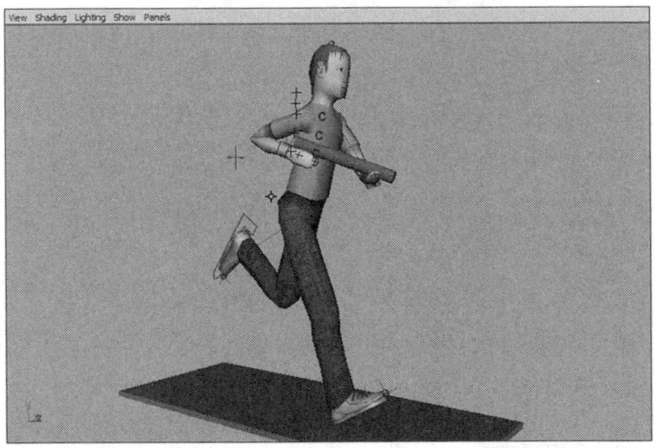

FIGURE 23.71 The character at frame 8. The pose is opposite from frame 1 and 16.

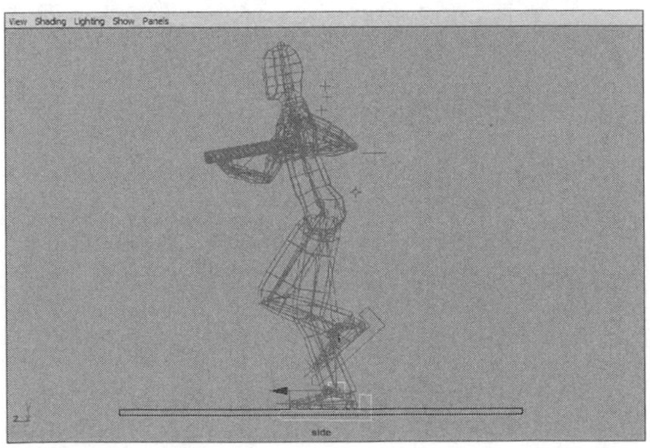

FIGURE 23.72 Plant the left foot at frame 4.

31. Go to frame 5.

32. Adjust the Ball RX and Toe RX custom attributes to give the appearance of the character pushing off with his foot, as shown in **FIGURE 23.74**. You will need to adjust the translate attributes as well. Keyframe all translate and custom attributes.

33. Repeat these steps for the right leg. The target frames are 9 and 13. Play through the animation and make any tweaks necessary.

34. Now you need to enhance the Character_Root motion. Select the Character_Root and go to frame 4.

35. Move the root down in the Y-axis. It is important to create the effect of a character pushing off when running. When one foot is passing the other, often referred to as the passing stage, the character should be at his lowest point. As the foot kicks off the ground, the character should then reach his highest point and begin to fall with gravity within a frame or two as the foot leaves the ground (see **FIGURE 23.75**).

36. Fix the arms so that they accommodate the root change.

37. Keyframe all changed attributes.

38. Adjust hands and neck as needed.

39. The steps provided have helped you rough in a character run cycle. It is up to you to fine-tune the animation so that the cycle looks good. Don't forget to use the Graph Editor to finesse the in-between motion generated by Maya.

END TUTORIAL 23.15

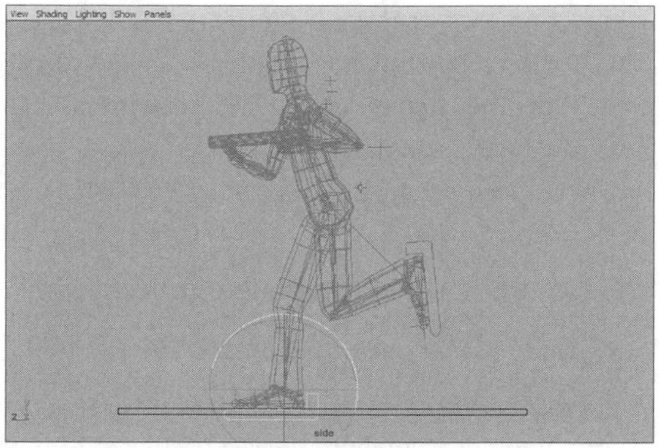

FIGURE 23.73 Rotating the foot until it is flat. This helps give the appearance of the foot helping hold the character's weight.

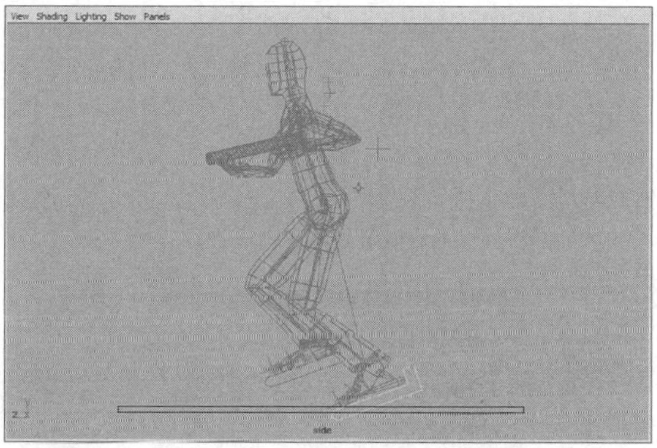

FIGURE 23.74 Adjusting the foot so that it appears to kick off.

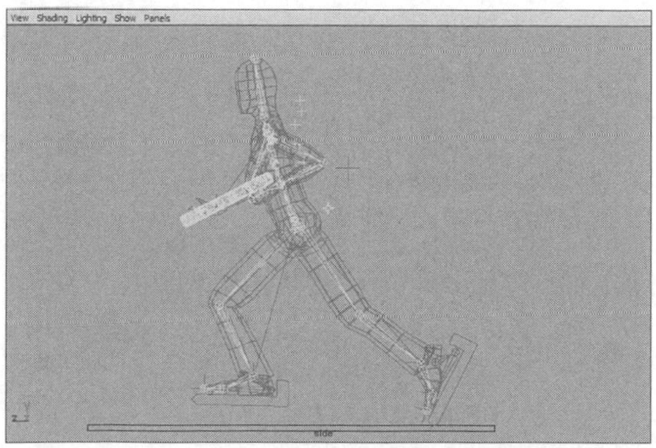

FIGURE 23.75 As the foot kicks off the ground, the character is at his highest point.

The second cycle that we are going to create is the Idle_Rest animation. This animation is played when a character stops moving for a second or two. There are several idle cycles that need to be created for the character to look natural in-game, but as mentioned in the beginning of this section, our focus is on only two cycles, and from these foundations you should be able to create any cycle you need for your character. In **TUTORIAL 23.16**, we will create this idle cycle.

TUTORIAL 23.16: Creating an Idle Cycle

23

1. Open the file Animation Cycles Idle Start.mb or continue from **TUTORIAL 23.15**.
2. For the Idle_Rest cycle, we need a larger number of frames. This will allow us to create a smoother animation. We will be using 24 frames:

   Set End Time to 41.

   Set Start Playback Time to 17.

   Set End Playback Time to 41.
3. Set the time slider to frame 17.
4. Activate the UTCharacter Character Set.
5. Create a resting pose:
   - Move the left leg forward.
   - Move the right leg back and rotate it outward.
   - Make sure the feet are flat on the ground.
   - Rotate the Character_Root so that it splits the difference between the left and right feet.
   - Adjust the arms accordingly so that the gun is held slightly downward (remember, this is a resting pose).
   - Rotate the head so that the character is looking forward.
   - Set a keyframe. You can see the result of this pose in **FIGURE 23.76**.

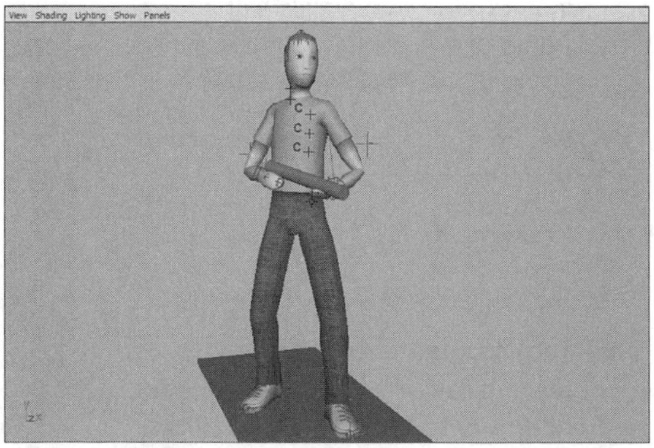

FIGURE 23.76 The `Idle_Rest` pose should have the character with the left leg forward with the hips rotated toward the right leg.

6. Using the techniques demonstrated in step 12 of **TUTORIAL 23.15**, copy this pose to frame 41. Again, this will make a perfect cycle.

7. Create the breathing effect:
   - Move the time slider to frame 29.
   - Move the Character_Root in the X-axis a small amount.
   - Move the BackControl_3 cluster back in the Z-axis a very small amount.
   - Adjust the hands so that the character is still holding the gun properly.
   - Set a keyframe.
8. Fine-tune the cycle:
   - Set the Character Set to None.
   - Play back through the animation and look for problem areas. The goal is to achieve a very subtle swaying/breathing effect.
   - You will most likely find that the animation is a bit jerky as it loops from the last frame to the first frame of the cycle. This can be fixed by changing the tangents at frame 17 and frame 41 so that they are flat. This will allow an ease-in and ease-out effect that will make the blending much smoother. Tweak the animation as needed.

END TUTORIAL 23.16

Before we can export the animation to UnrealEd, we need to put each of the animation cycles into a clip. We will then need to place the clips into the Trax Editor. The exporter plug-in will sample the animation from these clips during the exporting phase. In **TUTORIAL 23.17**, we use the Trax Editor to create animation clips from our cycles.

TUTORIAL 23.17: Creating Clips for the Animation Cycles

1. Activate the UTCharacter Character Set.
2. Select the Character_Root.
3. From the main menu, choose Window > Animation Editors > Trax Editor. The Trax Editor is Maya's nonlinear animation editor, which enables animators to package their animation into clips. Clips can then be reused, sped up, slowed down, split, merged, and so on. You can see the Trax Editor in **FIGURE 23.77**.
4. From the Trax Editor's menu bar, choose Create > Clip > Options Group.
5. In the Create Clip Options dialog, set the following settings and then click Create Clip (see **FIGURE 23.78**):

   Name: RunF

   Check the Leave Keys in Timeline check box.

   Time Range: Start/End

   Start Time: 1

   End Time: 15

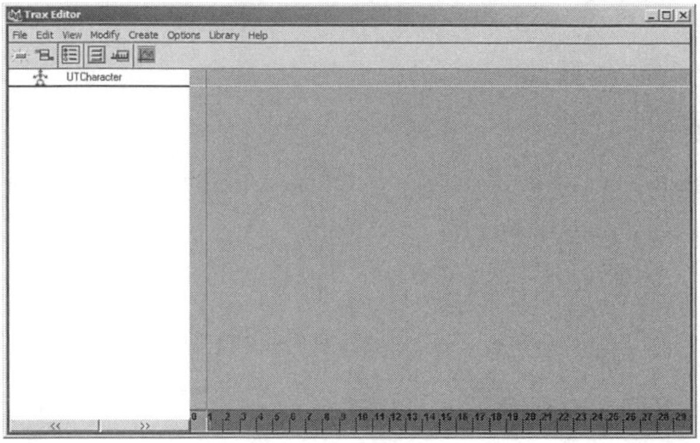

FIGURE 23.77 The Trax Editor is used to create nonlinear animation.

6. Create another clip setting the following options:

   Name: RunF

   UNCHECK the Leave Keys in Timeline check box.

   Time Range: Start/End

   Start Time: 17

   End Time: 41

7. From the Trax Editor's menu bar, choose File > Visor. From within the Visor dialog, click the Character Clips tab. This is where you will find the two clips that were just created, as shown in **FIGURE 23.79**.

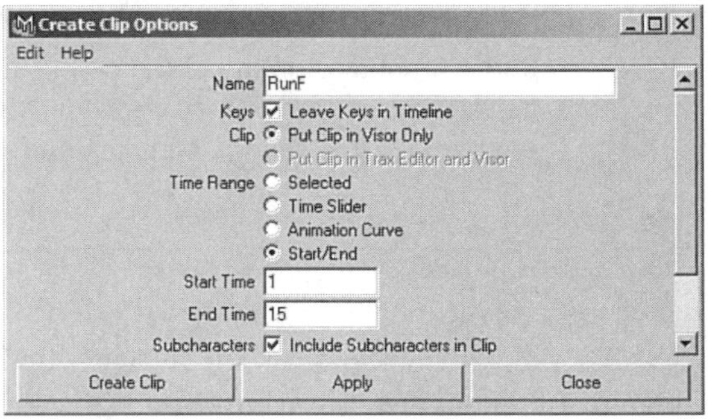

FIGURE 23.78 Creating the clip for the Run Forward animation cycle.

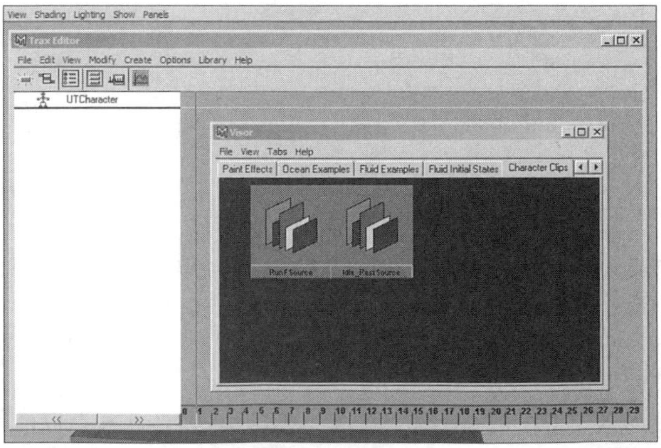

FIGURE 23.79 The Visor contains all clips that have been created along with other assets available for Maya.

8. From the Visor dialog, hold down the middle mouse button and drag each clip to the Trax Editor's timeline. You can navigate the timeline in Trax the same way you do all other panels in Maya. This may be necessary to see all of the clips.

9. Select each clip in the Visor and move them left or right so that they start at the appropriate place. The RunF clip should start at frame 1 and the Idle_Rest clip should start at frame 16. In **FIGURE 23.80**, you see both clips in the Trax Editor.

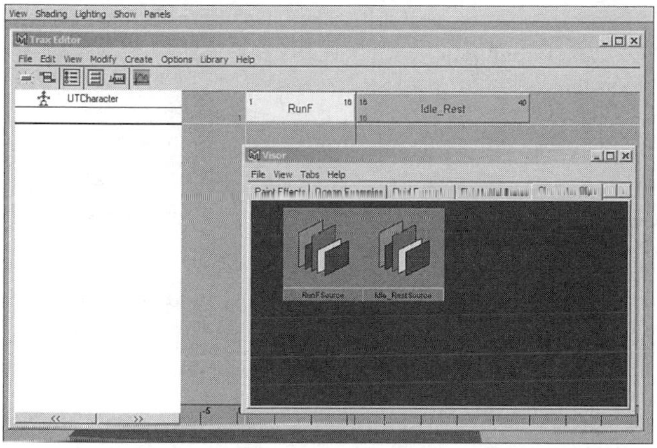

FIGURE 23.80 The two clips have been added to the Trax Editor.

10. Close the Trax Editor. You are now ready to export the character and the animation cycles to UnrealEd.

END TUTORIAL 23.17

Exporting Custom Animations into UnrealEd

In this section, we will discuss how to take your custom animation clips into Unreal. We will be focusing on doing this with the plug-in included with Unreal Tournament 2004. Also, we will mention a few considerations you must keep in mind when implementing your own animations in UnrealEd.

In **TUTORIALS 23.18** and **23.19**, we will assume that you have completed the various exporting tutorials in the last chapter. In **TUTORIAL 23.18**, we will take the animation from Maya and export it into UnrealEd.

TUTORIAL 23.18: Exporting Custom Animation into UnrealEd

1. Continue from **TUTORIAL 23.17**.
2. Make sure UnrealEd is open and that Maya and UnrealEd are synched.
3. Select and delete the cylinder that was used as a weapon stand-in.
4. Select Character_Root.
5. Click the Skeletal Mesh Export Window icon from the Shelf. The dialog looks a bit different than it did in the last chapter. With custom animation in place, the dialog now shows a list of cycles that are available for export.
6. Create a new package named UTCustomGuy.
7. Now that we are using our own custom animations, we no longer need to check the Underscore to Space check box. In the last chapter, this was necessary because we were using names from within other characters from Unreal.
8. Select both sequences in the list and click the Export button. The Command Feedback line should say: Result: Export Complete.
9. Save your Maya scene.

END TUTORIAL 23.18

Now that the character and his animation have been successfully exported to UnrealEd, several properties need to be adjusted for the character to work properly in the game. We will address this in **TUTORIAL 23.19**.

TUTORIAL 23.19: Adjusting the Custom Character's Properties in UnrealEd

1. Continue from **TUTORIAL 23.18**.
2. Switch to UnrealEd.
3. Open the Animations browser and switch to the UTCustomGuy package, as shown in **FIGURE 23.81**.
4. As you did in the last chapter, import the head, body, and portrait textures into a package named UTGuyTextures, and save this textures package.
5. Assign the body and head textures to the character.
6. Look in the Animation Sequences list. You will see that both animations have been imported from Maya. You will also notice that the Idle_Rest animation name has been messed up. This is because the plug-in has a problem with underscores in the name. We have left this in to demonstrate how to rename sequences when they have been imported.
7. In the Properties section, click the Sequence tab.
8. Select the rest of the animation in the sequence list.

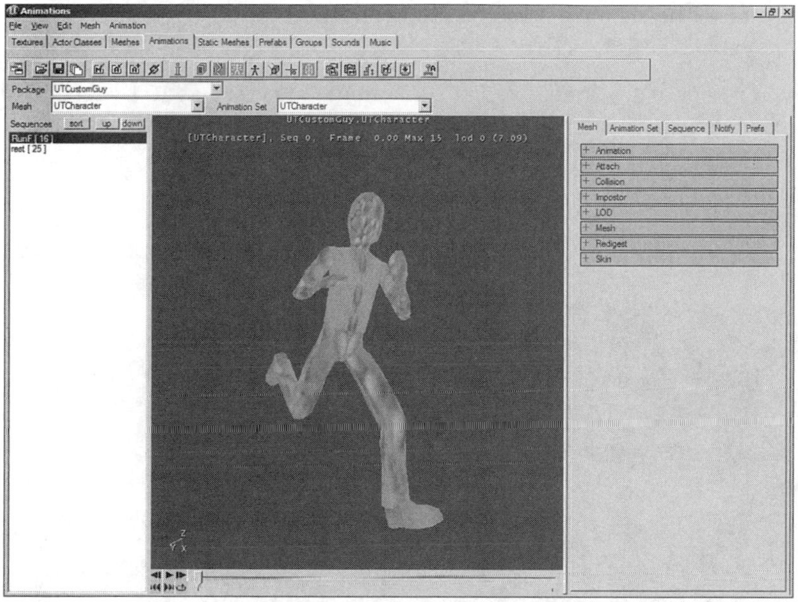

FIGURE 23.81 The Animations browser shows the character has been successfully imported into UnrealEd.

9. Under the SequenceProperties category, change the SequenceName to Idle_Rest and press Enter. Note that the name changes in the sequence list, as shown in **FIGURE 23.82**.

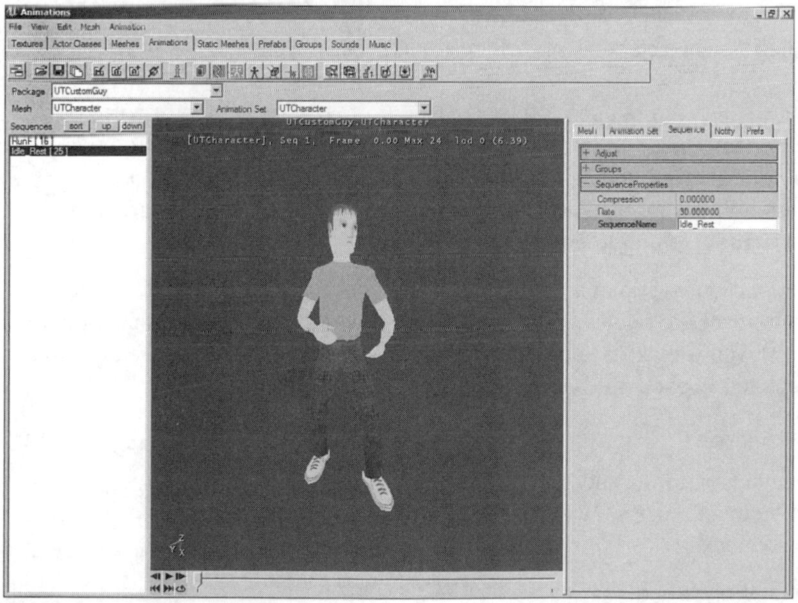

FIGURE 23.82 You can change sequence names in the SequenceProperties category under the Sequence tab.

10. The Scale of the Character needs to be adjusted. Switch back to the Mesh tab and expand the Mesh property category.

11. Expand the `Scale` property and set Scale X, Y, and Z to 1. It will always be at 10 by default. A size of 1 will match the typical size of an Unreal character, as shown in **FIGURE 23.83**.

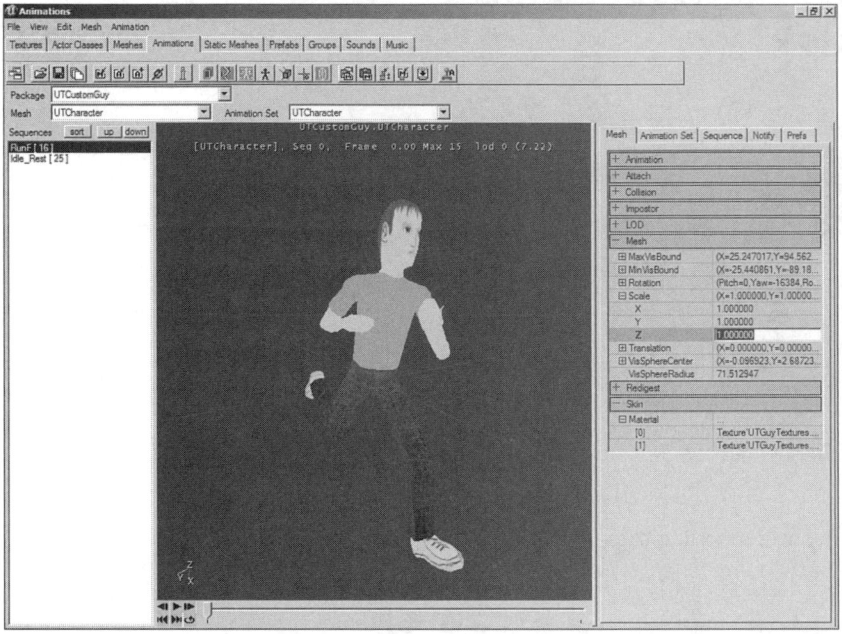

FIGURE 23.83 **Scaling the character to 1 so that its size matches a typical Unreal character.**

12. Now you are going to align the weapon to his hand. To do this we will need to create a socket. In the last chapter, we only had to adjust sockets because we borrowed them from another character. But because this is our own character, we will need to create a few. Remember, sockets are how we can identify specific bones for the Unreal Engine to use to attach weapons, flags, and so on to during gameplay.

    Before we add the socket, let's load all of the weapons into memory. To do this, switch over to the Weapons package and click the Load Entire Package icon. If you click on the Mesh drop-down list, you will see a listing of all weapons available in this package. Switch back to the UTCustomGuy package.

13. Expand the Attach category.

14. Click the plus symbol next to Sockets to reveal the Add button. Click the Add button to add a new socket.

15. Set the AttachAlias to righthand.

16. Set the BoneName to Right_Hand.

> **NOTE**
>
> **If your character is not in the center of the world, you will need to adjust the Translation properties to center the character there. Our character was never moved, so his alignment is perfect.**

17. To load a test model to help with alignment, enter **`AssaultRifle_3rd`** into the `TestMesh` property and press Enter. You will not see the weapon by default. Set the `ContinuousUpdate` property to `True`. This will cause the editor to continuously update all entries made to sockets in real time. When this property is set to `True`, you can see in **FIGURE 23.84** that the position, orientation, and scale are way off.

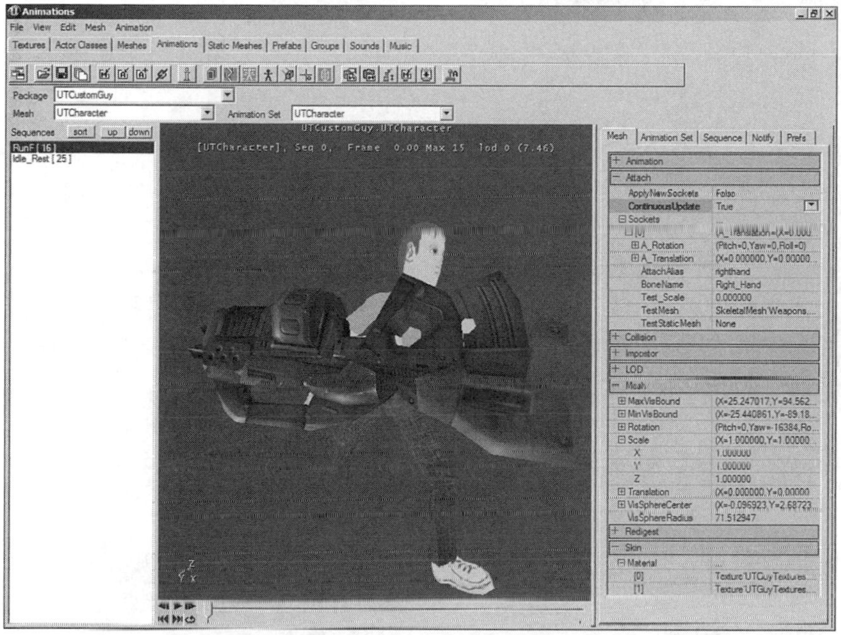

FIGURE 23.84 **The test weapon has been imported. As you can see, the positioning and orientation are way off.**

18. Set the TestScale to 0.3. We are using 0.3 because this is the DrawScale size that is used for this weapon internally in Unreal. Now the gun is a normal size, but the orientation is still way off.

19. Expand A_Rotation and set the following:

Pitch: -2000

Roll: 32768

Yaw: -32768

20. Expand A_Translation and set the following:

X: -2

Y: -1

Z: 0

The weapon should now be properly positioned and oriented, as shown in **FIGURE 23.85**.

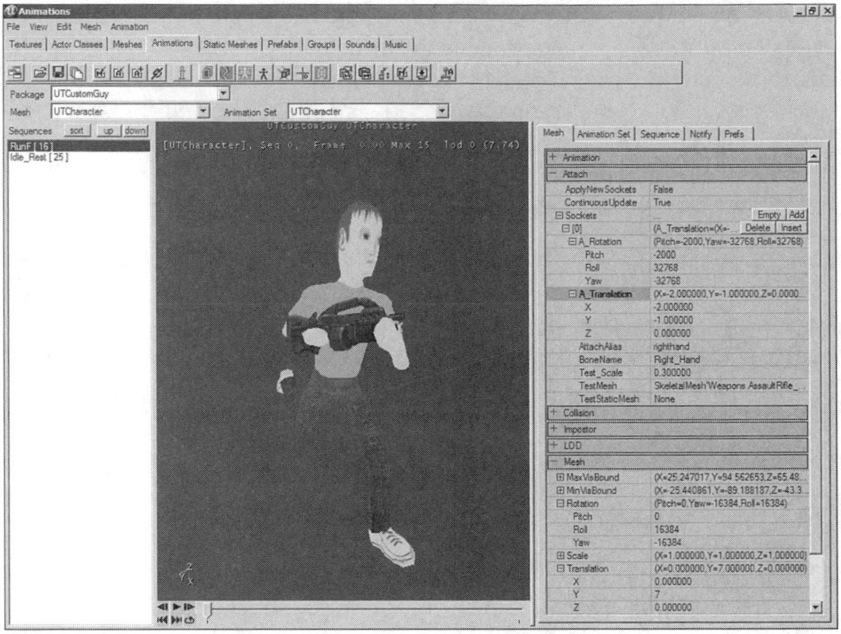

FIGURE 23.85 The test weapon has now been properly positioned.

20. Next we need to add a socket for the Flag attachment. Add another socket.

21. Set the following properties (see **FIGURE 23.86**):

`AttachAlias`: FlagHand

`BoneName`: Right_Hand

`TestMesh`: VertMesh'XGame_rc.FlagMesh'

`A_Rotation`:

Pitch: 0

Roll: 4000

Yaw: 0

`A_Translation`:

X: 2

Y: -1

Z: 0

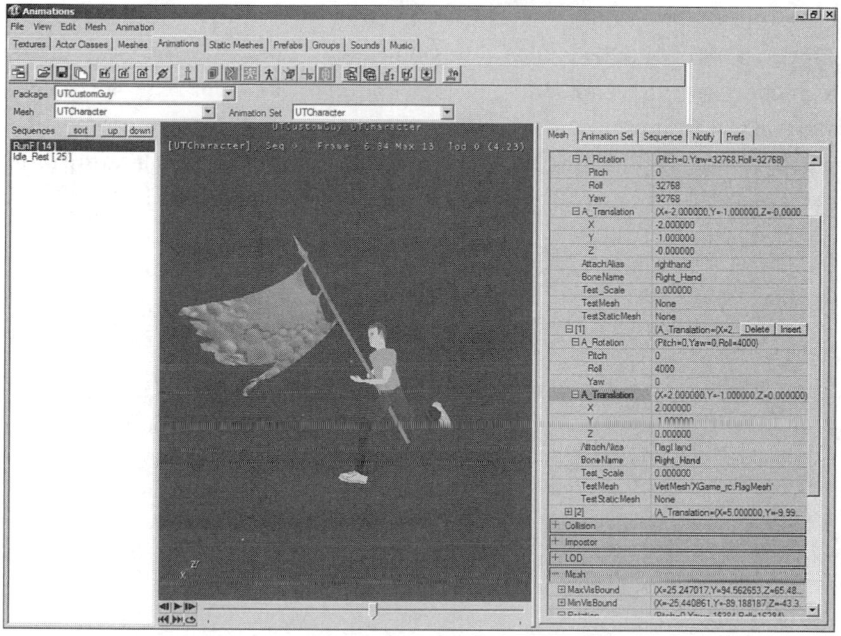

FIGURE 23.86 Using sockets to align the flag.

22. For good measure, set `ApplyNewSockets` to `True` to make 100% sure that the socket's settings have been accepted. Save the animation package.

23. Create the UPL file as shown in the last chapter and test your character in-game.

END TUTORIAL 23.19

Summary

In this chapter, we have introduced you to a vast number of new concepts concerning animation in Maya. We have covered the basics of animation, keyframes, and reactive animation scenarios, as well as the many animation constraints available. We also discussed Inverse and Forward Kinematics animation methods, as well as the three IK solvers available in Maya. From there, we demonstrated the creation of a complete character control system, or rig, to control your character's animation in a fluid and intuitive manner. Finally, we discussed how this rig can be used to animate cycles, how these cycles can be transferred to Trax clips, and how that animation can then be sent into Unreal for use with your game character.

With the completion of this chapter, you are now ready to create your own Unreal characters completely from scratch, and make them fully compatible with Unreal Tournament 2004. Combining this information with the many other chapters found in this book, you now know how to greatly expand the Unreal universe by re-creating the game in your own image. We sincerely hope that you have enjoyed reading this book, and that you are successful in all future projects and endeavors you may encounter with the Unreal Engine. Thanks, and good luck!

Part IV

Appendix A

The UnrealEd Manual

Welcome to Appendix A. The purpose of this Appendix is to act as a reference point for using UnrealEd. You will find a complete overview of the program, along with many detailed descriptions of its components, in this Appendix. Keep in mind that as the Unreal Engine has grown and progressed, certain parts of the editor's functionality have been changed or removed altogether. This Appendix has been created using UnrealEd build version 3236. **FIGURE A.1** shows the full user interface for UnrealEd.

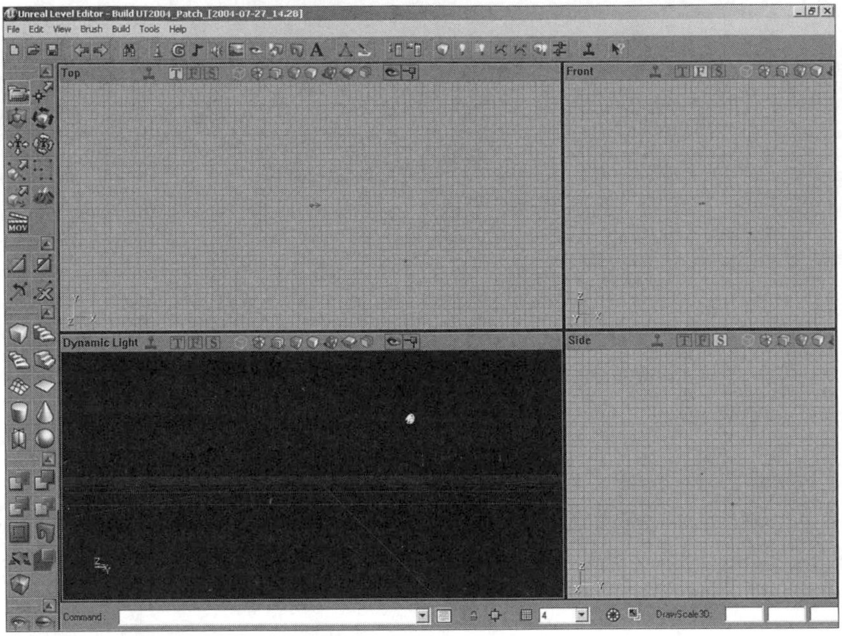

FIGURE A.1 The UnrealEd User Interface.

The Main Menu Bar

This area is common to many computer applications, and in UnrealEd it is very similar to what you've come to expect. There are seven menus across the menu bar (see **FIGURE A.2**), and the functions of each one are covered in **TABLE A.1**.

FIGURE A.2 The main menu bar.

TABLE A.1 The UnrealEd Menus

File	This menu is typical to most modern programs, and functions the same way. Here, you have access to opening files and saving them, as well as importing and exporting files. The bottom of the menu contains an area for opening recently used files.
Edit	This menu allows for access to Undo and Redo, as well as a variety of selection methods. It also holds the Search for Actors command, used to locate any Actor in your level. The menu includes the Cut, Copy, and Paste commands, which will work with any Actors in the level, as well as the Duplicate and Delete commands. At the bottom, the menu gives access to a wide variety of selection methods, such as Select All Actors, Select All Surfaces, and also several conditions for surface selections, such as Select All Surfaces with Matching Groups or with Matching Textures.

TABLE A.1 Continued

View	The View menu offers a tentative list of all of the windows available in UnrealEd, along with some options for the viewports in the program itself. Here you can access all of the browser windows, as well as all of the properties and options windows for the objects in your level, including the overall properties for the level itself. The menu also has an area where you can float or fix your viewports, as well as adjust their configurations, or their placement on the interface. You may also create a new viewport from this menu, as well as import background images for the viewports.
Brush	This menu contains a wide variety of options for your brushes. Using the choices on the Brush menu, you may edit your brushes by clipping or altering their normals, open, save, import, and export different brushes that you create, and add a wide variety of brushes into your level. Among these are additive and subtractive brushes, movers, Antiportals, and more. The menu also allows you to intersect and deintersect brushes. These actions are covered in detail in Chapters 3 and 4.
Build	The Build menu allows you to rebuild specific aspects of your level, in order to update them if changes have been made. Among the objects you can rebuild are geometry, lights, and AI paths. You may also establish settings to rebuild these only if changes have been made, as well as adjust rebuilding options. The menu also allows for you to play-test your level within the game itself.
Tools	The Tools menu contains a variety of utilities to help you as you construct your levels. Among these are tools for scaling the map, scaling lights, removing any particles that exist in your level (this, in effect, will reset a particle emitter), and a rotation tool for rotating Actors.
Help	This menu contains access to toggling on and off the Tip of the Day feature, as well as a link to the Unreal Developer's Network site (`www.udn.epicgames.com`). It also contains a contextual help system, which, at the time of this writing, is nonfunctional.

The Toolbar

Underneath the main menu bar, you will find the toolbar (see **FIGURE A.3**). This contains several buttons for quick access to many of the commands found in the menus. The buttons are divided into groups, and the following sections describe each of these groups.

FIGURE A.3 The toolbar.

File Options

The first three buttons across the toolbar contain the File options (see **FIGURE A.4**). Going from left to right, these allow the user to create a new file, open an existing file, and save the current file. These work exactly like the corresponding commands found in the File menu.

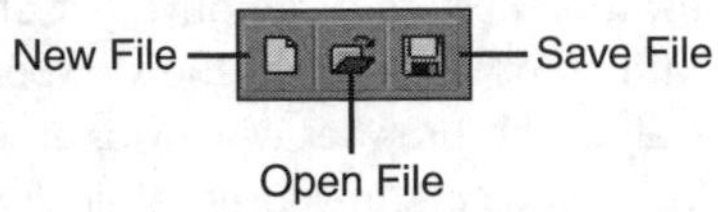

FIGURE A.4 File Options area.

Undo and Redo

The next two buttons on the toolbar allow you to undo and redo actions in your level (see **FIGURE A.5**). You have many levels of Undos in UnrealEd, and numerous Redos as well. These commands can also be found in the Edit menu.

FIGURE A.5 Undo and Redo area.

Search for Actor

This tool (see **FIGURE A.6**) is designed to help you find specific Actors within your scene in a fast and easy manner. For more information on this tool and how to use it go to the section called "Search for Actors" near the end of this appendix.

FIGURE A.6 Search for Actor button.

Browsers

The browsers are a series of dialogs that give access to most of UnrealEd's functionality (see **FIGURE A.7**). They will each be covered in more depth in the "Browsers" section later in this appendix.

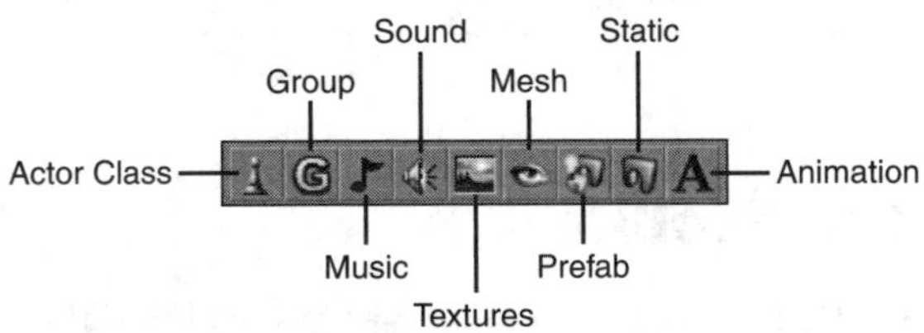

FIGURE A.7 Browsers area.

The browser buttons, from left to right, are

- Actor Class Browser
- Group Browser
- Music Browser
- Sound Browser
- Textures Browser
- Mesh Browser
- Prefab Browser
- Static Mesh Browser
- Animation Browser

Editors

The editors are covered in the "Editor Windows" section of this appendix. The button on the left in **FIGURE A.8** is for the 2D Script Editor; the button on the right is for the UnrealScript Editor.

FIGURE A.8 Editors area.

Properties

These windows allow you to view and adjust many of the parameters for your Actors. We will go into more depth on them in the "Property Windows" section later in this Appendix. The button on the left in **FIGURE A.9** is for the Actor Properties window; the button on the right is for the Surface Properties window.

FIGURE A.9 Properties area.

Building

This area allows for the updating of many aspects of the level when they are changed. **TABLE A.2** describes the buttons in the Building area shown in **FIGURE A.10** from left to right.

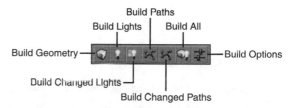

FIGURE A.10 Building Area

TABLE A.2 The Build Commands

Build Geometry	Building the geometry of your level will allow the Unreal Engine to construct the actual geometry of your level using the data created from your BSP brushes.
Build Lights	This recalculates all of the lights and shadows cast in your level. This must be done whenever new geometry is added, and whenever light properties are changed.
Build Changed Lights	This alternative to the Build Lighting button allows you to only rebuild the lights that have been added or altered in your level. This can greatly speed up rebuild time, especially on larger levels.
Build Paths	This command will allow you to construct the paths that AI-controlled creatures and bots use to navigate the level. Paths can be constructed from a variety of Actors, and it is the location of these that is used to calculate the path.
Build Changed Paths	Just like Build Changed Lights, this will only build the paths that have been modified or had an Actor added to them.

TABLE A.2 Continued

Build All	This button rebuilds Geometry, Lights, and AI Navigation paths in the level. This can take considerable time depending on system speed and the size of your level.
Build Options	This button initializes the Build Options window, within which you can change a variety of options on how levels are rebuilt. You can then use the Build button at the bottom to rebuild the level instantly, or use the settings later when you click the Build All button.

Play Level

This button (see **FIGURE A.11**) will launch your map inside Unreal, so that it can be play-tested. This will become one of your favorite buttons on the interface.

FIGURE A.11 Play Level button.

Help

This button (**SEE FIGURE A.12**) accesses the contextual help, which, at the time of this writing, is non-functional.

FIGURE A.12 Help button.

The Toolbox

The toolbox (see **FIGURE A.13**) contains a huge selection of necessary tools for constructing levels inside UnrealEd. Many of these you will use numerous times throughout the level design process. In this section, we will cover each of the buttons on the toolbox, and their various uses and parameters. The toolbox is broken up into five sections, and each section is expandable and collapsible. Also note that along the right side of the toolbox is a very thin green scrollbar for moving through the list of tools if your window is not big enough to see them all.

The following sections will walk you through the numerous tools and utilities available in each section of the toolbox.

FIGURE A.13 The toolbox.

Camera and Utilities Area

This area of the toolbox contains several tools for controlling your camera and other utilities that are used for a variety of functions within UnrealEd. See **FIGURE A.14**. Each of these tools and their settings will be covered in the following sections.

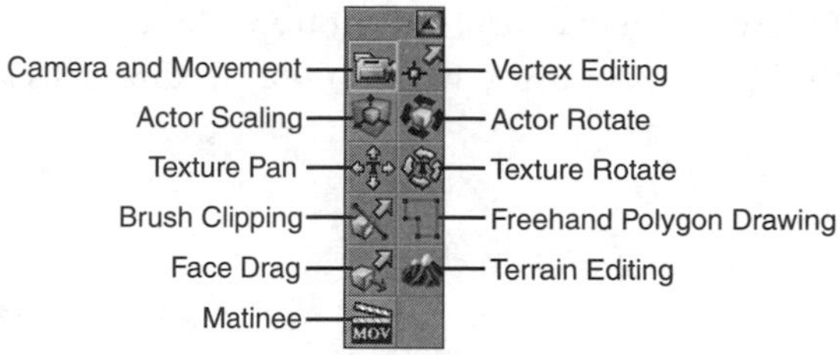

FIGURE A.14 Camera and Utilities area.

Camera and Movement

This tool is designed for manipulating the camera. At first, this may seem a bit curious, as you can always manipulate the camera with the proper mouse controls. However, aside from allowing you to move the camera as all modes do, this is a general editing mode, which allows you to place, move, select, edit, and delete actors and brushes.

Vertex Editing

Activating this tool will allow you to manipulate the vertices on a brush by selecting the vertices, holding the Ctrl key, and left-dragging.

Actor Scaling

As the name suggests, this tool allows you to scale Actors. To use the tool, simply activate it, and select a brush or other Actor. Then, hold down Ctrl and the right or left mouse button, and drag to adjust scale. Dragging with the left mouse will scale in the X axis, right will scale in Y, and left and right together will scale in Z. In this way, you can quickly and easily scale your Actors in the 3D and 2D views.

Actor Rotate

This tool allows you to rotate your Actors. It may be used in the 2D or 3D views, and works in a very similar fashion to the Actor Scaling tool, in that it allows for transformation on all three axes. To use it, activate Actor Rotate, hold down Ctrl, and then drag with the mouse buttons. Left mouse allows you to rotate in Y, right mouse allows you to rotate in Z, and left and right together allow for rotation in X. You can rotate Actors without this tool by using Ctrl+right-drag, but that only allows for rotation in one axis.

Texture Pan

This tool allows for panning of textures across the surface of a brush. It can only be used in the 3D view, as that is the only viewport in which textures can be seen. To use the tool, activate it in the toolbox, and select a texture by left-clicking on the surface to which it has been applied. Then, holding down Ctrl, drag with the left or right mouse button to slide the texture. Holding the left mouse button will pan the texture in the U direction, and the right mouse button will pan it in the V direction. If you have multiple textures selected, you can pan them simultaneously.

Texture Rotate

With this tool you can change the orientation of textures across a surface. Functionally, it works much like the Texture Pan tool. Simply invoke the tool, select any number of textures by left-clicking them in the 3D view (Ctrl+clicking if you want more than one), and then holding Ctrl and dragging with either left or right mouse to rotate the texture.

> **NOTE**
>
> **When you rotate a texture, you also rotate its axis. This means that, for example, if you rotate a texture 45 degrees to the right, when you use the Texture Pan tool, that texture will pan at that angle and not in the same direction it did prior to rotation.**

Brush Clipping

This tool can be used to dramatically change the shape of a brush by clipping it, or, in effect, cutting off one end of it. For more information on this tool, see Chapter 4.

Freehand Polygon Drawing

With this tool, you can create more complex brushes by placing a series of vertices to create the outline of a shape, and then extruding it outward, or adding depth (thickness) to it. For more information on this tool, see Chapter 4.

Face Drag

This tool allows you to pull the faces of a brush, so that you can sculpt the shape of your brush quickly. For more information on this tool see Chapter 4.

Terrain Editing

This button brings up the Terrain Editor window, which will allow you to create various types of natural-looking terrains by creating 2D monochromatic height maps. This window and all of its functionality are covered in Chapter 5.

Matinee

This button invokes the Matinee window, which allows for the creation of animated movies and cutscenes using the Unreal Engine. Matinee is covered thoroughly in Chapter 13.

Brush Clipping Area

This area (see **FIGURE A.15**) contains a few tools to control how brushes can be manipulated through clipping. Clipping brushes can be a great way to create unique simple shapes for your level quickly, without having to resort to a static mesh. The tools in this area are covered thoroughly in Chapter 4.

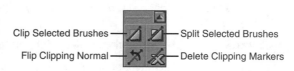

FIGURE A.15 Brush Clipping area.

Brush Primitives Area

This area (see **FIGURE A.16**) contains all of the primitive shapes that can be applied to the Builder brush in order to add or subtract matter and thereby shape your level. In this section, we will cover all of these primitives in detail. Right-clicking on any of the buttons in this area will bring up a dialog from which you can adjust the parameters for that specific primitive shape. After a description of each of the primitives, their respective parameters will be explained. If a parameter is repeated on another primitive, it will only be explained once, rather than repeating a definition.

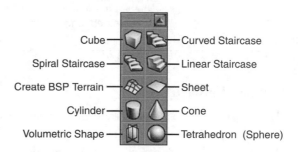

FIGURE A.16 Brush Primitives area.

Cube

The Cube button will change the Builder brush into a cube for you to use to create your level. Cubes will usually be one of the most frequently used shapes in your level-building arsenal. In **TABLE A.3** you can see the construction parameters for the cube, available in the CubeBuilder window.

TABLE A.3 CubeBuilder Parameters

`Height`	Naturally, this controls the height of the cube from which the Builder brush will be created. This height is defined in the direction of the Z-axis.
`Width`	This controls the width of the brush that will be created. The width is defined in the direction of the Y-axis.
`Breadth`	This controls the breadth of the resulting Builder brush. Breadth is defined by the direction of the X-axis.

TABLE A.3 Continued

`WallThickness`	This controls the thickness of each of the sides of the brush. The value of `WallThickness` is only relevant if the `Hollow` parameter is set to `True`.
`GroupName`	This option allows you to place your brush into a group.
`Hollow`	This parameter works in tandem with the `WallThickness` setting. When this parameter is activated, or set to `True`, your cube will be constructed like an empty box, rather than a constant object.
`Tessellated`	This divides each of the faces of the object into triangles rather than quadrangles. Tessellating your brush is a key step if you plan to do vertex editing, as such actions can cause the faces of your object to possibly become nonplanar, resulting in the Hall of Mirrors effect. If each face is three-sided, and not four, it becomes impossible to generate a nonplanar face.

Curved Staircase

The Curved Staircase is a set of stairs that run all the way up from the floor. As such, it should not be used to create staircases that spiral upward and wrap over themselves numerous times. For such staircases, use the Spiral Staircase brush described in **TABLE A.4**. Also, keep in mind that this particular brush will create a large number of BSP tessellations, which can quickly slow down your level. As such, this brush is rarely used in modern Unreal games, and a static mesh is used whenever such an object is needed.

TABLE A.4 CurvedStairBuilder Parameters

`InnerRadius`	This controls the inside radius of the Curved Staircase. It must have a value of at least 1. You would want this to be large if you wanted your staircase to travel around an object or area.
`StepHeight`	This value controls the height of each step. This value, multiplied by the number of steps, is the total height of the staircase.
`StepWidth`	This value is used to determine the width of each step. Adding this value to the `InnerRadius` will give you the total radius of the staircase. For instance, if you had an `InnerRadius` value of 128, and a `StepWidth` value of 256, the total radius, or radius from the center of the staircase, would be 384 units.
`AngleOfCurve`	As the name states, this gives you control over the curve angle of the staircase. Because the stairs are solid and extend up from the ground level, a curve angle greater than 270 degrees would cause the stairs to wrap over themselves.

TABLE A.4 Continued

`NumSteps`	This value controls the total number of stairs on the staircase. Multiplying this value by the height of each step will give you the total height of the staircase.
`AddToFirstStep`	This parameter basically offsets the entire staircase by the number of units entered. For example, if you need your staircase to begin 256 units in the air, you can enter that value here, and it will be added to the height of the first step and to every step thereafter.
`GroupName`	**See Table A.3.**
`CounterClockwise`	When this value is set to `True`, your staircase will wind in a counterclockwise direction. If this value is set to `False`, your stairs will wind clockwise instead.

Spiral Staircase

This primitive is similar to the Curved Staircase described in the preceding section, but does not extend from the floor. Rather, each section of the staircase is only as thick as each individual stair, meaning that you can create a staircase that wraps over itself numerous times, rotating greater than 360 degrees. As with the Curved Staircase, you will usually want to use a static mesh whenever you need such a shape. In **TABLE A.5** you can see the parameters for creating the Spiral Staircase.

TABLE A.5 SpiralStairBuilder Parameters

`InnerRadius`	**See Table A.4.**
`StepWidth`	**See Table A.4.**
`StepHeight`	**See Table A.4.**
`StepThickness`	This value will define how thick each step will be. This does not have any effect on the height of the staircase, only on the way the staircase appears. For instance, if the `StepHeight` value is 16, and the `StepThickness` value is set to 8, each of the steps would be 8 units thick, and there would be an 8-unit gap between each step.
`NumStepsPer360`	This value controls the number of steps in a single 360-degree revolution. For example, if this value is set to 60, it would take exactly 60 steps to complete one full 360-degree revolution.

TABLE A.5 Continued

`NumSteps`	This will be the actual number of stairs in the staircase. It is used in combination with the `NumStepsPer360` value to control how far the staircase will revolve as it goes up. For example, if our `NumStepsPer360` was still set to 60, and `NumSteps` was only 26, we would get half of one revolution, or a 180-degree spiral staircase. However, we have to add one extra stair into this value to get the desired rotation. So we would actually need 61 stairs to get one full 360-degree revolution. As a side note, you can solve for the total number of steps you need to get a certain rotation with the following math equation: ((`NumStepsPer360` * <desired rotation angle>) / 360)+1 = `NumSteps` So, if 60 steps were in each full 360-degree rotation, and we needed 270 degrees of rotation, the equation would solve like this: ((60 * 270) / 360) +1 = 46 This means that we would need exactly 46 stairs in our staircase to achieve precisely 270 degrees of rotation.
`GroupName`	**See Table A.3.**
`SlopedCeiling`	If this value is set to `True`, the underside of the staircase will be a smooth ramp. If, however, it is set to `False`, the underside of the stairs will be stepped instead. Essentially, this aligns the two vertices at the bottom rear of each stair to the two vertices at the bottom front of the next stair.
`SlopedFloor`	Very much like `SlopedCeiling`, but this value actually controls whether the bottom surfaces of the stairs are sloped. In effect, this creates a spiral ramp, rather than a staircase as such.
`CounterClockwise`	**See Table A.4.**

Linear Staircase

This will change the Builder brush into a staircase that moves in a straight line, rather than curving at all. As such, it is quite simple to use. Still, it will be far more efficient for your level to use a static mesh instead of this brush. **TABLE A.6** shows the parameters for the Linear Staircase.

TABLE A.6 LinearStairBuilder Parameters

`StepLength`	This value sets the length, from front to back, for each step. Multiplying this by the `NumSteps` value will give you the total length of the staircase.
`StepWidth`	**See Table A.5.**
`StepHeight`	**See Table A.5.**

TABLE A.6 Continued

NumSteps	See Table A.5.
AddToFirstStep	See Table A.4.
GroupName	See Table A.3.

Create BSP Terrain

This will allow you to create a basic terrain, or many other possible objects. The brush itself is essentially a cube in which one side has been tessellated so that you may safely and easily edit its vertices to form an object. Keep in mind that it will almost always be a better idea to use the actual terrain system to create landforms. For more information on UnrealEd's terrain system, please refer to Chapter 5. **TABLE A.7** lists the parameters for the Terrain Builder.

TABLE A.7 TerrainBuilder Parameters

Height	See Table A.3.
Width	See Table A.3.
Breadth	See Table A.3.
WidthSegments	This value controls the number of divisions that are tessellated along the width of the brush.
DepthSegments	This value controls the number of divisions that are tessellated along the breadth of the brush.
GroupName	See Table A.3.

Sheet

This command changes the Builder brush into a single plane, or four-sided polygon. It will be created as a rectangle, but its vertices can be edited later. This brush can never block a player. **TABLE A.8** shows the parameters for this brush.

TABLE A.8 SheetBuilder Parameters

Height	See Table A.3.
Width	See Table A.3.
HorizBreaks	This value controls the number of divisions in the surface along its width. For instance, setting this to 3 would divide the plane into four equal segments along its width.

TABLE A.8 Continued

`VertBreaks`	This parameter is exactly like `HorizBreaks`, except that it adds divisions along the height of the plane instead of the width.
`Axis`	This setting controls the orientation of the brush at the time of its creation.
`GroupName`	**See Table A.3.**

Cylinder

This will generate a cylindrical Builder brush, good for pillars, pipes, soda cans, raised daises, and just about anything else that is...well...cylindrical. In most modern Unreal games, however, it will be used mostly for cylindrically shaped rooms, and objects like pipes, pillars, soda cans, and so forth will be created with static meshes. **TABLE A.9** shows the parameters for the Cylinder brush.

TABLE A.9 CylinderBuilder Parameters

`Height`	**See Table A.3.**
`OuterRadius`	This is the overall radius of the cylinder, calculated from its center.
`InnerRadius`	This setting is similar to `WallThickness` on the Cube primitive, except that this will not cap off the ends. The effect is a pipe-like object. This setting is only relevant if `Hollow` is set to `True`.
`Sides`	This controls the number of polygons that will be created around the cylinder. It must have a value of at least 3.
`GroupName`	**See Table A.3.**
`AlignToSide`	If this setting is `True`, the cylinder will be oriented so that the bottom-most face is parallel to the XY plane, which means that the bottom of the brush would essentially be a flat face. If the value is `False`, however, the bottom of the brush will be a corner.
`Hollow`	**See Table A.3.**

Cone

You can think of this primitive as a cylinder in which all of the faces at one end have been collapsed down to a single point. **TABLE A.10** shows the Cone brush's creation parameters.

TABLE A.10 Cone Brush Creation Parameters

`Height`	**See Table A.3.**
`CapHeight`	This setting is only valid if `Hollow` is set to `True`. This controls how high the inside cap of the brush is. For example, if you were creating a cone-shaped room from a hollow cone, this setting would control the thickness of the floor.
`OuterRadius`	This is the total radius of the cone, as calculated from the center.
`InnerRadius`	This value is equal to the distance in units from the center of the cone to the inside edge of the cone. Naturally, this is only valid if `Hollow` is set to `True`.
`Sides`	**See Table A.9.**
`GroupName`	**See Table A.3.**
`AlignToSide`	**See Table A.9.**
`Hollow`	**See Table A.3.**

Volumetric Shape

This primitive is a great tool for creating various texture effects, such as fire, smoke, plasma, trees, and chains, where perfect three-dimensional detail is not necessary or the excess geometric detail would become suboptimal. It actually consists of a number of sheet brushes rotated about their pivot point in the Z-axis. **TABLE A.11** shows the creation parameters for the Volumetric Shape.

TABLE A.11 VolumetricBuilder Parameters

`Height`	**See Table A.3.**
`Radius`	This setting controls the distance each sheet will extend from the center of the brush.
`NumSheets`	This is the number of actual sheet brushes used to generate the volumetric shape.
`GroupName`	**See Table A.3.**

Tetrahedron (Sphere)

This is the closest object to a sphere that you can achieve with a brush. It is a spherical brush composed completely of triangles. As such, it can potentially form a very dense surface, geometrically speaking, but provides very smooth results. **TABLE A.12** shows the creation parameters for the Tetrahedron.

TABLE A.12 TetrahedronBuilder Parameters

`Radius`	See Table A.11.
`SphereExtrapolation`	This setting controls how smooth the sphere will be by adjusting the size of the triangles that it is composed of. The higher the number, the more triangles are in the sphere, and the smaller those triangles will be. You could think of this as the resolution of the tetrahedron. This setting raises the density of the tetrahedron's geometry exponentially, so you will find that a value of 7 will give you a ridiculously dense sphere.
`GroupName`	See Table A.3.

A

CSG Operations Area

The tools in this area (see **FIGURE A.17**) are designed to allow you to construct your level through the volumetric modeling method of Constructive Solid Geometry (CSG). In essence, this is where you go to add, subtract, intersect, or deintersect your brushes from the world of mass that exists within your level. Also in this area, you will find commands for adding a variety of special-purpose brushes and static meshes. For more information on CSG, see Chapter 4.

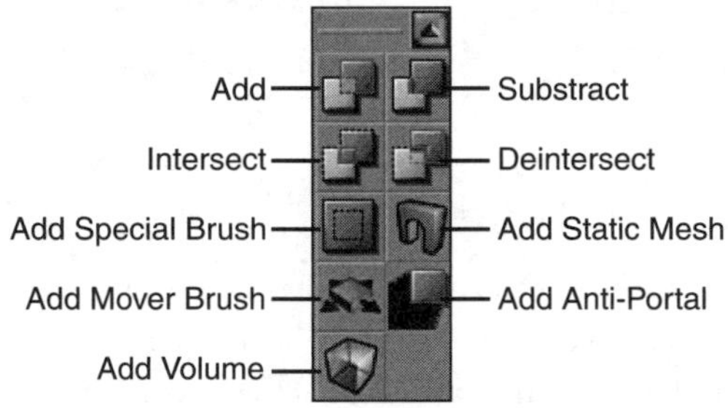

FIGURE A.17 CSG Operations area.

Add

This command will create an additive brush in the world, basically inserting mass back into a negative space that you have created. The new brush will be generated in the exact same location and shape as the Builder brush. Also, the texture that you have selected in the Textures browser will be applied to the new brush. The resulting additive brush will have a tell-tale blue wireframe, so that you are able to identify it as additive in a 2D view.

Subtract

This command is essentially the inverse of Add. Rather than inserting volume into your level, this command will take it away. This command is typically the first one used to create a level, as you need to remove volume from the solid mass of the Unreal universe to create a space within which to build a level. As with Add, the new brush will be in the same position and shape as the Builder brush, but will have a yellow wireframe in the 2D view to distinguish it as a subtractive brush. Also, the selected texture within the Textures browser will be applied to the inside of the object.

Intersect

The Intersect command only affects the Builder brush. It checks the BSP geometry within your level to see where the brush is intersecting, or passing into another brush. The command then performs a Boolean operation on the Builder brush, based on whether the brush that is intersecting with the Builder brush is additive or subtractive.

If the Builder brush is intersecting with an additive brush at the time of the command, only the area of the Builder brush that is actually passing into the additive brush will remain. The rest of the Builder brush, or the area of the brush that existed outside the additive brush, will be deleted.

If, instead, the brush that is intersecting with the Builder brush is subtractive, the result will be exactly the opposite. The area of the Builder brush that falls within the intersecting subtractive brush will be deleted, and only the area that was outside of the subtractive brush will remain. For tutorials involving this function, see Chapter 4.

> **NOTE**
>
> **Your Builder brush can be intersecting both an additive and subtractive brush simultaneously when you perform this command. This can yield some very interesting results. Experiment, and see what you can come up with.**

Deintersect

This command is, in effect, the exact opposite of Intersect. It essentially performs the same checks on the geometry surrounding the Builder brush, but performs an opposite Boolean operation than Intersect. This means that when the Builder brush is passing into a subtractive brush, only the area of the Builder brush that falls within the subtractive brush will be kept, and the area that falls outside the subtractive brush will be deleted.

Conversely, if the Builder brush is intersecting an additive brush, the area of the Builder brush that falls outside of the additive shape will be kept, and the area of actual intersection will be deleted.

Add Special Brush

This command will bring up the Add Special dialog (see **FIGURE A.18**). From here, you can create a variety of brushes for specific effect and optimization purposes. Because these types of brushes are not used very often, they have all been grouped within this single command, rather than each having a separate command of their own.

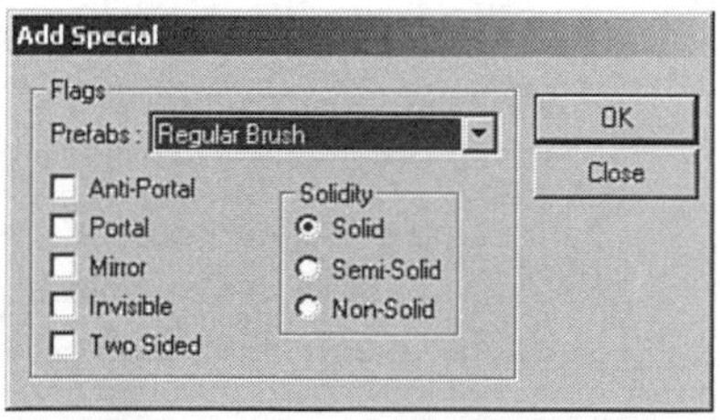

FIGURE A.18 Add Special dialog.

A variety of special brushes can be created from this dialog by either selecting one or more check boxes and a radio button for solidity, or selecting a Prefab from the drop-down list. **TABLE A.13** shows the options found under the Add Special dialog.

TABLE A.13 Add Special Options

Check Boxes	
Anti-Portal	This option turns your Special brush into an Antiportal. An Antiportal speeds up the rendering of a level by occluding geometry that falls behind it. This works to speed up your level in that objects in your scene may still be rendering, even though they are not visible in your view. As long as an Actor falls on the opposite side of an Antiportal, it will not render at all. You will not want these to be within the open space of your level, but hidden within another object. For example, if you have two bases that are built on opposite sides of a hill in your level, the rendering engine will still be rendering those objects, even though you are on the opposite side of the hill and cannot see them. If you were to place an Anti-Portal sheet inside the hill, the base on the opposite side of the hill will not render, and your level will move faster. For more information see Chapter 15.
Portal	Having this option selected will allow you to create a portal. Portals are used for zoning levels into separate areas to optimize the speed of rendering, or to designate certain areas of the map. Essentially, if no part of the portal is visible (whether the Invisible setting is checked or not), what is located behind it will not render. As such, it is a good idea to place these in corridors that separate rooms, so that the room at the other end of the corridor will not render if you do not see the portal. These are covered in finer detail in Chapter 15.
Mirror	This makes it so that all faces of a brush are tagged as Mirror. Doing this will cause all the faces to reflect the environment like a mirror.
Invisible	Simply put, this setting will disable visibility for your selected Special brush. Several of the prefabs use this feature. The wireframe for brushes created with this setting alone will be pink.
Two Sided	This setting will cause your Special brush to be double-sided, which means it will have a front and back side. This will cause the effect of your Special brush to be visible regardless of on which side you are positioned. For example, if you create a sheet brush without checking Two Sided, you will only be able to see one side of the brush, the positive side of the polygons. If you check Two Sided, both sides will be visible.

A

Solidity

Solidity for brushes does not immediately mean exactly what you may assume, in that it does not *only* specify whether an Actor can interact or pass through an object. It also deals with the way your BSP is divided in your level. Because the standard brushes created in your level are solid by default, a solid brush created from the Add Special window will work exactly like a normal added brush. For more information on brush solidity, see Chapter 4.

Prefabs

Prefabs are predesigned combinations of various settings from the Add Special dialog that are commonly used together. **TABLE A.14** lists the Prefabs in the Add Special window with a brief description, as well as the settings that are activated to create each one. You can then review the setting descriptions in **TABLE A.13** to get a thorough explanation of how each brush works.

TABLE A.14 Add Special Prefabs

Invisible Collision Hull	This brush is used to either create a surface over a non-collidable object to serve as a basis for collisions, or to simplify the collisions of a complex object, such as a static mesh. Note: These are overly complicated and can cause BSP problems; therefore, use Blocking Volumes instead. Settings: Invisible, Semi-Solid
Zone Portal	This is a portal specially designed to help zone your levels for optimization or to designate certain areas (such as the Blue Base). For more information see Chapter 15. Settings: Portal, Invisible, Non-Solid
Anti-Portal	As mentioned in **TABLE A.13**, these will obscure any Actors that fall behind them. For more information see Chapter 15. Settings: Anti-Portal, Invisible, Non-Solid
Regular Brush	Using this brush is the same as creating a normal additive brush. Settings: Solid
Semi-Solid Brush	As the name suggests, this simply creates a regular semi-solid brush with no other special attributes. Settings: Semi-Solid
Non-Solid Brush	This generates a Non-Solid brush with no other special attributes. Settings: Non-Solid

Add Static Mesh

This can be used to convert a brush into a static mesh. To use it, just click on a brush or static mesh, and a dialog appears so that you may choose the package, group, and name for your new static mesh. Keep in mind that this is a rather inefficient way to create static meshes, and in no way should be used to replace a 3D application such as Alias Maya.

Add Mover Brush

Although the name of this tool suggests that you are creating a brush, Add Mover actually creates a special kind of static mesh that can move throughout your scene. These can be a wide variety of objects in your level: doors, elevators, moving platforms, and so on. These objects and the methods for using them are covered in Chapter 9.

Add Anti-Portal

This tool generates an Antiportal actor. This actor gives you increased control over the Antiportal, allowing you to toggle it on and off as well as associating it with Movers. Otherwise, it works much the same as the Antiportal brush described in **TABLE A.14**. The wireframe for these objects is orange. For more information see Chapter 15.

Add Volume

This tool allows you to create a volume. These are used to specify three-dimensional areas within the level where environmental conditions can be altered, such as underwater areas. These are covered in depth in Chapter 6.

Selections and Movement Area

This area has a variety of commands that you can use to control what you see in the viewport, as well as change the behavior of the camera. See **FIGURE A.19**.

Show Selected Actors Only

This operation allows you to hide all actors that are not currently selected. The BSP brushes within the level will be hidden in the 2D views, but will remain visible in the 3D view. This form of isolated viewing is good for fine-tuning specific areas without having to deal with the clutter of surrounding actors.

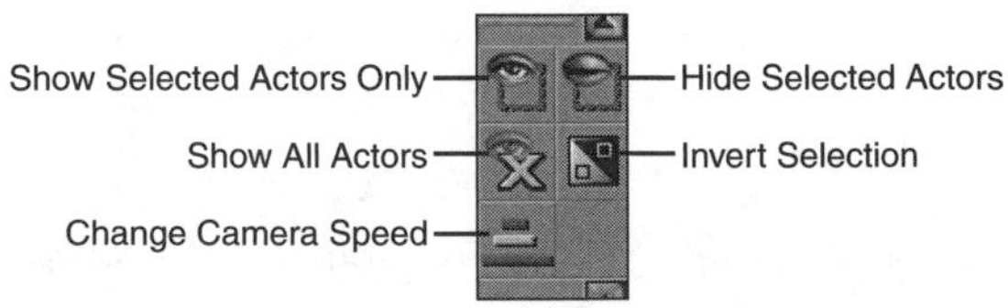

FIGURE A.19 Selections and Movement area.

Hide Selected Actors

This will hide only those Actors that are selected in a level. This is convenient if you are finished tweaking the locations, settings, textures, and so on of a set of Actors and need to move on to another area. You can hide the Actors you are finished with, and move on to others without filling your view needlessly. As with the Show Selected Actors Only command, the BSP brushes within the level will still be visible in the 3D view.

Show All Actors

This command will unhide all Actors in your level. If you have been hiding Actors, and seem to have misplaced one or two, be sure you click this button before you replace them.

Invert Selection

This is another of those special commands where the name really seems to say it all. This will deselect any currently selected actors, and instead select all actors that were not included in the original selection.

Change Camera Speed

This button gives you direct control over the speed at which your camera moves through the viewports. It has three separate settings, which you can switch through by clicking the button repeatedly. The second, or middle speed, is the default setting.

Mirroring and Miscellaneous Area

The commands in this area are designed to allow you to mirror your brushes along all three axes to achieve symmetry in your level. Also within this area are some tools to simplify the selection of several different objects as you work. See **FIGURE A.20**.

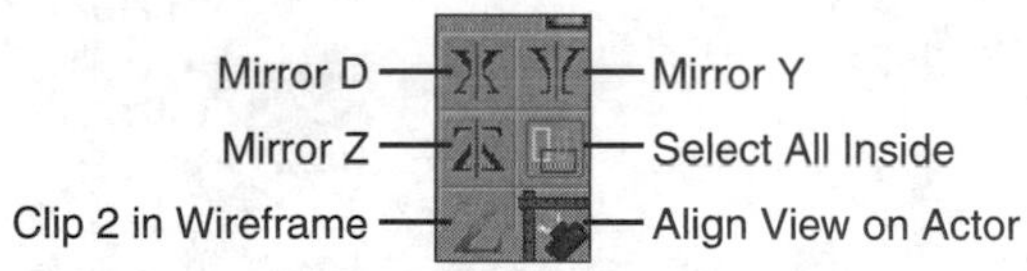

FIGURE A.20 Mirroring and Miscellaneous area.

Mirror X

This tool will mirror your Builder brush in the X-axis.

Mirror Y

This tool will mirror your Builder brush in the Y-axis.

Mirror Z

You guessed it! This mirrors your Builder brush in the Z-axis. (Never saw *that* coming, did you?)

Select All Inside

This handy little command will select all objects that either intersect with or fall within the 3D area of the Builder brush.

Clip Z in Wireframe

In newer versions of UnrealEd, this has been disabled.

Align View on Actor

This will position the cameras of all viewports to view the selected actor. This is extremely handy when you're in Vertex Editing mode.

The Viewports

One of the most important aspects of the UnrealEd interface is the viewport. Viewports are our windows into the Unreal world (see **FIGURE A.21**). We use them to see our work, verify placement of objects, and to preview our levels as we construct. This section will discuss the UnrealEd viewports along with their various capabilities.

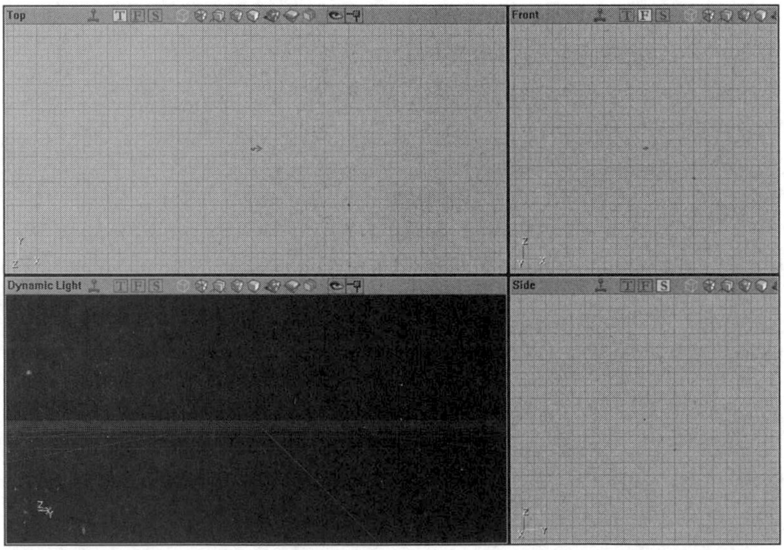

FIGURE A.21 The viewports.

The viewports in UnrealEd basically come in two different flavors. The first one that strikes our attention is the Dynamic Lighting view, often called the 3D view for short. This is, by default, the viewport in the lower left, and is the only view that actually offers us a perspective view of our level, meaning that it displays depth. It also displays the textures and lighting that have been applied to the Actors within the level. The 3D view, however, does have a weakness: It is very difficult (if not impossible) to gauge the precise location of specific objects, such as brushes and static meshes, within this viewport.

It is for this reason that the 2D views exist. They do not display depth of any kind, nor do they display any of the textures applied to your level. So, although your level will appear very much as if it were in blueprint form, you will have very precise control over exactly where each object is located within your level. These views display from three different angles: Top, Front, and Side.

You will notice that in the lower-left corner of each of the viewports you see a small icon representing the direction of the world coordinate axes. These will display the direction that each axis is pointing at all times, which will become very important as you work. This is especially true in the perspective window, in which you are constantly moving and rotating the camera.

Viewport Controls

There are many places within the editor that you can control the viewports. One of the first of these is within the View menu. In this menu, you will see the Viewports submenu near the bottom (see **FIGURE A.22**). From this submenu you can access a few commands to control various aspects of your viewports. These are described in **TABLE A.15**.

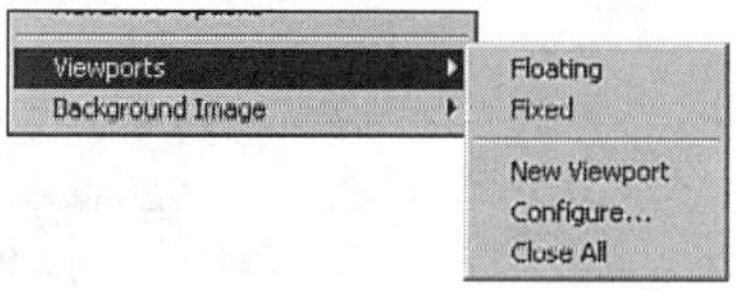

FIGURE A.22 Viewport controls.

TABLE A.15 Viewports Submenu Options

Floating	This command turns each of the viewports into separate windows that can be moved anywhere on the screen. This can be very handy if you want to maximize a particular viewport to fill your screen, or just need to move the viewports out of your way when working.
Fixed	This is the opposite of *floating*. This locks your viewports back into their original positions.
New Viewport	This command is only accessible when the viewports are floating. It allows you to create a new viewport, and set its display properties just as you would any other. In this way, you may have as many viewports as you feel you need.
Configure	This brings up the Viewport Configuration window. Here, you can adjust the layout of your viewports in the manner illustrated on each button. This will work whether your viewports are floating or fixed.
Close All	You can use this to close all of the viewports... if, for some reason, you should feel the need to do that.

Just below the Viewports submenu, you will find one of the less practical (but still pretty cool) features in UnrealEd. This is the Background Image submenu. This allows you to insert a bitmap into UnrealEd that actually displays *behind* the viewports. If you've got all of your viewports opened up or maximized, you won't get to see it, but it can still be a neat way to personalize your workspace a little.

Viewport Control Bar

Each of the viewports has a bar across the top with a selection of buttons. These invoke different view modes and options for each viewport. The following is a list of each of these available controls and what their uses are.

A

From left to right, the first thing you will see in the Viewport Control bar is the current mode of the viewport you're looking at. Examples would be Dynamic Lighting, Lighting Only, Texture Usage, and so on. You can read more about each of these view modes in the following sections. **FIGURE A.23** shows this bar and various modes available from it.

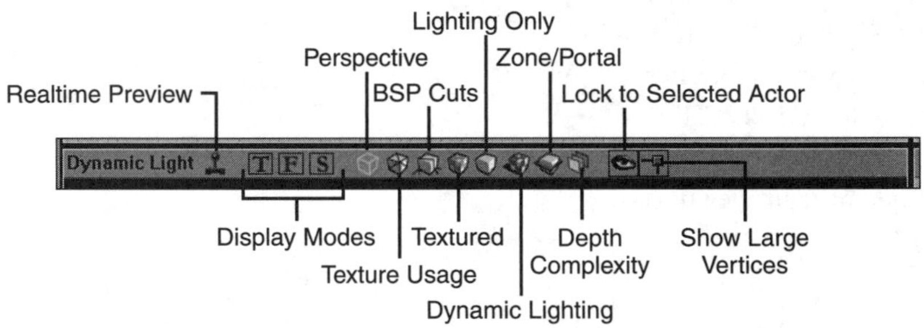

FIGURE A.23 Viewport Control bar.

Realtime Preview

This button will allow you to view any animated effects and textures in motion, as they will appear in the game. This only has a dramatic effect in the 3D view.

Display Modes

The first three Display Mode buttons control the type of 2D view you would like to use. The T, F, and S icons represent Top, Front, and Side, respectively. These will allow you to switch quickly between these three modes.

The next several buttons across the Viewport Control bar control a variety of display modes, which work specifically for the 3D View.

Perspective

This display mode will show your level in a three-dimensional wireframe. The brushes in your scene will be color-coded as they are in the 2D views. The hotkey combination for enabling this mode is Alt+1.

Texture Usage

This display mode will remove all lighting and show a different color for each individual texture displayed in your level. It has no effect on static meshes. This can be a good way to diagnose whether there are areas of the map that have perhaps too many textures, which could possibly be making high demands on the graphics engine. The hotkey for this display mode is Alt+3.

BSP Cuts

In previous versions of UnrealEd, this was used to display the locations in your map where cuts or tessellations in the BSP had been made. This mode is no longer completely functional, and will only display your BSP in white. The hotkey for this mode is Alt+4.

Textured

This display mode will show only the textures on your objects, not the lighting. This is a good way to ascertain texture placement without having to worry about how lights are affecting your scene. You must be careful, however, as many textures will look dramatically different when lighting is applied to them. The hotkey for this is Alt+6.

Lighting Only

This display mode will strip away all textures on your level and show only how light is playing on each surface. All surfaces, BSP or otherwise, will be rendered in white, and are only affected by the color and type of light that is striking them. This is especially useful for controlling the exact effect of shadows in your level. The hotkey for this is Alt+0.

Dynamic Lighting

This is the default display mode for the 3D view. It displays all lighting and texturing within the level. This is exactly how you would see the level within the game while you play. Despite the name, however, this will not show dynamic lighting effects, such as triggered flashes. To see these kinds of effects, you need to enable Realtime Preview, explained under "Realtime Preview." The hotkey to enable this mode is Alt+5.

Zone/Portal

This display mode will show each zone of your level in a different color. This is an invaluable mode for level optimization, and is discussed thoroughly in Chapter 15. Incidentally, this mode will also display any BSP cuts in your level in varying shades of the color in which the current zone is rendering. Therefore, if you need to see cuts in your BSP, be sure to use this mode rather than BSP Cuts mode. The hotkey for this display mode is Alt+2.

Depth Complexity

When using the Depth Complexity mode, you see how many textures are being drawn over a given part of the screen. This is useful when determining where terrain layers, deco layers, particles, and so on have become too dense. After you switch over to this mode, a bar appears on the right side of the viewport with a gradient from green to red. Green areas of the viewport represent areas that have but one texture. When an area is covered with more and more textures, that area will shift towards red. If the area goes beyond red, it simply loops back through the gradient to start again. If this happens, you may want to consider decreasing the amount of textures covering the same area.

Lock to Selected Actor

The next button in the Viewport Control bar is not a display mode; rather, it is a very handy tool to relocate objects in your level. This tool snaps the camera to the location of the selected object, and then attaches that object to the camera. In effect, it's a lot like dragging your Actor around with a tow truck. To use the Lock to Selected Actor function, click on it to enable it, and then left-click on an actor within your level. Your camera will jump to the current location and orientation of the Actor that you selected. Then, move your camera around using your standard viewport controls. When your camera is in the desired location for your Actor, disable Lock to Selected Actor, and move your camera. You will see that the Actor is now in the position the camera was when Lock to Selected Actor was disabled.

Show Large Vertices

This will display the vertices of a selected object as large, white, two-dimensional squares, making their selection very easy. This is a very convenient option for vertex editing.

Viewport Control Bar Context Menu

If you right-click on any of the control bars of any viewport, you will see a menu pop up that has a wide range of tools for controlling the behavior of your viewport. See **FIGURE A.24**. Because some of these have already been covered in the buttons described in the preceding section, we will only describe those that are entirely new.

Mode

This will set the current display mode for the viewport. These are the same as their corresponding buttons, described in the "Viewport Control Bar" section.

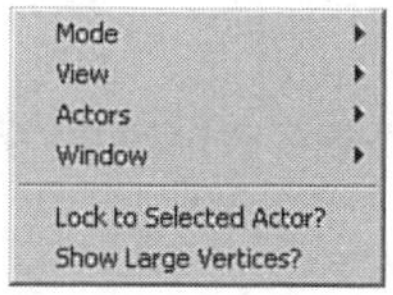

FIGURE A.24 Viewport Control Bar context menu.

View

This will control visibility for a variety of objects within your level. **TABLE A.16** lists and briefly describes each one of the options found in the View submenu.

TABLE A.16 View Submenu Options

Show Active Brush	Shows or hides the Builder brush.
Show Static Meshes	Shows or hides static meshes.
Show Moving Brushes	Shows or hides Movers.
Show Volumes	Shows Volume brushes such as waters and ladders.
Show Backdrop	Controls the visibility of the skybox. Skyboxes are covered in Chapter 5.
Show Coordinates	This option is not currently functional.
Show Paths	Shows AI Navigation paths.
Show Event Lines	Displays lines that connect Actors together who have matching `Tag` and `Event` properties.
Show Selection Highlight	Activates the effect on selected surfaces and Actors, which highlights them when selected. Surfaces are blue when selected, and Actors are green.
Show Terrain	Controls visibility of Terrain actors.
Show Distance Fog	Activates visibility for distance fog, provided you have generated it within your scene.
Matinee Rotations	At the time of this writing, this menu item is non-functional.
Matinee Paths	Activates visibility for Matinee interpolation paths.
Show Fluid Surfaces	Shows and hides Fluid Surfaces, which are tessellated planes that ripple like liquid.
Show Karma Primitives	Controls visibility of Karma objects, which are influenced by the Karma Physics engine.
Show Collision	Displays the collision wireframe around static meshes.

Actors

The context menu also offers an Actors submenu. Within this submenu, you will find the options shown in **TABLE A.17.**

TABLE A.17 Actors Submenu Options

Full Actor View	This resets the view to its default setting, deactivating any of the following options.
Information	This shows each Actor's name, as well as the values of their `Event` and `Tag` properties.
Icon View	This places an Eagle icon at the location of all Actors.
Radii View	For lights, this shows the `LightRadius` as a circle or sphere depending on whether you're in an orthographic viewport or perspective viewport respectively. For other colliding actors, it will show the collision height and radius as a cylinder.
Hide Actors	This hides all Actors, including static meshes, from the viewport.

Window

This submenu allows you to switch the viewport between 16- and 32-bit color. As the editor requires 32-bit color to run, this setting is irrelevant, and will not change.

The Console Bar

The final part of the UnrealEd user interface is the console bar (see **FIGURE A.25**). This strip across the bottom of the UI contains several tools for controlling UnrealEd's behavior, and methods to speed up level construction workflow.

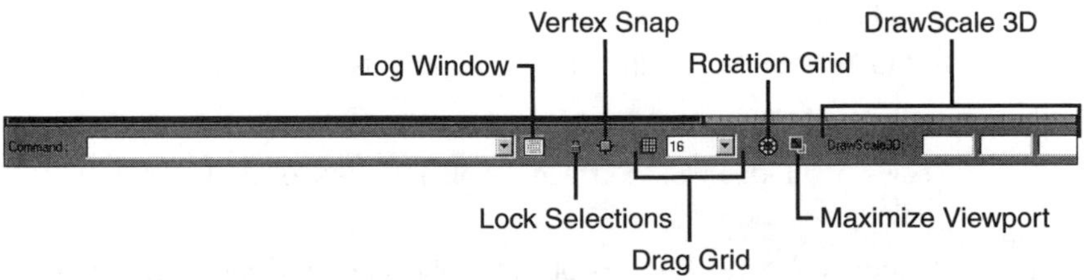

FIGURE A.25 The console bar.

The Text Field

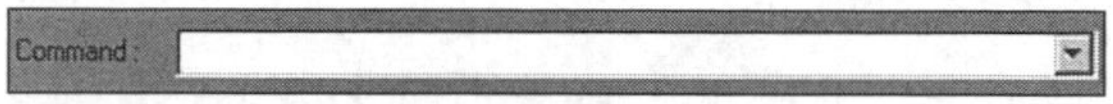

FIGURE A.26 The text field.

The text field (see **FIGURE A.26**) allows you to input console commands directly into UnrealEd. There are many of these, and they accomplish a wide variety of tasks, including returning feedback in the log or directly in the viewport. The prompt also works as a drop-down menu so that you may access commands that have been previously entered without having to rewrite them.

The Log Window

The Log window provides you with constant feedback from what is actually going on inside the editor as you work. There are many commands and queries in UnrealEd that only return data to the log.

Lock Selections

When this button is enabled, all Actors that were selected will remain selected and nothing else can be added or removed from the selection. When you are selecting surfaces with this button enabled, surface selection will behave as though you were holding down the Ctrl key.

Vertex Snap

In recent versions of Unreal, this is no longer used.

Drag Grid

This setting will snap entire brushes to points on the grid as they are moved around the level. This setting is dependent on the current Grid Size, which controls the distance that objects will snap when being moved. This is a very important option to have activated when constructing your level. Miniscule (or even imperceptible) distances that occur when aligning objects will have the same effect as tremendous distances. For example, if you are trying to connect two subtractive brushes to form a corridor, and there is a space between them that is even a fraction of a unit wide, the distance will still render as a wall, and will be completely impassible. Conversely, if your two subtractive brushes were intersecting into each other, you run the risk of creating BSP holes in your level.

Rotation Grid

This is another vital setting when creating your level. This setting will snap all rotations to a rotational grid composed of 64 grid divisions. This means that rotating one grid unit is equal to exactly 5.625 degrees (360 / 64 = 5.625). This is an invaluable tool when rotating objects in your level, as freely rotating to exact values is likely to be almost impossible. Even though your rotations might seem correct, there could be minor differences that would cause errors.

Maximize Viewport

This button will maximize the currently selected viewport, and it will restore a viewport to regular size if it is already maximized. This button is non-functional for older builds of Unreal.

DrawScale3D

This tool provides you with a simple method of object scaling. Each of the three numeric fields provides percentage-based scaling in the X, Y, and Z axes, respectively. The percentage system works such that 1.00 is equal to 100%, 0.5 would be equal to 50%, and so on.

Browsers

The assets needed to construct an Unreal level can all be accessed within the browsers. In this section you will see a description of each of these browsers, along with their respective functionality.

The Actor Class Browser

The Actor Class browser shown in **FIGURE A.27** lists all of the Actor classes available within Unreal. These Actor classes are used as a method of inserting Actors into your level. To do this, merely select the type of Actor you want from the list of classes, and then right-click in your viewport where you want the Actor to be placed. Then, from the popup menu, choose the third option, which will be "Add <*your selected Actor*> Here."

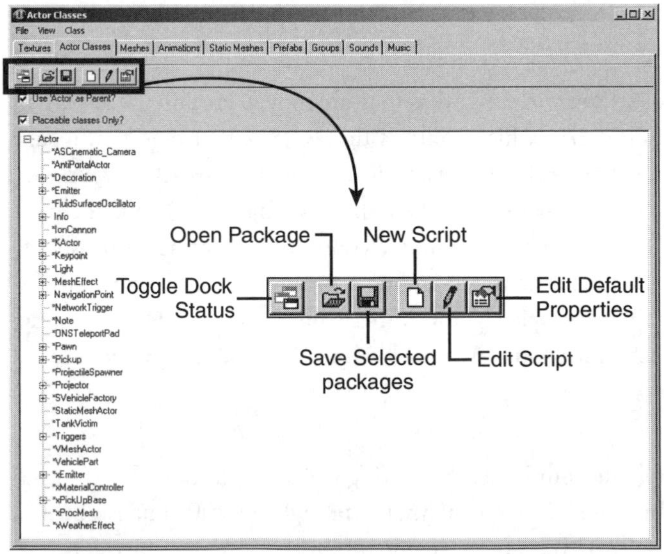

FIGURE A.27 The Actor Class browser.

The browser also has interface buttons and check boxes across the top. **TABLE A.18** lists each of these buttons and check boxes, and their functionality.

TABLE A.18 Actor Class Browser Options

Toggle Dock Status	This docks and undocks the browser from the Browser window. If undocked, the browser becomes a free-floating window that can be placed anywhere on the interface, and the browser's tab is removed from the main Browser window.
Open Package	This allows you to open packages of Actors so that you can insert their contents into your level. For more info on packages, please see the corresponding section in Chapter 1.
Save Selected Packages	This allows you to save packages if you have made any changes to their contents. To select a package for saving, you must first turn on Show Packages from the View menu at the top of the browser.
New Script	This allows you to create a new class using the UnrealScript Editor.
Edit Script	This allows you to access the source code for specific Actors and classes. This is the same as double-clicking the item in the list.
Edit Default Properties	This brings up the Properties window, and allows you to adjust what the settings of a specific Actor will be by default when it is added into your level.
Use Actor as Parent check box	This displays the head of the hierarchy tree as Actor, instead of Object.
Placeable Classes Only check box	This displays only classes containing Actors that can be placed in the scene.

Across the top of the browser is also a menu bar. **TABLE A.19** gives a comprehensive list of the menus and their functions. Any commands that were already covered in the interface buttons in **TABLE A.18** will be skipped.

TABLE A.19 Actor Class Browser Menus

File Menu	
Open Package	**Same as button described in Table A.18.**
Save Selected Packages	**Same as button described in Table A.18.**
Export Changed Scripts	Exports any class or Actor scripts that you might have changed to a folder containing .uc files so that they can be edited and rebuilt later.
Export All Scripts	Exports all Actor and class scripts to a series of folders and .uc files, so that you may edit them and rebuild them later.

TABLE A.19 Continued

View Menu	
Docked (Toggle)	**Same as Toggle Dock Status button described in Table A.18.**
Show Packages	Displays a check box list of all of the available packages. You must select a package by checking its box if you want to save it.
Class Menu	
New	**Same as New Script button described in Table A.18.**
New From Selection	Creates a new class within a selected package.
Edit Script	**Same as button described in Table A.18.**
Default Properties	**Same as Edit Default Properties button described in Table A.18.**

You may also double-click any Actor or class within the browser to access its source code. This is very handy if you need to quickly edit part of the programming code for a specific Actor or class. This is a great way to see "behind the scenes" of certain Actors and classes in order to see what makes them tick. It's also a good way to see how undocumented properties of an Actor or class work.

The Group Browser

The Group browser (see **FIGURE A.28**) allows you to create and manage groups of Actors in your scene. This can greatly increase the efficiency of your level as you work, as these groups can be hidden from within this browser. After you make a group, you can add objects into it, take them back out again, and edit the properties of objects within the group.

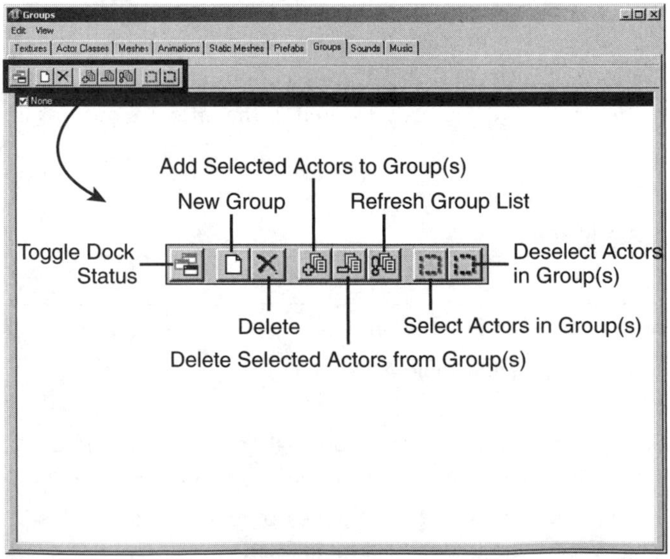

FIGURE A.28 The Group browser.

TABLE A.20 lists the buttons across the top of the browser.

TABLE A.20 Group Browser Buttons

Toggle Dock Status	This docks and undocks the browser from the Browser window. If undocked, the browser becomes a free-floating window that can be placed anywhere on the interface, and the browser's tab is removed from the main browser window.
New Group	This creates a new group that you can add Actors into, remove them from, edit, and so forth. A dialog appears that allows you to name the group. You may have one or several objects selected when you click this, and all will be added to the group.
Delete	This clears the selected group from the list.
Add Selected Actors to Group(s)	As the name suggests, this allows you to add selected objects into the group.
Delete Selected Actors from Group(s)	Once again, the name says it all here. This will remove any selected objects from the Group or Groups.
Refresh Group List	This button is intended to allow you to refresh the groups as you make changes in them. However, in more recent versions of the editor, this button is superfluous as the groups will update automatically as you perform actions upon them.
Select Actors in Group(s)	This selects Actors in the selected group.
Deselect Actors in Group(s)	Naturally, this deselects all Actors in the selected group.

Above these buttons on the browser is also a menu bar. **TABLE A.21** is an overview of those menus. Any commands that were already covered in the interface buttons in **TABLE A.20** will be skipped.

TABLE A.21 Group Browser Menus

Edit Menu	
New Group	**Same as button described in Table A.20.**
Rename Group	Changes the name of the selected group.
Delete Group	Removes the selected group.
Add Selected Actors to Group	**Same as button described in Table A.20.**
Delete Selected Actors from Group	**Same as button described in Table A.20.**

TABLE A.21 Continued

Edit Menu	
Selected Actors	**Same as Select Actors in Group(s) button described in Table A.20.**
Deselect Actors	**Same as Deselect Actors in Group(s) button described in Table A.20.**
View Menu	
Docked (toggle)	**See Toggle Dock Status in Table A.20.**
Refresh	Refreshes the group list.

Within the group list inside the browser, you will see check boxes next to each group. Checking these will activate visibility for the corresponding group. In this way, you can quickly hide and show grouped Actors in your scene, in order to speed up the viewport, or just to stay organized. The major exception to this, however, is BSP brushes. These do not turn invisible in the 3D view, but will be hidden in the 2D view.

Selecting all Actors within a group can be quite beneficial to speed of workflow. For example, let's say you have a series of lights in your scene that all require the same effect. You can group them all together, select all Actors within the group, and make your changes to all of the lights simultaneously, rather than having to go light by light.

Actors can be members of more than one group at a time. In fact, a single Actor can exist within any number of groups. The main rule that must be kept in mind, however, is that if an Actor is a member of numerous groups, if *any* of those groups are hidden, that Actor will be hidden as well, regardless of whether or not the other groups to whom the Actor belongs are hidden. Let's say, for example, that you have an Actor that has been added to GroupOne, GroupTwo, and GroupThree. If you hide GroupOne, the Actor will also be hidden, even if GroupTwo and GroupThree are visible.

The Music Browser

This browser is not used in Unreal Tournament 2003 or Unreal Tournament 2004. This window allows you to access music packages, as well as play music (see **FIGURE A.29**). it was used in the original Unreal Tournament (UT99) and the original Unreal game.

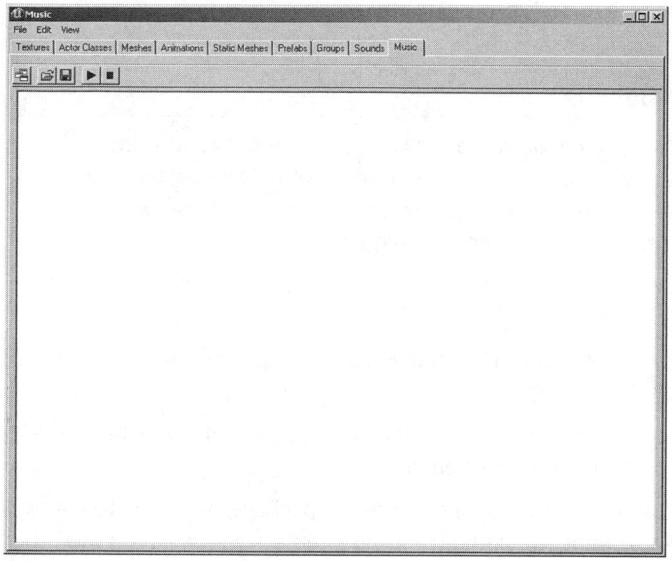

FIGURE A.29 The Music browser.

The Sound Browser

The Sound browser (see **FIGURE A.30**) allows you to access sound packages, and sample their contents. You may also save new sound packages that can be made up of your own sound effects. The top of the browser contains the following interface buttons and menus.

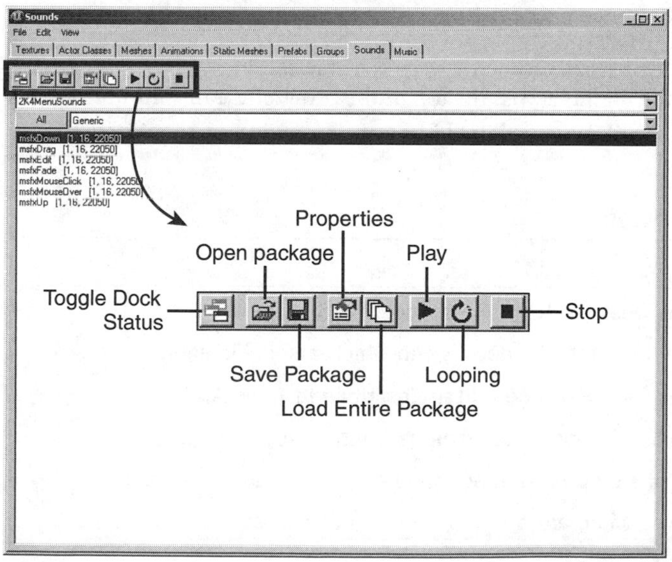

FIGURE A.30 The Sound browser.

TABLE A.22 describes the interface buttons of the Sound browser.

TABLE A.22 Sound Browser Buttons

Toggle Dock Status	This docks and undocks the browser from the Browser window. If undocked, the browser becomes a free-floating window that can be placed anywhere on the interface, and the browser's window is removed from the main browser window.
Open Package	This allows you to open packages of sounds and access their contents.
Save Package	This allows you to save new packages and packages that you have edited.
Properties	This button will display the Properties window for the selected sound, and allow you to edit those properties.
Load Entire Package	This button allows you to load the entire package of a selected sound effect. An example would be if you open up a level that you have been working on, or have already completed. The level contains three sounds that came out of a package. You will only see those three sounds in the browser when you open the window, but perhaps you wanted to see what other sounds were available in this package. This button will bring in all of the other sounds that are included in the package from which the first three sounds originated.
Play	This plays the selected sound effect.
Looping	This activates looping for the specific sound effect.
Stop	This button stops playback.

Next, **TABLE A.23** takes a look at the menus across the top of the browser. Again, any commands that have been covered in Table A.22 will be mentioned but not described.

TABLE A.23 Sound Browser Menus

File Menu	
Open	**Same as Open Package button described in Table A.22.**
Load Entire Package	Loads in the rest of a package to which a specific sound belongs.
Save	**Same as Save Package button described in Table A.22.**
Import	Allows you to import .wav files as sound effects.
Export	Allows for exporting Unreal sound effects out as .wav files.
New Sound Group	Allows you to create a new group to organize your sounds within a package.
New Procedural Sound	This is not being used in the current version of Unreal.

TABLE A.23 Continued

Edit Menu	
Properties	**Same as button described in Table A.22.**
Delete	Deletes the currently selected sound effect.
Play	**Same as button described in Table A.22.**
Looping	**Same as button described in Table A.22.**
Stop	**Same as button described in Table A.22.**
View Menu	
Docked (toggle)	**See Toggle Dock Status in A.22.**

There are two drop-down menus underneath the toolbar area on this browser. The first of these is the Package Selection menu. From here, you can access all of the packages loaded into Unreal. Beneath that is the Groups menu, which displays all of the groups contained within the specific package. To the left of the Group menus is the All button. This overrides the Group menu by displaying all sounds in the package, regardless of what group they're in.

The Textures Browser

Unreal already contains a wide variety of textures, and the Textures browser gives you access to them all (see **FIGURE A.31**). From here, you can open packages of textures, sort through them, add textures to new packages, and select textures to be applied to surfaces in the level.

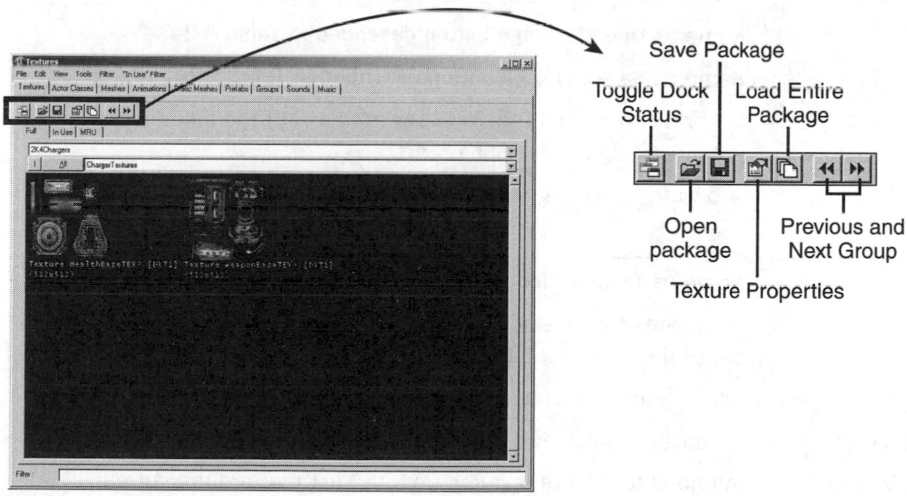

FIGURE A.31 The Textures browser.

TABLE A.24 lists the buttons and menus for this browser's interface.

TABLE A.24 Textures Browser Buttons

Toggle Dock Status	This docks and undocks the browser from the main browser window. If undocked, the browser becomes a free-floating window that can be placed anywhere on the interface, and the browser's tab is removed from the main browser window.
Open Package	This allows you to open and access packages of textures for browsing, relocating into other packages, and placing on surfaces.
Save Package	This allows you to save new packages, and to save any changes you might have made to the current package.
Texture Properties	This brings up the Properties window for the selected texture. From this window, you can create various shaders for your surfaces.
Load Entire Package	If you have a texture that came out of a specific package, and want to see the other textures available in that package, just click this button.
Previous and Next Group	These buttons switch between Groups of textures within packages.

The menu bar across the top of the browser contains the menus described in **TABLE A.25**.

TABLE A.25 Textures Browser Menus

File Menu	
New	Allows you to create a new material, and create shaders for it. For more information on this, turn to Chapter 8.
Open	**Same as Open Package button described in Table A.24.**
Save	**Same as Save Package button described in Table A.24.**
Import	Imports textures into the browser from any of the following formats: .bmp, .pcx, .tga, .dds, .upt, or .dxt.
Export	Allows for exporting out individual textures.
Edit Menu	
Properties	**Same as Texture Properties button described in Table A.24.**
Duplicate	Duplicates the selected texture to another texture and group, and under the name you specify.
Rename	Allows you to rename a selected texture.
Remove from Level	Removes a selected texture from a level.
Cull Unused Textures	Intended to remove textures from the list that are not currently in your level. At the time of this writing, however, this feature is not completely functional.
Load Entire Package	**Same as button described in Table A.24.**

TABLE A.25 Continued

Edit Menu	
Detail Hack	Replaces the texture's mipmap with one that gradually fades out to gray.
Replace Textures	Allows you to find certain textures within your level, and replace them with any other texture. Essentially, it works just like the find and replace commands found in most word processing programs.
Prev and Next Group	Allows you to sort through the groups of textures within your selected package.
Delete	Removes selected texture.
View Menu	
Docked (Toggle)	**See Toggle Dock Status in Table A.24.**
Zooms	The other options within this menu offer various levels of size and detail for which to view the textures in the browser.
Tools Menu	
Compress	Offers three different compression modes. These will be covered in more depth in Chapter 8.
Filters Menu	
This menu includes a variety of filters for including or excluding several different objects in the texture browser window. The filters include the following:	
Textures	
Shaders	
Modifiers	
Combiners	
Final Blends	
Show All	
Show None	
"In Use" Filter	
This menu offers several visibility filters for the In Use tab of the browser:	
Actors	
Sprites	
Brushes	
Static Meshes	
Terrain	
Show All	
Show None	

The browser also contains three different tabs for accessing textures that you have already been working with. The first tab is the Full tab. This contains all of the textures available based on the settings you have established within the tab. The first drop-down of the Full tab is the Package menu, from which you can select any of the texture packages that are loaded into Unreal. Beneath that is another drop-down for selecting any groups of textures that might be within that package. To the left of that drop-down are two buttons. The All button will override the Group menu by allowing you access to all textures within a package, regardless of their group. The "!" button allows you to see a realtime preview of any textures that are animated.

The next tab is the InUse tab. This allows you to see which texture you currently have selected. At first, that might not sound very handy, but when you consider that a texture list can be quite extensive and irregular, it can be very nice not to have to dig through a massive list of textures to see which one is current.

The MRU tab, which stands for Most Recently Used, allows you to view and select only the most recently accessed textures. This is very useful if you need to see which texture you applied to a specific surface a few commands prior.

The Mesh Browser

The objects displayed in this browser (see **FIGURE A.32**) are known as "vertex meshes" and are called such because they are driven by vertex animation. In other words, each vertex can transform over time as opposed to being driven by bones as in skeletal meshes.

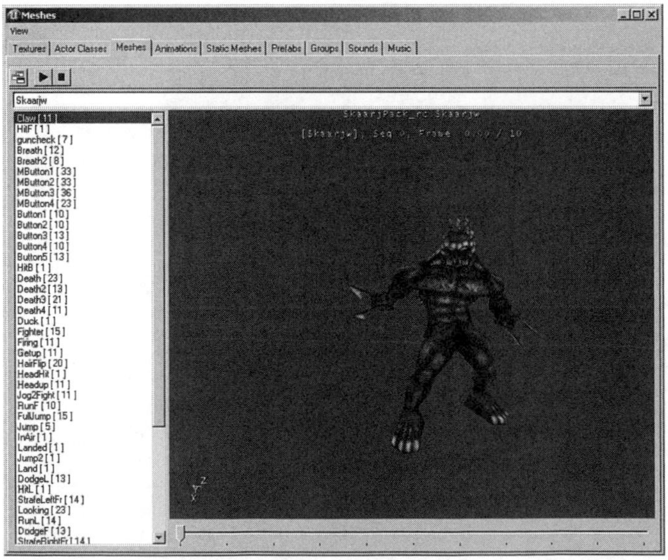

FIGURE A.32 The Mesh browser.

These can consist of many things, such as characters, flags, and more. A vertex mesh is a model, typically used for decoration, which is usually animated. Vertex meshes are not used as frequently as they were in the original Unreal and Unreal Tournament. They have almost completely been replaced by static meshes and skeletal meshes.

The Prefab Browser

This brings up the Prefab browser (see **FIGURE A.33**), which allows you to place prebuilt combinations of Actors. A Prefab can consist of just about anything: brushes, meshes, static meshes, lights, and so on. For example, you could build a crashed spacecraft, complete with particle emitters, lights, sound Actors, and so on, save that out as a Prefab, and then call it into the scene whenever you happened to need one. Inserting Prefabs causes no extra overhead, as the operation is internally recorded as if you had called in all of the objects individually. So, in effect, it's no different than just rebuilding a specific object again, only faster. This also means that if you bring a prefab into a level, adjusting one of the Actors in that Prefab will have no effect on the other Actors within the Prefab.

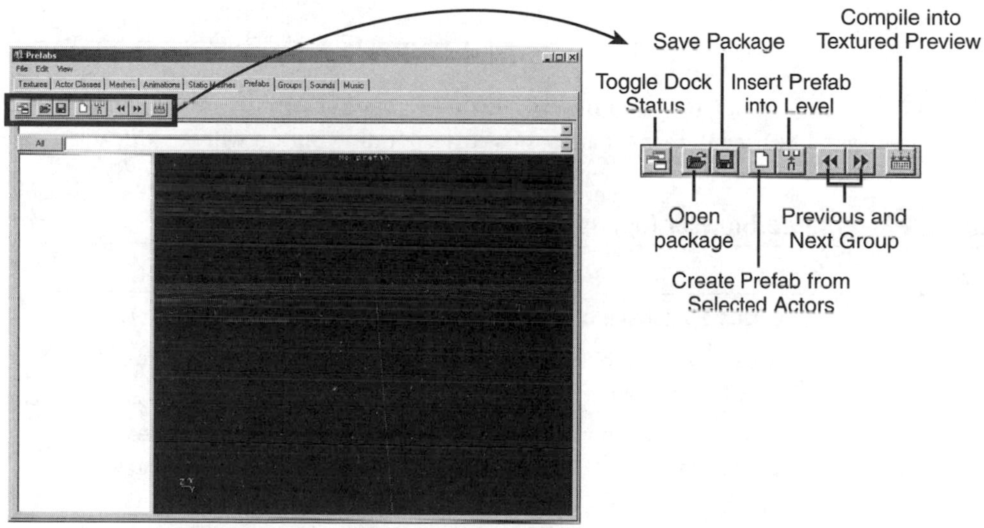

FIGURE A.33 The Prefab browser.

TABLE A.26 lists the interface buttons along the top of the browser, and their respective functionalities.

TABLE A.26 Prefab Browser Buttons

Toggle Dock Status	This docks and undocks the browser from the main browser window. If undocked, the browser becomes a free-floating window that can be placed anywhere on the interface, and the browser's tab is removed from the main browser window.
Open Package	This opens packages of Prefabs that you have created.
Save Package	This allows you to save a new package of Prefabs, or to save changes you have made to a prefab.
Create Prefab from Selected Actors	This is another one of those buttons where the name really says it all. Use this to create a new prefab from any number of Actors that are currently selected in your level.
Insert Prefab into Level	Again, sort of a no-brainer. This brings a selected prefab into your level.
Previous and Next Group	These buttons allow you to sort through the groups of Prefabs within the selected package.
Compile into Textured Preview	This was non-functional at the time of this writing.

TABLE A.27 lists the menus across the browser's menu bar, and the commands within them. As before, any command bearing the same name as its corresponding button will be skipped.

TABLE A.27 Prefab Browser Menus

File Menu	
Open	Opens a package of Prefabs for you to browse.
Save	Allows you to save new packages or save any changes you've made to a specific package.
Import	Allows you to import from a .t3d file, which is essentially a text file containing information for Unreal levels, Actors, or just brushes.
Export	Allows you to export your current Prefab out to a .t3d file.
Edit Menu	
Delete	Removes the selected Prefab.
Rename	Allows you to change the name of a selected prefab.
Prev and Next Group	**Same as the Previous and Next Group buttons.**
Add to Level	**Same as Insert Prefab into Level button.**
Create from Selections	**Same as Create Prefab from Selected Actors button.**
Compile into Textured Preview	**Same as button described in Table A.26.**

TABLE A.27 Continued

View Menu	
Docked (Toggle)	**See Toggle Dock Status in Table A.26.**

By default, Unreal Tournament 2004 installs with no Prefabs. Don't let this make you think that they aren't useful, though. Prefabs can be a great tool in speeding up level construction, especially if you're building a level that has many similar areas. For instance, you could build a Prefab of meshes, brushes, and lights for a computer workstation, and insert that Prefab wherever you happened to need another workstation in the level.

The Static Mesh Browser

The Static Mesh browser (see **FIGURE A.34**) gives you access to all available static meshes on your computer. Just as with the mesh browser, you may view the static mesh in the browser just as you would in a viewport. As with all browsers, the static mesh selected in this window will be the one placed if you right-click in your scene and choose Add Static Mesh.

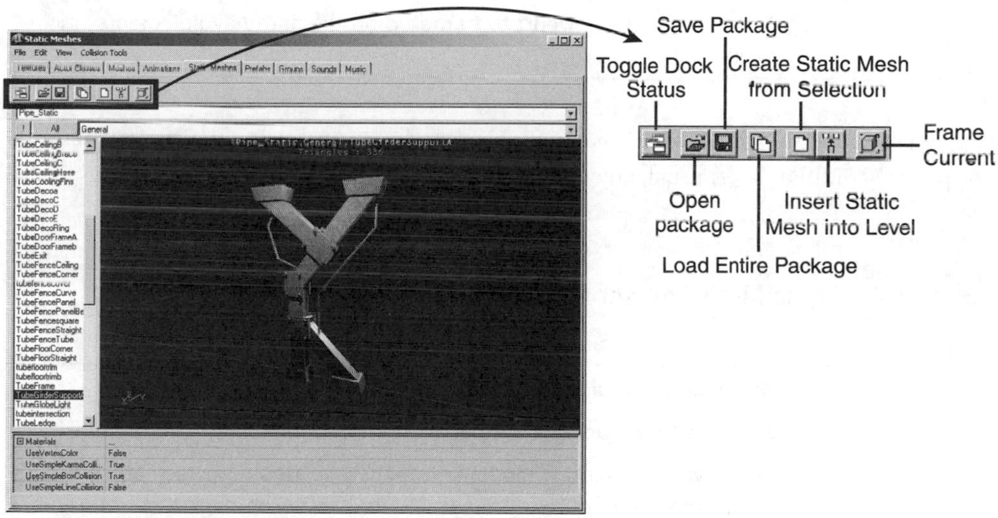

FIGURE A.34 The Static Mesh browser.

TABLE A.28 lists the interface buttons along the top of the browser, and their respective functionalities.

TABLE A.28 Static Mesh Browser Buttons

Toggle Dock Status	This docks and undocks the browser from the main browser window. If undocked, the browser becomes a free-floating window that can be placed anywhere on the interface, and the browser's tab is removed from the main browser window.
Open Package	This allows you to open a package of static meshes and browse its contents.
Save Package	With this button, you can save new packages, or save changes to a particular package.
Load Entire Package	This loads in the rest of a package from which a particular static mesh originated. This is useful if you find a static mesh within a level that you particularly like, and want to see if there are any more that look similar.
Create Static Mesh from Selection	This takes the selected static meshes or BSP brushes and makes them into a single static mesh. However, converting a BSP brush into a static mesh will often cause undesired results, and is not recommended.
Insert Static Mesh into Level	This allows you to place the selected static mesh into your level.
Frame Current	This causes the viewport to frame up on the currently selected static mesh.

Above the toolbar on the browser is also a menu bar. **TABLE A.29** lists each of the menus and their respective commands. As usual, any commands already covered in the buttons will not be covered.

TABLE A.29 Static Mesh Browser Menus

File Menu	
Open	**Same as Open Package button.**
Save	**Same as Save Package button.**
Import	Allows you to import a model into the Static Mesh browser. You can import models in either the .ase file format, which originates from 3ds max or the ActorX for Maya plug-in. It also accepts Lightwave's .lwo file format.
Edit Menu	
Delete	Removes the selected static mesh from the package.
Rename	Renames the selected static mesh.
Load Entire Package	**Same as button described in Table A.28.**
Add To Level	Adds the selected static mesh to the level.

TABLE A.29 Continued

Edit Menu	
Create From Selection	**Same as Create Static Mesh from Selection button.**
Prev and Next Group	Allows you to navigate through the available groups inside the package.
Copy Karma Properties to Clipboard	Copies the KInertiaTensor and KCOMOffset properties to the clipboard. You can then paste this information into your favorite text editor. You may want to use this as a starting point to adjust these properties after placing the object in the level. For more information on these properties go to Chapter 11.
View Menu	
Docked (Toggle)	**See Toggle Dock Status in Table A.28.**
Show Collision	Toggling this on will display the collision geometry for the selected static mesh.
Show Karma Primitives	When this is toggled, the Karma primitives for the selected static mesh will be displayed. For more information on Karma primitives, go to Chapter 11.
Show Karma Mass Primitives	When this is toggled, the Karma Mass primitives for the selected static mesh will be displayed.
Auto Frame Selection	When this is on, selecting a static mesh will cause the viewport to automatically frame up on the static mesh. Note: This feature is only implemented in later versions of Unreal Tournament 2004.
Collision Tools Menu	
Fit 6-DOP (Box)	This fits a box around the static mesh to be used as the collision geometry.
Fit 10-DOP	This creates a box with four beveled edges to be used as the collision geometry. The axis projected from will depend on whether you select X, Y, or Z.
Fit 18-DOP	This creates a box where every edge is beveled to better fit around the static mesh to be used as the collision geometry.
Fit 26-DOP	This creates a box where not only every edge, but also every corner, is beveled to better fit around the static mesh to be used as the collision geometry. This often works better for static meshes with sharp edges.
Fit Auto-OBB	This fits a box around the static mesh. If necessary, it will rotate the box to better fit the mesh, unlike the Fit 6-DOP (Box) command.
Import .ASE As Collision	This feature is non-functional.

TABLE A.29 Continued

Collision Tools Menu	
Fit Karma Primitive	This modifies the Karma primitive. The following are the available submenus: Sphere Cylinder-X Cylinder-Y Cylinder-Z Sphere will fit a sphere around the static mesh for a Karma primitive, and so on.
Refresh Karma Primitives	This duplicates the collision geometry and uses it as the Karma primitives.
Clear Karma Primitives	This removes all Karma primitives.

For information on how to create static meshes and import them into UnrealEd, go to Chapter 20.

The Animation Browser

The Animation browser (see **FIGURE A.35**) is by far the most complex browser in the editor. It allows you to preview animated meshes and characters, as well as import skeletal animated characters from third-party software packages, and adjust character settings.

1. Toggle Dock Status
2. Open Animation Package
3. Save Animation Package
4. Load Entire Package
5. Import Skeletal Mesh
6. Import Skeletal Animation
7. Import Additional Animation Data
8. Link Animation to Mesh
9. Info
10. View Bounds
11. View Bones
12. View Bones Names
13. View Reference Pose
14. View Influences
15. Toggle Raw Offset Display
16. View Wireframe
17. Copy Mesh Properties
18. Past Mesh Properties
19. Cycle Through LOD Mesh Levels
20. Import a Single LOD Mesh
21. Redigest LOD Levels
22. Forced Synchronous In-Level Animation

FIGURE A.35 The Animation browser.

As with the previous browsers, there's a menu along the top and a toolbar below that. Underneath that are three combo boxes: Package, Mesh, and Animation Set. Package shows you a list of the currently loaded animation packages. Mesh will show the list of meshes that are located inside the selected package. The Animation Set list will show all of the animations sets that are available in the package.

Below that on the left, there's a sequences list containing all animations for the object. In the middle, there's a perspective viewport that displays the skeletal mesh currently selected. And finally, on the right, you see a properties window that lets you change a series of properties of the currently selected skeletal mesh.

TABLE A.30 lists the toolbar buttons and the functions of each.

TABLE A.30 Animation Browser Buttons

Toggle Dock Status	This docks and undocks the browser from the main browser window. If undocked, the browser becomes a free-floating window that can be placed anywhere on the interface, and the browser's tab is removed from the main browser window.
Open Animation Package	This allows you to open a package of Skeletal Meshes and browse its contents.
Save Animation Package	With this button, you can save new packages, or save changes to a particular package.
Load Entire Package	This loads in the rest of a package from which a particular skeletal mesh originated. This is useful if you find a skeletal mesh within a level that you particularly like, and want to see if there are any more that look similar.
Import Skeletal Mesh	This allows you to import a .psk file as a skeletal mesh.
Import Skeletal Animation	This allows you to import animation from a .psa file.
Import Additional Animation data	This imports animation as well, but all new animation is appended to the existing ones.
Link Animation To Mesh	When this button is clicked, the currently selected mesh will be connected to the current set of animations.
Info	This button will open a window full of useful information about the currently selected mesh and its animation. Everything from the number of faces, vertices, and uvs, to the number of joints is displayed in this window.
View Bounds	This displays the visibility boundary of the currently selected mesh. As long as some part of this boundary is within the player's field of view and isn't completely blocked by an Antiportal, this mesh will be rendered.
View Bones	This toggles between three different display modes: bones of the skeletal mesh along with the mesh, just the bones, or just the mesh.
View Bone Names	This displays the bone names of the skeletal mesh.

TABLE A.30 Continued

<table>
<tr><td>View Reference Pose</td><td>This puts the skeletal mesh into the reference, or default, pose.</td></tr>
<tr><td>View Influences</td><td>This allows you to view the normals and influences on the mesh. Influence, in this case, means how many bones “influence” a particular vertex. This is represented by the color of the normal projecting out of each vertex.
<table>
<tr><th>Color</th><th>Number of Influences</th></tr>
<tr><td>Green</td><td>1</td></tr>
<tr><td>Red</td><td>2</td></tr>
<tr><td>Pink</td><td>3</td></tr>
<tr><td>Light Blue</td><td>4</td></tr>
<tr><td>White</td><td>5</td></tr>
</table>
The more influences each vertex has, the slower it is to render. Also, if you are developing for consoles, which support hardware skinning, you can only have a total of three or four influences. Therefore, you should try, as a rule, to ensure that each vertex has at most three influences.</td></tr>
<tr><td>Toggle Raw Offset Display</td><td>This causes the skeletal mesh to snap back to its default position, disregarding any transformations from the Mesh properties.</td></tr>
<tr><td>View Wireframe</td><td>This displays the skeletal mesh in wireframe mode.</td></tr>
<tr><td>Copy Mesh Properties</td><td>This copies all of the mesh properties, located under the Mesh tab, of the currently selected mesh. After doing this, you can paste them into another mesh.</td></tr>
<tr><td>Paste Mesh Properties</td><td>After copying the mesh properties, use this command to paste them into the selected mesh.</td></tr>
<tr><td>Cycle Through the LOD (Level of Detail) Mesh Levels</td><td>As the name suggests, this cycles through the four levels of detail (LOD [0], LOD [1], LOD [2], and LOD [3]) as well as the default view. LOD levels cause the mesh to appear simpler as you move away from them.</td></tr>
<tr><td>Import a Single LOD Mesh</td><td>With one of the LOD levels selected, click this button to import a .psk file for the mesh. This allows you to import simpler versions of meshes to be used as your own custom LOD levels.</td></tr>
<tr><td>Redigest LOD levels</td><td>This recalculates the actual geometry and skinning for the current LOD settings. You will need to do this whenever you add or edit LODLevels.</td></tr>
<tr><td>Forced Synchronous In-Level Animation</td><td>If there are instances of the currently selected mesh in the level, this will force those instances to play in sync with the animation browser.</td></tr>
</table>

TABLE A.31 lists the menus across the browser's menu bar, and the commands within them. As before, any command bearing the same name as its corresponding button will be skipped.

TABLE A.31 Animation Browser Manus

File Menu	
Open	**Same as Open Animation Package button.**
Save	**Same as Save Animation Package button.**
Mesh Import	**Same as Import Skeletal Mesh button.**
Animation Import	**Same as Import Skeletal Animation button.**
Animation Append	**Same as Import Additional Animation data button.**
Mesh LOD Import	**Same as Import a Single LOD Mesh button.**
View Menu	
Animation Set Info	**Same as Info button.**
Bones	**Same as View Bones button.**
Influences	**Same as View influences button.**
Bounds	**Same as View bounds button.**
BackFace	This is here for debugging purposes only and is non-functional in the retail build of Unreal Tournament 2004.
Wireframe	**Same as View Wireframe button.**
RefPose	**Same as VIew Reference Pose button.**
Raw Offset	**Same as Toggle Raw Offset Display button.**
BoneNames	**Same as View Bone Names button.**
Collision	This shows the collision geometry of the selected skeletal mesh.
Karma	This shows the karma primitives of the selected skeletal mesh.
Sync Level Actors	**Same as Forced Synchronous In-Level Animation button.**
Refresh	This refreshes the animation browser and the controls within.
Edit Menu	
Linkup Anim and Mesh	**Same as Link Animation to Mesh button.**
Unlink Animation and Mesh	This removes the link between the animation and currently selected mesh.
Load Entire Package	**Same as Load Entire Package button.**
Apply	At the time of this writing, this menu item was non-functional.
Undo	At the time of this writing, this menu item was non-functional.
Copy Karma Properties To Clipboard	This copies the `KInertiaTensor` and `KCOMOffset` properties to the clipboard. You can then paste this information into your favorite text editor. For more information on these properties go to Chapter 11.

TABLE A.31 Continued

Mesh Menu	
Mesh Properties	This changes the properties to the Mesh tab.
Copy Mesh Properties	**Same as Copy Mesh Properties button.**
Paste Mesh Properties	**Same as Paste Mesh Properties button.**
Rename Mesh	This command allows you to change the name of the currently selected mesh.
Delete Mesh	As long as the currently selected mesh is not in use, this command will delete it from the package.
Redigest LOD	**Same as Redigest LOD Levels button.**
Cycle Forced LODS	**Same as Cycle Through the LOD Mesh Levels button.**
Import LOD	**Same as Import a Single LOD Mesh button.**
Animation Menu	
Preferences	This changes the properties to the Prefs tab.
Animation Set Properties	This changes the properties to the Animation Set tab.
Sequence Properties	This changes the properties to the Sequence tab.
Notifications	This changes the properties to the Notify tab.
Add Notify	At the time of this writing, this menu item was non-functional.
Copy All Notifications	At the time of this writing, this menu item was non-functional.
Paste All Notifications	At the time of this writing, this menu item was non-functional.
Clear Notifications	At the time of this writing, this menu item was non-functional.
Edit Sequence Groups	This changes the properties to the Sequence tab.
Clear Groups	At the time of this writing, this menu item was non-functional.
Copy All Groups	This copies all of the groups, located under the Sequence tab, of the currently selected sequence. After doing this, you can paste it into another sequence.
Paste All Groups	After copying the groups, use this command to paste them into the selected sequence.
Rename Animation Set	As the name suggests, this allows you to modify the name of the currently selected Animation Set.
Delete Animation Set	This allows you to delete the currently selected Animation Set. However, the Animation Set can not have any DefaultAnim references.

Editor Windows

The editor windows provide you with two very different yet extremely useful tools for working on your levels. These are the Search for Actors editor window and the 2D Shape Editor.

Search for Actors

The Search for Actors command allows you to find and select a specific Actor in your level. The command initiates a dialog containing a list of all the Actors that currently exist in your level, and you may filter that list by entering text into any of the three text fields on the right of the window. The list of Actors will be filtered as you type. For example, let's say you want to find an Actor named BrightLight5. If you just type the first two letters into the name text field, the list will automatically shorten to include Actors that have names starting with "br." In this case, you would probably get a list containing most of your brushes (as their default name tends to be "brush" and a number), and your BrightLight5 object would also be listed. If, however, you continued to type the name out completely, only Actors with that name would be listed, in this case, the desired object. **FIGURE A.36** shows the Search for Actors window.

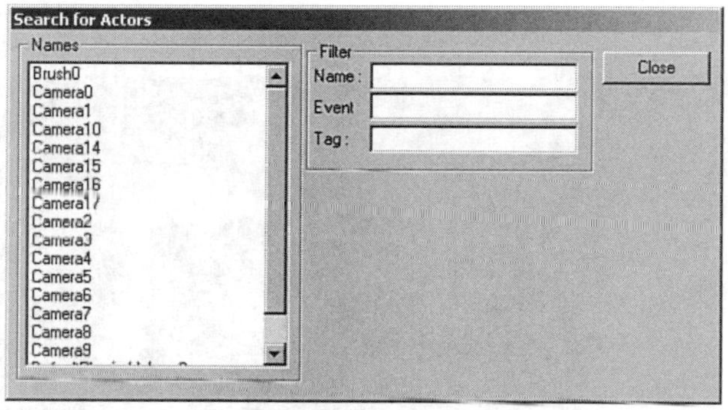

FIGURE A.36 Search for Actors.

This tool can also be accessed from the Edit menu.

The 2D Shape Editor

The 2D Shape Editor (see **FIGURE A.37**) allows you to create shapes out of linear and Bezier curves. It cannot create highly complex shapes, but does allow for objects that are more interesting than standard primitives. You can read more information about this editor in Chapter 4.

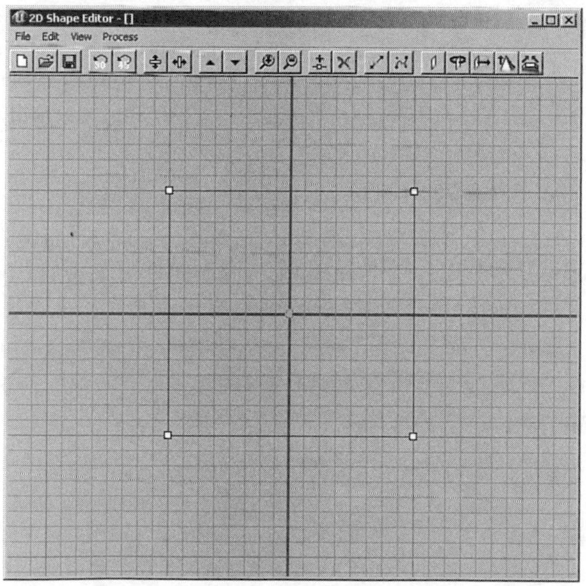

FIGURE A.37 The 2D Shape Editor.

The UnrealScript Editor

The UnrealScript Editor (see **FIGURE A.38**) gives you limited access to entering commands via UnrealScript. It is slightly limited, in that it will not allow for massive amounts of code to be input. Instead, it is designed to allow you to insert smaller areas of code, or to change existing code. It also allows for compiling of scripts into packages.

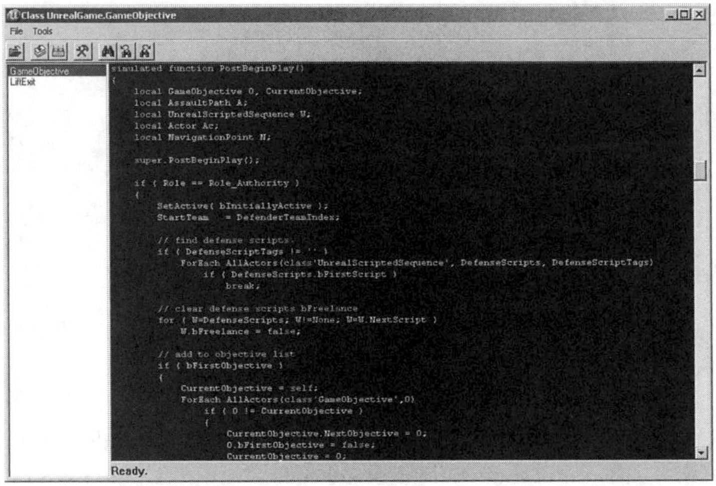

FIGURE A.38 The UnrealScript Editor.

Property Windows

The property windows give you access to the many properties inherent to any actor or surface in your level. As you construct your Unreal worlds, you will find yourself using these quite often.

Actor Properties

This brings up the Actor Properties window, which gives you access to a tremendous number of parameters for a specific Actor (see **FIGURE A.39**). The properties available will change depending on which Actor you have selected. It is divided into a series of categories, some of which are standard and can be found on any actor, such as the Display category. Other categories are Actor sensitive, such as the ZoneInfo category, which can only be found on the ZoneInfo actor, for example.

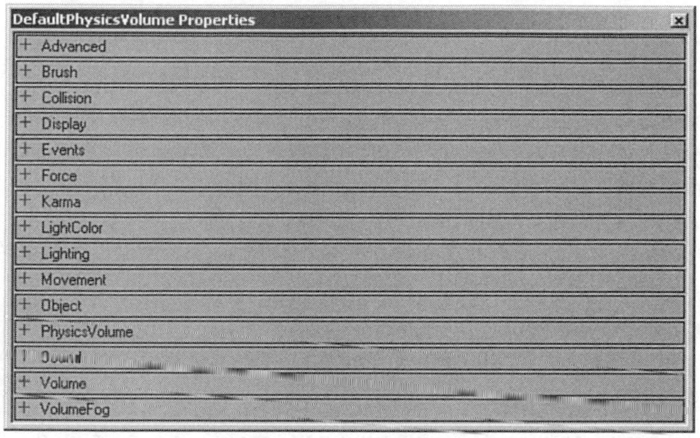

FIGURE A.39 Actor Properties window.

Surface Properties

This accesses the Surface Properties window, which is used to control how textures are placed on surfaces (see **FIGURE A.40**). From here, you can pan your textures in the U and V directions, as well as rotate them. The following sections show the options found under each of the four tabs found in the window: Flags, Pan/Rot/Scale, Alignment, and Scale.

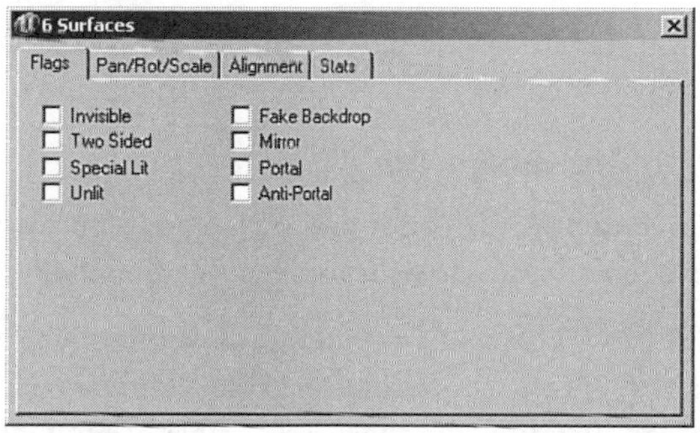

FIGURE A.40 Surface Properties window.

Flags Tab

The Flags tab provides a series of Boolean options you can activate for given surfaces. Each of these is described in **TABLE A.32**.

TABLE A.32 Surface Properties Flags

Option	Description
Invisible	The surface will not show in-game.
Two-Sided	The surface can be seen from both sides, though collisions will only occur on the positive side of the surface.
Special Lit	This allows the surface to receive lighting from lights in which the `bSpecialLit` property is set to `True`.
Unlit	The surface will not receive light for any reason.
Fake Backdrop	This will cause the surface to show the outside of the level; a vital setting for using skyboxes.

TABLE A.32 Continued

Option	Description
Mirror	This causes the surfaces to be mirrored, meaning that they reflect their environment. Keep in mind, though, that in a first-person view, your player character will not render. In order to see the effect, you must first change one of the rendering settings. To do this, open the `UT2004.ini` file under the System folder of your Unreal Tournament 2004 installation, go to the `D3DDrv.D3DRenderDevice` section, and set `UseStencil=True`. You can also set this property from within the game. To do this, use the console command `preferences`. Under the Rendering category, set the `UseStencil` setting to `True`.
Portal	This turns the surface into a portal, which is useful mostly when applied to a sheet brush for the purposes of zoning a level.
Anti-Portal	This turns the surface into an Antiportal, which will occlude anything found on its opposite side.

Pan/Rot/Scale Tab

This area provides you with a series of tools for panning (moving), rotating, and scaling your textures on a surface to help you align them properly.

The Pan group contains buttons for panning, which allow you to move the texture in increments of 1, 4, 16, and 64 in either the U or V direction. Clicking one of the buttons will move the texture in that direction the given number of units. Shift-clicking the button will move the texture in the opposite direction.

The Rotation group will rotate the texture either 45 or 90 degrees, as well as allow you to flip the texture in either U or V.

The Scaling group allows two different methods for scaling. The first is a simple method that is applied uniformly to the entire surface in both axes, and you can choose a number from the drop-down box. The second allows you to specify your own values for scaling in each axis. The Relative check box allows you to toggle between either absolute scaling or relative scaling based on the texture's previous scale. For example, if Relative is checked and you enter a value of 1 into the U and V fields, the texture will not scale, regardless of how it has been previously scaled.

The Light Map section allows you to control how detailed the shadows in your level will be. Remember that a lower setting will tighten your shadows, giving them more detail, whereas lower values will soften your shadows. Oversharpening your light maps on larger levels can lead to slowdown on some systems, as the textures for the light maps get larger.

Alignment

This section allows you to control how the textures are projected onto each surface. The Default system simply allows you to control how the textures will tile (repeat) in the U and V directions. The Planar method will project the texture onto all selected faces from the same direction, which can lead to stretching on some surfaces. The Box method will project the texture from six sides, such as a cube. Finally, the Face method will produce a separate projection of the texture on to each face of the surface.

State

The properties available in this tab are non-functional at the time of this writing.

Index

Symbols

A

B

D

F

M

O

P

Q - R

S

T

V

W

X - Y - Z